Strategic Management

Strategic Management

State of the Field and Its Future

Editors

Irene M. Duhaime
Michael A. Hitt
Marjorie A. Lyles

OXFORD
UNIVERSITY PRESS

Oxford University Press is a department of the University of Oxford. It furthers the University's objective of excellence in research, scholarship, and education by publishing worldwide. Oxford is a registered trade mark of Oxford University Press in the UK and certain other countries.

Published in the United States of America by Oxford University Press
198 Madison Avenue, New York, NY 10016, United States of America.

© Oxford University Press 2021

All rights reserved. No part of this publication may be reproduced, stored in a retrieval system, or transmitted, in any form or by any means, without the prior permission in writing of Oxford University Press, or as expressly permitted by law, by license, or under terms agreed with the appropriate reproduction rights organization. Inquiries concerning reproduction outside the scope of the above should be sent to the Rights Department, Oxford University Press, at the address above.

You must not circulate this work in any other form
and you must impose this same condition on any acquirer.

Library of Congress Cataloging-in-Publication Data
Names: Duhaime, Irene M., editor. | Hitt, Michael A., editor. |
Lyles, Marjorie A., editor.
Title: Strategic management : state of the field and its future / editors,
Irene M. Duhaime, Michael A. Hitt, Marjorie A. Lyles.
Description: New York, NY : Oxford University Press, [2021] |
Includes bibliographical references and index. |
Identifiers: LCCN 2021008277 (print) | LCCN 2021008278 (ebook) |
ISBN 9780190090890 (paperback) |
ISBN 9780190090883 (hardback) | ISBN 9780190090913 (epub) |
ISBN 9780190090920
Subjects: LCSH: Strategic planning.
Classification: LCC HD30.28 .S729286 2021 (print) | LCC HD30.28 (ebook) |
DDC 658.4/012—dc23
LC record available at https://lccn.loc.gov/2021008277
LC ebook record available at https://lccn.loc.gov/2021008278

DOI: 10.1093/oso/9780190090883.001.0001

3 5 7 9 8 6 4 2

Paperback printed by LSC Communications, United States of America
Hardback printed by Bridgeport National Bindery, Inc., United States of America

To Walter for your constant love and support. To my wonderful family, lifelong friends, and outstanding colleagues in the field of strategic management. To my doctoral faculty and fellow graduate students at the University of Pittsburgh, especially John H. Grant, for providing a learning environment both challenging and nurturing for the start of an academic career.

I.M.D.

To my professors and mentors during my graduate education at the Leeds School of Business, University of Colorado (PhD), and the Rawls College of Business, Texas Tech University (MBA), who prepared me for my career as an academic researcher and teacher. I was honored to receive a Distinguished Alumni Award from both institutions in recent years.

M.A.H.

To my fellow co-editors and chapter authors for their lifelong dedication to encouraging innovative and thoughtful work that has allowed the field of strategic management and SMS to flourish. Also to my professors and fellow doctoral students at the University of Pittsburgh for their love and patience with me—especially Ian Mitroff. I congratulate them for encouraging a young single mom to get a PhD in Business when other schools suggested she would be a great secretary. To my faculty at Carnegie-Mellon University who provided a basis for my research on organizational learning.

M.A.L.

Table of Contents

List of Contributors

Agarwal, Rajshree University of Maryland, USA

Aguilera, Ruth V. Northeastern University, USA

Amit, Raphael University of Pennsylvania, USA

Barnett, Michael L. Rutgers University, USA

Barney, Jay B. University of Utah, USA

Ben-Menahem, Shiko M. ETH Zurich, Switzerland

Burgelman, Robert A. Stanford University, USA

Chang, Sea-Jin National University of Singapore, Singapore

Child, John University of Birmingham, UK

Coff, Russell University of Wisconsin, USA

Connelly, Brian Auburn University, USA

Crossan, Mary University of Western Ontario, Canada

Cuervo-Cazurra, Alvaro Northeastern University, USA

Duhaime, Irene M. Georgia State University, USA

Durand, Rodolphe HEC Paris, France

Eisenhardt, Kathleen M. Stanford University, USA

Feldman, Emilie R. University of Pennsylvania, USA

Floyd, Steven W. University of Massachusetts, USA

Foss, Nicolai J. Copenhagen Business School, Denmark

Furr, Nathan R. INSEAD, France

Garg, Sam The Hong Kong University of Science and Technology, Hong Kong

Graebner, Melissa E. University of Illinois, USA

Greve, Henrich R. INSEAD, Singapore

Hambrick, Donald C. Pennsylvania State University, USA

Harrison, Jeffrey S. University of Richmond, USA

Helfat, Constance E. Dartmouth College, USA

Henriques, Irene York University, Canada

Hernsberger, Joshua S. University of California, Irvine, USA

Hitt, Michael A. Texas A&M University, USA

Hoskisson, Robert E. Rice University, USA

Howard, Michael Texas A&M University, USA

Husted, Bryan W. Technologico de Monterrey, Mexico

Huy, Quy N. INSEAD, Singapore

Ireland, R. Duane Texas A&M University, USA

Kim, Seojin University of Maryland, USA

Laamanen, Tomi University of St. Gallen, Switzerland

Lavie, Dovev Bocconi University, Italy

Lyles, Marjorie A. Florida International University, USA

Mack, Daniel Z. Singapore Management University, Singapore

Mackey, Alison Clarkson University, USA

Mantere, Saku McGill University, Canada

Pathak, Seemantini University of Missouri–St. Louis, USA

Pfarrer, Michael D. University of Georgia, USA

Puranam, Phanish INSEAD, Singapore

Reger, Rhonda K. University of North Texas, USA

Rickley, Marketa University of North Carolina–Greensboro, USA

Santos, José F.P. INSEAD, France

Schneidmuller, Tatjana LUISS Business School, Italy

Shaver, J. Myles University of Minnesota, USA

Shrestha, Yash Raj ETH Zurich, Switzerland

Sirmon, David G. University of Washington, USA

Tallman, Stephen University of Richmond, USA

Vaara, Eero University of Oxford, UK

Vera, Dusya University of Houston, USA

Volberda, Henk W. University of Amsterdam, The Netherlands

von Krogh, Georg ETH Zurich, Switzerland

Westney, D. Eleanor Massachusetts Institute of Technology, USA, and York University, Canada

Westphal, James D. University of Michigan, USA

Whittington, Richard University of Oxford, UK

Wiersema, Margarethe F. University of California, Irvine, USA

Williamson, Peter J. University of Cambridge, UK

Withers, Michael C. Texas A&M University, USA

Wowak, Adam J. University of Notre Dame, USA

Zadeh, Taghi University of Amsterdam, The Netherlands

Zhang, Yan (Anthea) Rice University, USA

Zott, Christoph IESE Business School, Spain

Editor Bios

Irene M. Duhaime is Professor Emeritus of the Robinson College of Business at Georgia State University, where she held the Robinson Distinguished Leadership Professorship and served as Senior Associate Dean. She received her PhD from the University of Pittsburgh. Her research has been published in the leading journals of the field. She has held leadership positions in professional associations, including the Strategic Management Society's Board of Directors, and led its 25th Anniversary Conference, first SMS Doctoral Workshop, and Entrepreneurship and Strategy Interest Group. She has served the Academy of Management as Chair of the Career Achievement Awards Committee and the Business Policy and Strategy Division, and as panelist and faculty resource on consortia and other developmental activities for doctoral students and junior faculty. She is deeply committed to the Ph.D. Project as a doctoral student mentor and frequent presenter at their annual conference. She was elected as a member of the SMS Fellows in 2010 and served as the elected Dean of the SMS Fellows group for 2017 and 2018. She received the Trailblazer Award from the Management Doctoral Student Association of the Ph.D. Project in 2015, and the Distinguished Service Award of the Academy of Management in 2014 and Strategic Management Society in 2017.

Michael A. Hitt is a University Distinguished Professor Emeritus at Texas A&M University. He received his PhD from the University of Colorado. His work has been published in many of the top scholarly journals, and the Times Higher Education listed him among the top scholars in economics, finance, and management. An article in the *Academy of Management Perspectives* lists him as one of the top two management scholars in terms of the combined impact of his work both inside (i.e., citations in scholarly journals) and outside of academia. He is a former editor of the *Academy of Management Journal*, a former co-editor of the *Strategic Entrepreneurship Journal*, and the current editor-in-chief of the *Oxford Research Encyclopedia of Business and Management*. He is a Fellow in the Academy of Management, the Strategic Management Society, and the Academy of International Business. He is a former President of both the Academy of Management and the Strategic Management Society. He has received honorary doctorates from the Universidad Carlos III de Madrid and Jönköping University. He has received the Irwin Outstanding Educator Award from the BPS Division and the Distinguished Service Award and the Distinguished Educator Award from the Academy of Management. He has been listed as a Highly Cited Researcher in the Web of Science (top 2 percent in citations) each year since 2014.

Marjorie A. Lyles is International Business Distinguished Research Fellow at the Florida International College of Business. She graduated from Carnegie-Mellon University and received her PhD from the University of Pittsburgh. She is Past President of the Strategic Management Society. She's an Emeritus Professor of Global Strategic Management at Indiana University Kelley School of Business and Adjunct Professor IU Lilly Family School of Philanthropy. She was given the John W. Ryan Award for exceptional contributions to IU's international programs. She received an Honorary Doctorate from Copenhagen Business School. She is a Fellow of both SMS and the Academy of International Business. Her teaching and research focused on emerging economies since the mid-1980s. She did projects, teaching, and work in China since 1985 when she was a consultant with the U.S. Department of Commerce in the Dalian programs. Her research includes mixed methods, which required her to seek research grants and includes two from National Science Foundation. Her work has helped the development of organizational learning and the knowledge-based perspectives. Her research has appeared in top journals such as SMJ, ASQ, JIBS, AMR, AMJ, OSci, and JMS. Lyles has also worked with governmental, nonprofit, and corporate entities. She has consulted with the USIS, World Bank, and UNDP.

INTRODUCTION

Irene M. Duhaime, Michael A. Hitt, and Marjorie A. Lyles

In 1977, a conference titled "Business Policy and Planning Research: The State-of-the-Art" was held at and hosted by the University of Pittsburgh, followed in 1979 by the publication of Schendel and Hofer's edited book, *Strategic Management: A New View of Business Policy and Planning*. That conference and the publication of the associated Schendel-Hofer book are widely viewed as landmark events that were turning points from what was referred to as "Business Policy and Planning," largely viewed in academia as a teaching field and area of management practice (Whittington, 2019), to the research-based discipline of Strategic Management we know today.

The Schendel-Hofer book, published by Little, Brown and Company, captured the field of Strategic Management as it existed in 1979, spanning the major areas envisioned as the scope of "Strategic Management." With primary contributions and commentaries enriched by the discussions and debates of the nearly 100 academics, business executives and consultants attending the conference, the book addressed what were then seen as the major issues encompassed by strategic management, and how research on those issues could develop the field as a scholarly discipline as well as enhance teaching in the field. It laid out a fairly comprehensive and well-organized representation of what was then known in the field and the major debates on the issues in the field. It concluded with an extensive set of research questions on each of those areas, providing a rich research agenda for then-current and future researchers in the fledgling field of Strategic Management.

Following the conference and book publication, a number of developments led to a flourishing field. The founding in 1980–1981 of the *Strategic Management Journal* (SMJ) and the Strategic Management Society (SMS), both through the efforts of Dan Schendel, provided strategic management researchers opportunities for presentation, discussion, and broad dissemination of their research. These in turn led to the rapid growth in numbers of doctoral programs in strategic management, faculty positions devoted to the discipline, and theoretical and empirical research to advance the field. The Schendel-Hofer book had significant impact on the development of the field of Strategic Management because it was widely used in doctoral seminars, influencing the research agendas of generations of strategic management scholars. The high impact of that edited book was attributable in large part to (1) the breadth of the book's coverage of the field as it was known at that time, and (2) the reputations, visibility, and quality of the editors and of the scholars who authored the sections and subsections of the book.

Over the last four decades, strategic management research has advanced significantly in a number of important areas, resulting in a field that is richer and more developed but is also more fine-grained in its focus. At the same time, the growing breadth of the field and the increasingly specialized nature of research can result in fragmentation, thus slowing the progress of critically important research contributions by limiting intradisciplinary research conversations and the identification of exciting and promising research directions.

After many years of development, there is a need to reassess the field of Strategic Management: to examine the current state of the field and to consider its future. As such, the need also arises to define the content and boundaries of the field. There are limited alternatives for obtaining a comprehensive overview of the field as it exists today and to identify promising directions for the field's further development. This volume assesses progress of the field, the content and boundaries of the field after more than 40 years of research, and the areas with the most promise for fruitful research to advance our knowledge in the future. Our purpose is to help scholars in the field, new and more established, by integrating the significant knowledge that has been created and by providing a base for research in the Strategic Management field over the coming decades.

In this book we address the major streams of research and major research approaches that have helped to develop the field to its current state. But perhaps the book's highest potential value is the extensive and insightful discussion of promising future opportunities and research agendas. Many chapter authors have devoted nearly half of their space to the discussion of promising pathways for future research, and have identified numerous research questions that, when addressed, will add significant value to research knowledge and to the strategic management of firms. We believe that the discussion of historical roots and the analysis of the field's development to its current state will be important resources for doctoral students and for young scholars whose careers began in recent decades without benefit of an up-to-date resource like this book, and that the extensive discussion of future research opportunities will benefit all. Another extremely helpful aspect of the book is that the chapters have extensive reference lists that can help the readers find the major past writings on the topics. In its examination of the future of strategic management, the book offers the perspectives of scholars who are widely regarded as leaders in the field. We hope that readers will be assisted in theory building and in identification and pursuit of new areas of exploration.

The book has 11 Parts, along with this introductory chapter by the editors. Each of the book's Parts covers a major topic area and is led by one or more prominent scholars whose research is specialized in the area on which the Part focuses. Those scholars have provided lead chapters on the primary research focus for their Parts of the book. In those lead chapters, the authors present an overview of that research (Part), including major theoretical perspectives present in the work to date, and commentary on the future of research in that area, identifying new directions as well as exciting interdisciplinary opportunities. Each Part also includes chapters on more focused topics, representing some of the major streams of research related to the primary foci in that Part. The chapters are authored by a mix of well-established scholars and scholars who are rising stars whose work is already well known and respected in their area.

The model for this book has been designed to consider the current breadth and depth of the field, both significantly greater than when the Schendel-Hofer book was published in 1979. In 1979, the research agenda being outlined and research questions suggested had the objective of defining Strategic Management as a research discipline and establishing its structure as a field. By contrast, this book examines theoretical perspectives and research methods for a field of far greater breadth and depth, with the challenge of assessing what possible avenues are likely most promising for research efforts in the coming decades. We believe that the works contributed by leading scholars can provide a blueprint for the future, offering significant value for readers seeking to make meaningful and valuable contributions to strategic management research and to have important and positive impacts on the field. By provoking creative thinking about productive future research agendas, these chapters are thus likely to have a major impact on the scholarly field of Strategic Management.

Overview of the Book

Evolution of strategic management research: theory and methods

In Part 1, the book begins with an examination of the major theoretical streams and research methods used in strategic management research. In their lead chapter, Hoskisson and Harrison emphasize the importance of conversation in strategic management—especially across disciplines, because the field draws on multiple disciplines. They argue that such interaction has advanced research in the field by moving from the broader "swings of the pendulum" between an internal firm focus and a focus on the external environment of the firm observed a few decades ago (Hoskisson et al., 1999) to narrower swings of the pendulum by applying external perspectives to internal questions, and vice versa. They argue that research integrating multiple theoretical perspectives (i.e., at the middle of the pendulum) is most promising for strategic problem solving and to advance knowledge in the field. Their overview is followed by two chapters presenting the evolution of major theoretical perspectives and future theoretical foci in strategic management research and two chapters addressing a variety of important research methods (quantitative and qualitative) that have been used in strategy research and/or are promising for future research development.

In his chapter on organizational perspectives, Greve discusses institutional theory, network theory, learning theory, and resource dependence theory in relation to individuals, groups, and societal influences on organizations. He argues there is significant value in theories that recognize how organizational processes and human judgment affect organizational decisions. In her chapter on the economic perspectives, Helfat presents economic foci in two categories: (1) "homegrown" theories (such as the resource-based view of the firm [RBV] and ordinary and dynamic capabilities) that rely on economic logic but have been developed largely within strategic management and (2) theories (such as economies of scope, expanded to intertemporal economies of scope, and transaction cost economics) that originated in the economics field but have been developed in new directions within strategic management research. She identifies interesting directions for future research, in particular questions involving interactions between theories and new perspectives on the relationship of the firm to its external environment.

The chapter by Shaver focuses on quantitative research methods and proposes practices to advance the rigor and impact of future such research. He emphasizes the importance of rigorous, evidence-based research to aid decision-makers, and of endogeneity and causal identification. Yet he recognizes the tension between designing research for causal identification and research that examines meaningful strategy questions, and recommends pathways for researchers' pursuit of these often-conflicting research objectives. Graebner's chapter reviews a variety of qualitative research methods used in strategic management research and those with promise for future research. She emphasizes the high value of qualitative research methods for exploring and understanding novel phenomena, particularly through the richness and nuance of qualitative data. She reviews qualitative research approaches that are well established in the strategy literature, approaches that are growing in use, and approaches that are used rarely but hold promise. Her discussion of promising future uses of qualitative research methods includes the study of strategy during crisis and examination of strategic decision-making in the era of machine learning and artificial intelligence.

Corporate strategy

Part 2 focuses on the strategic choices firms make about the breadth and scope of their businesses, resource allocation across those businesses, and management across those businesses. In his lead chapter, Chang identifies major dimensions of corporate strategy, including diversification, mergers and acquisitions, vertical integration, divestitures and spin-offs, and internal control systems to share resources across business boundaries. He highlights research focused on the potential positive effects of synergy and work exploring the internal coordination costs of sharing, adapting, and transferring resources (Helfat and Eisenhardt, 2004) to creating that synergy. Chang ends his chapter with discussion of the need for research in diverse cultural and institutional environments, such as emerging markets and family ownership; the business group structure; and the growing influence of tech giants and platform owners.

The chapter by Ireland and Withers explains the importance and different attributes of acquisitive growth as a key element of firms' corporate strategies. The authors explore research on factors influencing firm growth, including managerial capabilities, corporate governance, and firms' environments, as well as research on outcomes of acquisitive growth and issues in managing such growth. Ireland and Withers offer suggestions for promising future research on resource orchestration to drive corporate growth and on the role of acquisitive growth during crisis as a means to drive economic recovery. In her chapter, Feldman reviews research on the contractionary strategies firms engage in as they restructure their corporate portfolios through divestitures, identifying four main categories of such research: drivers of divestiture decision-making, actors that undertake and influence those decisions, interdependencies between divestitures and other modes of corporate strategy, and the implications of divestiture for divested units. She calls for needed research on these contractionary actions, pointing to promising areas such as modularity in organizational design, how divesting firms reconfigure organizational resources and processes after divestiture, and the role of interorganizational knowledge and learning spillovers within the context of divestitures. Feldman notes that divestitures are increasingly used in practice as value-adding strategic tools rather than merely as solutions to corporate problems, and she urges scholars to view them as part of holistic corporate strategies over time rather than as discrete events (Feldman, 2020).

Strategic entrepreneurship and technology

In her lead chapter for Part 3, Eisenhardt describes strategic entrepreneurship as emphasizing "how technologies, industries, and firms emerge, and why some firms (but also technologies and industries) succeed while others do not." Her chapter focuses on strategy in nascent markets, which she characterizes as ambiguous, uncertain, and fast-paced—all of which can pose significant challenges. Eisenhardt argues that in such an environment, a focus on *strategy formation* is critical; thus she takes an organizational view that emphasizes "thinking" and "doing." She notes that current research has advanced from an emphasis on founding teams to one on managerial cognition and from organizational processes to learning processes. Among the many questions to be addressed in the future, she identifies promising avenues for research in "shaping strategies" that attempt to restructure industry architectures and in exploration of different types of nascent markets, such as ecosystems, platforms, and markets with strong institutional forces, such as energy and defense as well as the medical profession and universities.

In their chapter, Agarwal and Kim explore research on industry emergence, emphasizing insights from research on industry evolution as well as from research on founding and top management teams. They explain the developmental stages of nascent industries and research on transition among those stages, combining insights drawn from those research streams with those from work on founding individuals and teams to identify challenging and valuable *puzzles* they recommend as opportunities for future research contributions. Those puzzles include a shift in focus from human and relational capital to human enterprise, the role of product champions and intrepreneurs in the evolution of firms and industries, the effect of institutional constraints on human enterprise and the markets for talent, and how industries emerge in developing-country contexts. Furr addresses technology entrepreneurship, calling for increased focus on technology strategy as the use of technology to create and capture value. His chapter argues that the most powerful firms today are those with technology positions rather than our more common focus on firms' industry and resource positions. Furr examines contributions to our understanding of technology entrepreneurship from the literatures on technology management, industry evolution, entrepreneurship, and strategy in dynamic environments. He calls for attention to the innovation and commercialization process, using a more behavioral lens and analyzing how entrepreneurs learn and adapt in a new market. He ends his chapter with discussions of the need for a technology strategy view and a theory of uncertainty in relation to technology entrepreneurship.

Competitive and cooperative strategy

Part 4 addresses competitive and cooperative strategy, long recognized as core topics of importance in strategic management research. In their lead chapter, Child, Durand, and Lavie define competitive and cooperative strategies, as well as coopetitive strategy, in which firms simultaneously compete and cooperate with each other. The authors identify four new contexts for research on competitive and cooperative strategies: the rise of emerging economies, increasing protectionism and political intervention stemming from the dominance of politics over economics, technological disruption, and increasing social demands on business. Child *et al.* explore the implications of these new contexts for the study and understanding of competitive and cooperative strategy.

Durand addresses competitive advantage in his chapter, reviewing research that examines links between competitive advantage and firm performance. He identifies three factors that explain firms' ability to earn and maintain a competitive advantage: barriers to the mobility of their productive factors, resource heterogeneity, and differences in managerial analytical capabilities. He argues that understanding of the important relationship between competitive advantage and firm performance can be enhanced by future research that better defines both *industry* and *performance* and utilizes new research methods from his many suggestions. Lavie's chapter addresses the roles of alliances and networks in cooperative and coopetitive strategy. He explores existing work and suggests future research opportunities regarding key dimensions of alliances and networks, including motivation for alliance formation, mechanisms for alliance partner relations, value creation and capture in alliances, managing alliance portfolios, partnering experience and learning in alliances, and multiparty alliances and ecosystems, as well as structural embeddedness in networks. Among the many questions to be addressed in the future are the microfoundations of alliance relationships, failure of relational mechanisms, and the trade-off between routinization and flexibility in alliance management.

Global strategy

Global strategy is a topic, like strategic entrepreneurship, that has such importance that the Strategic Management Society dedicated a journal to it. Tallman and Cuervo-Cazurra (founding and current coeditors, respectively, of the *Global Strategy Journal*) provide an overview of global strategy, organized around firms' decisions regarding expansion (whether to internationalize, country selection, and entry mode selection), management of foreign activities (how to structure, coordinate, and control operations for efficiency), and capitalizing on the advantage(s) sought (building scale, learning, and arbitrage across activities and operations). The authors suggest that fruitful future research will address changes in the context of international firms, including the context of countries (globalization, emerging markets, and government activism), industries (digitalization, big data, and global value chains), and companies (global expertise, remote collaboration, and the gig economy). Tallman and Cuervo-Cazurra end their chapter with a call to address grand global changes in the environment as the ultimate measure of success of the field.

Westney's chapter explains key aspects of multinational corporations (MNCs), companies whose operations are distributed across countries, and demonstrates their importance in global strategy and cross-border management. Westney describes the strategic challenge for MNCs as "*where* to do *what* and *how*." She explains the considerations of global integration and local responsiveness (GI/LR) through the GI/LR framework and explores MNC capabilities for innovation and cross-border learning. She suggests four areas as important for future research: the changing balance of global integration and local responsiveness, management of regional strategies, cross-border learning in the face of increasing resistance to globalization, and MNC's responses to global challenges such as climate change. Williamson and Santos address the opportunities and challenges presented by emerging economies, for the leading domestic firms in those economies and multinationals evolving from those economies, as well as for the strategies of multinationals from developed economies. Williamson and Santos characterize emerging economies as those for which novel interactions between market and nonmarket forces are widespread across the economy, while the economy is undergoing continued transformation. This results in a dynamic business environment as well as an opportunity-rich yet also challenging research environment. Williamson and Santos identified many interesting avenues for research, concluding their chapter with discussion of opportunities with suggestions for topics, specific questions, and research methods that hold promise for future research value.

Strategic leadership

Strategic leadership is a core construct in the field of Strategic Management. In their lead chapter, Hambrick and Wowak focus on three key topics in strategic leadership: executive attributes (including executive personality and experiences as well as CEO tenure), managerial discretion (to meaningfully influence firm strategy and thus performance), and executive compensation (including implications of pay dispersion among members of the top management team [TMT]). The authors suggest future research that pairs or reconciles managerial discretion and managerial attributions (the extent to which observers such as stakeholders *believe* managers matter). Additional suggestions for fruitful future research include examination of the relationships between CEOs and their top management teams.

Wiersema and Hernsberger's chapter examines the roles of top management teams and their influence in strategic decision-making in firms. They discuss TMT composition—demographic attributes, relative homogeneity or heterogeneity, and TMT structure—and research examining relationships between these factors and firm outcomes. Limitations of past research and research challenges for scholars are identified and some solutions are proposed. Promising avenues for future research are also suggested, including work drawing on sociocognitive theories as well as exploration of influence within the TMT and of the relationship between the CEO and the TMT. In her chapter, Zhang focuses on the other critical player in strategic leadership of firms, the CEO, specifically on a topic of significant impact for firms and for the CEOs themselves; CEO succession. She explains the different types of CEO candidates and decision-making by boards of directors about CEO succession. Zhang notes recent developments in this stream of research, including more fine-grained categorization of the CEO succession event and its related processes, the issue of limited information for board decisions, the roles of board evaluation and social approval in CEO succession, and limited representation of female and ethnic-minority CEOs. Among the many questions to be addressed in the future, she suggests that attention be given to the postsuccession transition process, incentives for CEOs to leave office, and the postsuccession careers of departed CEOs.

Governance and Boards of Directors

Governance and Boards in organizations, the topic of Part 7, bears some relationship to the topics of strategic leadership in Part 6. In her lead chapter, Aguilera describes corporate governance as "choices on who makes decisions in organizations (who governs), how those decision-makers are monitored and rewarded, and how the created value is appropriated and distributed among the different interest groups" (i.e., stakeholders such as shareholders, employees, customers, and society more broadly). She reviews corporate governance research, with particular attention to areas that have received the most attention in recent years, such as shareholder engagement and international corporate governance (including business groups and comparative corporate governance), as well as internal and external corporate governance mechanisms. Additionally, she identifies three themes for future research: the purpose of the firm in light of the ongoing debate on shareholder versus stakeholder maximization; increasing demands for corporate social responsibility accountability through the UN Global Sustainability Goals and the Environmental, Social, and Governance (ESG) ratings; and the corporate governance of artificial intelligence (AI) in organizations.

Westphal and Garg's chapter examines the role of Boards of Directors, with attention to corporate Boards as well as the Boards of new ventures. The authors report that their comparison of recent work on Boards in those different contexts showed a "common emphasis on behavioral processes in the boardroom, in dyadic CEO-board interactions ... and in relations between directors and external constituents." They recommend that future research link these behavioral processes to issues facing corporations and new ventures, including Board diversity, the role of technology and innovation in strategic decision-making and investor communication, and differences across cultures and institutions. In his chapter, Connelly reviews the roles of different types of owners (including institutional investors, inside owners, blockholders, and state ownership) in the governance of the firm, describing ways in which those different types of owners affect firm-level outcomes. He identifies and discusses the status of five unresolved debates among governance scholars: the competitive influence of common shareholding, the costs and benefits of excess control, the consequences of share repurchases, the threat of short sellers, and the value-creating prospects of shareholder-nominated directors. Each of these debates offer rich opportunities for future work contributing to these research conversations.

Knowledge and innovation

Knowledge and innovation is an area of growing importance in the Strategic Management field. Volberda, Schneidmuller, and Zadeh's lead chapter for this Part suggests that trends in knowledge and innovation research demonstrate that innovation has been moving from an earlier path-dependent (and thus incremental and passive) view toward a more active managerial agency of innovation view. Their citation analysis of Cohen and Levinthal's (1990) paper on absorptive capacity, a key concept in knowledge and innovation, finds subsequent work to be clustered around five concepts: international knowledge transfer, organizational capabilities and learning, networks and ties, regional clusters, and open innovation. Volberda *et al.* observe that research on knowledge and innovation has been changing from a more macro view to one that integrates microfoundations and from a focus only on managerial cognition to include the role of managerial attention. The authors note that more research is needed in four areas critical to the advancement of knowledge and innovation: diverse audiences (as a source of legitimacy but also as a source of knowledge and innovative ideas), regulation and regulators (not as inhibitors but as instruments of innovation), misalignment capabilities (for firms to embrace inconsistencies in progress for change), and internal agents such as middle managers (as active agents in creating change as opposed to sources of organizational inertia).

Crossan, Vera, and Pathak's chapter emphasizes the importance of organizational learning, particularly in the face of "the grand challenges facing our world, requiring strategy to extend beyond organizations to society." Among the areas of research they recommend for further development are (1) exploration, exploitation, and ambidexterity; (2) the processes of organizational learning in relation to strategic renewal and agility; and emerging frontiers at the interface between the human and nonhuman aspects of organizational learning and strategy, including artificial intelligence. In his chapter, Howard addresses the management of innovation and knowledge sharing with an emphasis on how new knowledge is developed and shared within and between organizations. He highlights research developments in the areas of absorptive capacity, knowledge recombination, and the emergence of innovation networks and ecosystems. Howard identifies three important areas rich for future research contributions: socially constructed nature of knowledge, the continuing trend toward knowledge complexity, and the emergence of machine learning as a tool for technological innovation.

Strategy processes and practices

Strategy processes and strategy practices are both important but sometimes overlooked areas of the strategic management field. In their lead chapter, Burgelman, Floyd, Laamanen, Mantere, Vaara and Whittington describe the broad array of topics addressed in the strategy process and strategy practice arenas. The authors argue that strategy process research and strategy practice research are complementary to each other, and they call for future research that combines the insights of the two areas. Interestingly these areas are currently separate interest groups of the Strategic Management Society. Among the many interesting questions to be addressed in the future, Burgelman *et al.* focus on four topics of high promise: temporality and spaciality, actors and agency, cognition and emotionality, and language and meaning. Their chapter identifies numerous opportunities to combine theoretical perspectives and methodological approaches from the strategy process and strategy practice arenas to advance knowledge on these and other valuable topics that will contribute to the improvement of strategy processes and strategy practice.

The chapter by Reger and Pfarrer explores research on strategic decision-making and organizational actors, using a sociocognitive perspective to understand how organizational actors' cognition, attention, and other factors influence organizational actions and thus organizational outcomes. The authors note a shift over time toward more inclusion of social issues such as communication, from an earlier focus on cognition, and observe the resulting diversity of theoretical bases and methodological approaches that have characterized recent research on organizational actors, actions, and outcomes. The authors identify promising avenues for future research, including communication-based research on organizational actors, study of the strategic management process in an age of social media and rapidly increasing digitalization, and alternative views of rational cognition in organizational actors. In their chapter, Huy and Mack identify patterns in existing research that can have a limiting effect on the breadth and speed of knowledge development on strategic renewal and change. These include a relatively narrow research focus on phases of the strategic change process as well as particular actors in that process. They argue that broader integration of these fragmented research interests, as well as application of multiple theoretical lenses, are needed to advance research frontiers on strategic change and renewal, a critical area of strategic management research in light of ever-accelerating rates of change in organizations' environments. Huy and Mack note that more research is needed to examine the links between the formulation and execution phases of the strategic change process, as well as the organizational actors characterized as agents of change and recipients of change; the authors also call for future research that gives more nuanced attention to temporality issues in strategic change and renewal.

Microfoundations and behavioral strategy

Microfoundations and behavioral strategy has received increased attention in strategic management research over the past decade. In his lead chapter, Foss explains the contributions possible from research that links individual-level actions with collective-level (organizational or firm-level) constructs. The importance of this type of research is demonstrated by the fact that organizations do not make decisions, people do. Among the contributions of microfoundational approaches in strategy research is the emphasis on choice as a concept in strategic management. Foss discusses insights available from a microfoundational approach to future research in behavioral strategy, strategic human capital, and other relevant strategic management topics, and highlights needed advances in methodological approaches to realize the promise offered by a microfoundations approach.

Coff and Rickley examine the importance and different aspects of human capital in strategic management within firms, explaining how human capital contributes to firms' competitive advantage. They discuss the tension of human capital specificity, with benefits and liabilities of firm-specific human capital, and explore the challenges of assortative matching between firms and their workers who constitute the firm's human capital, including issues of human capital selection and compensation as well as employee mobility. Areas of promise for future research are identified in the chapter, such as the impact of human capital aggregation on firm-level capabilities and the role of artificial intelligence and other technologies in altering the dynamics of value creation and value capture in regard to human capital. Sirmon's chapter on the development and utilization of organizational capabilities explores the microfoundations of capability-related processes, focusing on the roles of agentic technology and identity-based community. Through this approach, he demonstrates how links between individual factors, process factors, and structural factors affecting organizational capability processes can lead to a richer understanding of these important organizational processes. Among the many issues that need to be addressed in future research, Sirmon highlights options for enlarging what is considered under the "individual" and "structural" components of research on organizational capabilities.

Critical factors affecting strategy in the future

Throughout this volume, authors have placed significant emphasis on and devoted a major share of their chapter's space to future research needs within the field of strategic management research. In addition to providing a forum for future-oriented thinking and research on topics in areas of growing importance and others of long-standing and continuing criticality to strategic management in firms, this book offers a closing Part focused on critical factors affecting strategy in the future. Although other topics could be included in this Part of the book, we are confident that the topics of artificial intelligence, sustainability strategy, the stakeholder perspective, and business model innovation strategy will be highly significant for the successful strategic management of firms in future years.

In his lead chapter for Part 11, Puranam discusses both digitalization and sustainability, together with issues surrounding deglobalization as well as diversity and inclusion. He considers the theoretical implications of research on these topics, including questions about the basic objective function of firms, the need for new tools and frameworks for industry analysis, and perhaps new conceptualizations of resources and capabilities in organizations as well as alternatives to hierarchy in collaborative relationships.

In their chapter on artificial intelligence (AI) in strategizing, von Krogh, Ben-Menahem, and Shrestha explain AI and its current and possible future applications in firms' strategizing processes, considering how machine learning and related technologies are likely to affect various aspects of firms' strategic analysis, strategy formulation, and strategy implementation processes. The authors offer insights into opportunities for AI's application to achieve competitive advantage, along with the challenges and risks AI poses for firms' strategizing processes. Barnett, Henriques, and Husted, in their chapter on sustainability strategy, explore a range of strategies that firms pursue in relation to the sustainability of our socioecological system; they offer guidance on how firms can shift to a more active and critically needed role in sustaining the environment. The authors also provide a framework for levels of problems faced as well as solutions undertaken, and urge strategic management scholars to engage in research to assist firms' commitments to the socioecological systems of which they are part. Barney and Mackey's chapter explores the question of how serious consideration of the stakeholder perspective would shift strategic management theories such as the resource-based view, positioning theory, and the theory of the firm, exploring the necessary changes in those theories to more fully account for stakeholders. They posit that integration of a stakeholder perspective would have implications for numerous areas of strategic management research, and discuss corporate diversification, mergers and acquisitions, and corporate governance as examples. In their chapter on business model innovation (BMI) strategy, Amit and Zott focus on the continuing need for entrepreneurial leaders to design and redesign, implement, and manage the systems of activities in order to achieve, sustain, and improve their firms' competitive advantage. They argue that having a BMI perspective is essential to achieving transformative innovation and offer guidance on developing BMI strategy for firms' value creation and capture.

Strategic Management Knowledge in a Non-Ergodic World

The field of strategic management has undergone significant development since its inception more than 40 years ago. The breadth and depth of strategic management knowledge are ably demonstrated by the chapters in this book, authored by some of the most highly respected scholars and the field's brightest minds. The work provided herein shows the richness and diversity of strategic management knowledge that scholars in the field and executives now possess. Yet the world in which organizations operate today is considerably different from at the inception of the field, because organizations exist in what Nobel Laureate Douglass North (1999) refers to as a non-ergodic world, which is in a state of continuous change. Of course, major disruptions such as the financial crisis of 2008 and the COVID-19 pandemic of 2020-2021 create substantial changes, even altering industries and creating significant disequilibria in the competitive landscape and the environment surrounding it. But even in "normal" times, change is continuous because of new technologies, sociopolitical trends and disruptions, and changing institutional environments (especially new formal institutions). Ahlstrom et al. (2020) refer to this as the New Normal. As a result, executives and firms are continuously trying to achieve new states of equilibrium, but these states represent points of dynamic equilibrium, which as the term suggests are temporary and will in fact change. Thus, although knowledge in the field has developed significantly and might be described by some as mature, it cannot remain static. We can celebrate our successful development, but it must continue in order to achieve negative entropy. That is why this book is focused not only on the state of the strategic management field but also on its future. As such, chapter authors often focused 40 to 50 percent of their effort on describing their vision of the future, identifying research questions that when addressed can help us better achieve that vision.

Kobrin (2017) predicted a prolonged period of political instability and economic uncertainty, trends that the global pandemic have only exacerbated. The instability and uncertainty have been derived partly or largely because of sociopolitical pressures. For example, economic and political uncertainties in certain regions of the world have led to an increasing number of immigrants entering or trying to enter more economically and politically stable regions, producing heightened immigration concerns. Additionally, the unequal distribution of the benefits from globalization, especially in developed economies, is becoming an increasingly important issue. These concerns have led to nationalistic pressures. These pressures and political instabilities in other regions have resulted in a growing number of institutional changes. A major review of prior research demonstrated that home and host country institutions have major effects on firms' international strategies (Xu *et al.*, 2021). Likewise, country institutional environments strongly influence industry environments, which in turn affect firm strategies in domestic markets (Hitt *et al.*, 2021). Likewise, major technological developments have changed industry boundaries, enabled the sharing of resources, and expanded competition, thereby having a significant effect on firms' strategies (Ahlstrom, 2010; Jones, 2019). Fareed Zakaria echoes Kobrin's warnings, suggesting that major disruptions (technological, economic, and political) are occurring more frequently. Zakaria states, "As the worst passes, we emerge into the 'dead cold light of tomorrow'" (2020: 3).

Zakaria's quote suggests significant challenges requiring perhaps new and substantial managerial capabilities, but opportunities exist as well. For example, the uncertainties allow managers and entrepreneurs to "shape" their opportunities using a proactive strategy rather than simply reacting to environmental demands. Managers can build hybrid organizations that integrate strategies, multiple logics, and structural forms (e.g., platform organizations) that help them to manage complex problems, integrate multiple stakeholders' demands, and orchestrate a diverse resource portfolio. This type of organization can provide the agility needed to design and implement innovative strategies, demonstrating the resilience needed in these challenging environments (Hitt, Arregle, and Holmes, 2021).

Building the knowledge necessary to understand the complexity of these strategic situations and thereby facilitate the practice of strategic management will likely require new and/or more complex theories. For example, Hoskisson and Harrison in the lead chapter in Part 1 suggest that stakeholder theory can help us better understand the strategic approaches required in the future. And in the last Part of the book, Barney and Mackey (Chapter 11.3) compare stakeholder theory to other prominent theories used in strategic management, demonstrating its superior value. Harrison (2020) argues that stakeholder theory and other more systemic theories are needed to identify the most effective strategic approaches to deal with the current and forthcoming challenges. Increasing emphases will be placed on innovative technologies such as artificial intelligence (von Krogh *et al.*, Chapter 11.1) and sustainability strategy (Barnett *et al.*, Chapter 11.2) to help firms deal with the environmental complexity, critical nature of climate changes, and the substantial demands of multiple important stakeholders. In turn, the new technological approaches, new organizational forms for delivery of goods and services, and new strategies will require business model innovations (Amit and Zott, Chapter 11.4). All of these issues and more are addressed in chapters in the last Part of this book. Although significant challenges and potential pitfalls exist, we believe that there is substantial opportunity to move our field forward as demonstrated by the content of the chapters in this book. We hope that you enjoy reading and learning about this exciting field and also hope that the book provides the base for your own contributions to the Strategic Management field's continued development.

References

Ahlstrom D. 2010. Innovation and growth: how business contributes to society. *Academy of Management Perspectives* 24(3): 11–24.

Ahlstrom D, Arregle J-L, Hitt MA, Qian G, Ma X, Faems D. 2020. Managing technological, sociopolitical, and institutional change in the New Normal. *Journal of Management Studies* 57(3): 411–437.

Cohen WM, Levinthal DA. 1990. Absorptive capacity: a new perspective on learning and innovation. *Administrative Science Quarterly* 35(1): 128-152.

Feldman ER. 2020. Corporate strategy: past, present, and future. *Strategic Management Review* 1(1): 179–206.

Harrison, JS. 2020. *Sustaining High Performance in Business.* Business Expert Press: New York, NY.

Helfat CE, Eisenhardt KM. 2004. Inter-temporal economies of scope, organizational modularity, and the dynamics of diversification. *Strategic Management Journal* 25(13): 1217–1232.

Hitt MA, Arregle J-L, Holmes RM Jr. 2021. Strategic management theory in a post-pandemic and non-ergodic world. *Journal of Management Studies* 58(1): 259-264.

Hitt MA, Sirmon DG, Li Y, Ghobadian A, Arregle J-L, Xu K. 2021. Institutions, industries, and entrepreneurial versus advantage-based strategies: how complex, nested environments affect strategic choice. *Journal of Management and Governance* 25(1): 147-188.

Hoskisson RE, Hitt MA, Wan WP, Yiu D. 1999. Swings of a pendulum: theory and research in strategic management. *Journal of Management* 25(3): 417–456.

Jones CI. 2019. Paul Romer: ideas, nonrivalry, and endogenous growth. *Scandinavian Journal of Economics* 121(3): 859–883.

Kobrin SJ. 2017. Bricks and mortar in a borderless world: globalization, the backlash, and the multinational enterprise. *Global Strategy Journal* 7(2): 159–171.

North DC. 1999. Dealing with a non-ergodic world: institutional economics, property rights, and the global environment. *Duke Environmental Law and Policy Forum* 10(1): 1–12.

Schendel DE, Hofer CW. 1979. *Strategic Management: A New View of Business Policy and Planning.* Little, Brown, and Company: Boston, MA.

Whittington R. 2019. *Opening Strategy: Professional Strategists and Practice Change, 1960 to Today.* Oxford University Press: Oxford, U.K.

Xu K, Hitt MA, Brock DM, Pisano V, Huang L. 2021. Country institutional environments and international strategy: review and analysis. *Journal of International Management* 27(1): https://m/science/article/abs/pii/S1075425320305834www.sciencedirect.co.

Zakaria F. 2020. *Ten Lessons for a Post-Pandemic World.* W. W. Norton: New York, NY.

PART 1

EVOLUTION OF
STRATEGIC MANAGEMENT RESEARCH

Robert E. Hoskisson and
Jeffrey S. Harrison, Leads

1.0

KEEP THE CONVERSATION GOING: THEORY AND METHOD IN STRATEGIC MANAGEMENT

Robert E. Hoskisson and Jeffrey S. Harrison

In 1993, Joseph Mahoney wrote an article published in the *Journal of Management Studies* titled "Strategic Management and Determinism: Sustaining the Conversation." He wrote the article to defend the field against calls for more deterministic research with strong theory using deductive logic, emphasizing empirical falsification (Camerer, 1985). He also warned against taking too seriously the idea that " 'research progress is a continuous expansion of knowledge involving the generation, refutation, and application of theories' (Montgomery, Wernerfelt, and Balakrishnan, 1989: 189)." These suggestions on the surface are what strategy scholars often think they are doing. However, Mahoney (1993) indicates that following these pronouncements too strictly could lead the field into a dilemma that others have described as the "normal science straitjacket" (Bettis, 1991; Daft and Lewin, 1990).

In finance, for example, there seems to be a dominant paradigm accepted and method employed, based on a view of the firm stemming from the work of Alchian and Demsetz (1972) and Jensen and Meckling (1976). They define the firm as a nexus of explicit contracts, which provides clear insights regarding for whom a firm should be managed. Because employees (through their wages), as well as customers and suppliers (through their prices), have explicit contracts, shareholders are the only ones who bear the cost of decisions (e.g., have residual contracts). As such, the firm should be governed to maximize shareholders' value. At the same time, because any change in total value can be measured by changes in the value of the shareholders' residual contract, the impact of decisions on stock prices can be used to evaluate the social consequences of decisions, such as a corporate investment, a new product, or a merger announcement. Hence, there is a proliferation of event studies in finance. But this leads to few citations from outside the fields of finance and economics. How often do you see strategic management citations in finance journals? It is a rarity.

Instead, Mahoney (1993) suggests that we pursue conversation because, as McCloskey (1985) argues, "good science is good conversation." Accordingly, Mahoney suggests advancement will come through "conversation" among strategic management scholars and with scholars in other disciplines, such as economics, sociology, psychology, and political science. In another paper, he uses the resource-based view of the firm as an example of how a field can advance theoretically and have an influence on other fields through the suggested "conversation" analogy (Mahoney and Pandian, 1992).

In retrospect, we think he was right and that our conversations in strategic management have led to significant advances in our field over the last 40 years. They have also allowed us to stay focused on our purpose of learning why some organizations outperform others and then conveying this knowledge to managers. For instance, the interest groups of the Strategic Management Society focus on topics of interest to strategic managers: Corporate Governance, Strategic Leadership, Corporate Strategy, Innovation, Strategic Entrepreneurship, and Global Strategy, among others. Inevitably, however, the conversation approach and the growing number of problems that strategic managers face leads to topic fragmentation and the need for integration of theories and methods in order to make better scientific progress (Durand, Grant, and Madsen, 2017). As seen in the four chapters following in this Part of the book, that conversation continues. A broad number of theories and methods, both inductive and deductive, have allowed the field to grow theoretically and empirically, and have a strong influence on other fields.

In 1999, Hoskisson, Hitt, Wan, and Yiu published an article focused on the history of theory and methods in strategic management titled "Theory and Research in Strategic Management: Swings of a Pendulum" (Hoskisson *et al.*, 1999). The article demonstrated how the field of strategic management began with an internal firm focus and then swung more toward the external environment of the firm, followed by another swing toward the internal resources of a firm. As the article was published over 20 years ago, for this introduction we intend to provide a succinct update of some of the "swings of the pendulum" in research and methods that have happened since, and point to the future where we think strategic management scholars can make the most contributions to advancing theory, method and practice.

Historical Background

Hoskisson *et al.* (1999) provides the background and illustrates the various historical emphases in the field using the metaphor of swings of a pendulum. In the early periods, works by Ansoff (1965) and Andrews (1971), among others, emphasized the normative aspect of business knowledge and were chiefly interested in identifying and developing "best practices" that were useful for managers and students. The most appropriate method for accomplishing this objective was inductive, focused on in-depth case studies of single firms or industries. Case studies have remained the main pedagogical tool for strategy courses, but also a prominent tool for strategy process research and inductive theory development.

During the next developmental period, strategic management departed significantly both theoretically and methodologically from the early period and moved toward industrial organization economics, especially as Porter's (1980) book became popular. With Porter's (1981) exposition for a strategy and management audience, this swing largely changed strategy research from inductive case studies to deductive, large-scale statistical analyses using cluster analysis to find strategic groups within an industry (Hatten, Schendel, and Cooper, 1978) or to validate scientific hypotheses, based on models abstracted from the structure-conduct-performance (S-C-P) paradigm (Porter, 1981).

The field then swung back toward an intermediate position, using theories from organizational economics, specifically transaction cost economics (Williamson, 1975, 1985) and agency theory (Fama, 1980; Jensen and Meckling, 1976). This move was important because it shifted the field away from the industry or strategic group-level emphasis of the S-C-P paradigm and toward a firm level of analysis, which is more in line with firm-level strategies and associated implementation. Transaction cost economies (TCE) provided the background for studies about diversification strategy and the multidivisional form (M-form) of organization (Hill and Hoskisson, 1987), hybrid forms of organization (i.e., joint ventures) (Hennart, 1988), and international strategy (Buckley and Casson, 1981) to provide significant insights for the field. Likewise, agency theory was employed and fostered studies on corporate governance and boards of directors (Zahra and Pearce, 1989), executive compensation (Tosi and Gomez-Mejia, 1989), and the market for corporate control (Kosnik, 1990).

The resource-based view (RBV) of the firm was an important swing of the pendulum back toward the roots of strategic management. RBV focuses on internal resources and capabilities that lead to a competitive advantage that is potentially sustainable (i.e., cannot be replicated easily). The significance of the RBV was recognized in 1994 when Birger Wernerfelt's (1984) "A Resource-Based View of the Firm" was selected as the best paper published in the *Strategic Management Journal* within the previous ten years. In 1991, Barney presented a more concrete and comprehensive framework to identify the characteristics firm resources need in order to generate sustainable competitive advantage. Four criteria were proposed to assess the economic implications of the resources: value, rareness, inimitability, and nonsubstitutability. Although the RBV is applied theoretically in many studies using regression analysis, one of the problems is finding a method beyond case studies to examine firm idiosyncrasies that lead to better performance. As Hansen, Perry, and Reese note, "A statistically significant, positive association between a resource and performance in a study using regression analysis indicates that, on average, the more of that resource a firm possesses, the more positive the economic performance of that firm. Such a result provides evidence that a relationship exists between a resource and performance, and it informs us about the confidence we can have in the relationship existing across repeated samples (Cohen and Cohen, 1983). However, no comment can be made as to a specific probability that such a relationship exists in a given firm" (2004: 1283). As such, Hansen *et al.* (2004) propose Bayesian analysis to provide a solution, and although there are some studies (e.g., Mackey, Barney and Dotson, 2017), the method has not been widely applied in RBV studies.

Where can strategic management scholars contribute the most?

The field of strategic management examines how firms can formulate and implement strategies that lead to positive and sustained firm performance. So what phenomena should we study to accomplish this objective? Externally we have disciplines such as economics where there is no theory of the firm; it examines industry-level phenomena with the objective of setting policy that makes firms within the industry more competitive, and so that no firm can derive monopoly profits. Porter (1980) turned this paradigm on its head and asked how a firm can manage the competitive forces in its industry to gain market power and earn above-normal economic profits while avoiding the scrutiny of regulators. But still this is an external view of the firm, where the firm is dependent on external forces and derives the generic strategies of differentiation or low-cost leadership to manage these forces the best it can.

On the other hand, the RBV suggests that idiosyncratic resources and capabilities of the firm with the four essential attributes allow the firm to maintain sustainable profits. Furthermore, dynamic capabilities should allow the firm to maintain sustainable profits as the environment changes. As Helfat *et al.* suggest, "To survive and prosper under conditions of change, firms must develop the 'dynamic capabilities' to create, extend, and modify the ways in which they operate" (2007: 1). As such, dynamic capabilities may allow the firm to maintain Barney's (1991) four criteria, notwithstanding changes in the environment.

Although the RBV and the dynamic capabilities paradigm are at the heart of strategic management (that is, they are firm-level phenomena that pertain directly to firm performance and sustained competitive advantage), their usefulness as tools in developing strategies is limited by the weaknesses noted previously. Perhaps it is time to focus even more on the middle of the pendulum. Developing theories and addressing topics at the intersection of the environment and the firm should allow strategic management to make more progress and address more significant problems confronting the firm. As such, "the swing of the pendulum" that we review in the remaining pages focuses on topics at the intersection of the inside and the outside. In doing so, we consider some of the topics developed by Helfat (2021) from the economics perspective and by Greve (2021) on the organizational side.

Economics-Oriented Strategic Management Theory and Method at the Intersection

Because we have already touched on the strategies associated with industrial organization (IO) economics (e.g., Porter, 1980), we elaborate on the work in strategic groups and competitive dynamics a little more, even though it is, on the face, associated with IO economics. In doing so, we briefly evaluate some of the same top-ics found in the chapter by Helfat (2021). The aim of these sections is to point to topics that future research might address.

Strategic groups and competitive dynamics research

One of the reasons that strategic groups research was interesting to strategic man-agement scholars was that it showed that firms could be placed in strategic groups and that a firm's membership based on strategic characteristics contributed to a par-ticular firm's performance. Barney and Hoskisson (1990), however, showed that strategic groups could be a statistical artifact because most research at the time used cluster analysis to place firms in groups (McGee and Thomas, 1986). Cluster analysis, whether the groups are meaningful or not, divides firms into groups based on the input variables used.

The more interesting research on strategic groups, however, was produced through the lens of managerial or customer perceptions (Gur and Greckhamer, 2019). Early research in this area found that managers in the Scottish knitwear industry acted upon cognitive maps of their industry that constrained their strategic focus and rivals' com-petitive responses (Porac *et al.*, 1995). Many others identified strategic groups based on managerial perceptions (e.g., Reger and Huff, 1993). Because perception is reality, these approaches are likely to be more useful than strategic groups of rivals identified by cluster analysis of archival data. Likewise, close competitors have been identified by the nature and position of their approaches to customer preferences (Cooper and Inoue, 1996); this literature has mostly come from marketing.

Developing from this literature have been examinations of competitive dynamics, which analyze the nature of competitive interactions by rivals, asking questions about when a competitor will react to a significant competitive move (such as an acqui-sition) or a more tactical move (such as a change in price) (Chen, 1996; Chen and Miller, 2012). This area has also applied traditional game theory, and contributions continue (Menon and Yao, 2017). Chen, Su, and Tsai (2007) take a further step by suggesting that managerial perceptions of competitor awareness, motivation, and the capabilities of a rival, as well as their own, also contribute to tension leading to rival-rous action.

Interestingly, the most cutting-edge research both in strategic groups and compet-itive dynamics comes from a swing of the pendulum toward managerial cognitions and perceptions, as well as competitive actions and reactions (inside) from archival analysis to form strategic groups (outside) through formal game theory models. The exciting thing about this research is its reach into areas such as identifying compe-tition among start-up firms (Ireland, Hitt, and Sirmon, 2003) and even in under-standing corporate governance actions (Connelly, Shi, Hoskisson, and Ketchen, 2019). The work on managerial cognitions and perceptions indicates a shift inward. In the future, researchers might also consider moving outward in examining how institutional norms and industry conditions influence the perceptions of decision-makers and their decisions regarding the competitive tactics their firms pursue.

Institutional economics, market institutions, and government

North (1990) discussed the importance of formal and informal market institutions that facilitate business transactions. Countries with weak market institutions tend to have a lack of transparency in economic reporting, often associated with weak equity markets and weak legal contract law that leads to insecure property rights and corruption. As such, firms tend to internalize transactions into a single firm or business group where relationships among transacting parties are based on trust. In this regard, Wan and Hoskisson (2003) found that firms in Western European countries with relatively less-developed market institutions experienced a positive relationship between diversification and performance, whereas diversification was negatively related to performance in countries with more developed market institutions.

More specifically, Kim and Hoskisson (2015) argue that strong country institutional environments and factor markets allow firms to gain stronger resource bases. For instance, in a South Korean context, Kim, Hoskisson, and Lee (2015) found that pursuing an internationalization strategy into economies that were less developed than South Korea was positively related to performance, but internationalization into more developed countries than South Korea produced a negative relationship to performance early on and then a positive relationship later as the South Korean firm learned to adapt. Similarly, in India, Ramaswamy, Purkayastha, and Petitt (2017) found that business group–unrelated diversification was positively related to performance, but as market-related reforms took root, unrelated diversification led to lower performance and related diversification improved performance. This latter study suggests that as market institutions improve, related diversification outperforms unrelated diversification, as Rumelt (1974) found in his classic study in the United States. This suggests that factor markets and market institutions lead to better resource formation, thus an environmental contingency to the RBV. These studies and others from emerging economies provide a clear picture of the necessity to tie the RBV to an environmental context.

When countries have weak market institutions, governments often substitute as a source of resource provision. As such, government political connections are especially pertinent in emerging economies such as China. Research finds that networks such as business groups can facilitate entrepreneurial enterprise development and internationalization (Kim, Kim, and Hoskisson, 2010). However, in China, political connectedness allows a firm to survive and thrive better than a firm that only has a strong network (Burt and Opper, 2020). But once a firm seeks to expand overseas, such domestic political resources are less helpful (Guillen, 2000), and success requires firms to develop resources and capabilities that are comparable to those employed by other firms in the host country receiving the foreign direct investment (Kim and Hoskisson, 2015). Because there is so much variance across nations, the influence of government structures and policies on firm resource acquisition and the effectiveness of various strategies holds tremendous potential for additional research.

Transaction cost economics, the RBV, and property rights

Continuing with research at the intersection, we examine a few representative studies on the integration of transaction cost economics, property rights theory, and the RBV. Vertical integration is one of the topics in TCE, suggesting that transaction costs determine whether a firm uses an organization or market to make or buy needed resources. Research suggests that vertical integration is not only determined by TCE but may also be the product of a firm seeking to keep its capabilities tacit (Argyres, 1996). Diversification strategy also can be determined by transaction costs. However, the type and direction of diversification might be determined by technological resources and capabilities (Silverman, 1999) in addition to transaction costs. Chi (1994) also integrates TCE and the RBV to suggest when an acquisition versus a joint venture will take place to meet the criteria established for both theories when trading strategic assets that are less tradeable, as defined by the RBV.

Establishing property rights to firm assets and managing them appropriately can save costs and add to value beyond what the resources provide. In this way, governance can also be a capability that adds value to the firm (Foss and Foss, 2005). Likewise, Kim and Mahoney (2010) suggest that creating bundles of property rights associated with firm resources allows us to gain a better understanding of dynamic capabilities because the firm becomes a nexus of incomplete contracts. As noted above, dynamic capabilities allow resources and capabilities to evolve, overcoming the static nature of the RBV. For instance, firm human capital cannot be owned by the firm, nor does its human capital have residual claimant status. But there is a co-specialized interaction between the firm and specialized human capital, which is continuously reconfigured to more fully capture economic value created from both sides (Coff, 1999). "Defining the firm as a nexus of *incomplete* contracts enables this process of continuous adaptation," according to Kim and Mahoney (2010: 819).

In the future, researchers may want to delve into decision-makers' perceptions of the completeness of their contracts to predict their behavior. For example, a customer firm may perceive that its contract with a focal firm is incomplete, and expect additional compensation in the form of added services or future discounts, whereas the focal firm may consider that the contracted transactions represent the totality of their relationship with the customer. This sort of analysis is closely tied to property rights. The literature on reciprocity between stakeholders more generally could inform this research (Bosse, Phillips, and Harrison, 2009; Bridoux and Stoelhorst, 2014).

Agency theory, behavioral agency theory, stakeholder theory, and other perspectives

As suggested earlier, agency theory has defined the firm as a nexus of explicit contracts, except for the shareholders who take on risk with an incomplete contract as the residual claimants. Agency theory also suggests that because managers cannot diversify their wealth like shareholders can, they are naturally risk averse. Accordingly, governance devices are established to monitor and incentivize managers through executive compensation, which boards of directors employ to encourage adequate managerial risk taking (Fama and Jensen, 1983).

However, risk taking is influenced by other factors besides governance structures. Wiseman and Gomez-Mejia (1998) coined the term *behavioral agency theory* and integrated agency theory with prospect theory. They suggest that positive agency theory is deficient in that managers are more loss averse than risk averse. Since being established, behavioral agency theory has spawned a number of studies. For example, Martin, Wiseman, and Gomez-Mejia (2016) found that CEOs with significant option wealth pursue long-term investments. But with a large number of recently granted options, the CEO is likely to implement a short-term strategy to gain wealth more rapidly. When the firm has significant retained earnings (slack or wealth that can be lost by strategic action), the long-term and short-term effects are both reduced. Using this information, boards can anticipate strategic actions by CEOs and seek to monitor potential negative consequences. Moreover, Pepper and Gore (2015) updated the theory by incorporating other behavioral aspects, such as leader motivation and goal setting, in examining influences on executive compensation. Research using this stream of theory can foster future research that will allow predictions more helpful to managers and governance actors.

Stakeholder theory is gaining attention by incorporating more stakeholder involvement in value creation and value capture (Amis, Barney, Mahoney, and Wang, 2020). One of the most-cited papers combining stakeholder theory and the RBV (Harrison, Bosse, and Phillips, 2010) suggests that treating stakeholders particularly well leads to competitive advantage. More recently, Jones, Harrison, and Felps (2018) apply the standard RBV criteria to the relationships that firms develop with stakeholders when they treat them very well to demonstrate that such "close relationships" can lead to sustainable competitive advantage. That is, those relationships are valuable, rare, nonsubstitutable, and extremely difficult to imitate. Also, Hoskisson, Gambeta, Green, and Li (2018) integrate stakeholder theory and the RBV by seeking to overcome a dilemma in the RBV. They discuss how to incentivize stakeholders to make firm-specific investments (FSIs, those not transferable to other firms), which is a central issue in the RBV. In particular, their model provides suggestions regarding how the firms ensure that such investment by stakeholders can receive a return from their investment without worry about being held hostage or having their investments appropriated by the firm.

Accordingly, stakeholder theory extends the RBV to creating competitive advantage through relationships both inside (e.g., employee stakeholders) as well as outside (through supplier and customer stakeholders). This notion is similar to what Dyer and Singh (1998) have termed "the relational view of the firm," where firms create "relation-specific assets" through cooperative agreements such as joint ventures. The stakeholder conceptualization, however, moves the pendulum closer to outside the firm with relationship-specific assets, and simultaneously makes governance more difficult because we move from explicit contracts as assumed by agency theory with insiders and outsiders to evolving incomplete contracts (Barney, 2018). Stakeholder theory also focuses on the goals that firms set, as explained in the next section on organization-oriented strategic management research. However, we believe there is a need for more research integrating stakeholder theory into other strategic management topics, such as corporate governance, cooperative strategies, strategic human capital, global strategy, and strategy process. Indeed, stakeholder theory provides a plausible alternative to agency theory, and can be applied everywhere that theory has been applied.

Evolutionary economics and Penrosian economics

Joseph Schumpeter (1911, 1950) is the father of Austrian economics. He created the theory of economic development and established the idea that "creative destruction" is the primary way that economic growth and progress are advanced. However, there was an intellectual battle with modeling and equilibrium using neoclassical theory based on perfect competition, and Schumpeter's theory lost that battle as the driving theory of economic thought. Schumpeter's model was based on disequilibrium, and he provided no modeling solution, so the neoclassical view prevailed, apparently because of its modeling properties (Winter, 2012). But a resurgence of Austrian economics has taken place in association with the RBV and evolutionary economics (Nelson and Winter, 1982; Nelson, 2012). Evolutionary economics has permeated both strategy (Jacobson, 1992) and strategic entrepreneurship (Keyhani, Lévesque, and Madhok, 2015) because of the focus on evolution through innovation and potential "Ricardian rents" (Barney and Arikan, 2001). Interestingly, a popular book in strategy by Clayton Christiansen (1997), *The Innovator's Dilemma: When New Technologies Cause Great Firms to Fail*, is inherently about creative destruction even though it did not cite Schumpeter. However, these innovations are driven by entrepreneurs who create a new business (Kirchoff, 1991) or by top leaders (CEOs) who innovate by marshaling firm resources to exploit new opportunities (Castanias and Helfat, 1991).

Also on the economic front, Edith Penrose's (1959) book titled *The Theory of the Growth of the Firm* suggested that firms could be modeled individually as a simple production function rather than traditional economic models that assumed firms observe supply and demand conditions in the market and translate these into levels of production that maximize profits. Furthermore, she assumed that the growth of the firm was limited by productive opportunities that exist under the administrative framework of an organization and a firm's bundle of productive resources to address these opportunities. Additionally, she observed that there are a variety of entrepreneurial skills, such as raising capital, risk-taking ambition, and superior decision-making judgment. A number of scholars have written about the association of Penrose's work to the resource-based view of the firm (Rugman and Verbeke, 2002), especially with regard to using firm resources to diversify into new businesses (Hansen *et al.* 2004) and when resources have changed and require business divestment (Vidal and Mitchell, 2018). Similar to evolutionary economics, Penrosian opportunity exploration is driven by managers who head the "administrative framework." Scholars may find some interesting topics for future research by integrating the work of Penrose with the tenets of Austrian economics.

Organization-Oriented Strategic Management Theory at the Intersection

Our main point thus far is that moving more internally oriented research outward and externally oriented research inward is likely to bring the most fruitful explanations of phenomena pertinent to the strategic management domain. In this section we highlight topics that had an inward organizational focus at the inception of the strategy field but have benefited from shifting the pendulum toward the outside, including some mentioned in the chapter by Greve (2021). What is interesting, of course, is that many of the topics that Helfat's (2021) chapter (generally an outward topic) discusses are also discussed by Greve's (2021) chapter (generally an inward topic). This fact alone is evidence of movement toward the middle of the pendulum.

Person, team, situation fit

Over the years there has been a significant amount of research regarding the CEO and top management team (TMT) fit with the organization and strategy of the firm. For instance, Michel and Hambrick (1992) found that a number of top management team characteristics, such as long tenure, fit the type of diversification strategy being pursued. In particular, when there is interdependence between the divisions, such as in vertical integration or related diversification, long tenure in the TMT fosters better performance. Likewise, Chen and Hambrick (2012) found that when a significant turnaround is required, a successor CEO with operations or accounting experience to emphasize cost control and efficiency is more likely to lead to a successful strategic change than one with marketing (or output) experience. However, Blettner, Chaddad, and Bettis (2012) argued that the complexity of firm performance is not as simple as many studies have suggested. Blettner *et al.* (2012) argue that there are a number of variables that fit into a complex system to predict performance—and sometimes the variables are loosely fitting and sometimes they are closely knit together, making the overall performance system more complex. As such, more research is needed from a causal system perspective to determine the appropriate action(s) needed.

Organizational structure

Organizational structure—reflected in the numbers and types of departments or groups within an organization as well as lines of communication, decision-making, and reporting—was a central topic in the early strategic management literature (Chandler, 1962; Galbraith and Nathanson, 1979). Based on a historical study of 70 US firms, Chandler hypothesized that the primary influence on a firm's structure is its growth strategy, and that firms do not significantly change their structures unless prompted to do so due to inefficiency. His internally focused sequence of events involves creation of a new strategy that makes the existing structure inefficient, followed by a decline in performance that prompts adjustments to structure that then results in improved performance. This logic led to a number of studies of strategy, structure, and economic performance. One of the most important was by Rumelt (1974), who is best known for classifying and testing the performance implications of various types of diversification strategies, but his research also provides results on structures. He found, "The data gave strong support for Chandler's proposition that 'structure follows strategy,' but forced the addition of 'structure also follows fashion' " (149). In this statement we find evidence of an outward or institutional influence on structures.

Rumelt (1974) also found that firms with product-division structures grew faster, but he did not specifically test the idea that a strategy-structure fit is associated with higher performance. However, others did test this idea. For example, Hoskisson (1987) found that adoption of a multidivisional structure increased performance for unrelated diversifiers but decreased performance for vertically integrated firms (see also Hoskisson, Harrison, and Dubofsky, 1991).

Aupperle, Acar, and Mukherjee (2014) published a large-scale longitudinal study that examined the same firms that Chandler (1962) included. Aupperle *et al.* studied the changes these firms made to their structures as their strategies evolved. They found evidence of mismatch between strategy and structure, followed by changes to the structure, such that strategy and structure were matched again. Surprisingly, they found that mismatched firms generally had higher financial performance than firms that matched structure to strategy. This is due, perhaps, to recent or future-oriented structural adaptations necessary to deal with the tremendous shifts in the external environment that have made traditional structures less valuable.

As research moved into the 21st century, strategic management scholars began to recognize that traditionally defined organizational structures were no longer as viable in a tumultuous and global organizational environment (Hitt, Keats, and DeMarie, 1998; Keats and O'Neill, 2001). Previously, Jack Welch, longtime CEO of General Electric, was famously known for describing what he called a "boundaryless" organization based on principles of flexibility and adaptability (Ashkenas, Ulrich, Jick, and Kerr, 2002). Managing a boundaryless organization means leveraging resources, and this sort of management requires learning, sharing, and redeploying knowledge, and bundling both intellectual and physical assets in new ways. Hitt *et al.* (1998) refer to managing the firm as "bundles of assets." The people in this sort of organization work on projects and share information and resources broadly across the organization as well as with stakeholders outside of traditional firm boundaries. Today the most extreme forms of this organization tend to be internet based. Although many are smaller start-ups, these characteristics are also found in larger, platform-based firms such as Amazon, Apple, Uber, and Facebook.

The realities of a turbulent global environment—and firms' attempts to structure work to create more flexibility, given the instability—enhanced the popularity of network theory, cooperative strategies, and industrial districts (e.g., Silicon Valley). However, these topics deal with how a firm structures its relationships with external stakeholders. There is little research regarding how to actually structure and manage the internal firm to take advantage of changes in the external environment. For example, although organization structures are still an important topic in many of the mainstream strategic management textbooks (e.g., Harrison and St. John, 2013; Hitt, Ireland, and Hoskisson, 2020), these discussions continue to incorporate much of the very early literature on the topic. Although we progress in understanding "platform" strategies and how firms can use a common platform to take advantage of network effects and complementors (McIntyre and Srinivasan, 2017), such internet-based organization structures seem to have unique characteristics that make it difficult to describe them in terms that can apply across the population of firms. As Greve (2021) points out, companies can be reorganized based on an institutional logic as we observe within industries, and studying this sort of phenomenon is likely to result in theoretically rich and managerially useful findings.

In this research stream, a concerted effort is needed to find patterns in the data—to identify characteristics upon which the newer structural forms can be classified, and match these identifying characteristics to a variety of external contexts to determine the best way to produce outcomes such as innovation, customer satisfaction, employee satisfaction, and ultimately higher performance. Many research areas relevant to strategic management provide a foundation for this area of inquiry, to include network theory, industry structure, competitive dynamics, cooperative strategies, team production, corporate governance, top management teams, and organizational culture, among others.

Adaptation, enactment, and nonmarket strategies

Greve (2021) suggests that how organizations develop strategies to adapt to their environment is a central question in organization theory. While this deterministic view was popular during the early development of the strategy field, we soon realized that the relationship between a firm and its environment is highly interactive, and that firms can enact (i.e., influence) their environments through strategic actions (Bourgeois, 1984; Smircich and Stubbart, 1985). This move puts the pendulum square in the middle between internal and external. As Greve (2021: 44) put it, "The field of strategy appears to be making a gradual transition in research interest from the formation and understanding of environments, through environmental effects on the organization, to organizational interaction with the environment." In this light, network theory and learning theory both deal with the important subject of how firms use their interorganizational network to learn as they innovate to develop new products and services, new technologies and structures, and better ways to approach markets (Greve, 2009; Ingram and Baum, 1997; Jain, 2013).

Greve's chapter (2021) also suggests that one of the most important topics in this area of the strategy literature is societal groups, including governments, and their influence on strategic decisions. Mass media outlets, social media, nongovernmental organizations (NGOs), special interest groups, government regulators, and other nonmarket stakeholders can have a huge impact on firm strategies, especially when they represent a popular social movement such as sustainability or equal treatment and rights for people of all genders, races, religions, and national origins. From a strategic perspective, what seems most valuable is helping firms learn how to genuinely manage these influences to the advantage of the firm, or at least to reduce or eliminate harm. Approaches highlighted by Greve include evading regulation (Funk and Hirschman, 2014), lobbying (Rudy and Johnson, 2016), or use of social media to influence external stakeholders (Yue, Wang, and Yang, 2019).

Researchers are barely scratching the surface of what are often called *nonmarket strategies*. Mellahi, Frynas, Sun, and Siegel (2016) did a comprehensive review of the nonmarket literature and developed a multitheoretic framework to help advance research. The moral underpinning of nonmarket strategy is among the most interesting topics. Some of these strategies, such as engaging in corporate social responsibility or extolling a firm's virtues to pacify societal interests, are less controversial. Yet others have what might be called a dark side. For example, Amazon lobbied legislators in Washington State (where the company is headquartered) to make noncompete clauses enforceable. Also, after a public relations debacle concerning a harmful chemical used in apple orchards, agricultural firms and their representative groups persuaded several states to pass laws that restrict speech disparaging agricultural practices (Sutton and Bosse, 2019). Of course, these sorts of actions are risky because they can be exposed by social media. The tradeoffs between the risk of damaging a reputation through such actions and the financial payoffs if the nonmarket strategy is successful seem to be a fruitful research area. How far can a firm go in manipulating the societal and political environments before any positive performance benefits are exceeded by reputational damage, which reduces firm legitimacy and may also reduce firm performance?

Organizational goals

Goal setting has traditionally been considered an internal process, albeit one that is influenced by the external environment (Schendel and Hofer, 1979: 14; Smith, Locke, and Barry, 1990). As Greve (2021) noted, research on goals falls into three general categories: goals related to profitability, managerial preferences, and societal or stakeholder benefit. In strategic management, and in many corporations, the most widely accepted superordinate goal has been to increase profits for the welfare of the shareholders—a norm called *shareholder primacy* (Rönnegard and Smith, 2019). This norm has driven much of the research in strategic management. In contrast is the perspective that the firm exists to satisfy the interests of a broad group of stakeholders— the *stakeholder perspective* briefly explored in the previous section.

The debate between shareholder primacy and the stakeholder perspective predates the formation of the strategic management field (Harrison, Phillips, and Freeman, 2020). In the 1930s, Adolph Berle and Merrick Dodd debated it, with Berle arguing for shareholder primacy and Dodd representing a broader stakeholder perspective. Berle conceded later that Dodd had won the debate (Berle, 1954). However, the pendulum shifted in the other direction in the 1970s as free market economists at the University of Chicago, including Milton Friedman, led an effort to put profits at the center of top executive goal setting (Harrison *et al.*, 2020). Shareholder primacy was reinforced by agency theory and the argument that managers serve as agents of the shareholders, who are the principals of the firm (Jensen and Meckling, 1976). Strategic management scholars increasingly embraced both agency theory and shareholder primacy. Furthermore, the doctrine became dogma in many business organizations (Rönnegard and Smith, 2019).

In spite of the tremendous popularity of shareholder primacy among scholars and business executives, there is a strong shift underway toward the stakeholder perspective. Pertinent to our discussion here, much of the current movement can be explained by shifting societal interests. The stakeholder perspective is consistent with the global movement toward corporate accountability associated with the environment, society, and governance (ESG). Additionally, scholars have found substantial evidence that firms pursuing goals consistent with serving the interests of a broad group of stakeholders have higher, not lower, financial performance (i.e., Choi and Wang, 2009; Henisz, Dorobantu, and Nartey, 2014; Hillman and Keim, 2001), which is appealing to strategy scholars. Also, in an important development, Barney (2018) argued that resource-based theory will not work under an assumption of shareholder primacy. Barney and Mackey's chapter (2021) extended this argument further in a later chapter herein. In addition, in 2019, members of the Business Roundtable, a large group of top US CEOs, signed a statement declaring that the purpose of a corporation is to serve its primary stakeholders, including employees, customers, suppliers, communities, and the shareholders (Harrison *et al.*, 2020). Moving forward, there is a great deal of work to do in strategic management to reconcile existing theories and research to a new perspective that is not shareholder centric. Whether societal pressure reinforces this approach will be interesting to see.

A Note on Empirical Methods in Strategic Management

All of the promising research topics identified in the previous sections require rigorous theoretical development, but empirical research is also necessary. Interestingly, in Hatten's (1979) review of quantitative research methods in strategic management, he observed, "Quantitative research methods have had little impact on Business Policy, so far" (448). So much has changed since then. In the top strategy journals, empirical papers that use quantitative methods significantly outnumber those using qualitative methods. Nonetheless, rigorous qualitative methods are equally as important, especially for the development of new integrative theories and perspectives. The qualitative methods and quantitative methods are well explained by Graebner's (2021) and Shaver's (2021) chapters in this Part of the book.

Extending the Conversation through Theoretical Integration

We began this chapter by highlighting the importance of an open conversation in the field of strategic management, and avoiding widespread adoption of a particular paradigm that, like a straitjacket, could stifle forward progress. We also reviewed the notion that the field, in its first few decades, shifted back and forth from an internal organizational focus to an external environmental focus. The most meaningful research in the future will be at the middle of the pendulum—basically, research that relies on and integrates multiple theoretical perspectives. In particular, we view that strategic management is about problems that top managers face; thus, the best approach will be to integrate theories focused on understanding and solving the thorniest problems that managers experience to sustain their competitive advantage (Nickerson, Yen, and Mahoney, 2012). The best way to tackle problems is to have a conversation with diverse disciplines and theories relevant to these problems. As a result, continued fragmentation is likely in the field as noted previously (Durand *et al.*, 2017). However, the conversation approach focused on strategic problem solving has provided the field with progress and influence, both with other fields and with strategic managers. However, we see two other possibilities for moving forward.

First, researchers may adopt a theoretical perspective that, by its nature, is able to incorporate and even integrate multiple other theoretical perspectives (e.g., Blettner *et al.* 2012). For example, Harrison (2020) uses systems theory to integrate the essential concepts from industrial organization economics, resource-based theory, and stakeholder theory into a useful model for formulating strategy. He models the firm as a value-creating system that relies on its stakeholder network (internal and external stakeholders) to obtain and develop resources within the context of an external environment. He applies a variety of internal and external tools to diagnose the firm's system and find the weak area or areas that constrain the creation of additional value in the entire system. Harrison bases this notion on the systems theory idea that it is not the total sum of resources that restricts the creation of more value, but the scarcest resource (Liebig, 1840). Strategies to address weaknesses are formulated based on a variety of internal and external approaches, and using data collected during the diagnostic process. Harrison argues that many managers instinctively use a decision-making process that shares similarities with his model, and this accounts for many of the firms that have sustained high performance even without possessing a valuable resource that is rare and difficult to imitate. As this example suggests, we may create a larger paradigm that allows for integration at the intersection of the internal firm view and external environmental conditions.

Another way forward is to establish norms within research schools regarding hiring faculty with diverse theoretical foundations. In the early years of the field, many organizational behavior researchers moved into the field, which in part resulted in an internal focus. Then economists became interested in strategic management phenomena, and the pendulum swung externally. Thus, adding researchers with diverse and strong disciplinary backgrounds can stimulate new research perspectives as their core ideas are integrated into the existing theories in strategy. In fact, some schools have pursued hiring faculty with PhDs in the basic disciplines such as economics, sociology, psychology, anthropology, or even the hard sciences, seeking to build a stronger disciplinary research base. Whether this approach will build stronger collaborations that contribute to strategic management remains to be seen. The Department of Management at Texas A&M University in the 1980s and 1990s had three strong disciplinary groups: organization behavior (based in psychology), strategic management, and public policy (based in economics and law). There was enough critical mass in each group to foster quality research, but the best work entailed integrative research among the groups. The strategy group flourished there because they were able to draw on colleagues with strong disciplinary backgrounds from organizational behavior and from economics and legal backgrounds. However, the potential existed for more contention than light (academic productivity), and careful individual selection was needed to maintain a collaborative culture and strong departmental leadership.

In conclusion, although there may be different integrative theoretical approaches for pursuing strategic management research as well as different ways to organize strategic management researchers, we feel that the discipline can maintain its grounding by producing research that solves significant managerial and societal problems, while allowing organizations to sustain high performance.

References

Alchian A, Demsetz H. 1972. Production, information costs, and economic organization. *American Economic Review* 62(5): 777–795.

Amis J, Barney J, Mahoney JT, Wang H. 2020. From the editors—why we need a theory of stakeholder governance—and why this is a hard problem. *Academy of Management Review* 45(3): 499–503.

Andrews K. 1971. *The Concept of Corporate Strategy*. Dow Jones-Irwin: Homewood, IL.

Ansoff HI. 1965. *Corporate Strategy*. McGraw Hill: New York, NY.

Argyres N. 1996. Evidence on the role of firm capabilities in vertical integration decisions. *Strategic Management Journal* 17(2): 129–150.

Ashkenas R, Ulrich D, Jick T, Kerr S. 2002. *The Boundaryless Organization: Breaking the Chains of Organizational Structure*. Jossey-Bass: San Francisco, CA.

Aupperle, KE, Acar W, Mukherjee D. 2014. Revisiting the fit-performance thesis half a century later: a historical financial analysis of Chandler's own matched and mismatched firms. *Business History* 56(3): 341–371.

Barney JB. 1991. Firm resources and sustained competitive advantage. *Journal of Management* 17(1): 99–120.

Barney JB. 2018. Why resource-based theory's model of profit appropriation must incorporate a stakeholder perspective. *Strategic Management Journal* 39(13): 3305–3325.

Barney JB, Arikan A. 2001. The resource-based view: origins and implications. In *The Blackwell Handbook of Strategic Management*, Hitt MA, Freeman RE, Harrison JS (eds). Blackwell Publishers: Oxford, U.K.; 124–188.

Barney JB, Hoskisson RE. 1990. Strategic groups: untested assertions and research proposals. *Managerial and Decision Economics* 11(3): 187–198.

Barney JB, Mackey, A. 2021. What would the field of strategic management look like if it took the stakeholder perspective seriously? In *Strategic Management: State of the Field and Its Future*, Duhaime IM, Hitt MA, Lyles MA (eds). Oxford University Press: New York, NY; 663–678.

Berle AA Jr. 1954. *The 20th-Century Capitalist Revolution*. Harcourt, Brace: New York, NY.

Bettis RA. 1991. Strategic management and the straightjacket: an editorial essay. *Organization Science* 2(3): 315–319.

Blettner DP, Chaddad FR, Bettis RA. 2012. The CEO performance effect: statistical issues and a complex fit perspective. *Strategic Management Journal* 33(8): 986–999.

Bosse DA, Phillips RA, Harrison JS. 2009. Stakeholders, reciprocity, and firm performance. *Strategic Management Journal* 30(4): 447–456.

Bourgeois J III. 1984. Strategic management and determinism. *Academy of Management Review* 9(4): 586–596.

Bridoux F, Stoelhorst JW. 2014. Microfoundations for stakeholder theory: managing stakeholders with heterogeneous motives. *Strategic Management Journal* 35(1): 107–125.

Buckley PJ, Casson MC. 1981. *The Future of Multinational Enterprise*. Macmillan: London, U.K.

Burt RS, Opper S. 2020. Political connection and disconnection: still a success factor for Chinese entrepreneurs. *Entrepreneurship Theory and Practice* 44(6): 1199–1228.

Camerer CF. 1985. Redirecting research in business policy and strategy. *Strategic Management Journal* 6(1): 1–15.

Castanias RP, Helfat CE. 1991. Managerial resources and rents. *Journal of Management* 17(1): 155–172.

Chandler AD. 1962. *Strategy and Structure: Chapters in the History of the American Industrial Enterprise.* MIT Press: Cambridge, MA.

Chen G, Hambrick DC 2012. CEO replacement in turnaround situations: executive (mis)fit and its performance implications. *Organization Science* 23(1): 225–243.

Chen MJ. 1996. Competitor analysis and interfirm rivalry: toward a theoretical integration. *Academy of Management Review* 21(1): 100–134.

Chen MJ, Miller D. 2012. Competitive dynamics: themes, trends, and a prospective research platform. *Academy of Management Annals* 6: 135–210.

Chen MJ, Su KH, Tsai WP. 2007. Competitive tension: the awareness-motivation-capability perspective. *Academy of Management Journal* 50(1): 101–118.

Chi T. 1994. Trading in strategic resources: necessary conditions, transaction cost problems, and choice of exchange structure. *Strategic Management Journal* 15(4): 271–290.

Choi J, Wang H. 2009. Stakeholder relations and the persistence of corporate financial performance. *Strategic Management Journal* 30(8): 895–907.

Christiansen CM. 1997. *The Innovator's Dilemma: When New Technologies Cause Great Firms to Fail.* Harvard Business School Press: Boston, MA.

Coff RW. 1999. When competitive advantage doesn't lead to performance: resource-based theory and stakeholder bargaining. *Organization Science* 10(2): 119–133.

Cohen J, Cohen P. 1983. *Applied Multiple Regression / Correlation Analysis for the Behavioral Sciences.* Erlbaum: Hillsdale, NJ.

Connelly B, Shi W, Hoskisson RE, Ketchen DJ. 2019. Portfolio spillover of institutional investor activism: an awareness-motivation-capability perspective. *Academy of Management Journal.* Available at https://doi.org/10.5465/amj.2018.0074.

Cooper L, Inoue A. 1996. Building market structures from consumer preferences. *Journal of Marketing Research* 33(3): 293–306.

Daft RL, Lewin AY. 1990. Can organization studies begin to break out of the normal science straitjacket? An editorial essay. *Organization Science* 1(1): 1–9.

Durand R, Grant RM, Madsen TL. 2017. The expanding domain of strategic management research and the quest for integration. *Strategic Management Journal* 38(1): 4–16.

Dyer JH, Singh H. 1998. The relational view: cooperative strategy and sources of interorganizational competitive advantage. *Academy of Management Review* 23(4): 660–679.

Fama EF. 1980. Agency problems and the theory of firm. *Journal of Political Economy* 88(2): 288–307.

Fama EF, Jensen MC. 1983. Separation of ownership and control. *Journal of Law and Economics* 26(2): 301–325.

Foss K, Foss NJ. 2005. Resources and transaction costs: how property rights economics furthers the resource-based view. *Strategic Management Journal* 26(6): 541–553.

Funk RJ, Hirschman D. 2014. Derivatives and deregulation: financial innovation and the demise of Glass–Steagall. *Administrative Science Quarterly* 59(4): 669–704.

Galbraith JR, Nathanson DA. 1979. The role of organizational structure and process in strategy implementation. In *Strategic Management: A New View of Business Policy and Planning,* Schendel DE, Hofer CW (eds). Little, Brown and Company: Boston, MA; 249–283.

Graebner ME. 2021. Evolution of qualitative methods in strategic management. In *Strategic Management: State of the Field and Its Future,* Duhaime IM, Hitt MA, Lyles MA (eds). Oxford University Press: New York, NY; 99–114.

Greve HR. 2009. Bigger and safer: the diffusion of competitive advantage. *Strategic Management Journal* 30(1): 1–23.

Greve HR. 2021. The organizational view of strategic management. In *Strategic Management: State of the Field and Its Future,* Duhaime IM, Hitt MA, Lyles MA (eds). Oxford University Press: New York, NY; 43–59.

Guillen M. 2000. Business groups in emerging economies: a resource-based view. *Academy of Management Journal* **43**(2): 362–381.

Gur FA, Greckhamer T. 2019. Know thy enemy: a review and agenda for research on competitor identification. *Journal of Management* **45**(5): 2072–2100.

Hansen MH, Perry LT, Reese CS. 2004. A Bayesian operationalization of the resource-based view. *Strategic Management Journal* **25**(13): 1279–1295.

Harrison JS. 2020. *Sustaining High Performance in Business: Systems, Resources, and Stakeholders.* Business Expert Press: New York, NY.

Harrison J, Bosse D, Phillips RA. 2010. Managing for stakeholders, stakeholder utility functions, and competitive advantage. *Strategic Management Journal* **31**(1): 58–74.

Harrison JS, Phillips RA, Freeman RE. 2020. On the 2019 "Business Roundtable Statement on the Purpose of a Corporation." *Journal of Management* **46**(7): 1223–1237.

Harrison JS, St. John CH. 2013. *Foundations in Strategic Management,* 6th ed. Cengage: Boston, MA.

Hatten KJ. 1979. Quantitative research methods in strategic management. In *Strategic Management: A New View of Business Policy and Planning,* Schendel DE, Hofer CW (eds). Little, Brown and Company: Boston, MA; 448–466.

Hatten KJ, Schendel DE, Cooper AC. 1978. A strategic model of the U.S. brewing industry: 1952–1971. *Academy of Management Journal* **21**(4): 592–619.

Helfat CE. 2021. The economic view of strategic management. In *Strategic Management: State of the Field and Its Future,* Duhaime IM, Hitt MA, Lyles MA (eds). Oxford University Press: New York, NY; 61–79.

Helfat CE, Finkelstein S, Mitchell W, Peteraf MA, Singh H, Teece DJ, Winter SG. 2007. *Dynamic Capabilities: Understanding Strategic Change in Organizations.* Blackwell: Malden, MA.

Henisz WJ, Dorobantu S, Nartey LJ. 2014. Spinning gold: the financial returns to stakeholder engagement. *Strategic Management Journal* **35**(12): 1727–1748.

Hennart JF. 1988. A transactions costs theory of equity joint ventures. *Strategic Management Journal* **9**(4): 361–374.

Hill CWL, Hoskisson RE. 1987. Strategy and structure in the multiproduct firm. *Academy of Management Review* **12**(2): 331–341.

Hillman AJ, Keim GD. 2001. Shareholder value, stakeholder management, and social issues: What's the bottom line? *Strategic Management Journal* **22**(2): 125–139.

Hitt MA, Ireland RD, Hoskisson RE. 2020. *Strategic Management: Competitiveness and Globalization,* 13th ed. Cengage: Boston, MA.

Hitt MA, Keats BW, DeMarie SM. 1998. Navigating in the new competitive landscape: building strategic flexibility and competitive advantage in the 21st century. *Academy of Management Executive* **12**(4): 22–42.

Hoskisson RE. 1987. Multidivisional structure and performance: the contingency of diversification strategy. *Academy of Management Journal* **30**(4): 625–644.

Hoskisson RE, Gambeta E, Green CD, Li TX. 2018. Is my firm-specific investment protected? Overcoming the stakeholder investment dilemma in the resource-based view. *Academy of Management Review* **43**(2): 284–306.

Hoskisson RE, Harrison JS, Dubofsky D. 1991. Capital market evaluation of M-form implementation and diversification strategy. *Strategic Management Journal* **12**(4): 271–279.

Hoskisson RE, Hitt MA, Wan WP, Yiu D. 1999. Swings of a pendulum: theory and research in strategic management. *Journal of Management* **25**(3): 417–456.

Ingram P, Baum JAC. 1997. Opportunity and constraint: organizations' learning from the operating and competitive experience of industries. *Strategic Management Journal* **18** (Summer): 75–98.

Ireland R, Hitt M, Sirmon D. 2003. A model of strategic entrepreneurship: the construct and its dimensions. *Journal of Management* **29**(6): 963–989.

Jacobson R. 1992. The "Austrian" school of strategy. *Academy of Management Review* 17(4): 782–807.

Jain A. 2013. Learning by doing and the locus of innovative capability in biotechnology research. *Organization Science* 24(6): 1683–1700.

Jensen MC, Meckling W. 1976. Theory of the firm: managerial behavior, agency costs and capital structure. *Journal of Financial Economics* 3(4): 305–360.

Jones TM, Harrison, JS, Felps W. 2018. How applying instrumental stakeholder theory can provide sustainable competitive advantage. *Academy of Management Review* 43(3): 371–391.

Keats BW, O'Neill HM. 2001. Organization structure: looking through a strategy lens. In *The Blackwell Handbook of Strategic Management*, Hitt MA, Freeman RE, Harrison JS (eds). Blackwell: Oxford, U.K.; 520–542.

Keyhani M, Lévesque M, Madhok A. 2015. Toward a theory of entrepreneurial rents: a simulation of the market process. *Strategic Management Journal* 36(1): 76–96.

Kim H, Hoskisson RE. 2015. A resource environment view of competitive advantage. In *Advances in International Management*, Tihanyi L, Pedersen T, Devinney T (eds). Emerald Group: Bingley, U.K.; 95–140.

Kim H, Hoskisson RE, Lee S-H. 2015. Why strategic factor markets matter: "new" multinationals' geographic diversification and firm profitability. *Strategic Management Journal* 36(4): 518–536.

Kim H, Kim H, Hoskisson RE. 2010. Does market-oriented institutional change in an emerging economy make business group-affiliated multinationals perform better? An institution-based view. *Journal of International Business Studies* 41(7): 1141–1160.

Kim J, Mahoney JT. 2010. A strategic theory of the firm as a nexus of incomplete contracts: a property rights approach. *Journal of Management* 36(4): 806–826.

Kirchhoff BA. 1991. Entrepreneurship's contribution to economics. *Entrepreneurship: Theory and Practice* 16(2): 93–112.

Kosnik RD. 1990. Effects of board demography and directors' incentives on corporate greenmail decisions. *Academy of Management Journal* 33(1): 129–150.

Liebig J. 1840. *Organic Chemistry in Its Application to Agriculture and Physiology*. Playfair: London, U.K.

Mackey TB, Barney JB, Dotson JP. 2017. Corporate diversification and the value of individual firms: a Bayesian approach. *Strategic Management Journal* 38(2): 322–341.

Mahoney JT. 1993. Strategic management and determinism: sustaining the conversation. *Journal of Management Studies* 30(1): 173–191.

Mahoney JT, Pandian JR. 1992. The resource-based view within the conversation of strategic management. *Strategic Management Journal* 13(5): 363–380.

Martin GP, Wiseman RM, Gomez-Mejia LR. 2016. Going short-term or long-term? CEO stock options and temporal orientation in the presence of slack. *Strategic Management Journal* 37(12): 2463–2480.

McCloskey D. 1985. *The Rhetoric of Economics*. University of Wisconsin Press: Madison, WI.

McGee J, Thomas H. 1986. Strategic groups: theory, research and taxonomy. *Strategic Management Journal* 7(2): 141–160.

McIntyre DP, Srinivasan A. 2017. Networks, platforms, and strategy: emerging views and next steps. *Strategic Management Journal* 38(1): 141–160.

Mellahi K, Frynas JG, Sun P, Siegel D. 2016. A review of the nonmarket strategy literature: toward a multi-theoretic integration. *Journal of Management* 42(1): 143–173.

Menon AR, Yao DA. 2017. Elevating repositioning costs: strategy dynamics and competitive interactions. *Strategic Management Journal* 38(10): 1953–1963.

Michel JG, Hambrick DC. 1992. Diversification posture and top management team characteristics. *Academy of Management Journal* 35(1): 9–37.

Montgomery CA, Wernerfelt B, Balakrishnan S. 1989. Strategy content and the research process: a critique and commentary. *Strategic Management Journal* 10(2): 189–197.

Nelson R. 2012. Why Schumpeter has had so little influence on today's main line economics, and why this may be changing. *Journal of Evolutionary Economics,* 22(5): 901–916.

Nelson RR, Winter S. 1982. *An Evolutionary Theory of Economic Change.* Harvard University Press: Cambridge: MA.

Nickerson J, Yen CJ, Mahoney JT. 2012. Exploring the problem-finding and problem-solving approach for designing organizations. *Academy of Management Perspectives* 26(1): 52–72.

North DC. 1990. *Institutions, Institutional Change, and Economic Performance.* Cambridge University Press: New York, NY.

Penrose E. 1959. *The Theory of the Growth of the Firm.* Oxford University Press: Oxford, U.K.

Pepper A, Gore J. 2015. Behavioral agency theory: new foundations for theorizing about executive compensation. *Journal of Management* 41(4): 1045–1068.

Porac J, Thomas H, Wilson F, Paton D, Kanfer A. 1995. Rivalry and the industry model of Scottish knitwear producers. *Administrative Science Quarterly* 40(2): 203–227.

Porter ME. 1980. *Competitive Strategy.* Free Press: New York, NY.

Porter ME. 1981. The contribution of industrial organization to strategic management. *Academy of Management Review* 6(4): 609–620.

Ramaswamy K, Purkayastha S, Petitt BS. 2017. How do institutional transitions impact the efficacy of related and unrelated diversification strategies used by business groups? *Journal of Business Research* 72(1): 1–13.

Reger RK, Huff AS. 1993. Strategic groups: a cognitive perspective. *Strategic Management Journal* 14(2): 103–123.

Rönnegard D, Smith NC. 2019. Shareholder primacy vs. stakeholder theory: the law as constraint and potential enabler. In *Cambridge Handbook of Stakeholder Theory,* Harrison JS, Barney JB, Freeman RE, Phillips RE (eds). Cambridge University Press, Cambridge, U.K.; 117–131.

Rudy BC, Johnson AF. 2016. Performance, aspirations, and market versus nonmarket investment. *Journal of Management* 42(4): 936–959.

Rugman AM, Verbeke A. 2002. Edith Penrose's contribution to the resource-based view of strategic management. *Strategic Management Journal* 23(8): 769–781.

Rumelt RP. 1974. *Strategy, Structure, and Economic Performance.* Harvard University Press: Cambridge, MA.

Schendel DE, Hofer CW. 1979. *Strategic Management: A New View of Business Policy and Planning.* Little, Brown and Company: Boston, MA.

Schumpeter J. 1911. *Theory of Economic Development.* Transaction: Piscataway, NJ.

Schumpeter J. 1950. *Capitalism, Socialism, and Democracy.* Harper Perennial: New York, NY.

Shaver JM. 2021. Evolution of quantitative research methods in strategic management. In *Strategic Management: State of the Field and Its Future,* Duhaime IM, Hitt MA, Lyles MA (eds). Oxford University Press: New York, NY; 83–97.

Silverman BS. 1999. Technological resources and the direction of corporate diversification: toward an integration of the resource-based view and transaction cost economics. *Management Science* 45(8): 1109–1124.

Smircich L, Stubbart C. 1985. Strategic management in an enacted world. *Academy of Management Review* 10(4): 724–736.

Smith KG, Locke EA, Barry D. 1990. Goal setting, planning, and organizational performance: an experimental simulation. *Organizational Behavior and Human Decision Processes* 46(1): 118–134.

Sutton T, Bosse D. 2019. Shareholder value creation, constrained stakeholder reciprocity, and nonmarket strategy. Paper presented at the annual meeting of the Academy of Management, Boston, MA.

Tosi HL, Gomez-Mejia LR. 1989. The decoupling of CEO pay and performance: an agency theory perspective. *Administrative Science Quarterly* 34(4): 169–189.

Vidal E, Mitchell W. 2018. Virtuous or vicious cycles? The role of divestitures as a complementary Penrose effect within resource-based theory. *Strategic Management Journal* 39(1): 131–154.

Wan WP, Hoskisson R. 2003. Home country environments, corporate diversification strategies, and firm performance. *Academy of Management Journal* 46(1): 27–45.

Wernerfelt B. 1984. A resource-based view of the firm. *Strategic Management Journal* 5(2): 171–180.

Williamson OE. 1975. *Markets and Hierarchies*. Free Press: New York, NY.

Williamson OE. 1985. *The Economic Institutions of Capitalism*. Free Press: New York.

Winter SG. 2012. Capabilities: their origins and ancestry. *Journal of Management Studies* 49(8): 1402–1406.

Wiseman R, Gomez-Mejia L. 1998. A behavioral agency model of managerial risk taking. *Academy of Management Review* 23(1): 133–153.

Yue LQ, Wang J, Yang B. 2019. Contesting commercialization: political influence, responsive authoritarianism, and cultural resistance. *Administrative Science Quarterly* 64(2): 435–465.

Zahra S, Pearce, JA. 1989. Boards of directors and corporate financial performance: a review and integrative model. *Journal of Management* 15(2): 291–334.

Evolution of Theory in Strategic Management

1.1

THE ORGANIZATIONAL VIEW OF STRATEGIC MANAGEMENT

Henrich R. Greve

Introduction

To paraphrase Cyert and March (1963: 1), an interest in how the firm makes economic decisions implies a need to examine organizational structures and processes, and to understand how decisions are made in an organizational context. This interest leads to an organizational view of strategic management. Not all organizational theory concerns strategic management and not all strategy theories are organizational, but every strategic decision that we study is a product of an organizational context. The organizational theory most relevant to strategy has a 40-year history, and it has gradually increased in its volume of research and connection to strategy. This chapter gives a selective review of its history and current state before suggesting promising future developments. This discussion is selective because it reflects my preference for presenting research streams that are large and highly relevant to strategic management.

The organizational view has three important premises. First, formal organizations are the central actors. Second, organizational actions are the product of decisions made by boundedly rational individuals acting alone or in groups, with goals and information structured by the organization. Third, organizations must be understood in relation to their environment, which provides a broad range of resources that organizations depend on along with regulatory and social constraints. A central question in organizational theory is how organizations adapt to their environment—in other words, how firms choose strategies. Other central questions are how organizations affect their members and society, but these questions are not treated here.

Foundations of the Organizational View

Although organizational theory is older, the organizational view of strategy dates back to the 1970s, which saw the appearance of major research streams examining organizational responses to the environment, which is defined as external actors and processes that could affect organizational actions or outcomes (e.g., Scott, 1987). Theory and evidence of how organizations come to understand the environment, face the opportunities and constraints it generates, and interact with it are inherently strategic, so this period built the foundations of the organizational view of strategy.

Although each major organizational theory addresses a wide range of topics and phenomena, they can be roughly divided by emphasis. The main theories of how the environment is formed and made known to the organization are organizational ecology and network theory (Brass *et al.*, 2004; Carroll and Hannan, 2000; Shipilov and Gawer, 2020). The main theory of how the environment imposes or constrains organizational action is institutional theory (Scott, 2001). The main theories of how the organization interacts with the environment are resource dependence theory and learning theory (Gavetti *et al.*, 2012; Wry, Cobb, and Aldrich, 2013).

Taking *Strategic Management Journal* articles as a measure of the presence of each organizational theory in strategic management, network theory has had a steady and large representation in the last 20 years, indicating significant interest in environmental formation and discovery. Institutional theory has had a significant presence for a little more than 10 years, showing more recent, but similar levels of interest in environmental opportunities and constraints. Organizational learning has had a significant presence for more than 20 years and a recent increase that shows long-lasting and growing interest in organizational interaction with the environment. The field of strategy appears to be making a gradual transition in research interest from the formation and understanding of environments, through environmental effects on the organization, to organizational interaction with the environment. The trend is toward organizational theories that give the firm an active role in forming its strategy and adapting it to the environment. Organizational theory is becoming more strategic.

The history of organizational theory in strategic management is best introduced by selected phenomena that we now understand better thanks to earlier work. For example, it is now well known that industries have a temporary period of rapid growth driven by density-dependent founding and failure (e.g., Hannan *et al.*, 1995; Perretti, Negro, and Lomi, 2008), and firm movement into new product or market niches is driven by similar factors (Carroll *et al.*, 1996; Dobrev and Kim, 2006; Ruef, 2000). The fragmentation of industries that have had a period of high concentration is understood to be a function of organizations discovering and exploiting the market niche structure (Boone, Brocheler, and Carroll, 2000; Carroll and Swaminathan, 2000).

Early research on institutional theory started by explaining how organizations adopt symbols that legitimize them in the eyes of external evaluators without making actual strategic or operational changes (Meyer and Rowan, 1977), but the research has since moved on to investigate how the environment directs strategic change. Pioneering findings showed that emergent industries become established through a variety of political and social processes that make the function and reliability of the product or service better known (Rao, 1994; Zelizer, 1978). Firms gain opportunities to enter new markets through new ideologies offered by social movements or other firms in the industry (Haveman, Rao, and Paruchuri, 2007; Negro, Hannan, and Rao, 2011; Rao, Monin, and Durand, 2003; Weber, Heinze, and DeSoucey, 2008). Changes in societal belief systems are entrepreneurial opportunities, which industry participants know and exploit (Delmestri and Greenwood, 2016).

Network theory views interorganizational ties as a sensory system that lets firms discover and evaluate innovations through observation and communication, and many studies address how major changes diffuse through network ties among organizations. Strategic actions that diffuse through interorganizational ties include innovative market positions, production assets, and business practices (Greve, 2009; Haunschild and Beckman, 1998; Westphal, Seidel, and Stewart, 2001). An important part of the theory and evidence is a movement away from the observation-only idea that firms imitate what they observe without careful consideration of the consequences. Multiple studies have examined how controversial or uncertain innovations have limited or slow diffusion while firms assess their value (Fligstein, 1991; Jonsson, 2009). The role of communication is especially clear in the diffusion of practices that organizations try to conceal. Learning of effective internal operations is facilitated by network ties across competitors (Ingram and Baum, 1997), and deception and collusion are also learned through network ties (Baker and Faulkner, 1993).

Learning theory has a significant research record showing how firms improve their operations through their own experience and vicarious learning from other firms, and how these processes can serve as either complements or substitutes (Baum and Ingram, 1998; Kim and Miner, 2007; Madsen, 2009; Simon and Lieberman, 2010). More recently, a research stream has developed on how the timing and content of strategic changes are shaped by environmental feedback in the form of performance relative to aspiration levels (Baum et al., 2005; Gaba and Joseph, 2013; Greve, 1998; Tarakci et al., 2018). There is also significant research on how learning contributes to innovations through directing the organization toward exploration (Daneels, 2002; McGrath, 2001) and improving its capabilities (Jain, 2013; Lane and Lubatkin, 1998).

These brief examples indicate how the organizational view of strategy has led to many findings that are important for understanding strategic change. They were chosen for their relevance to strategic management and contain only a sample of cites from larger research streams. They effectively exemplify the history of the organizational view of strategy because they share two central features of past research. First, the theory and evidence were developed with an eye to understanding organizations, with little concern for strategic management. Second, because many organizational actions are strategic, the theory and evidence produced knowledge of value to the field of strategic management. Currently, organization theory and strategic management are better aligned than in the past, so much theory and evidence in organizational research are developed with the intent of informing strategic management.

Current Research Streams in the Organizational View

The main organizational theories have changed little in recent years, so we can treat the theoretical foundations as stable but with growing detail and evidence. Thus, elaboration of recent theoretical developments is less fruitful than a discussion of the applied research topics that are currently popular. If we take articles in *Administrative Science Quarterly*, the *Academy of Management Journal*, and *Organization Science* as indicators of active organizational research relevant to strategic management, inspection of recently published articles shows that the following research topics are important:

1. Societal groups influence strategic decisions, especially through actors such as social movements and the state.
2. Individual actors and groups influence strategic decisions, including but not limited to the CEO, top management team, and board of directors. This research is discussed in Parts 6, 7, and 9 of this volume and is not treated here.
3. Organizations choose strategic actions that maneuver complex institutional and power structures such as institutional logics, community relations, and symbolic or linguistic effects.
4. Organizations mobilize and direct the strategy to pursue multiple goals, including environmentally imposed goals.

Societal groups

Social movements can inflict damage on targeted firms, so they are capable of changing key parts of strategy and operations (Bartley and Child, 2011), and they can eliminate or reduce specific opportunities by pressuring political institutions (Hiatt, Grandy, and Lee, 2015; Ingram and Rao, 2004). These activities are especially powerful when directed at low-performing organizations and when amplified by coverage in the press (King, 2008) or social media (Zhang and Luo, 2013). Firms are not passive recipients of such pressure, however, and seek to counteract it by making their good deeds better known, in order to compensate or distract (McDonnell and King, 2013).

While social movements are often sources of political pressures, there is also research examining how the state, parties, or other political actors make firms comply with costly demands of actions to benefit society (Reid and Toffel, 2009). Firms' relationships with political actors can be quite close when the firms are seen as important solutions to societal problems (Tihanyi and Hegarty, 2007) or the political actors are powerful (Stark and Vedres, 2012). Again, firms are not passive recipients of such pressure and can counteract it through actions that evade regulatory constraints (Funk and Hirschman, 2014; Joseph, Ocasio, and McDonnell, 2014) or through lobbying to shape regulation or enforcement (Rudy and Johnson, 2016).

Mass media outlets voice and organize public pressure on firms and have gained increased attention in current organizational research. They can lead to adoption of highly consequential organizational practices (Shipilov, Greve, and Rowley, 2019), as well as changes in the firm's strategy (Bednar, Boivie, and Prince, 2013). This happens in part because media coverage often provides increased attention to the firm by stakeholders, including mobilization for change (Kölbel, Busch, and Jancso, 2017). Mass media effects are exploited by firms, too, because efforts to be covered by news media can result in increased access to funding (Petkova, Rindova, and Gupta, 2013). Social media postings by individuals are also an important part of the organizational environment, and their evaluations affect product and firm outcomes (Goldberg, Hannan, and Kovács, 2016; Greve and Song, 2017; Wang, Wezel, and Forgues, 2016). Our knowledge of firm responses to this part of the environment is still incomplete, but we know that organizations make use of media to influence other actors, such as the state (Yue, Wang, and Yang, 2019).

Environmental structures

Industries can be reorganized according to new principles for organizing firms and competition, known as institutional logics (Thornton, 2002). Firms can be similarly reorganized, as institutional logics compete to determine structures and processes such as corporate governance (Joseph et al., 2014; Shipilov, Greve, and Rowley, 2010), innovation practices (Pahnke, Katila, and Eisenhardt, 2015), and use of occupations (Lounsbury, 2002). Communities also have different requirements for firm behaviors, leading to community-firm matching both on business and social behaviors (Greve and Rao, 2012; Lee and Lounsbury, 2015; Schneiberg, King, and Smith, 2008). For example, communities with experience organizing voluntary associations and businesses with mutual ownership (e.g., thrifts and cooperatives) are difficult competitive arenas for regular business firms. Some of these distinctions are related to symbols such as the language used to describe products and firms; firms that carefully position themselves in the symbolic environment gain advantages (Barlow, Verhaal, and Hoskins, 2016; Granqvist, Grodal, and Woolley, 2013; Hsu and Grodal, 2015). Positioning a firm can be complex, however, as shown by research on coexisting institutional logics in conflict with each other. These pose a special problem for firms, which are left with the options of committing to one or making a compromise between multiple logics (Greenwood et al., 2011).

Organizational goals

Organizational pursuit of basic goals such as survival and profitability has seen much research in organizational theory (Shinkle, 2012), and a research stream now gaining increased focus examines how organizations react to multiple goals, or to goals that are separate from profitability. This research has emphasized three broad types of goals. The first is goals that are related to profitability in the short or long run, such as market share (Greve, 1998), network ties (Baum *et al.*, 2005), or innovations (Tyler and Caner, 2016). The second is goals that are mainly related to managerial preferences, such as firm growth (Greve, 2008). The third is goals that are mainly related to societal or stakeholder benefit, such as safety (Baum and Dahlin, 2007; Gaba and Greve, 2019) or corporate governance (Rowley, Shipilov, and Greve, 2017). There is increased interest in discovering what goals organizations pursue and how they choose between them, and preliminary findings indicate that firms are multigoal actors, but with survival and profitability emphasized, as one would expect.

Future of the Organizational View

In the past, the abundance of organizational theories and their emphasis on environmental effects on organizations served as barriers against integration with strategic management. These barriers are now lower. The modern synthesis of organization theory and strategy is that problem and opportunity discovery by internal decision-makers directs strategic change. The behavioral theory of the firm is a good example of this synthesis. It has inspired a growth in research combining performance feedback, problem identification, solutions search, and solution sellers, all of which form inputs to a dominant coalition of decision-makers. The environment in turn constrains, facilitates, and responds, just as current theory and evidence hold, and starts a new round of adaptation. The modern synthesis differs from earlier organization theory in seeing an interactive relationship between organizations and their environment, rather than unidirectional influence. In the modern synthesis, the firm initiates actions based on internal and external signals; it has an active role in searching for alternatives but is also provided alternatives from external actors; and its decision-making is premised on internal goals but also influenced by the external experiences of decision-makers.

Similar movement toward the firm interacting with the environment can be seen in other parts of organizational theory and will become a growing part of the organizational view of strategy. There has long been ecological research on how firms attract founding of other firms with complementary products, leading to regional specialization that crosses industries (Audia, Freeman, and Reynolds, 2006; Sorenson and Audia, 2000). Interorganizational ties with suppliers, especially, are seen as sufficiently important that firms adding manufacturing locations sometimes encourage existing suppliers to follow rather than use the existing suppliers in the new location (Martin, Swaminathan, and Mitchell, 1998). This research has given rise to work on how firms partially create organizational environments, and the consequences of this creation for competition. One branch of this research examines how employees become entrepreneurs (spin-outs) and use knowledge gained from their work to improve their venture (Argyres and Mostafa, 2016; Dencker and Gruber, 2015). Another branch examines how corporations seek to fold external ventures into their organization through corporate venture capital and acquisitions, and also gain advantages from selective spin-offs of parts of their business (Gaba and Bhattacharya, 2012; Katila, Rosenberger, and Eisenhardt, 2008; McKendrick, Wade, and Jaffee, 2009; Vidal and Mitchell, 2015).

Each of these branches is early in its development and will see significant new research. In addition, the current evidence on how organizational founding and other events that modify the ecology of firms affect communities (e.g., Greve and Rao, 2014) can be extended by examining whether and how communities become specialists in founding specific kinds of firms, or alternatively, whether such events make communities more entrepreneurial in general. Because the origins of such community differences are not yet well known, but are presumably related to an ecology of organizations that have either direct synergies or synergies through their effects on the labor market, the duration of such community effects should be explored as well. Research so far indicates that the effects can endure for decades (Greve and Rao, 2014), which adds strategic significance to location choices.

Research on how firms establish network ties with other firms that hold complementary capabilities has been done for some time, and this research has examined strategic considerations and different forms of social similarity or proximity (Chung, Singh, and Lee, 2000; Mitsuhashi and Greve, 2009; Powell et al., 2005). Elaborations of this research include an increased focus on how network ties are broken when they are no longer useful or when better alternatives become available (Greve et al., 2010; Greve, Mitsuhashi, and Baum, 2013). There is also increased work on how firms can adjust their network tie formation to fit their current strategy (Shipilov, Li, and Greve, 2011; Sytch, Tatarynowicz, and Gulati, 2012). Current network research is discovering that firms selectively use the common principles for tie creation found in earlier research depending on their fit to strategic goals. For example, network ties connecting firms of different status may be coupled with asymmetric resource exchanges because high-status firms extract resources from low-status firms in exchange for the benefit of associating with them (Castellucci and Ertug, 2010).

With network theory having examined the benefits of different network positions and firm actions to rearrange their networks, the next step forward is to address a crucial missing piece in network theory and evidence. For parsimony, network theory starts with the assumption of identical nodes (firms), deviating from this mainly through controls for firm differences. This assumption is contrary to the evidence on firm differences accumulated in strategic management research. It is also a missed opportunity because scholars still know too little about the joint effect of firm characteristics and network positions on strategic outcomes. Nor is much known about how firm characteristics affect the tendency to change firm network positions and draw benefits from such changes. Gaining and exploiting beneficial network positions are widely recognized as important strategic actions, but we should examine more closely whether firms differ in their ability to take these actions, either as a result of consciously building up a network management capability or as a side effect of other firm characteristics. Exploring these questions is a significant research opportunity for scholars in organizational theory and strategic management.

Research using institutional theory has increasingly focused on the firm shaping the institutional environment or maneuvering within its constraints. Work on how firms act as institutional entrepreneurs seeking to shape institutions to fit their business has old origins (Dobbin, 1995), and has led to significant research on the formation of institutions to support new products or services in emerging industries (Hargadon and Douglas, 2001; Munir and Phillips, 2005). An important discovery is that firms' formation of the institutional environment is done not only in emerging industries but also in mature industries (Greenwood and Suddaby, 2006). In an industry as old as banking, partially contradictory institutional constraints complicate the work of teams seeking to found a bank, but when resolved well improve its chances of success (Almandoz, 2012). Similar balancing has also been observed in other contexts (Jonsson and Regnar, 2009; Smets *et al.*, 2015). Conflicting demands on the organization can be used to delay reactions to institutional demands and better calibrate the response (Raaijmakers *et al.*, 2015; Zhang and Greve, 2018).

An important area for future research lies in recognizing that the emphasis in early institutional theory on firms decoupling symbolic actions from actual production was a parsimonious simplification. The reality is that institutions reach into firms, affecting the costs and benefits of strategic actions and even altering firm goals. Consider, for example, the increase in environmental, social, and governance (ESG) goals imposed on firms and the rise of ESG funds as investors (Odziemkowska and Henisz, 2020). Given the importance of the resources that are released to actors fulfilling ESG goals and the sophistication of actors checking whether firms truly fulfill such goals, it would be surprising if ESG goals were not added to the internal firm goal structure. Such goal additions are an institutional effect that is so important that we need to know much more about it. Generic examination of how institutions affect closely related behaviors (e.g., ESG pressures affecting corporate social responsibility (CSR) reports) is not enough: researchers should examine the effects on strategic decision-making processes and actual organizational changes. This is only an example of an institution that reaches deep into firm decision-making, and we can expect future research to uncover many more like it.

Resource dependence theory suggests that firms interact with the environment in order to avoid costly dependency (Pfeffer and Salancik, 1978), and this work has continued to produce new findings on organizational actions to avoid dependence or gain power (Casciaro and Piskorski, 2005; Howard, Withers, and Tihanyi, 2016). It includes work on the defense mechanisms that entrepreneurial ventures put in place to gain resources from more powerful firms without exposing themselves to takeover attempts or other uses of power (Hallen, Katila, and Rosenberger, 2014; Katila *et al.*, 2008). Resource dependence theory has also shown the cost of firm actions to rearrange dependence relations, because the counterparts of these relations observe the firm and act to neutralize or overturn attempts to gain power over them (Rogan and Greve, 2015). Moreover, recent research has found that organizations seek to control demands from their institutional environment through mechanisms such as establishing political or administrative ties with the state (Hillman, 2005; Zhang and Greve, 2018).

Because resource dependence between pairs of firms can be conceptualized as a specific type of network tie, resource dependence theory and network theory have always been related. It naturally follows that each of them can also inform the other in future research. A notable gap in current research is that resource dependence theory has produced much less knowledge than one might expect on the rearrangement of interfirm ties that result in resource dependence, given the quick progress in network theory. It would be easy to follow up with research examining how much firms modify their exchange ties (and other ties producing dependence), how effective these changes are, and whether the changes are connected to firm differences. Indeed, among organizational theories examined in the last decades, resource dependence theory has always been distinctively strategic in its predictions and implications for practice, suggesting that it should be a high-priority research effort.

A recent development in learning theory suggests that external goals the institutional environment seeks to impose are not necessarily adopted by the organization but may instead be ignored or altered. Thus, changing institutional environments make performance measures less important for determining organizational decisions (Wezel and Saka-Helmhout, 2006). In particular, institutional pressures in favor of specific goals fail if the goal is not universally adopted and firm decision-makers are opposed (Shipilov et al., 2010) or need to attend to more critical performance goals (Desai, 2008). Indeed, quick adoption of goals is usually associated with support from powerful actors internally (Crilly, Zollo, and Hansen, 2012; Sauder and Espeland, 2009) or externally (e.g., Luo et al., 2015). This idea ties learning theory more closely to theories on power sources and use in organizations, such as resource dependence theory. It also suggests that the research streams outlined in this chapter can be combined with learning theory to produce knowledge on how each organization adjusts to changes in network position and resource dependence. After all, the bounded rationality of decision-makers suggests that organizational changes that may be beneficial in the longer run still require learning to produce higher performance.

An important discovery in current learning theory research is how organizations rely on performance feedback to choose the timing and form of major corporate decisions such as acquisitions and divestments (Haleblian, Kim, and Rajagopalan, 2006; Kuusela, Keil, and Maula, 2017; Vidal and Mitchell, 2015) as well as smaller-scale decisions like resource acquisition and product line trimming (Greve, 2011; Joseph, Klingebiel, and Wilson, 2016; Parker, Krause, and Covin, 2017). Many of the findings can be interpreted as learning shaped by political events within the organization, because changes in the performance influences the relative power of different coalitions as well as the fit of alternatives to situations characterized by abundant or scarce resources (Gaba and Joseph, 2013; Kuusela et al., 2017; Zhang and Greve, 2019). If a firm is experiencing low performance following a series of expansion decisions (such as acquisitions), top managers who favor further expansion will have difficulty implementing it because they face resource scarcity and increased resistance from other top managers. Organizational changes following these events are likely to maintain or reduce the firm size.

Performance feedback followed by problemistic search is a well-documented process, but so far little research has documented its consequences for attaining or maintaining competitive advantage. The answers to two key questions are currently not well understood. First, problemistic search is not required for organizations to change, because organizations can also innovate following slack search (search using available resources). We do not know whether changes made following problemistic search perform better than those made after slack search. We are also not sure how often changes are made after slack search, and under what conditions. Second, a key element of performance feedback theory is that organizations search and change in response to problems, not in response to opportunities. Although the theory is clear on this point, the empirical evidence shows that organizations also change when the performance is above the aspiration level, though less often than when it is below. We do not know whether the changes made when performing above the aspiration level are in response to opportunities, and whether they perform better than changes made in response to problems. Initial evidence suggests that making changes such as market position (Greve, 1999) and production technology (Desai, 2010) below the aspiration level gives better performance than changing them above the aspiration level. These findings on the benefits of problemistic search go against our fascination with entrepreneurial search for opportunities and should be studied further. The evidence on when firms make changes is presently so rich that we should now investigate the consequences of the change timing as well as the change content.

These recent changes and additions within the field of organizational theory have the common theme of exploring the interaction of organization and environment in more detail. The firm makes changes that are targeted toward the environment or even seeks to alter the environment; actors in the environment seek to reach into the firm and influence its decision-making. This adaptive cycle keeps modifying the strategic and operational decisions of each firm, leading to a dynamic view of firm strategies and market competition.

Discussion and Conclusions

Strategic decision-making and execution are done by organizations and for organizations, making organizational theory a central part of strategy. Organizational theory and strategy are interrelated like two ends of a string. Ask an organizational question, and a strategic answer will follow. Ask a strategic question, and an organizational answer will follow. This close relationship means that the two fields will continue to develop in tandem, as has been increasingly true in recent years.

The close relationship of these fields has not always been recognized, and indeed some of the theory in each of these sister disciplines has been constructed in ways that make it appear less relevant for the other than it is. Organizational theories focusing on unidirectional effects from the environment to the organization give the impression that strategy cannot be formed because the environment is determinate. The reality is that environmental influences give opportunities and constraints that the strategist must choose from; moreover, they are malleable. Strategic management theories emphasizing rationality and optimization as the central premise look implausible to organizational researchers because they ignore findings on how organizational processes and human judgment affect decisions. The reality is that organizations can often be shown to make smart choices if the researcher considers how their decision-makers understand the world.

The modern synthesis of organization theory and strategy is that problem and opportunity discovery by internal decision-makers directs strategic change. This definition is the root of a broad variety of important research projects, including the creation of modification of problems and opportunities, the focus on external versus internal problems and opportunities, the selection of decision-makers and their relative influence on the decision, and their ability to direct strategic change. Although much is already known about these topics, their importance for organizational strategy and the wide areas still not explored ensure that the organizational view of strategy has many research opportunities.

References

Almandoz J. 2012. Arriving at the starting line: the impact of community and financial logics on new banking ventures. *Academy of Management Journal* 55(6): 1381–1406.

Argyres N, Mostafa R. 2016. Knowledge inheritance, vertical integration, and entrant survival in the early U.S. auto industry. *Academy of Management Journal* 59(4): 1474–1492.

Audia PG, Freeman JH, Reynolds P. 2006. Organizational foundings in community context: instrument manufacturers and their interrelationship with other organizations. *Administrative Science Quarterly* 51(September): 381–419.

Baker WE, Faulkner RR. 1993. The social organization of conspiracy: illegal networks in the heavy electrical equipment industry. *American Sociological Review* 58(December): 837–860.

Barlow MA, Verhaal JC, Hoskins JD. 2016. Guilty by association: product-level category stigma and audience expectations in the U.S. craft beer industry. *Journal of Management* 44(7): 2934–2960.

Bartley T, Child C. 2011. Movements, markets, and fields: the effects of anti-sweatshop campaigns on U.S. firms, 1993–2000. *Social Forces* 90(2): 425–451.

Baum JAC, Dahlin KB. 2007. Aspiration performance and railroads' patterns of learning from train wrecks and crashes. *Organization Science* 18(3): 368–385.

Baum JAC, Ingram P. 1998. Survival-enhancing learning in the Manhattan hotel industry, 1898–1980. *Management Science* 44(7): 996–1016.

Baum JAC, Rowley TJ, Shipilov AV, Chuang Y-T. 2005. Dancing with strangers: aspiration performance and the search for underwriting syndicate partners. *Administrative Science Quarterly* 50(4): 536–575.

Bednar MK, Boivie S, Prince NR. 2013. Burr under the saddle: how media coverage influences strategic change. *Organization Science* 24(3): 910–925.

Boone C, Brocheler V, Carroll GR. 2000. Custom service: application and tests of resource-partitioning theory among Dutch auditing firms from 1896 to 1992. *Organization Studies* 21(2): 355.

Brass DJ, Galaskiewicz J, Greve HR, Tsai W. 2004. Taking stock of networks and organizations: a multi-level perspective. *Academy of Management Journal* 47(6): 795–814.

Carroll GR, Bigelow LS, Seidel M-D, Tsai LB. 1996. The fates of de novo and de alio producers in the American automobile industry, 1885–1981. *Strategic Management Journal* 17(Summer Special Issue): 117–137.

Carroll GR, Hannan MT. 2000. *The Demography of Corporations and Industries*. Princeton University Press: Princeton, NJ.

Carroll GR, Swaminathan A. 2000. Why the microbrewery movement? Organizational dynamics of resource partitioning in the U.S. brewing industry. *American Journal of Sociology* 106(3): 715–762.

Casciaro T, Piskorski MJ. 2005. Power imbalance, mutual dependence, and constraint absorption: a closer look at resource dependence theory. *Administrative Science Quarterly* 50(June): 167–199.

Castellucci F, Ertug G. 2010. What's in it for them? Advantages of higher-status partners in exchange relationships. *Academy of Management Journal* 53(1): 149–166.

Chung S, Singh H, Lee K. 2000. Complementarity, status similarity, and social capital as drivers of alliance formation. *Strategic Management Journal* 21(1): 1–22.

Crilly D, Zollo M, Hansen MT. 2012. Faking it or muddling through: understanding decoupling in response to stakeholder pressures. *Academy of Management Journal* 55(6): 1429–1448.

Cyert RM, March JG. 1963. *A Behavioral Theory of the Firm*. Prentice-Hall: Englewood Cliffs, NJ.

Daneels E. 2002. The dynamics of product innovation and firm competences. *Strategic Management Journal* 23(12): 1095.

Delmestri G, Greenwood R. 2016. How Cinderella became a queen: theorizing radical status change. *Administrative Science Quarterly* 61(4): 507–550.

Dencker JC, Gruber M. 2015. The effects of opportunities and founder experience on new firm performance. *Strategic Management Journal* 36(7): 1035–1052.

Desai V. 2010. Do organizations have to change to learn? Examining the effects of technological change and learning from failures in the natural gas distribution industry. *Industrial and Corporate Change* 19(3): 713–739.

Desai VM. 2008. Constrained growth: how experience, legitimacy, and age influence risk taking in organizations. *Organization Science* 19(4): 594–608.

Dobbin FR. 1995. The origins of economic principles: railway entrepreneurs and public policy in 19th-century America. In *The Institutional Construction of Organizations: International and Longitudinal Studies*, Scott WR, Christensen S (eds). Sage: Thousand Oaks, CA; 277–301.

Dobrev SD, Kim TY. 2006. Positioning among organizations in a population: moves between market segments and the evolution of industry structure. *Administrative Science Quarterly* 51(2): 230–261.

Fligstein N. 1991. The structural transformation of American industry: an institutional account of the causes of diversification in the largest firms, 1919–1979. In *The New Institutionalism in Organizational Analysis*, Powell WW, DiMaggio PJ (eds). University of Chicago Press: Chicago, IL; 311–336.

Funk RJ, Hirschman D. 2014. Derivatives and deregulation: financial innovation and the demise of Glass–Steagall. *Administrative Science Quarterly* 59(4): 669–704.

Gaba V, Bhattacharya S. 2012. Aspirations, innovation, and corporate venture capital: a behavioral perspective. *Strategic Entrepreneurship Journal* 6(2): 178–199.

Gaba V, Greve HR. 2019. Safe or profitable? the pursuit of conflicting goals. *Organization Science* 30(4): 647–667.

Gaba V, Joseph J. 2013. Corporate structure and performance feedback: aspirations and adaptation in M-form firms. *Organization Science* 24(4): 1102–1119.

Gavetti G, Greve HR, Levinthal DA, Ocasio W. 2012. The behavioral theory of the firm: assessment and prospects. *Academy of Management Annals* 6: 1–40.

Goldberg A, Hannan MT, Kovács B. 2016. What does it mean to span cultural boundaries? Variety and atypicality in cultural consumption. *American Sociological Review* 81(2): 215–241.

Granqvist N, Grodal S, Woolley JL. 2013. Hedging your bets: explaining executives' market labeling strategies in nanotechnology. *Organization Science* 24(2): 395–413.

Greenwood R, Raynard M, Kodeih F, Micelotta ER, Lounsbury M. 2011. Institutional complexity and organizational responses. *Academy of Management Annals* 5: 317–371.

Greenwood R, Suddaby R. 2006. Institutional entrepreneurship in mature fields: the big five accounting firms. *Academy of Management Journal* 49(1): 27–48.

Greve HR. 1998. Performance, aspirations, and risky organizational change. *Administrative Science Quarterly* 44(March): 58–86.

Greve HR. 1999. The effect of change on performance: inertia and regression toward the mean. *Administrative Science Quarterly* 44(September): 590–614.

Greve HR. 2008. A behavioral theory of firm growth: sequential attention to size and performance goals. *Academy of Management Journal* 51(3): 476–494.

Greve HR. 2009. Bigger and safer: the diffusion of competitive advantage. *Strategic Management Journal* 30(1): 1–23.

Greve HR. 2011. Positional rigidity: low performance and resource acquisition in large and small firms. *Strategic Management Journal* 32(1): 103–114.

Greve HR, Baum JAC, Mitsuhashi H, Rowley TJ. 2010. Built to last but falling apart: cohesion, friction, and withdrawal from interfirm alliances. *Academy of Management Journal* 53(2): 302–322.

Greve HR, Mitsuhashi H, Baum JAC. 2013. Greener pastures: outside options and strategic alliance withdrawal. *Organization Science* 24(1): 79–98.

Greve HR, Rao H. 2012. Echoes of the past: organizational foundings as sources of an institutional legacy of mutualism. *American Journal of Sociology* 118(3): 635–675.

Greve HR, Rao H. 2014. History and the present: institutional legacies in communities of organizations. *Research in Organizational Behavior* 34: 27–41.

Greve HR, Song SY. 2017. Amazon warrior: how a platform can restructure industry power and ecology. *Advances in Strategic Management* 37: 299–335.

Haleblian J, Kim J-YJ, Rajagopalan N. 2006. The influence of acquisition experience and performance on acquisition behavior: evidence from the U.S. commercial banking industry. *Academy of Management Journal* 49(2): 357–370.

Hallen BL, Katila R, Rosenberger JD. 2014. How do social defenses work? A resource-dependence lens on technology ventures, venture capital investors, and corporate relationships. *Academy of Management Journal* 57(4): 1078–1101.

Hannan MT, Carroll GR, Dundon EA, Torres JC. 1995. Organizational evolution in a multinational context: entries of automobile manufacturers in Belgium, Britain, France, Germany, and Italy. *American Sociological Review* 60(August): 509–528.

Hargadon AB, Douglas Y. 2001. When innovations meet institutions: Edison and the design of the electric light. *Administrative Science Quarterly* 46(3): 476–501.

Haunschild PR, Beckman CM. 1998. When do interlocks matter?: Alternate sources of information and interlock influence. *Administrative Science Quarterly* 43(December): 815–844.

Haveman HA, Rao H, Paruchuri S. 2007. The winds of change: the progressive movement and the bureaucratization of thrift. *American Sociological Review* 72(1): 117–142.

Hiatt SR, Grandy JB, Lee BH. 2015. Organizational responses to public and private politics: an analysis of climate change activists and U.S. oil and gas firms. *Organization Science* 26(6): 1769–1786.

Hillman AJ. 2005. Politicians on the board of directors: do connections affect the bottom line? *Journal of Management* 31(3): 464–481.

Howard M, Withers M, Tihanyi L. 2016. Knowledge dependence and the formation of director interlocks. *Academy of Management Journal* 60(5): 1986–2013.

Hsu G, Grodal S. 2015. Category taken-for-grantedness as a strategic opportunity: the case of light cigarettes, 1964 to 1993. *American Sociological Review* 80(1): 28–62.

Ingram P, Baum JAC. 1997. Opportunity and constraint: organizations' learning from the operating and competitive experience of industries. *Strategic Management Journal* 18(Summer): 75–98.

Ingram P, Rao H. 2004. Store wars: the enactment and repeal of anti-chain-store legislation in America. *American Journal of Sociology* 110(2): 446–487.

Jain A. 2013. Learning by doing and the locus of innovative capability in biotechnology research. *Organization Science* 24(6): 1683–1700.

Jonsson S. 2009. Refraining from imitation: professional resistance and limited diffusion in a financial market. *Organization Science* 20(1): 172–186.

Jonsson S, Regnar P. 2009. Normative barriers to imitation: social complexity of core competences in a mutual fund industry. *Strategic Management Journal* 30(5): 517–536.

Joseph J, Klingebiel R, Wilson AJ. 2016. Organizational structure and performance feedback: centralization, aspirations, and termination decisions. *Organization Science* 27(5): 1065–1083.

Joseph J, Ocasio W, McDonnell M-H. 2014. The structural elaboration of board independence: executive power, institutional logics, and the adoption of CEO-only board structures in U.S. corporate governance. *Academy of Management Journal* 57(6): 1834–1858.

Katila R, Rosenberger JD, Eisenhardt KM. 2008. Swimming with sharks: technology ventures, defense mechanisms, and corporate relationships. *Administrative Science Quarterly* 53(2): 295–332.

Kim J-YJ, Miner AS. 2007. Vicarious learning from the failures and near-failures of others: evidence from the U.S. commercial banking industry. *Academy of Management Journal* 50(3): 687–714.

King BG. 2008. A political mediation model of corporate response to social movement activism. *Administrative Science Quarterly* 53(3): 395–421.

Kölbel JF, Busch T, Jancso LM. 2017. How media coverage of corporate social irresponsibility increases financial risk. *Strategic Management Journal* 38(11): 2266–2284.

Kuusela P, Keil T, Maula M. 2017. Driven by aspirations, but in what direction? Performance shortfalls, slack resources, and resource-consuming vs. resource-freeing organizational change. *Strategic Management Journal* 38(5): 1101–1120.

Lane PJ, Lubatkin M. 1998. Relative absorptive capacity and interorganizational learning. *Strategic Management Journal* 19(5) (May): 461–477.

Lee M-DP, Lounsbury M. 2015. Filtering institutional logics: community logic variation and differential responses to the institutional complexity of toxic waste. *Organization Science* 26(3): 847–866.

Lounsbury M. 2002. Institutional transformation and status mobility: the professionalization of the field of finance. *Academy of Management Journal* 45(1): 255–266.

Luo X, Wang H, Raithel S, Zheng Q. 2015. Corporate social performance, analyst stock recommendation, and firm future returns. *Strategic Management Journal* 36(1): 123–136.

Madsen PM. 2009. These lives will not be lost in vain: organizational learning from disaster in U.S. coal mining. *Organization Science* 20(5): 861–875.

Martin X, Swaminathan A, Mitchell W. 1998. Organizational evolution in the interorganizational environment: incentives and constraints on international expansion strategy. *Administrative Science Quarterly* 43(September): 566–601.

McDonnell M-H, King B. 2013. Keeping up appearances: reputational threat and impression management after social movement boycotts. *Administrative Science Quarterly* 58(3): 387–419.

McGrath RG. 2001. Exploratory learning, innovative capacity, and the role of managerial oversight. *Academy of Management Journal* 44(1): 118–131.

McKendrick DG, Wade JB, Jaffee J. 2009. A good riddance? Spin-offs and the technological performance of parent firms. *Organization Science* 20(6): 979–992.

Meyer JW, Rowan B. 1977. Institutionalized organizations: formal structure as myth and ceremony. *American Journal of Sociology* 83: 340–363.

Mitsuhashi H, Greve HR. 2009. A matching theory of alliance formation and organizational success: complementarity and compatibility. *Academy of Management Journal* 52(5): 975–995.

Munir KA, Phillips N. 2005. The birth of the "Kodak moment": Institutional entrepreneurship and the adoption of new technologies. *Organization Studies* 26(11): 1665–1687.

Negro G, Hannan MT, Rao H. 2011. Category reinterpretation and defection: modernism and tradition in Italian winemaking. *Organization Science* 22(6): 1449–1463.

Odziemkowska K, Henisz WJ. 2020. Webs of influence: secondary stakeholder actions and cross-national corporate social performance. *Organization Science*, forthcoming.

Pahnke EC, Katila R, Eisenhardt KM. 2015. Who takes you to the dance? How partners' institutional logics influence innovation in young firms. *Administrative Science Quarterly* 60(4): 596–633.

Parker ON, Krause R, Covin JG. 2017. Ready, set, slow: how aspiration-relative product quality impacts the rate of new product introduction. *Journal of Management* 43(7): 2333–2356.

Perretti F, Negro G, Lomi A. 2008. E pluribus unum: framing, matching, and form emergence in U.S. television broadcasting, 1940–1960. *Organization Science* 19(4): 533–547.

Petkova AP, Rindova VP, Gupta AK. 2013. No news is bad news: sensegiving activities, media attention, and venture capital funding of new technology organizations. *Organization Science* 24(3): 865–888.

Pfeffer J, Salancik GR. 1978. *The External Control of Organizations*. Harper and Row: New York, NY.

Powell WW, White DR, Koput KW, Owen-Smith J. 2005. Network dynamics and field evolution: the growth of interorganizational collaboration in the life sciences. *American Journal of Sociology* 110(4): 1132–1205.

Raaijmakers AGM, Vermeulen PAM, Meeus MTH, Zietsma C. 2015. I need time! Exploring pathways to compliance under institutional complexity. *Academy of Management Journal* 58(1): 85–110.

Rao H. 1994. The social construction of reputation: certification contests, legitimation, and the survival of organizations in the American automobile industry, 1895–1912. *Strategic Management Journal* 15(S2): 29–44.

Rao H, Monin P, Durand R. 2003. Institutional change in Toque Ville: nouvelle cuisine as an identity movement in French gastronomy. *American Journal of Sociology* 108(4): 795–843.

Reid EM, Toffel MW. 2009. Responding to public and private politics: corporate disclosure of climate change strategies. *Strategic Management Journal* 30(11): 1157–1178.

Rogan M, Greve HR. 2015. Resource dependence dynamics: partner reactions to mergers. *Organization Science* 26(1): 239–255.

Rowley TI, Shipilov AV, Greve HR. 2017. Board reform versus profits: the effect of rankings on the adoption of governance practices. *Strategic Management Journal* 38(4): 815–833.

Rudy BC, Johnson AF. 2016. Performance, aspirations, and market versus nonmarket investment. *Journal of Management* 42(4): 936–959.

Ruef M. 2000. The emergence of organizational forms: a community ecology approach. *American Journal of Sociology* 106(3): 658–714.

Sauder M, Espeland WN. 2009. The discipline of rankings: tight coupling and organizational change. *American Sociological Review* 74(1): 63–82.

Schneiberg M, King M, Smith T. 2008. Social movements and organizational form: cooperative alternatives to corporations in the American insurance, dairy, and grain industries. *American Sociological Review* 73(4): 635–667.

Scott WR. 1987. *Organizations: Rational, Natural, and Open Systems, 2nd ed.* Prentice-Hall: Englewood Cliffs, NJ.

Scott WR. 2001. *Institutions and Organizations.* Sage: Thousand Oaks, CA.

Shinkle GA. 2012. Organizational aspirations, reference points, and goals. *Journal of Management* 38(1): 415–455.

Shipilov A, Gawer A. 2020. Integrating research on inter-organizational networks and ecosystems. *Academy of Management Annals* 14(1): 92–121.

Shipilov AV, Greve HR, Rowley TJ. 2010. When do interlocks matter? Institutional logics and the diffusion of multiple corporate governance practices. *Academy of Management Journal* 53(4): 846–864.

Shipilov AV, Greve HR, Rowley TJ. 2019. Is all publicity good publicity? The impact of direct and indirect media pressure on the adoption of governance practices. *Strategic Management Journal* 40(9): 1368–1393.

Shipilov AV, Li SX, Greve HR. 2011. The prince and the pauper: search and brokerage in the initiation of status-heterophilous ties. *Organization Science* 22(6): 1418–1434.

Simon DH, Lieberman MB. 2010. Internal and external influences on adoption decisions in multi-unit firms: the moderating effect of experience. *Strategic Organization* 8(2): 132–154.

Smets M, Jarzabkowski P, Burke GT, Spee P. 2015. Reinsurance trading in Lloyd's of London: balancing conflicting-yet-complementary logics in practice. *Academy of Management Journal* 58(3): 932–970.

Sorenson O, Audia PG. 2000. The social structure of entrepreneurial activity: geographic concentration of footwear production in the U.S., 1940-1989. *American Journal of Sociology* 106(2): 424–462.

Stark D, Vedres B. 2012. Political holes in the economy: the business network of partisan firms in Hungary. *American Sociological Review* 77(5): 700–722.

Sytch M, Tatarynowicz A, Gulati R. 2012. Toward a theory of extended contact: the incentives and opportunities for bridging across network communities. *Organization Science* 23(6): 1658–1681.

Tarakci M, Ateş NY, Floyd SW, Ahn Y, Wooldridge B. 2018. Performance feedback and middle managers' divergent strategic behavior: the roles of social comparisons and organizational identification. *Strategic Management Journal* 39(4): 1139–1162.

Thornton PH. 2002. The rise of the corporation in a craft industry: conflict and conformity in institutional logics. *Academy of Management Journal* 45(1): 81–101.

Tihanyi L, Hegarty WH. 2007. Political interests and the emergence of commercial banking in transition economies. *Journal of Management Studies* 44(5): 788–813.

Tyler BB, Caner T. 2016. New product introductions below aspirations, slack, and R&D alliances: a behavioral perspective. *Strategic Management Journal* 37(5): 896–910.

Vidal E, Mitchell W. 2015. Adding by subtracting: the relationship between performance feedback and resource reconfiguration through divestitures. *Organization Science* 26(4): 1101–1118.

Wang T, Wezel FC, Forgues B. 2016. Protecting market identity: when and how do organizations respond to consumers' devaluations? *Academy of Management Journal* 59(1): 135–162.

Weber K, Heinze KL, DeSoucey M. 2008. Forage for thought: mobilizing codes in the movement for grass-fed meat and dairy products. *Administrative Science Quarterly* 53(3): 529–567.

Westphal JD, Seidel M-D, Stewart KJ. 2001. Second-order imitation: uncovering latent effects of board network ties. *Administrative Science Quarterly* 46(December): 717–747.

Wezel FC, Saka-Helmhout A. 2006. Antecedents and consequences of organizational change: "institutionalizing" the behavioral theory of the firm. *Organization Studies* 27(2): 265–286.

Wry T, Cobb JA, Aldrich HE. 2013. More than a metaphor assessing the historical legacy of resource dependence and its contemporary promise as a theory of environmental complexity. *Academy of Management Annals* 7(1): 441–488.

Yue LQ, Wang J, Yang B. 2019. Contesting commercialization: political influence, responsive authoritarianism, and cultural resistance. *Administrative Science Quarterly* 64(2): 435–465.

Zelizer VA. 1978. Human values and the market: the case of life insurance and death in 19th-century America. *American Journal of Sociology* 84(3): 591–610.

Zhang CM, Greve HR. 2018. Delayed adoption of rules: a relational theory of firm exposure and state cooptation. *Journal of Management* 44(8): 3336–3363.

Zhang CM, Greve HR. 2019. Dominant coalitions directing acquisitions: different decision makers, different decisions. *Academy of Management Journal* 62(1): 44–65.

Zhang J, Luo XR. 2013. Dared to care: organizational vulnerability, institutional logics, and MNCs' social responsiveness in emerging markets. *Organization Science* 24(6): 1742–1764.

1.2

THE ECONOMIC VIEW OF STRATEGIC MANAGEMENT

Constance E. Helfat

Research in strategic management has traditionally distinguished between strategy "content" (what a strategy consists of) and strategy "process" (how a firm or other organization formulates and implements its strategy). Although scholars sometimes have the perception that theory in strategic management that relies on the logic of economics deals only with strategy content, some economics-based theories also deal with strategy process. In addition, because strategic management is an interdisciplinary field, economics-based theories of strategic management have many touchpoints with organizational and psychological theory.

Economics-based theories in strategic management can be grouped into two categories: (1) homegrown theories developed within the field of strategic management that rely on economic logic, and (2) theories that originated in the field of economics but that have been applied and often developed more extensively in the field of strategic management. The discussion in this chapter emphasizes foundational theories and provides selected examples of subsequent work of both types, before turning to emerging areas of interest. The survey does not focus on modeling approaches in economics such as game theory, which scholars have used to develop theory in many areas of strategic management.[1] In addition, although theory leads to empirical work and vice versa, this chapter focuses primarily on theory.

Homegrown Economics-Based Theory in Strategic Management

Given the centrality of supply and demand in economics, it is not surprising that economics-based theories in strategic management fall naturally into those that focus on either supply or demand or their interaction. Many of the homegrown economics-based theories in strategic management focus on supply, especially firms' use of resources and capabilities for the production of goods and services, which is largely a black box in economics. In recent years, theory in strategic management has also focused on demand, and on the interaction of supply and demand viewed through the lens of value creation and capture.

Resources

The *resource-based view* of the firm (RBV) is one of the earliest and most widely used of the homegrown economics-based theories. The RBV has as a central concern the contribution of firm resources to competitive advantage, including tangible, intangible, and human assets (Grant, 2019) and capabilities (together referred to simply as "resources" in the remainder of this section).[2] The economist Edith Penrose in 1959 proposed the idea that firms are a "collection of productive resources" in her seminal work, *The Theory of the Growth of the Firm* (1959; third edition, 1995: 24). However, the idea largely lay fallow until strategic management scholars developed theory that linked firm resources to differential firm performance. Early theoretical contributions to the RBV included the work of Wernerfelt (1984), Rumelt (1984), Barney (1986, 1991), Mahoney and Pandian (1992), Peteraf (1993), and Amit and Schoemaker (1993), followed by many others.

The economic principle of scarcity is central to the RBV—otherwise, resources (or bundles of resources) cannot serve as sources of advantage. Firms also require *isolating mechanisms* that make resource imitation or substitution by other firms difficult (Rumelt, 1984). These mechanisms include *causal ambiguity*, which refers to the difficulty that firms face in understanding how particular resources produce the outcomes that they do (Rumelt, 1984). The resulting *uncertain imitability* can produce above-normal industry profits as well as heterogeneity in profitability across firms (Lippman and Rumelt, 1982). Additional isolating mechanisms include *time compression diseconomies* (high costs that arise when firms try to speed up resource development and imitation) (Dierickx and Cool, 1989; Pacheco de Almeida and Zemsky, 2007), among others. For these reasons, valuable, rare, inimitable, and nonsubstitutable (VRIN) resources are potential sources of competitive advantage (Barney, 1991).

A variety of resources fit the VRIN criteria, and perhaps none more so than some types of knowledge. *Tacit knowledge* in particular is difficult to purchase in the marketplace and difficult to imitate (Nelson and Winter, 1982; Winter, 1987). What is known as the *knowledge-based view* (KBV) of the firm deals with the role of knowledge as a critical intangible asset that underpins the ability of firms to survive, prosper, and innovate (Kogut and Zander, 1992; Grant, 1996). Moreover, recombination of knowledge is a fundamental source of innovation that can propel firm growth and confer competitive advantage (Kogut and Zander, 1992).

Firms also require access to human assets. Research has focused on the ability of firms to generate rents from human capital (Coff, 1997) and appropriate the returns; the latter depends in part on the bargaining power of management, employees, and shareholders (Coff, 1999; Castanias and Helfat, 1991). Campbell, Coff, and Kryscynski (2012) further argued that both firm-specific and general human capital (Becker, 1964) may serve as sources of competitive advantage, and that firm-specific incentives for firm-specific human capital are required (Kryscynski, Coff, and Campbell, 2020).

Other theory related to the RBV includes the *relational view*, which incorporates resources that are embedded in interfirm relationships and can lead to above-normal profits (Dyer and Singh, 1998). For example, partners may invest in relation-specific assets such as equipment that is specialized to a particular production process (Dyer and Singh, 1998). In addition, *complementary assets* that are required for the commercialization of an innovation (e.g., manufacturing technology) and that are specialized to the innovation can defend against imitation when a firm lacks strong legal property rights (Teece, 1986). Taking this one step further, using cooperative game theory Lippman and Rumelt (2003a) argued that complementarities among resources are critical for excess (above-zero-profit) returns from trading (buying and selling) resources (see also Barney, 1988; Conner, 1991). In addition, research has examined the relationship between factor markets for resources (Barney, 1986) and competition in the product market (e.g., Chatain, 2014).

Capabilities

Like tangible, intangible, and human assets, firm capabilities can also serve as sources of above-normal profits and help firms to innovate and survive. An organizational capability is generally viewed as a coordinated bundle of routines—a set of rules, procedures, or techniques (Nelson and Winter, 1982)—that provides the capacity to make decisions or perform an activity (Winter, 2000). Capabilities relate directly to strategy process (Maritan and Peteraf, 2007), in that routines and capabilities are part and parcel of strategic decision-making and implementation (Dosi, Nelson, and Winter, 2000).

Firms in the same industry often differ in their capabilities. Amit and Schoemaker (1993) pointed to psychological factors such as heterogeneous beliefs and biases that affect decisions to develop and deploy resources. In addition, a path-dependent process of capability accumulation through experiential and deliberate learning (Zollo and Winter, 2002) of firms that have different initial capabilities reinforces heterogeneity of capabilities across firms (Helfat and Peteraf, 2003).

The literature distinguishes between *operational* or *ordinary capabilities* and *dynamic capabilities* (Teece, Pisano, and Shuen, 1997; Eisenhardt and Martin, 2000; Winter, 2003). Operational capabilities enable a firm to maintain how it currently makes its living (Winter, 2003) "using more or less the same techniques on the same scale to support existing products and services for the same customer population" (Helfat and Winter, 2011: 1244). Dynamic capabilities refer to firm capabilities directed toward strategic and organizational change, including capabilities for innovation (Teece *et al.*, 1997), acquisitions (Capron, Anand, and Mitchell, 2007; Capron and Mitchell, 2009), and alliances (Dyer, Kale, and Singh, 2007).

Teece *et al.* (1997: 516) defined firm dynamic capabilities as "the ability to integrate, build, and reconfigure internal and external capabilities" (for related definitions, see Winter, 2003, and Helfat *et al.*, 2007). Managers may also have *dynamic managerial capabilities* directed toward strategic change (Adner and Helfat, 2003). Key dynamic managerial capabilities include those for *resource management* (Sirmon, Hitt, and Ireland, 2007) and *asset orchestration* (Helfat *et al.*, 2007) that involve building and (re)configuring firm resources (Sirmon and Hitt, 2009). Teece (2007) elaborated on the core functions that dynamic capabilities perform: *sensing* new opportunities and threats, *seizing* new opportunities through investment and construction of business models, and *transforming/reconfiguring* the organization. Like Amit and Schoemaker's (1993) analysis of capabilities in general, Teece (2007) brought in cognitive elements, especially with respect to the sensing and seizing functions of dynamic capabilities. More generally, the firm's capacity to absorb new knowledge and employ it—*absorptive capacity* in the terminology of Cohen and Levinthal (1990)—is critical for dynamic capabilities (Zahra and George, 2002).

Demand-based view and value creation and capture

To complement strategic management theory focused on the supply side of the market, an important body of theoretical work put forward a *demand-based view* of strategy. Adner (2002) modeled consumer preferences in order to understand competition between technologies and the emergence of competition from disruptive technologies (Christensen, 1997). Adner and Zemsky (2006) expanded the demand-based view to show how consumer heterogeneity across market segments, in combination with resource heterogeneity, affects the sustainability of competitive advantage. Lippman and Rumelt (2003a) also brought together demand and supply (of resources) in arguing that the value of both priced and unpriced resources stems from demand for the products that the resources produce. Priem (2007) then emphasized the importance of strategies that maximize the value of goods and services to consumers. Makadok and Ross (2013) further analyzed the effect on profits of product differentiation, which influences consumer demand, in combination with the effect of rivalry.

Whether from the perspective of the demand or the supply side, research in strategic management often focuses on capturing value, that is, profits. Drawing on industrial organization economics, Porter (1979) laid out a framework for understanding how the relative bargaining power between different "forces" in an industry affects the ability of industry incumbents as a group to capture profits. Then, using the tools of cooperative game theory, Brandenburger and Stuart (1996) developed a theory of *value-based strategy*, in which bargaining among different players in an industry affects which players capture value, and how much.

Brandenburger and Stuart (1996) defined *economic value* as the difference between consumer willingness-to-pay and supplier opportunity costs. This definition has been widely adopted in strategic management, including in the resource-based view (Peteraf and Barney, 2003) and the demand-based view (Adner and Zemsky, 2006). How much value each player captures depends in part on how much value each player adds to the total value created, and in part on each player's bargaining ability (Brandenburger and Stuart, 1996, 2007; MacDonald and Ryall, 2004). Building on this work, Lieberman, Balasubramanian, and Garcia-Castro (2018) introduced the concept of *economic gain*, defined as the increase in economic value created by a firm, including through innovation or displacement of one firm by another.

Economic Theory Applied and Expanded in Strategic Management

In addition to homegrown theories that rely on economic logic, some prominent theories used in strategic management originated in the field of economics but have been substantially expanded in new directions within strategic management. These include theories focused on the scale and scope of the firm, the boundary of the firm, and strategic adaptation and change.

Scale and scope of the firm

The scale and scope of the firm is a core topic of research in strategic management, beginning with early empirical investigations of product-market diversification by scholars such as Rumelt (1974), Bettis (1981), and Christensen and Montgomery (1981). As research on diversification proceeded in strategic management, Penrose's (1959) work in economics on firm growth came to provide an important theoretical foundation (Mahoney and Pandian, 1992).[3] Penrose argued that firms have incentives to expand through what Rumelt (1974) later termed *related diversification*, in order to (1) fully utilize indivisible resources, (2) efficiently utilize resources specialized to a particular task, and (3) take advantage of opportunities uncovered through the accumulation of and search for knowledge. This logic underpins arguments made in numerous empirical studies that related diversification is more likely to have a positive effect on firm performance than *unrelated diversification*.

Many years later, Panzar and Willig (1981) introduced the concept of *economies of scope*, in which the total cost of producing two products jointly is less than the total cost of producing them separately, including for reasons proposed by Penrose (1959) (see Bailey and Friedlander, 1982). Teece (1980, 1982) further argued that economies of scope on their own do not provide a basis for related diversification, and that market failure is also required. In addition, Montgomery and Wernerfelt (1988) developed a model showing that resources that are more specialized to particular uses (reminiscent of Penrose) form the basis for related diversification into a narrower set of markets but generate higher rents than more fungible resources.

More recently, Helfat and Eisenhardt (2004) introduced the concept of *intertemporal economies of scope* that derive from *resource redeployment* across products and businesses over time, in contrast to sharing resources contemporaneously as in standard (intratemporal) economies of scope. Levinthal and Wu (2010) subsequently distinguished between *scale-free* and *non-scale-free resources*, arguing that diversification through redeployment is more likely to rely on the latter type of resources. Subsequent research has used *real options* theory to model resource redeployment as a source of value in product-market diversification (Sakhartov and Folta, 2014, 2015), and to model business exit by diversified firms (Lieberman, Lee, and Folta, 2017).

The organizational form of multibusiness firms also affects their performance. Williamson (1970, 1975) proposed that a multidivisional form (*M-form*), in which the firm decentralizes decisions to divisions that participate in different product-markets, is most efficient. The canonical M-form, however, does not provide a mechanism for achieving economies of scope through resources shared across divisions. Hill, Hitt, and Hoskisson (1992) argued that in order to realize such economies of scope, related diversified firms require greater centralized control and coordination between divisions than in the pure M-form. In contrast, achieving intertemporal economies of scope through resource redeployment does not require contemporaneous coordination across divisions, so a modular approach such as the M-form may be efficient (Helfat and Eisenhardt, 2004).

Boundary of the firm

Another important question concerns where the boundary of the firm lies, and the limits to scale and scope. One prominent answer to this question comes from *transaction cost economics*, developed by the Nobel Prize–winning economist Oliver Williamson.[4] With respect to vertical integration, Williamson (1975, 1985) argued that when standalone entities face high transaction costs of contracting in markets, organizing production internally is more efficient (all else being equal). It is often prohibitively costly to craft contracts when uncertainty and complexity are high. In addition, firms face a high risk of *ex post opportunism*, in which one party acts opportunistically to "hold up" the other to obtain better terms after having entered into a contract, when there are *small numbers* of parties with whom to contract and *asset specificity* is high (i.e., a buyer requires inputs that are specialized to its output or a supplier tailors its output to a buyer's input requirements). These principles spawned a large number of empirical studies on vertical integration in strategic management.

Teece (1980, 1982) applied this logic to product-market diversification, arguing that in the absence of market failures such as those due to high transaction costs, joint production of multiple products need not take place within the same firm. In addition, firms may utilize strategic alliances and joint ventures when high transaction costs make contracting for goods and services infeasible and acquiring the requisite assets outright or building them internally is difficult (Hennart, 1988, 1991; Oxley, 1997).

A related stream of research brought together work on transaction costs and resources/capabilities. Monteverde and Teece (1982) argued that transaction-specific knowledge is more efficiently organized internally. Hennart (1988, 1991) and Oxley (1997) made a similar point about the difficulty of using market contracts for the exchange of tacit knowledge. Teece (1988, 1996) further argued that *systemic innovations*, which require alignment and coordinated adjustment across different stages in a vertical chain, raise the transaction costs of using markets (see also Armour and Teece, 1980). Monteverde (1995) then proposed that systemic innovations are facilitated by in-house *unstructured technical dialogue*—"unstructured, uncodifiable, generally verbal and often face-to-face communication" (Monteverde, 1995: 1629). More generally, research has argued that asset specificity in the form of firm-specific routines and communication codes may facilitate vertical integration (Armour and Teece, 1980; Conner and Prahalad, 1996; Kogut and Zander, 1992).

Building on this work, Helfat and Campo-Rembado (2016) proposed that when firms have strong *integrative capabilities* for communication and coordination (see also Iansiti and Clark, 1994; Henderson, 1994; Helfat and Raubitschek, 2000; Chen, Williams, and Agarwal, 2009), they may remain integrated even when transaction costs are low in order to retain the potential to develop systemic innovations. Argyres and Zenger (2012) also brought together transaction cost and resource-based logic in arguing that the boundary of the firm is driven by unique complementarities among resources and activities. Taking a different approach, Jacobides and Winter (2005) developed a theory of the co-evolution of firm capabilities and transaction costs, in which transaction costs fall endogenously and formerly integrated firms disintegrate. Complementary research has proposed that firms may develop *contract design capabilities* that enable firms to use contracts rather than internalize transactions (Mayer and Argyres, 2004; Argyres and Mayer, 2007).

Strategic adaptation and change

The interlinked questions of firm boundaries and firm expansion relate to the broader issue of strategic change. *Evolutionary economics* (Nelson and Winter, 1982) is fundamentally concerned with economic change, particularly with technological innovation (Nelson et al., 2018). Evolutionary economics followed Simon (1957) and Cyert and March (1963) in basing firm behavior on bounded rationality and routines, key features of the *behavioral theory of the firm*. From this starting point, evolutionary economics went in new directions, adding greater flexibility in routines, along with more attention to their replication and imitation. Evolutionary economics also incorporated the skills of individuals, including with respect to tacit knowledge and cognition, and put forth the concept of firm capabilities. The theory further incorporated the capacity of the firm to search for new knowledge and techniques, to innovate, and to respond to changing market conditions through profit-seeking behavior (Nelson, 2020).

In addition to providing a foundation for research on capabilities in strategic management as discussed earlier, evolutionary economics served as an important foundation for the knowledge-based view of the firm (Kogut and Zander, 1992). Evolutionary theory has also come into play in numerous studies of technology strategy. In addition, the concept of *local search* from evolutionary economics and the behavioral theory of the firm has featured prominently in strategic management research, especially in the analysis of innovative activity (e.g., Rosenkopf and Nerkar, 2001; Katila and Ahuja, 2002). Evolutionary economics has strong implications for heterogeneity among firms as well. Local search and cumulative learning, in combination with tacit and firm-specific knowledge, lead to persistent differences in firm capabilities, activities, and performance (Nelson, 1991; Rumelt, Schendel, and Teece, 1991; Helfat, 1994).

Beginning with the work of Levinthal (1997), a stream of theoretical research on firm adaptation to changing environments has used NK simulation modeling (Kauffman, 1993, 1995) to incorporate both local and distant search. (For a discussion of NK methodology and its use in strategic management research, see Ganco and Hoetker, 2009.) Models of this type have investigated firms' search for organizational forms (Levinthal, 1997), strategies (Rivkin, 2000), and innovations (Ethiraj and Levinthal, 2004), and compared experiential and cognitive search for firm policies and practices (Gavetti and Levinthal, 2000). Nickerson and Zenger (2004) also used the logic of NK models to propose a *problem-solving perspective* on knowledge generation that has implications for firm boundaries, drawing on evolutionary economics, the resource-based and knowledge-based views, and transaction cost economics. Recent work has used NK modeling to incorporate not only the search for new policies but also firms' *shaping* of their external environments, which affects competitive advantage (Gavetti, Helfat, and Marengo, 2017).

Another approach to strategic change draws from work on *real options* in economics (Dixit and Pindyck, 1994), a concept first introduced by Myers (1977), in which firms' organizational investments provide preferential access to opportunities in the future. In one of the first applications of real options theory in strategic management, Kogut (1991) proposed that joint ventures provide real options for strategic responses to opportunities for future growth while limiting downside investment risk. Bowman and Hurry (1993: 763) argued more generally that a firm's resources provide real options for strategic choices and are particularly valuable under conditions of uncertainty. Kogut and Kulatilaka (2001) subsequently expanded on the real options characteristics of capabilities and the learning that underpins them (see also Baldwin and Clark [1992] on real options valuation of investments in capabilities). In addition, Kogut and Kulatilaka (1994) modeled multinational operations as providing real options that firms can use to shift operations across countries in response to future developments. This and other work on real options has provided a lens through which to understand a wide range of strategic issues, including managing risk, developing resources and capabilities, market entry and exit, growth, diversification (including through resource redeployment), vertical integration, international business, and strategic alliances and joint ventures (for a review, see Trigeorgis and Reuer, 2017).

Additional economic theories and concepts used in strategic management

Beyond the theoretical work already discussed, strategic management research has benefited from many other economic theories and concepts. For example, agency theory (Jensen and Meckling, 1976) has been used to analyze corporate governance (boards of directors and executives), strategic actions such as mergers and acquisitions, and resource allocation. Research on competitive actions and outcomes has relied on signaling theory (Spence, 1974) and information economics more generally, oligopoly theory (Shapiro, 1989), auction theory (Wilson, 1992), and economic analysis of first mover advantage (for a review, see Lieberman and Montgomery, 1988), strategic groups (Caves and Porter, 1977), multimarket contact (Bernheim and Whinston, 1990), and product differentiation (Hotelling, 1929; Mussa and Rosen, 1978). Models of industry evolution (Jovanovic, 1982; Klepper, 1996; Malerba *et al.*, 1999), research and development (Nelson, 1961), and the learning curve (Arrow, 1962; Lieberman, 1987) have also proved useful. In addition, strategic management research concerned with risk has utilized the concept of Knightian uncertainty (Knight, 1921), as well as prospect theory (Kahneman and Tversky, 1979). Although this is not a complete list, it provides a sense of additional economics-based theories and concepts used in strategic management.

Emergent Theoretical Research and Future Directions

Theoretical research in strategic management is on the upswing—advancing existing theory in new directions and providing theoretical understanding of new phenomena. In what follows, I discuss a sampling of recent research that points to directions for future work. I also highlight an understudied but important issue in strategic management that would benefit from additional theoretical as well as empirical research.

Advancing existing theory in new directions

New theory is emerging in the foundations of, and interactions between, the resource-based view (RBV), transaction cost theory, and value-based strategy, as well as new directions for evolutionary theory. Barney (2018) put forth the argument that the model of profit generation in the resource-based view requires a stakeholder perspective in which shareholders are not the only residual claimants to firm profits. He used transaction cost and property rights theories to show that shareholders cannot be unique claimants to economic profits when firms generate economic profits through resources. Barney (2018) then drew additional implications for a stakeholder approach to the RBV, including with respect to profit appropriation. Future research could model a resource-based stakeholder view from the perspective of value-based strategy, building on the *payments perspective* of Lippman and Rumelt (2003b), and building out the stakeholder view in other ways.

Another new perspective that is closely related to the RBV comes from Wernerfelt's (2016, 2020) *adaptation-cost theory*. Wernerfelt focused on the extent to which workers (and other resources) must adapt as they provide services to different users or uses, in an effort to provide a microfoundation (Felin and Foss, 2005) for the theory of the firm. He then linked this need for adaptation to the cost of contracting for the services of resources, and to economies of scale in contracting. The analysis has implications for the types of resources that are likely to be housed within firms. In future research, it may be helpful to ask: how do contract design capabilities (Argyres and Mayer, 2007) affect adaptation costs, and what implications does this have for the boundary of the firm? Wernerfelt's analysis also has implications for firm scope that hark back to Penrose's (1959) original ideas about individual resources as the basis for related diversification. As Wernerfelt (2020) notes, different resources may provide different paths for scope expansion. This observation suggests questions for future research. For example: How do resources affect the choices that firms make among multiple paths for scope expansion? Can firms pursue multiple expansion paths simultaneously, and if so, under what conditions? What effect does the potential to redeploy existing resources have on the expansion paths that firms choose?

Another avenue for further exploration concerns the relationship of the firm to its external environment. Prior research has brought together resource-based theorizing with competitive interactions and rivalry (e.g., Makadok, 2010; Chatain, 2014). New work along these lines would be valuable to further unpack the effects of resource development on competitive positions in the marketplace and the ability to appropriate profits (for a recent example, see Asmussen *et al.*, 2020).

In addition, strategic management research is only beginning to focus on a different aspect of a firm's relationship to its environment, namely that a firm can shape its external environment by taking actions such as developing innovative new products (Gavetti *et al.*, 2017; Eisenhardt, 2021; Rindova and Courtney, 2020). That is, instead of a firm seeking a competitive advantage within a predetermined (exogenous) payoff structure and adapting to exogenous events after they unfold, the firm may be able to create or alter the payoff structure for all firms to its advantage (Gavetti *et al.*, 2017). For example, a firm that introduces a disruptive innovation (Bower and Christensen, 1995) may be able to reshape the payoff structure in its favor. There are many interesting questions to ask about shaping. For example, how does shaping interact with exogenous changes in technologies, customer tastes, competitors, and nonmarket factors? How does shaping affect competitive advantage as firms and their external environments coevolve? How does shaping differ in existing markets versus nascent markets?

Theoretical understanding of new phenomena

Several areas of research in strategic management have emerged or become more prominent in recent years as firms contend with strategic issues that have taken on greater importance. These include corporate social responsibility (CSR) and non-market strategy, as well as business ecosystems and digital platforms.

Research on corporate social responsibility has been largely empirical, but new work is emerging that seeks to provide a stronger theoretical foundation. For example, Kaul and Luo (2018) developed a formal model that explains the conditions under which it is efficient for firms rather than not-for-profit entities to provide social goods, which depends in part on a firm's cost advantage from its resources and capabilities. Firms may also use nonmarket strategy (Dorobantu, Kaul, and Zelner, 2017), including through collective action (Ostrom, 1990), to cope with external pressures to increase activities directed toward CSR, and to deal with a world in which government actions around the globe affect firm performance. In new theoretical work, it would be helpful to ask: how do firms use CSR activities, and nonmarket actions more generally, to shape the external environment rather than simply adapt to it?

It is also truer now more than ever that firms cannot do everything on their own, and often rely on partners in business *ecosystems*. Adner (2017) provided a theoretical framework for understanding ecosystems, with subsequent analysis by Jacobides, Cennamo, and Gawer (2018). With the rise of ecosystems as well as greater openness in innovation (Chesbrough, 2003), firms draw more frequently on resources outside of their boundaries. Alexy *et al.* (2018) provided an analysis of resource-based competitive advantage when important resources come from outside the firm. New technology has also made possible an important type of ecosystem based on a digital platform. The economics of multisided platforms (Rochet and Tirole, 2003) have proved helpful in understanding platform strategy, together with theoretical work in strategic management on platforms (Gawer, 2014, 2020), including with respect to the firm boundaries of platform owners (Boudreau, 2017). Recent work has also proposed that integrative capabilities (Helfat and Raubitscheck, 2018) and dynamic capabilities more generally play an important role in platform and ecosystem strategy (Teece, 2018). All of these issues would benefit from more attention in a digitally enabled world. Examining core strategic management issues would be especially fruitful in future research. For example, what are the sources of heterogeneity in the resources and capabilities of firms operating in business ecosystems, and how does this affect competitive advantage? How do economies of scope affect diversification by different types of firms in business ecosystems?

An understudied issue in strategic management

Finally, I would like to highlight an important issue in strategic management that is rarely examined as a separate topic in its own right: firm growth. A great deal of research has implicitly examined firm growth through the study of diversification, and many other topics studied in strategic management have implications for firm growth; these topics include vertical integration, market entry and exit, resource redeployment, real options, divestment (including through spinoffs), technological innovation and diffusion, the evolution of firms and industries, and firm strategy in nascent industries, to name just a few. However, we know much less about firm growth overall and its effect on financial performance. This seems important to remedy, given the emphasis that firms place on growth, and the importance of profitable firm growth to the growth of the economy. Some unanswered questions include: How do firms choose among and combine different avenues for growth? What determines heterogeneity in the ways in which firms pursue growth? How do these choices affect real options that firms may be able to capitalize on in the future? And what is the effect on financial performance?

Conclusion

As strategic management has grown into a thriving field of academic inquiry during the past 50 years, theory that relies on the logic of economics has played a pivotal role. Homegrown theory has been instrumental to the growth of the field, paving the way for a large amount of empirical work. Theoretical work in the field of economics has also had a substantial effect on strategic management research, both empirical and theoretical. Scholars today are pushing forward theory development in strategic management to address gaps in existing theories, to improve the understanding of new phenomena, and to investigate fundamental questions not yet addressed. New theory development holds great promise for the field of strategic management in the years to come.

Notes

1. See Hannah, Tidhar, and Eisenhardt (2020) for a survey of modeling approaches from economics used in theoretical models in strategic management.
2. The meaning of "competitive advantage" has been the subject of debate in the strategic management literature. It has been used to refer to both the creation of rents and its appropriation in the form of profits. See Coff (1999) and the discussion of value creation and capture later in this chapter.
3. Although Penrose included only physical and human resources in her analysis, her arguments apply to other types of resources.

4. The seminal paper of Ronald Coase (1937), "The Nature of the Firm," served as a springboard for Williamson's theory. As in transaction cost theory, the incompleteness of contracts is central to property rights theory (Grossman and Hart, 1986; Hart and Moore, 1990). Although property rights theory has been used less in strategic management, many applications are possible (Kim and Mahoney, 2005).

References

Adner R. 2002. When are technologies disruptive? A demand-based view of the emergence of competition. *Strategic Management Journal* 28(8): 667–688.

Adner R. 2017. Ecosystem as structure: an actionable construct for strategy. *Journal of Management* 43(1): 39–58.

Adner R, Helfat CE. 2003. Corporate effects and dynamic managerial capabilities. *Strategic Management Journal* 24(10): 1011–1025.

Adner R, Zemsky P. 2006. A demand-based perspective on sustainable competitive advantage. *Strategic Management Journal* 27(3): 215–239.

Alexy O, West J, Klapper H, Reitzig M. 2018. Surrendering control to gain advantage: reconciling openness and the resource-based view of the firm. *Strategic Management Journal* 39(1): 1704–1727.

Amit R, Schoemaker PJH. 1993. Strategic assets and organizational rent. *Strategic Management Journal* 14(1): 33–46.

Argyres N, Mayer KJ. 2007. Contract design as a firm capability: an integration of learning and transaction cost perspectives. *Academy of Management Review* 23(4): 1060–1077.

Argyres NS, Zenger TR. 2012. Capabilities, transaction costs, and firm boundaries. *Organization Science* 23(6): 1643–1657.

Armour HO, Teece DJ. 1980. Vertical integration and technological innovation. *Review of Economics and Statistics* 62(3): 470–474.

Arrow KJ. 1962. The economic implications of learning by doing. *The Review of Economic Studies* 29(3): 155–173.

Asmussen CG, Foss K, Foss NJ, Klein P. 2020. Economizing and strategizing: how coalitions and transaction costs shape value creation and appropriation. *Strategic Management Journal*, forthcoming.

Bailey EE, Friedlander A. 1982. Market structure and multiproduct industries. *Journal of Economic Literature* 20(3): 1024–1048.

Baldwin C, Clark K. 1992. Capabilities and capital investment: new perspectives on capital budgeting. *Journal of Applied Corporate Finance* 5: 67–82.

Barney JB. 1986. Strategic factor markets: expectations, luck, and business strategy. *Management Science* 32(10): 1231–1241.

Barney JB. 1988. Returns to bidding firms in mergers and acquisitions: reconsidering the relatedness hypothesis. *Strategic Management Journal* 9(Summer): 71–78.

Barney JB. 1991. Firm resources and sustained competitive advantage. *Journal of Management* 17: 99–120.

Barney JB. 2018. Why resource-based theory's model of profit appropriation must incorporate a stakeholder perspective. *Strategic Management Journal* 39: 3305–3325.

Becker G. 1964. Human Capital: *A Theoretical and Empirical Analysis, with Special Reference to Education*. University of Chicago Press: Chicago, IL.

Bernheim BD, Whinston MD. 1990. Multimarket contact and collusive behavior. *RAND Journal of Economics* 21: 1–26.

Bettis RA. 1981. Performance differences in related and unrelated firms. *Strategic Management Journal* 2(4): 379–393.

Boudreau KJ. 2017. Platform boundary choices and governance: opening up while still coordinating and orchestrating. *Entrepreneurship, Innovation, and Platforms, Advances in Strategic Management* 37: 227–297.

Bower JL, Christensen CM. 1995. Disruptive technologies: catching the wave. *Harvard Business Review* (January–February): 43–53.

Bowman EH, Hurry D. 1993. Strategy through the option lens: an integrated view of resource investments and the incremental-choice process. *Academy of Management Review* 18(4): 760–782.

Brandenburger AM, Stuart HW. 1996. Value-based business strategy. *Journal of Economics and Management Strategy* 5: 5–25.

Brandenburger A, Stuart H. 2007. Biform games. *Management Science* 53(4): 537–549.

Campbell B, Coff R, Kryscynski D. 2012. Re-thinking sustained competitive advantage from human capital. *Academy of Management Review* 37(3): 376–395.

Capron L, Anand J, Mitchell W. 2007. Acquisition-based dynamic capabilities. In *Dynamic Capabilities: Understanding Strategic Change in Organizations*, Helfat CE, Finkelstein S, Mitchell W, Peteraf MA, Singh H, Teece DJ, Winter SG. Blackwell Publishing: Malden, MA; 80–99.

Capron L, Mitchell W. 2009. Selection capability: how capability gaps and internal social frictions affect internal and external strategic renewal. *Organization Science* 20(2): 294–312.

Castanias RP, Helfat CE. 1991. Managerial resources and rents. *Journal of Management* 17(1): 155–171.

Caves RE, Porter ME. 1977. From entry barriers to mobility barriers: conjectural decisions and contrived deterrence to new competition. *Quarterly Journal of Economics* 91(2): 241–262.

Chatain O. 2014. How do strategic factor markets respond to rivalry in the product market? *Strategic Management Journal* 35(13): 1952–1971.

Chen P-L, Williams C, Agarwal R. 2009. Growing pains: pre-entry experience and the challenge of transition to incumbency. *Strategic Management Journal* 33: 252–276.

Chesbrough HW. 2003. *Open Innovation: The New Imperative for Creating and Profiting from Technology*. Harvard Business School Publishing: Boston, MA.

Christensen C. 1997. *The Innovator's Dilemma: When New Technologies Cause Great Firms to Fail*. Harvard Business School Press: Boston, MA.

Christensen HK, Montgomery CA. 1981. Corporate economic performance: diversification strategy versus market structure. *Strategic Management Journal* 2(4): 327–343.

Coase R. 1937. The nature of the firm. *Economica* (November): 386–405.

Coff RW. 1997. Human assets and management dilemmas: coping with hazards on the road to resource-based theory. *Academy of Management Review* 22(2): 374–402.

Coff RW. 1999. When competitive advantage doesn't lead to performance: the resource-based view and stakeholder bargaining power. *Organization Science* 10(2): 119–133.

Cohen WM, Levinthal DA. 1990. Absorptive capacity: a new perspective on learning and innovation. *Administrative Science Quarterly* 35: 128–152.

Conner KR. 1991. A historical comparison of resource-based theory and five schools of thought within industrial organization economics: do we have a new theory of the firm? *Journal of Management* 17: 121–154.

Conner KR, Prahalad CK. 1996. A resource-based theory of the firm: knowledge versus opportunism. *Organization Science* 7(5): 477–501.

Cyert RM, March JG. 1963. *A Behavioral Theory of the Firm*. Prentice-Hall: Englewood Cliffs, NJ.

Dierickx I, Cool K. 1989. Asset stock accumulation and the sustainability of competitive advantage. *Management Science* 35: 1504–1511.

Dixit A, Pindyck R. 1994. *Investment under Uncertainty*. Princeton University Press: Princeton, NJ.

Dorobantu S, Kaul A, Zelner B. 2017. Nonmarket strategy research through the lens of new institutional economics: an integrative review and future directions. *Strategic Management Journal* **38**(1): 114–140.

Dosi G, Nelson RR, Winter SG (eds). 2000. *The Nature and Dynamics of Organizational Capabilities*. Oxford University Press: New York, NY.

Dyer J, Kale P, Singh H. 2007. Relational capabilities: drivers and implications. In *Dynamic Capabilities: Understanding Strategic Change in Organizations*, Helfat CE, Finkelstein S, Mitchell W, Peteraf MA, Singh H, Teece DJ, Winter SG. Blackwell Publishing: Malden, MA; 65–79.

Dyer JH, Singh H. 1998. The relational view: cooperative strategy and sources of interorganizational competitive advantage. *Academy of Management Review* **23**(4): 660–679.

Eisenhardt KM. 2021. Strategy in nascent markets and entrepreneurial firms. In *Strategic Management: State of the Field and Its Future*, Duhaime I, Hitt MA, Lyles M (eds). Oxford University Press: New York, NY; .

Eisenhardt KM, Martin JA. 2000. Dynamic capabilities: what are they? *Strategic Management Journal* **21**(10): 1105–1121.

Ethiraj SK, Levinthal D. 2004. Modularity and innovation in complex systems. *Management Science* **50**: 159–173.

Felin T, Foss NJ. 2005. Strategic organization: a field in search of microfoundations. *Strategic Organization* **3**(4): 441–455.

Ganco M, Hoetker G. 2009. NK modeling methodology in the strategy literature: bounded search on a rugged landscape. In *Research Methodology in Strategy and Management*, vol. 5., Bergh DD, Ketchen DJ (eds). Emerald Publishing Limited: Bingley, U.K.: 237–268.

Gavetti G, Helfat CE, Marengo L. 2017. Searching, shaping, and the quest for superior performance. *Strategy Science* **2**(3): 194–209.

Gavetti G, Levinthal D. 2000. Looking forward and looking backward: cognitive and experiential search. *Administrative Science Quarterly* **45**: 113–137.

Gawer A. 2014. Bridging differing perspectives on technological platforms: toward an integrative framework. *Research Policy* **43**(7): 1239–1249.

Gawer A. 2020. Digital platforms' boundaries: the interplay of firm scope, platform sides, and digital interfaces. *Long Range Planning*, forthcoming.

Grant RM. 1996. Toward a knowledge-based theory of the firm. *Strategic Management Journal* **17**(Winter Special Issue): 109–122.

Grant RM. 2019. *Contemporary Strategy Analysis*, 10th ed. John Wiley and Sons: Hoboken, NJ.

Grossman S, Hart O. 1986. The costs and benefits of ownership: a theory of vertical and lateral integration. *Journal of Political Economy* **94**: 691–719.

Hannah DP, Tidhar R, Eisenhardt KM. 2020. Analytic models in strategy, organizations, and management research: a guide for consumers. *Strategic Management Journal*, forthcoming.

Hart O, Moore J. 1990. Property rights and the nature of the firm. *Journal of Political Economy* **98**: 1119–1158.

Helfat CE. 1994. Evolutionary trajectories in petroleum firm R&D. *Management Science* **40**(12): 1720–1747.

Helfat CE, Campo-Rembado MA. 2016. Integrative capabilities, vertical integration, and innovation over successive technology lifecycles. *Organization Science* **27**(2): 249–264.

Helfat CE, Eisenhardt KM. 2004. Inter-temporal economies of scope, organizational modularity, and the dynamics of diversification. *Strategic Management Journal* **25**(13): 1217–1232.

Helfat CE, Finkelstein S, Mitchell W, Peteraf MA, Singh H, Teece DJ, Winter SG. 2007. *Dynamic Capabilities: Understanding Strategic Change in Organizations*. Blackwell Publishing: Malden, MA.

Helfat CE, Peteraf MA. 2003. The dynamic resource-based view: capability lifecycles. *Strategic Management Journal* 24(10): 997–1010.

Helfat CE, Raubitschek RS. 2000. Product sequencing: co-evolution of knowledge, capabilities, and products. *Strategic Management Journal* 21(10–11): 961–980.

Helfat CE, Raubitschek RS. 2018. Dynamic and integrative capabilities for profiting from innovation in digital platform-based ecosystems. *Research Policy* 47(8): 1391–1399.

Helfat CE, Winter SG. 2011. Untangling dynamic and operational capabilities: strategy for the (n)ever-changing world. *Strategic Management Journal* 32(11): 1243–1250.

Henderson R. 1994. The evolution of integrative capability: innovation of cardiovascular drug discovery. *Industrial and Corporate Change* 3(3): 607–630.

Hennart J-F. 1988. A transaction cost theory of equity joint ventures. *Strategic Management Journal* 9(4): 361–374.

Hennart J-F. 1991. The transaction cost theory of joint ventures: an empirical study of Japanese subsidiaries in the United States. *Management Science* 37(4): 483–497.

Hill CWL, Hitt MA, Hoskisson RE. 1992. Cooperative versus competitive structures in related and unrelated diversified firms. *Organization Science* 3(4): 501–521.

Hotelling H. 1929. Stability in competition. *Economic Journal* 39: 41–57.

Iansiti M, Clark KB. 1994. Integration and dynamic capability: evidence from product development in automobiles and mainframe computers. *Industrial and Corporate Change* 3(3): 557–605.

Jacobides MG, Cennamo C, Gawer A. 2018. Towards a theory of ecosystems. *Strategic Management Journal* 39: 2255–2276.

Jacobides MG, Winter SG. 2005. The co-evolution of capabilities and transaction costs: explaining the institutional structure of production. *Strategic Management Journal* 26: 395–413.

Jensen MC, Meckling WH. 1976. Theory of the firm: managerial behavior, agency costs, and ownership structure. *Journal of Financial Economics* 3(4): 305–360.

Jovanovic B. 1982. Selection and the evolution of industry. *Econometrica* 50(3): 649–670.

Kahneman D, Tversky A. 1979. Prospect theory: an analysis of decision under risk. *Econometrica* 47: 313–327.

Katila R, Ahuja G. 2002. Something old, something new: a longitudinal study of search behavior and new product introduction. *Academy of Management Journal* 45(6): 1183–1194.

Kauffman SA. 1993. *The Origins of Order: Self-Organization and Selection in Evolution.* Oxford University Press: Oxford, U.K.

Kauffman SA. 1995. *At Home in the Universe.* Oxford University Press: Oxford, U.K.

Kaul A, Luo J. 2018. An economic case for CSR: the comparative efficiency of for-profit firms in meeting consumer demand for social goods. *Strategic Management Journal* 39: 1650–1677.

Kim J, Mahoney JT. 2005. Property rights theory, transaction costs theory, and agency theory: an organizational economics approach to strategic management. *Managerial and Decision Economics* 26: 223–242.

Klepper S. 1996. Entry, exit, growth, and innovation over the product life cycle. *American Economic Review* 86(3): 562–583.

Knight FH. 1921. *Risk, Uncertainty, and Profit.* Houghton Mifflin: Boston, MA.

Kogut B. 1991. Joint ventures and the option to expand and acquire. *Management Science* 37(1): 19–33.

Kogut B, Kulatilaka N. 1994. Operating flexibility, global manufacturing, and the option value of multinationality. *Management Science* 40: 123–139.

Kogut B, Kulatilaka N. 2001. Capabilities as real options. *Organization Science* 12(6): 744–758.

Kogut B, Zander U. 1992. Knowledge of the firm, combinative capabilities, and the replication of technology. *Organization Science* 3(3): 383–397.

Kryscynski D, Coff R, Campbell B. 2020. Charting a path between firm-specific incentives and human capital-based competitive advantage. *Strategic Management Journal*, forthcoming.

Levinthal DA. 1997. Adaptation on rugged landscapes. *Management Science* 43: 934–950.

Levinthal DA, Wu W. 2010. Opportunity costs and non-scale free capabilities: profit maximization, corporate scope, and profit margins. *Strategic Management Journal* 31(7): 780–801.

Lieberman MB. 1987. The learning curve, diffusion, and competitive strategy. *Strategic Management Journal* 8(5): 441–452.

Lieberman MB, Balasubramanian N, Garcia-Castro R. 2018. Toward a dynamic notion of value creation and appropriation in firms: the concept and measurement of economic gain. *Strategic Management Journal* 39: 1546–1572.

Lieberman MB, Lee GK, Folta TB. 2017. Entry, exit, and the potential for resource redeployment. *Strategic Management Journal* 38(3): 526–544.

Lieberman MB, Montgomery DB. 1988. First-mover advantages. *Strategic Management Journal* 9(S1): 41–58.

Lippman SA, Rumelt RP. 1982. Uncertain imitability: an analysis of interfirm differences under competition. *Bell Journal of Economics* 13: 418–438.

Lippman SA, Rumelt RP. 2003a. A bargaining perspective on resource advantage. *Strategic Management Journal* 24: 1069–1086.

Lippman SA, Rumelt RP. 2003b. The payments perspective: micro-foundations of resource analysis. *Strategic Management Journal* 24: 903–927.

MacDonald G, Ryall RD. 2004. How do value creation and competition determine whether a firm appropriates value? *Management Science* 50: 1319–1333.

Mahoney JT, Pandian JR. 1992. The resource-based view within the conversation of strategic management. *Strategic Management Journal* 13: 363–380.

Makadok R. 2010. The interaction effect of rivalry restraint and competitive advantage on profit: why the whole is less than the sum of the parts. *Management Science* 56(2): 356–372.

Makadok R, Ross D. 2013. Taking industry structuring seriously: a strategic perspective on product differentiation. *Strategic Management Journal* 34(5): 509–532.

Malerba F, Nelson R, Orsenigo L, Winter S. 1999. "History-friendly" models of industry evolution: the computer industry. *Industrial and Corporate Change* 8(1): 3–40.

Maritan C, Peteraf MA. 2007. Dynamic capabilities and organizational processes. In *Dynamic Capabilities: Understanding Strategic Change in Organizations*, Helfat CE, Finkelstein S, Mitchell W, Peteraf MA, Singh H, Teece DJ, Winter SG. Blackwell Publishing: Malden, MA; 30–45.

Mayer KJ, Argyres NS. 2004. Learning to contract: evidence from the personal computer industry. *Organization Science* 15(4): 394–410.

Monteverde K. 1995. Technical dialog as an incentive for vertical integration in the semiconductor industry. *Management Science* 41(10): 1624–1638.

Monteverde K, Teece DJ. 1982. Supplier switching costs and vertical integration. *Bell Journal of Economics* 25: 321–328.

Montgomery CA, Wernerfelt B. 1988. Diversification, Ricardian rents, and Tobin's q. *Rand Journal of Economics* 19(4): 623–632.

Mussa M, Rosen S. 1978. Monopoly and product quality. *Journal of Economic Theory* 18(2): 301–317.

Myers SC. 1977. Determinants of corporate borrowing. *Journal of Financial Economics* 5: 147–176.

Nelson RR. 1961. Uncertainty, learning, and the economics of parallel research and development efforts. *Review of Economics and Statistics* 43(4): 351–364.

Nelson RR. 1991. Why do firms differ and how does it matter? *Strategic Management Journal* 12(S2): 61–74.

Nelson, RR. 2020. A perspective on the evolution of evolutionary economics. *Industrial and Corporate Change*, forthcoming.

Nelson RR, Dosi G, Helfat CE, Pyka A, Winter SG, Saviotti P, Lee K, Malerba F, Dopfer K. 2018. *Modern Evolutionary Economics: An Overview.* Cambridge University Press: Cambridge, U.K.

Nelson RR, Winter SG. 1982. *An Evolutionary Theory of Economic Change.* The Belknap Press of Harvard University Press: Cambridge, MA.

Nickerson JA, Zenger TR. 2004. A knowledge-based theory of the firm—the problem-solving perspective. *Organization Science* 15(6): 617–734.

Ostrom E. 1990. *Governing the Commons: The Evolution of Institutions for Collective Action.* Cambridge University Press: Cambridge, U.K.

Oxley JE. 1997. Appropriability hazards and governance in strategic alliances: a transaction cost approach. *Journal of Law, Economics, & Organization.* 13(2): 387–409.

Pacheco de Almeida G, Zemsky P. 2007. The timing of resource development and sustainable competitive advantage. *Management Science* 53(4): 651–666.

Panzar JC, Willig RD. 1981. Economies of scope. *American Economic Review* 71(2): 268–272.

Penrose ET. 1959. *The Theory of the Growth of the Firm.* Oxford University Press: Oxford, U.K.

Penrose ET. 1995. *The Theory of the Growth of the Firm,* 3rd ed. Oxford University Press: Oxford, U.K.

Peteraf MA. 1993. The cornerstones of competitive advantage: a resource-based view. *Strategic Management Journal* 14(3): 179–191.

Peteraf MA, Barney JB. 2003. Unraveling the resource-based tangle. *Managerial and Decision Economics* 24: 309–323.

Porter ME. 1979. How competitive forces shape strategy. *Harvard Business Review* 57(2): 137–145.

Priem RL. 2007. A consumer perspective on value creation. *Academy of Management Review* 32(1): 219–235.

Rindova V, Courtney H. 2020. To shape or adapt: knowledge problems, epistemologies, and strategic postures under Knightian uncertainty. *Academy of Management Review,* forthcoming.

Rivkin J. 2000. Imitation of complex strategies. *Management Science* 46: 824–844.

Rochet JC, Tirole J. 2003. Platform competition in two-sided markets. *Journal of the European Economic Association* 1: 990–1029.

Rosenkopf L, Nerkar A. 2001. Beyond local search: boundary-spanning, exploration, and impact in the optical disk industry. *Strategic Management Journal* 22(4): 287–306.

Rumelt RP. 1974. *Strategy, Structure, and Economic Performance.* Harvard Business School Press: Boston, MA.

Rumelt RP. 1984. Towards a strategic theory of the firm. In *Competitive Strategic Management,* Lamb B (ed). Prentice-Hall: Englewood Cliffs, NJ; 556–570.

Rumelt RP, Schendel D, Teece DJ. 1991. Strategic management and economics. *Strategic Management Journal* 12: 5–29.

Sakhartov AV, Folta TB. 2014. Resource relatedness, redeployability, and firm value. *Strategic Management Journal* 35(12): 1781–1797.

Sakhartov AV, Folta TB. 2015. Getting beyond relatedness as a driver of corporate value. *Strategic Management Journal* 36(13): 1939–1959.

Shapiro C. 1989. Theories of oligopoly behavior. In *Handbook of Industrial Organization,* vol. 1, Schalmensee R, Willig R (eds). Elsevier: Oxford, U.K.; 329–414.

Simon H. 1957. *Models of Man: Social and Rational.* Wiley and Sons: New York, NY.

Sirmon DG, Hitt MA. 2009. Contingencies within dynamic managerial capabilities: interdependent effects of resource investment and deployment on firm performance. *Strategic Management Journal* 30: 1375–1394.

Sirmon DG, Hitt MA, Ireland RD. 2007. Managing firm resources in dynamic environments to create value: looking inside the black box. *Academy of Management Review* 32(1): 273–293.

Spence AM. 1974. *Market Signaling: Informational Transfer in Hiring and Related Practices*. Harvard University Press: Cambridge, MA.

Teece DJ. 1980. Economies of scope and the scope of the enterprise. *Journal of Economic Behavior and Organization* 1(3): 223–247.

Teece DJ. 1982. Towards and economic theory of the multiproduct firm. *Journal of Economic Behavior and Organization* 3(1): 39–63.

Teece DJ. 1986. Profiting from technological innovation: implications for integration collaboration, licensing, and public policy. *Research Policy* 15: 285–305.

Teece DJ. 1988. Technological change and the nature of the firm. In *Technical Change and Economic Theory*, Dosi G, Freeman C, Nelson RR, Silverberg G, Soete L (eds). Pinter Publishers: New York, NY; 256–281.

Teece DJ. 1996. Firm organization, industrial structure, and technological innovation. *Journal of Economic Behavior and Organization* 31: 537–556.

Teece DJ. 2007. Explicating dynamic capabilities: the nature and microfoundations of (sustainable) enterprise performance. *Strategic Management Journal* 28(13): 1319–1350.

Teece DJ 2018. Profiting from innovation in the digital economy: enabling technologies, standards, and licensing models in the wireless world. *Research Policy* 47(8): 1367–1387.

Teece DJ, Pisano G, Shuen A. 1997. Dynamic capabilities and strategic management. *Strategic Management Journal* 18(7): 509–534.

Trigeorgis L, Reuer JJ. 2017. Real options theory in strategic management. *Strategic Management Journal* 38(1): 42–63.

Wernerfelt B. 1984. A resource-based view of the firm. *Strategic Management Journal* 5(2): 171–180.

Wernerfelt B. 2016. *Adaptation, Specialization, and the Theory of the Firm: Foundations of the Resource-Based View*. Cambridge University Press: Cambridge, U.K.

Wernerfelt B. 2020. A possible micro-foundation for the RBV and its implications. *Strategic Management Review* 1(1): 145–158.

Williamson OE. 1970. *Corporate Control and Business Behavior*. Prentice Hall: Englewood Cliffs, NJ.

Williamson OE. 1975. *Markets and Hierarchies: Analysis and Antitrust Implications*. Free Press: New York, NY.

Williamson OE. 1985. *The Economic Institutions of Capitalism: Firms, Markets, Relational Contracting*. Free Press: New York, NY.

Wilson R. 1992. Strategic analysis of auctions. In *Handbook of Game Theory with Economic Applications*, vol. 1, Aumann RJ, Hart S (eds). Elsevier: Amsterdam, The Netherlands; 227–279.

Winter SG. 1987. Knowledge and competence as strategic assets. In *The Competitive Challenge: Strategies for Industrial Innovation and Renewal*, Teece DJ (ed). Ballinger: Cambridge, MA; 159–184.

Winter SG. 2000. The satisficing principle in capability learning. *Strategic Management Journal* 21(10–11): 981–996.

Winter SG. 2003. Understanding dynamic capabilities. *Strategic Management Journal* 24(10): 991–995.

Zahra SA, George G. 2002. Absorptive capacity: A review, reconceptualization, and extension. *Academy of Management Review* 27(2): 185–203.

Zollo M, Winter SG. 2002. Deliberate learning and the evolution of dynamic capabilities. *Organization Science* 13(3): 339–351.

Evolution of Research Methods in Strategic Management

1.3
EVOLUTION OF QUANTITATIVE RESEARCH METHODS IN STRATEGIC MANAGEMENT

J. Myles Shaver

Introduction

Quantitative empirical research in the strategic management field continues to evolve. In this chapter, I discuss elements of its evolution and provide observations of where we stand today. My approach is to highlight research trends and not provide an exhaustive review of the literature. As a result, the work I cite draws heavily on domains of study in which I am most familiar.

A large portion of the chapter is forward looking and presents ways in which quantitative research has the potential to evolve further. Rather than focus on specific estimation methods and statistical approaches, I attend to broader issues related to research design. I ground this discussion on two principles. First, the ultimate goal of strategic management scholarship is to inform the action of many decision-makers, including managers, owners, and policymakers. Second, our advantage as scholars, compared to others who wish to inform these decision-makers, comes from the insights we bring through rigorous evidence-based research.

Quantitative Research in Strategic Management: An Evolutionary Perspective

The field of strategic management is relatively nascent. Moreover, scholarship in the field overlaps with many other fields of study within management (e.g., organization theory and organization behavior) and within the social sciences (e.g., economics and sociology). As a result, scholarship in the field is not confined to a single outlet or area of study. However, to draw insights into the evolution of quantitative research in the field, I focus my discussion from the launch of the *Strategic Management Journal* (*SMJ*) in 1980. Also, many examples and generalizations I make stem from the nature of the research in *SMJ*.

Prevalence of quantitative research

Quantitative empirical work constituted an important element in the early days of the *SMJ*. In the first three volumes of the journal—volumes 1–3, 1980–1982—there are 74 research papers. Thirty (41 percent) employ quantitative methods.[1] The scholarly output in the *SMJ* has shifted even more toward quantitative research over the last 40 years. It now accounts for the vast majority of papers in the journal. In the latest full volume of the *SMJ*—volume 40, 2019—there are 81 research papers. Sixty-eight (85 percent) employ quantitative methods.

Research approach: descriptive versus theory testing

In addition to the increased prevalence of quantitative research, the nature of the work evolved. One pronounced change is that early empirical work in the field reflected a more even balance between descriptive and hypothesis-testing analyses. The general structure of descriptive empirical papers is to use a large data sample and employ quantitative techniques to describe companies or phenomena. The focal insight is to create an empirical picture for scholars. Susuki (1980) described the strategies and structures of Japanese firms and compared them to Western firms, an example of descriptive quantitative work in the early years of *SMJ*. In contrast, hypothesis-testing work presents theoretically derived hypotheses (sometimes formally stated as a hypothesis and sometimes not) and uses statistical tests to infer support or rejection of the hypotheses (for a recent example see Chai and Freeman, 2019).

This balance from the early years of *SMJ* now leans very heavily toward hypothesis testing. Although descriptive papers still exist, over time they became increasingly rare—so rare that scholars noted this and encouraged the field to focus on, and journals to be open to, descriptive quantitative work (e.g., Helfat, 2007; Hambrick, 2007; Oxley, Rivkin, and Ryall, 2010).

Data

There have also been a number of trends in the evolution of quantitative empirical work with respect to the nature of data employed. First, to my reading, quantitative empirical work in the early years of the *SMJ* primarily drew upon secondary data sources; however, seeing survey-based quantitative work or survey-augmented secondary sources was notable. Over time, the reliance on secondary versus primary sources appears to have become even more pronounced. For example, over the last 20 years, *SMJ* published, on average, approximately four papers a year with primary survey data.[2] For 2019, this is about 6 percent of the quantitative papers.

Second, the amount of data and sample sizes employed increased dramatically over the last 40 years. This reflects a number of trends. One is the wider availability of secondary datasets with relevant information (e.g., the National Bureau of Economic Research [NBER] patent database). Moreover, scholars' data collection strategies now often enhance data from widely available secondary sources with less-widely available data collected from secondary sources. For example, Kim (2019) combines data from commonly used sources (e.g., Orbis, Capital IQ, Worldscope, and Zephyr) with data on U.S. Department of Defense weapons systems prime contracts, corporate lobbying activities, and corporate campaign contributions. We also observe data collection strategies that focus on securing secondary data that are large in sample but not publicly available (e.g., Oldroyd, Morris, and Dotson, 2019). Finally, a notable trend over time is the use of panel data instead of purely cross-sectional data.

Third, from its founding, quantitative research in the field draws on datasets from beyond the United States. Part of this reflects that scholars from North America, Europe, and Asia were active in publishing quantitative empirical work in the early volumes of the *SMJ*. This trend has continued over time and has arguably broadened—especially with the scope of countries from which strategy scholars draw data. Therefore, although many strategy papers draw on U.S. data, it would be in error to say that quantitative research in the field is U.S.-centric.

Fourth, in terms of level of analysis, a preponderance of research over the last 40 years focuses on firms or subunits of firms (e.g., business units)—especially in studies that examine performance. Nevertheless, strategic management research addresses a broader array of questions than those related to firm performance. In many of these studies, quantitative work initially included studies at the industry level of analysis and at the manager or managerial-team level of analysis. However, this has changed over time reflecting two underlying theoretical trends. An increased focus on microfoundations of firms' decisions, married with moving away from theories situated at the industry level (such as Bain-Mason industrial organization economics), resulted in the reduction of industry-level studies and an increase in within-firm level studies (e.g., individuals or teams).

Acknowledging endogeneity concerns

Probably the most profound change in the approach to quantitative work in the field is the explicit consideration of endogeneity concerns following Shaver (1998). Until then, the accepted approach to identify superior strategies was to regress a measure of performance on an indicator of strategy choice. If the coefficient estimate of this indicator was positive and statistically significant, then the strategy was considered superior. Studies often concluded with normative implications that companies should adopt these superior strategies.

However, such inference is warranted only if companies randomly choose strategies—which is not consistent with strategic management literature documenting how firms systematically choose strategies—or if all systematic determinants of performance are controlled for in statistical analyses—which is unlikely because many key strategy theories focus on unobservable constructs (Godfrey and Hill, 1995). Therefore, an observed correlation (or partial correlation in a regression context) between performance and strategy choice can reflect systematic differences in the attributes of companies that select those strategies and is not necessarily an indication of a superior strategy.

The ideal counterfactual to assess the superiority of a strategy is not to compare companies that adopt a strategy to those who do not. Rather, it is to compare the performance of companies that adopt a strategy to what would have occurred had they not adopted the strategy. Of course, such comparisons are not directly observable or measurable. Therefore, efforts to mitigate spurious conclusions due to endogeneity concerns took greater hold in the literature. Examples include the adoption of statistical techniques that acknowledge the concern, research design choices to mitigate the concern, and more nuanced interpretations of results to assess the potential for the concern.

Contemporary Issues

As the preceding discussion highlights, quantitative empirical work is central and pervasive in strategic management research. The current approach in the field is predominantly hypothesis testing using secondary data sources—many of which are not widely available. Samples have become larger, longitudinal, and increasingly international. The field evolved from ignoring endogeneity concerns to making this a central consideration. Nevertheless, the following five issues reflect elements of quantitative research that are unfolding or are in flux.

Beyond endogeneity to causal identification

The notion of causal identification is determining the underlying cause-and-effect relationship between correlated variables (e.g., strategy choice and performance)—should one exist. Addressing endogeneity is an element of this. The key point is that, in a setting where firms choose strategies, strategy choice or characteristics of firms that make those choices can lead to the correlation between strategy and performance. However, causal identification goes beyond the endogeneity concern. Because many different theoretical mechanisms can lead to the same empirical relationship, discerning which theory or theories are at play is another key element of causal identification.

Focusing on causal identification not only conceptually expands the endogeneity concern, it also provides a useful reframing for the following reasons. First, this mirrors research trends and discussions in many social science disciplines, where scholars increasingly seek to identify underlying cause and effect. This includes sociology (e.g., Gangl, 2010), economics (e.g., Angrist and Pischke, 2010), political science (e.g., Samii, 2016), and psychology (e.g., Rohrer, 2018). Second, this focuses on the conceptual issue that underlies the endogeneity problem. This, in turn, highlights that addressing endogeneity concerns should go beyond the adoption of a specific estimation algorithm. When viewed this way, it reinforces the need for clarity in theorizing and clarity in research design. Third, it helps link our research to practice. If we wish to effectively guide decision-makers, then we have to know the underlying cause and effect levers at their disposal. Fourth, and most importantly, when viewed this way it becomes apparent that there are many approaches to help address the issue of causal identification, and statistical techniques are but one set of tools that we have—a point I expand upon in the section on future directions.

Tension of seeking causal identification and examining meaningful strategy questions

Although I see many desirable outcomes from the increased attention to designing research for causal identification, it has created tension in the field. There is a tension between the push for causal identification and the importance of gaining insight into meaningful strategy questions. Elements that make strategic management research important for practice also make addressing causal identification difficult (Shaver, 2020). We study outcomes, such as firm performance, that have many determinants. We tend to study business organizations, which are complex entities and where managers purposely manage to the outcomes that we study. Focusing exclusively on identification can draw us away from the phenomena we wish to inform. Ignoring identification can lead us to make unsubstantiated or harmful recommendations for decision-makers.

As a result, I fear the field could bifurcate into scholars who are adamant about focusing on causal identification and scholars who are adamant about examining important and complex phenomena. The latter look at the former as the "endogeneity police" who are more interested in finding desirable research settings than they are asking important strategy questions. The former look at the latter as being sloppy in their empirical work and afraid to conduct meaningful tests of their preferred theories. This tension reflects the underlying difficulties of doing empirical strategy research; however, should it become pronounced it will be detrimental to the field. Although there are indications of the existence of this tension, I believe we can avoid this outcome if the field moves towards the issues I detail in the section on future directions.

Fully leveraging panel data

Employing panel data gives rise to many statistical complications because these data often violate the assumptions of basic statistical methods. However, once accounting for this, panel data estimation techniques can be very powerful—especially how they map to important strategy concepts and address some complications of assessing strategy outcomes.

The key element in panel data is that they measure variables across firms and within firms over time. Therefore, panel estimators provide the ability to isolate within-firm and across-firm variance in empirical estimates (Certo, Withers, and Semadeni, 2017). This can be powerful; nevertheless, doing so often requires nuanced interpretations of results. As scholars become more cognizant of these underlying sources of variance in panel data, they have become more explicit in how they leverage the advantages of panel data designs, while better recognizing the limitations and nuances of interpretation in these approaches (Shaver, 2019).

The benefit of using panel data to isolate within-firm variance is that these analyses (a) map more directly to theories of firm-level dynamics, (b) help rule out alternative explanations that stem from differences across firms, and (c) provide a way to isolate and estimate firm effects that are not otherwise measurable (e.g., Henderson and Cockburn, 1994). Moreover, recent advances in panel data estimators allow for the ability to test if effects of variables (i.e., coefficient estimates) are universal or vary across firms (e.g., Alcácer et al., 2018; Knott, 2008). This latter point is a powerful way to identify how firm heterogeneity affects outcomes of interest.

Reintroducing descriptive quantitative work and the importance of abduction

There is a recent resurgence in quantitative empirical work that is descriptive and not hypothesis testing in focus. Two notable examples are the *SMJ* Special Issue on Question-Driven and Phenomenon-Based Empirical Strategy Research and the launch of *Academy of Management Discoveries*. This resurgence is important because non-hypothesis-testing quantitative work facilitates the understanding of important strategy issues by looking at large samples. Moreover, much of the current work is explicitly abductive in reasoning. In other words, papers that start by identifying an important phenomena, go to the data (often iteratively), and, from the data, identify plausible causes for the relationships that they find, while eliminating plausible causes for the relationship that are not consistent with the relationships that they find (e.g., Benner and Waldfogel, forthcoming; Guadalupe, Li, and Wulf, 2014). Such work is beneficial because it highlights that data-informed theory building is not solely the realm for qualitative work. Moreover, by acknowledging and isolating the role of abduction in quantitative work, it reinforces the importance of causal identification when testing theory.

Buzzwords or statistical "fixes" as approaches to causal identification

Some authors recognize the actions taken by other scholars to address causal identification; however, they do not have a good appreciation for the underlying reasons for these actions. In other words, some authors invoke (often incorrectly) statistical cures or buzzwords without having an appreciation of the underlying motivation. As a result, papers employ (and reviewers request) statistical techniques and use terminology that are consistent with many best practices, but do not reflect the nature of the data or the theory being tested. For example, some papers advance theories that hypothesize differences between firms. However, they test the theory by employing panel data and fixed-effects models, which suppresses the across-firm variance that is central to their arguments. Although such approaches can be valid in some situations, there is no recognition or discussion of this. Rather, such papers apply standard fixes or buzzwords without a good comprehension of the underlying problem and the nature of data required to effectively test the underlying theory.

Future of Quantitative Empirical Research

In this section, I present practices that, if embraced, should advance the rigor and heighten the impact of quantitative strategy research. This set of practices is shaped by the view that the primary goal of strategy research is to inform action. Therefore, our work must ultimately speak to and influence managers, owners, policymakers, or other decision-makers. However, we are not the only ones trying to have such influence. As scholars, we compete in a market for ideas with many others who try to influence these actors. This includes management consultants, authors of popular management books, and practicing managers, among others. As strategic management scholars, our competitive advantage in this market for ideas stems from the rigor of an evidence-based approach.

The approaches described herein are central to evidence-based research aimed at influencing practice. If we fail to embrace these approaches, our impact may be minimized and our relevance for practice questioned. Part of this reflects the fact that we would give up our source of advantage in the market for ideas. Moreover, many of the elements reflect broader trends in social science research. Failing to adopt these approaches will marginalize the field in the broader domain of social science scholars. Our field will suffer if we are marginalized in our impact on practice and in our scholarly assessment by other social scientists.

Causal identification through a cumulative body of research

If our goal is to inform action, then we need to understand the levers that decision-makers can wield to achieve their desired outcomes. In other words, we have to know what causes the outcomes that decision-makers wish to accomplish. This is the notion of causal identification. For this reason, the recent trend toward focusing on causal identification is important and must play a central role moving forward.

As I described previously, a tension often exists between addressing key strategy questions and our ability to advance causal identification. If our goal is to provide informed and credible answers to important strategy questions, then we are not aided by poor identification of important problems or good identification of trivial problems. As such, we must take on the tension of good identification of important—but hard to identify—problems. How do we do that?

We have to view identification as the outcome from a cumulative empirical research program. No single study will get us to the goal of causal identification for important strategy questions, but a collection of studies that build toward more sound identification can pave a way forward. We must not view perfect identification as a requirement for studies of important phenomena, but we cannot claim that the importance of the question inoculates us from seriously considering identification. A cumulative body of research requires many different types of tests of important theories. It also requires that we revisit and replicate existing findings (e.g., Bettis, Helfat, and Shaver, 2016). We have to value novel approaches to testing existing theories (e.g., Bikard, 2020; Pillai, Goldfarb, and Kirsh, 2020) as much as we value addressing novel research questions or advancing novel theories. A cumulative body of research has to span many scholars, studies, approaches, and years. Although I detail specific elements of this approach and current research norms that constrain its adoption in Shaver (2020), the following three elements should play an important role in future quantitative work.

Focus on research design

The key issue in addressing causal identification is research design. Research design, in its essence, is about one concept: variance. The key to designing research for causal identification requires attention to three sources of variance. First, we must be able to invoke variance in the underlying causal mechanism (i.e., the independent variable). And central to this, we must understand how the variance is invoked. Is it imposed or chosen? And if chosen, by whom? Second, there must be the potential for variance in the dependent variable and we must have a way to measure it. It is possible that the dependent variable does not respond to the hypothesized mechanism, but it must have the potential to respond. Third, we must try to isolate the variation of the causal mechanism from all other sources of variance. Namely, ideally we hold everything else constant when we evaluate a causal mechanism.

Statistical techniques are too often confounded as research design. Statistical techniques are an element—but only one part. When thinking of causal identification as research design, we can see that scholars have many choices and can take many actions to try and build causal identification. These range from choices in measurement, sampling, statistical technique, and interpretation.

Plurality of approaches

An important implication of building a cumulative body of research with an eye for causal identification is that it will require a plurality of approaches. Many research design choices can help advance causal identification, but it is unlikely that all can be implemented in one study. Therefore, this calls for a plurality of approaches—within the profession. I stress "within the profession" because working to one's skill set and interest often means that individual scholars specialize in their approach to quantitative research. Evidence that the field is evolving to causal identification through a cumulative body of research means we should see a greater variety of approaches for a set of focal and important questions and theories—not a single approach to study an ever-expanding set of questions.

To deal with causal identification, a recent trend is to adopt more experimental research designs in strategy research, such as natural experiments and field experiments (e.g., Chatterji *et al.*, 2016). These are useful approaches—within the plurality of approaches required to build a cumulative body of research. Like all research design choices, they have advantages and disadvantages. In particular, some of these studies assess unique settings that might not generalize or test against null hypotheses that might not be informative.

Also, leveraging the plurality of approaches requires that we be transparent about our research design choices, which includes issues of measurement and sampling. It is difficult to build a cumulative body of research if scholars cannot understand prior research design choices. This is especially salient with the use of non–publicly available data and trends to process large volumes of data to create variables. An example of framing data collection, measurement, and statistical approach within an overall research design can be seen in Hernandez and Shaver (2019). Likewise, an example of detailing how research design and measurement efforts relate to an empirical testing strategy can be seen in Simcoe and Waguespack (2011).

Importance of detailed interpretation of findings

Another element of empirical research—especially in our quest to build a cumulative body of research—is accurately assessing the effects that we find. For decision-makers, it is not only important that they know if an action has an impact on an outcome; it is also important that they understand the nature and magnitude of its impact, particularly because decision-makers often weigh different actions and trade off one activity versus another. When faced with multiple actions that are beneficial, but the resources to only undertake a subset of them, they must know the impact of one action versus another. This highlights the importance of carefully interpreting our findings.

To demonstrate the importance of such interpretation, we need look no further than the assessment of predictive models during the COVID-19 pandemic. On May 13, 2020, of the seven major models that predicted the pandemic spread, the model with the lowest predicted deaths for June 6 was 103,000 and the highest 120,000 (https://projects.fivethirtyeight.com/covid-forecasts/ [accessed May 14, 2020]). This is a difference of approximately 20 percent—and differences from models at the beginning of the pandemic were much more pronounced. All models predict increased loss of life; however, the magnitude of the prediction has important implications for decision-makers. Although there is agreement in the direction of the effect, there is substantive difference in the magnitude of the effect. Findings in our field are often simply described as directional. However, as the COVID example demonstrates, agreeing on direction is not necessarily beneficial for making decisions if the magnitude is not well understood.

The importance of not confounding evidence with hypotheses or assumptions

Because a central goal of our research should be to build a body of evidence-based knowledge, it becomes important that we not confound evidence with theory and assumptions. Within our literature, we often see statements of empirical relationships supported by theoretical claims or assumptions, rather than by empirical assessments. Without attribution to the source articles, because such statements frequently occur in the literature, the following examples demonstrate this practice:

> *"Due to bounded rationality, executives filter and interpret situations based on their personal characteristics (Hambrick and Mason, 1984)."*
>
> *"However, the entrepreneur's weaker position in an investment relationship gives them little control over their partner's subsequent decisions (Garg, 2013)."*
>
> *"Prior research has shown, for example, that more independent boards are less susceptible to escalation of commitment (Buchholtz, Lubatkin, and O'Neill, 1999)."*

Each statement reads as a statement of fact or finding. However, in each case, the evidence cited for these claims are theory papers. None provide evidence for those statements. Rather, such citations are references to propositions, hypotheses, or assumptions, instead of empirical findings.

We need to rectify this practice because it has several detrimental effects. First, it undermines the value of doing high-quality empirical work. It suggests that we are willing to accept assertion as much as evidence. That works against being an evidence-based scholarly discipline. Second, to the extent that hypothesized relationships are subsequently empirically investigated, it does not give credit to those who do the empirical lifting. Designing and executing high-quality empirical work requires creativity, thoughtfulness, effort, and skill. We should reward empirical design and execution as much as theorizing because we need both elements to build toward causal identification. Third, accepting assertions as evidence works against building a cumulative body of knowledge because we take an initial assumption or hypothesis and treat it as our knowledge on a topic.

This practice might occur because it eliminates having to deal with the ambiguity of conflicting or mixed empirical findings. However, working through conflicting or mixed findings—as a field—is an important element of building a cumulating body of research. By avoiding this, we minimize the level of our understanding and our impact.

Skepticism rather than celebration of counterintuitive findings

In line with the importance of a detailed interpretation of our findings, it is important to take a skeptical eye to, rather than celebrate, counterintuitive findings. Building a cumulative body of research means that converging to a finding and calibrating to a magnitude of that finding is a good thing. However, this is often perceived as uninteresting or unimportant in our literature (Davis, 2015). Surprising or counterintuitive findings are considered more important—especially within the publication process. However, this approach is problematic because seeking counterintuitive findings might be biasing us to report and publish statistical aberrations rather than representative estimates (Goldfarb and King, 2016). Of particular concern is Kalnins's (2018) insight that several counterintuitive findings in the literature are likely manifestations of multicollinearity between regressors that are correlated with an unobservable or hard-to-measure common factor.

In addition, being skeptical of counterintuitive findings might mitigate the degree to which we find conflicting results across studies. When we incent counterintuitive versus cumulative research, in essence, we are asking scholars to generate a set of inconsistent results. If we remove this incentive, we might discover greater convergence and commonality in empirical insight than what we see in current published work.

Limitations and potential benefits of big datasets

Over time, there has been a greater volume of data collected, with greater frequency, and more granularity. While this big data can provide quantitative research design advantages, it alone does not aid in causal identification. The reason is that causal identification is an issue about the nature of the data we use—not its quantity. For example, endogeneity biases are not "small sample" bias; they hold asymptotically. Therefore, big data sets are beneficial when they allow us to advance research design considerations for hypothesis-testing studies.

Nevertheless, large data sets, in their own right, can be an important tool for descriptive quantitative work. The advantage of quantitative research in theory building or abduction, compared to qualitative research, is the scope of the data employed. Large data sets aid this. In addition, large data sets facilitate the use of tools like machine learning algorithms, which can be a powerful way to advance descriptive quantitative research by documenting patterns not detectable by traditional research methods (e.g., Choudhury, Allen, and Endres, 2020).

Conclusion

Schendel and Hofer (1979) is an important volume that set the stage for the scholarly field of strategic management; research methods are among the many topics discussed in the volume. To conclude, I reflect on that volume's commentary with respect to quantitative research. Schwenk (1982: 213) nicely summarizes key points Schendel and Hofer made as to how they thought the field should advance with respect to quantitative research methods.

> *First, more empirical ... [since] we do not want for theories, but we do want for theories that have been adequately tested against empirical data. Second ... normative in character [although] purely descriptive research is also needed and welcome.... Third, ... [making] greater efforts to build on the work of others.... Finally ... more rigorous, in a scientific sense, than it has been in the past. (Schendel and Hofer, 1979: 394)*

There are many reasons to claim success in light of these proposed directions. Quantitative research played a demonstrative role in the initial volumes of *SMJ*, and the proportion of quantitative empirical papers in *SMJ* has increased substantively over the last 40 years. Moreover, there is greater emphasis on hypothesis testing relative to descriptive work over this time frame. Likewise, the research methods, nature of the data, and research designs have all advanced—and this advancement is not just relative to the state of the field in the late 1970s. It also reflects advances in quantitative social science research generally over the period. Many papers in our field reflect best practices in social science research.

At the same time, the future directions that I highlight in this chapter map directly to these four points. Therefore, while the field has progressed—and we should celebrate these accomplishments—it is too early to declare victory in our approach.

Schendel and Hofer's first point is a charge to test theories. As the focus on identification has become more pronounced in all social science research, we now accept that adequately testing a theory requires that we expend efforts to distinguish if a theory causes an empirical relationship versus plausible alternative theories. Therefore, focusing on causal identification is a reflection of how current research practices relate to Schendel and Hofer's desire for the field.

Likewise, their second point is that our empirical work should be normative, which means that our research should aid decision-makers. This requires that we empirically identify what levers affect important strategic outcomes and what type of impact moving these levers will have. This approach reflects also that we should aim toward causal identification in our work. It also requires that we carefully interpret and understand the nature and magnitude of the causal mechanisms we document.

Consistent with their third point, causal identification in strategic management must be the outcome of a cumulative body of research: we must build upon the research of others and in doing so be careful not to confound evidence with theory or assumptions. We must also not disincent cumulative research efforts by rewarding or glorifying new theory or counterintuitive findings. The field will not progress if we all advance disparate research agendas or disproportionately reward contradictory findings in the publication process.

Finally, and related to their final point, our work must continue to be more rigorous. This does not mean just the application of advanced statistical or econometric techniques. Rather, we need to think of rigor as better matching research designs to the underlying theoretical elements that we wish to test.

Are there tangible steps to help direct the evolution of the field in these directions? I see two. First, we focus more on describing the research design choices that underpin our quantitative empirical work. The norm in most published quantitative strategy research is to describe "data and methods." However, there is often little discussion of why authors chose the data and methods—and how this choice maps to research design considerations. While accurately and transparently describing data and methods is important, describing how these choices reflect the underlying research design will bring to the forefront many elements that I discuss. In turn, explicitly describing research design increases the transparency of the choices we make and has the potential to advance rigor and promote novelty of our research design approaches.

Second, it is important that the strategic management field recognize that advancing quantitative empirical research requires creativity in many aspects of research design, including measurement, research settings, estimation algorithms, and data collection strategies, among other elements. Many authors and reviewers in our journals strive for formulaic approaches to quantitative research—for example, expecting that a specific estimation method or a specific source of data is used. This can help advance the adoption of desirable research practices and simplify the evaluation of papers. However, formulaic approaches can be detrimental when they inhibit the novelty and creativity required to advance quantitative research in our field.

As a member of the strategy research community, I am impressed with our advances in quantitative empirical research. Nevertheless, we still have to progress so that we can effectively aid decision-makers by providing rigorous evidence-based strategic management research.

Acknowledgment

I thank Aseem Kaul, Irene Duhaime, Mike Hitt, and Marjorie Lyles for comments.

Notes

1. I tally the number of papers in *SMJ* employing quantitative research designs, qualitative research designs, and papers that solely focus on conceptual issues or theory development. A few papers employ quantitative and qualitative designs, and I considered them to demonstrate scholarship reflecting both categories.
2. I make this assessment by examining key words in the abstract.

References

Alcácer J, Chung W, Hawk A, Pacheco-de-Almeida G. 2018. Applying random coefficient models to strategy research: identifying and exploring firm heterogeneous effects. *Strategy Science* 3(3): 533–553.

Angrist JD, Pischke, JS. 2010. The credibility revolution in empirical economics: how better research design is taking the con out of econometrics. *Journal of Economic Perspectives* 24(2): 3–30.

Benner MJ, Waldfogel J. Forthcoming. Changing the channel: digitization and the rise of "middle tail" strategies. *Strategic Management Journal*, DOI: 10.1002/smj.3130.

Bettis RA, Helfat CE, Shaver JM. 2016. The necessity, logic, and forms of replication. *Strategic Management Journal* 37: 2193–2203.

Bikard M. 2020. Idea twins: simultaneous discoveries as a research tool. *Strategic Management Journal* 41:1528–1543.

Buchholtz AK, Lubatkin M, O'Neill HM. 1999. Seller responsiveness to the need to divest. *Journal of Management* 25(5): 633–652.

Certo ST, Withers MC, Semadeni, M. 2017. A tale of two effects: Using longitudinal data to compare within- and between-firm effects. *Strategic Management Journal*, 38: 1536–1556.

Chai S, Freeman RB. 2019. Temporary colocation and collaborative discovery: Who confers at conferences. *Strategic Management Journal*, 40: 2138–2164.

Chatterji AK, Findley M, Jensen NM, Meier S, Nielson D. 2016. Field experiments in strategy research. *Strategic Management Journal*, 37(1): 116–132.

Choudhury P, Allen R, Endres MG. 2020. Machine learning for pattern discovery in management research. *HBS working paper*.

Davis GF. 2015. Editorial essay: what is organizational research for? *Administrative Science Quarterly* 60(2): 179–188.

Gangl M. 2010. Causal inference in sociological research. *Annual Review of Sociology* 36: 21–47.

Garg S. 2013. Venture boards: distinctive monitoring and implications for firm performance. *Academy of Management Review* 38: 90–108.

Godfrey PC, Hill CWL. 1995. The problem of unobservables in strategic management research. *Strategic Management Journal* 16: 519–533.

Goldfarb B, King AA. 2016. Scientific apophenia in strategic management research: significance tests and mistaken inference. *Strategic Management Journal* 37: 167–176.

Guadalupe M, Li L, and Wulf J. 2014. Who lives in the C-suite? Organizational structure and the division of labor in top management. *Management Science* 60(4): 824–844.

Hambrick DC. 2007. The field of management's devotion to theory: Too much of a good thing? *Academy of Management Journal* 50 (6): 1346–1352.

Hambrick DC, Mason PA. 1984. Upper echelons: the organization as a reflection of its top managers. *Academy of Management Review* 9(2): 193–206.

Helfat, C. 2007. Stylized facts, empirical research, and theory development in management. *Strategic Organization* 5(2): 185–192.

Henderson R, Cockburn I. 1994. Measuring competence? Exploring firm effects in pharmaceutical research. *Strategic Management Journal* 15(S1): 63–84.

Hernandez E, Shaver JM. 2019. Network synergy. *Administrative Science Quarterly* 64(1): 171–202.

Kalnins, A. 2018. Multicollinearity: how common factors cause Type 1 errors in multivariate regression. *Strategic Management Journal* 39: 2362–2385.

Kim JH. 2019. Is your playing field unleveled? U.S. defense contracts and foreign firm lobbying. *Strategic Management Journal* 40: 1911–1937.

Knott AM. 2008. R&D/returns causality: absorptive capacity or organizational IQ. *Management Science* 54(12): 2054–2067.

Oldroyd JB, Morris SS, Dotson JP. 2019. Principles or templates? The antecedents and performance effects of cross-border knowledge transfer. *Strategic Management Journal* 40: 2191–2213.

Oxley JE, Rivkin, JW, Ryall MD, Strategy Research Initiative. 2010. The strategy research initiative: recognizing and encouraging high-quality research in strategy. *Strategic Organization* 8(4): 377–386.

Pillai SD, Goldfarb, B, Kirsh, DA. 2020. The origins of firm strategy: learning by economic experimentation and strategic pivots in the early automobile industry. *Strategic Management Journal* 41: 369–399.

Rohrer JM. 2018. Thinking clearly about correlations and causation: graphical causal models for observational data. *Advances in Methods and Practices in Psychological Science* 1(1): 27–42.

Samii, C. 2016. Causal empiricism in quantitative research. *Journal of Politics* 78(3): 941–955.

Schendel DE, Hofer CW (eds). 1979. *Strategic Management: A New View of Business Policy and Planning.* Little, Brown and Company: Boston, MA.

Schwenk CR. 1982. Why sacrifice rigour for relevance? A proposal for combining laboratory and field research in strategic management. *Strategic Management Journal* 3: 213–225.

Shaver JM. 1998. Accounting for endogeneity when assessing strategy performance: does entry mode choice affect FDI survival? *Management Science* 44(4): 571–585.

Shaver JM. 2019. Interpreting interactions in linear fixed-effect regression models: when fixed-effect estimates are no longer within-effects. *Strategy Science* 4(1): 25–40.

Shaver JM. 2020. Causal identification through a cumulative body of research in the study of strategy and organizations. *Journal of Management* 46(7): 1244–1256.

Simcoe TS, Waguespack DM. 2011. Status, quality, and attention: what's in a (missing) name? *Management Science* 57(2): 274–290.

Susuki Y. 1980. The strategy and structure of top 100 Japanese industrial enterprises, 1950–1970. *Strategic Management Journal* 1: 265–291.

1.4
EVOLUTION OF QUALITATIVE RESEARCH METHODS IN STRATEGIC MANAGEMENT

Melissa E. Graebner

Introduction

The contributions of qualitative scholarship to the field of strategic management are "wide and deep" (Bettis *et al.*, 2015). The open-endedness of qualitative data frees scholars from imposing prespecified constructs and measures, making qualitative research invaluable for understanding novel phenomena, inductively developing new theory, and authentically capturing strategists' thought processes and lived experiences (Graebner, Martin, and Roundy, 2012). The vividness of qualitative data inspires creativity in researchers and helps to communicate ideas, complementing more abstract research approaches like analytic models (Hannah, Tidhar, and Eisenhardt, forthcoming) and computational simulations (Davis, Eisenhardt, and Bingham, 2007). The richness and nuance of qualitative data help illuminate the intricacies of complex organizational processes that defy traditional statistical analysis (Langley, 2007). Taken together, these qualities foster a more sophisticated and ecologically valid understanding of organizational strategies and strategy making, creating a close link between theory and practice that is fitting for an applied field such as strategic management.

Of course, qualitative research is not without its difficulties. Qualitative studies remain relatively rare in the field of management in general (Pratt, Kaplan, and Whittington, 2020), and in strategic management in particular. Misunderstandings regarding the diverse forms and uses of qualitative research methods often emerge during the review process, creating hurdles for authors (Graebner *et al.*, 2012; Eisenhardt, Graebner, and Sonenshein, 2016). Nonetheless, qualitative research remains essential to advancing the strategy field. This chapter outlines the past and present contributions of qualitative work to strategic management and suggests challenges and promising opportunities for future qualitative scholarship.

Foundational Contributions

Qualitative research has a rich history in strategic management. Scholars including Chandler (1962), Bower (1970), Pettigrew (1973), and Mintzberg and colleagues (Mintzberg, 1979; Mintzberg, Raisinghani, and Theoret, 1976) demonstrated the unique potential of qualitative research methods even before the creation of the *Strategic Management Journal* and the publication of Michael Porter's bestselling *Competitive Strategy* (1980), events that many view as ushering in the modern strategy field. Chandler's (1962) longitudinal case studies of large industrial firms illustrated the power of open-ended, fine-grained data, offering "as much richness of detail as possible, without the limiting filter of a narrow theory-testing focus" (Teece, 2010: 297). Bower's (1970) in-depth study of resource allocation processes revealed that strategy involves multiple organizational levels (front-line workers, middle managers, and top managers) and is shaped by both rational (measurement systems, incentives) and behavioral (cognitive and political) forces. As Bower later wrote, "The reality of resource allocation is that it is a complex process involving technical, economic and financial, organizational, cultural, and interpersonal forces that are fundamentally interrelated" (2017: 2428). Qualitative data are ideally suited to shed light on these intricacies. Mintzberg *et al.*'s (1976) field study of 25 strategic decision processes in a diverse set of organizations yielded insights that had been overlooked in the artificial environment of laboratory experiments. The authors noted, "Because the structure of the strategic decision process is determined by its very complexity, oversimplification in the laboratory removes the very element on which the research should be focused" (1976: 247). Taken together, these early works exemplified how qualitative data could contribute nuanced, empirically grounded descriptions and theoretical models to the field of strategy.

In the 1980s, qualitative researchers extended their contributions to strategic management through ambitious new projects. Pettigrew's (1985) study of strategic change at chemical manufacturer ICI was published the same year that the Centre for Corporate Strategy and Change was founded at Warwick Business School. The ICI study helped shape the longitudinal approach of the Centre's projects, as Pettigrew later recalled: "I took the view that theoretically sound and practically useful research on change therefore needed to involve the simultaneous analysis of the contexts, content, and the process of change. This kind of analysis was only possible if the strategic change processes were examined over very long periods of time" (Starkey, 2002: 21). Accordingly, one of the Centre's first projects was a comparison of high- and low-performing firms in four industry sectors over a 30-year period (Pettigrew and Whipp, 1991). Andrew Van de Ven and colleagues' seminal work through the Minnesota Innovation Research Program was narrower in temporal scope but included a larger and more diverse set of organizations. The data collection effort involved 15 faculty and 19 doctoral students from eight different academic departments at the University of Minnesota (Van de Ven and Poole, 1990). Few such expansive projects have been implemented since.

The 1980s also saw the emergence of a new generation of qualitative strategy scholars, including Robert Burgelman, Ann Langley, and Kathleen Eisenhardt. Burgelman's (1983, 1985) in-depth case study of "GAMMA" corporation's new venture division generated a multilevel and multistage process model of internal corporate venturing that elaborated on Bower's (1970) model of resource allocation. Whereas Burgelman focused on developing a deep understanding of a single, large, multibusiness firm, Eisenhardt and coauthor Jay Bourgeois (Bourgeois and Eisenhardt, 1988; Eisenhardt and Bourgeois, 1988; Eisenhardt, 1989a) conducted a multiple-case study of computer firms, enabling comparisons across organizations. They focused on explaining variation in outcomes such as overall firm performance (Bourgeois and Eisenhardt, 1988), the emergence of political behavior (Eisenhardt and Bourgeois, 1988), and the speed of strategic decision-making (Eisenhardt, 1989a). Eisenhardt summarized her approach in a methodological article (1989b) that continues to be one of the most highly cited publications in management.

Like Eisenhardt, Langley's early works involved multiple organizations (Langley, 1988, 1989). Langley selected three disparate organizations to represent Mintzberg's (1979) typology of structural types: machine bureaucracy, professional bureaucracy, and adhocracy. She used an embedded research design, studying eight to 10 strategic issues within each of the organizations. The major contribution of this work was a typology of the purposes served by formal analysis within organizations, ranging from generating information to symbolizing rational decision-making (Langley, 1989) and providing a form of "group therapy" (1988). These emerging scholars thus illustrated the broad range of contributions that can be generated by qualitative studies, including models of a single process (Burgelman), explanations of variance in outcomes (Eisenhardt), and insightful typologies of organizational activities (Langley).

Increasing Diversity and Broadening Impact

Despite representing a relatively small proportion of published research in strategic management, in recent decades qualitative studies have continued to generate an outsized impact on the field. Qualitative research has added to our understanding of alliances (de Rond and Bouchikhi, 2004; Ariño and Ring, 2010; Ozcan and Eisenhardt, 2009), mergers and acquisitions (Graebner, 2004, 2009; Graebner and Eisenhardt, 2004; Schweizer, 2005; Vaara and Tienari, 2011), responses to technological change (Tripsas, 2009; Benner, 2010; Gilbert, 2006), corporate governance (Garg and Eisenhardt, 2017; Hoppmann, Naegele, and Girod, 2019), strategy development in entrepreneurial ventures (Kirtley and O'Mahony, forthcoming; McDonald and Eisenhardt, 2020; Oliver and Vough, 2020), managerial cognition (Porac, Thomas, and Baden-Fuller, 1989; Tripsas and Gavetti, 2000; Kaplan, 2008), competitive behavior (Irwin, Lahneman, and Parmigiani, 2018; Jarzabkowski and Bednarek, 2018), business model innovation (Berends et al., 2016; Snihur and Zott, 2020) and dynamic capabilities (Huy and Zott, 2019; Rindova and Kotha, 2001). The textured findings that emerge from qualitative analyses have counterbalanced the simplifying assumptions of economic models and highlighted behavorial influences such as social embeddedness and sensemaking in interorganizational relationships (Davis, 2016; Seidl and Werle, 2018), heuristics in strategic decision-making (Bingham and Eisenhardt, 2011), symbolic actions in resource acquisition (Zott and Huy, 2007), and organizational identity in strategic change (Tripsas, 2009; Sasaki *et al.*, 2019; Wenzel *et al.*, 2020).

These diverse contributions have emerged from an array of different qualitative research designs. The next section of this chapter surveys the range of approaches to qualitative research in strategy, with the caveat that the authors, topics, and research designs presented here are certainly not exhaustive. This brief review includes two approaches that are relatively well established and often overlapping in the strategy literature (multicase theory building and process analysis), two approaches that are rapidly growing (strategy-as-practice and narrative, discursive, and rhetorical analyses), and two approaches that have been used more rarely (deductive and illustrative case studies).

Multicase theory building

In keeping with strategic management's traditional interest in firm performance, many qualitative studies in strategy have attempted to explain variance in organizational outcomes, typically through inductive comparison of multiple case studies. This approach is most closely associated with Kathleen Eisenhardt, whose *Academy of Management Review* article (1989b) provided a roadmap of the method that was elaborated in subsequent *Academy of Management Journal* essays (Eisenhardt and Graebner, 2007; Eisenhardt *et al.*, 2016). Eisenhardt (1989b) focused on building theory by identifying concepts, exploring the relationships between them, and explicating mechanisms that underlie those relationships. She recommended investigating a small number of cases (between four and 10 cases is common) chosen through theoretical rather than random sampling, engaging in constant comparison between theory and data, and using "replication logic" (Yin, 1984) to ensure robust findings across cases and to generate parsimonious theory. Cases may center on entire firms, decisions or projects within a single firm (Galunic and Eisenhardt, 1996), or relationships involving multiple firms (e.g., Hallen and Eisenhardt, 2012; Davis, 2016). Many studies have embedded units of analysis. For example, Martin and Eisenhardt (2010) examined two cross-business collaborations within each of six firms. Eisenhardt and others who use the method (e.g., Gilbert, 2005; Zuzul and Tripsas, 2020) have relied on a variety of data sources, but frequently emphasize interviews with key informants.

Process analysis

"Process" research refers to "considering phenomena dynamically—in terms of movement, activity, events, change and temporal evolution" (Langley, 2007: 271). The hallmark of this approach is its emphasis on time, which requires gathering and analyzing

rich longitudinal data that may include interviews, archival documents, and/or ethnographic observations (Gehman *et al.*, 2018). A key methodological reference for
process research in strategic management is Langley's (1999) explication of ways to
analyze process data, including temporal bracketing, visual mapping, and comparing
alternate templates. Process studies have been conducted at the individual (Shah and
Tripsas, 2007), team (Bresman, 2013), firm (Jacobides and Billinger, 2006), community or platform (O'Mahony and Karp, forthcoming), and industry (Jacobides,
2005) levels and have examined an eclectic set of strategic phenomena. For example,
Jacobides (2005) conducted a longitudinal case study of the process of vertical disintegration in the mortgage banking industry over a 20-year period, while Monin *et al.*
(2013) examined the postmerger integration process in a single merger over a five-year
period. Many multicase theory-building studies also describe temporal processes (e.g.,
Graebner, 2009; Hallen and Eisenhardt, 2012; Martin and Eisenhardt, 2010), although
not all process studies involve multiple-case theory building, or vice versa.

Strategy-as-practice

The growing literature on strategy-as-practice is concerned with the microprocesses
through which strategy is enacted. Jarzabkowski *et al.* (2015) describe the "what," "who,"
and "how" of practice—what practices are adopted by organizations, who performs
those practices ("practitioners"), and how the practices are enacted in context ("praxis").
Strategy is "a situated, socially accomplished activity," and strategizing "comprises those
actions, interactions and negotiations of multiple actors and the situated practices that
they draw upon in accomplishing that activity" (Jarzabkowski, Balogun, and Seidl,
2007: 7–8). This perspective highlights the importance of detailed observation to avoid
simplistic, superficial descriptions. In keeping with this focus, many strategy-as-practice
studies supplement interview and documentary data with extended periods of on-site
fieldwork. For example, Jarzabkowski (2008) observed 51 strategy meetings involving
top managers from three universities, and Kaplan (2008) observed 33 meetings within
a firm as well as conducting 80 interviews and gathering archival data. The strategy-as-
practice perspective has also opened the field up to unusual data sources such as diaries
and focus groups (Balogun and Johnson, 2004) and videos of micro-interactions (Gylfe
et al., 2016). For their study of a firm undergoing a major organizational restructuring,
Balogun and Johnson asked 26 middle managers to write diary entries every two weeks,
answering questions such as, "What problems do you foresee? What have been the significant events? What rumors and stories are circulating?" (2004: 526).

Narrative, discursive, and rhetorical approaches

Qualitative data are central to strategy research focusing on linguistic phenomena
such as narratives, discourse, and rhetoric (Graebner *et al.*, 2012). Scholars interested

in these phenomena may examine texts such as conference presentations (Kahl and Grodal, 2016), initial public offering prospectuses (Martens, Jennings, and Jennings, 2007), media reports (Vaara and Tienari, 2011), or transcripts of strategy meetings (Jalonen, Schildt, and Vaara, 2018). For example, Dalpiaz and di Stefano (2018) examined corporate biographies and monographs to understand how narratives enabled transformational change in the Italian manufacturing firm Alessi. An array of analytical techniques are available, ranging from simple word counts to thematic analyses to dynamic temporal models. Sillince, Jarzabkowski, and Shaw (2012) collected interviews, meeting transcripts, emails, and other documents related to a strategic change. They coded the arguments presented in these texts into six rhetorical categories, and then analyzed how each type of rhetoric generated ambiguity. Finally, the authors developed a process model of the "evolving relationship between strategic ambiguity and strategic action" (2012: 645).

Deductive qualitative studies

Although the approaches mentioned above often use qualitative data for inductive or abductive theory development, it is also possible, though less common, to use qualitative data deductively. Greenwood, Hinings, and Brown (1994) used prior literature on mergers and acquisitions to develop two hypotheses: that premerger activities would reflect lack of attention to organizational fit, and that ambiguous agreements made in the early stages of a merger would lead to escalating conflicts. A longitudinal case study of a merger found that, surprisingly, significant attention was paid to organizational issues during the "courtship" phase, yet nevertheless, consistent with the second hypothesis, significant conflict emerged during implementation. Similarly, Benner (2010) drew upon prior research regarding responses to new technologies to develop a hypothesis regarding security analysts' reactions to incumbent firm strategies that depart from existing technologies. She examined analyst reports covering incumbent firms in the photography and wireline telecommunications industries during periods of technological transformation, finding consistent support for the hypothesis.

Illustrative case studies

Rather than forming the basis for either inductive or deductive reasoning, qualitative data may be used to bring an abstract idea or model to life, making it more persuasive and credible. As Siggelkow noted when reflecting on his study of Liz Claiborne (Siggelkow, 2001), "The framework proposed in the paper emerged more from a conceptual exercise.... However, the case turned out to be a very helpful illustration and was used in that manner" (Siggelkow, 2007: 22). De Rond and Bouchikhi (2004) developed a theory regarding dialectics in alliance relationships that they then illustrated with a small case study. They explained that the case study "is intended to be an empirical illustration of the dialectical forces to which alliances are likely to be subject. It was never our intention to use this as a dataset from which to inductively construe a new theory of alliances" (2004: 60). More recently, Jarzabkowski and Kaplan (2015) developed a framework for examining how strategy tools are used within organizations. After developing their conceptual framework, the authors "illustrate some of the dynamics" (548) using a vignette drawn from a wider study of strategy making.

While presented here separately, the approaches listed above are not mutually exclusive. Studies taking a temporal process perspective can also explain variance in outcomes (e.g., Graebner, 2009). Strategy process and strategy-as-practice research have many commonalities, as explored in a recent special issue of the *Strategic Management Journal* (Burgelman *et al.*, 2018). The ethnographic approach that is typical of strategy-as-practice research can provide a window into linguistic phenomena like framing contests (Kaplan, 2008). Deductive and inductive analyses may also appear within a single study. Indeed, such flexibility has traditionally been a distinctive advantage of qualitative methods.

Challenges for Qualitative Strategy Research

In many ways, qualitative research in strategy is thriving, with its rich assortment of methodological approaches bringing fresh perspectives to the field. Nonetheless, challenges exist. Some of these challenges are inherent to the method. Qualitative research is laborious and unpredictable, and the holistic and iterative process of qualitative data analysis does not lend itself to sharing the workload across a large author team. As Van de Ven and Poole noted three decades ago, "Systematic and creative data analysis often involves a sequential set of tasks best performed by one or two individuals, who can increase their probabilities of learning and generating significant insights by performing all these tasks from beginning to end" (1990: 315).

Other challenges are not intrinsic to qualitative research, but result from the fact that qualitative studies remain relatively rare in strategy scholarship. This rarity generates hurdles in the publication process and barriers to the accumulation of knowledge.

Publication hurdles

Despite the fact that flexibility is a key feature of qualitative research methods, many qualitative strategy scholars have noted a growing rigidity in the journal review process (Eisenhardt *et al.*, 2016; Pratt *et al.*, 2020). As leading qualitative authors have described their methodological approaches, some readers have treated these approaches as prescriptive templates (cf. Langley and Abdallah,

2011) to be strictly followed in the name of "rigor" or "transparency." An illustration is the "Gioia method." Originally developed for interpretive studies of organizational identity, the method prioritizes giving "extraordinary voice to informants" by preserving their wording during the analytical process (Gioia, Corley, and Hamilton, 2013: 26). The method generates a comprehensive, hierarchical categorization system with first-, second-, and third-order codes, presented in a standardized diagram. Some strategy scholars find the method very useful, particularly when examining the intersection of strategy and organizational identity (e.g., Wenzel *et al.*, 2020).

Yet by virtue of offering a ready template of analytical steps and formatted outputs, the Gioia method is appealing to some journal reviewers (particularly those who are not familiar with the full range of qualitative methods) even when it is not appropriate (Eisenhardt *et al.*, 2016). Gioia and colleagues did not view their method as a universally applicable approach, writing, "To force fit data into the 1st-order/2nd-order rubric when not called for ... sacrifices the benefits of qualitative research's flexibility in applying different approaches to fit different phenomenological needs" (2013: 25). For example, the focus on preserving informants' words during the analytical process may not be suitable for ethnographic studies. Ethnographers' "truth claims" are "not primarily based in what research participants have said to researchers" (Jarzabkowski and Bednarek, 2014: 275), but rather in the researchers' observations, based on their "experience of deep immersion in the field" (2014: 276). As another example, multi-case, variance-oriented studies aim to home in on constructs with explanatory power for an outcome of interest. Since parsimony is often regarded as a feature of good theory, scholars who are inductively building variance theory will aim for simplicity rather than comprehensiveness.

Overall, checklists of methodological steps deprive qualitative scholars of the ability to craft approaches that are tailored to the goals of their specific research projects. The trend toward rigidity in qualitative research may be collateral damage from the "replication crisis" that has emerged in social psychology. Yet as Pratt *et al.* (2020) have pointed out, the proposed solutions to the replication crisis—namely, preregistration of hypotheses, sharing detailed research protocols, and making data publicly available—are not feasible for most qualitative research. They wrote, "[T]he first is often inappropriate, the second can be problematic, and the third is potentially unethical when considering inductive qualitative management research" (2020: 6). More fundamentally, exact replication is neither realistic nor, in general, even desirable for qualitative studies, given their goals.

Accumulation of knowledge

While exact replication is rarely germane for qualitative studies, the broader issue of knowledge accumulation remains an important challenge. Qualitative studies receive many accolades such as best paper awards, but other scholars sometimes overlook these studies' insights. For example, two literature reviews on "strategy process research" excluded all qualitative work (Hutzschenreuter and Kleindienst, 2006; Bromiley and Rau, 2016), leading to some puzzling conclusions. The first review identified "strategy process as dynamic capability" as a future research area, arguing, "process research has hardly witnessed any application" of the concept of dynamic capabilities. This claim disregarded, among others, qualitative studies by Rindova and Kotha (2001) on the process of continuous "morphing" and by Galunic and Eisenhardt (2001) on architectural innovation through divisional charter change—both of which explicated strategic processes and explicitly used the term "dynamic capabilities" in their framing.

It should be straightforward for literature reviews to include both qualitative and quantitative studies, and for quantitative studies to acknowledge relevant qualitative work. A more formidable task is developing approaches to synthesize multiple qualitative studies without losing their rich insights. One path forward is offered by Majchrzak, Jarvenpaa, and Bagherzadeh (2015) in their analysis of published studies of interorganizational collaboration dynamics. The authors analyzed scholarly case studies from prominent journals, finding 22 longitudinal cases that were described in sufficient detail for their purposes. The authors then inductively analyzed each case, characterizing the types and causes of change in each interorganizational relationship over time. The result of this analysis was a typology of six distinct patterns that included recursive feedback loops and other nuanced processual dynamics. Habersang *et al.* (2019) offer another example of "meta-synthesis" of case studies in the context of organizational failure. Further refining such approaches would be valuable for advancing knowledge on topics that have been the subject of multiple qualitative studies, such as resource redeployment, entrepreneurial strategy formation, and international expansion.

Future Opportunities

New organizational phenomena and global challenges continue to call for the type of nuanced and open-ended inquiry that qualitative research offers. Accordingly, the final section of this chapter highlights several areas that would benefit from future qualitative research. This section places particular emphasis on topics at the intersection of strategic management and broader societal concerns.

Strategy during crisis

As this is written, the world is facing crises including a global pandemic, economic upheaval, and a reckoning regarding racial injustice. These come in the midst of ongoing challenges including digital transformation and climate change. All of these issues have implications for the field of strategy, and present opportunities for qualitative research. Qualitative methodologies offer a unique ability to examine sensemaking and other complex social and cognitive processes under conditions of risk and ambiguity. Indeed, Graham Allison's (1971) qualitative analysis of the Cuban Missile Crisis was a seminal contribution to understanding decision-making in high-stakes, time-sensitive settings. However, in the ensuing decades, qualitative studies of strategic decision-making during crisis have been relatively few. In 2020 the Strategic Management Society published a Virtual Special Issue on "Strategic Responses to Crisis," which comprised 13 articles that had appeared in the Society's three journals (see https://onlinelibrary.wiley.com/doi/toc/10.1002/(ISSN)1097-0266.strategic-responses-to-crisis). Of the 13, only one (from the *Strategic Entrepreneurship Journal*) used a qualitative methodology.

Yet the current set of crises has distinctive characteristics that raise new questions and call for open-ended approaches to scholarship. In the era of globalization and social media, crises may escalate rapidly in severity and scope as information (not all of it accurate) spreads with unprecedented speed. How do these characteristics influence how leaders manage strategic decisions amid crisis? The COVID-19 pandemic has also created unique challenges. Work and family life collide as parents conduct business from home alongside children who are attending school remotely. How does the overlap of work and family responsibilities influence managerial attention and shape the ways in which strategic decisions are made and implemented? The isolation and stress created by a pandemic can trigger depression and other mental illnesses. How might the emergence of widespread mental health challenges influence strategic decisions? The breadth of the COVID-19 pandemic is unparalleled in modern times. How are businesses coping when one or more senior leaders are quarantined, hospitalized, or incapacitated by lingering symptoms? These are all critical issues to understand.

Strategy and the "new normal"

Much speculation is occurring about what the world will look like post-COVID. The emerging consensus is that some changes will be permanent, likely including greater use of technology to enable remote work. Qualitative research methods are ideal for exploring the implications of this shift. For example, how do top management team interactions differ when they take place online? Will the technological affordances of services like Zoom (e.g., video recording, automated generation of transcripts, private chat during meetings) shift the dynamics of board meetings and influence corporate governance? Social interaction is a central aspect of the formation of interorganizational relationships (e.g., Graebner, 2009). If partnership or merger talks occur over Zoom rather than on the golf course, what will be the impact upon whether deals are closed? Will greater use of videoconferencing enable better postmerger integration or alliance implementation processes? Or will lack of in-person interaction lead to mutual suspicion and misunderstanding? These questions remain unanswered.

Strategy, diversity, and inclusion

The reckoning taking place in the United States with regard to race generates an important set of questions at the intersection of strategy and diversity, equity and inclusion. Acknowledging the racial overtones of long-standing product names such as "Uncle Ben's" rice and "Aunt Jemima's" pancake mix, companies are making changes after decades of inaction. What creates the tipping point that motivates such change within an organization? What narratives and discourses surround these decisions, both within and outside of the organization? Moreover, much of what we know about the links between demographic diversity and senior leadership has relied upon survey and archival methods (e.g., McDonald, Keeves, and Westphal, 2018). While these methods are invaluable for observing broad patterns, observational and interview studies may reveal more nuance regarding the ways that diversity influences the tenor of strategic discussions, how strategic ideas are received, which voices have influence, and how strategies are implemented. How can women and people of color be effective participants in framing contests (Kaplan, 2008)? What are the lived experiences of racial minority executives who are involved with strategic processes? These questions have important societal as well as strategic implications.

Strategy, machine learning, and artificial intelligence

Finally, advanced analytics designed to exploit the exponential growth of business data are likely to play an increasing role in firms' strategic decisions. The rapid diffusion of big data analytics into firms' strategy processes raises a new set of questions about how actors will guide, interpret, and act upon the results of these analyses. For instance, given the emergence of specialized business analytics degree programs, will big data tools upend hierarchical structures, increasing the influence of junior analysts over the decisions of senior executives (see Barley, 1986)? Like other analytical approaches, machine learning requires assumptions and judgment calls that can shape results. In what ways will traditional power dynamics influence such seemingly "objective" analyses? Individuals' prior experiences and knowledge will still exist alongside new analyses that make use of massive data sets. How will domain expertise be used to supplement the results of automated analyses (e.g., Choudhury, Starr, and Agarwal, 2020)? How will firm leaders use their own judgment to deal with results of large-scale analyses that produce results that are racially biased or problematic in other ways? All of these questions would benefit from qualitative research approaches.

Conclusion

Qualitative research has made seminal contributions to strategic management since the inception of the field. In recent years, qualitative research has flourished across a range of topic areas and methodological approaches, despite a variety of challenges. New phenomena continue to fuel opportunities for qualitative scholars to build theory, describe complex social processes, and investigate linguistic patterns. Big data and machine learning will surely be important to the strategy field, yet fine-grained analyses of individual top management teams, firms, and industries will continue to provide invaluable insights to strategy scholarship. In the words of Amazon founder Jeff Bezos (Bort, 2018), "when the anecdotes and the data disagree, the anecdotes are usually right."

References

Allison GT. 1971. *Essence of Decision: Explaining the Cuban Missile Crisis*. Little, Brown: Boston, MA.

Ariño A, Ring PS. 2010. The role of fairness in alliance formation. *Strategic Management Journal* 31: 1054–1087.

Balogun J, Johnson G. 2004. Organizational restructuring and middle manager sensemaking. *Academy of Management Journal* 47(4): 523–549.

Barley SR. 1986. Technology as an occasion for structuring: evidence from observations of CT scanners and the social order of radiology departments. *Administrative Science Quarterly* 31: 78–108.

Benner MJ. 2010. Securities analysts and incumbent response to radical technological change: evidence from digital photography and Internet telephony. *Organization Science* 21(1): 42–62.

Berends H, Smits A, Reymen I, Podoynitsyna K. 2016. Learning while (re)configuring: business model innovation processes in established firms. *Strategic Organization* 14(3): 181–219.

Bettis RA, Gambardella A, Helfat C, Mitchell W. 2015. Qualitative empirical research in strategic management. *Strategic Management Journal* 35: 637–639.

Bingham CB, Eisenhardt KM. 2011. Rational heuristics: the "simple rules" that strategists learn from process experience. *Strategic Management Journal* 32: 1437–1464.

Bort J. 2018. Amazon founder Jeff Bezos explains why he sends single character "?" emails. *Inc*. https://www.inc.com/business-insider/amazon-founder-ceo-jeff-bezos-customer-emails-forward-managers-fix-issues.html.

Bourgeois LJ III, Eisenhardt KM. 1988. Strategy decision processes in high-velocity environments: four cases in the microcomputer industry. *Management Science* 34: 816–835.

Bower JL. 1970. *Managing the Resource Allocation Process: A Study of Corporate Planning and Investment*. Harvard Business School Press: Boston, MA.

Bower JL. 2017. Managing resource allocation: personal reflections from a managerial perspective. *Journal of Management* 43(8): 2421–2429.

Bresman H. 2013. Changing routines: a process model of vicarious group learning in pharmaceutical R&D. *Academy of Management Journal* 56: 35–61.

Bromiley P, Rau D. 2016. Social, behavioral, and cognitive influences on upper echelons during strategy process: a literature review. *Journal of Management* 42(1): 174–202.

Burgelman RA. 1983. A process model of internal corporate venturing in the diversified major firm. *Administrative Science Quarterly* 28: 223–244.

Burgelman RA. 1985. Managing the new venture division: research findings and implications for strategy management. *Strategic Management Journal* 6: 39–54.

Burgelman RA, Floyd SW, Laamanen T, Mantere S, Vaara E, Whittington R. 2018. Strategy processes and practices: dialogues and intersections. *Strategic Management Journal* 39: 531–558.

Chandler AD. 1962 *Strategy and Structure: Chapters in the History of the Industrial Enterprise.* MIT Press: Cambridge, MA.

Choudhury P, Starr E, Agarwal R. 2020. Machine learning and human capital complementarities: experimental evidence on bias mitigation. *Strategic Management Journal* 41: 1381–1411.

Dalpiaz E, Di Stefano G. 2018. A universe of stories: mobilizing narrative practices during transformative change. *Strategic Management Journal* 39(3): 664–696.

Davis JP. 2016. The group dynamics of interorganizational relationships. *Administrative Science Quarterly* 61(4): 621–661.

Davis JP, Eisenhardt KM, Bingham CB. 2007. Developing theory through simulation methods. *Academy of Management Review* 32(2): 480–499.

de Rond M, Bouchikhi H. 2004. On the dialectics of strategic alliances. *Organization Science* 15(1): 56–69.

Eisenhardt KM. 1989a. Making fast strategic decisions in high-velocity environments. *Academy of Management Journal* 32: 543–576.

Eisenhardt KM. 1989b. Building theories from case study research. *Academy of Management Review* 14(4): 532–550.

Eisenhardt KM, Bourgeois LJ III. 1988. Politics of strategic decision making in high-velocity environments: toward a midrange theory. *Academy of Management Journal* 31: 737–770.

Eisenhardt KM, Graebner ME. 2007. Theory building from cases: opportunities and challenges. *Academy of Management Journal* 50(1): 25–32.

Eisenhardt KM, Graebner ME, Sonenshein S. 2016. Grand challenges and inductive methods: rigor without rigor mortis. *Academy of Management Journal* 59(4): 1113–1123.

Galunic DC, Eisenhardt KM. 1996. The evolution of intracorporate domains: divisional charter losses in high-technology, multidivisional corporations. *Organization Science* 7(3): 255–282.

Galunic DC, Eisenhardt KM. 2001. Architectural innovation and modular corporate forms. *Academy of Management Journal* 44(6): 1229–1249.

Garg S, Eisenhardt KM. 2017. Unpacking the CEO-board relationship: how strategy making happens in entrepreneurial firms. *Academy of Management Journal* 60(5): 1828–1858.

Gehman J, Glaser VL, Eisenhardt KM, Gioia D, Langley A, Corley KG. 2018. Finding theory-method fit: a comparison of three qualitative approaches to theory building. *Journal of Management Inquiry* 27(3): 284–300.

Gilbert CG. 2005. Unbundling the structure of inertia: resource versus routine rigidity. *Academy of Management Journal* 48(5): 741–763.

Gilbert CG. 2006. Change in the presence of residual fit: can competing frames coexist? *Organization Science* 17(1): 150–167.

Gioia DA, Corley KG, Hamilton AL. 2013. Seeking qualitative rigor in inductive research: notes on the Gioia methodology. *Organizational Research Methods* 16(1): 15–31.

Graebner ME. 2004. Momentum and serendipity: how acquired leaders create value in the integration of technology firms. *Strategic Management Journal* 25: 751–777.

Graebner ME. 2009. Caveat venditor: trust asymmetries in acquisitions of entrepreneurial firms. *Academy of Management Journal* 52(3): 435–472.

Graebner ME, Eisenhardt KM. 2004. The seller's side of the story: acquisition as courtship and governance as syndicate in entrepreneurial firms. *Administrative Science Quarterly* 49: 366–403.

Graebner ME, Martin JA, Roundy PT. 2012. Qualitative data: cooking without a recipe. *Strategic Organization* 10(3): 276–284.

Greenwood R, Hinings CR, Brown J. 1994. Merging professional services firms. *Organization Science* 5(2): 239–257.

Gylfe P, Franck H, LeBaron C, Mantere S. 2016. Video methods in strategy research: focusing on embodied cognition. *Strategic Management Journal* 37(1): 133–148.

Habersang S, Küberling-Jost J, Reihlen M, Seckler C. 2019. A process perspective on organizational failure: a qualitative meta-analysis. *Journal of Management Studies* 56(1): 19–56.

Hallen BL, Eisenhardt KM. 2012. Catalyzing strategies and efficient tie formation: how entrepreneurial firms obtain investment ties. *Academy of Management Journal* 55(1): 35-70.

Hannah DP, Tidhar R, Eisenhardt KM. Forthcoming. Analytic models in strategy, organizations, and management research: a guide for consumers. *Strategic Management Journal.*

Hoppmann J, Naegele F, Girod B. 2019. Boards as a source of inertia: examining the internal challenges and dynamics of boards of directors in times of environmental discontinuities. *Academy of Management Journal* 62(2): 437–468.

Hutzschenreuter T, Kleindienst I. 2006. Strategy-process research: what have we learned and what is still to be explored. *Journal of Management* 32(5): 673–720.

Huy Q, Zott C. 2019. Exploring the affective underpinnings of dynamic managerial capabilities: how managers' emotion regulation behaviors mobilize resources for their firms. *Strategic Management Journal* 40: 28–54.

Irwin J, Lahneman B, Parmigiani A. 2018. Nested identities as cognitive drivers of strategy. *Strategic Management Journal* 39: 269–294.

Jacobides MG. 2005. Industry change through vertical disintegration: How and why markets emerged in mortgage banking. *Academy of Management Journal* 48(3): 465–498.

Jacobides MG, Billinger S. 2006. Designing the boundaries of the firm: from "make, buy, or ally" to the dynamic benefits of vertical architecture. *Organization Science* 17(2): 249–261.

Jalonen K, Schildt H, Vaara E. 2018. Strategic concepts as micro-level tools in strategic sensemaking. *Strategic Management Journal* 39: 2794–2826.

Jarzabkowski P. 2008. Shaping strategy as a structuration process. *Academy of Management Journal* 51(4): 621–650.

Jarzabkowski P, Balogun J, Seidl D. 2007. Strategizing: the challenges of a practice perspective. *Human Relations* 60(1): 5–27.

Jarzabkowski P, Bednarek R. 2014. Demystifying ethnographic textwork in strategy and organization research. *Strategic Organization* 12(4): 274–287.

Jarzabkowski P, Bednarek R. 2018. Toward a social practice theory of relational competing. *Strategic Management Journal* 39(3): 794–829.

Jarzabkowski P, Kaplan S. 2015. Strategy tools-in-use: a framework for understanding "technologies of rationality" in practice. *Strategic Management Journal* 36: 537–558.

Jarzabkowski P, Kaplan S, Seidl D, Whittington R. 2015. On the risk of studying practices in isolation: linking what, who, and how in strategy research. *Strategic Organization* 14(3): 248–259.

Kahl SJ, Grodal S. 2016. Discursive strategies and radical technological change: multilevel discourse analysis of the early computer. *Strategic Management Journal* 37: 149–166.

Kaplan S. 2008. Framing contests: strategy making under uncertainty. *Organization Science* 19(5): 729–752.

Kirtley J, O'Mahony S. Forthcoming. What is a pivot? Explaining when and how entrepreneurial firms decide to make strategic change and pivot. *Strategic Management Journal.*

Langley A. 1988. The roles of formal strategic planning. *Long Range Planning* 21(3): 40–50.

Langley A. 1989. In search of rationality: the purposes behind the use of formal analysis in organizations. *Administrative Science Quarterly* 34: 598–631.

Langley A. 1999. Strategies for theorizing from process data. *Academy of Management Review* 24(4): 691–710.

Langley A. 2007. Process thinking in strategic organization. *Strategic Organization* 5(3): 271–282.

Langley A, Abdallah C. 2011. Templates and turns in qualitative studies of strategy and management. In *Research Methodology in Strategy and Management*, Vol. 6, Bergh D, Ketchen D (eds). Emerald Publishing Group: Bingley, U.K.; 201–235.

Majchrzak A, Jarvenpaa SL, Bagherzadeh M. 2015. A review of interorganizational collaboration dynamics. *Journal of Management* 41(5): 1338–1360.

Martens ML, Jennings JE, Jennings PD. 2007. Do the stories they tell get them the money then need? The role of entrepreneurial narratives in resource acquisition. *Academy of Management Journal* 50(5): 1107–1132.

Martin JA, Eisenhardt KM. 2010. Rewiring: cross-business-unit collaborations in multibusiness organizations. *Academy of Management Journal* 53(2): 265–301.

McDonald RM, Eisenhardt KM. 2020. Parallel play: startups, nascent markets, and effective business model design. *Administrative Science Quarterly* 65(2): 483–523.

McDonald ML, Keeves GD, Westphal JD. 2018. One step forward, one step back: white male top manager organizational identification and helping behavior toward other executives following the appointment of a female or racial minority CEO. *Academy of Management Journal* 61(2): 405–439.

Mintzberg H. 1979. *The Structuring of Organizations*. Prentice-Hall: Englewood Cliffs, NJ.

Mintzberg H, Raisinghani D, Theoret A. 1976. The structure of "unstructured" decision processes. *Administrative Science Quarterly* 21: 246–275.

Monin P, Noorderhaven N, Vaara E, Kroon D. 2013. Giving sense to and making sense of justice in postmerger integration. *Academy of Management Journal* 56(1): 256–284.

Oliver D, Vough HC. 2020. Practicing identity in emergent firms: how practices shape founders' organizational identity claims. *Strategic Organization* 18(1): 75–105.

O'Mahony S, Karp R. Forthcoming. From proprietary to collective governance: how do platform participation strategies evolve? *Strategic Management Journal*.

Ozcan P, Eisenhardt KM. 2009. Origin of alliance portfolios: entrepreneurs, network strategies, and firm performance. *Academy of Management Journal* 52(2): 246–279.

Pettigrew AM. 1973. *Politics of Organizational Decision-Making*. Tavistock: London, U.K.

Pettigrew AM. 1985. *Awakening Giant: Continuity and Change in ICI*. Basil Blackwell: Oxford, U.K.

Pettigrew AM, Whipp R. 1991. *Managing Change for Competitive Success*. Blackwell Publishers: Oxford, U.K.

Porac JF, Thomas H, Baden-Fuller C. 1989. Competitive groups as cognitive communities: the case of Scottish knitwear manufacturers. *Journal of Management Studies* 26(4): 397–416.

Porter ME. 1980. *Competitive Strategy*. Free Press: New York.

Pratt MG, Kaplan S, Whittington R. 2020. Editorial essay: the tumult over transparency: decoupling transparency from replication in establishing trustworthy qualitative research. *Administrative Science Quarterly* 65(1): 1–19.

Rindova VP, Kotha S. 2001. Continuous "morphing": competing through dynamic capabilities, form, and function. *Academy of Management Journal* 44(6): 1263–1280.

Sasaki I, Kotlar J, Ravasi D, Vaara E. 2019. Dealing with revered past: historical identity statements and strategic change in Japanese family firms. *Strategic Management Journal* 41: 590–623.

Schweizer L. 2005. Organizational integration of acquired biotechnology companies into pharmaceutical companies: the need for a hybrid approach. *Academy of Management Journal* 48(6): 1051–1074.

Seidl D, Werle F. 2018. Inter-organizational sensemaking in the face of strategic meta-problems: requisite variety and dynamics of participation. *Strategic Management Journal* **39**: 830–858.

Shah SK, Tripsas M. 2007. The accidental entrepreneur: the emergent and collective process of user entrepreneurship. *Strategic Entrepreneurship Journal* **1**: 123–140.

Siggelkow N. 2001. Change in the presence of fit: the rise, the fall, and the renaissance of Liz Claiborne. *Academy of Management Journal* **44**(4): 838–857.

Siggelkow N. 2007. Persuasion with case studies. *Academy of Management Journal* **50**(1): 20–24.

Sillince J, Jarzabkowski P, Shaw D. 2012. Shaping strategic action through the rhetorical construction and exploitation of ambiguity. *Organization Science* **23**(3): 630–650.

Snihur Y, Zott C. 2020. The genesis and metamorphosis of novelty imprints: how business model innovation emerges in young ventures. *Academy of Management Journal* **63**(2): 554–583.

Starkey K. 2002. Andrew Pettigrew on executives and strategy: an interview by Kenneth Starkey. *European Management Journal* **20**(1): 20–25.

Strategic responses to crisis. 2020. Strategic Management Society Virtual Special Issue, https://onlinelibrary.wiley.com/doi/toc/10.1002/(ISSN)1097-0266.strategic-responses-to-crisis.

Teece DJ. 2010. Alfred Chandler and "capabilities" theories of strategy and management. *Industrial and Corporate Change* **19**(2): 297–316.

Tripsas M. 2009. Technology, identity, and inertia through the lens of "The Digital Photography Company." *Organization Science* **20**(2): 441–460.

Tripsas M, Gavetti G. 2000. Capabilities, cognition, and inertia: evidence from digital imaging. *Strategic Management Journal* **21**: 1147–1161.

Vaara E, Tienari J. 2011. On the narrative construction of multinational corporations: an ante-narrative analysis of legitimation and resistance in a cross-border merger. *Organization Science* **22**(2): 370–390.

Van de Ven AH, Poole MS. 1990. Methods for studying innovation development in the Minnesota Innovation Research Program. *Organization Science* **1**(3): 313–335.

Wenzel M, Cornelissen JP, Koch J, Hartmann M, Rauch M. 2020. (Un)Mind the gap: how organizational actors cope with an identity-strategy misalignment. *Strategic Organization* **18**(1): 212–244.

Yin R. 1984. *Case Study Research*. Sage Publications: Beverly Hills, CA.

Zott C, Huy QN. 2007. How entrepreneurs use symbolic management to acquire resources. *Administrative Science Quarterly* **52**(1): 70–105.

Zuzul T, Tripsas M. 2020. Start-up inertia versus flexibility: the role of founder identity in a nascent industry. *Administrative Science Quarterly* **65**(2): 395–433.

PART 2
CORPORATE STRATEGY

Sea-Jin Chang, Lead

2.0

CORPORATE STRATEGY: OVERVIEW AND FUTURE CHALLENGES

Sea-Jin Chang

Corporate strategy can be defined as the choices firms make in allocating resources across multiple lines of business in order to create competitive advantage. Corporate strategy has been central to the strategy field from its inception. Ansoff (1965) envisioned corporate strategy as a firm's growth plan and analyzed the risks associated with pursuing growth in both product and market. As corporate strategy involves diverse decisions by top management teams and CEOs, including diversification, international expansion, divestiture, spinoff, strategic alliances, vertical integration, mergers and acquisitions, and internal control systems to share resources beyond business boundaries, corporate strategy research tends to be phenomena driven.[1] The field also embraces a variety of theoretical perspectives in order to explain various value creation mechanisms through which corporate strategy can add or destroy value. This chapter offers a brief historical overview of corporate strategy before turning to avenues for future research.

Historical Overview

Early works on diversification

Early works on corporate strategy focused on understanding the performance implications of diversification strategies. Rumelt (1974) classifies the diversification patterns of large U.S. corporations into several types and shows that related, as opposed to unrelated, diversification drives superior performance. Rumelt's work, along with others examining similar relationships in other countries (e.g., Channon, 1973, for the United Kingdom), spurred interest among scholars in the burgeoning strategy field. The managerial implications from this line of research are clear: firms should pursue related, not unrelated, diversification. Numerous subsequent publications examined the so-called diversification-performance relationship.[2] Researchers typically come up with various measures to capture the degree of diversification and estimate the impact on several performance indicators, like return on assets (ROA), sales growth, risk reduction, and Tobin's q. For instance, one may create a Herfindahl index of diversification with a firm's sales revenue by two-digit Standard Industry Classification

(SIC) codes in order to capture unrelated diversification, while calculating the firm's sales revenue by four-digit SIC codes within the same two-digit SIC codes to capture related diversification (Berry, 1974; Jacquemin and Berry, 1979; Palepu, 1985).[3] Economies of scope (Panzar and Willig, 1981), also commonly known as synergy, serve as a key mechanism for superior performance of related diversification. That is, by sharing common inputs in related businesses, firms can either lower costs or increase revenue from diversification. Transferring skills and leveraging learnings or know-how, a type of intangible resource with value that does not diminish with use, also serve as important sources of value creation from diversification.

Despite the vast literature on the diversification-performance relationship, results are largely mixed. While some find a positive relationship (e.g., Rumelt, 1974; Christensen and Montgomery, 1981), others find a negative or no significant relationship (e.g., Amit and Livnat, 1988). More recent research sought to improve measures and methodology to generate more consistent results. Researchers often use the SIC scheme to determine whether resources from a business in an industry can be shared or leveraged in another industry. As the SIC scheme is partly based on technology and market similarity, related diversification within the same two-digit SIC industry is assumed to share resources, thereby creating synergy. The term "relatedness," however, may mean many things within the common two-digit SIC code. Relatedness can come from common physical assets and common inputs, which are conventionally assumed to capture synergy. Relatedness can also come from technological knowledge that can be leveraged to other businesses. For example, Robins and Wiersema (1995) measure technological similarities using the structural equivalences of inter-industry technology flow. Miller (2006) operationalizes technology diversity using breadth of firms' patent stocks. Relatedness can also come from the similarity of human resource profiles among businesses (Chang, 1996; Farjoun, 1994). Given that each business may be similar to other businesses in each of these relatedness dimensions, any measure in one dimension may capture the relatedness construct in an imperfect, partial way. Furthermore, a diversification measure, defined at the corporate level, imposes the same level of synergies across diverse lines of business, which can be too constraining, as synergy may be high within set of related businesses but low in a different set of businesses (Brush and Bromiley, 1997; Brush, Bromiley, and Hendrickx, 1999).

Diversification discount and the size of corporate effects

Early works in diversification mainly explored correlations without proper endogeneity controls. A positive coefficient in the relationship between related diversification and performance does not necessarily mean that if a firm pursues related diversification it will enjoy superior performance. Yet a reversed causality is equally plausible: highly performing firms may pursue related diversification while poorly performing firms may pursue unrelated diversification as a defensive strategy (Montgomery and Wernerfelt, 1986). As diversification strategy is not randomly adopted, such highly endogenous diversification strategies should affect subsequent firm performance, thus creating endogeneity issues when studying diversification.

Corporate finance researchers have also actively studied the performance implications of diversification, as rooted in the broader interest in diversification (or conglomerate) discounts. That is, diversified conglomerates are often traded at a discount because the capital market suspects that conglomerates are too diversified and, thus, unwieldy. The hostile takeovers and proxy fights of the 1980s proved that the broken-up value of conglomerates is often higher than the actual value of conglomerates. Corporate finance scholars such as Berger and Ofek (1995) and Lang and Stulz (1994) calculate imputed firm values using the weighted average of segments, based on the values of single-business firms in the same segment, and find a significantly negative impact of diversification, that is, a diversification discount. Campa and Kedia (2002), however, point out that after controlling for endogenous choices inherent to diversification, the diversification discount disappears or even converts to a premium. Villalonga (2004) similarly finds evidence of a diversification premium, based on a sample of U.S. census data that includes many small-sized firms, after controlling for endogeneity. In other words, poorly performing firms pursue unrelated diversification, but not vice versa. This may be because poorly performing firms lack competencies in their own and related businesses. For these firms, it is not practical to diversify in related businesses. Rather, unrelated areas may prove to be more promising opportunities.

The size of corporate effects in determining business-level performance has also been hotly debated in the strategy field. Schmalensee (1985) decomposed variances in profitability across firms from the 1975 Federal Trade Commission (FTC) line of business data to find that industry effects were the most important factor in explaining a firm's profitability, while corporate effects were negligible. Rumelt (1991) reanalyzed the FTC data using four years of time-series data (1974–1977). This pooled sample enabled him to add a major component: a business-unit dummy variable. Further, Rumelt used the random effects model, while Schmalensee used the fixed effects model. Rumelt finds that business-unit and industry effects, not corporate effects, are the main sources of firm profitability, thus implying that corporate strategy may not matter. That is, corporate strategy may be so similar across sample firms in the FTC database that it does not have any impact on business performance.

Rumelt's controversial finding prompted several subsequent works to qualify Rumelt's findings. Using the Compustat business segment database, McGahan and Porter (1997) find nontrivial corporate effects. This divergence in findings may be attributable to differences in samples. First, the Compustat database is more recent than the FTC database. Second, the Compustat database includes many small companies, while the FTC database consists mainly of large, diversified corporations. Third, Bowman and Helfat (2001) argue that the inclusion of single-business firms masks the true size of corporate effects, as it is not possible to distinguish corporate effects from business-unit effects for these firms. Similarly, Chang and Singh (2000) demonstrate that different industry definitions, inclusion/exclusion of small business units, and firm size systematically change the populations from which we draw samples of corporations, industries, and businesses, thus significantly influencing results. Fourth, institutional context also matters. Chang and Hong (2002) indicate that corporate parents, such as business groups, play a more important role in developing countries with market inefficiencies. Makino, Isobe, and Chan (2004) further show that corporate and subsidiary effects tend to be more critical in explaining the variance in foreign subsidiary performance in developed countries, as country and industry effects are more salient in developing countries.

In addition, several researchers highlight important methodological constraints. The random effects model is specified in a way that assumes corporations have equal impact on the profitability or market share of each strategic business unit (SBU). It does not allow corporate effects to be stronger for some SBUs than others, even though operating synergies may only exist with select SBUs. Brush and Bromiley (1997) and Brush, Bromiley, and Hendrickx (1999) demonstrate, via simulation, that the sizes of corporate effects diminish rapidly in a nonlinear fashion when the corporate effects apply only to part of the entire set of SBUs.

To summarize, prior works on corporate strategy, represented by diversification strategy, find that diversification indeed matters for firm performance. Zooming out to the bigger picture, the literature as a whole suggests that corporate strategy matters. Specifically, the diversification discount disappears after controlling for endogenous choice to diversify, while the corporate effects in determining business-level performance can be larger for smaller firms and smaller businesses, in developing countries, and when relaxing various methodological constraints.

Future Challenges and Directions

Corporate strategy, as briefly summarized so far in this chapter, presents many challenges for the field to explore going forward. Prior works in corporate strategy focused mostly on the contemporaneous sharing of resources across businesses, employed rough measures for resources, and suffered from data and methodological constraints. In the rest of this chapter, I outline several areas for the future direction of corporate strategy research, calling for new theoretical angles, a more dynamic approach, better measures and methodology, attention to internal coordination costs and control systems, and expansion to more diverse institutional environments.

New theory and value creation mechanisms

As corporate strategy is made at the corporate level by top management, essentially interacting between a firm's internal and external environments, there can be several alternative theoretical perspectives and several mechanisms through which corporate strategy can create value. Prior works use four main theoretical mechanisms to understand corporate strategy. First, as discussed earlier, common inputs or resources that create economies of scope are the main driver for diversification, which is also consistent with the prediction of resource-based theory (Penrose, 1959; Barney, 1991). Second, vertically integrated firms, that is, those that diversified in vertical value chains from upstream to downstream operations, can benefit from better coordination while also saving on market transactions costs from opportunistic behaviors of buyers or sellers. The vertical scope of firms (indicated by vertical integration or by the extent of outsourcing, for example) have been also studied from the perspective of transaction cost theory (Williamson, 1975). Third, diversified firms can use profits from one business to subsidize losses from another business, particularly when the latter is a newly entered business or facing competition (Scherer, 1980). Diversified firms can also engage in predatory pricing, that is, driving out competitors by undercutting their prices with subsidies from other businesses (Areeda and Turner, 1975). Last, diversification lowers risk by generating stable income streams from diverse lines of businesses, although such risk reduction often benefits managers more than shareholders (Amit and Livnat, 1988).

In particular, scholars point out that corporate strategy may not always be motivated by efficiency. Managers often pursue growth for their own benefit, creating agency costs (Jensen and Meckling, 1976; Amihud and Lev 1981; Lane, Cannella, and Lubatkin, 1998). For example, many conglomerate mergers in the 1960s and 1970s were likely motivated by empire building, which led to divestitures and restructuring in the 1980s (Duhaime and Grant, 1984). As such, corporate governance factors like board composition, interlocking directorates, and executive compensation structures are important in understanding the underlying managerial motivations for corporate strategy (Baysinger and Hoskisson, 1990). More recent works by both strategy and finance scholars have substantially contributed to this line of research from the agency theory perspective.

For example, recent works have focused on executives who make corporate strategy decisions. Kaplan, Klebanov, and Sorensen (2012) examine how CEOs' personal characteristics, like resoluteness and overconfidence, impact firm performance. CEOs' past experiences also may matter. For example, Dittmar and Duchin (2016) examine how CEOs' past experience with negative corporate outcomes, like bankruptcy and financial difficulties, often lead them to implement more conservative strategies. Nakauchi and Wiersema (2015) conclude that nonroutine succession, wherein retiring CEOs leave firms without any official titles, often leads to strategic changes. Several other studies examine CEOs' overconfidence in their own strategic judgment and leadership capabilities (e.g., Park, Westphal, and Stern, 2011)

Organization theory and economic sociology can also help us better understand corporate strategy. Zuckerman (1999) offers a new theoretical angle to explain the diversification discount, as he argues that the diversification discount derives from a lack of identity and legitimacy as stock analysts tend to focus on specialized sectors and so neglect conglomerates that span multiple sectors. From this perspective, a diversification discount may really exist, not rooted in actual value destruction but instead coming from wrong perceptions by audiences, namely stock analysts. According to this line of research, conformity to the institutional norm—that is, related diversification or a focus on the core business—should improve stock market valuation. Corporate strategy that conforms to environmental constraints may be more pronounced when firms are more concerned about broader stakeholders other than shareholders. For example, corporate-level resource allocations to corporate social responsibility initiatives may be driven by institutional environments. Lee (2020) shows that the level of corporate social responsibility engagement is significantly lower for U.S. firms headquartered in tax havens compared to those headquartered in the United States.

Levinthal and Wu (2010) advance an alternative explanation of the observed conglomerate discount, arguing that diversifying firms that allocate non-scale-free resources in diversified lines of business should consider the opportunity cost of their use in one business or another. As the productive opportunity to use non-scale-free resources in a mature business is lower, profit-maximizing firms would better reallocate them to new or growing businesses. Levinthal and Wu show that such profit-maximizing decisions lower profitability (profit margins) but increase total profit. In other words, the diversification discount is actually consistent with profit maximization. Maksimovic and Phillips (2002) also provide evidence consistent with this claim using plant-level data to show that the observed conglomerate discount is consistent with profit maximization but not necessarily with agency theory, as conglomerates create value by reallocating resources from declining businesses, characterized by lower productivity, to growing businesses.

These more recent works demonstrate that strategy scholars can always revisit important issues in corporate strategy with a new theoretical angle to generate alternative explanations that are consistent with observed patterns, thus enriching managerial implications. Strategy scholars should therefore broaden their theoretical perspectives by adopting new theoretical insights from other areas like economics, finance, sociology, and psychology, to feed new theories that deepen our understanding of corporate strategy.

Dynamic approach

Strategy scholars traditionally invested much effort into understanding "intratemporal scope economies"—the (static) synergy created by contemporaneously sharing resources across businesses. In doing so, this research essentially takes a snapshot of a firm's pattern of diversification and tries to relate it to performance. More recent literature, however, pays closer attention to how resources can be transferred to other businesses over time, especially from exited to newly entered businesses, thereby creating "intertemporal economies of scope" or dynamic synergy (Helfat and Eisenhardt, 2004; Anand and Singh, 1997).

Why, though, do we need a more dynamic approach in the future? In reality, a firm's pattern of diversification is not static. While exogenous shocks like technological change or intensified competition surely prompt resource redeployment, profit-maximizing firms should be constantly engaged in resource redeployment to generate maximum services from the resources they possess (Penrose, 1959). In fact, firms are very active in changing their business portfolios with new business entries and exits. Almost half of U.S. manufacturing firms are known to alter their mix of five-digit standard industry classification (SIC) products every five years (Bernard, Redding, and Schott, 2010). From an analysis of high-tech U.S. firms, Miller and Yang (2016) show that firms often show resource redeployment via simultaneous entry and exit, particularly among small and medium-sized firms, as they tend to be more resource-constrained. Kaul (2012) similarly shows that technological innovation both by focal firms and competitors encourages firms to redeploy resources to enter new businesses and exit marginal businesses. Uzunca (2018) also shows that incumbents faced with technological and market disruption tend to reposition themselves by entering and exiting submarkets. Lee and Parachuri (2016) point out that the threat of substitution encourages new entry by resource redeployment, which is mediated by the similarity between a focal firm's existing business and new businesses. Firms are also observed to pursue reorganization of units they plan to divest, that is, shifting resources to other units before their divestitures (Karim, 2006). Stagni, Santalo, and Giarratana (2020) show that diversified firms reallocate internal non-scale-free resources to a business faced with international competition from unaffected businesses.

By taking a dynamic perspective, we may gain a deeper understanding of how corporate strategy creates value. A smooth resource reallocation, as just outlined, is one such example, as firms can orchestrate their resource reconfigurations in a timely manner, given the fast-moving environment. Because not all firms have the same level of dynamic capabilities (Helfat and Eisenhardt, 2004; Teece, 2007), we may find a stronger effect of corporate strategy by examining dynamic resource reallocation. Dynamic capabilities, which enable firms to adapt to a fast-changing environment, evolve from three key managerial capabilities: (1) sensing: recognizing opportunities and anticipating competitive threats; (2) seizing: taking advantage of opportunities and responding to emerging threats; and (3) reconfiguring: orchestrating assets to maintain strategic fit among organizational assets as conditions change (Helfat and Peteraf, 2015: 837). Intertemporal scope economies are critically conditioned by such dynamic capabilities (Karim and Capron, 2016). To this end, Lee (2008) shows that if a firm can adjust its capabilities within a newly entered product category, it can overcome the initial disadvantage of dissimilarity between current capabilities and those required to compete in a focal category. Vidal and Mitchell (2015) further show that firms can use divestiture to free up resources that can be used for future growth, which may improve performance.

Another benefit of a dynamic approach is that it captures the uncertain nature of corporate strategy. Diversifying firms may not always be sure they can be successful in a newly entered businesses. Therefore, they often test the water with experimental entry and exit before making a big move. In that regard, entry can be conceived as a real option, either scale up or exit, upon receiving feedback from the market. Lieberman, Lee, and Folta (2017) find that business relatedness supports resource redeployment from incumbent businesses to a new business, as well as from a new business back to other businesses, thus encouraging experimental entry and early exit if the performance of the newly entered business fails to meet expectations. O'Brien and Folta (2009) demonstrate that the negative effect of sunk cost on the probability of exit diminishes when firms enter highly related industries, as firms can reenter previously exited businesses without paying a reentry cost.

Furthermore, firms may use prior entry as a platform when moving sequentially toward a business of more dissimilar resource profiles (Chang, 1996). Based on learning from prior entry experiences, firms may approach their next entries with more appropriate strategies (March, 1991; Nelson and Winter, 1982). Similarly, firms show a sequential exit pattern, divesting businesses of more dissimilar resource profiles to the rest of businesses over time. Therefore, corporate strategy naturally shows path dependency—that is, a firm's prior choices have a significant impact on its subsequent choices. Firms also make serial entries to strengthen their newly entered businesses, as in the case of internet giants. Google, for example, made a series of acquisitions in artificial intelligence, like PittPatt in 2011, DeepMind in 2014, and Onward in 2019.

The dynamic approach can shed further light on the simultaneous pursuit of competition and cooperation in platform competition (Hoffmann *et al.*, 2018). For example, platform participants, who cooperate with platform owners, may hedge against being locked into a particular platform and thus make their products and services available for rival platforms, which will in turn invite competitive responses from a focal platform owner. In response, some platforms may focus only on platform technology while avoiding direct competition with platform participants, which may then constrain its diversification strategy. Likewise, the dynamic approach can shed new light on how corporate strategy can add value to individual businesses over time by constantly interacting with ever-changing external environments.

Better measures and methodology

While prior works have examined synergies from resource sharing, the resources themselves have yet to be precisely measured. Resources are distinctive factors that can differentiate firms from competitors. When resources are valuable, rare, inimitable, and irreplaceable, firms can generate significant and sustainable competitive advantages (Barney, 1991). Despite these rather clear conceptual definitions, researchers often rely on rough expenditure-based measures like research and development (R&D) and advertising intensities, mainly due to data constraints.

Technological resources are often captured by patents, thereby measuring only patentable technology.

Such rough proxies for resources and their assumed sharing have been obstacles to a more precise understanding of the inner workings of corporate strategy. In order to push the corporate strategy field forward, future studies should measure resources and the extent of their sharing more precisely. In that regard, Anand, Kim, and Lu's (2016) four characteristics of resources are helpful: (1) fungibility, (2) scale-free nature, (3) decomposability, and (4) tradability. Fungibility indicates whether resources are substitutable for other uses without sacrificing productive value.[4] Some intangible resources, like brand, may be fungible, while physical and other intangible resources can be used only in related businesses characterized by a similar set of resources. Scale-free resources occur when the value of resources does not shrink due to the magnitude of usage, like well-documented knowledge such as patents. On the other hand, the value of non-scale-free resources, like the working hours of engineers, decreases when multiple businesses have to share them simultaneously. Decomposability indicates how easily resources can be separated into individual chunks without a strong interrelationship to other parts of the company. Less decomposable resources are difficult to transfer to other businesses. Tradability means that resources can be sold or bought in factor markets (Dierickx and Cool, 1989). If resources are tradable, firms do not have to rely on internal synergies. Rather, they can get the maximum value out of resources by selling them to external buyers. Future research should seek measures that more directly capture these characteristics of resources in order to enable a more meaningful discussion of resource sharing and redeployment across businesses.

To capture resource characteristics and measure them precisely, we may need to conduct research in a more narrowly defined context, like a single industry setting where there are more detailed product categories with distinctive technology and market characteristics, like the semiconductor (e.g., Uzunca, 2018; Chang and Matsumoto, 2020), biotech (Baum, Calabrese, and Silverman, 2000), or medical device (e.g., Mitchell, 1989) industries. On the other hand, studying a population of all public firms from which financial data are available may be more useful in understanding firms' broader choices, including unrelated diversification. For example, if resources are non-scale-free, firms need to consider how to allocate limited resources among businesses, not only at the same time but also during two different time periods. One can study how non-scale-free resources like engineers and machinery may be transferred from mature businesses to a newly entered business. Furthermore, resource redeployment can take place among incumbent businesses without necessarily incurring entry and exit costs. Burgelman (1994) shows that Intel gradually transferred resources from Dynamic Random Access Memory businesses (DRAMs) to the growing microprocessor and Erasable Programmable Read Only Memory (EPROM) businesses, long before its formal exit from the former.

The field should also measure fungibility or decomposability more directly by examining how individual resources can be used in newly entered businesses. Anand (2004) finds that firms conducting civilian business, such as computers, communications, or instruments, are more likely to redeploy resources than firms conducting defense-related business, like aircraft, missiles, or ships. By concentrating on one industry, researchers may be able to collect more detailed data on resources like human capital to illustrate how talent can be shared or transferred to create a corporate advantage. Such a closer look at how each resource, with its own unique characteristics, can be either shared or redeployed among businesses will help us understand how corporate strategy can create value.

In tandem, future strategy research should employ empirical research designs that better handle the thorny endogeneity issue. In general, research conducted in the fields of economics and finance has been more careful in managing endogeneity. Yet, it is also important for strategy scholars to clarify causality in order to provide practical advice to managers. As mentioned earlier, it is difficult to advise managers to pursue related diversification if one is not sure whether related diversification leads to higher performance or high-performing firms often pursue related diversification.

In reality, however, it is actually hard to fully control endogeneity issues in corporate strategy, as decisions at the corporate level are often intertwined. As I browse papers published in the *Strategic Management Journal* for the last decade, it is clear that strategy researchers are now fully aware of the challenges of establishing causality in corporate strategy research. While aware, it remains difficult to find a good instrument or natural experiment. Yet a variety of new techniques enable quasi-experimental design, including matching technique, regression discontinuity, and various selection models. For example, the propensity score matching technique, combined with differences-in-difference methodology, can create a quasi-experimental setting in which there is a clear treatment, that is, a strategic decision. For example, Chang, Chung, and Moon (2013) examined the effects of conversion from joint venture to wholly owned subsidiary by matching converted wholly owned subsidiaries with continuing joint ventures of similar ex ante likelihood of conversion. As such, and in the absence of good instruments, researchers can devise research designs so that they can carefully rule out obvious alternative hypotheses or reverse causality. While researchers may not be able to fully control endogeneity with methods alone, strong theory and careful empirical research design can minimize endogeneity issues. For example, in the above case of joint venture conversion, propensity score matching could be more effective when we can specify the first-stage conversion decision more precisely, as *matched* treatment and control groups can be considered identical. In order to better specify the first-stage conversion decision, it is important to rely on the joint ventures termination literature to identify key variables to consider in matching.

Another possibility is to design an empirical study based on an exogenous shock or natural experiment. For example, Contigiani, Hsu, and Barankay (2018) use U.S. state-level legislation on protecting trade secrets as a natural experiment to inventor mobility. Likewise, the COVID-19 pandemic is an exogenous shock that might have a fundamental impact on how firms conduct business. Exploiting such exogenous shocks will certainly help relieve endogeneity concerns.

Internal coordination costs

Prior works tended to focus on positive synergies, while paying less attention to the potential costs associated with creating synergy. In fact, sharing or transferring resources is not free but subject to different types of costs, namely "adjustment costs" and "coordination costs" (Helfat and Eisenhardt, 2004; Hashai, 2015). The former costs are incurred from transferring and adapting resources to different categories; the latter arise when firms try to share and create connections between resources used for different categories. If the adjustment or coordination costs exceed any benefit from diversification, we may not be able to observe any performance improvement associated with diversification. Several prior empirical works show that managing interdependencies among businesses incurs high coordination costs (Rawley and Simcoe, 2010; Maritan and Brush, 2003). In order to enjoy economies of scope, firms need to manage interdependencies between businesses that share inputs (Zhou, 2011).

As Penrose (1959: 22) points out, "Strictly speaking, it is never *resources* themselves that are the 'inputs' in the production process, but only the *services* that the resources can render" (emphasis in original). Even if resources have the potential to contribute to a firm's sustainable competitive advantage, the firm cannot realize its full potential unless it generates and utilizes services from those resources. Therefore, there should be a lot of variation in a firm's ability to lower adjustment or coordination costs. In general, the more similar two businesses are, the lower the adjustment and coordination costs, though there has not been sufficient work that captures cost factors in a precise way. Furthermore, the benefits and costs of sharing and redeploying resources are not necessarily evenly shared among businesses. While relatedness is beneficial at the company level, it may reward core businesses, while related business segments suffer (Kumar, 2013). Even though the benefits of diversification may outweigh the costs at the time of diversification, these benefits may soon evaporate when an external shock occurs. This causes costs to persist longer, which in turn causes poorer long-term performance (Natividad and Rawley, 2016).

In particular, utilizing a pool of unused productive services from resources in large, diversified lines of business has proven to be an inherently difficult task. Chandler's (1962) historical analysis indicates that executives in these firms find it difficult to address the conflicting pressures of long-term strategic considerations and short-term operational administrative activities. In response, these firms created the multidivisional structure referred to as the M-form. In the M-form, business divisions operate as autonomous profit centers, often organized by product or region, thereby freeing up time and resources for the general office to spend on long-term strategic decision-making (Williamson, 1975). While the M-form is designed to address corporate-wide coordination and control over businesses, business divisions can easily become silos that hoard resources and fail to share with other divisions. Interdivisional coordination within diversified corporations can be further constrained due to the limited and uneven attention of top management (Ocasio, 1997). Hill, Hitt, and Hoskisson

(1992) argue that related diversified firms need more cooperative structures to promote mutual support, while unrelated diversified firms may need more competitive structures to maintain discipline in capital allocation.

Wulf (2002) likewise shows that the likelihood of distorting information by division is higher when executive compensation is more strongly tied to division—as opposed to corporate—performance, and when businesses are unrelated to each other. In a similar vein, Belenzon, Hashai, and Patacconi (2019) suggest that corporate groups often suffer from miscommunication and governance frictions, that is, distortions of information transmitted through communication channels and actions that are beneficial to the focal division while suboptimal for the group. As such, compensation policies and incentive systems may affect not only the motivations behind corporate strategy but also their effective implementation. Future studies should delve further into the internal operations of diversified firms and focus on how managerial initiatives create corporate advantages. For example, future studies may want to examine the role of executives, who play a crucial role in coordinating activities in diversified multidivisional firms. Executives can function as the catalysts that translate unused resources into productive services for corporate advantage by actively interacting with various types of resources across organizational units. Interdivisional coordination and control through executive transfer will differ by type of resource to be shared or transferred—that is, scalable intangible resources such as technological knowledge and nonscalable tangible resources such as financial capital.

Diverse institutional environments

The degree to which corporate strategy can add value depends on the institutional environments in which firms operate. Prior works in corporate strategy were often based on the context of more developed economies, such as the United States. For firms operating in less developed countries, where external capital or labor markets are in earlier stages, there will be more room to create value via internal capital or labor markets (Leff, 1978; Chang and Choi, 1988; Williamson, 1975). As mentioned earlier, the size of corporate effects tends to be larger in developing countries than in developed countries (Chang and Hong, 2002). During the last several decades, we have witnessed the rise of strong emerging-market competitors like Samsung, Hyundai, TSMC, Haier, Huawei, and Alibaba, which challenged developed-country-market multinationals.

While a significant amount of research has taken place on the role of corporate strategy of emerging-market competitors—for example, new business entry, global strategy, mergers and acquisitions (M&As), and divestiture—certainly there are still areas for further research on this topic. For example, prior works demonstrate that market imperfections in emerging markets create ample opportunities for the corporate level to create value by sharing resources internally (Khanna and Yafeh, 2007). Khanna and Palepu (1997) even argued that unrelated diversification is the best choice in emerging markets. It is not clear whether unrelated diversification will continue to create value through resource sharing and redeployment, even when markets are developed over time. Furthermore, many firms in emerging markets are in transition from first-generation founders to second-generation family managers or professional managers. It would be interesting to examine whether family heirs or professional managers perform better, and how we can design governance systems to better guide future corporate strategy.

Fortunately for strategy researchers, the diverse cultural and institutional environments that firms face provide a rich context in which to explore corporate strategy (North, 1990). As cultural norms and institutional environments vary greatly by country, comparative studies using firms facing different institutional constraints could generate interesting insights. For example, corporate strategy can differ greatly depending on the identity of dominant shareholders. While a large portion of the prior work in corporate strategy has been conducted in the context of publicly owned enterprises with dispersed ownership in the United States, the findings may or may not be applicable to other countries with different governance structures. For example, in many countries, families or governments are large, dominant shareholders. Obviously, families and governments may have different preferences from individual shareholders, who tend to be motivated by short-term profit.

Family owners may have a long-term time horizon, but this can create agency problems that exploit minority shareholders. Family ownership can create nepotism, family legacy, and succession issues, which can have important implications for corporate strategy in those firms (Bertrand *et al.*, 2008: Bennedsen *et al.*, 2007; Chang and Shim, 2015). On the other hand, in countries like China and Singapore, government ownership is high, which has its own pros and cons. On the one hand, governments can be patient, long-term-oriented owners. On the other hand, government ownership may invite bureaucracy and cronyism. It will be interesting to further explore how different ownership types may lead to different corporate strategies in a cross-country setting. Surroca *et al.* (2020) show that firms' simultaneous adoption of managerial entrenchment provisions and corporate social responsibilities creates shareholder values in liberal market economies but destroys shareholder value in coordinating market economies.

Furthermore, business groups, a form of diversified firm prevalent in many developing countries, offer a unique opportunity to examine whether corporate strategy plays a more important role in developed countries. *Business groups* are defined as collections of legally independent firms under single common administrative and financial control (Colpan, Hikino, and Lincoln, 2010; Khanna and Yafeh, 2007). Affiliate companies of a business group, though legally separate, are bound together in formal and informal ways. For example, group affiliates in Korean business groups function like operating divisions in the M-form, while group-level staff organizations function like corporate headquarters in diversified conglomerates in the United States to support the group CEOs' strategic decisions at the group level (Chang and Hong, 2002). While some business groups are ultimately controlled by families, like those in Korea or Taiwan, others are owned by the government or government-owned financial firms, as in the case of Chinese business groups.

A key empirical advantage of business groups as a research context is the accessibility of full data on its member affiliates, that is, business divisions in a typical M-form. As each group affiliate is legally independent (unlike the business division in fully consolidated corporations), the group provides financial information, as well as interaffiliate business transactions data. Such division-level information is not usually accessible in fully consolidated corporations in the United States. While Korean business groups may be an exemplary case of the M-form organization because they are hierarchical business groups, Taiwanese or Japanese groups may function more like an alliance structure, wherein affiliates cooperate voluntarily (Colpan, Hikino, and Lincoln, 2010). As business groups may face different cultural and institutional environments unique to each country, a cross-country research setting would further our understanding of corporate strategy. For example, Korean business groups are strong in executing strategy, since they are ultimately controlled by shareholders; it is also easier for Korean business groups to create synergies across businesses. Yet their weaknesses lie in a weak corporate governance system that cannot prevent wrong decisions by those ultimate shareholders. Likewise, it would be interesting to see how distinctive forms of business groups in each country have their own strengths and weaknesses.

Conclusions

In recent years, we have witnessed the rise of platform giants like Alphabet, Facebook, and Neflix, whose business models are based on their user bases. For example, Alphabet is adding a variety of new businesses to its core search engine business (Google), exhibiting network externality and an increasing return to scale and scope. Customers become increasingly dependent on new Google services, thus increasing traffic and providing more data to Google and its parent, Alphabet. Given the unprecedented scale, one wonders if there is any limit to Alphabet's growth. A more detailed characterization of resources of these firms would be needed to understand the strategies of these tech giants. As discussed earlier, as many of these tech giants are platform owners, it would be interesting to examine the effectiveness of the strategic alliances and M&A strategies used to maintain and reinforce their platforms. It would also be interesting to see how these platform owners balance cooperation and competition over time.

Furthermore, firm environments are undergoing drastic changes. In the first decades of the 21st century, we have witnessed a widening income gap in most countries. People increasingly mistrust business, as the Occupy Wall Street movement showed. The conventional notion of shareholder maximization is being widely challenged. Therefore, firms are required to pay attention to a broader spectrum of stakeholders, like employees, the community, and the natural environment. With the increased influence of stakeholder perspective, social performance should be recognized alongside shareholder value. It is, however, debatable whether the pursuit of social performance has any trade-off with the pursuit of shareholder value maximization, as there is evidence that well-governed firms that suffer from fewer agency concerns engage in more corporate social responsibility (e.g., Ferrell, Liang, and Renneboog, 2016). It will be a great challenge for managers and strategy researchers alike to find a way to harmonize the conflicting demands of various stakeholders, which will greatly benefit from a cross-national comparison (e.g., Surroca *et al.*, 2020). In that regard, Harrison and Wicks (2019) argue that strategies that benefit some stakeholders but harm others can be considered unethical and may eventually backfire.

In sum, corporate strategy remains an exciting area for future research with ever more interesting new phenomena and changes in external environments to study. New theories, more dynamic approaches, better measurement and methodology, more internal scrutiny of organizational issues, and better incorporation of diverse institutional factors will be crucial to generating important insights for managers.

Notes

1. See the chapter by Feldman in this book for more detailed discussion of divestiture and spinoff and the chapter by Ireland and Wither on mergers and acquisitions.
2. See Ahuja and Novelli's (2017) review of the diversification-performance relationship.
3. Many researchers highlight the inherent limitations of these measures (e.g., Robins and Wiersema, 2003; Davis and Duhaime, 1992).
4. Sakhartov and Folta (2014) show that the value of fungibility (redeployability) grows with industry uncertainty.

References

Ahuja G, Novelli El. 2017. Redirecting research efforts on the diversification-performance linkage: the search for synergy. *Academy of Management Annals* 11(1): 342–390.

Amihud Y, Lev B. 1981. Risk reduction as a managerial motive for conglomerate mergers. *Bell Journal of Economics* 12(2): 605–617.

Amit R, Livnat J. 1988. Diversification strategies, business cycles, and economic performance. *Strategic Management Journal* 9(2): 99–110.

Anand J. 2004. Redeployment of corporate resources: a study of acquisition strategies in the US defense industries, 1978–1996. *Managerial and Decision Economics* 25(6–7): 383–400.

Anand J, Kim H, Lu S. 2016. Resource characteristics and redeployment strategies: Toward a theoretical synthesis. In *Resource Redeployment and Strategic Management* (Advances in Strategic Management, Volume 35), Folta TB, Helfat CE, Karim S (eds). Emerald Group Publishing: Bingley, U.K.; 155–184.

Anand J, Singh H. 1997. Asset redeployment, acquisitions and corporate strategy in declining industries. *Strategic Management Journal* 18(Summer Special Issue): 99–118.

Ansoff I. 1965. *Corporate Strategy: An Analytic Approach to Business Policy for Growth and Expansion.* McGraw-Hill: New York, NY.

Areeda P, Turner D. 1975. Predatory pricing and related practices under Section 2 of the Sherman Act. *Harvard Law Review* 88(4): 697–733.

Barney J. 1991. Firm resources and sustained competitive advantage. *Journal of Management* 17(1): 99–120.

Baum J, Calabrese T, Silverman B. 2000. Don't go it alone: alliance network composition and startups' performance in Canadian biotechnology. *Strategic Management Journal* 21(3): 267–294.

Baysinger B, Hoskisson B. 1990. The composition of board of directors and strategic control: effect on corporate strategy. *Academy of Management Review* 15(1): 72–87.

Belenzon S, Hashai N, Patacconi A. 2019. The architecture of attention: group structure and subsidiary autonomy. *Strategic Management Journal* 40: 1610–1643.

Bennedsen M, Nielsen KM, Perez-Gonzalez F, Wolfenzon D. 2007. Inside the family firm: the role of families in succession decisions and performance. *Quarterly Journal of Economics* 122: 647–691.

Berger P, Ofek E. 1995. Diversification effect on firm value. *Journal of Financial Economics* 37: 39–65.

Bernard A, Redding S, Schott P. 2010. Multiple-product firms and product switching. *American Economic Review* 100(1): 70–97.

Berry CH. 1974. Corporate diversification and market structure. *Bell Journal of Economics* 5: 196–204.

Bertrand M, Johnson S, Samphantharak K, Schoar A. 2008. Mixing family with business: a study of Thai business groups and the families behind them. *Journal of Financial Economics* 88: 466–498.

Bowman E, Helfat C. 2001. Does corporate strategy matter? *Strategic Management Journal* 22(1): 1–23.

Brush T, Bromiley P. 1997. What does a small corporate effect mean? A variance components simulation of corporate and business effects. *Strategic Management Journal* 18(10): 825–835.

Brush T, Bromiley P, Hendrickx M. 1999. The relative influence of industry and corporation on business unit performance: an alternative estimate. *Strategic Management Journal* 20(6): 519–547.

Burgelman RA. 1994. Fading memories: a process theory of strategic business exit in dynamic environments. *Administrative Science Quarterly* 39(1): 24–56.

Campa JM, Kedia S. 2002. Explaining the diversification discount. *Journal of Finance* 57(4): 1731–1762.

Chandler AD. 1962. *Strategy and Structure: Chapters in the History of the Industrial Enterprise.* MIT Press: Cambridge, MA.

Chang SJ. 1996. An evolutionary perspective on diversification and corporate restructuring: entry, exit, and economic performance during 1981–89. *Strategic Management Journal* 17(8): 587–611.

Chang SJ, Choi U. 1988. Strategy, structure and performance of Korean business groups: a transactions cost approach. *Journal of Industrial Economics* 37: 141–158.

Chang SJ, Chung J, Moon J. 2013. When do wholly owned subsidiaries perform better than joint ventures? *Strategic Management Journal* 34(3): 317–337.

Chang S, Hong J. 2002 How much does the business group matter in Korea? *Strategic Management Journal* 23(3): 265–274.

Chang SJ, Matsumoto Y. 2020. Resource redeployment in global semiconductor industry. Working Paper.

Chang SJ, Shim J. 2015. When does transitioning from family to professional management improve performance? *Strategic Management Journal* 36: 1297–1316.

Chang S, Singh H. 2000. Corporate and industry effects on business unit competitive position. *Strategic Management Journal* 21(7): 739–752.

Channon D. 1973. *Strategy and Structure of British Enterprise*. Harvard University Graduate School of Business Administration, Boston, MA.

Christensen H, Montgomery C. 1981. Corporate economic performance: diversification strategy versus market structure. *Strategic Management Journal* 2(4): 327–343.

Colpan AM, Hikino T, Lincoln JR. 2010. *The Oxford Handbook of Business Groups*. Oxford University Press, Oxford, U.K.

Contigiani A, Hsu D, Barankay I. 2018. Trade secrets and innovation: evidence from the "inevitable disclosure" doctrine. *Strategic Management Journal* 39(11): 2921–2942.

Davis R, Duhaime I. 1992. Corporate diversification, vertical integration, and industry analysis: new perspectives and measurement. *Strategic Management Journal* 13(7): 511–524.

Dierickx I, Cool K. 1989. Asset stock accumulation and sustainability of competitive advantage. *Management Science* 35(12): 1504–1511.

Dittmar A, Duchin R. 2016. Looking in the rearview mirror: the effect of managers' professional experience on corporate financial policy. *Review of Financial Studies* 29(3), 565–602.

Duhaime I, Grant J. 1984. Factors influencing divestment decision-making: evidence from a field study. *Strategic Management Journal* 5(4): 301–318.

Farjoun M. 1994. Beyond industry boundaries: human expertise, diversification, and resource-related industry groups. *Organization Science* 5(2): 185–199.

Ferrell A, Liang H, Renneboog L. 2016. Socially responsible firms. *Journal of Financial Economics* 122(3): 585–606.

Harrison J, Wicks A. 2019. Harmful stakeholder strategies. *Journal of Business Ethics* 104(1): 59–75.

Hashai, N. 2015. Within-industry diversification and firm performance: an S-shaped hypothesis. *Strategic Management Journal* 36(9): 1378–1400.

Helfat CE, Eisenhardt KM. 2004. Inter-temporal economies of scope, organizational modularity, and the dynamics of diversification. *Strategic Management Journal* 25(13): 1217–1232.

Helfat CE, Peteraf MA. 2015. Managerial cognitive capabilities and the microfoundations of dynamic capabilities. *Strategic Management Journal* 36(6): 831–850.

Hill C, Hitt M, Hoskisson R. 1992. Cooperative versus competitive structures in related and unrelated diversified firms. *Organization Science* 3(4): 501–521.

Hoffmann W, Lavie D, Reuer J, Shipilov A. 2018. The interplay of competition and cooperation. *Strategic Management Journal* 39(12): 3033–3052.

Jacquemin AP, Berry CH. 1979. Entropy measure of diversification and corporate growth. *Journal of Industrial Economics* 27: 359–369.

Jensen M, Meckling W. 1976. Theory of the firm: managerial behavior, agency cost, and ownership structure. *Journal of Financial Economics* 3: 305–360.

Kaplan SN, Klebanov MM, Sorensen M. 2012. Which CEO characteristics and abilities matter? *Journal of Finance* 67(3): 973–1007.

Karim S. 2006. Modularity in organizational structure: the reconfiguration of internally developed and acquired business units. *Strategic Management Journal* 27(9): 799–823.

Karim S, Capron L. 2016. Reconfiguration: adding, redeploying, recombining, and divesting resources and business units. *Strategic Management Journal* 37(13): E54–E62.

Kaul A. 2012. Technology and corporate scope: firm and rival innovation as antecedents of corporate transactions. *Strategic Management Journal* 33(4): 347–367.

Khanna T, Palepu K. 1997 Why focused strategies may be wrong for emerging markets. *Harvard Business Review* 75(4): 41–51.

Khanna T, Yafeh Y. 2007. Business groups in emerging markets: paragons or parasites? *Journal of Economic Literature* 45: 331–372.

Kumar MVS. 2013. The costs of related diversification: the impact of the core business on the productivity of related segments. *Organization Science* 24(6): 1827–1846.

Lane P, Cannella A, Lubatkin M. 1998. Agency problems as antecedents to unrelated mergers and diversification: Amihud and Lev reconsidered. *Strategic Management Journal* 19(6): 557–578.

Lang LHP, Stulz RM. 1994. Tobin's q, corporate diversification, and firm performance. *Journal of Political Economy* 102: 1248–1280.

Lee D. 2020 Corporate social responsibility of U.S.-listed firms headquartered in tax havens. *Strategic Management Journal* 41(9): 1547–1571.

Lee GK. 2008. Relevance of organizational capabilities and its dynamics: what to learn from entrants' product portfolios about the determinants of entry timing. *Strategic Management Journal* 29(12): 1257–1280.

Lee GK, Parachuri S. 2016. Resource redeployment through exit and entry: threats of substitution as inducements. In *Resource Redeployment and Strategic Management* (Advances in Strategic Management, Volume 35), Folta TB, Helfat CE, Karim S (eds). Emerald Group Publishing: Bingley, U.K.; 89–124.

Leff N. 1978. Industrial organization and entrepreneurship in the developing countries: the economic group. *Economic Development and Cultural Change* 26(4): 661–675.

Levinthal DA, Wu B. 2010. Opportunity costs and non-scale free capabilities: profit maximization, corporate scope, and profit margins. *Strategic Management Journal* 31(7): 780–801.

Lieberman MB, Lee GK, Folta TB. 2017. Entry, exit, and the potential for resource redeployment. *Strategic Management Journal* 38(3): 526–544.

Makino S, Isobe T, Chan C. 2004. Does country matter? *Strategic Management Journal* 25: 1027–1043.

Maksimovic V, Phillips G. 2002. Do conglomerate firms allocate resources inefficiently across industries? Theory and evidence. *Journal of Finance* 57(2): 721–767.

March J. 1991. Exploration and exploitation in organizational learning. *Organization Science* 2:71–87.

Maritan CA, Brush TH. 2003. Heterogeneity and transferring practices: implementing flow manufacturing in multiple plants. *Strategic Management Journal* 24(10): 945–959.

McGahan A, Porter M. 1997 How much does industry matter, really? *Strategic Management Journal* 18(S1): 15–30.

Miller DJ. 2006. Technological diversity, related diversification, and firm performance. *Strategic Management Journal* 27(7): 601–619.

Miller DJ, Yang HS. 2016. The dynamics of diversification: market entry and exit by public and private firms. *Strategic Management Journal* 37(11): 2323–2345.

Mitchell W. 1989. Whether and when: probability and timing of incumbent entry into emerging industrial subfields. *Administrative Science Quarterly* 34: 208–230.

Montgomery C, Wernerfelt B. 1986. What is an attractive industry? *Management Science* 32(10): 1223–1370.

Nakauchi M, Wiersema MF. 2015. Executive succession and strategic change in Japan. *Strategic Management Journal* 36(2): 298–306.

Natividad G, Rawley E. 2016. Interdependence and performance: a natural experiment in firm scope. *Strategy Science* 1(1): 12–31.

Nelson R, Winter S. 1982. *The Evolutionary Theory of the Economic Change*. Belknap Press of Harvard University Press: Cambridge, MA.

North DC. 1990. *Institutions, Institutional Change, and Economic Performance*. Cambridge University Press, Cambridge, U.K.

O'Brien JP, Folta TB. 2009. Sunk costs, uncertainty and market exit: real options perspective. *Industrial and Corporate Change* 18(5): 807–833.

Ocasio W. 1997. Toward an attention-based view of the firm. *Strategic Management Journal* 18(S1): 187–206.

Palepu K. 1985. Diversification strategy, profit performance, and the entropy measure. *Strategic Management Journal* 6(3): 239–255.

Panzar JC, Willig RD. 1981. Economies of scope. *American Economic Review* 71(2): 268–272.

Park SH, Westphal JD, Stern I. 2011. Set up for a fall: the insidious effects of flattery and opinion conformity toward corporate leaders. *Administrative Science Quarterly* 56(2): 257–302.

Penrose ET. 1959. *The Theory of the Growth of the Firm.* Wiley: New York, NY.

Rawley E, Simcoe TS. 2010. Diversification, diseconomies of scope, and vertical contracting: evidence from the taxicab industry. *Management Science* 56(9): 1534–1550.

Robins J, Wiersema MF. 1995. A resource-based approach to the multibusiness firm: empirical analysis of portfolio interrelationships and corporate financial performance. *Strategic Management Journal* 16: 277–299.

Robins J, Wiersema M. 2003. The measurement and corporate portfolio strategy: analysis of the content validity of related diversification indexes. *Strategic Management Journal* 24(1): 39–59.

Rumelt RP. 1974. *Strategy, Structure, and Economic Performance.* Harvard University Press: Boston, MA.

Rumelt R. 1991. How much does industry matter? *Strategic Management Journal* 12: 167–185.

Sakhartov AV, Folta TB. 2014. Resource relatedness, redeployability, and firm value. *Strategic Management Journal* 35(12): 1781–1797.

Scherer FM. 1980. *Industrial Market Structure and Economic Performance.* Rand-McNally: Chicago, IL.

Schmalensee R. 1985. Do markets differ much? *American Economic Review* 75(3): 341–351.

Stagni R, Santalo J, Giarratana M. 2020. Product-market competition and resource redeployment in multi-business firms. *Strategic Management Journal* 41: 1799–1836.

Surroca J, Aguilera R, Desender K, Tribo J. 2020. Is managerial entrenchment always bad and corporate social responsibilities always good? A cross-national examination of their combined influences of shareholder value. *Strategic Management Journal* 41(5): 891–920.

Teece DJ. 2007. Explicating dynamic capabilities: The nature and microfoundations of (sustainable) enterprise performance. *Strategic Management Journal* 28(13): 1319–1350.

Uzunca B. 2018. A competence-based view of industry evolution: the impact of submarket convergence on incumbent-entrant dynamics. *Academy of Management Journal* 61(2): 738–768.

Vidal E, Mitchell W. 2015. Adding by subtracting: the relationship between performance feedback and resource reconfiguration through divestitures. *Organization Science* 26(4): 1101–1118.

Villalonga B. 2004. Diversification discount or premium? New evidence from the business information tracking series. *Journal of Finance* 59(2): 479–506.

Williamson O. 1975. *Markets and Hierarchies.* Free Press: New York, NY.

Wulf J. 2002. Internal capital markets and firm-level compensation incentives for division managers. *Journal of Labor Economics* 20(S2): S219–S262.

Zhou YM. 2011. Synergy, coordination costs, and diversification choices. *Strategic Management Journal* 32(6): 624–639.

Zuckerman E. 1999. The categorical imperative: securities analysts and the illegitimacy discount. *American Journal of Sociology* 104(5): 1398–1438.

2.1
CORPORATE GROWTH AND ACQUISITION

R. Duane Ireland and Michael C. Withers

Introduction

For most corporations of varying sizes, growth remains an important strategic objective. Some scholars even argue that growth should be the central objective of public corporations (Penrose, 1959; Rugman and Verbeke, 2002). Reflecting this perspective, Ahlstrom (2010: 12) suggests that "Innovation-driven growth, particularly through disruptive innovation, should be the main goal of business." In this regard, growth is an important strategic outcome that is associated with a firm's ability to gain and potentially sustain a competitive advantage (Zander and Zander, 2005). Growth also determines long-term organizational survival and viability (e.g., Pe'er, Vertinsky, and Keil, 2016). In market-based economies, corporate growth contributes directly to the economy and society as a whole because of the employment opportunities and wealth creation that derive from growth (Ahlstrom, 2010). In part, the study of corporate growth is necessary for a broad theoretical perspective of strategic management (Zollo, Minoja, and Coda, 2018).

In the corporate context, firms pursue growth in several ways (Gilbert, McDougall, and Audretsch, 2006; McKelvie and Wiklund, 2010), including organically through innovation (Ireland *et al.*, 2001), hybrid approaches such as alliances and franchising systems (Sarkar, Echambadi, and Harrison, 2001; Shane, 1996), and acquiring other companies (Lockett *et al.*, 2011; Lockett and Wild, 2013). This literature generally suggests that existing corporations often pursue growth through acquisitions (Hitt, Hoskisson, and Ireland, 1990; McKelvie and Wiklund, 2010). Given this recognition and this chapter's general focus on corporate strategy, we offer a review of acquisitive growth—or corporate growth occurring through acquisition activity (Hitt and Ireland, 1985; Lockett *et al.*, 2011). We first provide an overview of the theoretical perspectives employed to consider acquisitive growth. We then discuss the general findings regarding the antecedents and outcomes of acquisitive growth. Finally, we offer a research agenda for the acquisitive growth literature.

Theoretical Perspectives on Acquisitive Corporate Growth

Given its strategic importance, several theoretical perspectives have been developed or leveraged to understand and explain corporate growth (Bogner and Bansal, 2007; Nason and Wiklund, 2018). Much of the early work in the strategic management field leveraged biological and ecological perspectives on growth and development to propose stages of firm growth (Kazanjian, 1988). For example, scholars apply organizational life-cycle models to understand the growth stages that firms may enter (for a review, see Whetten, 1987). Early empirical research in this area, however, finds that firms need not follow these direct patterns (Birley and Westhead, 1990).[1] As such, research often focused on leveraging other theoretical perspectives that take into consideration the nature of organizations to explain growth.

Penrose's (1959) theory of firm growth provides the theoretical foundations for much of the work on corporate growth (Kor and Mahoney, 2000; Lockett and Thompson, 2004; Nason and Wiklund, 2018; Rugman and Verbeke, 2002, 2004). In breaking from many of the arguments associated with economic theories at the time, Penrose (1960) focused on actual organizations. Growth derived from developing and using internal organizational resources. In particular, versatile resources—those with internal or external fungibility—are associated with higher levels of growth than nonversatile resources (Nason and Wiklund, 2018). While much of Penrose's classic work focuses on organic growth, her theory also contributes to the development of ideas concerning acquisitive growth (Lockett et al., 2011; Lockett and Wild, 2013).

Penrose's early theorizing is the foundation for a number of strategic management theories, such as the resource-based theory (Barney, 1991; Wernerfelt, 1984), the knowledge-based view (Grant, 1996; Kogut and Zander, 1992), and dynamic capabilities (Eisenhardt and Martin, 2000; Helfat et al., 2007; Teece, Pisano, and Shuen, 1997). Each of these perspectives shares a view of growth that "implies that the firm takes unto itself the activities associated with the opportunities for production and marketing that it perceives in its own capabilities and in its environment" (Penrose, 2008: 1119). Following in the Penrosian tradition, these resource-based perspectives recognize firms as unique bundles of heterogeneous resources (Barney, 1991; Wernerfelt, 1984). As a direct extension of the resource-based perspective, the knowledge-based view provides that knowledge is an important factor that creates opportunity for growth (Bogner and Bansal, 2007). From this perspective, firms leverage knowledge to recognize and exploit growth opportunities (Kogut and Zander, 1992).

The dynamic capability perspective is also a prominent framework employed to understand firm growth (Wilden, Devinney, and Dowling, 2016). Dynamic capabilities researchers focus on the alignment of organizational activities to capitalize on firm-specific resources to compete in rapidly changing environments (Teece et al., 1997). Dynamic capabilities enable a firm to "profitably build and renew resources and assets that lie both within and beyond its boundaries, reconfiguring them to respond to (or bring about) changes in the market" (Teece, 2014: 332). As Helfat and her colleagues (2007: 1) observe, "Some dynamic capabilities enable firms to enter new businesses and extend old ones through internal growth, acquisitions, and strategic alliances." In the context of acquisitive growth, acquisition targets can be an important means of obtaining new resources necessary to alter a firm's resource base and create dynamic capabilities (Chatterji and Patro, 2014). In a related stream applying this perspective, research suggests that some firms possess selection and integration capabilities that enable them to leverage the resources of acquisition targets to produce greater growth (Zollo and Singh, 2004).

While these resource-based perspectives focus on developing and/or leveraging resources to achieve growth, other perspectives consider the uncertainty surrounding growth. Real options theory is particularly important to analyze firms' strategic decisions under conditions of uncertainty (e.g., Tong and Reuer, 2007). Real options are rights, without obligations, on real assets to undertake actions at a future date (Dixit and Pindyck, 1994). With real options, managers possess the ability to wait for uncertainty about the value of a decision to be reduced to an acceptable point rather than commit to costly-to-reverse actions (O'Brien and Folta, 2009). From the real options perspective, much of the work concerned with growth focuses on "growth options" (Alessandri, Tong, and Reuer, 2012) with acquisitions being an example of such options (Brouthers and Dikova, 2010). A growth option "involves one, or more likely several, discretionary investments to expand the business" (Folta and Miller, 2002: 78). From this perspective, "the option to grow gains its value from the possibility that early investment will help the firm to develop a 'capability' that will allow it to take better advantage of future growth opportunities in the industry" (Folta and O'Brien, 2004: 121).

The behavioral theory of the firm (BToF) is another perspective applied to understand acquisitive growth as it explains managerial decisions when facing uncertain environments or conditions (e.g., Cyert, DeGroot, and Holt, 1979; Cyert and March, 1963; Greve, 2003). Specifically, the BToF examines the factors that influence managers' decision-making processes and outcomes, recognizing that managers cannot or do not employ a perfect calculus to make optimal decisions. Scholars in this area suggest that managers make decisions based on how their firm is performing relative to expectations, aspirations, or peer firms (Arrfelt, Wiseman, and Hult, 2013; Greve, 2003). In turn, these expectations and aspirations can influence corporate growth (Greve, 2008a, 2008b). With the various perspectives[2] described, we turn to an abbreviated review of the current state of research on acquisitive growth.

The Current State of Research on Acquisitive Corporate Growth

As prior reviews on firm growth observe, research on acquisitive growth remains rather limited relative to the work on firm growth in general and organic growth specifically (Gilbert et al., 2006; Lockett and Wild, 2013; McKelvie and Wiklund, 2010). As Gilbert et al. (2006: 939) state, "This absence in the literature is striking because clearly, growth resulting from internal or external mechanisms differentially influences the growth outcomes firms realize." While work concerned specifically with acquisitive growth remains limited, some studies examine the mode of growth (Lockett et al., 2011; Lockett and Wild, 2013; Tan et al., 2020). In addition, the general work on acquisition activity can be informative when examining whether acquisition activity drives growth or not (for reviews see Devers et al., in press; Haleblian et al., 2009). Given these considerations, we highlight the research focused on managerial capabilities and other resources, the role of corporate governance, and environmental factors.

Managerial capabilities and other resources

As suggested earlier, resources have been a focal point for growth research. From Penrose's theory of firm growth, managerial capabilities were important determinants of growth. CEO and executive team characteristics are important determinants of firm growth strategies (e.g., Eisenhardt and Schoonhoven, 1990) and can have a significant influence on how firms approach acquisitive growth (Steinbach et al., 2016). For example, CEO scanning emphasis and attention processes can spur corporate growth (e.g., Joseph and Wilson, 2018). Similarly, the cognitive simplification process that decision-makers use in response to the complexity of acquisition decisions may influence acquisitive growth (Duhaime and Schwenk, 1985).

Organizational resources also influence corporate growth. As Lei, Hitt, and Bettis (1996: 549) explain, "A firm's core competence(s) is defined as a set of problem-defining and problem-solving insights that fosters the development of idiosyncratic strategic growth alternatives." When examining acquisitive growth, financial constraints are an important determinate of growth prospects (Chaddad and Reuer, 2009). A corporation's ability to recombine existing and acquired resources to solve new problems (i.e., entrepreneurial bricolage) can be an important determinant of its ability to create or exploit opportunities for acquisitive growth (Baker and Nelson, 2005). Firms with prior acquisition experience also may be in a better position to grow using this strategy (Barkema and Schijven, 2008). Relatedly, the quality of a firm's acquired knowledge resources and the ability to manage the activities around knowledge also may affect firm growth (Bogner and Bansal, 2007). Network position is an important determinant of growth as well and may help firms determine and select acquisition targets (Zaheer, Hernandez, and Banerjee, 2010). Finally, restructuring resource portfolios, through acquisition and divestiture activities, in accordance with environmental demands, can be a growth path (Clarysse, Bruneel, and Wright, 2011).

The role of corporate governance

Given the potential agency issues that arise from acquisition activity (e.g., Amihud and Lev, 1981), corporate governance is an important consideration when examining acquisitive corporate growth (Hitt et al., 1989). Research finds that boards of directors, executive compensation, and concentrated ownership can influence growth strategies (Chen *et al.*, 2017). For example, Hoskisson *et al.* (2002) find that outside directors may be associated more with acquisitive growth. Through their human and social capital, boards can be an important driver of growth (Kor and Sundaramurthy, 2009) and influence acquisition decisions (Kroll, Walters, and Wright, 2008). Managerial incentives aligned with growth options are more likely to lead to increases in overall firm growth (Alessandri *et al.*, 2012). In turn, equity-based compensation is more likely to increase firm growth (Oxley and Pandher, 2016). Finally, investor influence often derives from concentrated ownership in which an investor owns a large percentage of a firm's shares (Shleifer and Vishny, 1986). Recent research recognizes that concentrated ownership often arises in the form of institutional investors. From this perspective, investor influence must be understood in terms of the heterogeneity of investor preferences and time horizons (e.g., Bushee, 1998). The differences in time horizons may lead investors to emphasize differing levels of strategic versus financial controls. For example, some investors may prefer short-term payoffs and emphasizing financial controls, preferences with the potential to reduce growth prospects (Thomsen and Pedersen, 2000). Those with short-term time horizons may be more likely to prefer acquisitive growth to organic growth (Hoskisson *et al.*, 2002).

Environmental factors

Environmental factors are an important determinant of corporate growth (Kotha and Nair, 1995). High-growth industries generally have a positive association with firm growth (McDougall *et al.*, 1994). Economic shocks can also influence growth prospects and the outcomes from growth strategies (Chakrabarti, 2015). Industry factors may matter more for established firms in comparison to new ventures when it comes to firm growth (Short *et al.*, 2009). For example, given its relative growth potential, firm-level factors may influence a new venture's growth more than industry conditions in comparison to an established firm. We might anticipate the influence of firm-level factors to be even stronger than industry effects when experienced entrepreneurs lead a new venture. For acquisitive growth, a number of external factors, such as acquisition waves, can influence a firm's likelihood of employing an acquisition strategy to grow (Haleblian *et al.*, 2009). The institutional and regulatory environments can influence general firm growth in complex ways. For example, institutional intermediaries established to foster the creation of new firms may at the same time also hinder new firm growth (Eberhart and Eesley, 2018). For acquisitive growth, the environment can be an important factor in determining whether an acquisition strategy is pursued for growth and what type of acquisition a firm chooses to use (Haleblian *et al.*, 2009)

Outcomes of Acquisitive Growth

Acquisitive growth also has a relationship with a number of important organizational outcomes (Devers *et al.*, in press; Haleblian *et al.*, 2009). Firm growth generally has a positive association with firm performance; however, a number of contingencies may influence this relationship (Brush, Bromiley, and Hendrickx, 2000). When employing acquisitive growth modes, the organization may be able to gain market power and enhanced competitiveness (Bird and Zellweger, 2018). In turn, market growth has a negative association with competitive inertia as firms expanding their markets engage in more strategic actions seeking to outperform rivals in doing so (Miller and Chen, 1994). Growth also may influence a firm's entrepreneurial orientation (Eshima and Anderson, 2017) as well as its likelihood to pursue other forms of growth (Hitt et al., 1990). Acquisitive growth, in most cases, leads to increases in firm size (Josefy et al., 2015). Relatedly, corporate growth generally allows firms to recruit employees more easily as it provides internal opportunities for upward employment mobility (Ahlstrom, 2010).

Corporate growth can also lead to some negative consequences. For example, Pierce and Aguinis (2013: 322) state, "The evidence suggests that too much growth too fast leads to diminishing positive returns up to a point after which growth rate has a negative impact on firm success." Acquisitive growth specifically may create organizational challenges often associated with agency issues and managing acquisition integration (Datta, 1991). For example, firms desperate for growth may overpay for acquisition targets (Kim, Haleblian, and Finkelstein, 2011). Similarly, while executive compensation can be an important incentive driving corporate growth, corporate growth also increases CEO compensation (Kroll, Simmons, and Wright, 1990).

Managing Acquisitive Growth

A key decision is how firms manage corporate growth (Carman and Langeard, 1980). With acquisitive growth, the acquisition integration strategy can be an important factor that determines ultimate value creation (Datta, 1991). Given their potential use of this growth mode, growth management and associated integration efforts are particularly important within diversified firms (Chandler, 1991). Research suggests that multidivisional firms exist, in part, because corporate managers possess superior internal information regarding potential business-unit synergies that the market would not possess if the business units were separate firms (Hoskisson, 1987). Early work in this area focused on growth management tools (Hambrick, MacMillan, and Day, 1982). More recently, the work has moved to a focus on capital allocation strategies in general (Busenbark et al., 2017). In this regard, corporate headquarters can facilitate market-like dynamics between strategic business units that enable innovation and growth (Knott and Turner, 2019). In the diversified firm, divesting can also lead to growth opportunities by making resources available along with enhanced prospects for leveraging them. For example, in a study of Japanese spinoffs, Ito (1995) finds that such divestitures lead to the achievement of growth objectives.

Future Research Directions in Acquisitive Growth

Despite the importance of this outcome, we echo prior reviews about growth that research has only begun to consider fully the theoretical and empirical nuances surrounding growth (Davidsson, Delmar, and Wiklund, 2006; Gilbert *et al.*, 2006; McKelvie and Wiklund, 2010; Tan *et al.*, 2020). We also concur with McKelvie and Wiklund's (2010) perspective that future research on growth would benefit from a focus on the growth modes pursued. We hope this chapter contributes to the broader understanding of different modes of growth by focusing specifically on acquisitive corporate growth. Beyond these general points, though, we offer the following research agenda on acquisitive corporate growth to spur scholarly development in this area.

Acquisitive corporate growth in the new competitive landscape

As prior reviews of growth indicate, there have been substantial shifts in the competitive landscape since Penrose developed her early theory of firm growth (Lockett *et al.*, 2011). Environmental changes—including increasing technological developments and globalization—are blurring industry boundaries (Withers *et al.*, 2018). Acquisitive growth may be an important factor driving this reality. As Penrose (1959: 126) states, "Acquisitions can be a means of obtaining the productive services and knowledge that are necessary for a firm to establish itself in a new field."

For example, Google's prowess as a technology company with search-engine and advertising capability and Apple's expanding and innovative product offerings initially rendered the two firms more like complementors than competitors. In 2007, Google and Apple even shared board interlocks, with Google's CEO, Eric E. Schmidt, sitting on Apple's board and Arthur Levinson serving on both. However, in subsequent years, the firms' competitive interactions increased. For both, acquisitive growth was an important driver in this change in the relationship. As Google became involved in mobile computing through its 2005 acquisition of Android, it moved more directly into Apple's traditional market space. Similarly, Apple developed a stronger presence in the search-engine market space through products and applications within its ecosystem, particularly when it acquired start-up Siri in 2010. Relatedly, both firms acquired other companies and resources that caused them to compete against each other with greater intensity. Through their acquisitive growth actions, Google and Apple now perceive one another as firms engaging more directly in competition against each other. The competitive interactions between Google and Apple provide just one of many recent examples of entrepreneurial actions firms take to grow that cause them to compete against each other with additional specificity. As such, future research may look to acquisitive growth to understand changes in competitive interactions (Withers *et al.*, 2018). For example, what are the implications for new competitive interactions when a firm's acquisitive growth actions drive its rivalry with competitors? How might acquisitive growth allow a firm to change its resource endowment to challenge new competitors? Finally, might acquisitive growth actions result in a firm becoming less of a direct rival with a company with whom it has been a direct competitor historically?

Applying resource orchestration to understand acquisitive corporate growth

To understand the process of managing resources from acquisitions to drive corporate growth, research may look to the work on resource orchestration. Resource orchestration extends resource-based theory by considering the active role of management in bundling, structuring, and leveraging resources to build competitive advantage (Helfat *et al.*, 2007; Sirmon, Hitt, and Ireland, 2007). In this regard, the theoretical focus is on the managerial actions used to exploit available resources in the marketplace (Sirmon *et al.*, 2011). These actions include managing and allocating resources between activities concentrated on pursuing the known best alternatives and those focused on investigating unknown alternatives (Hitt *et al.*, 2011).

Within their discussion of the structuring of resources, Sirmon and colleagues (2007) recognize acquiring resources as the initial step of the orchestration process. From this perspective, acquiring resources is "[t]he process of purchasing resources from strategic factor markets" (2007: 277). The authors suggest that the environment has a direct effect on managers' ability to assess the value of resources acquired in strategic factor markets and increases the likelihood of different resource expectations across firms in a particular market. This suggestion may be particularly helpful in developing theoretical perspectives to understand and explain acquisitive growth. For example, how might managerial ability to orchestrate resources influence a firm's likelihood to use acquisitive growth? Relatedly, acquisitive growth opportunities may influence how managers make decisions regarding the orchestration of resources (Eshima and Anderson, 2017; Rahmandad, 2012). For instance, how might firms engaging in acquisitive growth differ in their approach to orchestrating their resource endowments in comparison to firms engaging in organic growth?

The relationship between acquisitive growth and other forms of growth

Research on growth has long recognized the tradeoffs between different growth modes (Capron and Mitchell, 2004; McKelvie and Wiklund, 2010). For example, Hitt *et al.* (1990) propose that acquisitive growth may have a negative relationship with future organic growth. Recently, work suggests that prior acquisitive growth may influence organic growth positively (Lockett *et al.*, 2011). Other research suggests relationships that are more complex such that firms may use acquisitions to gain access to resources and capabilities needed to grow organically (Hitt *et al.*, 1996; Makri, Hitt, and Lane, 2010). In her theory of firm growth, Penrose "never explicated how acquisitive growth would affect the firm's ability to continue to expand organically" (Lockett and Wild, 2013). However, the application of multiple modes may provide the largest number of growth opportunities. In particular, Bingham *et al.* (2015: 1821) find that "growth may be enhanced when firms do not skew towards the use of one particular growth process, but rather use multiple ones in a balanced approach." In part, employing a balance of these modes of growth enables a firm to modify its resource base in several different ways to take advantage of growth opportunities (Bingham *et al.*, 2015).

To better understand the complex interaction of different growth modes, research may leverage the strategic entrepreneurship (SE) perspective (Hitt *et al.*, 2002). Ireland, Hitt, and Simon's (2003) conceptualization of SE and its underlying model provides arguments framed around how firms identify opportunities and then exploit them to produce innovation by using the strategic management process as a perspective and guide to actions. Given SE's dual focus on advantage- and opportunity-seeking behaviors, it may be particularly apt for considering the balance between growth modes. For example, those firms with a strong SE capability would possess an entrepreneurial mindset, which is "a growth-oriented perspective through which individuals promote flexibility, creativity, continuous innovation, and renewal" (Ireland *et al.*, 2003: 968). These firms would also possess an entrepreneurial culture and practice entrepreneurial leadership, which enable organizations to engage in and support behaviors aligned with entrepreneurial imperatives (Covin and Slevin, 2002). Firms engaged in SE have the ability to manage and orchestrate their resources strategically to recognize and exploit opportunities as a foundation for growing, creating wealth, and developing and maintaining competitive advantages (Sirmon *et al.*, 2007). Firms using SE successfully may be particularly adept at balancing the different modes of growth and ensuring that acquisitive growth does not become a substitute for organic growth (Hitt *et al.*, 1990). As such, future research may seek to apply this perspective to examine acquisitive growth as well as how firms manage growth modes. For example, how might firms using SE pursue acquisitive growth differently than firms not using it? Are firms using SE better able to balance acquisitive and organic growth than other firms? How might different growth modes interact within a firm, and what might be the optimum combination of modes?

Acquisitive corporate growth during crisis

As we write this chapter, the world is facing unprecedented challenges derived from the COVID-19 pandemic. At this point, the economic devastation of this crisis is broad and deep (Atkeson, 2020). While substantial uncertainty remains about how business and the world's economies will recover from this crisis, we believe corporate growth, as is the case historically, will play a critically important role in the recovery. In part, the societal impact of corporate growth may only increase as we begin to experience economic recovery and renewal (Ahlstrom, 2010). For strategy researchers, this may be an important time and opportunity to revisit theories of firm growth (Lockett *et al.*, 2011) with the hope of having a broader impact on society (Tihanyi, 2020). Acquisitive corporate growth, in particular, may be a primary mechanism to help spur economic growth as well as save and grow employment opportunities for individuals. For firms facing financial difficulties, a decision by other companies to acquire them may represent an option and outcome that avoids broader economic losses. Firms considering acquisitions in this manner must understand the underlying value creation potential embedded within acquisition targets in the context of a global business environment that the pandemic has altered.

While considering theories with the potential to enhance our understanding of corporate growth, scholars can contextualize their work by forming indigenous theories. Some argue that historically, the theories scholars use to understand organizational phenomena have a foundation in North American and European settings (Bruton *et al.*, 2020). While valuable, we can question if these theories allow researchers to develop appropriate arguments and testable relationships given the greater diversity and complexity in today's business environments and economies. More specifically, theory should be appropriate to the context in which scholars apply it to maximize the likelihood of understanding the phenomena under analysis. Moreover, as Davison and Díaz Andrade (2018: 759) indicate, "an inappropriately applied theory could be very dangerous since the assumptions that frame the theory may not exist in a context different to the one where it was created." To better study corporate growth in different regions and economies, scholars can consider developing theory that captures the context within which relationships exist that they seek to examine. For example, what theory would help scholars study the different contexts within which firms extend efforts to grow within informal economies (Webb *et al.*, 2009)? Indigenous research, grounded in indigenous theory, studies "local phenomena using local language, local subjects, and locally meaningful constructs, with the aim to build or test theories that can explain and predict the phenomena in their local social and cultural contexts" (Van de Ven, Meyer, and Jing, 2018: 451). Given corporate growth's complexity, indigenous theories may have the potential to facilitate scholars' efforts to untangle and understand acquisitive growth's complex and intertwined relationships.

Conclusion

Corporate growth remains a central topic in strategic management research. The market punishes firms that do not grow, causing them to potentially lose human capital in that employees believe that fewer internal opportunities are available to them (Ahlstrom, 2010). Given the turbulence encountered recently in global economies from events such as the COVID-19 pandemic, corporate growth will continue to be a critical factor in determining economic and societal gains. Given its importance as a strategy for firm growth, acquisitive growth remains a critical topic for future research. We hope our chapter helps in moving this research area forward through our review and research agenda.

Acknowledgments

We would like to thank the editors, Irene Duhaime, Mike Hitt, and Marjorie Lyles, for their helpful comments and guidance through the process of writing this chapter. We also thank Brittney Zhang for her research assistance in the preparation of this chapter.

Notes

1. Similarly, Penrose (1952) argues for the application of economic theories and concepts rather than relying on such approaches. As she stated, "Biological analogies contribute little . . . to the theory of growth and development of the firm" (804).
2. Beyond these theoretical perspectives, scholars use other theories, such as transaction cost economics and agency theory, with less of a focus on growth outcomes, to consider growth (e.g., Chandler, McKelvie, and Davidsson, 2009; Chittenden, Hall, and Hutchinson, 1996). Similarly, as with a great deal of strategy research, researchers use contingency perspectives that take into consideration strategic and environmental factors to examine and understand growth (Slevin and Covin, 1997).

References

Ahlstrom D. 2010. Innovation and growth: how business contributes to society. *Academy of Management Perspectives* 24(3): 11–24.

Alessandri TM, Tong TW, Reuer JJ. 2012. Firm heterogeneity in growth option value: the role of managerial incentives. *Strategic Management Journal* 33(13): 1557–1566.

Amihud Y, Lev B. 1981. Risk reduction as a managerial motive for conglomerate mergers. *Bell Journal of Economics* 12(2): 605–617.

Arrfelt M, Wiseman R, Hult GTM. 2013. Looking backward instead of forward: aspiration-driven influences on the efficiency of the capital allocation process. *Academy of Management Journal* 56(4): 1081–1103.

Atkeson A. 2020. What will be the economic impact of COVID-19 in the U.S.? Rough estimates of disease scenarios. National Bureau of Economic Research.

Baker T, Nelson RE. 2005. Creating something from nothing: resource construction through entrepreneurial bricolage. *Administrative Science Quarterly* 50(3): 329–366.

Barkema HG, Schijven M. 2008. How do firms learn to make acquisitions? A review of past research and an agenda for the future. *Journal of Management* 34(3): 594–634.

Barney JB. 1991. Firm resources and sustained competitive advantage. *Journal of Management* 17(1): 99–120.

Bingham CB, Heimeriks KH, Schijven M, Gates S. 2015. Concurrent learning: how firms develop multiple dynamic capabilities in parallel. *Strategic Management Journal* 36(12): 1802–1825.

Bird M, Zellweger T. 2018. Relational embeddedness and firm growth: comparing spousal and sibling entrepreneurs. *Organization Science* 29(2): 264–283.

Birley S, Westhead P. 1990. Growth and performance contrasts between "types" of small firms. *Strategic Management Journal* 11(7): 535–557.

Bogner WC, Bansal P. 2007. Knowledge management as the basis of sustained high performance. *Journal of Management Studies* 44(1): 165–188.

Brouthers KD, Dikova D. 2010. Acquisitions and real options: the greenfield alternative. *Journal of Management Studies* 47(6): 1048–1071.

Brush TH, Bromiley P, Hendrickx M. 2000. The free cash flow hypothesis for sales growth and firm performance. *Strategic Management Journal* 21(4): 455.

Bruton G, Zahara SA, Van de Ven AH, Hitt MA, Ireland, RD, Filatotchev I. 2020. From comparative management to indigenous research and theory: uses, abuses, and the future. Working paper.

Busenbark JR, Wiseman RM, Arrfelt M, Woo H-S. 2017. A review of the internal capital allocation literature: piecing together the capital allocation puzzle. *Journal of Management* 43(8): 2430–2455.

Bushee BJ. 1998. The influence of institutional investors on myopic R&D investment behavior. *Accounting Review* 73(3): 305–333.

Capron L, Mitchell W. 2004. Where firms change: internal development versus external capability sourcing in the global telecommunications industry. *European Management Review* 1(2): 157–174.

Carman JM, Langeard E. 1980. Growth strategies for service firms. *Strategic Management Journal* 1(1): 7–22.

Chaddad FR, Reuer JJ. 2009. Investment dynamics and financial constraints in IPO firms. *Strategic Entrepreneurship Journal* 3(1): 29–45.

Chakrabarti A. 2015. Organizational adaptation in an economic shock: the role of growth reconfiguration. *Strategic Management Journal* 36(11): 1717–1738.

Chandler AD. 1991. The functions of the HQ unit in the multibusiness firm. *Strategic Management Journal* 12: 31–50.

Chandler GN, McKelvie A, Davidsson P. 2009. Asset specificity and behavioral uncertainty as moderators of the sales growth: employment growth relationship in emerging ventures. *Journal of Business Venturing* 24(4): 373–387.

Chatterji A, Patro A. 2014. Dynamic capabilities and managing human capital. *Academy of Management Perspectives* 28(4): 395–408.

Chen PL, Kor Y, Mahoney JT, Tan D. 2017. Pre-market entry experience and post-market entry learning of the board of directors: implications for post-entry performance. *Strategic Entrepreneurship Journal* 11(4): 441–463.

Chittenden F, Hall G, Hutchinson P. 1996. Small firm growth, access to capital markets, and financial structure: review of issues and an empirical investigation. *Small Business Economics* 8(1): 59–67.

Clarysse B, Bruneel J, Wright M. 2011. Explaining growth paths of young technology-based firms: structuring resource portfolios in different competitive environments. *Strategic Entrepreneurship Journal* 5(2): 137–157.

Covin JG, Slevin DP. 2002. The entrepreneurial imperatives of strategic leadership. In *Strategic Entrepreneurship: Creating a New Mindset.* Hitt MA, Ireland RD, Camp SM, Sexton DL (eds), Blackwell Publishers: Oxford, U.K.; 309–327.

Cyert RM, DeGroot MH, Holt CA. 1979. Capital allocation within a firm. *Behavioral Science* 24(5): 287–295.

Cyert RM, March JG. 1963. *A Behavioral Theory of the Firm.* Prentice-Hall: Englewood Cliffs, NJ.

Datta DK. 1991. Organizational fit and acquisition performance: effects of post-acquisition integration. *Strategic Management Journal* 12(4): 281–297.

Davidsson P, Delmar F, Wiklund J. 2006. *Entrepreneurship and the Growth of Firms.* Edward Elgar: Cheltenham, U.K.

Davison RM, Díaz Andrade A. 2018. Promoting indigenous theory. *Information Systems Journal* 28(5): 759–764.

Devers CE, Wuorinen S, McNamara G, Haleblian J, Gee IH, Kim J. In press. An integrative review of the emerging behavioral acquisition literature: charting the next decade of research. *Academy of Management Annals.*

Dixit AK, Pindyck RS. 1994. *Investment under Uncertainty.* Princeton University Press: Princeton, NJ.

Duhaime IM, Schwenk CR. 1985. Conjectures on cognitive simplification in acquisition and divestment decision making. *Academy of Management Review* 10(2): 287–295.

Eberhart RN, Eesley CE. 2018. The dark side of institutional intermediaries: junior stock exchanges and entrepreneurship. *Strategic Management Journal* 39(10): 2643–2665.

Eisenhardt KM, Martin JA. 2000. Dynamic capabilities: what are they? *Strategic Management Journal* 21: 1105–1121.

Eisenhardt KM, Schoonhoven CB. 1990. Organizational growth: linking founding team, strategy, environment, and growth among U.S. semiconductor ventures, 1978–1988. *Administrative Science Quarterly* 35(3): 504–529.

Eshima Y, Anderson BS. 2017. Firm growth, adaptive capability, and entrepreneurial orientation. *Strategic Management Journal* 38(3): 770–779.

Folta TB, Miller KD. 2002. Real options in equity partnerships. *Strategic Management Journal* 23(1): 77–88.

Folta TB, O'Brien JP. 2004. Entry in the presence of dueling options. *Strategic Management Journal* 25(2): 121–138.

Gilbert BA, McDougall PP, Audretsch DB. 2006. New venture growth: a review and extension. *Journal of Management* 32(6): 926–950.

Grant RM. 1996. Toward a knowledge-based theory of the firm. *Strategic Management Journal* 17(S2): 109–122.

Greve HR. 2003. Investment and the behavioral theory of the firm: evidence from shipbuilding. *Industrial and Corporate Change* 12(5): 1051–1076.

Greve HR. 2008a. A behavioral theory of firm growth: sequential attention to size and performance goals. *Academy of Management Journal* 51(3): 476–494.

Greve HR. 2008b. Multimarket contact and sales growth: evidence from insurance. *Strategic Management Journal* 29(3): 229–249.

Haleblian J, Devers CE, McNamara G, Carpenter MA, Davison RB. 2009. Taking stock of what we know about mergers and acquisitions: a review and research agenda. *Journal of Management* 35(3): 469–502.

Hambrick DC, MacMillan IC, Day DL. 1982. Strategic attributes and performance in the BCG matrix: a PIMS-based analysis of industrial product businesses. *Academy of Management Journal* 25(3): 510–531.

Helfat CE, Finkelstein S, Mitchell W, Peteraf MA, Singh H, Teece D, Winter SG. 2007. *Dynamic Capabilities: Understanding Strategic Change in Organizations.* Blackwell: Oxford, U.K.

Hitt MA, Hoskisson RE, Ireland RD. 1990. Mergers and acquisitions and managerial commitment to innovation in M-form firms. *Strategic Management Journal* 11(4): 29–47.

Hitt MA, Hoskisson RE, Ireland RD, Harrison J. 1989. Acquisitive growth strategy and relative R&D intensity: the effects of leverage, diversification, and size. *Academy of Management Proceedings* 1989(1): 22–26.

Hitt MA, Hoskisson RE, Johnson RA, Moesel DD. 1996. The market for corporate control and firm innovation. *Academy of Management Journal* 39(5): 1084–1119.

Hitt MA, Ireland RD. 1985. Strategy, contextual factors, and performance. *Human Relations* 38(8): 793–812.

Hitt MA, Ireland RD, Camp SM, Sexton DL. 2002. *Strategic Entrepreneurship: Creating a New Mindset*, Wiley-Blackwell: Oxford, U.K.

Hitt MA, Ireland RD, Sirmon DG, Trahms CA. 2011. Strategic entrepreneurship: creating value for individuals, organizations, and society. *Academy of Management Perspectives* 25(2): 57–75.

Hoskisson RE. 1987. Multidivisional structure and performance: the contingency of diversification strategy. *Academy of Management Journal* 30(4): 625–644.

Hoskisson RE, Hitt MA, Johnson RA, Grossman W. 2002. Conflicting voices: the effects of institutional ownership heterogeneity and internal governance on corporate innovation strategies. *Academy of Management Journal* 45(4): 697–716.

Ireland RD, Hitt MA, Camp SM, Sexton DL. 2001. Integrating entrepreneurship and strategic management actions to create firm wealth. *Academy of Management Executive* 15(1): 49–63.

Ireland RD, Hitt MA, Sirmon DG. 2003. A model of strategic entrepreneurship: the construct and its dimensions. *Journal of Management* 29(6): 963–989.

Ito K. 1995. Japanese spinoffs: unexplored survival strategies. *Strategic Management Journal* 16(6): 431–446.

Josefy M, Kuban S, Ireland RD, Hitt MA. 2015. All things great and small: organizational size, boundaries of the firm, and a changing environment. *Academy of Management Annals* 9(1): 715–802.

Joseph J, Wilson AJ. 2018. The growth of the firm: an attention-based view. *Strategic Management Journal* 39(6): 1779–1800.

Kazanjian RK. 1988. Relation of dominant problems to stages growth in technology-based new ventures. *Academy of Management Journal* 31(2): 257–279.

Kim J-Y, Haleblian J, Finkelstein S. 2011. When firms are desperate to grow via acquisition: the effect of growth patterns and acquisition experience on acquisition premiums. *Administrative Science Quarterly* 56(1): 26–60.

Knott AM, Turner SF. 2019. An innovation theory of headquarters value in multibusiness firms. *Organization Science* 30(1): 19–39.

Kogut B, Zander U. 1992. Knowledge of the firm, combinative capabilities, and the replication of technology. *Organization Science* 3(3): 383–397.

Kor YY, Mahoney JT. 2000. Penrose's resource-based approach: the process and product of research creativity. *Journal of Management Studies* 37(1): 109–139.

Kor YY, Sundaramurthy C. 2009. Experience-based human capital and social capital of outside directors. *Journal of Management* 35(4): 981–1006.

Kotha S, Nair A. 1995. Strategy and environment as determinants of performance: evidence from the Japanese machine tool industry. *Strategic Management Journal* 16(7): 497–518.

Kroll M, Simmons SA, Wright P. 1990. Determinants of chief executive officer compensation following major acquisitions. *Journal of Business Research* 20(4): 349–366.

Kroll M, Walters BA, Wright P. 2008. Board vigilance, director experience, and corporate outcomes. *Strategic Management Journal* 29(4): 363–382.

Lei D, Hitt MA, Bettis R. 1996. Dynamic core competences through meta-learning and strategic context. *Journal of Management* 22(4): 549–569.

Lockett A, Thompson S. 2004. Edith Penrose's contributions to the resource-based view: an alternative perspective. *Journal of Management Studies* 41(1): 193–203.

Lockett A, Wiklund J, Davidsson P, Girma S. 2011. Organic and acquisitive growth: re-examining, testing and extending Penrose's growth theory. *Journal of Management Studies* 48(1): 48–74.

Lockett A, Wild A. 2013. A Penrosean theory of acquisitive growth. *Business History* 55(5): 790–817.

Makri M, Hitt MA, Lane PJ. 2010. Complementary technologies, knowledge relatedness, and invention outcomes in high-technology mergers and acquisitions. *Strategic Management Journal* 31(6): 602–628.

McDougall PP, Covin JG, Robinson RB Jr, Herron L. 1994. The effects of industry growth and strategic breadth on new venture performance and strategy content. *Strategic Management Journal* 15(7): 537–554.

McKelvie A, Wiklund J. 2010. Advancing firm growth research: a focus on growth mode instead of growth rate. *Entrepreneurship Theory and Practice* 34(2): 261–288.

Miller D, Chen M-J. 1994. Sources and consequences of competitive inertia: a study of the U.S. airline industry. *Administrative Science Quarterly* 39(1): 1–23.

Nason RS, Wiklund J. 2018. An assessment of resource-based theorizing on firm growth and suggestions for the future. *Journal of Management* 44(1): 32–60.

O'Brien J, Folta T. 2009. Sunk costs, uncertainty and market exit: a real options perspective. *Industrial and Corporate Change* 18(5): 807–833.

Oxley J, Pandher G. 2016. Equity-based incentives and collaboration in the modern multibusiness firm. *Strategic Management Journal* 37(7): 1379–1394.

Pe'er A, Vertinsky I, Keil T. 2016. Growth and survival: the moderating effects of local agglomeration and local market structure. *Strategic Management Journal* 37(3): 541–564.

Penrose ET. 1952. Biological analogies in the theory of the firm. *American Economic Review* 42(5): 804–819.

Penrose E. 1959. *The Theory of the Growth of the Firm.* Oxford University Press: Oxford, U.K.

Penrose ET. 1960. The growth of the firm—a case study: the Hercules Powder Company. *Business History Review* 34(1): 1–23.

Penrose E. 2008. Strategy/organization and the metamorphosis of the large firm. *Organization Studies* 29(8/9): 1117–1124.

Pierce JR, Aguinis H. 2013. The too-much-of-a-good-thing effect in management. *Journal of Management* 39(2): 313–338.

Rahmandad H. 2012. Impact of growth opportunities and competition on firm-level capability development trade-offs. *Organization Science* 23(1): 138–154.

Rugman AM, Verbeke A. 2002. Edith Penrose's contribution to the resource-based view of strategic management. *Strategic Management Journal* 23(8): 769.

Rugman AM, Verbeke A. 2004. A final word on Edith Penrose. *Journal of Management Studies* 41(1): 205–217.

Sarkar MB, Echambadi RAJ, Harrison JS. 2001. Alliance entrepreneurship and firm market performance. *Strategic Management Journal* 22(6/7): 701.

Shane SA. 1996. Hybrid organizational arrangements and their implications for firm growth and survival: a study of new franchisors. *Academy of Management Journal* 39(1): 216–234.

Shleifer A, Vishny RW. 1986. Large shareholders and corporate control. *Journal of Political Economy* 94(3, Part 1): 461–488.

Short JC, McKelvie A, Ketchen DJ, Chandler GN. 2009. Firm and industry effects on firm performance: a generalization and extension for new ventures. *Strategic Entrepreneurship Journal* 3(1): 47–65.

Sirmon DG, Hitt MA, Ireland RD. 2007. Managing firm resources in dynamic environments to create value: looking inside the black box. *Academy of Management Review* 32(1): 273–292.

Sirmon DG, Hitt MA, Ireland RD, Gilbert BA. 2011. Resource orchestration to create competitive advantage: breadth, depth, and life cycle effects. *Journal of Management* 37(5): 1390–1412.

Slevin DP, Covin JG. 1997. Strategy formation patterns, performance, and the significance of context. *Journal of Management* 23(2): 189.

Steinbach A, Devers Cynthia E, McNamara G, Li J. 2016. Peering into the executive mind: expanding our understanding of the motives for acquisitions. In *Advances in Mergers and Acquisitions*. Emerald Group Publishing Limited, Bingley, U.K.; 145–160.

Tan D, Su W, Mahoney JT, Kor Y. 2020. A review of research on the growth of multinational enterprises: a Penrosean lens. *Journal of International Business Studies* 51(4): 498–537.

Teece DJ. 2014. The foundations of enterprise performance: dynamic and ordinary capabilities in an (economic) theory of firms. *Academy of Management Perspectives* 28(4): 328–352.

Teece DJ, Pisano G, Shuen A. 1997. Dynamic capabilities and strategic management. *Strategic Management Journal* 18(7): 509–533.

Thomsen S, Pedersen T. 2000. Ownership structure and economic performance in the largest European companies. *Strategic Management Journal* 21(6): 689–705.

Tihanyi L. 2020. From "that's interesting" to "that's important." *Academy of Management Journal* 63(2): 329–331.

Tong TW, Reuer JJ. 2007. Real options in strategic management. In *Advances in Strategic Management: Real Options Theory*, Reuer JJ, Tong TW (eds). Elsevier: Amsterdam, the Netherlands; 3–28.

Van de Ven AH, Meyer AD, Jing R. 2018. Opportunities and challenges of engaged indigenous scholarship. *Management and Organization Review* 14(3): 449–462.

Webb JW, Tihanyi L, Ireland RD, Sirmon DG. 2009. You say illegal, I say legitimate: entrepreneurship in the informal economy. *Academy of Management Review* 34(3): 492–510.

Wernerfelt B. 1984. A resource-based view of the firm. *Strategic Management Journal* 5(2): 171–180.

Whetten DA. 1987. Organizational growth and decline processes. *Annual Review of Sociology* 13: 335–358.

Wilden R, Devinney TM, Dowling GR. 2016. The architecture of dynamic capability research. *Academy of Management Annals* 10(1): 997–1076.

Withers MC, Ireland RD, Miller D, Harrison JS, Boss DS. 2018. Competitive landscape shifts: the influence of strategic entrepreneurship on shifts in market commonality. *Academy of Management Review* 43(3): 349–370.

Zaheer A, Hernandez E, Banerjee S. 2010. Prior alliances with targets and acquisition performance in knowledge-intensive industries. *Organization Science* 21(5): 1072–1091.

Zander I, Zander U. 2005. The inside track: on the important (but neglected) role of customers in the resource-based view of strategy and firm growth. *Journal of Management Studies* 42(8): 1519–1548.

Zollo M, Minoja M, Coda V. 2018. Toward an integrated theory of strategy. *Strategic Management Journal* 39(6): 1753–1778.

Zollo M, Singh H. 2004. Deliberate learning in corporate acquisitions: post-acquisition strategies and integration capability in U.S. bank mergers. *Strategic Management Journal* 25(13): 1233–1256.

2.2

RESTRUCTURING AND DIVESTITURES

Emilie R. Feldman

Introduction

Research in corporate strategy fundamentally seeks to address the question "How do managers set and oversee the scope of their firms?" (Feldman, 2020), a key component of which is the issue of which businesses they choose to participate in and which they do not. Managers can pursue a range of strategies to make such decisions, which can generally be grouped into two categories: (1) expansionary strategies, such as mergers and acquisitions, alliances, joint ventures, and corporate venture capital, which allow firms to increase their scope; and (2) contractionary strategies, such as selloffs, spinoffs, carveouts, and asset restructuring, which enable firms to reduce their boundaries.

Despite the fact that expansionary and contractionary corporate strategies are inverses of one another, significantly more academic research has been conducted about the former than the latter. In the last 10 years, for example, the *Strategic Management Journal* published 144 articles about acquisitions, alliances, and joint ventures versus 20 articles about divestitures.[1] This pattern is echoed in practice as well. My analyses show that in 2019, U.S.-based firms undertook nearly three acquisitions for every one divestiture they implemented. Nonetheless, contractionary strategies have a significant potential for value creation, perhaps even more so than expansionary strategies. For instance, my analyses of U.S.-based acquisitions and divestitures over the last 10 years reveal that the shareholder returns to divestiture announcements are more than double the shareholder returns to acquisition announcements, and my review of recent literature indicates that the average abnormal return to divesting firms upon divestiture announcements is +3.0 percent,[2] as compared to a –0.7 percent abnormal return to acquiring firms upon acquisition announcements.[3]

Together, these points suggest that contractionary strategies such as divestitures and restructuring (henceforth, I refer to both as divestitures) are a very fruitful area for investigation. In this chapter, I present an agenda for research into these phenomena by surveying past and current literature about them and laying out some productive directions for future research in this domain.

Past Research

Past research on divestitures largely conceptualized these strategies as reactions to negative occurrences that had previously happened either inside or outside of firms. Some examples of internal problems that have been shown to prompt managers to divest include declining firm or business unit performance (e.g., Duhaime and Grant, 1984; Duhaime and Schwenk, 1985; Jain, 1985; Hoskisson and Turk, 1990; Ravenscraft and Scherer, 1991; Barker and Duhaime, 1997; Desai and Jain, 1999; Schlingemann, Stulz, and Walkling, 2002); unsuccessful mergers and acquisitions (e.g., Kaplan and Weisbach, 1992; Weisbach, 1995); over-diversification, especially when driven by empire building (e.g., Jensen, 1986; Hoskisson and Turk, 1990; Markides 1992, 1995; Hoskisson and Hitt, 1994; Comment and Jarrell, 1995; Daley, Mehrotra, and Sivakumar, 1997); and other manifestations of agency conflicts, including managerial entrenchment or inefficient internal capital markets (e.g., Shleifer and Vishny, 1989; Scharfstein, 1998). Analogously, some external factors that have been shown to induce managers to divest include industry decline (e.g., Harrigan, 1980); information asymmetry vis-à-vis external constituents like securities analysts and investors (e.g., Zuckerman, 1999; Gilson *et al.*, 2001); hostile takeover attempts (e.g., Bhagat, Shleifer, and Vishny, 1990; Berger and Ofek, 1999); and regulatory requirements such as antitrust (Joskow, 2002).

In turn, much of the early literature on divestitures documented that these transactions are beneficial for divesting firms, in terms of operating performance (e.g., Hoskisson and Turk, 1990; John and Ofek, 1995; Daley *et al.*, 1997), short- and long-term stock market performance (e.g., Montgomery, Thomas, and Kamath, 1984; Hoskisson and Turk, 1990; Comment and Jarrell, 1995; John and Ofek, 1995; Desai and Jain, 1999), and analyst coverage and forecast accuracy (e.g., Krishnaswami and Subramaniam, 1999; Zuckerman, 2000; Gilson *et al.*, 2001). These favorable consequences are often portrayed as evidence that divestitures succeed at resolving the problems that prompted managers to undertake these transactions in the first place.

It is interesting to note that a significant portion of the above-described body of research is published in finance journals. This at least in part reflects this literature's use of divestitures as a context in which to measure the existence and magnitude of the diversification discount (a topic of significant debate in the late 1990s and early 2000s), in that the value gains resulting from divestitures could be interpreted as evidence of value destruction within the diversified firms that undertook those transactions (Villalonga, 2003). Having said this, much more of the current research on divestitures is appearing in strategy journals, reflecting a reconceptualization of these strategies as proactive, forward-looking ways for managers to reshape their boundaries rather than as reactive, backward-looking solutions to problems. I discuss this shift in the next section, emphasizing the point that a key way for strategy scholars to differentiate their work from that of finance scholars (even though both sets of researchers often use similar data, measures, and methodological approaches) is to focus on the proactive, forward-looking aspects of divestitures as part of companies' corporate strategy toolkits.

Current Research

Current strategy research about divestitures can be grouped into four main categories: the drivers of divestiture decision-making, the actors that undertake and influence those decisions, the interdependences between divestitures and other modes of corporate strategy, and the implications of divestitures for divested units. I describe each of these in turn.

First, per the earlier discussion, divestiture decisions were historically thought to be driven largely by economic considerations, such as industry decline or ill-fated expansion strategies. Increasingly, though, strategy scholars have come to realize that a host of totally different, non-economic considerations can and do affect divestiture decisions. For example, such factors as historical connections (Feldman, 2014), organizational inertia (Shimizu and Hitt, 2005), unit interdependency (Duhaime and Grant, 1984; Duhaime and Grant, 1985), behavioral biases (Hayward and Shimizu, 2006; Shimizu, 2007; Vidal and Mitchell, 2015), prior transaction experience (Bergh and Lim, 2008; Villalonga and McGahan, 2005), internal social comparison costs (Feldman, Gartenberg, and Wulf, 2018), and even public stigma against these transactions (Dranikoff, Koller, and Schneider, 2002) all have a significant influence on divestiture decision-making.

Second, and further to the previous point, the identity and characteristics of various organizational actors have also been shown to affect divestiture decisions. The characteristics of managers and directors—such as their age and tenure (Wiersema and Bantel, 1992; Shimizu and Hitt, 2005; Feldman, 2014), share ownership (Bergh, 1995; Hoskisson, Johnson, and Moesel, 1994), and experience and power (Bigley and Wiersema, 2002)—have all been shown to be key drivers of decision-making. More recently, research on divestitures has also begun to attend to the role of various corporate owners, such as activist investors (Chen and Feldman, 2018; Shimizu and Hitt, 2005), other large blockholders (Bethel and Liebeskind, 1993; Bergh, 1995; Bergh and Sharp, 2015; Bergh *et al.*, 2019), and founding families (Feldman, Amit, and Villalonga, 2016).

Third, a rich stream of research, primarily rooted in the resource reconfiguration literature (Karim and Capron, 2016), has emerged about interdependences between divestitures and other modes of corporate strategy. Scholars in this domain are exploring how managers may sequentially use divestitures and other modes of corporate strategy to proactively reshape firm scope (Teece *et al.*, 1994; Chang, 1996; Capron, Mitchell, and Swaminathan, 2001; Helfat and Eisenhardt, 2004; Bennett and Feldman, 2017; Vidal and Mitchell, 2018), and also when and how these modes may be complements to or substitutes for one another (Berry, 2010; Kaul, 2012; Miller and Yang, 2016; Lieberman, Lee, and Folta, 2017; Feldman and Sakhartov, 2021).

Fourth, and finally, while much current strategy research about divestitures has taken the perspective of the divesting firm, scholars have also begun examining the implications of these transactions, especially spinoffs, for the units that are divested. Within this domain, questions about how divested businesses constitute their boards of directors (Semadeni and Cannella, 2011; Feldman, 2016a), structure managerial incentives (Seward and Walsh, 1996; Feldman, 2016b), establish independent identities (Corley and Gioia, 2004; Wiedner and Mantere, 2019), secure relevant analyst coverage (Feldman, Gilson, and Villalonga, 2014), and even experience the divestiture process (Moschieri, 2011) have all become paramount.

Future Research

Having surveyed the landscape of past and current divestiture research, it now becomes possible to articulate my views about the future of research in this domain. In seeking to address the foundational question of how managers set and oversee the scope of their firms, I proposed a framework for corporate strategy in Feldman (2020) that comprises three levels of analysis: intraorganizational, whereby managers must coordinate relationships and resources within the boundaries of their firms; interorganizational, whereby managers must coordinate interactions with other companies across firm boundaries; and extraorganizational, whereby managers must decide which businesses belong within the boundaries of their firms and which ones do not. I structure my discussion of future research on divestitures around these three levels of analysis.

Intraorganizational

Beginning with an intraorganizational perspective, three key facets of how divestitures influence and are influenced by resource allocation within firm boundaries merit further research attention. The first looks at the firm through the lens of stakeholder theory. Stakeholder theory holds that the firm lies at the center of a network of stakeholders (such as customers, employees, suppliers, local communities, shareholders, and other providers of financial capital) that contribute specialized and socially complex assets and resources to the firm (Barney, 2018). The issue that immediately becomes apparent from this perspective is that divestitures are likely to disrupt the ongoing resource contributions of one or more of these stakeholders (especially employees, who may experience the dislocations resulting from divestitures most acutely[4]), with potentially significant consequences for the firm's ongoing operations. Bettinazzi and Feldman (2020) began exploring this very point by conceptualizing divestitures (and different types of divestitures) as arising endogenously in firms where those transactions are less costly to stakeholders than the internal resolution of conflicts among those stakeholders (Klein *et al.*, 2019). Building from this premise, future research could usefully explore when and how divestitures disrupt the contribution and allocation of resources by various stakeholders, as well as the implications that this has for the anticipation and proactive management of conflicts among stakeholders, and hence, for firm performance and other outcomes.

A second key direction for future research taking an intraorganizational perspective on divestitures is to introduce organization design into the mix. With the exception of only a few prior studies (e.g., Arora, Belenzon, and Rios, 2014), the literatures on organization design and corporate strategy have largely remained separate from one another, despite the obvious parallel that the former explores internal boundary decisions while the latter explores external boundary decisions. As noted in Feldman and McGrath (2016), modularity is one facet of organization design that could interact with divestitures, particularly in terms of the ease with which divesting firms may be able to cleave off divested units. For instance, it may be more straightforward for companies to divest previously acquired rather than internally developed units, to the extent that the former are less integrated with, and hence, more modular, than the latter. Another facet of organization design that could interact with divestitures is the firm's degree of centralization or decentralization. For example, in a recent working paper, Eklund and Feldman (2021) show that the degree of centralization of divesting firms' research and development (R&D) units has significant implications for the manner in which firms apply the resources that are freed up by divestitures (e.g., cash, human resources, physical capital) to future innovation opportunities. Scholars would be well served to continue mining the rich literature on organization design for potentially interesting intersections with research on divestitures.

Third, future research could investigate how divesting firms reconfigure existing resources and processes within their organizations following the completion of divestitures. These transactions can be enormously disruptive events for firms, and existing studies have begun to contemplate how divestitures may impel firms to reorganize internal processes and practices like compensation (Pathak, Hoskisson, and Johnson, 2014; Feldman, 2016b), capital allocation (Feldman, 2016c), and innovation (Eklund and Feldman, 2021). A few papers have also begun to consider how divestitures might disrupt key interdependencies within divesting firms (Feldman, 2014; Natividad and Rawley, 2016; de Figueiredo, Feldman, and Rawley, 2019), prompting a reconsideration of where synergistic value is generated within multibusiness firms. Future research could usefully continue to explore these issues in greater depth.

Interorganizational

From an interorganizational perspective, a key direction for future research about divestitures is to study how divesting firms manage their post-divestiture relationships with divested businesses. In particular, it would be very valuable to understand how various resources, processes, capabilities, physical assets, and human capital are divided between divesting firms and divested businesses, especially because practitioners have articulated that these entities often need to continue sharing such resources following the completion of divestitures (e.g., Alaix, 2014). A few published papers and some work in progress have begun to pursue this approach, for example, by exploring the allocation of board members, management, and other employees (Semadeni and Cannella, 2011; Feldman, 2016a, 2016b; Bodner and Feldman, 2021); the establishment of distinct identities and cultures (Corley and Gioia, 2004; Wiedner and Mantere, 2019); and even the use of transition services agreements to manage the separation process (McGlinch and Feldman, 2021). Having said this, many other aspects of the process of division remain unaddressed, including the allocation of patents and other intellectual property; reputational assets such as brands, logos, and names; plants and machinery; debt, overhead, and other centralized corporate expenses; contracts with suppliers and customers; and even alliance relationships. The literature on post-merger integration may have useful insights into these issues, since this body of research, at its core, considers the inverse question of how to *unite* resources, capabilities, physical assets, human capital, and cultures that originate from distinct organizations (Graebner *et al.*, 2017; Bodner and Capron, 2018).

A second way in which one might approach the interorganizational question of how managers coordinate relationships with other companies across the boundaries of their firms is to consider the role of counterparties to divestiture transactions (i.e., the acquiring entities that buy divested businesses). As noted in Feldman, Amit, and Villalonga (2019), divestitures and acquisitions are bilateral transactions, in that one company buys an asset or a business from another company that is selling that asset or that business. A few recent studies have shown that conceptualizing divestitures in this way has significant performance implications (Capron and Shen, 2007; Laamanen, Brauer, and Junna, 2014; Kaul, Nary, and Singh, 2018; Feldman *et al.*, 2019). As Feldman (2020) points out, one useful extension of these ideas might be to examine corporate strategy transactions—divestitures in particular—trilaterally, in that they involve an acquiring firm, a divesting firm, and the business unit that is changing hands. This approach could be used to generate novel insights into how interorganizational relationships between divesting firms and their counterparties influence divestiture performance. Another important extension to the idea of conceptualizing divestitures bilaterally or trilaterally is to consider the role of private equity firms versus traditional corporations as buyers and sellers in divestitures (and acquisitions). Kaul *et al.* (2018) began to do this in their study of which divested assets are bought by private equity firms versus companies, but many more opportunities remain in this line of inquiry, especially given the recent prevalence of private equity as a major player in the market for corporate transactions. This point could be extended even further into an exploration of which acquirers (private equity vs. companies) buy the assets that are removed by full versus partial divestitures (e.g., Vidal and Mitchell, 2015).

Finally, it would be valuable for scholars to study the role of interorganizational knowledge and learning spillovers within the context of divestitures. While existing research has shown that the repeated execution of transactions like acquisitions and divestitures leads to the accumulation of valuable capabilities and, in turn, better transaction performance (e.g., Haleblian and Finkelstein, 1999; Bergh and Lim, 2008), it is readily evident that learning and experience may accumulate due to interactions and relationships *between* firms as well. Thus, one might consider, for example, whether firms that have more acquisition experience perform better when they undertake divestitures (and vice versa), as well as when and why this might or might not be the case. Further to this point, one could also explore whether and how interactions with intermediaries like investment bankers, lawyers, and consultants result in the accumulation of divestiture capabilities, as articulated, for example, in McGrath's (2016) dissertation on this topic. These and related ideas raise intriguing questions about how interorganizational relationships between firms and their intermediaries might influence divestiture decision-making and performance.

Extraorganizational

From an extraorganizational perspective, one important direction for future inquiry is for scholars to continue to incorporate the insight into their research that divestitures are a key part of the intertemporal process of resource reconfiguration and scope change. As mentioned previously, the notion of using divestitures sequentially with other corporate strategy transactions is not new, especially in terms of acquisitions preceding divestitures (Kaplan and Weisbach, 1992; Teece *et al.*, 1994; Chang, 1996; Capron *et al.*, 2001; Shimizu and Hitt, 2005; Hayward and Shimizu, 2006; Shimizu, 2007) and divestitures preceding acquisitions (Dranikoff *et al.*, 2002; Bennett and Feldman, 2017; Vidal and Mitchell, 2018).

Having said this, however, many opportunities remain available to explore this issue in greater depth. For example, researchers might examine the different configurations of corporate strategy transactions that exist, incorporating acquisitions, alliances, divestitures, joint ventures, corporate venture capital, and even internal resource redeployment (e.g., Feldman and Sakhartov, 2021) and organic growth (e.g., Tang and Feldman, 2021) into their analyses. To facilitate this, scholars must embrace the notion that corporate strategy is a dynamic and holistic process that unfolds over time and involves series of transactions rather than discrete events (Feldman, 2020), and they must begin to explicitly conceptualize and model longer-term sequences of corporate strategy transactions, as a few scholars have begun to do (e.g., Chang, 1996; Teece *et al.*, 1994; Feldman and Sakhartov, 2021).

Another important research direction from an extraorganizational perspective is to understand how various internal and external constituents might influence the divestiture decision. Much of the existing literature about divestitures has been built around the assumption that managers decide to divest or not to divest particular businesses. Recently, though, some studies have begun to explore how external actors, such as activist investors (Chen and Feldman, 2018) and securities analysts (Feldman *et al.*, 2014; Feldman, 2016d), might influence or equally be influenced by these decisions. As an extension of these findings, it would be interesting to understand how other external constituents—such as the press, social activists, debtholders, and even other kinds of equity owners—might exert pressure on firms to divest or not to divest certain businesses, with significant implications for the divesting firms.

Extending this idea a step further, one could even consider the role of internal constituents along this dimension as well. For example, Feldman *et al.* (2018) articulate that firms may undertake divestitures in response to high pay inequality and its resulting social comparisons among their employees. Although these authors do not argue that employees *demand* divestitures in response to high pay inequality, there could be situations in which such demands are made in response to some sort of dissatisfaction within the organization. Investigating these kinds of questions could be very interesting, especially in the current business environment where such expressions are becoming increasingly commonplace and where companies are increasingly responsive to them. This could form an important link to the literature on entrepreneurial spin-offs, which explicitly considers the separation of employee-led ventures into freestanding entities (e.g., Klepper and Sleeper, 2005; Agarwal *et al.*, 2004). There are obvious parallels between entrepreneurial spin-offs and corporate divestitures, creating a potentially fascinating opportunity for cross-fertilization across fields of research.

Last but not least, one final area of inquiry taking an extraorganizational perspective could be to consider the interplay between divestitures and industry conditions. A few studies have examined industry divestiture waves, documenting significant industry clustering of divestiture activity as well as performance consequences deriving from the point in an industry divestiture wave at which a focal transaction is situated (Mulherin and Boone, 2000; Brauer and Wiersema, 2012). One could usefully extend some of these ideas by considering macroeconomic and even social trends (per the earlier discussion) as significant drivers of divestiture decisions and divestiture performance. This leads to an additional possibility, which might be to explore the implications of divestitures for competition and industry characteristics. For example, when one company sells a business unit to another firm that is already in that line of business, market concentration increases in the industry in which that business operates (since the acquiring firm now holds a larger share of the market). It would be useful to consider the competitive implications of divestitures for different industries, which would represent an important marriage of the competitive and corporate strategy literatures.

Conclusion

This chapter has reflected on the historical development, current status, and future trajectory of research on divestitures. Against the backdrop of the central question in corporate strategy—how do managers set and oversee the boundaries of their firms?—it is evident that divestitures play as integral a role as the expansionary strategies that have heretofore received more attention in the academic literature and in managerial practice. Having said this, the tide is beginning to turn, as scholars increasingly see divestitures as interesting and worthy of investigation, and as numerous studies document the significant implications that divestitures have for divesting firms, divested businesses, and the other actors and entities that are involved in or affected by these transactions. This is also reflected in the rich opportunities for future inquiry about divestitures that I have presented in this chapter.

Divestiture activity reached an all-time high between 2014 and 2019, with over $1 trillion of transactions completed annually during this period and close to $1.5 trillion in 2015 alone. This trend is likely to have been driven by a number of factors, including the rise of activist investors demanding that managers proactively reshape their firms' corporate scope as well as major consulting firms actively promoting the use of these transactions.[5] In the wake of the coronavirus pandemic, managers are likely to turn to divestitures to restructure and reconfigure their portfolios of businesses with an eye toward retrenchment and efficiency gains in the face of performance decline,[6] just as they did after the 2007–2009 financial crisis. Among managers, this may prompt some regression to the view that divestitures are merely solutions to problems, intended primarily to be used in times of distress or decline. The forward-thinking executive, however, will continue to look to divestitures as a proactive, strategic tool with which to manage corporate scope in a value-additive manner. Thus, I close this chapter with a call to the academic community, especially scholars in the field of corporate strategy, to continue producing robust knowledge and insights about how and why divestitures can fulfill this function and accomplish these objectives.

Notes

1. I conducted this analysis using Web of Science, with the following keywords (presented with their variants): merg*, acqui*, M&A, ally, alliance*, joint ventur*, divest*, asset sale, spinoff, spin-off, selloff, and sell-off.
2. The following articles were used to generate this figure: John and Ofek (1995), Comment and Jarrell (1995), Daley, Mehrotra, and Sivakumar (1997), Krishnaswami and Subramaniam (1999), Desai and Jain (1999), Bergh, Johnson, and DeWitt (2008), Feldman (2014, 2016d).
3. The following articles were used to generate this figure: Asquith, Bruner, and Mullins (1983), Bradley, Desai, and Kim (1988), Lang, Walkling, and Stulz (1989), Servaes (1991), Kaplan and Weisbach (1992), Mulherin and Boone (2000), and Mitchell and Stafford (2000).
4. "For example, when DowDuPont announced that it would divide the newly-merged company into three independent firms, employees in the divesting firm were angered by the prospect of having to move to the different geographic locations where the divested businesses would be headquartered" (Bettinazzi and Feldman, 2020: 10–11).
5. https://advisory.kpmg.us/content/dam/advisory/en/pdfs/2020/think-like-an-activist.pdf
6. https://www.carpenterwellington.com/post/corporate-divestiture-plans-placed-on-hold-during-pandemic

References

Agarwal R, Echambadi R, Franco AM, Sarkar MB. 2004. Knowledge transfer through inheritance: spin-out generation, development, and survival. *Academy of Management Journal* 47(4): 501–522.

Alaix JR. 2014. How I did it … the CEO of Zoetis on how he prepared for the top job. *Harvard Business Review* 92: 41–44.

Arora A, Belenzon S, Rios, LA. 2014. Make, buy, organize: the interplay between research, external knowledge, and firm structure. *Strategic Management Journal* 35(3): 317–337.

Asquith P, Bruner RF, Mullins DW Jr. 1983. The gains to bidding firms from merger. *Journal of Financial Economics* 11(1-4): 121–139.

Barker VL III, Duhaime IM. 1997. Strategic change in the turnaround process: theory and empirical evidence. *Strategic Management Journal* 18(1): 13–38.

Barney JB. 2018. Why resource-based theory's model of profit appropriation must incorporate a stakeholder perspective. *Strategic Management Journal* 39(13): 3305–3325.

Bennett VM, Feldman ER. 2017. Make room! Make room! A note on sequential spinoffs and acquisitions. *Strategy Science* 2(2): 100–110.

Berger PG, Ofek E. 1999. Causes and effects of corporate refocusing programs. *Review of Financial Studies* 12(2): 311–345.

Bergh DD. 1995. Size and relatedness of units sold: an agency theory and resource-based perspective. *Strategic Management Journal* 16(3): 221–239.

Bergh DD, Johnson RA, Dewitt RL. 2008. Restructuring through spin-off or sell-off: transforming information asymmetries into financial gain. *Strategic Management Journal* 29(2): 133–148.

Bergh DD, Lim E. 2008. Learning how to restructure: absorptive capacity and improvisational views of restructuring actions and performance. *Strategic Management Journal* 29(6): 593–616.

Bergh DD, Peruffo E, Chiu WT, Connelly B, Hitt MA. 2020. Market response to divestiture announcements: a screening theory perspective. *Strategic Organization* 18(4): 547–572.

Bergh DD, Sharp BM. 2015. How far do owners reach into the divestiture process? Blockholders and the choice between spin-off and sell-off. *Journal of Management* 41(4): 1155–1183.

Berry H. 2010. Why do firms divest? *Organization Science* 21(2): 380–396.

Bethel JE, Liebeskind J. 1993. The effects of ownership structure on corporate restructuring. *Strategic Management Journal* 14(S1): 15–31.

Bettinazzi ELM, Feldman ER. 2020. Stakeholder orientation and divestiture activity. *Academy of Management Journal*, forthcoming.

Bhagat S, Shleifer A, Vishny RW. 1990. Hostile takeovers in the 1980s: the return to corporate specialization. *Brookings Papers on Economic Activity: Microeconomics* 1990: 1–84.

Bigley GA, Wiersema MF. 2002. New CEOs and corporate strategic refocusing: how experience as heir apparent influences the use of power. *Administrative Science Quarterly* 47(4): 707–727.

Bodner J, Capron L. 2018. Post-merger integration. *Journal of Organization Design* 7(3): 1–20.

Bodner J, Feldman ER. 2021. Employee redeployment in the divestiture process. Working paper.

Bradley M, Desai A, Kim EH. 1988. Synergistic gains from corporate acquisitions and their division between the stockholders of target and acquiring firms. *Journal of Financial Economics* 21(1): 3–40.

Brauer MF, Wiersema MF. 2012. Industry divestiture waves: how a firm's position influences investor returns. *Academy of Management Journal* 55(6): 1472–1492.

Capron L, Mitchell W, Swaminathan A. 2001. Asset divestiture following horizontal acquisitions: a dynamic view. *Strategic Management Journal* 22(9): 817–844.

Capron L, Shen JC. 2007. Acquisitions of private vs. public firms: private information, target selection, and acquirer returns. *Strategic Management Journal* 28(9): 891–911.

Chang SJ. 1996. An evolutionary perspective on diversification and corporate restructuring: entry, exit, and economic performance during 1981–89. *Strategic Management Journal* 17(8): 587–611.

Chen S, Feldman ER. 2018. Activist-impelled divestitures and shareholder value. *Strategic Management Journal* 39(10): 2726–2744.

Comment R, Jarrell GA. 1995. Corporate focus and stock returns. *Journal of Financial Economics* 37(1): 67–87.

Corley KG, Gioia DA. 2004. Identity ambiguity and change in the wake of a corporate spin-off. *Administrative Science Quarterly* 49(2): 173–208.

Daley L, Mehrotra V, Sivakumar R. 1997. Corporate focus and value creation evidence from spinoffs. *Journal of Financial Economics* 45(2): 257–281.

de Figueiredo RJ Jr, Feldman ER, Rawley E. 2019. The costs of refocusing: evidence from hedge fund closures during the financial crisis. *Strategic Management Journal* 40(8): 1268–1290.

Desai H, Jain PC. 1999. Firm performance and focus: long-run stock market performance following spinoffs. *Journal of Financial Economics* 54(1): 75–101.

Dranikoff L, Koller T, Schneider A. 2002. Divestiture: strategy's missing link. *Harvard Business Review* 80(5): 74–83.

Duhaime IM, Grant JH. 1984. Factors influencing divestment decision-making: evidence from a field study. *Strategic Management Journal* 5(4): 301–318.

Duhaime IM, Grant JH. 1985. Divestment decisions involving interdependencies, unit strength and management attachment. In *Advances in Strategic Management*. Lamb R, Shrivastava P (eds.), JAI Press, Inc. 3: 305–322.

Duhaime IM, Schwenk CR. 1985. Conjectures on cognitive simplification in acquisition and divestment decision making. *Academy of Management Review* 10(2): 287–295.

Eklund JC, Feldman ER. 2021. Understanding the relationship between divestitures and innovation. Working paper.

Feldman ER. 2014. Legacy divestitures: motives and implications. *Organization Science* 25(3): 815–832.

Feldman ER. 2016a. Dual directors and the governance of corporate spinoffs. *Academy of Management Journal* 59(5): 1754–1776.

Feldman ER. 2016b. Managerial compensation and corporate spinoffs. *Strategic Management Journal* 37(10): 2011–2030.

Feldman ER. 2016c. Corporate spin-offs and capital allocation decisions. *Strategy Science* 1(4): 256–271.

Feldman ER. 2016d. Corporate spinoffs and analysts' coverage decisions: the implications for diversified firms. *Strategic Management Journal* 37(7): 1196–1219.

Feldman ER. 2020. Corporate strategy: past, present, and future. *Strategic Management Review* 1(1): 179–206.

Feldman ER, Amit R, Villalonga B. 2016. Corporate divestitures and family control. *Strategic Management Journal* 37(3): 429–446.

Feldman ER, Amit R, Villalonga B. 2019. Family firms and the stock market performance of acquisitions and divestitures. *Strategic Management Journal* 40(5): 757–780.

Feldman ER, Gartenberg C, Wulf J. 2018. Pay inequality and corporate divestitures. *Strategic Management Journal* 39(11): 2829–2858.

Feldman ER, Gilson SC, Villalonga B. 2014. Do analysts add value when they most can? Evidence from corporate spin-offs. *Strategic Management Journal* 35(10): 1446–1463.

Feldman ER, McGrath PJ. 2016. Divestitures. *Journal of Organization Design* 5(1): 1–16.

Feldman ER, Sakhartov AV. 2021. Resource redeployment and divestiture as strategic alternatives. *Organization Science*, forthcoming.

Gilson SC, Healy PM, Noe CF, Palepu KG. 2001. Analyst specialization and conglomerate stock breakups. *Journal of Accounting Research* 39(3): 565–582.

Graebner ME, Heimeriks KH, Huy QN, Vaara E. 2017. The process of post-merger integration: a review and agenda for future research. *Academy of Management Annals* 11(1): 1–32.

Haleblian J, Finkelstein S. 1999. The influence of organizational acquisition experience on acquisition performance: a behavioral learning perspective. *Administrative Science Quarterly* 44(1): 29–56.

Harrigan KR. 1980. Strategy formulation in declining industries. *Academy of Management Review* 5(4): 599–604.

Hayward ML, Shimizu K. 2006. De-commitment to losing strategic action: evidence from the divestiture of poorly performing acquisitions. *Strategic Management Journal* 27(6): 541–557.

Helfat CE, Eisenhardt KM. 2004. Inter-temporal economies of scope, organizational modularity, and the dynamics of diversification. *Strategic Management Journal* 25(13): 1217–1232.

Hoskisson RE, Hitt MA. 1994. *Downscoping: How to Tame the Diversified Firm*. Oxford University Press: New York, NY.

Hoskisson RE, Johnson RA, Moesel DD. 1994. Corporate divestiture intensity in restructuring firms: effects of governance, strategy, and performance. *Academy of Management Journal* 37(5): 1207–1251.

Hoskisson RE, Turk TA. 1990. Corporate restructuring: governance and control limits of the internal capital market. *Academy of Management Review* 15(3): 459–477.

Jain PC. 1985. The effect of voluntary sell-off announcements on shareholder wealth. *Journal of Finance* 40(1): 209–224.

Jensen MC. 1986. Agency costs of free cash flow, corporate finance, and takeovers. *American Economic Review* 76: 323–329.

John K, Ofek E. 1995. Asset sales and increase in focus. *Journal of Financial Economics* 37(1): 105–126.

Joskow PL. 2002. Transaction cost economics, antitrust rules, and remedies. *Journal of Law, Economics, and Organization* 18(1): 95–116.

Kaplan SN, Weisbach MS. 1992. The success of acquisitions: evidence from divestitures. *Journal of Finance* 47(1): 107–138.

Karim S, Capron L. 2016. Reconfiguration: adding, redeploying, recombining, and divesting resources and business units. *Strategic Management Journal* 37(13): E54–E62.

Kaul A. 2012. Technology and corporate scope: firm and rival innovation as antecedents of corporate transactions. *Strategic Management Journal* 33(4): 347–367.

Kaul A, Nary P, Singh H. 2018. Who does private equity buy? Evidence on the role of private equity from buyouts of divested businesses. *Strategic Management Journal* 39(5): 1268–1298.

Klein PG, Mahoney JT, McGahan AM, Pitelis CN. 2019. Organizational governance adaptation: who is in, who is out, and who gets what. *Academy of Management Review* 44(1): 6–27.

Klepper S, Sleeper S. 2005. Entry by spinoffs. *Management Science* 51(8): 1291–1306.

Krishnaswami S, Subramaniam V. 1999. Information asymmetry, valuation, and the corporate spin-off decision. *Journal of Financial Economics* 53(1): 73–112.

Laamanen T, Brauer M, Junna O. 2014. Performance of acquirers of divested assets: evidence from the US software industry. *Strategic Management Journal* 35(6): 914–925.

Lang LH, Walkling RA, Stulz RM. 1989. Managerial performance, Tobin's Q, and the gains from successful tender offers. *Journal of Finance* 24: 137–154.

Lieberman MB, Lee GK, Folta TB. 2017. Entry, exit, and the potential for resource redeployment. *Strategic Management Journal* 38(3): 526–544.

McGlinch J, Feldman ER. 2021. Intra-shift information costs: transition services agreements in corporate spinoffs. Working paper.

McGrath PJ. 2016. *Three Essays on Firm Learning and Performance in the Context of Corporate Divestiture.* PhD dissertation, University of Pennsylvania.

Markides CC. 1992. Consequences of corporate refocusing: ex ante evidence. *Academy of Management Journal* 35(2): 398–412.

Markides CC. 1995. Diversification, restructuring, and economic performance. *Strategic Management Journal* 16(2): 101–118.

Miller DJ, Yang H. 2016. Product turnover: simultaneous product market entry and exit. *Advances in Strategic Management* 35: 49–87.

Mitchell ML, Stafford E. 2000. Managerial decisions and long-term stock price performance. *Journal of Business* 73(3): 287–329.

Montgomery CA, Thomas AR, Kamath R. 1984. Divestiture, market valuation, and strategy. *Academy of Management Journal* 27(4): 830–840.

Moschieri C. 2011. The implementation and structuring of divestitures: the unit's perspective. *Strategic Management Journal* 32(4): 368–401.

Mulherin JH, Boone AL. 2000. Comparing acquisitions and divestitures. *Journal of Corporate Finance* 6(2): 117–139.

Natividad G, Rawley E. 2016. Interdependence and performance: a natural experiment in firm scope. *Strategy Science* 1(1): 12–31.

Pathak S, Hoskisson RE, Johnson RA. 2014. Settling up in CEO compensation: the impact of divestiture intensity and contextual factors in refocusing firms. *Strategic Management Journal* 35(8): 1124–1143.

Ravenscraft DJ, Scherer FM. 1991. Divisional sell-off: a hazard function analysis. *Managerial and Decision Economics* 12(6): 429–438.

Scharfstein DS. 1998. The dark side of internal capital markets II: evidence from diversified conglomerates. NBER working paper w6352, National Bureau of Economic Research, Cambridge, MA. Available at: https://www.nber.org/papers/w6352.

Schlingemann FP, Stulz RM, Walkling RA. 2002. Divestitures and the liquidity of the market for corporate assets. *Journal of Financial Economics* 64(1): 117–144.

Semadeni M, Cannella AA Jr. 2011. Examining the performance effects of post spin-off links to parent firms: should the apron strings be cut? *Strategic Management Journal* 32(10): 1083–1098.

Servaes H. 1991. Tobin's Q and the gains from takeovers. *Journal of Finance* 46(1): 409–419.

Seward JK, Walsh JP. 1996. The governance and control of voluntary corporate spin-offs. *Strategic Management Journal* 17(1): 25–39.

Shimizu K. 2007. Prospect theory, behavioral theory, and the threat-rigidity thesis: combinative effects on organizational decisions to divest formerly acquired units. *Academy of Management Journal* 50(6): 1495–1514.

Shimizu K, Hitt MA. 2005. What constrains or facilitates divestitures of formerly acquired firms? The effects of organizational inertia. *Journal of Management* 31(1): 50–72.

Shleifer A, Vishny RW. 1989. Management entrenchment: The case of manager-specific investments. *Journal of Financial Economics* 25(1): 123–139.

Tang L, Feldman ER. 2021. The strategic complementarity between M&A and R&D. Working paper.

Teece DJ, Rumelt R, Dosi G, Winter S. 1994. Understanding corporate coherence: theory and evidence. *Journal of Economic Behavior and Organization* 23(1): 1–30.

Vidal E, Mitchell W. 2015. Adding by subtracting: the relationship between performance feedback and resource reconfiguration through divestitures. *Organization Science* 26(4): 1101- 1118.

Vidal E, Mitchell W. 2018. Virtuous or vicious cycles? The role of divestitures as a complementary Penrose effect within resource-based theory. *Strategic Management Journal* 39(1): 131–154.

Villalonga B. 2003. Research roundtable discussion: the diversification discount. Working paper. Available at: https://papers.ssrn.com/sol3/papers.cfm?abstract_id=402220.

Villalonga B, McGahan AM. 2005. The choice among acquisitions, alliances, and divestitures. *Strategic Management Journal* 26(13): 1183–1208.

Weisbach MS. 1995. CEO turnover and the firm's investment decisions. *Journal of Financial Economics* 37(2): 159–188.

Wiedner R, Mantere S. 2019. Cutting the cord: mutual respect, organizational autonomy, and independence in organizational separation processes. *Administrative Science Quarterly* 64(3): 659–693.

Wiersema MF, Bantel KA. 1992. Top management team demography and corporate strategic change. *Academy of Management Journal* 35(1): 91–121.

Zuckerman EW. 1999. The categorical imperative: securities analysts and the illegitimacy discount. *American Journal of Sociology* 104(5): 1398–1438.

Zuckerman EW. 2000. Focusing the corporate product: securities analysts and de-diversification. *Administrative Science Quarterly* 45(3): 591–619.

PART 3

STRATEGIC ENTREPRENEURSHIP AND TECHNOLOGY

Kathleen M. Eisenhardt, Lead

3.0
STRATEGY IN NASCENT MARKETS AND ENTREPRENEURIAL FIRMS

Kathleen M. Eisenhardt

This Part focuses on strategic entrepreneurship with an emphasis on how technologies, industries, and firms emerge, and why some firms (but also technologies and industries) succeed while others do not. Strategic entrepreneurship is a significant topic for several reasons. One is that it seeks to understand some of the most substantial influences on contemporary society—that is, how life-altering technologies (e.g., artificial intelligence, gene sequencing, quantum computing) and game-changing firms (e.g., Amazon, Google, Airbnb, Tesla, Apple) arise and compete. A second reason is that strategic entrepreneurship revitalizes traditional theories of strategy. Strategic entrepreneurship shifts the research conversation from traditional, more static perspectives to dynamic ones. These latter perspectives reflect the information challenges of high uncertainty, such as the inability to interpret surroundings, loss of predictability about the future, and compressed time, that reshape the fundamental assumptions and logics of strategy theories that apply.

The primary context of strategic entrepreneurship is *nascent markets*. Nascent markets are often new markets, but can also be existing markets that are experiencing significant technical, regulatory, or institutional shifts that fundamentally disrupt market order. These settings are characterized by incomplete or fleeting market structures (Eisenhardt, 1989; Fombrun and Rindova, 2001), unclear or contested product definitions (Hargadon and Douglas, 2001), competing technologies (Furr, 2019), ambiguous or uncertain demand (Hiatt and Carlos, 2019; Ozcan and Eisenhardt, 2009), and often a lack of legitimated categories (Navis and Glynn, 2010; Suarez, Grodal, and Gotsopoulos, 2015).

The primary actors in nascent markets are *entrepreneurs*—that is, individuals, ventures, and established firms whose common denominator is emphasis on engagement in creating new businesses and novel ways of competing. Although regulatory and institutional change can matter, technological innovation frequently drives the emergence of nascent markets. By *technological innovation*, we mean the creation of new knowledge or combinations of existing knowledge based in science, mathematics, and/or engineering that may have commercial potential. Innovators can be found in universities, firms, user communities, or even working on their own. Entrepreneurs attempt to realize this commercial potential.

In nascent markets, traditional strategy approaches like positioning and resource logics are often less relevant because they do not fit with the ambiguity, uncertainty, and velocity of these markets (Bingham and Eisenhardt, 2008). Rather, these logics implicitly assume relatively stable or slowly changing markets (i.e., relatively low uncertainty) that can be reasonably interpreted and often well predicted, and seek long-term competitive advantage. In contrast, opportunity logic is germane in nascent markets. This logic centers on shaping or capturing novel, ambiguous, and often fleeting opportunities (Bingham and Eisenhardt, 2008; Bingham, Eisenhardt, and Furr, 2007). Here, although strategy is relevant, so too is the strategy formation process. Indeed, strategy formation is central to why some firms succeed in nascent markets while others do not. By *strategy*, I mean how a firm attempts to create and capture value. Simply, strategy is about winning. *Strategy formation* is then the process by which entrepreneurs and others create or design this strategy.

A salient feature of competitive advantage in nascent markets is its unpredictability. Advantage may be long-term, but it may also end tomorrow. So slogans like, "Snooze, you lose," and "Only the paranoid survive," capture strategy in nascent markets. As recent illustrations like air taxis (Zuzul and Tripsas, 2020), solar power (Furr, 2019), agricultural biotechnology (Moeen and Agarwal, 2017), and fintech (McDonald and Eisenhardt, 2020) reveal, nascent markets are typically business settings in which firms (often but not always ventures) try to successfully navigate a "high velocity" (i.e., uncertain, ambiguous, and often fast-paced) landscape.

A further distinction of nascent markets is between emergent and growth markets. Waves of innovation and change stimulate the birth of *emergent markets*. These markets are young, small, and particularly ill formed. Here the strategic challenge is coping with ambiguity (Davis, Eisenhardt, and Bingham, 2009). By *ambiguity*, I mean very high (i.e., extreme) uncertainty (i.e., Knightian uncertainty) where it is often impossible to identify even basic market features like industry structure. These markets are particularly challenging for strategists because they are open to multiple interpretations and because it is virtually impossible to anticipate when, if ever, these markets will coalesce and gain traction. Ventures and individuals, in particular, may not have the resources to survive this early period.

Some emergent markets, of course, become *growth markets*. Here, the industry structure is congealing. Yet the market is still highly *uncertain* (i.e., while strategists may be able to interpret more accurately than in emergent markets, they still cannot predict well) (Furr and Eisenhardt, 2021). Indeed, growth markets are characterized by high uncertainty and often rapid pace as incumbents innovate, rivals enter, buyers shift, substitutes emerge, and so on (Eisenhardt, 1989). The strategic challenge is coping with high uncertainty and velocity. Strategists can be very successful in growth markets by riding or even triggering a wave of accelerating growth. But they can also make mistakes, fall behind, and fail (Tidhar and Eisenhardt, 2020).

The strategic entrepreneurship chapters share a similar understanding of technology, entrepreneurs, strategy, and nascent markets. They spotlight common topics from past research, such as founding teams, technology, and industry evolution, and organizational actions, such as alliances, acquisitions, and fundraising. At the same time, the chapters are unique. Agarwal and Kim bring a more economics-based lens, and a deep understanding of how industries emerge. Blending strategy and technology perspectives, Furr explores significant new insights regarding both technology evolution and innovation processes. Eisenhardt takes a more organizational perspective that looks inside firms to understand strategy formation in terms of managerial cognition and learning—or, more simply, "thinking" and "doing." Finally, each chapter offers a compelling future agenda, such as understanding the human enterprise broadly (Agarwal and Kim), fresh theories of technology strategy and uncertainty (Furr), and exploration of shaping versus adapting strategies, strategies in nascent markets with distinct "games" (e.g., ecosystem, marketplace), and scaling profitable growth (Eisenhardt).

With this introduction as background, I turn now to this chapter, "Strategy in Nascent Markets and Entrepreneurial Firms." It begins by laying out several themes of the early research, including founding teams and organizational processes. It then continues with a discussion of current work and an agenda for future research.

Early Research

Founding entrepreneurs and teams

Early work on strategy in nascent markets focuses on the *founding entrepreneur*, who is often portrayed as a heroic figure who sets the course for many years. For example, Mintzberg and Waters (1982), who studied Steinberg's grocery chain, attribute much of its success to the unique abilities of its entrepreneur, Sam Steinberg. Later research explores *founding teams*, finding that larger, diverse, and more experienced teams are likely to be more successful (Roure and Maidique, 1986). For example, Eisenhardt and Schoonhoven (1990) find that larger teams, with heterogeneous industry experience (a proxy for a mix of ages and industry backgrounds), who had previously worked together (a proxy for spinoffs) are more likely to start ventures that survive and grow than other teams. Further, the interaction of these superior teams with founding during a growth market is associated with dramatically higher growth than similarly superior teams in emergent and mature markets. Thus, superior teams seem particularly able to take advantage of (and perhaps create) surges in growth. Indeed, the gap between high and low performers amplifies (not dissipates) over time. More broadly, founding teams appear to imprint their strategies on their firms (Boeker, 1989). Finally, these findings are contingent on market competition. Eesley, Hsu, and Roberts (2016) find, for example, that functionally diverse teams have higher performance (e.g., IPO, acquisition) in competitive markets. But when commercialization with a partner is crucial, teams composed solely of scientists and engineers are more effective.

More recent work emphasizes *prior firm and industry affiliations* of founding teams that create templates for later strategies and organizational structures. For example, Benner and Tripsas (2012) study the strategies of entrants into the nascent digital camera industry. They find that industry experience (e.g., computing, photography) influences key strategic choices like product features. In a related study, Beckman (2006) demonstrates that teams whose members previously worked for the same company often converged quickly on exploitative strategies such as ones focused on cost. In contrast, teams with diverse prior employers were slower and more likely to pursue exploration strategies such as ones focused on innovation. These affiliations also affect performance. Beckman (2006), for example, finds that the highest-growth firms combine common and diverse firm backgrounds, reiterating the benefits of diverse yet similar firm backgrounds among team members from earlier research (Eisenhardt and Schoonhoven, 1990; Roure and Maidique, 1986). See Furr (2019) for related insights.

Organizational processes

A second stream centers on organizational processes such as acquisition, product development, internationalization, and broadly, strategic decision-making including speed (Eisenhardt, 1989) and politics (Eisenhardt and Bourgeois, 1988). A particularly well-studied process is *alliance formation*, which is associated with successful performance in nascent markets (Baum, Calabrese, and Silverman, 2000). Much of this work explores why strategists form alliances. Traditional explanations like transaction costs typically fail to capture the strategic and social factors that shape alliance formation in nascent markets. For example, Shan (1990) emphasizes strategic factors like extensive competition, which is associated with alliance formation in nascent biotechnology markets. Eisenhardt and Schoonhoven (1996) confirm earlier work on the strategic advantages of alliance formation, but also add the social basis. That is, strategists pursue alliances when their firms are in vulnerable strategic positions like competing in emergent or highly competitive markets, or attempting pioneering technical strategies. But they are better able to form alliances when they are led by large, experienced, and well-connected top management teams. Finally, Katila, Rosenberger, and Eisenhardt (2008) find that alliances are more likely when firms are able to protect their technology through patenting, trade secrets, or a market presence.

Another well-studied organizational process is *fundraising*. Here, storytelling and symbols of quality and legitimacy—particularly when engaging potential stakeholders—are beneficial (Lounsbury and Glynn, 2001). For example, Zott and Huy (2007) find that projecting symbols of personal credibility (e.g., educational credentials), achievement, and stakeholder quality (e.g., high-status investors) is advantageous when meeting would-be funders. Extending this work, Hallen (2008) finds that well-connected and previously successful entrepreneurs can take a relatively easy path to gain investments. In contrast, less-connected and novice teams must follow a more complex path using symbolic and relational actions termed "catalyzing strategies" to be successful in their fundraising. See also Hallen and Eisenhardt (2012).

Summary

Early research on strategy in nascent markets emphasizes (1) founding entrepreneurs and teams with their often long-lived influence on strategy, organization, and performance, and (2) organizational processes like alliance formation, fundraising, internationalization, product development, and broadly, strategic decision-making. When effective, these processes can become dynamic capabilities that enable flexible strategic actions and improve firm performance (Eisenhardt and Martin, 2000).

Recent Research

Recent research on strategy in nascent markers extends these earlier themes. The prior emphasis on founding teams flows into managerial cognition. While some work continues to examine founding team demographics and relies on cognitive mechanisms, substantial work explores cognition directly. It studies how holistic cognitive structures like identity, analogy, and framing influence strategy formation. Similarly, the emphasis on organizational processes flows into learning processes and their influence on strategy formation. Overall, strategy formation (rather than strategy per se) takes center stage in much of the recent research on strategy in nascent markets.

Managerial cognition

Managerial cognition closely informs the strategy formation process in nascent markets. While this literature includes cognitive processes, it emphasizes cognitive structures that provide integrative representations (Helfat and Peteraf, 2015). Thus, while action matters, this perspective emphasizes "strategizing by thinking"—that is, using cognitive structures to guide formation of strategy (Ott, Eisenhardt, and Bingham, 2017; Raffaelli, Glynn, and Tushman, 2019). In particular, effective strategists rely on holistic representations such as accurate mental models (Gary and Wood, 2011) and relevant analogies (Gavetti, Levinthal, and Rivkin, 2005) to form strategy. These holistic representations can also guide strategists in building multiple activities— relating to demand, supply, logistics, and so forth—that can fit into a complex strategy (i.e., multiple distinct yet connected elements) of activities (Ott and Eisenhardt, 2020).[1] Fit among activities often improves a strategy's effectiveness and inimitability (Rivkin, 2000). There are several relevant cognitive structures.

Broadly, a *mental model* is a simplified cognitive structure by which individuals organize knowledge into a rough representation or map of a more complex reality (Gary and Wood, 2011). Mental models are relevant to strategy because strategists (like other individuals) often think through their choices by using them. The core argument is that strategists with more holistic and accurate mental models form more effective strategies. An illustration is Gary and Wood (2011), who look at the relationship between mental models and performance. Specifically, they study MBA students playing a business simulation. Students with more accurate mental models (i.e., correct understanding of the deep structure of relationships among strategic domains and their causal logic) form better strategies and achieve higher performance. Similarly, Kiss and Barr (2015) study executives in technology-based firms. By analyzing their letters to shareholders, the authors find that executives with more complex models and more causal links are likely to form strategies with more diverse actions and higher performance.

Other research centers on a *holistic vision* that may emerge from formal planning or creative imagination of possible futures. This vision is, in effect, a lay theory that describes the strategist's understanding of strategy and performance. For example, strategists may conceptualize a blueprint of a nascent market with roles for different types of firms. An example is Ozcan and Eisenhardt (2009), who examine strategy formation by entrepreneurs in six mobile gaming ventures as their industry began. Successful strategists envisioned an industry architecture that gave roles to different types of firms, including their own (e.g., publishers [the focus of the study], game developers, brand owners, software platforms, phone makers, and wireless carriers). Guided by their holistic vision, more successful strategists built complete ecosystems and succeeded. In contrast, those strategists without a vision of the nascent market were less successful. They myopically formed incomplete ecosystems, and incremental and fewer relationships.

Other research on cognitive structures explores how strategists use *analogy* to guide strategy formation. An analogy provides a simplified representation of a previous situation to improve understanding of the current one. A classic example comes from the founders of Netflix, who began by using an analogy to an offline rival, Blockbuster, to form key aspects of their business model and related strategy. Analogies can come from various sources, including personal experience (Gavetti and Menon, 2016), personal values (Gavetti and Rivkin, 2007), and knowledge of exemplar firms (Rindova and Kotha, 2001).

A core insight is that analogies can improve strategy formation by providing a set of coherent and relevant touchpoints. For example, Gregoire, Barr, and Shepherd (2010) examine how executives form strategies for introducing new technologies into nascent markets. Those who use analogies were also more able to recognize opportunities and form superior strategies. NK simulations that explore how analogies work indicate that starting with an initial map (like an analogy) accelerates the pace of finding an optimal peak (Gavetti et al., 2005). Yet since analogies are never perfect fits for the target situation, analogies are typically more effective when individuals can distinguish the differences between the analogical source and the target. Further, individuals are better able to make these distinctions when they use several analogies, not just one (Lovallo, Clarke, and Camerer, 2012). Finally, analogies are most useful early on and diminish in value with time (Gavetti *et al.*, 2005). Thus, analogies work best when they fit the target reasonably well, multiple analogies are used, and they are used primarily at the outset of strategy formation.

Other research on cognitive structures emphasizes how strategists may draw on *identity* to form strategy. This identity can be personal for the strategist—such as the conception of "who I am"—or organizational for the firm—such as the conception of "who we are." Personal identity operates by affecting how strategists filter information and incorporate their values and personal motivations as they form strategy. For example, Fauchart and Gruber (2011) develop a typology of founders and their related motivations, such as missionaries who see themselves as drivers of social change. These identities guide subsequent strategy formation. Similarly, Powell and Baker (2014) study strategy formation and find that the personal identities of founders shape their strategic response to adversity. Consistent with their identities, some founders saw adversity as an opportunity and formed strategies that took advantage of the negative situation. Others did not. Organizational identity can also influence strategy formation. For example, Tripsas (2009) observes that the organizational identity of Lynco as a "digital camera" company shaped strategy and influenced the understanding of the firm by its stakeholders. This led to a shared view that any digital photography opportunity could be relevant to Lynco's strategy.

Other research on cognitive structures emphasizes *framing*. Framing is particularly relevant in nascent markets where uncertainty and ambiguity make alternative framings likely (Uzunca, Rigtering, and Ozcan, 2018). For example, Anthony, Nelson, and Tripsas (2016) examine firms in the nascent music synthesizer industry. The four principal firms entered with different framings of product meaning, despite products with similar technical features and pricing. Some framed the synthesizer as a "new musical instrument" for creating unique "synth" sounds while others framed it as an "imitator" of existing instruments. These different product framings, in turn, influenced product positioning strategy. Framing also emerges in the Gurses and Ozcan (2015) study of the successful and unsuccessful strategies of entrepreneurs attempting to introduce pay TV into a highly regulated market. Entrepreneurs who adopted framing that avoided directly attacking incumbents were more successful.

A final concept is *optimal distinctiveness*, by which entrepreneurs attempt to balance between being novel and being similar to what already exists (and is thus legitimate) (Navis and Glynn, 2010). Although not a cognitive structure per se, optimal distinctiveness attempts to find a framing balance point. Hargadon and Douglas (2001), for example, describe how Edison positioned his lightbulb as both novel yet familiar such as by using a lampshade that was consistent with traditional gas lighting, but actually unnecessary for electric lights. Similarly, Santos and Eisenhardt (2009) examine five highly successful firms in the internet boom. They find that the founders of these Internet stars engaged in storytelling and other symbolic actions to convey their optimal distinctiveness relative to the offline world and reinforce their emerging legitimacy. Further, in their study of video gaming, Zhao and colleagues (2017) find that conforming is helpful early on while being unique matters later.

Organizational learning

A second perspective on strategy formation in nascent markets examines learning processes. Processes such as trial and error (Rindova and Kotha, 2001), experimentation (Murray and Tripsas, 2004), and bricolage (Baker and Nelson, 2005) enable strategists to learn about nascent markets and adjust their actions. While thinking occurs, this literature emphasizes "strategizing by doing"—that is, flexibly taking actions and learning (Ott *et al.*, 2017).

Trial-and-error is a learning process by which individuals adjust their behaviors and learn in response to what they do (Bingham and Davis, 2012). Thus, strategists who use trial-and-error (sometimes termed *local search*) form their strategies incrementally based on the results of their actions. Rindova and Kotha (2001), for example, describe the "continuous morphing" of Yahoo as these entrepreneurs gained experience from trial-and-error learning. Similarly, Gavetti and Rivkin (2007) chronicle how entrepreneurs at Lycos blended trial-and-error learning with cognitive structures like analogies to form strategy. Further, Bingham and Eisenhardt (2011) find that more successful strategists codified trial-and-error learning into "simple rules" heuristics for later use as a repeatable formula, while the less successful ones create few if any rules.

Experimentation is another learning process by which executives form strategy. Experimentation research has a long history (Brown and Eisenhardt, 1997; Thomke, 2003; Murray and Tripsas, 2004), but has more recently undergone a resurgence in strategy formation research (Andries, Debackere, and Van Looy, 2013; McDonald and Eisenhardt, 2020; Camuffo *et al.*, 2020). Experimentation involves purposeful and controlled variation of experiences in order to mitigate uncertainties such as from technical, market, or business model sources (Ott *et al.*, 2017). Experimentation can be sequential, parallel, or both (Thomke, 2003; Bremner and Eisenhardt, 2021). Its scale can be modest, like A/B testing, or more substantial, like experiments to decide between business model templates (McDonald and Eisenhardt, 2020). Andries and colleagues (2013), for example, describe how entrepreneurs in high-performing ventures conduct parallel experiments to compare competing business models and choose the best. Finally, experimentation in the form of hypothesis testing (i.e., proposing a hypothesis such as an appropriate price and then confirming it [or not] with data) is at the heart of the lean start-up model (Contigiani and Levinthal, 2019; McDonald and Gao, 2019).

Bricolage is a related process that is commonly observed in nascent markets. Bricolage is simply "making do by applying combinations of resources at hand to new problems and opportunities" (Baker and Nelson, 2005: 333) and is central to effectuation (Reymen *et al.*, 2015; Sarasvathy, 2001). When entrepreneurs engage in bricolage, they may ignore the usual meanings and uses of objects and instead re-imagine them. Thus, they form strategy by taking actions that use existing resources in unexpected ways to create new sources of value. For example, Baker and Nelson (2005) study 29 resource-constrained entrepreneurs. The more effective ones were bricoleurs who created "something from nothing." One illustration is a farmer who reimagined seemingly worthless methane as a product to be sold to a local utility. Next he used this methane to provide heat for a new hydroponic vegetable business, and then later commercially raised fish in the warm water. An important insight is that using bricolage occasionally (selective bricolage) to exploit scalable opportunities works well for forming a successful strategy. In contrast, continuous bricolage (parallel bricolage) creates too much change and so makes it difficult to develop a coherent strategy.

Much of the learning research on strategy formation centers on one or maybe two learning processes. More recent research explores multiple processes at once (Ott and Eisenhardt, 2020). For example, McDonald and Eisenhardt (2020) explore the contingent use of a repertoire of learning approaches. Specifically, they examine strategy formation by focusing on how strategists design effective business models. Their sample is five fintech ventures that begin at about the same time with similar top management teams and professional funding. While trial-and-error, bricolage, and experimentation are all present, so too are new and neglected learning processes. Passive learning is gaining knowledge by pausing for some period of time to simply observe what is happening. Passive learning thus generates the counterintuitive insight that even when trying to form strategy quickly, strategists can move fast and learn more by doing nothing. Learning by borrowing (i.e., imitation) is an often-neglected learning process that can accelerate strategy formation, reduce risk, and conserve resources for use in more value-creating ways. Finally, a broad repertoire of learning processes, contingently applied, is often most effective. For example, experimentation is particularly valuable at "forks in the road" where sharply defined uncertainties can be mitigated or even resolved (McDonald and Eisenhardt, 2020).

Summary

Recent research on strategy in nascent markets emphasizes strategy formation, particularly related to cognitive structures and learning processes. While specific cognitive structures and learning processes are often studied individually, they often appear together in practice (Gavetti and Rivkin, 2007; Ozcan and Eisenhardt, 2009; Santos and Eisenhardt, 2009). Moreover, while cognitive structures can be sources of inertia (Tripsas, 2009; Zuzul and Tripsas, 2020), they can also be useful guides that lead to better and faster strategy formation. Moreover, optimal distinctiveness is often valuable, especially in emergent markets where ambiguity is particularly salient. Finally, a repertoire of learning processes, used contingently, is also likely to lead to better and faster strategy formation.

Future of Research

There are multiple avenues for future research on strategy in nascent markets. One is extension of the strategy formation literature into strategy per se, notably shaping versus adapting strategies. While adapting strategy is consistent with recent research on "thinking" and "doing," shaping strategy is less explored and presents an intriguing contrast with adapting. Another avenue is taking seriously the implications for strategy posed by distinct market types like ecosystems and marketplaces. A third is examining growth—a critical performance outcome in nascent markets, yet also a process that is not well understood.

Shaping versus Adapting Strategies

Two contrasting strategies deal with the uncertainty of nascent markets—shaping and adapting (Rindova and Courtney, 2020). Adapting views uncertainty as a problem to resolve while shaping sees it as an opportunity to exploit. As Rindova and Courtney (2020) note, this distinction between strategies then drives related differences in epistemologies and execution.

Adapting strategies are those that seek to learn about uncertainties and form strategy in response to those insights. Adapting strategies rely on a scientific epistemology, and are "truth seeking" in the sense that they treat uncertainty as exogenous and often resolvable (Rindova and Courtney, 2020). They rely on experimentation and other learning processes (often guided by cognitive structures) to figure out a potentially winning strategy. In contrast, *shaping strategies* are those that seek to exploit uncertainties and form strategy that organizes (or reorganizes) uncertain and ambiguous markets (Eisenhardt and Bingham, 2017). Shaping strategies rest on a design epistemology, and are "truth making" in the sense that they attempt to endogenously structure (or restructure) a market (Rindova and Courtney, 2020). They seek to order relationships, roles, competition, and product categories. Design processes like sensemaking (Cattani *et al.*, 2018), imagining (Rindova and Martins, 2018), and storytelling (Lounsbury and Glynn, 2001) are germane. Other processes like persuasion, timing, and use of soft (and hard) power become relevant in order to entice others to follow the shaper's lead (Ozcan and Eisenhardt, 2009; Santos and Eisenhardt, 2009; Suarez *et al.*, 2015). These processes may focus on particular end states like category creation (Navis and Glynn, 2010; Suarez *et al.*, 2015) and may involve acquisitions and alliances to structure the new market order (Santos and Eisenhardt, 2009; Ozcan and Eisenhardt, 2009). Overall, shaping strategies attempt to restructure both the industry architecture and the cognitive understanding of that architecture.

The shaping-versus-adapting dichotomy suggests several paths for future research. A key one is unpacking the design processes that underlie the less-explored shaping strategy. For example: How does imagination work? How do individuals gain break-through insights? Schilling (2018) argues that superior strategists engage in more abstract thinking than others. Is this true? Ott and Eisenhardt (2020) note the importance of integrative thinking and creativity. Yet how do these processes operate in strategy formation? What is not a shaping strategy?

Another possibility is to explore when strategists shape versus adapt. On the one hand, some work argues that shaping is relevant in ambiguous markets where uncertainty is extreme (Davis *et al.*, 2009). Here there are more degrees of freedom, and more scope for new industry architectures, particularly those shaped by skilled executives who prefer to manage uncertainty over ambiguity. In support, for example, Ozcan and Eisenhardt (2009) find that the initial entrants into the emergent mobile gaming market were able to be shapers while later entrants were adapters to the now existing architecture of what had become a growth market. Thus, the choice to shape versus adapt depends on market uncertainty and ambiguity. On the other hand, others argue that shaping is a strategic choice that strategists make based on factors like their attitude toward uncertainty (Rindova and Courtney, 2020). For example, Zuzul and Tripsas (2020) describe how some strategists in the nascent air taxi market chose to be "revolutionaries" and so shapers while others chose to be "discoverers" and so adapters. Similarly, Rindova and Martins (2018) argue that value-driven strategies are often distinctive and, thus, more likely to involve shaping. An important research path is exploring these differing arguments and examining how strategists might blend shaping and adapting strategies, oscillate between them, or shape some aspects of strategy but not others. This path may be fruitful because many strategists likely mix shaping and adapting.

A third path is to sharpen how to form more successful shaping strategies. On the one hand, high-level accounts of shaping strategies often return to the hero-entrepreneur of early research on strategy in nascent markets by describing icons like Charlie Merrill, Elon Musk, and Walt Disney (Gavetti and Menon, 2016; Felin and Zenger, 2017). Yet these accounts are often based on relatively thin, often distant, and even anecdotal accounts. Do these accounts miss the degree to which these iconic executives blend shaping with adapting? Do they miss the challenges of shaping strategies that may be glossed over in mythic stories? On the other hand, more granular and proximate accounts suggest that shaping strategies are not easy to enact (Kalkus *et al.*, 2020). For example, shapers are prone to strategic inertia and perform poorly in the Zuzul and Tripsas (2020) study of the nascent air taxi market. When the primary strategist's identity (and motivation) was as a revolutionary shaper, firms remained locked into an inflexible (even inertial) shaping strategy. In contrast, when the primary strategist's identity was as an adaptive discoverer seeking to build a viable enterprise, firms successfully adjusted strategy as events unfolded and learning occurred. These observations suggest the relevance of questions such as, How do executives form successful strategies? What are the major pitfalls of shaping strategies?

Types of nascent markets

Another avenue for future research is to explore strategies and strategy formation processes in different types of nascent markets. Here the notion is that superior strategists play the "right" game (e.g., marketplace, product, ecosystem) (Eisenhardt and Bingham, 2017). They recognize the underlying economics of distinct types of markets and business models, and form strategies accordingly. Yet prior research often posits broad frameworks like positioning, resource, and opportunity that fail to consider the specific mechanisms at work in particular types of markets.

One such market type is an *ecosystem*. Here complementors as well as upstream and downstream firms influence the strategy of a focal firm by expanding the relevant technical and competitive dynamics (Adner and Kapoor, 2010). Innovations, for example, may require co-invention and cooperation with partners and suppliers (Ozcan and Hannah, 2020). Yet incentives can be problematic. Casadesus-Masanell and Yoffie (2007), for example, analyze two complementors that depend on each other for value creation, but have conflicting preferences regarding pricing and new product timing. Thus, an attractive technology for one partner may not work well for the other. Such incentive misalignments can undermine even the formation of an ecosystem (Ozcan and Santos, 2015). Research questions include: How do these collaborations emerge? What makes them successful? Another research question might ask about the conditions under which particular ecosystem strategies will be preferred. As Hannah and Eisenhardt (2018) observe in their study of the emergent residential solar market, ecosystems have multiple winning strategies. Their three high-performing firms, for example, pursued different strategies. The successful component strategist excelled in one part of the ecosystem, but also developed productive collaborative relationships with complementors in the other components. Another followed a systems strategy and so entered all components. A third firm was a bottleneck strategist that moved around the ecosystem to ensure favorable positioning in the most critical component over time. While these descriptions are compelling, more deeply: How do these strategies work? When should each be used?

Another market type is one with *strong institutional forces*, such as commercial markets that also involve the government, like energy and defense, or involve other institutions like the medical profession and universities. These markets are often critical for meeting grand challenges such as addressing climate change and democratizing education (Volmar and Eisenhardt, 2020). Prior work finds that firms in these markets typically require hybrid organizations and strategies that combine institutional logics, often in novel ways. Battilana and Dorado (2010), for example, compare two commercial microfinance organizations and identify the importance of hiring and socialization processes. These processes can create a common identity that balances social mission and commercial logics. Similarly, Pache and Santos (2013) explore how social welfare organizations that begin with one logic (social mission or commercial) proceed to then adopt attributes of the other. Further research questions could ask about the viability of other logic combinations, such as medical, education, or defense logics with commercial. How might these combinations be structured so that they are more likely to succeed? Another path is to ask: How can commercial firms influence strong institutions? Gao and McDonald (2020) make a start in looking at how personal genomics firms attempt to work with federal agencies to influence regulatory policy, and succeed with a strategy of regulatory co-creation. There is, however, more research to do. Another path is to examine how firms with different institutional logics like social mission and commercial might compete with one another for users and resources. For example, how do organizations with a social mission compete for users against commercial firms?

Another market type is *platforms* such as marketplaces like Airbnb and Uber and product platforms like Intuit Quickbooks and iTunes. Platforms are central to many high-growth companies (e.g., Google, Facebook, Apple) and have distinct economics like network effects that influence strategy. While there is progress on understanding the strategy of established platforms, less is known about the initial strategies by which these platforms begin (often in nascent markets). Ott and Eisenhardt (2020) suggest the importance of decision weaving—that is, starting with the bottleneck domain (often supply) and then sequentially focusing on other strategic domains before attempting to scale dramatic growth. But does decision weaving work in other marketplaces? In contrast with marketplaces, product platforms seem to begin with different strategic moves, and depend upon first building a strong product that has stand-alone value. What are these strategic moves? Is a strong product a necessary antecedent?

Other market types include those with extreme technology challenges, like space travel (e.g., SpaceX, Blue Origin), and tech-enabled businesses that combine AI and physical goods such that inventory and profitable unit economics are critical (e.g., StitchFix, Rent-the-Runway) (Tidhar and Eisenhardt, 2020). The overall point is that nascent markets involve distinct economic "games" such that the rules of strategy and strategy formation may be quite different across games. The research questions here (and others) might then broadly answer: What are the rules of particular games? How can entrepreneurs succeed in playing a given game?

Growth processes of firms

A third opportunity for future research is exploring the growth process of firms in nascent markets. Traditional strategic logics like positioning and resources emphasize profitability over growth or growth by entering adjacencies in modestly changing markets, respectively. Yet growth is a common and often primary objective of firms in nascent markets. Indeed, a well-known mantra is "grow or die." Some work on nascent markets emphasizes antecedents of growth like team characteristics (Beckman, 2006; Eisenhardt and Schoonhoven, 1990), while other work highlights outcomes like routinizing structures (DeSantola and Gulati, 2017). Yet the process of *how* firms grow remains underexplored. Some recent work points to the importance of resolving successive bottlenecks like dominant design and product-market fit that unlock market growth and spur the growth of individual firms (Eisenhardt and Bingham, 2017; Bremner and Eisenhardt, 2021). Deeper examination of bottlenecks is one path forward. For example: What precisely is a bottleneck? Do all firms in a given nascent market face the same bottlenecks? Another path is to study the transition from a venture (a well-studied phenomenon) to an adolescent firm (an understudied next step). For example: What are the critical changes that occur in this transition? At what point does profitability, not just growth, become relevant? How do firms scale, and so achieve profitable growth?

Conclusion

This chapter centers on strategy in nascent markets, a unique entrepreneurial setting characterized by an ambiguous, uncertain, and fast-paced landscape. Earlier and recent research explores top management teams and their cognitive structures, and organizational and learning processes. Fruitful next steps likely focus on alternative strategies (shaping vs. adapting) in nascent markets, unpacking the implications of the underlying "games" in different types of nascent markets, and revealing the growth of firms. Overall, an exciting future lies ahead for one of the most critical and richest areas of strategy.

Note

1. In more certain markets where positioning and leverage logics are relevant, a distinction is made between choosing strategy and then implementing it. This distinction is, however, not germane in nascent markets, where they blend together in strategy formation. Indeed, unique activities are central to the ultimate strategy, and the activity system is the means by which value is created. We appreciate an editor raising this point.

References

Adner R, Kapoor R. 2010. Value creation in innovation ecosystems: how the structure of technological interdependence affects firm performance in new technology generations. *Strategic Management Journal* 30(3): 306–333.

Andries P, Debackere K, Van Looy B. 2013. Simultaneous experimentation as a learning strategy: business model development under uncertainty. *Strategic Entrepreneurship Journal* 7: 288–310.

Anthony C, Nelson A, Tripsas M. 2016. "Who are you? … I really wanna know": product meaning and competitive positioning in the nascent synthesizer industry. *Strategy Science* 1: 163–183.

Baker T, Nelson RE. 2005. Creating something from nothing: resource construction through entrepreneurial bricolage. *Administrative Science Quarterly* **50**(3): 329–366.

Battilana J, Dorado S. 2010. Building sustainable hybrid organizations: the case of commercial microfinance organizations. *Academy of Management Journal* **53**(6): 1419–1440.

Baum JAC, Calabrese T, Silverman BS. 2000. Don't go it alone: alliance network composition and startups' performance in Canadian biotechnology. *Strategic Management Journal* **21**: 267–294.

Beckman CM. 2006. The influence of founding team company affiliations on firm behavior. *Academy of Management Journal* **49**(4): 741.

Benner MJ, Tripsas M. 2012. The influence of prior industry affiliation on framing in nascent industries: the evolution of digital cameras. *Strategic Management Journal* **33**(3): 277–302.

Bingham CB, Davis JP. 2012. Learning sequences: their existence, effect and evolution. *Academy of Management Journal* **55**(3): 611–641.

Bingham CB, Eisenhardt KM. 2008. Position, leverage, and opportunity: a typology of strategic logics linking resources with competitive advantage. *Managerial Decisions and Economics* **29**(2/3): 241–256.

Bingham CB, Eisenhardt KM. 2011. Rational heuristics: the "simple rules" that strategists learn from process experience. *Strategic Management Journal* **32**(13): 1437–1464.

Bingham CB, Eisenhardt KM, Furr NR. 2007. What makes a process a capability? Heuristics, strategy, and effective capture of opportunities. *Strategic Entrepreneurship Journal* **1**(November): 27–47.

Boeker W. 1989. Strategic change: the effects of founding and history. *Academy of Management Journal* **32**: 489–515.

Bremner RP, Eisenhardt KM. 2021. Organizing form, experimentation, and performance: innovation lessons from the nascent civilian drone industry. *Organization Science*, conditional acceptance.

Brown SL, Eisenhardt KM. 1997. The art of continuous change: linking complexity theory and time-paced evolution in relentlessly shifting organizations. *Administrative Science Quarterly* **42**(1): 1–34.

Camuffo A, Cordova A, Gambardella A, Spina C. 2020. A scientific approach to entrepreneurial decision making: evidence from a randomized control trial. *Management Science* **66**(2): 564–586.

Casadesus-Masanell R, Yoffie D. 2007. Wintel: cooperation and conflict. *Management Science* **53**: 584–598.

Cattani G, Sands D, Porac J, Greenberg J. 2018. Competitive sensemaking in value creation and capture. *Strategy Science* **3**: 632–657.

Contigiani A, Levinthal DA. 2019. Situating the construct of lean start-up: adjacent conversations and possible future directions. *Industrial and Corporate Change* **28**(3): 551–564.

Davis JP, Eisenhardt KM, Bingham CB. 2009. Optimal structure, market dynamism, and the strategy of simple rules. *Administrative Science Quarterly* **54**(3): 413–452.

DeSantola A, Gulati R. 2017. Scaling: organizing and growth in entrepreneurial ventures. *Academy of Management Annals* **11**(2): 640–668.

Eesley CE, Hsu DH, Roberts EB. 2016. The contingent effects of top management teams on venture performance: aligning founding team composition with innovation strategy and commercialization environment. *Strategic Management Journal* **35**(12): 1798–1817.

Eisenhardt KM. 1989. Making fast strategic decisions in high-velocity environments. *Academy of Management Journal* **32**(3): 543–576.

Eisenhardt KM, Bingham CB. 2017. Superior strategy in entrepreneurial settings: Thinking, doing, and the logic of opportunity. *Strategy Science* **2**(4): 246–257.

Eisenhardt KM. Bourgeois LJ III. 1988. Politics of strategic decision making in high-velocity environments: towards a mid-range theory. *Academy of Management Journal* 31(4): 737–770.

Eisenhardt KM, Martin JA. 2000. Dynamic capabilities: what are they? *Strategic Management Journal* 21: 1105–1121.

Eisenhardt KM, Schoonhoven CB. 1990. Organizational growth: linking founding team, strategy, environment, and growth among U.S. semiconductor ventures, 1978–1988. *Administrative Science Quarterly* 35(3): 504–529.

Eisenhardt KM, Schoonhoven CB. 1996. Resource-based view of strategic alliance formation: strategic and social effects in entrepreneurial firms. *Organization Science* 7: 136–150.

Fauchart E, Gruber M. 2011. Darwinians, communitarians, and missionaries: the role of founder identity in entrepreneurship. *Academy of Management Journal* 54(5): 935–957.

Felin T, Zenger TR. 2017. The theory-based view: economic actors as theorists. *Strategy Science* 2: 258–271.

Fombrun CJ, Rindova VP. 2001. Fanning the flame: corporate reputations as social constructions of performance. In *Constructing Markets and Industries*. Oxford University Press: New York, NY; 5–14.

Furr NR. 2019. Product adaptation during new industry emergence: the role of the start-up team pre-entry experience. *Organization Science* 30(5): 1076–1096.

Furr NR, Eisenhardt KM. 2021. Strategy and uncertainty: resource-based view, strategy-creation view and the hybrid between them. *Journal of Management*: forthcoming.

Gao C, McDonald R. 2020. Shaping nascent industries: innovation strategy and regulatory uncertainty in personal genomics. Working paper, University of Michigan.

Gary MS, Wood RE. 2011. Mental models, decision rules, and performance heterogeneity. *Strategic Management Journal* 32(6): 569–594.

Gavetti G, Levinthal D, Rivkin JW. 2005. Strategy making in novel and complex worlds: the power of analogy. *Strategic Management Journal* 26(8): 691–712.

Gavetti G, Menon A. 2016. Evolution cum agency: toward a model of strategic foresight. *Strategy Science* 1(3): 207–233.

Gavetti G, Rivkin JW. 2007. On the origin of strategy: action and cognition over time. *Organization Science* 18(3): 420–439.

Gregoire D, Barr P, Shepherd D. 2010. Cognitive processes of opportunity recognition: the role of structural alignment. *Organization Science* 21: 413–431.

Gurses K, Ozcan P. 2015. Entrepreneurship in regulated markets: framing contests and collective action to introduce Pay TV in the U.S. *Academy of Management Journal* 58(6): 1709–1739.

Hallen BL. 2008. The causes and consequences of initial network positions of new organizations: from whom entrepreneurs receive investments. *Administrative Science Quarterly* 53: 685–718.

Hallen BL, Eisenhardt KM. 2012. Catalyzing strategies and efficient tie formation: how entrepreneurial firms obtain investment ties. *Academy of Management Journal* 55(1): 35–70.

Hannah D, Eisenhardt KM. 2018. How firms navigate cooperation and competition in nascent ecosystems. *Strategic Management Journal* 39: 3163–3192.

Hargadon AB, Douglas Y. 2001. When innovations meet institutions: Edison and the design of the electric light. *Administrative Science Quarterly* 46(3): 476–501.

Helfat CE, Peteraf MA. 2015. Managerial cognitive capabilities and the microfoundations of dynamic capabilities. *Strategic Management Journal* 36(6): 831–850.

Hiatt SR, Carlos WC. 2019. From farms to fuel tanks: stakeholder framing contests and entrepreneurship in the emergent U.S. biodiesel market. *Strategic Management Journal* 40(6): 865–893.

Kalkus KM, Eisenhardt KM, Tidhar R, Volmar E. 2020. Decoding the double helix: shaping v. adapting strategies in the U.S. personal genomics market. *Academy of Management Proceedings* 1: 16652–16662.

Katila R, Rosenberger J, Eisenhardt KM. 2008. Swimming with sharks: technology ventures and corporate relationships. *Administrative Science Quarterly* 53: 295–332.

Kiss AN, Barr PS. 2015. New venture strategic adaptation: the interplay of belief structures and industry context. *Strategic Management Journal* 36(8): 1245–1263.

Lounsbury M, Glynn MA. 2001. Cultural entrepreneurship: stories, legitimacy, and the acquisition of resources. *Strategic Management Journal* 22: 545–564.

Lovallo D, Clarke C, Camerer C. 2012. Robust analogizing and the outside view: two empirical tests of case-based decision making. *Strategic Management Journal* 33(5): 496–512.

McDonald RM, Eisenhardt KM. 2020. Parallel play: startups, nascent markets, and effective business-model design. *Administrative Science Quarterly* 65(2): 483–523.

McDonald RM, Gao C. 2019. Pivoting isn't enough? Managing strategic reorientation in new ventures. *Organization Science* 30: 1289–1318.

Mintzberg H, Waters J. 1982. Tracking entrepreneurial strategy. *Academy of Management Journal* 25: 465–499.

Moeen M, Agarwal R. 2017. Incubation of an industry: heterogenous knowledge bases and modes of value capture. *Strategic Management Journal* 38(3): 566–587.

Murray F, Tripsas M. 2004. The exploratory processes of entrepreneurial firms: the role of purposeful experimentation. *Advances in Strategic Management* 21: 45–76.

Navis C, Glynn MA. 2010. How new market categories emerge: temporal dynamics of legitimacy, identity, and entrepreneurship in satellite radio, 1990–2005. *Administrative Science Quarterly* 55: 439–471.

Ott TE, Eisenhardt KM. 2020. Decision weaving: forming novel, complex strategy in entrepreneurial settings. *Strategic Management Journal*, 41(12): 2275-2314.

Ott TE, Eisenhardt KM, Bingham CB. 2017. Strategy formation in entrepreneurial settings: past insights and future directions. *Strategic Entrepreneurship Journal* 11(3): 306–325.

Ozcan P, Eisenhardt KM. 2009. Origin of alliance portfolios: entrepreneurs, network strategies, and firm performance. *Academy of Management Journal* 52(2): 246–279.

Ozcan P, Hannah D. 2020. Forced ecosystems and digital stepchildren: reconfiguring advertising suppliers to realize disruptive social media technology. *Strategy Science* 5(3): 193–217.

Ozcan P, Santos F. 2015. The market that never was: turf wars and failed alliances in mobile payments. *Strategic Management Journal* 36(10): 1486–1512.

Pache A-C, Santos F. 2013. Inside the hybrid organization: selective coupling as a response to competing institutional logics. *Academy of Management Journal* 56(4): 972–1001.

Powell E, Baker T. 2014. It's what you make of it: founder identity and enacting strategic responses to adversity. *Academy of Management Journal* 57(5): 1406–1433.

Raffaelli R, Glynn MA, Tushman M. 2019. Frame flexibility: the role of cognitive and emotional framing in innovation adoption by incumbent firms. *Strategic Management Journal* 40(7): 1013–1039.

Reymen IMMJ, Andries P, Berends H, Mauer R, Stephan U, van Burg E. 2015. Understanding dynamics of strategic decision-making in venture creation: a process study of effectuation and causation. *Strategic Entrepreneurship Journal* 9(4): 351–379.

Rindova VP, Courtney H. 2020. Shape or adapt: knowledge problems, epistemologies and strategic postures under Knightian uncertainty. *Academy of Management Review*, forthcoming.

Rindova VP, Kotha S. 2001. Continuous "morphing": competing through dynamic capabilities, form, and function. *Academy of Management Journal* 44(6): 1263–1280.

Rindova VP, Martins LL. 2018. From values to value: value rationality and the creation of great strategies. *Strategy Science* 3(1): 323–334.

Rivkin JW. 2000. Imitation of complex strategies. *Management Science* 46(6): 824–844.

Roure J, Maidique MA. 1986. Linking prefunding factors and venture success: an exploratory study. *Journal of Business Venturing* 1: 295–306.

Santos FM, Eisenhardt KM. 2009. Constructing markets and shaping boundaries: entrepreneurial power in nascent fields. *Academy of Management Journal* 52(4): 643–671.

Sarasvathy S. 2001. Causation and effectuation: toward a theoretical shift from economic inevitability to entrepreneurial contingency. *Academy of Management Review* 26(2): 243–263.

Schilling MA. 2018. The cognitive foundations of visionary strategy. *Strategy Science* 3: 335–342.

Shan W. 1990. An empirical analysis of organizational strategies by entrepreneurial high-technology firms. *Strategic Management Journal* 11: 129–139.

Suarez F, Grodal S, Gotsopoulos A. 2015. Perfect timing? Dominant category, dominant design, and the window of opportunity for firm entry. *Strategic Management Journal* 36: 437–448.

Thomke SH. 2003. *Experimentation Matters: Unlocking the Potential of New Technologies for Innovation*. Harvard Business Press, Cambridge, MA.

Tidhar R, Eisenhardt KM. 2020. Measure twice, cut once: scaling novel business models in the nascent online fashion industry. Working paper, Stanford University.

Tripsas M. 2009. Technology, identity, and inertia through the lens of "the digital photography company." *Organization Science* 20(2): 440–461.

Uzunca B, Rigtering JPC, Ozcan P. 2018. Sharing and shaping: A cross-country comparison of how sharing economy firms shape their institutional environment to gain legitimacy. *Academy of Management Discoveries* 4(3): 248–272.

Volmar E, Eisenhardt KM. 2020. Mavericks and diplomats: contrasting paths for strategy formation in nascent markets with strong institutional forces. Working paper, Stanford University.

Zhao EY, Fisher G, Lounsbury M, Miller D. 2017. Optimal distinctiveness: broadening the interface between institutional theory and strategic management. *Strategic Management Journal* 38: 93–113.

Zott C, Huy Q. 2007. Symbolic emphasizing: how entrepreneurs use symbolism to acquire resources. *Administrative Science Quarterly* 52: 70–105.

Zuzul T, Tripsas M. 2020. Start-up inertia vs. flexibility: the role of founder identity in a nascent industry. *Administrative Science Quarterly* 65: 395–433.

3.1

INDUSTRY EMERGENCE: A MARKETS AND ENTERPRISE PERSPECTIVE

Rajshree Agarwal and Seojin Kim

> *The more you know, the more you know what you don't know.*
> —*Sir Anthony Leggett, 2003 Nobel Laureate in Physics* (**Leggett, 2007**)

The emergence of industries has been an enduring theme in scholarly research. At the macro level, scholars have identified stages of emergence based on patterns of firm entry and exit, rates and types of innovation, and heterogeneity in demand. At the micro level, scholars have examined fountainheads of emergence—be they established firms seeking to renew themselves or new ventures formed by individuals and teams—as each seeks to leverage preentry knowledge to create and grow altogether new industries and technologies. As reflected in the quote at the beginning of the chapter, our intent here is to build on what we know, and to identify what is yet unknown but that which represents fruitful future avenues. Our stylized depiction of insights uses a "market" and an "enterprise" perspective, with a focus on how one engine of change interacts and informs the other for path-dependent outcomes in industry emergence. We define *markets* in the broadest sense of trade—to capture interactions among any two parties for exchange of knowledge, products, or services. Similarly, the term *enterprise* denotes purposeful activity undertaken by individuals, teams, or firms. The synthesis across research using different theoretical perspectives, methodologies, and levels of analysis sets the stage for a discussion of theoretical puzzles deserving scholarly attention.

What Do We Know?

From decades of work in industry evolution

An *industry* is defined as a distinct group of enterprises that engage in the provision of a specific product or service. At base is a technological system that brings together component pieces in specific ways that characterize the product or service. Industry evolution literature took steam in the 1980s following seminal work in economics (Gort and Klepper, 1982), sociology (Hannan and Freeman, 1977), and technology management (Abernathy and Utterback, 1978). Here we distill three critical insights from four decades of research, focusing on the nascent (pregrowth) stages of industry evolution.

Insight 1: Industries emerge through distinct temporal stages of incubation, pre-firm takeoff, and pre-sales takeoff

Nascent industries exhibit three distinctive developmental stages: incubation, pre-firm takeoff, and pre-sales takeoff (Agarwal and Bayus, 2002; Moeen and Agarwal, 2017). The incubation period is the period between a trigger event—a technological discovery or identification of unmet need—and the first commercial introduction of a product (Agarwal, Moeen, and Shah, 2017; Moeen and Agarwal, 2017). Sampling from successful industries (i.e., industries that achieved high growth) introduced during the 20th century, scholars document the incubation period to have an average duration of approximately 30 years, though with notable variation across industries (Agarwal and Bayus, 2002; Golder, Shacham, and Mitra, 2009). Until recently, the incubation period did not garner significant scholarly attention, in part because of the implicit assumption that it consisted of lone inventors. However, the decades of the incubation period are characterized by vibrant enterprising activity (Moeen, Agarwal, and Shah, 2020) that is critical to the endogenous progression to commercialization. In agricultural biotechnology, for example, three times more firms made technological investments during the incubation period than firms that ultimately commercialized a product (Moeen and Agarwal 2017).

The second stage of pre-firm takeoff commences with commercialization and ends with a sharp "hockey-stick" increase in the number of firms. Across 46 industries, Agarwal and Gort (2001) report this stage to last on average 14 years, though with high variation. Though the technology embodied in these first instances of commercialization represent significant breakthroughs, the often primitive designs during this "monopoly" period cater largely to few users, resulting in very low overall industry sales (Abernathy and Utterback, 1978).

The third nascent stage of pre-sales takeoff begins with a stark increase in the number of commercializing firms (Gort and Klepper, 1982), and ends with a similar sharp hockey-stick pattern in industry sales. Scholars note that across numerous nascent industries, firm takeoff always precedes sales takeoff (Agarwal and Bayus, 2002). Accelerated net entry rates are characterized by heterogeneous firms whose different experiences and knowledge foster the inflows of diverse information and capabilities (Gort and Klepper, 1982; Klepper and Simons, 2000). Such diversity legitimizes the industry due to increased density (Hannan and Freeman, 1977) that enables social sensemaking (Anthony, Nelson, and Tripsas, 2016) and product innovation (Kapoor and Furr, 2015; Rosenberg, 1982), which in turn grows user bases with different design features (Abernathy and Utterback, 1978; Agarwal and Bayus, 2002), resulting in sales takeoff. Scholars have documented the mean duration to be about eight years, again with substantial variance (Agarwal and Bayus, 2002). Industries that experience sales takeoff then transition into growth and maturity periods.

Insight 2: Experimentation and knowledge acquisition/release by enterprising actors enable the building of industries through the building of knowledge.

This insight centers on what activities enable the above transitions of an industry from one stage to another. Importantly, relative to growth and mature industries, nascent industries are characterized by high levels of uncertainty of the industry's structural fundamentals (Moeen *et al.*, 2020). Building on Knight's (1921) definition of uncertainty as characterized by a state of partial knowledge, Moeen *et al.*'s (2020) synthesis of the literature on nascent industries links enterprising activity to resolution of four dimensions of uncertainty that enable transitions in nascent stages. These dimensions include technology, demand, ecosystem, and institutions.[1]

Uncertainty resolution is not exogenous; rather, enterprising actors purposefully undertake knowledge creation and exchange within and across the four environmental dimensions. It is only if and when such activities are successful that industries may transition through stages of emergence and achieve subsequent growth. Enterprising actors include individuals and firms that have prerequisite knowledge and capabilities, but also extend to universities and government agencies. Each generates new knowledge, either independently or in collaboration with other actors. Aggregation mechanisms facilitate knowledge exchange; these include market transactions for economic gain or spillover mechanisms that diffuse knowledge in uncompensated ways. For instance, in the case of the nascent bionic prosthetic market (Kim, Agarwal, and Goldfarb, 2020), knowledge aggregation occurred not only through interorganizational transactions but also through knowledge spillovers from firms that incubated the core technology but were focused on other downstream markets. Also, knowledge aggregation required coordinated research and development (R&D) efforts among diverse actors including start-ups, incumbents, universities, and the Department of Defense.

Furthermore, actors focus on different dimensions of uncertainty across stages. Integrating across research that has collectively examined almost 100 single-industry case studies, Moeen *et al.* (2020) theorize that during incubation, enterprising actors focus attention on building the technological and demand knowledge. Relatedly, aggregation mechanisms are used to weave disparate pieces of knowledge; while some of these represent transactions that can be priced, many transactions rely on open and reciprocal sharing norms. After commercialization, there is an increase in attention to ecosystem and institutional uncertainty and interdependencies across the four dimensions. During the pre-firm and pre-sales takeoff stages, aggregation mechanisms shift toward market-based exchange and appropriability. Importantly, while open knowledge sharing may still be observed, competitive and selection pressures significantly increase as industries advance to sales takeoff.

Insight 3: Nascent industries represent vibrant markets for commercialization ("end" products and services), "knowledge/resources" (alliances), and corporate control (acquisitions)

The early industry evolution literature focused on markets for commercialization, consistent with their definition and sampling of industry actors as only those who commercialized end products and services. Accordingly, scholars drew on diverse theoretical lenses to investigate entry, competition, and exit of commercializing firms (Gort and Klepper, 1982; Hannan and Freeman, 1977). During pre-firm takeoff and pre-sale takeoff, increased entry of firms results in an inflow of new information (Gort and Klepper, 1982), selection of firms (Hannan and Freeman, 1977), vigorous technological experimentation and product innovation (Abernathy and Utterback, 1978), and growth in demand size (Agarwal and Bayus, 2002).

Early industry evolution scholars often invoked the limited size of the market prior to sales takeoff to assume that markets for technology/resources (e.g., licensing, alliances) or corporate control (e.g., acquisitions) were largely absent during industry emergence stages (Stigler, 1957; Gort and Klepper 1982).[2] This assumption seemed justifiable, given that commercializing firms—diversifying entrants and start-ups alike—had integrated capabilities upon entry (Helfat, 2015; Qian, Agarwal, and Hoetker, 2012). However, recent work on incubation shows such integration was enabled by extensive use of markets for technology/resources and corporate control in configuring capabilities (Moeen, 2017; Moeen and Mitchell, 2020). Postcommercialization, firms rely on knowledge alliances with existing suppliers (Hoetker, 2005) and owners of requisite complementary assets (Kapoor and Furr, 2015).

Inclusion of these markets expands enterprising actors beyond those who commercialized products and services, and additionally allows for the possibility that markets are leveraged by entrants for collaboration, not just competition. Well-functioning markets for technology/resources and corporate control are important aggregation mechanisms. Hence, firm strategy and performance are better understood through firm positioning in the evolving industry structure: heterogeneous "investing" firms then become important conduits for diverse sets of capabilities to coalesce and form the knowledge base of new industries.

Moreover, vibrant markets for technology/resources and corporate control provide firms with alternative channels to create and capture value (Conti, Gambardella, and Novelli, 2019; Moeen and Agarwal, 2017). Not only can firms capture value while building the industry knowledge base through alliances or seeking acquisitions by commercializing firms (Moeen and Mitchell, 2020), they may also use these markets to shape organizational scope, with subsequent impact on nascent industry structures. As Conti et al. (2019) suggest, innovative firms in the emerging laser industry chose to "specialize in knowledge generality," eschewing direct market entry in favor of intermediate markets. Similarly, in the nascent mobile money industry, startups from developing countries created and traded their unique and valuable bundled knowledge to build mobile money platforms through alliances with established mobile network operators, and their strategy resulted in far greater impact on global sales takeoff than strategies that relied on internal expansion (Wormald *et al.*, 2021).

From decades of work on founding and top management teams

Firms do not make decisions; people do. At the heart of organizations contributing to industry emergence are talented and purposeful individuals in action. These individuals, be they founders of new ventures or intrapreneurs in established firms, bring into industries their human capital—defined as knowledge, ideas, and skills gained from prior education and experience. While there is a dearth of research on intrapreneurs, a growing body of work has examined the role of founders in industry emergence. The next three insights delve deeper into individuals and teams as microfoundations of firm and industry emergence.

Insight 4: The knowledge context of founders affects their identification of ideas, access to complementary assets, and conditions through which they can appropriate value

While early industry evolution scholars focused on the firm level to distinguish between diversifying entrants and start-ups (Carroll *et al.*, 1996; Klepper and Simons, 2000), later scholars recognized that prior experience of founders also benefits start-ups (Agarwal and Shah, 2014). As noted in Insight 2 earlier, heterogeneity of enterprising actors is a critical element for building an industry's knowledge base and resolving uncertainty. Parallel literature streams in academic, employee, and user entrepreneurship noted these three important knowledge contexts. Specifically, founders of new ventures include scientists who apply research conducted in university settings, employees who identify technological and market opportunities when working in industrial firms, and users who seek to address their unmet needs through innovation. Agarwal and Shah (2014) integrate across these literature streams and connect the different knowledge contexts of entrepreneurship and associated human capital of founders to the industry life cycle. Expanding on Teece's (1986) framework on profiting from innovation, Agarwal and Shah note that endogenous increases in appropriability regimes and importance of complementary assets as industries evolve from inception to maturity have important implications for entry by founders from each knowledge context, whether their start-ups have complementary or competing relationships with established firms, and firm performance.

When technological discoveries in university settings serve as a trigger for industry incubation, scientists who develop these inventions for commercial application initially bring their open sharing norms to build knowledge, and form start-ups during the pre-firm and pre-sales takeoff stages to create and capture value (Merton, 1973; Sanderson and Simons, 2014). When unmet needs trigger industry incubation, users innovate and share knowledge within user communities, and later create firms to capitalize on a wider demand for their products and services (Franke and Shah, 2003; Mody, 2006). Moreover, employees in firm settings benefit from access to either R&D or unmet customer needs, and additionally have operational knowledge and social networks to create new ventures to capitalize on their knowledge (Holbrook et al., 2000).

Heterogeneity in the founder knowledge context has two direct implications for industry emergence. First, differences in founders' prior knowledge bases imply that different individuals may perceive different applications for the same underlying technology, enabling greater diversity in use. For example, emerging 3D technology was used by entrepreneurs with different prior knowledge to pursue different entrepreneurial opportunities (Shane, 2000). Similarly, emerging commercial drone manufacturers draw on different prior experiences and exhibit significant differences in the features included in their designs (Shermon and Moeen, 2020). Second, different prior knowledge bases can complement each other—not only to resolve different dimensions of uncertainty, but also as components that fit together to form solutions for any one dimension. For instance, Kim (2020) documents the complementarities between academic, user, and employee entrepreneurs when situated within the technological system of the prosthetic limb industry. In addition to showing how each knowledge context enables identification of opportunities, her study reveals that the heterogeneity manifests in the start-ups' technological positioning and level of product integration.

Insight 5: Founding teams are formed through either resource seeking or interpersonal-attraction strategies; more successful firms are associated with founding teams that use both strategies.

Although Insight 4 may suggest that founders go solo, new ventures often have founding teams at their helm (Wasserman, 2012). Moreover, founders who pursue complex technological ideas venture forth as a team, given greater interdependencies and linkages (Ganco, 2013). Thus, how founding teams form in the first place is very relevant for industry emergence. We summarize insights from Lazar et al. (2020), who reviewed the budding literature on entrepreneurial team formation, even as we note a dearth of work that has directly examined entrepreneurial team formation in nascent industry stages.

Drawing on economics, psychology, and sociology perspectives, Lazar et al. (2020) provide several insights on entrepreneurial team formation. An entrepreneurial team may originate either because an individual (ringleader) identifies an opportunity and then seeks cofounders, or because teams working together identify an opportunity and create a firm. Formation strategies focus on identifying cofounders with requisite complementary resources or capitalizing on prior ties through interpersonal attraction, or both. Regardless of origin or formation strategy, the search for cofounders occurs in a "small world" rather than random network. Thus, entrepreneurial team formation is constrained or enabled by the context within which founders emanate (i.e., preentry experience, social networks, and sociocultural environment). Importantly, Lazar *et al.* (2020) note that entrepreneurial team formation is an interactive process wherein team characteristics, internal routines, and initial performance feedback result in entry and exit of individuals in the early founding team; moreover, the formation strategies may iterate between interpersonal attraction and resource seeking. While fewer founding teams are created with simultaneous attention to interpersonal attraction and resource needs, these ventures consistently outperform ventures based on a singular strategy (Forbes *et al.*, 2006; Grossman, Yli-Renko, and Janakiraman, 2012; Shah, Agarwal, and Echambadi, 2019).

While many of the studies reviewed in Lazar *et al.* (2020) do not explicitly focus on nascent industry stages, they lend themselves to conjectures regarding the importance of entrepreneurial team formation to industry emergence. For example, the academic start-ups reviewed by Lazar *et al.* (2020) engaged in a sequential process, first selecting cofounders based on interpersonal attraction within their narrow networks. These start-ups struggled due to resource gaps and negative environmental feedback and had to shift to resource-seeking strategies (often forced by external stakeholders) to bring in complementary knowledge and resources. If also true for user innovators and their founding teams, industry emergence may be delayed because founding teams emanating from these critical knowledge contexts lack requisite complementary resources to navigate a highly uncertain environment.

Importantly, Lazar *et al.*'s (2020) cross-disciplinary review also reveals that much of the work on industry emergence reviewed in Insight 4 has focused primarily on capabilities and networks of founders, drawing predominantly from an economics or sociology lens. However, entrepreneurial teams also require strong internal processes that facilitate communication and coordination, and engender trust and cohesiveness. The lack of these internal processes could result in failure of the start-up and/or attrition of founding members, particularly if founding teams lack goal alignment and shared workplace values. Indeed, Shah *et al.*'s (2019) study of the evolving disk drive industry lends credence to this conjecture; the paper indicates that ringleaders who paid careful attention to value alignment and complementary expertise when seeking cofounders created start-ups that systematically outperformed start-ups where cofounders exhibited only complementary expertise.

Insight 6: Stable shared leadership arises when founding teams manage conflict constructively, and is associated with firms that grow to become centers of gravity in industries.

Path dependencies from entrepreneurial team formation that then become top management teams (TMTs) also have critical implications for firms as they evolve and grow within nascent industries. Industry emergence and growth are strongly linked to underlying firm evolution (Chen, Williams, and Agarwal, 2012), and TMTs are critical for managing firm growth and evolution (Eisenhardt and Schoonhoven, 1990; Williams, Chen, and Agarwal, 2017). Within economics, managerial diseconomies of scale have long been recognized as a limit to firm growth (Penrose, 1959; Chandler,

1992). Using an organizational behavior lens, scholars have defined the concept of shared leadership—the extent to which authority for strategic decision-making is shared by two or more individuals (Carson, Tesluk, and Marrone, 2007), and related the stability of founding teams/TMTs to firm and industry evolution (Agarwal, Braguinsky, and Ohyama, 2020).

In the linkages between firm and industry growth, on the one hand, strategic disagreements among founders and key employees of existing firms are a critical source of new entrepreneurial entry (Agarwal *et al.*, 2004; Klepper and Thompson, 2010). Underexploited opportunities and strategic disagreements result in an increase in economic experiments, which is particularly important for resolving uncertainty in nascent industries (Rosenberg, 1982). Thus, at an industry level, individuals exiting a firm, or even entire firm dissolutions, contribute to diversity of ideas, crucial for nascent industries to transition into the next developmental stages and achieve subsequent growth.

On the other hand, founding teams that later transition into top management teams may also experience interpersonal frictions or ethical conflicts (Agarwal, Braguinsky *et al.*, 2020; Chandler *et al.*, 2005; Forbes *et al.*, 2006; Ucbasaran *et al.*, 2003). Such differences not only hurt focal firm performance but also result in delays in industry emergence if pervasive across firms. In their study of the nascent Japanese cotton spinning industry, Agarwal, Braguinsky *et al.* (2020) document that most firms experienced significant turnover in leadership due to TMT discords. The five start-ups that emerged as centers of gravity in the industry maintained stable shared leadership—not because of the absence of discord, but because they resolved these discords early by adhering to fundamental principles for long-term value creation, adoption of merit-based promotion in defiance of social norms, and honorable resolution of ethical breaches.

What Do We Not Fully Know?

Building off these six insights, we now turn to theoretical puzzles that provide opportunities for future research, particularly those that arise at the intersection of disciplinary perspectives and levels of analysis.

Puzzle 1: How might a shift in focus from human and relational capital to human enterprise yield novel insights?

Insights 4 through 6 reviewed the literature on individuals and teams as critical fountainheads of firm and industry emergence. Drawing predominantly from economics and sociology perspectives, current research privileges pursuit of economic gains of human capital from prior experience and relational capital arising from social networks. However, humans are more than just their capabilities, and are driven by more than just economic incentives. Missing in the literature on industry emergence is the critical role of psychological drivers. In spite of rich parallel literature streams on psychological drivers of entrepreneurship, there is almost no mention of motivation theories such as *expectancy* (Vroom, 1964), *reinforcement* (Skinner, 1971), *equity* (Goodman, 1977), *need* (Maslow, 1954), and *goal-setting* (Locke, 1968).

Incorporating motivations may require a shift from human capital to *human enterprise*, defined as "systematic, purposeful activity that may be daring or difficult, based on the combination of an individual's abilities and aspirations" (Agarwal, 2019: 488–489). Human enterprise is forward looking rather than merely path dependent, in that it incorporates how aspirations may shape both current and future investments in knowledge and capabilities. Such a shift will allow for the study of the main and interaction effects of individual motivation and purpose on the emergence and evolution of not only their own capabilities but also how these factors map onto the emergence and evolution of teams, firms, and industries.

At least three lines of research inquiry could be pursued with a lens of human enterprise (Agarwal, 2019). First, investigating human enterprise would require taking (self)-selection more seriously. For example, adding to the "treatment effect theories of knowledge context" discussed in Insight 4, future work could examine how and why individuals coming from similar knowledge contexts choose to (not) engage in shaping industry emergence. Second, industry emergence is intertwined with mobility of individuals within and across organizations, and existing work has largely adopted a knowledge-based perspective: it privileges entrepreneurial ideas or innovation projects as the genesis for mobility and entrepreneurship, and additionally draws upon opportunistic or agency-theory-based motivations using an economics cost-benefit calculus. Building on Insight 5, a refocus on people as the genesis for new venture formation and formal incorporation of motivation theories may enable new insights regarding the antecedents and consequences of new ventures' team formation, processes, and strategic decisions (Agarwal, 2019; Lazar *et al.*, 2020).

Third, investigating human enterprise would enable scholars to develop theories by integrating the existing focus on complementary capabilities with the role of creating and maintaining an alignment of aspirations and purpose. As noted in Insight 6, recent research examines the role of managing conflict for firm and industry evolution, but important questions remain unaddressed, including the role of key individuals in developing organizational ethos and factors that ensure maintaining that ethos as firms grow.

Puzzle 2: What role do product champions and intrapreneurs play in evolution of firms and industries?

Although existing research has examined how enterprising individuals create new ventures and contribute to industry emergence, less work exists on the role of individuals who choose to remain at existing firms. These product champions and intrapreneurs equally deserve our attention as fountainheads of established firms' decisions to create and enter new industries. For example, while Walt Disney was an iconic founder whose human enterprise critically shaped the early animated film industry, the subsequent history of Disney Inc. illustrates that its ability to introduce several new technologies and create new industries (e.g., theme parks) relied on internal product champions such as Marty Sklar and Martin Buehler (Pransky, 2015; Sklar, 2015). Similarly, Wormald *et al.* (2021) showcase that worldwide diffusion of mobile money stemmed not only from founders such as Carol Realini (Obopay) and Hannes van Rensburg (Fundamo), but also from intrapreneurs such as Nick Hughes and Susan Lonie (M-Pesa launch by Vodafone). Coff (2010) sheds light on Tony Fadell, who invented Apple's iPod. Interestingly, Apple did not possess many of the capabilities essential to the design, manufacturing, and marketing of the iPod. Fadell had conceptualized the idea independently and persevered through the failure of his entrepreneurial venture before seeking work as a contractor and then as an employee at Apple. An opportunity for future research is to examine enterprising individuals who choose not to leave existing organizations. For example, how and why do enterprising individuals seek to innovate within existing firms to create new industries? Complementing studies of incumbent inertia due to cognitive inattention to new industries or markets (Tripsas and Gavetti, 2000; Klepper and Thompson, 2010), scholars could open the black box of established firms' entry into nascent markets to ask how intrapreneurs access resources and create internal buy-in to enable established firms to pioneer new industries.

Importantly, the career histories of Fadell, van Rensburg and Buehler reveal that they transitioned in and out of start-ups and established firms, and spanned across industries. Fadell left Apple to found Nest Technologies (an early entrant in smart homes), and later sought synergies through acquisition of Nest by Google when continuing at the helm. Similarly, van Rensburg worked in South Africa's second-largest life insurance company prior to creating Fundamo (a pioneer in mobile money), and later sought acquisition by Visa. Buehler helped develop Roomba (the robotic vacuum cleaner) and Creator (a robotic burger cook) earlier in his career, and is now the chief technology officer at incubator Wavemaker Labs. Such anecdotes underscore that rather than making a one-off decision of founding start-ups versus choosing paid employment, enterprising individuals may navigate in and out of start-ups and established firms, and seamlessly cross industry boundaries even as they create a lasting impact in each nascent context.

Yet we lack systematic evidence on how and why entrepreneurial careers may spawn multiple industries. One reason is that scholars have focused on single-industry contexts and only examine related *prior* industry experience. Switching the focus to enterprising individuals may allow scholars to overlay firm and industry histories on individual career life cycles in order to examine questions such as: What are the motivations and capabilities associated with career switches that enable industry emergence versus career transitions within existing industries? Do these motivations and capabilities evolve over career age, and if so, what are some consistent patterns? In their pursuit of pioneering new industries, is there a disproportionate incidence of individuals having to engage in entrepreneurship (e.g., van Rensburg for Fundamo) relative to seeking established firm resources (e.g., Fadell joining Apple)? Moreover, what are the similarities and differences among serial entrepreneurs and serial pioneers?

Puzzle 3: How do institutional constraints affect human enterprise and markets for talent?

So far, our discussion implicitly assumes that enterprising individuals can exercise their preferences and leverage their human capital freely as they move across organizations, create new ventures, or both. Scholars have always noted that such choices are subject to factors shaping demand and supply in human capital markets, which in turn are critically shaped by institutional constraints. As asserted in Insight 2, while enterprising actors can and do address institutional uncertainty in nascent industries, more work is needed to examine how pervasive institutional constraints may limit human enterprise in fostering new industries. Creating a stronger link between human enterprise and industry emergence requires scholars to carefully study the impediments that institutional constraints pose on human capital markets. For example, noncompete covenants may constrain innovation activities, knowledge spillovers, mobility of talent, and new venture creation (Marx, Strumsky, and Fleming, 2009; Samila and Sorenson, 2011). However, there may also be nuanced effects, such as when institutional constraints create selection pressures. For example, Starr, Balasubramanian, and Sakakibara (2018) note that while reducing rates of industry spinout formation, noncompetes "screen out" low-quality individuals from pursuing entrepreneurship, thus creating faster-growing, larger start-ups. Ganco, Ziedonis, and Agarwal (2015) find similar effects when established firms use legal instruments for intellectual property enforcement. A fruitful avenue for future research includes: How and why may use of institutional instruments in human capital markets shape product market emergence and growth?

Another important research avenue is the role of immigration-related work constraints; this has implications at industry and economy-wide levels. For example, immigration-related work constraints suppress early career entrepreneurship in the United States and redirect highly educated individuals toward paid employment (Agarwal, Ganco, and Raffiee, 2020; Roach, Sauermann, and Skerntny, 2019). Such constraints also increase offshoring of high-skilled jobs by U.S. multinationals (Glennon, 2020). We need additional research, asking: How do barriers and facilitators of international mobility and entrepreneurship shape industry emergence through individual mobility and entrepreneurship? How might restrictions in one country constrain or enable increased opportunities for talented individuals in other countries? Potentially, industries of the future may no longer conform to the typical

North-South model of industry emergence and diffusion, wherein industries are first created in developed-economy contexts, and later diffuse to developing economies (Grossman and Helpman, 1991; Krugman, 1979; Vernon, 1966).

Puzzle 4: What market institutions do we take for granted when we examine industry emergence in developed-country contexts, and how do industries emerge in developing-country contexts?

Continuing the chapter's theme, the country context of almost all the nascent industries examined is the United States. Understudied are factors that may be more salient for industry emergence in emerging and developing countries. For example, studies of industry emergence take many market institutions (e.g., impersonal rule of law) for granted, and focus on the role of market failures in nascent settings (see Insight 2 regarding institutional uncertainty) arising due to lack of foundational conditions of a competitive market (Mahoney and Qian, 2013). However, the pervasiveness of market institutional voids in developing and emerging economies implies that uncertainty facing enterprising actors is qualitatively different from that in developed countries (North, 1990; Rosenberg, 1982). Historically, scholars have implicated such lack of institutions for the dearth in developing economies of both physical infrastructure and a pool of specialized talent necessary for industry emergence (Rosenberg, 1982). An important corollary of the North-South diffusion model is that it privileges user needs that are most acute in developed economies, and there are lost opportunities for industries that cater to unmet needs in developing countries.

At least two research avenues are worthwhile to pursue in this context. First, scholars can relax the implicit assumption of "taken-for-granted" market institutions. This approach extends issues discussed in Puzzle 3. There is value in theory building and thought experiments that explicate which market institutions are critical and ancillary to industry emergence. Dutt *et al.* (2016) document how business incubators may create alternative intermediaries that provide different types of capital and foster capability development in emerging economies. Moreover, government and nonprofit sectors may be more important for creating market institutions in developing economies. For example, Shah, Agarwal, and Sonka (2017) document that aid agencies were critical in seeding entrepreneurial firms and redirecting established firms to attend to unmet needs in developing economies. The strategies of the aid agencies consisted of circumventing those voids that were essential to address for focused industry emergence, rather than focusing on *all* institutional constraints in the economy. Additional research is needed to test, build, and extend the formative insights from these studies.

Second, the winds of globalization and technological change imply that institutional voids and unmet needs represent *opportunities* for industry emergence in developing countries. Portable water filters that remove parasites and impurities from water are being created to serve billions of the underprivileged population in developing economies without easy access to clean water (LifeStraw, 2020). Similarly, the mobile money industry has helped address unique needs in developing economies arising from the lack of stable financial institutions (Jack and Suri, 2014). Wormald *et al.* (2021) show that although pioneering mobile money platforms were launched almost equally in developed and developing countries, their traction was much stronger in developing countries. Moreover, start-ups emanating from developing countries tended to expand internationally and had an outsized influence on industry growth relative to multinational diversifying entrants and developed-country start-ups. Additional work will be useful in building the same corpus of knowledge as currently exists for developed contexts.

Conclusion

This chapter discusses decades of work on nascent industries and human enterprise and identifies promising avenues for future research on industry emergence. Shifting focus from human capital to human enterprise will likely lead to promising areas of research, including the microfoundations of firms and industry emergence (e.g., intrapreneurs). Work and institutional conditions (e.g., noncompete covenants, immigration policy) that influence human enterprise and subsequently entrepreneurship and industry emergence are other fruitful areas of research. Embracing developing-economy contexts will uncover implicit assumptions regarding the role that market institutions play in industry emergence and deepen our understanding of entrepreneurial processes that cater to different needs. These theoretical puzzles may well require researchers to expend creative efforts to compile novel datasets, combine quantitative and qualitative/historical data for inference, and synthesize insights across different single-industry studies.

Just as industries emerge through dedicated efforts by enterprising actors to identify and address knowledge gaps that are then aggregated through trade in markets, so can scholarly effort undertaken by (teams) of enterprising scholars generate new knowledge that, in the aggregate, builds our collective knowledge base on industry emergence.

Notes

1. Technological uncertainty results from limited knowledge of necessary components and their assembly for creating appropriate technical designs (Gort and Klepper, 1982; Rosenberg, 1982). Demand uncertainty results from lack of critical information about customers' preferences for products and services and willingness to pay (Christensen and Bower, 1996). Ecosystem uncertainty stems from lack of well-defined structures to enable collaboration with related industries for the focal industry's value chain or provide

complementary products and services (Adner and Kapoor, 2010). Institutional uncertainty arises because of lack of formal and social institutions that foster efficient market exchanges and legitimize a nascent product (North, 1990).

2. Gort and Klepper (1982: 632) explicitly state frictions in markets for technology (information) "may leave innovator with no option but to enter" markets for commercialization; similarly, Teece (1986: 291) states that in early industry stages, "complementary assets do not loom large" and markets for specialized assets are not relevant.

References

Abernathy WJ, Utterback JM. 1978. Patterns of industrial innovation. *Technology Review* 80(7): 40–47.

Adner R, Kapoor R. 2010. Value creation in innovation ecosystems: how the structure of technological interdependence affects firm performance in new technology generations. *Strategic Management Journal* 31(3): 306–333.

Agarwal R. 2019. Human enterprise. In *Handbook of Research on Strategic Human Capital Resources*. Edward Elgar Publishing.

Agarwal R, Bayus BL. 2002. The market evolution and sales takeoff of product innovations. *Management Science* 48(8): 1024–1041.

Agarwal R, Braguinsky S, Ohyama A. 2020. Centers of gravity: the effect of stable shared leadership in top management teams on firm growth and industry evolution. *Strategic Management Journal* 41(3): 467–498.

Agarwal R, Echambadi R, Franco AM, Sarkar MB. 2004. Knowledge transfer through inheritance: spin-out generation, development, and survival. *Academy of Management Journal* 47(4): 501–522.

Agarwal R, Ganco M, Raffiee J. 2020. Immigrant entrepreneurship: the effect of early career immigration constraints and job-education match on science and engineering workforce. Available at SSRN: https://ssrn.com/abstract=3640401.

Agarwal R, Gort M. 2001. First-mover advantage and the speed of competitive entry, 1887–1986. *Journal of Law and Economics* 44(1): 161–177.

Agarwal R, Moeen M, Shah SK. 2017. Athena's birth: triggers, actors, and actions preceding industry inception. *Strategic Entrepreneurship Journal* 11(3): 287–305.

Agarwal R, Shah SK. 2014. Knowledge sources of entrepreneurship: firm formation by academic, user, and employee innovators. *Research Policy* 43(7): 1109–1133.

Anthony C, Nelson AJ, Tripsas M. 2016. "Who are you? ... I really wanna know": product meaning and competitive positioning in the nascent synthesizer industry. *Strategy Science* 1(3): 163–183.

Carroll GR, Bigelow LS, Seidel MDL, Tsai LB. 1996. The fates of de novo and de alio producers in the American automobile industry, 1885–1981. *Strategic Management Journal* 17(S1): 117–137

Carson JB, Tesluk PE, Marrone JA. 2007. Shared leadership in teams: an investigation of antecedent conditions and performance. *Academy of Management Journal* 50(5): 1217–1234.

Chandler AD. 1992. Organizational capabilities and the economic history of the industrial enterprise. *Journal of Economic Perspectives* 6(3): 79–100.

Chandler GN, Honig B, Wiklund J. 2005. Antecedents, moderators, and performance consequences of membership change in new venture teams. *Journal of Business Venturing* 20(5): 705–725.

Chen PL, Williams C, Agarwal R. 2012. Growing pains: pre-entry experience and the challenge of transition to incumbency. *Strategic Management Journal* 33(3): 252–276.

Christensen CM, Bower JL. 1996. Customer power, strategic investment, and the failure of leading firms. *Strategic Management Journal* 17(3): 197–218.

Coff RW. 2010. The coevolution of rent appropriation and capability development. *Strategic Management Journal* 31(7): 711–733.

Conti R, Gambardella A, Novelli E. 2019. Specializing in generality: firm strategies when intermediate markets work. *Organization Science* 30(1): 126–150.

Dutt N, Hawn O, Vidal E, Chatterji A, McGahan A, Mitchell W. 2016. How open system intermediaries address institutional failures: the case of business incubators in emerging-market countries. *Academy of Management Journal* 59(3): 818–840.

Eisenhardt KM, Schoonhoven CB. 1990. Organizational growth: linking founding team, strategy, environment, and growth among U.S. semiconductor ventures, 1978–1988. *Administrative Science Quarterly* 35(3): 504–529.

Forbes DP, Borchert PS, Zellmer–Bruhn ME, Sapienza HJ. 2006. Entrepreneurial team formation: an exploration of new member addition. *Entrepreneurship Theory and Practice* 30(2): 225–248.

Franke N, Shah S. 2003. How communities support innovative activities: an exploration of assistance and sharing among end-users. *Research Policy* 32(1): 157–178.

Ganco M. 2013. Cutting the Gordian knot: the effect of knowledge complexity on employee mobility and entrepreneurship. *Strategic Management Journal* 34(6): 666–686.

Ganco M, Ziedonis RH, Agarwal R. 2015. More stars stay, but the brightest ones still leave: job hopping in the shadow of patent enforcement. *Strategic Management Journal* 36(5): 659–685.

Glennon B. 2020. How do restrictions on high-skilled immigration affect offshoring? Evidence from the H-1B program (No. w27538). National Bureau of Economic Research (February 21).

Golder PN, Shacham R, Mitra D. 2009. Findings—innovations' origins: when, by whom, and how are radical innovations developed? *Marketing Science* 28(1): 166–179.

Goodman PS. 1977. Social comparison processes in organizations. *New Directions in Organizational Behavior* 1: 97–132.

Gort M, Klepper S. 1982. Time paths in the diffusion of product innovations. *Economic Journal* 92(367): 630–653.

Grossman EB, Yli-Renko H, Janakiraman R. 2012. Resource search, interpersonal similarity, and network tie valuation in nascent entrepreneurs' emerging networks. *Journal of Management* 38(6): 1760–1787.

Grossman GM, Helpman E. 1991. Trade, knowledge spillovers, and growth. *European Economic Review* 35(2–3): 517–526.

Hannan MT, Freeman J. 1977. The population ecology of organizations. *American Journal of Sociology* 82(5): 929–964.

Helfat CE. 2015. Vertical firm structure and industry evolution. *Industrial and Corporate Change* 24(4): 803–818.

Hoetker G. 2005. How much you know versus how well I know you: selecting a supplier for a technically innovative component. *Strategic Management Journal* 26(1): 75–96.

Holbrook D, Cohen WM, Hounshell DA, Klepper S. 2000. The nature, sources, and consequences of firm differences in the early history of the semiconductor industry. *Strategic Management Journal* 21(10–11): 1017–1041.

Jack W, Suri T. 2014. Risk sharing and transactions costs: evidence from Kenya's mobile money revolution. *American Economic Review* 104(1): 183–223.

Kapoor R, Furr NR. 2015. Complementarities and competition: unpacking the drivers of entrants' technology choices in the solar photovoltaic industry. *Strategic Management Journal* 36(3): 416–436.

Kim S. 2020. Pre-entry knowledge of entrepreneurs and market strategy. Working Paper, University of Maryland, College Park, MD.

Kim S, Agarwal R, Goldfarb, B. 2020. Creating competencies for radical technologies: revisiting "incumbent-entrant" dynamics in the bionic prosthetic industry. Working Paper, University of Maryland, College Park, MD.

Klepper S, Simons KL. 2000. Dominance by birthright: entry of prior radio producers and competitive ramifications in the U.S. television receiver industry. *Strategic Management Journal* 21(10-11): 997–1016.

Klepper S, Thompson P. 2010. Disagreements and intra-industry spinoffs. *International Journal of Industrial Organization* 28(5): 526–538.

Knight FH. 1921. *Risk, Uncertainty, and Profit* (Vol. 31). Houghton Mifflin: New York, NY.

Krugman PR. 1979. Increasing returns, monopolistic competition, and international trade. *Journal of International Economics* 9(4): 469–479.

Lazar M, Miron-Spektor E, Agarwal R, Erez M, Goldfarb B, Chen G. 2020. Entrepreneurial team formation. *Academy of Management Annals* 14(1): 29–59.

Leggett AJ. 2007. Sir Anthony Leggett—Keynote Address: The University of Illinois Regional FIRST LEGO Competition. Chicago, IL.

LifeStraw® Corporate Website. 2020. *About LifeStraw®: we make water safe to drink.* Retrieved July 31, 2020, from https://www.lifestraw.com/pages/about-us.

Locke EA. 1968. Toward a theory of task motivation and incentives. *Organizational Behavior and Human Performance* 3(2): 157–189.

Mahoney JT, Qian L. 2013. Market frictions as building blocks of an organizational economics approach to strategic management. *Strategic Management Journal* 34(9): 1019–1041.

Marx M, Strumsky D, Fleming L. 2009. Mobility, skills, and the Michigan non-compete experiment. *Management Science* 55(6): 875–889.

Maslow AH. 1954. The instinctoid nature of basic needs. *Journal of Personality* 22: 326–347.

Merton RK. 1973. *The Sociology of Science: Theoretical and Empirical Investigations.* University of Chicago Press: Chicago, IL.

Mody CC. 2006. Corporations, universities, and instrumental communities: commercializing probe microscopy, 1981–1996. *Technology and Culture* 47(1): 56–80.

Moeen M. 2017. Entry into nascent industries: disentangling a firm's capability portfolio at the time of investment versus market entry. *Strategic Management Journal* 38(10): 1986–2004.

Moeen M, Agarwal R. 2017. Incubation of an industry: heterogeneous knowledge bases and modes of value capture. *Strategic Management Journal* 38(3): 566–587.

Moeen M, Agarwal R, Shah SK. 2020. Building industries by building knowledge: uncertainty reduction over industry milestones. *Strategy Science* 5(3): 218–244.

Moeen M, Mitchell W. 2020. How do pre-entrants to the industry incubation stage choose between alliances and acquisitions for technical capabilities and specialized complementary assets? *Strategic Management Journal* 41(8): 1450–1489.

North DC. 1990. The path of institutional change. In *Institutions, Institutional Change and Economic Performance*, North, DC (ed). Cambridge University Press: Cambridge, U.K.; 92–104.

Penrose ET. 1959. *The Theory of the Growth of the Firm.* John Wiley: New York, NY.

Pransky J. 2015. The Pransky interview: Dr Martin Buehler, Executive R & D Imagineer at Walt Disney Imagineering and renowned expert in advanced robotics. *Industrial Robot: An International Journal* 42(6): 497–501.

Qian L, Agarwal R, Hoetker G. 2012. Configuration of value chain activities: the effect of pre-entry capabilities, transaction hazards, and industry evolution on decisions to internalize. *Organization Science* 23(5): 1330–1349.

Roach M, Sauermann H, Skrentny J. 2019. Are foreign stem Phds more entrepreneurial? Entrepreneurial characteristics, preferences and employment outcomes of native and foreign science and engineering Phd studies. NBER Working paper No. w26225. Available at SSRN: https://ssrn.com/abstract=3450251.

Rosenberg N. 1982. *Inside the Black Box: Technology and Economics.* Cambridge University Press: Cambridge, U.K.

Samila S, Sorenson O. 2011. Venture capital, entrepreneurship, and economic growth. *Review of Economics and Statistics* **93**(1): 338–349.

Sanderson SW, Simons KL. 2014. Light emitting diodes and the lighting revolution: the emergence of a solid-state lighting industry. *Research Policy* **43**(10): 1730–1746.

Shah S, Agarwal R, Sonka ST. 2017. A time and a place: non-profit engagement in the creation of markets and industry emergence. Available at SSRN: https://ssrn.com/abstract=2959714 or http://dx.doi.org/10.2139/ssrn.2959714.

Shah SK, Agarwal R, Echambadi R. 2019. Jewels in the crown: exploring the motivations and team building processes of employee entrepreneurs. *Strategic Management Journal* **40**(9): 1417–1452.

Shane S. 2000. Prior knowledge and the discovery of entrepreneurial opportunities. *Organization Science* **11**(4): 448–469.

Shermon A, Moeen M. 2020. Zooming in or Zooming out: entrants' product usage breadth in the nascent drone industry. Working Paper, University of North Carolina, Chapel Hill, NC.

Skinner BF. 1971. *Beyond Freedom and Dignity.* Alfred A. Knopf: New York, NY.

Sklar M. 2015. *One Little Spark!: Mickey's Ten Commandments and the Road to Imagineering.* Disney Editions: New York, NY.

Starr E, Balasubramanian N, Sakakibara M. 2018. Screening spinouts? How noncompete enforceability affects the creation, growth, and survival of new firms. *Management Science* **64**(2): 552–572.

Stigler GJ. 1957. Perfect competition, historically contemplated. *Journal of Political Economy* **65**(1): 1–17.

Teece DJ. 1986. Profiting from technological innovation: implications for integration, collaboration, licensing, and public policy. *Research Policy* **15**(6): 285–305.

Tripsas M, Gavetti G. 2000. Capabilities, cognition, and inertia: evidence from digital imaging. *Strategic Management Journal* **21**(10-11): 1147–1161.

Ucbasaran D, Lockett A, Wright M, Westhead P. 2003. Entrepreneurial founder teams: factors associated with member entry and exit. *Entrepreneurship Theory and Practice* **28**(2): 107–128.

Vernon R. 1966. International trade and international investment in the product cycle. *Quarterly Journal of Economics* **80**(2): 190–207.

Vroom VH. 1964. *Work and Motivation.* Wiley: New York, NY.

Wasserman N. 2012. *The Founder's Dilemmas: Anticipating and Avoiding the Pitfalls That Can Sink a Startup.* Princeton University Press: Princeton, NJ.

Williams C, Chen PL, Agarwal R. 2017. Rookies and seasoned recruits: How experience in different levels, firms, and industries shapes strategic renewal in top management. *Strategic Management Journal* **38**(7): 1391–1415.

Wormald A, Agarwal R, Braguinsky S, Shah SK. 2021. David overshadows Goliath: specializing in generality for internationalization in the global mobile money industry. *Strategic Management Journal*, forthcoming. Available at: https://doi.org/10.1002/smj.3270.

3.2
TECHNOLOGY ENTREPRENEURSHIP, TECHNOLOGY STRATEGY, AND UNCERTAINTY

Nathan R. Furr

Introduction

At its core, strategy focuses on the question of why one firm outperforms another firm, and scholars have offered industry-based, resource-based, and opportunity-based views of competitive advantage. But few of these models directly address a fundamental activity at the heart of strategy: the use of technology to create and capture value. Technology entrepreneurship, and by extension technology strategy, is the study of how firms use technology to create and capture value. While this area draws on multiple domains, including literatures describing the evolution of technology, firms, and industries, few dedicated efforts have been made to integrate these domains to describe technology strategy more broadly. Yet today, many firms' products, services, business models, and competitive advantage are built upon technology or depend upon technology to capture that advantage. Indeed, arguably the most powerful firms today are not those with industry or resource positions but those with technology positions.

Although technology positions can become industry and resource positions, ignoring the technologies and processes that create those positions is like having a theory of produce markets without a theory of farming. Accordingly, the goal of this chapter is twofold. First, this chapter unpacks the theoretical and empirical foundations of technology entrepreneurship as it relates to strategy, summarizes current research, and highlights important unanswered questions, foremost of which is the role of uncertainty in our theories of strategy. But second, this chapter asks the question: given the growing centrality of technology in almost every area of economic life, should technology entrepreneurship, and by extension technology strategy, take a more central role in the canon of strategy frameworks alongside industry, resource, network, and knowledge-based views?

Past Research: The Contributing Literatures to Technology Entrepreneurship

First, it is important to define technology entrepreneurship and, by extension, technology strategy. Arthur (2009) defined technology as a phenomenon put to use. However, most people think of technology in terms of a more tangible instantiation that allows us to achieve something. For example, a microprocessor, a smartphone, artificial intelligence, and CRISPR would be technologies that we put to use to achieve outcomes, such as smart factories, the internet of things, therapeutic treatments, and so forth. But whether viewed more abstractly or concretely, it is clear that in today's world, as Rosenberg (1976) argued, technology is fundamentally interwoven with almost every human domain, including strategy, not just scientific or engineering domains. Thus, even firms that do not view themselves as technology-based are so deeply affected by technology that it seems strange to not have a technology view. Even the farmer lives by technology, driving a smart tractor and using computer-aided visualization for planting, drones for crop management, and online platforms for obtaining supplies and selling output. But on a larger scale, firms are having to answer how to invest in and operate by technologies as evidenced by the conversations around digital transformation, the fourth industrial revolution, and specific technologies such as artificial intelligence.

Likewise, entrepreneurship cannot be defined simply as a person (e.g., an entrepreneur) or a thing (e.g., a start-up). Rather entrepreneurship is an action taken to address a problem or opportunity. It can occur outside an organization (e.g., a start-up, spinout) or inside an organization (e.g., corporate venture) and when successful often results in new or adapted goods and services (e.g., products, services, or platforms). With that said, it can also have other outcomes, such as knowledge generation, social movements, institutional change, or cultural influence. As such, *technology entrepreneurship* can be defined as entrepreneurial action to apply a technology to achieve some end, often an economic or social end. Thus, technology entrepreneurship incorporates both start-ups and corporations that engage in entrepreneurial activity.

As such, technology entrepreneurship may be the most fundamental form of economic action shaping modern economic life now and in the future—the water of the waves of creative destruction described by Schumpeter (1942). Indeed, it is hard and perhaps impossible to find a sector of economic activity not increasingly influenced by technology, if not transformed by it. Thus, in the sense that technology entrepreneurship is the *action* of applying technology to create new value, and perhaps capture it as well, then *technology strategy*, as an umbrella concept incorporating technology entrepreneurship, can be defined as a firm's strategy for creating and capturing value with technology as well as the firm's strategy in a world shaped and reshaped by technology. With these definitions in mind, we can explore some of the contributing literatures to technology entrepreneurship and ultimately to a technology strategy view.

Multiple research domains contribute to the conversation on technology entrepreneurship as well as to technology strategy.[1] Work in the fields of technology management, evolutionary economics, entrepreneurship, and dynamic strategy represent four particularly important contributing literatures. First, the technology management literature provides a starting point by describing the evolution of technology from a basic scientific invention (Eggers and Kaul, 2018; Fleming and Sorenson, 2001; Katila and Ahuja, 2002) through pre-industry emergence (Cattani, 2005; Moeen and Agarwal, 2017), the competition of multiple technology variants during an era of ferment (Suarez, Grodal, and Gotsopoulos, 2015; Utterback and Suarez, 1993), the emergence of a dominant design that consolidates competition (Anderson and Tushman, 1990; Suarez and Utterback, 1995), and the competition to capture value from these technologies as they mature (Agarwal and Tripsas, 2011; Teece, 1986). The strength of this literature has traditionally been the focus on technology itself, and grand patterns of technology evolution. For example, the literature has underscored how differences in the capabilities required to produce a technology (Abernathy and Clark, 1985; Tushman and Anderson, 1986), the architecture of the technology (Henderson and Clark, 1990), and even the customers for a technology (Adner, 2002; Christensen and Bower, 1996) create challenges for firms adapting to a new technology generation. But the tradeoff is that this literature, with some notable exceptions already cited, puts more emphasis on the technology than the firm's capabilities and strategies. Only recently have researchers started to more explicitly combine views of technology with firm capabilites, for example, by showing how the interaction of available complementary assets and firm capabilities determine which technologies firms choose when entering an industry (Kapoor and Furr, 2015). Likewise, Hannah and Eisenhardt (2018) describe how a firm strategy of migrating to the evolving bottlenecks in a technology ecosystem yields higher performance than a strategy focusing on a component where the firm has specific capabilities or on integrating the systems as a whole.

By contrast, the industry evolution literature places a heavy emphasis on the nature of firms (Agarwal and Tripsas, 2011; Helfat and Eisenhardt, 2005; Helfat, 2000) and the differences in their capabilities derived from history. This literature describes how different types of firms (e.g., start-ups versus diversifiers [Agarwal *et al.*, 2004; Agarwal and Shah, 2014; Holbrook *et al.*, 2000; Klepper and Simons, 2000]), coming from different industries (e.g., related versus unrelated capabilities [Helfat and Lieberman, 2002; Klepper and Simons, 2000]), and with different backgrounds (e.g., science versus industry capabilities [Howard-Grenville *et al.*, 2017; Roach and Sauermann, 2010; Shah, Agarwal, and Echambadi, 2019]) perform differently. The strength of this literature has been the focus on how differences in firm capabilities shapes competitive outcomes and industry evolution, but the tradeoff has been that although such studies are often set in technology industries, they pay limited attention to the issues of technology itself.

In addition, the entrepreneurship literature provides the frame for entrepreneurial action, in terms of individuals, start-ups, and corporate entrepreneurship.

This literature presents broad-brushstroke portraits about the nature of opportunity, through debates about opportunity discovery versus creation (Alvarez and Barney, 2007; Shane, 2000) as well as entrepreneurial processes such as effectuation, brico-lage, and assembly (Baker and Nelson, 2005; Garud and Karnøe, 2003; Miner, Bassoff, and Moorman, 2001; Sarasvathy, 2001). Furthermore, this literature details entrepre-neurial elements that contribute to opportunity capture, such as teams, financing, and resources (Beckman, Burton, and O'Reilly, 2007; Hallen, 2008; Hallen and Eisenhardt, 2012; Shah et al., 2019; Wasserman, 2003). While this literature provides foundations for entrepreneurship, it rarely focuses on the technology element and has historically been ambiguous about the specifics of the entrepreneurial process, for example, by suggesting that entrepreneurs experiment but without unpacking such processes until recently (Furr, 2019).

Finally, the literature on strategy in dynamic environments examines how firms nav-igate changing environments (Brown and Eisenhardt, 1997). This literature draws on foundations from complexity theory (Anderson, 1999; Padgett and Ansell, 1993), psy-chology (Gigerenzer and Brighton, 2009; Goldstein and Gigerenzer, 2009), and product development (Brown and Eisenhardt, 1995; Eisenhardt and Tabrizi, 1995) to argue that in dynamic environments, strategy is more about the logic of opportunity capture than industry or resource position (Davis, Eisenhardt, and Bingham, 2009). This view focuses more on the iterative creation and evolution of business models (McDonald and Eisenhardt, 2019), dynamic capabilities (Eisenhardt, Furr, and Bingham, 2010; Eisenhardt and Martin, 2000; Rindova and Kotha, 2001), forming industry boundaries (Ozcan and Eisenhardt, 2009; Santos and Eisenhardt, 2009), and navigating ecosystems (Bremner and Eisenhardt, 2021; Hannah and Eisenhardt, 2018) than on fortifying firm resources or position. This literature emphasizes creating a series of temporary advan-tages (Brown and Eisenhardt, 1997; Eisenhardt et al., 2010)—a compelling alternative to the model of sustained competitive advantage based on industry structure (Porter, 1980) or resource ownership (Barney, 1991; Wernerfelt, 1984).

These four, somewhat overlapping literatures provide the foundations for under-standing technology entrepreneurship and strategy. Naturally, a focus on these four does not do credit to additional contributing literatures, such as the work on inven-tion (Bikard, 2018; Kaplan and Vakili, 2015), intellectual property (Arora, Fosfuri, and Gambardella, 2001; Dushnitsky and Lenox, 2005; Knott, Bryce, and Posen, 2003), and innovation ecosystems (Adner, 2017; Jacobides, Cennamo, and Gawer, 2018; Kapoor, 2018) among others, which are important but cannot be summarized here.

Current Research Directions and Unanswered Questions

Contemporary research focuses on several questions at the intersection of these liter-atures that also represent opportunities for future research, some of which are sum-marized below.

Are existing models of technology evolution oversimplified?

Although early models of technology evolution served to simplify the world in hopes of yielding accurate predictions, current research has focused on unpacking the relevant but potentially oversimplified dimensions of these earlier models. One key area is the stylistic description of technology emergence with frameworks like the S-curve (Christensen, 1992; Foster, 1986) or technology adoption life cycle (Abernathy and Utterback, 1978; Utterback, 1996). Although these frameworks have provided useful descriptions of the evolution of technologies from an era of ferment, competition toward a dominant design, and then industry stabilization, these patterns oversimplify important elements of technology dynamics.

For example, these frameworks rarely account for how the ecosystem shapes the ability of firms to create and capture value (Adner, 2017; Jacobides *et al.*, 2018; Kapoor, 2018). But the ecosystem—or the interdependent actors required for an innovation to deliver value to an end user—shapes which technologies firms choose when they enter the industry (Kapoor and Furr, 2015), how they allocate innovative investment (Bremner and Eisenhardt, 2021; Ethiraj, 2007; Hannah and Eisenhardt, 2018), and the performance of firms (Adner and Kapoor, 2010). Moreover, firms enter the industry with capabilities brought from other ecosystems that shape if firms enter an industry (Moeen, 2017), which technology features they pay attention to (Benner and Tripsas, 2012; Kapoor and Furr, 2015), and the strategies firms use to introduce them (Moeen and Agarwal, 2017). Likewise, the model of technologies competing during an era of ferment until the emergence of a dominant design is useful, but some have argued that this competition can occur asynchronously, yet interdependently, across different levels of the technology stack, from components to systems (Murmann and Frenken, 2006).

Just as importantly, not all technologies have the same impact on the evolution of the innovation or the same relevance to firm strategy. For example, some technologies create bottlenecks that limit the performance of the system and that shape firm investments (Baldwin, 2015; Ethiraj, 2007; Furr, Kapoor, and Eisenhardt, 2020; Hannah and Eisenhardt, 2018). Moreover, as Furr *et al.* argue (2021), bottlenecks differ: technology bottlenecks arise from the challenge of discovering "good enough" solutions and require search-focused strategies to resolve, whereas capacity bottlenecks arise from investment and cooperation problems that result in undersupply and require coordination strategies to resolve. Likewise, some technologies are simple inputs to an innovation, whereas others are enabling technologies that facilitate the emergence of the entire industry (Furr *et al.*, 2021). Moreover, the structure of interdependence of these technologies, such as how central components are or how locally connected they are, affects the performance of the firms using them (Burford, Shipilov, and Furr, 2021).

Furthermore, prior models of technology generation transition have provided critical insight into how established firm capabilities are undermined by new technology regimes (Abernathy and Clark, 1985; Christensen and Bower, 1996; Utterback, 1996), creating cognitive, technical, and capability obstacles for incumbents to adapt to the new technology regime (Henderson and Clark, 1990; Tripsas and Gavetti, 2000; Tushman and Anderson, 1986). But recent research has begun to unpack the complexity hidden within this simple pattern (Furr and Snow, 2021). For example, old technologies have a surprising persistence (Adner and Snow, 2010; Henderson, 1995; Tripsas, 2008), often exhibiting surprising leaps, or "last gasps" in performance that can delay a discontinuity (Furr and Snow, 2021)—or, by tapping into other dimensions of demand, lead to the reemergence of a technology (Raffaelli, 2019). Likewise, when threatened by a new technology generation, firms do not always have to adapt immediately. Sometimes firms can create hybrid technologies that serve as defenses against the new technology (Furr and Snow, 2015b) or bridges between old and new by allowing firms to develop knowledge and capabilities in the threatening technology generation (Cohen and Tripsas, 2018; Furr and Snow, 2015a). This has led to the proposal of an alternative model to the dominant, more deterministic post-hoc view of technology discontinuity, namely an ex-ante view of how firms significantly influence if, when, and where new technologies ultimately substitute for old (Furr and Snow, 2021).

Finally, recent research explores the field-level dynamics that shape technology evolution. For example, research has underscored the malleable, co-creative nature of industry emergence (Santos and Eisenhardt, 2005), particularly in how entrepreneurial action legitimizes the conceptual categories within an industry (Navis and Glynn, 2010); how the regulations that control the industry are often co-created (McDonald and Gao, 2020); and how much firms influence the approval of new products (Hiatt and Park, 2013), shape the boundaries of products (Anthony, Nelson, and Tripsas, 2016), and even kill innovations (Cunningham, Ederer, and Ma, 2021). Likewise, recent research has shown how institutional actors such as start-up accelerators facilitate critical activities necessary to create new innovations, including raising capital and gaining customer traction (Hallen, Cohen, and Bingham, 2020), overcoming premature satisficing through feedback mechanism design (Cohen, Bingham, and Hallen, 2019), and helping founders more quickly evaluate the future success of the start-up (Yu, 2020).

This brief review suggests how current research continues to enrich existing models but also reveals gaps for future research. For example, in our study of technology discontinuity, far too few accounts examine threatening discontinuities that never occur. Perhaps by accounting for this survivor bias in our existing theories, we may discover a different model of technology transition that leaves more room for technology false starts, restarts, and reemergence, or that more fully accounts for the complexity of creating new markets with technology. Alternatively, it may be that our existing models are too narrow and do not account for the full scope of technology processes that may occur outside the scope of industry commercialization (Arthur, 2009; Levinthal, 1998).

Do we really understand the innovation and commercialization process?

Although technology entrepreneurship implies action, prior literature has been vague about the specifics of the process behind that action. Prior work has outlined high-level processes such as effectuation or bricolage, and a few notable accounts describe "what happened" during the technology entrepreneurship process (e.g., Van de Ven and Garud, 1993), but only recently has research explored the process of experimentation and change at the core of technology entrepreneurship.

For example, research has just started to analyze how entrepreneurs learn and adapt in a new market. Although Eisenhardt and Tabrizi (1995) laid the foundations for this idea, arguing that an iterative, adaptive approach to product development increased success, recent research delves into the nature of experimentation. For example, Camuffo *et al.* (2019) used a field experiment to provide evidence that entrepreneurs who learned to frame and test hypotheses employing the scientific method outperformed those who did not. But at the same time we start to unpack the mechanisms of experimentation, research is exploring types of experimentation. For example, Sommer, Loch, and Dong (2009) use a simulation to suggest that when an innovation project is characterized by uncertainty, trial-and-error learning works well, but when it is both uncertain and complex, parallel trials may be more effective. Likewise, Bremner and Eisenhardt (2021) explore complex experimentation at the intersection of firm and community boundaries. Last, research is exploring how firms adapt to these changes. Furr (2019) showed how the types of experience in the team shaped whether they adapt, and Kirtley and O'Mahony (2021) found that this adaption occurs as a series of iterative strategy changes that build over time. These studies reveal a research opportunity to explore experimentation processes: what they are, when they are most appropriate, and what forces shape how experimenters design, enact, and interpret them.

Another opportunity is to apply a more integrated behavioral lens to understand the innovation and commercialization process. For example, Furr and Eggers (2021) argue that the evolutionary variation-selection-retention (VSR) framework is an overly rational, risk-based view of innovation processes—and that as uncertainty and ambiguity increase, it is necessary to take a more integrated behavioral view of innovation to understand it properly. Specifically, Furr and Eggers focus on introducing additional "stages" to a latent VSR model, such as a "motivation" stage to acknowledge that innovation starts with and is shaped by many different motivations. Likewise, the authors identify key behavioral issues that shape the innovation process, such as the fuzzy nature of designing, executing, and gathering feedback from experimentation, the depth and complexity of organizational filters that shape which innovations are selected, and the biasing forces that shape retention and maintenance of an innovation. Most importantly, they call for research that goes beyond simply identifying a list of behavioral biases to designing remedies for these biases—an issue critical to any organization seeking renewal through innovation.

Although a brief summary, these papers highlight the gap. The process at the core of innovation and entrepreneurship needs to be unpacked in significantly greater detail.

Big Questions for the Future

Do we need a technology strategy view?

Technology entrepreneurship draws on multiple domains to describe how individuals and organizations engage in entrepreneurial action to create and capture value using technology. Technology management, industry evolution, entrepreneurship, and dynamic strategy have featured prominently in this review, but so have the literatures on ecosystems, platforms, accelerators, open innovation, user communities, and other topics.

But technology is playing an increasingly central role in all elements of organizational life. Whereas information technology was once a support function, with the rise of digital transformation (Adner, Puranam, and Zhu, 2019; Furr and Shipilov, 2019), growth of enabling technologies, and dominance of new technology firms, it is hard to imagine how any firm can formulate a strategy without taking technology into account. Yet while we have an industry-structure, resource-based, relational-view, and other such views of strategy, we do not have a cohesive technology strategy view. The closest would be the technology management perspective, which some may see as synonymous with technology strategy.

But does technology management, for all its many contributions to how technology evolves, provide the answers to how a firm creates and captures value in a world shaped by technology? Certainly, the S-curve provides rough guidance, but even popular frameworks like disruptive innovation (Christensen, 1997) are mostly descriptive rather than predictive. Moreover, they give only a partial picture: far too many firms invest too early in threatening technologies as opposed to too late (for an example of the dangers of premature investments, see Gilbert's [2005] account of newspapers investing in media portal precursors). Likewise, stories of technologies that threaten but never disrupt are grossly undersampled in our literature, as are how firms extend technologies, forestalling discontinuity for long periods. (Consider for a moment how pundits have predicted the disruption of silicon microprocessors, both in terms of materials and architectures, and yet Intel has managed to defer these threats seemingly indefinitely.) In sum, do our existing views fully answer questions such as, how do you acquire, integrate, and compete with or against technology?

Moreover, this view could raise interesting questions, such as whether technology is a product, resource, capability, or structure, or all at the same time. Even if we categorize technology as a resource, it has some strange properties in the conditions under which it becomes or retains value. For example, if data can be replicated at zero cost, is it still valuable? Perhaps, if it is kept proprietary. But a second challenge arises in that proprietary data in one setting may be valueless in another setting, or it may be valueless unless it is recombined with other data, which if it is owned by another firm runs the risk of becoming nonproprietary or worthless. Perhaps our theories of resources, or Arrow's paradox, help us explain these, but are we overlooking issues by doing so?

Alternatively, we know that firm structure tends to resemble the structure of production, but contemporary technology developments are pushing this idea to extremes. For example, in 2006, Amazon.com CEO Jeff Bezos sent a memo to the company that all internal and external activities would be performed via a common software interface—application program interfaces (APIs). Adopting this modularity in technology design has enabled an unusual level of modularity in organization design, allowing Amazon.com to scale, enter new industries, and compete in domains normally limited by diseconomies of scale. We could dismiss this as a more extreme form of firm structure imitating technology, but then we would be missing the new structural and competitive implications revealed by this and other technologies.

This review highlights the benefits of integrating insights from related fields—including industry evolution, entrepreneurship, dynamic strategy, and others—to fully understand technology entrepreneurship. Perhaps a similar approach is required to develop a technology strategy view. Although Teece (1986, 2006) provides some important answers, such as the role of complementary assets, this is just the beginning. Perhaps only an integration of these many contributing literatures can accurately describe what we might call a "technology strategy view" of how firms integrate with, compete with, and create advantage from technology.

Do we need a theory of uncertainty?

Related to the rise of technology is an increase in the pace of change and uncertainty (Knight, 1921). Recent research has highlighted how increasing uncertainty has decreased the length and predictability of a firm's competitive advantage (Agarwal and Gort, 2001; D'Aveni, 1994; Davis *et al.*, 2009; Wiggins and Ruefli, 2005). It seems logical that the rise of technology could be a major precipitating factor, whether due to an increasing pace of technology change, technology lowering entry barriers and thus increasing competition, technology increasing connectivity and interdependence, or other reasons. Whatever the cause, the important question is what impact uncertainty has on what we know about strategy and management.

Although many strategy studies often cite uncertainty as a contingency, one could ask, are we really taking uncertainty seriously enough as a field? Whether we recognize it or not, many of our theoretical and empirical tools are rooted in a risk-based, expected-outcome, "on average" view of the world based on probability theory and statistics (Cavarretta and Furr, 2010). But fundamental differences between risk and uncertainty affect the nature of knowing, decision-making, action, and outcomes (for a review and definitions, see Rindova and Courtney, 2021).

For example, Furr and Eggers (2021) argue that as uncertainty increases, so does the degree of behavioral bias in the innovation process, but it can also change the nature of the innovation process itself. Although we can analyze the antecedents to radical innovation, it is nearly impossible to predict if a radical innovation will occur. Moreover, the appropriate tools for dealing with the uncertainty characterizing radical innovation may be different from lower uncertainty contexts. This is illustrated by the scientist who stumbled upon the breakthrough that led to the LED lighting industry. Shuji Nakamura recounts presenting at academic conferences to nearly empty rooms and then finally being ordered by his employer to stop working on his approach. Notably, Nakamura's breakthrough would be unlikely to emerge from the kind of low-cost "lean start-up" experimentation striving to eliminate "bias," which has become popular today. Rather, a population-level search process that allowed individuals like Nakamura to follow their bias to the bitter end led to a discovery worthy of a Nobel Prize.

The differences between risk and uncertainty are not isolated to innovation processes alone. Rather uncertainty creates boundary conditions on our most familiar strategy theories (Furr and Eisenhardt, 2021) and underscores key activies such as experimentation, learning, cognition, and creation as strategy activities. To illustrate, Rindova and Courtney (2021) argue that uncertainty changes the character of strategy by creating fundamental challenges to the act of knowing. Whereas many extant strategy theories rest on the economic logic of choice (e.g., choice of resources, market position, options, etc.), under uncertainty firms cannot choose because they must first create the knowledge, resources, and opportunities. Rindova and Courtney (2021) contend that under uncertainty, strategy is more about shaping the future rather than choosing and defending a position.

Recognizing the differences between risk and uncertainty-based theories does not diminish the value of prior research. Rather it reveals interesting research opportunities and helps avoid the risk of inappropriate theory borrowing (Whetten, Felin, and King, 2009). As the LED breakthrough case suggests, there are rich opportunities to explore the different types of experimentation regimes that may be more or less appropriate for uncertainty (Bremner and Eisenhardt, 2021; Camuffo et al., 2019; Sommer et al., 2009). Moreover, much of the work on experimentation makes the latent assumption that experimenters can rationally design, enact, and interpret the results of experiments, but as uncertainty increases, experimenters are increasingly biased in their search; in some cases, the act of experimentation may change the search landscape (Furr, Nickerson, and Wuebker, 2016; Shelef, Wuebker, and Barney, 2020).

Perhaps the most interesting implication of uncertainty and ambiguity may be this thought experiment: do we need a theory of strategy under uncertainty? Consider for a moment that most theories of strategy are described with words like *ownership*, *competition*, *scarcity*, *contracts*, *barriers*, and other control-oriented terms. This makes sense in the economics, risk-based world at the heart of our core theories. But what if uncertainty and ambiguity, like that from which came the solid-state lighting breakthrough, aren't to be controlled or managed in the same sense? Thus, better themes to think about them might be words such as *unlock* or *activate*. Key themes for strategy under uncertainty include activities such as experimentation, learning, cognition, shaping and generativity. Certainly, the way scholars have described simple rules is not about how these rules control or manage competition but more about how they enable firms to unlock new opportunities (Brown and Eisenhardt, 1997; Eisenhardt *et al.*, 2010; Rindova and Kotha, 2001).

The thought experiment is not to condemn our current theories as wrong, but rather to ask, if we take uncertainty seriously, how would we re-see or reinvent our theories? Furr and Eisenhardt (2021) suggest several building blocks for a "strategy-creation view". Further developing this "theory of uncertainty" will be critical for the future of strategy in a world of potentially ever-greater change and dynamism.

Note

1. Notably this is a selective review that mixes "classics" with contemporary research. There is not space to conduct a comprehensive review.

References

Abernathy W, Clark K. 1985. Innovation: mapping the winds of creative destruction. *Research Policy* 14(1): 3–22.

Abernathy W, Utterback J. 1978. Patterns of industrial innovation. *Technology Review* 80(7): 40–47.

Adner R. 2002. When are technologies disruptive? A demand-based view of the emergence of competition. *Strategic Management Journal* 23(8): 667–688.

Adner R. 2017. Ecosystem as structure: an actionable construct for strategy. *Journal of Management* 43(1): 39–58.

Adner R, Kapoor R. 2010. Value creation in innovation ecosystems: how the structure of technological interdependence affects firm performance in new technology generations. *Strategic Management Journal* 31(3): 306–333.

Adner R, Puranam P, Zhu F. 2019. What is different about digital strategy? From quantitative to qualitative change. *Strategy Science* 4(4): 253–261.

Adner R, Snow D. 2010. Old technology responses to new technology threats: demand heterogeneity and technology retreats. *Industrial and Corporate Change* 19(5): 1655–1675.

Agarwal R, Echambadi R, Franco AM, Sarkar MB. 2004. Knowledge transfer through inheritance: spin-out generation, development, and survival. *Academy of Management Journal* 47(4): 501–522.

Agarwal R, Gort M. 2001. First-mover advantage and the speed of competitive entry, 1887–1986. *Journal of Law and Economics* 44(1): 161–177.

Agarwal R, Shah SK. 2014. Knowledge sources of entrepreneurship: firm formation by academic, user, and employee innovators. *Research Policy* 43(7): 1109–1133.

Agarwal R, Tripsas M. 2011. Technology and industry evolution. In *Handbook of Technology and Innovation Management,* Shane S (ed). John Wiley & Sons: Hoboken, NJ; 3–53.

Alvarez SA, Barney JB. 2007. Discovery and creation: alternative theories of entrepreneurial action. *Strategic Entrepreneurship Journal* 1(1–2): 11–26.

Anderson P. 1999. Complexity theory and organization science. *Organization Science* 10(3): 216–232.

Anderson P, Tushman M. 1990. Technological discontinuities and dominant designs: a cyclical model of technological change. *Administrative Science Quarterly* 35(4): 604–633.

Anthony C, Nelson AJ, Tripsas M. 2016. "Who are you? ... I really wanna know": product meaning and competitive positioning in the nascent synthesizer industry. *Strategy Science* 1(3): 163–183.

Arora A, Fosfuri A, Gambardella A. 2001. Markets for technology and their implications for corporate strategy. *Industrial and Corporate Change* 10(2): 419–451.

Arthur WB. 2009. *The Nature of Technology: What It Is and How It Evolves.* Simon and Schuster: New York, NY.

Baker T, Nelson RE. 2005. Creating something from nothing: resource construction through entrepreneurial bricolage. *Administrative Science Quarterly* 50(3): 329–366.

Baldwin C. 2015. Bottlenecks, modules, and dynamic architectural capabilities. Working Paper. HBS Working Paper Series, Harvard University.

Barney J. 1991. Firm resources and sustained competitive advantage. *Journal of Management* 17(1): 99.

Beckman CM, Burton MD, O'Reilly C. 2007. Early teams: the impact of team demography on VC financing and going public. *Journal of Business Venturing* 22(2): 147–173.

Benner MJ, Tripsas M. 2012. The influence of prior industry affiliation on framing in nascent industries: the evolution of digital cameras. *Strategic Management Journal* 33(3): 277–302.

Bikard M. 2018. Made in academia: the effect of institutional origin on inventors' attention to science. *Organization Science* 29(5): 818–836.

Bremner RP, Eisenhardt KM. 2021. Experimentation, bottlenecks, and organizational form: innovation and growth in the nascent drone industry. *Organization Science,* forthcoming.

Brown SL, Eisenhardt KM. 1995. Product development: past research, present findings, and future directions. *Academy of Management Review* 20(2): 343–378.

Brown SL, Eisenhardt K. 1997. The art of continuous change: linking complexity theory and time-paced evolution in relentlessly shifting organizations. *Administrative Science Quarterly* 42(1): 1–34.

Burford N, Shipilov A, Furr N. 2021. How ecosystem structure affects firm performance in response to a negative shock to interdependencies. Working Paper, INSEAD.

Camuffo A, Cordova A, Gambardella A, Spina C. 2019. A scientific approach to entrepreneurial decision making: evidence from a randomized control trial. *Management Science* 66(2): 564–586.

Cattani G. 2005. Preadaptation, firm heterogeneity, and technological performance: a study on the evolution of fiber optics, 1970–1995. *Organization Science* 16(6): 563–580.

Cavarretta F, Furr N. 2010. Too much of a good thing? Extreme outcomes and the resource curse. Working Paper. Available at: https://www.researchgate.net/publication/254555941_Too_much_of_a_good_thing_Resources_effects_in_new_ventures.

Christensen C. 1992. Exploring the limits of the technology S-curve. Parts I and II. *Production and Operations Management* 1(4): 334–366.

Christensen C. 1997. *The Innovator's Dilemma.* Harvard Business School Press: Boston, MA.

Christensen C, Bower JL. 1996. Customer power, strategic investment, and the failure of leading firms. *Strategic Management Journal* 17(3): 197–218.

Cohen S, Bingham CB, Hallen BL. 2019. The role of accelerator designs in mitigating bounded rationality in new ventures. *Administrative Science Quarterly* 64(4): 810–854.

Cohen S, Tripsas M. 2018. Managing technical transitions by building bridges. *Academy of Management Journal* 61(6): 2319–2342.

Cunningham C, Ederer F, Ma S. 2021. Killer acquisitions. *Journal of Political Economy* 129(3): 649–702.

D'Aveni RA. 1994. *Hypercompetition: Managing the Dynamics of Strategic Maneuvering*. Free Press: New York, NY.

Davis J, Eisenhardt K, Bingham C. 2009. Optimal structure, market dynamism, and the strategy of simple rules. *Administrative Science Quarterly* 54(3): 413–452.

Dushnitsky G, Lenox MJ. 2005. When do firms undertake R&D by investing in new ventures? *Strategic Management Journal* 26(10): 947–965.

Eggers J, Kaul A. 2018. Motivation and ability? A behavioral perspective on the pursuit of radical invention in multi-technology incumbents. *Academy of Management Journal* 61(1): 67–93.

Eisenhardt K, Furr N, Bingham C. 2010. Micro-foundations of performance: balancing efficiency and flexibility in dynamic environments. *Organization Science* 21(6): 1263–1273.

Eisenhardt K, Martin J. 2000. Dynamic capabilities: What are they? *Strategic Management Journal* 21(10–11): 1105–1121.

Eisenhardt K, Tabrizi B. 1995. Accelerating adaptive processes: product innovation in the global computer industry. *Administrative Science Quarterly* 40(1): 84–110.

Ethiraj SK. 2007. Allocation of inventive effort in complex product systems. *Strategic Management Journal* 28(6): 563–584.

Fleming L, Sorenson O. 2001. Technology as a complex adaptive system: evidence from patent data. *Research Policy* 30(7): 1019–1039.

Foster R. 1986. The s-curve: a new forecasting tool. In *Innovation: The Attacker's Advantage*, Foster, RN (ed). Simon and Schuster: New York, NY; 87–112.

Furr N. 2019. Product adaptation during new industry emergence: the role of start-up team pre-entry experience. *Organization Science* 30(5): 1076–1096.

Furr N, Eggers JP. 2021 Behavior innovation and corporate renewal. *Strategic Management Review*, forthcoming.

Furr N, Eisenhardt KM. 2021. Strategy and uncertainty: resource-based view, strategy-creation view, and the hybrid between them. *Journal of Management*, forthcoming.

Furr N, Kapoor R, Eisenhardt KM. 2021. Bottlenecks and technology industry emergence. Working Paper, INSEAD.

Furr N, Nickerson JA, Wuebker R. 2016. A theory of entrepreneuring. Working Paper, INSEAD.

Furr N, Shipilov A. 2019. Digital doesn't have to be disruptive. *Harvard Business Review* 97(4): 94–104.

Furr N, Snow D. 2015a. Inter-generational hybrids: spillbacks, spillforwards, and surviving technological discontinuities. *Organization Science* 6(2): 475–493.

Furr N, Snow D. 2015b. The Prius approach: how hybrid technologies help companies survive disruption and shape the future. *Harvard Business Review* 93(11): 103–109.

Furr N, Snow D. 2021. Unpacking technology substitution: last gasp, hybrids, and retreat. Working Paper, INSEAD.

Garud R, Karnøe P. 2003. Bricolage versus breakthrough: distributed and embedded agency in technology entrepreneurship. *Research Policy* 32(2): 277.

Gigerenzer G, Brighton H. 2009. Homo heuristicus: why biased minds make better inferences. *Topics in Cognitive Science* 1(1): 107–143.

Gilbert C. 2005. Unbundling the structure of inertia: resource versus routine rigidity. *Academy of Management Journal* 48(5): 741–763.

Goldstein DG, Gigerenzer G. 2009. Fast and frugal forecasting. *International Journal of Forecasting* 25(4): 760–772.

Hallen BL. 2008. The causes and consequences of the initial network positions of new organizations: from whom do entrepreneurs receive investments? *Administrative Science Quarterly* 53(4): 685–718.

Hallen BL, Cohen SL, Bingham CB. 2020. Do accelerators work? If so, how? *Organization Science* 31(2): 378–414.

Hallen BL, Eisenhardt KM. 2012. Catalyzing strategies and efficient tie formation: how entrepreneurial firms obtain investment ties. *Academy of Management Journal* 55(1): 35–70.

Hannah DP, Eisenhardt KM. 2018. How firms navigate cooperation and competition in nascent ecosystems. *Strategic Management Journal* 39(12): 3163–3192.

Helfat CE. 2000. The evolution of firm capabilities. *Strategic Management Journal* 21(10–11): 955–959.

Helfat C, Eisenhardt K. 2005. Inter-temporal economies of scope, organizational modularity, and the dynamics of diversification. *Strategic Management Journal* 25(13): 1217–1232.

Helfat C, Lieberman M. 2002. The birth of capabilities: market entry and the importance of pre-history. *Industrial and Corporate Change* 11(4): 725–760.

Henderson R. 1995. Of life cycles real and imaginary: the unexpectedly long old age of optical lithography. *Research Policy* 24(4): 631–643.

Henderson RM, Clark KB. 1990. Architectural innovation: the reconfiguration of existing product technologies and the failure of established firms. *Administrative Science Quarterly* 35(1): 9–30.

Hiatt SR, Park S. 2013. Lords of the harvest: third-party influence and regulatory approval of genetically modified organisms. *Academy of Management Journal* 56(4): 923–944.

Holbrook D, Cohen WM, Hounshell DA, Klepper S. 2000. The nature, sources, and consequences of firm differences in early history of the semiconductor industry. *Strategic Management Journal* 21(10–11): 1017–1041.

Howard-Grenville J, Nelson AJ, Earle AG, Haack JA, Young DM. 2017. "If chemists don't do it, who is going to?" Peer-driven occupational change and the emergence of green chemistry. *Administrative Science Quarterly* 62(3): 524–560.

Jacobides MG, Cennamo C, Gawer A. 2018. Towards a theory of ecosystems. *Strategic Management Journal* 39(8): 2255–2276.

Kaplan S, Vakili K. 2015. The double-edged sword of recombination in breakthrough innovation. *Strategic Management Journal* 36(10): 1435–1457.

Kapoor R. 2018. Ecosystems: broadening the locus of value creation. *Journal of Organization Design* 7(1): 1–16.

Kapoor R, Furr N. 2015. Complementarities and competition: unpacking the drivers of entrants' technology choices in the solar photovoltaic industry. *Strategic Management Journal* 36(3): 416–436.

Katila R, Ahuja G. 2002. Something old, something new: a longitudinal study of search behavior and new product introduction. *Academy of Management Journal* 45(6): 1183–1194.

Kirtley J, O'Mahony S. 2021. What is a pivot? Explaining when and how entrepreneurial firms decide to make strategic change and pivot. *Strategic Management Journal*, forthcoming.

Klepper S, Simons KL. 2000. Dominance by birthright: entry of prior radio producers and competitive ramifications in the U.S. television receiver industry. *Strategic Management Journal* 21(10–11): 997–1016.

Knight F. 1921. *Risk, Uncertainty, and Profit*. Houghton Mifflin: Boston, MA.

Knott AM, Bryce DJ, Posen HE. 2003. On the strategic accumulation of intangible assets. *Organization Science* 14(2): 192–207.

Levinthal D. 1998. The slow pace of rapid technological change: gradualism and punctuation in technological change. *Industrial and Corporate Change* 7(2): 217–247.

McDonald R, Eisenhardt KM. 2019. Parallel play: startups, nascent markets, and effective design of a business model. *Administrative Science Quarterly* 65(2): 483–523.

McDonald R, Gao C. 2020. Shaping nascent industries: innovation strategy and regulatory uncertainty in personal genomics. Working Paper. Available at: https://www.hbs.edu/faculty/Pages/item.aspx?num=57720.

Miner AS, Bassoff P, Moorman C. 2001. Organizational improvisation and learning: a field study. *Administrative Science Quarterly* **46**(2): 304–337.

Moeen M. 2017. Entry into nascent industries: disentangling a firm's capability portfolio at the time of investment versus market entry. *Strategic Management Journal* **38**(10): 1986–2004.

Moeen M, Agarwal R. 2017. Incubation of an industry: heterogeneous knowledge bases and modes of value capture. *Strategic Management Journal* **38**(3): 566–587.

Murmann JP, Frenken K. 2006. Toward a systematic framework for research on dominant designs, technological innovations, and industrial change. *Research Policy* **35**(7): 925–952.

Navis C, Glynn MA. 2010. How new market categories emerge: temporal dynamics of legitimacy, identity, and entrepreneurship in satellite radio, 1990–2005. *Administrative Science Quarterly* **55**(3): 439–471.

Ozcan P, Eisenhardt K. 2009. Origin of alliance portfolios: entrepreneurs, network strategies, and firm performance. *Academy of Management Journal* **52**(2): 246–279.

Padgett JF, Ansell C. 1993. Robust action and rise of the Medici. *American Journal of Sociology* **98**(6): 1259–1319.

Porter ME. 1980. *Competitive Strategy*. Free Press: New York, NY.

Raffaelli R. 2019. Technology reemergence: creating new value for old technologies in Swiss mechanical watchmaking, 1970–2008. *Administrative Science Quarterly* **64**(3): 576–618.

Rindova V, Courtney H. 2021. To shape or adapt: knowledge problems, epistemologies, and strategic postures under Knightian uncertainty. *Academy of Management Review*, forthcoming. Available at: https://doi.org/10.5465/amr.2018.0291.

Rindova V, Kotha S. 2001. Continuous "morphing": competing through dynamic capabilities, form, and function. *Academy of Management Journal* **44**(6): 1263–1280.

Roach M, Sauermann H. 2010. A taste for science? PhD scientists' academic orientation and self-selection into research careers in industry. *Research Policy* **39**(3): 422–434.

Rosenberg N. 1976. *Perspectives on Technology*. Cambridge University Press: New York, NY.

Santos FM, Eisenhardt KM. 2005. Organizational boundaries and theories of organization. *Organization Science* **16**(5): 491–508.

Santos FM, Eisenhardt K. 2009. Constructing markets and shaping boundaries: entrepreneurial power and agency in nascent fields. *Academy of Management Journal* **52**(4): 643–671.

Sarasvathy SD. 2001. Causation and effectuation: toward a theoretical shift from economic inevitability to entrepreneurial contingency. *Academy of Management Review* **26**(2): 243.

Schumpeter J. 1942. *Capitalism, socialism, and democracy*. Harper: NewYork, NY.

Shah SK, Agarwal R, Echambadi R. 2019. Jewels in the crown: exploring the motivations and team building processes of employee entrepreneurs. *Strategic Management Journal* **40**(9): 1417–1452.

Shane S. 2000. Prior knowledge and the discovery of entrepreneurial opportunities. *Organization Science* **11**(4): 448–469.

Shelef O, Wuebker R, Barney J. 2020. Heisenberg effects on business ideas. Working Paper. Available at SSRN: https://papers.ssrn.com/sol3/papers.cfm?abstract_id=3581255.

Sommer SC, Loch CH, Dong J. 2009. Managing complexity and unforeseeable uncertainty in startup companies: an empirical study. *Organization Science* **20**(1): 118–133.

Suarez FF, Grodal S, Gotsopoulos A. 2015. Perfect timing? Dominant category, dominant design, and the window of opportunity for firm entry. *Strategic Management Journal* **36**(3): 437–448.

Suarez FF, Utterback JM. 1995. Dominant designs and the survival of firms. *Strategic Management Journal* **16**(6): 415–430.

Teece DJ. 1986. Profiting from technological innovation: implications for integration, collaboration, licensing, and public policy. *Research Policy* 15(2): 285–305.

Teece DJ. 2006. Reflections on "profiting from innovation." *Research Policy* 35(8): 1131–1146.

Tripsas M. 2008. Customer preference discontinuities: a trigger for radical technological change. *Managerial and Decision Economics* 29(2–3): 79–97.

Tripsas M, Gavetti G. 2000. Capabilities, cognition, and inertia: evidence from digital imaging. *Strategic Management Journal* 21(10–11): 1147–1161.

Tushman ML, Anderson P. 1986. Technological discontinuities and organizational environments. *Administrative Science Quarterly* 31(3): 439–465.

Utterback JM. 1996. *Mastering the Dynamics of Innovation: How Companies Can Seize Opportunities in the Face of Technological Change.* Harvard Business School Press: Boston, MA.

Utterback JM, Suarez FF. 1993. Innovation, competition, and industry structure. *Research Policy* 22(1): 1–21.

Van de Ven AH, Garud R. 1993. Innovation and industry development: the case of cochlear implants. *Research on Technological Innovation, Management and Policy* 5(1): 1–46.

Wasserman N. 2003. Founder-CEO succession and the paradox of entrepreneurial success. *Organization Science* 14(2): 149–172.

Wernerfelt B. 1984. A resource-based view of the firm. *Strategic Management Journal* 5(2): 171–180.

Whetten DA, Felin T, King BG. 2009. The practice of theory borrowing in organizational studies: current issues and future directions. *Journal of Management* 35(3): 537–563.

Wiggins RR, Ruefli TW. 2005. Schumpeter's ghost: is hypercompetition making the best of times shorter? *Strategic Management Journal* 26(10): 887–911.

Yu S. 2020. How do accelerators impact the performance of high-technology ventures? *Management Science* 66(2): 530–552.

PART 4

COMPETITIVE AND COOPERATIVE STRATEGY

John Child, Rodolphe Durand, and
Dovev Lavie, Leads

4.0

COMPETITIVE AND COOPERATIVE STRATEGY

John Child, Rodolphe Durand, and Dovev Lavie

Introduction

Strategy is about defining ways to outperform rivals in a given environment; rivals are firms that offer the same products or services as those of the focal firm. Strategy as a research field flourished after World War II, when firms expanded globally and as product and financial markets professionalized. The early view of strategy underscored a firm's position in a value chain that enables it to either access production factors at a lower cost or offer buyers differentiated products or services (e.g., Porter, 1985). Another view proposed that firms, embodying heterogeneous sets of resources, can extract rents by better leveraging these resources and combining them to shape value propositions and support transactions (e.g., Barney, 1991).

With the opening of more global markets following the collapse of the Soviet Union and the surge of revolutionary technologies, firms began facing new realities in their quest to outperform rivals and formulate and implement their strategies. In these turbulent contexts, securing a position in a value chain and protecting rent-accruing resources may still be necessary—but not sufficient. Competition has intensified and become more dynamic. Cooperative strategies with local partners or technology vendors have become essential, resulting in coopetition—allying with rivals while also competing with them in the same or other market segments, or in different markets.

This lead chapter offers an overview of the theories that have been used to account for competitive and cooperative strategies. Taking stock of the new realities of the competitive landscape, we unravel the challenges and opportunities for strategy research that these new realities harbor. This is followed by two subsequent chapters: "Competitive Advantage = Strategy, Reboot" and "Alliances and Networks." Each of these chapters provides a focused reading on the constitutive nature of how firms seek to outperform rivals. The chapter on competitive advantage accounts for the determinants of rent creation and appropriation for a firm vis-à-vis its rivals. The chapter on alliances and networks embeds the firm in a web of interactions that benefit the firm but could also derail its operations and undercut its profitability if not managed properly. The current chapter is structured as follows: we review the basic theories used in research on competitive and cooperative strategies; then we uncover primary challenges that strategy research faces; and finally, mirroring these challenges, we preview the theoretical and empirical opportunities for strategy research in the coming decade.

Competitive and Cooperative Strategies: Definitions and Theoretical Blocks

Defining competitive, cooperative, and coopetitive strategies

Competitive strategies characterize the goal setting and behaviors that firms implement to take advantage of their industry positions and resources. Competition occurs between firms as they strive to access and defend their value and cost positions in their industry and to maintain their offerings' attractiveness and inimitability (Besanko *et al.*, 2009). Firms can vie for better market positions by improving product features and accessing superior resources (Hoopes, Madsen, and Walker, 2003). The success of these competitive actions depends on the awareness, motivations, and capabilities of the firms that engage in competitive interactions (Chen, Su, and Tsai, 2007). While the primary goal of strategy is above-average returns, that goal can be reached in multiple ways, which firms decompose into strategic objectives. In devising competitive strategies, firms rely on the results of industry and competitor analyses. These strategies include cost and differentiation strategies at the product and business levels, which complement corporate strategies of make-or-buy choices, horizontal and vertical integration, and other forms of diversification in different products and geographies. The bulk of strategy research has focused on explaining which firm characteristics—for example, top management team (TMT) composition and experience, nature of resources, financial slack, and organizational aspiration—lead to specific decisions that in turn affect financial performance.

Cooperative strategy refers to the attempt by firms to realize their objectives through cooperation with other firms, which can take various forms of collaboration and partnership. Many of these can be described as "strategic alliances." An *alliance* is a voluntary relationship between two or more independent firms that is intended to achieve the firms' individual and mutual objectives. The firms share or exchange resources such as key brands, information, technology, production facilities, and finance, and obtain benefits from connections with governments, politicians, and other external stakeholders. Alliances are termed "strategic" when they are formed to help the partner firms achieve their strategic objectives, often as a direct response to major challenges or opportunities. The range of cooperative forms now used to implement a cooperative strategy has expanded considerably beyond the dyads typical in the early days of cooperation, namely joint ventures, co-production, licensing, and franchising. Today, cooperation often takes place between multiple partners, crosses sector boundaries, brings together different contributors to integrated value chains, and utilizes technology platforms as a basis for transactional networks (Beamish and Lupton, 2016; Child *et al.*, 2019).

While cooperation may take place between firms that do not compete directly in any sphere of activity, firms often agree to cooperate in certain defined spheres while remaining competitors in others (Dussauge and Garrette, 1999). Thus, although cooperation would appear in principle to be incompatible with competition, in practice, some firms simultaneously compete and cooperate with each other in markets and value chain functions, a process labeled *coopetition* (Bengtsson and Kock, 2000; Nalebuff and Brandenburger, 1996). For instance, firms may jointly develop a new technology while competing for its commercialization. Although partners typically compete for their value share in an alliance, coopetition entails their market competition beyond the alliance's scope. Coopetition can evolve in distinct paths: rivals may enter into an alliance, or alliance partners may enter each other's product markets.

Whereas scholars have studied horizontal alliances within an industry, such alliances do not necessarily entail coopetition, because partners may occupy distinct market niches outside their alliance. Furthermore, this activity-centered view focuses on dyads, whereas an actor-centered framework considers the creation and distribution of value in a network (Bengtsson and Raza-Ullah, 2016), suggesting that coopetition can emerge within firms, in alliances, in strategic groups, and at the industry or ecosystem level. Early research on coopetition focused on competitive tension between partners in an alliance and discussed circumstances that prompt firms to simultaneously compete and cooperate (Dagnino and Padula, 2002). More recently, scholars have paid more attention to coopetition across levels of analysis and begun to discern the dynamics of coopetition at each level. For example, bilateral coopetition in an alliance differs from multilateral coopetition in an ecosystem wherein complex interdependencies emerge across different actors that operate under loose governance. Yet the interplay between competition and cooperation merits further attention, especially with respect to reconciling the conflicting pressures imposed by competition and cooperation (Hoffmann *et al.*, 2018). Recent reviews (Bengtsson and Raza-Ullah, 2016; Bouncken *et al.*, 2015; Devece, Ribeiro-Soriano, and Palacios-Marqués, 2019; Dorn, Schweiger, and Albers, 2016) seek coherence in this fragmented body of research.

Theoretical approaches to competitive and cooperative strategies

While the strategy research field may appear fragmented today (Durand, Grant, and Madsen, 2017), five decades ago it seemed more coherent. Over the period from the 1960s to 1980s, a series of theoretical approaches enabled management scholars to move beyond the broad-brush application of economics and political science palettes to reflect on firms' behaviors as shaping the world reality.

Early theoretical perspectives on competitive strategy derived from the more general body of orthodox and heterodox economic scholarship. Market-power, transaction cost, and resource-based theories were used to identify the motives for firms to compete and cooperate (Contractor and Lorange, 1988; Nelson, 1991), while other theories, such as agency theory and game theory, were applied mostly when studying risk and control loss arising when undertaking a cooperative strategy.

Market-power theory (MPT) is concerned with ways in which firms can improve their competitive success by securing stronger positions in their markets. It forms the basis for analyzing firms' competitive landscapes (Porter, 1980). MPT has been refined to explain how competitive advantage shaped by industry and firm conditions accounts for how a firm can sustainably outperform its competition. Competitive position is thus understood as the difference between customers' willingness to pay and price—the larger this difference, the more competitive a firm is (Besanko *et al.*, 2009). A firm's superior competitive position results from securing value drivers—such as quality, services, access, and delivery—and minimizing costs through means such as economies of scale, scope, and learning. The firm can also attract and retain customers by reducing their search, identification, and transaction costs, while preventing rivals from emulating the firm by using property rights and idiosyncratic processes. Beyond a given geography, MPT and its derivatives also help to account for a firm's entry into new foreign markets to enhance its global market position, in which case the risks and consequent costs of entering such a market independently may favor cooperation with a local partner.

Writing in 1937, Coase (1991) was the pioneer of transaction cost economics (TCE), which was later refined by Williamson (1981, 1985). At the hands of scholars such as Hennart (1988), Dyer (1997), Poppo and Zenger (1998), and Judge and Dooley (2006), TCE became one of the most influential perspectives within the field of strategy, addressing issues such as make-or-buy decisions, the choice between expansion through alliances rather than mergers and acquisitions (M&A), new market entry modes and alliance governance structures, and the costs of safeguarding against guile and opportunism on the part of transaction partners. The TCE approach contributed to explaining firm boundaries by delineating the conditions for integrating activities or relying on market transactions (Leiblein and Miller, 2003). The TCE perspective on cooperative relationships shed new light on the relevance of partners' motives, the nature of the investments they commit to the collaboration, and the specific character of their transactions. Whereas MPT emphasizes motives for cooperative strategy that relate to market power and profit attainment, TCE stresses transaction governance efficiency rationales for cooperation. The combination of these two perspectives gives rise to the transaction-value perspective, which balances the opportunities against transaction costs.

The resource-based view (RBV), dating back to Penrose (1959) and Wernerfelt (1984), has been a trailblazing approach to revisiting how firms compete. MPT and TCE depart from the idea that firms are quasi-identical and that competitive advantage results from a temporary disequilibrium in market conditions or is a converging but transitory interpretation of a firm's superior productive capacity (e.g., Powell, 2001). By contrast, the RBV considers that firms can use their resources to take advantage of ex ante and ex post imperfections in competitive markets to garner benefits, maintain their intrinsic heterogeneity, and alter market structures to prolong rent accruing to them (Durand, 2002; Peteraf, 1993). Resources and capabilities have been seen as contributing to a firm's ability to reach and defend better market positions rather than providing superior advantages in and of themselves (Hoopes *et al.*, 2003). Moreover, the RBV draws attention to another motive for adopting a cooperative strategy that has remained prominent: it highlights the potential mutual benefits to be gained from collaborative interfirm relationships through the sharing of complementary resources between alliance partners that maintain their independent status. The sharing of knowledge can have synergistic benefits for innovation despite the risks of its misappropriation, through promoting mutual learning, speeding up the research and development (R&D) process, and reducing the financial burden it places on each partner firm.

Theorists have acknowledged that interactions between rivals lead to unexpected firm behaviors. For instance, Lieberman and Asaba (2006) detail the reasons why firms imitate each other, while Chen and Miller (2015) reflect on the possibility of mutual forbearance as firms' market positions overlap. Likewise, Child and Rodrigues (2004) document the inherent risks of a cooperative strategy. Some risks, such as the leakage of proprietary knowledge, arise from the poor character and trustworthiness of partners, as highlighted in Williamson's (1985) elaboration of TCE. Agency theory and game theory point to the more structural risks when the partners' objectives are not completely aligned, as in cooperation between competing firms. Agency theory points out that when cooperating, firms become partial agents for the realization of each other's interests and goals. This gives rise to a concern over the governance and monitoring mechanisms that are appropriate within a cooperative partnership (e.g., Geringer and Hébert, 1989). Game theory identifies the dilemma that arises because while cooperation will maximize joint interest, it does not necessarily maximize the self-interest of partners, at least for a given transaction at a given time. Hence, game theory points to the tradeoffs between short- and long-term benefits in cooperative relationships (Parkhe, 1993).

New Contexts for Studying Competitive and Cooperative Strategy

Following our brief review of the subject's principal theoretical underpinnings and their historical origins, we proceed to considering the impact of the changing context of strategy. Key developments in the new context are (1) the rise of emerging economies, (2) increasing protectionism and political intervention associated with a dominance of politics over economics, (3) technological disruption, and (4) the growing pressure of social demands on business. Each of these developments has stimulated interest in applying noneconomic theories to the understanding of competitive and cooperative strategies.

The rise of emerging economies

As emerging economies have come to play a larger role in world business (Meyer and Grosse, 2019), new sources of production factors have spawned. Costs of factors such as labor, production, inventory, transportation, and delivery have been dramatically affected, leading firms to rethink their areas of competencies and value chains. Where to source from, what to produce, why specialize, whom to serve, and how to distribute have become essential questions for competitive strategy at the business level. Economies of scale become vastly larger when a firm considers its natural market not as its domestic market but the world. Economies of scope and innovative ideas travel across business lines and accrue vastly more rents when broadening an offerings portfolio as new ingredients, components, or inputs become available. Yet the institutional contexts of emerging economies generally contrast with those of the Western contexts assumed in established analyses (Rotting, 2016). Hence, multinational enterprises (MNEs) need to rethink how to manage knowledge flows between entities (Subramaniam and Venkatraman, 2001) and business groups that compensate for the shortcomings of institutional voids. They also need to develop diversification strategies that protect them in the long run (Khanna and Palepu, 2000) and reinforce their global competitiveness (Guillén and García-Canal, 2009).

Paralleling this opening of strategic opportunities from a competitive strategy perspective, alliances between developed- and emerging-economy firms have become more common, as has cooperation between firms located in different emerging economies (Anand and Kale, 2006). This has stimulated research into the respective benefits derived from collaboration by developed- and emerging-economy MNEs (Juasrikul et al., 2018). In these relationships, an important issue is the implications for the risks and transaction costs of cooperation posed by the institutional voids that characterize many emerging economies (Doh et al., 2017). Another theme is the effects of national institutional distance between alliance partners, which can influence the choice of their alliance governance mode (Choi and Contractor, 2016; Hitt et al., 2004). Finally, the microfoundations of effective relationship management are a necessary condition for the successful implementation of a cooperative strategy, especially in emerging economies where good relations with government agencies and political leaders can be vital. Elg et al.'s (2017) investigation of Swedish MNEs operating in emerging markets identifies the microfoundations and routines for managing regulative, normative, and cultural-cognitive institutional pressures in order to develop a firm's capability to achieve a legitimate and environmentally sustainable position in those markets.

Ascendancy of politics over economics

While public and political agencies, such as government agencies and nongovernmental organizations (NGOs), have always had a role in setting the boundary conditions for viable competitive and cooperative strategies, their significance in this respect has grown, reflecting two broad trends.

First is the recognition that nonmarket strategies (i.e., firms' proactive activities outside their product or resource markets, such as lobbying and political engagements) are as important in enabling firms to acquire and allocate resources as are their profit-driven market strategies (cf. Dorobantu, Kaul, and Zelner, 2017). The recognition that multiple stakeholders contribute to the creation of value for the firm's shareholders and that the state intervenes conditionally to favor emerging industries has been pervading research on competitive strategy (Georgallis, Dowell, and Durand, 2019; Tantalo and Priem, 2016; Vasi and King, 2012). However, the generally higher degree of state intervention in the business systems of emerging economies creates the potential for state agencies in emerging-economy host countries to shape the conditions under which cooperative strategy unfolds, for example, how an international alliance can operate (Xu and Meyer, 2013). If it is prey to the vagaries of politics, state intervention and control can discourage international business cooperation by elevating uncertainty and perceived risk. By contrast, bilateral intergovernmental agreements that relax restrictions, such as local employment laws, can provide favorable operating conditions for foreign-investing firms collaborating with host-country enterprises (Child and Marinova, 2014).

Second, the increasing ascendancy of politics over economics is disrupting the former market-guided global economic order. This latter trend is reflected in several developments: the shift toward greater political management of international trade; the rise of "techno-nationalism" evident in inter-nation competition to build innovation capacity (Petricevic and Teece, 2019); and deglobalization, as manifest by reshoring and declining levels of foreign direct investment and driven further by a widespread sociopolitical backlash against globalization. A significant development has been the Trump administration's resort to economic sanctions and tariffs for political ends, while Brexit is another political shift likely to result in additional barriers to free trade. The lockdown of national borders and disruption of international travel following the COVID-19 outbreak are additional reminders of state intervention. These developments create constraints on trade and foreign investment that reduce strategic choice in opportunities for competition and cooperation and the forms these can take.

Technological disruption

Innovations in technology have disruptive consequences that are fundamentally reshaping established firms' strategies (Christensen, 1997). The significant competitive advantage offered by innovation has spread research on capabilities and promoted the sharing and development of joint intellectual property. From a research standpoint, the position in a value system (inspired by MPT) or the ownership of valuable and nontransferable resources (inspired by the RBV) falls short in accounting for the variegated phenomena taking place around innovation and technological disruption. In an effort to cope with and account for these phenomena, researchers developed new concepts—such as dynamic capabilities, adjustable and evolutive—that nurture competitiveness (Eisenhardt and Martin, 2000). Innovation emanates from a controlled openness vis-à-vis parties previously seen as excluded from internal firm processes (e.g., buyers, suppliers, and third parties). It combines these parties' knowledge flows within the firm (Laursen and Salter, 2006; Rosenkopf and Nerkar, 2001). This, in turn, encourages more cooperative ventures. KPMG (2017: 3) concluded from a survey of alliance experts that "for many organizations, strategic alliances are becoming a fundamental part of corporate strategy as a means of keeping abreast of disruptive technologies." At the same time, contractual alliances are becoming more attractive than equity joint ventures in many situations, as improvements in information and communication technologies (ICT), contract law, and collaborative experience reduce the transactional risks of cooperation (Child et al., 2019).

More advanced digital applications have become possible, such as the internet of things, big data analytics, blockchain, and servitization—the last being the digital integration of services with products (Gomes et al., 2019), a trend that is driving a dramatic increase in the number of cross-sector alliances such as those between automobile manufacturers and ICT firms (KPMG, 2017). Likewise, many firms have formed alliances and partnerships in order to capitalize on the potential of digital platforms such as the blockchain technology. Its application has expanded beyond fintech to global supply chains, such as for food and pharmaceuticals, where it can facilitate greater transparency, traceability, and accountability among multiple suppliers, intermediaries, and retailers (Child et al., 2019). For many, the growing significance of disruptive manufacturing technologies and unanticipated problems in managing the complexity of global value chains are among other reasons given for re-shoring and taking greater managerial control in-house (Barbieri et al., 2018). Insofar as global value chains have become an important form of networked cooperation, re-shoring represents a retreat from this domain of cooperative strategy.

Social demands on business

In many societies, trust in business and its leaders has fallen to a low ebb (Edelman, 2020). An increasing number of companies are responding through amplifying their claims to espouse principles of responsible conduct and broadening the referents for that responsibility to a wider set of stakeholders than just shareholders. Competitive strategy must consider reputational and operational effects of corporate social responsibility (CSR) on performance (Durand, Paugam, and Stolowy, 2019; McWilliams and Siegel, 2000; Surroca, Tribó, and Waddock, 2010). Firms also seek cooperation with public authorities to help rebuild public trust in business that has been damaged by corporate scandals, exploitation of consumers, and self-serving executive behavior.

One of the avenues for demonstrating CSR is to commit expertise and resources to public projects in cooperation with public authorities and NGOs (Quelin *et al.*, 2019). Although former models of public-private partnership have come in for considerable criticism, such as burdening public organizations like hospitals with crippling levels of debt, greater cooperation on a broader plane between business and government is being called for to deal with the growing tensions and threats within contemporary societies.

Many areas for collaboration between business and public authorities are emerging. One is to combat threats from malevolent actors such as cybercriminals and terrorists. Another is climate change, with the specific challenge of implementing the 2015 Paris Agreement. To this end, the UN Climate Change secretariat announced that it "seeks to engage in mutually beneficial, collaborative partnerships with non-party stakeholders such as states, regions, cities, companies, investors, and citizens" (UN, n.d.). A third area is urban management and the growing requirement for cities to become smart in dealing with challenges such as air pollution, traffic congestion, cybersecurity, and fresh food supply.

These challenges encourage collaboration between firms and public authorities as much as they open opportunities for developing competitive strategies. An example is Mobility as a Service (MaaS) partnerships (MaaS, 2018). A city's public municipality partners with private sector actors who provide the smartphone apps, bicycles, and vehicles, and together they serve the public. The contribution of MaaS is to integrate different forms of transport services into a single mobility service that is accessible on demand (Goodall *et al.*, 2017). Autonomous electric vehicles, pervasive networks of cameras and sensors, and automated roof gardens are examples of disruptive technologies aimed at providing other solutions for urban living, which involve collaboration between technology firms and city authorities, as in the Australian Government's Smart Cities and Suburbs Program. Other areas in which firms are increasingly collaborating with government institutions include social infrastructure, such as educational and training initiatives, and environmental protection.

The Future of Competitive and Cooperative Strategy Research

The theoretical perspectives on which the early frameworks of competitive and cooperative strategies were grounded offered relevant explanations. However, the new conditions for strategy—for example, emerging economies, nonmarket forces, technology disruptions, and social demands on firms—increase the diversity of competitive conditions and cooperative arrangements. These developments have implications for the future focus of theoretical and empirical research on competitive and cooperative strategies. We next discuss potentially fruitful areas of future research for competitive strategy, cooperative strategy, and coopetition.

Future research in competitive strategy

The aforementioned trends question three basic assumptions underlying the research traditions in competitive strategy: (1) the scope of firm activities and usefulness of classical strategy concepts, (2) the new responsibilities of firms and the nature of competition, and (3) the behavioral and motivational aspects of competitiveness.

First, under the pressure of globalization and technology trends, the erstwhile simple depiction of a firm as a compilation of businesses with a few shared activities is incomplete. Firms develop complex networks of activities that cut across their various businesses, generating new economic dependencies among actors grouped in adaptive ecosystems (Jacobides, Cennamo, and Gawer, 2018). In this context, can the traditional concepts of economies of scale, scope, and learning; those associated with TCE; and the definition of resources as valuable, rare, non-imitable, and non-substitutable, still hold and contribute to explaining firms' strategic decisions and outcomes? When interdependencies impose a multipartite engagement to build platforms in a winner-takes-all model of competition (Cennamo and Santalo, 2013); when states' interests and regulations impinge on firms' technological and geographical expansion plans (Dorobantu *et al.*, 2017); when (big) data flow into "data oceans" and "data lakes" open to suppliers, clients, and other parties, for example, universities, students, and individuals, to revive innovation (Boudreau and Lakhani, 2013)—new concepts are needed to theorize about competitive strategy.

Second, as the scope of firm activities changes, the responsibilities of firms evolve as well. More intense economic activity and exchanges at a global scale, and exacerbated exploitation of natural and human resources, both weigh on firms and raise questions about their responsibilities beyond profitability for shareholders. Stakeholders' demands do not coincide; firms and their decision-makers confront the situation of optimizing under complexity and prioritizing objectives. For a long time, CSR has been considered a nice add-on, and research questioned its benefits for financial performance (e.g., Surroca *et al.*, 2010) and attractiveness for investors (Durand *et al.*, 2019; Ioannou and Serafeim, 2015). As natural, environmental, and health crises unfurl and upend our productive systems on a regular basis, should competitive strategy not begin including environmental and social externalities in a more systematic fashion? This would lead us to reconsider performance as not purely financial but nonfinancial as well, posing puzzles about optimization of dual- or multipurpose organizations (Gaba and Greve, 2019) and considering CSR to be just as core to strategy as other nonmarket strategies (Lyon *et al.*, 2018).

Third, we need to amend behavioral and motivational assumptions about competitiveness. More research is needed to investigate the microfoundations of strategy and the behavioral determinants leading to competitiveness (Powell, Lovallo, and Fox, 2011). Managers' cognitive abilities become essential for adjusting to and anticipating environmental changes (Helfat and Peteraf, 2015). Beyond cognitive abilities, motivational profiles of organizations that assemble pro-self and pro-social individuals determine value creation and competitive edge (Bridoux, Coeurderoy, and Durand, 2011). In a context where trusting employees is core to strategy implementation, and the purpose of firms underlies how employees' engagement affects performance (Gartenberg, Prat, and Serafeim, 2019), competitive strategy must include behavioral and motivational components as the bedrock of innovativeness, execution, and performance—all the more so if one is to consider financial and nonfinancial performance dimensions concurrently. A significant topic for future research is therefore whether organizational policies that permit a greater participation of employees, especially knowledge workers, in the decision-making process contribute to firm competitiveness. Another topic concerns the alignment between firms' or their entities' moral values, the implementation of strategic practices (e.g., Bitektine and Haack, 2015; Jacqueminet and Durand, in press), and the resulting impact on firm performance.

Future research in cooperative strategy

Theorizing about cooperative strategy has become even more challenging in the light of ongoing contextual changes (Contractor and Reuer, 2019). Decades ago, Tallman and Shenkar (1994: 92) argued that "the selection of cooperative strategies, organizational forms and partners, is not strictly economic, but also a social, psychological and emotional phenomenon." Similarly, Klijn *et al.* (2010) reported that, in practice, partners normally have a combination of rationales for joint venture formation and that an explanation of this issue consequently requires multiple theoretical perspectives. With the notable exception of culturally informed studies, early perspectives on cooperative strategy were generally predicated on the rationality assumptions of economic reasoning and did not take account of further insights offered by other disciplines. Such insights bring new research questions onto the agenda. These include how psychological factors such as trust affect the quality of cooperation between firms (Zhong *et al.*, 2017) and how political factors in the alliance context, such as national institutional policies and ideologies, can constrain alliance policy options.

The changing context of cooperation not only continues to speak for the combination of existing theories, but it also brings into prominence other perspectives that have not until recently held center stage. The contextual developments just outlined carry the clear implication that theorizing on cooperative strategy has to embrace contributions from a broader range of perspectives, particularly the political, sociological, and technological. Research is required into how managers of alliances and cooperative ecosystems individually and collectively cope with the complexity that this broader view exposes.

A political perspective draws attention to the growing relevance of governments and NGOs for the implementation of cooperative strategy, especially in infrastructural and environmentally sensitive areas of business. The negotiation of strategic opportunities within a context of the heightened public and institutional expectations now being placed on business is a significant issue for future research on international alliances operating in different jurisdictions. It could benefit from a "political action" perspective that examines initiatives to construct "relational frameworks" between MNEs and their alliance units, on the one hand, and external agencies, on the other. The bases of power and the processes under which these translate into influence within relational frameworks—such as the cultivation of social legitimacy—are central to this line of inquiry, which brings into theoretical play insights from both political science and sociology (Child, Tse, and Rodrigues, 2013). The role played by general managers as well as dedicated "alliance managers" (Kale and Singh, 2009) in establishing relational frameworks both with external institutions and between alliance partners themselves is a question deserving further research, as noted later in the "Alliances and Networks" chapter.

A sociological perspective is concerned with the future role of business within society as a whole. It draws attention to the implications of a changing definition of the social role of business for the concept of cooperative strategy. The future legitimacy of business may depend on its adoption of a strategy that turns away from the wasteful and exploitative ethos of "free" market–based competition toward a more communitarian approach. This would define a strategic role for business in partnership with community and public agencies to leverage the complementary strengths of both parties directed at achieving environmentally and socially constructive ends.

The power of disruptive technologies such as artificial intelligence presents fundamental choices relevant to cooperative strategy, choices that bring the technological perspective to the fore. Within that perspective, a long-running debate has weighed whether the transformative power of new technologies lends them a determining influence over human behavior and social organization, or whether the effects of technology are socially constructed (Leonardi and Barley, 2010). If technology appears to be a force in its own right, that status lies in the economics of its development and application. For example, innovation is a driver of social change because it is a significant source of competitive advantage. This is why when cooperative strategy has taken technology into account, it has tended to be with reference to the knowledge-sharing synergies in innovation that technology alliances or partnerships could bring. Now and into the future, the innovation perspective will also inform other developments in cooperative strategy that are deserving of more study. Prominent among these are the integrative potential of new communication and accountability technologies (such as blockchain) for facilitating the process of cooperation per se within alliances and value chains, and the compelling logic of a cooperative strategy for achieving the integration of artificial intelligence into products and services across a wide range of sectors. Moreover, as the rate of technology development accelerates, cooperative arrangements will increasingly be designed to foreshadow a flexible reconfiguration of objectives and partners, and probably shorter life cycles, so as to achieve the necessary dynamic capabilities.

The Future of Coopetition Research

Future research should bring more clarity to the multifaceted nature of coopetition, distinguishing coopetition in the product market from coopetition in the resource market, and acknowledging informal and implicit coopetition (e.g., via collusion), which can be contrasted with explicit coopetition via alliances and product market overlap. Research should consider various aspects of coopetition, such as coopetition for identity (jointly maintaining a collective and individual corporate identities), in addition to the traditional coopetition for resources. When considering various dimensions of coopetition, scholars may examine how the implications of overlap in product functionality and service offerings differ from those relating to geographical proximity and reliance on similar resources and technologies. How does product-market coopetition shape patterns of competition and cooperation in these other dimensions?

Scholars may also discern the unique dynamics of coopetition in horizontal versus vertical or complementary relations. They may examine how firms' transition from cooperation to competition with former partners differs from their transition toward more cooperation with former rivals, highlighting the unique processes by which simultaneous competition and cooperation emerge or dissipate. Studying the temporal dynamics of coopetition is also worthwhile: competition can precede cooperation (e.g., alliances formed to attenuate competitive pressure) or be prompted by it (e.g., following learning races), while cooperation may drive out competition (e.g., collusion) or substitute for it (e.g., explicit alliances replacing implicit cooperation among multimarket rivals). How do these distinct scenarios vary with respect to their mechanisms and implications? Another extension concerns a firm's competition with a rival that partners with a third party, or a firm's cooperation with a partner of its competitor. The dynamics of value creation and value capture manifest even in such indirect coopetition, but raise the question of how the association between the firm and such third parties shapes the firm's coopetitive relations.

Antecedents and consequences of coopetition

Literature on the antecedents of coopetition echoes that on alliances (see the "Alliances and Networks" chapter), covering environmental, organizational, and motivational drivers. For example, rivals enter alliances to improve their competitive positions in markets with intermediate rivalry: at low rivalry intensity, they have little incentive to change the status quo, while at high intensity, they risk opportunistic behavior. Coopetition is also typical in R&D-intensive industries in which firms strive for complementary resources, cost sharing, and shorter time-to-market (e.g., Gnyawali, He, and Madhavan, 2008). Seeking scale efficiencies and coping with uncertainty, industry dynamism, and regulatory changes are also important antecedents (e.g., Gnyawali and Park, 2011). Finally, coopetition is more likely when rivals exhibit a partner-friendly culture (Das and Teng, 1998) and may be motivated by attempts to lock out rivals (Gimeno, 2004), enter new markets (Gnyawali *et al.*, 2008), or learn from a rival (Gnyawali and Park, 2011).

However, many studies neither specify unique antecedents that distinguish coopetition from cooperation, nor fully disentangle the underlying mechanisms. Future research on the microfoundations of coopetition may study how personality traits, values, culture, and friendship ties influence firms' tendencies to simultaneously cooperate and compete (e.g., Han, Shipilov, and Greve, 2017). Scholars may also go beyond the emergence of coopetition to study its evolution. Does coopetition follow a life-cycle pattern with observable phases (e.g., Dorn *et al.*, 2016)? What tilts the balance between competition and cooperation or enables firms to strive toward balance? How do various stakeholders shape firms' coopetitive relations? How do a firm's alliances with and competitive actions against third parties influence the nature of coopetition? These questions among others merit further attention.

Research on the consequences of coopetition has been split between studies that focus on its virtues and those highlighting its risks and challenges. The first stream predicts its positive implications for learning, innovation, knowledge exchange, value creation, and financial performance. Nevertheless, empirical findings are mixed, pointing to potential contingencies. For instance, whereas some studies reveal that coopetition enhances innovation (e.g., Ritala, 2012), others suggest divergent effects for radical versus incremental innovation (e.g., Bouncken and Fredrich, 2012). The second stream relates to the hazards of coopetition, alluding to tensions and conflicts both with the partner and internally because of incongruence between the logics of competition and cooperation. This stream of research discusses the misalignment of objectives, lack of commitment, knowledge leakage, and opportunism that characterize coopetition, which is depicted as a double-edged sword.

Hence, scholars should consider the benefits and costs of coopetition, and study boundary conditions for coopetition effects. For example, do technological relatedness and geographical proximity between parties in an alliance facilitate knowledge exchange and cooperation or rather reinforce the competitive tension between these parties? More broadly, theories should be elaborated to explain how competitive and cooperative logics can coexist and be reconciled (e.g., Chen and Miller, 2015). Future research may carefully map the types of tensions and outcomes of coopetition, because, for example, certain tensions may affect market entry and growth, while others may matter for innovation or the survival of alliances. Such research should study the implications of coopetition not only for performance but also for corporate strategy. For example, how does coopetition drive acquisitions, diversification, divestitures, and internationalization? Scholars may also seek to explain how firms can mitigate opportunism and other noncooperative behaviors in coopetition: should they invest in formalizing contracts, in building trust, or in other measures? Finally, future research may examine the tradeoffs between value creation and capture, answering questions such as, How can firms share knowledge while protecting their proprietary assets from potential rivals in alliances? Should firms nurture routines for restricting knowledge leakage to their partners or rather encourage such spillover while developing routines for recapturing the gains from subsequent inventions using that leaked knowledge?

Managing the tensions between competition and cooperation

Recent research on coopetition draws from the literature on paradoxes to study how firms manage the tensions between competition and cooperation (e.g., Schad *et al.*, 2016). In addition to the tension between knowledge sharing and protection, tensions arise from parties' disparate agendas. To resolve the paradox resulting from the need to cooperate while competing, scholars have identified alternative approaches for buffering these contradictory activities or developing capabilities for managing them simultaneously. According to Hoffmann *et al.* (2018), the tensions can be managed by devoting separate organizational units to either cooperating or competing with the partner (organizational separation); switching between competition and cooperation with the partner over time (temporal separation); focusing on cooperation in certain domains (products, markets, or value chain activities) while competing in others (domain separation); or developing capabilities for synthesizing competition and cooperation via differentiation and integration in the same unit (contextual integration). The last entails coping with uncertainty and complexity while nurturing trust and commitment, thus calling for managerial expertise, a cooperative mindset, and dedicated routines, which are embodied in coopetition capabilities (e.g., Gnyawali and Park, 2011).

Future research may examine the relative effectiveness of these alternative approaches for managing coopetition using qualitative and quantitative research methods. Besides documenting firms' approaches for managing coopetition, scholars should elaborate on how these approaches enable firms to mitigate tensions and overcome coopetition challenges. Under what conditions would one approach outperform others? What are the cognitive and behavioral processes that underlie these tensions? What role do individuals play in managing the tensions between competition and cooperation, and what personality profile and skills can help cope with these tensions? Finally, and more substantially, what does "balancing" competition and cooperation mean, and what is the appropriate level of balance given various organizational and environmental contingencies?

Conclusion

The changing context of competitive and cooperative strategies—for example, emerging economies, nonmarket forces, technology disruptions, and social demands on firms—is bringing new themes to the fore of strategy research. These include newer forms of competition, cooperation, and coopetition as a result of partaking in eco-systems, pursuing the maximization of multiple objectives, and the appreciation of different assumptions about cognitive abilities and motivational profiles. Examples of new phenomena raising theoretical and empirical puzzles for competitive and cooperative strategies are global value chains, cross-sector alliances, technologically based platforms, and new models of public-private collaboration. The theoretical support for these themes is likely to draw increasingly from insights complementary to well-established perspectives in strategy—for example, MPT, TCE, the RBV, and agency theory—including those offered by political science, sociopsychology, and technology studies. Coopetition is an emerging theme that merits further attention and elaboration.

References

Anand J, Kale P. 2006. International joint ventures in emerging economies: Past drivers and emerging trends. In *Handbook of Strategic Alliances*, Shenkar O, Reuer JJ (eds). Sage: Thousand Oaks, CA; 297–311.

Barbieri P, Ciabuschi F, Fratocchi L, Vignoli M. 2018. What do we know about manufacturing reshoring? *Journal of Global Operations and Strategic Sourcing* 11(1): 79–122.

Barney J. 1991. Firm resources and sustained competitive advantage. *Journal of Management* 17(1): 99–120.

Beamish PW, Lupton NC. 2016. Cooperative strategies in international business and management: reflections on the past 50 years and future directions. *Journal of World Business* 51(1): 163–175.

Bengtsson M, Kock S. 2000. "Coopetition" in business networks—to cooperate and compete simultaneously. *Industrial Marketing Management* 29(5): 411–426.

Bengtsson M, Raza-Ullah T. 2016. A systematic review of research on coopetition: toward a multilevel understanding. *Industrial Marketing Management* 57: 23–39.

Besanko D, Dranove D, Shanley M, Schaefer S. 2009. *Economics of Strategy*. Wiley: New York, NY.

Bitektine A, Haack P. 2015. The "macro" and the "micro" of legitimacy: toward a multilevel theory of the legitimacy process. *Academy of Management Review* 40(1): 49–75.

Boudreau KJ, Lakhani KR. 2013. Using the crowd as an innovation partner. *Harvard Business Review* 91(4): 60–69.

Bouncken RB, Fredrich V. 2012. Coopetition: performance implications and management antecedents. *International Journal of Innovation Management* 16(05): 12500281–1250028.

Bouncken RB, Gast J, Kraus S, Bogers M. 2015. Coopetition: a systematic review, synthesis, and future research directions. *Review of Managerial Science* 9(3): 577–601.

Bridoux F, Coeurderoy R, Durand R. 2011. Heterogeneous motives and the collective creation of value. *Academy of Management Review* 36(4): 711–730.

Cennamo C, Santalo J. 2013. Platform competition: strategic trade-offs in platform markets. *Strategic Management Journal* 34(11): 1331–1350.

Chen MJ, Miller D. 2015. Reconceptualizing competitive dynamics: a multidimensional framework. *Strategic Management Journal* 36(5): 758–775.

Chen M-J, Su K-H, Tsai W. 2007. Competitive tension: the awareness-motivation-capability perspective. *Academy of Management Journal* 50: 101–118.

Child J, Faulkner D, Tallman S, Hsieh L. 2019. *Cooperative Strategy*. 3rd ed. Oxford University Press: Oxford, U.K.

Child J, Marinova ST. 2014. The role of contextual combinations in the globalization of Chinese firms. *Management and Organization Review* 10(3): 347–371.

Child J, Rodrigues SB. 2004. Corporate governance in international joint ventures: toward a theory of partner preferences. In *Corporate Governance and Firm Organization*, Grandori A (ed). Oxford University Press: Oxford, U.K.; 89–112.

Child J, Tse KK-T, Rodrigues SB. 2013. *The Dynamics of Corporate Co-Evolution*. Edward Elgar: Cheltenham, U.K.

Choi J, Contractor F. 2016. Choosing an appropriate alliance governance mode: the role of institutional, cultural, and geographical distance in international research and development (R&D) collaborations. *Journal of International Business Studies* 47(2): 210–232.

Christensen C. 1997. *The Innovator's Dilemma: When New Technologies Cause Great Firms to Fail.* Harvard Business Review Press: Boston, MA.

Coase RH. 1991. The nature of the firm (1937). In *The Nature of the Firm: Origins, Evolution, and Development*, Williamson OE, Winter SJ (eds). Oxford University Press: New York, NY; 18–33.

Contractor FJ, Lorange P. 1988. Why should firms cooperate? The strategy and economics basis for cooperative ventures. In *Cooperative Strategies in International Business*, Contractor FJ, Lorange P (eds). Lexington Books: New York, NY; 3–28.

Contractor FJ, Reuer JJ. 2019. Frontiers of alliance research. In *Frontiers of Strategic Alliance Research: Negotiating, Structuring, and Governing Partnerships*, Contractor FJ, Reuer JJ (eds). Cambridge University Press: Cambridge, MA, 3–39.

Dagnino GB, Padula G. 2002. Coopetition strategic: towards a new kind of interfirm dynamics. Paper presented at the Second Annual European Academy of Management Conference on Innovative Research in Management, Stockholm, May 9–11, 2002.

Das TK, Teng BS. 1998. Between trust and control: developing confidence in partner cooperation in alliances. *Academy of Management Review* 23(3): 491–512.

Devece C, Ribeiro-Soriano DE, Palacios-Marqués D. 2019. Coopetition as the new trend in inter-firm alliances: literature review and research patterns. *Review of Managerial Science* 13(2): 207–226.

Doh JP, Rodrigues SB, Saka-Helmhout A, Makhija M. 2017. International business responses to institutional voids. *Journal of International Business Studies* 48(3): 293–307.

Dorn S, Schweiger B, Albers S. 2016. Levels, phases, and themes of coopetition: a systematic literature review and research agenda. *European Management Journal* 34(5): 484–500.

Dorobantu S, Kaul A, Zelner B. 2017. Nonmarket strategy research through the lens of new institutional economics: an integrative review and future directions. *Strategic Management Journal* 38(1): 114–140.

Durand R. 2002. Competitive advantages exist: a critique of Powell. *Strategic Management Journal* 23(9): 867–872.

Durand R, Grant RM, Madsen TL. 2017. The expanding domain of strategic management research and the quest for integration. *Strategic Management Journal* 38: 4–16.

Durand R, Paugam L, Stolowy H. 2019. Do investors actually value sustainability indices? Replication, development, and new evidence on CSR visibility. *Strategic Management Journal* 40(9): 1471–1490.

Dussauge P, Garrette B. 1999. *Cooperative Strategy: Competing Successfully through Strategic Alliances.* Wiley: Chichester, U.K.

Dyer JH. 1997. Effective interim collaboration: how firms minimize transaction costs and maximise transaction value. *Strategic Management Journal* 18(7): 535–556.

Edelman. 2020. *2020 Edelman Trust Barometer.* https://www.edelman.com/trustbarometer [22 February 2020].

Eisenhardt KM, Martin JA. 2000. Dynamic capabilities: what are they? *Strategic Management Journal* 21(10–11): 1105–1121.

Elg U, Ghauri P, Child J, Collinson S. 2017. MNEs' microfoundations and routines for building a legitimate and sustainable position on emerging markets. *Journal of Organizational Behavior* 38(9): 1320–1337.

Gaba V, Greve HR. 2019. Safe or profitable? The pursuit of conflicting goals. *Organization Science* 30(4): 647–667.

Gartenberg C, Prat A, Serafeim G. 2019. Corporate purpose and financial performance. *Organization Science* 30(1): 1–18.

Georgallis P, Dowell G, Durand R. 2019. Shine on me: industry coherence and policy support for emerging industries. *Administrative Science Quarterly* 64(3): 503–541.

Geringer JM, Hébert L. 1989. Control and performance of international joint ventures. *Journal of International Business Studies* 20(2): 235–254.

Gimeno J. 2004. Competition within and between networks: the contingent effect of competitive embeddedness on alliance formation. *Academy of Management Journal* 47(6): 820–842.

Gnyawali DR, He J, Madhavan R. 2008. Co-opetition: promises and challenges. In *21st-Century Management: A Reference Handbook,* Wankel C. (ed). Sage: Thousand Oaks, CA; 386–398.

Gnyawali DR, Park BJR. 2011. Co-opetition between giants: collaboration with competitors for technological innovation. *Research Policy* 40(5): 650–663.

Gomes E, Bustinza OF, Tarba S, Khan Z, Ahammad M., 2019. Antecedents and implications of territorial servitization. *Regional Studies* 53(3): 410–423.

Goodall W, Fishman TD, Bornstein J, Bonthron B. 2017. The rise of mobility as a service: reshaping how urbanites get around. *Deloitte Review* 20: 113–129.

Guillén MF, García-Canal E. 2009. The American model of the multinational firm and the "new" multinationals from emerging economies. *Academy of Management Perspectives* 23(2): 23–35.

Han JY, Shipilov AV, Greve HR. 2017. Unequal bedfellows: gender role-based deference in multiplex ties between Korean business groups. *Academy of Management Journal* 60(4): 1531–1553.

Helfat CE, Peteraf MA. 2015. Managerial cognitive capabilities and the microfoundations of dynamic capabilities. *Strategic Management Journal* 36(6): 831–850.

Hennart JF. 1988. A transaction costs theory of equity joint ventures. *Strategic Management Journal* 9(4): 361–374.

Hitt MA, Ahlstrom D, Dacin MT, Levitas E, Svobodina L. 2004. The institutional effects on strategic alliance partner selection in transition economies: China vs. Russia. *Organization Science* 15(2): 173–185.

Hoffmann W, Lavie D, Reuer JJ, Shipilov A. 2018. The interplay of competition and cooperation. *Strategic Management Journal* 39(12): 3033–3052.

Hoopes DG, Madsen TL, Walker G. 2003. Guest editors' introduction to the special issue: why is there a resource-based view? Toward a theory of competitive heterogeneity. *Strategic Management Journal* 24(10): 889–902.

Ioannou I, Serafeim G. 2015. The impact of corporate social responsibility on investment recommendations: analysts' perceptions and shifting institutional logics. *Strategic Management Journal* 36(7): 1053–1081.

Jacobides MG, Cennamo C, Gawer A. 2018. Towards a theory of ecosystems. *Strategic Management Journal* 39(8): 2255–2276.

Jacqueminet, A, Durand R. In press. Ups and downs: the role of legitimacy judgment cues in practice implementation. *Academy of Management Journal.*

Juasrikul S, Sahaym A, Hyunsoon Y, Liu RL. 2018. Do cross-border alliances with MNEs from developed economies create firm value for MNEs from emerging economies? *Journal of Business Research* 93: 98–110.

Judge WQ, Dooley R. 2006. Strategic alliance outcomes: a transaction-cost economics perspective. *British Journal of Management* 17(1): 23–37.

Kale P, Singh H. 2009. Managing strategic alliances: what do we know now, and where do we go from here? *Academy of Management Perspectives* 23(3): 45–62.

Khanna T, Palepu K. 2000. The future of business groups in emerging markets: long-run evidence from Chile. *Academy of Management Journal* 43(3): 268–285.

Klijn E, Reuer JJ, Buckley PJ, Glaister KW. 2010. Combinations of partners' joint venture formation motives. *European Business Review* 22(6): 576–590.

KPMG. 2017. *Strategic Alliances: A Real Alternative to M&A?* KPMG International. https://assets.kpmg.com/content/dam/kpmg/xx/pdf/2017/11/strategic-alliances-toolkit.pdf [14 March 2020].

Laursen K, Salter A. 2006. Open for innovation: the role of openness in explaining innovation performance among UK manufacturing firms. *Strategic Management Journal* 27(2): 131–150.

Leiblein MJ, Miller DJ. 2003. An empirical examination of transaction- and firm-level influences on the vertical boundaries of the firm. *Strategic Management Journal* 24(9): 839–859.

Leonardi PM, Barley SR. 2010. What's under construction here? Social action materiality, and power in constructivist studies of technology and organizing. *Academy of Management Annals* 4(1): 1–51.

Lieberman MB, Asaba S. 2006. Why do firms imitate each other? *Academy of Management Review* 31(2): 366–385.

Lyon TP, Delmas MA, Maxwell JW, Bansal P, Chiroleu-Assouline M, Crifo P, Durand R, *et al*. 2018. CSR needs CPR: corporate sustainability and politics. *California Management Review* 60(4): 5–24.

MaaS. 2018. What is MaaS? https://maas-alliance.eu/homepage/what-is-maas [15 August 2018].

McWilliams A, Siegel D. 2000. Corporate social responsibility and financial performance: correlation or misspecification? *Strategic Management Journal* 21(5): 603–609.

Meyer KE, Grosse R. 2019. Introduction to managing in emerging markets. In *Oxford Handbook of Managing in Emerging Markets*, Grosse R, Meyer KE (eds). Oxford University Press: New York, NY; 3–34.

Nalebuff BJ, Brandenburger A. 1996. *Co-opetition*. Harper Collins Business: London, U.K.

Nelson RR. 1991. Why do firms differ, and how does it matter? *Strategic Management Journal* 12(S2): 61–74.

Parkhe A. 1993. Strategic alliance structuring: a game theoretic and transaction cost examination of interfirm cooperation. *Academy of Management Journal* 36(4): 794–829.

Penrose ET. 1959. *The Theory of the Growth of the Firm*. Blackwell: Oxford, U.K.

Peteraf MA. 1993. The cornerstones of competitive advantage: a resource-based view. *Strategic Management Journal* 14(3): 179–191.

Petricevic O, Teece DJ. 2019. The structural reshaping of globalization: implications for strategic sectors, profiting from innovation, and the multinational enterprise. *Journal of International Business Studies* 50(9): 1487–1512.

Poppo L, Zenger T. 1998. Testing alternative theories of the firm: transaction cost, knowledge-based, and measurement explanations for make-or-buy decisions in information services. *Strategic Management Journal* 19(9): 853–877.

Porter ME. 1980. *Competitive Strategy: Techniques for Analyzing Industries and Competitors*. Free Press: New York, NY.

Porter ME. 1985. *The Competitive Advantage: Creating and Sustaining Superior Performance*. Free Press: New York, NY.

Powell TC. 2001. Competitive advantage: logical and philosophical considerations. *Strategic Management Journal* 22(9): 875–888.

Powell TC, Lovallo D, Fox CR. 2011. Behavioral strategy. *Strategic Management Journal* 32(13): 1369–1386.

Quelin BV, Cabral S, Lazzarini S, Kivleniece I. 2019. The private scope in public-private collaborations: an institutional and capability-based perspective. *Organization Science* 30(4): 831–846.

Ritala P. 2012. Coopetition strategy—when is it successful? Empirical evidence on innovation and market performance. *British Journal of Management* 23(3): 307–324.

Rosenkopf L, Nerkar A. 2001. Beyond local search: boundary-spanning, exploration, and impact in the optical disk industry. *Strategic Management Journal* 22(4): 287–306.

Rotting D. 2016. Institutions and emerging markets: effects and implications for multinational corporations. *International Journal of Emerging Markets* 11(1): 2–17.

Schad J, Lewis MW, Raisch S, Smith WK. 2016. Paradox research in management science: looking back to move forward. *Academy of Management Annals* 10(1): 5–64.

Subramaniam M, Venkatraman N. 2001. Determinants of transnational new product development capability: testing the influence of transferring and deploying tacit overseas knowledge. *Strategic Management Journal* 22(4): 359–378.

Surroca J, Tribó JA, Waddock S. 2010. Corporate responsibility and financial performance: the role of intangible resources. *Strategic Management Journal* 31(5): 463–490.

Tallman SB, Shenkar O. 1994. A managerial decision model of international cooperative venture formation. *Journal of International Business Studies* 25(1): 91–113.

Tantalo C, Priem R L. 2016. Value creation through stakeholder synergy. *Strategic Management Journal* 37(2): 314–329.

UN (United Nations). n.d. *UN Climate Change Partnerships.* https://unfccc.int/about-us/un-climate-change-partnerships [10 March 2020].

Vasi IB, King BG. 2012. Social movements, risk perceptions, and economic outcomes: the effect of primary and secondary stakeholder activism on firms' perceived environmental risk and financial performance. *American Sociological Review* 77: 573–596.

Wernerfelt B. 1984. A resource-based view of the firm. *Strategic Management Journal* 5(2): 171–180.

Williamson OE. 1981. The economics of organization: the transaction cost approach. *American Journal of Sociology* 87(3): 548–577.

Williamson OE. 1985. *The Economic Institutions of Capitalism.* Free Press: New York, NY.

Xu D, Meyer KE. 2013. Linking theory and context: "strategy research in emerging economies" after Wright et al. 2005. *Journal of Management Studies* 50(7): 1322–1346.

Zhong W, Su C, Peng J, Yang Z. 2017. Trust in interorganizational relationships. a meta-analytic integration. *Journal of Management* 43(4): 1050–1075.

4.1

COMPETITIVE ADVANTAGE = STRATEGY, REBOOT

Rodolphe Durand

Introduction

In markets, some firms, at any given time of observation, perform better than others. The persistence of performance heterogeneity is the core question of strategy as a research (and practice) field. When firms maintain their performance superiority over time, they are said to possess a competitive advantage. Logically, a direct association relates competitive advantage to strategy. For many scholars and most practitioners, competitive advantage = strategy; put another way, the essence of strategy is to act in ways that build and maintain competitive advantages. This chapter reviews the conditions whereby this equivalence holds true (or not), elaborates on the extant research's limitations, and offers questions for investigating competitive advantage anew—reverberating back and questioning the strategy research field as a whole.

Competitive Advantage Defined

Superior profit = CA

A starting point, nurtured by both theory and experience, is that superior profits relative to competitors and accumulated over time do not last long because rivals, attracted by evidence of profit and rent potential, will work to deplete that potential (Oster, 1999; D'Aveni, Dagnino, and Smith, 2010). Competition is a force that attracts rivals who nullify the advantages obtained by some actors from a set of various circumstances, which is why many qualify competitive advantage (CA) as leading to superior or abnormal returns (Jacobsen, 1988).

An industry's structural conditions (e.g., the number of rivals, access to inputs, and the cost of entry) can favor or hinder the likelihood of firms earning abnormal returns (Porter, 1980). Interindustry comparisons enable the disentangling of factors that lead firms to prolong their capacity to earn abnormal profits (McGahan and Porter, 1997). Furthermore, within-industry analyses help to identify the specific factors that lead to some firms—or groups of firms, known as strategic groups—being more likely than their rivals to accrue rents (Roquebert, Phillips, and Westfall, 1996). Finally, firms differ in their organizational structures (Chandler, 1962) and generic types of strategy, which generates heterogeneity in profit making.

As a result, most researchers conceive of competitive advantage as being conducive to superior economic performance. Thus, having a competitive advantage means having the ability to outperform rivals (Wiggins and Ruefli, 2002; Newbert, 2008).

CA is not random and results from firm action

The very possibility of firms experiencing above-average performance may be random: in any population, individuals have some odds to under- or overperform others. Describing a process analogous to biological evolution, Alchian (1950) expressed the possibility that successive rounds of (firms') overperformance are not due to (human) intervention but to luck. Stochastic models where firms are subject to random walks have found groups of firms with long-lasting superior and lower performance (Denrell, 2004). While anecdotal evidence and practitioner-oriented books portray firms and leaders as exceptional performers, they "may reflect the inherent ingenuity of their authors rather than the validity of the case study data that they employed" (Henderson, Raynor, and Ahmed, 2012: 401). Henderson *et al.* (2012) adjusted a random-walk model to account for a firm's variable duration to stay at a given level of performance. They reproduced patterns of superior performance persistence without assuming any special form of firm performance distribution. Comparing their simulated data with real Compustat data, they found that "for both ROA [return on assets] and Tobin's q, and for both top 10 percent and top 20 percent outcomes, there were many more sustained superior performers than we could expect through a time-homogenous Markov process on the percentile state space" (Henderson *et al.*, 2012: 400).

This result lends support to the premise that something more than luck probably explains the persistence of greater profitability over time. Responding to Alchian (1950), Penrose (1952) famously objected and refused to apply biological constructs and stochastic reasoning to companies. Instead, she highlighted the importance of human rationality (including its limitations) and motivation in determining a firm's behavior, growth potential, and survival odds (Durand, 2006). Hence, while stochastic models can mimic observable patterns in firm performance, they do not exhaust the reality that some firms consistently and intentionally overperform their rivals. While the majority of strategic decisions result in patterns that are amenable to random-walk modeling, some true positives emerge in firms that systematically beat the odds. In their modeled case, Henderson *et al.* (2012) estimated 300 such firms among the 20,000 firms listed in Compustat, or 1.5 percent.

CA = strategy

Derived from observations and extant theories, a strategy credo states that "a fundamental objective of firms is to sustain profits superior to those of competitors" (Madsen and Walker, 2017: 184). As firms can defeat the forces that may lead them to regress toward the mean, strategy's intent is to bolster firms in building and maintaining a competitive advantage. Hence, for many, the equivalence between CA and strategy holds, as strategy embodies the set of actions that produce CA.

Competitive Advantage Explained

Broadly speaking, three factors explain a firm's ability to earn and defend a competitive advantage: barriers to the mobility of factors, resource heterogeneity, and managerial analytical differences.

Barriers to mobility

The most famous and seminal explanation of competitive advantage lies in the analysis of the microeconomic environment where firms cohabit and compete. Porter (1980, 1991) interpreted imperfect competition in markets as firms' competitive advantage. Market structure determines firm positions in a value system and the respective portion of value that each category of actors can appropriate. Some competitors' assets and characteristics place them in favorable transactional positions (i.e., with suppliers or buyers). Economic actors cannot smoothly modify their positions within the value system—vertical integration, mergers, and exits take time and money— neither can they transform their operations rapidly. As a result, positions are gained and lost with some delay, which explains the persistence and sustainability of competitive advantages.

A source of advantage, therefore, consists in a series of barriers imposed on the mobility of productive factors within the value system. Depending on the approach, barriers that help preserve favorable positions address different aspects of the transactional system. For instance, laws, norms, and standards rule every sector of the economy, thereby imposing constraints on asset specificity and exchange. As such, barriers to mobility exist within and across industries, and assets cannot be used or transferred indifferently (or at zero cost) across usages (Waring, 1996; Madsen and Walker, 2017). Other approaches identify the environmental dynamism that leads to varying degrees of entry and churn rates within an industry, which reduce the persistence of abnormal returns (Wiggins and Ruefli, 2002; D'Aveni et al., 2010).

Resource heterogeneity and optimal ownership

The analysis of competitive advantage in terms of position and barriers to mobility is not specific to any firm. Reacting to the undifferentiated treatment of interfirm differences, complementary veins of research propose alternative explanations for the existence of competitive advantage. First and foremost, while concerned by the exclusion of rivals from economic opportunities, the resource-based view (RBV) focuses more on the rent potential of resources that individual firms own and control than on the competition imperfections due to market structure characteristics (Barney, 1986). A firm is a collection of resources, and when a resource's properties isolate a firm from competitive pressures, that firm can extract rents inaccessible to its rivals (Barney, 1991). As such, ex ante and ex post barriers to competition exist, as resources are more valuable for their owner, less imitable for rivals, and less transferable to other market actors (Peteraf, 1993; Newbert, 2008). Thus, relative to its rivals, a resource owner can derive a greater amount of rents and sustain its competitive advantage through learning and capability development (Helfat and Peteraf, 2003; Hatch and Dyer, 2004).

Second, value capture theory considers firms as contributing to and being rewarded by a value network that comprises all transactions relating to economic agents that produce value—that is, the sum of the differences between individual actors' utility minus their costs associated with producing and transacting (Gans and Ryall, 2017). Actors can, in theory, contribute to different value networks and be rewarded through their participation. Depending on the value their participation generates, they will need to capture a minimum value to participate in a given network, essentially the minimum value they could capture in any of the available value networks.

For some scholars, firms bargain over resources necessary in the production process, and the competition results in the most efficient user becoming the owner of the resources (Lippman and Rumelt, 2003). Hence, there exists an optimal ownership that implies that the transfer of a given resource to another owner will lower the total value created in the economic system. According to this view, competitive advantage results from the value surplus that accrues to the optimal owner of resources relative to the marginal competitor (Peteraf and Barney, 2003).

Resources' characteristics generate value differentials, as modeled by pure or combined models from property right theory (Hart and Moore, 1990; Bel, 2018) and cooperative game theory (Brandenburger and Stuart, 2007; Gans and Ryall, 2017). Resources that are likely to generate more rents are valuable for the organization (firm i as the best owner), and difficult to imitate or substitute. Other characteristics contribute to this advantage without depreciating the total value present in the system, such as the presence of scale-free resources (Asmussen, 2015) or complementarity across resources, which leads to envisaging strategies beyond resource ownership (Bel, 2018). For instance, increasing the degree of complementarity of the focal firm's resources or building relationships with other firms with complementary assets will likely increase the total value generated and appropriated by the focal firm, which, all other conditions being equal, reinforces not only the focal firm's original advantage but also that no other firm would be better off by being the owner of another firm's resource.

Managerial analytical differences

Generally, market failures are seen as a necessary condition for a competitive advantage to endure. However, many strategy scholars object, and consider instead the firm-level determinants of profit heterogeneity. To these scholars, the premise that assets and capabilities are not entirely decomposable in their full utility value suffices to imply the existence of competitive advantages (Penrose, 1959/1995). Had we to simplify to the maximum the underlying conditions for the presence of competitive advantage, we could imagine a world of transacting actors valuing identical assets in a market. That every actor (i.e., every buyer) perceives and attributes a unique (and hence subjective) value to the same assets offered by sellers is sufficient to generate performance heterogeneity.

A dividing line separates those research streams that suggest that the perceptual and interpretative nature of valuation is a necessary and sufficient condition for profit heterogeneity to endure (e.g., Porac, Thomas, and Baden-Fuller, 1989), and those that associate the different pricings of these assets—and the corresponding profits—with the complementarities estimated by each buyer—that is, the supplemental value that a given asset generates as a function of the preexisting resources controlled by the buyer (Makadok, 2001; Adegbesan, 2009). For the former, performance differentials between firms result from sociocognitive heterogeneity at the firm level, whereas, for the latter, performance differentials stem from intrinsic differences in firms' resource endowments that provide (or do not provide) additional value in combination with the new asset.

Notwithstanding this distinction, decision-makers process the available information differently. Biases constrain them in their attention, interpretation, and analysis of available information (Schwenk, 1984). As decision-makers reduce these biases, they are more susceptible to taking advantage of revealed opportunities. As firms improve their capabilities, the potential value they create likely increases (Cockburn, Henderson, and Stern, 2000). Yet no direct correlation suggests that their capacity to appropriate this value creation increases correspondingly (Coff, 1999). Chatain (2011) found evidence that developing client-specific knowledge favors new contracts when clients need new services that involve this knowledge, but not otherwise. In the latter case, special capabilities do not enable the supplier to appropriate the extra-value potentially contained in them. Overall, some evidence points to managerial analytical differences in acquiring and processing information that situate firms in better or worse positions to generate and appropriate value from similar assets and opportunities, thereby representing a major source of competitive advantage.

Competitive Advantage Contested

The number of *Strategic Management Journal* articles with "competitive advantage" in their titles is surprising: 22 in the decade from 1990 to 1999, 15 from 2000 to 2009, and only nine from 2010 to 2019. While anecdotal, this reduced interest in competitive advantage at the center of the research agenda coincides with a mounting contestation of the notion on multiple accounts: conceptual, theoretical, contextual, and methodological.

Conceptual critique

The widespread definition for *competitive advantage*—consisting in any positive cause of superior performance—raises issues.

First, as noted earlier, a long-standing problem in strategy research has been the conflation between the notions of competitive advantage and superior profit. Indeed, the above definition verges on tautology. If any cause leading to superior performance is a competitive advantage, the utility of the concept of competitive advantage is questioned (Powell, 2001). Superior performance is sufficient for developing theory, and competitive advantage is not a concept but describes a situation theorized otherwise. Reciprocally, if, in some situations, positive causes of superior returns are not equivalent to competitive advantage, can we logically infer that sustainable competitive advantage generates superior performance?

Second, such a definition appears flawed on another account—the ignorance that a firm's competitive advantage could result from a firm being less disadvantaged than its rivals. Hence, a correct definition of competitive advantage needs to include relative levels of contributing and hindering factors (Powell, 2001; Arend, 2003). Sirmon *et al.* (2010) expose the implications of integrating a firm's strong and weak positions. Strategic weakness does not mean that a resource or capability per se has a negative value, only that its value is inferior to rivals' similar resources or capabilities. It follows that a low relative weakness set combined with a low relative strength set is conducive to a neutral performance effect, whereas two high relative sets lead to a "precarious advantage" position.

Overall, an appropriate definition of competitive advantage must account for the negative forces hindering the manifestation of positive causes into positive outcomes (Arend, 2008). *Competitive advantage* is therefore the manifested capability of an organization to perform better than its rivals in a sustained and systematic manner—that is, above and beyond what luck would permit. Note that this definition entails two logical consequences: (1) that firms can be reasonably well compared with their rivals—that is, that some market categories enable comparison among economic actors; and (2) that all players (shareholders, managers, and third parties) agree on a definition and measure of performance. These two conditions were not questioned for decades, yet since the 2008 financial crisis and even more since the COVID-19 pandemic, the two conditions have been challenged.

Theoretical critique

A first important assumption of the theories of competitive advantage reverts to the intentional nature of strategy. Most strategy scholars would agree that competitive advantage results from firms' choices about resource acquisition and allocation. However, others argue that extrinsic forces select firms' organizational forms, resources, and products based on their fitness values (Durand, 2001, 2006). A long-standing debate between environmental selection and strategic choice (Hrebiniak and Joyce, 1985; Hannan and Freeman, 1989; Child, 1997) questions the essence of competitive advantage as either the result of an intention or as the outcome of a selection process.

Is there such a thing as a (unified) theory of competitive advantage? So many factors play a role in explaining a sustained manifestation of superior returns that perhaps no such theory exists. Hence, a second critique poses that, at best, research should cumulate contextual studies that document the influence of various factors specific to the context under study. For instance: not all industries follow the same natural evolutionary path, and some (de)regulations affect which firms—incumbents or new entrants—might outperform rivals (Madsen and Walker, 2017); the role of technology in procuring cost or differentiation advantages functions not independently of rivals' and industries' network structure (Greve, 2009). As illustrated by these examples, it seems that an endless list of factors contributes to explaining competitive advantage—and for some scholars, the quest for a metatheory of competitive advantage is moot.

A third critique concerns the ignorance of demand-side effects. For instance, some scholars wonder whether the resource-based view can be a complete theory without theorizing demand (Priem and Butler, 2001). More generally, a series of studies associated supply-side characteristics—in terms of resource productivity, technological trajectories, and learning capacities—with functional descriptions of demand. Most notably, how is competitive advantage affected when consumers' marginal utility from a firm's performance improvements is decreasing slowly or quickly (Adner and Levinthal, 2001)? Furthermore, if consumers' taste for quality is heterogeneous versus homogeneous, the sources and sustainability of competitive advantage must vary—and they do, as modeled by Adner and Zemsky (2006). Therefore, the degree to which customers value specific differentiation and appreciate levels of product quality is of fundamental importance for the existence and durability of competitive advantage.

Finally, at the center of strategy research, an implicit underlying postulate assumes that competition is the best mechanism for resource allocation. For six decades or more, as mentioned earlier, strategy scholars considered that "a fundamental objective of firms is to sustain profits superior to those of competitors" (Madsen and

Walker, 2017: 184). Strategy research reveals market and resource properties that isolate companies from competitive pressures, and strategists striving to erect these isolating properties to preserve and increase their firm's profits (Mahoney and Pandian, 1992). However, this posture raises questions about the economic and moral foundations of competitive advantage. When referring to Penrose (1959/1995) as a seminal inspiration, strategy scholars forget that Penrose condemned the undue appropriation of rents, and that her theory of firm growth addressed an anomaly in markets that needed correction (Rugman and Verbeke, 2002). Hence, successive scholarly works have reinterpreted Penrose's theory on competitive advantage. More broadly, whereas economics pay heed to welfare, strategy scholars focus on rent-seeking and private forms of value appropriation, assuming that the economic system (and its regulation) is conducive to welfare. Said differently, the business of welfare is not the business of strategy, which in return interrogates the moral underpinnings of competitive advantage.

Methodological critique

Of the variety of methodological critiques that have been addressed in an attempt to evidence competitive advantage, I list five of the most common:

1) *Assimilation issue 1* [dependent variable]. While the theoretical arguments strive to distinguish competitive advantage from superior returns, most of the empirical work skips the competitive advantage's operationalization and measures only superior returns, once more assimilating superior returns with competitive advantage.

2) *Assimilation issue 2* [independent variable]. While the theoretical arguments rely on the isolating properties of assets, resources, and capabilities, most of the empirical work approximates the levels of assets, resources, and capabilities, and not their isolating properties, assuming that more of such assets (i.e., more marketing expenses) transpires into better rent potential (i.e., higher differentiation), hence assimilating resource levels with their properties.

3) *Correlational analyses.* The bulk of the empirical research cannot eschew the main limitations of correlational analyses. Among many: Average effects do not characterize any actual entity. Evidenced relationships need not be symmetric. Outliers tend to be ignored in regression models, while extreme cases are of interest to strategists. Correlation is not causality. For these reasons, observed associations between firm characteristics, strategic moves, and performance represent supporting evidence for competitive advantage but not irrefutable proof.

4) *Exogeneity.* For many, correlational analyses are flawed because the factors assumed to determine competitive advantage result from prior choices that were neither independent nor observable. But how can differences in resource

levels or properties be demonstrated to lead to differences in performance when all resource levels and properties depend on the same antecedents? A firm's resource differential vis-à-vis each of its rivals covaries with their respective past performances. Hence, endogeneity plagues research on competitive advantage.

5) *Causal identification*. Many studies neither pose counterfactual hypotheses clearly nor test the counterfactual hypotheses. Luck is rarely excluded as an explanatory factor. Causal identification is thorny. No paper can bring together a formal model explicating the relationships between the multiple factors, a simulation ruling out luck, and an empirical study identifying causality between factors.

Advantage Research Reboot

Despite these criticisms, multiple avenues exist for new research around competitive advantage. Many of the difficulties encountered are rooted in the relatively inexplicit definitions for *industry* and *performance*, which are fundamental for competitive advantage theorizing and testing. A potential source of regeneration for competitive advantage research lies, therefore, in better defining these root notions and in finding inspiration from adjacent fields.

Overcoming the industry divide: what category research can bring to competitive advantage research

The definition of *industry* separates researchers. Some researchers start their analyses with industry as being the logical and unquestioned theater in which competition occurs. Indeed, industrial structure conditions the possibility for performance differentials to endure or not. Other researchers do not negate that industries exist but view them as sedimented, postcompetition categories. For instance, McGrath (2013) warns decision-makers that their successes rely on old assumptions, and that "industry" is not the playing level where competition occurs; she instead prefers "arenas," which characterize particular connections between customers and solutions in a local market. More broadly, the whole resource-based view has induced strategists to depart from their resource bundle and envisage opportunities inside out, that is, in existing or nonexisting markets where this bundle could disrupt or create competition. There are theoretical possibilities to overcome this divide about industry definition and transit back and forth between the two sides, and in so doing, to offer a new perspective for competitive advantage research.

One such metatheorization is the market category research stream, which has roots in sociopsychology as applied to organizations and markets (Porac *et al.*, 1989; Durand and Paolella, 2013), organizational ecology (Hannan, Pólos, and Carroll,

2007), and economics (Cattani, Porac, and Thomas, 2017). Categories in the context of markets "provide a cognitive infrastructure that enables evaluations of organizations and their products, drives expectations, and leads to material and symbolic exchanges" (Durand and Paolella, 2013: 1102). Category research accommodates situations where categories are crisp and stable, utilities are well defined, associations among (productive) factors are established, and expectations are unambiguous. These situations characterize mature industries with known rates of entry, objectified economies of scale, factor productivity, and so forth. Several approaches to competitive advantage pertain well to this depiction. Furthermore, category research is amenable to situations where categories emerge under the impetus of intruders, innovators, or incumbents (Durand and Khaire, 2017). These situations characterize nascent industries where products proliferate, factor productivity is unknown or unstable, and demand is not yet specified (Suarez, Grodal, and Gotsopoulos, 2015).

From this brief description, competitive advantage, its antecedents, and its consequences appear to vary greatly in their function of industry category features, such as the grade of membership of firms within the category, the existence of a prototypical offer, the contrast between adjacent categories, the fluidity or stability of the category system within which the industry category is nested, and more. Thus, it seems promising that a theoretical account can be developed whereby competitive advantage will morph in its nature, and its antecedents will gain or lose significance as the industry category emerges, matures, and senesces. Such an endeavor could revitalize important but relatively idle strategic notions related to performance differentials. For instance, what is the most desirable level of differentiation, and how does it compare with optimal distinctiveness (Haans, 2019; Zhao et al., 2017)? What new insights are to be gained in diversification research by integrating categorical spanning research (Paolella and Durand, 2016)? Can vertical and horizontal integrations be better explained through category merging and collapse?

Enriching competition

Second, competition remains undertheorized. However, the notion of competition can be conceived through multiple levels and in myriad ways. Competition can be a cognitive disposition of individuals—here, decision-makers—in terms of what they perceive as opportunities and threats (Kilduff, Elfenbien, and Staw, 2010). Competition can be a property of markets and operate at the level of both resources and firms (Makadok, 2001; Barney, 1986).

Some authors have suggested that what matters for competitive advantage to manifest is not resource ownership alone but the set of properties that a firm's resource instantiates. Logically, a falsifiable theory of competitive advantage compels researchers to separate resources from their properties and analyze these properties as being selected by the environment—that is, as providing a fitness advantage to their possessors (Durand, 2006; Durand and Vaara, 2009). While, in the 1990s, cross-fertilization with evolutionary economics advanced strategy research (Montgomery, 1995; Levinthal, 1997), each stream reverted to its riverbed. The time is ripe for a novel convergence between the two streams that will tackle the conceptual distinction between competition and selection and benefit research into the sustainability of competitive advantage.

Furthermore, one perspective for rethinking competitive advantage is to fill competition with more cognitive and institutional nuances (Durand, 2012). For decision-makers, competition might not instantiate the same content but might instead be tainted by personal resentment, local rivalry, or nationalistic sentiments (Meyer and Rowan, 1977; Vaara and Monin, 2010). To understand why firms with immense resources fail in given contexts, one must realize that distinct institutional factors and pressures weigh on resource allocation, usage, and productivity (Oliver, 1997). Nonmarket strategies then become part and parcel with the understanding of competitive advantage not only because they determine the context for resources and organizations to materialize their competitive potential but also because firms can directly influence the very force of competition per se (Durand, 2006; Dorobantu, Kaul, and Zelner, 2017). Hence, how do institutional factors (nationalism, regulations, and international treaties) mesh with individual perceptions (cognitive and emotional) to determine market and nonmarket decisions and superior competitive outcomes?

Broadening performance definition when rethinking competitive advantage

Another potential route to a land full of new explorations concerns the definition of *performance*. There are mounting debates about what a firm's performance comprises. A full domain of research has centered on the nonfinancial (also known as extrafinancial) dimensions of performance and their connection with financial performance. Increasingly, financial markets, shareholders, and managers pay more heed to societal demands and economic risks related to nonfinancial domains, such as the environmental and social impacts of their activities. As such, because firms compete substantially and symbolically on nonfinancial performance indicators, shouldn't we expand the notion of *performance* to include financial and extrafinancial indicators (e.g., DesJardine and Durand, 2020)? What are the strategic implications for a firm to compete in two distinct, and likely connected, domains? As some positive and negative interdependencies exist between the usage of resources for one or the other domain, extremely puzzling questions emerge for strategy research: How to pursue conflicting goals (Gaba and Greve, 2019)? How to sustain advantage when some resources contribute to one objective and degrade the other, or when indirect positive effects cumulate (Obloj and Sengul, 2020)? Finally, what new theorizations are necessary for strategy research when stakeholders sit around the competitive advantage table (Harrison, Bosse, and Phillips, 2010; Jones, Harrison, and Felps, 2018)?

Mobilizing new methodologies to observe better effects

In the previous section, we listed methodological critiques, each of which opens new research avenues, enriched by the prior conceptual and theoretical suggestions.

1) *Assimilation issue 1* [dependent variable]. Several possibilities exist to disentangle the conflation of competitive advantage and superior returns. One possibility is to study intermediary dependent variables, such as the effectiveness of business processes (Ray, Barney, and Muhanna, 2004) or reputation (Durand, Rao, and Monin, 2007), which are known to lead to superior performance. Another possibility is to use nonparametric methods such as the efficient frontier calculations of data envelopment analysis (Chen, Delmas, and Lieberman, 2015), and then associate the obtained measure of efficiency with financial or economic performance. A third possibility is to study the effect of a factor or an event simultaneously on distinct dimensions of performance (e.g., in Durand, Paugam, and Stolowy, 2019: stock price, volume of transactions, analysts' attention, and shareholder composition).

2) *Assimilation issue 2* [independent variable]. Most strategy studies use an ordinary least squares (OLS) reasoning in approaching the measures of resource levels or properties. To approach subjective interpretation of a firm's resources (and the subjective opportunities they represent; see Penrose, 1959/1995), experimental methods are useful. To avoid the traps associated with the comparison between individual levels of resources and industry averages, several new ways to measure similarities are available. First, market category research and associated methods offer a toolkit to evaluate the grade of membership, fuzzy-logic category belonging and spanning, and contrast between categories (Hannan *et al.*, 2007; Paolella and Durand, 2016). Second, natural language processing techniques enable researchers to assess cosine distances between firms' vectors (which represent the full semantic content of each firm's textual corpus) within a common semantic space: instead of considering predetermined industry categories, firms cluster in a rich and dense semantic space wherein their idiosyncratic characteristics are captured in a highly fine-grained manner (Gouvard, 2020; Corritore, Goldberg, and Srivastava, 2020).

3) *Correlational analyses*. At least three routes exist to complement correlational analyses. First, modeling approaches offer promising perspectives, and can be formal modeling combined with observed and/or simulated data (Adner and Zemsky, 2006; Chatain, 2011). Second, Bayesian approaches avoid the liabilities of classical statistical methods (e.g., that an average association is not specific to any given observation; that outliers must be eliminated from empirical models on the grounds that they bias estimations) and allow for a full estimation of individual effects, a prediction of "what-if" results, and robust results with small samples or skewed data (e.g., Hahn and Doh, 2006; Hansen, Perry,

and Reese, 2004). Third, in-depth case analyses, when properly conducted and following historical counterfactual methods, provide important insights into the sources and processes leading to competitive advantage (Durand and Vaara, 2009; Danneels, 2011).

4) *Exogeneity and causal identification.* New methods enable strategy scholars to get closer to causal analyses. The following examples should be combined to offer better testing of competitive advantage theory. For instance, instrumental variables ensure unbiased coefficient estimations; matching and difference-in-difference techniques, while not fully tackling endogeneity, contrast treated and control observations; and regression discontinuity designs reveal quasi-causal relationships through event-based counterfactual models (Flammer and Bansal, 2017; Durand *et al.*, 2019).

Indeed, this list is brief. Yet it stresses that multiple methods can help us collectively to tackle the multiple conceptual, theoretical, and methodological challenges implied by competitive advantage research.

Future research on competitive advantage

Beset by multiple challenges, "competitive advantage" risks becoming a shell term, and this chapter aimed to pave the way for addressing criticisms and rejuvenating competitive advantage research. As stressed in the previous chapter, "Competitive and Cooperative Strategy," economic interdependence, nonmarket forces, technological prowess, and new social demands reconfigure the meaning of competition. Collectively, we therefore need to return to the drawing board and consider anew what *competitive advantage* is and has become, and the new determinants to explain its occurrence and disappearance. As I write these lines, for the first time in recent human history, the worldwide economic system is hurt globally, both in its supply and demand functions simultaneously, opening up opportunities for strategy scholars to reset a new research program around competitive advantage. I conclude this chapter with a series of questions, circling back to the research opportunities delineated in the previous section, and to the overarching purpose of strategy research more generally.

If competitive advantage is equal to abnormal returns, what is competitive advantage equal to in abnormal times such as during the COVID-19 crisis? What exactly do *performance* and *superior performance* mean in our current times? Can *performance* mean minimizing the usage of short-supply resources for a higher impact that need not be only monetary? When considering that natural resources are depleting, does competitive advantage imply an overappropriation of resources? Next, is strategy research ultimately about helping firms build and defend a competitive advantage? In a world of inequalities and resource shortages, should we consider the highest mark of strategy research to be the value extracted from the chain of transactions and contracts that bind economic actors? If so, aren't we hitting the moral principles that constitute the bedrock of our discipline?

Further, how do we integrate extrafinancial dimensions into the definition of *performance*? And how does doing so also modify our definitions of *competition* and *competitive advantage*? While competition represents the best allocative mechanism in normal times, 2020 marks the passage to a new normal historic time. Hence, are there conditions when competition may become less optimal than other economic coordination mechanisms? What are the implications for a definition of *competitive advantage*? If *sustainable* means both durable (i.e., repeated over time in a nonrandom way) and not depriving future generations from essential planetary resources, what new constructs and models are necessary to theorize and measure sustainable competitive advantage, the best strategies, and their benefits to the multiple parties contributing to its actualization?

References

Adegbesan JA. 2009. On the origins of competitive advantage: strategic factor markets and heterogeneous resource complementarity. *Academy of Management Review* 34(3): 463–475.

Adner R, Levinthal D. 2001. Demand heterogeneity and technology evolution: implications for product and process innovation. *Management Science* 47(5): 611–628.

Adner R, Zemsky P. 2006. A demand-based perspective on sustainable competitive advantage. *Strategic Management Journal* 27(3): 215–239.

Alchian AA. 1950. Uncertainty, evolution, and economic theory. *Journal of Political Economy* 58(3): 211–221.

Arend RJ. 2003. Revisiting the logical and research considerations of competitive advantage. *Strategic Management Journal* 24(3): 279–284.

Arend RJ. 2008. Differences in RBV strategic factors and the need to consider opposing factors in turnaround outcomes. *Managerial and Decision Economics* 29(4): 337–355.

Asmussen CG. 2015. Strategic factor markets, scale free resources, and economic performance: the impact of product market rivalry. *Strategic Management Journal* 36(12): 1826–1844.

Barney JB. 1986. Strategic factor markets: expectations, luck, and business strategy. *Management Science* 32(10): 1231–1241.

Barney JB. 1991. Firm resources and sustained competitive advantage. *Journal of Management* 17(1): 99–120.

Bel R. 2018. A property rights theory of competitive advantage. *Strategic Management Journal* 39(6): 1678–1703.

Brandenburger A, Stuart H. 2007. Biform games. *Management Science* 53(4): 537–549.

Cattani G, Porac JF, Thomas H. 2017. Categories and competition. *Strategic Management Journal* 38(1): 64–92.

Chandler AD. 1962. *Strategy and Structure: Chapters in the History of American Industrial Enterprises*. MIT Press: Cambridge, MA.

Chatain O. 2011. Value creation, competition, and performance in buyer-supplier relationships. *Strategic Management Journal* 32(1): 76–102.

Chen CM, Delmas MA, Lieberman MB. 2015. Production frontier methodologies and efficiency as a performance measure in strategic management research. *Strategic Management Journal* 36(1): 19–36.

Child J. 1997. Strategic choice in the analysis of action, structure, organizations and environment: retrospect and prospect. *Organization Studies* 18(1): 43–76.

Cockburn IM, Henderson RM, Stern S. 2000. Untangling the origins of competitive advantage. *Strategic Management Journal* 21(10–11): 1123–1145.

Coff RW. 1999. When competitive advantage doesn't lead to performance: the resource-based view and stakeholder bargaining power. *Organization Science* 10(2): 119–133.

Corritore M, Goldberg A, Srivastava SB. 2020. Duality in diversity: how intrapersonal and interpersonal cultural heterogeneity relate to firm performance. *Administrative Science Quarterly* 65(2): 359–394.

Danneels E. 2011. Trying to become a different type of company: dynamic capability at Smith Corona. *Strategic Management Journal* 32(1): 1–31.

D'Aveni RA, Dagnino GB, Smith KG. 2010. The age of temporary advantage. *Strategic Management Journal* 31(13): 1371–1385.

Denrell J. 2004. Random walks and sustained competitive advantage. *Management Science* 50(7): 922–934.

DesJardine MR, Durand R. 2020. Disentangling the effects of hedge fund activism on firm financial and social performance. *Strategic Management Journal* 41(6): 1054–1082.

Dorobantu S, Kaul A, Zelner B. 2017. Nonmarket strategy research through the lens of new institutional economics: an integrative review and future directions. *Strategic Management Journal* 38(1): 114–140.

Durand R. 2001. Firm selection: an integrative perspective. *Organization Studies* 22(3): 393–417.

Durand R. 2002. Competitive advantages exist: a critique of Powell. *Strategic Management Journal* 23(9): 867–872.

Durand R. 2006. *Organizational Evolution and Strategic Management*. Sage Publications: London, U.K.

Durand R. 2012. Advancing strategy and organization research in concert: towards an integrated model? *Strategic Organization* 10(3): 297–303.

Durand R, Khaire M. 2017. Where do market categories come from and how? Distinguishing category creation from category emergence. *Journal of Management* 43(1): 87–110.

Durand R, Paolella L. 2013. Category stretching: reorienting research on categories in strategy, entrepreneurship, and organization theory. *Journal of Management Studies* 50(6): 1100–1123.

Durand R, Paugam L, Stolowy H. 2019. Do investors actually value sustainability indices? Replication, development, and new evidence on CSR visibility. *Strategic Management Journal* 40(9): 1471–1490.

Durand R, Rao H, Monin P. 2007. Code and conduct in French cuisine: impact of code changes on external evaluations. *Strategic Management Journal* 28(5): 455–472.

Durand R, Vaara E. 2009. Causation, counterfactuals, and competitive advantage. *Strategic Management Journal* 30(12): 1245–1264.

Flammer C, Bansal P. 2017. Does a long-term orientation create value? Evidence from a regression discontinuity. *Strategic Management Journal* 38(9): 1827–1847

Gaba V, Greve HR. 2019. Safe or profitable? The pursuit of conflicting goals. *Organization Science* 30(4): 647–667.

Gans J, Ryall MD. 2017. Value capture theory: a strategic management review. *Strategic Management Journal* 38(1): 17–41.

Gouvard P. 2020. The (relative) effects of typicality on volatility: A study using word embeddings. Dissertation, HEC Paris.

Greve, HR. 2009. Bigger and safer: the diffusion of competitive advantage. *Strategic Management Journal* 30(1): 1–23.

Haans RFJ 2019. What's the value of being different when everyone is? The effects of distinctiveness on performance in homogeneous versus heterogeneous categories. *Strategic Management Journal* **40**(1): 3–27.

Hahn ED, Doh JP. 2006. Using Bayesian methods in strategy research: an extension of Hansen et al. *Strategic Management Journal* **27**(8): 783–798.

Hannan MT, Freeman J. 1989. *Organizational Ecology*. Harvard University Press: Cambridge, MA.

Hannan MT, Pólos L, Carroll GR. 2007. *Logics of Organization Theory: Audiences, Codes, and Ecologies*. Princeton University Press: Princeton, NJ.

Hansen MH, Perry LT, Reese CS. 2004. A Bayesian operationalization of the resource-based view. *Strategic Management Journal* **25**(13): 1279–1295.

Harrison JS, Bosse DA, Phillips RA. 2010. Managing for stakeholders, stakeholder utility functions, and competitive advantage. *Strategic Management Journal* **31**(1): 58–74.

Hart O, Moore J. 1990. Property rights and the nature of the firm. *Journal of Political Economy* **98**(6): 1119–1158.

Hatch NW, Dyer JH. 2004. Human capital and learning as a source of sustainable competitive advantage. *Strategic Management Journal* **25**(12): 1155–1178.

Helfat CE, Peteraf MA. 2003. The dynamic resource-based view: capability lifecycles. *Strategic Management Journal* **24**(10): 997–1010.

Henderson AD, Raynor ME, Ahmed M. 2012. How long must a firm be great to rule out chance? Benchmarking sustained superior performance without being fooled by randomness. *Strategic Management Journal* **33**(4): 387–406.

Hrebiniak LG, Joyce WF. 1985. Organizational adaptation: strategic choice and environmental determinism. *Administrative Science Quarterly* **30**(3): 336–349.

Jacobsen R. 1988. The persistence of abnormal returns. *Strategic Management Journal* **9**(5): 415–430.

Jones TM, Harrison JS, Felps W. 2018. How applying instrumental stakeholder theory can provide sustainable competitive advantage. *Academy of Management Review* **43**(3): 371–391.

Kilduff GJ, Elfenbein HA, Staw BM. 2010. The psychology of rivalry: a relationally dependent analysis of competition. *Academy of Management Journal* **53**(5): 943–969.

Levinthal DA. 1997. Adaptation on rugged landscapes. *Management Science* **43**(7): 934–950.

Lippman SA, Rumelt RP. 2003. A bargaining perspective on resource advantage. *Strategic Management Journal* **24**(11): 1069–1086.

Madsen TL, Walker G. 2017. Competitive heterogeneity, cohorts, and persistent advantage. *Strategic Management Journal* **38**(2): 184–202.

Mahoney JT, Pandian JR. 1992. The resource-based view within the conversation of strategic management. *Strategic Management Journal* **13**(5): 363–380.

Makadok R. 2001. Toward a synthesis of the resource-based and dynamic-capability views of rent creation. *Strategic Management Journal* **22**(5): 387–401.

McGahan AM, Porter ME. 1997. How much does industry matter, really? *Strategic Management Journal* **18**(S1): 15–30.

McGrath R. 2013. *The End of Competitive Advantage: How to Keep Your Strategy Moving as Fast as Your Business*. Harvard Business Review Press: Boston, MA.

Meyer JW, Rowan B. 1977. Institutionalized organizations: formal structure as myth and ceremony. *American Journal of Sociology* **83**(2): 340–363.

Montgomery CA (ed). 1995. *Resource-Based and Evolutionary Theories of the Firm: Towards a Synthesis*. Kluwer Academic Publishers: Norwell, MA.

Newbert SL. 2008. Value, rareness, competitive advantage, and performance: a conceptual-level empirical investigation of the resource-based view of the firm. *Strategic Management Journal* **29**(7): 745–768.

Obloj, T., Sengul, M. 2020. What do multiple objectives really mean for performance? Empirical evidence from the French manufacturing sector. *Strategic Management Journal* 41(13): 2518–2547.

Oliver C. 1997. Sustainable competitive advantage: combining institutional and resource-based views. *Strategic Management Journal* 18(9): 697–713.

Oster SM. 1999. *Modern Competitive Analysis*. Oxford University Press: New York, NY.

Paolella L, Durand R. 2016. Category spanning, evaluation, and performance: revised theory and test on the corporate law market. *Academy of Management Journal* 59(1): 330–351.

Penrose ET. 1952. Biological analogies in the theory of the firm. *American Economic Review* 42(5): 804–819.

Penrose E. 1959/1995. *The Theory of the Growth of the Firm*. John Wiley and Sons: New York, NY.

Peteraf MA. 1993. The cornerstones of competitive advantage: a resource-based view. *Strategic Management Journal* 14(3): 179–191.

Peteraf MA, Barney JB. 2003. Unraveling the resource-based tangle. *Managerial and Decision Economics* 24(4): 309–323.

Porac JF, Thomas H, Baden-Fuller C. 1989. Competitive groups as cognitive communities: the case of Scottish knitwear manufacturers. *Journal of Management Studies* 26(4): 397–416.

Porter ME. 1980. Industry structure and competitive strategy: keys to profitability. *Financial Analysts Journal* 36(4): 30–41.

Porter ME. 1991. Towards a dynamic theory of strategy. *Strategic Management Journal* 12(S2): 95–117.

Powell TC. 2001. Competitive advantage: logical and philosophical considerations. *Strategic Management Journal* 22(9): 875–888.

Priem RL, Butler JE. 2001. Is the resource-based "view" a useful perspective for strategic management research? *Academy of Management Review* 26(1): 22–40.

Ray G, Barney JB, Muhanna WA. 2004. Capabilities, business processes, and competitive advantage: Choosing the dependent variable in empirical tests of the resource-based view. *Strategic Management Journal* 25(1): 23–37.

Roquebert JA, Phillips RL, Westfall PA. 1996. Markets vs. management: what drives profitability? *Strategic Management Journal* 17(8): 653–664.

Rugman AM, Verbeke A. 2002. Edith Penrose's contribution to the resource-based view of strategic management. *Strategic Management Journal* 23(8): 769–780.

Schwenk CR. 1984. Cognitive simplification processes in strategic decision-making. *Strategic Management Journal* 5(2): 111–128.

Sirmon DG, Hitt MA, Arregle JL, Campbell JT. 2010. The dynamic interplay of capability strengths and weaknesses: investigating the bases of temporary competitive advantage. *Strategic Management Journal* 31(13): 1386–1409.

Suarez FF, Grodal S, Gotsopoulos A. 2015. Perfect timing? Dominant category, dominant design, and the window of opportunity for firm entry. *Strategic Management Journal* 36(3): 437–448.

Vaara E, Monin P. 2010. A recursive perspective on discursive legitimation and organizational action in mergers and acquisitions. *Organization Science* 21(1): 3–22.

Waring GF. 1996. Industry differences in the persistence of firm-specific returns. *American Economic Review* 86(5): 1253–1265.

Wiggins RR, Ruefli TW. 2002. Sustained competitive advantage: temporal dynamics and the incidence and persistence of superior economic performance. *Organization Science* 13(1): 81–105.

Zhao EY, Fisher G, Lounsbury M, Miller D. 2017. Optimal distinctiveness: broadening the interface between institutional theory and strategic management. *Strategic Management Journal* 38(1): 93–113.

4.2
ALLIANCES AND NETWORKS

Dovev Lavie

Alliances and networks are a central theme in cooperative strategy research. *Alliances* are voluntary arrangements among independent firms that exchange resources for the co-development or provision of products and services. They include equity joint ventures and nonequity alliances, encompassing various value chain activities. Scholars have studied their formation and performance, shifting focus from dyadic relations to structural properties of networks (Gulati, Nohria, and Zaheer, 2000). They have accounted for multilateral interdependencies in multiparty alliances, portfolios, and ecosystems. While drawing from diverse theoretical foundations, this research has been mostly phenomenon-driven. It has enhanced the understanding of alliance formation and evolution, partner selection, value creation and capture, alliance governance, portfolio configuration, and the dynamics of alliance networks (e.g., Contractor and Reuer, 2019; Lumineau and Oliveira, 2018). Nevertheless, this conversation has left some open questions for future research. This chapter discusses major streams of research on alliances and networks and identifies future research opportunities in each stream.

Theoretical Foundations of Alliance Research

Early research on joint ventures has considered the choice of governance mode from a transaction cost economics perspective (e.g., Hennart, 1988). In turn, resource-dependence theory has suggested alliances as a vehicle for accessing resources and reducing the firm's dependence on stakeholders (e.g., Mitchell and Singh, 1996). The relational view (Dyer and Singh, 1998) has extended this logic from internally owned resources to partners' network resources, explaining how value creation is driven by resource combinations, relational mechanisms, and informal governance. Social network theories have directed attention to how the social structure of alliance relations facilitates alliance formation, partner selection, and information flows (e.g., Gulati and Gargiulo, 1999). Learning theories have elaborated on the processes of searching for, acquiring, exchanging, and generating knowledge in alliances (Ingram, 2002), given partners' absorptive capacities and routines (Lane, Salk, and Lyles, 2001). Game theories have modeled cooperation and conflict as a function of partners' expected payoffs (e.g., Parkhe, 1993), whereas real options theory has explained partners' resource commitments and governance choices (e.g., Folta and Miller, 2002).

There remains an opportunity for process theories on the evolution and dynamics of alliances and networks (e.g., Ahuja, Soda, and Zaheer, 2012; Doz, 1996). For example, the interaction of senior management with business units can shape the responsibility for partner selection and negotiations, thus affecting alliance formation. Additionally, a microfoundations perspective may draw attention to the characteristics, behavior, and decisions of managers (Felin, Foss, and Ployhart, 2015) and inform research, which has paid less attention to behavioral tendencies. In turn, institutional theory (DiMaggio and Powell, 1983; Scott, 1995), stakeholder theory (Freeman, 2010), or political theories (e.g., Dryzek, Honig, and Phillips, 2008) can explain how alliance partners strive for legitimacy and adhere to conflicting expectations of industry, state, and global actors.

Motivation for Alliance Formation

Scholars have identified environmental, organizational, and motivational antecedents of alliance formation. Environmental conditions encompass industry structure, dynamics, and regulations. In particular, alliance formation is linked to rivalry intensity (e.g., Ang, 2008), with alliances formed to mitigate competitive tension. Additionally, alliance formation may be prompted by a bandwagon effect (Tallman and Shenkar, 1994), followed by a decline, as firms exhaust partnering opportunities. Alliances are driven by scale economies, technology development, market growth, resource scarcity, uncertainty, and dynamism in the industry (e.g., Park, Chen, and Gallagher, 2002). The institutional environment mitigates relational risk and thus facilitates alliances (e.g., Roy and Oliver, 2009). The appropriability regime may encourage firms with intellectual property to partner, while discouraging firms that seek it. Finally, national culture and cultural differences shape alliance formation (e.g., Pothukuchi et al., 2002).

A central theme underscores organizational motivations such as resource access (e.g., Singh and Mitchell, 2005), yet firms need sufficient managerial resources to support alliances and attract partners (e.g., Stern, Dukerich, and Zajac, 2014). Firms seek scale and scope economies (e.g., Mowery, Oxley, and Silverman, 1998) and endorsements from reputable partners (Brass et al., 2004) when accessing resources via alliances. Alliance formation has also been tied to firms' ownership structure and age (e.g., Mitsuhashi and Greve, 2009), but mostly to their partnering experience (e.g., Gulati, 1999). However, some studies reveal diminishing returns to partnering experience, with variance in alliance formation tied to firms' network positions (e.g., Rowley, Behrens, and Krackhardt, 2000). These studies hint that relational embeddedness reduces search, coordination, and monitoring costs, thus reinforcing alliances with existing partners. Other studies refer to structural embeddedness, noting that centrality in the network of direct and indirect ties provides information on prospective partners (e.g., Ahuja, 2000), while structural holes offer brokerage positions (Gnyawali and Madhavan, 2001). A learning motivation involves internalizing a partner's knowledge or jointly developing knowledge (e.g., Grant and Baden-Fuller, 2004). Horizontal alliances may be formed to improve industry positions, mitigate competitive pressure, counter a common rival, create barriers to entry, or respond to alliances of peers (e.g., Powell *et al.*, 2005). Finally, firms ally to reduce uncertainty or performance gaps (e.g., Beckman, Haunschild, and Phillips, 2004).

Needed is research on the interplay of environmental, organizational, and motivational antecedents. Scholars occasionally confuse antecedents with consequences when studying alliance formation. Moreover, some claims have yet to be tested empirically, and in light of mixed findings, scholars should focus on boundary conditions and develop process perspectives on alliance life cycles (e.g., Ariño and de la Torre, 1998). We know little about how alliances evolve and terminate, with most studies focusing on alliance success rather than failure. While some alliances have a preset duration and others achieve their objectives, many terminate prematurely. In the absence of reliable data about terminations, research on alliance termination is mostly limited to case studies or focuses on joint ventures. The difficulty in assessing when an alliance is terminated and whether termination is indicative of success or failure has implications for research that assumes a set alliance duration. Some progress has been made in predicting termination as a consequence of adverse events (e.g., Bruyaka, Philippe, and Castañer, 2018), yet scholars should examine how alliances are renegotiated, reconfigured, and terminated by monitoring material changes in alliances over their life cycles.

Relational Mechanisms

Scholars have studied the dynamics of alliances and partners' interactions by alluding to relational mechanisms such as embeddedness, trust, commitment, and problem solving (e.g., McEvily and Marcus, 2005), which are interdependent and counter opportunism. These mechanisms enhance coordination and learning (e.g., Kale, Singh, and Perlmutter, 2000), and motivate knowledge exchange and investments in relation-specific assets. They also nurture relation-specific routines, mitigate conflict, and increase the reliability of outcomes, while reducing governance costs (e.g., Dyer and Singh, 1998). Relational mechanisms emerge via interpersonal interaction, partners' organizational and cultural fit, or joint experience (e.g., Lavie, Haunschild, and Khanna, 2012).

Although we know much about the evolution and implications of relational mechanisms, they remain a topic for debate. One debate concerns the interplay of informal and formal governance (e.g., Cao and Lumineau, 2015; Puranam and Vanneste, 2009). Some contend that formal governance signals distrust and may prompt opportunistic behavior, while others claim that contractual control facilitates trust by reassuring partners' behaviors. Resolving this debate may require distinguishing calculative trust from relational trust (Poppo, Zhou, and Li, 2016) and unpacking the dynamics of governance and trust in alliances. Another question is how interpersonal trust relates to interorganizational trust (e.g., Zaheer, McEvily, and Perrone, 1998), given that managers may trust a partner to different extents. Future research may study the implications of incoherent trust in a partner. Furthermore, most studies do not distinguish mutual trust from trustworthiness of a partner, and assume symmetry of trust, while inferring about trust by surveying one partner (Lumineau and Oliveira, 2018). By surveying both parties and relying on multiple informants, scholars can study the implications of trust asymmetry and incoherence in partners' perceptions of the alliance.

A related avenue centers on the individual's perspective. In particular, extant research disregards the inherent conflict in the role of alliance managers as boundary spanners who face the dilemma of "dual citizenship": should they advocate for the alliance, or rather represent the interests of their firm? Another question is how cognitive constraints and managers' experience, expertise, and character shape the prospects of alliances. A microfoundations approach can uncover personality catalysts of trust or opportunism in alliances. Whereas transaction cost economics assumes opportunistic individuals and the relational view assumes their cooperative intentions, an approach rooted in individual inclinations can go beyond field research and surveys to offer a more subtle answer.

Finally, there is room for studying failure of relational mechanisms, such as breakdown of trust. It is difficult to foresee such breakdown at the outset of alliances, but some research relates it to organizational change. For instance, when a firm's partner acquires a target that operates in the firm's business domain, competitive tension, dissatisfaction, and distrust may lead to reduced commitment and termination of the alliance (e.g., Rogan and Greve, 2015). Hence, scholars should study the pathology of failure and examine not only the evolution of trust and the design of conflict resolution mechanisms, but also the application of such mechanisms and the recovery and renewal of trust in alliances.

Value Creation and Capture in Alliances

A central theme in alliance research concerns the creation of value. Scholars have distinguished common benefits, which are jointly created by the partners, from private benefits, which they produce unilaterally at the other partner's expense by gaining from unintended knowledge spillover or by using shared resources beyond the alliance's scope (e.g., Khanna, Gulati, and Nohria, 1998). This perspective underscores the value of network resources that reside beyond the firm's boundaries but are accessible via alliances (Gulati, 2007). According to the relational view (e.g., Dyer, Singh, and Hesterly, 2018), the potential value of an alliance depends on the partners' complementarity resources and their relation-specific assets and knowledge-sharing routines, which in turn generate common benefits. A firm can create value by extending its market opportunities using network resources that are unavailable internally (enrichment), integrating network resources with its own resources or other partners' resources (combination), or internalizing network resources to grow its own resources (absorption) (Lavie, 2007). Nevertheless, scholars should pay more attention to the tradeoffs between common benefits and private benefits. For instance, rich network resources or knowledge sharing increase common benefits, but may restrict private benefits. In contrast, opportunistic behavior increases private benefits at the expense of common benefits. Common benefits and private benefits are interdependent, and their expected value shapes partners' behaviors (e.g., Arslan, 2018).

Whereas scholars have made progress in studying value creation in alliances, less is known about value capture. With few exceptions, studies do not disentangle value creation from capture, but rather examine their net effect. *Value capture* refers to the distribution of common benefits and to a firm's appropriation of private benefits from the partner's shared and nonshared resources. Scholars have associated value capture with the relative scale and scope of the parties' resources, relative bargaining power, relative absorptive capacity, opportunistic behavior, and isolating mechanisms (Lavie, 2006). Value creation and capture in alliances is typically measured with abnormal stock market returns around alliance announcements and the total returns to the partners (Gulati and Wang, 2003). However, this approach cannot discern value creation from capture, nor separate a firm's private benefits from its share of common benefits. Moreover, stock market returns can predict the expected value but not the realized value in an alliance.

To disentangle value creation from capture, future research may develop refined measures and methodologies to account for interdependencies between common and private benefits and for postformation dynamics in alliances. A dynamic perspective can explain how expected benefits guide the partners' behaviors, which in turn affect the resulting benefits. Game theoretical approaches may account not only for the expected payoffs to a firm but also for the payoffs to a partner and hence for their resulting behaviors. Unpacking the interdependence in the parties' value creation and capture is a way forward. Other opportunities involve switching from a dyad to a portfolio perspective in studying value creation and capture (Wassmer, 2010) and considering organizational attributes of partners, besides their network resources, such as their national origin (Lavie and Miller, 2008). The next step then is to study the interplay of the parties' attributes with relational and structural properties of alliance networks. Empirically examining the firm's receptivity, reach, and richness of network resources (Gulati, Lavie, and Madhavan, 2011) can provide a better understanding of how value is created and captured in alliances.

Structural Embeddedness in Networks

The network resources perspective relates to partners' characteristics, while the relational view explains how the nature of relations and resource flows drives economic benefits. A related tradition alludes to structural embeddedness, according to which the configuration of ties and positions of firms in networks influence their behaviors and outcomes (Kilduff and Brass, 2010). Following this tradition, scholars examine patterns of relations, referring to properties such as network centrality, cohesion, and structural holes, which contribute to value creation in distinctive ways. Alliance research has adopted methods for social network analysis (e.g., Baum, Calabrese, and Silverman, 2000; Schilling and Phelps, 2007; Zaheer and Bell, 2005), yet this structuralist approach assumes away heterogeneity in partner attributes and alliance relations.

Recent research acknowledges the merits of juxtaposing relational and structural aspects of networks, while studying heterogeneity in network resources. For instance, Lavie (2007) relates the performance effect of network resources to relational aspects such as relative bargaining power and competitive tension with partners; Sytch and Tatarynowicz (2014) examine how network structure evolves with collaborative versus conflictual relations; and Aggarwal (2020) studies how resource constraints of direct and indirect ties shape collaborative benefits. These studies bring together network structure, the nature of relations, and firms' attributes. To enhance understanding of the evolution and performance of alliance networks, future research can consider how organizing alliances and allocating internal resources influence the gains from structural and relational embeddedness. Going forward, scholars can explore the dark side of embeddedness, for example, how unintended resource leakage to partners, as well as efficient absorption of network resources, can lead to inertia and decline in the richness of network resources.

Additionally, scholars may revisit the mechanisms of value creation in alliance networks, which are rooted in interpersonal networks. Friendships and personal attachment (e.g., Uzzi, 1996) matter in alliances, but do not fully explain the economic rationale of business exchange. Although network analytics have linked network structure to firm performance, the theoretical reasoning has been underdeveloped. Future research may also elaborate on the implications of multiplex networks that embed several types of relations (e.g., Shipilov, 2012), whereby engaging in one relation affects the parties' behavior and prospects with other types of relations. Finally, whereas scholars have explored the emergence and evolution of alliance networks (e.g., Ahuja *et al.*, 2012), a question remains concerning the origin of networks. If network structure evolves from preceding network structures (e.g., Gulati and Gargiulo, 1999), then what motivates tie formation where no prior ties exist, and how can firms dislodge from inertial network structures? Relatedly, how do cognitive biases and behavioral inclinations shape network evolution? Social network scholars assume an almost involuntary reaction to structural properties of networks. Nevertheless, managers cannot always map their network nor comprehend its complex implications, thus limiting their concern to immediate network ties.

Managing Alliance Portfolios

Research on alliance portfolios assumes a firm-centric perspective for studying the evolution, configuration, and interdependencies in immediate alliance relations

(Wassmer, 2010). Besides structural properties, interdependencies encompass complementarity and competitive tension with partners, which shape the firm's ability to create and capture value from alliances. For example, besides bilateral competition between the firm and its partners, a portfolio approach studies the multilateral competition among the firm's partners (Lavie, 2007). Scholars have studied the emergence of alliance portfolios, seeking to explain a firm's tendency to form particular types of alliances, its partner choice, and changes in the portfolio configuration, which may be guided by its cooperative strategy or reaction to exogenous trends (e.g., Ozcan and Eisenhardt, 2009). Research on the configuration of alliance portfolios relates to the number of partners, the proportion of exploration versus exploitation alliances, and diversity of value chain activities, types of partners, and their characteristics (e.g., Hoffmann, 2007). A related focus is the performance effects of portfolio configuration. For example, scholars have studied the performance effects of network resources (Stuart, 2000), cross-national distance to partners (Lavie and Miller, 2008), balance between exploration and exploitation alliances (Lavie, Kang, and Rosenkopf, 2011), and portfolio diversity (Jiang, Tao, and Santoro, 2010). However, relational mechanisms such as trust are inherently dyadic: trusting one partner does not entail trusting another. Hence, trust, cultural fit, and joint experience should not be aggregated across the portfolio. Similarly, network properties such as structural holes are not informative at the portfolio level if indirect ties are excluded.

A fruitful research stream has centered on managing alliance portfolios. Portfolio interdependencies can generate synergies but also lead to discontent, withheld cooperation, and alliance termination. Firms can reduce their dependence on a partner by establishing ties to competing partners (Lavie, 2007), but managing competing alliances entails separation, segmentation, or coordination of alliance operations and tradeoffs with the firm's internal organization (Lavie, 2009). A firm may develop a capability for managing collaborative relations with partners by accumulating, codifying, disseminating, and applying alliance management know-how (Kale, Dyer, and Singh, 2002; Kale and Singh, 2007). This is typically achieved by instituting a dedicated alliance function, managerial tools, and practices that facilitate coordination (Heimeriks and Duysters, 2007). In particular, a dedicated function can leverage partnering experience, codify tacit know-how and disseminate it to managers, obtain corporate support, monitor alliances, and enhance their visibility (Kale et al., 2002), which improves alliance performance (e.g., Schilke and Goerzen, 2010). However, scholars should demonstrate how the alliance management capability shapes corporate performance, while disentangling firm-specific practices from relation-specific routines.

In particular, scholars have underscored the role of a dedicated function in standardizing, formalizing, and centralizing alliance management practices (Albers, Wohlgezogen, and Zajac, 2016), which can be systematically applied with different partners. However, recent research (e.g., Findikoglu and Lavie, 2019) suggests that coherent routines that support best practices may preclude adaptation that is essential in recurrent alliances with the same partners. The formality of the dedicated function may also drive out relational mechanisms such as trust (Das and Teng, 2001). Hence, scholars should examine how firms can balance the efficiency of firm-specific routines and the adaptation of relation-specific routines.

Although the dedicated function can be valuable, it may pay off only under certain circumstances, which remain to be studied. Future research may also study how the firm and its partner's dedicated functions sync despite inconsistent practices and inherent rigidities. Such research may also examine how the configuration of the alliance portfolio affects the firm's partners. Moreover, there remains the question of how centralized the alliance function should be to reconcile the conflicting needs of its corporate management and alliance managers. The broader question concerns the trade-off between routinization and flexibility of alliance management. Related to that is the need to assess how technologies facilitate alliance management, and when they undermine interpersonal exchange. Does digitalization enhance calculative trust while impeding relational trust? Scholars should separate the effect of technology from that of practices for managing alliances. Prior research has also focused on the design of alliances, but changes in partners' strategies and industry conditions may affect the power balance and behavior in alliances. Research on the dynamics of relational mechanisms might track changes in alliance governance and firms' recurrent alliances. A microfoundations approach that brings the alliance manager to the foreground can also shed light on these issues.

Partnering Experience and Learning in Alliances

Partnering experience contributes to alliance management capabilities by generating know-how that supports practices for partner selection, coordination, and governance. It enables firms to specialize, avoid pitfalls, and nurture best practices that create value in alliances (Gulati, Lavie, and Singh, 2009; Hoang and Rothaermel, 2005). Whereas most studies reveal its positive effects (e.g., Anand and Khanna, 2000; Child and Yan, 2003), others show negative (Reuer, Zollo, and Singh, 2002) or insignificant effects (e.g., Merchant and Schendel, 2000). To reconcile these findings, scholars have proposed a curvilinearly diminishing effect (e.g., Sampson, 2005) or underscored contingencies. They have also distinguished this general partnering experience (GPE) from partner-specific experience (PSE). GPE accounts for all prior alliances irrespective of the partners' identities, while PSE refers to experience gained in recurrent alliances with the same partner (Gulati *et al.*, 2009). Whereas GPE contributes to a firm's alliance management capability, PSE fosters relational mechanisms such as trust and embeddedness with certain partners and facilitates relation-specific routines for knowledge exchange. Still, whereas some studies report positive PSE effects (e.g., Gulati *et al.*, 2009), others show insignificant (Hoang and Rothaermel, 2005) or negative effects (Goerzen, 2007), thus leaving room for exploring boundary conditions.

Learning how to manage alliances is distinct from content learning. Content learning from partners entails motivation and the ability to learn, relational mechanisms, and certain features of partners and their knowledge (Lyles and Salk, 1996). Specifically, a firm can design deliberate structures to actively internalize its partner's skills and apply them beyond the scope of their alliance. When both parties intend to learn, a learning race transpires in which each seeks to hinder the other's learning. This race's outcomes depend on the parties' relative absorptive capacity (Lane and Lubatkin, 1998). A certain overlap in their knowledge facilitates learning, but they can rely on boundary spanners, knowledge codification, and relational mechanisms to facilitate receptivity. But learning also depends on the firm's ties to diverse and distant partners (reach) and on the potential value of its partners' knowledge (richness) (Gulati et al., 2011). The transparency of knowledge makes it accessible, while the partners' efforts to protect their proprietary knowledge restrict learning (Kale et al., 2000). If a partner's knowledge is easily transported and interpreted, the firm can learn it more easily, but the partner can regulate knowledge flows by limiting the scope of agreements, relying on legal protection, restricting the presence of the firm's personnel, and training gatekeepers to withhold information.

Research on alliances tends to assume that when a partner possesses complementary knowledge, learning follows, but scholars should carefully document knowledge flows to verify that learning indeed occurs and that it can be related to the alliance as opposed to alternative channels. Scholars should step away from alliance counts and investigate learning by documenting knowledge flows, for example, using patent citations. Moreover, there is a latent assumption that experience is beneficial, but firms may encounter negative experience or fail to learn from their experience. Future research may consider how learning from failure differs from learning from success in alliances, and the conditions under which a firm indeed learns from its experience. For instance, research on negative transfer learning suggests that learned knowledge may be misapplied because of unwarranted assumptions of isomorphism that prevent the recognition of critical contextual differences, for example, knowledge learned in domestic alliances may be misapplied in international alliances (Lavie and Miller, 2008). Perhaps firms that manage to develop dynamic learning abilities—that is, learn how to learn in alliances—are better off, but this has been understudied.

Future research may identify conditions under which learning in alliances can be effective, while acknowledging learning challenges. More attention should be paid to tradeoffs. For example, facilitating joint knowledge creation in a joint venture may restrict the partners' learning outside the venture. Most studies highlight the benefits of investing in personnel and practices for learning, but this should be weighed against the costs while considering the extent to which knowledge is fungible across alliances. Moreover, thus far, scholars have focused on the firm, dyad, or network, but learning takes place in the minds of individuals who are biased and cognitively constrained. What are the implications? For instance, research on learning from performance feedback suggests that alliance performance may affect learning in alliances, but this has been understudied. Another question concerns the role of expatriates. In a learning race, is a firm better off hosting the alliance, or sending expatriates? More broadly, in managing learning races, how can firms simultaneously facilitate collaboration while restricting their partners' opportunism? This is especially relevant in open innovation, wherein there are greater learning opportunities, but centralized alliance governance is ill suited. In contrast, a decentralized structure makes it difficult to coordinate decisions.

Multiparty Alliances and Ecosystems

In multiparty alliances, several firms interact multilaterally in pursuit of common objectives, while maintaining their interests and competing for their share of the common benefits. The alliance organization is typically governed in a democratic fashion, with the partners specifying problems and their solutions, which they then collectively promote in their industry. Scholars have studied the formation of research consortia (e.g., Sakakibara, 2002), decision-making and practices in standards associations (e.g., Ranganathan and Rosenkopf, 2014), and the distribution of benefits to multiparty alliance members as a function of their involvement, timing of entry, and competitive aspirations (e.g., Lavie, Lechner, and Singh, 2007; Lazzarini, 2007). They have also studied governance and strategic behavior in these alliances in light of the interplay of cooperative and competitive motives (e.g., Li *et al.*, 2012; Ranganathan, Ghosh, and Rosenkopf, 2018).

The recent research on ecosystems focuses on "the alignment structure of the multilateral set of partners that need to interact in order for a focal value proposition to materialize" (Adner, 2017: 40), discerning business ecosystems from innovation and platform ecosystems (Jacobides, Cennamo, and Gawer, 2018). Ecosystem members lack formal agreements, but their performance is driven by complementarities and interdependent decisions (Shipilov and Gawer, 2020). Some ecosystems are led by orchestrators that facilitate coordination and set rules for other members. Yet the ecosystem organization and its dynamics evolve as bottlenecks shift (Adner and Kapoor, 2016; Hannah and Eisenhardt, 2018). Scholars have studied the emergence, evolution, strategies, and performance of ecosystems, but this research is still in its infancy.

Future research should disentangle the unique characteristics and organizational dynamics of multiparty alliances and ecosystems, paying attention to their antecedents, complex governance, and tradeoffs. It is essential to isolate archetypes of governance mechanisms that work effectively under different market conditions and member configurations. It is also worth studying how the balance of power in constellations with different structures affects the distribution of benefits to members. Scholars may also uncover how multiparty alliances and ecosystems emerge and how they evolve as a function of their members' strategic behavior. How do cooperative and competitive behaviors at the dyad level impact the functioning and performance of the multiparty alliance or ecosystem, and how do multilateral interactions affect bilateral alliance decisions? How do the dynamics within the multiparty alliance or ecosystem affect its overall competitiveness, and how does the behavior within one alliance or ecosystem affect the prospects for another? Given the complexity and interdependencies, there is room for studying how cognitive constraints and biases shape decisions and outcomes in these constellations. Whereas case studies have shed light on the inner working of multiparty alliances and ecosystems, formal modeling and simulations can offer systematic recommendations. However, when drawing from theories on traditional alliances and networks, scholars should revisit their underlying assumptions.

Conclusion

Research on alliances and networks has flourished in the past 30 years, and while much is known about their formation, management, and performance implications, many questions remain underexplored. Although it is not possible to effectively review the vast literature on the topic, this chapter has sought to highlight promising themes, identify relevant opportunities, and guide future research in this exciting domain of cooperative strategy.

References

Adner R. 2017. Ecosystem as structure: an actionable construct for strategy. *Journal of Management* 43(1): 39–58.

Adner R, Kapoor R. 2016. Innovation ecosystems and the pace of substitution: re-examining technology S-curves. *Strategic Management Journal* 37(4): 625–648.

Aggarwal VA. 2020. Resource congestion in alliance networks: how a firm's partners' partners influence the benefits of collaboration. *Strategic Management Journal*: 41(4): 627–655.

Ahuja G. 2000. The duality of collaboration: inducements and opportunities in the formation of interfirm linkages. *Strategic Management Journal* 21(3): 317–343.

Ahuja G, Soda G, Zaheer A. 2012. The genesis and dynamics of organizational networks. *Organization Science* 23(2): 434–448.

Albers S, Wohlgezogen F, Zajac EJ. 2016. Strategic alliance structures: an organization design perspective. *Journal of Management* 42(3): 582–614.

Anand BN, Khanna T. 2000. Do firms learn to create value? The case of alliances. *Strategic Management Journal* 21(3): 295–315.

Ang SH. 2008. Competitive intensity and collaboration: impact on firm growth across technological environments. *Strategic Management Journal* 29(10): 1057–1075.

Ariño A, de la Torre J. 1998. Learning from failure: towards an evolutionary model of collaborative ventures. *Organization Science* 9(3): 306–325.

Arslan B. 2018. The interplay of competitive and cooperative behavior and differential benefits in alliances. *Strategic Management Journal* 39(12): 3222–3246.

Baum JAC, Calabrese T, Silverman BS. 2000. Don't go it alone: alliance network composition and startups' performance in Canadian biotechnology. *Strategic Management Journal* 21(3): 267–294.

Beckman CM, Haunschild PR, Phillips DJ. 2004. Friends or strangers? Firm-specific uncertainty, market uncertainty, and network partner selection. *Organization Science* 15(3): 259–275.

Brass DJ, Galaskiewicz J, Greve HR, Tsai W. 2004. Taking stock of networks and organizations: a multilevel perspective. *Academy of Management Journal* 47(6): 795–817.

Bruyaka O, Philippe D, Castañer X. 2018. Run away or stick together? The impact of organization-specific adverse events on alliance partner defection. *Academy of Management Review* 43(3): 445–469.

Cao Z, Lumineau F. 2015. Revisiting the interplay between contractual and relational governance: a qualitative and meta-analytic investigation. *Journal of Operations Management* 33: 15–42.

Child J, Yan Y. 2003. Predicting the performance of international joint ventures: an investigation in China. *Journal of Management Studies* 40(2): 283–320.

Contractor FJ, Reuer JJ (eds). 2019. *Frontiers of Alliance Research*. Cambridge University Press: Cambridge, MA.

Das TK, Teng BS. 2001. Trust, control, and risk in strategic alliances: an integrated framework. *Organization Studies* 22(2): 251–283.

DiMaggio PJ, Powell WW. 1983. The iron cage revisited: institutional isomorphism and collective rationality in organizational fields. *American Sociological Review* 48(2): 147–160.

Doz YL. 1996. The evolution of cooperation in strategic alliances: initial conditions or learning processes? *Strategic Management Journal* 17(S1): 55–83.

Dryzek JS, Honig B, Phillips A (eds). 2008. *The Oxford Handbook of Political Theory* (Vol. 1). Oxford University Press: New York, NY.

Dyer JH, Singh H. 1998. The relational view: cooperative strategy and sources of interorganizational competitive advantage. *Academy of Management Review* 23(4): 660–679.

Dyer JH, Singh H, Hesterly WS. 2018. The relational view revisited: a dynamic perspective on value creation and value capture. *Strategic Management Journal* 39(12): 3140–3162.

Felin T, Foss NJ, Ployhart R. 2015. The microfoundations movement in strategy and organization theory. *Academy of Management Annals* 9(1): 575–632.

Findikoglu M, Lavie D. 2019. The contingent value of the dedicated alliance function. *Strategic Organization* 17(2): 177–209.

Folta TB, Miller KD. 2002. Real options in equity partnerships. *Strategic Management Journal* 23(1): 77–88.

Freeman RE. 2010. *Stakeholder Theory: The State of the Art*. Cambridge University Press: New York, NY.

Gnyawali DR, Madhavan R. 2001. Cooperative networks and competitive dynamics: a structural embeddedness perspective. *Academy of Management Review* 26(3): 431–445.

Goerzen A. 2007. Alliance networks and firm performance: the impact of repeated partnerships. *Strategic Management Journal* 28(5): 487–509.

Grant RM, Baden-Fuller C. 2004. A knowledge accessing theory of strategic alliances. *Journal of Management Studies* 41(1): 61–84.

Gulati R. 1999. Network location and learning: the influence of network resources and firm capabilities on alliance formation. *Strategic Management Journal* 20(5): 397–420.

Gulati R. 2007. *Managing Network Resources: Alliances, Affiliations, and Other Relational Assets*. Oxford University Press: New York, NY.

Gulati R, Gargiulo M. 1999. Where do interorganizational networks come from? *American Journal of Sociology* 104(5): 1439–1493.

Gulati R, Lavie D, Madhavan RR. 2011. How do networks matter? The performance effects of interorganizational networks. *Research in Organizational Behavior* 31: 207–224.

Gulati R, Lavie D, Singh H. 2009. The nature of partnering experience and the gains from alliances. *Strategic Management Journal* 30(11): 1213–1233.

Gulati R, Nohria N, Zaheer A. 2000. Strategic networks. *Strategic Management Journal* 21(3): 203–215.

Gulati R, Wang LO. 2003. Size of the pie and share of the pie: implications of network embeddedness and business relatedness for value creation and value appropriation in joint ventures. *Research in the Sociology of Organizations* 20(1): 209–242.

Hannah DP, Eisenhardt KM. 2018. How firms navigate cooperation and competition in nascent ecosystems. *Strategic Management Journal* 39(12): 3163–3192.

Heimeriks KH, Duysters G. 2007. Alliance capability as a mediator between experience and alliance performance: an empirical investigation into the alliance capability development process. *Journal of Management Studies* 44(1): 25–49.

Hennart JF. 1988. A transaction costs theory of equity joint ventures. *Strategic Management Journal* 9(4): 361–374.

Hoang H, Rothaermel FT. 2005. The effect of general and partner-specific alliance experience on joint R&D project performance. *Academy of Management Journal* 48(2): 332–345.

Hoffmann WH. 2007. Strategies for managing a portfolio of alliances. *Strategic Management Journal* 28(8): 827–856.

Ingram P. 2002. Interorganizational learning. In *The Blackwell Companion to Organizations*, Baum JAC (ed). Blackwell Publishers: Malden, MA; 642–663.

Jacobides MG, Cennamo C, Gawer A. 2018. Towards a theory of ecosystems. *Strategic Management Journal* 39(8): 2255–2276.

Jiang RJ, Tao QT, Santoro MD. 2010. Alliance portfolio diversity and firm performance. *Strategic Management Journal* 31(10): 1136–1144.

Kale P, Dyer JH, Singh H. 2002. Alliance capability, stock market response, and long-term alliance success: the role of the alliance function. *Strategic Management Journal* 23(8): 747–767.

Kale P, Singh H. 2007. Building firm capabilities through learning: the role of the alliance learning process in alliance capability and firm-level alliance success. *Strategic Management Journal* 28(10): 981–1000.

Kale P, Singh H, Perlmutter H. 2000. Learning and protection of proprietary assets in strategic alliances: building relational capital. *Strategic Management Journal* 21(3): 217–237.

Khanna T, Gulati R, Nohria N. 1998. The dynamics of learning alliances: competition, cooperation, and relative scope. *Strategic Management Journal* 19(3): 193–210.

Kilduff M, Brass DJ. 2010. Organizational social network research: core ideas and key debates. *Academy of Management Annals* 4(1): 317–357.

Lane PJ, Lubatkin M. 1998. Relative absorptive capacity and interorganizational learning. *Strategic Management Journal* 19(5): 461–477.

Lane PJ, Salk JE, Lyles MA. 2001. Absorptive capacity, learning, and performance in international joint ventures. *Strategic Management Journal* 22: 1139–1161.

Lavie D. 2006. The competitive advantage of interconnected firms: an extension of the resource-based view. *Academy of Management Review* 31(3): 638–658.

Lavie D. 2007. Alliance portfolios and firm performance: a study of value creation and appropriation in the U.S. software industry. *Strategic Management Journal* 28(12): 1187–1212.

Lavie D. 2009. Capturing value from alliance portfolios. *Organizational Dynamics* 1(38): 26–36.

Lavie D, Haunschild P, Khanna P. 2012. Organizational differences, relational mechanisms, and alliance performance. *Strategic Management Journal* 33(13): 1453–1479.

Lavie D, Kang J, Rosenkopf L. 2011. Balance within and across domains: the performance implications of exploration and exploitation in alliances. *Organization Science* 22(6): 1517–1538.

Lavie D, Lechner C, Singh H. 2007. The performance implications of timing of entry and involvement in multipartner alliances. *Academy of Management Journal* 50(3): 578–604.

Lavie D, Miller SR. 2008. Alliance portfolio internationalization and firm performance. *Organization Science* 19(4): 623–646.

Lazzarini SG. 2007. The impact of membership in competing alliance constellations: evidence on the operational performance of global airlines. *Strategic Management Journal* 28(4): 345–367.

Li D, Eden L, Hitt MA, Ireland RD, Garrett RP. 2012. Governance in multilateral R&D alliances. *Organization Science* 23: 1191–1210.

Lumineau F, Oliveira N. 2018. A pluralistic perspective to overcome major blind spots in research on interorganizational relationships. *Academy of Management Annals* 12(1): 440–465.

Lyles MA, Salk, JE. 1996. Knowledge acquisition from foreign parents in international joint ventures: an empirical examination in the Hungarian context. *Journal of International Business Studies* 27(5): 877–903.

McEvily B, Marcus A. 2005. Embedded ties and the acquisition of competitive capabilities. *Strategic Management Journal* 26(11): 1033–1055.

Merchant H, Schendel D. 2000. How do international joint ventures create shareholder value? *Strategic Management Journal* 21(7): 723–737.

Mitchell W, Singh K. 1996. Survival of businesses using collaborative relationships to commercialize complex goods. *Strategic Management Journal* 17(3): 169–195.

Mitsuhashi H, Greve HR. 2009. A matching theory of alliance formation and organizational success: Complementarity and compatibility. *Academy of Management Journal* 52(5): 975–995.

Mowery DC, Oxley JE, Silverman BS. 1998. Technological overlap and interfirm cooperation: implications for the resource-based view of the firm. *Research Policy* 27(5): 507–523.

Ozcan P, Eisenhardt KM. 2009. Origin of alliance portfolios: entrepreneurs, network strategies, and firm performance. *Academy of Management Journal* 52(2): 246–279.

Park SH, Chen R, Gallagher S. 2002. Firm resources as moderators of the relationship between market growth and strategic alliances in semiconductor start-ups. *Academy of Management Journal* 45(3): 527–545.

Parkhe A. 1993. Strategic alliance structuring: a game theoretic and transaction cost examination of interfirm cooperation. *Academy of Management Journal* 36(4): 794–829.

Poppo L, Zhou KZ, Li JJ. 2016. When can you trust "trust"? Calculative trust, relational trust, and supplier performance. *Strategic Management Journal* 37(4): 724–741.

Pothukuchi V, Damanpour F, Choi J, Chen CC, Park SH. 2002. National and organizational culture differences and international joint venture performance. *Journal of International Business Studies* 33(2): 243–265.

Powell WW, White DR, Koput KW, Owen-Smith J. 2005. Network dynamics and field evolution: the growth of interorganizational collaboration in the life sciences. *American Journal of Sociology* 110(4): 1132–1205.

Puranam P, Vanneste BS. 2009. Trust and governance: untangling a tangled web. *Academy of Management Review* 34(1): 11–31.

Ranganathan R, Ghosh A, Rosenkopf L. 2018. Competition-cooperation interplay during multifirm technology coordination: the effect of firm heterogeneity on conflict and consensus in a technology standards organization. *Strategic Management Journal* 39(12): 3193–3221.

Ranganathan R, Rosenkopf L. 2014. Do ties really bind? The effect of knowledge and commercialization networks on opposition to standards. *Academy of Management Journal* 57(2): 515–540.

Reuer JJ, Zollo M, Singh H. 2002. Post-formation dynamics in strategic alliances. *Strategic Management Journal* 23(2): 135–151.

Rogan M, Greve HR. 2015. Resource dependence dynamics: partner reactions to mergers. *Organization Science* 26(1): 239–255.

Rowley T, Behrens D, Krackhardt D. 2000. Redundant governance structures: an analysis of structural and relational embeddedness in the steel and semiconductor industries. *Strategic Management Journal* 21(3): 369–386.

Roy JP, Oliver C. 2009. International joint venture partner selection: the role of the host-country legal environment. *Journal of International Business Studies* 40(5): 779–801.

Sakakibara M. 2002. Formation of R&D consortia: industry and company effects. *Strategic Management Journal* 23(11): 1033–1050.

Sampson RC. 2005. Experience effects and collaborative returns in R&D alliances. *Strategic Management Journal* 26(11): 1009–1031.

Schilke O, Goerzen A. 2010. Alliance management capability: an investigation of the construct and its measurement. *Journal of Management* 36(5): 1192–1219.

Schilling MA, Phelps CC. 2007. Interfirm collaboration networks: the impact of large-scale network structure on firm innovation. *Management Science* 53(7): 1113–1126.

Scott WR. 1995. *Institutions and Organizations: Ideas, Interests and Identities.* Sage Publications: Los Angeles, CA.

Shipilov A. 2012. Strategic multiplexity. *Strategic Organization* 10(3): 215–222.

Shipilov A, Gawer A. 2020. Integrating research on interorganizational networks and ecosystems. *Academy of Management Annals* 14(1): 92–121.

Singh K, Mitchell W. 2005. Growth dynamics: the bidirectional relationship between interfirm collaboration and business sales in entrant and incumbent alliances. *Strategic Management Journal* 26(6): 497–521.

Stern I, Dukerich JM, Zajac E. 2014. Unmixed signals: how reputation and status affect alliance formation. *Strategic Management Journal* 35(4): 512–531.

Stuart TE. 2000. Interorganizational alliances and the performance of firms: a study of growth and innovation rates in a high-technology industry. *Strategic Management Journal* 21(8): 791–811.

Sytch M, Tatarynowicz A. 2014. Friends and foes: the dynamics of dual social structures. *Academy of Management Journal* 57(2): 585–613.

Tallman SB, Shenkar O. 1994. A managerial decision model of international cooperative venture formation. *Journal of International Business Studies* 25(1): 91–113.

Uzzi B. 1996. The sources and consequences of embeddedness for the economic performance of organizations: the network effect. *American Sociological Review* 61(4): 674–698.

Wassmer U. 2010. Alliance portfolios: a review and research agenda. *Journal of Management* 36(1): 141–171.

Zaheer A, Bell GG. 2005. Benefiting from network position: firm capabilities, structural holes, and performance. *Strategic Management Journal* 26(9): 809–825.

Zaheer A, McEvily B, Perrone V. 1998. Does trust matter? Exploring the effects of interorganizational and interpersonal trust on performance. *Organization Science* 9(2): 141–159.

PART 5

GLOBAL STRATEGY

Stephen Tallman and Alvaro Cuervo-Cazurra, Leads

5.0
GLOBAL STRATEGY

Stephen Tallman and Alvaro Cuervo-Cazurra

Introduction

Global strategy, as a field, "involves the study of cross-border activities of economic agents or the strategies and governance of firms engaged in such activity" (Tallman and Pedersen, 2015: 273) to ensure success. The distinctive attribute of global strategy (also called "international strategy"—terms treated as equivalent herein) is that its study gives explicit recognition to the importance of the cross-border context in the design, execution, and success of strategy, that is, "strategy in context." Global strategy cannot be abstracted from the complex, varied, dynamic setting of the international business environment or from the effects of operating in multiple national settings. Global trends in technology, society, politics, and economics alter the relative standing among countries and ease of operating across borders. Variations in the sociocultural, politico-legal, techno-economic, and geographic characteristics of countries combine to make every national market idiosyncratic, even unique. All this demands that firms modify their goals, strategies, competitive advantage sources, and structures across countries and time. Global strategy scholars recognize that these contextual variations alter how firms approach national markets, coordinate activities and operations across locations, and the performance outcomes of these decisions.

In this chapter, we review the state of the art of global strategy. We start with an overview of the historical evolution of the field, and then we review the literature on global strategy around three major decisions: (1) expansion (whether to internationalize and how to select countries and entry modes to ensure effectiveness), (2) management (how to structure, coordinate, and control operations dispersed across countries to achieve efficiency), and (3) advantage (how to build an advantage in scale, learning, and arbitrage across locations to guarantee success). Future research can provide novel insights on these decisions by analyzing the impact of changes in three contexts: (1) countries, and the dynamics in cross-border interactions emerging from globalization, emerging markets, and government activism; (2) industries, and the reorganization of firm boundaries arising from digitalization, big data, and global value chains; and (3) organizations, and the reconsideration of the nature of work derived from global expertise, remote collaboration, and the gig economy. Figure 1 illustrates these ideas.

This chapter, together with Westney's (2021) study of the multinational as an organization and Williamson and Santos's (2021) analysis of emerging-market multinationals, offers a unique vision of the current and future global strategy scholarship

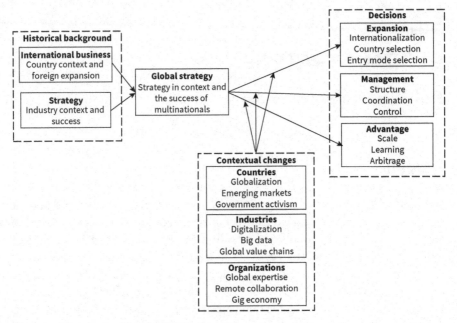

Figure 1 The past and future of global strategy research

directions. They provide an overview of global strategy as directed action. The organization both limits strategic possibilities and is changed as new foreign strategies are attempted, while firm resources provide the basis for competitive advantage and are altered by ventures into new countries. The chapters highlight the importance of national home and host context, resources and competitive advantage, and the diversity within and across national markets.

A Short History of the Field of Global Strategy

Global strategy emerged as a major field of strategy by integrating insights from international business and competitive strategy. Although some studies analyzed global strategy topics since the 1960s, the field of global strategy took form in the 1980s (see an overview in Ghoshal, 1987) and became established in the 2000s (see the review in Tallman and Yip, 2008), leading to the launch of *Global Strategy Journal* in 2011.

Historical antecedent: international business, country context, and foreign expansion

The field of international business emerged in the 1960s to explain foreign direct investment, highlighting the importance of cross-country differences. Hymer (1976) used the concept of monopolistic advantage from industrial organization economics to explain foreign direct investment. Vernon's (1966) international product life cycle model borrowed from marketing studies to explain sales and production movements across countries. Stopford and Wells's (1972) model of international diversification and structure helped shift the focus from country-level trade and investment to the multinationals' actions. Buckley and Casson (1976), Hennart (1982), and Teece (1986) used transaction cost economics to explain multinationals' selection of modes for coordinating cross-border transactions. Johanson and Vahlne's (1977) incremental internationalization or Uppsala model was built on behavioral economics to explain the evolution in selecting countries and entry modes. Dunning's (1977) eclectic or OLI model explained international production from the existence of three advantages: ownership, location, and internalization.

Although establishing a critical base, international business studies were not quite global strategy analyses. Most explained the decisions to expand across borders but not the success of such decisions. These early studies did not speak much of strategies for building sources of advantage, focusing instead on explaining how to use existing sources of advantage abroad.

Taking form: Strategic management, industry context, and success

Strategy as a field of inquiry evolved concurrently with these models of the multinational and provided an explanation of the sources of advantage and success. The strategy field emerged from industrial organization economics and its structure-conduct-performance model (Bain, 1956), which proposed that the (competitive) structure of the industry determined the (strategic) conduct of firms and their subsequent performance. Porter (1985) popularized this view and the generic strategies of low costs and differentiation that enable firms' superior profitability. Williamson (1975) explained how firms' boundaries and governance supported efficiency. The resource-based view (Barney, 1991) identified the conditions that enable firms' resources and capabilities to become sources of competitive advantage.

By the early 1990s, scholars recognized that strategic management concepts mapped closely onto models of the multinational, and began applying them to analyzing cross-border activities (Fladmoe-Lindquist and Tallman, 1994; Tallman, 1991, 1992) and the relationship between internationalization and performance (Hitt, Hoskisson, and Kim, 1997; Tallman and Li, 1996). This cross-pollination resulted in the identification of various international strategies based on the (organizational) coordination and (geographic) configuration of activities (Porter, 1986), challenging the view that global strategy was simply about standardizing products across countries (Levitt, 1983) to benefit from the integration of global operations (Yip, 1995).

Establishment: Strategy in context and the success of multinationals

The integration of ideas from international business and strategy gave rise to global strategy as a field, or "strategy in context"—that is, identifying strategies appropriate for the context that would support firms' success. One set of studies focused on the global industry context's impact on strategy. Prahalad and Doz's (1987) integration-responsiveness model classified industries according to their relative pressures for global integration and responsiveness to local markets. Bartlett and Ghoshal (1989) built on this idea to identify four strategies (international, global, multidomestic, and transnational) and introduced international learning as an additional source of success for multinational firms. Ghemawat's (2007) aggregation-adaptation-arbitrage model extended the integration-responsiveness approach and reintroduced arbitrage (Kogut, 1985) as the third dimension of global strategy. These models engaged with organizational structure and coordination to solve the competing demands between headquarters and local contexts (Rosenzweig and Singh, 1991). Another set of studies analyzed the influence of country context on strategies and their success. Differences between home and host countries deterred exports in gravity models explaining international trade (Tinbergen, 1962) and investments in the incremental internationalization model (Johanson and Vahlne, 1977). In the 2000s, country differences were narrowed to institutional differences as the drivers of the internationalization and success of multinationals (Cuervo-Cazurra and Genc, 2008; Khanna and Palepu, 2010; Henisz, 2000; Peng, 2002). However, it was not just absolute but rather relative differences between countries that drove country selection (Shenkar, 2001). Additionally, changes in the global context—including emerging markets and the international expansion of their multinationals (Cuervo-Cazurra and Ramamurti, 2014), digital technologies and the reconfiguration of interactions across borders (Banalieva and Dhanaraj, 2019), and global value chains and the disaggregation of activities across borders (Pananond, Gereffi, and Pedersen, 2020)—reinforced the importance of contextual influence on strategy.

The analysis of the impact of global strategy on performance complemented these studies of strategy in context. Early studies compared multinationals to nonmultinational firms, finding that the former did better (Agmon and Lessard, 1977). Later studies explored two decisions. One was how internationalization affected profitability, suggesting various relationships, such as linear, U-shaped, inverted U-shaped, and S-shaped (Lu and Beamish, 2004; Contractor, Kundu, and Hsu, 2003; Geringer, Beamish, and DaCosta, 1989). Another decision was the impact of entry mode on performance, examining which entry mode (greenfield, alliance, acquisition) supported superior performance and under what circumstances (Hennart and Park, 1993). Although the analyses were critiqued for weak measures (Wiersema and Bowen, 2011), theoretical imprecision (Hennart, 2011), and self-selection biases

(Shaver, 1998), many confirmed that internationalization contributes to performance, especially in the presence of firm-specific assets (Kirca *et al.*, 2011).

Decisions in Global Strategy: Expansion, Management, and Advantage

In the 2020s, global strategy is an established subfield of study, combining insights from international business and its understanding of contextual differences across countries and ideas from strategic management and its analysis of companies' success in competition with others. We organize our discussion of global strategy around three significant managerial decisions: (1) expansion, that is, the decision on whether to expand across borders and the subsequent selection of countries and entry modes to accomplish effectiveness; (2) management, that is, the decision on how to structure, coordinate, and control operations dispersed across countries to achieve efficiency; and (3) advantage, that is, the decision on how to build sources of advantage from scale, learning, and arbitrage across activities and operations that ensure the multinationals' success and performance.

Expansion: internationalization, country selection, and entry mode selection for effectiveness

The first set of strategic decisions for managers in a firm that wants to operate internationally is (1) taking the firm abroad, (2) selecting the best countries to enter, and (3) choosing the entry modes for each of the foreign markets that are most effective for achieving the desired goals.

Internationalization
Essential to understanding global strategy is identifying why individual companies choose to expand abroad. Early models, relying on industrial organization economics, argue that firms become multinationals to counter the moves of local competitors and build on their market power (Knickerbocker, 1973). Marketing models explain the export decision as the outcome of a shift in managerial attitudes toward foreign markets from reactive to proactive as their firms are increasingly exposed to foreign market demands (Cavusgil, 1980). The model of the growth of the firm indicates that companies grow to increase the efficiency of their productive assets and that, as they reach a level of dominance at home, they start expanding abroad in search of additional growth (Penrose, 1959). Once a firm has created a stock of unique resources, it can extract additional profitability from applying these resources in foreign markets (Hitt *et al.*, 1997; Tallman and Li, 1996).

The diversity of foreign expansion motives complicates the internationalization decision, however. Most of the models assume that companies expand abroad in search of new markets to sell more, and in such a situation, the critical strategic challenge is to identify and transfer abroad existing sources of advantage (Cuervo-Cazurra, Maloney, and Manrakhan, 2007). However, companies also expand abroad to buy better inputs, obtaining new sources of advantage in the form of strategic resources like technology or marketing skills, or reducing costs by accessing country endowments like unexploited natural resources, skilled inexpensive labor, abundant finance, or reduced taxation (Dunning and Lundan, 2008). These decisions require identifying the desired country endowments and negotiating access with their owners (Hennart, 2012).

Country selection

The diversity of economic-technological, politico-legal, sociocultural, and geographic conditions across countries requires managers to make a concerted effort in selecting the country that is most likely to facilitate internationalization success. Opportunities vary with the objective of the firm—whether to increase sales, for which a large customer market is preferred; lower production costs, for which low-cost factors of production are desired; or improve competitiveness, requiring sophisticated technology or marketing. Balancing country opportunities with the costs of managing cross-border operations drives the selection.

The incremental internationalization process model (Johanson and Vahlne, 1977) is an influential explanation of country selection. This model, which assumes internationalization in search of markets, proposes that managers choose countries depending on the psychic distance between the home and host countries, that is, the factors that limit the cross-country transfer and use of knowledge. As a result, managers select countries that are closer to the home country so that they can use more of their knowledge and expertise. After the firm expands into closer countries and managers learn how to operate there, they then select countries that are more distant for further expansion.

Success in the host country depends on how well managers solve three sources of costs (Eriksson *et al.*, 1997): competing in the host country, operating in the host country, and coordinating activities across countries. These three costs create the liability of internationalization, that is, the additional costs of foreign operations in comparison to home country ones. This concept is often confused with the liability of foreignness (Zaheer, 1995) or the cost of doing business abroad (Hymer, 1976), which refers to the disadvantages and costs, respectively, that subsidiaries of foreign firms face in comparison to established domestic competitors in the host country.

Entry mode selection

Having decided to expand the firm abroad and selected a country, managers must choose the entry mode that will enable them to reach their internationalization objectives. This commonly requires picking among contractual entry modes in which the firm establishes contracts but does not invest in the host country (international trade, licensing and franchising, or subcontracting), and investment entry modes in which the multinational invests and exerts controls over a host country operation (cross-border greenfield, alliances, or acquisitions).

Transaction cost economics is commonly used to explain entry mode decisions. The selection of licensees, partners, and ownership is driven by the characteristics of the assets and cross-border transaction (Hennart, 2009), including information asymmetry and uncertainty about the local market and partners, expropriation concerns, and the strength of the contractual system (Anderson and Gatignon, 1986). Entry mode decisions are also driven by contextual conditions that increase uncertainty about host markets, such as political risk (Kobrin, 1979), geography (Chakrabarti and Mitchell, 2013), culture (Kogut and Singh, 1988), and institutions (Meyer, 2001), affecting the commitment choices and altering the rent-earning potential of firm resources and capabilities from market to market (Tallman, 1992).

An alternative explanation of entry mode selection is based on a learning approach found in the incremental internationalization model (Johanson and Vahlne, 1977). In this model, risk-averse managers select methods that limit exposure to the host country while they learn how to operate there. This results in firms starting with exports, then using intermediaries to distribute products, later establishing sales subsidiaries to facilitate interactions with customers, and finally creating production subsidiaries if the market is sufficiently important and they have learned how to operate there.

Another dynamic explanation of entry mode selection is Dunning's (1988) internationalization model. It expects that firms with ownership advantages use exports to access foreign markets, shift to using overseas licensees if location advantages become salient, and make direct foreign investments when internalization advantages render internal control of host country production advantageous.

Success in the host country leads to increased investments and a change to more engaged modes (Chang and Rosenzweig, 2001). Poor performance results in a reduction of operations or eventual divestment (Benito, 2005). Although the study of international divestments is usually done by looking at one operation or country at a time (Duhaime and Grant, 1984), it can also be part of the overall reorganization of a multinational firm. Such a change may not be driven by the host country conditions and local success, but rather by relative changes in the operation in comparison to other operations elsewhere.

Management: structure, coordination, and control of operations for efficiency

The second strategic decision is to manage the network of foreign activities, establishing (1) structure, (2) coordination, and (3) control mechanisms to facilitate the achievement of efficiency. Westney (2021) discusses these decisions in detail.

Structure

The early strategic management discussions on the interdependence between strategy and structure (Chandler, 1962) have informed research on multinationals. As firms move from being exclusively domestic concerns to increasingly engaging in international markets, they alter their formal structures to improve efficiency (Malnight, 1996; Martinez and Jarillo, 1989). The selection among these alternatives depends on the relative importance of international markets for the firm (Stopford and Wells, 1972). The usual sequence is serving foreign markets with the same structure used for the domestic setting until the foreign business becomes too significant. This prompts the creation of an international department that coordinates foreign activities and is staffed with managers and employees with international experience. The continued growth of foreign business leads to the transformation of the structure to coordinate operations more efficiently, following two alternatives. One is a geographic structure in which important markets or regions are managed independently; this facilitates responsiveness to local conditions. Another is a product structure in which important products are managed separately; this facilitates global coordination of product innovation and sales.

Coordination

The coordination of activities across countries ensures the identification, transfer, and use of best practices that support efficiency and innovation. At the beginning of the firm's internationalization, home operations tend to be the main source of advantage, with managers designing strategies to transfer best practices to host country subsidiaries (Kostova, 1999). However, as the multinational expands into a variety of countries, some subsidiaries undertake initiatives to build their capabilities and become centers of excellence (Birkinshaw, Hood, and Jonsson, 1998; Rugman and Verbeke, 2001). This requires the coordination of operations across countries to facilitate local innovation and the transfer of best practices across subsidiaries (Bartlett and Ghoshal, 1989). Additionally, some multinationals disperse activities across countries to benefit from local endowments (Kogut, 1985), further requiring the coordination of intracompany trade and knowledge to achieve global efficiency (Gereffi, Humphrey, and Sturgeon, 2005).

Control

Control within the multinational ensures that subsidiary managers and operations behave as expected to achieve efficiency. While common to all large firms, this issue is a more pronounced challenge in multinationals because differences across countries create knowledge gaps between headquarters and subsidiaries, altering the role that subsidiaries play within the multinationals as users and providers of knowledge and innovation (Gupta and Govindarajan, 1991). Local managers are tasked with ensuring the success of their operations, while headquarters managers aim to ensure the overall success of the multinational. The knowledge gap and divergence in objectives (Roth and O'Donnell, 1996) lead to conflict in the decisions within the multinational and tension between the desire for centralization from headquarters managers and for decentralization from subsidiary managers (Kostova, Marano, and Tallman, 2016).

Solving control challenges depends on the governance modes selected in each country and the overall governance of the multinational. Unlike domestic firms, multinationals tend to use a wide variety of entry modes across countries, resulting in a diversity of governance arrangements that adds complexity to control decisions (Tallman and Shenkar, 1994). Headquarters managers may be able to impose controls in wholly owned subsidiaries, but they will be less able to control alliances or non-equity contractual operations in host countries, resulting in instability (Inkpen and Beamish, 1997).

Advantage: building scale, learning, and arbitrage across activities and operations for success

The third set of decisions that managers make addresses building the sources of the multinational's advantage across activities and operations to ensure success. Managers need to decide how to leverage the multinational's presence in multiple locations to create a multinational advantage that is superior to the sum of advantages of individual locations to compensate for the additional complexity of managing across borders. We group the creation of advantages into three types based on the underlying strategy: scale, learning, and arbitrage.

Advantage from scale

Multinationals build advantages from the economies of scale in the global use of resources. Economies of scale are a common initial source of advantage for the internationalizing firm. The company innovates products or processes and obtains additional returns on previous knowledge investments by selling more abroad. Moreover, once the multinational expands into multiple countries, it generates additional economies of scale from the local operations and their cross-border coordination, helping the firm reinforce its advantage. The multinational can operate production facilities on a much larger scale than domestic competitors because it serves multiple markets. It can specialize its production facilities across locations so that they manufacture at a global scale. It can also achieve economies of scale in purchasing, extracting better terms from suppliers of raw materials, parts, and intermediate products that supply it on a global scale. This logic underpins the global strategy of multinationals (Levitt, 1983; Yip, 1995), which, thanks to similarities across countries, can sell globally.

Advantage from learning

Another way for multinationals to build advantage is by promoting global learning. To create such an advantage, managers take a proactive approach to knowledge creation and diffusion, using the multinational's exposure to the variety of consumers, competitors, and innovation systems across countries to promote a culture of learning and innovation (Doz, Santos, and Williamson, 2001). The diversity of knowledge across countries enables the multinational to achieve novel combinations of newly acquired and long-held knowledge. The multinational achieves superior innovativeness because it provides the supportive context and incentives that facilitate the transfer, integration, and development of knowledge across borders in a manner that is not possible via contractual relationships (Kogut and Zander, 1993; Lyles and Salk, 1996). The multinational can further this advantage by supporting subsidiaries to become centers for excellence that generate innovations that other subsidiaries use later (Birkinshaw and Hood, 1998). This is, for example, the case with reverse innovations, which are new products and services developed to serve the needs of poor customers in emerging economies and that are later used in advanced nations as well (Govindarajan and Ramamurti, 2011).

Advantage from arbitrage

A third way of building advantage is by actively benefiting from the diversity of location endowments across nations. The multinational's presence in multiple countries provides it with access to a diverse set of factors of production that are in better conditions than those available in the home country, enabling the multinational to profit from these differences. Country differences can take a large variety of dimensions, from economic to political to cultural to geographic (Berry, Guillen, and Zhou, 2010; Ghemawat, 2001). The multinational reorganizes operations to benefit from these differences. For example, it obtains low-cost finance from operations in countries with advanced capital markets, reduces its tax burden from subsidiaries in offshore financial centers, lowers production costs by establishing labor-intensive activities in countries with skilled and low-cost labor, or reduces input costs by obtaining raw materials in locations with abundant and inexpensive natural resources. This ability to arbitrage country differences (Kogut, 1985) is built by creating an organization that can identify, access, and transfer favorable endowments better than through market intermediaries.

Where to Next in Global Strategy Studies?

The global marketplace has become highly dynamic. Technological advances have created new industries that have little resemblance to the manufacturing industries that existed when much of the theory of the multinational was built. Even traditional industries are being transformed through digitization and platforms and a changing globalization environment to the point that the old assumptions are no longer tenable. Novel conditions demand new approaches to old problems and innovative studies of emergent situations. As we noted before, the essence of international strategy is strategy in context. Incorporating the effects of the changing context is vital to understanding evolving multinational strategies and offering novel directions for research.

We outline three areas where the study of global strategy seems to be heading as a result of changes in the context of international firms: (1) countries, and changes in cross-border interactions arising from globalization, the rise of emerging markets, and government activism; (2) industries, and the reorganization of firm boundaries from digitalization, big data, and global value chains; and (3) companies, and the reconsideration of the nature of work from global expertise, remote collaboration, and the gig economy.

Changes in the context of countries: globalization, emerging markets, and government activism

Changes in the context of the country alter global strategies by modifying the relative advantages of locations. Notable changes in the context of the countries are (1) the globalization process that facilitates international trade and investment and the recent rise in skepticism of globalization, (2) the growth of emerging markets and their firms, and (3) increasing government activism and influence on firms' internationalization.

Globalization and antiglobalization

Most models of global strategy are built on the assumption of a supportive global context in which the liberalization of economies and technological advances in communication and transportation facilitate the international expansion of firms (Cuervo-Cazurra, Gaur, and Singh, 2019). However, antiglobalization feelings have started to undermine cross-border trade and investment flows (Witt, 2019). Although multinationals have redesigned their strategies to adapt to and get around some of these new constraints to cross-border flows (Cuervo-Cazurra, Doz, and Gaur, 2020), antiglobalization has created new sources of uncertainty that force multinationals to rethink their global operations, and researchers to reconsider their theoretical predictions.

These trends provide novel conditions under which to observe evolving global strategies. How might the balance of global integration and local responsiveness change for market-focused strategies? Will the ability of multinationals to transfer inputs, technologies, and even brands across borders be compromised? On the upstream end, how have challenges to offshoring of production activities led to greater diversification in value-adding locations through relocation to newly emerging nations; an increase in nearshoring, especially within redefined free trade areas; and reshoring? How might multinationals redesign the relationships among operating units and with suppliers in response to sudden increases in cross-border tariffs and regulatory constraints, or plan investments in the face of political opposition, or more fundamentally, continue to serve customers that are increasingly skeptical of foreign products and multinationals?

Emerging markets and their multinationals

The 1980s and 1990s witnessed the rapid transformation and growth of many emerging markets, forcing their companies to upgrade their capabilities to face new competitive conditions (Luo and Tung, 2007; Williamson *et al.*, 2013). Those companies that survived this transformation benefited from growing home markets and supportive global conditions that enabled some to become leading global players and a new source of competition for established multinationals from advanced economies (Guillén and Garcia-Canal, 2012; Ramamurti and Singh, 2009). The unanticipated success of emerging-market multinationals has led to a fundamental rethinking of existing theories and models of the multinational and its sources of competitive advantage (Cuervo-Cazurra, 2012; Cuervo-Cazurra and Ramamurti, 2014). Williamson and Santos (2021) review this topic in more detail.

New research lines have opened to address topics such as, How do advanced-economy multinationals counter the advantages of emerging-market multinationals? How can managers in emerging markets build a globally competitive company from an unsupportive home country? How should these emerging-market firms rethink coordination and control when subsidiaries rather than headquarters are at the technological frontier?

Government activism

Another change in country context is the increase of government activism in their economies and sometimes the direct support of firms and their internationalization. The pro-market reforms that accompanied the Washington Consensus (Williamson, 2009) led governments to take a hands-off approach, privatizing firms, deregulating industries, and dropping industrial policy and plans that propped up preferred national companies in favor of providing a stable macroeconomic environment and light-touch regulation (Cuervo-Cazurra *et al.*, 2019). However, the Great Recession of 2008 led advanced-country governments to invest in firms to facilitate their survival, and the 2020 pandemic has resulted in massive government support for firms. At the same time, the relative success of the Chinese government in navigating these crises has lent credence to a new model of government guidance of the economy, that is, the Beijing Consensus (Ramo, 2004), in which governments actively support firms, including their internationalization (Aggarwal and Agmon, 1990; Luo, Xue, and Han, 2010). This government activism has also resulted in the comeback of state-owned multinationals in global markets (Cuervo-Cazurra *et al.*, 2014; Musacchio and Lazzarini, 2014), leading to new theories of the advantages and disadvantages of state ownership (Cuervo-Cazurra and Li, 2021).

Government activism should force a rethinking of models of the multinational that have tended to assume a passive, or sometimes negative, impact of governments on advantage. Instead, governments increasingly intervene in the global business context. This reconsideration of governments' role in global strategy provides new conditions for scholarly research, such as, How can multinationals design strategies to compete against government-supported firms and state-owned multinationals? How can managers design political strategies to counter government activism or build a government-supported advantage? How can firms include government activism as a new source of advantage and driver of internationalization?

Changes in the context of industries: digitalization, big data, and global value chains

Variations in the context of global industries are another source of future development of global strategy studies. Changes in the industry context are usually driven by technological advances that undermine the competitiveness of established competitors and enable the entry of new players with uncommon business models. The most significant ones, which are likely to modify the predictions of existing models, are digitalization, big data, and global value chains.

Digitalization

Advances in information and communication technologies have enabled the expansion of multinationals and the coordination of distant operations. At the same time, many of the large investments made by multinationals are being undermined by the rapid advancement of digital technologies via the internet and smartphones, which have given rise to new business models (Brynjolfsson and McAfee, 2014). Digital technologies lead to the emergence of born-global firms (Knight and Cavusgil, 2004; Oviatt and McDougall, 1994). They also give rise to new competitors that revolutionize industries with asset-light business models, raising questions about the traditional explanations of the multinational firm and foreign direct investment (Tallman, Luo, and Buckley, 2018). Their market position as platform businesses—connecting producers and consumers through the auspices of the digital platform (Cusumano, Gawer, and Yoffie, 2019)—alters the conceptualization of the multinational as a company that produces goods and distributes them to dispersed consumers.

The digitalization revolution also has transformed the role of information in established firms (Rogers, 2016). The costs of seeking information, vetting partners, accessing foreign markets, coordinating and defending alliance networks, and monitoring operations have dropped dramatically. All this has radically modified the costs and risks of international market transactions, and of global hierarchies and networks. The tools and metrics used to analyze multinationals and their global strategies and structures are fundamentally changed.

All this requires scholars to reconsider, challenge, and test existing concepts and propose innovative approaches to the global marketplace. We might ask, for instance, How should internationalization and the selection of countries and entry modes be reconceptualized in the digital environment? How should multinationals reconsider operations and investments to counter digital competitors, or how might they implement a digital transformation across dispersed operations?

Big data

Traditional models of the multinational were built on manufacturing multinationals that produced and distributed products across markets. Big data is changing the relationship between firms and their products and customers as data become the main source of value creation in economic relationships (Marr, 2015). Technological advances have led many firms to redesign their business models toward services, gathering data from customers' usage and redesigning payment based on the continued collaboration with customers rather than from a single market transaction. The many services that support the production and sale of final goods are being de-integrated and priced separately, often by specialist service providers. Big data has also led to new business models in which companies provide services for free to consumers in exchange for access to very detailed data on their behavior that is sold to other companies. All this has increased concerns about national security by governments and privacy by individuals, leading to calls for restricting cross-border data transfer and requiring local data storage, potentially undermining the open and global internet system.

Big data thus opens new research lines. We might ask, How do firms design data collection, analysis, and use for competing across borders, especially if these actions are being challenged in some countries? How do we rethink the models of the multinational when data rather than physical assets are the source of advantage? How do vast amounts of detailed data enable the adaptation of products and services not just to the country but to the individual customer within that country?

Global value chains

Technological advances in transportation, communication, and production have altered global value chains. The traditional configuration of global value chains—in which firms from advanced countries act as lead firms and concentrate on technology and marketing and subcontract assembly to companies in emerging economies—has started to be undermined from the upgrading of emerging-market suppliers (Pananond et al., 2020). Emerging-market firms aim to move into high-value-added activities to avoid being stuck in the low-value-added segments of the global supply chain (Mudambi, 2008). The ease of the diffusion of advanced manufacturing technologies through licensing, access to sophisticated technology through alliances and acquisitions (Mudambi and Tallman, 2010) and sometimes imitation (Luo, Sun, and Wang, 2011), and a better understanding of customers through integration enable supplier firms to expand into new value chain segments and to become lead firms. Global value chains are also increasingly based on outsourcing large sets of activities, even those that were considered essential in the recent past, to alliance partners or contractors (Kano, Tsang, and Yeung, 2020).

This challenges our theoretical models and past empirical findings because sophisticated technology is no longer the sole realm of lead multinationals from advanced countries and instead is increasingly being created in emerging-market suppliers. How do theories of global advantage need to evolve? What are the new configurations of value-adding networks and the new governance styles and structures that emerge from evolving industries? How can we better analyze the design transformation strategies that connect suppliers to lead firms in global value chains? How should global value chains be rethought with technological advances in manufacturing and coordination? How should lead multinationals reconsider the activities they control in the face of increasingly sophisticated suppliers?

Changes in the context of organizations: global expertise, remote collaboration, and the gig economy

Finally, changes in the context of the organization alter the management of global operations and future research. These are part of the microfoundations of strategy (Contractor *et al.*, 2019; Foss and Linder, 2019) that are leading the field to a refocus on individual decision-makers. Changes in the organizational context that alter future global strategies are (1) the redefinition of international expertise in individuals, (2) the possibility of remote collaboration across individuals, and (3) the rise of the gig economy.

Global expertise

The concept of global experience has been redefined as increasing numbers of individuals visit, study, and work abroad. This international expertise has facilitated the transfer of knowledge across countries and eased the subsequent internationalization of established firms (Choudhury, 2016), as well as the creation of new firms by entrepreneurs who have direct experience with a variety of countries (Kulchina, 2016). Growing diaspora populations from emerging markets in the industrialized world are the source of new business concepts targeting their countries of origin (Hernandez, 2014). Additionally, the internet and its vast store of easily searchable information have made researching foreign locations, regulations, firms, and individuals simpler, cheaper, and more transparent. The declining costs of transactions have rendered unclear the selection among alternative modes of entry and governance.

As a result, many of the predictions of previous models on the internalization decision and selection of countries and entry modes need rethinking, given that even small firms can start operations with a large supply of global expertise. How does the availability of global expertise alter the traditional internationalization patterns for firms? How does the ease of access to global expertise redefine the characteristics and use of expatriate managers in multinationals? How does the availability of global expertise redefine the consideration of differences across countries in internationalization and entry decisions?

Remote collaboration

The availability of information on suppliers and the existence of platform firms that facilitate remote collaboration among dispersed individuals have given rise to new models of multinationals. In some cases, the new multinationals are merely sets of individuals located in a variety of countries who work and collaborate for particular projects, redefining the concept of the multinational (Maznevski and Chudoba, 2000). In other cases, entrepreneurs define a business model and outsource production to offshore suppliers with whom they have no previous connections, while they focus on establishing a brand and customer connections. The idea of the network firm has stretched far beyond the original conceptualization of a network of subsidiaries belonging to a multinational (Ghoshal and Bartlett, 1990). The network of subsidiaries controlled by headquarters has been externalized to a digitally monitored and incentivized cloud of suppliers, partners, and consultants who collaborate in the creation and distribution of new products and services.

This remote collaboration can lead to new thinking on how the multinational is conceptualized in the absence of joint assets, how managers design incentives and controls for coordinating relationships across borders, or how the boundaries of the multinational change from project to project, among a variety of possible research questions.

The gig economy

The gig economy has emerged, in which individuals are no longer employees and instead work on short-term projects for a variety of clients (Sundararajan, 2017). The gig economy has moved from locally to globally provided services, with platforms connecting skilled individuals to companies in need of help, service providers to those in need of their skills, or one business to another. These arrangements have redefined the global workforce and the activities within the multinational. Activities have been split into simple tasks that can be offshored and/or outsourced to individual providers dispersed around the globe. Employment relationships within the multinational, global careers, and expatriate management need to be reconsidered in the face of these changes in the nature of work in organizations. At the same time, these changes at the micro level of employment have driven increasing numbers of sociopolitical entities—countries, states, even cities—to advocate new regulations for economic activity that force change into a still unformed sector (Parente, Geleilate, and Rong, 2018).

National and regional boundaries are being reinforced with new rules to influence the digitally enabled tide of new businesses, business models and strategies, industries, and economics, creating tremendous opportunities for original and innovative global strategy research. We can ask, How do managers design work and coordinate activities across a network of globally dispersed independent contractors? How are the boundaries of the multinational defined when relying on gig work for many of its activities? How do individuals consider their careers in multinationals with flexible organizational boundaries? How do service providers combine with platform providers to build businesses in many varied markets?

Conclusions

We began this chapter by providing a critical overview of the literature on global strategy, as illustrated in Figure 1. We addressed the evolution of this literature by dividing its history into three periods that reflect its dual roots in international business and strategic management to become the current "strategy in context" approach. We then organized the literature around three key decisions that managers take when designing their firms' global strategy: how to expand, manage, and build advantage across borders. We concluded with an overview of how recent changes in the context of countries, industries, and organizations alter the main decisions and will lead to new explanations and suggested possible themes for future research.

Global strategy is highly contingent on the global context of operation and competition, and as such, changes to this context create opportunities for rethinking past models and adapting or introducing new explanations that provide a better account of the reality of firms and help managers guide their companies to be successful. Global strategy is well positioned not just to help managers improve their firms' value creation abilities but also to contribute to solving grand global challenges (Buckley, Doh, and Benischke, 2017; George *et al.*, 2016). These grand challenges will require a reconceptualization of firms' objectives and the recognition of their impact on society worldwide. The contribution of global strategy research to grand global challenges—in the environment, such as solving the climate crisis and ensuring a sustainable planet for future generations; in society, such as equitable and distributed human development; and in governance, such as increasing democracy and power redistribution—would be the ultimate measure of success of the field. We hope that this chapter offers at least the beginnings of an organized approach to innovative research in global strategy that will provide answers to some of these grand challenges.

References

Aggarwal R, Agmon T. 1990. The international success of developing country firms: role of government-directed comparative advantage. *Management International Review* 30(2): 163–180.

Agmon T, Lessard DR. 1977. Investor recognition of corporate international diversification. *Journal of Finance* 32(4): 1049–1055.

Anderson E, Gatignon H. 1986. Modes of foreign entry: a transaction cost analysis and propositions. *Journal of International Business Studies* 17(3): 1–26.

Bain JS. 1956. *Barriers to New Competition: The Character and Consequences in Manufacturing Industries*. Harvard University Press: Cambridge, MA.

Banalieva ER, Dhanaraj C, 2019. Internalization theory for the digital economy. *Journal of International Business Studies* 50(8): 1372–1387.

Barney J. 1991. Firm resources and sustained competitive advantage. *Journal of Management* 17(1): 99–120.

Bartlett CA, Ghoshal S. 1989. *Managing Across Borders*. Harvard Business School Press: Boston, MA.

Benito GR. 2005. Divestment and international business strategy. *Journal of Economic Geography* 5(2): 235–251.

Berry H, Guillen M, Zhou N. 2010. An institutional approach to cross-national distance. *Journal of International Business Studies* 41(9): 1460–1480.

Birkinshaw J, Hood N. 1998. Multinational subsidiary evolution: capability and charter change in foreign-owned subsidiary companies. *Academy of Management Review* 23(4): 773–795.

Birkinshaw J, Hood N, Jonsson S. 1998. Building firm-specific advantages in multinational corporations: the role of subsidiary initiative. *Strategic Management Journal* 19(3): 221–242.

Brynjolfsson E, McAfee A. 2014. *The Second Machine Age: Work, Progress, and Prosperity in a Time of Brilliant Technologies*. W. W. Norton & Company: New York, NY.

Buckley PJ, Casson MC. 1976. *The Future of the Multinational Enterprise*. Macmillan: London, U.K.

Buckley PJ, Doh JP, Benischke MH. 2017. Towards a renaissance in international business research? Big questions, grand challenges, and the future of IB scholarship. *Journal of International Business Studies* 48(9): 1045–1064.

Cavusgil ST. 1980. On the internationalization process of the firm. *European Research* 6: 273–281.

Chakrabarti A, Mitchell S. 2013. The persistent effect of geographic distance in acquisition target selection. *Organization Science* 24(6): 1805–1826.

Chandler AD. 1962. *Strategy and Structure: Chapters in the History of American Industrial Enterprises*. MIT Press: Cambridge, MA.

Chang SJ, Rosenzweig PM. 2001. The choice of entry mode in sequential foreign direct investment. *Strategic Management Journal* 22(8): 747–776.

Choudhury P. 2016. Return migration and geography of innovation in MNEs: a natural experiment of knowledge production by local workers reporting to return migrants. *Journal of Economic Geography* 16(3): 585–610.

Contractor F, Foss NJ, Kundu S, Lahiri S. 2019. Viewing global strategy through a microfoundations lens. *Global Strategy Journal* 9(1): 3–18.

Contractor FJ, Kundu SK, Hsu CC. 2003. A three-stage theory of international expansion: the link between multinationality and performance in the service sector. *Journal of International Business Studies* 34(1): 5–18.

Cuervo-Cazurra A. 2012. Extending theory by analyzing developing country multinational companies: solving the Goldilocks debate. *Global Strategy Journal* 2(3): 153–167.

Cuervo-Cazurra A, Doz Y, Gaur A. 2020. Skepticism of globalization and global strategy: increasing regulations and countervailing strategies. *Global Strategy Journal* 10(1): 3–31.

Cuervo-Cazurra A, Gaur A, Singh D. 2019. Pro-market institutions and global strategy: the pendulum of pro-market reforms and reversals. *Journal of International Business Studies* 50(4): 598–632.

Cuervo-Cazurra A, Genc M. 2008. Transforming disadvantages into advantages: developing-country MNEs in the least developed countries. *Journal of International Business Studies* 39(6): 957–979.

Cuervo-Cazurra A, Inkpen A, Musacchio A, Ramaswamy K. 2014. Governments as owners: state-owned multinational companies. *Journal of International Business Studies* 45(8): 919–942.

Cuervo-Cazurra A, Li C. 2021. State ownership and internationalization: the advantage and disadvantage of stateness. *Journal of World Business* 56(1): 101112.

Cuervo-Cazurra A, Maloney MM, Manrakhan S. 2007. Causes of the difficulties in internationalization. *Journal of International Business Studies* 38(5): 709–725.

Cuervo-Cazurra A, Ramamurti R (eds). 2014. *Understanding Multinationals from Emerging Markets*. Cambridge University Press: New York, NY.

Cusumano MA, Gawer A, Yoffie DB. 2019. *The Business of Platforms: Strategy in the Age of Digital Competition, Innovation, and Power*. Harper Business: New York, NY.

Doz Y, Santos J, Williamson P. 2001. *From Global to Metanational: How Companies Win in the Knowledge Economy*. Harvard Business School Press: Boston, MA.

Duhaime IM, Grant JH. 1984. Factors influencing divestment decision-making: evidence from a field study. *Strategic Management Journal* 5(4): 301–318.

Dunning JH. 1977. Trade, location of economic activity, and the MNE: a search for an eclectic approach. In *The International Allocation of Economic Activity*, Ohlin B, Hesselborn PO, Wiskman PJ (eds). Palgrave Macmillan: London, U.K.; 395–418.

Dunning JH. 1988. The eclectic paradigm of international production: a restatement and some possible extensions. *Journal of International Business Studies* 19(1): 1–31.

Dunning JH, Lundan SM. 2008. *Multinational Enterprises and the Global Economy*. Edward Elgar Publishing: Northampton, MA.

Eriksson K, Johanson J, Majkgård A, Sharma DD. 1997. Experiential knowledge and cost in the internationalization process. *Journal of International Business Studies* 28(2): 337–360.

Fladmoe-Lindquist K, Tallman SB. 1994. Resource-based strategy and competitive advantage among multinationals. *Advances in Strategic Management* 10: 45–72.

Foss NJ, Linder S. 2019. *Microfoundations in Management Research*. Cambridge University Press: Cambridge, U.K.

George G, Howard-Grenville J, Joshi A, Tihanyi L. 2016. Understanding and tackling societal grand challenges through management research. *Academy of Management Journal* 59(6): 1880–1895.

Gereffi G, Humphrey J, Sturgeon T. 2005. The governance of global value chains. *Review of International Political Economy* 12(1): 78–104.

Geringer JM, Beamish PW, DaCosta RC. 1989. Diversification strategy and internationalization: implications for MNE performance. *Strategic Management Journal* 10(2): 109–119.

Ghemawat P. 2001. Distance still matters: the hard reality of global expansion. *Harvard Business Review* 79(8): 137–147.

Ghemawat P. 2007. *Redefining Global Strategy: Crossing Borders in a World Where Differences Still Matter*. Harvard Business School Press: Boston, MA.

Ghoshal S. 1987. Global strategy: an organizing framework. *Strategic Management Journal* 8(5): 425–440.

Ghoshal S, Bartlett CA. 1990. The multinational corporation as an interorganizational network. *Academy of Management Review* 15(4): 603–626.

Govindarajan V, Ramamurti R. 2011. Reverse innovation, emerging markets, and global strategy. *Global Strategy Journal* 1(3–4): 191–205.

Guillén MF, García-Canal E. 2012. *Emerging Markets Rule: Growth Strategies of the New Global Giants*. McGraw Hill: New York, NY.

Gupta AK, Govindarajan V. 1991. Knowledge flows and the structure of control within multinational corporations. *Academy of Management Review* 16(4): 768–792.

Henisz WJ. 2000. The institutional environment for multinational investment. *Journal of Law, Economics, and Organization* 16(2): 334–364.

Hennart JF. 1982. *A Theory of Multinational Enterprise*. University of Michigan Press: Ann Arbor, MI.

Hennart JF. 2009. Down with MNE-centric theories! Market entry and expansion as the bundling of MNE and local assets. *Journal of International Business Studies* 40: 1432–1454.

Hennart JF. 2011. A theoretical assessment of the empirical literature on the impact of multinationality on performance. *Global Strategy Journal* 1(1–2): 135–151.

Hennart JF. 2012. Emerging market multinationals and the theory of the multinational enterprise. *Global Strategy Journal* 2(3): 168–187.

Hennart JF, Park YR. 1993. Greenfield vs. acquisition: the strategy of Japanese investors in the United States. *Management Science* 39: 1054–1070.

Hernandez E. 2014. Finding a home away from home: effects of immigrants on firms' foreign location choice and performance. *Administrative Science Quarterly* 59(1): 73–108.

Hitt MA, Hoskisson RE, Kim H. 1997. International diversification: effects on innovation and firm performance in product-diversified firms. *Academy of Management Journal* 40(4): 767–798.

Hymer SH. 1976. *A Study of Direct Foreign Investment*. MIT Press: Cambridge, MA.

Inkpen AC, Beamish PW. 1997. Knowledge, bargaining power, and the instability of international joint ventures. *Academy of Management Review* 22(1): 177–202.

Johanson J, Vahlne JE. 1977. The internationalization process of the firm—a model of knowledge development and increasing foreign market commitments. *Journal of International Business Studies* 8(1): 23–32.

Kano L, Tsang EW, Yeung HWC. 2020. Global value chains: a review of the multi-disciplinary literature. *Journal of International Business Studies* 51(4): 577–622.

Khanna T, Palepu KG. 2010. *Winning in Emerging Markets: A Road Map for Strategy and Execution*. Harvard Business School Press: Boston, MA.

Kirca AH, Hult GT, Roth K, Cavusgil ST, Perryy MZ, Akdeniz MB, Deligonul SZ, Mena JA, Pollitte WA, Hoppner JJ, Miller JC, White RC. 2011. Firm-specific assets, multinationality, and financial performance: a meta-analytical review and theoretical integration. *Academy of Management Journal* 54: 47–72.

Knickerbocker FT. 1973. Oligopolistic reaction and multinational enterprise. *International Executive* 15(2): 7–9.

Knight GA, Cavusgil ST. 2004. Innovation, organizational capabilities, and the born-global firm. *Journal of International Business Studies* 35(2): 124–141.

Kobrin SJ. 1979. Political risk: a review and reconsideration. *Journal of International Business Studies* 10(1): 67–80.

Kogut B. 1985. Designing global strategies: comparative and competitive value-added chains. *Sloan Management Review* 26(4): 15.

Kogut B, Singh H. 1988. The effect of national culture on the choice of entry mode. *Journal of International Business Studies* 19(3): 411–432.

Kogut B, Zander U. 1993. Knowledge of the firm and the evolutionary theory of the multinational corporation. *Journal of International Business Studies* 24(4): 625–645.

Kostova T. 1999. Transnational transfer of strategic organizational practices: a contextual perspective. *Academy of Management Review* 24(2): 308–324.

Kostova T, Marano V, Tallman S. 2016. Headquarters-subsidiary relationships: 50 years of evolving research. *Journal of World Business* 51(1): 176–184.

Kulchina E. 2016. A path to value creation for foreign entrepreneurs. *Strategic Management Journal* 37(7): 1240–1262.

Levitt T. 1983. The globalization of markets. *Harvard Business Review* 61(3): 92–102.

Lu JW, Beamish PW. 2004. International diversification and firm performance: the S-curve hypothesis. *Academy of Management Journal* 47(4): 598–609.

Luo Y, Sun J, Wang SL. 2011. Emerging economy copycats: capability, environment, and strategy. *Academy of Management Perspectives* 25(2): 37–56.

Luo Y, Tung RL. 2007. International expansion of emerging market enterprises: a springboard perspective. *Journal of International Business Studies* 38(4): 481–498.

Luo Y, Xue Q, Han B. 2010. How emerging market governments promote outward FDI: experience from China. *Journal of World Business* 45(1): 68–79.

Lyles MA, Salk JE. 1996. Knowledge acquisition from foreign parents in international joint ventures: an empirical examination in the Hungarian context. *Journal of International Business Studies* 27(5): 877–903.

Malnight TW. 1996. The transition from decentralized to network-based MNC structures: an evolutionary perspective. *Journal of International Business Studies* 27(1): 43–65.

Marr B. 2015. *Big Data: Using SMART Big Data, Analytics and Metrics to Make Better Decisions and Improve Performance.* John Wiley and Sons: Chichester, West Sussex, U.K.

Martinez JI, Jarillo JC. 1989. The evolution of research on coordination mechanisms in multinational corporations. *Journal of International Business Studies* 20(3): 489–514.

Maznevski ML, Chudoba KM. 2000. Bridging space over time: global virtual team dynamics and effectiveness. *Organization Science* 11(5): 473–492.

Meyer KE. 2001. Institutions, transaction costs, and entry mode choice in Eastern Europe. *Journal of International Business Studies* 32(2): 357–367.

Mudambi R. 2008. Location, control, and innovation in knowledge-intensive industries. *Journal of Economic Geography* 8(5): 699–725.

Mudambi S, Tallman S. 2010. Make, buy, or ally? Theoretical perspectives on knowledge process outsourcing through alliances. *Journal of Management Studies* 47: 1434–1456.

Musacchio A, Lazzarini SG. 2014. *Reinventing State Capitalism.* Harvard University Press: Cambridge, MA.

Oviatt BM, McDougall PP. 1994. Toward a theory of international new ventures. *Journal of International Business Studies* 25(1): 45–64.

Pananond P, Gereffi G, Pedersen T. 2020. An integrative typology of global strategy and global value chains: the management and organization of cross-border activities. *Global Strategy Journal* 10(3): 421–443.

Parente RC, Geleilate JMG, Rong K. 2018. The sharing economy globalization phenomenon: a research agenda. *Journal of International Management* 24(1): 52–64.

Peng MW. 2002. Towards an institution-based view of business strategy. *Asia Pacific Journal of Management* 19(2–3): 251–267.

Penrose ET. 1959. *The Theory of the Growth of the Firm.* Oxford University Press: Oxford, U.K.

Porter ME. 1985. *Competitive Advantage: Creating and Sustaining Superior Performance.* Free Press: New York, NY.

Porter ME. 1986. Competition in global industries: a conceptual framework. In *Competition in Global Industries,* Porter ME (ed). Harvard Business School Press: Boston, MA; 15–60.

Prahalad CK, Doz YL. 1987. *The Multinational Mission: Balancing Global Integration with Local Responsiveness.* Free Press: New York, NY .

Ramamurti R, Singh JV (eds). 2009. *Emerging Multinationals in Emerging Markets.* Cambridge University Press: Cambridge, U.K.

Ramo JC. 2004. *The Beijing Consensus.* Foreign Policy Centre: London, U.K.

Rogers DL. 2016. *The Digital Transformation Playbook: Rethink Your Business for the Digital Age.* Columbia University Press: New York, NY.

Rosenzweig PM, Singh JV. 1991. Organizational environments and the multinational enterprise. *Academy of Management Review* 16(2): 340–361.

Roth K, O'Donnell S. 1996. Foreign subsidiary compensation strategy: an agency theory perspective. *Academy of Management Journal* 39(3): 678–703.

Rugman AM, Verbeke A. 2001. Subsidiary-specific advantages in multinational enterprises. *Strategic Management Journal* 22(3): 237–250.

Shaver M. 1998. Accounting for endogeneity when assessing strategy performance: does entry mode choice affect FDI survival? *Management Science* 44(4): 571–585.

Shenkar O. 2001. Cultural distance revisited: towards a more rigorous conceptualization and measurement of cultural differences. *Journal of International Business Studies* 32(3): 519–535.

Stopford JM, Wells LT. 1972. *Strategy and Structure of the Multinational Enterprise*. Basic Books: New York, NY.

Sundararajan A. 2017. *The Sharing Economy: The End of Employment and the Rise of Crowd-Based Capitalism*. MIT Press: Cambridge, MA.

Tallman SB. 1991. Strategic management models and resource-based strategies among MNEs in a host market. *Strategic Management Journal* 12(S1): 69–82.

Tallman SB. 1992. A strategic management perspective on host country structure of multinational enterprises. *Journal of Management* 18(3): 455–471.

Tallman SB, Li J. 1996. Effects of international diversity and product diversity on the performance of multinational firms. *Academy of Management Journal* 39(1): 179–196.

Tallman SB, Luo Y, Buckley PJ. 2018. Business models in global competition. *Global Strategy Journal* 8(4): 517–535.

Tallman SB, Pedersen T. 2015. What is international strategy and what is not? *Global Strategy Journal* 5: 273–277.

Tallman SB, Shenkar O. 1994. A managerial decision model of international cooperative venture formation. *Journal of International Business Studies* 25(1): 91–113.

Tallman SB, Yip GS. 2008. Strategy and the multinational enterprise. In *The Oxford Handbook of International Business*, Rugman A (ed.) Oxford University Press: Oxford, U.K.; 307–340.

Teece DJ. 1986. Transactions cost economics and the multinational enterprise: an assessment. *Journal of Economic Behavior and Organization* 7(1): 21–45.

Tinbergen J. 1962. *The World Economy: Suggestions for an International Economic Policy*. Twentieth Century Fund: New York, NY.

Vernon R. 1966. International investment and international trade in the product cycle. *Quarterly Journal of Economics* 80(2): 190–207.

Westney E. 2021. MNCS and cross-border strategic management. In *Strategic Management: State of the Field and Its Future*, Duhaime IM, Hitt MA, Lyles MA (eds). Oxford University Press: New York, NY; 301–318.

Wiersema MF, Bowen HP. 2011. The relationship between international diversification and firm performance: why it remains a puzzle. *Global Strategy Journal* 1(1–2): 152–170.

Williamson J. 2009. A short history of the Washington Consensus. *Law and Business Review of the Americas* 15(1): 7–23 .

Williamson OE. 1975. *Markets and Hierarchies*. Free Press: New York, NY.

Williamson P, Santos J. 2021. Emerging economies. In *Strategic Management: State of the Field and Its Future*, Duhaime IM, Hitt MA, Lyles MA (eds). Oxford University Press: New York, NY; 319–334.

Williamson PJ, Ramamurti R, Fleury A, Fleury MTL (eds). 2013. *The Competitive Advantage of Emerging Market Multinationals*. Cambridge University Press: New York, NY.

Witt MA. 2019. De-globalization: theories, predictions, and opportunities for international business research. *Journal of International Business Studies* 50(7): 1053–1077.

Yip GS. 1995. *Total Global Strategy*. Prentice-Hall: Englewood Cliffs, NJ.

Zaheer S. 1995. Overcoming the liability of foreignness. *Academy of Management Journal* 38(2): 341–363.

5.1

MNCS AND CROSS-BORDER STRATEGIC MANAGEMENT

D. Eleanor Westney

Introduction

Multinational corporations (MNCs) in some form have existed for centuries (Wilkins, 2009), but the challenges of strategic management in MNCs only became a major focus of interest for researchers and managers in the 1960s, with the rapid international expansion of American companies. Over the decades since then, the international business environment in which MNCs operate has changed dramatically, and MNCs have both responded to and shaped this evolving strategic environment (for an overview, see Lessard, 2021). From the early 1970s (e.g., Mccrae, 1972) to the present day, the business press has carried recurrent warnings that MNCs are too geographically extended and too complex to be effectively managed, and that technological change is reducing their advantages of scale and geographic scope (e.g., *The Economist* 2017). In spite of these challenges, however, very large MNCs have continued to dominate international business, and do so to this day, in no small part because how they are organized and managed has changed significantly over time. In 2020, with increasing threats of disruption to cross-border trade and the pandemic-induced dislocation of the global economy, we are witnessing yet another period of apparently discontinuous change, challenging both the practice and analysis of MNC strategic management to evolve to meet the changing context.

The defining feature of MNCs is that their operations, in whatever form (factories, development labs, offices), are distributed across countries. The dispersion of activities in locations that are often far apart and that differ in their economic, regulatory, political, social, and cultural features highlights strategic management challenges of differentiation, coordination, and integration that are relevant for all multiunit enterprises but are distinctively salient for MNCs. Most notably, the challenges of managing within and across different societies highlights the political and cultural aspects of strategic management, which are relevant for all firms but are impossible to set aside in MNCs.

One of the central issues in theories of the MNC has been the potential advantages of operating in multiple countries that can compensate for the costs and complexity of managing across distances and differences (see Chapter 5.0). The generic *potential* advantages of multinationality, however, can only be realized by effectively organizing and managing in order to develop competitive advantage from those advantages—the core issue in MNC cross-border management (Teece, 2014).

The strategic challenges of doing so can be summed up in a deceptively simple phrase: *where* to do *what* and *how*. *Where* focuses on the choice of geographic location; *what* concerns which activities or bundle of activities to conduct in each location. These constitute the geographic footprint of the MNC. *How* involves organizing and managing those activities within each location and across locations so as to create and capture value. It is the most complex of these three strategic challenges, involving choices about organization design in the broadest sense, from drawing the boundaries of the firm to incentive structures and performance assessment. It is this last set of challenges, effectively organizing and managing an MNC that has an extensive geographic footprint, on which this chapter focuses. The following sections briefly summarize four of the foundational concepts in MNC cross-border management, and then survey the changes in MNCs and in the trajectory of research in recent years, before turning to the contemporary challenges facing MNCs and some potentially promising areas for future research.

Conceptual Foundations

As in many management-related fields, from finance to organization studies, the 1980s saw the development of innovative concepts in MNC strategic management that have continued to influence research to this day. Four interdependent contributions in particular stand out: the global integration and local responsiveness framework, the identification of the capabilities of innovation and cross-border learning as the central advantage of the established MNC, the concept of the MNC as a network, and the focus on process rather than structure. All were anchored in intensive case studies of (and deep interactions with) a number of established MNCs originating in Western Europe and North America and with a smaller number of rapidly expanding Japanese MNCs (Prahalad and Doz, 1987; Bartlett and Ghoshal, 1989; Hamel and Prahalad, 1990).

Global integration / local responsiveness

The global integration / local responsiveness (GI/LR) framework took a central theme of the first two decades of MNC strategy research—the tension between the global and the local—and separated what had been regarded as a dichotomy into two vectors, global integration (GI) and local responsiveness (LR). Developed in the late 1970s and early 1980s by C. K. Prahalad, Yves Doz, and Christopher Bartlett (Bartlett, 1986; Doz, Bartlett, and Prahalad, 1981; Prahalad, 1976; Prahalad and Doz, 1981), the framework identified two sets of industry-level external pressures on MNC capabilities: those demanding global integration on the one hand and those requiring responsiveness to country-level differences on the other. Both vectors were multi-factor. The resulting two-dimensional map of industry pressures provided a tool for assessing both industry dynamics and the current position of the industry relative to others. The concepts played a double role in MNC strategic management—they provided a way to map the strategic environment, but they also identified *organizational capabilities*: global integration and local responsiveness. The level of capabilities of local responsiveness and cross-border integration could (and probably should) differ not only by product/business unit but also by function and even by activity within a function. For example, in marketing, value might be created by high local responsiveness and low global integration in product promotions, low LR and high GI for product policy, and high levels of both on pricing and advertising (Bartlett and Ghoshal, 1989: 96–98). How to organize and manage in order to develop and leverage these capabilities was the core focus of much of this seminal research.

MNC competitive advantage: learning and innovation

By the end of the 1980s, scholars increasingly agreed that the core potential competitive advantage of large established MNCs is what Bartlett and Ghoshal called a "worldwide learning capability" (Bartlett and Ghoshal, 1989: 16)—that is, leveraging the differences across its multiple environments and across the capabilities of its subunits to learn and to innovate (see also Kogut, 1989; Kogut and Zander, 1993). This potential for multidirectional learning stretches across activities, from identifying trends in one local market that have value-creating potential in others to the capacity for pooling different but complementary location-based skills and knowledge in global product development projects (Ghoshal, 1987).

The MNC as an integrated network

The third enduring contribution of the 1980s is the model of the MNC as an integrated network, in contrast to the hierarchical model of MNC organization prevalent in the 1960s and 1970s. The model emerged in the mid-1980s as Chris Bartlett's model of the "transnational" MNC in the United States (Bartlett, 1986; Bartlett and Ghoshal, 1989), and Gunnar Hedlund's "heterarchy," developed at the Stockholm School of Economics (Hedlund, 1986), but quickly took on the less idiosyncratic term of a *network MNC* (Ghoshal and Bartlett, 1990). The network concept made explicit the growing importance of horizontal flows of resources and information across subsidiaries as well as the increasingly two-way vertical flows between headquarters and subsidiaries. The strategic management of the MNC network involved differentiated subunit roles in the network, based on differences across their locational advantages and their capabilities. This meant differentiated structures, interactions with other subunits, and different levels and kinds of HQ control (Bartlett and Ghoshal, 1989; Nohria and Ghoshal, 1997).

Process focus

The process focus was a deliberate repudiation of the first generation of MNC management research, much of which built on the Chandlerian strategy-structure paradigm (Hedlund and Rolander, 1990). This research had focused on the top-level reporting structure for country units, which were then the basic building blocks of MNC architecture: that is, whether the country units reported to an international division, regional divisions, worldwide business units, or a matrix with geography as one of the two vectors (e.g., Stopford and Wells, 1972; Egelhoff, 1982). The process focus differed from this earlier work in two aspects. The first was portraying processes rather than top-level reporting structures as the key design instrument in the strategic management of MNCs. While continuing the earlier work's emphasis on organization design as a strategic management instrument, this work focused on organizational processes (such as information management, conflict management, and human resource management) and on lower-level coordinating structures and systems (such as cross-border committees, task forces, and integrator roles that crossed internal organizational boundaries). In addition, the focus shifted from *strategy* to *strategizing* as a process in which strategic initiatives were developed (within the context of dynamic and complex environmental pressures) not just by top management but also at multiple levels of the organization, including subsidiaries.

All four of these concepts proved to be remarkably resilient over the next three decades, accommodating dramatic changes in MNCs and the emergence of new challenges in strategic management.

Established MNCs in the Globalization Era: Changing Footprints and the Return of Structure

During the decades following the disintegration of the Soviet bloc at the beginning of the 1990s, the geographic footprint of established MNCs changed significantly, as geopolitical and economic shifts greatly increased the array of potentially attractive locations for MNC activities. In particular, the growing attractiveness of emerging-market countries not only in terms of markets but also resources and capabilities in production and even technology development (see the chapter in this volume by Williamson and Santos) led many established MNCs to reduce or even eliminate activities in some countries in which they had a long-established presence and expand their activities in emerging-market countries (Flores and Aguilera, 2007; Vahlne,

Ivarsson, and Alvstam, 2018). Moreover, technological innovations in transport (Levinson, 2006) and information and communications technologies (ICT) (Zaheer and Manrakhan, 2001) greatly reduced the costs and difficulties of coordinating activities across long distances and enabled major structural changes in MNCs. This reconfiguration of MNC geographic footprints was aided by a rapid expansion of the institutional infrastructure for cross-border mergers and acquisitions.

The geographic scope of established MNCs was also affected by the expansion of their external networks. The early and mid-1990s saw a number of high-profile strategic alliances between competing MNCs, raising challenges of how to manage them so as to make them vehicles for learning and for enhancing core competences (Hamel, 1991; Doz and Hamel, 1998). By the mid-1990s, attention shifted to global outsourcing of support activities and elements of value chains deemed to be noncore (Quinn and Hilmer, 1994), a general trend that MNCs quickly adopted. The growing geographical specialization of external sourcing provided MNCs with a mode of leveraging location advantages that did not involve direct ownership—and expanded the network MNC concept to include external as well as internal networks. However, this fostered the global expansion of supporting industries providing business services to MNCs, such as management consulting (e.g., McKinsey, Accenture, and BCG) and an array of more focused consulting firms (in engineering, human resources [HR], information technology [IT], logistics, and even corporate social responsibility [CSR]), executive search firms, accounting firms, advertising agencies and media companies, logistics firms, ICT companies, and the global institutional infrastructure of financial institutions and investment companies. One unanticipated consequence of strategic outsourcing by MNCs was that domestic and emerging-market firms had access to these providers, enabling them to learn from them and become increasingly formidable competitors to established MNCs.

In the second half of the 1990s and well into the next decades, structure reemerged as a key instrument of MNC strategic management, as many MNCs adopted the "front/back" architecture (Galbraith, 2000; Mees-Buss, Welch, and Westney, 2019). Originating in the early 1990s in IT industries in which customers wanted to buy integrated systems rather than the separate products and components produced by individual business units, the structure had two differentiated organizations. One was a customer-facing front end organized by market (originally customer segment, but usually based on geography in MNCs); the other was a technology-focused back end with subunits specialized by product or even component and centered on production, sourcing, and in many industries, incremental product development (basic research was usually a corporate function). The specialized subunits in both front and back were aided and monitored by centrally directed global support functions—not only the traditional support functions such as finance, IT, and HR but also functional units such as global supply chain, global manufacturing, and global marketing. A feature of this structure was the internal "fine-slicing" of activities into highly specialized subunits that paralleled the increasingly specialized external outsourcing networks. For an MNC, this meant breaking country subsidiaries into a number of specialized subunits that were more closely integrated with related subunits in other locations than with other specialized units in the same country (Birkinshaw, 2001).

The front/back architecture provided a structural solution to the challenges of balancing global integration, local responsiveness, and cross-border learning identified in the 1980s. Bartlett and Ghoshal (1989) had based their rejection of structure on the impossibility of matrixing on three dimensions, and had pointed out that different activities could and should balance these three demands differently. In somewhat oversimplified terms, the front/back structure was an architecture that addressed this challenge: the front end could focus on the appropriate level of local responsiveness in different markets, with significant global integration on pricing and product positioning; the back end could focus on the efficiencies of global integration, with local responsiveness primarily on the external supplier network; and the global support functions could focus on cross-unit learning and the appropriate level of local adaptations within their assigned activity. Each could develop and manage a distinctive external network. This architecture also changed the political dynamics of established MNCs, dismantling long-established, multifunction country subsidiaries—"the powerful geographic fiefdoms with duplicate infrastructure in each country," in the words of Lou Gerstner (2002: 42), describing IBM in the mid-1990s—making it easier for headquarters to drive the reconfiguration of the firm's geographic footprint.

Research Trajectories

Much of the MNC research of the last three decades has focused on mapping and explaining the geographic footprints of MNCs: what do they do where, and *why* (drawing on economic geography and theories of location advantage). Less research attention has been devoted to the "how" question that was central to the influential work of the 1980s: how to organize and manage dispersed subunits so as to achieve a value-creating balance of global integration, local responsiveness, and cross-border learning. MNC management research became increasingly specialized into streams that focused on one particular set of activities, most notably product and technology innovation (e.g., Doz and Wilson, 2012; Monteiro and Birkinshaw, 2017), production and global supply chains (e.g., Buckley and Strange, 2015), HR management (e.g., Stahl, Björkman, and Morris, 2012), and CSR (e.g., Henisz, 2016). Much of the work on organizing and managing MNCs and developing cross-border capabilities thus focused on a particular aspect of MNC organization.

However, one reason that issues of the entire MNC organization drew less research attention may be that the concepts developed in the 1980s proved remarkably resilient in the ensuing decades. The network model easily accommodated the growing importance of external networks at multiple levels of the MNC, and the focus on processes rather than structures was well suited to addressing the challenges of effectively developing and managing those networks. On the other hand, the adaptability of the network model and the process focus had some disadvantages for advancing the research agenda on MNC strategic management: they disguised the significance of the structural changes in many MNCs described in the preceding section and the consequent narrowing range of activities in subunits. The practice among researchers of continuing to use the traditional term "subsidiary" for MNC subunits may also have been a contributing factor disguising changes in and differences across MNCs.

Managing subsidiaries

Subsidiary-level organization and management has consistently been an important theme in MNC research, and one that has broad implications for the strategic management of subunits below the business-division level more generally (for a recent survey of the extensive literature on MNC subsidiary management, see Meyer, Li, and Schotter, 2020). One of the key elements of the MNC network model is that subunits have different roles, which can be formalized, through "mandates" or the designation of certain subsidiaries as "centres of excellence" (Frost, Birkinshaw, and Ensign, 2002), or emergent, as subsidiaries deepen and expand their internal capabilities, develop strategically useful external networks, and build relationships with other subsidiaries and with headquarters.

A very substantial body of work has addressed the questions of why and how subsidiaries actively develop strategic initiatives and contribute to MNC cross-border learning (Birkinshaw, 1997; Tippmann et al., 2018). A central focus has been the entrepreneurial role of subunit managers and the political and social skills they develop in order to leverage internal subunit capabilities and external local networks to identify opportunities, negotiate with headquarters, and build relationships with other subunits in order to gain mandates and deliver effectively on them (e.g., O'Brien et al., 2019). Subsidiary entrepreneurship has remained central to the learning capabilities of MNCs (Teece, 2014), even though the internal and external fine-slicing of MNCs during the late 1990s and the first decade of the 21st century narrowed the scope of such mandates in many MNCs to within-function value adding rather than developing the full value chain (Birkinshaw, Hood, and Young, 2005; Rugman, Verbeke, and Yuan, 2011). Recent work on subsidiary mandates has highlighted both the growing centralization of the processes involved in upgrading subsidiary mandates in the context of current MNC structures and the ongoing importance of strategic subsidiary initiatives, increasingly focused on upgrading capabilities to secure enhanced mandates (Riviere, Bass, and Andersson, 2020; Ryan et al., 2020).

Role of headquarters

Just as much of the empirical research on MNC cross-border management in the past two decades has focused on a specialized aspect of MNC activity and organization, the substantial body of research on the role of MNC headquarters (HQ) has tended to examine that role in one of the MNC networks, most notably innovation, human resource management, and corporate social responsibility. A common finding of this research is that HQs need to employ a wide variety of influence tools, from simple attention to legitimation strategies, to align their subunits with corporate initiatives: internalization does not necessarily confer control (Kostova, Marano, and Tallman, 2016). HQ needs a wider range of influence strategies for the largest and most capable subunits, which can more openly contest corporate initiatives, but even small, narrowly focused subunits can effectively resist those initiatives by relying on ritual compliance or even simply ignoring them (Schotter and Beamish, 2011). This research has broader relevance for the strategy field: how the MNC HQ performs its role as the architect and orchestrator of a complex nested network of subunits and of multiple levels of external relationships can provide an anchor for research on both the governance of global value chains and the strategic management of a firm's ecosystem (Williamson and De Meyer, 2012; De Meyer and Williamson, 2020).

Beyond the transnational: typologies of MNCs

A large and growing body of research on MNC management, especially the transfer of management systems and processes across countries, draws on organization theory. However, the implications for strategic management have been difficult to make, partly because of the absence of a parsimonious way to categorize MNCs and make comparisons across different types. A research community has developed and used widely only two typologies since that proposed in the 1980s by Bartlett and Ghoshal: the Metanational/Projector typology of Doz, Santos, and Williamson (2001) and the region-based characterization developed by Rugman and Verbeke (2004).

Grounded in fieldwork in MNCs whose home country was not an advantaged location in their industry ("born in the wrong place" MNCs), the Metanational ideal type exemplified the capabilities of building both internal and external networks to sense and mobilize geographically dispersed knowledge of different kinds (technology, process, market) and to use that knowledge to generate innovations and leverage them through different combinations of internal and external networks (Doz et al., 2001; Lessard, Teece, and Leih, 2016). Doz et al. (2001) contrasted this with the Projector model of the MNC, which leveraged its home-base advantage in multiple locations (and which could evolve into a multiple home base organization), locating the core location for each business in the most advantaged location and projecting that advantage through an operating network. Their model recognized the growing importance of external networks and incorporated them into the network model of the MNC, and challenged the prevailing emphasis in the international business (IB) field on location advantage as the determining factor in the development of MNC competitive advantage. This model also developed at considerable length the organizational design and management features of the Metanational.

Alan Rugman and Alain Verbeke, in contrast, challenged the concept of global strategy and the global extension of MNC footprints, arguing that most MNCs were regional rather than global in terms of the geographic distribution of their activities, and that most MNCs (and MNC researchers) should therefore focus on regional rather than global strategies. Rugman and Verbeke (2004) defined four categories of MNCs—home-region-oriented, host-region-oriented, biregional, and global—and found that the overwhelming majority were home-region-oriented. Researchers have continued to use this categorization for studies of performance (e.g., Banalieva and Dhanaraj, 2013) and geographic footprint (Jeong and Siegel, 2020; see also Rosa, Gugler, and Verbeke 2020 for a recent overview). Relatively little of the research, however, addressed the relationships between MNC regional strategy and organization and management. Even the considerable literature on regional headquarters focused more on their existence and location and less on how they were organized and the scope of their activities. Ghemawat pointed out that MNC organizational architecture was rarely aligned effectively with regional strategies, and that "a regional headquarters is not enough" (Ghemawat, 2005: 104), but research on regional organization in MNCs is only beginning.

Processes and people

Since the earliest days of MNC strategic management research to the present, responding to the challenges of managing across differences in MNCs is a capability that has been vested in people (e.g., Perlmutter, 1969) and in the processes by which MNCs develop competencies in spanning the many boundaries within an MNC and its external networks (e.g., Schotter *et al.*, 2017; Birkinshaw, Ambos, and Bouquet, 2017). Bartlett and Ghoshal (1989: 175–195) argued that, since matrix structures could only accommodate two dimensions, the key to managing the transnational was to build a matrix in the minds of the managers through international assignments, training programs, and cross-border committees. In 1991, the CEO of ABB, a company widely regarded as an exemplar of the transnational networked MNC, famously declared that he only needed 500 of his 15,000 employees to be "global"—the rest needed to be focused on the local (Taylor, 1991). As cross-border networks grew in number and penetrated more deeply into MNCs, however, more and more employees at middle and even lower levels of the organization interacted across borders (Pedersen, Soda, and Stea, 2019). MNCs expanded their international management development and training programs dramatically. Some attempted to reduce the difficulties of working across borders by adopting English as the official corporate language (e.g., Neeley 2012, 2019), though this can bring its own problems in making English-language facility a key factor in upward mobility in MNCs (Piekkari, Welch, and Welch, 2014; Brannen, Piekkari, and Tietze, 2014).

Future Challenges for MNCs and for Strategic Management Research

The 2007–2008 global financial crisis led to a growing realization of the risks of global integration (Guillén, 2015), and in 2016, the Brexit vote and the U.S. election of Donald Trump dramatically focused business and academic attention on the rising tide of antiglobalization (Butzbach, Fuller, and Schnyder, 2020). Since then, the threats to global integration raised by growing populism, trade tensions, economic slowdown, and, most recently, the COVID-19 pandemic have grown. They pose particular challenges to established MNCs, which have spent the last quarter-century building globally integrated enterprises. The changing global context highlights some gaps in established areas of strategic management research on MNCs and raises new research challenges. The following section identifies potentially promising lines of future research in terms of four interrelated topics:

- The changing balance of global integration and local responsiveness (GI/LR)
- Regional and global strategic management challenges
- Cross-border learning
- Responding to global external challenges: climate change and pandemics

The changing balance of GI/LR

When the GI/LR model was first developed, what became the local responsiveness (LR) axis was defined as responsiveness to host government demands (Doz, 1980; Prahalad and Doz, 1981). By the late 1980s, as governments began their retreat from protectionism and market intervention, pressures for LR were increasingly defined in narrower terms: the distinctiveness and strength of the local market and differences in local cultures and business practices for which adaptation created value (Bartlett and Ghoshal, 1989). Today, governments are again becoming significant sources of demands for local responsiveness.

MNC strategic management has built on Bartlett and Ghoshal's insight that different MNC functions and activities require different levels of integration and responsiveness. The internal fine-slicing of the globally integrated enterprise of the late 1990s and 2000s intensified the trend for local responsiveness to take different forms in different parts of the MNC, varying in kind and not simply degree. For research and development (R&D) and technology development, local responsiveness meant developing networks with local external sources of knowledge (such as universities and local research institutes) and attracting local technical talent. For production subunits, it involved building relationships with the local supply base that makes the location an advantaged one for production activities. For marketing units, it meant tailoring distribution, product positioning, and pricing to local market conditions.

In addition, the growing capacity of ICT enabled MNCs to separate local responsiveness from local presence. MNCs can provide various forms of customer support from outside a country, analyze market data in central locations, identify preferred suppliers from global databases, and use open innovation systems to gain access to local sources of technical knowledge.

Today's MNCs have well-developed capabilities for tailoring marketing strategies to cope with rising cultural populism, but may be less well positioned for coping with political and economic populism and demands on other functions, as the COVID-related challenges in MNCs in the medical supplies sectors have demonstrated (Gereffi, 2020). Santos and Williamson (2015) suggested that, in emerging markets, MNCs need to recognize the difference between immediate local responsiveness in terms of adaptation to local market conditions on the one hand and more value-creating "local embeddedness" on the other—the identity and the understanding of local contexts that come from extensive and integrated local relationships. Today this is increasingly true not just for emerging-market countries but also for many developed countries (Lorenzen, Mudambi, and Schotter, 2020).

Researchers on strategic management in MNCs therefore face some challenging research questions:

- Has the large established MNCs' focus on global integration eroded their capabilities for the kind and variety of local responsiveness they may require for creating value in the context of rising populism and growing restrictions on cross-border flows of goods and data?
- In which activities does a physical local presence create increased value? How does this vary across industries?
- Do MNC networks of widely dispersed and highly specialized subunits need to be reconfigured to respond effectively to "a prolonged period of political-economic instability and uncertainty" (Kobrin, 2017), or are they still a source of competitive advantage?
- Do differences across countries in the manifestations of rising cultural, political, and socioeconomic populism create significant differences in the activities that create value in local responsiveness across MNC locations? If so, does this increase the internal differentiation of strategies by location within the MNC (revisiting the concept of "requisite complexity" in MNC organization proposed by Ghoshal and Nohria [1993])?

Regional and global strategic management challenges

MNC executives and researchers alike are wrestling today with strategic questions of whether competitive advantage increasingly derives from focusing on creating and capturing value regionally, whether there is still important value to be captured by integrating and learning on a multiregional or global basis, and how to develop the capabilities to develop and deliver on their strategies. There is some evidence that cross-border supply chains have become more regional since 2011, and may well become more so in the near future (*The Economist*, 2019).

Among the issues rarely addressed in the existing research on regional MNCs are the implications for strategic management of difference across regions. These differences include the number of countries (three in North America, assuming Central America is not included, compared to 14 in South America and 44 in Europe); the level of economic and regulatory integration across national borders within the region (relatively high in Europe, very low in Africa); and cultural, economic, and institutional variation across countries within a region (much higher in Southeast Asia, for example, than in North America). Given these differences, MNCs are likely developing different strategies in different regions, in terms of geographic footprint and strategies for creating and delivering value through local responsiveness and regional integration. The gaps in the research on regional versus global strategies raises interesting possibilities for future research, including the following questions:

- Are MNCs currently reconfiguring their activities within and across regions in response to growing constraints on cross-border integration, and if so, are industry-level or firm-level factors more important in explaining the speed and nature of these changes?
- Do strategic organization and regional footprint differ across MNCs within a given region, and if so, what factors explain such differences (e.g., industry, home region, or firm-level factors such as experience within the region over time and/or strategic positioning)?
- Does an MNC operating across several regions develop a regional template for strategic management across all regions, with only minor variations, or does it adjust the strategic management approach by region? If so, what factors influence this internal variation?
- What are the implications of regional strategies and organizations for cross-regional learning in multiregional MNCs?

Cross-border learning

The ability to learn across locations has for decades been recognized as one of the MNC's key competitive advantages. The internal fine-slicing of activities into highly specialized subunits and the externalization of supply chains increased the challenges of identifying and sharing value-creating knowledge across the MNC's complex internal networks. One response of MNCs in the 21st century has been the growing role of global functional organizations. Most large established MNCs have multiple headquarters: geographic, business, and increasingly, functional (Ciabuschi, Dellastrand, and Holm, 2012). According to Bartlett and Ghoshal (1989), cross-border learning—identifying and sharing value-creating innovations in products and processes—is the key role of global functions (just as the role of the geographic dimension of the organization is local responsiveness and the business division is efficiency-driven integration). In addition, cross-border learning in MNCs has been facilitated by the fostering of cross-border networks via training programs, cross-border and cross-unit transfers, committees and task forces, and international projects that bring people from different locations together in shared tasks and environments.

In a provocative recent article, Buckley and Hashai (2020) argued that growing restrictions on work visas and increasing nationalistic efforts to restrict the outflow of intellectual property will erode MNCs' innovation advantages over domestic firms. The constraints on cross-border learning faced by MNCs dramatically increased in 2020, as the disruption of international travel by COVID-19 created an unanticipated "natural experiment" in cross-border interaction, with the abrupt cancellation of training programs and the substitution of virtual interactions for the in-person meetings that provided opportunities for informal learning as well as formal information exchange.

How MNCs respond to the increasing challenges of cross-border learning opens new topics for research, including the following:

- What steps do MNCs take to maintain or even increase their capabilities in cross-border learning as constraints on travel, international assignments, and cross-border transfers of intellectual property increase?
- In MNCs that move to an increasingly regional organizational architecture, what measures do they take to build capabilities in cross-regional learning? Do global functions take on an enhanced role, or are they superseded by regional functional organizations? What variations do we observe across MNCs by sector and by strategic positioning within an industry?
- As COVID-related restrictions on travel are relaxed, which cross-border programs and face-to-face coordination mechanisms are reinstated first? And what does this indicate about the strategic importance of various cross-border integration mechanisms?

Responding to global external challenges: climate change and pandemics

Finally, large established MNCs are very likely to be key actors in efforts to address climate change, both as targets and as change agents (Henderson, 2020). Although in 2020, the pandemic took precedence in public discourse over the threat of climate change, the devastation from wildfires, catastrophic storms, floods, and crop destruction rooted in rising global temperatures continues to mount. The environmental costs of MNCs' complex, multilocation global value chains are likely to draw increasing criticism from environmental groups and, in the future, from policymakers concerned with having rapid access to resources for dealing with pandemics, as will their mixed track record on environmental regulation (Bartley, 2018). MNCs will be faced with demands to respond not only individually but also collectively. How they organize to address this internally and in terms of their external networks will be a major cross-border management challenge in the coming years. More specifically,

- In which sectors (if any) will MNCs collectively engage in initiatives to address climate and pandemic challenges?
- Will MNC initiatives to address climate change and pandemic challenges follow similar patterns across their distributed operations, or will a greater national government assertiveness on pandemic policies create a divergence in MNC strategies at the individual and collective levels?
- Is such collective action more likely in some regions than in others? In some industries than others?
- Will newer emerging-market MNCs cooperate with established MNCs to address climate issues, or will patterns of rivalry emerge?

Each reader can undoubtedly identify additional areas and topics for future research, and more will continue to emerge as MNCs face the challenges posed by rapidly evolving technologies, changing and often unpredictable business environments, and developments in management practice. MNCs will continue to offer complex but rewarding opportunities for strategic management researchers.

Acknowledgments

I would like to acknowledge the very significant contribution of Yves Doz to this chapter. Over the last four years I have benefited enormously from extended conversations with him as we have tried to develop papers on the evolving challenges facing MNC managers in the changing global environment. My thanks are also due to Elizabeth Rose, who read and provided invaluable feedback on successive chapter drafts.

References

Banalieva ER, Dhanaraj C. 2013. Home-region orientation in international expansion strategies. *Journal of International Business Studies* 44(2): 89–116.
Bartlett CA. 1986. Building and managing the transnational: the new organizational challenge. In *Competition in Global Industries*, Porter, ME (ed). Harvard Business School Press: Cambridge, MA: 367–404.
Bartlett CA, Ghoshal S. 1989. *Managing across Borders: The Transnational Solution*. Harvard Business School Press: Boston, MA.
Bartley T. 2018. Transnational corporations and global governance. *Annual Review of Sociology* 44: 145–165.

Birkinshaw J. 1997. Entrepreneurship in multinational corporations: the characteristics of subsidiary initiatives. *Strategic Management Journal* 18(3): 207–229.

Birkinshaw J. 2001. Strategy and management in MNE subsidiaries. In *The Oxford Handbook of International Business,* Rugman AM, Brewer TL (eds). Oxford University Press: Oxford, U.K.: 380–401.

Birkinshaw J, Ambos TC, Bouquet C. 2017. Boundary spanning activities of corporate HQ executives: insights from a longitudinal study. *Journal of Management Studies* 54(4): 422–454.

Birkinshaw J, Hood N, Young S. 2005. Subsidiary entrepreneurship, internal and external competitive forces, and subsidiary performance. *International Business Review* 14(2): 227–248.

Brannen MY, Piekkari R, Tietze S. 2014. The multifaceted role of language in international business: unpacking the forms, functions, and features of a critical challenge in MNC theory and performance. *Journal of International Business Studies* 45(5): 495–507.

Buckley PJ, Hashai N. 2020. Skepticism toward globalization, technological knowledge flows, and the emergence of a new global system. *Global Strategy Journal* 10(1): 94–122.

Buckley PJ, Strange R. 2015. The governance of the global factory: location and control of world economic activity. *Academy of Management Perspectives* 29(2): 237–249.

Butzbach O, Fuller DB, Schnyder G. 2020. Manufacturing discontent: national institutions, multinational firm strategies, and anti-globalization backlash in advanced economies. *Global Strategy Journal* 10(1): 67–93.

Ciabuschi F, Dellestrand H, Holm U. 2012. The role of headquarters in the contemporary MNC. *Journal of International Management* 18(3): 213–223.

De Meyer A, Williamson PJ. 2020. *Ecosystem Edge: Sustaining Competitiveness in the Face of Disruption.* Stanford University Press: Stanford, CA.

Doz Y. 1980. Strategic management in multinational companies. *Sloan Management Review* 21(2): 27–46.

Doz YL, Bartlett CA, Prahalad CK. 1981. Global competitive pressures vs. host country demands: managing tensions in multinational corporations. *California Management Review* 23(1): 15–29.

Doz YL, Hamel G. 1998. *Alliance Advantage: The Art of Creating Value through Partnering.* Harvard Business School Press: Boston, MA .

Doz YL, Santos J, Williamson, P. 2001. *From Global to Metanational: How Companies Can Win in the Global Economy.* Harvard Business School Press: Boston, MA.

Doz YL, Wilson K. 2012. *Managing Global Innovation: Frameworks for Integrating Capabilities around the World.* Harvard Business School Press: Boston, MA.

Egelhoff WG. 1982. Strategy and structure in multinational corporations: an information-processing approach. *Administrative Science Quarterly* 27(3): 435–458.

Flores RG, Aguilera RV. 2007. Globalization and location choice: an analysis of US multinational firms in 1980 and 2000. *Journal of International Business Studies* 38(7): 1187–1210.

Frost TS, Birkinshaw JM, Ensign PC. 2002. Centers of excellence in multinational corporations. *Strategic Management Journal* 23: 997–1018.

Galbraith JR. 2000. *Designing the Global Corporation.* Jossey-Bass: San Francisco, CA.

Gereffi G. 2020. What does the COVID-19 pandemic teach us about global value chains? The case of medical supplies. *Journal of International Business Policy* 3(3): 287–301.

Gerstner LV. 2002. *Who Says Elephants Can't Dance? Inside IBM's Historic Turnaround.* HarperCollins: New York, NY.

Ghemawat P. 2005. Regional strategies for global leadership. *Harvard Business Review* 83(12): 98–108.

Ghoshal S. 1987. Global strategy: an organizing framework. *Strategic Management Journal* 8(5): 425–440.

Ghoshal S, Bartlett CA. 1990. The multinational corporation as an interorganizational network. *Academy of Management Review* 15(4): 603–626.

Ghoshal S, Nohria N. 1993. Horses for courses: organizational forms for multinational corporations. *MIT Sloan Management Review* 34(2): 23–35.

Guillén MF. 2015. *The Architecture of Collapse: The Global System in the 21st Century.* Oxford University Press: New York, NY.

Hamel G. 1991. Competition for competence and interpartner learning within international strategic alliances. *Strategic Management Journal* 12(S1): 83–103.

Hamel G, Prahalad CK. 1990. The core competence of the corporation. *Harvard Business Review* 68(3): 79–91.

Hedlund G. 1986. The hypermodern MNC—a heterarchy? *Human Resource Management* 25(1): 9–25.

Hedlund G, Rolander D. 1990. Action in heterarchies—new approaches to managing the MNC. In *Managing the Global Firm,* Bartlett CA, Doz Y, Hedlund G (eds). Routledge: London, U.K.; 15–46.

Henderson RM. 2020. *Reimagining Capitalism in a World on Fire.* Public Affairs: New York.

Henisz WJ. 2016. The dynamic capability of corporate diplomacy. *Global Strategy Journal* 6(3): 183–196.

Jeong Y, Siegel JI. 2020. How important is regional vs. global scope? An examination of U.S. multinationals. *Journal of International Business Studies* 51: 1142–1160.

Kobrin SJ. 2017. Bricks and mortar in a borderless world: globalization, the backlash, and the multinational enterprise. *Global Strategy Journal* 7(2): 159–171.

Kogut B. 1989. Research notes and communications a note on global strategies. *Strategic Management Journal* 10(4): 383–389.

Kogut B, Zander U. 1993. Knowledge of the firm and the evolutionary theory of the multinational corporation. *Journal of International Business Studies* 24(4): 625–645.

Kostova T, Marano V, Tallman S. 2016. Headquarters-subsidiary relationships in MNCs: fifty years of evolving research. *Journal of World Business* 51(1): 176–184.

Lessard DR. 2021. Global strategic analysis and multi-level institutional change. In *The Multiple Dimensions of Institutional Complexity* (Progress in International Business Research, Vol. 15), Verbeke A, Tulder RV, Rose EL, Wei Y (eds). Emerald Publishing: Bingley, U.K.; 45–62.

Lessard D, Teece DJ, Leih S. 2016. The dynamic capabilities of meta-multinationals. *Global Strategy Journal* 6(3): 211–224.

Levinson M. 2006. *The Box: How the Shipping Container Made the World Smaller and the World Economy Bigger.* Princeton University Press, Princeton NJ.

Lorenzen M, Mudambi R, Schotter A. 2020. International connectedness and local disconnectedness: MNE strategy, city-regions, and disruption. *Journal of International Business Studies* 51: 1199–1222 https://doi.org/10.1057/s41267-020-00339-5.

Macrae N. 1972. The future of international business. *The Economist,* January 22: v–xxxvi.

Mees-Buss J, Welch C, Westney DE. 2019. What happened to the transnational? The emergence of the neo-global corporation. *Journal of International Business Studies* 50(9): 1513–1543.

Meyer KE, Li C, Schotter AP. 2020. Managing the MNE subsidiary: advancing a multi-level and dynamic research agenda. *Journal of International Business Studies* 51(9): 538–576.

Monteiro F, Birkinshaw J. 2017. The external knowledge sourcing process in multinational corporations. *Strategic Management Journal* 38(2): 342–362.

Neeley TB. 2012. Global business speaks English. *Harvard Business Review* 90(5): 116–124.

Neeley T. 2019. *The Language of Global Success: How a Common Tongue Transforms Multinational Organizations.* Princeton University Press: Princeton, NJ.

Nohria N, Ghoshal S. 1997. *The Differentiated Network: Organizing Multinational Corporations for Value Creation.* Jossey-Bass Publishers: San Francisco, CA.

O'Brien D, Sharkey Scott P, Andersson U, Ambos T, Fu N. 2019. The microfoundations of subsidiary initiatives: how subsidiary manager activities unlock entrepreneurship. *Global Strategy Journal* 9(1): 66–91.

Pedersen T, Soda G, Stea D. 2019. Globally networked: Intraorganizational boundary spanning in the global organization. *Journal of World Business* 54(3): 169–180.

Perlmutter H. 1969. The tortuous evolution of the multinational corporation. *Columbia Journal of World Business* 4(1): 9–18.

Piekkari R, Welch D, Welch LS. 2014. *Language in International Business: The Multilingual Reality of Global Business Expansion*. Edward Elgar Publishing: Cheltenham, U.K.

Prahaalad CK. 1976. Strategic choices in diversified MNCs. *Harvard Business Review* 54(4): 67-78.

Prahalad CK, Doz Y. 1981. An approach to strategic control in MNCs. *Sloan Management Review* 22(4): 5–13.

Prahalad CK, Doz YL. 1987. *The Multinational Mission: Balancing Local Demands and Global Vision*. Free Press: New York, NY.

Quinn JB, Hilmer FG. 1994. Strategic outsourcing. *MIT Sloan Management Review* 35(4): 43–55.

Riviere M, Bass AE, Andersson U. 2020. Dynamic capability development in multinational enterprises: reconciling routine reconfiguration between the headquarters and subsidiaries. *Global Strategy Journal,* https://doi.org/10.1002/gsj.1389.

Rosa B, Gugler P, Verbeke A. 2020. Regional and global strategies of MNEs: revisiting Rugman & Verbeke (2004). *Journal of International Business Studies* 51(7): 1045–1053.

Rugman AM, Verbeke A. 2004. A perspective on regional and global strategies of multinational enterprises. *Journal of International Business Studies* 35(1): 3–18.

Rugman A, Verbeke A, Yuan W. 2011. Re-conceptualizing Bartlett and Ghoshal's classification of national subsidiary roles in the multinational enterprise. *Journal of Management Studies* 48(2): 253–277.

Ryan P, Buciuni G, Giblin M, Andersson U. 2020. Subsidiary upgrading and global value chain governance in the multinational enterprise. *Global Strategy Journal* 10(3): 496–519.

Santos JF, Williamson PJ. 2015. The new mission for multinationals. *MIT Sloan Management Review* 56(4): 45–54.

Schotter A, Beamish PW. 2011. Performance effects of MNC headquarters-subsidiary conflict and the role of boundary spanners: The case of headquarter initiative rejection. *Journal of International Management* 17(3): 243–259.

Schotter AP, Mudambi R, Doz YL, Gaur A. 2017. Boundary spanning in global organizations. *Journal of Management Studies* 54(4): 403–421.

Stahl GK, Björkman I, Morris S (eds). 2012. *Handbook of Research in International Human Resource Management*. Edward Elgar Publishing: Cheltenham, U.K.

Stopford JM, Wells LT. 1972. *Managing the Multinational Enterprise: Organization of the Firm and Ownership of the Subsidiaries*. Basic Books: New York, NY.

Taylor W. 1991. The logic of global business: an interview with Percy Barnevik. *Harvard Business Review* 69(2): 91–105.

Teece DJ. 2014. A dynamic capabilities-based entrepreneurial theory of the multinational enterprise. *Journal of International Business Studies* 45(1): 8–37.

The Economist. 2017. Multinationals: The retreat of the global company. January 28. Available at   https://www.economist.com/briefing/2017/01/28/the-retreat-of-the-global-company [18 December 2018].

The Economist. 2019. Globalisation has faltered. Available at: https://www.economist.com/briefing/2019/01/24/globalisation-has-faltered [28 August 2020].

Tippmann E, Scott PS, Reilly M, O'Brien D. 2018. Subsidiary coopetition competence: navigating subsidiary evolution in the multinational corporation. *Journal of World Business* 53(4): 540–554.

Vahlne JE, Ivarsson I, Alvstam CG. 2018. Are multinational enterprises in retreat? *Multinational Business Review* 26(2): 94–110.

Wilkins M. 2009. The history of the multinational enterprise. In *The Oxford Handbook of International Business*, 2nd ed., Rugman A (ed). Oxford University Press: Oxford, U.K.; 3–38.

Williamson PJ., De Meyer A. 2012. Ecosystem advantage: How to successfully harness the power of partners. *California Management Review 55*(1): 24–46.

Zaheer S, Manrakhan S. 2001. Concentration and dispersion in global industries: remote electronic access and the location of economic activity. *Journal of International Business Studies 32*(4): 667–686.

5.2

EMERGING ECONOMIES: THE IMPACT OF CONTEXT ON GLOBAL STRATEGIC MANAGEMENT

Peter J. Williamson and José F.P. Santos

Introduction

In this chapter, we begin by exploring what defines emerging economies based on how they are different from the viewpoint of strategy making. Contrary to the common practice of describing emerging-market economies based on some combination of their level of development and GDP growth, we argue that their key distinguishing features from a strategy perspective lie in the fact that their path and pace of economic development are nonlinear, unstable, and unpredictable, stretching over decades. Emerging economies can be characterized as complex, dynamic systems at a stage of development where novel interactions between market and nonmarket forces are widespread across the economy. As a result, new, systemic properties of these economies are a powerful force in shaping the overall economic environment. Based on this characterization, we examine how global strategic management might need to differ in theory and practice from approaches that have been successful in more stable, developed markets.

We then turn to explore the strategies of leading domestic firms in emerging economies. Understanding their strategies is important for the study and practice of global strategic management for a number of interrelated reasons. First, we recognize that domestic firms, rather than other multinationals, are increasingly becoming the most important competitors that multinational enterprises (MNEs) face in emerging economies (Santos and Williamson, 2015).

Second, much of the body of theory concerning MNEs was established by examining firms that amassed competitive advantages at home in well-resourced developed economies and then began to expand abroad in a world where national markets were separated by significant barriers to trade, investment, and knowledge flows (Vernon, 1966). Now, by contrast, when domestic firms think about internationalizing, as many firms from emerging economies are today, they must take into account a context that is already highly globalized (Williamson, 2014).

In the third section of the chapter, we examine the implications for global strategic management of the potential for market disruption from emerging-market multinationals.

Fourth, we explore the implications of the emerging economies context for the strategies of multinationals from developed economies—an underresearched field, despite the growing importance of emerging economies in the global economy.

Finally, we conclude by proposing seven different avenues for future research on how emerging economies impact global strategic management.

The strategic significance of emerging economies for the global economy is now unquestionable, whether in terms of market size, capabilities, or as a cradle of powerful competitors. The GDP of the International Monetary Fund's list of emerging and developing economies, measured at purchasing power parity (PPP), is now at almost 60 percent of world GDP (International Monetary Fund, 2020). By 2030, India and China will be home to about 1.5 billion people each. Indonesia, Nigeria, Pakistan, and Brazil will each be home to more than 200 million people. Together these six emerging economies will have a population of four billion people, or 47 percent of the world population. China produced 21 percent of all science and technology articles published in peer-reviewed journals in the world in 2018, with the United States second with 17 percent; and the BRIC nations (Brazil, Russia, India, and China) as a whole produced 30 percent, just shy of the U.S., Germany, Japan, and U.K. total, with 33 percent (National Science Board, National Science Foundation, 2019). Meanwhile, multinationals from emerging economies have advanced strongly as competitors in global markets: in 1999, there were 23 emerging-economy companies in the *Fortune* Global 500, a number that grew to 176 in 2019 (*Fortune*, 2019). In 2019, in *Fortune*'s list of 52 companies that "change the world," there were six from emerging economies.

The emerging-economy context also has significant implications for the theory of international business and global strategy. In the next sections of this chapter, we seek to highlight what existing literature has taught us about these implications, as well as what the literature suggests are fruitful directions for future research.

What Distinguishes Emerging Economies?

Emerging economies are often described as economies with low to middle per capita incomes that are undergoing a process of economic development that allows them to "emerge" toward higher living standards and global competitiveness (Hoskisson *et al.*, 2000; Meyer and Grosse, 2019).

This emphasis on national income per capita has led many practitioners, international institutions, and researchers to use definitions based on GDP growth, an increase in the size of the middle class, and a potential for rapid growth and investment as proxies to identify emerging markets (EMs). As a result, shorthand categorizations of emerging economies—such as the "BRICs" for Brazil, Russia, India, and China (O'Neill, 2001) or the 26 "Emerging Markets" currently in the Morgan Stanley Capital

International Index (MSCI Inc., 2020)—have been popularized. Such shorthand classifications, however, risk obscuring a number of key features of emerging economies, and in particular the markets within them (hereafter "emerging markets"), that are important for global strategic management to take into account.

First among these features is the diversity of emerging markets in many dimensions beyond income, growth, and volatility. Such differences among emerging markets and compared with developed markets that are particularly significant for global strategy include: different endowments of natural resources, different demographics, and cultural differences, especially between East and West (Barkema *et al.*, 2015); differences which impact local comparative advantage, ranging from levels of technological sophistication to institutional infrastructure, (Redding, 2005); and different histories and associated path dependencies. The histories of many emerging markets have been shaped by long periods of foreign domination, extensive state intervention, institutional inefficiencies, and extended turbulence, resulting in variations in the way business is organized, including the role of the informal economy, family businesses, large business groups, and considerations of corporate social responsibility (CSR) (Austin, Dávila, and Jones, 2017).

Second, it matters that emerging markets are at very different stages of development and where they are in the transition toward more fully developed, and more stable, economic and institutional environments. These timing differences are relevant for strategic management when making international comparisons. It is also worth remembering that, at different times, economies such as the United States' (in the second half of the 19th century) and Japan's (in the 1970s and 1980s during the so-called era of high-speed growth) were themselves emerging or reemerging economies. It might, therefore, be useful to look for lessons from their histories at similar stages of development (Kosai, 1986).

Third, researchers as well as strategists need to be cognizant of the fact that the context within an emerging market will change rapidly. Louis T. Wells, in a recent retrospective of his pioneering 1983 book *Third World Multinationals*, concluded, "I fear that many of us assume that the context is simply a given and thus we fail to be explicit about the significance of a specific setting to our findings. We fail to imagine changes that may be just around the corner. Yet, those changes have a profound impact on the phenomenon we are studying" (Wells, 2017: 3). This underlines the importance for research into the dynamics of emerging markets and of longitudinal studies as we explore more fully below.

What Makes Emerging Markets Different for Global Strategic Management?

Despite the variations, emerging markets have three key characteristics in common (beyond their huge market potential) that are relevant to global strategic management theory and practice.

First, as the term suggests, *emerging* markets sit within an economy undergoing a process of continued transformation—an evolution toward some unique, as yet unknown, but more stable economy and business system. At the core of the concept of emergence is the fact that the properties and behavior of a new whole will be different from the sum of the properties of its constituents. The process of emergence is nonlinear, unpredictable, and irreversible. It is shaped both by bottom-up and top-down forces that involve many different types of constituents and ever-changing interconnections among them (Holland, 1998; Bunge, 2000). Economic development consists of a myriad of changes over time, some incremental and some disruptive: new institutions, new policies, new rules and practices, new technologies and skills, new offerings and preferences, new industries and product markets. An emerging market is "emerging" exactly because the combinations of such changes are dynamic and turbulent, with outcomes that are unforeseeable.

The presence of these dynamics in emerging markets means that global strategic management not only faces the traditional problem of how to transfer and adapt a firm's ownership advantages to a different foreign market setting (Dunning, 2001). Global strategic management also faces the considerably more challenging problem of how to build and evolve its competitive advantage against a backdrop of unpredictable emergence that is systemic and hence cannot be understood by aggregating the behavior of its constituents nor simply "rewound" once it has taken place. For example, bottom-up effects during emergence mean that firm strategies have the potential to shape their market and even nudge the country as a whole (Santos and Williamson, 2015).

Arthur (2014) described such process dynamics in an economy. Expectations and actions of the economic agents change endogenously as a result of the systemic patterns they generate over time, hence nonequilibrium and irreversibility. Agents face absolute uncertainty. Technology keeps changing through combinations of existing technologies. This environment contrasts sharply with the concerns, assumptions, and tools that underlie classic economic analysis: resource allocation, optimization, deduction, and comparative statics, on which much strategic management research has been based. Arguably "complexity economics" (Arthur, 2014) that emphasizes models of contingency, indeterminacy, and path dependency are more appropriate to future research into the development and re-formation of economies. It also alerts us to the need to study the active role of institutions, not just when markets fail, but also in their creation and evolution.

Second, as an emerging economy develops, the variety and scope of its own technological capability base grows. Hidalgo and Hausmann (2009) observed that developed countries exhibit diversified portfolios of exclusive products while underdeveloped countries exhibit nondiversified portfolios of ubiquitous, standard products. Hidalgo and Hausmann (2009) argued that the productivity of a country is directly and positively related to its nontradable capabilities and their interactions, which they defined as the country's level of "economic complexity" and measured using international trade data to construct each country's Economic Complexity

Index (ECI) (Hausmann *et al.*, 2011). Importantly, positive deviations from the trend relationship between ECI and GDP are predictive of future growth (Hidalgo and Hausmann, 2009). Building on this insight to allow for nonlinearity, Cristelli *et al.* (2013) have developed the concept of a country's competitive "fitness."

These indicators of economic complexity are potentially very useful for global strategic management both as a frame of reference and as a prospective tool for firms as they assess the future potential of a particular emerging market as a location for sourcing, as a market, and as incubators of new competition. They suggest, for example, that over the past few decades, Brazil and Russia have remained heavily dependent on natural resources, with falling rankings, while China and India have progressed substantially by expanding their technological capabilities and competing internationally in a growing number of different categories of products and services. Firms operating in the latter markets, therefore, need to adopt strategies to augment their own stock of capabilities and use these to further differentiate their offerings to the market.

Third, given the rapid pace of change in emerging markets, dynamic capabilities are key sources of competitive advantage. In their seminal article, Teece, Pisano, and Shuen (1997: 516) define *dynamic capabilities* "as the firm's ability to integrate, build, and reconfigure internal and external competences to address rapidly changing environments." Eisenhardt and Martin (2000) went further to argue that dynamic capabilities in "moderately dynamic markets" and in "high-velocity markets" are categorically distinct. In markets changing at "moderate" speed, detailed and analytic routines with predictable outcomes that evolve only gradually are sufficient to maintain a firm's competitiveness. High-velocity markets with the kinds of ambiguity, nonlinearity, and unpredictability characteristic of emerging markets, by contrast, require dynamic capabilities involving highly experiential and unstable processes with unpredictable outcomes, guided by managed selection (Eisenhardt and Martin, 2000: 1115). Reconciling these different conceptions (Peteraf, Di Stefano, and Verona, 2013) and understanding the nature of dynamic capabilities required to thrive in different emerging markets and industries, therefore, merit serious future research.

Beyond their high velocity of change, it is also worth noting that emerging markets have experienced faster rates of innovation than developed markets (DMs) in some businesses, particularly in the digital arena (despite the popular notion that Silicon Valley necessarily leads). Innovation in digital payment systems, including M-Pesa in Kenya and Alipay and WeChat Pay in China, are good examples. It may be that these kinds of strategic innovations are enabled by the combination of an emerging environment and the higher-order dynamic capabilities that firms already need to stay competitive in an emerging market. The context of rising economic complexity and opportunities for leapfrogging (such as Chinese policies favoring ecommerce instead of building the costly infrastructure of "modern" bricks-and-mortar retail) drastically reduces the constraints on realizing novel possibilities. The endless possibilities to make new economic connections that characterize emerging markets may make them particularly fertile ground for breakthrough innovation, especially for new customer solutions and business models. This would suggest that the study of leading domestic firms in emerging markets and the way they innovate are new and important areas for future research in global strategic management.

Domestic Firms' Strategies in Emerging Markets

In addition to uncovering potentially novel innovation processes, understanding the strategies of leading domestic firms in emerging markets is important to global strategic management for two other reasons. First, domestic firms in emerging markets are now important competitors to MNEs in emerging markets. Second, domestic firms in emerging markets are internationalizing in a new context for strategy making in the guise of markets that are already globalized, in contrast to MNEs that globalized in the less integrated world of the past.

A combination of modularization of product designs and outsourcing has opened up once closed value chains, enabling local players to source "plug-and-play" modules that can be combined to create products very similar and sometimes superior to those of MNEs. Meanwhile, increasingly efficient global markets for resources, capabilities, and knowledge mean that companies based in emerging markets can now access or acquire brands, product modules, technologies, and talent overseas through strategic asset seeking (Luo and Tung, 2007, 2018).

The evolution of global value chains has also played a role in helping emerging-market firms amass capabilities unavailable locally. In the initial development of most global value chains, "lead" firms tend to monopolize high-rent activities such as design, distribution, and marketing while outsourcing low-value-added, low-return functions such as assembly and basic manufacturing to firms from emerging markets (Gereffi, 1999). Over time, however, firms from emerging markets often use their entry into global value chains to enhance their position through product, process, functional, and intersectoral upgrading underpinned by learning and incremental investment (Humphrey and Schmitz, 2002). Although the magnitude of this effect is a matter of debate (Pietrobelli and Rabellotti, 2011), it has been found that the international expansion of emerging-market firms is a possible mechanism for economic upgrading, allowing domestic firms to capture more value from their participation in global value chains (Pananond, 2013) while benefiting from global value chains as a gateway into the global market (Williamson and Zeng, 2009).

At the same time, domestic firms in emerging markets can enjoy "home team" advantage by using a dynamic capability dubbed "local integration," which includes engaging deeply with and educating customers and end users, partnering and co-creating with local suppliers, fostering the development of the local talent pool, shaping the regulatory and institutional environment, and participating in the broader development of the local society (Santos and Williamson, 2015). Local integration requires a high degree of embeddedness in local networks that MNEs often lack (Johanson and Vahlne, 2011) and a symbiotic relationship with the local society.

As leading domestic firms in emerging markets have augmented their ordinary capabilities through "learning from the world" (Doz, Santos, and Williamson, 2001), they have moved to use their enhanced set of capabilities in combination with local integration so as to reinforce their local competitive advantage. This is creating a new challenge for global strategic management because no amount of local adaptation by MNEs can deliver the competitive benefits of global learning combined with local integration pursued by leading domestic firms in emerging markets.

Faced with this new reality, one option for MNEs is to build on their "assets of foreignness" (Mallon and Fainshmidt, 2017) as a source of differentiation to become "cultural exporters" (just as Levi Strauss and Co. sells a piece of American lifestyle, Prada Italian fashion sense, and Porsche and BMW German engineering). The other option is to create new layers of advantage beyond the global strategies that have dominated their thinking over the past decades and embrace a new mission founded on two dynamic capabilities: the ability to integrate locally and adapt globally (Santos and Williamson, 2015). Global adaptation calls, for example, for the ability to lead global ecosystems (De Meyer and Williamson, 2020), a role that even leading domestic firms from emerging markets will find difficult to perform due to limited international experience. This "new mission" for MNEs opens up a new avenue for global strategy research in the context of emerging markets.

It is also worth considering whether domestic firms in emerging markets are better placed than MNEs to take advantage of the dynamic environment in emerging markets to build new sources of competitive advantage. It has also long been recognized that country-specific advantages (CSAs) play a role in underpinning the competitive advantages of individual firms (Rugman and Verbeke, 2001). Historically these CSAs have been characterized as Ricardian-type endowments such as land, labor, and capital, along with aspects of the legal and commercial environment in which the firm is based, such as market structure, government legislation, and policies (Dunning, 1980). In emerging markets, however, some of the most important CSAs may take the form of the opportunity for locals to understand fast-paced changes happening there, including new types of customer behavior, new distribution channels, new institutional environments, and new potential partners and suppliers.

Access to the new potential CSAs being created in emerging markets has implications for global strategic management because some CSAs are not freely and fully available to all firms operating in the same location (Hennart, 2009). Domestic firms may have better access to some CSAs at home than MNEs as a result of their greater stocks of experiential and context-dependent, complementary local knowledge; closer relationships with related industries and local government; and home-focused strategies. The last of these disadvantages for foreign MNEs is the price they pay for the chance to exploit ownership advantages imported from overseas (Rugman, 1981).

Better access to the new CSAs being generated in emerging markets combined with the possibility that they may be transformed into new, firm-specific advantages, augmented by learning from the world, raises the possibility that domestic firms may be able to improve their competitive advantage at a faster rate than MNEs are able to overcome their "liability of foreignness" (Zaheer, 1995; Miller and Eden, 2006). In this case, domestic firms would gain and retain an upper hand against MNEs competing in emerging markets (Wan, Williamson, and Pandit, 2020).

In sum, the improved access that domestic firms in emerging markets now enjoy to the world stock of knowledge as an indirect result of globalization, their superior ability to pursue "local integration," their better access to new CSAs arising in emerging markets, and their dynamic capabilities suited to volatile, high-velocity emerging-market environments present new challenges for incumbent MNEs. This suggests the need to reevaluate and extend the received characterization in global strategic management that MNEs need to find the appropriate trade-off between global integration and local responsiveness to compete in the global market (Prahalad and Doz, 1987).

The Rise of Emerging-Market Multinationals

Profitable internationalization by firms from emerging economies (EMNEs) appears unconventional and even paradoxical when viewed through the lens of traditional theories of internationalization, such as Vernon (1966) or Dunning (1980). In businesses such as home appliances, telecom systems, consumer electronics, software, information technology (IT) services, or ecommerce, they seemingly lack ownership of the rich stocks of intangible assets that could underpin international expansion. Yet they were able to compete abroad successfully against established MNEs that benefited from global capabilities and networks built over many decades (Mathews, 2002; Fleury and Fleury, 2011).

A number of possible explanations have been advanced, including the ability of EMNEs to create business models that enable them to combine CSAs from home (such as low labor costs) with asset-seeking investments overseas to fill capability gaps they face as "late-comers" to the global market (Williamson, 2016b). But this argument seems to be only part of the story (Williamson, 2015). A number of other researchers have raised the intriguing possibility that some of the best EMNEs have converted their original CSAs and learning from their home-market contexts into firm-specific advantages that could underpin competitive advantage in global markets. Foremost among these are "cost innovation" (the strategy of using cost advantage in radically new ways to offer customers in mass markets dramatically more for less [Zeng and Williamson, 2007]) and "frugal innovation" (a resource-scarce solution that is good enough to meet the basic needs of customers who would otherwise remain unserved [Prabhu and Jain, 2015]). Other possible advantages include a particular capability to manage uncertainty (Cuervo-Cazurra et al., 2018), the ability to unlock latent demand in low-end segments (Prahalad, 2006), optimizing products and processes for emerging markets (Ramamurti and Singh, 2009), capabilities in dealing with weak institutions and infrastructure (Cuervo-Cazurra and Genc, 2008), and filling institutional voids (Khanna, Palepu, and Sinha, 2005) in the emerging markets they entered.

These firm-specific advantages differ from those enjoyed by established multinationals and are not necessarily substitutes for them, but they are potentially powerful sources of advantage in 21st-century markets. These advantages are very relevant to the needs of emerging and frontier economies, which, as we have already noted, now account for the majority of world demand, while also appealing to the growing market segment of consumers in developed countries forced by income stagnation to look for value-for-money products (Ramamurti and Williamson, 2019). Moreover, as discussed, putative EMNEs may be equipped with distinctive dynamic capabilities that afford them competitive advantage in global markets undergoing rapid change (Williamson, 2016a). Successful Chinese EMNEs, for example, have developed dynamic capabilities that can be used to disrupt and undermine the strategies of incumbent multinationals and local firms (Abernathy and Clark, 1985; Santos, 2007; Wan, Williamson, and Yin, 2015). Moreover, EMNE's dynamic capabilities may enable them to spawn a continuous series of innovations in their offerings and business models that enable them to "run faster" as they adapt to evolving market demands and hence stay ahead of competitors for an extended period (Williamson, 2016a).

Nonetheless, it remains true that EMNEs often face particular "capability holes" as they internationalize from an emerging-market home base (Ramamurti and Williamson, 2019). These might be filled by adopting the "springboard" strategy—using asset-seeking foreign investments to provide a springboard to penetrating overseas markets—proposed by Luo and Tung (2007). But, unlike the classic internationalization process proposed by Johanson and Vahlne (1977), the springboard model is "not path dependent nor evolutionary in selecting entry modes and project locations" (Luo and Tung, 2007: 482). This begs the question of how these models can be integrated (Ramamurti, 2012; Luo and Tung, 2018). An important, unanswered question here is whether strategic assets accessed abroad should be integrated and leveraged back in the home market first before attempting to exploit their expanded portfolio of capabilities abroad (Williamson, 2016b).

EMNEs also face the issue of how to gain legitimacy in host countries they enter (Kostova and Zaheer, 1999), burdened by liabilities as a result of country-of-origin effects. Overcoming these barriers, especially given increasing emphasis on risks to national security, is another area ripe for future research.

Opportunities and Challenges for Foreign Multinationals

MNEs from developed markets (DMNEs) have advantages in brands, proprietary technologies, and cutting-edge innovation acquired at home. Because such established DMNEs are linked with two sets of ties—one internal to their multinational organization and the other with the local environment where they operate (Nachum and Keeble, 2003)—they also can benefit from the opportunity to learn from other markets and access sources of research and development (R&D) across borders (Foss and Santos, 2011). These links enable DMNEs to create what Doz *et al.* (2001) termed "metanational advantage," with breakthrough innovations realized by melding technical, market, and user knowledge embedded in different locations around the world (Santos, Doz, and Williamson, 2004).

Despite these advantages, DMNEs also face challenges in emerging markets. We have already mentioned many of the most common ones, including failure to exploit local CSAs and falling short on local integration. But perhaps the greatest challenge for DMNEs is that the competitive demands of emerging markets keep changing in uncertain ways, usually at a rapid pace. Many of the core capabilities that DMNEs enjoy have been accumulated primarily in their stable and predictable home markets. This is likely to make them ill-suited to emerging markets, so that DMNEs also face capability holes relative to the demands of today's global markets.

The paradigm of EMNEs striving to catch up with DMNEs, so pervasive in the literature (Meyer, 2018), is therefore a misnomer because both EMNEs and DMNEs have capability holes—albeit different ones. As a result, the strategic management challenge of global competition needs to be recast as a learning race to the future between EMNEs and DMNEs (Ramamurti and Williamson, 2019).

Nonetheless, DMNEs can be successful in emerging markets, although cases are rarer than many MNEs' chief executives might hope and assume. Critical to success is active participation in the development of emerging economies (Santos and Williamson, 2015), the further study of which may improve our understanding of how global strategic management can rise to the challenges presented by emerging markets.

Conclusion: Looking Forward

We conclude by stepping back and reviewing the implications of our findings about emerging economies and the state of the art in global strategic management in the emerging-market context for future research in the field.

The main distinguishing feature of emerging markets for global strategic management is that they are *complex dynamic systems*—far from equilibrium, and unpredictable—whose systemic behavior cannot be understood by reductionist methodologies. This suggests the need for further research on

- The dynamic process of emergence at various levels (firm, market, industry, economy) in emerging economies, with particular attention to upward and downward causalities.
- Developing classifications of emerging markets based on the key dynamics at play.

- The consequences of focusing on the interactions between culture, institutions, and business systems in emerging markets over time, rather than adopting static indicators such as cultural or institutional distance on effective emerging-market strategies.
- Longitudinal studies with a focus on processes and timing with a systems perspective.
- How analysis using comparative statics, reductionism, and assumptions about convergence to market equilibrium or punctuated equilibrium in emerging markets limits our understanding of global competitive advantage.

The development of emerging markets is usually accompanied by an increase in *economic complexity* and variations in country rankings. Therefore, we could usefully examine these questions:

- How can we appropriately measure and incorporate into global strategic management the implications of changes in economic complexity that occur in emerging markets as they develop? Does it create the need for greater firm specialization? New ecosystems? Geographic concentration of particular activities? Does it have meaningful impacts on how to build competitive advantage? And why?
- What are the implications of levels and changes in economic complexity for innovation by domestic firms in an emerging market and their access to new technologies, demanding customers, and lead users?

Because of the dynamic and volatile nature of emerging markets, a firm's *dynamic capabilities* are key to competitive advantage and, hence future research could valuably explore these questions:

- What kinds of dynamic capabilities are most powerful in creating competitive advantage in the context of emerging markets? Are these different for domestic and foreign firms?
- Should a DMNE move to high-velocity emerging markets early in its internationalization path in order to develop and extend its range of dynamic capabilities?
- What forms of governance foster dynamic capabilities? Does the dynamic and coevolutionary nature of an "ecosystem" fit an emerging market better than more stable forms of interorganizational cooperation?

Dynamic emergence, less legacy, and fewer constraints suggest that emerging markets will be a very fertile ground for *innovation*, especially those types of innovation, such as new business models, that are fueled by contextual change (including new types of consumer behavior, rapid adoption of new technologies, deepening capabilities in the supply chain, and changing institutional environment). This suggests a number of research questions:

- What differences in types of innovation and innovation processes are observed in emerging markets relative to developed markets? Why?
- How are innovations shaped by the dynamics of a changing local environment?
- What processes of search and learning are more common in an emerging market? Does experimentation, for example, have a larger role to play relative to investment in R&D in the dynamic and uncertain setting of emerging markets?

The strategies of *domestic firms* in emerging markets are importantly shaped by the fact that they are developing in an environment that is already highly globalized. As such, their sources of competitive advantage are formed by a mix of the strategic assets they are able to obtain overseas and a home-team advantage due to local integration.

- How do local entrepreneurs best leverage strategic asset-seeking abroad?
- Can involvement in global value chains assist with improving capabilities to underpin upgrading and internationalization?
- How do the processes of local integration differ from local adaption?
- How does a firm's liability of foreignness change over time in a dynamic host emerging market?

EMNEs are gaining *competitive advantage* not only from the CSAs in their home markets (country-of-origin effects) but also from the dynamic processes at work in their emerging-market home markets.

- How do the dynamics of emerging markets help EMNEs create competitive advantage?
- When and why are FSAs developed in emerging markets location-bound, constraining EMNEs' ability to compete globally?

Given the dynamic nature of emerging markets and their impacts on the evolution of global markets, DMNEs also exhibit *capability holes* relative to future requirements for success.

- What changes in the global environment are impacting the relevance of firm-specific assets enjoyed by incumbent DMNEs?
- What needs to change to enable incumbent DMNEs to compete more effectively with domestic firms in emerging markets?
- Does "universalism" and the paradigms endemic in many Western developed markets and DMNEs limit their competitiveness in the face of emerging markets?

Clearly, the unique context of emerging economies poses many, still largely unanswered questions and challenges for both research and practice in the field of global strategic management. Perhaps even more fundamentally, our analysis of implications of economic and market emergence suggests we may need to adopt a new paradigm based on systems and complexity theory in order to improve our understanding of global strategy in a world of dynamic, far-from-equilibrium, and unpredictable emerging-market economies.

References

Abernathy W, Clark KB. 1985. Innovation: mapping the winds of creative destruction. *Research Policy* 14(1): 3–22.

Arthur BW. 2014. *Complexity and the Economy*. Oxford University Press: New York, NY.

Austin G, Dávila C, Jones G. 2017. Emerging markets and the future of business history. Working Paper 18–012, Harvard Business School. Available at: https://www.hbs.edu/ris/Publication%20Files/18-012_47e98088-6b60-4630-bf51-f6ca5abfe766.pdf / [11 March 2020].

Barkema HG, Chen X-P, George G, Luo Y, Tsui AS. 2015. West meets East: new concepts and theories. *Academy of Management Journal* 58(2): 460–479.

Bunge M. 2000. Systemism: the alternative to individualism and holism. *Journal of Socio-Economics* 29: 147–157.

Cristelli M, Gabrielli A, Tacchella A, Caldarelli G, Pietronero L. 2013. Measuring the intangibles: a metrics for the economic complexity of countries and products. *PLoS ONE* 8(8): e70726.

Cuervo-Cazurra A, Ciravegna L, Melgarejo M, Lopez L. 2018. Home country uncertainty and the internationalization-performance relationship: building an uncertainty management capability. *Journal of World Business* 53: 209–221.

Cuervo-Cazurra A, Genc M. 2008. Transforming disadvantages into advantages: developing-country MNEs in the least developed MNEs. *Journal of International Business Studies* 39: 957–979.

De Meyer A, Williamson PJ. 2020. *Ecosystem Advantage: How to Successfully Harness the Power of Partners*. Stanford University Press: Palo Alto, CA.

Doz Y, Santos J, Williamson P. 2001. *From Global to Metanational: How Companies Win in the Global Knowledge Economy*. HBS Press: Boston, MA.

Dunning JH. 1980. Toward an eclectic theory of international production: some empirical tests. *Journal of International Business Studies* 11(1): 9–31.

Dunning JH. 2001. The eclectic (OLI) paradigm of international production: past, present and future. *International Journal of the Economics of Business* 8(2): 173–190.

Eisenhardt KM, Martin JA. 2000. Dynamic capabilities: What are they? *Strategic Management Journal* 21(10–11): 1105–1121.

Fleury A, Fleury MTL. 2011. *Brazilian Multinationals: Competences for Internationalization*. Cambridge University Press: Cambridge, U.K.

Fortune. 2019. "Global 500" List. www.fortune.com/global500/ [23 May 2020].

Foss N, Santos J. 2011. A knowledge system approach to the multinational company: conceptual grounding implications for research. *Advances in International Management* 24: 425–453.

Gereffi G. 1999. International trade and industrial upgrading in the apparel commodity chain. *Journal of International Economics* 48(1): 37–70.

Hausmann R, Hidalgo CA, Bustos S, Coscia M, Chung S, Jimenez J, Simoes A. 2011. *Atlas of Economic Complexity: Mapping the Path to Prosperity*. Yildirim / Puritan Press: Boston, MA.

Hennart J. 2009. Down with MNE-centric theories! Market entry and expansion as the building of MNE and local assets. *Journal of International Business Studies* **40**(9): 1432–1454.

Hidalgo CA, Hausmann R. 2009.The building blocks of economic complexity *Proceedings of the National Academy of Sciences* **106**(26): 10570–10575.

Holland JH. 1998. *Emergence: From Chaos to Order*. Oxford University Press: Oxford, U.K.

Hoskisson RE, Eden L, Lau CM, Wright M. 2000. Strategy in emerging economies. *Academy of Management Journal* **43**(3): 249–267.

Humphrey J, Schmitz H. 2002. How does insertion in global value chains affect upgrading in industrial clusters? *Regional Studies* **36**(9): 1017–1027.

International Monetary Fund. 2020. *World Economic Outlook, April 2020: The Great Lockdown*. Washington, DC: International Monetary Fund.

Johanson J, Vahlne J. 1977. The internationalization process of the firm: a model of knowledge development and increasing foreign market commitments. *Journal of International Business Studies* **8**(1): 25–34.

Johanson J, Vahlne J. 2011. Markets as networks: implications for strategy-making. *Journal of the Academy of Marketing Science* **39**(4): 484–491.

Khanna T, Palepu KG, Sinha J. 2005. Strategies that fit emerging markets. *Harvard Business Review* **83**(6): 63–76.

Kosai Y. 1986. *The Era of High-Speed Growth: Notes on the Post-War Japanese Economy*. University of Tokyo Press: Tokyo, Japan.

Kostova T, Zaheer S. 1999. Organizational legitimacy under conditions of complexity: the case of the multinational enterprise. *Academy of Management Review* **24**(1): 64–81.

Luo Y, Tung RL. 2007. International expansion of emerging market enterprises: a springboard perspective. *Journal of International Business Studies* **38**(4): 481–498.

Luo Y, Tung RL. 2018. A general theory of springboard MNEs. *Journal of International Business Studies* **49**: 129–152.

Mallon M, Fainshmidt S. 2017. Assets of foreignness: a theoretical integration and agenda for future research. *Journal of International Management* **23**(1): 43–55.

Mathews JA. 2002. *Dragon Multinational: A New Model for Global Growth*. Oxford University Press: Oxford, U.K.

Meyer KE. 2018. Catch-up and leapfrogging: emerging economy multinational enterprises on the global stage. *International Journal of the Economics of Business* **25**(1): 19–30.

Meyer KE, Grosse R. 2019. Introduction to managing in emerging markets. In *Oxford Handbook of Management in Emerging Markets*, Grosse R, Meyer KE (eds). Oxford University Press: New York, NY; 3–34.

Miller SR, Eden L. 2006. Local density and foreign subsidiary performance. *Academy of Management Journal* **49**: 341–355.

MSCI Inc. 2020. https://www.msci.com/emerging-markets [10 May 2020].

Nachum L, Keeble D. 2003. MNE linkages and localised clusters: foreign and indigenous firms in the media cluster of Central London. *Journal of International Management* **9**: 171–192.

National Science Board, National Science Foundation. 2019. Publication output: U.S. trends and international comparisons. *Science and Engineering Indicators 2020*. NSB-2020-6. Alexandria, VA. Available at https://ncses.nsf.gov/pubs/nsb20206/ [22 December 2019].

O'Neill J. 2001. *Building Better Global Economic BRICs. Global Economics Paper No: 66*. Goldman Sachs: London, U.K.

Pananond P. 2013. Where do we go from here? Globalizing subsidiaries moving up the value chain. *Journal of International Management* **19**(3): 207–221.

Peteraf M, Di Stefano G, Verona G. 2013. The elephant in the room of dynamic capabilities: bringing two diverging conversations together. *Strategic Management Journal* 34: 1389–1410.

Pietrobelli C, Rabellotti R. 2011. Global value chains meet innovation systems: are there learning opportunities for developing countries? *World Development* 39(7): 1261–1269.

Prabhu J, Jain S. 2015. Innovation and entrepreneurship in India: understanding jugaad. *Asia Pacific Journal of Management* 32(4): 843–868.

Prahalad CK. 2006. *The Fortune at the Bottom of the Pyramid.* Wharton School Publishing: Philadelphia, PA.

Prahalad CK, Doz Y. 1987. *The Multi-National Mission: Balancing Local Demands and Global Vision.* Free Press: New York, NY.

Ramamurti R. 2012. What is really different about emerging market multinationals? *Global Strategy Journal* 2(1): 41–47.

Ramamurti R, Singh JV. 2009. *Emerging Multinationals in Emerging Markets.* Cambridge University Press: Cambridge, U.K.

Ramamurti R, Williamson PJ. 2019. Rivalry between emerging-market MNEs and developed-country MNEs: capability holes and the race to the future. *Business Horizons* 62(2): 157–169.

Redding G. 2005. The thick description and comparison of societal systems of capitalism. *Journal of International Business Studies* 36: 123–155.

Rugman A. 1981. A test of internalization theory. *Managerial and Decision Economics* 2: 211–219.

Rugman A, Verbeke A. 2001. Subsidiary-specific advantages in multinational enterprises. *Strategic Management Journal* 22: 237–250.

Santos J. 2007. Strategy lessons from left field. *Harvard Business Review*, April: 20–21.

Santos J, Doz Y, Williamson P. 2004. Is your innovation process global? *MIT Sloan Management Review* 45(4): 31–37.

Santos JF, Williamson PJ. 2015. The new mission for multinationals. *MIT Sloan Management Review* 56(4): 45–55.

Teece DJ, Pisano G, Shuen A. 1997. Dynamic capabilities and strategic management. *Strategic Management Journal* 18(7): 509–533.

Vernon R. 1966. International investment and international trade in the product cycle. *Quarterly Journal of Economics* 80(2): 190–207.

Wan F, Williamson P, Pandit, NR. 2020. MNE liability of foreignness versus local firm-specific advantages: the case of the Chinese management software industry. *International Business Review* 29(1): 2–10.

Wan F, Williamson P, Yin E. 2015. Antecedents and implications of disruptive innovation: evidence from China. *Technovation* 39–40: 94–104.

Wells LT. 1983. *Third World Multinationals: The Rise of Foreign Direct Investment from Developing Countries.* MIT Press: Cambridge, MA.

Wells LT. 2017. Third world multinationals: a retrospective. *Progress in International Business Research* 11: 3–16.

Williamson PJ. 2014. The global expansion of EMNCs: paradoxes and directions for future research. In *Understanding Multinationals from Emerging Markets*, Cuervo-Cazurra A, Ramamurti R (eds). Cambridge University Press, Cambridge, U.K.; 155–168.

Williamson PJ. 2015. The competitive advantages of emerging market multinationals: a reassessment. *Critical Perspectives on International Business* 11(3/4): 216–235.

Williamson PJ. 2016a. Building and leveraging dynamic capabilities: insights from accelerated innovation in China. *Global Strategy Journal* 6(3): 197–210.

Williamson PJ. 2016b. Chinese acquisitions in Europe: absorptive capability and impacts on competitive advantage. *International Relations* 13(49): 61–83.

Williamson PJ, Zeng M. 2009. Chinese multinationals: emerging through new global gateways. In *Emerging Multinationals in Emerging Markets*, Ramamurti R, Singh J (eds). Cambridge University Press: Cambridge, U.K.; 81–109.

Zaheer S. 1995. Overcoming the liability of foreignness. *Academy of Management Journal* **38**: 341–363.

Zeng M, Williamson PJ. 2007. *Dragons at Your Door: How Chinese Cost Innovation Is Disrupting Global Competition*. Harvard Business School Press: Boston, MA.

PART 6

STRATEGIC LEADERSHIP

Donald C. Hambrick and Adam J. Wowak, Leads

6.0

STRATEGIC LEADERSHIP

Donald C. Hambrick and Adam J. Wowak

> *Strategy is a human construction.*
>
> —Andrews (1971: 107)

Introduction and Overview

Scholars have long recognized that the strategic behaviors of firms do not strictly, or even primarily, stem from technical calculation. Instead, as Kenneth Andrews, a forefather of the field of strategic management, noted in the chapter epigraph, the formulation and implementation of strategic initiatives are the results of human enterprise—or the interpretations, insights, talents, and foibles of strategists themselves. As such, strategy researchers have had an abiding interest in top executives and their influences on companies' actions and performance.

This important topical domain has been formalized under the label *strategic leadership*, which is the study of "the executives who have overall responsibility for an organization—their characteristics, what they do, how they do it, and particularly how they affect organizational outcomes" (Finkelstein and Hambrick, 1996: 2). Over the past few decades, scholarly interest in strategic leadership has flourished. For instance, the Strategic Leadership and Governance Interest Group of the Strategic Management Society is thriving, and nearly every issue of every top journal in management contains one or more articles on some aspect of strategic leadership.

Within this broad scope, researchers devote attention to chief executive officers (CEOs), top management teams (TMTs), division heads, entrepreneurs, and boards of directors. Far from glorifying these figures, strategic leadership researchers build their theories and studies upon the premise that business leaders are utterly human, replete with personal blinders, biases, jealousies, fatigue, and other limitations, while in some cases also possessing remarkable degrees of creativity and boldness. For good or for ill, these factors all shape executive actions.

This is not to say that all business leaders, in every instance, have complete latitude to alter the trajectories of their companies. In fact, researchers have made substantial progress in understanding the conditions that confer, or conversely restrict, the discretion available to CEOs and other top managers (for a review, see Wangrow, Schepker, and Barker, 2015). Strategic leadership scholars have shown, for example, that CEOs in some industries have far more discretion than in other industries (Hambrick and Abrahamson, 1995), that CEOs under some corporate governance arrangements have more discretion than their peers under different arrangements (Quigley and Hambrick, 2012), and that CEOs themselves vary in the degree to which they can envision alternative courses of action (Carpenter and Golden, 1997).

This chapter serves two main purposes. First, we provide an overview of recent developments in the strategic leadership domain. We roughly follow the organizing scheme of Finkelstein, Hambrick, and Cannella (2009) in their comprehensive book on the topic, particularly highlighting works that have appeared since that volume. As such, we trace recent theory and research on managerial discretion, CEO attributes, and executive compensation. Two other topics that we might have included—CEO succession and TMTs—are addressed in accompanying chapters in this volume by Anthea Zhang and by Margarethe Wiersema and Joshua Hernsberger, respectively, so we leave it to them to assess those domains. We likewise omit consideration of CEO-board relations and other aspects of governance, even though these topics are generally viewed as an element of the scope of strategic leadership; another Part of this volume addresses these matters.

Our second purpose in this chapter is to suggest priorities for future research in strategic leadership. Here we are driven both by our sense of major voids and inconsistencies in the academic literature as well as by our perception of significant trends in the business world that call out for fresh scholarly insights.

Current State of the Field

As noted earlier, the strategic leadership domain is profuse and robust, far exceeding what can be comprehensively reviewed within the framework of this chapter; indeed, to do so properly would warrant its own book, a task twice undertaken already (Finkelstein and Hambrick, 1996; Finkelstein et al., 2009). As such, our focus in this section is on recent themes, trends, and representative examples as opposed to an exhaustive cataloging of studies.

Executive attributes

In the decades since Hambrick and Mason's introduction of upper echelons theory (1984), research on executive attributes has thrived. This perspective holds that executives' decisions and actions are manifestations of their individual values, personalities, and experiences. It thus makes sense that the vast majority—indeed, virtually all—of the research in the upper echelons literature has focused on executive characteristics as independent variables. (As we discuss in a later section, we see great potential in examining executive attributes as outcomes in their own right.) We now review some recent developments in this area.

While the original formulation of upper echelons theory stressed the importance of executives' personal values in the strategic decision process, only in recent years have scholars begun to explore this idea in earnest. The impetus for this trend is clear: the public availability of political donation data, which allows researchers to approximate executives' political ideologies based on the party affiliations of the candidates to which they donate. Political ideologies are closely tied to individuals' personal values, as one's position on the liberalism-conservatism spectrum says a lot about the types of goals and outcomes they seek (Jost, Federico, and Napier, 2009).

One of the first major studies in this stream was conducted by Chin and colleagues (2013), who found that liberal-leaning CEOs were more likely than their conservative-leaning peers to emphasize corporate social responsibility (CSR) initiatives. Their study opened the floodgates, and research on executive (and more recently, board) ideologies has flourished ever since. Besides affecting CSR, executive ideology has been shown to influence outcomes such as firm risk taking (Christensen *et al.*, 2015), TMT pay arrangements (Chin and Semadeni, 2017), and corporate resource allocation (Gupta, Briscoe, and Hambrick, 2018). Scholars also have begun to explore the implications of political ideology at the board level, as when Gupta and Wowak (2017) found that more conservative-leaning boards tend to pay their CEOs more while also tying pay more closely to performance. Overall, this is among the most active arenas in the strategic leadership domain.

Researchers also have continued to gain new insights into executive personality and its implications for firms. Some of this work has focused on aspects of the CEO-TMT leadership dynamic, as when Ou and colleagues (2014) demonstrated that CEO humility had a positive effect on TMT behavioral integration, or the degree to which the TMT engages in "mutual and collective interaction" (Hambrick, 2007: 336). TMT behavioral integration also tends to be higher when CEOs have a more collectivist orientation (Simsek *et al.*, 2005). Other work in this stream emphasizes the link between CEO personality (and to a lesser extent, TMT members' personalities) and strategic decisions. For instance, CEOs' Big Five personality traits have been demonstrated to play an important role in determining their firms' ability to adapt quickly to changes in the environment (Nadkarni and Herrmann, 2010). Researchers also have begun to explore the effects of CEO emotions, which Delgado-Garcia and De La Fuente-Sabaté (2010) found to be meaningful predictors of a firm's likelihood of mimicking competitors' strategies.

The other major topical area in this stream emphasizes executives' experiences as antecedents of organizational outcomes. Many of these studies have focused on CEO tenure stage, which has long been thought to play a key role in shaping CEOs' decisions (Finkelstein *et al.*, 2009). For instance, research suggests that newer CEOs are likelier than longer-tenured CEOs to sell off a firm's original or "legacy" businesses without fully understanding the interdependencies between the legacy units and the firm's remaining operations (Feldman, 2014). Tenure can also offer a window into how executives' influences on strategy change over time, as when Wowak and colleagues (2016) showed that the effect of CEO charisma varied over the course of a

CEO's tenure, becoming alternately weaker (in the case of strategic dynamism) and stronger (in the case of CSR and strategic distinctiveness relative to rivals) over time, depending on the outcome in question.

CEO tenure is not the only aspect of experience to have important consequences for firm strategy. For instance, one recent study found that CEOs with upper and lower social-class origins engaged in greater strategic risk taking than their middle-class peers (Kish-Gephart and Campbell, 2015). Career histories also play a role in shaping executives' decisions, as CEOs with more diverse work backgrounds (which covaries with openness to experience) are more likely to engage in year-over-year strategic change while also favoring strategies that deviate more widely from industry norms (Crossland et al., 2014). Scholars have also explored the firm-level implications of executive educational experience, as when Troy, Smith, and Domino (2011) offered evidence that CEOs without business degrees are more likely to rationalize accounting fraud as an acceptable decision. According to the authors, this tendency is attributable to these CEOs being relatively less knowledgeable about accounting fundamentals, the monitoring role of the board, and the potential repercussions of financial misconduct.

Managerial discretion

To understand the implications of strategic leadership for organizations and their stakeholders, it is necessary to first consider the extent to which corporate leaders can meaningfully influence firm strategy and, by extension, firm performance. This is the key idea underlying the concept of managerial discretion, or latitude of action, which Hambrick and Finkelstein (1987) introduced as a way to bridge opposing views of managers, either as the central drivers of firm strategy (e.g., the strategic choice perspective [Andrews, 1971]) or as interchangeable pieces whose influence on strategy pales in comparison to inertial and institutional forces (e.g., the population ecology perspective [Hannan and Freeman, 1977]). The reality is that executives vary widely in their capacity to affect change in their organizations, and research on managerial discretion attempts to gain insight into when and why some executives—especially CEOs—matter more than others.

Discretion, which is at its highest in situations characterized by substantial means-ends ambiguity and a relative absence of constraint, is thought to emanate from three sources: the environment (e.g., industry, national context), the internal organization (e.g., inertial forces, resource availability), and the executive him- or herself (e.g., locus of control, cognitive complexity). Surprisingly little research has examined discretion as a dependent variable, though, as most studies conceptualize the construct as an antecedent (e.g., greater discretion leads to higher CEO pay [Finkelstein and Boyd, 1998]) or as a moderator (for instance, the relationship between poor performance and CEO dismissal is stronger in high-discretion contexts [Crossland and Chen, 2013]). But scholars have begun to address this absence. For instance, Parker, Krause, and Devers (2019) developed a model exploring the relationship between firm reputation and executives' perceived discretion. In another example, Gupta, Nadkarni, and Mariam (2018) demonstrated that CEO personality traits such as extraversion and narcissism are positively associated with both perceived and actual discretion. More work here is needed, but these studies are indicative of progress.

A more typical approach to studying discretion conceptualizes it as an independent variable. Some of this research focuses on CEOs' impact on performance, as when Hambrick and Quigley (2014) found evidence of a stronger "CEO effect" (e.g., the proportion of variance in firm performance attributable to individual CEOs) in higher-discretion industries than in lower-discretion industries. This is also a central theme in studies of national-level discretion (Crossland and Hambrick, 2011), which suggest that institutional factors such as individualism and tolerance of uncertainty influence the degree to which CEOs matter for firm performance.

The other common approach involves modeling discretion as a moderator (or less frequently, a mediator) of another relationship or set of relationships. Numerous studies have shown that discretion amplifies the association between executive attributes and firm outcomes (Wangrow et al., 2015)—which makes sense, given that executives' characteristics can only manifest in firm strategies when executives have the leeway to steer the firm in their preferred direction. When executives' hands are tied, on the other hand, their personal values and preferences are relatively inconsequential for firm outcomes. Most of this research has focused on CEOs, but not all. For instance, one recent study found that firms with female chief financial officers (CFOs) had a lower likelihood of financial misreporting, and that this relationship was more pronounced in situations characterized by greater discretion (as reflected in governance arrangements) (Gupta et al., 2020). As strategic leadership researchers increasingly focus on non-CEO members of TMTs and their influences on firm outcomes—a trend we applaud—it will be important to account for differences in the extent to which these individuals matter for firm strategy and performance (cf. Finkelstein, 1992).

Executive compensation

Last, the topic of executive compensation has long been central in the strategic leadership domain, and—perhaps more than any of the topics discussed so far—is truly multidisciplinary in nature. One major stream of research in this domain examines executive pay as the dependent variable, while another focuses on executives' responses to pay (i.e., where pay is the independent variable). The first of these streams deals mainly with corporate governance, and as such is discussed at more length in that Part of this book. Here we focus primarily on research investigating the consequences of executive pay (for a more comprehensive review, see Wowak, Gomez-Mejia, and Steinbach, 2017).

Much of the research in the executive compensation domain draws upon agency theory (Jensen and Meckling, 1976), which centers on the conflicts of interest between managers and owners (shareholders) that characterize most public corporations. According to this view, equity-based pay (e.g., restricted stock and stock options) promotes shareholder value–creating decisions and actions, as the executive's pay is linked to the company's stock price. While some studies offer support for this idea—for example, higher CEO pay-performance sensitivity ("delta") has been found to lead to more optimal outsourcing decisions (Sedatole, Vrettos, and Widener, 2012)—the evidence remains decidedly mixed. For example, TMT equity pay has been associated with shorter-term temporal orientation in managers (as measured by asset durability), which runs counter to agency theory predictions (Souder and Bromiley, 2012). Along these lines, scholars have found evidence of a negative relationship between inside stock ownership and capital investment (Panousi and Papanikolaou, 2012). These are just a few of many examples of mixed/contradictory findings in this literature, which points to the complex motivational properties of pay.

Among the other theoretical perspectives in this area are the behavioral agency model (BAM) (Wiseman and Gomez-Mejia, 1998) and stewardship theory (Davis, Schoorman, and Donaldson, 1997). The BAM differs from agency theory in its emphasis on executive loss aversion (as opposed to agency theory's assumption of risk aversion), which refers to the idea from prospect theory (Kahneman and Tversky, 1979) that people have a stronger desire to avoid losses than to realize equivalent gains. As such, to the extent that specific pay instruments compel executives to perceive themselves to be in a loss frame (e.g., abundant out-of-the-money options) or a gain frame (e.g., abundant in-the-money options), their decisions—and particularly the risk profiles of those decisions—will fluctuate accordingly (Martin, Gomez-Mejia, and Wiseman, 2013). Stewardship theory, on the other hand, downplays the role of extrinsic motivation in influencing CEOs' and top executives' decisions, assuming instead that their intrinsic desires to serve their organizations will reduce the need for strict monitoring and incentive-laden pay arrangements. This perspective has not received as much attention as the others, although scholars have explored stewardship theory as it applies in the family firm context (Le Breton-Miller, Miller, and Lester, 2011).

The other notable stream worth mentioning concerns the TMT-level implications of pay dispersion, or differences in pay between and among members of the TMT. Studies in this area often explore the tension between (a) equity theory (Adams, 1963) / social comparison theory (Festinger, 1954), which predicts that large pay differentials will cause lower-paid executives to perceive unfair treatment, and (b) tournament theory (Lazear and Rosen, 1981), which argues that such large differences serve as motivation for lower-paid executives to work harder to attain higher levels of pay and promotions. While early studies tended to focus on straightforward tests of the two (e.g., O'Reilly, Main, and Crystal, 1988), recent work has taken more of a contingency approach in examining the situational characteristics that determine whether one or the other applies more readily in a given context (e.g., Ridge, Aime, and White, 2015; Ridge, Hill, and Aime, 2017).

What's Needed Next?

Our discussion of recent research developments indicates the richness of the strategic leadership domain, highlighting that many opportunities lie ahead for scholars interested in the effects of top executives on business outcomes. In our remaining pages we identify several particularly promising research avenues. Recognizing that others will have their own sensible ideas for future priorities, we are drawn to topics that we believe have been understudied relative to their apparent theoretical and practical importance.

Reconciliation of managerial discretion and managerial attributions

There is a major need for research that pairs, or reconciles, two of the most fundamental constructs in strategic leadership theory: managerial discretion and managerial attributions. Stated concisely, managerial discretion refers to the degree to which managers matter, while managerial attributions refer to the degree to which observers, especially stakeholders, *believe* managers matter. We might reasonably expect the two to covary, with stakeholders pointing at managers, particularly CEOs, in proportion to how much discretion they possess (Quigley, Crossland, and Campbell, 2017). But there are reasons to expect that the relationship might actually be slight, as stakeholders may erroneously inflate, or conversely deflate, their assessments of the potency of company leaders—with major implications for an array of important phenomena.

The concept of managerial attributions was brought to the fore by Meindl, Ehrlich, and Dukerich (1985), particularly through their ideas and evidence regarding "the romance of leadership." In a series of archival and lab studies, the authors showed that observers attribute extreme organizational performance outcomes, both positive and negative, to the actions of managers. Observers tend to blame managers for very poor performance and credit managers for great performance, while pointing to other factors, such as the environment or organizational constraints, when performance is neutral—even when provided no information about any of these potentially causal factors.

Regrettably, these preliminary ideas about managerial attributions have largely lain dormant since Meindl and colleagues proposed them. This void is striking because a host of major strategic leadership phenomena hinge on stakeholders' attributions about managers, particularly CEOs. For example, compensation adjustments and dismissals are reflections of post hoc attributions regarding CEOs (Wowak,

Hambrick, and Henderson, 2011), as are journalists' glowing portrayals (or criticisms) of CEOs (Hayward, Rindova, and Pollock, 2004). Similarly, CEOs' initial pay packages and boards' payments to executive search firms are reflections of ex ante attributions regarding CEOs (Quigley, Wowak, and Crossland, 2020).

Ostensibly, these attributions should bear a strong correspondence to the actual degree of discretion the CEOs possess. For example, CEOs in high-discretion countries should be more subject to praise and blame than those in low-discretion countries (Crossland and Hambrick, 2011); CEOs in high-discretion industries should be held more responsible than those in low-discretion industries (Finkelstein and Hambrick, 1990); and CEOs operating under high-discretion governance arrangements should be feted and vilified to a greater degree than those operating under more restrictive governance arrangements (Adams, Almeida, and Ferreira, 2005). But do these strong relationships exist?

Our prediction is that CEO discretion and CEO attributions do indeed covary, but far less than they logically should. On the one hand, stakeholders may have a rough or implicit sense of the discretion afforded a given CEO, which they imprecisely factor into their attributions regarding the CEO. On the other hand, though, stakeholders are susceptible to a host of psychological biases, including the romance of leadership, and are furthermore subject to impression management tactics by CEOs (Graffin, Haleblian, and Kiley, 2016; Westphal *et al.*, 2012), such that their attributions about CEOs may bear only a faint relationship with the actual degree of discretion that CEOs possess. Understanding of such mismatches between managerial attributions and managerial discretion could help improve insights about human gullibility regarding leaders, fairness toward leaders, and other matters of great consequence.

Heightened attention to strategic leaders as leaders

In our estimation, far more attention needs to be paid to strategic leaders in their roles as, well, organizational leaders. The great majority of strategic leadership studies examines the effects of CEOs or TMTs on quantum strategic actions—acquisitions, divestitures, research and development (R&D) spending, technology adoption, and so on—as well as the effects of such actions on firm performance. However, if we bear in mind that firm performance is shaped by the talents and motivations of employees at all levels (Cowherd and Levine, 1992), along with the fact that many strategic insights originate in the middle ranks of organizations (Burgelman, 1996), it becomes exceedingly clear that there exists a great need to understand the roles of strategic leaders in stimulating and directing the collective energy of their employee populations.

Indeed, strategic leadership scholars can bring their understanding of macro phenomena to the study by executive charisma, executive symbolism, organizational culture, and change leadership (e.g., Gioia and Chittipeddi, 1991; Hambrick and Lovelace, 2018; Huy, Corley, and Kraatz, 2014). Perhaps in collaboration with micro scholars, strategic leadership researchers should redouble their efforts to shed light on how some CEOs, far more than others, are able to generate exceptional energy and commitment throughout their organizations.

As part of this agenda, researchers might fruitfully cast their lights on the relationships between CEOs and their top management teams. CEOs vary greatly in how they configure and motivate their TMTs. For example, some CEOs try to tightly integrate their TMTs, while others prefer to engage in bilateral exchanges with individual executives and for the overall executive group to be relatively atomistic (Hambrick, 1994; Simsek *et al.*, 2005). Some CEOs are eager to have chief operating officers (COOs), who oversee line operating units (and their associated executives), while others strongly resist having COOs, preferring to directly oversee all TMT members themselves (Hambrick and Cannella, 2004). We can readily envision that these respective choices, along with other unexplored aspects of CEO-TMT dynamics, greatly affect TMT members' outlooks and actions, in ways that cascade throughout organizational ranks. More broadly, we encourage exploration of the interpersonal leadership behaviors of top executives.

Greater understanding of the antecedents of strategic leadership phenomena

Strategy scholars have an abiding interest in the consequences, particularly the performance consequences, of whatever phenomena they are studying. And similarly, strategic leadership scholars have focused overwhelmingly on the outcomes associated with the various CEO and TMT attributes they have examined. This focus on outcomes, however, has squeezed out needed attention to *antecedents* of strategic leadership phenomena. In short, we need to know much more about why CEOs and TMTs look the way they do in the first place.

Consider the classic question of whether an insider or an outsider will be selected as a given company's CEO. Folklore has always said that outsiders will tend to be chosen when performance is poor and the board wants change. The reality of it is more complex (Boeker and Goodstein, 1993; Dalton and Kesner, 1985), however, and the conventional wisdom may be less valid today than ever. The executive labor market has become so fluid, and outside hires so prevalent, that such appointments are no longer necessarily signals of board frustration with the status quo. Instead, boards might hire outsider CEOs for any number of reasons, including a simple lack of any suitable internal candidates. That is, the appointment of outsider CEOs might be due more to poor succession planning than to a desire for strategic change. Of course, the antecedents of such CEO selections greatly affect their consequences.

Similar questions can be asked about numerous other CEO attributes. For instance, how does a highly narcissistic individual become a high-level executive? And what prompts a board to select such a person as the company's leader? Under what circumstances do boards appoint their CFOs, who typically lack operating experience, to be

CEOs? What gives rise to the selection of someone who has already been a CEO elsewhere as a company's new leader? In every one of these illustrative cases, an improved understanding of underlying antecedents will allow for more accurate predictions of consequences.

Counterpart questions can be asked about the composition and processes of top management teams. For example, what determines turnover rates within TMTs? What determines the proportion of women in TMTs? What enters into a given CEO's decision to appoint a COO to oversee internal operational affairs? What are the factors that influence whether executives' bonuses are largely based on company-wide performance versus subunit performance? Why do some TMTs engage in a great deal of face-to-face interactions, while others rarely meet? Here again, answers to these questions about determinants are essential for framing questions about outcomes.

The attributes of business leaders are not randomly distributed properties, but instead are traceable to complex institutional, social psychological, and instrumental forces. These underlying forces need to be better understood. We are suggesting a need for far more than the inclusion of now-obligatory instrumental variables for handling endogeneity, or inclusion of cursory first-stage models in two-stage analyses. Instead, we are proposing the need for focused theorizing about why CEOs and TMTs possess the attributes they do. Only after we begin generating such insights will we be able to cogently explore or interpret potential consequences.

Temporal dynamics of strategic leadership phenomena

For the most part, strategic leadership researchers have adopted static perspectives in their studies of executives, even though the outlooks and orientations of CEOs and TMTs change considerably over time. Accordingly, there is an abundant need to know more about the temporal dynamics—ebbs and flows, learning and obsolescence, tests and achievements—that business leaders encounter during their time in office.

The most apparent opportunity is to leverage and advance prior theories about the evolution of CEOs' mindsets as their tenures advance, or "the seasons" of CEOs' tenures (Hambrick and Fukutomi, 1991; Miller, 1991). For instance, we thus far have only relatively coarse insights about the mounting rigidity of CEOs over their time in office, but we still lack deep understanding of why this occurs or how it might be prevented or forestalled. Recently adding to this puzzle, Graf-Vlachy, Bundy, and Hambrick (2020) demonstrated that the cognitive complexity of CEOs increases monotonically with tenure, which is distinctly at odds with the prevailing depiction of long-tenured CEOs as cognitively impoverished. It is intriguing to consider the possibility that cognitive simplicity is an aid to action (and to getting others to act), and that long-tenured CEOs become behaviorally rigid because their thoughts are too complex.

Relatedly, we know far too little about how CEOs navigate the early days of their tenures. Gabarro (1987) documented the extraordinary pressures on new leaders to become oriented and gain legitimacy. Since then, researchers have confirmed that CEOs are highly vulnerable to dismissal in their early years in office (Fredrickson, Hambrick, and Baumrin, 1988; Zhang, 2008). So far, however, we have very little granularity in our understanding of the available options, or tendencies, of new CEOs to surmount their early vulnerability. These options might encompass strategic and staffing moves, information gathering, expectation-setting tactics, or other impression management endeavors.

As a logical extension of focusing on the evolution of CEOs over time, researchers might also focus on the evolution of top management teams (e.g., Ma and Seidl, 2018). Unlike CEOs, TMTs do not have clear starting points. TMTs are thus more difficult to assess temporally, but perhaps new insights can be gained by considering TMTs over the course of CEOs' tenures. After all, if CEOs traverse their own "seasons," these must surely be transmitted into the evolving makeup and dynamics of their TMTs over time. Moreover, CEOs tend to have strong personal preferences regarding TMT composition and processes (e.g., Crossland *et al.*, 2014; Simsek *et al.*, 2005), which should become more and more vividly manifested as CEOs' own tenures advance. In short, there is considerable opportunity to study the temporal dynamics of CEOs and their teams.

New theorizing about CEOs and sociopolitical influence of firms

Recognizing that business corporations have considerable influence over governmental policies, scholars in multiple fields have sought to assess the role of firms in the political arena (e.g., Cooper, Gulen, and Ovtchinnikov, 2010; Hillman and Hitt, 1999; Ridge, Ingram, and Hill, 2017; Sheng, Zhou, and Li, 2011). So far, the prevailing logic has been that firms promote political outcomes that suit their economic interests. Only recently have researchers considered the dual premises that (1) company executives, not inanimate "firms," make decisions about corporate political activity (CPA), and (2) these executives inject their own personal values, as well as their assessments of various stakeholders' values, into their judgments about CPA (summarized in Hambrick and Wowak, 2021). In short, strategic leadership scholars are now bringing their lenses to the study of the sociopolitical influence of firms. Far more such work needs to be done.

The most direct opportunity is to examine the role of executives' personal values in shaping corporate lobbying and political donation actions, the mainstay behaviors of interest to CPA scholars. There is already some tantalizing evidence that CEOs direct their firms' political action committee (PAC) contributions in ways that align with their personal political ideologies (Chin *et al.*, 2013), but far more needs to be known about how business leaders use their positions as platforms to pursue their own public policy agendas.

Additionally, there is abundant opportunity to analyze CEOs' decisions to engage in a relatively new and increasingly prevalent form of political influence: CEO activism. In recent years, CEOs have increasingly spoken out about social matters, some of which are only tangentially connected to their firms' near-term prosperity, such as transgender rights, gun control, same-sex marriage, and race relations (e.g., Chatterji and Toffel, 2018, 2019; Mayer, 2017; *The Economist*, 2017; Weber Shandwick / KRC Research, 2017). It is important to know more about the motivations driving these (often risky) behaviors as well as their consequences—for the CEOs themselves, their firms, and society (Hambrick and Wowak, 2021).

In a related vein, it is essential to know more about how business leaders establish and leverage coalitions for pursuing their political agendas. As Mizruchi (2013) documented, America's business leaders once spoke with a unified voice when it came to political matters. But their dominant vehicles for doing so—the Committee for Economic Development and (less so) the U.S. Chamber of Commerce—have lost much of their potency, and modern executives tend to operate through narrower, more factionalized alliances when attempting to advance political agendas. What are the foundations of these alliances? To what extent do they reflect the ideologies of the business leaders who constitute them, rather than strictly the instrumental aims of their firms? What are the tactics of such alliances? And how effective are they?

CEOs might end up creating alliances to save capitalism from itself. Just recently, 181 CEOs of major American firms, under the auspices of the Business Roundtable, signed a public letter asserting the importance of non-owner stakeholders in the American capitalist system (Business Roundtable, 2019). Widely seen as a collective response to mounting disdain for the current system, especially among young Americans, this letter engendered various responses (Kotter, 2019; Mackintosh, 2020; Rosenbaum, 2019). Some applauded it, seeing the statement as a sign that business leaders are ready for major reform of America's system of capitalism. Others saw the letter as hollow rhetoric, an effort to forestall reforms and buy time. How this initiative will play out remains to be seen, but it clearly illustrates the potential for business leaders to influence sociopolitical outcomes. In turn, it illustrates the potential for strategic leadership scholars to contribute substantially toward understanding such activities.

Conclusion

An organization's strategy is inextricably linked with the people who devise and implement it, and the myriad studies focusing in one way or another on the individuals atop the firm are a testament to the prominent position of strategic leadership within the broader field of strategy. We have outlined a number of avenues that scholars might pursue in the interest of moving the domain forward, but these are just the tip of the iceberg, as our ideas are—like the strategies we study—the product of our own personal preferences, biases, and limitations. As is the case within organizations, only through the collective efforts of many is true progress realized.

References

Adams JS. 1963. Toward an understanding of inequity. *Journal of Abnormal and Social Psychology* 67: 422–436.

Adams RB, Almeida H, Ferreira D. 2005. Powerful CEOs and their impact on corporate performance. *Review of Financial Studies* 18(4): 1403–1432.

Andrews KR. 1971. *The Concept of Corporate Strategy*. Dow Jones-Irwin: Homewood, IL.

Boeker W, Goodstein J. 1993. Performance and successor choice: the moderating effects of governance and ownership. *Academy of Management Journal* 36(1): 172–186.

Burgelman RA. 1996. A process model of strategic business exit: implications for an evolutionary perspective on strategy. *Strategic Management Journal* 17: 193–214.

Business Roundtable. 2019. Business Roundtable redefines the purpose of a corporation to promote "an economy that serves all Americans." https://www.businessroundtable.org/business-roundtable-redefines-the-purpose-of-a-corporation-to-promote-an-economy-that-serves-all-americans [21 January 2020].

Carpenter MA, Golden BR. 1997. Perceived managerial discretion: a study of cause and effect. *Strategic Management Journal* 18(3): 187–206.

Chatterji AK, Toffel MW. 2018. The new CEO activists. *Harvard Business Review* 96: 78–89.

Chatterji AK, Toffel MW. 2019. Assessing the impact of CEO activism. *Organization and Environment* 32(2): 159–185.

Chin MK, Hambrick DC, Treviño LK. 2013. Political ideologies of CEOs: the influence of executives' values on corporate social responsibility. *Administrative Science Quarterly* 58(2): 197–232.

Chin MK, Semadeni M. 2017. CEO political ideologies and pay egalitarianism within top management teams. *Strategic Management Journal* 38(8): 1608–1625.

Christensen DM, Dhaliwal DS, Boivie S, Graffin SD. 2015. Top management conservatism and corporate risk strategies: evidence from managers' personal political orientation and corporate tax avoidance. *Strategic Management Journal* 36(12): 1918–1938.

Cooper MJ, Gulen H, Ovtchinnikov AV. 2010. Corporate political contributions and stock returns. *Journal of Finance* 65(2): 687–724.

Cowherd DM, Levine DI. 1992. Product quality and pay equity between lower-level employees and top management: an investigation of distributive justice theory. *Administrative Science Quarterly* 37(2): 302–320.

Crossland C, Chen G. 2013. Executive accountability around the world: sources of cross-national variation in firm performance–CEO dismissal sensitivity. *Strategic Organization* 11(1): 78–109.

Crossland C, Hambrick DC. 2011. Differences in managerial discretion across countries: how nation-level institutions affect the degree to which CEOs matter. *Strategic Management Journal* 32(8): 797–819.

Crossland C, Zyung J, Hiller NJ, Hambrick DC. 2014. CEO career variety: effects on firm-level strategic and social novelty. *Academy of Management Journal* 57(3): 652–674.

Dalton DR, Kesner IF. 1985. Organizational performance as an antecedent of inside/outside chief executive succession: an empirical assessment. *Academy of Management Journal* 28(4): 749–762.

Davis JH, Schoorman FD, Donaldson L. 1997. Toward a stewardship theory of management. *Academy of Management Review* 22(1): 20–47.

Delgado-García JB, De La Fuente-Sabaté JM. 2010. How do CEO emotions matter? Impact of CEO affective traits on strategic and performance conformity in the Spanish banking industry. *Strategic Management Journal* 31(5): 562–574.

Feldman ER. 2014. Legacy divestitures: motives and implications. *Organization Science* 25(3): 815–832.

Festinger L. 1954. A theory of social comparison processes. *Human Relations* 7: 117–140.

Finkelstein S. 1992. Power in top management teams: dimensions, measurement, and validation. *Academy of Management Journal* 35(3): 505–538.

Finkelstein S, Boyd BK. 1998. How much does the CEO matter? The role of managerial discretion in the setting of CEO compensation. *Academy of Management Journal* 41(2): 179–199.

Finkelstein S, Hambrick DC. 1990. Top-management-team tenure and organizational outcomes: the moderating role of managerial discretion. *Administrative Science Quarterly* 35(3): 484–503.

Finkelstein S, Hambrick DC. 1996. *Strategic Leadership: Top Executives and Their Effects on Organizations.* West: St. Paul, MN.

Finkelstein S, Hambrick DC, Cannella AA. 2009. *Strategic Leadership: Theory and Research on Executives, Top Management Teams, and Boards.* Oxford University Press: New York, NY.

Fredrickson JW, Hambrick DC, Baumrin S. 1988. A model of CEO dismissal. *Academy of Management Review* 13(2): 255–270.

Gabarro J. 1987. *The Dynamics of Taking Charge.* Harvard Business School Press: Boston, MA.

Gioia DA, Chittipeddi K. 1991. Sensemaking and sensegiving in strategic change initiation. *Strategic Management Journal* 12(6): 433–448.

Graf-Vlachy L, Bundy J, Hambrick DC. 2020. Effects of an advancing tenure on CEO cognitive complexity. *Organization Science* 31(4): 936-959.

Graffin SD, Haleblian J, Kiley JT. 2016. Ready, AIM, acquire: impression offsetting and acquisitions. *Academy of Management Journal* 59(1): 232–252.

Gupta A, Briscoe F, Hambrick DC. 2018. Evenhandedness in resource allocation: CEO ideology, organizational discretion, and firm performance. *Academy of Management Journal* 61(5): 1848–1868.

Gupta A, Nadkarni S, Mariam M. 2018. Dispositional sources of managerial discretion: CEO ideology, CEO personality, and firm strategies. *Administrative Science Quarterly* 64(4): 855–893.

Gupta A, Wowak AJ. 2017. The elephant (or donkey) in the boardroom: how board political ideology affects CEO pay. *Administrative Science Quarterly* 62(1): 1–30.

Gupta VK, Mortal S, Chakrabarty B, Guo X, Turban DB. 2020. CFO gender and financial statement irregularities. *Academy of Management Journal,* 63(3): 802-831.

Hambrick DC. 1994. Top management groups: a conceptual integration and reconsideration of the "team" label. In Staw BM, Cummings LL (eds). *Research in Organizational Behavior.* JAI Press: Greenwich, CT; 171–213.

Hambrick DC. 2007. Upper echelons theory: an update. *Academy of Management Review* 32(2): 334–343.

Hambrick DC, Abrahamson E. 1995. Assessing managerial discretion across industries: a multimethod approach. *Academy of Management Journal* 38: 1427–1441.

Hambrick DC, Cannella AA. 2004. CEOs who have COOs: contingency analysis of an unexplored structural form. *Strategic Management Journal* 25(10): 959–979.

Hambrick DC, Finkelstein S. 1987. Managerial discretion: a bridge between polar views of organizational outcomes. In *Research in Organizational Behavior,* Cummings LL, Staw BM (eds). JAI Press: Greenwich, CT; 369–406.

Hambrick DC, Fukutomi GDS. 1991. The seasons of a CEO's tenure. *Academy of Management Review* 16(4): 719–742.

Hambrick DC, Lovelace JB. 2018. The role of executive symbolism in advancing new strategic themes in organizations: a social influence perspective. *Academy of Management Review* 43(1): 110–131.

Hambrick DC, Mason PA. 1984. Upper echelons: the organization as a reflection of its top managers. *Academy of Management Review* 9(2): 193–206.

Hambrick DC, Quigley TJ. 2014. Toward more accurate contextualization of the CEO effect on firm performance. *Strategic Management Journal* 35(4): 473–491.

Hambrick DC, Wowak AJ. 2021. CEO sociopolitical activism: a stakeholder alignment model. *Academy of Management Review* 46(1): 33-59.

Hannan MT, Freeman J. 1977. The population ecology of organizations. *American Journal of Sociology* 82(5): 929–964.

Hayward MLA, Rindova VP, Pollock TG. 2004. Believing one's own press: the antecedents and consequences of CEO celebrity. *Strategic Management Journal* 25(7): 637–653.

Hillman AJ, Hitt MA. 1999. Corporate political strategy formulation: a model of approach, participation, and strategy decisions. *Academy of Management Review* 24(4): 825–842.

Huy QN, Corley KG, Kraatz MS. 2014. From support to mutiny: shifting legitimacy judgments and emotional reactions impacting the implementation of radical change. *Academy of Management Journal* 57(6): 1650–1680.

Jensen MC, Meckling WH. 1976. Theory of the firm: managerial behavior, agency costs and ownership structure. *Journal of Financial Economics* 3(4): 305–360.

Jost JT, Federico CM, Napier JL. 2009. Political ideology: its structure, functions, and elective affinities. *Annual Review of Psychology* 60(1): 307–337.

Kahneman D, Tversky A. 1979. Prospect theory: an analysis of decisions under risk. *Econometrica* 47(2): 263–291.

Kish-Gephart JJ, Campbell JT. 2015. You don't forget your roots: the influence of CEO social class background on strategic risk taking. *Academy of Management Journal* 58(6): 1614–1636.

Kotter J. 2019. This one document may have just changed Corporate America forever. MarketWatch. https://www.marketwatch.com/story/this-one-document-may-have-just-changed-corporate-america-forever-2019-09-23 [21 January 2020].

Lazear EP, Rosen S. 1981. Rank-order tournaments as optimum labor contracts. *Journal of Political Economy* 89(5): 841–864.

Le Breton-Miller I, Miller D, Lester RH. 2011. Stewardship or agency? A social embeddedness reconciliation of conduct and performance in public family businesses. *Organization Science* 22(3): 704–721.

Ma S, Seidl D. 2018. New CEOs and their collaborators: divergence and convergence between the strategic leadership constellation and the top management team. *Strategic Management Journal* 39(3): 606–638.

Mackintosh J. 2020. In stakeholder capitalism, shareholders are still king. *Wall Street Journal*. https://www.wsj.com/articles/in-stakeholder-capitalism-shareholders-are-still-king-11579462427 [21 January 2020].

Martin GP, Gomez-Mejia LR, Wiseman RM. 2013. Executive stock options as mixed gambles: revisiting the behavioral agency model. *Academy of Management Journal* 56(2): 451–472.

Mayer D. 2017. The law and ethics of CEO social activism. *Journal of Law, Business, and Ethics* 23: 21–44.

Meindl JR, Ehrlich SB, Dukerich JM. 1985. The romance of leadership. *Administrative Science Quarterly* 30(1): 78–102.

Miller D. 1991. Stale in the saddle: CEO tenure and the match between organization and environment. *Management Science* 37(1): 34–52.

Mizruchi MS. 2013. *The Fracturing of the American Corporate Elite*. Harvard University Press: Cambridge, MA.

Nadkarni S, Herrmann P. 2010. CEO personality, strategic flexibility, and firm performance: the case of the Indian business process outsourcing industry. *Academy of Management Journal* 53(5): 1050–1073.

O'Reilly CA, Main BG, Crystal GS. 1988. CEO compensation as tournament and social comparison: a tale of two theories. *Administrative Science Quarterly* 33(2): 257–274.

Ou AY, Tsui AS, Kinicki AJ, Waldman DA, Xiao Z, Song LJ. 2014. Humble chief executive officers' connections to top management team integration and middle managers' responses. *Administrative Science Quarterly* 59(1): 34–72.

Panousi V, Papanikolaou D. 2012. Investment, idiosyncratic risk, and ownership. *Journal of Finance* 67(3): 1113–1148.

Parker O, Krause R, Devers CE. 2019. How firm reputation shapes managerial discretion. *Academy of Management Review* 44(2): 254–278.

Quigley TJ, Crossland C, Campbell RJ. 2017. Shareholder perceptions of the changing impact of CEOs: market reactions to unexpected CEO deaths, 1950–2009. *Strategic Management Journal* 38(4): 939–949.

Quigley TJ, Hambrick DC. 2012. When the former CEO stays on as board chair: effects on successor discretion, strategic change, and performance. *Strategic Management Journal* 33(7): 834–859.

Quigley TJ, Wowak AJ, Crossland C. 2020. Board predictive accuracy in executive selection decisions: How do initial board perceptions of CEO quality correspond with subsequent CEO career performance? *Organization Science* 31(3): 720–741.

Ridge JW, Aime F, White MA. 2015. When much more of a difference makes a difference: social comparison and tournaments in the CEO's top team. *Strategic Management Journal* 36(4): 618–636.

Ridge JW, Hill AD, Aime F. 2017. Implications of multiple concurrent pay comparisons for top-team turnover. *Journal of Management* 43(3): 671–690.

Ridge JW, Ingram A, Hill AD. 2017. Beyond lobbying expenditures: how lobbying breadth and political connectedness affect firm outcomes. *Academy of Management Journal* 60(3): 1138–1163.

Rosenbaum E. 2019. Steve Mnuchin dissed 181 major CEOs in a new battle over the future of profits. *CNBC*. https://www.cnbc.com/2019/09/20/steve-mnuchin-disses-181-ceos-in-new-battle-over-future-of-profits.html [21 January 2020].

Sedatole KL, Vrettos D, Widener SK. 2012. The use of management control mechanisms to mitigate moral hazard in the decision to outsource. *Journal of Accounting Research* 50(2): 553–592.

Sheng S, Zhou KZ, Li JJ. 2011. The effects of business and political ties on firm performance: evidence from China. *Journal of Marketing* 75(1): 1–15.

Simsek Z, Veiga JF, Lubatkin MH, Dino RN. 2005. Modeling the multilevel determinants of top management team behavioral integration. *Academy of Management Journal* 48(1): 69–84.

Souder D, Bromiley P. 2012. Explaining temporal orientation: evidence from the durability of firms' capital investments. *Strategic Management Journal* 33(5): 550–569.

The Economist. 2017. America Inc gets woke. https://www.economist.com/news/business/21731855-left-leaning-employees-leave-many-bosses-little-choice-mount-barricades [11 January 2018].

Troy C, Smith KG, Domino MA. 2011. CEO demographics and accounting fraud: who is more likely to rationalize illegal acts? *Strategic Organization* 9(4): 259–282.

Wangrow DB, Schepker DJ, Barker VL. 2015. Managerial discretion: an empirical review and focus on future research directions. *Journal of Management* 41(1): 99–135.

Weber Shandwick / KRC Research. 2017. CEO activism in 2017: high noon in the C-suite. https://www.webershandwick.com/news/article/ceo-activism-in-2017-high-noon-in-the-c-suite [9 January 2018].

Westphal JD, Park SH, McDonald ML, Hayward MLA. 2012. Helping other CEOs avoid bad press: social exchange and impression management support among CEOs in communications with journalists. *Administrative Science Quarterly* 57(2): 217–268.

Wiseman RM, Gomez-Mejia LR. 1998. A behavioral agency model of managerial risk taking. *Academy of Management Review* 23(1): 133–153.

Wowak AJ, Gomez-Mejia LR, Steinbach AL. 2017. Inducements and motives at the top: a holistic perspective on the drivers of executive behavior. *Academy of Management Annals* 11(2): 669–702.

Wowak AJ, Hambrick DC, Henderson AD. 2011. Do CEOs encounter within-tenure settling up? A multiperiod perspective on executive pay and dismissal. *Academy of Management Journal* 54(4): 719–739.

Wowak AJ, Mannor MJ, Arrfelt M, McNamara G. 2016. Earthquake or glacier? How CEO charisma manifests in firm strategy over time. *Strategic Management Journal* 37(3): 586–603.

Zhang Y. 2008. Information asymmetry and the dismissal of newly appointed CEOs: an empirical investigation. *Strategic Management Journal* 29(8): 859–872.

6.1

TOP MANAGEMENT TEAMS

Margarethe F. Wiersema and Joshua S. Hernsberger

Introduction

The study of top management teams (TMTs) is one of the most significant streams of research in strategic management. The interest in TMTs is due to the fact that it is not just the CEO, but also the executives who report to the CEO who are responsible for the strategic and operational decisions that ultimately determine firm outcomes. Scholars have long recognized that the firm's top management plays a key role in enabling organizations with the ability to adapt to changes in their environment. While earlier work recognized that organizational decision-making is not just the domain of the firm's CEO but is influenced by a "dominant coalition" (Cyert and March, 1963), research prior to the mid-1980s was predominantly focused on the role of the CEO in determining firm strategy and performance. The upper-echelon perspective introduced by Hambrick and Mason in 1984, one of the most highly cited articles in management, provided the basis for examining how attributes of the firm's executives may influence organizational outcomes. Scholarly interest in the firm's top management continues to be an important research topic given executives' influence on strategic decision-making and firm outcomes, as well as increased media attention and activist investor scrutiny on the firm's executives.

The theoretical perspectives used in examining the firm's executives as a team stem from cognitive psychology, organizational demography theory, and social psychology research on groups. Theoretical insights gained from cognitive psychology are based on studying individual behavior to better understand cognition and mental processes. Pfeffer (1983) was the first to propose that scholars use the demographic attributes of the individuals within the group to capture underlying psychological and sociological processes that cannot be directly observed, while social psychology group research has provided significant insights into understanding both intergroup and intragroup behavior. These theoretical perspectives have provided much of the basis for TMT research over the past 35 years. The implicit assumption is that the insights gained from studying individuals and teams at lower levels of the organization are applicable at the executive level. However, it is important to recognize that a firm's executives are unlike other employees of the firm or individuals at large and that TMTs may differ from organizational teams. These differences may undermine the applicability of existing theories to examine the relationship of TMTs to firm outcomes in several respects.

First, a firm's executives represent an elite and exclusive group of individuals—each with their own set of responsibilities and decision-making authority over their domain. A firm's top management includes the chief executive officer (CEO), chief operating officer (COO), and/or president as well as the direct reports to these individuals. Executive positions can vary in terms of stature and responsibility. They include staff positions such as the chief financial officer, chief technology officer, and the chief human resources officer, as well as line positions such as the executives in charge of major businesses, who often also hold the title of CEO (e.g., Kieran Murphy, the president and CEO of General Electric Healthcare). Executives in staff roles are responsible for support functions at the corporate level, while line executives have distinct responsibilities for specific product and/or geographic markets, acting as CEOs of the business. The level of responsibility and authority of the executives who make up the TMT differs considerably from the firm's other employees according to both their titles and their compensation. Thus, members of TMTs are not comparable to the firm's other employees or individuals at large in that they are high-level executives with significant decision-making responsibility. The distinct characteristics of executives are likely to have ramifications for understanding their individual behavior as well as their team dynamics.

Second, a firm's executives may not even constitute a functioning team. A *team* is a group of individuals who are responsible for accomplishing a common task or goal, engage in frequent interaction, and report to and are evaluated by management. This characterization of a team may not always hold for TMTs. According to Hambrick (2015: 459), TMTs can be "highly fragmented" and "vary widely in the degree to which they have the properties of a 'team.'" To qualify as a team, the group of individuals must be "behaviorally integrated" in that they make decisions jointly based on communication and interaction (Hambrick, 1995). Yet, for many firms, there may be limited interaction and exchange among executives. Furthermore, different businesses within a firm can operate as silos, with little or no exchange or interaction among them. Thus, a firm's executives may not really constitute a decision-making team.

Lastly, there is the issue of the distinct characteristics of the firm's CEO, who is a member of the TMT. The CEO determines the structure and composition of the TMT in terms of the formal positions reporting to the CEO as well as the individuals assigned to these executive positions.

In this chapter, we provide a brief overview of the current state of research on TMTs. We then address limitations of this research on TMTs before proposing an agenda for future research. Our intent is to suggest avenues of scholarly inquiry to better understand how the firm's TMT, through its interactions, attributes, and behavior, influences strategic decision-making. In doing so, we hope to encourage future research that will provide practical insight on how companies and boards can have more effective executive teams.

Current State of Research

Management research interest on top management teams is predicated on the assumption that, in order to understand firm outcomes, it is important to understand the decision-makers in the organization. Research on TMTs could be broadly classified into research examining the antecedents to TMT composition and turnover, and research on the consequences of TMT composition on firm outcomes. Many studies also include an examination of factors that might moderate the relationship of interest. In examining TMT composition, there are two aspects of particular interest—the team's demographic composition and the team's structure.

With regard to TMT composition, researchers have focused on demographic attributes such as age, gender, national origin, educational level, and specialization, as well as managers' career experiences in terms of their functional background, organizational tenure, top management team tenure, and international exposure (e.g., work experience abroad). In examining the traits of the TMT, researchers use psychological theories to infer how demographic attributes are likely to influence one's cognitive perspective. For instance, age is associated with the level of risk taking. Risk aversion increases with one's age (Vroom and Pahl, 1971), while organizational tenure is linked to adherence to the status quo by leading to a commitment to past decision-making and therefore less change (Staw and Ross, 1980). Similarly, research has also found that educational level and specialization, functional background, and international exposure have a bearing on an executive's cognitive perspective (e.g., Bantel and Jackson, 1989; Takeuchi et al.2005). Thus, TMT demographic traits are used to infer the cognitive perspectives that are brought to bear on decision-making.

In addition to specific traits of the TMT, research also focuses on the relative homogeneity or heterogeneity within the TMT along particular attributes. Theoretically, greater homogeneity on a specific attribute is indicative of greater similarity among individuals on the team, resulting in interpersonal attraction (Lott and Lott, 1965), facilitating communication and thus leading to group integration (O'Reilly, Caldwell, and Barnett, 1989). Heterogeneity, on the other hand, brings diverse cognitive perspectives and increased levels of information, which facilitates greater points of views and debate (Hoffman and Maier, 1961). There is no single ideal composition with regard to the homogeneity/heterogeneity of the TMT along a specific attribute since heterogeneity may negatively impact communication within the group (Pfeffer, 1983), whereas homogeneity may result in a lack of openness to information (Lott and Lott, 1965).

With regard to TMT structure, research has predominantly focused on the size of the team, given the ramifications of size on the extent of homogeneity/heterogeneity. Larger teams, by being composed of more individuals, have the potential for greater diversity in cognitive perspectives. Team size is also likely to influence communication and coordination, with smaller teams benefiting from their diminished size. Research has indicated that the size of the executive team in large (Fortune 500) U.S. firms has increased significantly since the mid-1980s—from five to 10 direct reports to the CEO—as a result of more corporate staff positions (Guadalupe, Li, and Wulf, 2014).

Researchers have also focused on the demographic characteristics and structure of the TMT as influences on strategic decision-making. The majority of this research has focused on strategic outcomes, including the scope of the firm in terms of its global strategic posture (Carpenter and Fredrickson, 2001) and strategic change (Wiersema and Bantel, 1992), as well as firms' competitive behavior (Hambrick, Cho, and Chen, 1996). Other studies have examined the consequences of TMT composition and structure on innovation (Bantel and Jackson, 1989) and research and development (R&D) expenditures (Kor, 2006), alliance formation (Eisenhardt and Schoonhoven, 1996), and the quality and extent of the firm's financial reporting (Plockinger *et al.,* 2019). Finally, much research has examined the effect of TMT demographic composition on financial performance, where the results have been found to be equivocal (Certo *et al.,* 2006).

Research has further examined how contextual conditions may moderate the linkage between TMT demographic composition and firm outcomes. The firm's industry environment in terms of its stability, munificence, complexity, and uncertainty has been found to moderate the relationship. Similarly, the extent of managerial discretion can moderate the relationship between TMT composition and firm outcomes (Finkelstein and Hambrick, 1990). Sociocultural differences may also accentuate or diminish the effects of TMT demography on firm outcomes (Wiersema and Bird, 1993). Thus, the firm's environment and organizational context have ramifications for the degree of influence that managers exert in their organizations and the degree to which TMT composition is likely to influence firm outcomes.

In addition to the consequences of TMT demographics and structure on firm outcomes, research has also examined antecedents to the composition of the TMT. In particular, the factors that influence executive turnover have been the most frequent focus of research. Scholars in both management and finance have conducted numerous studies linking the firm's financial performance to executive turnover (e.g., Coughlan and Schmidt, 1985; Puffer and Weintrop, 1991). These studies provide strong evidence that boards take into account the financial performance of the firm, as well as investor and financial analysts' perceptions when it comes to evaluating the firm's executives. The linkage, however, can be attenuated by contextual factors as well as the board's perception as to whether to attribute poor firm performance to management or external factors beyond their control. Corporate misconduct and the social context surrounding misconduct have also been found to be a factor in explaining executive turnover (Wiersema and Zhang, 2012). Finally, similar to research on employee turnover at lower levels of the organization, dissimilarity on demographic attributes between individuals on a TMT, such as age, can lead to turnover.

Limitations of Past Research

TMT scholars rely on attributes of the team as surrogates for the psychological and sociological processes that underlie decision-making. This approach, however, cannot fully infer what transpires within TMTs. Thus, we are limited in our understanding of the underlying processes—such as communication and interaction among the firm's executives or the relative influence of certain individuals within the team, as well as the cognitive perspectives of individuals on the team. Thus, demographic attributes do not capture the actual psychological attributes of the individuals on the team nor the sociological processes that influence managerial decision-making. A recent review and critique of upper echelon theory highlights the problems in utilizing demographic attributes for inferring managerial behavior and provides an assessment of the current state of research in addressing these issues (Neely *et al.*, 2020).

One further research challenge for scholars is clarifying the question of who constitutes the firm's TMT. The TMT is generally defined as the small group of executives at the apex of the firm, consisting of the CEO and his or her direct reports (Finkelstein, Hambrick, and Cannella, 1996). However, companies vary extensively on this, with Amazon having just five executives reporting to CEO Jeff Bezos, while General Electric and General Motors each have 19 direct reports to the CEO. The wide disparity in how companies compose their TMTs makes it extremely difficult to draw inferences or generalizations about them.

There is also the issue of comparability across organizations and countries. Is the TMT of a multibusiness, global corporation comparable to the management team of a small privately owned company with few employees? Yet many TMT studies have used private, small organizations or nonprofit organizations (e.g., hospitals) as their research settings. The firm's institutional context is also likely to be important in our understanding of TMTs. Corporate governance codes, regulations, and ownership of the firm varies across countries. Most research has been conducted in the United States, where publicly traded companies with high levels of institutional investor stock ownership and boards comprising a majority of independent directors characterize the institutional context. In the rest of the world, public firm ownership is more commonly controlled by families, banks, or governments, and boards often have ownership ties—all factors that are likely to influence not just TMT decision-making but also the composition of the TMT. How similar is a TMT in Japan to that of its U.S. or European counterparts? In Japan, the firm's TMT has a formal designation, the *jomukai*. Unlike TMTs in the United States and Europe, the *jomukai* is the executive committee of the board, and thus all members of the TMT are also board directors. While it is noteworthy that TMT research seeks to have a global perspective, we should be aware of the substantial differences that may exist in institutional context that may influence the nature of the TMT as well as its ability to influence firm outcomes.

Agenda for Future Research

A key challenge for many organizations is adapting under conditions of change, which is based on the firm's *dynamic capabilities*, defined as the ability to "integrate, build, and reconfigure internal and external competencies" (Teece, Pisano, and

Shuen, 1997: 517). The literature identifies managerial human capital, managerial social capital, and managerial composition as three drivers of dynamic managerial capabilities (Adner and Helfat, 2003). Kor and Mesko (2013) further elaborate on the determination of managerial capabilities by identifying the orchestration role of the CEO in facilitating productive TMT interactions. Thus, the composition of the firm's top management and the dynamics within the team are key to understanding how firms differ in their dynamic capabilities. In what follows, we propose several avenues for research that may prove insightful in gaining a better understanding of how top management teams influence strategic decision-making and firm outcomes.

Sociocognitive properties

As our brief summary of the current state of the research has shown, many studies have linked demographic attributes of the TMT as factors influencing the team's strategic decision-making. However, in addition to demographic composition, social psychology research would suggest that, to understand intragroup behavior, one needs to understand the properties of the group in terms of its cohesiveness and structure. Cohesiveness is an important property of the TMT because it reflects how tightly knit the group is and has implications for decision-making. Group cohesiveness is influenced by interpersonal attraction and social capital, as well as by social identity. According to Lott and Lott (1965), interpersonal attraction between members of the group is a major determinant of cohesiveness. Homophily theory proposes that demographic similarity between individuals leads to enhanced interpersonal attraction (Byrne, 1971; Montoya and Horton, 2004) and to greater trust and mutual understanding (Ibarra, 1992). This can further lead to positive bias and favoritism (McPherson, Smith-Lovin, and Cook, 2001; Pulakos and Wexley, 1983). Thus, individuals favor those who are similar to themselves in terms of their background and experiences, which leads to greater interpersonal attraction and group cohesiveness.

In addition to homophily, social capital in the form of interpersonal ties from common affiliations and backgrounds may also result in interpersonal attractions due to greater levels of trust and better mutual understanding (Cross and Parker, 2004). Prior research has shown that managers with greater ties to the CEO are more likely to be promoted in Korea (Kim and Cannella, 2008), while Wiersema, Nishimura, and Suzuki (2018) found that executives' relational social capital to the CEO determines who succeeds the CEO in Japan. Greater social ties, by leading to interpersonal attraction, thus also play a role in group cohesiveness. Lastly, social identity theory (Ashforth and Mael, 1989: 20) is likely to be highly applicable in understanding TMTs since how members perceive each other is based on how they categorize themselves as well as others, based on the team members' characteristics. According to social identity theory, individuals perceived as members of the "ingroup" are viewed more favorably than nonmembers (Martin and Hewstone, 2001). Research has shown that identification with the group leads to conforming to the group's preferences, attitudes, and behavior (Hogg, 1992). Thus, sociocognitive theories of homophily, social ties, and social identity can shed light on how members of the TMT interact and relate with each other.

While research indicates that social network ties influence perceptions of minority board directors within the board (Westphal and Milton, 2000), the utilization of sociocognitive theories to study TMTs can position researchers to investigate new questions regarding the dynamics of the TMT. Specifically, based on social capital and social identity theories, who is likely to have influence within the TMT? Furthermore, what are the ramifications of in-group and out-group distinctions within the TMT on strategic decision-making? Applying sociocognitive theories of intragroup behavior to TMTs provides an opportunity to better understand team processes and the dynamics within the team that can shed light on decision-making and firm outcomes.

Who has influence within the TMT?

Prior research has shown that not all members of the TMT have an equal say—with those having greater power likely to have a greater influence (Finkelstein, 1992). While most research has focused on horizontal differences between TMT members (e.g., differences based on demographic characteristics), Bunderson and Van der Vegt (2018) highlight the importance of vertical differences between TMT members. Vertical differences refer to inequality (Blau, 1977) and can be due to hierarchies of power, status, prestige, or privilege that exist within organizations. Vertical differences are inherent in TMTs because executives who constitute the team have different responsibilities and oversight as reflected in their positions and compensation. In Japan, these distinctions can be quite important—as when certain members of the *jomukai* (the Japanese TMT) have "representative rights" that provide them with the legal right to represent the company in third-party dealings and to make decisions delegated by the firm's board. Status characteristics theory (Berger, Cohen, and Zelditch, 1972) may shed light on how vertical differences within a TMT may influence decision-making. According to this theory, differences among members of the team in terms of their status as well as their characteristics (e.g., gender, tenure, and functional expertise) can lead to deference, where individuals yield to another's opinion because they seek to climb up the hierarchy or be treated more favorably. This leads to a question of whether differences in social status may have an influence on TMT decision-making and firm outcomes.

While vertical differences may indeed lead to deference, this may be a constrained view of hierarchy (Bunderson et al., 2016). Even differences relating to functional background, education, or work experience that are typically used to examine TMT diversity can be sources of inequality within the TMT (Bunderson and Van der Vegt, 2018). Joshi and Knight (2015) propose a model of deference in teams by which one needs to examine the dyadic relationships between team members—specifically, how demographic attributes, by conferring relative status as well as contributing to the degree of similarity, influence deference between individuals within a team. Differences in influence among team members may also be due to an individual's subject expertise and its importance to the firm, as well as to the characteristics of the person and the preferences or cognitive biases of the rest of the team members. Differences in influence thus need to be considered in terms of how each individual relates to others on the TMT. A potential research question is, then, whether the possession of knowledge and expertise that the firm needs to achieve its objectives provides an executive with a basis of power and greater influence within the TMT.

While power within the management literature has been conceptualized as the property of a person based on position and title, power is also relative and can stem from interpersonal interaction and exchange. For example, as data analytics has become a critical driver of business value, chief technology officers (CTOs), once relegated to a support role function, are now important TMT members. Finally, the nature of the decision under consideration is also likely to play a role as to who will have influence. Recent work by Tang (2019) proposes and finds that, when it comes to mergers and acquisitions (M&As), corporate development executives are the ones who influence the determinants and outcomes of these important strategic decisions. Past research on TMTs has focused on attributes of the team, neglecting the fact that individuals are likely to vary as to their influence on the TMT. Research that focuses on individual executives could address questions such as, How important are certain managerial capabilities to the firm's strategy and competitiveness? Under what conditions are executives with a specific type of background or skills likely to have greater influence in strategic decision-making?

TMTs and the CEO

Research on CEOs and TMTs constitute two disparate literature streams—one focusing on a single actor, the CEO, and the other on the TMT. The CEO is a rather distinct TMT member, as the rest of the team directly reports to the CEO. Yet not much research attention has focused on the influence of the CEO on the TMT.

The CEO plays a significant role in influencing TMT composition and behavior, and the dynamics within the team. The CEO determines the organization's reporting structure in terms of the top management positions that report directly to him or her and which executives hold these positions. The CEO defines his or her TMT, as well as how frequently the team meets and the topics of discussion. Thus, the extent to which a company has a group of executives who make decisions jointly and thus function as a TMT is the CEO's call. In addition, given the position and its power, the CEO is not an equal team member and is likely to have significant influence on the level of communication, integration, and dynamics, as well as the cohesiveness of the team. Sociocognitive theories would suggest that the CEO is not likely to view all TMT members equally and that there are likely to be different levels of interpersonal attraction, which has consequences for TMT dynamics. Given these sociocognitive theories of intragroup behavior, what are the ramifications for the utilization of the TMT as a strategic decision-making body when the CEO is highly similar or dissimilar to executives on the team? Are executives who are highly similar to the CEO more likely to have the CEO's trust and thus have greater influence on strategic decisions than other TMT members?

The behavior of the TMT and its decision-making processes are also likely to be functions of the CEO's personal characteristics. Using a variety of means, scholars have assessed CEOs' personal characteristics, such as hubris, overconfidence, and narcissism. At the individual level, hubris reflects a high level of self-esteem and can lead to an overestimation of one's abilities, outcomes, and probability of success as well as fostering a risk-taking attitude (Sitkin and Pablo, 1992). Hubris reflects psychological biases of overconfidence, self-attribution, optimism, and illusion of control that will influence decision-making (March and Shapira, 1987). Research has provided strong evidence that CEO hubris influences firm decision-making (e.g., Hayward and Hambrick, 1997; Chatterjee and Hambrick, 2007). The psychological biases of the CEO are likely to influence not just decision-making but also the dynamics within the TMT. A CEO with hubris, for example, may view him- or herself as the smartest person in the room and be less willing to listen to those who provide dissenting ideas, perspectives, or opinions. Executives within the TMT are likely to adopt behaviors to cull favor and avoid interpersonal conflict with a hubristic CEO and thus be more agreeable and supportive and less likely to offer differences in opinion. As a result, executives may not relay their own knowledge when it differs from that of the CEO, leading to suboptimal decision-making. GE's acquisition of Alstom in 2015 for $13.7 billion, for example, was an abysmal blunder on the part of GE CEO Jeff Immelt, contributing to his resignation two years later. The CEO was determined to make the acquisition, despite internal analysis that the acquisition would not pencil out. As recounted in a *Fortune* article,

> The transaction has been a debacle and an embarrassment. A former senior leader recalls that as GE Power cratered, "People looked at us and said, 'You've been in this business a hundred years, right?'" GE nonetheless defended the deal stoutly as long as Immelt was around. Then, a few weeks after he stepped down as board chairman, Flannery acknowledged what everyone already knew, telling investors, "Alstom has clearly performed below our expectations, clearly. I don't need to tell you that." (Colvin, 2018)

Given the power and position of the CEO, the personality of the individual can have a significant influence on all aspects of the firm, including the TMT. The CEO, to a large extent, determines the composition of the TMT, and not surprisingly, CEO succession lead to changes to the TMT (see Hutzschenreuter, Kleindienst, and Greger [2012] for a review). How the CEO's personality influences the composition and structure of the TMT is an unexplored research domain. Thus, we propose that scholars investigate the questions, How does the CEO's personality influence the selection of executives to the TMT? Are hubristic CEOs more likely to choose executives who are similar in perspectives and background to themselves and less likely to favor the appointment of executives with capabilities and perspectives that differ? And if so, what are the ramifications for strategic decision-making?

The composition of the TMT is determined by the CEO and thus reflects his or her attention and focus, which we know from theory is likely to influence decision-making (Ocasio, 2011). Examining how the composition of the TMT has changed at Google over time, for example, reflects significant changes in the company's strategic focus and the breadth and scope of issues that it deems important. A change in leadership at the top can also lead to subsequent changes in the firm's TMT. This effect is especially evident when an external CEO is appointed, as he or she seeks to assemble an executive team not involved with past decision-making. This occurred, for example, when Dara Khosrowshahi became CEO of Uber in 2017 after founder Travis Kalanick was forced aside by the board. Research could address the question, how does CEO succession have an impact on TMT composition and the ability of the firm to adapt to changing competitive conditions?

The managerial human and social capital and cognition residing in the TMT are the underlying drivers of the firm's dynamic managerial capabilities (Adner and Helfat, 2003). The past experiences, knowledge, and skills of the individuals in the TMT represent the stock of the firm's strategic human capital, which, along with their social capital and cognitive perspectives, influence decision-making, which in turn determines the firm's competitive strategy and performance. By determining the composition of the TMT, the CEO alters the firm's dynamic managerial capabilities and provides the means by which the firm will compete and adapt to a changing contextual environment. Thus, we propose that scholars address the question, how do the CEO's personality and personal attributes influence who is selected to the TMT?

In addition to determining the composition of the TMT, the CEO plays a significant role in influencing TMT dynamics. Shedding light on the interplay of the CEO and TMT offers an opportunity to provide insight into the behavioral context operating within TMTs. This potential avenue of research can address the questions, How do the CEO's personality and characteristics influence the behavior of the TMT? Do certain types of CEOs have more effective TMTs? Given the increased scrutiny, as well as the recognized importance, of the firm's leadership, greater understanding of the CEO's influence on the composition of the TMT and the dynamics within the team present areas that deserve greater scholarly inquiry.

Conclusion

Our chapter has provided a brief overview of the literature on TMTs, highlighting the limitations of past studies and proposing an agenda for research that identifies some avenues that have been relatively unexplored. Despite the importance of better understanding the impact of the firm's leadership on strategic decision-making and firm outcomes, scholars face some significant challenges, such as the difficulty of gaining access to executives, the problem of relying on demographic attributes as surrogates for cognitive perspectives and group behavior of the TMT, and the fact that there is a lack of consistency across firms in how the TMT is defined or the degree to which its members make decisions as a team. These issues are not easily overcome, given that the number of direct reports to the CEO has expanded over time (Guadalupe, Li, and Wulf, 2014), and that some of the CEO's advisers may actually be outsiders to the firm rather than the firm's top executives (Ma and Seidl, 2018). Understanding strategic decision-making within organizations has never been an easy task. However, in light of the increased scrutiny on firms' leadership, and the pressures that firms face to meet the various demands from their constituents, a renewed focus on examining firms' top management is warranted.

References

Adner R, Helfat CE. 2003. Corporate effects and dynamic managerial capabilities. *Strategic Management Journal* 24(10): 1011–1025.

Ashforth BE, Mael F. 1989. Social identity theory and the organization. *Academy of Management Journal* 14(1): 20–39.

Bantel KA, Jackson SE. 1989. Top management and innovations in banking: does the composition of the top team make a difference? *Strategic Management Journal* 10(1): 107–124.

Berger J, Cohen B, Zelditch M. 1972. Status characteristics and social interaction. *American Sociological Review* 37(3): 241–255.

Blau PM. 1977. *Inequality and Heterogeneity: A Primitive Theory of Social Structure.* Free Press: New York, NY.

Bunderson JS, Van der Vegt GS. 2018. Diversity and inequality in management teams: a review and integration of research on vertical and horizontal member differences. *Annual Review of Organizational Psychology and Organizational Behavior* 5: 47–73.

Bunderson JS, Van Der Vegt GS, Cantimur Y, Rink F. 2016. Different views of hierarchy and why they matter: hierarchy as inequality or as cascading influence. *Academy of Journal* 59(4): 1265–1289.

Byrne D. 1971. *The Attraction Paradigm.* Academic Press: New York, NY.

Carpenter M, Fredrickson J. 2001. Top management teams, global strategic posture, and the moderating role of uncertainty. *Academy of Management Journal* 44(3): 533–545.

Certo T, Lester R, Dalton C, Dalton D. 2006. Top management teams, strategy, and financial performance: a meta-analytic examination. *Journal of Management Studies* 43(4): 813–839.

Chatterjee A, Hambrick DC. 2007. It's all about me: narcissistic chief executive officers and their effects on company strategy and performance. *Administrative Science Quarterly* 52(3): 351–386.

Colvin, G. 2018. What the hell happened at GE? *Fortune Magazine* 24 May. https://fortune.com/longform/ge-decline-what-the-hell-happened/

Coughlan AT, Schmidt RM. 1985. Executive compensation, management turnover, and firm performance. *Journal of Accounting and Economics* 7: 43–66.

Cross RL, Parker A. 2004. *The Hidden Power of Social Networks: Understanding How Work Really Gets Done in Organizations.* Harvard Business School Press: Boston, MA.

Cyert RM, March JG. 1963. *A Behavioral Theory of the Firm.* Prentice-Hall: Englewood Cliffs, NJ.

Eisenhardt K, Schoonhoven C. 1996. Resource-based view of strategic alliance formation: strategic and social effects in entrepreneurial firms. *Organization Science* 7(2): 136–150.

Finkelstein S. 1992. Power in top management teams: dimensions, measurement, and validation. *Academy of Management Journal* 35(3): 505–538.

Finkelstein S, Hambrick D. 1990. Top management team tenure and organizational outcomes: the moderating role of managerial discretion. *Administrative Science Quarterly* 35(3): 484–503.

Finkelstein S, Hambrick D, Canella A. 1996. *Strategic Leadership: Top Executives and Their Effects on Organizations*. West Publishing Co.: Minneapolis, MN.

Guadalupe M, Li H, Wulf J. 2014. Who lives in the C-suite? Organizational structure and the division of labor in top management. *Management Science* 60(4): 824–844.

Hambrick DC. 1995. Fragmentation and the other problems CEOs have with their top management teams. *California Management Review* 37(3): 110–127.

Hambrick DC. 2015. Top management teams. In *Wiley Encyclopedia of Management*, Flood PC, Freeney Y (eds). https://doi.org/10.1002/9781118785317.weom110276

Hambrick D, Cho TS, Chen M. 1996. The influence of top management team heterogeneity on firms' competitive moves. *Administrative Science Quarterly* 41(4): 659–684.

Hambrick DC, Mason PA. 1984. Upper echelons: the organization as a reflection of its top managers. *Academy of Management Review* 9: 193–206.

Hayward MLA, Hambrick D. 1997. Explaining the premiums paid for large acquisitions: evidence of CEO hubris. *Administrative Science Quarterly* 42(1): 103–127.

Hoffman LR, Maier NRF. 1961. Quality and acceptance of problem solutions by members of homogeneous and heterogeneous groups. *Journal of Abnormal and Social Psychology* 62(2): 401–407.

Hogg MA. 1992. *The Social Psychology of Group Cohesiveness: From Attraction to Social Identity*. Harvester Wheatsheaf: London, U.K.

Hutzschenreuter T, Kleindienst I, Greger C. 2012. How new leaders affect strategic change following a succession event: a critical review of the literature. *Leadership Quarterly* 23(5): 729–755.

Ibarra H.1992. Homophily and differential returns: sex differences in network structure and access in an advertising firm. *Administrative Science Quarterly* 37(3): 422–447.

Joshi A, Knight AP. 2015. Who defers to whom and why? Dual pathways linking demographic differences and dyadic deference to team effectiveness. *Academy of Management Journal* 58(1): 59–84.

Kim Y, Cannella AA. 2008. Toward a social capital theory of director selection. *Corporate Governance: An International Review* 16(4): 282–293.

Kor Y. 2006. Direct and interaction effects of top management team and board compositions on R&D investment strategy. *Strategic Management Journal* 27(11): 1091–1999.

Kor YY, Mesko A. 2013. Dynamic managerial capabilities: configuration and orchestration of top executives' capabilities and the firm's dominant logic. *Strategic Management Journal* 34(2): 233–244.

Lott AJ, Lott BE. 1965. Group cohesiveness as interpersonal attraction: a review of relationships with antecedent and consequent variables. *Psychological Bulletin* 64(4): 259–309.

Ma S, Seidl D. 2018. New CEOs and their collaborators: divergence and convergence between the strategic leadership constellation and the top management team. *Strategic Management Journal* 39(3): 606–638.

March JG, Shapira Z. 1987. Managerial perspectives on risk and risk taking. *Management Science* 33(11): 1404–1418.

Martin R, Hewstone M. 2001. Conformity and independence in groups: Majorities and minorities. In *Blackwell Handbook of Social Psychology: Group Processes*, Hogg MA, Tindale RS (eds). Blackwell Publishers: Malden, MA; 209–234.

McPherson M, Smith-Lovin L, Cook JM. 2001. Birds of a feather: homophily in social networks. *Annual Review of Sociology* 27(1): 415–444.

Montoya RM, Horton RS. 2004. On the importance of cognitive evaluation as a determinant of interpersonal attraction. *Journal of Personality and Social Psychology* 86(5): 696–712.

Neely BH, Lovelace JB, Cowen AP, Hiller NJ. 2020. Metacritiques of upper echelons theory: verdicts and recommendations for future research. *Journal of Management* 46(6): 1029–1062.

Ocasio W. 2011. Attention to attention. *Organization Science* 22: 1121–1367.

O'Reilly C, Caldwell D, Barnett W. 1989. Work group demography, social integration, and turnover. *Administrative Science Quarterly* 34(1): 21–37.

Pfeffer J. 1983. Organizational demography. *Research in Organizational Behavior* 5: 99–357.

Plockinger M, Aschauer E, Hiebl M, Rohatschek R. 2019. The influence of individual executives on corporate financial reporting: a review and outlook from the perspective of upper echelons theory. *Journal of Accounting Literature* 37: 55–75.

Puffer SM, Weintrop JB. 1991. Corporate performance and CEO turnover: the role of performance expectations. *Administrative Science Quarterly* 36(1): 1–19.

Pulakos ED, Wexley KN. 1983. The relationship among perceptual similarity, sex, and performance ratings in manager-subordinate dyads. *Academy of Management Journal* 26(1): 129–139.

Sitkin SB, Pablo AL. 1992. Reconceptualizing the determinants of risk behavior. *Academy of Management Review* 17(1): 9–38.

Staw BM, Ross J. 1980. Commitment in an experimenting society: a study of the attribution of leadership from administrative scenarios. *Journal of Applied Psychology* 65(3): 249–260.

Takeuchi R, Tesluk P, Yun S, Lepak D. 2005. An integrative view of international experience. *Academy of Management Journal* 48(1): 85–100.

Tang KN. 2019. *Leadership and Change Management*. Springer: Singapore, Singapore.

Teece D, Pisano G, Shuen A. 1997. Dynamic capabilities and strategic management. *Strategic Management Journal* 18(7): 509–533.

Vroom VH, Pahl B. 1971. Relationship between age and risk taking among managers. *Journal of Applied Psychology* 55(5): 399–405.

Westphal JD, Milton LP. 2000. How experience and network ties affect the influence of demographic minorities on corporate boards. *Administrative Science Quarterly* 45(2): 366–398.

Wiersema M, Bantel K. 1992. Top management team demography and corporate strategic change. *Academy of Management Journal* 35(1): 91–121.

Wiersema M, Bird A. 1993. Organizational demography in Japanese firms: group heterogeneity, individual dissimilarity, and top management team turnover. *Academy of Management Journal* 36(5): 996–1025.

Wiersema M, Nishimura Y, Suzuki K. 2018. Executive succession: the importance of social capital in CEO appointments. *Strategic Management Journal* 39(5): 1473–1495.

Wiersema M, Zhang Y. 2012. Executive turnover in the stock option backdating wave: the impact of social context. *Strategic Management Journal* 34(5): 590–609.

6.2
CEO SUCCESSION

Yan (Anthea) Zhang

CEO succession, in which an incumbent chief executive officer (CEO) is replaced by a successor CEO, is perhaps one of the most crucial events in the life of a firm because of the substantive and symbolic importance of the CEO position. Due to its importance, scholars have paid significant attention to the topic. Kesner and Sebora (1994) and Finkelstein, Hambrick, and Cannella (2009) have provided excellent reviews of the literature. In this chapter, I start with a brief summary of the early literature, review the current status of the field, and offer suggestions on possible future research directions.

A Brief Summary of Early Research on CEO Succession

CEO turnover—the departure of an incumbent CEO—can be divided into two types: voluntary turnover and involuntary turnover (i.e., dismissal). As indicated in the name, *voluntary CEO turnover* refers to a situation in which an incumbent CEO voluntarily leaves office, often due to age, health issues, or family-related issues, or for better career opportunities. In contrast, *CEO dismissal* refers to "a situation in which the CEO's departure is ad hoc (e.g., not part of a mandatory retirement policy) and against his or her will" (Fredrickson, Hambrick, and Baumrin, 1988: 255). Based upon where successor CEOs come from, successor CEOs' origin has been commonly divided into two types: insiders (referring to those promoted from within the firm) and outsiders (referring to those hired from outside).

Based upon these categorizations, the early literature on CEO succession focused mainly on the following questions: (1) When do CEOs leave office, especially leave office against their will? In other words, what are the antecedents of CEO turnover and dismissal? (2) Where do successor CEOs come from? In other words, what are the antecedents of successor CEOs' origin? (3) Does CEO turnover, dismissal, and successor CEO's origin affect the firm's performance—and how? While these questions are different, there are common threads across previous studies that investigate these questions.

Firm performance has been proposed and found to be the most important single factor that explains CEO turnover and dismissal (Fredrickson *et al.*, 1988). The argument is that when a firm does not perform well, the firm tends to replace its CEO in order to have needed change to turn around the poor performance. Firm performance is also an important factor predicting the origin of successor CEOs. An outside successor is more likely to be appointed when firm performance is poor, because an outside CEO tends to bring in new skills and perspectives and initiate strategic change (Cannella and Lubatkin, 1993). In general, these explanations are consistent with the behavioral theory of firms, suggesting that when facing adversity, firms tend to engage in problematic searches for solutions (Cyert and March, 1963).

While these arguments are appealing, examples exist of CEOs who stayed in office through years of poor performance (e.g., Jeff Immelt, CEO of General Electric [GE] in 2001–2017: during his tenure, GE's shares dropped 30 percent whereas the S&P 500 had risen by over 130 percent). It appears that other factors besides firm performance may also affect CEO succession. Management scholars thus turn their attention to social and political factors that may affect CEO succession (e.g., Cannella and Lubatkin, 1993; Fredrickson *et al.*, 1988). The argument is that while poor firm performance makes it necessary to replace a CEO, poor performance by itself is not sufficient; instead, a CEO will be replaced or dismissed under condition of poor firm performance only when the board of directors has sufficient power to replace or dismiss the CEO.

Fredrickson *et al.* (1988) developed a theoretical model on CEO dismissal. In this model, a firm's actual current performance is the primary predictor for the firm's decision on retention or dismissal of its CEO. Four groups of social and political factors are proposed to moderate the performance–CEO dismissal relationship: the board's expectations and attributions of firm performance, the board's allegiances and values, the availability of alternative CEO candidates, and the incumbent CEO's power. This framework provides a foundation for subsequent empirical work on antecedents of CEO dismissal (and CEO turnover in general). In the same vein, Cannella and Lubatkin (1993) argued that CEO succession is a sociopolitical process, and there are internal impediments to the selection of an outside CEO even when the firm is performing poorly. They found that poor performance leads to the selection of an outside CEO only when sociopolitical forces are weak.

In summary, the early work focused on the joint effect of firm performance and social and political factors on CEO succession. Empirically, firm performance has been measured in various ways, including (industry-adjusted) accounting performance and stock return performance (Cannella and Lubatkin, 1993), as well as actual firm performance relative to the board's expectation of firm performance, which may be shaped by financial analysts' earnings forecasts (Puffer and Weintrop, 1991). For social and political factors, Fredrickson *et al.* (1988: 261) suggested various observable indicators of a board's expectations and attributions of firm performance, a board's allegiances and values, the availability of alternative CEO candidates, and the incumbent CEO's power. Among these social and political factors, the incumbent CEO's power has received the most empirical attention. CEO power has been commonly measured by the following dimensions: CEO–board chair duality, CEO tenure (relative to outside directors' average tenure), CEO ownership (relative to outside directors' average ownership), and the ratio of independent outside directors on the board (Zajac and Westphal, 1996).

Management scholars are interested in performance consequences of CEO succession—the "so what" question. This is related to an early debate on a fundamental question: do managers matter, or are they simply "scapegoats" (Gamson and Scotch, 1964; Grusky, 1963)? Examining the relationship between CEO change and firm performance in large corporations, Beatty and Zajac (1987) argued that the CEO succession–firm performance relationship is a function of two distinct, complementary effects: succession effect and manager effect. *Succession effect* refers to whether the stock market may react to the announcements of CEO changes, while *manager effects* refers to whether successor CEOs may significantly influence their firms' production and investment decisions. Their empirical results supported both the succession effect and the manager effect, providing evidence to suggest that managers do matter in large publicly listed corporations.

Current State of the Field

An overall observation

Figures 1 and 2 summarize the papers on CEO succession that were published in the past 20 years (2000–2019) in the *Academy of Management Journal* (*AMJ*) and *Strategic Management Journal* (*SMJ*), two flagship academic journals for strategy research. There are 84 papers in total, with 27 published in *AMJ* and 57 in *SMJ*. Relatively, the second 10-year period saw more papers published (57 papers in 2010–2019) than the first 10-year period (27 papers in 2000–2009). This trend suggests that scholarly interest in CEO succession has continued to rise.

Figure 1 summarizes the major outcome variables examined in the studies published in 2000–2009 and 2010–2019, respectively. The two lists are quite consistent. In both decades, firm performance and CEO succession/turnover are the most widely used outcome variables, followed by firm strategies and new CEO appointment. A noticeable difference is that executive compensation (to a lesser extent, top management team [TMT] / board process) attracts greater attention in the second decade than in the first decade. Overall, scholars studying CEO succession remain interested in the same questions: when will CEOs be replaced/dismissed, who will be appointed as successor CEOs, and how does it matter to firm performance and firm strategies?

Figure 2 summarizes the common predictors used in the studies published in the two decades, respectively. Again, there are some similar patterns between the two decades. CEO succession/turnover, demographic attributes (of CEO, TMT, and board of directors), firm performance, CEO origin, and CEO power are the most common predictors used in both decades. However, the two lists show some noticeable differences. Relatively speaking, fewer studies use corporate governance as predictors in

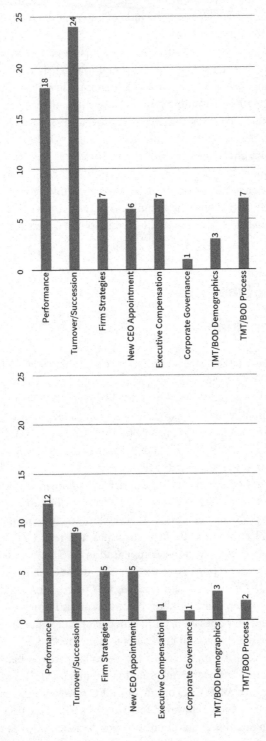

Figure 1 Outcomes examined in *AMJ*/*SMJ* articles on CEO succession (2000–2019); Left panel: outcomes in 27 articles on CEO succession (2000–2009); Right panel: outcomes in 57 articles on CEO succession (2010–2019)

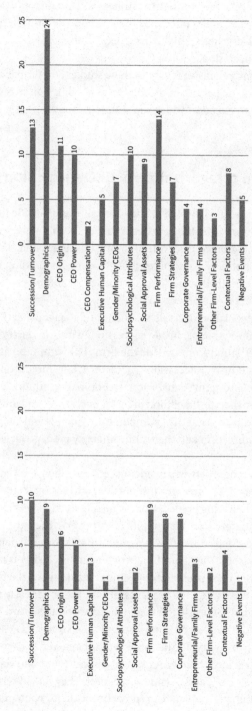

Figure 2 Predictors used in *AMJ/SMJ* articles on CEO succession (2000–2019); Left panel: predictors in 27 articles on CEO succession (2000–2009); Right panel: predictors in 57 articles on CEO succession (2010–2019)

the second decade, relative to the first decade. Adjusted for the number of publications in the two decades, the salience of firm strategies as predictors also declines in the second decade. Instead, studies published in the second decade pay greater attention to social and social-psychological factors in explaining CEO succession and the consequences of CEO succession.

Instead of giving a comprehensive review of these studies and the papers published in other journals in the same period, in the following sections I discuss some themes emerging in the past two decades, which are different from the early literature on CEO succession.

More fine-grained categorization of CEO succession

As noted earlier, the distinction between inside succession and outside succession has attracted scholarly attention from the very beginning of the literature. Recent studies have provided more fine-grained categorization of CEO succession. The more fine-grained categorization not only contributes to a better understanding of the differences among new CEOs in their experiences, knowledge, and power bases but also helps identify various succession processes.

To distinguish among outside successions, Zhang and Rajagopalan (2003) divided CEO successions into three groups: inside succession, within-industry outside succession (successor CEOs hired from outside the firms but within the firms' primary industry), and outside-industry succession (successor CEOs hired from outside the firms' primary industry). Adopting a managerial labor market argument, the authors proposed and supported that the likelihood of inside succession and the likelihood of within-industry outside succession depend upon the demands and supplies of managerial talents in the within-firm and the within-industry managerial labor markets, respectively.

Focusing on the differences between inside successions, Shen and Cannella (2002) divided CEO successions into three groups: outsider succession, contender succession (inside succession following predecessor dismissal), and follower succession (inside succession following predecessor voluntary turnover). They argued that these two types of inside successions differ fundamentally in the power dynamics between successors and predecessors. They found that contender succession is more likely to occur when a predecessor is in a vulnerable position, that is, when the predecessor is hired from outside the firm, when the predecessor is in his or her early tenure, when there is a larger proportion of non-CEO inside directors on the board (who may be alternative candidates for the CEO position), and/or when non-CEO executives own a large proportion of firm equity. In the same vein, Zhang and Rajagopalan (2004) divided CEO successions into three groups: relay succession, non-relay inside succession (internal "horse race"), and outside succession. They linked relay succession to CEO succession planning, in which firms proactively identify potential candidates and groom the selected candidate (i.e., the heir apparent) for the top position. They found that relay succession is associated with better postsuccession performance than both non-relay inside succession and outside succession.

Moreover, recent studies have examined temporary succession practices. As a widely spread practice of public companies in the United States, the board of directors designates an incumbent executive as "interim CEO" or "acting CEO" until a permanent successor is appointed. Ballinger and Marcel (2010) found that such a temporary leadership arrangement may be detrimental to firm performance. Their findings suggest that an interim CEO does not have the authority to be effective unless the interim CEO is the chair of the board of directors.

Information issues surrounding CEO succession

Boards of directors are the key decision-makers regarding CEO turnover and the selection of successor CEOs. However, boards typically make such decisions with limited information, under pressure, and even in secrecy. Thus, information—or more precisely, lack of information—can have an important impact on the process and outcome of CEO succession. Adopting the adverse selection logic of agency theory, Zhang (2008) argued that information asymmetry between the hiring firm's board of directors and CEO candidates increases the chance that the board makes a poor CEO selection decision. With updated information after succession, the board may need to dismiss the newly appointed CEO to correct its wrong selection decision. Therefore, Zhang (2008) proposed that the level of information asymmetry at the time of succession is positively related to the likelihood of dismissing a newly appointed CEO. Information asymmetry may stem from various sources. Relative to inside succession, outside succession is characterized by a higher level of information asymmetry between the board and the selected CEO. Dismissal of the predecessor CEO tends to bypass a normal succession planning process and thus amplify the information problems. Meanwhile, having an independent nomination committee and/or a focused nomination committee (i.e., committee members who have few other external directorships) on the board helps reduce the information problems. Zhang (2008) found that all these factors affect the likelihood of dismissing a newly appointed CEO (i.e., dismissed within three years after succession).

Of course, the board of directors is not the only party facing information problems in CEO succession. Investors, as external parties, are at an informational disadvantage relative to corporate insiders, including the board of directors. Such information asymmetry allows firms to conduct impression management targeting investors as well as other stakeholders. In exploring this idea, Graffin, Carpenter, and Boivie (2011) introduced the notion of "strategic noise." They argued that the board of directors might manage investors' (potential negative) reactions to a new CEO appointment announcement by simultaneously releasing confounding information about other important events—namely, "strategic noise." They found that strategic noise is more likely to be released when the new CEO does not have previous CEO experience and/or comes from a less well-regarded firm. In the same vein, Davidson *et al.* (2004) found that earnings management occurs more frequently after CEO successions that put the same person in both the CEO and board chair positions (i.e., duality-creating succession) than otherwise. They argued that CEOs who also hold the board chair title face higher performance expectation and have greater control of the impressions created by their firms' financial reports. Therefore, such CEOs have both incentive and power to conduct earnings management after succession.

Overall, these studies highlight the roles of various information issues surrounding CEO succession. On the one hand, with limited information, boards of directors may make suboptimal decisions on CEO turnover/dismissal and new CEO appointments. On the other hand, firms can take advantage of information asymmetry for "window dressing" their otherwise underwhelming CEO succession processes and new CEO appointments.

Role of board evaluation in CEO succession

Due to the information problems just discussed, it is difficult, if not impossible, for boards of directors to make "objective" evaluations of the incumbent CEOs or CEO candidates. Therefore, contextual factors play a critical role in the evaluation processes, which in turn affect the boards' decisions on the incumbent CEOs' turnover/dismissal as well as the appointments of new CEOs. Such contextual factors include the characteristics of the incumbent CEO and of CEO candidates, the board's own attributes, and the relational factors between the board and the incumbent CEO or CEO candidates.

Graffin, Boivie, and Carpenter (2013) examined boards' evaluation of early-stage CEOs as reflected in the CEOs' compensation changes and the CEOs' survival prospects. They argued that in the first years of CEO tenure, traditional performance metrics are less diagnostic of CEO quality; thus, contextual elements of the CEO succession process can influence the heuristics that directors use in the evaluation. Such contextual factors include the status of the predecessor (is the predecessor a "star" or a founder of the firm?), the new CEO's own track record (does the new CEO have previous CEO experience?), and investors' reactions to the new CEO appointment announcement. Graham, Harvey, and Puri (2017) conducted multiple experiments to examine how people perceive CEOs' competence based on the CEOs' facial traits. They found that CEO compensation is related to the perceived "competence" ratings; however, they found no evidence that the firms of competent-looking CEOs perform better than others.

The board's own attributes also play an important role in its evaluation of the incumbent CEO or CEO candidates. The similarity attraction theory suggests that people like and are attracted to others who are similar to themselves. In an early study, Zajac and Westphal (1996) argued that board members prefer to choose a successor CEO who is demographically similar to themselves, whereas the incumbent CEO prefers a successor who is demographically similar to him- or herself. In support of their argument, they found that if a firm's board of directors is more powerful in relation to the incumbent CEO, CEO characteristics are more likely to change when succession occurs, and the new CEO is demographically more similar to the existing board members. Recent studies go beyond the similarity in conventional dimensions (such as industry backgrounds, education backgrounds, and demographic characteristics) and examine other aspects of "homophily." Damaraju and Makhija (2018), in the context of India, examined caste/religion-based hiring of CEOs. They proposed that caste and religion might matter in the CEO selection process for two different reasons: caste and religion are used as information sources (positive discrimination) and/or caste and religion are used to pursue taste-based preferences (negative discrimination). The authors' empirical evidence suggests that caste and religion play important roles in the CEO selection process as information sources.

Focusing on directors' political ideology, Park, Boeker, and Gomulya (2020) asked why some boards refuse to take serious actions against CEOs who have committed financial misconduct. They found that politically conservative boards are more likely than liberal boards to respond by dismissing the CEO. The authors explained that this is because relative to liberals, conservatives are more likely to feel morally offended by norm violators and have a more punitive attitude toward norm violators.

The incumbent CEO certainly plays an important role in the appointment of a new CEO. As Zajac and Westphal (1996) noted, an incumbent CEO prefers to select a new CEO who is demographically similar to him- or herself. Extending this line of research, Wiersema, Nishimura, and Suzuki (2018) examined the roles of two forms of connections between the incumbent CEO and CEO candidates in new CEO appointment: "bonding" (personal relationships developed through a history of interactions) and "bridging" (informal connections that exist between two actors). They found that both forms of connections help CEO candidates to be appointed.

Role of social approval assets in CEO succession

Scholars have begun to recognize the role of social approval assets accrued to top executives—for example, status, reputation, and social network—in explaining the occurrence and consequences of CEO succession. *Social approval assets* refer to socially constructed, collective assessments by external audiences (Pollock *et al.*, 2019). Although they are not observable and not directly controlled by the focal individuals or organizations, these intangible assets affect how people exchange resources as well as interpret information (Pollock *et al.*, 2019).

Taking a network-embedded perspective, Jiang *et al.* (2017) argued that in declining firms, CEOs' social capital, their peer executives' social capital, and their firms' alliance networks can affect the CEOs' cost-benefit trade-offs in their decisions on whether to leave the firms—that is, "jumping ship." Regarding the CEOs' own social capital, those with a low level of social capital do not have many external career opportunities and thus are less likely to jump ship. Those with a high level of social capital may bring in external resources and support to "save the ship" and thus are also less likely to jump ship. Jiang *et al.* (2017) proposed and found that CEOs with a moderate level of social capital are the most likely to leave their declining firms. In addition, CEOs' peer executives' social capital and their firms' alliance network may also bring in external resources and support to save the ship, thus also reducing the CEOs' incentives to jump ship.

Status, referring to "the social ranking and esteem accorded to an executive," is another form of social approval asset (Westphal and Khanna, 2003). Studies have found that non-CEO executives get a higher chance of promotion both inside and outside their current companies if they gain directorships (Boivie *et al.*, 2016), because serving in directorships provides CEO candidates with certification of their quality as well as access to resources. Status has also been shown to safeguard CEOs during performance downturns (Flickinger *et al.*, 2016).

While social approval assets can offer benefits to CEOs, their concern about maintaining their status or reputation may bind their footsteps in initiating strategic changes. By building an analytical model, Sliwka (2007) demonstrated that it may be optimal to replace executives of higher ability when firms seek strategic changes. Sliwka's (2007) model was based upon several assumptions. First, managers and firm owners have different goals: while both managers and firm owners (and boards of directors as the representatives of the firm owners) care for the firm's long-term success, managers are also interested in maintaining their own reputation. Second, managers with higher abilities are more likely to choose a successful strategy initially, and when the initial strategy no longer works, they are reluctant to change it since a publicly observable correction of their past strategic decision would reveal that they had chosen a bad strategy, damaging their reputation. Sliwka (2007) demonstrated that it might be optimal to dismiss managers of higher ability while those with lower ability may be kept, when strategic change has to be enforced.

Female and ethnic-minority CEOs

While women's representation in boardrooms has significantly increased in the past decade, the glass ceiling for women remains in the executive suites, especially the C-suites of large corporations (Dezső, Ross, and Uribe, 2016). According to a recent report,[1] only 38 of the Fortune 500 companies had female chief executives at the start of August 2020. Meanwhile, as shown in Figure 2, there is increasing research interest in female and ethnic-minority CEOs. Studies have examined the gender and ethnic-minority issues at various stages of the succession process. Hill, Upadhyay, and Beekun (2015) tested whether female and ethnic-minority CEOs would endure inequalities or benefit from their minority status, compared to the majority CEOs (i.e., white males). The authors found that female CEOs and ethnic-minority CEOs are both paid more than white male CEOs. However, while ethnic-minority CEOs are less likely to exit than white male CEOs, female CEOs are more likely to exit than white male CEOs. The authors' findings suggest that minority status does not necessarily hurt CEOs and indeed may benefit those who have successfully broken the corporate glass ceiling. More important, the results demonstrated that gender minority and ethnic minority may have different implications in CEO succession.

Regarding the effect of gender on promotions to leadership positions, Cook and Glass (2014) developed a glass cliff theory, suggesting that females are more likely to be promoted to leadership positions when the organizations are facing performance problems. In examining female representation in executive teams in S&P 1500 companies, Dezső et al. (2016) found evidence of an implicit quota that female executives face—that is, the presence of a woman on an executive team reduces the likelihood of other females being appointed to that same team.

Another group of studies examined the consequences of executive turnover that involve female/minority-status predecessors or successors. Zhang and Qu (2016) found that CEO succession with gender change, a situation in which the predecessor and the successor CEOs have different genders, is associated with lower postsuccession firm performance and a higher likelihood of the successor's early departure. McDonald, Keeves, and Westphal (2018) showed how minority and female CEOs had difficulties in their transition due to their white male managers being unwilling to help in this process. In the same vein, Dwivedi, Joshi, and Misangyi (2018) found that the gatekeeping behaviors of the (mostly) male predecessors that promote gender inclusion during succession can enhance the performance of the incoming female CEOs after succession.

In addition, some studies analyzed third parties' perceptions of CEO successions involving female or minority predecessors or successors by investigating stock market reactions to such successions. Lee and James (2007) and Dixon-Fowler, Ellstrand, and Johnson (2013) found that executive succession involving females generally receives negative stock market reactions.

Suggestions for Future Research Directions

Addressing the endogeneity issue in CEO succession research

Previous studies have significantly advanced our understanding of CEO succession. However, a critical challenge facing CEO succession research is the endogeneity issue. For example, poor firm performance may increase the likelihood of CEO succession, which, in turn, may be related to firm performance after succession. In this sense, CEO succession is endogenous to presuccession performance and other contextual factors. The same concern exists for research on the origin of successor CEOs. Without carefully addressing the endogeneity issue, we cannot claim causality in terms of how CEO succession or appointment of new CEO may affect firm performance.

Recent studies on executives in entrepreneurial firms provide some hints on how to address the challenge. Kulchina (2017) examined whether foreign entrepreneurs would perform better by managing their ventures, compared to hiring domestic professional managers. She used Russia's visa policy change as an instrument variable to predict the owner-manager choice in foreign entrepreneurial firms in Russia. In examining the impact of CEO change on initial public offering (IPO) valuation, Chahine and Zhang (2020) used the distance between a venture and its lead venture capital (VC) investor as an instrument variable to predict whether the venture would change CEO before the IPO. These studies' research designs allow the authors to draw causal conclusions regarding the research questions they investigated.

Publicly listed companies, on which most studies on CEO succession focus, are different from and more complicated than entrepreneurial firms. While it might be difficult to find strong instrument variables for the occurrence of CEO succession, researchers may examine specific succession practices (e.g., whether a firm has a formalized CEO succession process) and/or the selection of certain types of successor CEOs (e.g., female CEOs) that may allow researchers to address the endogeneity issues in such choices.

Postsuccession transition

The postsuccession transition process is not easy for new CEOs because it takes time for them to demonstrate credibility and to assemble an effective and supportive team. However, how new CEOs manage the postsuccession transition period has largely remained as a black box. Ma and Seidl (2018) found that new CEOs would establish a group of close collaborators to support their leadership initiatives. Lam *et al.* (2018) suggested that both the new CEO and his or her team's proactive personalities are significant factors in increasing the new leaders' identification with the team and organization. New CEOs can also engage in social influence behaviors: ingratiation toward the predecessors and self-promotion of their own capabilities, which may reduce their vulnerabilities from various sources and accordingly improve their early survival prospects (Yi, Zhang, and Windsor, 2020).

Future research may further explore questions related to the leadership transition period. For example, while it is important for new CEOs to build a group of close collaborators, how can they establish such a group, and who tend to be the new CEOs' close collaborators? Should the new CEO, if hired from outside the firm, bring in former colleagues to fill the executive positions of the current firm? If they do so, what might be the consequences for the new CEO and for other top managers (existing ones and newly hired ones)? Moreover, it has been well noted that new CEOs may have going-in mandates, which have been decided by the board of directors or other key stakeholders such as investors. Meanwhile, new CEOs also need to start their own strategic initiatives. How should they pace the transition from the going-in mandates to their own strategic initiatives? These important questions have remained unexplored because researchers did not have needed data. Luckily, data sources—such as conference call transcripts as well as CEOs' public speeches—now are widely available and offer rich opportunities for scholars to examine what new CEOs say and what they (plan to) do, as well as how analysts, shareholders, and employees react to what the CEOs say and what they do.

Postsuccession careers

The average CEO tenure has become shorter in the past couple of decades. As a result, many CEOs leave office, voluntarily or involuntarily, before they are willing to fully retire. A recent study (Lee, Yoon, and Boivie, 2020) found that many founder CEOs voluntarily leave their firms after their firms' IPOs—many of them leave the CEO position at a relatively young age. Then an interesting question arises: what do CEOs do after succession? Many former CEOs sit on the boards of directors of other public corporations as well as private institutions. Directorships, especially directorships in public corporations, provide opportunities for these former CEOs to extend their corporate careers.

However, it is well noted that corporate failure, including poor firm performance, during a CEO's tenure can lead to professional devaluation of the individual, which reduces the chance that she or he can find an equivalent executive position or directorship in another public corporation after succession (Wiesenfeld, Wurthmann, and Hambrick, 2008). Is it possible that different types of corporate failures will have different impacts on CEOs' postsuccession career prospects? Organizational failures may be categorized into competence failures and integrity failures (Connelly et al., 2016). While competence failures occur when a firm falls short of performance, integrity failures occur when "a firm's motives, honesty, and/or character fall short" (Connelly et al., 2016: 2136). Future research may examine whether competence failures and integrity failures may have different impacts on CEOs' postsuccession careers.

Moreover, Sliwka's (2007) model showed that if a (talented) manager is fired to pave the way for the firm to enforce strategic change, the dismissal may not hurt the manager's reputation badly in the managerial labor market. As an example, Bernd Pischetsrieder, who was fired from the CEO position of BMW (for his unwillingness to sell the loss-making Rover business) in 1999 was appointed as CEO of Volkswagen in 2002 (Sliwka, 2007). Future research may investigate what factors may signal a manager's ability even if he or she is dismissed and thus maintain his or her professional valuation in the managerial labor market.

In addition to corporate failures or misconduct, CEOs may be dismissed for their personal misconduct. For example, McDonald's fired its CEO Steve Easterbrook in November 2019 after it was found that he engaged in a consensual relationship with an employee, which violated the company's policy. It would be interesting for future research to examine the career prospects of CEOs who are fired for their personal misconduct. Is it possible that these CEOs would be penalized more severely by the managerial labor market than those who are fired for corporate failures and misconduct since corporate failures and misconduct offer greater room for different interpretation and attribution?

Many former CEOs, equipped with the financial prowess accumulated during their corporate careers, are actively involved in charitable activities. Other CEOs pursued poltical career opportunities after leaving their corporate executive positions. For example, Carly Fiorina, who was ousted from the CEO and board chair positions in Hewlett-Packard Company in 2005, ran unsuccessfully for the U.S. Senate in 2010 and the Republican presidential nomination in 2016. We have not seen studies examining people's charitable activities or their pursuit of political careers after leaving the CEO position. What factors may affect their charitable activities after succession? The amount of the person's wealth certainly matters. Does how the person made the money matter as well? Does easy money—for example, a windfall of cash from exercised stock options—make a departed CEO more generous? Does money made from "sin" businesses—for example, tobacco and alcohol businesses—make people feel guilty and thus prompt them to engage more in charitable activities? Moreover, as shown in Carly Fiorina's case, as a former corporate executive pursues a political career, how transferable is former corporate experience to the new field?

Incentives for CEOs to leave office

When McDonald's fired Steve Easterbrook from its CEO position, the company allowed its ex-CEO to walk away with severance pay worth up to $57 million (McDonald's later was suing its ex-CEO on the basis that he lied about multiple affairs with employees).[2] When WeWork fired its founder CEO, Adam Neumann, in October 2019, the company offered its ex-CEO a severance package that could be valued over $1 billion. (In October 2020, WeWork said that the consulting deal with its ex-CEO was no longer in place.)[3]

A lucrative severance payment to a CEO who is dismissed for poor firm performance, organizational misconduct, and/or personal misconduct is controversial and causes public outcry. Media outlets often depict such payments as "pay to go away" or "rewards for failure." Despite the controversy of severance pay, it is commonly included as a component in CEO compensation contracts. Although severance payment is triggered only when an executive is dismissed "without cause or for good reason" (Schwab and Thomas, 2006), almost all dismissed CEOs are eligible to receive severance payments as "for-cause" exits are very rare, as shown in the examples of CEO dismissals in McDonald's and WeWork.

If severance pay is so controversial, why do many firms include it in their CEO compensation contracts? Essentially, severance pay provides insurance against a CEO's job risk (Klein, Chaigneau, and Devers, 2019). Future research may examine how severance pay affects CEO turnover. Does a lucrative severance pay contract make it easy for a firm to remove its incumbent CEO when needed? Previous studies have noted that incumbent CEOs have a strong incentive to stay in office, and therefore only when the board is more powerful in relation to the CEO can the board dismiss the CEO when needed (Fredrickson *et al.*, 1988). Severance pay may ease the difficulty in removing the incumbent CEO. It would be interesting to examine how boards of directors balance the cost of paying out severance packages and the potential benefit of replacing the incumbent CEO. Moreover, severance payments to CEOs upon their dismissal often lead to negative reactions from firms' shareholders (Bebchuk and Fried, 2004). How do firms manage the tension between the need to replace the incumbent CEO and potential pushback from shareholders?

Conclusion

CEO succession has been an important and exciting research topic for management scholars. Whereas some conventional topics (such as the antecedents and organizational consequences of CEO succession and new CEO selection) deserve continued attention, new topics are emerging. New data sources, such as a significant expansion of data from social media and corporate-generated files, call for more sophisticated analyses of CEO succession processes and offer opportunities to analyze CEO succession at a more granular level.

Acknowledgments

I am grateful to Sung H. "Brian" Chung, Yoon Jung "Jenny" Kwon, and Yiying Zhu for their help in collecting the data on the papers on CEO succession and creating the figures.

Notes

1. https://www.theguardian.com/business/2020/sep/10/citigroup-wall-street-bank-female-ceo-jane-fraser.
2. https://www.businessinsider.com/mcdonalds-ceo-steve-easterbrook-57-million-severance-package-2020-8
3. https://www.wsj.com/articles/the-fall-of-wework-how-a-startup-darling-came-unglued-11571946003

References

Ballinger GA, Marcel JJ. 2010. The use of an interim CEO during succession episodes and firm performance. *Strategic Management Journal* 31(3): 262–283.

Beatty RB. Zajac EJ. 1987. CEO change and firm performance in large corporations: succession effects and manager effects. *Strategic Management Journal* 8(4): 305–317.

Bebchuk LA, Fried JM. 2004. *Pay without Performance: The Unfulfilled Promise of Executive Compensation.* Harvard University Press: Cambridge, MA.

Boivie S, Graffin SD, Oliver AG, Withers MC. 2016. Come aboard! Exploring the effects of directorships in the executive labor market. *Academy of Management Journal* 59(5): 1681–1706.

Cannella AA, Lubatkin M. 1993. Succession as a sociopolitical process: internal impediments to outsider selection. *Academy of Management Journal* 36(4): 763–793.

Chahine S, Zhang YA. 2020. Changing gears before speeding up: the roles of CEO human capital and VC monitoring in CEO change before IPO. *Strategic Management Journal* 41(9): 1653–1681.

Connelly BL, Ketchen DJ Jr, Gangloff KA, Shook CL. 2016. Investor perceptions of CEO successor selection in the wake of integrity and competence failures: a policy capturing study. *Strategic Management Journal* 37(10): 2135–2151.

Cook A, Glass C. 2014. Above the glass ceiling: when are women and racial/ethnic minorities promoted to CEO? *Strategic Management Journal* 35(7): 1080–1089.

Cyert RM, March JG. 1963. *A Behavioral Theory of the Firm.* Prentice Hall: Englewood Cliffs, NJ.

Damaraju NL, Makhija AK. 2018. The role of social proximity in professional CEO appointments: evidence from caste/religion-based hiring of CEOs in India. *Strategic Management Journal* 39(7): 2051–2074.

Davidson WN III, Jiraporn P, Kim YS, Nemec C. 2004. Earnings management following duality-creating successions: ethnostatistics, impression management, and agency theory. *Academy of Management Journal* 47(2): 267–275.

Dezső CL, Ross DG, Uribe J. 2016. Is there an implicit quota on women in top management? A large-sample statistical analysis. *Strategic Management Journal* 37(1): 98–115.

Dixon-Fowler HR, Ellstrand AE, Johnson JL. 2013. Strength in numbers or guilt by association? Intragroup effects of female chief executive announcements. *Strategic Management Journal* 34(12): 1488–1501.

Dwivedi P, Joshi A, Misangyi VF. 2018. Gender-inclusive gatekeeping: how (mostly male) predecessors influence the success of female CEOs. *Academy of Management Journal* 61(2): 379–404.

Finkelstein S, Hambrick DC, Cannella AA. 2009. *Strategic Leadership: Theory and Research on Executives, Top Management Teams, and Boards.* Oxford University Press: New York, NY.

Flickinger M, Wrage M, Tuschke A, Bresser R. 2016. How CEOs protect themselves against dismissal: a social status perspective. *Strategic Management Journal* 37(6): 1107–1117.

Fredrickson JW, Hambrick DC, Baumrin S. 1988. A model of CEO dismissal. *Academy of Management Review* 13(2): 255–270.

Gamson WA, Scotch, NA. 1964. Scapegoating in baseball. *American Journal of Sociology* 70: 69–72.

Graffin SD, Boivie S, Carpenter MA. 2013. Examining CEO succession and the role of heuristics in early-stage CEO evaluation. *Strategic Management Journal* 34(4): 383–403.

Graffin SD, Carpenter MA, Boivie S. 2011. What's all that (strategic) noise? Anticipatory impression management in CEO succession. *Strategic Management Journal* 32(7): 748–770.

Graham JR, Harvey CR, Puri M. 2017. A corporate beauty contest. *Management Science* 63(9): 3044–3056.

Grusky O. 1963. Managerial succession and organizational effectiveness. *American Journal of Sociology* 69: 21–31.

Hill AD, Upadhyay AD, Beekun RI. 2015. Do female and ethnically diverse executives endure inequity in the CEO position or do they benefit from their minority status? An empirical examination. *Strategic Management Journal* 36(8): 1115–1134.

Jiang H, Cannella AA Jr, Xia J, Semadeni M. 2017. Choose to fight or choose to flee? A network embeddedness perspective of executive ship jumping in declining firms. *Strategic Management Journal* 38(10): 2061–2079.

Kesner IF, Sebora TC. 1994. Executive succession: Past, present, and future. *Journal of Management* 20(2): 327–372.

Klein FB, Chaigneau P, Devers CE. 2019. CEO gender-based termination concerns: evidence from initial severance agreements. *Journal of Management*. https://doi.org/10.1177/0149206319887421 [14 April 2021].

Kulchina E. 2017. Do foreign entrepreneurs benefit their firms as managers? *Strategic Management Journal* 38(8): 1588–1607.

Lam W, Lee C, Taylor MS, Zhao HH. 2018. Does proactive personality matter in leadership transitions? Effects of proactive personality on new leader identification and responses to new leaders and their change agendas. *Academy of Management Journal* 61(1): 245–263.

Lee JM, Yoon D, Boivie S. 2020. Founder CEO succession: the role of CEO organizational identification. *Academy of Management Journal* 63(1): 224–245.

Lee PM, James EH. 2007. SHÉ-E-OS: gender effects and investor reactions to the announcements of top executive appointments. *Strategic Management Journal* 28(3): 227–241.

Ma S, Seidl D. 2018. New CEOs and their collaborators: divergence and convergence between the strategic leadership constellation and the top management team. *Strategic Management Journal* 39(3): 606–638.

McDonald ML, Keeves GD, Westphal JD. 2018. One step forward, one step back: white male top manager organizational identification and helping behavior toward other executives following the appointment of a female or racial minority CEO. *Academy of Management Journal* 61(2): 405–439.

Park UD, Boeker W, Gomulya D. 2020. Political ideology of the board and CEO dismissal following financial misconduct. *Strategic Management Journal* 41(1): 108–123.

Pollock TG, Lashley K, Rindova VP, Han J-H. 2019. Which of these things are not like the others? Comparing the rational, emotional, and moral aspects of reputation, status, celebrity, and stigma. *Academy of Management Annals* 13(2): 444–478.

Puffer SM. Weintrop JB. 1991. Corporate performance and CEO turnover: the role of performance expectation. *Administrative Science Quarterly* 36(1): 1–19.

Schwab SJ, Thomas RS. 2006. Empirical analysis of CEO employment contracts: what do top executives bargain for? *Washington and Lee Law Review* 63: 231–270.

Shen W, Cannella AA. 2002. Power dynamics within top management and their impacts on CEO dismissal followed by inside succession. *Academy of Management Journal* 45(6): 1195–1206.

Sliwka D. 2007. Managerial turnover and strategic change. *Management Science* 53(11): 1675–1687.

Westphal JD, Khanna P. 2003. Keeping directors in line: social distancing as a control mechanism in the corporate elite. *Administrative Science Quarterly* 48(3): 361–398.

Wiersema MF, Nishimura Y, Suzuki K. 2018. Executive succession: the importance of social capital in CEO appointments. *Strategic Management Journal* 39(5): 1473–1495.

Wiesenfeld BA, Wurthmann KA, Hambrick DC. 2008. The stigmatization and devaluation of elites associated with corporate failures: a process model. *Academy of Management Review* 33(1): 231–251.

Yi X, Zhang YA, Windsor D. 2020. You are great and I am great (too): examining new CEOs' social influence behaviors during leadership transition. *Academy of Management Journal* 63(5): 1508–1534.

Zajac EJ, Westphal JD. 1996. Who shall succeed? How CEO/board preferences and power affect the choice of new CEOs. *Academy of Management Journal* 39(1): 64–90.

Zhang Y. 2008. Information asymmetry and the dismissal of newly appointed CEOs: an empirical investigation. *Strategic Management Journal* 29(8): 859–872.

Zhang Y, Qu H. 2016. The impact of CEO succession with gender change on firm performance and successor early departure: evidence from China's publicly listed companies in 1997–2010. *Academy of Management Journal* 59(5): 1845–1868.

Zhang Y, Rajagopalan N. 2003. Explaining new CEO origin: firm versus industry antecedents. *Academy of Management Journal* 46(3): 327–338.

Zhang Y, Rajagopalan N. 2004. When the known devil is better than an unknown god: An empirical study of the antecedents and consequences of relay CEO successions. *Academy of Management Journal* 47(4): 483–500.

PART 7

GOVERNANCE AND BOARDS OF DIRECTORS

Ruth V. Aguilera, Lead

7.0
CORPORATE GOVERNANCE

Ruth V. Aguilera

Corporate Governance in Strategy

Corporate governance refers to the strategiwc bundle of mechanisms and practices that guide how decisions are made within an organization among its different interest groups (shareholders, managers, boards, and employees) and its broader stakeholders (customers, suppliers, communities, regulators, etc.). Corporate governance entails delineating the rights and responsibilities of each of these interest groups (or stakeholders) relative to firm decisions and resources. Corporate governance is not a new topic, as it concerns fundamental choices on who makes decisions in organizations (who governs), how these decision-makers are monitored and rewarded, and how the created value is appropriated and distributed among the different interest groups (shareholders, stakeholders, and society more broadly). Some new dimensions of corporate governance have emerged such as the salience of the interest groups, the practices for relating with each other, the mechanisms and tactics available to exercise power and voice, the sense of timing and urgency, the interest groups' competitive environment, and the institutional norms within which these groups operate. Corporate governance evolves with strategic corporate needs, individual capabilities, and societal expectations.

Companies and organizations have always been governed. Why is this more complicated than it appears? Simply because individuals and interest groups operate under bounded rationality (Simon, 1991). That is, organizational and societal interest groups do not always share the same values, goals, or logics, and the decisions to reach an agreement, to enforce it, or to voluntarily internalize it can be complex. In addition, there is a clear codependence and coevolution between firm governance and country institutions. For instance, country-level managerial discretion shapes the key strategic decisions that firms make and contributes to their performance and long-term survival. Conversely, governance decisions such as shareholder activism by certain hedge funds can potentially affect an entire ecosystem of financial market institutions and regulations regarding director selection, and institutions and their norms might in turn be trespassed or revised to match firms' corporate governance behavior (Aguilera and Jackson, 2003). This makes most corporate governance research challenging to properly identify and account for the multilevel effects.

The study of corporate governance is highly interdisciplinary, drawing from a variety of scholarly and applied fields with some specialization in the level of analysis (finance, law, sociology, ethics, political science, accounting, economics, and psychology); spans industries and countries; and tackles issues that range from employee representation on the board and CEO incentives in family versus state-owned firms to institutional investors' shareholders' proposals for greater environmental and social disclosure. These governance decisions are all consequential for firms' strategic behavior.

A simple bibliometric search of corporate governance research in four selected top-tier journals publishing strategy research (*Academy of Management Annals, Academy of Management Journal, Journal of Management*, and *Strategic Management Journal*) with the term "corporate governance" in the title, keywords, and abstract reveals that during the last 20 years (2000–2020), there were a total of 283 articles published—10, 64, 75, and 134 in the five-year periods, respectively. However, it is noticeable that in the 2010–2020 decade, there has been a significant increase in corporate governance articles in all these journals. For example, *SMJ* went from 36 in the 2000s to 98 articles in the 2010s. The main governance areas of these articles center around the board and its directors, the CEO, and financial performance. As a second set of keywords, we find, on the one hand, articles drawing on different perspectives of *institution*-related issues such as institutional context, institutional logics, formal institutions, and institutional fit (see Aguilera and Grøgaard, 2019), and on the other hand, on *social*-focused areas, such as corporate social responsibility (CSR) and social performance. More recent topics are institutional owners and shareholder engagement, activism, and stewardship.

There have also been a number of comprehensive review articles; a selected sample since 2010 is listed in Table 1. In addition to the themes already described, additional areas of research emerge: different owners such as family business and state-owned enterprises and their governance, wrongdoing as a governance failure, and comparative corporate governance. The time is possibly right to think about corporate governance of stakeholder voice, particularly organized employees, independent contractors in the platform economy, and new shareholders (e.g., responsible investors and sovereign wealth funds). Interestingly, there is also a large vacuum of corporate governance studies outside the for-profit organizations, such as social enterprises, B-corporations, non-for-profit organizations, and the entire array of hybrid organizations. In a flourishing number of new or revised corporate governance books written from a strategic point of view and targeted to both, academics and practitioners offer different disciplinary perspectives on corporate governance research and practice (e.g., Gordon and Ringe, 2018; Hermalin and Weisbach, 2017; Larcker and Tayan, 2020a; Mallin, 2019; Tricker, 2019; Westphal and Park, 2020; Zattoni, 2020). Similarly, nongovernmental agencies such as the Organisation for Economic Co-operation and Development (OECD; Organisation for Economic Co-operation and Development, 2019), international organizations such as the World Bank and its governance quality index, and different investor agencies such as the Big Four (e.g., PcW, 2020) and

Table 1 Selected review articles from three journals (by publication year order)

Author	Year	Title	Journal	Main focus
Ma, Kor, and Seidl	2020	"CEO Advice Seeking: An Integrative Framework and Future Research Agenda"	JoM	CEO
Neville, Byron, Post, and Ward	2019	"Board Independence and Corporate Misconduct: A Cross-National Meta-Analysis"	JoM	Wrongdoing
Tihanyi, Aguilera, Heugens, van Essen, Sauerwald, Duran, and Turturea	2019	"State Ownership and Political Connections"	JoM	SOE
Brauer, and Wiersema	2018	"Analyzing Analyst Research: A Review of Past Coverage and Recommendations for Future Research"	JoM	Analysts
Schnatterly, Gangloff, and Tuschke	2018	"CEO Wrongdoing: A Review of Pressure, Opportunity, and Rationalization"	JoM	Wrongdoing
Boyd, Gove, and Solarino	2017	"Methodological Rigor of Corporate Governance Studies: A Review and Recommendations for Future Studies"	CGIR	Methods
Uhde, Klarner, and Tuschke	2017	"Board Monitoring of the Chief Financial Officer: A Review and Research Agenda"	CGIR	Boards
Boivie, Bednar, Aguilera, and Andrus	2016	"Are Boards Designed to Fail? The Implausibility of Effective Board Monitoring"	Annals	Boards
Busenbark, Krause, Boivie, and Graffin	2016	"Toward a Configurational Perspective on the CEO: A Review and Synthesis of the Management Literature"	JoM	CEO
Colli, and Colpan	2016	"Business Groups and Corporate Governance: Review, Synthesis, and Extension"	CGIR	BGs
Cuomo, Mallin, and Zattoni	2016	"Corporate Governance Codes: A Review and Research Agenda"	CGIR	Codes
Gabaldon, de Anca, Mateos de Cabo, and Gimeno	2016	"Searching for Women on Boards: An Analysis from the Supply and Demand Perspective"	CGIR	Diversity
Grosman, Wright, and Okhmatovskiy	2016	"State Control and Corporate Governance in Transition Economies: 25 Years on from 1989"	CGIR	SOE

Continued

Table 1 *Continued*

Author	Year	Title	Journal	Main focus
Jain, and Jamali	2016	"Looking inside the Black Box: The Effect of Corporate Governance on Corporate Social Responsibility"	*CGIR*	CSR
Schiehll, and Martins	2016	"Cross-National Governance Research: A Systematic Review and Assessment"	*CGIR*	Cross-national
Aguilera, Desender, Bednar, and Lee	2015	"Connecting the Dots: Bringing External Corporate Governance into the Corporate Governance Puzzle"	*Annals*	CG
Krause, Semadeni, and Cannella	2014	"CEO Duality: A Review and Research Agenda"	*JoM*	CEO
Johnson, Schnatterly, and Hill	2013	"Board Composition beyond Independence: Social Capital, Human Capital, and Demographics"	*JoM*	Boards
McNulty, Zattoni, and Douglas	2013	"Developing Corporate Governance Research through Qualitative Methods: A Review of Previous Studies"	*CGIR*	Methods
Gedajlovic, Carney, Chrisman, and Kellermanns	2012	"The Adolescence of Family Firm Research: Taking Stock and Planning for the Future"	*JoM*	Family Firm
Gomez-Mejia, Cruz, Berrone, and De Castro	2011	"The Bind That Ties: Socioemotional Wealth Preservation in Family Firms"	*Annals*	Family Firm
Aguilera, and Jackson	2010	"Comparative and International Corporate Governance"	*Annals*	CG

Note: Annals (Academy of Management Annals), CGIR (Corporate Governance: An International Review), and JoM (Journal of Management); BG (Busiess Group); CEO (Chief Executive Officer); CG (Corporate Governance),CSR (Corporate Social Responsibility), and SOE (State owned Enterprise).

consulting firms (McKinsey, 2018) continue to produce surveys and issue increasingly detailed reports on boards, compensation, diversity, sustainability, geopolitical tensions, and digital preparedness.

Highlights of Existing Corporate Governance Research

Corporate governance and its dimensions and processes have been studied mostly as precursors to multiple organizational outcomes (e.g., cost of debt, product and geographic diversification, investments in research and development (R&D) and CSR), although a great deal of attention in strategy research has been devoted to firm financial performance and firm survival. Larcker and Tayan (2020b: 5) state that good corporate governance is a "set of processes or organizational features that, on average, improve decision-making and reduce the likelihood of poor outcomes arising from strategic, operating, or financial choices, or from ethical or behavioral lapses within an organization."

Thus, the quality of a company's corporate governance is believed to be a key component contributing to its success because it is the engine that decides where to invest, how to share dividends, how much risk to take, which chief executive officer (CEO) to hire, how much to pay her or him, when to comply with regulations, to whom political contributions are given, and a long list of firm strategic decisions. These decisions are typically shared among owners, the board of directors, the top management team (TMT), and employees, although with differing actor weights across these decisions depending on the type, location, and industry of the firm. Firm success is attributed to good governance, including leadership—see the strategic leadership Part in this volume. Conversely, corporate scandals, such as the Boeing 737 MAX 8's safety violations and "Dieselgate" on emissions testing, are often seen as the outcome of corporate governance failures in terms of internal controls, robust materiality process, and transparency.

Even though sociologists have long written about the distribution of power and authority within organizations, legal scholars have given a lot of thought to the nexus of property rights (Berle and Means, 1932), and economists have studied the costs of contracts within the firm (Williamson, 1996), it was not until the enlightened combination of strong stock markets, managers gaining more control over firm's decisions, and dispersed ownership that the popularity of agency theory exploded (Jensen and Meckling, 1976). Many strategy scholars studying corporate governance have been heavily influenced by agency theory, focusing mostly on internal governance mechanisms (ownership, boards, and incentives). These are indeed critical pieces of the corporate governance puzzle, and the next two chapters in this volume are dedicated to boards and owners.

Internal and external corporate governance mechanisms

The tripod in the early corporate governance studies was owners-boards-managers, and the problems that corporate governance had to solve were their potential conflicts of interest. The large missing insider piece was employees, which was left to the field of industrial relations and later human resource management. Given the changing nature of employment relationships—for example, as independent contractors, knowledge workers, or collective pension fund holders—the role of employees in the corporate governance equation deserves more attention. The relationship between the structure (not as much the behavior) of boards and managers, particularly the CEO, has been well researched (Daily and Schwenk, 1996). These studies focus on an array of topics, such as political ideology (Park, Boeker, and Gomulya, 2020), board diversity (Guldiken *et al.*, 2019; Knippen, Shen, and Zhu, 2019), monitoring (Desender *et al.*, 2016), corporate misconduct and lack of transparency (Lungeanu, Paruchuri, and Tsai, 2018; Gomulya and Boeker, 2016), board-TMT relations such as lone insider boards (Zorn *et al.*, 2017), and dual leadership (Krause, 2017). Studies include an agency theory perspective, sociocognitive approaches, and now board behavior as well as institutional forces shape the board-management relationship and in turn organizational outcomes.

Interestingly, the other side of the insider corporate governance link—the owner-board relationship—has not received as much attention, possibly because early studies were more interested in publicly traded firms with widely held ownership where the relationship was more at arm's length. Recent research has focused on the different types of owners, as presented in Connelly's (2021) chapter in this volume. Yet less attention has been given to how these different owners influence boards. The first premise is the acknowledgment that owners and shareholders are not homogeneous, as they differ in their concentration, type, and control rights. In a review, Federo *et al.* (in press) examine how different types of owners (pertaining to family, lone founder, corporation, institutional investor, state, and venture capitalist) influence board governance practices, defined as board structure (visible board design features), composition (directors' characteristics), and processes (boards' practices and behavioral patterns to fulfill their functions). The authors also look at how ownership type influences board functional performance in terms of monitoring, resource provision, and strategic involvement. They show that organizational outcomes from this owner-board governance are highly contingent on the type of owners' behaviors and interests as well as the country in which the firm is operating. This research confirms the rejection of the "one-size-fits-all" best-practice approach in board governance advocated by some policymakers, scholars, and corporate governance activists. Also the research underscores the significance of contingent effects of different types of owners' behaviors and interests in shaping and assessing board governance.

Outside the firm, a series of external corporate governance mechanisms interact with the internal mechanisms. Walsh and Seward (1990) focus mostly on the market for corporate control as a disciplinary tool, albeit a credible threat. Aguilera *et al.* (2015) expand on and discuss the list of the following external corporate governance mechanisms: the legal system, external audits, rating organizations, stakeholder activism, and the media. Then the authors explore whether and how different external mechanisms interact with internal ones to shape firms' governance in terms of protection of stakeholder rights and enforceability, managing stakeholder relations, information disclosure and strategy, and ethical guidance.

Business groups

Organizational structures such as business groups are very much part of the economic landscape of a great number of countries, including South Korea and Italy, and particularly in emerging markets. Scholars have studied business groups extensively, and they continue to evolve and reinvent themselves. Originally, they were created for organic growth through diversification as well as to be more resilient to risk. While business groups have at times been used to expropriate minority shareholders and to artificially sustain unprofitable businesses, particularly state-owned enterprises, their strategic structure equips them with some unique capabilities. For example, in a review article on the relationship between business groups and internationalization, Aguilera, Crespí-Cladera, *et al.* (in press) show that the structure of these business groups' ownership and group affiliation determines internationalization patterns. In addition, the authors also discovered that director and CEO characteristics are associated with the likelihood of pursuing internationalization strategies. Chittoor, Aulakh, and Ray (2019) also show that CEOs tend to pursue international strategies when firms underperform, and this effect is smaller for business groups, as CEOs have more autonomy in the decision-making in stand-alone firms. The business group organizational structure has been taken for granted, but many multinational corporations have adopted it, and it is also common with family and state-owned firms. More research is needed to understand the effectiveness of business groups and whether and how they achieve the purposes for which they were intended.

Shareholder engagement and stewardship

There is a growing stream of research within corporate governance examining how different types of shareholders express their voice or pressure firms to pursue their financial and nonfinancial interests. Some of the engagement mechanisms are included in the following. First, an entire body of work, in parallel with finance studies, focuses on institutional investors' engagement or lack thereof (for instance, index funds). Particularly exciting is research on activist hedge funds, their governance requests (e.g., board seats) and subsequent consequences of their activism for firms (e.g., Ahn and Wiersema, in press; DesJardine and Durand, 2020). A second growing line of research studies the unique corporate governance of responsible investment funds (Yan, Ferraro, and Almandoz, 2019) as well as socially oriented shareholder activism (Hadani, Doh, and Schneider, 2018). They look at market mechanisms such as alignment of managerial pay with sustainability practices (Flammer, Hong, and Minor, 2019) and nonmarket mechanisms borrowed from social movements such as boycotts (McDonnell and King, 2013).

Third, many countries have adopted soft regulation to enact stewardship codes following the initial codes of good governance in the United Kingdom in 2012. These codes encourage deliberate interactions on matters such as strategy, performance, risk, capital structure, and corporate governance between companies and institutional investors and asset managers toward more responsible and long-term-oriented value creation. Fourth, research on shareholder voting and shareholder proposals has also proliferated as there is more access to the data as well as interest groups such as unions, religious organizations, and socially conscientious investors that express their voice (Iliev et al., 2015). There are research opportunities to further explore the influence of shareholder voting in corporate governance, particularly in different proposals. Fifth, as a form of engagement, some French companies are issuing loyalty shares to shareholders who are long-term oriented (Bolton and Samama, 2013). Finally, there is a set of investment assets such as the sovereign wealth fund of Norway and the pension fund of California that engage in activism by warning investee companies of the potential risk of delisting them from their large portfolios if they do not adhere to certain corporate governance and sustainability rules. Shareholder activism is an area of corporate governance that should receive more strategic attention, given the increasing power of shareholders with access to information and more impactful and less costly tactics such as social media exposure.

Corporate political activism

Governments and companies have a symbiotic relationship. There is work that examines the nonmarket strategies that firms and governments undertake, such as inviting politicians to the board or having CEOs advise the government. In the case of state-owned companies, it is more apparent (Tihanyi et al., 2019), but these interconnections occur across all types of ownership. A specific kind of corporate political activism is when companies contribute to political parties or engage in lobbying (Hadani and Schuler, 2013; Hillman, Keim, and Schuler, 2004). The motivation for this corporate political spending is generally attributed to minimizing the environmental uncertainty when government changes the rules of the game. This is confirmed in a study by Shi, Gao, and Aguilera (in press) where they analyze the political spending of U.S. firms with foreign institutional investors as part owners. They find that the greater the level of foreign ownership, the greater the spending, and that this relationship is contingent on the firms' dependence on government contracting and the strategic nature of the industry. Following the Citizens United ruling in the United States, political spending there is expected to keep growing and to interfere with other firm governance decisions.

Theoretical innovations

In terms of theoretical innovations, in addition to multiple developments and extensions to resource dependency theory (Marquis and Qian, 2014), stakeholder theory (Freeman et al., 2010), and actor-center institutionalism (Aguilera and Jackson, 2003), three perspectives contribute to existing debates in corporate governance. The first one, team production, is an old idea transplanted from economics into the governance setting. Blair and Stout's (1999) team production model of governance departs from the premise that shareholders are the only ones to contribute to the corporation;

rather, other members of the production function also contribute to value creation, therefore suggesting a team production model of internal and external members with the board as a mediating hierarchy for distributing the surplus of team production and resolving the disputes among stakeholders. Lan and Heracleous (2010) contrast team production theory with agency theory to explain the superior bargaining power of the board vis-à-vis shareholders.

The second perspective is the development of behavioral theory to understand corporate governance processes, with a strong reliance on sociocultural dynamics, decision-making, and political bargaining. For example, Van Ees, Gabrielsson, and Huse (2009) propose that a behavioral theory of boards and corporate governance should focus on interactions inside and outside the firm—decisions are made by coalitions of actors, and outcomes are the result of political bargaining—thus, cooperation is part of the process of board decision-making. Westphal and Park's (2020) book draws on symbolic management to integrate the different components of behavioral processes into one agentic, political process by which "organizational actors leverage norms, values, beliefs, and assumptions in the broader culture to exert influence over perceptions and behavior of organizational stakeholders" (1). Westphal and Garg (2021) discuss further these fruitful theoretical insights and its contribution to corporate governance research in this volume.

The third perspective is deliberative corporate governance, which draws from political philosophy and seeks to introduce greater democracy into the governance process (Scherer and Voegtlin, 2020). It encompasses bringing into the public discourse all the stakeholders and having reflexivity and participation as the building blocks toward reaching authentic, inclusive, and consequential responsible decisions. According to Scherer and Voegtlin (2020), deliberation can help corporations define the right goals, choose the appropriate means, and secure social acceptance. Acosta, Acquier, and Gond (2019) tested this perspective against coercive norms within a Colombian supplier company during the implementation of a client's global CSR program. It is a powerful perspective particularly in the processes that require stakeholder involvement and seek social innovations to tackle grand societal challenges.

Comparative corporate governance

Comparative corporate governance research focuses on the nature of the country's corporate governance to understand how firms' governance differs across countries (Aguilera and Jackson, 2010). A related area of research is that of the corporate governance of the multinational corporation (MNC) and how, as its subsidiaries cross borders, they adopt their host countries' governance practices (Aguilera, Marano, and Haxhi, 2019). Comparative capitalism work in political economy has categorized advanced industrialized countries into coordinated (Germany and Japan, civil law) and liberal market economies (United Kingdom and United States, common law) (Hall and Soskice, 2001). The argument is that the institutional environment of these market economies defines the coalitions among corporate governance actors (Aguilera and Jackson, 2003), the ownership firm concentration (La Porta, Lopez-de-Silanes, and Shleifer, 1999), employee rights, and most other governance practices. Building on this institutional and actor-centered perspective, Fainshmidt and colleagues (2018) classified understudied countries in terms of their institutions and corresponding corporate governance systems.

The argument is that corporate governance systems are the product of the history of the industry and country in which an organization is embedded. Specifically, the industrial and national institutional settings define the political and economic power of different interest groups, their voice, authority, and exit. While most of the corporate governance research has been conducted in the U.S. context, the United States is an outlier in terms of its unique ownership structure, developed and sophisticated financial intermediaries, strong minority shareholder rights, weak employee rights, open labor market, aggressive corporate political activism, and lack of welfare state, to mention just a few aspects of American exceptionalism. It is now more imperative that we examine alternative corporate governance systems that have proven resilient to financial crises (possibly Canada) that are built on egalitarian values (Nordic countries), religious tenets (Middle Eastern countries), or strong family/clan values (Asian countries).

Three areas of research in the linkage between country and firm governance require attention, particularly from a comparative corporate governance perspective. First is the belief that the quality of corporate governance at the country level leads to more competitive economies. For example, the OECD claims that "[Good] corporate governance is an essential means to create an environment of market confidence and business integrity that supports capital market development and corporate access to equity capital for long-term productive investments. As a matter of fact, the quality of a country's corporate governance framework is of decisive importance for the dynamics and the competitiveness of a country's business sector" (Organisation for Economic Co-operation and Development, 2019: 9). This strong relationship requires further empirical work, particularly outside the United States, to demonstrate the country-firm governance relationship and its causality, along with the definition and measurement of a high quality of corporate governance and for whom. Some societies might be more effective with informal governance norms because they are more effective than formal rules. It also remains to be answered whether the country or the organization has the most influence on firm governance.

A second line of research that emanates from this country-versus-firm governance discussion is how transportable governance practices are across countries. On the one hand, one area that needs more research is the efforts that firms make to change their governance by going to other countries. For example, *bonding* is where firms become listed on foreign market exchanges to borrow the quality of the country's corporate governance and gain governance legitimacy. Alternatively, *governance arbitrage* is when firms locate in a country with lower-quality corporate governance to bypass stringent home-country corporate governance practices such as disclosure requirements or independent boards. Alternatively, there are studies on the diffusion of corporate governance practices around the world, which started with codes of good governance, contingent pay, and more recently have addressed diverse boards and TMTs. The challenge here is that many corporate governance practices do not translate well across borders and might be only symbolically adopted.

Finally, most countries fall in some ideal type of corporate governance system where its different pieces are in equilibrium to reinforce each other—such as strong employee voice, strong internal labor markets, and employee training, or weak minority shareholder rights, ownership concentration, and weak capital markets (Aguilera and Jackson, 2003). However, further empirical research is needed to identify when some firms enjoy significant degrees of freedom or governance deviance in their corporate practices, and how they exercise them (Aguilera, Judge, and Terjesen, 2018). Firms might choose to operate outside of the zone of acceptance of a given country's corporate governance system because it gives them a competitive advantage. As firms become more global, we need to better understand whether national governance systems will evolve to a new hybrid or will converge, as there are only a few golden rules of corporate governance.

Salient Corporate Governance Themes for Changing Times

The significant technological, environmental, socioeconomic, and geopolitical changes in the last two decades—topped off with the 2008 global financial crisis and the 2020 global health crisis—have highlighted the potential for firms and their corporate governance as possible rescuers and mitigators, particularly as public governance is facing its own challenges given the urgency of these global grand social challenges. In turn, firms and financiers are realizing that paying attention to these grand social challenges can buffer their long-term risk. Boards, shareholders, and other governance actors lead the shifting nature of value creation as new demands and societal expectations arise. Three critical themes emerge: the debate on the purpose of the corporation, raising demands for CSR accountability in light of the UN Global Sustainability Goals and other transnational initiatives, and the need to rein in the digital economy and its companies.

The purpose of the firm and rekindling the debate on shareholder-stakeholder maximization

The world is at a crossroads in terms of political, economic, and social turmoil. Regular citizens, whether shareholders through their pensions, the Sisters of St. Francis Philadelphia, or part-time baristas or Uber drivers without benefits, now have more information on what firms do, how their CEOs think, where they source their products, and so on. In addition, global institutional investors are increasingly aware of the financial significance of companies' environmental and social strategies, bringing much greater attention to companies' societal responsibilities. It is possible that we are returning to the roots of capitalism, where corporations were expected to not simply maximize shareholder value but also to safeguard nonshareholder stakeholder interests. These pressures have led to a growing number of corporate and institutional advocates around the world calling for firms to think about their purpose.

In Europe and other parts of the world, this debate has not been as prominent because stakeholders are typically protected in the law or by stronger social norms. In the United States, the movement toward safeguarding the stakeholders started in the 1980s with Martin Lipton's corporate governance innovation of the poison pill to protect companies from hostile takeovers (Lipton and Rosenblum, 1991), and reemerged in 2016 when he started collaborating with the World Economic Forum to design a "new paradigm" for corporate governance. The debate about the purpose of the firm beyond shareholders was heightened with Larry Fink's (CEO of the world's largest asset manager, BlackRock) letter to shareholders in January 2018 asking companies to find a "sense of purpose." This was followed by a cascading trend of strategic leaders becoming societal leaders for advancing social change (Krause and Miller, 2021) such as the U.S. Business Roundtable's (BRT) revised statement in August 2019 on the purpose of the corporation beyond maximizing shareholder value (Harrison, Phillips, and Freeman, 2020) and the Davos Manifesto of 2020: The Universal Purpose of the Company in the Fourth Industrial Revolution. Scholars such as Colin Mayer in his 2018 book *Prosperity*, and the subsequent report titled "Principles for Purposeful Business," have articulated innovative ideas to reinvent capitalism to be more socially and environmentally focused. Along the same line, France introduced a regulation in its commercial code that firms were required to publicly state their purpose (Filatotchev, Aguilera, and Wright, 2020). In the questioning of the purpose of the corporation and shared value initiatives, new organizations are constituted as social enterprises, for-benefit corporations, and other hybrid models that seek to pursue simultaneously economic and noneconomic goals.

This stakeholder orientation based on the stakeholder perspective (see the chapter by Barney and Mackey in this volume on the stakeholder perspective) has heavily influenced corporate governance research and given rise to proponents of stakeholder capitalism, particularly in corporate law. Stakeholder capitalism rests on the premise that firms' value creation cannot be achieved solely by maximizing short-term shareholder value as it also requires the management and oversight of long-term risks and opportunities. Similarly, stakeholder capitalism incorporates the idea that simply attending to shareholders is myopic because the firm is created as a system that depends also on the broader stakeholders for its survival. This perspective rejects the idea of maximizing one interest group to the exclusion of all others.

Questions have been raised about stakeholderism from different fronts. First, there is the question of whether focusing on stakeholders and firm purpose beyond maximizing shareholder value might be a rhetorical strategy. Second, the Council on

Institutional Investors (CII) stated that the BRT statement shows a potential lack of accountability to firms' shareholders, and Bebchuk and Tallarita's (in press) article argues that this call has no teeth because, among other things, it was not consulted on by the board and firms do not seem to change their practices beyond words.

The once-sharp distinction between shareholder and stakeholder systems of corporate governance has become blurred, at least regarding rhetorical commitments to broader stakeholder interests and overall responsibility, with important implications for corporate governance. Two implications of this inward focus are (1) investors' heightened responsible engagement and (2) further requests for environmental, social, and governance (ESG) disclosure. Future research should analyze the mechanisms of stakeholder engagement and their success, as well as bring much-needed clarity to the materiality and roadblocks to nonfinancial disclosure. These two areas are possibly more advanced outside the United States, where regulation has been debated at the transnational level, such as the European Union.

The visibility of environmental, social, and governance (ESG) rating and reporting and its challenges moving forward

As an almost separate movement from the "purpose of the corporation" and triggered by imminent societal grand challenges—particularly concerning climate change, economic inequality, and diversity issues—there has been a tremendous interest and increase in corporate social responsibility (CSR) and financial instruments of responsible investments. For instance, in the United States, 1,243 institutions jointly having $14 trillion in assets have pledged to divest of fossil fuels (GoFossilFree.org), and globally a total of $32 trillion in assets is managed under the broadest definition of responsible investment. Corporate governance is at the core of sustainability decisions, yet little research has been conducted at the intersection of corporate governance and CSR (an exception being Jain and Jamali, 2016; Zaman *et al.*, in press). In a recent systematic review of 124 articles focusing on corporate governance and environmental sustainability, Aguilera, Marano, *et al.* (in press) discuss the contribution of each corporate governance actor (shareholders, managers, directors, and employees) to environmental sustainability outcomes, broken down into environmental strategy (e.g., proactivity, reactivity, and inertia), environmental performance (e.g., emissions, improvement, and violations), and environmental disclosure (e.g., voluntary vs. mandatory). We suggest developing a wholistic perspective that explores how the different corporate governance actors engage with each other regarding environmental decisions, the need to explore further the risks of greenwashing related to the adoption of symbolic as opposed to substantive practices, and scant attention to the global dimension and scalability of environmental issues.

There are important cross-national differences in CSR measurement, requirements, enforcement, and compliance because firms operate in different institutional environments. A study by Surroca *et al.* (2020) analyzes the types of CSR investments (symbolic vs. substantive) that managers with different shareholder orientations (shareholder vs. stakeholder value maximization) pursue if alleviated from short-termism pressure by different entrenchment governance practices (i.e., golden parachutes, poison pills, staggered boards, etc.). The authors find that, in short-term and shareholder-maximizing countries such as the United States, when managers are relieved from short-term pressures they are more likely to invest in substantial CSR that contributes to ultimate firm financial value. Instead, it seems that in countries with more patient capital and a longer-term view, managers are more likely to ally with majority owners and invest in symbolic CSR that does not necessarily contribute to financial performance. We know that corporate governance practices do not travel well across countries as they operate in tandem with other practices in the corporate governance bundle.

The main risk of these sustainability efforts from the corporate governance point of view is greenwashing—decoupling the sustainability efforts into mere symbolic actions but not fully adopting them, thereby conveying a false impression that the firm is engaging in sustainable practices. This risk could be minimized with proper measurement, standardized reporting, and mandatory disclosure that enable corporate governance actors to make better sustainability investments. Three challenges stand out when it comes to reporting: (1) the insufficient materiality of some of the items disclosed (Khan, Serafeim, and Yoon, 2016), (2) the fragmentation in reporting standards, and (3) the lack of integration of ESG and data stewardship into mainstream financial reporting. The International Business Council and the Big Four accounting firms have developed a joint framework for ESG reporting that they hope companies will adopt in their future accounting for non-financial reporting. This still is not fully convergent with existing reporting frameworks such as the Task Force on Climate-Related Financial Disclosure, the Sustainability Accounting Standards Board, and the Global Reporting Initiative. Given the urgency of the issues related to ESG, the primary concern for future research would seem to be to understand how ESG works around the world and to assess its impact for firms and society. Future research could examine the relationship between quality of reporting and substantive corporate change and its effects on a firm's long-term value creation. Another interesting question to explore is what types of governance might facilitate the coordination of different stakeholders to persuade firms to become heroic leaders in this space.

Corporate governance of artificial intelligence

The unprecedented growth in digital innovation beyond "the internet as we know it" is creating new business opportunities and business models that bring in economic value by transforming existing companies (Kellogg, Valentine, and Christin, 2020). This is especially prevalent in strategic industries, such as health care, transportation, and energy, which have incorporated applications of artificial intelligence (AI) into their operations and processes—for example, robotics and autonomous vehicles, computer vision, virtual agents, and machine learning have become more efficient. Stanford University's AI Index 2019 Annual Report (Perrault *et al.,* 2019) reveals that global private AI investment in 2019 was over US$70 billion, and global investment in AI start-ups rose from a total of US$1.3 billion in 2010 to over US$40.4 billion in 2018. This AI revolution fed with big data generates a new socioeconomic fabric, sometimes referred to as "surveillance capitalism" (Zuboff, 2019), and—with calls to rein in unsupervised algorithms (Hosanagar, 2020)—will continue to shape and disrupt organizational activities (Wright and Schultz, 2018). Effectively exploiting AI will require not only operational innovations but also new governance practices and mechanisms that support complex and responsible cross-sector and cross-border AI collaborations, and that protect governments, companies, and users. Possibly triggered by the COVID-19 pandemic, AI decisions have been elevated to the board of directors because of their systemic impact and potential risks. It is important to think about frameworks that can help us govern AI in a responsible and ethical way that contributes to firm value and societal progress.

Emerging markets will likely play a disproportionate role in driving digital innovation because of their high GDP growth rates, competitive cost structures, and relatively lax regulations. Ideally, AI innovations will help close the traditional digital divide and narrow the economic inequality within and across countries. However, new or enhanced institutions, legal frameworks, and global governance structures will be necessary to facilitate and regulate the responsible widespread use of digital innovation and AI in research and development, intellectual property, data management, and privacy domains. Companies in emerging markets can use corporate governance to better structure their AI and, in turn, use AI to strengthen corporate governance. Future research needs to help identify supportive corporate governance systems that allow the deployment of low-cost innovative solutions with widespread impact.

The main challenges include the fact that technology often advances much faster than rules and norms to regulate the results of it (Flyverbom, Deibert, and Matten, 2019) and that technological growth is occurring on a global scale, that is, across national boundaries. Additionally, advances in technology make it possible to collect and process vast amounts of data with increasing smartphone adoption, internet access, and social media activity. Online user activity (in the forms of clicks, purchases, GPS location tracking, etc.) leading to generation of big data gives rise to a new problem—that of privacy and user consent. At the regulatory level, the European Union (EU) has made the most progress with the General Data Protection Regulation (GDPR) law on data protection and privacy covering all European companies and companies operating in the EU and European Economic Area. The primary goal of this EU law is to harmonize and simplify existing EU regulation on data protection and processing, allowing individuals to control their personal data. A close follower is the California Consumer Privacy Act (CCPA), which was signed in 2018 and came into effect on January 1, 2020. These two regulations are much needed in a world replete with digital transactions and may prove to be a harbinger of regulatory change in guiding boards, managers, and customers.

Aguilera and Chhillar (2020) review the existing management and strategy literature on AI and conclude that we are in the embryonic stages of this research in this field, with more questions than answers. The Von Krogh, Ben-Menahem, and Shrestha chapter in this volume provides more detail on digital strategies and artificial intelligence. From the point of view of corporate governance, the two main challenges are bias and opacity. First, as data get bigger and algorithms become smarter, organizations often end up with unintended consequences, such as biased outcomes due to biased training data or agents strategically self-learning to alter the functioning and output of the algorithm (Choudhury, Starr, and Agarwal, in press; Lambrecht and Tucker, 2019). For example, Amazon discontinued its machine learning–based hiring platform due to a gender bias that occurred as a result of biased training data. The machine learning model disproportionately favored male applicants based on its training based on résumés of candidates received by Amazon in the last 10 years, which contained an overrepresentation of male candidates (Shrestha, Ben-Menahem, and von Krogh, 2019). Moreover, often there is *opacity* about how the algorithm produces a given efficient outcome. This leaves little room for monitoring and revising, suggesting a greater need for self-governing and external mechanisms to promote accountability and responsibility.

The corporate governance of AI in organizations is a fruitful area of study, both conceptually and empirically, given the need to address imminent questions. Suggestions for future research include the following: How is AI-created value distributed among the different users? How can the boundaries be designed where the firm ends and the user starts? Who has the responsibility over the algorithms and the data that are fed into them? How can digital audits be structured to allow for greater disclosure and transparency? Who should regulate boards to responsibly use AI to create value? In sum, it is time to add a D to ESG for digital stewardship (ESGD) and into the corporate governance equation.

Conclusion

This chapter cannot be closed without noting that COVID-19 represents an inflection point in the role of corporations in society and its stakeholder expectations. Many companies have shifted their shareholder value focus to give high priority to the health and safety of their employees (Paine, 2020: 4) and customers. Thus, in the pandemic and postpandemic periods, recent calls for corporations to give a stronger voice to nonshareholder stakeholders will require that boards recalibrate their strategic oversight and decision-making processes. Future research should take an interdisciplinary approach and evaluate whether companies are "walking the talk," not only from a communications point of view but also in how they structure their stakeholders' incentives for value creation in the long term and guarantee sustained accountability, both moral as well as legal. In a nutshell, boards almost have no choice if they want to survive but to attend to an array of stakeholders in addition to shareholders.

It is also clear that the current grand societal systemic challenges—wealth inequality, climate change, environmental degradation, racial and ethnic discrimination, cyber fraud, food security, and so on—which are global and exacerbated by both the pandemic and the digital divide, are affecting how owners, boards, managers, employees, and related stakeholders resolve trade-offs in decision-making about firm market and nonmarket strategies. Future research should examine these decision-makers as interrelated actors and ask, What is the purpose of a given firm or set of firms? What incentives and punishments are in place to guide that purpose? Would diversity alone be the purpose of the corporation—aligned with a racially diverse board? How can we better measure governance processes and their outcomes? How can we account for the industry, sector, regional, national, transnational, or virtual environment in which these corporations operate? To explore these questions, it is often helpful to find intermediate organizational outcomes, such as R&D investment, training, and diversification, that in turn might lead to enhancing financial and non-financial firm performance. In all, the future is replete with research opportunities to continue to explore how, when, and why effective corporate governance practices and processes are key to healthy, long-term firm sustainability and value creation for shareholders and beyond.

References

Acosta P, Acquier A, Gond JP. 2019. Revisiting politics in political CSR: how coercive and deliberative dynamics operate through institutional work in a Colombian company. *Organization Studies*. https://doi.org/10.1177/0170840619867725.

Aguilera RV, Chhillar D. 2020. An eye for AI: insights into the governance of artificial intelligence and vision for future research. Working Paper, Northeastern University.

Aguilera RV, Crespí-Cladera R, Infantes PM, Pascual-Fuster B. In press. Business groups and internationalization: effective identification and future agenda. *Journal of World Business* 55(4): https://doi.org/10.1016/j.jwb.2019.101050.

Aguilera, RV, Desender K, Bednar MK, Lee JH. 2015. Connecting the dots: bringing external corporate governance into the corporate governance puzzle. *Academy of Management Annals* 9(1): 483–573.

Aguilera, RV, Grøgaard B. 2019. The dubious role of institutions in international business: a road forward. *Journal of International Business Studies* 50(1): 20–35.

Aguilera RV, Jackson G. 2003. The cross-national diversity of corporate governance: dimensions and determinants. *Academy of Management Review* 28(3): 447–465.

Aguilera RV, Jackson G. 2010. Comparative and international corporate governance. *Academy of Management Annals* 4(1): 485–556.

Aguilera RV, Judge WQ, Terjesen SA. 2018. Corporate governance deviance. *Academy of Management Review* 43(1): 87–109.

Aguilera RV, Marano V, Aragon-Correa A, Tashman P. In press. The corporate governance of environmental sustainability: a review and proposal for more integrated research. *Journal of Management*.

Aguilera RV, Marano V, Haxhi I. 2019. International corporate governance: a review and opportunities for future research. *Journal of International Business Studies* 50(3): 457–498.

Ahn A, Wiersema M. In press. Activist hedge funds: beware the new titans. *Academy of Management Perspectives*. https://doi.org/10.5465/amp.2018.0059

Bebchuk L, Tallarita R. In press. The illusory promise of stakeholder governance. *Cornell Law Journal*.

Berle AA, Means GC. 1932. *The Modern Corporation and Private Property*. Transaction: New Brunswick, NJ.

Blair MM, Stout LA. 1999. A team production theory of corporate law. *Virginia Law Review* 85(2): 247–328.

Boivie S, Bednar MK, Aguilera RV, Andrus JL. 2016. Are boards designed to fail? The implausibility of effective board monitoring. *Academy of Management Annals* 10(1): 319–407.

Bolton P, Samama F. 2013. Loyalty-shares: rewarding long-term investors. *Journal of Applied Corporate Finance* 25(3): 86–97.

Boyd BK, Gove S, Solarino AM. 2017. Methodological rigor of corporate governance studies: a review and recommendations for future studies. *Corporate Governance: An International Review* 25(6): 384–396.

Brauer M, Wiersema M. 2018. Analyzing analyst research: a review of past coverage and recommendations for future research. *Journal of Management* 44(1): 218–248.

Busenbark JR, Krause R, Boivie S, Graffin, SD. 2016. Toward a configurational perspective on the CEO: a review and synthesis of the management literature. *Journal of Management* 42(1): 234–268.

Chittoor R, Aulakh PS, Ray S. 2019. Microfoundations of firm internationalization: the owner CEO effect. *Global Strategy Journal* 9(1): 42–65.

Choudhury P, Starr E, Agarwal R. In press. Machine learning and human capital complementarities: experimental evidence on bias mitigation. *Strategic Management Journal*.

Colli A, Colpan AM. 2016. Business groups and corporate governance: review, synthesis, and extension. *Corporate Governance: An International Review* 24(3): 274–302.

Connelly, B. 2021. Ownership and governance. In *Strategic Management: State of the Field and Its Future*, Duhaime IM, Hitt MA, Lyles MA (eds). Oxford University Press: New York, NY; 427–441.

Cuomo F, Mallin C, Zattoni A. 2016. Corporate governance codes: a review and research agenda. *Corporate Governance: An International Review* 24(3): 222–241.

Daily CM, Schwenk C. 1996. Chief executive officers, top management teams, and boards of directors: congruent or countervailing forces? *Journal of Management* 22(2): 185–208.

Desender KA, Aguilera RV, Lópezpuertas-Lamy M, Crespi R. 2016. A clash of governance logics: foreign ownership and board monitoring. *Strategic Management Journal* 37(2): 349–369.

DesJardine MR, Durand R. 2020. Disentangling the effects of hedge fund activism on firm financial and social performance. *Strategic Management Journal* 41(6): 1054–1082.

Fainshmidt S, Judge WQ, Aguilera RV, Smith A. 2018. Varieties of institutional systems: a contextual taxonomy of understudied countries. *Journal of World Business* 53(3): 307–322.

Federo R, Ponomareva Y, Aguilera RV, Saz-Carranza A, Losada C. In press. Bringing owners back on board: a review of the role of ownership type in board governance. *Corporate Governance: An International Review*.

Filatotchev I, Aguilera RV, Wright M. 2020. From governance of innovation to innovations in governance. *Academy of Management Perspectives* 34(2): 173–181.

Flammer C, Hong B, Minor D. 2019. Corporate governance and the rise of integrating corporate social responsibility criteria in executive compensation: effectiveness and implications for firm outcomes. *Strategic Management Journal* 40(7): 1097–1122.

Flyverbom M, Deibert R, Matten D. 2019. The governance of digital technology, big data, and the internet: new roles and responsibilities for business. *Business and Society* 58(1): 3–19.

Freeman RE, Harrison JS, Wicks AC, Parmar BL, De Colle S. 2010. *Stakeholder Theory: The State of the Art*. Cambridge University Press: Cambridge, U.K.

Gabaldon P, De Anca C, Mateos de Cabo R, Gimeno R. 2016. Searching for women on boards: an analysis from the supply and demand perspective. *Corporate Governance: An International Review* 24(3): 371–385.

Gedajlovic E, Carney M, Chrisman JJ, Kellermanns FW. 2012. The adolescence of family firm research: taking stock and planning for the future. *Journal of Management* 38(4): 1010–1037.

Gomez-Mejia LR, Cruz C, Berrone P, De Castro J. 2011. The bind that ties: socioemotional wealth preservation in family firms. *Academy of Management Annals* 5(1): 653–707.

Gomulya D, Boeker W. 2016. Reassessing board member allegiance: CEO replacement following financial misconduct. *Strategic Management Journal* 37(9): 1898–1918.

Gordon JN, Ringe WG (eds). 2018. *The Oxford Handbook of Corporate Law and Governance*. Oxford University Press: Oxford, U.K.

Grosman A, Wright M, Okhmatovskiy I. 2016. State control and corporate governance in transition economies: 25 years on from 1989. *Corporate Governance: An International Review* 24(3): 200–221.

Guldiken O, Mallon MR, Fainshmidt S, Judge WQ, Clark CE. 2019. Beyond tokenism: how strategic leaders influence more meaningful gender diversity on boards of directors. *Strategic Management Journal* 40(12): 2024–2046.

Hadani M, Doh, JP, Schneider MA. 2018. Corporate political activity and regulatory capture: how some companies blunt the knife of socially oriented investor activism. *Journal of Management* 44(5): 2064–2093.

Hadani M, Schuler DA. 2013. In search of El Dorado: the elusive financial returns on corporate political investments. *Strategic Management Journal* 34(2): 165–181.

Hall PA, Soskice D. 2001. *Varieties of Capitalism: The Institutional Foundations of Comparative Advantage*. Oxford University Press: Oxford, U.K.

Harrison JS, Phillips RA, Freeman RE. 2020. On the 2019 Business Roundtable "Statement on the Purpose of a Corporation." *Journal of Management* 46(7): 1223–1237.

Hermalin B, Weisbach M (eds). 2017. *The Handbook of the Economics of Corporate Governance*. Elsevier: Amsterdam, the Netherlands.

Hillman AJ, Keim, GD, Schuler D. 2004. Corporate political activity: a review and research agenda. *Journal of Management* 30(6): 837–857.

Hosanagar K. 2020. *A Human's Guide to Machine Intelligence: How Algorithms are Shaping Our Lives and How We Can Stay in Control*. Penguin Books: New York, NY.

Iliev P, Lins KV, Miller DP, Roth L. 2015. Shareholder voting and corporate governance around the world. *Review of Financial Studies* 28(8): 2167–2202.

Jain T, Jamali D. 2016. Looking inside the black box: the effect of corporate governance on corporate social responsibility. *Corporate Governance: An International Review* 24(3): 253–273.

Jensen MC, Meckling WH. 1976. Theory of the firm: managerial behavior, agency costs, and ownership structure. *Journal of Financial Economics* 3(4): 305–360.

Johnson SG, Schnatterly K, Hill AD. 2013. Board composition beyond independence: social capital, human capital, and demographics. *Journal of Management* 39(1): 232–262.

Kellogg KC, Valentine MA, Christin A. 2020. Algorithms at work: the new contested terrain of control. *Academy of Management Annals* 14(1): 366–410.

Khan M, Serafeim G, Yoon A. 2016. Corporate sustainability: first evidence on materiality. *Accounting Review* 91(6): 1697–1724.

Knippen JM, Shen W, Zhu Q. 2019. Limited progress? The effect of external pressure for board gender diversity on the increase of female directors. *Strategic Management Journal* 40(7): 1123–1150.

Krause R. 2017. Being the CEO's boss: an examination of board chair orientations. *Strategic Management Journal* 38(3): 697–713.

Krause R, Miller TL. 2021. From strategic leaders to societal leaders: on the expanding social role of executives and boards. *Journal of Management*. DOI: 0149206320950439.

Krause R, Semadeni M, Cannella AA Jr. 2014. CEO duality: a review and research agenda. *Journal of Management* 40(1): 256–286.

Lambrecht A, Tucker C. 2019. Algorithmic bias? An empirical study of apparent gender-based discrimination in the display of STEM career ads. *Management Science* 65(7): 2966–2981.

Lan LL, Heracleous L. 2010. Rethinking agency theory: the view from law. *Academy of Management Review* 35(2): 294–314.

La Porta R, Lopez-de-Silanes F, Shleifer A. 1999. Corporate ownership around the world. *Journal of Finance* 54(2): 471–517.

Larcker DF, Tayan B. 2020a. *Corporate Governance Matters: A Closer Look at Organizational Choices and Their Consequences*. Pearson Education: Old Tappan, NJ.

Larcker DF, Tayan B. 2020b. Loosey-goosey governance: 4 misunderstood terms. *Corporate Board* 41(241): 5–11.

Lipton M, Rosenblum SA. 1991. A new system of corporate governance: the quinquennial election of directors. *University of Chicago Law Review* 58(1): 187–253.

Lungeanu R, Paruchuri S, Tsai W. 2018. Stepping across for social approval: ties to independent foundations' boards after financial restatement. *Strategic Management Journal* 39(4): 1163–1187.

Ma S, Kor YY, Seidl D. 2020. CEO advice seeking: an integrative framework and future research agenda. *Journal of Management* 46(6): 771–805.

Mallin C. 2019. *Corporate Governance*. Oxford University Press: Oxford, U.K.

Marquis C, Qian C. 2014. Corporate social responsibility reporting in China: symbol or substance? *Organization Science* 25(1): 127–148.

Mayer C. 2018. *Prosperity: Better Business Makes the Greater Good*. Oxford University Press: Oxford, U.K.

McDonnell MH, King B. 2013. Keeping up appearances: reputational threat and impression management after social movement boycotts. *Administrative Science Quarterly* 58(3): 387–419.

McKinsey. 2018. A time for boards to act. https://www.mckinsey.com/business-functions/strategy-and-corporate-finance/our-insights/a-time-for-boards-to-act [1 December 2020].

McNulty T, Zattoni A, Douglas T. 2013. Developing corporate governance research through qualitative methods: a review of previous studies. *Corporate Governance: An International Review* 21(2): 183–198.

Neville F, Byron K, Post C, Ward A. 2019. Board independence and corporate misconduct: a cross-national meta-analysis. *Journal of Management* 45(6): 2538–2569.

Organisation for Economic Co-operation and Development. 2019. *OECD Corporate Governance Factbook*. OECD: Paris, France.

Paine LS. 2020. COVID-19 is rewriting the rules of corporate governance. *Harvard Business Review*, October 6, 2020. https://hbr.org/2020/10/covid-19-is-rewriting-the-rules-of-corporate-governance.

Park UD, Boeker W, Gomulya D. 2020. Political ideology of the board and CEO dismissal following financial misconduct. *Strategic Management Journal* 41(1): 108–123.

PcW. 2020. PcW Annual Corporate Director Survey. https://www.pwc.com/us/en/services/governance-insights-center/library/annual-corporate-directors-survey.html [1 December 2020].

Perrault R, Shoham Y, Brynjolfsson E, Clark J, Etchemendy J, Grosz B, Lyons T, Manyika J, Mishra S, Niebles JC. 2019. *The AI Index 2019 Annual Report*. Stanford University: AI Index Steering Committee, Human-Centered AI Institute: Stanford, CA.

Scherer AG, Voegtlin C. 2020. Corporate governance for responsible innovation: approaches to corporate governance and their implications for sustainable development. *Academy of Management Perspectives* **34**(2): 182–208.

Schiehll E, Martins HC. 2016. Cross-national governance research: a systematic review and assessment. *Corporate Governance: An International Review* **24**(3): 181–199.

Schnatterly K, Gangloff, KA, Tuschke A. 2018. CEO wrongdoing: a review of pressure, opportunity, and rationalization. *Journal of Management* **44**(6): 2405–2432.

Shi W, Gao C, Aguilera R. In press. The liabilities of foreign institutional ownership: managing political dependence through corporate political spending. *Strategic Management Journal*.

Shrestha YR, Ben-Menahem SM, Von Krogh G. 2019. Organizational decision-making structures in the age of artificial intelligence. *California Management Review* **61**(4): 66–83.

Simon HA. 1991. Bounded rationality and organizational learning. *Organization Science* **2**(1): 125–134.

Surroca JA, Aguilera RV, Desender K, Tribó JA. 2020. Is managerial entrenchment always bad and corporate social responsibility always good? A cross-national examination of their combined influence on shareholder value. *Strategic Management Journal* **41**(5): 891–920.

Tihanyi L, Aguilera RV, Heugens P, van Essen M, Sauerwald S, Duran P, Turturea R. 2019. State ownership and political connections. *Journal of Management* **45**(6): 2293–2321.

Tricker B. 2019. *Corporate Governance: Principles, Policies, and Practices.* Oxford University Press: Oxford, U.K.

Uhde, DA, Klarner P, Tuschke A. 2017. Board monitoring of the chief financial officer: a review and research agenda. *Corporate Governance: An International Review* **25**(2): 116–133.

Van Ees H, Gabrielsson J, Huse M. 2009. Toward a behavioral theory of boards and corporate governance. *Corporate Governance: An International Review* **17**(3): 307–319.

Walsh JP, Seward JK. 1990. On the efficiency of internal and external corporate control mechanisms. *Academy of Management Review* **15**(3): 421–458.

Westphal JD, Garg S. 2021. Boards of directors and strategic management in public firms and new ventures. In *Strategic Management: State of the Field and Its Future*, Duhaime IM, Hitt MA, Lyles MA (eds). Oxford University Press: New York, NY; 411–426.

Westphal J, Park SH. 2020. *Symbolic Management: Governance, Strategy, and Institutions.* Oxford University Press: Oxford, U.K.

Williamson OE. 1996. *The Mechanisms of Governance.* Oxford University Press: Oxford, U.K.

World Economic Forum. Davos Manifesto 2020: The Universal Purpose of a Company in the Fourth Industrial Revolution. World Economic Forum: Davos, Switzerland.

Wright SA, Schultz AE. 2018. The rising tide of artificial intelligence and business automation: developing an ethical framework. *Business Horizons* **61**(6): 823–832.

Yan S, Ferraro F, Almandoz J. 2019. The rise of socially responsible investment funds: the paradoxical role of financial logic. *Administrative Science Quarterly* **64**(2): 466–501.

Zaman R, Jain T, Samara G, Jamali D. In press. Corporate social responsibility meets corporate governance: mapping the interface. *Business and Society*.

Zattoni A. 2020. *Corporate Governance. How to Design Good Companies.* Egea, S.p.A.: Milan, Italy.

Zorn ML, Shropshire C, Martin JA, Combs JG, Ketchen DJ Jr. 2017. Home alone: the effects of lone-insider boards on CEO pay, financial misconduct, and firm performance. *Strategic Management Journal* **38**(13): 2623–2646.

Zuboff S. 2019. *The Age of Surveillance Capitalism: The Fight for a Human Future at the New Frontier of Power.* PublicAffairs: New York, NY.

7.1

BOARDS OF DIRECTORS
AND STRATEGIC MANAGEMENT
IN PUBLIC FIRMS AND NEW VENTURES

James D. Westphal and Sam Garg

The board of directors plays a foundational role in strategic management due to its boundary-spanning position at the top of business organizations (Thompson, 1967; Pfeffer and Salancik, 1978). It has the potential to influence each phase of the strategic decision-making process, and the broader process of strategy formation (Mintzberg and Waters, 1985; Garg and Eisenhardt, 2017), from setting strategic goals, to identifying strategic alternatives, to communicating and legitimating the strategy with organizational stakeholders, to monitoring and evaluating its success. The board exerts this broad influence over strategy through multiple means: providing information, input, and analysis; setting incentives; and requisitioning the capital needed for implementation, whether social, human, or financial. Yet, in part because early research on boards was conducted by sociologists who had relatively little interest in strategy, corporate governance scholars are only beginning to examine the full range of the board's influence on strategic management. We briefly review the evolution of research on corporate boards and strategic management, describe contemporary perspectives and emerging topics in the literature, and identify a range of future research opportunities. We then turn to the rapidly growing literature on venture boards and strategy. Our review of recent research on boards of public companies and new ventures reveals a common focus on micro-level behavioral processes in the boardroom, in dyadic CEO-board interactions outside the boardroom, and in relations between directors and external constituents. We describe numerous opportunities to extend these complementary literatures in interesting new directions.

Three Stages of Early Research

The literature on corporate boards and strategy has developed in three overlapping stages. Beginning in the 1980s, financial economists and management scholars applied agency theory to explain the influence of boards on strategy. A central theme in this economics-based literature is that top managers, if left to their own devices, tend to develop strategies that further their own personal interests but fail to max-imize shareholder returns. Another theme is that boards function to constrain self-interested strategies by developing incentive plans that align management and shareholder interests, and by directly monitoring decision-making processes and outcomes (Fama and Jensen, 1983). Moreover, boards are more likely to carry out these functions effectively to the extent that they are independent of management (Hoskisson, Johnson, and Moesel, 1994).

Beyond agency theory: incorporating social structure, strategic knowledge, and different forms of board involvement

While agency theory provided a simple and elegant normative model to assess the impact of boards on strategy and performance, it was criticized by organization theorists for failing to describe social and psychological influences on director be-havior, and for not incorporating variation in directors' strategic knowledge and experience. In the second stage of development, researchers began to correct this "under-embedded" view of boards and strategy by examining the interorganizational diffusion of strategic information through board interlock ties (e.g., Haunschild, 1993; Geletkanycz and Hambrick, 1997). This literature not only showed that director ties to other boards were an important determinant of business and corporate strat-egies, but it addressed how the composition of interlock ties, such as the diversity of directors' strategic experiences on other boards, interacted with features of the busi-ness environment, such as its dynamism, to affect the level and quality of board in-volvement in strategy (e.g., Carpenter and Westphal, 2001; Beckman and Haunschild, 2002). These studies began to incorporate social structure and strategic knowledge and experience into models of board behavior and effectiveness. They also broadened prevailing conceptions of board influence over strategy to include a cooperative form of involvement in which directors provided strategic advice and input to executives, rather than exercising independent control.

At the same time, another stream of research explored micro-social and psycho-logical determinants of the board's contributions to strategy. For example, studies showed how social similarity, friendship ties, and social influence tactics in CEO-director relationships reduce the independence of outside directors and compromise their influence over corporate strategy (e.g., Westphal, 1998).

Bringing culture in: boards and symbolic management

The third stage of development in research on boards and strategy, which con-tinues to the present day, is the incorporation of sociocultural factors into models of board influence over strategic decision-making. One stream of research in this vein reconceives widespread theories of governance such as agency theory as institutional logics, or sets of value-laden assumptions and beliefs about appropriate governance structures, policies, and practices. Studies have provided evidence for symbolic decoupling in which firms adopt board reforms that give the appearance of conforming to agency prescriptions, such as board independence from management, but which are decoupled from actual board behavior (Westphal and Graebner, 2010; Joseph, Ocasio, and McDonnell, 2014). Boards often appear to constrain managerial decision-making on behalf of shareholders, while actually protecting managerial discretion over strategy. Such symbolic decoupling is shown to reduce outside interference in strategic decision-making by powerful institutional investors, especially when accompanied by verbal impression management directed at information intermediaries (e.g., security analysts and journalists) and institutional fund managers (Westphal and Park, 2020). This ongoing stream of research suggests that boards play an important role in the legitimation of strategy.

Other research examines how the cultural norms that prevail in corporate leadership preserve managerial discretion and limit stakeholder influence over strategy. A number of studies have provided evidence for a segmented director labor market in which directors on boards that appear to exercise independent control over management and strategy are more likely to gain appointments on other independent boards, while directors on boards that defer to management tend to gain appointments on similarly deferential boards (Zajac and Westphal, 1996; Benton, 2016; Levit and Malenko, 2016; Li et al., 2018). Moreover, this research generally suggests that the segment that rewards director deference is considerably larger than the segment that rewards independent control (Westphal and Stern, 2007). Prevailing norms of deference to top management, which are particularly strong on issues of corporate strategy, appear to be maintained by informal mentoring and socialization of first-time directors (McDonald and Westphal, 2013), combined with social control of deviant behavior. Directors who participate in board reforms that increase the board's ability to exercise independent control over strategy at a particular firm, such as separating the CEO and board chair positions, are more likely to experience social distancing or informal ostracism at other companies where they serve as director: they are less likely to be invited to informal meetings, their advice is solicited less often, and other directors are less likely to build on their comments and suggestions (Westphal and Khanna, 2003).

New Directions

Boards are both agents and subjects of symbolic management, which might raise concerns about the sincerity and credibility of their accounts. However, scholars are beginning to examine cooperative forms of symbolic management that may have more influence on stakeholder assessments of governance and strategy than firm-level impression management by directors about their own board's involvement in strategy.

For example, recent research has documented the spread of symbolic management support, in which board members and top managers make positive remarks about the leadership, governance, and/or strategy of particular other firms in their communications with information intermediaries such as journalists and analysts (Westphal and Park, 2020). Symbolic management support is a kind of generalized social exchange: leaders who receive such support feel socially obligated to pay it forward when given the opportunity, such that cooperative forms of symbolic management have diffused among corporate leaders over time.

Moreover, there is evidence that cooperative symbolic management has not only influenced stakeholder beliefs about individual firms and their leaders, but over time it may have had a deeper influence on normative assumptions about governance, including the criteria by which stakeholders evaluate boards and their contributions to strategy. The rhetoric of symbolic management support reinterprets major prescriptions of agency theory in ways that reassert the final decision-making authority of top management. In particular, board involvement in strategic planning was redefined as participative decision-making and democratic governance, and board independence from management was reinterpreted as a means of giving objective advice and counsel to executives, rather than as a means of exercising control over top management to mitigate agency problems created by self-interested strategies. This rhetoric draws normative legitimacy from the social logic of democratic process (Westphal, Zhu, and Kunapuli, 2020), rather than from the economic logic of independent monitoring and control.

There are many opportunities to conduct further research on the ways in which boards legitimize corporate governance and strategy. For example, there is a need for research on an emerging form of symbolic management in which corporate directors, in communicating with journalists at general media outlets, highlight the sparsity of board interlock ties between firms in their industry as part of a narrative of competition (Westphal and Park, 2020). Such rhetoric is often put forth in the context of corporate disclosures that might arouse antitrust concerns, such as merger announcements in concentrated industries. Research could examine whether these communications contribute to the prevailing impression among many journalists that firm leaders have become increasingly independent of one another.

Such impression management is important, because the appearance of independence and competition between leaders may belie a persistently high level of relational and structural embeddedness. Although board interlock ties between competitors are indeed rare, top executives are often connected by two-step network ties in which the friends of a firm's CEO serve on the board of a competitor firm (Westphal and Zhu, 2019). There is a need for systematic research on whether and how such "board-friendship ties" reduce the intensity of competition between firms. Executives and directors are connected by other kinds of indirect ties as well, including shared ties to headhunters and other management consultants (Westphal and Park, 2020). There is a multifaceted decoupling between appearances and reality in the social structure of firm leadership, including corporate directors, and it has increased over time. Whereas board interlocks have become more sparse, informal and less visible connections such as board-friendship ties have become more common. Future studies can examine whether symbolic management by corporate directors plays a role in the increasing separation between stakeholder assumptions about the relations among firm leaders and the reality inside corporate leadership, as well as the consequences of this decoupling for firm strategy and performance.

Symbolic management about strategic decision-making and governance processes

While boards are an agent of symbolic management about governance and strategy in their communications with stakeholders, they are also an audience of symbolic management about strategy in their communications with managers. Recent research has identified a potent form of symbolic action in which top executives adopt participative strategic decision-making (PSDM) programs that purportedly use crowdsourcing technology to solicit input from lower-level managers about strategic options available to the firm, but decouple the programs from actual strategic decision-making, in the sense that executives decide on a strategic option *before* soliciting input under the program (Westphal, Zhu, and Kunapuli, 2020). Executive communication about PSDM programs reduces the propensity for outside directors to raise questions about strategic decisions, even decisions that were communicated to the board more than a year later (and which were not the subject of participation under the program). Thus, impression management in relations between managers and directors, including impression management about strategy processes, is an important topic of future research on boards and strategy; such communication is increasing, and there is a need to better understand the mechanisms and consequences of such behavior.

There is also a need for further research on the symbolic management of governance processes. Among the most prominent governance innovations in recent years is the lead independent director. Krause, Withers, and Semadeni (2017) found that appointing a lead independent director positively affects the recommendations of security analysts, and also positively influences stock returns and return on investment when CEO power is low, but not when it is high. The authors suggest that lead independent directors can enhance the legitimacy of board governance, even though powerful CEOs may circumvent the lead director's monitoring efforts (Semadeni and Krause, 2020). Krause *et al.*'s (2017) results also suggest that the widespread appointment of lead independent directors may have forestalled pressures for more substantial reforms in board leadership structure, such as separating the CEO and board chair positions.

The role of new technology in decision-making processes, governance, and symbolic management

The symbolic management of PSDM programs reveals another important trend that merits further research attention: the growing use of technology in strategic decision-making and corporate governance processes, and the tendency to *highlight* the use of new technologies in communicating about strategy and governance processes with directors and external stakeholders. In recent years, rhetoric about strategic decision-making has increasingly referenced "new" techniques and processes that ostensibly complement or enhance crowdsourcing, such as machine learning. References to machine learning in crowdsourcing and other participatory decision-making processes obscure the substantial role of consultants and top executives in processing and aggregating strategic input. By highlighting the use of technological innovations in decision-making, executives associate their leadership and strategies with technological progress, triggering an optimistic mindset and focusing attention away from evaluating the performance consequences of previous decisions.

In communicating with activist investors, executives increasingly refer to the use of information technologies such as machine learning and artificial intelligence in corporate governance processes, including director selection (Westphal and Park, 2020). These technologies are ostensibly used to search more broadly for qualified board candidates and predict their performance as directors, in response to pressure from activist investors to increase board diversity and enhance the capacity of boards to monitor and advise management (Zhu, Shen, and Hillman, 2014). There is a need for systematic research on the use of information technologies in director search and selection processes, and the consequences for board effectiveness. In principle, big data technologies could be a valuable tool in increasing the diversity, depth, and relevance of board members' strategic expertise. On the other hand, these technologies may contain implicit biases (Filatotchev, Aguilera, and Wright, 2020) that perpetuate homophily. There is also the potential for a kind of decoupling, akin to the decoupling of PSDM programs, in which information technology is portrayed as guiding the search and selection process, when it actually serves to rationalize choices already made. Moreover, advertising the use of these technologies lends a veneer of objectivity to board processes that are known to be chronically vulnerable to similarity and attraction biases.

Board diversity and strategic management

There is long-standing evidence that diversity on such dimensions as functional background, education, and strategic experience is linked to the level and quality of board involvement in strategic decision-making, especially in changing business environments (e.g., Carpenter and Westphal, 2001; Haynes and Hillman, 2010;

Hambrick, Misangyi, and Park, 2015). However, corporate stakeholders increasingly gauge diversity in firm leadership according to the representation of women and racial minorities on corporate boards (Perrault, 2015; Knippen, Shen, and Zhu, 2019), and we still know relatively little about how diversity in these dimensions affects strategy and performance. Diversity does not guarantee inclusion, and in fact female and racial-minority directors often face significant barriers to having an equal influence on strategy and policy, particularly under conditions of low firm performance when diverse input is most needed (Westphal and Milton, 2000). Moreover, research on the "glass cliff" phenomenon suggests that minority directors may face a greater risk of dismissal. Main and Gregory-Smith (2018) showed that female directors in the United Kingdom tend to have shorter tenures than men, and they face a much higher risk of dismissal after serving nine years, when they lose their status as independent directors.

At the same time, while minority directors are less likely to be included in informal policy discussions when firm performance is poor, firm leaders are particularly likely to highlight the firm's commitment to diversity in their communications with infomediaries and other corporate stakeholders under these conditions (Westphal and Park, 2020). Such communications tend to include broad claims about the benefits of diversity to strategy, firm leadership, and/or performance. What's more, minority directors are sometimes enlisted to help with these communications. In response to open-ended questions about the contributions of fellow directors, white men were more likely to mention contributions to strategy- or policy-related issues by their white male colleagues, while mentioning participation in external communications with certain stakeholders (e.g., security analysts) by female and racial-minority colleagues (Westphal and Park, 2020). The overall pattern of evidence suggests that, especially under conditions of poor performance, minority directors are often valued more for their contributions to symbolic management, and less for their substantive contributions to strategic decision-making.

As the racial and gender diversity of boards has taken on greater symbolic significance—not only as an indication of leaders' commitment to organizational diversity, but as a signal of trustworthiness and responsiveness to corporate stakeholders (Perrault, 2015)—decoupling between diversity and inclusion increasingly threatens the moral legitimacy of corporate leadership and governance. While a growing literature has compared the effectiveness of different policies and procedures in promoting goals related to diversity, equity, and inclusion at lower levels of organizations, scholars have devoted little attention to the effectiveness of such interventions in corporate leadership and governance. There is a clear need and opportunity to conduct systematic research on policy and practice interventions that promote greater inclusiveness in boards and strategic decision-making.

A major focus in the strategy literature on boards has been to increase our understanding of strategic processes at different levels of analysis, including social and psychological processes within boards, and the content of relations between boards and external constituents. A long-standing criticism of the empirical literature, however, is that it focuses mainly on public companies. In the following section, we describe a rapidly growing body of research on the boards of venture firms, that is, privately owned, professionally funded entrepreneurial companies (Garg, 2013), which is beginning to fill the gap with new theoretical and empirical insights. This literature has also extended prior research on public-firm boards by deepening our understanding of behavioral processes in the boardroom and outside, with a particular focus on the multiple roles played by directors and how CEOs can harness their boards effectively in the strategic management of technology-based ventures. We identify plentiful opportunities to extend this literature in future theory and empirical research.

Venture Boards and Strategy

Venture boards play a critical role in the strategic management of ventures through both active monitoring and resource provisioning (Garg and Furr, 2017). Recent empirical evidence suggests they are involved in a range of strategic outcomes, such as alliances, innovation, mergers and acquisitions (M&As), and initial public offerings (IPOs) (Amornsiripanitch, Gompers, and Xuan, 2019; Garg, Howard, and Pahnke, 2019). Several factors promote the strategic involvement of venture boards. First, venture directors (many of whom are investors) are financially motivated to pursue rapid growth and ultimately lucrative M&As or IPOs (Garg, 2013); they are also often knowledgeable about the firm's sector and structurally powerful to push forward their ideas (Fried and Ganor, 2006). Second, the agency problem is not central in ventures because venture CEOs are often well aligned (Garg, 2020b), and so the board's focus can be on firm growth through innovation and strategic management. Third, small board size, frequent board meetings (every four to six weeks), and general absence of formal board structures (e.g., board committees) tend to promote relatively high levels of director participation in the key strategic issues (Garg and Eisenhardt, 2017). Venture boards can also focus on strategy because there is simply less regulatory compliance work (Fried, Bruton, and Hisrich, 1998).

Research finds that directors are involved in strategic management of ventures through their active monitoring, especially when ventures are geographically proximate (Lerner, 1995) and accessible by direct flights (Bernstein, Giroud, and Townsend, 2016), and when directors perceive CEO goals as not well aligned (Sapienza and Gupta, 1994). However, research also suggests that venture boards are distinctive in their approach to monitoring (Garg, 2013, 2014), and do not monitor as agency theory might suggest. For example, the CEOs can be replaced not only when the venture is performing poorly but also when it is performing well (Boeker and Karichalil, 2002; Wasserman, 2003). In their monitoring, venture boards often suffer from a "principal problem," as opposed to the classic agency problem (Garg, 2013, 2020b). That is, although the investor-directors are interested in firm success, they gravitate toward optimizing at the portfolio level; independent directors who are often their allies in the ecosystem tend to defer. Thus, venture directors may press the firm to accept low valuations for M&As (Garg and Eisenhardt, 2017), push for early IPOs to improve their own performance record for future fundraising (Gompers, 1996), and accept lower valuation to maintain relationships with investment bankers for future IPOs (Arthurs *et al.*, 2008). Board members can also be conflictual with executives at the time of fundraising, especially when the new valuations are unattractive (Forbes, Korsgaard, and Sapienza, 2010).

But while these role conflicts of directors as investors can become particularly stark during an equity sale, much research emphasizes that boards are involved in providing resources to advance the firm's strategic goals. Venture boards can be a critical source of advice (Knockaert, Bjornali, and Erikson, 2015; Zahra and Filatotchev, 2004). They can facilitate ties that lead to acquisitions (Graebner and Eisenhardt, 2004) and alliances (Beckman *et al.*, 2014). They can also assist in venture professionalization by hiring key personnel and formalizing human resource policies, and by stimulating rapid product commercialization (Hellmann and Puri, 2000). Finally, directors can signal greater prestige for ventures (Chen, Hambrick, and Pollock, 2008) and thereby lead to better-performing IPOs, especially in highly uncertain environments and industries (Gulati and Higgins, 2003).

Yet research on venture boards also indicates that accessing potential resources through directors can be challenging. For example, Garg and Eisenhardt (2017) find that board members can offer helpful advice and resources, but they may also provide poor advice when there are conflicts among the interests of different ventures in their portfolios, which can lead to suboptimal strategic decisions for the focal venture. Beckman and colleagues (2014) find that ventures build their alliance portfolios more quickly when their directors possess diverse, multiplex relationships and central network positions. Although noninvestor outside directors who have central network positions help form alliance portfolios more quickly, the pace of alliance formation slows, interestingly, when central investor-directors like venture capitalists dominate the board. Similarly, Katila and colleagues (2017) find in the medical device industry that the user (i.e., physician)-board members, despite their skills, have an inverted-U, not a linear positive, relationship with venture innovation. Garg, Howard, and Pahnke (2019) examine the effects of different categories of directors (venture capital [VC]–directors, corporate venture capital [CVC]–directors, and founder-directors) on three strategic outcomes: (1) interorganizational ties (R&D, licensing, supply-chain), (2) innovation (patenting, product launch), and (3) exits (M&As and IPOs). They show that directors—not investors per se—are better predictors of key venture outcomes. But in contrast to the potential struggle between CVCs and VCs as investors suggested in the literature (e.g., Alvarez-Garrido and Dushnitsky, 2016), the authors find that CVC-directors and VC-directors appear to have a truce and defer to each other in prespecified domains (e.g., VC-directors lead in commercialization, and CVC-directors lead in alliances). The results also suggest the tussle may exist among directors of the *same* type (i.e., VC-directors), rather than different types of directors. Founder-directors are associated with a greater likelihood of first product introduction and lower levels of technological licensing, but surprisingly do not necessarily have significant influence over other outcomes. Overall, these findings suggest the usefulness of examining different types of venture directors and their incentives, power, and capabilities to assess their contributions to strategic outcomes.

Some research on strategic management of venture boards brings back the original conception of resource dependence as an exchange theory (Emerson, 1962), which suggests that directors can provide critical resources for a firm's adaptation to the environment, but in exchange the directors also gain power over the firm (Pfeffer and Salancik, 1978). That is, a *resource-power trade-off* exists such that power must be extended to the directors in exchange for the resources they bring to the firm (Garg and Eisenhardt, 2017). In a survey-based study, Wasserman (2017) finds that some founder-CEOs may ex ante choose to retain control over the board and the CEO position by not accepting external equity and other resources from potential board members. He finds that such a trade-off often leads to poor firm performance. Using rare process data from board meeting observations and multiwave interviews, Garg and Eisenhardt (2017) examine how venture CEOs can ex-post behaviorally resolve this resource-power trade-off, and gain resources like advice from directors *and* yet also retain power. In particular, they find that CEOs who have more effective strategy-making processes with their boards (1) have unique, role-based, dyadic interactions with directors; (2) propose a single decision alternative (not multiple proposals) in board meetings; (3) use board meetings primarily for updates but hold separate meetings for strategy brainstorming; and (4) use political action to close the strategy-making process. Overall, this study advances understanding of the venture CEO–board relationship for strategy-making by highlighting the *CEO perspective* and by reconceptualizing boards of directors as CEO-director dyads (not as monolithic groups). It suggests that effective CEOs flip the principal-agent roles in the strategy process—that is, directors are more misaligned than the CEOs, and it is the CEOs who shepherd them to draw the best possible advice while retaining power over strategy.

For effective strategic involvement of the boards, a positive CEO-board relationship is essential. In an inductive study, Garg (2020a) examines how first-time venture CEOs learn to develop a positive CEO-board relationship, where positive relationships are defined as those where the central goals of *both* parties in the relationship are addressed and can lead to more satisfactory relationships and positive firm-level outcomes (Dutton and Heaphy, 2003). Garg identifies the emergence of two CEO-board relationship cycles—positive and negative—based on behaviors during the three types of learning occasions: (1) board meeting previews, (2) board meetings, and (3) board meeting follow-ups. He finds that first-time CEOs begin by drawing analogies for the CEO-board relationship from their recent work experiences (e.g., consulting, general management)—without referring to models such as "agents" or "stewards"—but CEOs who successfully foster a positive relationship learn specific behaviors. In particular, they learn to conduct board-meeting previews by sending a brief asynchronous note to the directors rather than conducting interactive personal meetings or sending elaborate slide-decks. For board meetings, instead of presenting materials themselves, they learn to bring their well-coached management team to deliver the presentations and let founder-executives on the board freely express their divergent views. For board meeting follow-ups, they learn to conduct personal follow-ups with the directors, not use executives or a director for buffering themselves. These behaviors offer adequate transparency for directors and a perception that they could influence the firm; they also help the CEOs with their goals of autonomy and signaling competence to the board. These behaviors in three key learning occasions mutually reinforce each other, thereby generating positive or negative cycles of CEO-board relationship. Unexpectedly, despite an initial expectation of positive relationships by all the CEOs and their respective boards, the CEOs receive limited formal feedback by their boards on how to develop a positive work relationship that is ultimately so consequential for their cooperation.

Future research on venture boards

There are many important research opportunities relating to the relationship between boards and strategic management in the nascent literature on venture boards, and venture governance more broadly.

Board process

There is an opportunity to understand board processes more closely, looking beyond the agency problem and the simple conception of boards as automatic resource providers in new ventures. Scholars may investigate further implications of the principal problem. For example, there is an opportunity to investigate the trade-off investor-directors face in pressing the ventures for their own financial interests and the consequent negative reputation they may accumulate in the market for new investment deals and board seats. Relatedly, venture boards are also likely to have principal subgroups—based, for example, on different financial incentives in the focal firm and other professional and social relationships with fellow directors. Financing rounds are considered a positive feature of ventures because they can avoid potential shirking by the founders and executives. Yet the more funding rounds a venture has, the more subgroups may be added on the board and the more factious the board may become. Finally, while venture boards often do not have much formal leadership structure, such as board committees or even board chairs, they may install these formal leadership structures at the time of the IPO with long-term consequences as these newly public firms evolve into S&P 1500 firms (Garg, Li, and Shaw, 2018, 2019). Scholars may investigate how venture board process (and related characteristics) shape the adoption and effectiveness of the formal governance structures. This can help develop insights into the possible imprinting effects of venture governance on corporate governance, and thus link the literatures on venture boards and corporate boards.

Diversity in venture boards

While a growing literature has examined the determinants and strategic consequences of board diversity in public companies, there has been much less attention to the issue of racial and gender diversity of directors and CEOs in ventures. The venture capital industry in the United States remains dominated by white males, and diversity in venture boards is much less than that in large, public firms. Given the private nature of ventures, symbolic management through board composition may be less relevant, and minorities may be selected for more substantive reasons. Although homogeneity at the top possibly leads to faster decision-making that can be useful in ventures, it may also result in numerous biases and errors in strategic and organizational decisions. In what ways do board and executive diversity pay off—socially and financially—for ventures? As public firm boards grow more diverse in some dimensions, are the ventures compelled to be more diverse at the board and leadership level if they work with public firm customers or are funded by corporate venture capital? Although there are many immigrant founders in Silicon Valley, what is the likelihood of their survival in CEO positions as ventures grow? Scholars could investigate how minority CEOs work together effectively with their boards, which may not always comprise coethnics. Likewise, scholars may investigate how female CEOs, particularly without a female director ally, can work effectively with their boards.

Societal culture and institutions

Another timely research opportunity is the exploration of the role of societal culture and institutions. Much of the nascent venture boards literature is focused on U.S. ventures. For research on board behaviors on strategic issues, there is a significant opportunity to investigate the role of societal/country culture and institutions. These factors are likely to shape what CEOs and boards expect of each other, how much monitoring is deemed feasible and appropriate, what kind of resources are valued, and what behaviors and organizational structures are relevant for more effective board involvement in strategic management of ventures. For example, in contrast to routine CEO dismissal in Silicon Valley, CEOs are rarely dismissed in China, which is among the largest markets for venture capital. Similarly, venture boards in Asia are not as involved in professionalizing the management teams, even though the founders privately admit they could benefit from the board's help (Rhee and Garg, 2020). Understanding the antecedents and consequences of board behaviors related to CEO dismissal and venture team scaling are likely to reveal unique board dynamics in non-U.S. cultural and institutional settings. Siblings and spouses as cofounders are common in India. How do boards harness such kinship ties and deal with potential fallouts? For example, do they install their own affiliates to keep a close eye on the executives? There is also the issue of dominant investors in Asia. While much of the extant literature focuses on U.S. ventures where VC investors are the primary financiers, corporate investors such as Tencent and Alibaba are increasingly important and even dominant investors in Asia. In many cases, they are better placed than high-status VCs because of deep connections with the governments and the international distribution channels they can provide. How do they impact the innovation and growth trajectory of ventures, and how do venture CEOs work with their CVC-led boards to retain power and avoid misappropriation? Overall, there is a significant opportunity to study rich phenomena that may not be present in the United States, and thereby to develop and test wider theories on boards and strategic management.

Conclusion

The literature on boards of directors is among the most interdisciplinary in strategic management. The development of theories that integrate sociological, social psychological, political, and economic perspectives has significantly advanced our understanding of board processes and effectiveness. Yet, while our theories and empirical studies have shed considerable light on the behavioral processes that occur in and around boards, both in corporations and private ventures, our understanding of how these processes influence the content of corporate and business strategies remains incomplete. There is a major opportunity for researchers to examine how the social and psychological processes that are known to occur on boards affect the quality of strategic decisions in such domains as technology and innovation, competitive strategy, and strategic alliances. There is also a significant opportunity to explore beyond the traditional samples of public U.S. firms. Privately held ventures, including those outside the United States, are especially promising because boards tend to be particularly influential in shaping firm strategy and innovation trajectories in these firms. In some ways, ventures provide a new horizon for corporate governance scholars (Garg, 2020b)—social and psychological processes identified in public firm boards may manifest differently in venture boards, and researchers are likely to identify entirely new processes that can enrich our understanding of public firm boards. There is much to explore at the intersection of boards and strategy over the next several decades!

References

Alvarez-Garrido E, Dushnitsky G. 2016. Are entrepreneurial venture's innovation rates sensitive to investor complementary assets? Comparing biotech ventures backed by corporate and independent VCs. *Strategic Management Journal* 37(5): 819–834.

Amornsiripanitch N, Gompers PA, Xuan Y. 2019. More than money: venture capitalists on boards. *Journal of Law, Economics, and Organization* 35(3): 513–543.

Arthurs JD, Hoskisson RE, Busenitz LW, Johnson RA. 2008. Managerial agents watching other agents: multiple agency conflicts regarding underpricing in IPO firms. *Academy of Management Journal* 51(2): 277–294.

Beckman CM, Haunschild PR. 2002. Network learning: the effects of partners' heterogeneity of experience on corporate acquisitions. *Administrative Science Quarterly* 47(1): 92–124.

Beckman CM, Schoonhoven CB, Rottner RM, Kim SJ. 2014. Relational pluralism in de novo organizations: boards of directors as bridges or barriers to diverse alliance portfolios? *Academy of Management Journal* 57(2): 460–483.

Benton RA. 2016. Corporate governance and nested authority: cohesive network structure, actor-driven mechanisms, and the balance of power in American corporations. *American Journal of Sociology* 122(3): 661–713.

Bernstein S, Giroud X, Townsend RR. 2016. The impact of venture capital monitoring. *Journal of Finance* 71(4): 1591–1622.

Boeker W, Karichalil R. 2002. Entrepreneurial transitions: factors influencing founder departure. *Academy of Management Journal* 45(4): 818–826.

Carpenter MA, Westphal JD. 2001. The strategic context of external network ties: examining the impact of director appointments on board involvement in strategic decision making. *Academy of Management Journal* 44(4): 639–660.

Chen G, Hambrick DC, Pollock TG. 2008. Puttin' on the Ritz: pre-IPO enlistment of prestigious affiliates as deadline-induced remediation. *Academy of Management Journal* 51(5): 954–975.

Dutton JE, Heaphy ED. 2003. The power of high-quality connections. *Positive Organizational Scholarship: Foundations of a New Discipline* 3: 263–278.

Emerson RM. 1962. Power-dependence relations. *American Sociological Review* 27(1): 31–41.

Fama EF, Jensen MC. 1983. Separation of ownership and control. *Journal of Law and Economics* 26(2): 301–325.

Filatotchev I, Aguilera RV, Wright M. 2020. From governance of innovation to innovations in governance. *Academy of Management Perspectives* 34(2): 173–181.

Forbes DP, Korsgaard MA, Sapienza HJ. 2010. Financing decisions as a source of conflict in venture boards. *Journal of Business Venturing* 25(6): 579–592.

Fried JM, Ganor M. 2006. Agency costs of venture capitalist control in startups. *New York University Law Review* 81: 967–1025.

Fried VH, Bruton GD, Hisrich RD. 1998. Strategy and the board of directors in venture capital-backed firms. *Journal of Business Venturing* 13(6): 493–503.

Garg S. 2013. Venture boards: distinctive monitoring and implications for firm performance. *Academy of Management Review* 38(1): 90–108.

Garg S. 2014. Microfoundations of board monitoring: the case of entrepreneurial firms. *Academy of Management Review* 39(1): 114–117.

Garg S. 2020a. CEO-board relationship cycles in new ventures. Working Paper, Hong Kong University of Science and Technology (HKUST).

Garg S. 2020b. Venture governance: a new horizon for corporate governance. *Academy of Management Perspectives* 34(2): 252–265.

Garg S, Eisenhardt KM. 2017. Unpacking the CEO–board relationship: how strategy making happens in entrepreneurial firms. *Academy of Management Journal* 60(5): 1828–1858.

Garg S, Furr N. 2017. Venture boards: past insights, future directions, and transition to public firm boards. *Strategic Entrepreneurship Journal* 11(3): 326–343.

Garg S, Howard MD, Pahnke EC. 2019. An empirical examination of board of directors in technology ventures. Working Paper, HKUST.

Garg S, Li Q, Shaw JD. 2018. Undervaluation of directors in the board hierarchy: impact on turnover of directors (and CEOs) in newly public firms. *Strategic Management Journal* 39(2): 429–457.

Garg S, Li QJ, Shaw JD. 2019. Entrepreneurial firms grow up: board undervaluation, board evolution, and firm performance in newly public firms. *Strategic Management Journal* 40(11): 1882–1907.

Geletkanycz MA, Hambrick DC. 1997. The external ties of top executives: implications for strategic choice and performance. *Administrative Science Quarterly* 42: 654–681.

Gompers PA. 1996. Grandstanding in the venture capital industry. *Journal of Financial Economics* 42(1): 133–156.

Graebner ME, Eisenhardt KM. 2004. The seller's side of the story: acquisition as courtship and governance as syndicate in entrepreneurial firms. *Administrative Science Quarterly* 49(3): 366–403.

Gulati R, Higgins MC. 2003. Which ties matter when? The contingent effects of interorganizational partnerships on IPO success. *Strategic Management Journal* 24(2): 127–144.

Hambrick DC, Misangyi VF, Park CA. 2015. The quad model for identifying a corporate director's potential for effective monitoring: toward a new theory of board sufficiency. *Academy of Management Review* 40(3): 323–344.

Haunschild PR. 1993. Interorganizational imitation: the impact of interlocks on corporate acquisition activity. *Administrative Science Quarterly* 38: 564–592.

Haynes KT, Hillman A. 2010. The effect of board capital and CEO power on strategic change. *Strategic Management Journal* 31(11): 1145–1163.

Hellmann T, Puri M. 2000. The interaction between product market and financing strategy: the role of venture capital. *Review of Financial Studies* 13(4): 959–984.

Hoskisson RE, Johnson RA, Moesel DD. 1994. Corporate divestiture intensity in restructuring firms: effects of governance, strategy, and performance. *Academy of Management Journal* 37(5): 1207–1251.

Joseph J, Ocasio W, McDonnell M-H. 2014. The structural elaboration of board independence: executive power, institutional logics, and the adoption of CEO-only board structures in U.S. corporate governance. *Academy of Management Journal* 57(6): 1834–1858.

Katila R, Thatchenkery S, Christensen MQ, Zenios S. 2017. Is there a doctor in the house? Expert product users, organizational roles, and innovation. *Academy of Management Journal* 60(6): 2415–2437.

Knippen JM, Shen W, Zhu Q. 2019. Limited progress? The effect of external pressure for board gender diversity on the increase of female directors. *Strategic Management Journal* 40(7): 1123–1150.

Knockaert M, Bjornali ES, Erikson T. 2015. Joining forces: top management team and board chair characteristics as antecedents of board service involvement. *Journal of Business Venturing* 30(3): 420–435.

Krause R, Withers MC, Semadeni M. 2017. Compromise on the board: investigating the antecedents and consequences of lead independent director appointment. *Academy of Management Journal* 60(6): 2239–2265.

Lerner J. 1995. Venture capitalists and the oversight of private firms. *Journal of Finance* 50(1): 301–318.

Levit D, Malenko N. 2016. The labor market for directors and externalities in corporate governance. *Journal of Finance* 71(2): 775–808.

Li W, Krause R, Qin X, Zhang J, Zhu H, Lin S, Xu Y. 2018. Under the microscope: an experimental look at board transparency and director monitoring behavior. *Strategic Management Journal* 39(4): 1216–1236.

Main BG, Gregory-Smith I. 2018. Symbolic management and the glass cliff: evidence from the boardroom careers of female and male directors. *British Journal of Management* 29(1): 136–155.

McDonald ML, Westphal JD. 2013. Access denied: low mentoring of women and minority first-time directors and its negative effects on appointments to additional boards. *Academy of Management Journal* 56(4): 1169–1198.

Mintzberg H, Waters JA. 1985. Of strategies, deliberate and emergent. *Strategic Management Journal* 6(3): 257–272.

Perrault E. 2015. Why does board gender diversity matter and how do we get there? The role of shareholder activism in deinstitutionalizing old boys' networks. *Journal of Business Ethics* 128(1): 149–165.

Pfeffer J, Salancik GR. 1978. *The External Control of Organizations: A Resource Dependence Perspective.* Harper and Row: New York, NY.

Rhee C, Garg S. 2020. Remedies to growing pains: conflicts with new executives in scaling ventures and founders' effective resolution behaviors. Working Paper, HKUST.

Sapienza HJ, Gupta AK. 1994. Impact of agency risks and task uncertainty on venture capitalist–CEO interaction. *Academy of Management Journal* 37(6): 1618–1632.

Semadeni M, Krause R. 2020. Innovation in the boardroom. *Academy of Management Perspectives* 34(2): 240–251.

Thompson JD. 1967. *Organizations in Action.* Transaction Publishers: London, U.K.

Wasserman N. 2003. Founder-CEO succession and the paradox of entrepreneurial success. *Organization Science* 14(2): 149–172.

Wasserman N. 2017. The throne vs. the kingdom: founder control and value creation in start-ups. *Strategic Management Journal* 38(2): 255–277.

Westphal JD. 1998. Board games: how CEOs adapt to increases in structural board independence from management. *Administrative Science Quarterly* 43: 511–537.

Westphal JD, Graebner ME. 2010. A matter of appearances: How corporate leaders manage the impressions of financial analysts about the conduct of their boards. *Academy of Management Journal* 53(1): 15–44.

Westphal JD, Khanna P. 2003. Keeping directors in line: Social distancing as a control mechanism in the corporate elite. *Administrative Science Quarterly* 48(3): 361–398.

Westphal JD, Milton LP. 2000. How experience and network ties affect the influence of demographic minorities on corporate boards. *Administrative Science Quarterly* 45(2): 366–398.

Westphal JD, Park SH. 2020. *Symbolic Management: Governance, Strategy, and Institutions.* Oxford University Press: Oxford, U.K.

Westphal JD, Stern I. 2007. Flattery will get you everywhere (especially if you are a male Caucasian): how ingratiation, boardroom behavior, and demographic minority status affect additional board appointments at US companies. *Academy of Management Journal* 50(2): 267–288.

Westphal JD, Zhu DH. 2019. Under the radar: How firms manage competitive uncertainty by appointing friends of other chief executive officers to their boards. *Strategic Management Journal* 40(1): 79–107.

Westphal JD, Zhu DH, Kunapuli R. 2020. Seeking input when the train has left the station: the symbolic management of participative strategic decision making. Working Paper, University of Michigan.

Zahra SA, Filatotchev I. 2004. Governance of the entrepreneurial threshold firm: A knowledge-based perspective. *Journal of Management Studies* 41(5): 885–897.

Zajac EJ, Westphal JD. 1996. Director reputation, CEO-board power, and the dynamics of board interlocks. *Administrative Science Quarterly* 41: 507–529.

Zhu DH, Shen W, Hillman AJ. 2014. Recategorization into the in-group: the appointment of demographically different new directors and their subsequent positions on corporate boards. *Administrative Science Quarterly* 59(2): 240–270.

7.2

OWNERSHIP AND GOVERNANCE

Brian L. Connelly

In his groundbreaking Broadway musical *Hamilton*, Lin Manuel Miranda wrote about "the room where it happens." He describes how most people do not have access to that important room, and as a result "no one really knows how the game is played, the art of the trade, how the sausage gets made" (Miranda and McCarter, 2016: 187). In the organizational context, the room where it happens might be the corporate boardroom, the CEO's office, the offices of the top management team, or perhaps even the company's break room or shop floor. The problem for the firm's owners (i.e., shareholders) is that they are *almost never* in the room where it happens.

Berle and Means (1932) were among the first to draw attention to this problem when they noted that the control of companies (i.e., the room where it happens) had become separated from those who hold legal ownership over the company. Since that time, policymakers have tinkered with a wide range of mechanisms to restore balance with respect to company control, and academics have responded by investigating the various consequences of those approaches. The main concern of this line of study has been on understanding how a firm's owners affect managerial behavior and firm-level outcomes. Through the years, ownership structures have become increasingly complex, and mechanisms designed to empower, or shield against, them have evolved to match these changes. The topic of ownership and governance has received extensive attention in the literature (Boyd and Solarino, 2016), and is garnering special consideration in management journals.

Ownership Structures

For publicly traded companies, ownership is about shareholders, and *institutional investors* are central to this body of work because they control about 80 percent of the U.S. equity market. This group of shareholders is characterized by a dual-agency structure where many small, heterogeneous investors sign over their voting rights to owner agents. Early attempts to understand their influence on firms classified them into owner types based on their relationship to the firm, legal category, or trading behavior. The classification approach has been useful for examining the broad influence of most of the largest institutional investors, such as mutual funds, pension funds, endowments, and banks. For example, institutional investors are consequential to a firm's competitive behavior (Connelly *et al.*, 2017), international diversification (Tihanyi *et al.*, 2003), innovation (David, Hitt, and Gimeno, 2001), executive compensation (Connelly, Haynes, *et al.*, 2016), and corporate social responsibility (CSR) (Eesley, DeCelles, and Lenox, 2016).

Within the firm, *inside owners* can also hold appreciable shares, and in fact many would argue that inside ownership helps solve the agency problem because it ensures that insider interests are aligned with those of external shareholders (Dalton *et al.*, 2007). It is assumed that when executives own shares in the firm, they are likely to focus their effort and resources on creating long-term value for shareholders. There are, however, potential negative externalities that arise when executives have large ownership stakes. Managers could become entrenched or motivated to engage in nefarious behavior, such as stock options backdating or earnings manipulation, owing largely to greed (Haynes, Campbell, and Hitt, 2017). The same logic applies to the firm's directors, who have a fiduciary duty to shareholders but may be more inclined to fulfill that duty when it aligns with their own interests. Some extend interest alignment to all firm employees, noting how ownership motivates employees to work hard and display good organizational citizenship (Wilson, 2016).

Shareholders with large stakes in a firm (more than 5 percent), referred to as *blockholders*, often look more toward controlling firm outcomes as opposed to relying on interest alignment. This special set of owners wields more power over management than minority shareholders. The most common form of blockholders is family owners, who have received considerable research attention (Cannella, Jones, and Withers, 2015). The term *family owners* might appear to suggest a small company, but such large, publicly traded companies as Walmart, Novartis, and Ford all have large blocks of family ownership. Some suggest that family owners do not create value for the firm, except when the founder serves as CEO (Villalonga and Amit, 2006), while others find positive characteristics in family ownership (Sirmon and Hitt, 2003). New ventures, especially pre–initial public offering (IPO), present a unique set of owners and blockholders (for a recent review, see Drover *et al.*, 2017). Corporations can also be blockholders if they buy a minority share of another firm, which often precedes an acquisition.

State ownership is common in emerging countries with poor property rights protection and has become more common in many developed countries as well. The large economies of China and Russia have extensively used state ownership as a policy instrument. Management researchers have considered the efficacy of state ownership from many different angles. Most studies reveal a liability of stateness, wherein state ownership has a negative effect on firm financial performance (Li, Li, and Wang, 2019). However, the contingencies and mediating strategic factors in this relationship suggest more complex relationships. At a minimum, firms with high levels of state ownership appear to be risk averse, exhibiting lower financial leverage, R&D investment, and internationalization than those with low levels of state ownership (Tihanyi *et al.*, 2019). This might explain, in part, why financial fraud is often lower at state-owned, as compared to privately owned, firms (Shi, Aguilera, and Wang, 2020).

Many studies investigate the governance influence of one or more of these types of owners in isolation, but some consider how they *work together*. Business groups, such as those found in Korea, India, and a variety of Southeast Asian and Latin American countries, are confederations of legally independent owners. Participation in the group can confer benefits that have enduring consequences for firm behavior and performance but come at a high cost (Khanna and Rivkin, 2001). Some have also considered how various types of shareholders cooperate in coalitions or interact to affect firm outcomes without explicit agreements (Connelly et al., 2019).

Owner Influence

The mark of a good investor used to be one who could pick the winners. Today, the most influential shareholders are no longer just trying to identify which firms will outperform others; now they are more concerned with identifying firms where they can add value by introducing change (David et al., 2001). If firms do not comply with shareholder demands, shareholders hold the threat of exit. Increasingly, though, shareholders are exercising their voice to impose their will and ensure that managers are acting in shareholders' interest.

Shareholder activism

The main mechanism by which shareholders bring about change is through activism (Goranova and Ryan, 2014). *Shareholder activism* refers to actions shareholders take with the intent of influencing corporate policy and practice. Historically shareholders have exercised their voice by voting at shareholder meetings, and that could involve introducing issues about which they seek a vote or working to gather votes in support of, or opposition to, individuals or actions. Powerful shareholders engage in private activism, which might include letters, phone calls, meetings, and dialogue with management with a view toward swaying their decision-making about matters that concern the shareholder (Boss et al., 2013). This quiet diplomacy typically occurs behind the scenes, but there is little research about how it takes shape or how well it works. When private activism is ineffective, shareholders turn to a range of public tactics, such as publishing letters or organizing media campaigns, to force managerial compliance. The effectiveness of either private or public activism depends on the power of the shareholder initiating the activism and the legitimacy and urgency of the demand (Mitchell, Agle, and Wood, 1997).

Researchers investigating the broad influence of institutional investors sometimes overlook niche types of activists who require special attention. For instance, some have begun to investigate the intense pressure imposed by hedge funds, which are aggressively managed funds not subject to the same regulations as other institutional investors. This is important work because some of the largest hedge funds control over \$100 billion, so perhaps not surprisingly research shows they hold considerable sway over managerial decisions (DesJardine, Marti, and Durand, in press). Others have investigated shareholders with specific interests, such as those who have environmental or religious concerns (Eesley *et al.*, 2016). Activism is a costly endeavor, so it is informative to consider the motivations of activists and how their activism impacts not only the target firm but also other firms that are not yet targeted (Shi, Connelly, *et al.*, in press).

Possible research questions:

- How do "celebrity activists," such as Carl Icahn, Bill Ackman, and Daniel Loeb, use their status to engage with management in unique ways?
- In what ways does shareholder activism spill over to other firms, creating an invisible influence on firms that are not even targets of activism?

Cross-border influence

Some forms of owner influence are most prevalent in particular countries or regions. For example, shareholder activism is strongest in the United States, Canada, the United Kingdom, and Japan. Powerful blockholders with dual-class shares, on the other hand, are more common in Europe and a range of emerging economies. Some research, though, considers how owner influence reaches across national borders (Bena *et al.*, 2017). This line of study is becoming increasingly important as shareholders increasingly look for investment and influence beyond geographic boundaries. Management researchers have found that foreign institutional investors infuse their own governance logic into firms, which changes managerial decision-making (Aguilera *et al.*, 2017).

Firms can facilitate foreign ownership through global depository receipts (GDRs), which allow them to cross-list on stock exchanges in, and outside of, the country in which they are headquartered. This can be beneficial, for example, if a firm headquartered in a country with weak or poorly defined institutional controls wishes to rent the legitimacy of another country's strict reporting standards (Ribstein, 2005). GDRs facilitate cross-border trading, but also make the firm subject to the influence of shareholders outside their own country, who are likely to have different priorities and means of engagement than in their home country.

Sovereign wealth funds (SWFs), which are investment vehicles owned and operated by a national government, represent a powerful set of investors that exercise cross-border influence (Aguilera, Capapé, and Santiso, 2016). For example, the Pension Fund of Norway, Abu Dhabi Investment Authority, and China Investment Corporation collectively control over \$2 trillion, much of which is in foreign assets. The number, size, and influence of SWFs are growing quickly, but research on SWFs is nascent (Bernstein, Lerner, and Schoar, 2013). This class of ownership allows nations to extend their reach, but their lack of transparency introduces difficulties in understanding their potential sway over managers, and research remains siloed within disciplines (Balding, 2012). As publicly traded companies gain increasing levels of SWF ownership, it could introduce strategic concerns about where and how the firm competes. For instance, in the months following the outbreak of COVID-19, Saudi Arabia's Public Investment Fund poured billions into U.S. stocks that had suddenly decreased in value, and some question how their presence might affect firm strategies (Jones and Said, 2020).

Possible research questions:

- When non-U.S. firms list on a U.S. stock exchange via American Depository Receipts (ADRs), what are the consequences for executive compensation and pay gaps (both of which are higher in the United States compared to other countries)?
- If a firm takes on a high level of SWF ownership, how does that affect their foreign direct investment (FDI), internationalization, and location decisions?

Behavioral aspects of owner influence

Most of the work on the governance of corporate ownership is based on archival data (Boyd and Solarino, 2016). As a field, we have an overabundance of studies relying on archival data that theorize about, but do not measure, owner influence. Few researchers, though, talk to shareholders or do qualitative studies of shareholder behavior. One exception is Connelly, Ketchen, and colleagues (2016), who conducted a scenario study with participants who were "principal managers of major investment funds, with median assets of $1.8 billion." Similarly, Westphal and Bednar (2008) conducted a large-scale study of institutional investors to learn about how managers engaged with them. Another recent study found that female CEOs face more scrutiny from institutional investors than their male counterparts, making them more likely to be a target for shareholder activism (Gupta et al., 2018). These studies, and others like them, offer the potential to uncover the processes by which owners engage with management and reveal nuances of their social interactions with managers.

The theories and methods we use to explain owner influence are evolving. For example, the long-dominant agency theory has expanded to multiple agency theory (Arthurs et al., 2008) and given way to new theories, such as cognitive evaluation theory (Shi, Connelly, and Hoskisson, 2017), social identity theory (Cannella, Jones, and Withers, 2015), and the awareness-motivation-capability perspective (Shi, Connelly, et al., in press). Methodologically, we increasingly see studies using research designs that are event- or contingency-oriented, that focus on construct development, and that consider matters of causality or endogeneity, which have long been a major concern in the field.

Stated simply, a behavioral understanding of owner governance might be called the wild west of ownership research insofar as there are wide-open opportunities for those willing to stake their claim. For example, future research might incorporate the notion of psychological ownership (Pierce, Kostova, and Dirks, 2001) to help explain why some investors feel differently than others about their sense of obligation and responsibility to firms they own. Scholars are investigating ways in which shareholders exercise power, so it seems reasonable to view their power through the lens of French and Raven's (1959) bases of power. Further investigation of shareholder influence should also explore the role played by groups who may be pulling the strings, such as Glass-Lewis, the Council of Institutional Investors (CII), and Institutional Shareholder Services (ISS). In addition to studying owner influence on managerial conduct, we also need to know more about how shareholders affect potential misconduct, including unethical behavior, and negative organizational events, such as product recalls.

Possible research questions:

- What are the factors (e.g., owning few firms, holding them for a long time) that create feelings of psychological ownership among shareholders, and how might those feelings affect their monitoring and engagement with managers?
- How do different types of shareholders affect ethical decision-making, such as product safety design decisions and willingness to recall?

Emerging Debates for Future Study

Tihanyi, Graffin, and George (2014) call for management researchers to design studies that account for emerging ownership arrangements as they spring up and evolve over time. Owners are in the process of shifting from a primarily defensive governance strategy, focused on structures and prevention, to an offensive strategy, focused on shareholder power and engagement (Boyd and Solarino, 2016). As this change has occurred, several topics have sparked considerable debate and demand more research attention.

Common shareholders

Investors who hold appreciable shares of competing firms have become the focal point of an "ongoing transatlantic debate" in corporate governance (Tzanaki, 2019). One group makes a case that common ownership is an "economic blockbuster" that constitutes the greatest antitrust problem of our time (Posner, Scott Morton, and Weyl, 2016). Empirical work on common ownership began with a study by Azar, Schmalz, and Tecu (2018, but appearing on SSRN in 2014), who found that common ownership results in airline ticket prices that are approximately 5 percent higher than they would be under separate ownership. This spawned a battery of studies that examine the economic consequences of, regulatory implications for, and managerial responses to common ownership (e.g., Connelly *et al.*, 2019; Hemphill and Kahan, 2019). Researchers go so far as to suggest that firms with high levels of common ownership will reward (i.e., compensate) managers when their competitors perform well. Elhauge (2021: *forthcoming*) concludes that "dozens of empirical studies have now confirmed this economic reality that common shareholding alters corporate behavior."

Others, though, contest this body of research on both conceptual and empirical grounds. Lambert and Sykuta (2018) suggest that "the purported competitive problem is overblown" and even contend "that the theory of competitive harm from institutional investors' common ownership is implausible and that the empirical studies supporting the theory are methodologically unsound." One of the problems that detractors point to is that empirical studies fail to capture the mechanisms by which common owners supposedly reduce competition, and detractors believe that the incentives for them to pressure firms to reduce competition are not conceptually sound. Empirically, they point to weaknesses in measures used to capture common ownership and endogeneity in the relationships these studies investigate (Gilje, Gormley, and Levit, 2019). Their conclusion is that proposed policy solutions, which typically engender restrictions on shareholder power for intra-industry holdings, would do more harm than good.

The growth of common ownership is likely to continue. In 2010, just 10 percent of firm pairs in the S&P 500 had at least one common owner with more than a 5 percent stake in both companies, but by 2019 that number grew to over 90 percent. It is imperative, therefore, that debate on the topic continue and scholars on both sides of the argument thoroughly examine the phenomenon to explain how common ownership may, or may not, affect managerial decisions. Future research might consider how common ownership affects a range of strategic outcomes. For example, research shows that common owners benefit when they are on both sides of an acquisition deal (Goranova, Dharwadkar, and Brandes, 2010), but we do not yet know whether or how common owners affect target selection decisions, or the extent to which common owners might expedite the acquisition process after a target is selected. Moreover, research on common ownership is limited almost exclusively to consideration of firm dyads. We do not yet know whether shareholders leverage knowledge gained via ownership of firms in one industry to benefit firms in other industries, or how common ownership of all or most firms in an industry might affect competitive activity.

Possible research questions:

- How do the effects of common ownership change when the common owner is a dedicated, as opposed to transactional, institutional investor?
- If we imagine a network of firms interconnected by common shareholdings, what are the organizational consequences of being central or peripheral in the network?

Excess control

One of the most talked about, and most controversial, ownership practices worldwide is the advent of stock offerings where shareholders have voting rights that differ from the number of shares they hold (i.e., voting rights exceed cash-flow rights for some shareholders, but not others). Investors, analysts, and the media have levied criticism against such ownership arrangements. Armed with research that almost universally pans dual- and multi-class stock structures, these groups charge that excess control rights are dangerous and value reducing (Council of Institutional Investors, 2020). Despite considerable pushback, many high-profile companies still offer dual or multiple share classes, and the practice is especially common among newly public firms. The egregiousness of the separation between share classes reached a high point in 2017 with the initial public offering (IPO) of Snap, which offered shares with no voting rights at all. In response, some major stock exchanges ban companies that offer dual-class shares, and top institutional investors BlackRock, Vanguard, and T. Rowe Price limit investment in firms that do not offer shareholder voting rights in proportion to their economic interest.

Research on the topic has centered mainly around what happens when specific groups of shareholders (e.g., family members, founders, early investors) have control rights that exceed their cash-flow rights. Disproportionate allocation of control rights between shareholders creates potential legal, economic, and strategic problems for firms that allow such ownership arrangements (Wasserman, 2017). From an agency perspective, privileged shareholders may expropriate value from minority investors when they have excess control rights, which creates principal-principal conflicts. Problems arise because shareholders with limited voting rights cannot remove directors, approve extraordinary transactions (e.g., acquisitions, material asset sales), amend bylaws, or have an equitable voice in decisions on managerial compensation. As a result, firms with high levels of excess control for specific shareholders exhibit a range of inefficiencies, such as high borrowing costs, reduced value of excess cash, and low market-to-book value (Lin *et al.*, 2011). Many corporate insiders, though, still want dual-class shares, so some stock exchanges (e.g., Singapore, Hong Kong) allow them as a means to woo firms to list on their exchange. This has sparked a global debate about restricting dual-class shares, with each side looking for empirical support about the potential harm or benefit of excess control rights (Govindarajan *et al.*, 2018).

Possible research questions:

- Are there hidden benefits to excess control rights, such as consolidation of monitoring responsibility or creation of an ownership block that will be highly sensitive to retaining the firm's long-term reputation?
- If firms have dual-class shares at IPO, what are the benefits and risks associated with offering a time-based "sunset period" to eliminate the share classes?

Share repurchases

Repurchasing a firm's own shares of stock is a popular method of distributing cash to shareholders (Zajac and Westphal, 2004). This activity simultaneously changes the makeup of a firm's ownership structure and constitutes an action that a firm's owners govern. There are many forms of stock buybacks, but the vast majority occur in the open market of the listing exchange. Firms use buybacks as a defensive tactic to prevent a takeover, but they are also a pervasive means of shoring up a firm's stock price (Benner and Ranganathan, 2012). In fact, from 2017 to 2019, firms in the S&P 500 bought back more than $2 trillion of their own stock. This has raised questions about the value of stock buybacks and what they communicate to capital markets.

The rapid escalation of stock buybacks has captured the attention of regulators. The main rationale for buying back stock derives from signaling theory, which suggests that managers use buybacks as an observable signal to communicate about the firm's unobservable quality. Managers have private information about the firm, so buying back their own stock serves as a credible signal that the firm's strategy is sound, and their stock is underpriced. The problem is that managers own appreciable shares of the firm's stock and can thus exploit inside information to maximize personal wealth creation without violating securities laws (Bonaime and Ryngaert, 2013). This problem is exacerbated when managers initiate a repurchase offering but then either do not follow through on the repurchase (which sometimes happens) or sell their own shares, enriching themselves and reducing their proportional ownership stakes (Firth, Leung, and Rui, 2010). For this reason, lawmakers providing firms with funds to assist with COVID-19 attached to the terms a temporary prohibition on stock buybacks at firms that received the funds so that managers could not enrich themselves. Though some are wary of stock buybacks, scholars have just begun to unpack the managerial motivations and long-term consequences of the practice.

Possible research questions:

- What are the consequences of stock buybacks for competitive dynamics in the industry and for long-term investor value appropriation (LIVA)?
- Stock buybacks presumably reflect managerial confidence, so how do they affect morale, perceived organizational support, and organizational citizenship?

Short sellers

Investors can short a stock by borrowing shares and selling them on the open market, with the expectation they can buy them back and return the borrowed shares at a lower price. Short sellers constitute one of the greatest ownership threats facing firms today as they seek temporary dips in a firm's stock price (Shi, Ndofor, and Hoskisson, in press). Short sellers actively engage with firm owners in a public battle sometimes referred to as "short-and-distort." They use all means at their disposal to cast doubt on the firm, its managers, and its strategy in an effort to create downward price pressure on the firm's stock (Jiao, Massa, and Zhang, 2016). Policymakers have, from time to time, introduced regulations that restrict the practice. In the wake of the COVID-19 crisis, several European and Asian stock exchanges even banned short selling entirely. Investors, though, have continued to demand access to short sales to hedge their bets, and debates about the topic largely revolve around whether and how short sales should be restricted.

Short sellers have become an increasingly powerful form of corporate governance. They are sophisticated investors (technically not "owners" since they loan out their shares) who possess superior information about firms they sell short. They have considerable influence over managers, boards, and even other investors (Hughes-Morgan and Ferrier, 2017). Top managers pay close attention to short sellers because they directly affect compensation and job security. When short sellers target a firm, managers respond with protective behavior. Studies show they restructure their organization, reduce long-term investment, and dial back on growth activities (Shi, Connelly, and Cirik, 2018). Short sellers are generally good predictors of fiscal problems, and managers respond to short selling by being fiscally prudent (Fang, Huang, and Karpoff, 2016).

The amount that we do *not* know about the influence of short sellers on managerial activity is greater than what we know. For example, studies suggest that managers will take some actions in response to increased levels of short interest, but it takes time to implement those actions, and managerial response to short sellers must be swift and convincing. Future research might consider not only what managers are doing in response to short sellers, but also what they are saying. Moreover, short selling is typically a predictor as researchers examine firm responses, but it could also be the dependent variable if researchers were to consider what firms are doing to keep short sellers at bay and reduce the likelihood of being sold short. Most research examines increases or decreases in short interest, but short selling is often punctilious and followed with immediate public-facing attacks. An opportunity for future research could be to examine short attacks in more depth, exploring how firms respond in the immediate aftermath of the attacks and how the attacks on one firm affect other firms in the industry. Also, our understanding of short selling as a form of governance to date is largely mechanical, with studies investigating relationships between short sales and various financial or firm-level outcomes. We know less about managerial cognitions and how top executives feel when their company is sold short.

Possible research questions:

- How do managers respond to increased levels of short selling of their suppliers or competitors within the industry?
- What do managers say (e.g., in earnings conference calls) and do (e.g., their immediate strategic reactions) in response to short attacks, and are their methods effective?

Shareholder-nominated directors

Shareholders have become increasingly frustrated with managerial nominees to the board of directors and are thus asking to choose their own representatives to serve on the board (Campbell *et al.*, 2012). This phenomenon arose because director behavior often falls short of shareholder expectations. Consequently, many shareholders want their own voice in the boardroom. This creates an entirely new type of director, a shareholder-nominated director, that has become increasingly prevalent but received little academic attention.

There are two distinct factions with opposing views about shareholder representation on the board. Proponents assert that a manager's responsibility is to return value to the firm's shareholders. This group argues that managerial entrenchment reduces shareholder value, and high levels of shareholder involvement in key organizational decisions helps keep managers in check (Bebchuk *et al.*, 2020). Institutional investors—such as BlackRock, CalPERS, and TIAA-CREF—and influential advisory firms such as Glass Lewis, the CII, and ISS—all state as policy that they advocate for shareholders being able to nominate their own representatives to the board.

Opponents disagree, asserting that the board of directors is a legally independent entity that must not be beholden to any one shareholder (Strine, 2006). These groups often question the judgment and motivation of shareholder nominees. They argue that shareholder representatives are disruptive to the firm's long-term goals (Sharfman, 2012). For example, shareholder-nominated directors could be more concerned about financial indicators than value creation. A director who represents a single shareholder could skew board decision-making and force the board to devote inordinate attention to narrow agendas as opposed to strategic objectives.

Despite the rhetoric from both sides, few have empirically evaluated the strategic consequences of shareholder-nominated directors. This is a critical omission because many shareholders obtain board seats with a view toward strict governance. For instance, one institutional investor put representatives on the board of the Tuesday Morning Corporation to "instill accountability," and another put representatives on the board of Dillard's owing to "disappointment with the company's poor operating performance and governance" (Gow, Shin, and Srinivasan, 2014). Management scholars must consider how this special new group of directors affects firm-level outcomes, such as competitive actions, stakeholder relations, and organizational misconduct. As they do so, political theories of representation could provide useful explanatory mechanisms for understanding the consequences of shareholders being able to nominate their own representatives to the board.

Possible research questions:

- What are the consequences of having shareholder-nominated directors for non-shareholding stakeholders, such as employees, suppliers, and the community?
- How do annual director elections (i.e., declassified boards) work together with, or in place of, shareholder nominations to affect board decision-making?

Conclusion

A case can be made that ownership was first launched as a form of governance in 1926. In that year, Benjamin Graham met with senior management of Northern Pipeline to request a special dividend to shareholders. Management refused, telling Graham, "You must give us credit for knowing better than you what is best for the company and its stockholders" (Gramm, 2015: 9). Graham responded by contacting other shareholders, making his case that they should have a say in how the firm deployed excess capital—the dawn of shareholder cooperation with a view toward influencing managerial decision-making. Graham also secured enough proxy votes to capture two board seats—perhaps the first instance of a shareholder forcing one's way onto the board of directors. Soon thereafter, Northern Pipeline distributed cash to shareholders (Chatman, 1996).

Over the subsequent 100 years, ownership as a form of corporate governance has been characterized by an exponential rate of change. For most of that time, the governance role of shareholders slowly simmered. Types of ownership grew more complex over time, and owner influence evolved to engender more engagement with management. The 1980s and 1990s saw a faster rate of change as corporate raiders entered the picture and shareholder activism became more public. In the past two decades, though, the landscape of shareholder governance has burst wide open. Hedge fund managers, activist shareholders, and short sellers capture headlines in the business press and demand the attention of managers. Change is occurring at a furious pace, and the task before us as academics is to consider how to incorporate these new developments into our theories of corporate governance.

References

Aguilera RV, Capapé J, Santiso J. 2016. Sovereign wealth funds: a strategic governance view. *Academy of Management Perspectives* **30**(1): 5–23.

Aguilera RV, Desender KA, Lamy ML, Lee JH. 2017. The governance impact of a changing investor landscape. *Journal of International Business Studies* **48**(2): 195–221.

Arthurs JD, Hoskisson RE, Busenitz LW, Johnson RA. 2008. Managerial agents watching other agents: multiple agency conflicts regarding underpricing in IPO firms. *Academy of Management Journal* **51**(2): 277–294.

Azar J, Schmalz MC, Tecu I. 2018. Anticompetitive effects of common ownership. *Journal of Finance* **73**(4): 1513–1565.

Balding C. 2012. *Sovereign Wealth Funds: The New Intersection of Money and Politics*. Oxford University Press: Oxford, U.K.

Bebchuk LA, Brav A, Jiang W, Keusch T. 2020. Dancing with activists. *Journal of Financial Economics* **137**(1): 1–41.

Bena J, Ferreira MA, Matos P, Pires P. 2017. Are foreign investors locusts? The long-term effects of foreign institutional ownership. *Journal of Financial Economics* **126**(1): 122–146.

Benner MJ, Ranganathan R. 2012. Offsetting illegitimacy? How pressures from securities analysts influence incumbents in the face of new technologies. *Academy of Management Journal* 55(1): 213–233.

Berle A, Means G. 1932. *The Modern Corporation and Private Property*. Macmillan: New York, NY.

Bernstein S, Lerner J, Schoar A. 2013. The investment strategies of sovereign wealth funds. *Journal of Economic Perspectives* 27(2): 219–238.

Bonaime AA, Ryngaert MD. 2013. Insider trading and share repurchases: do insiders and firms trade in the same direction? *Journal of Corporate Finance* 22: 35–53.

Boss DS, Connelly BL, Hoskisson RE, Tihanyi L. 2013. Ownership interests, incentives, and conflicts. In *The Oxford Handbook of Corporate Governance*, Wright DM, Siegel DS, Keasey K, Filatotchev I (eds). Oxford University Press: Oxford, U.K.; 246–268.

Boyd BK, Solarino AM. 2016. Ownership of corporations: a review, synthesis, and research agenda. *Journal of Management* 42(5): 1282–1314.

Campbell JT, Campbell TC, Sirmon DG, Bierman L, Tuggle CS. 2012. Shareholder influence over director nomination via proxy access: implications for agency conflict and stakeholder value. *Strategic Management Journal* 33(12): 1431–1451.

Cannella AA, Jones CD, Withers MC. 2015. Family versus lone-founder-controlled public corporations: social identity theory and boards of directors. *Academy of Management Journal* 58(2): 436–459.

Chatman S. 1996. *Benjamin Graham: The Memoirs of the Dean of Wall Street*. McGraw-Hill: New York, NY.

Connelly BL, Haynes KT, Tihanyi L, Gamache DL, Devers CE. 2016. Minding the gap: antecedents and consequences of top management-to-worker pay dispersion. *Journal of Management* 42(4): 862–885.

Connelly BL, Ketchen DJ Jr, Gangloff KA, Shook CL. 2016. Investor perceptions of CEO successor selection in the wake of integrity and competence failures: a policy capturing study. *Strategic Management Journal* 37(10): 2135–2151.

Connelly BL, Shi W, Hoskisson RE, Koka BR. 2019. Shareholder influence on joint venture exploration. *Journal of Management* 45(8): 3178–3203.

Connelly BL, Tihanyi L, Ketchen DJ, Carnes CM, Ferrier WJ. 2017. Competitive repertoire complexity: governance antecedents and performance outcomes. *Strategic Management Journal* 38(5): 1151–1173.

Council of Institutional Investors. 2020. https://www.cii.org/dualclass_stock [9 March 2021].

Dalton DR, Hitt MA, Certo ST, Dalton CM. 2007. The fundamental agency problem and its mitigation: independence, equity, and the market for corporate control. *Academy of Management Annals* 1(1): 1–64.

David P, Hitt MA, Gimeno J. 2001. The influence of activism by institutional investors on R&D. *Academy of Management Journal* 44(1): 144–157.

DesJardine MR, Marti E, Durand R. In press. Why activist hedge funds target socially responsible firms: the reaction costs of signaling corporate social responsibility. *Academy of Management Journal*. doi.org/10.5465/amj.2019.0238

Drover W, Busenitz L, Matusik S, Townsend D, Anglin A, Dushnitsky G. 2017. A review and road map of entrepreneurial equity financing research: venture capital, corporate venture capital, angel investment, crowdfunding, and accelerators. *Journal of Management* 43(6): 1820–1853.

Eesley C, DeCelles KA, Lenox M. 2016. Through the mud or in the boardroom: examining activist types and their strategies in targeting firms for social change. *Strategic Management Journal* 37(12): 2425–2440.

Elhauge E. 2021. The causal mechanisms of horizontal shareholding. *Ohio State Law Journal* 82: forthcoming. https://papers.ssrn.com/sol3/papers.cfm?abstract_id=3370675.

Fang VW, Huang AH, Karpoff JM. 2016. Short selling and earnings management: a controlled experiment. *Journal of Finance* 71(3): 1251–1294.

Firth M, Leung TY, Rui OM. 2010. Double signals or single signal? An investigation of insider trading around share repurchases. *Journal of International Financial Markets, Institutions, and Money* 20(4): 376–388.

French JR, Raven B. 1959. The bases of social power. In *Classics in Organization Theory*, Shafritz JM, Ott JS, Jang YS. Cengage: Boston, MA; 150–167.

Gilje EP, Gormley TA, Levit D. 2019. Who's paying attention? Measuring common ownership and its impact on managerial incentives. *Journal of Financial Economics* 137(1): 152–178.

Goranova M, Dharwadkar R, Brandes P. 2010. Owners on both sides of the deal: mergers and acquisitions and overlapping institutional ownership. *Strategic Management Journal* 31(10): 1114–1135.

Goranova M, Ryan LV. 2014. Shareholder activism: a multidisciplinary review. *Journal of Management* 40(5): 1230–1268.

Govindarajan V, Rajgopal S, Srivastava A, Enache L. 2018. Should dual class shares be banned? *Harvard Business Review*, December 3, 2018. https://hbr.org/2018/12/should-dual-class-shares-be-banned.

Gow ID, Shin SP, Srinivasan S. 2014. Activist directors: determinants and consequences. Harvard Business School Working Paper Series No. 14–120.

Gramm J. 2015. *Dear Chairman: Boardroom Battles and the Rise of Shareholder Activism*. HarperCollins: New York, NY.

Gupta VK, Han S, Mortal SC, Silveri SD, Turban DB. 2018. Do women CEOs face greater threat of shareholder activism compared to male CEOs? A role congruity perspective. *Journal of Applied Psychology* 103(2): 228–236.

Haynes KT, Campbell JT, Hitt MA. 2017. When more is not enough: executive greed and its influence on shareholder wealth. *Journal of Management* 43(2): 555–584.

Hemphill CS, Kahan M. 2019. The strategies of anticompetitive common ownership. *Yale Law Journal* 2: 18–29.

Hughes-Morgan M, Ferrier WJ. 2017. Short interest pressure and competitive behaviour. *British Journal of Management* 28(1): 120–134.

Jiao Y, Massa M, Zhang H. 2016. Short selling meets hedge fund 13F: an anatomy of informed demand. *Journal of Financial Economics* 122(3): 544–567.

Jones R, Said S. 2020. Saudi sovereign wealth fund buys stakes in Facebook, Boeing, Cisco Systems. *Wall Street Journal*, May 17. https://www.wsj.com/articles/saudi-sovereign-wealth-fund-buys-stakes-in-facebook-boeing-cisco-systems-11589633300?mod=-searchresults&page=1&pos=4

Khanna T, Rivkin JW. 2001. Estimating the performance effects of business groups in emerging markets. *Strategic Management Journal* 22(1): 45–74.

Lambert TA, Sykuta ME. 2018. The case for doing nothing about institutional investors' common ownership of small stakes in competing firms. University of Missouri School of Law Legal Studies Research Paper No. 2018–2021.

Li J, Li P, Wang B. 2019. The liability of opaqueness: state ownership and the likelihood of deal completion in international acquisitions by Chinese firms. *Strategic Management Journal* 40(2): 303–327.

Lin C, Ma Y, Malatesta P, Xuan YH. 2011. Ownership structure and the cost of corporate borrowing. *Journal of Financial Economics* 100(1): 1–23.

Miranda LM, McCarter J. 2016. *Hamilton: The Revolution*. Grand Central Publishing: New York, NY.

Mitchell RK, Agle BR, Wood DJ. 1997. Toward a theory of stakeholder identification and salience: defining the principle of who and what really counts. *Academy of Management Review* 22(4): 853–886.

Pierce JL, Kostova T, Dirks KT. 2001. Toward a theory of psychological ownership in organizations. *Academy of Management Review* 26(2): 298–310.

Posner EA, Scott Morton FM, Weyl EG. 2016. A proposal to limit the anti-competitive power of institutional investors. *Antitrust Law Journal*, 81: 669-728.

Ribstein LE. 2005. Cross-listing and regulatory competition. *Review of Law and Economics* 1(1): 97–148.

Sharfman BS. 2012. What's wrong with shareholder empowerment? *Journal of Corporation Law* 37(4): 903–909.

Shi W, Aguilera R, Wang K. 2020. State ownership and securities fraud: a political governance perspective. *Corporate Governance: An International Review* 28(2): 157–176.

Shi W, Connelly BL, Cirik K. 2018. Short seller influence on firm growth: a threat rigidity perspective. *Academy of Management Journal* 61(5): 1892–1919.

Shi W, Connelly BL, Hoskisson RE. 2017. External corporate governance and financial fraud: cognitive evaluation theory insights on agency theory prescriptions. *Strategic Management Journal* 38(6): 1268–1286.

Shi W, Connelly BL, Hoskisson RE, Ketchen DJ. In press. Portfolio spillover of institutional investor activism: an awareness-motivation-capability perspective. *Academy of Management Journal*, doi.org/10.5465/amj.2018.0074.

Shi W, Ndofor HA, Hoskisson RE. In press. Disciplining role of short sellers: evidence from M&A activity. *Journal of Management*, doi.org/10.1177%2F0149206320912307.

Sirmon DG, Hitt MA. 2003. Managing resources: linking unique resources, management, and wealth creation in family firms. *Entrepreneurship Theory and Practice* 27(4): 339–358.

Strine LE. 2006. Toward a true corporate republic: a traditionalist response to Bebchuk's solution for improving corporate America. *Harvard Law Review* 119(6): 1759–1783.

Tihanyi L, Aguilera RV, Heugens P, van Essen M, Sauerwald S, Duran P, Turturea R. 2019. State ownership and political connections. *Journal of Management* 45(6): 2293–2321.

Tihanyi L, Graffin S, George G. 2014. Rethinking governance in management research. *Academy of Management Journal* 57(6): 1535–1543.

Tihanyi L, Johnson RA, Hoskisson RE, Hitt MA. 2003. Institutional ownership differences and international diversification: the effects of boards of directors and technological opportunity. *Academy of Management Journal* 46(2): 195–211.

Tzanaki A. 2019. The Common Ownership Boom. *CPI Antitrust Chronicle*, May 2019, 2-10.

Villalonga B, Amit R. 2006. How do family ownership, control, and management affect firm value? *Journal of Financial Economics* 80(2): 385–417.

Wasserman N. 2017. The throne vs. the kingdom: founder control and value creation in start-ups. *Strategic Management Journal* 38(2): 255–277.

Westphal JD, Bednar MK. 2008. The pacification of institutional investors. *Administrative Science Quarterly* 53(1): 29–72.

Wilson N. 2016. *ESOPs: Their Role in Corporate Finance and Performance*. Springer: New York, NY.

Zajac EJ, Westphal JD. 2004 The social construction of market value: institutionalization and learning perspectives on stock market reactions. *American Sociological Review* 69(3): 433–457.

PART 8

KNOWLEDGE AND INNOVATION

Henk W. Volberda, Tatjana Schneidmuller,
and Taghi Zadeh, Leads

8.0
KNOWLEDGE AND INNOVATION: FROM PATH DEPENDENCY TOWARD MANAGERIAL AGENCY

Henk W. Volberda, Tatjana Schneidmuller, and Taghi Zadeh

Introduction

In the strategic management literature, knowledge and innovation are two central and inseparable concepts. In fact, over time, with the increased pace of technological advancement and rapid obsolescence of information, knowledge acquisition and organizational learning have become vital sources of competitive advantage, enabling companies to stay abreast of technological developments (Cohen and Levinthal, 1989, 1990). But what is knowledge? And how does it relate to innovation?

Knowledge can be broadly and simply defined as "that which is known" (Grant, 1996). This general definition, however, raises important questions not only with regard to the properties of knowledge itself but also concerning its origins, carriers, and underlying processes, such as knowledge creation, acquisition, and transfer, and its maintenance and utilization. *Innovation*, on the other hand, is the process whereby firms tap into learning and knowledge to create new products and services (Chesbrough, 2003). As such, knowledge is a vital and necessary precondition for innovation. Knowledge and innovation both continue to occupy the minds of many researchers, resulting in a diverse and vibrant research field.

Founding theories in knowledge and innovation contend that, from a strategist's perspective, innovation is either path-dependent, and thus incremental and largely passive, or is active and radical, with strategists playing a decisive role in shaping and influencing innovation outcomes. Those taking a macro perspective and a path-dependency view would argue that firms' embeddedness in their past and current networks has a confining effect on their external relationships and social context (Soda, Usai, and Zaheer, 2004), trapping them in certain ways of behaving (David, 2001). Path-creating theories, on the other hand, assume a microfoundations perspective. Such theories emphasize the role and importance of managerial agency in steering innovation trajectories (Jones, 2006), and the focus is on individuals as autonomous and self-directing actors and on their managerial capabilities (Dosi, Faillo, and Marengo, 2008).

Recent developments in the knowledge and innovation literature echo the original tension between path dependency and managerial agency at different levels of analysis (i.e., micro, meso, and macro). Moving on from foundational theories of knowledge and innovation, the field has evolved organically and has become more diverse in line with organizational priorities and wider societal developments. As our citation analysis of Cohen and Levinthal's (1990) seminal paper indicates, current research is clustered around five interrelated and partially overlapping areas: (1) international knowledge transfer, (2) organizational capabilities and learning, (3) networks and ties, (4) regional clusters, and (5) open innovation.

When we look back at traditional innovation theories, in which strategists are seen as passive bystanders driven by path dependency, we can clearly see that over time there has been a shift away from static, path-dependent assumptions toward more dynamic theories, which embrace the role of agency and agents in knowledge and innovation. For instance, we observe that current work is increasingly moving away from a purely macro-level view and is now considering also the microfoundations; there is a shift away from thinking only about cognition to examining also the part played by managerial attention. Similarly, there is a notable shift in focus from stakeholders to a broader conceptualization of critical audiences, from routine dynamics to dynamic capabilities, and from closed innovation systems to open innovation and ecosystems perspectives.

In this more active managerial agency view, strategists can make real choices, explicitly or implicitly, and thereby shape innovation trajectories of a firm. Important macro developments such as the growing democratization of knowledge and innovation, advances in machine learning and artificial intelligence, and the progressive digitalization of industries are not only accelerating this shift away from path-dependent views, but also increasingly calling into question our existing assumptions about what will be needed for successful innovation in the future. Thus we believe that a number of key areas will be central to future knowledge and innovation studies: (1) diverse audiences, which serve not only as a source of legitimacy and social evaluation but more importantly and increasingly also as a fount of knowledge and innovative ideas, as well as architects of new technology; (2) regulation and regulators, which can be not inhibitors but rather instruments and accelerators of innovation; (3) capabilities to embrace misalignment, namely organizational competencies that enable firms to be comfortable with contextual paradoxes and force them to continuously innovate and change; and (4) internal agents, such as front-line or middle managers, who can be active movers and shakers of innovation, rather than a source of organizational inertia.

The overarching goal of this introductory chapter is to prepare for the future by auditing the past and examining current theories of innovation and knowledge. We look at the historical development of the field, starting with a brief review of foundational theories. We then move on to highlight key developments in the current literature and conclude by outlining some directions for future research. In line with the evolutionary shift from path dependency to path creation, throughout this chapter we address central questions relating to the role of strategy and strategists in knowledge and innovation.

Foundational Theories of Knowledge and Innovation: Innovation as Path-Dependent or as Actively Shaped by Strategists

In our review here we note two dominant streams on knowledge and innovation. These two streams appear to lie at opposite ends of a continuum, between processes of selection and processes of adaptation. At one extreme, there are evolutionary theories emphasizing tight selection and path dependencies. They stress that organizations and their units accumulate know-how in the course of their existence and become repositories of skills that are unique and often difficult to copy. According to *population ecology theory*, these skills are a source of both inertia and distinctive competence (Hannan and Freeman, 1977, 1984). The inertia is due to sunk costs in past investments and entrenched social structures, as well as those within the organization becoming attached to particular cognitive styles, behavioral dispositions, and decision heuristics. The accumulated skills that lead to inertia in firms or in individual units also provide opportunities to strengthen their unique advantages and to further improve their know-how. The potential benefits are that firms may become better at consistently delivering sound, well-designed products, and their processes and routines may become more efficient (Miller and Chen, 1994). In a similar vein, *institutional theories* stress the coercive, normative, and mimetic behavior of organizations in the face of environmental forces for change. Institutional theories also stress how difficult it is for existing firms to create the requisite variety in routines and behavior (DiMaggio and Powell, 1983).

In their *Evolutionary Theory of Economic Change*, Nelson and Winter (1982) present firms as repositories of routines that endow them with a capacity to search. Yet these same routines limit managers' attention span and their capacity to absorb new information by reinforcing behavior that permits search only for new ideas that are consistent with prior learning. According to this theory, innovations are contingent on proximity to tacit knowledge and to prior skills. They have an inner logic of their own and give rise to natural trajectories. Given that much knowledge is tacit and cumulative in nature, experience of previous generations of a technology is often essential for future innovative success (Cohen and Levinthal, 1990). On the other hand, the "switching costs," or the cost of changing direction and acquiring knowledge unrelated to the asset base, can be quite high (Henderson and Clark, 1990). In a similar way, in the *resource-based theory* the firm is seen as a bundle of tangible and intangible resources and tacit know-how that must be identified, selected, developed, and deployed to generate superior performance (Wernerfelt, 1984). These scarce, firm-specific assets lead to a focused innovation process where there is limited capacity to change; firms are stuck with what they have and have to live with what they lack (Teece, Pisano, and Shuen, 1997).

In the above selection and path-dependent theories on knowledge accumulation and innovation, firms do best when they try not to reverse their history but instead allow evolution to take its course. At the opposite extreme, however, theories focusing on adaptation and managerial intentionality argue that innovation journeys are more varied and are less determined by tight selection and path dependencies. A large body of work suggests that organizations can and do change, overcoming their own rigidities. For instance, Teece *et al.* (1997) have suggested it is not only the bundle of resources that matter but also the mechanisms by which firms accumulate and disseminate new skills and new capabilities. They propose that *dynamic capabilities* represent the firm's latent abilities to renew its core competences over time. The *behavioral theory of the firm* (Cyert and March, 1963) argues that a firm's ability to innovate is determined primarily by the availability and control of organizational slack and by the firm's strategic intent to allocate slack to renewal. The theory describes how structural inertia comes about and shows why periodic innovation through restructuring and rationalization may be needed (Lewin and Volberda, 1999). In addition, the *strategic choice perspective* (Miles and Huberman, 1994) argues that organizations are not always passive recipients of environmental influence but also have the opportunity and power to reshape the environment. Hrebiniak and Joyce (1985), Khandwalla (1977), Mintzberg (1979), and many other neocontingency theorists assert that innovation is a dynamic process that is affected by both managerial action and environmental forces. Finally, *learning theories* assume that innovation processes are both adaptive and manipulative, in the sense that organizations adjust defensively to reality and use the resulting knowledge offensively to improve their fit to the environment (Fiol and Lyles, 1985).

The theories just discussed seem to describe innovation as processes of either selection or adaptation (see Table 1). Certain theoretical lenses, such as the behavioral theory of the firm, strategic choice, and learning perspectives, attempt to further elaborate the role of managerial intentionality. Other theoretical lenses—such as population ecology, institutionalism, and, to some extent, evolutionary theories—discount the ability of organizations to deliberately reinvent themselves in a significant way. Using variables such as resource scarcity, industry norms and shared logics, static routines, and structural inertia, those adopting these selection perspectives argue that the potential for fundamental innovation and developing new knowledge is highly restricted.

While use of these theoretical lenses has shown us either adaptive or selective innovation journeys, we think there is much more pluralism (Lewin and Volberda, 1999). Instead of focusing purely on selection or adaptation processes, perhaps one should look at how they work in combination. With a few exceptions (e.g., Baum and Singh, 1994), researchers have tended not to address the interrelationships between processes of firm-level adaptation and population-level selection pressures. Adaptation and selection are not entirely different processes but are fundamentally interrelated.

Table 1 Theoretical lenses for examining innovation: path dependency versus managerial agency

Theories on Knowledge and Innovation	
Path dependency theories	Managerial agency theories
• *Population ecology*: Innovations are based on and limited to the accumulation of structural and procedural baggage through retention processes (Hannan and Freeman, 1977, 1984; Aldrich and Pfeffer, 1976). • *Institutional theory*: Innovation results from coercive, normative, and mimetic isomorphism. Innovation is achieved by maintaining congruence with shifting industry norms and shared logics (DiMaggio and Powell, 1983; Greenwood and Hinings, 1996). • *Evolutionary theory*: Innovations are based on proliferation of routines and lead to incremental improvements (Nelson and Winter, 1982) • *Resource-based theory*: Innovations are built on exploitation of unique core competencies (Penrose 1959; Learned *et al.*, 1969; Wernerfelt, 1984).	• *Dynamic capability theory*: Innovations are promoted by firms' latent abilities to renew, augment, and adapt their core competences over time (Teece, Pisano, and Shuen, 1997). • *Behavioral theory of the firm*: Innovations are determined primarily by the availability and control of organizational slack and by the strategic intent to allocate slack to new knowledge (Cyert and March, 1963). • *Learning theories*: Innovations derive from processes of alignment of firm and environment based on unique skills for learning, unlearning, or relearning (Argyris and Schön, 1978; Fiol and Lyles, 1985; Huber, 1991). • *Strategic choice theories*: Innovation and knowledge development is a dynamic process that is subject to managerial action and environmental forces (Child, 1972, 1997; Hrebiniak and Joyce, 1985; Miles and Snow, 1978).

Such a coevolutionary approach assumes that innovation is not an outcome of managerial adaptation or environmental selection but rather the joint outcome of managerial intentionality and environmental effects.

Current Strategy Themes in the Innovation Field

It is undeniable that knowledge (Grant, 1996 and tapping into external knowledge stocks for innovation are key for innovation, superior firm performance (e.g., Geroski, Machin, and Reenen, 1993) and competitive advantage (Chesbrough, 2003). However, as external knowledge is not always easily accessible, organizations need to be able to source critical knowledge internally (Nonaka, 1994). Both approaches call for a capacity to absorb knowledge. In their seminal papers, Cohen and Levinthal define absorptive capacity (AC) as the "ability to identify, assimilate, and exploit knowledge from the environment" (1989: 589, 1990),. As a property of units—that is, individuals, groups, or organizations (van Wijk, Van den Bosch, and Volberda, 2011)—AC enables firms (Zahra and George, 2002) to utilize different forms of knowledge (Nonaka, 1991) embedded in their network (Reagans and

McEvily, 2003) and environment (Argote, McEvily, and Reagans, 2003) for the purposes of innovation.

In earlier studies, the focus on "knowledge stickiness," "knowledge stock," knowledge routines, research and development (R&D) efforts, and patent counts highlighted the path dependency of AC and innovation. Studies in this tradition explored AC in relation to static features of organizational design (Jansen, Van den Bosch, and Volberda, 2005), as well as internal (Tsai and Ghoshal, 1998) and external organizational ties (Mowery, Oxley, and Silverman, 1996; Simonin, 1999). However, relying on path-dependent capabilities alone can result in inadequate evaluations of new external knowledge (Theeke, Polidoro, and Fredrickson, 2018). This is particularly troublesome, given the exponential rise in new and pathbreaking technologies, on the one hand, and the rapid decline and obsolescence of knowledge stocks, on the other.

Consequently, researchers have begun to explore the role of strategy and strategists, and managers in particular, in AC and innovation processes. This has led to a proliferation of microfoundational studies (Distel, 2019). Among the various topics considered are managerial human capital, social capital, and cognition in innovation (Helfat and Martin, 2015), and also the mobility of strategic human resources, as both carriers of knowledge (Fang et al., 2010) and entrepreneurial agents (Knight and Cavusgil, 2004).

Centered around knowledge creation, transfer, and accumulation, AC was originally closely tied to learning and foundational theories of innovation. Over the subsequent 30 years of active research the field has diversified significantly in terms of theoretical perspectives, and five interrelated and overlapping areas have emerged: (1) international knowledge transfer, (2) organizational capabilities and learning, (3) networks and ties, (4) regional clusters, and (5) open innovation.

Each of these research clusters provides perspectives on different elements of the knowledge-based systems of firms and their activities. These include knowledge and its characteristics (von Hippel, 1994; Szulanski, 1996), the knowledge networks and knowledge-based relationships (Dyer and Singh, 1998; Mowery et al., 1996; Phelps, Heidl, and Wadhwa, 2012; Powell, Koput, and Smith-Doerr, 1996), the ability to learn and to utilize new knowledge (Argote et al., 2003; Grant, 1996; Todorova and Durisin, 2007; Zahra and George, 2002), and innovation outcomes. Clusters 1 and 4 deal mainly with knowledge stickiness and the significance of where the knowledge is located. Clusters 1 and 3 are concerned with the role of the network in which the knowledge is embedded. Cluster 2 concerns the ability of the firm to acquire and utilize new knowledge. Clusters 3 and 5 deal with how the previous elements lead to innovative outcomes. Below we provide a short overview of each cluster.

Cluster 1: international knowledge transfer

Knowledge transfer has been a concern for both international business and international management research. Informed by the notion of knowledge stickiness

(Szulanski, 1996), researchers have investigated how AC influences cross-country knowledge transfer and have theorized about the international orientation (Bagheri *et al.*, 2019), network and operations (Alcácer, Cantwell, and Piscitello, 2016), strategic human resource management (Minbaeva *et al.*, 2014), speed of internationalization (Knight and Cavusgil, 2004), and the pace, rhythm, success, and performance of multinationals (Vermeulen and Barkema, 2002). Gaur, Kumar, and Singh (2014), for instance, show how human mobility within and between multinationals and their subsidiaries (Fang *et al.*, 2010) contributes to innovation. Highlighting the role of managers in AC and innovation (Nuruzzaman, Gaur, and Sambharya, 2019), recent research has called for more microfoundational studies in innovation to explicate managerial agency in international contexts (Contractor *et al.*, 2019; Foss and Pedersen, 2019).

Cluster 2: organizational capabilities and learning

The organizational capability perspective is path-creating (Zahra and George, 2002). Here, scholars underscore the importance of managerial agency and creativity for radical innovations (Cohen and Tripsas, 2018). Managers use their networks (Floyd and Wooldridge, 1999), incorporate new knowledge into the knowledge base of the firm, and develop its knowledge capabilities (Omidvar, Edler, and Malik, 2017). As a knowledge-based capability that is developed and accumulated over time (Zahra and George, 2002), AC is associated with a stronger entrepreneurial orientation, because it increases managers' confidence in their ability to exploit the potential of new technology effectively (Ireland, Hitt, and Sirmon, 2003), and it makes those technologies and markets feel less uncertain and makes managers less risk-averse (Eshima and Anderson, 2017). Managers with higher levels of AC have been found to be more motivated to explore and innovate as they often set ambitious technological goals (Eggers and Kaul, 2018), irrespective of their firm's current performance (Cohen and Levinthal, 1990).

In the organizational learning literature, on the other hand, there is a focus on value recognition (Gavetti and Levinthal, 2000; Tripsas and Gavetti, 2000) and application (i.e., acquiring, assimilating, transforming, and exploiting) of external knowledge. This results in a rich learning model that includes feedback loops between different parts of the process as well as contingency factors, such as power, appropriability regimes, and mechanisms for social integration. Highlighting the importance and impact of the source of knowledge and the organization's prior knowledge stocks (Todorova and Durisin, 2007), this view is essentially one of path dependency. To understand the importance of AC for learning and innovation, strategy scholars have investigated the relationship between organization-level characteristics and AC, including organization design elements (Jansen *et al.*, 2005), incentive structures, the informal social context, and internal communication (Argote, 2012). Recent research has shown that when developing and using knowledge for innovation, particularly in ambiguous and uncertain environments (Boumgarden, Nickerson, and Zenger, 2012; Khanagha *et al.*, 2018), managers oscillate between exploration and exploitation in organizational learning (March, 1991).

Cluster 3: networks and ties

According to Cohen and Levinthal (1990), AC depends on the links between intraorganizational (Tsai, 2001) and interorganizational networks of knowledge (Dyer and Singh, 1998). The focus is on networks and intra- and interfirm ties, as well as on how firms use these ties for innovation by tapping into knowledge embedded within those networks. Path-dependent examples include work on strategic alliances (Lane and Lubatkin, 1998) and (international) joint ventures (Dhanaraj *et al.*, 2004). Research adopting an agency perspective has explored network structures and knowledge transfer in relationships between members of the same organization (Reagans and McEvily, 2003) or between members and their external networks (Tortoriello, 2015). In particular, the effect of entrepreneurial managers' networking (Kelley, Peters, and O'Connor, 2009) on organizational knowledge and breakthrough innovations (Hoskisson *et al.*, 2011) has attracted scholarly attention. Recent research has also examined how corporate innovators utilize the knowledge stock of the firm, thereby affecting the intraorganizational diffusion of knowledge and the recombinant possibilities of the firm (Brennecke and Rank, 2017).

Cluster 4: regional clusters

Informed by the idea of knowledge spillovers (Audretsch and Feldman, 1996), this research stream examines how different types of proximity can affect innovation. It has been established that proximity can generally improve coordination and interactive learning (Boschma, 2005). Geographical proximity can also help clustered firms create and make use of formal and informal networks (Dahl and Pedersen, 2004), while firms outside the cluster have limited access to the knowledge embedded in the networks. Knowledge spillovers within clusters can be further facilitated through community interactions (Crevoisier, 2004) and human resource mobility within a cluster (Almeida and Kogut, 1999). In regional clusters, the focus is on high-tech innovation, research excellence, attracting global firms to join the cluster, and stimulation of spin-offs (Tödtling and Trippl, 2005). Although higher levels of social capital in an industrial region have generally been found to complement internal and external R&D effectiveness (Laursen, Masciarelli, and Prencipe, 2012), scholars have also recognized that there is a two-way relationship between firms and clusters. Findings suggest that the AC of clustered firms enhances the intra- and extra-cluster knowledge systems (Giuliani and Bell, 2005) and contributes to regional growth (Huggins and Thompson, 2013).

Cluster 5: open innovation

The concept of open innovation is built on the idea that all resources required for innovation are not present within the same organization. Hence, the organization collaborates with external parties at different stages of the innovation process in order to exchange information (Chesbrough, 2003). Open innovation theorists conceptualize innovation as a multiagent process (Alexy, George, and Salter, 2013), which is powered by digital information transfer methods (Dodgson, Gann, and Salter, 2006) and can result in better innovative outcomes compared to internal R&D efforts (Terwiesch and Xu, 2008). This research stream is path-creating, as it emphasizes strategists' agency in decision making with regard to the level of openness and the way in which resources are used for innovation (Bogers *et al.*, 2019). Strategists are key in open innovation, because firms' decisions on when and how to open up the innovation process are largely driven by how managers react to and shape rapid and unprecedented changes in the environment (Alexy and Reitzig, 2013).

The research areas discussed briefly here are no longer strictly path-dependent or path-creating. However, we can still see the original tension between static and active perspectives on strategy and strategists in knowledge and innovation. Research streams such as organizational capabilities, networks, and ties, and open innovation are further along the continuum toward managerial agency, as they clearly acknowledge the importance and role of strategy and strategists as dynamos for innovation and path creators. Other streams, including those on international knowledge transfer and regional clusters, remain largely path-dependent, placing more importance on static characteristics and components of the innovation process; strategists are therefore regarded as more passive bystanders (Contractor *et al.*, 2019; Foss and Pedersen, 2019). While recent studies have shown the importance of agency and the key role of strategists as agents, we believe there is more to be learned from research that takes account of and balances both perspectives, accentuating and uniting existing knowledge and managerial agency. Such research can, for example, take the form of microfoundational studies (Nuruzzaman *et al.*, 2019; Volberda, Foss, and Lyles, 2010) and embrace a coevolutionary perspective (Lewin, Massini, and Peeters, 2011; Lewin and Volberda, 1999).

Future Perspectives in Knowledge and Innovation

Comparing the foundational theories of knowledge and innovation on which current research is based, we observe a shift away from antistrategy theories, where managers and strategists are seen as passive actors driven by path dependency, toward an active path-creation perspective that emphasizes the prominent role of strategists in shaping innovation outcomes. We suggest that, in the future, institutionalized and taken-for-granted assumptions about knowledge and innovation will continue to be questioned and tested in light of societal and technological developments, including changes in behavioral norms and in perceptions of what is desirable or acceptable (e.g., hyperconnectivity and social media). Recent examples, including the rise of open innovation and ecosystems, are already posing important questions regarding the locus and scope of knowledge creation and innovation.

Going forward, access to new knowledge and continuous innovation, once hailed as sources of competitive advantage, may quickly turn into absolute necessities for organizational survival in the digital era. Collaborations for innovation and knowledge sourcing are likely to transcend traditional boundaries and organizational contexts. As knowledge and innovation are becoming increasingly democratized and the pace of technology breakthroughs is accelerating, strategists and strategy are likely to become more important than ever. We thus propose that management scholars' focus and attention will naturally continue to gravitate toward strategy, strategic agents, and strategists, away from purely path-dependent considerations. Specifically, we envisage that in the future knowledge and innovation scholars will increase their focus on changing societal and economic trends and the challenges these pose for innovation. We now discuss four exciting and potentially fruitful research avenues that we consider most important for future-proofing our field of study and ensuring that it remains relevant.

Diverse audiences

Recent trends such as crowdsourcing, crowdfunding, and the general idea of democratizing knowledge and innovation have put a spotlight on social actors and social collectives or audiences. The critical role and importance of social audiences during periods of technological change and innovation have long been acknowledged in diverse strands of literature, with scholars examining areas such as institutional change (Greenwood, Suddaby, and Hinings, 2002; Grodal, 2018; Maguire, Hardy, and Lawrence, 2004), categorization (e.g., Suarez, Grodal, and Gotsopoulos, 2015; Zunino, Suarez, and Grodal, 2019), incumbent responses (Benner, 2007; Gerstner *et al.*, 2013), and technological evolution (Kahl and Grodal, 2016; Kaplan and Tripsas, 2008).

The early stages of technological evolution—when the existing consensus is being challenged but no new paradigm has yet been established—are marked by a consensus-challenging (Bitektine and Haack, 2015), sociocognitive process of contestation and divergence (Garud and Rappa, 1994), with different self-interested field communities (Wooten and Hoffman, 2008) or audiences (Bitektine, 2011; Hoefer and Green, 2016) experimenting with competing ideas and approaches (Abernathy and Utterback, 1978; Anderson and Tushman, 1990). In this initial state of confusion and flux (Bitektine and Haack, 2015), audiences' interpretations of technologies and attention are still fluid (Kennedy, 2008) and are likely to ebb and flow between established rationalizations and emerging ideas (Green, Babb, and Alpaslan, 2008). The resulting discursive chaos and confusion not only create a temporary state of flux (Swanson and Ramiller, 1997), they also generate a sense that incumbents need to respond and take action (Eggers and Park, 2018; Sinha and Noble, 2008). Consequently, important and potentially far-reaching investment decisions are being made while social consensus has still not been reached (Kennedy, 2008; Swanson and Ramiller, 1997). Prior research suggests that such decisions are not made solely on the basis of the economic potential for the firm (Kennedy and Fiss, 2009) but in fact require some form of external approval (Clemente and Roulet, 2015). What we currently do not know is, Whose approval matters and when? And, more generally, to whom do firms turn for guidance, and at what point? And does this vary according to the type of innovation or the stage of technological evolution?

In addition, our current understanding of how audiences engage with emerging technologies and with innovation more broadly does not take sufficient account of the possibility that they may revise and significantly change their evaluation as new technologies become available or evolve, nor of the consequences this may have for the industry and the actions of incumbents. This is particularly because most studies focus on later stages of technological evolution (Eggers and Park, 2018), where social evaluations are comparably stable (Kennedy, 2008), and more information is generally available or accessible. As such, existing explanations and models of audience engagement usually assume that all audiences engage with emerging technologies from the start (Kaplan and Tripsas, 2008).

However, audiences are undeniably heterogeneous (Dorobantu, Henisz, and Nartey, 2017). Their interest in and knowledge about emerging technologies and innovation will therefore vary significantly, and so too will their engagement with them. We assert that this heterogeneity cannot be explained by the prevailing theories alone (Kaplan and Tripsas, 2008; Pfarrer *et al.*, 2019). What we need to know is when, how, and why do audiences engage with emerging technologies? And what audience characteristics matter in this process?

While in the past we have observed a focus predominantly on managerial cognition and agency, the future, we believe, will be much more diverse and uncertain. With the rise and dominance of social media, it is no longer just top management steering innovation and knowledge; others inside and outside the firm are increasingly assuming the role of strategists. How do these diverse audiences relate to each other? What part do they play in knowledge creation and innovation? What is the role of social media in knowledge and innovation, and what are the dynamics of that interaction? Considering a wider range of critical audiences as agentic social actors and co-creators of knowledge and innovation could significantly advance our current understanding of the processes involved.

Regulation and regulators

Allowing for the possibility that strategy and strategists in knowledge and innovation can exist *outside* the firm enables us to consider other audiences, including regulators, as agentic drivers and accelerators of innovation. Even though the relationships between regulation, innovation, and competitiveness have been debated for decades, there is still no coordinated empirical research that explores the impact of existing regulation on innovation (Blind, 2012). There are, however, studies that explore the effects of different types of regulation on innovation (e.g., Bassanini and Ernst, 2002; Prieger, 2002; Swann, 2005). In knowledge and innovation specifically, studies often only look at patents and other ways of protecting intellectual property rights, or consider how new regulation can be an impediment to innovation for incumbents within established industries. This is in line with regulation increasingly being used as a means of promoting innovation (Blind *et al.*, 2004), especially in industries that have traditionally been more conservative (e.g., financial services, the legal sector, or health care). While Porter and van der Linde (1995) assert that regulation has a positive effect on innovation, others struggle to confirm these findings or find the opposite effect (Blind, 2012, 2016).

As recent technological developments and advances in machine learning, AI, and increasing digitalization are blurring industry boundaries, the importance and role of industry regulation and regulators is growing. At the same time, however, the democratization of knowledge and innovation and disintermediation of products and services may, in the long run, call into question the need for regulation in general. How will technological advances such as smart contracts affect the notion and importance of industry regulation in knowledge and innovation processes? What might the future of intellectual property protection look like?

Consequently, both current and new regulation and its effects on innovation warrant considerably more attention. We need a more thorough examination of the role of regulators and regulatory action, and specifically to consider what effect existing and new regulation aimed at promoting innovation might have, and what tensions it may create. Similarly, more attention needs to be given to regulation more generally and how it is enforced, and particularly to the differing agendas of regulators and enforcement bodies (Grandy and Hiatt, 2020). While strategists can do relatively little to influence enforcement mechanisms, research has shown that organizations can lobby and have a significant influence on what new legislation is passed. In particular, innovators with knowledge and expertise can sway regulators in their favor (Ernkvist, 2015). At the same time, new regulation that is meant to level the competitive playing field for new entrants and accelerate innovation within an industry may create compliance costs for new entrants, thus discouraging them from innovating in the long run. It would be interesting to see whether regulatory initiatives and strategies actually deliver on their promise and spur innovation, and how organizational strategists navigate their regulatory environment.

Misalignment capabilities

In an age of disruption, the survival of firms often rests on their ability to address complexities and paradoxical situations that require technology adoption. Drawing on contingency theory, some scholars argue for the importance of internal fit, namely the alignment between internal aspects of the organization such as its strategy, structure, and activities (Peteraf and Reed, 2007). The universality of this strategic alignment perspective has recently been challenged by the idea that consistency becomes less viable when firms face diverse contingencies and conflicting requirements on the demand side as well as the supply side. How can innovation scholars incorporate supply-side and demand-side heterogeneity when studying incumbents' attempts to innovate? These questions are in line with the growing attention being given to multisided markets and platform ecosystems by strategy and innovation scholars who consider heterogeneity as an important, yet less examined, factor that influences innovation performance. It is argued that organizations are able to thrive by embracing misalignment between internal components and promoting inconsistent mentalities and structures. They should embrace inconsistencies (Poulis and Poulis, 2016) such as misalignment of their strategies, structure, and resources (Khanagha *et al.*, 2018). How can incumbent firms develop organizational capabilities that allow them to appreciate, nurture, and deal with the tensions associated with misalignment—that is, dynamic capabilities that could be argued to be crucial for innovation? Firms that are able to embrace misalignment can steer a path through their technological developments when they do not have a clear view of what the future may hold. They can accommodate differing visions of the future among their managers (Dattée, Alexy, and Autio, 2017), allowing them to ideate, incubate, and industrialize new core technologies.

Role of strategists

Developing misalignment capabilities requires an organization-wide flexible cognitive frame to cope with environmental ambiguity and uncertainty. Incumbents with a long history of success, however, are subject to path-dependent frame rigidity, for instance, in terms of their organizational identity (Raffaelli, Glynn, and Tushman, 2019). Organizational identity is the perception of organizational members about what is core and enduring in the business, and is shaped partially by the firm's technological knowledge stock and practice (Tripsas, 2009). If there is identity pluralism within an organization (Pratt and Foreman, 2000), this can be leveraged by strategists as a source or driver of innovation (Baker and Nelson, 2005). In the context of platform ecosystems, scholars with an interest in innovation and knowledge might address new research avenues from an organizational identity perspective. A business model that is based on a platform ecosystem provides a significantly different setting for innovation compared to a linear model (Volberda, Van den Bosch, and Heij, 2018). For instance, when faced with a volatile environment, those working within an ecosystem should be able to try out multiple identities and strategy processes (Ciborra, 1996; Khanagha *et al.*, 2018).

Studying multi-echelon strategy processes (Heyden *et al.*, 2017) in large, well-established firms and the multiple related identities in the top management team and at the middle and front-line manager levels might help scholars to understand better the complexities that these firms face when moving from pipeline to platform ecosystem business models. Innovation in a platform ecosystem needs multi-echelon strategy processes as well as collaboration with complementors and customers (Altman and Tushman, 2017). Little work has been done, however, on how strategists from different hierarchical organizational levels, given the established organizational identity, apply a platform innovation logic and "harness creativity outside the organization" (Yoo et al., 2012). For instance, because of their openness platforms provide multiple opportunities for innovation. Opening up the innovation process of an established business to external parties may create tensions with the firm's existing organizational identity (Nambisan et al., 2017). There are a number of key questions that could be addressed in future research. For example, how do strategists in incumbent firms manage the convergence of internal and external knowledge that is required to become a platform player? How do the organizational identities of incumbents facilitate or hinder this convergence of knowledge? And how can strategists reshape identities within a firm in order to foster innovation in a platform ecosystem?

Knowledge, cognition (e.g., organizational identity and attention), and innovation are interlinked in organizations: the knowledge stock and knowledge-based capabilities of a firm influence its organizational identity (Corley, Gioia, and Nag, 2011). Organizational identity determines what types of opportunities for innovation may attract the strategists' attention (Ocasio and Joseph, 2017). Without paying sustained attention to these opportunities, firms cannot exploit them (Shepherd, McMullen, and Ocasio, 2017). Research suggests that a flexible identity (Tripsas, 2009) and attention from managers at various hierarchical levels (Ocasio, 2011) foster a firm's innovativeness. Organizational identity has different dimensions, as it is multilevel, nested, and open to interpretation. Researchers have shown how strategists can make a firm's organizational identity more flexible in order to innovate (Anthony and Tripsas, 2016). Future studies could seek to explore the links between knowledge, cognition, and innovation in more depth. Researchers could investigate what role is played in this relationship by different knowledge-based strategies (e.g., interfirm knowledge transfer and investment in external and internal R&D, partnerships with complementors, and co-creation with customers in ecosystems) and capabilities (e.g., misalignment capability and absorptive capacity). They might address questions such as what configurations of organizational identity, knowledge-based strategy, and organizational capabilities may result in stronger innovative performance when using platform ecosystems compared to linear business models, and how might strategists modify the knowledge-cognition-innovation chain of a linear business model to help the firm become an innovation platform player.

Conclusion

We started this chapter by claiming that knowledge is essential for innovation, and that the two are in fact inseparable and interrelated in important ways. In our review of foundational theories we showed how these were based on the idea that firms possess knowledge stocks, which accumulate over time from the various activities that they carry out as a part of their innovation process. This in turn enables firms to tap into new knowledge that exists in their environment. This constituted a path-dependent perspective on knowledge and innovation. What we have then shown in the subsequent discussion is that our thinking has evolved from those early path-dependent views of innovation toward a managerial agency of innovation view in which managers are regarded as playing a more active role as strategists in knowledge development and innovation. Essentially, we endorse the view that managers and other social actors both inside and outside a firm can act as strategists, exercising their agency to influence the knowledge and technological trajectories not only of the firm itself but also of the wider ecosystem or industry. We discussed four exciting and potentially fruitful research avenues that we consider most important for the future of the field. They were derived from recent technological advancements and their sociocognitive influence on the business environment. We envisage that, in the future, knowledge and innovation scholars will increase their focus on changing societal and economic trends and the challenges these pose for innovation.

References

Abernathy WJ, Utterback JM. 1978. Patterns of industrial innovation. *Technology Review* 80(7): 40–47.

Alcácer J, Cantwell J, Piscitello L. 2016. Internationalization in the information age: a new era for places, firms, and international business networks? *Journal of International Business Studies* 47(5): 499–512.

Aldrich HE, Pfeffer J. 1976. Environments of organizations. *Annual Review of Sociology* 2: 121–140.

Alexy O, George G, Salter AJ. 2013. Cui bono? The selective revealing of knowledge and its implications for innovative activity. *Academy of Management Review* 38(2): 270–291.

Alexy O, Reitzig M. 2013. Private-collective innovation, competition, and firms' counterintuitive appropriation strategies. *Research Policy* 42(4): 895–913.

Almeida P, Kogut B. 1999. Localization of knowledge and the mobility of engineers in regional networks. *Management Science* 45(7): 905–917.

Altman EJ, Tushman ML. 2017. Platforms, open/user innovation, and ecosystems: a strategic leadership perspective. *Advances in Strategic Management* 37: 177–207.

Anderson P, Tushman ML. 1990. Technological discontinuities and dominant designs: a cyclical model of technological change. *Administrative Science Quarterly* 35(4): 604–633.

Anthony C, Tripsas M. 2016. Organizational identity and innovation. In *The Oxford Handbook of Organizational Identity*, Pratt MG, Schultz M, Ashforth BE, Ravasi D (eds). Oxford University Press: Oxford, U.K.; 417–435.

Argote L. 2012. *Organizational Learning: Creating, Retaining, and Transferring Knowledge.* 2nd ed. Springer: New York, NY.

Argote L, McEvily B, Reagans R. 2003. Managing knowledge in organizations: an integrative framework and review of emerging themes. *Management Science* 49(4): 571–582.

Argyris C, Schön D. 1978. *Organizational Learning.* Addison-Wesley: Reading, MA.

Audretsch DB, Feldman MP. 1996. Innovative clusters and the industry life cycle. *Review of Industrial Organization* 11(2): 253–273.

Bagheri M, Mitchelmore S, Bamiatzi V, Nikolopoulos K. 2019. Internationalization orientation in SMEs: the mediating role of technological innovation. *Journal of International Management* 25(1): 121–139.

Baker T, Nelson RE. 2005. Creating something from nothing: resource construction through entrepreneurial bricolage. *Administrative Science Quarterly* 50(3): 329-366.

Bassanini A, Ernst E. 2002. Labour market institutions, product market regulation, and innovation: cross-country evidence. OECD Economics Department Working Papers.

Baum JAC, Singh JV. 1994. *Evolutionary Dynamics of Organizations*. Oxford University Press: New York, NY.

Benner MJ. 2007. The incumbent discount: stock market categories and response to radical technological change. *Academy of Management Review* 32(3): 703–720.

Bitektine A. 2011. Toward a theory of social judgments of organizations: the case of legitimacy, reputation, and status. *Academy of Management Review* 36(1): 151–179.

Bitektine A, Haack P. 2015. The "macro" and the "micro" of legitimacy: toward a multilevel theory of the legitimacy process. *Academy of Management Review* 40(1): 49–75.

Blind K. 2012. The influence of regulations on innovation: a quantitative assessment for OECD countries. *Research Policy* 41(2): 391–400.

Blind K. 2016. The impact of regulation on innovation. In *Handbook of Innovation Policy*, Edler J, Cunningham P, Gök A, Shapira P (eds). Edward Elgar Publishing: Cheltenham, U.K.; 450–482.

Blind K, Bührlen B, Menrad K, Hafner S, Walz R, Kotz C. 2004. *New Products and Services: Analysis of Regulations Shaping New Markets*. Study financed by the European Commission, Fraunhofer Institute Systems and Innovation Research: Karlsruhe.

Bogers M, Chesbrough H, Heaton S, Teece DJ. 2019. Strategic management of open innovation: a dynamic capabilities perspective. *California Management Review* 62(1): 77–94.

Boschma R. 2005. Proximity and innovation: a critical assessment. *Regional Studies* 39(1): 61–74.

Boumgarden P, Nickerson JA, Zenger TR. 2012. Sailing into the wind: exploring the relationships among ambidexterity, vacillation, and organizational performance. *Strategic Management Journal* 33(6): 587–610.

Brennecke J, Rank O. 2017. The firm's knowledge network and the transfer of advice among corporate inventors—a multilevel network study. *Research Policy* 46(4): 768–783. http://dx.doi.org/10.1016/j.respol.2017.02.002.

Chesbrough HW. 2003. *Open Innovation: The New Imperative for Creating and Profiting from Technology*. Harvard Business School Press: Boston, MA.

Child J. 1972. Organizational structure, environment and performance: the role of strategic choice. *Sociology* 6(1): 1–22.

Child J. 1997. Strategic choice in the analysis of action, structure, organizations and environment: retrospect and prospect. *Organization Studies* 18(1): 43–76.

Ciborra CU. 1996. The platform organization: recombining strategies, structures, and surprises. *Organization Science* 7(2): 103–118.

Clemente M, Roulet T. 2015. Public opinion as a source of deinstitutionalization: a "spiral of silence" approach. *Academy of Management Review* 40(1): 96–114.

Cohen SL, Tripsas M. 2018. Managing technological transitions by building bridges. *Academy of Management Journal* 61(6): 2319–2342.

Cohen WM, Levinthal DA. 1989. Innovation and learning: the two faces of R&D. *Economic Journal* 99 (September): 569–596.

Cohen WM, Levinthal DA. 1990. Absorptive capacity: a new perspective on learning and innovation. *Administrative Science Quarterly* 35(1): 128–152.

Contractor F, Foss NJ, Kundu S, Lahiri S. 2019. Viewing global strategy through a microfoundations lens. *Global Strategy Journal* 9(1): 3–18.

Corley KG, Gioia DA, Nag R. 2011. Subtle learning and organizational identity as enablers of strategic change. In *Handbook of Organizational Learning and Knowledge Management*. 2nd ed., Easterby-Smith M, Lyles MA (eds). Wiley: Chichester, U.K.; 349–365.

Crevoisier O. 2004. The innovative milieus approach: toward a territorialized understanding of the economy? *Economic Geography* 80(4): 367–379.

Cyert RM, March JG. 1963. *A Behavioral Theory of the Firm*. Prentice-Hall: Englewood Cliffs, NJ.

Dahl MS, Pedersen CØR. 2004. Knowledge flows through informal contacts in industrial clusters: myth or reality? *Research Policy* 33(10): 1673–1686.

Dattée B, Alexy O, Autio E. 2017. Maneuvering in poor visibility: how firms play the ecosystem game when uncertainty is high. *Academy of Management Journal* 61(2): 466–498.

David PA. 2001. Path dependence, its critics and the quest for "historical economics." In *Evolution and Path Dependence in Economic Ideas: Past and Present*, Garrouste P, Ioannides S (eds). Edward Elgar: Cheltenham, U.K.; 15–40.

Dhanaraj C, Lyles MA, Steensma HK, Tihanyi L. 2004. Managing tacit and explicit knowledge transfer in IJVs: the role of relational embeddedness and the impact on performance. *Journal of International Business Studies* 35(5): 428–442.

DiMaggio P, Powell WW. 1983. The iron cage revisited: institutional isomorphism and collective rationality in organizational fields. *American Sociological Review* 48(2): 147–160.

Distel AP. 2019. Unveiling the microfoundations of absorptive capacity: a study of Coleman's Bathtub Model. *Journal of Management* 45(5): 2014–2044.

Dodgson M, Gann D, Salter A. 2006. The role of technology in the shift towards open innovation: the case of Procter and Gamble. *R and D Management* 36(3): 333–346.

Dorobantu S, Henisz WJ, Nartey L. 2017. Not all sparks light a fire: stakeholder and shareholder reactions to critical events in contested markets. *Administrative Science Quarterly* 62(3): 561–597.

Dosi G, Faillo M, Marengo L. 2008. Organizational capabilities, patterns of knowledge accumulation, and governance structures in business firms: an introduction. *Organization Studies* 29(8–9): 1165–1185.

Dyer JH, Singh H. 1998. The relational view: cooperative strategy and sources of interorganizational competitive advantage. *Academy of Management Review* 23(4): 660–679.

Eggers JP, Kaul A. 2018. Motivation and ability? A behavioral perspective on the pursuit of radical invention in multi-technology incumbents. *Academy of Management Journal* 61(1): 67–93.

Eggers JP, Park KF. 2018. Incumbent adaptation to technological change: the past, present, and future of research on heterogeneous incumbent response. *Academy of Management Annals* 12(1): 357–389.

Ernkvist M. 2015. The double knot of technology and business-model innovation in the era of ferment of digital exchanges: the case of OM, a pioneer in electronic options exchanges. *Technological Forecasting and Social Change* 99: 285–299.

Eshima Y, Anderson BS. 2017. Firm growth, adaptive capability, and entrepreneurial orientation. *Strategic Management Journal* 38(3): 770–779.

Fang Y, Jiang GLF, Makino S, Beamish PW. 2010. Multinational firm knowledge, use of expatriates, and foreign subsidiary performance. *Journal of Management Studies* 47(1): 27–54.

Fiol CM, Lyles MA. 1985. Organizational learning. *Academy of Management Review* 10(4): 803–813.

Floyd SW, Wooldridge B. 1999. Knowledge creation and social networks in corporate entrepreneurship: the renewal of organizational capability. *Entrepreneurship Theory and Practice* 23(3): 123–144.

Foss NJ, Pedersen T. 2019. Microfoundations in international management research: the case of knowledge sharing in multinational corporations. *Journal of International Business Studies* 50(9): 1594–1621.

Garud R, Rappa MA. 1994. A socio-cognitive model of technology evolution: the case of cochlear implants. *Organization Science* 5(3): 344–362. Available at: https://doi.org/10.1287/orsc.5.3.344.

Gaur AS, Kumar V, Singh D. 2014. Institutions, resources, and internationalization of emerging economy firms. *Journal of World Business* 49(1): 12–20. Available at: http://dx.doi.org/10.1016/j.jwb.2013.04.002.

Gavetti G, Levinthal DA. 2000. Looking forward and looking backward: cognitive and experiential search. *Administrative Science Quarterly* 45(1): 113–137.

Geroski PA, Machin S, Reenen J Van. 1993. The profitability of innovating firms. *RAND Journal of Economics* 24(2): 198–211.

Gerstner W-C, König A, Enders A, Hambrick DC. 2013. CEO narcissism, audience engagement, and organizational adoption of technological discontinuities. *Administrative Science Quarterly* 58(2): 257–291.

Giuliani E, Bell M. 2005. The micro-determinants of meso-level learning and innovation: evidence from a Chilean wine cluster. *Research Policy* 34(1): 47–68.

Grandy JB, Hiatt SR. 2020. State agency discretion and entrepreneurship in regulated markets. *Administrative Science Quarterly*: 1–40. Available at: http://journals.sagepub.com/doi/10.1177/000183922091102.

Grant RM. 1996. Toward a knowledge-based theory of the firm. *Strategic Management Journal* 17(Winter Special Issue): 109–122.

Green SE Jr, Babb M, Alpaslan CM. 2008. Institutional field dynamics and the competition between institutional logics: the role of rhetoric in the evolving control of the modern corporation. *Management Communication Quarterly* 22(1): 40–73.

Greenwood R, Hinings CR. 1996. Understanding radical organizational change: bringing together the old and the new institutionalism. *Academy of Management Review* 21(4): 1022-1054.

Greenwood R, Suddaby R, Hinings CRR. 2002. Theorizing change: the role of professional associations in the transformation of institutionalized fields. *Academy of Management Journal* 45(1): 58–80.

Grodal S. 2018. Field expansion and contraction: how communities shape social and symbolic boundaries. *Administrative Science Quarterly* 63(4): 783–818.

Hannan MT, Freeman J. 1977. The population ecology of organizations. *American Journal of Sociology* 82(5): 929–964.

Hannan MT, Freeman J. 1984. Structural inertia and organizational change. *American Sociological Review* 49(2): 149–164.

Helfat CE, Martin JA. 2015. Dynamic managerial capabilities: review and assessment of managerial impact on strategic change. *Journal of Management* 41(5): 1281–1312.

Henderson RM, Clark KB. 1990. Architectural innovation: the reconfiguration of existing product technologies and the failure of established firms. *Administrative Science Quarterly* 35(1): 9–30.

Heyden MLM, Fourné SPL, Koene BAS, Werkman R, Ansari S (Shaz). 2017. Rethinking "top-down" and "bottom-up" roles of top and middle managers in organizational change: implications for employee support. *Journal of Management Studies* 54(7): 961–985.

von Hippel E. 1994. "Sticky information" and the locus of problem solving: implications for innovation. *Management Science* 40(4): 429–439.

Hoefer R, Green S. 2016. A rhetorical model of institutional judgment and decision-making. *Academy of Management Review* 41(1): 130–150.

Hoskisson RE, Covin JG, Volberda HW, Johnson RA. 2011. Revitalizing entrepreneurship: the search for new research opportunities. *Journal of Management Studies* 48(6): 1141–1168.

Hrebiniak LG, Joyce WF. 1985. Organizational adaptation: strategic choice and environmental determinism. *Administrative Science Quarterly* 30(3): 336–349.

Huber GP. 1991. Organizational learning: the contributing processes and literatures. *Organization Science* 2(1): 88–115.

Huggins R, Thompson P. 2013. A network-based view of regional growth. *Journal of Economic Geography* 14(3): 511–545.

Ireland RD, Hitt MA, Sirmon DG. 2003. A model of strategic entrepreneurship: the construct and its dimensions. *Journal of Management* 29(6): 963–989.

Jansen JJP, Van den Bosch FAJ, Volberda HW. 2005. Managing potential and realized absorptive capacity: how do organizational antecedents matter? *Academy of Management Journal* 48(6): 999–1015.

Jones O. 2006. Developing absorptive capacity in mature organizations: the change agent's role. *Management Learning* 37(3): 355–376.

Kahl SJ, Grodal S. 2016. Discursive strategies and radical technological change: multilevel discourse analysis of the early computer (1947–1958). *Strategic Management Journal* 37(1): 149–166.

Kaplan S, Tripsas M. 2008. Thinking about technology: applying a cognitive lens to technical change. *Research Policy* 37(5): 790–805.

Kelley DJ, Peters L, O'Connor GC. 2009. Intra-organizational networking for innovation-based corporate entrepreneurship. *Journal of Business Venturing* 24: 221–235.

Kennedy MT. 2008. Getting counted: markets, media, and reality. *American Sociological Review* 73(2): 270–295.

Kennedy MT, Fiss PC. 2009. Institutionalization, framing, and diffusion: the logic of TQM adoption and implementation decisions among U.S. hospitals. *Academy of Management Journal* 52(5): 897–918.

Khanagha S, Ramezan Zadeh MT, Mihalache OR, Volberda HW. 2018. Embracing bewilderment: responding to technological disruption in heterogeneous market environments. *Journal of Management Studies* 55(7): 1079–1121.

Khandwalla PN. 1977. *The Design of Organizations.* McGill University Press: New York, NY.

Knight GA, Cavusgil ST. 2004. Innovation, organizational capabilities, and the born-global firm. *Journal of International Business Studies* 35(2): 124–141.

Lane PJ, Lubatkin M. 1998. Relative absorptive capacity and interorganizational learning. *Strategic Management Journal* 19(5): 461–477.

Laursen K, Masciarelli F, Prencipe A. 2012. Regions matter: how localized social capital affects innovation and external knowledge acquisition. *Organization Science* 23(1): 177–193.

Learned EP, Christensen CR, Andrews KR, Guth W. 1969. *Business Policy: Text and Cases.* R. Irwin: Homewood, IL.

Lewin AY, Massini S, Peeters C. 2011. Microfoundations of internal and external absorptive capacity routines. *Organization Science* 22(1): 81–98.

Lewin AY, Volberda HW. 1999. Prolegomena on coevolution: a framework for research on strategy and new organizational forms. *Organization Science* 10(5): 519–534.

Maguire S, Hardy C, Lawrence TB. 2004. Institutional entrepreneurship in emerging fields: HIV/AIDS treatment advocacy in Canada. *Academy of Management Journal* 47(5): 657–679.

March JG. 1991. Exploration and exploitation in organizational learning. *Organization Science* 2(1): 71–87.

Miles RE, Snow CC. 1978. *Organizational Strategy, Structure, and Process.* McGraw-Hill: New York, NY.

Miles MB, Huberman AM. 1994. *Qualitative Data Analysis: An Expanded Sourcebook*. SAGE Publications: Thousand Oaks, CA.

Miller D, Chen M-J. 1994. Sources and consequences of competitive inertia: a study of the US airline industry. *Administrative Science Quarterly* 39(1): 1–23.

Minbaeva DB, Pedersen T, Björkman I, Fey CF. 2014. A retrospective on: MNC knowledge transfer, subsidiary absorptive capacity, and HRM. *Journal of International Business Studies* 45(1): 52–62.

Mintzberg H. 1979. *The Structuring of Organizations*. Prentice Hall: Upper Saddle River, NJ.

Mowery DC, Oxley JE, Silverman BS. 1996. Strategic alliances and interfirm knowledge transfer. *Strategic Management Journal* 17(S2): 77–91.

Nambisan S, Lyytinen K, Majchrzak A, Song M. 2017. Digital innovation management: reinventing innovation management research in a digital world. *MIS Quarterly* 41(1): 223–238.

Nelson RR, Winter SG. 1982. *An Evolutionary Theory of Economic Change*. Belknap Press of Harvard University Press: Cambridge, MA.

Nonaka I. 1991. The knowledge-creating company. *Harvard Business Review* 69(6): 96–104.

Nonaka I. 1994. A dynamic theory of organizational knowledge creation. *Organization Science* 5(1): 14–37.

Nuruzzaman N, Gaur AS, Sambharya RB. 2019. A microfoundations approach to studying innovation in multinational subsidiaries. *Global Strategy Journal* 9(1): 92–116.

Ocasio W. 2011. Attention to attention. *Organization Science* 22(5): 1286–1296.

Ocasio W, Joseph J. 2017. The attention-based view of great strategies. *Strategy Science* 3(1): 289–294.

Omidvar O, Edler J, Malik K. 2017. Development of absorptive capacity over time and across boundaries: the case of R&D consortia. *Long Range Planning* 50(5): 665–683.

Penrose ET. 1959. *The Theory of Growth of the Firm*. Wiley: New York, NY.

Peteraf MA, Reed R. 2007. Managerial discretion and internal alignment under regulatory constraints and change. *Strategic Management Journal* 28(11): 1089–1112.

Pfarrer MD, Devers CE, Corley K, Cornelissen JP, Lange D, Makadok R, Mayer K, Weber L. 2019. Sociocognitive perspectives in strategic management. *Academy of Management Review* 44(4): 767–774.

Phelps C, Heidl R, Wadhwa A. 2012. Knowledge, networks, and knowledge networks. *Journal of Management* 38(4): 1115–1166.

Porter ME, Linde C van der. 1995. Toward a new conception of the environment-competitiveness relationship. *Journal of Economic Perspectives* 9(4): 97–118.

Poulis K, Poulis E. 2016. Problematizing fit and survival: transforming the law of requisite variety through complexity misalignment. *Academy of Management Review* 41(3): 503–527.

Powell WW, Koput KW, Smith-Doerr L. 1996. Interorganizational collaboration and the locus of innovation: networks of learning in biotechnology. *Administrative Science Quarterly* 41(1): 116–145.

Pratt MG, Foreman PO. 2000. Classifying managerial responses to multiple organizational identities. *Academy of Management Review* 25(1): 18–42.

Prieger JE. 2002. Regulation, innovation, and the introduction of telecommunications services. *Review of Economics and Statistics* 84(4): 704–715.

Raffaelli R, Glynn MA, Tushman M. 2019. Frame flexibility: the role of cognitive and emotional framing in innovation adoption by incumbent firms. *Strategic Management Journal* 40(7): 1013–1039.

Reagans R, McEvily B. 2003. Network structure and knowledge transfer: the effects of cohesion and range. *Administrative Science Quarterly* 48(2): 240–267.

Shepherd DA, McMullen JS, Ocasio W. 2017. Is that an opportunity? An attention model of top managers' opportunity beliefs for strategic action. *Strategic Management Journal* 38(3): 626–644.

Simonin BL. 1999. Ambiguity and the process of knowledge transfer in strategic alliances. *Strategic Management Journal* 20(7): 595–623.

Sinha RK, Noble CH. 2008. The adoption of radical manufacturing technologies and firm survival. *Strategic Management Journal* 29(9): 943–962.

Soda G, Usai A, Zaheer A. 2004. Network memory: the influence of past and current networks on performance. *Academy of Management Journal* 47(6): 893–906.

Suarez FF, Grodal S, Gotsopoulos A. 2015. Perfect timing? Dominant category, dominant design, and the window of opportunity for firm entry. *Strategic Management Journal* 36(3): 437–448.

Swann GMP. 2005. *Do Standards Enable or Constrain Innovation? The Empirical Economics of Standards*. Department of Trade and Industry, U.K.

Swanson EB, Ramiller NC. 1997. The organizing vision in information systems innovation. *Organization Science* 8(5): 458–474.

Szulanski G. 1996. Exploring internal stickiness: impediments to the transfer of best practice within the firm. *Strategic Management Journal* 17(S2): 27–43.

Teece DJ, Pisano G, Shuen A. 1997. Dynamic capabilities and strategic management. *Strategic Management Journal* 18(7): 509–533.

Terwiesch C, Xu Y. 2008. Innovation contests, open innovation, and multiagent problem solving. *Management Science* 54(9): 1529–1543.

Theeke M, Polidoro F, Fredrickson JW. 2018. Path-dependent routines in the evaluation of novelty: the effects of innovators' new knowledge use on brokerage firms' coverage. *Administrative Science Quarterly* 63(4): 910–942.

Todorova G, Durisin B. 2007. Absorptive capacity: valuing a reconceptualization. *Academy of Management Review* 32(3): 774–786.

Tödtling F, Trippl M. 2005. One size fits all?: Towards a differentiated regional innovation policy approach. *Research Policy* 34(8): 1203–1219.

Tortoriello M. 2015. The social underpinnings of absorptive capacity: the moderating effects of structural holes on innovation generation based on external knowledge. *Strategic Management Journal* 36(4): 586–597.

Tripsas M. 2009. Technology, identity, and inertia through the lens of "The Digital Photography Company." *Organization Science* 20(2): 441–460.

Tripsas M, Gavetti G. 2000. Capabilities, cognition, and inertia: evidence from digital imaging. *Strategic Management Journal* 21(10–11): 1147–1161.

Tsai W. 2001. Knowledge transfer in intraorganizational networks: effects of network position and absorptive capacity on business unit innovation and performance. *Academy of Management Journal* 44(5): 996–1004.

Tsai W, Ghoshal S. 1998. Social capital and value creation: the role of intrafirm networks. *Academy of Management Journal* 41(4): 464–476.

Vermeulen F, Barkema H. 2002. Pace, rhythm, and scope: process dependence in building a profitable multinational corporation. *Strategic Management Journal* 23(7): 637–653.

Volberda HW, Foss NJ, Lyles MA. 2010. Absorbing the concept of absorptive capacity: how to realize its potential in the organization field. *Organization Science* 21(4): 931–951.

Volberda H, Van den Bosch F, Heij K. 2018. *Reinventing Business Models: How Firms Cope with Disruption*. Oxford University Press: Oxford, U.K.

Wernerfelt B. 1984. A resource-based view of the firm. *Strategic Management Journal* 5(2): 171–180.

van Wijk R, Van den Bosch FAJ, Volberda HW. 2011. Absorptive capacity: taking stock of its progress and prospects. In *Handbook of Organizational Learning and Knowledge Management*, 2nd ed., Easterby-Smith M, Lyles MA (eds). Wiley: Chichester, U.K.; 273–304.

Wooten M, Hoffman AJ. 2008. Organizational fields: past, present and future. In *The Sage Handbook of Organizational Institutionalism*, Greenwood R, Oliver C, Sahlin K, Suddaby R (eds). SAGE: Thousand Oaks, CA; 131–147.

Yoo Y, Boland RJ, Lyytinen K, Majchrzak A. 2012. Organizing for innovation in the digitized world. *Organization Science* 23(5): 1398–1408.

Zahra SA, George G. 2002. Absorptive capacity: a review, reconceptualizations, and extension. *Academy of Management Review* 27(2): 185–203.

Zunino D, Suarez FF, Grodal S. 2019. Familiarity, creativity, and the adoption of category labels in technology industries. *Organization Science* 30(1): 169–190.

8.1
ORGANIZATIONAL LEARNING

Mary Crossan, Dusya Vera, and Seemantini Pathak

In spite of the rich history linking organizational learning (OL) and strategy, there is tremendous opportunity for strategy scholars and practitioners to tap into the deep reservoir of OL research to address: how is OL uniquely positioned to contribute to the advancement of strategic management? We advocate that the need to elevate OL in strategy research has never been more important, given the grand challenges facing our world, requiring strategy to extend beyond organizations to society. We structure our analysis around four sections.

The first section reveals that the underutilization of OL in strategy may arise because of other concepts in the nomological space that direct attention elsewhere, such as knowledge management, routines, resources, dynamic capabilities, strategy process, and strategy as practice. We call for strategy researchers to be more explicit in recognizing the interrelationships of these concepts and leverage the rich socio-cognitive processes that have been studied in OL, which can help to explain the mechanisms underlying competitive advantage in theories of strategy. We offer two important areas that can be leveraged more effectively in strategy and propose directions that merit deeper examination. Those two areas are (1) exploration, exploitation, and ambidexterity; and (2) the processes of OL as they relate to strategic renewal and agility, including multilevel theorizing. Although we outline prior research, our aim is to shed light on opportunities for future research, since our primary conclusion is that strategy researchers have only scratched the surface of OL theory.

Finally, we examine emerging frontiers for both OL and strategy that will serve to strengthen the first three sections, and challenge researchers to apply OL theory to even more compelling strategic challenges. Given that the context of strategy has been consistently described as dynamic, ambiguous, uncertain, and complex, we elevate the role of the agent and the quality of judgment and wisdom required within the domain of strategy. The interface between the human and nonhuman aspects of strategy, including artificial intelligence (AI), calls for the essential role of inserting judgment as a core construct linking OL and strategy. Throughout the chapter, we also offer research questions in the intersection of OL and strategy.

A Call to Leverage OL Processes as Part of the Strategy Nomological Net

OL theory, the knowledge-based view (KBV), the resource-based view (RBV), the evolutionary theory of economic change, dynamic capabilities, strategy process, and strategy as practice perspectives are intertwined, and the concepts of learning, knowledge, knowing, knowledge management, resources, capabilities, absorptive capacity, human and social capital, routines, and practices are interrelated (e.g., Lane, Koka, and Pathak 2006; Pettit, Crossan, and Vera, 2017; Vera, Crossan, and Apaydin, 2011). Although these links exist, rarely do researchers build on the insights arising from these related domains; essentially, as a research community we fail to learn from one another. As strategy researchers who have studied OL, we are well aware that OL tends to be considered as an organizational theory with strategic implications, while RBV, KBV, and dynamic capabilities, for example, are considered strategy theories with organizational content (e.g., Greve, 2021). Strategic renewal is an example of a phenomenon that is critical for organizations, industries, and economies (Agarwal and Helfat, 2009); however, many descriptions of strategic renewal that position it as a capability fail to acknowledge that the processes involved are learning processes previously discussed in OL theory. Our conclusion is that OL is frequently underutilized in strategy, or is mentioned in a superficial way.

Greve (2021) compared OL and RBV and observed that the fields have lived separate lives, with the *Strategic Management Journal* often publishing RBV papers and *Organization Science* often publishing learning theory. Greve (2021) noted three areas of overlap and three areas of differences between OL and RBV. The areas of overlap were (1) the assumption of organizational differences, (2) path dependence, and (3) complex social mechanisms, while the areas of differences were (1) focus on either resources or behaviors, (2) the detailed learning-theory treatment of own and others' experience as sources of learning, and (3) the greater interest in environmental change in learning theory (Greve, 2021). He concludes that OL can serve RBV in considering the implications of both sustainable competitive advantage and enduring competitive advantage, particularly with respect to diffusion of knowledge and vicarious learning. While sustainable advantage depends on a firm's resource base, the duration of that advantage depends on other firms' vicarious learning and ability to transfer knowledge (Greve, 2021).

Some links between OL and strategy are explicit. For example, learning capabilities are the ultimate second-order capabilities (Winter, 2003). Deliberate investments in OL, including experience accumulation, and knowledge articulation and codification, enable the creation and modification of dynamic capabilities (Zollo and Winter, 2002). In addition, for some, KBV is a useful extension of OL to strategy. However, Eisenhardt and Santos (2002) warn that not all knowledge is equally strategically valuable. They also argue that a theory of the firm is more likely going to be focused on knowing than on knowledge. An example of progress toward integration is Argote's

(2011) description of OL as having three subprocesses: creating, retaining, and transferring knowledge. She combines the learning and knowledge vocabulary to clearly explain that when organizations learn from experience, new knowledge is created. However, territorial battles still exist. Castaneda, Manrique, and Cuellar recently concluded in their review that "OL has been gradually absorbed within KM" (2018: 322). The evidence they provide is that the word "knowledge" (e.g., knowledge acquisition and creation) was included in OL studies. For us, that knowledge processes are included in OL definitions is not a sign of "absorption" but of integration.

We propose that OL is uniquely positioned to contribute to strategic management because OL theories are rich in explaining paradoxes, tensions, and multilevel phenomena (e.g., Crossan, Lane, and White, 1999), which are increasingly relevant in strategy as theories need to deal with extreme complexity and uncertainty. Words matter, and a first step is embracing a pluralistic vocabulary that recognizes that learning, knowledge, knowing, memory, resources, capabilities, routines, and strategy processes are in the same nomological net. An example of integration, linking OL, KM, and sensemaking (Thomas, Sussman, and Henderson, 2001) is the concept of "strategic learning" (Kuwada, 1998), which is a capability that aims to generate learning in support of future strategic initiatives that will, in turn, foster knowledge asymmetries that can lead to differences in firm performance (Thomas *et al.*, 2001). Mechanisms matter, and, as a second step, the sociocognitive processes studied in OL can help to explain the processes contributing to competitive advantage in strategy theories. That OL is fully utilized in strategy does not require the creation of models that link OL directly to firm performance. OL processes can be powerful mediating effects in strategy theories. Another example of integration is Beer *et al.*'s (2005) description of change as leading an OL process, which means holding an organization-wide conversation about the strategy and the organization's alignment with it. One of the seminal underpinnings of OL is the particular insights it reveals about the tension between exploration and exploitation as described in the next section.

Strategy Mechanisms: Exploration and Exploitation

James March's article on organizational exploration and exploitation in *Organization Science*'s seminal 1991 issue on OL has been cited over 26,000 times on Google Scholar, reflecting the importance of using limited organizational resources to balance the conflicting priorities of exploring new opportunities while leveraging existing knowledge. In strategy research, the exploration and exploitation perspective has been most prominent in the areas of organizational design, innovation, and alliances, which we unpack in this section. In the 30 years since March's article, scholars have engaged in a number of debates, such as: Are exploration and exploitation orthogonal or on a continuum? How is ambidexterity, that is, the ability of organizations to both explore and exploit, achieved? Should organizations seek a balance between the two (e.g., through structural ambidexterity), or specialize in one at a time (e.g., through punctuated equilibrium)? Rather than focusing on the nuances of studying exploration and exploitation (for reviews and discussions of central issues, see Lavie, Stettner, and Tushman, 2010; Gupta, Smith, and Shalley, 2006; Wilden *et al.*, 2018), here we offer a short overview of some important findings that the exploration and exploitation perspective has contributed to strategic management and opportunities for future research.

Organizational design

This substream of research focuses on how organizations can achieve exploration, or an effective balance between exploration and exploitation. For instance, Siggelkow and Rivkin (2006) study when exploration should be decentralized, and caution that doing so is only likely to help when decisions and departments are modularized. In general, ambidexterity scholars have focused extensively on features of organizational design— the structure and processes that can optimize the exploitation and exploration balance (e.g., Fang, Lee, and Schilling, 2010; O'Reilly and Tushman, 2013; Siggelkow and Levinthal, 2003, 2005).

Providing an integrative model of ambidexterity and its impact on performance, Úbeda-García *et al.* (2020) included (a) structural solutions, with differentiated organizational units focusing on specialized exploration or exploitation activities (e.g., Jansen *et al.*, 2009; Raisch *et al.*, 2009); (b) contextual solutions, with organizations creating a behavioral capacity to simultaneously explore and exploit within undifferentiated units (e.g., Raisch and Birkinshaw, 2008; Wang and Rafiq, 2014); and (c) interorganizational solutions that allow co-exploration and co-exploitation (e.g., Kauppila, 2010; Wilden *et al.*, 2018). Ubeda-Garcia *et al.* (2020) found that structural, contextual, and interorganizational factors can mutually reinforce one another. Temporal or sequential arrangements of ambidexterity have also been proposed; because such shifts can be highly disruptive, scholars suggest that they are most suitable for stable environments, or for smaller firms that may lack the resources necessary for structural ambidexterity (e.g., O'Reilly and Tushman, 2013; Rosenkopf and Nerkar, 2001).

The dynamic aspects of ambidexterity have just started to be examined. For example, Luger, Raisch, and Schimmer (2018) argued that not only firms pursuing one-sided exploration or exploitation orientations show self-reinforcing tendencies but also ambidextrous firms, and that reinforcing ambidexterity can be good or bad for firms' long-term performance, depending on the environment they face. In contexts of incremental change, firm performance benefits from the learning effects of maintaining ambidexterity, while in contexts of discontinuous change, firm performance suffers from the misalignment that reinforcement creates. Luger *et al.* (2018) propose reconceptualizing ambidexterity as the ability to dynamically balance exploration and exploitation, which involves combining capability-building processes (to balance exploration and exploitation) with capability-shifting processes (to adapt the exploration-exploitation balance). Time has come to dig deeper into the temporal aspects of the balance between exploration and exploitation. Thus,

Research Question 1: *How does organizational ambidexterity evolve across time?*

As ambidexterity research achieves a certain degree of maturity, we also see great opportunities for cross-fertilization in other strategy areas. Ambidexterity is intimately associated with innovation, and product introduction, development, and commercialization (e.g., Jansen, Van den Bosch, and Volberda, 2006; Rothaermel and Deeds, 2004; Katila and Ahuja, 2002). However, the balance of exploration and exploitation has also been positioned as the ultimate question of strategic renewal (Crossan and Berdrow, 2003), and, from this perspective, there is great potential to apply the ambidexterity lens to the diverse ways in which firms can pursue renewal. Thus,

Research Question 2: *How do firms balance exploratory and exploitative (a) entry modes, (b) acquisitions, (c) alliances, (d) divestitures, (e) economies of scale, and (f) economies of scope?*

Innovation

While there is general acknowledgment of a trade-off between exploration and exploitation, much research has focused on examining how organizations can best balance them through ambidextrous decoupling, so as to achieve greater innovation. For example, Stettner and Lavie (2014) show how focusing separately on exploration and exploitation in different modes of operation can help companies avoid common dangers with the attempt to balance the two, such as conflicting routines, negative transfer of learning, and limited specialization. Swift (2016) points to the perils associated with transitioning from exploitative to exploratory learning, and argues that maintaining high levels of absorptive capacity helps firms survive such significant changes in organizational focus; similarly, Mavroudi, Kesidou, and Pandza (2020) show that cycling back and forth too fast between exploration and exploitation decreases learning. Contextual factors such as problemistic search, presence of slack resources, path dependence, organizational attention, and environmental conditions shape firms' tendency to engage in exploitative versus exploratory learning (e.g., Alexiev *et al.*, 2010; Greve, 2007; Mavroudi *et al.*, 2020; Uotila *et al.*, 2009). Scholars have also divided exploitative and exploratory learning into various, more nuanced categories, and drawn conclusions about their effectiveness in encouraging innovation (e.g., Garriga, von Krogh, and Spaeth, 2013; Lavie and Rosenkopf, 2006; Piao and Zajac, 2016; Rosenkopf and Nerkar, 2001).

Interorganizational learning

Treating interorganizational relationships as a conduit to learning from external sources, researchers have examined the role of a firm's orientation toward exploration and exploitation, both as represented in its approach toward alliances and acquisitions, and in determining its learning performance. For instance, Lavie and Rosenkopf (2006) explain that firms can achieve equilibrium through ambidexterity, that is, by trading off exploration and exploitation in different alliance domains (e.g., function, structure, and attribute). Rothaermel and Deeds (2004), on the other hand, find support for a temporal separation approach, whereby small biotechnology firms begin with exploration alliances as they develop products, transitioning to exploitation alliances to bring products to market. While alliances represent real options for future exploration, Vassolo, Anand, and Folta (2004) explore the challenges associated with managing multiple potential exploration options. Yang, Zheng, and Zhao (2014) argue that small firms' fear of partner appropriation leads them to favor exploitation, rather than exploration, alliances with large firms; however, exploration alliances offer greater value potential if the trust issues can be managed through proper governance. Choi and McNamara (2018) demonstrate how acquirers' prior exploitation or exploration orientation influences their tendency to integrate their existing knowledge with the acquired firm's knowledge in innovative actions. Hoang and Rothaermel (2010) also examine the impact of prior exploration and exploitation experience, but in the context of alliances, and find that firms' internal research and development (R&D) experience moderates the relationship between joint R&D project performance and the firm's experience in exploitative and explorative alliances.

Ambidexterity and mechanisms of exploration and exploitation also have implications for the increasing research on how businesses, and organizations in general, can contribute to grand challenges such as climate change, poverty and hunger, and disease (e.g., Nowacki and Monk, 2020; Olsen, Sofka, and Grimpe, 2016). For instance, Olsen *et al.* (2016) argue that consortia addressing grand challenges are likely to see better exploration outcomes when they include advocacy groups within the coalition of organizations. Theorists have recommended collaborative partnerships among governmental and nongovernmental organizations as well as the private sector, given that responding to grand challenges requires a variety of capabilities and resources that are beyond the scope of any single organization (George *et al.*, 2016). However, due to the substantial potential for conflict and learning failures in such networks of partnerships, together with the urgency associated with grand challenges such as climate change (Arslan and Tarakci, 2020; Doh, Tashman, and Benischke, 2019; Greve, 2020; Wright and Nyberg, 2017), there is a compelling need for strategy scholars to examine how such coalitions can learn quickly and effectively so as to come up with innovative solutions. Thus,

Research Question 3: *What factors enable interorganizational coordinated exploration and exploitation in the search for solutions to grand societal challenges?*

In conclusion, we foreshadow a recurring insight in this chapter: progress arises from building on prior research, but by extending and deepening it, rather than repackaging it using different terms, which occurs more often than not, as described in our first section. We are pleased to see progress in the greater incorporation of nuanced measures and contextual considerations in strategy research that uses a learning perspective. At the same time, we suggest that *extending* means embracing a multilevel perspective of OL as described in our next section as it relates to strategy, and *deepening* refers to understanding the role of the agent within that multilevel framework as we describe in our final section.

Strategy Mechanisms: Learning Types and Processes

Research taking a learning perspective (Bapuji and Crossan, 2004) has examined how OL from experience impacts a variety of strategic actions and performance.

Learning by doing

Learning curve, or experience curve, research represents some of the earliest studies of learning by experience; as organizations accumulate repetitive experience, their efficiency and hence performance in that area goes up (Argote and Epple, 1990; Yelle, 1979). Strategy scholars have applied this insight to the incidence and performance of strategic actions such as alliances (Hoang and Rothaermel, 2005), acquisitions (Barkema, Bell, and Pennings, 1996; Hayward, 2002), divestitures (Bergh and Lim, 2008; Brauer, Mammen, and Luger, 2017), foreign entry mode (Belderbos, 2003), and responses to foreign political risk (Oh and Oetzel, 2017). Other research, however, has found nonpositive learning curve effects (Barkema and Schijven, 2008).

While learning curve research has traditionally focused on more accessible measures such as the number of times a strategic action has been carried out, or years of experience, in recent times there is a greater focus on the nuances and contingencies of learning from experience. For instance, Arthur and Huntley (2005) argue that organizations are much more likely to see learning curve benefits when they engage in *deliberate learning* practices to acquire, codify, and transfer relevant knowledge. Musaji, Schulze, and de Castro (2020) examine the organizational factors that reduce the time and cost required to reach the learning curve, and Wiersma (2007) studies how organizational practices shape whether mature firms can continue to receive learning curve benefits. The type of experience is an important contingency, which researchers have examined in terms of country and industry differences (Hoang and Rothaermel, 2005; Li, 1995; Shimizu and Hitt, 2005). Specificity of the experience matters, as similar and related experience leads to better subsequent outcomes for a range of strategic actions (e.g., Finkelstein and Haleblian, 2002; Porrini, 2004; Zollo, Reuer, and Singh, 2002). At the same time, firms may also be able to generate learning spillovers across activities (e.g., Nadolska and Barkema, 2007). Further, scholars have pointed out that problemistic search arising from performance below expectations, and slack-driven search from performance above expectations, differentially impact the nature of learning from failure and success (Aranda, Arellano, and Davila, 2017; Kim, Haleblian, and Finkelstein, 2011; Muehlfeld, Rao Sahib, and van Witteloostuijn, 2012). There also exists a very real possibility that organizations may fail to learn, or learn the wrong things (Brauer *et al.*, 2017; Finkelstein and Haleblian, 2002; Miller and Shamsie, 2001; Schilling and Fang, 2014). Levinthal and March (1993) point to the dangers of learning myopias—organizations are likely to learn better through experiences that are more recent and related to their existing expertise and priorities. All these considerations are particularly crucial for learning in the context of grand challenges. Thus,

> Research Question 4: *What factors enable organizations to learn by doing in the context of extreme events (e.g., a global pandemic) and nontraditional goals (e.g., grand societal challenges)?*

Learning from others

Firms may learn from the experience of others through either transfer of learning or vicarious learning. Haunschild's (1993, 1994) early research examined firms' imitation of acquisition-related actions carried out by other firms with which they have close interaction. Alliances are a potentially rich source of interfirm learning (Gulati, 1999; Lane and Lubatkin, 1998), and recent research has also begun to examine how firms learn from external advisers such as investment banks and lawyers (Brauer *et al.*, 2017; Pathak and Chiu, 2020). Vicarious learning does not involve direct interfirm knowledge transfer; instead, firms analyze the information of other firms to avoid mistakes and imitate successful actions (Terlaak and Gong, 2008). Similar to early research on learning by doing, researchers have often operationalized vicarious learning through the cumulative experience of a focal firm's industry peers (e.g., Brauer *et al.*, 2017; Guillen, 2002; Yang and Hyland, 2006). However, new, complex, and uncertain domains of learning—such as the COVID-19 pandemic—or grand societal challenges do not allow organizations to rely on traditional markers of success and relevance for them to learn from (Greve, 2020); such contexts also call for multilevel vicarious learning (e.g., Pahl-Wostl, 2009). Thus,

> Research Question 5: *Who do organizations learn from (e.g., public-private partnerships) in the context of extreme events (e.g., a global pandemic) and nontraditional goals (e.g., grand societal challenges)?*

Learning processes

Strategy researchers focusing on the learning perspective are also increasingly paying attention to the organizational processes that underlie learning from experience. Indeed, Crossan and Berdrow (2003) point to the importance of OL processes for strategy research and examine strategic renewal through four OL processes across organizational levels: intuiting, interpreting, integrating, and institutionalizing. Flores et al. (2012) divide OL into the five processes of information acquisition, information distribution, information interpretation, knowledge integration, and organizational memory, while Walter, Lechner, and Kellermanns (2016) conceptualize it as the four processes of searching, processing, codifying, and practicing. Van de Ven, Bechara, and Sun (2019) view OL as repeated cycles of action, assessment, and response on similar tasks over time, and find that organizational actors' power imbalance, as well as their extent of agreement on outcome assessments, impacts the learning process to give rise to different learning outcomes. Westbrock, Muehlfeld, and Weitzel (2019) divide learning processes into lower-level learning (occurring within a given set of norms, rules, and routines) and higher-level learning (that changes existing rules and frameworks). As the above examples demonstrate, there is little consensus as of yet within the field about the processes that constitute OL. Some scholars focus on OL processes specific to the strategic actions studied, such as alliances or mergers and acquisitions (e.g., Kale and Singh, 2007; Trichterborn, Zu Knyphausen-Aufseß, and Schweizer, 2016), while others point to the importance of temporal process-related factors, such as learning horizons, timing decisions, and the rhythm and frequency of change (Henderson and Cool, 2003; Klarner and Raisch, 2013; Mudambi and Swift, 2014; Rothaermel and Deeds, 2004).

Scholars have called for a greater appreciation of the social and cognitive processes involved (e.g., Crossan and Berdrow, 2003), but empirical focus on them is still rare. A focus on learning processes also includes attention to microfoundational issues relating to learning at various levels of the organization and beyond. Strategy scholars have examined how individual learning underlies outcomes of strategic actions such as alliances and acquisitions (e.g., Bresman, Birkinshaw, and Nobel, 1999; Inkpen and Crossan, 1995; Lakshman, 2011), and how individual propensity to distort information influences OL-driven outcomes (Fang, Kim, and Milliken, 2014). In a different vein, chief executive officers' (CEO) individual learning differs from that of lower-level employees in a number of ways. Clearly, the implications for the organization of CEO learning (or its failure) are immense. At the same time, CEOs also have access to resources (such as advice from the board of directors and the top management team, as well as external experts). Miller and Shamsie (2001) study the characteristics and implications of top executives' individual learning across their careers. Other scholars have studied strategic implications of learning at other levels of analysis, such as Alexiev et al.'s (2010) investigation of the relationship between the top management team's advice-seeking and the firm's exploratory innovation, and Pan, Wang, and

Weisbach's (2015) examination of how financial markets learn about CEO abilities over a CEO's tenure.

In summary, there is a danger that OL is treated as a reified construct, often equating something like experience or patents with learning. While there are interesting insights arising from such research, it neglects the depth of insight that OL research offers strategy, as exemplified here by our discussion of learning types and processes, and perhaps contributes to the very issues identified in our first section.

A Call to Bring the Judgment and Wisdom of the Agent Back to Strategy

Upper echelons theory (Hambrick and Mason, 1984) is the strategy theory that reminds us that organizations are a reflection of their top managers: CEOs, top management teams, and boards of directors. An aspect of top managers that is critical to strategy is their capacity to learn from mistakes and failures, and become wiser. While research has suggested that organizations can improve by investigating and learning from failures, some work has found that strategic leaders may draw the wrong conclusions, generate incorrect lessons (overly simplified, potentially misleading, or superficial lessons), or fail to learn. Research, for example, has looked into CEOs becoming obsolete (Henderson, Miller, and Hambrick, 2006). Learning misjudgments are learning traps that have important implications for competitive advantage. We do not know enough about why upper echelons draw the wrong conclusions. Although practitioners frequently talk about the "wisdom economy," wisdom is a concept that upper echelons theory, specifically, and strategy, as a whole, have seldom discussed (Antonacopoulou and Bento, 2018).

OL research reveals that the challenges and opportunities associated with learning represent not simply an upper echelons issue, but rather one that is fundamental to the learning of all individuals in the organization, with important implications for strategy. As Edmondson (2011) notes, learning from organizational failures is anything but straightforward because the attitudes and activities required to effectively detect and analyze failures are in short supply, and the need for context-specific learning strategies is underappreciated. For example, Desai (2015) studied the way in which decision-makers interpret information about where failures occurred or who was involved, and found that organizations learn less effectively when their failures are relatively concentrated in origin, meaning that failures typically involve a particular unit or even a specific individual, compared to when failures are more broadly dispersed. In fact, learning how to learn has been described as a neglected management ability (Dechant, 1990). Thus,

Research Question 6: *What processes influence whether organizational members, including those in upper echelons, learn what they think they are learning?*

We see great potential for OL and strategy to work synergistically in the area of wisdom. At the organizational level, Bierly, Kessler, and Christensen (2000) explain that a key to organizational wisdom is judgment and decision-making, and that success does not necessarily go to the firms that know the most, but to those that can make the best use of what they know, and those that know what is strategically most important to the firm and to society at large. That is, organizational wisdom relates to the judgment, selection, and use of specific knowledge for a specific context (Bierly et al., 2000). At the upper-echelon level, Kolodinsky and Bierly (2013) argue that, compared to their less prudent counterparts, wise executives recognize the strategic implications that their decisions can have on long-term organizational effectiveness and on salient stakeholders. Executive wisdom requires a unique combination of cognitive and behavioral processes that are intentionally reflective and appreciative of the complexities of multifaceted goals and stakeholders (Kolodinsky and Bierly, 2013). Thus,

Research Question 7: *What are the roles of judgment and wisdom, at the individual, group, and organizational levels, in strategy decisions (e.g., strategic renewal, diversification, divestitures)?*

An attribute of leaders that can be invaluable in this discussion of how upper echelons learn is leader character. Leader character encompasses an interconnected set of habituated patterns of thought, emotion, motivation or volition, and action (Bright, Winn, and Kanov, 2014) that satisfy very specific criteria identified by Peterson and Seligman (2004) as being virtuous. Crossan et al. (2017) proposed 10 character dimensions (drive, courage, accountability, justice, temperance, integrity, humility, humanity, transcendence, and collaboration) which support the 11th dimension, which is judgment. Strength of character is associated with strong judgment, or what Aristotle referred to as "practical wisdom." Studying the character of upper echelons will shed light on the quality of their judgment for decision-making. OL as a field has overlooked the role that strength or deficiency of character play in quality judgment within the OL processes, which, as described in our prior sections, have important implications for strategy because, acknowledged or not, OL processes are mechanisms in strategy theories. Furthermore, the character of the agent has implications for multilevel outcomes. In fact, Crossan et al. (2020) propose that the processes of character activation, character contagion, and character embedment are OL-rooted multilevel processes in organizations. Bringing the character of the agent back into OL and strategy theories is promising because character impacts what individuals can do and what they choose to do. Furthermore, we posit that strength of character may be a primary source of sustainable competitive advantage. Thus,

Research Question 8: *How is strategy altered by the character of the individuals at the center of OL and strategy processes?*

Finally, returning to the discussion of judgment and wisdom, we draw attention to areas such as AI, which by its very label speaks to this interplay. As Argote, Lee, and Park (2020) conclude, given the strengths and weaknesses of artificial and human intelligence, another promising research agenda centers on the relationship between AI and human intelligence in OL. This is particularly relevant as we encourage strategy research to apply the tools of OL to the pressing societal problems of the world. Thus,

Research Question 9: *What learning is captured by AI, and how is it strategically used?*

Conclusion

We conclude this chapter by drawing attention to the application of both OL and strategy research to the grand challenges facing the world and advocate that the nexus of OL and strategy offers important promise to extend the multilevel theorizing from organizations and industries to society at large. OL theory is particularly suited to bridge micro, meso, and macro levels, and it is also well suited to address the interplay between the human and the nonhuman—the learning that is intentionally or unintentionally embedded in artifacts and systems whether they be organizational or societal.

References

Agarwal R, Helfat CE. 2009. Strategic renewal of organizations. *Organization Science* 20(2): 281–293.

Alexiev AS, Jansen JJ, Van den Bosch FA, Volberda HW. 2010. Top management team advice seeking and exploratory innovation: the moderating role of TMT heterogeneity. *Journal of Management Studies* 47: 1343–1364.

Antonacopoulou E, Bento RF. 2018. From laurels to learners: leadership with virtue. *Journal of Management Development* 37(8): 624–633.

Aranda C, Arellano J, Davila A. 2017. Organizational learning in target setting. *Academy of Management Journal* 60(3): 1189–1211.

Argote L. 2011. Organizational learning research: past, present and future. *Management Learning* 42(4): 439–446.

Argote L, Epple D. 1990. Learning curves in manufacturing. *Science* 23: 920–924.

Argote L, Lee, S, Park, J. 2020. Organizational learning processes and outcomes: major findings and future research directions. *Management Science*, in press.

Arslan B, Tarakci M. 2020. Negative spillovers across partnerships for responsible innovation: evidence from the 2014 Ebola outbreak. *Journal of Management Studies*, in press.

Arthur JB, Huntley CL. 2005. Ramping up the organizational learning curve: assessing the impact of deliberate learning on organizational performance under gainsharing. *Academy of Management Journal* 48: 1159–1170.

Bapuji H, Crossan M. 2004. From questions to answers: reviewing organizational learning research. *Management Learning* 35(4): 397–417.

Barkema HG, Bell JHJ, Pennings JM. 1996. Foreign entry, cultural barriers, and learning. *Strategic Management Journal* 17: 151–166.

Barkema HG, Schijven M. 2008. How do firms learn to make acquisitions? A review of past research and an agenda for the future. *Journal of Management* 34: 594–634.

Beer M, Voelpel SC, Leibold M, Tekie EB. 2005. Strategic management as organizational learning: developing fit and alignment through a disciplined process. *Long Range Planning* 38(5): 445–465.

Belderbos R. 2003. Entry mode, organizational learning, and R&D in foreign affiliates: evidence from Japanese firms. *Strategic Management Journal* 24(3): 235–259.

Bergh DD, Lim ENK. 2008. Learning how to restructure: absorptive capacity and improvisational views of restructuring actions and performance. *Strategic Management Journal* 29: 593–616.

Bierly PE, Kessler EH, Christensen EW. 2000. Organizational learning, knowledge, and wisdom. *Journal of Organizational Change Management* 13(6): 595–618.

Brauer M, Mammen J, Luger J. 2017. Sell-offs and firm performance: a matter of experience? *Journal of Management* 43(5): 1359–1387.

Bresman H, Birkinshaw J, Nobel R. 1999. Knowledge transfer in international acquisitions. *Journal of International Business Studies* 30: 439–462.

Bright DS, Winn B, Kanov J. 2014. Reconsidering virtue: differences of perspective in virtue ethics and the positive social sciences. *Journal of Business Ethics* 119: 445–460.

Castaneda DI, Manrique LF, Cuellar S. 2018. Is organizational learning being absorbed by knowledge management? A systematic review. *Journal of Knowledge Management* 22(2): 299–325.

Choi S, McNamara G. 2018. Repeating a familiar pattern in a new way: the effect of exploitation and exploration on knowledge leverage behaviors in technology acquisitions. *Strategic Management Journal* 39(2): 356–358.

Crossan MM, Berdrow I. 2003. Organizational learning and strategic renewal. *Strategic Management Journal* 24(11): 1087–1105.

Crossan M, Byrne A, Seijts GH, Reno M, Monzani L, Gandz J. 2017. Toward a framework of character in organizations. *Journal of Management Studies* 54(7): 986–1018.

Crossan MM, Lane HW, White RE. 1999. An organizational learning framework: From intuition to institution. *Academy of Management Review* 24(3): 522–537.

Crossan M, Nguyen B, Sturm R, Vera D, Ruiz Pardo A, Maurer C. 2020. Organizational learning through character-enabled judgement. Working Paper, Ivey Business School, Western University, Canada.

Dechant K. 1990. Knowing how to learn: the neglected management ability. *Journal of Management Development* 9(4): 40–49.

Desai V. 2015. Learning through the distribution of failures within an organization: evidence from heart bypass surgery performance. *Academy of Management Journal* 58(4): 1032–1050.

Doh JP, Tashman P, Benischke MH. 2019. Adapting to grand environmental challenges through collective entrepreneurship. *Academy of Management Perspectives* 33: 450–468.

Edmondson AC. 2011. Strategies for learning from failure. *Harvard Business Review* 89: 48–55.

Eisenhardt KM, Santos FM. 2002. Knowledge-based view: a new theory of strategy. *Handbook of Strategy and Management* 1(1): 139–164.

Fang C, Kim J, Milliken FJ. 2014. When bad news is sugarcoated: information distortion, organizational search, and the behavioral theory of the firm. *Strategic Management Journal* 35(8): 1186–1201.

Fang C, Lee J, Schilling MA. 2010. Balancing exploration and exploitation through structural design: the isolation of subgroups and organizational learning. *Organization Science* 21: 625–642.

Finkelstein S, Haleblian J. 2002. Understanding acquisition performance: the role of transfer effects. *Organization Science* 13: 36–47.

Flores LG, Zheng W, Rau D, Thomas C. 2012. Organizational learning: subprocess identification, construct validation, and an empirical test of cultural antecedents. *Journal of Management* 38(2): 640–667.

Garriga H, von Krogh G, Spaeth S. 2013. How constraints and knowledge impact knowledge innovation. *Strategic Management Journal* 34(9): 1134–1144.

George G, Howard-Grenville J, Joshi A, Tihanyi L. 2016. Understanding and tackling societal grand challenges through management research. *Academy of Management Journal* 59: 1880–1895.

Greve HR. 2007. Exploration and exploitation in product innovation. *Industrial and Corporate Change* 16(5): 945–975.

Greve HR. 2020. Learning theory: the pandemic research challenge. *Journal of Management Studies* 57: 1759–1762.

Greve HR. 2021. The resource-based view and learning theory: overlaps, differences, and a shared future. *Journal of Management*. 0149206320967732.

Guillen M. 2002. Structural inertia, imitation, and foreign expansion: South Korean firms and business groups in China, 1987–95. *Academy of Management Journal* 45(3): 509–525.

Gulati R. 1999. Network location and learning: the influence of network resources and firm capabilities on alliance formation. *Strategic Management Journal* 20(5): 397–420.

Gupta AK, Smith KG, Shalley CE. 2006. The interplay between exploration and exploitation. *Academy of Management Journal* 49(4): 693–706.

Hambrick DC, Mason P. 1984. Upper echelons: the organization as a reflection of its top managers. *Academy of Management Review* 9(2): 193–206.

Haunschild P. 1993. Interorganizational imitation: the impact of interlocks on corporate acquisition activity. *Administrative Science Quarterly* 38: 564–592.

Haunschild P. 1994. How much is that company worth? Interorganizational relationships, uncertainty, and acquisition premiums. *Administrative Science Quarterly* 39(3): 391–411.

Hayward MLA. 2002. When do firms learn from their acquisition experience? Evidence from 1990–1995. *Strategic Management Journal* 23: 21–39.

Henderson AD, Miller D, Hambrick DC. 2006. How quickly do CEOs become obsolete? Industry dynamism, CEO tenure, and company performance. *Strategic Management Journal* 27(5): 447–460.

Henderson J, Cool K. 2003. Learning to time capacity expansions: an empirical analysis of the world petrochemical industry, 1975–95. *Strategic Management Journal* 24(5): 393–413.

Hoang H, Rothaermel FT. 2005. The effect of general and partner-specific alliance experience on joint R&D project performance. *Academy of Management Journal* 48(2): 332–345.

Hoang H, Rothaermel FT. 2010. Leveraging internal and external experience: exploration, exploitation, and R&D project performance. *Strategic Management Journal* 31: 734–758.

Inkpen A, Crossan M. 1995. Believing is seeing: joint ventures and organization learning. *Journal of Management Studies* 32(5): 595–618.

Jansen JJ, Tempelaar MP, Van den Bosch FA, Volberda HW. 2009. Structural differentiation and ambidexterity: the mediating role of integration mechanisms. *Organization Science* 20(4): 797–811.

Jansen JJ, Van den Bosch FA, Volberda HW. 2006. Exploratory innovation, exploitative innovation, and performance: effects of organizational antecedents and environmental moderators. *Management Science* 52(11): 1661–1674.

Kale P, Singh H. 2007. Building firm capabilities through learning: the role of the alliance learning process in alliance capability and firm-level alliance success. *Strategic Management Journal* 28(10): 981–1000.

Katila R, Ahuja G. 2002. Something old, something new: a longitudinal study of search behavior and new product introduction. *Academy of Management Journal* 45(6): 1183–1194.

Kauppila OP. 2010. Creating ambidexterity by integrating and balancing structurally separate interorganizational partnerships. *Strategic Organization* 8(4): 283–312.

Kim J, Haleblian J, Finkelstein S. 2011. When firms are desperate to grow via acquisition: the effect of growth patterns and acquisition experience on acquisition premiums. *Administrative Science Quarterly* 56(1): 26–60.

Klarner P, Raisch S. 2013. Move to the beat—rhythms of change and firm performance. *Academy of Management Journal* 56(1): 160–184.

Kolodinsky R, Bierly PE. 2013. Understanding the elements and outcomes of executive wisdom: a strategic approach. *Journal of Management and Organization* 19(1): 1–24.

Kuwada K. 1998. Strategic learning: the continuous side of discontinuous strategic change. *Organization Science* 2(6): 719–736.

Lakshman C. 2011. Postacquisition cultural integration in mergers and acquisitions: a knowledge-based approach. *Human Resource Management* 50(5): 605–623.

Lane P, Lubatkin M. 1998. Relative absorptive capacity and interorganizational learning. *Strategic Management Journal* 19(5): 461–477.

Lane PJ, Koka BR, Pathak S. 2006. The reification of absorptive capacity: a critical review and rejuvenation of the construct. *Academy of Management Review* 31(4): 833–863.

Lavie D, Rosenkopf L. 2006. Balancing exploration and exploitation in alliance formation. *Academy of Management Journal* 49(4): 797–818.

Lavie D, Stettner U, Tushman M. 2010. Exploration and exploitation within and across organizations. *Academy of Management Annals* 4(1): 109–155.

Levinthal D, March J. 1993. The myopia of learning. *Strategic Management Journal* 14: 95–112.

Li J. 1995. Foreign entry and survival: effects of strategic choices on performance in international markets. *Strategic Management Journal* 16: 333–351.

Luger J, Raisch S, Schimmer M. 2018. Dynamic balancing of exploration and exploitation: the contingent benefits of ambidexterity. *Organization Science* 29(3): 449–470.

March JG. 1991. Exploration and exploitation in organizational learning. *Organization Science* 2(1): 71–87.

Mavroudi E, Kesidou E, Pandza K. 2020. Shifting back and forth: how does the temporal cycling between exploratory and exploitative R&D influence firm performance? *Journal of Business Research* 110: 386–396.

Miller D, Shamsie J. 2001. Learning across the life cycle: experimentation and performance among the Hollywood studio heads. *Strategic Management Journal* 22(8): 725–745.

Mudambi R, Swift T. 2014. Knowing when to leap: transitioning between exploitative and explorative R&D. *Strategic Management Journal* 35(1): 126–145.

Muehlfeld K, Rao Sahib P, Van Witteloostuijn A. 2012. A contextual theory of organizational learning from failures and successes: a study of acquisition completion in the global newspaper industry, 1981–2008. *Strategic Management Journal* 33(8): 938–964.

Musaji S, Schulze WS, De Castro J. 2020. How long does it take to get to the learning curve? *Academy of Management Journal* 63(1): 205–223.

Nadolska A, Barkema HG. 2007. Learning to internationalise: the pace and success of foreign acquisitions. *Journal of International Business Studies* 38: 1170–1186.

Nowacki C, Monk A. 2020. Ambidexterity in government: the influence of different types of legitimacy on innovation. *Research Policy* 49(1): 103840.

Oh C, Oetzel J. 2017. Once bitten twice shy? Experience managing violent conflict risk and MNC subsidiary-level investment and expansion. *Strategic Management Journal* 38: 714–731.

Olsen AO, Sofka W, Grimpe C. 2016. Coordinated exploration for grand challenges: the role of advocacy groups in search consortia. *Academy of Management Journal* 59: 2232–2255.

O'Reilly CA, Tushman M. 2013. Organizational ambidexterity: past, present, and future. *Academy of Management Perspectives* 27(4): 324–338.

Pahl-Wostl, C. 2009. A conceptual framework for analyzing adaptive capacity and multi-level learning processes in resource governance regimes. *Global Environmental Change* 19(3): 354–365.

Pan Y, Wang TY, Weisbach MS. 2015. Learning about CEO ability and stock return volatility. *Review of Financial Studies* 28(6): 1623–1666.

Pathak S, Chiu S. 2020. Firm-advisor ties and financial performance in the context of corporate divestiture. *Journal of Business Research* 121: 315–328.

Peterson C, Seligman MEP. 2004. *Character Strengths and Virtues: A Classification and Handbook*. Oxford University Press and American Psychological Association: New York, NY.

Pettit K, Crossan, M, Vera D. 2017. Organizational learning and knowledge processes: a critical review. In *SAGE Handbook of Process Organization Studies*, Langley A, Tsoukas, H (eds). Sage Publications: London, U.K.; 481–496.

Piao M, Zajac E. 2016. How exploitation impedes and impels exploration: theory and evidence. *Strategic Management Journal* 37(7): 1431–1447.

Porrini P. 2004. Alliance experience and value creation in high-tech and low-tech acquisitions. *Journal of High Technology Management Research* 15: 267–292.

Raisch S, Birkinshaw J. 2008. Organizational ambidexterity: antecedents, outcomes, and moderators. *Journal of Management* 34(3): 375–409.

Raisch S, Birkinshaw J, Probst G, Tushman ML. 2009. Organizational ambidexterity: balancing exploitation and exploration for sustained performance. *Organization Science* 20: 685–695.

Rosenkopf L, Nerkar A. 2001. Beyond local search: boundary-spanning, exploration, and impact in the optical disk industry. *Strategic Management Journal* 22: 287–306.

Rothaermel FT, Deeds DL. 2004. Exploration and exploitation alliances in biotechnology: a system of new product development. *Strategic Management Journal* 25(3): 201–221.

Schilling M, Fang C. 2014. When hubs forget, lie, and play favorites: interpersonal network structure, information distortion, and organizational learning. *Strategic Management Journal* 35(7): 974–994.

Shimizu K, Hitt MA. 2005. What constrains or facilitates divestitures of formerly acquired firms? The effects of organizational inertia. *Journal of Management* 31: 50–72.

Siggelkow N, Levinthal D. 2003. Temporarily divide to conquer: centralized, decentralized, and reintegrated organizational approaches to exploration and exploitation. *Organization Science* 14(6): 650–669.

Siggelkow N, Levinthal D. 2005. Escaping real (non-benign) competency traps: linking the dynamics of organizational structure to the dynamics of search. *Strategic Organization* 3(1): 85–115.

Siggelkow N, Rivkin J. 2006. When exploration backfires: unintended consequences of multi-level organizational search. *Academy of Management Journal* 49(4): 779–795.

Stettner U, Lavie D. 2014. Ambidexterity under scrutiny: exploration and exploitation via internal organization, alliances, and acquisitions. *Strategic Management Journal* 35(13): 1903–1929.

Swift T. 2016. The perilous leap between exploration and exploitation. *Strategic Management Journal* 37(8): 1688–1698.

Terlaak A, Gong Y. 2008. Vicarious learning and inferential accuracy in adoption processes. *Academy of Management Review* 33(4): 846–868.

Thomas JB, Sussman SW, Henderson JC. 2001. Understanding "strategic learning": linking organizational learning, knowledge management, and sensemaking. *Organization Science* 12(3): 331–345.

Trichterborn A, Zu Knyphausen-Aufseß D, Schweizer L. 2016. How to improve acquisition performance: the role of a dedicated M&A function, M&A learning process, and M&A capability. *Strategic Management Journal* 37(4): 763–773.

Úbeda-García M, Claver-Cortés E, Marco-Lajara B, Zaragoza-Sáez P. 2020. Toward a dynamic construction of organizational ambidexterity: exploring the synergies between structural differentiation, organizational context, and interorganizational relations. *Journal of Business Research* 112: 363–372.

Uotila J, Maula M, Keil T, Zahra S. 2009. Exploration, exploitation, and financial performance: analysis of S&P 500 corporations. *Strategic Management Journal* 30: 221–231.

Van de Ven A, Bechara JP, Sun K. 2019. How outcome agreement and power balance among parties influence processes of organizational learning and nonlearning. *Journal of Management* 45(3): 1252–1283.

Vassolo R, Anand J, Folta T. 2004. Non-additivity in portfolios of exploration activities: a real options-based analysis of equity alliances in biotechnology. *Strategic Management Journal* 25(11): 1045–1061.

Vera D, Crossan M, Apaydin M. 2011. A framework for integrating organizational learning, knowledge, capabilities, and absorptive capacity. In *The Blackwell Handbook of Organizational Learning and Knowledge Management*, 2nd edition, Easterby-Smith M, Lyles MA (eds). John Wiley and Sons: Chichester, U.K.; 153–180.

Walter J, Lechner C, Kellermanns FW. 2016. Learning activities, exploration, and the performance of strategic initiatives. *Journal of Management* 42(3): 769–802.

Wang CL, Rafiq M. 2014. Ambidextrous organizational culture, contextual ambidexterity and new product innovation: a comparative study of UK and Chinese high-tech firms. *British Journal of Management* 25(1): 58–76.

Westbrock B, Muehlfeld K, Weitzel U. 2019. Selecting legal advisors in M&As: organizational learning and the role of multiplicity of mental models. *Journal of Management* 45: 2193–2224.

Wiersma E. 2007. Conditions that shape the learning curve: factors that increase the ability and opportunity to learn. *Management Science* 53(12): 1903–1915.

Wilden R, Hohberger J, Devinney TM, Lavie D. 2018. Revisiting James March (1991): whither exploration and exploitation? *Strategic Organization* 16(3): 352–369.

Winter SG. 2003. Understanding dynamic capabilities. *Strategic Management Journal* 24: 911–995.

Wright C, Nyberg D. 2017. An inconvenient truth: how organizations translate climate change into business as usual. *Academy of Management Journal* 60(5): 1633–1651.

Yang H, Zheng Y, Zhao X. 2014. Exploration and exploitation? Small firms' alliance strategies with large firms. *Strategic Management Journal* 35(1): 146–157.

Yang M, Hyland M. 2006. Who do firms imitate? A multilevel approach to examining sources of imitation in the choice of mergers and acquisitions. *Journal of Management* 32: 381–399.

Yelle LE. 1979. The learning curve: historical review and comprehensive survey. *Decision Sciences* 10: 302–328.

Zollo M, Reuer JJ, Singh H. 2002. Interorganizational routines and performance in strategic alliances. *Organization Science* 13: 701–713.

Zollo M, Winter SG. 2002. Deliberate learning and the evolution of dynamic capabilities. *Organization Science* 13: 339–351.

8.2

MANAGEMENT OF INNOVATION AND KNOWLEDGE SHARING

Michael Howard

The field of management strategy has provided important insights to enhance our understanding of how organizations learn, innovate, and manage their knowledge to create value and competitive advantage. There is much to gain from taking stock of key findings from this work and how they relate to emerging technological and societal changes, allowing us to chart a course for future scholarship. We accept as axiomatic the proposition that the pace of innovation continually accelerates. As a field, we have an opportunity and responsibility to help explain the dynamics and consequences of this trend. Perhaps our best hope is to proceed not simply as spectators or commentators, but by offering our help in guiding innovation to the advantage of society.

The goal of this chapter is to offer observations of key foundational elements of innovation management and knowledge sharing, to identify some of the critical insights from the current state of research in these topics, and to anticipate the direction of future developments and the corresponding role of scholars in this field. It may prove helpful to focus the discussion on some broad themes that have had a persistent influence on our understanding of innovation and knowledge, and in combination, may open the door for very different ideas and outcomes in the future. I would suggest that three specific aspects of innovation and knowledge development may serve this purpose: the socially constructed nature of knowledge, the demonstrable positive gradient in knowledge complexity, and the rise of computational knowledge search.

Foundational Work in Innovation and Knowledge Development

Though knowledge often appears to comprise objective elements, advanced and systematically recombined through rational processes of research and development (R&D), the reality is quite different. Prior research has explored how our conception of knowledge rests on a socially constructed fabric of perception and evaluation (Berger and Luckmann, 1967; Glynn, 1996). In an organizational setting, knowledge is advanced against a backdrop of socially embedded connections among individuals

(Kogut and Zander, 1992). The individuals involved in innovation and knowledge sharing exert an impactful, if sometimes unrecognized influence on how knowledge is perceived, organized, and applied for useful purposes (Spender, 1996; Polanyi, 2009). While our powerful tools of information technology can help in the process of retaining and organizing knowledge, human interaction and interpretation remain central to innovation.

Researchers bridging sociology and the development of science and technology have explored how shared understanding and interpretation impact and direct technological advancement. Pinch and Bijker (1984) offer an interesting example of the social construction of technology (SCOT) through the emergence of our common understanding of the bicycle. They describe that while many variations of human-powered wheeled vehicles existed in the late nineteenth century with a wide variety of configurations and components, relevant social groups played a key role in defining the bicycle as we know it today—the "low-wheeled bicycle with rear chain drive, diamond frame, and air tyres" (Pinch and Bijker, 1984: 416). Changes in culture, usage, and social perception have led to further evolution of this platform, for example, recently favoring the widespread use of the mountain bike as a preferred form (Rosen, 1993). As society changes, so will the understanding and perception of technologies it creates.

In management strategy research, these ideas are evident in the research streams on technology cycles and dominant designs (Utterback and Abernathy, 1975; Anderson and Tushman, 1990; Suarez and Utterback, 1995). Organizations pursue variations in technologies based on economic and social pressures (Dosi, 1982; Tushman and Murmann, 1998), working to influence technology cycles in their fields and define the dominant design. Innovation thus involves the application of new technologies in an interaction of social interpretation and understanding.

The increasing complexity of knowledge is another long-standing trend impacting innovation management and knowledge sharing. The field of computer science offers interesting and relevant insights into this trend. Computational complexity theory explores the difficulty of solving computational problems based on the number of finite components and potential combinations among them (Dean, 2016). In the exchange and calculation of new combinations, the interaction among different parties plays a fundamental role in determining this complexity (Goldwasser, Micali, and Rackoff, 1989; Goldreich and Petrank, 1999). Drawing from this view, knowledge complexity is thus driven by the introduction of new knowledge elements, the growing scale of possible combinations in their use, and the interaction of different parties in the application and combination of these knowledge elements.

Within management strategy, the knowledge search literature has addressed how the recombination of knowledge elements enables organizational learning and innovation (March and Simon, 1958; Nelson and Winter, 1982; Cohen and Levinthal, 1990). Fleming and Sorenson (2001) conceptualize the search for new knowledge as the traverse over topographic landscapes comprising different combinations of knowledge elements, with higher points in the search domain exhibiting greater fit or utility in satisfying the requirements or serving the needs of the design. Higher complexity equates to "rougher terrain" in this search space—more local maxima, with steeper gradients in fit or value of potential new innovations.

Over time, the development of new knowledge elements has dramatically increased the complexity of the knowledge search landscape. Trends in patented technologies help illustrate this phenomenon, offering important insights into the growth of knowledge stocks and the interdependencies between innovations (Trajtenberg, 1990). Data from the U.S. Patent and Trademark Office reveal the expansion of knowledge elements through the exponential increase in the introduction of new patent classifications (Lafond and Kim, 2019), resulting in more knowledge components and exponentially more potential combinations of these components. Furthermore, knowledge flow across organizations and institutions drives growth in new knowledge creation (Zucker *et al.*, 2007), increasing the complexity of both our underlying knowledge and the organizational structures and collaborations we develop to pursue innovation.

The third macro-level tendency impacting innovation and knowledge sharing is the rapid development of computational systems to hasten and augment the knowledge search process through machine learning. *Machine learning* refers to the use of computer algorithms that are "trained," improving their effectiveness in identifying patterns or making predictions through increased usage (Mitchell, 1997). Samuel (1959) exemplified early efforts in machine learning, with his development of a computer algorithm that learned to surpass human performance in the game of checkers through rote learning and through generalization, practicing game scenarios against itself. Self-improving algorithms have been applied to neural networks, self-forming systems of pattern recognition used to cluster or categorize raw data inputs (Haykin, 1994), and data mining, the further application of computational pattern recognition to the interpretation of large-scale datasets (Han, Pei, and Kamber, 2011). These automated systems may have tremendous influence on the pace and scale of knowledge search, enabling the examination of more complex systems of knowledge elements, while testing wider combinations for potential solutions in technological design.

The conceptual foundations relevant to machine learning in the management strategy field may arguably lie in the research literature on organizational learning. Viewing the organization as the "machine," there are many characteristics in common between computer and organizational algorithms used to drive knowledge development and innovation. Individuals within firms must usefully organize information into meaningful problems or opportunities (Herden and Lyles, 1981; Cowan, 1986). They must identify patterns linking the data (Crossan, Lane, and White, 1999), adapting them as new information is obtained (Denrell and March, 2001). As with the machine learning process, optimal combinations emerge, allowing organizations to develop beneficial, innovative solutions (Herriott, Levinthal, and March, 1985; Huber, 1991). Fiol and Lyles (1985) note the distinction between lower-level organizational learning characteristics of repetition, routines, rules, and structures in contrast with higher-level learning characteristics that involve nonroutine processes and ambiguity. These characteristics align with single-loop and double-loop models of organizational learning that either constrain or permit organizations to modify the underlying mental model applied in its learning or decision-making process (Argyris, 1976). The advancement of computational knowledge search capabilities may move from single-loop optimization of specific technological design challenges toward double-loop practices in which automated systems can reconsider the rules and parameters of the search itself. As I describe later, the strategy field has begun to integrate these ideas, more directly linking organizational learning and machine learning, and beginning to explain how these processes are combined to fundamentally change the nature of innovation.

Continuing Trends in Organizational Knowledge and Innovation

Current research in innovation management is beginning to recognize important aspects of the collective nature of knowledge development. The socially constructed nature of knowledge, as well as the increasing scale of technological complexity, place the forefront of innovation in collaborative, interactive structures that span organizational boundaries. Recent research has begun to characterize this emerging trend in several forms, building from theoretical foundations that view collective knowledge development through structural systems of organizational transactions and relational contracts (Williamson, 1975; Dyer and Singh, 1998) or affiliation and exchange based on coopetition and multiparty alliances (Nalebuff, Brandenburger, and Maulana, 1996; Zeng and Chen, 2003).

The literature on innovation ecosystems has added significant value and brought attention to the boundary-spanning nature of innovation. An ecosystem is "the alignment structure of the multilateral set of partners that need to interact in order for a focal value proposition to materialize" (Adner, 2017: 40). In earlier work from this structural perspective, Adner and Kapoor (2010) develop a framework characterizing the interdependencies of challenges faced by organizations operating in the environment of a focal firm. They find a relationship between the tendency for technology leaders to gain or lose advantage based on their location within the ecosystem. In subsequent work, they build from these ideas to broaden the level of analysis, examining how ecosystem characteristics help dictate which new technologies will emerge (and when) to supplant the existing paradigm (Adner and Kapoor, 2016). One plausible intuition from this view is that the structural characteristics of innovation ecosystems establish the framework necessary for the development and evolution of technology trajectories.

Another perspective on ecosystems emphasizes the network of affiliations and exchange between organizations (Iansiti and Levien, 2004). Through explicit ties or implicit dependencies, firms are impacted by the knowledge development of outside organizations, shaping the broader trajectory of technologies in ways that may enhance or detract from the value of their own core technologies (Howard, Withers, and Tihanyi, 2017). Operating within this system of ties and dependencies, the ecosystem boundary (rather than the individual organizational boundary) becomes more relevant to the exchange of knowledge and the advancement of innovation within an industry or field (Autio and Thomas, 2014). As Autio *et al.* (2018) describe, the advancement of digital technologies has further advanced this shift, through the effects of generativity, emergent innovation through the interaction of uncoordinated, geographically dispersed organizations. Linking recent scholarship to foundational concepts in knowledge development, coordination through exchange (either formal or informal) across organizational ecosystems may provide the driving force behind emergent dominant designs (Anderson and Tushman, 1990; Murmann and Frenken, 2006).

The concept of innovation ecosystems has also been linked to the multiparty alliance literature. Collaborative alliances among three or more organizational participants raise the social dilemma of balancing cooperation with competition (Zeng and Chen, 2003). The success of such arrangements, and arguably ecosystems as the broader phenomenon, depends on interaction among multiple actors. For example, Davis (2016) describes how a cyclical dyadic approach—dynamic, recurring exchange across many interlinked dyads within the system—leads to a more productive innovative exchange balancing goals and interests of the individual organizations with those of the broader group. In fact, core multiparty alliances may establish the basis for the construction of an innovation ecosystem (Jacobides, Cennamo, and Gawer, 2018). We can see the field of knowledge and innovation management moving from its early foundation of firm-level decision-making in a dyadic alliance framework toward an understanding of these broader dynamics of interaction that increasingly underlie knowledge development and technological innovation.

The trend toward increasing knowledge complexity is intertwined with the organizational complexity of innovation occurring through these broader social structures of interaction. Dougherty and Dunne (2011) observe the technological link between innovation in complex fields (such as pharmaceuticals and alternative energies) and the necessity of having a broader ecological framework of firms, universities, and nonprofits or private institutes. Thus, complex knowledge development requires increasingly complex interorganizational efforts and a conceptual framework focused on cross-firm structures of collaboration. As an example, the concept of absorptive capacity, the ability to recognize and assimilate new knowledge, was originally applied at the organizational level (Cohen and Levinthal, 1990), and then the dyadic level of analysis (Lane and Lubatkin, 1998). Recent research extends this more broadly, arguing that absorptive capacity is relevant and necessary at a collective level, across R&D consortia (Omidvar, Edler, and Malik, 2017).

We're beginning to understand that knowledge complexity also drives dynamism in collaborative networks of innovation. Uncertainty enhances the need for establishing and operating through such collaborative structures (Dattée, Alexy, and Autio, 2018). Furthermore, firms require a dynamic shuffling of ties in their collaborative networks in order to facilitate innovation performance in complex technological settings (Kumar and Zaheer, 2019). Ties may need to be formed, abandoned, or reconstituted with the changing and unpredictable interdependencies among knowledge elements and core technological skills of collaborating organizations. This dynamic restructuring of ties can have important consequences for governance and coordination in the collaborative system (O'Mahony and Karp, 2021). Future research may explore what types of interorganizational collaborative structures are optimal for new knowledge creation or how the pace of dynamic network restructuring may promote or hinder innovation.

Computational knowledge search techniques have also had a profound impact on processes of knowledge development and innovation. The health-care industry provides a number of interesting examples of how this is taking place. Adaptive computer systems increase the pace and scope of drug development (Dougherty and Dunne, 2012). From a clinical perspective, machine learning models enhance medical diagnosis through the interpretation of digitized images generated from radiological exams and also improve prognosis by processing large datasets of treatment and patient outcomes (Obermeyer and Emanuel, 2016). The tremendous potential of machine learning in the area of genomics has also been well established. Computer learning algorithms can be trained to recognize patterns in DNA sequences, enabling the development of targeted genomic treatments (Libbrecht and Noble, 2015).

Organizational research is beginning to explore the implications of the machine-human interface in the development and implementation of new innovations. The automation of R&D tasks is accelerating the rate of innovation and influencing the trajectory of new knowledge development by broadening the scope of ideas that are pursued (Furman and Teodoridis, 2020). Machine innovation changes the role and capabilities of human actors, exhibited in technology implementations such as robotic surgery (Sergeeva, Faraj, and Huysman, 2020). We can expect a corollary effect for R&D scientists, with machine learning and artificial intelligence enhancing and perhaps directing the process of knowledge creation.

The Future Is Digital, Complex, and Connected

We can extrapolate future developments from these ideas that have been established in foundational strategy research and advanced through recent work. Knowledge is socially constructed against a backdrop of increasingly complex information. It is driven by collective learning and development efforts across organizational boundaries, spanning the private and public sectors, bridging national boundaries, and increasingly incorporating human and machine techniques of knowledge search.

Looking to the future, we can anticipate that organizational leaders will act on our greater understanding of the socially constructed nature of knowledge in an increasingly complex system of innovation. I propose three specific ways we may see this transpire. Managers are likely to engage in more intentional design of internal collaboration networks, continue to broaden their engagement and strategic focus in external cooperative consortia of "fellow traveler" organizations, and seek opportunities for competitive advantage through open source systems of innovation. Each of these paths offers benefits for knowledge development and organizational learning by actively engineering the construction of knowledge and the pursuit of innovation.

Organizations will increasingly recognize internal social interaction as a finite resource, requiring development and optimization, as with any other resource that is critical to competitive advantage. Employees are limited in the time and attention they can apply to collaborative interaction. Social ties are expensive, in that they require effort and maintenance in order to facilitate the flow of information and enable knowledge development (Kim, Oh, and Swaminathan, 2006). Recognizing these limitations, managers are likely to be more proactive in monitoring and coordinating collaborative ties among employees. Research has provided the tools for organizations to actively manage internal collaborative innovation networks. Small world theory, for example, addresses the notion that actors within large networks can be surprisingly closely connected through intermediaries (Travers and Milgram, 1969; Borgatti and Halgin, 2011). It demonstrates that the path length of communication for actors in a social network quickly decreases through the proper balance of weak and strong ties. This aligns well with the observations that R&D networks balancing depth and breadth of knowledge—nodes of intense expertise in specific technologies loosely connected to each other—enhance innovation (Yayavaram and Ahuja, 2008). Combining these insights, firms will exhibit more intentional design in the network of ties within and between R&D teams. From a research standpoint, it will be important to explore the categories of intentional collaborative social network design and the conditions under which it provides significant benefits in terms of technology development, adaptability, and firm performance.

Beyond the traditional design of organizational hierarchy and formal reporting structure, firms are now in a position to craft the structure of *informal* social exchange among knowledge workers. For example, imagine a new employee orientation process that includes organized events to promote social exchange with specifically assigned contacts within the firm, encouraging specific informal paths of mentorship and advice-giving. These contacts can be optimized based on an individual's knowledge, expertise, and even social and demographic characteristics. Companies such as Cisco, Microsoft, and Collaboration.AI already offer this type of social network optimization service for firms seeking to craft effective teams (Gupta, 2020). Chosen correctly, these collaboration network structures may offer great advantages, not only in innovation productivity, but also in providing employees with greater social embeddedness and sense of belonging within the organization.

Decisions to form ties at the organizational level may also change as firms become aware of the importance of collaboration structure to knowledge and innovation outcomes. The theories and perspectives of researchers studying joint ventures and alliance engagement have often focused on the dyadic characteristics of exchange and the potential to obtain needed knowledge and resources from a specific partner

(Muthusamy and White, 2005). More research is needed to understand how collaborative network structure does and should shape these decisions beyond the dyad level. Furthermore, we can gain new theoretical insights by linking this concept to the other trends of increasing innovation complexity and the importance of computer-driven search processes. Given the increasing complexity of knowledge and the need for new capabilities in computers and machine learning, it is unlikely that individual organizational partners chosen through dyadic decision processes can fully meet the needs of firms in connecting to emergent technologies and gaining the ability to influence the direction of innovation within their fields.

In the future, organizations must increasingly account for the broader ecosystem of collaborative interactions and their position within it. This requires a broader understanding of the landscape of alliances and cooperative knowledge exchange among firms that comprise the fine-grained details of organizational ecosystems. Drawing from social network theory, subnetwork structures such as cliques or factions may continue to emerge, characterized by both a greater density of connections within the group and a lower density of connections to those outside the group (Borgatti and Everett, 2000). Members gain benefits in terms of access to broader information from their group counterparts and greater support in competition against outsiders. Driven by increasing complexity, the locus of innovation (Powell, Koput, and Smith-Doerr, 1996) in collaborative interfirm networks of the future is more likely to reside in these network clusters or multiplex cross-organizational structures, lending greater definition and intentionality to the structure of ecosystems. The trend could raise important research questions regarding the appropriation of rents from innovation activities. Which organizational network actors are likely to benefit within cliques or factions? How or under what conditions can firms operating in these collaborative structures share economic benefits to promote sustainable collaboration? Outside of the collaborative clusters, individual firms may less frequently possess the knowledge resources or scale to fully develop and capture the benefits of the most impactful new innovations. For these reasons, managers may increasingly consider not only the information resources and suitability of their direct partners, but also their partners' connections to others within intermediate network structures and how access through such indirect connections may lead to their own competitive advantage.

Participation in external innovation may increasingly extend beyond traditional alliance networks. Open source innovation captures an even broader base of knowledge and creativity, from technology experts to users and independent developers (Hippel and von Krogh, 2003). Firms such as Adobe, Facebook, Google, and IBM have embraced open source development in software projects, and similar trends are beginning to emerge in hardware design. Some authors suggest that the open source approach not only enhances innovation but creates incentives for participants to improve the stability and security of their designs (Pearce, 2018). Organizations may increasingly consider participating in open source projects to avoid being left behind in the development of new innovations.

Computer-Driven Search and the Development of New Knowledge

Many of the changes in organizational innovation due to the social construction of knowledge and the complexity gradient may be significantly accelerated through the growing use and importance of artificial intelligence (Faraj, Pachidi, and Sayegh, 2018). Machine learning and data analytics will play an increasingly important role in the advancement of knowledge and innovation at the field level. Computer systems are well suited in their application to specific aspects of the knowledge search process. In the future, automated systems will increasingly have the ability to extract meaningful patterns from the development of prior innovations. Absorbing information on technology keywords, incorporating references to prior art and prior basic science research, such systems will be able to recognize patterns of meaning in innovation development that may not be apparent to human actors. Having learned these patterns, optimization algorithms in computational search platforms may then be applied proactively, identifying promising new areas of knowledge recombination that should plausibly lead to new innovations.

We can observe a recent example of the application of computer-based knowledge search systems in the rapid response to the COVID-19 pandemic. BenevolentAI, an artificial intelligence firm, applied its technologies to quickly search vast stores of prior medical data for promising drugs, identifying new treatments that could be quickly brought forward into clinical trials (Simonite, 2020). Similarly, a startup developed by computer scientists from Columbia University leveraged automated computer technology to assess hundreds of millions of potential antibodies that might be beneficial in treating the virus (Kent, 2020). Drawing from the framework of knowledge exploration and exploitation, this and other emerging examples show how machine learning and computer-based systems make exploitation of existing data and previously developed solutions easier, narrowing the uncertainty of pursuing new knowledge areas by offering a superior design optimization to what would be humanly possible. Rather than scanning and assessing the broader knowledge search landscape, human knowledge workers will focus in areas recommended by their AI "collaborators," allowing them to spend more effort in the process of local optimization.

The trend toward computer-based knowledge search opens important paths for future research in strategic management. Extending models of organizational learning, scholars may explore how computer technologies change processes such as double-loop learning. For example, computers may use pattern recognition and automated analysis to absorb additional tasks in the learning process, going beyond simply optimizing solutions within a given search to guide and improve the rules and parameters of the search itself. Under such conditions, how should organizations be structured to appropriately balance benefits of automation with human capital capabilities in the innovation process?

Technological Tragedy of the Commons

While the benefits of broader collaboration and the application of machine learning in the face of technological complexity are evident, the future landscape of knowledge development and innovation may hold significant challenges. The new systems of innovation linking humans, organizations, and computers may struggle with incentives that derail progress toward new knowledge development.

As knowledge is increasingly built on a broader set of elements with greater interdependencies, the process of managing innovation and new knowledge may experience significant changes. The search space for new knowledge will become increasingly broad. The balance of ambidexterity at the organizational level may shift in favor of exploitation over exploration. For example, firms leveraging artificial intelligence to optimize knowledge recombination across the broad repository of collective knowledge gain efficiency advantages. This leads to the rise of knowledge integration firms, those that take advantage of AI-based systems to identify promising local regions of innovation in the knowledge search landscape. They will establish a de facto ambidexterity, the ability to balance knowledge exploitation and exploration (Raisch and Birkinshaw, 2008), by (1) relying on other firms to build intensive expertise in specific knowledge elements, and (2) applying computer-based knowledge search to more easily spot favorable new combinations of knowledge and even aid in the process of overcoming barriers historically encountered in areas of complex, tacit knowledge.

In markets where the intellectual property (IP) regime is strong (e.g., courts have upheld patent rights of assignees more vigorously), this trend will be less evident. True knowledge developers, those that blaze the trail to identify fundamentally new knowledge elements, will still appropriate rents from their efforts and remain encouraged to continue the basic research and development necessary to create this expertise. Many years ago, Heller and Eisenberg (1998) identified a potential crisis in biomedical research in which this dynamic could lead to a failure to diffuse knowledge that might otherwise provide greater benefit to society. They noted that "a resource is prone to underuse in a 'tragedy of the anticommons' when multiple owners each have a right to exclude others from a scarce resource and no one has an effective privilege of use" (Heller and Eisenberg, 1998: 698).

In markets in which IP appropriability is weak, society may experience the opposite effect. A *technological tragedy of the commons* may emerge, in which rents accrue to knowledge integrators, those that are able to quickly optimize the recombination of knowledge that has previously been developed. The knowledge developers, having based their innovation management strategy on developing deeper expertise in more narrow areas, will be at a fundamental disadvantage to the integrators. With limited protection of their IP and lacking the competencies at broad knowledge integration, knowledge developers will fail to gain rents from the innovations they develop. With more integrators and increasingly fewer knowledge developers, society may suffer as the pool of valuable knowledge elements stagnates, resulting in new technologies that are broad but increasingly shallow in their ability to advance the economy, improve standards of living, and provide solutions to problems facing society. Recent research has already highlighted the decline of basic science research in corporate R&D activities (Arora, Belenzon, and Patacconi, 2018). It will be critical to monitor these trends in the future, with strategy scholars, organizational leaders, and policymakers taking a much broader view in analyzing and guiding the health and strength of the innovation systems in our society.

From a research perspective, strategic management scholars have a number of ways to offer greater insight into this potential technological tragedy of the commons. Given the heterogeneity across industries and regulatory regimes, researchers may examine what institutional conditions result in healthier versus more stagnant environments for innovation. For example, specific government policies designed to support basic science research or offering new incentives for knowledge creation may serve as natural experiments to test ideas in this area. Scholars may also explore how or whether the collective actions of firms might enable knowledge creation ambidexterity at a broader system level. Perhaps factions of collaborative firms within technology fields may recognize the need for sustainable innovation practices. If so, is it possible to balance exploratory search with exploitation of existing knowledge across the entire ecosystem, rather than within individual organizations? Finally, university collaboration with commercial firms, often facilitated through technology transfer programs, has proven to be a valuable method for linking basic science development with commercialization of technology. Strategic management scholars may explore how greater involvement of university-driven science research may influence innovation productivity in technology fields where computer-based knowledge search is adopted.

Implications for Methods and Theory in Future Research

The field of management research must adopt methods that can adequately reflect the rich fabric of social connections and interdependencies underlying the process of innovation. Knowledge travels within and between organizations through many conduits, and our empirical tools must capture this elaborate multiplexity of knowledge exchange. While we can and should continue to leverage techniques such as longitudinal analysis of large patent datasets to understand trends in knowledge development, other approaches can provide complementary information in characterizing innovation ecosystems. Social network analysis through techniques such as exponential random graph models (ERGMs) or stochastic actor-oriented models (SAOMs) have the capacity to capture overlapping ties and knowledge flows in innovation networks, while also disentangling endogenous network structural effects (Snijders, 1996; Lusher, Koskinen, and Robins, 2013; Kim *et al.*, 2016). At the same time, the field must continue to pursue intensive qualitative research to understand the complexities of the innovation process that still rely on socially embedded human interaction (e.g., Fisher, Pillemer, and Amabile, 2018). Combining these different techniques will allow us to understand the true nature of social exchange involved in knowledge development and how it changes with increasing knowledge complexity and the integration of machine learning.

Our field also needs to develop theory to explain knowledge and innovation in light of the emerging trends. For example, the growth of machine-driven innovation raises important issues that management strategy scholars may help address (e.g., von Krogh, 2018). We need a framework to understand the dynamics and consequences of knowledge search increasingly conducted through artificial intelligence platforms. This could include adapting concepts such as ambidexterity and absorptive capacity to integrate computer-based knowledge search as a fundamental component of knowledge development and knowledge management capabilities. For example, Raisch and Krakowski (2020) offer an interesting theoretical discussion of the role of AI in either augmenting or automating human tasks within organizations. As they observe, it is critical that management scholars continue to engage the broader topic of AI from a theoretical perspective.

Research into organizational innovation and knowledge management must continue to look beyond the firm level. We must account for motivations, value appropriation, and social benefits of innovation processes that will increasingly occur at a field level. Much of the framework for strategy theory is housed within the traditional boundaries of the firm, and in fact has been developed to explain how and why these boundaries exist. We have an opportunity to build out more descriptive models of intermediate collaborative structures that develop within and across industries. Our work can inform how these structures are best organized and governed, balancing intellectual property appropriation incentives for innovators with benefits for society. Perhaps it is time to develop an interorganizational corollary to research in corporate social responsibility—organizational social and ethical policies in the context of their financial performance (McGuire, Sundgren, and Schneeweis, 1988)—adapted to the ecosystem level. As groups of organizations interface and align with technological platforms to achieve a collective competitive advantage for those platforms, perspectives on ecosystem social responsibility could begin to inform and balance how coordinated knowledge development and innovation behaviors can be best aligned with the greater good for all of society.

References

Adner R. 2017. Ecosystem as structure: an actionable construct for strategy. *Journal of Management* 43(1): 39–58.

Adner R, Kapoor R. 2010. Value creation in innovation ecosystems: how the structure of technological interdependence affects firm performance in new technology generations. *Strategic Management Journal* 31(3): 306–333.

Adner R, Kapoor R. 2016. Innovation ecosystems and the pace of substitution: re-examining technology S-curves. *Strategic Management Journal* 37(4): 625–648.

Anderson P, Tushman ML. 1990. Technological discontinuities and dominant designs: a cyclical model of technological change. *Administrative Science Quarterly* 35(4): 604–633.

Argyris C. 1976. Single-loop and double-loop models in research on decision making. *Administrative Science Quarterly* 21(3): 363–375.

Arora A, Belenzon S, Patacconi A. 2018. The decline of science in corporate R&D. *Strategic Management Journal* 39(1): 3–32.

Autio E, Nambisan S, Thomas LD, Wright M. 2018. Digital affordances, spatial affordances, and the genesis of entrepreneurial ecosystems. *Strategic Entrepreneurship Journal* 12(1): 72–95.

Autio E, Thomas L. 2014. Innovation ecosystems. In *The Oxford Handbook of Innovation Management*, Dodgson M, Gann DM, Phillips N (eds). Oxford University Press: Oxford, U.K.; 204–288.

Berger PL, Luckmann T. 1967. *The Social Construction of Reality: A Treatise in the Sociology of Knowledge*. Doubleday Anchor: Garden City, NY.

Borgatti SP, Everett MG. 2000. Models of core/periphery structures. *Social Networks* 21(4): 375–395.

Borgatti SP, Halgin DS. 2011. On network theory. *Organization Science* 22(5): 1168–1181.

Cohen WM, Levinthal DA. 1990. Absorptive capacity: a new perspective on learning and innovation. *Administrative Science Quarterly* 35(1): 128–152.

Cowan DA. 1986. Developing a process model of problem recognition. *Academy of Management Review* 11(4): 763–776.

Crossan MM, Lane HW, White RE. 1999. An organizational learning framework: from intuition to institution. *Academy of Management Review* 24(3): 522–537.

Dattée B, Alexy O, Autio E. 2018. Maneuvering in poor visibility: how firms play the ecosystem game when uncertainty is high. *Academy of Management Journal* 61(2): 466–498.

Davis JP. 2016. The group dynamics of interorganizational relationships: collaborating with multiple partners in innovation ecosystems. *Administrative Science Quarterly* 61(4): 621–661.

Dean W. 2016. Computational Complexity Theory. In *The Stanford Encyclopedia of Philosophy*, Zalta EN (ed). Metaphysics Research Lab, Stanford University: Stanford, CA.

Denrell J, March JG. 2001. Adaptation as information restriction: the hot stove effect. *Organization Science* 12(5): 523–538.

Dosi G. 1982. Technological paradigms and technological trajectories: a suggested interpretation of the determinants and directions of technical change. *Research Policy* 11(3): 147–162.

Dougherty D, Dunne DD. 2011. Organizing ecologies of complex innovation. *Organization Science* 22(5): 1214–1223.

Dougherty D, Dunne DD. 2012. Digital science and knowledge boundaries in complex innovation. *Organization Science* 23(5): 1467–1484.

Dyer JH, Singh H. 1998. The relational view: cooperative strategy and sources of interorganizational competitive advantage. *Academy of Management Review* 23(4): 665.

Faraj S, Pachidi S, Sayegh K. 2018. Working and organizing in the age of the learning algorithm. *Information and Organization* 28(1): 62–70.

Fiol CM, Lyles MA. 1985. Organizational learning. *Academy of Management Review* 10(4): 803–813.

Fisher CM, Pillemer J, Amabile TM. 2018. Deep help in complex project work: guiding and path-clearing across difficult terrain. *Academy of Management Journal* 61(4): 1524–1553.

Fleming L, Sorenson O. 2001. Technology as a complex adaptive system: evidence from patent data. *Research Policy* 30(7): 1019–1039.

Furman JL, Teodoridis F. 2020. Automation, research technology, and researchers' trajectories: evidence from computer science and electrical engineering. *Organization Science* 31(2): 330–354.

Glynn MA. 1996. Innovative genius: a framework for relating individual and organizational intelligences to innovation. *Academy of Management Review* 21(4): 1081–1111.

Goldreich O, Petrank E. 1999. Quantifying knowledge complexity. *Computational Complexity* 8(1): 50–98.

Goldwasser S, Micali S, Rackoff C. 1989. The knowledge complexity of interactive proof systems. *SIAM Journal on Computing* 18(1): 186–208.

Gupta S. 2020. Cognitive collaboration market projected to grow $1,660 million by 2024. https://www.marketsandmarkets.com/Market-Reports/cognitive-collaboration-market-245084124.html, accessed May 20, 2020.

Han J, Pei J, Kamber M. 2011. *Data Mining: Concepts and Techniques.* Elsevier: Waltham, MA.

Haykin S. 1994. *Neural Networks: A Comprehensive Foundation.* Prentice Hall PTR: Upper Saddle River, NJ.

Heller MA, Eisenberg RS. 1998. Can patents deter innovation? The anticommons in biomedical research. *Science* 280(5364): 698–701.

Herden RP, Lyles MA. 1981. Individual attributes and the problem conceptualization process. *Human Systems Management* 2(4): 275–284.

Herriott SR, Levinthal D, March JG. 1985. Learning from experience in organizations. *American Economic Review* 75(2): 298–302.

Hippel E, von Krogh G. 2003. Open source software and the "private-collective" innovation model: issues for organization science. *Organization Science* 14(2): 209–223.

Howard MD, Withers MC, Tihanyi L. 2017. Knowledge dependence and the formation of director interlocks. *Academy of Management Journal* 60(5): 1986–2013.

Huber GP. 1991. Organizational learning: the contributing processes and the literatures. *Organization Science* 2(1): 88–115.

Iansiti M, Levien R. 2004. Strategy as ecology. *Harvard Business Review* 82(3): 68–78, 126.

Jacobides MG, Cennamo C, Gawer A. 2018. Towards a theory of ecosystems. *Strategic Management Journal* 39(8): 2255–2276.

Kent J. 2020. Data scientists use machine learning to discover COVID-19 treatments. *Health IT Analytics*. https://healthitanalytics.com/news/data-scientists-use-machine-learning-to-discover-covid-19-treatments [20 May 2020].

Kim JY, Howard M, Cox Pahnke E, Boeker W. 2016. Understanding network formation in strategy research: exponential random graph models. *Strategic Management Journal* 37(1): 22–44.

Kim T-Y, Oh H, Swaminathan A. 2006. Framing interorganizational network change: a network inertia perspective. *Academy of Management Review* 31(3): 704–720.

Kogut B, Zander U. 1992. Knowledge of the firm, combinative capabilities, and the replication of technology. *Organization Science* 3(3): 383–397.

Kumar P, Zaheer A. 2019. Ego-network stability and innovation in alliances. *Academy of Management Journal* 62(3): 691–716.

Lafond F, Kim D. 2019. Long-run dynamics of the US patent classification system. *Journal of Evolutionary Economics* 29(2): 631–664.

Lane PJ, Lubatkin M. 1998. Relative absorptive capacity and interorganizational learning. *Strategic Management Journal* 19(5): 461–477.

Libbrecht MW, Noble WS. 2015. Machine learning applications in genetics and genomics. *Nature Reviews Genetics* 16(6): 321–332.

Lusher D, Koskinen J, Robins G. 2013. *Exponential Random Graph Models for Social Networks: Theory, Methods, and Applications.* Cambridge University Press: Cambridge, U.K.

March JG, Simon HA. 1958. *Organizations.* John Wiley and Sons: New York, NY.

McGuire JB, Sundgren A, Schneeweis T. 1988. Corporate social responsibility and firm finan-cial performance. *Academy of Management Journal* 31(4): 854–872.

Mitchell TM. 1997. *Machine Learning*. McGraw-Hill: New York, NY.

Murmann JP, Frenken K. 2006. Toward a systematic framework for research on dom-inant designs, technological innovations, and industrial change. *Research Policy* 35(7): 925–952.

Muthusamy SK, White MA. 2005. Learning and knowledge transfer in strategic alliances: a so-cial exchange view. *Organization Studies* 26(3): 415–441.

Nalebuff BJ, Brandenburger A, Maulana A. 1996. *Co-opetition*. HarperCollinsBusiness: London, U.K.

Nelson RR, Winter SG. 1982. *An Evolutionary Theory of Economic Change*. Belknap Press of Harvard University Press: Cambridge, MA.

Obermeyer Z, Emanuel EJ. 2016. Predicting the future—big data, machine learning, and clin-ical medicine. *New England Journal of Medicine* 375(13): 1216-1219.

O'Mahony S, Karp R. 2021. From proprietary to collective governance: how platform par-ticipation strategies evolve. *Strategic Management Journal*, forthcoming. https://doi.org/ 10.1002/smj.3150.

Omidvar O, Edler J, Malik K. 2017. Development of absorptive capacity over time and across boundaries: the case of R&D consortia. *Long Range Planning* 50(5): 665–683.

Pearce JM. 2018. Open-source hardware could defend against the next generation of hacking. *Salon*, 21 October. https: //salon.com/2018/10/20/open-source-hardware-could-defend-against-the-next-generation-of-hacking.

Pinch TJ, Bijker WE. 1984. The social construction of facts and artefacts: or how the sociology of science and the sociology of technology might benefit each other. *Social Studies of Science* 14(3): 399–441.

Polanyi M. 2009. *The Tacit Dimension*. University of Chicago Press: Chicago, IL.

Powell WW, Koput KW, Smith-Doerr L. 1996. Interorganizational collaboration and the locus of innovation: networks of learning in biotechnology. *Administrative Science Quarterly* 41(1): 116–145.

Raisch S, Birkinshaw J. 2008. Organizational ambidexterity: antecedents, outcomes, and mod-erators. *Journal of Management* 34(3): 375–409.

Raisch S, Krakowski S. 2021. Artificial intelligence and management: the automation-augmentation paradox. *Academy of Management Review* 46(1): 192–210.

Rosen P. 1993. The social construction of mountain bikes: technology and postmodernity in the cycle industry. *Social Studies of Science* 23(3): 479–513.

Samuel AL. 1959. Some studies in machine learning using the game of checkers. *IBM Journal of Research and Development* 3(3): 210–229.

Sergeeva AV, Faraj S, Huysman M. 2020. Losing touch: an embodiment perspective on coordi-nation in robotic surgery. *Organization Science* 31(5): 1248–1271.

Simonite T. 2020. AI uncovers a potential treatment for COVID-19 patients. *Wired*, April 17. https://www.wired.com/story/ai-uncovers-a-potential-treatment-for-covid-19-patients.

Snijders TA. 1996. Stochastic actor-oriented models for network change. *Journal of Mathematical Sociology* 21(1–2): 149–172.

Spender JC. 1996. Making knowledge the basis of a dynamic theory of the firm. *Strategic Management Journal* 17(S2): 45–62.

Suarez FF, Utterback JM. 1995. Dominant designs and the survival of firms. *Strategic Management Journal* 16(6): 415–430.

Trajtenberg M. 1990. A penny for your quotes: patent citations and the value of innovations. *Rand Journal of Economics* 21(1): 172–187.

Travers J, Milgram S. 1969. An experimental study of the small world problem. *Sociometry* 32(4): 425–443.

Tushman ML, Murmann JP. 1998. Dominant designs, technology cycles, and organizational outcomes. *Research in Organizational Behavior* 20: 213–266.

Utterback JM, Abernathy WJ. 1975. A dynamic model of process and product innovation. *Omega* 3(6): 639–656.

von Krogh G. 2018. Artificial intelligence in organizations: new opportunities for phenomenon-based theorizing. *Academy of Management Discoveries* 4(4): 404–409.

Williamson OE. 1975. Markets and hierarchies. *American Economic Review* 63(2): 316–325.

Yayavaram S, Ahuja G. 2008. Decomposability in knowledge structures and its impact on the usefulness of inventions and knowledge-base malleability. *Administrative Science Quarterly* 53(2): 333–362.

Zeng M, Chen X-P. 2003. Achieving cooperation in multiparty alliances: a social dilemma approach to partnership management. *Academy of Management Review* 28(4): 587–605.

Zucker LG, Darby MR, Furner J, Liu RC, Ma H. 2007. Minerva unbound: knowledge stocks, knowledge flows, and new knowledge production. *Research Policy* 36(6): 850–863.

PART 9

STRATEGY PROCESSES AND PRACTICES

Robert A. Burgelman, Steven W. Floyd,
Tomi Laamanen, Saku Mantere, Eero Vaara,
and Richard Whittington, Leads

9.0

STRATEGY PROCESSES AND PRACTICES

Robert A. Burgelman, Steven W. Floyd, Tomi Laamanen,
Saku Mantere, Eero Vaara, and Richard Whittington

Strategy process research and strategy-as-practice research have always shared one fundamental idea: a discomfort with the conception of strategy as being preeminently about the discrete "choices" of top management (Geletkanycz and Hambrick, 1997). As strategy-as-practice research emerged early in this century, however, the two traditions often saw themselves as distinct, with practice theory encouraging different levels of analysis than the organizational focus typical in process research (Vaara and Whittington, 2012). Given their fundamental commonality, this chapter argues that it is time that process and strategy-as-practice researchers combine their forces. Together they can deliver important insights into new research topics, ranging from the role of digital information technologies in strategy making to more inclusive modes of strategizing.

Strategy process research is about understanding strategy as an organizational phenomenon (Burgelman *et al.*, 2018; Hutzschenreuter and Kleindienst, 2006; Mintzberg and Waters, 1985; Pettigrew, 1992). Against the earlier, normative-rational view that strategy is the result of senior management choices articulated in a formal plan (Andrews, 1971; Ansoff, 1965; Hitt and Tyler, 1991), strategy process research builds on the premise that strategy is a coherent pattern of actions and incremental decisions taken over time across the organization (Mintzberg, 1978). Strategy-as-practice research embraces the concern for organizations (Jarzabkowski and Spee, 2009; Whittington, 1996). Where it diverges from strategy process research is to zoom inward and outward from the organization to examine strategy both as a form of micro-activity and as a product of institutional fields spanning countless actors and organizations (Jarzabkowski, 2004; Whittington, 2006). Thus for strategy-as-practice research, important units of analysis are not only the organization, but also micro-episodes of strategy work, the whole range of individual actors involved in this work, and the various practices they draw upon as they carry out their work.

The relationship between strategy process and strategy-as-practice research can be seen as the basis for mutual critique or as complementary views of closely related phenomena (Burgelman *et al.*, 2018). However, as evident from the above, they do fundamentally share a common interest in strategy making. Thus there are also grounds for a combinatory perspective on strategizing. By removing artificial boundaries between processes and practices, such as units and levels of analysis, we argue that a combinatory approach offers the most potential for holistic insight. Moreover, a shared "strong process ontology" (Chia, 1997; Langley *et al.*, 2013) provides a basis for seeing both processes and practices as ongoing activity and removes earlier incommensurability concerns between the two subjects of research.

The purpose of this chapter is to encourage future strategy research in the combinatory mode. Reviews of strategy process and strategy-as-practice research can be found elsewhere (Burgelman *et al.*, 2018; Hutzschenreuter and Kleindienst, 2006; Vaara and Whittington, 2012; Weiser, Jarzabkowski, and Laamanen, 2020; Wolf and Floyd, 2017), and the following subsection chapters provide detailed reviews of strategic decision-making and organizational actors and of strategic change and renewal, respectively. Here we offer an overview of the two perspectives. Then we review only the most recent work published from 2018 onward. We devote most of our effort to considering high-priority research questions, novel theorizing, and productive methodologies suggested by the combinatory approach and constituting our vision for the newly constituted strategy as processes and practices field.

A Brief History of Strategy Process Research

The historical foundations of the strategy process domain can be traced to early work on executive decision-making (Barnard, 1938), organizational change (Chandler, 1962; Pettigrew, 1985), formal strategic planning (Ansoff, 1965; Lorange, 1980), and the resource allocation process (Bower, 1970). Early scholars also benefited from the psychological perspective drawn out of Simon's concept of bounded rationality (Simon, 1957) and the recognition of the role that human behavior (Cyert and March, 1963) and cognition (Schwenk, 1984) play in explaining decision-making outcomes. While some of the early work was clearly normative and atheoretical in nature (Lorange, 1980), other studies provided descriptive or theory-based accounts (Pettigrew, 1985). All of the work was focused on answering the same core question: "Where do [or should] strategies come from?"

Bower's (1970) seminal research on the resource allocation process foregrounded middle managers as sources of strategic alternatives. In Bower's model, middle managers act as champions of capital investment projects, and strategy evolves out of the projects selected by top management. Thus, rather than a top-down view of planning where strategic choice drives organizational structure (cf. Chandler, 1962), for Bower the structure was used by top management to influence the planning process. Building on this structure-drives-strategy model, Burgelman's conceptual (1983) and empirical work (1991) described the strategy process in evolutionary terms and identified both induced (top-down) and autonomous (bottom-up) initiatives competing in the intraorganizational selection environment as the antecedents of corporate strategy and the basis of strategic renewal.

Mintzberg's early contributions resonate with the bottom-up influences in strategy. He defined *strategy* as a "pattern in a stream of decisions" (Mintzberg, 1978: 935) and distinguished between *deliberate* and *emergent strategies*, the latter defined as "patterns or consistencies realized despite, or in the absence of, intentions" (Mintzberg and Waters, 1985: 257). He argued that most organizations reflect a mix of deliberate and emergent forces in an "umbrella strategy." When environments are complex and uncertain, top management sets boundaries, but control over other actors is relaxed so that emergent strategies that fall within the boundaries may be realized. Mintzberg decried separation of strategy formulation and implementation and instead conceptualized strategy formation as a social learning process.

In addition to these theoretical contributions, Bower, Burgelman, and Mintzberg adopted a common method to study strategy processes. As described by Pettigrew (2012), they employed a processual approach marked by "combining the virtues of deductive intention with post-hoc inductive pattern recognition" (1309) and drawing on rich, longitudinal case data in order to surface context-process-outcome relationships. Langley (1999) elaborated seven different strategies for making sense of qualitative process data and evaluated these in terms of their accuracy, generality, and simplicity. While strategy process researchers also undertake quantitative, theory-testing research (Hutzschenreuter and Kleindienst, 2006; Wolf and Floyd, 2017), it is no coincidence that the foundational work relied on inductive research designs that are sensitive to the diverse logics and fine-grained activities that constitute organization process.

A Brief History of Strategy-as-Practice Research

As distinct from the organizational processes that have been the concern of strategy process research, strategy-as-practice research has from the beginning foregrounded activity, treating strategy not only as something an organization has, but also as "something people do" (Jarzabkowski, 2004; Whittington, 2004: 62). Accordingly, strategy-as-practice researchers initially emphasized closely observed, micro-level studies of managerial strategizing (Johnson, Melin, and Whittington, 2003). The approach was often to employ ethnographic methods of deep immersion (Rasche and Chia, 2009) to study particular episodes of activity within an overall strategy process—for example, board meetings or strategy retreats (Johnson *et al.*, 2010; Samra-Fredericks, 2003). This micro-level stream of research remains highly vigorous, with recent examples including Bencherki *et al.* (2020) and Whittle *et al.* (2020).

The introduction of the 3P model, with its emphasis on praxis, practices, and practitioners (Whittington, 2006), has helped to set this micro-level strategy activity within a wider context. While the 3P model does highlight activity in the form of *praxis*, that is, what people actually do, it also connects such activity to *practitioners*—in other words, the actors of strategy—and *practices*, that is, the tools, methods, and routines of strategy. Thus, strategy-as-practice research considers types of strategy practitioners, for example, chief strategy officers (Angwin, Paroutis, and Mitson,

2009), and increasingly focuses on how ordinary managers become strategists, by acquiring legitimacy (Paroutis and Heracleous, 2013), discursive skills (Dameron, Lê, and LeBaron, 2015), and self-identities (Mantere and Whittington, 2020). Researchers also consider material practices such as the use of PowerPoints (Kaplan, 2011) and social media (Neeley and Leonardi, 2018); symbolic and substantive practices, such as structural and symbolic changes (Hambrick and Lovelace, 2018; Weiser, 2020); and discursive practices, such as the strategy "talk" used to include or exclude managers (Mantere and Vaara, 2008) or to communicate strategic initiatives (Wenzel and Koch, 2018).

This emerging appreciation of practices has lately prompted a more macro-oriented shift in research. The discursive practices of strategy, particularly its jargon, are rooted at the societal level rather than at particular organizations (Vaara and Monin, 2010); similarly, material technologies (PowerPoint and Excel, for example) are liable to skew strategizing work in all kinds of organizations (Whittington, 2015). Researchers are increasingly aware of the dangers of an overabsorption in the particularities of single organizations (Seidl and Whittington, 2014; Zilber, 2020). Thus, Jarzabkowski and Bednarek (2018) study practices within the insurance industry on a global scale. Similarly, studies are increasingly likely to take the long view, reminiscent of the longitudinal orientation of strategy process research. For example, Pratap and Saha (2018) study changing strategy development practices across decades in an Indian steel company, while Whittington (2019) tracks changing practices within Western business as a whole from the 1960s to today.

The Emergence of the Strategy Processes and Practices Field: A Combinatory View

These brief histories of strategy process and strategy-as-practice research bring out strongly convergent themes. Recognizing this, Burgelman *et al.* (2018) called for research synthesizing the insights of the two research streams into a "combinatory model" based on a shared concern for activity. This focus on activity is underpinned by the emergence of what Langley and Tsoukas (2010) describe as a "strong process" ontology in which every aspect of the organization is seen as a product of activity. Any single set of activities is inextricably part of a larger, moving whole. Distinctions between levels of analysis blur. Micro-level episodes of strategizing, organizational-level strategy emergence, and macro-level strategic practices all involve the same fundamental phenomenon, the activity of human actors in the moment. The key elements of this combinatory model—strategy formation, actors, episodes, and practices—are compatible across process and practice traditions. The center of the combinatory model is the strategy formation process, where both process and practice researchers unite in their concern to understand the origins of strategy. Practice researchers share the original interest of process researchers in deliberate strategies, especially in strategic planning activities, while accepting that realized strategies are rarely direct and simple outcomes of these activities. Both process and practice scholars join in a concern for better understanding of the roles of different actors, especially middle managers and consultants. They see these actors as pursuing strategic issues and initiatives of their own and drawing upon a wide range of discursive and material tools. The combinatory model of strategy processes and practices thus allows process and practice researchers to work together, each enriching the other with different theoretical approaches and research methodologies.

Contemporary Research Trajectories

In this section, we discuss the trajectory of research following the publication of the *Strategic Management Journal* Special Issue on Strategy Processes and Practices in 2018. A keyword search of top strategy journals, using the terms "strategy process," "strategy processes," "strategy practices," and "strategy-as-practice," identifies 52 articles published in the period from 2018 to 2020. From among these, 20 predominantly focus on strategy processes and 20 on strategy practices. Already, however, there have been 12 articles that take the combinatory path. We first discuss the studies positioned in either strategy process or strategy practice research streams before addressing studies following the combinatory path.[1]

Studies on the strategy process path

One strong theme in recent process research is the role of different actors (Van den Steen, 2018) and their interface in the strategy process. For example, Simsek, Heavey, and Fox (2018) propose a conceptual framework of the interfaces of strategic leaders and call for more research on how these interfaces emerge, how they evolve over time, and how they relate to societal context. Similarly, Tarakci *et al.* (2018) examine the interfaces between middle and top managers. Based on a behavioral analysis of subunit performance feedback, the authors offer a multilevel explanation of the divergent behavior of middle managers. Schubert and Tavassoli (2020) examine the effects of relative diversity in top and middle management teams and its influence on product innovation. Finally, Gabaldon, Kanadli, and Bankewitz (2018) find that job-related diversity in corporate boardrooms influences the involvement of the board in the strategy process.

Another stream of research focuses on narratives. For example, Holstein, Starkey, and Wright (2018) argue that it is the "on-going interaction between historical and new narratives that gives the content of strategy its essential voice" (Holstein *et al.*, 2018: 61). Similarly, Jalonen, Schildt, and Vaara (2018) examine strategic concepts as micro-level tools in strategic sensemaking. They conclude that strategy concepts help managers make sense of the changing environment but that the ambiguity inherent in such concepts can hinder strategy implementation.

Finally, strategy process scholars have also revisited classic strategy process topic areas, such as strategic decision comprehensiveness (Miller and McKee, 2020), strategic consensus (Ateş *et al.*, 2020; Porck *et al.*, 2020), strategic issues management (Laamanen *et al.*, 2018), and strategic changes over time (Snihur, Thomas, and Burgelman, 2018). Many of these studies have been enhanced by improved methods for analyzing strategy processes as multilevel phenomena.

Studies on the strategy-as-practice path

Recent studies of strategy practice have examined a wide range of topics from materiality (Comi and Whyte, 2018; Palli, 2018) to performativity (Cabantous, Gond, and Wright, 2018), paradoxes (Schneider, Bullinger, and Brandl, 2020), rituals (van den Ende and van Marrewijk, 2018), and emotions (Vuori, Vuori, and Huy, 2018). While some of these themes have also appeared in process research, they have become especially prominent in research on strategy practices. We highlight here two themes that are particularly close to the strategy process tradition.

First, many of the recent strategy-as-practice studies focus on the role of language and discourse in strategizing, close to the narrative interest in process research. For example, Sasaki *et al.* (2020) examine how companies reconcile change in organizational identity with their original identity. The authors describe three discursive strategies (elaborating, recovering, and decoupling) that enable a sense of continuity in a time of change. Relatedly, Dalpiaz and Di Stefano (2018) show how strategy-makers influence acceptance of an ongoing transformation through a steady influx of "captivating narratives of transformative change."

Many recent papers on strategy practices have shown interest in temporal and processual dynamics (Kunisch *et al.*, 2017). For example, Gond, Cabantous, and Krikorian (2018) and Vogus and Rerup (2018) examine "how activities become strategic," Bencherki *et al.* (2020) examine "how strategy comes to matter," and Mantere and Whittington (2020) examine "how to become a strategist." Relatedly, Jarzabkowski and Bednarek (2018) apply practice theory to understanding how competitive dynamics unfold through microcompetitions over time, and Luoma, Laamanen, and Lamberg (2020) highlight the continuously evolving nature of competitive action routines.

Studies on the combinatory path

Most of the studies on the strategy process and the strategy practice paths that we have discussed so far can be seen as complementary (Burgelman *et al.*, 2018). While recent strategy process research has focused on *actors, interfaces, consensus, concepts,* and *narratives,* strategy practice research has focused on more micro-level dynamics: *performativity, materiality, rituals, paradoxes, routines, identity,* and *emotions.* Both these sets of topics can usefully inform each other. However, the interest in *narratives, communication,* and *language,* as well as the focus on *temporal dynamics* are more combinatory, representing shared topic areas across the two research streams.

While six of the 12 combinatory articles appearing in 2018–2020 were published in the *SMJ* Special Issue where we specifically called for intersections between strategy processes and practices, other scholars have been developing the combinatory approach. We highlight four areas that are receiving the most attention: (1) practices enabling and constraining participation in the strategy process (Dobusch, Dobusch, and Muller-Seitz, 2019; Hautz, Seidl, and Whittington, 2017; Mantere and Whittington, 2020); (2) the use of strategy tools and information technologies in the strategy process (Jarzabkowski and Kaplan, 2015; Knight, Paroutis, and Heracleous, 2018; Vuorinen *et al.*, 2018); (3) the dynamics of strategy emergence (Kannan-Narasimhan and Lawrence, 2018; Kaplan, 2008; Mirabeau and Maguire, 2014; Mirabeau, Maguire, and Hardy, 2018; Ocasio, Laamanen, and Vaara, 2018); and (4) adaptive strategy implementation, that is, the continuous interplay between conceptualization and enactment of strategies on multiple levels and in multiple units (Ahearne, Lam, and Kraus, 2014; Weiser *et al.*, 2020).

As the strategy process and practice literatures pursue deeper combinatory lines of research, strategy processes and practices themselves are changing. First, digitalization is transforming the processes and practices of strategy in ways that undermine traditional distinctions. Digital media stand to integrate the different elements of strategy formation—from the work of formulating strategy (Johnson *et al.*, 2010) to implementing it (Weiser *et al.*, 2020) and from micro activity (Balogun, Best, and Le, 2015) to macro, institutional structures (Whittington, 2006). Because of strategy-as-practice researchers' interest in materiality, and strategy process researchers' distrust of formulation-implementation distinctions, combinatory scholarship has unique insights to contribute here. Second, strategy processes and practices are becoming more inclusive. To a large extent, the wider participation in strategy processes is facilitated by new digital technologies (Morton, Wilson, and Cooke, 2020), but there are also societal and organizational developments in play—for example, the rise of highly educated workforces and the radical delayering of organizations (Whittington, 2019). Given their interest in bottom-up strategy and actors from outside top management, combinatory scholars are well positioned to explore greater inclusivity in strategy. Digitalization and inclusivity thus provide two issues that run through the research agenda that we see as emerging within the strategy as processes and practices perspective.

The Combinatory Research Agenda

Here we outline a research agenda that emerges both from the combinatory framework presented in Burgelman *et al.* (2018) and from this chapter's review of more recent research. These themes include *temporality and spatiality, actors and agency, cognition and emotionality*, and *language and communication*.

Temporality and spatiality

Strategy process research has demonstrated the importance of temporality in understanding strategy. This has been a key part of evolutionary views on strategy-making (Burgelman, 1983) and in defining strategic "emergence"' (Mintzberg and Waters, 1985). Recent methodological contributions (Kouame and Langley, 2018) provide guidance on how researchers can better deal with issues relating to temporality by combining correlation and progression methodologies of strategy process with the instantiation methodology of strategy-as-practice.

Recent work (Mirabeau and Maguire, 2014) has elucidated ways in which temporality is linked with strategy practices. Future research could focus on developing a better understanding of episodes in the context of longer processes of strategy-making routines (Jarzabkowski and Seidl, 2008) and continuous adaptation (Weiser *et al.*, 2020). Research could also focus on practices used by successive CEOs to harness the past and drive the future to secure corporate longevity. As a basis for this, strategy process research reveals that legacy and associated path dependencies left by predecessors affects the performance of successive CEOs (Burgelman, McKinney, and Meza, 2017). Future research could adopt an organization's successive CEOs as a unit of observation. Studies could document the unresolved challenges each CEO leaves for their successor and focus on practices successive CEOs use to resolve path dependencies and how the concomitance of these path dependencies shape the organization's adaptive capacity (Ma and Seidl, 2018).

Temporality and strategic change are inherently related as shown in research on acquisitions and alliances (Laamanen and Keil, 2008; Shi, Sun, and Prescott, 2012), divestment (Brauer, 2006; Vidal and Mitchell, 2018), and the role of headquarters in multinational corporations (Nell, Kappen, and Laamanen, 2017). These and other substantive areas could be enriched by studies combining strategy-as-practice's instantiation methodology with the progression methodology from strategy process (Kouame and Langley, 2018).

Finally, issues of temporality and spatiality connect to issues of digitalization and inclusivity. Digitalization has been predicted to drive strategizing practice toward greater fluidity and adaptability, challenging expectations about the pace of change (Schildt, 2020) and blurring further the divide between strategy formulation and implementation (Weiser *et al.*, 2020). Studying how strategy consultants help organizations use artificial intelligence and machine learning capabilities (Raisch and Krakowski, forthcoming) on business problems could produce valuable contributions.

The future is also likely to transform, or even disrupt, the roles of space and spatiality in strategizing. The boundaries between internal and external stakeholders, employees and customers, market and hierarchy are being redrawn. Organizations coauthor strategies, realize them conjointly (Mintzberg, Etzion, and Mantere, 2018), and contribute through platforms (Gawer, 2020). The boundary of an ecosystem may be a better focus to understand a pattern in a stream of action rather than the boundary of an organization (Jacobides, Cennamo, and Gawer, 2018; Snihur *et al.*, 2018). Through the trivialization of physical boundaries, expert personnel offer their contribution to employers around the globe without the cost and effort of traveling.

The trend toward open strategy and the erosion of physical space also links combinatory scholarship with understanding the potential impact of management and organizations on societal grand challenges (George *et al.*, 2016). While practices of open strategy do not themselves imply the democratization of organizational practice (Whittington, 2019), the inclusion of a larger number of stakeholders enabled by digital media is likely to challenge strategy to consider more than just economic values. Strategies spanning boundaries across several organizations and leveraging the scale and resources of networks and platforms (Jacobides *et al.*, 2018; Seidl and Werle, 2018) may be more likely to create partnerships designed to tackle grand challenges (Mintzberg *et al.*, 2018).

Actors and agency

As detailed in the following chapter, "Strategic Decision-Making and Organizational Actors," strategy process studies have allowed us to better understand how managers make decisions, and they have also focused attention on middle managers (Floyd and Wooldridge, 1992; Mantere, 2008; Wooldridge and Floyd, 1990; Wooldridge, Schmid, and Floyd, 2008). This stream of work has inspired strategy-as-practice scholars to study the roles and identities oof middle managers (Mantere, 2008) and their ability to participate (Mantere and Vaara, 2008) in strategy work. Future work could go further. Middle management represents a highly institutionalized profession, and yet there is scant research on how such macro influence relates to middle managers' identity and strategic roles. Moreover, as digitalization penetrates ever deeper into organizations, the middle managerial monitoring and control function is likely to decline. How will this affect the strategic roles? Will the lack of operational responsibility undermine the knowledge base and networks that are essential to middle managers' strategic agency (Floyd and Wooldridge, 2000)?

There is also a potential to combine insights from top and middle management focused dynamic process analysis with an understanding of "practitioners" as actors enabled or constrained by the sociohistorical practices of strategy work. For instance, further studies could focus on vertical (within CEO tenure) and horizontal (across CEO tenures) learning. Research on vertical learning could examine how higher levels of management learn from innovative initiatives undertaken by lower levels. Research on horizontal learning could examine how successive CEOs learn from the legacy of their predecessor(s). Other promising avenues include research on identity and subjectivity (Mantere and Whittington, 2020), including the question of who can be seen as a strategist. Future research could focus on how the profession of strategic management continues to develop and how specific conceptions of strategy enable or constrain how strategy-making is viewed or conducted (Whittington *et al.*, 2017).

Power and politics have played an early and important role in strategy process research (Pettigrew, 1973), and several studies include insights about the tensions and politics between top and middle managers (Burgelman, 2002; Floyd and Lane, 2000; Lechner and Floyd, 2012). A number of scholars have focused on power (Dick and Collings, 2014) and resistance in strategy-making (Alcadipani, Hassard, and Islam, 2018; Ezzamel, Willmott, and Worthington, 2001; Laine and Vaara, 2007). The digital transformation of strategy and organization can be expected to transform power relations in various ways. Indeed, organizations built on digital platforms transform many of the power-related aspects of organizing such as control and coordination, and as above, communication and physical structure. Artificial intelligence coordinates work by matching client demand with supply, rewards and punishes workers, and governs work contracts (Curchod *et al.*, 2020). Again, the influence of strategists and managers more broadly remains open in that technology may trivialize existing work roles and their associated power sources but create new ones in their place (Frey, 2019). However, while technologies may undermine existing forms of resistance because there is no arguing with an algorithm (Curchod *et al.*, 2020), all practices have the potential to be either enabling or constraining (Mantere and Whittington, 2020). It seems likely that the strategic control practices of distributed, digitalized organizations will be resisted in innovative ways (Suominen and Mantere, 2010).

Thus, there is an enormous need to describe changes in power and influence systematically and to develop theory that accounts for the effects of digitalization on strategy making. Research questions include: What new influence practices are enabled by digital media? How will these new technologies facilitate or inhibit strategic influence, change decision rights, and (dis-) empower strategic actors? Why does digitalization undermine participation in strategy making under some conditions and enable it in others?

Cognition and emotionality

Research on cognition has traditionally been an important part of strategy process research (Reger and Palmer, 1996; Walsh, 1995), as well as related streams such as microfoundations (Felin and Foss, 2005) and behavioral strategy (Gavetti, 2012). This tradition has been prominent, for example, in the research on framing contests (Kaplan, 2008; Kaplan and Henderson, 2005) and in the attention-based view (Ocasio, 1997; Ocasio and Joseph, 2005, 2008). Strategy practice research has rarely focused explicitly on cognition beyond the work on sensemaking (Balogun and Johnson, 2004) and the early research on the interplay of strategic planning and strategic action (Burgelman, 1983).

This body of work reveals a great deal of potential remaining in the analysis of cognition as distributed and mediated in and through social and socio-material practices—as in "cognition in the wild" (Hutchins, 1995). There are also examples of recent studies paving the way for combinatory research. For instance, Kaplan's (2011) work has shown how cognition develops over time with the use of PowerPoint and related practices. Attention-based research has recently been extended to include communication practices (Ocasio *et al.*, 2018).

The digital transformation is already transforming strategy practices in the executive suite with so-far unexplored consequences on managerial cognition (Fraser and Ansari, 2020; Seidl and Whittington, 2020). Schildt (2020: 9) predicts that the "systematic replacement of human judgment with algorithms [...] involves a new mindset and norms concerning the management and organization of businesses." Strategists will have far superior data for scanning the business landscape with tools to match, yet the role of the strategist may be radically diminished by those very tools. As new technologies create new work and destroy the old (Frey, 2019), practitioners of strategy are likely to be at least transformed in their skill sets and identities (Mantere and Whittington, 2020). One key cognitive capability might be the capacity to resolve paradoxes between competitive and collaborative mindsets (Karhu and Ritala, 2020) or between open strategies and proprietary ones (Whittington, 2019). Indeed, it does not take much of a thought experiment to predict that AI may dramatically transform the role of a strategist, particularly challenging the place of strategy professionals such as consultants or planners.

Alongside cognition exists emotionality. For instance, Liu and Maitlis (2014) have demonstrated that emotional dynamics are linked with particular types of strategizing processes. Vuori and Huy (2016) have shown that fear may have an impeding effect on strategy processes, and Balogun, Bartunek, and Do (2015) illustrate the role of the affective dimension of senior managers' change narratives. The emotional self-confidence to participate actively in strategy conversations is also a delicate element within efforts to foster greater inclusivity (Mantere and Whittington, 2020). Further research could examine the extent to which emotional disarray in top and middle management is cause or consequence of digitalization and/or of major crises facing organizations (Doz and Wilson, 2018; Vuori and Huy, 2016).

Language and communication

Research on language and communication has become a vibrant area of strategy practice research in recent years (Balogun *et al.*, 2014; Dalpiaz and Di Stefano, 2018; Ocasio *et al.*, 2018). We have seen a proliferation of research on the discursive (Phillips, Sewell, and Jaynes, 2008) or narrative underpinnings (Snihur *et al.*, 2018) of strategies and how strategy work is conducted in and through discussions and conversations (Spee and Jarzabkowski, 2011). The role of communication has also played a role in specific streams of strategy process research such as framing (Kaplan and Henderson, 2005) and the attention-based view (Ocasio, 1997).

Despite these advances, there is a need for a better micro-level understanding of how language is used in strategic interactions and how that use is based on discursive and rhetorical means. Snihur *et al.* (2018) identified the phenomenon of a "disruptor's gambit," where the disruptor (Marc Benioff of startup Salesforce.com) used new language—"software-as-a-service"—to communicate his strategic intent to disrupt Siebel's customer relationship management ecosystem. Benioff's successful use of this new language generated a virtuous framing-adaptation cycle, rapidly attracting new customers and partners.

Studies point to a number of important issues that warrant attention to better understand such communicative dynamics in strategic processes (Ocasio *et al.*, 2018). Research should move beyond analysis of strategic narratives per se to better understand the role of strategic storytelling (Küpers, Mantere, and Statler, 2013). Moreover, to capture attention dynamics there is a need for new kinds of discursive and rhetorical analysis that would focus on specific vocabularies and how they are (or are not) picked up by strategists or other actors. It will be important to understand transparent and inclusive forms of strategy language and communication, as too often the jargon of strategy can alienate and confuse would-be participants (Kornberger and Clegg, 2011; Mantere and Vaara, 2008). Scholars have also only recently started to focus attention on the role of the media—for instance, the mediatization of strategic decision-making and the discursive and rhetorical dynamics it involves (Ritvala, Granqvist, and Piekkari, 2020).

The discursive competences and skills of actors and their use of different types of digital media also deserve more research. Marshall McLuhan famously suggested that "the medium is the message" (McLuhan, 1964). The technology that is used for communicating shapes the meanings that are communicated (Yates and Orlikowski, 1992). This sentiment has been recognized as well. Consider the work on the semiotics of PowerPoint by Knight *et al.* (2018) who demonstrate that the graphical format of communication frames what it communicates. Future research should keep abreast with the development of new communication technologies as strategic practices (Whittington, 2019).

There also is research at the intersection of information systems research, strategic management and organization theory on the use of social media by strategists and other stakeholders (Leonardi and Vaast, 2017). Heavey *et al.* (2020) demonstrate that the strategic use of social media ranges from simple, unidirectional information sharing to dialogical interchange with stakeholders, community building, and even ideologically motivated obfuscation—a practice that Vaara and Monin (2010) label "sense-hiding." The transformation of strategy practice by digital media is not limited to managerial communication, however; it challenges practices of strategy formation as well. As strategy processes open up (Whittington, 2019), organizational boundaries between strategists and stakeholders are blurred (Schildt, 2020), and core assumptions about the nature of strategy tools are challenged (Gulbrandsen, Plesner, and Raviola, 2020).

New Methods

Strategy process and practice research has been characterized by a qualitative orientation, which has produced a wealth of longitudinal case studies as well as ethnographic analyses. As strategizing is transforming due to digitalization and parallel drivers of change, research methods need to enable the study of strategizing where and when it happens (Whittington, 2006). In recent years, we have also seen new methods enriching this area of research.

This includes a new interest in historical analysis, helping this area move beyond historical case studies by using more specific methods (Sasaki *et al.*, 2020; Vaara and Lamberg, 2016; Whittington, Cailluet, and Yakis-Douglas, 2011). Historical understanding has been a key part of strategy process studies, although not always explicitly recognized as such (Pettigrew, 1985). It has, however, remained a less important theme in strategy-as-practice research (Ericson, Melin, and Popp, 2015). Fortunately, recent papers have sketched ways in which historical approaches can be used in both strategy process and practice studies, including not only conventional historical methods but also counterfactual analysis, microhistory, and genealogy (Vaara and Lamberg, 2016). Combining historical (Gaddis, 2002) and comparative grounded theorizing (Glaser and Strauss, 1967) methods, for instance, may inspire strategy process and practice research to develop conceptual frameworks that bridge history and reductionism (Burgelman, 2011).

The field should continue to pursue methodological innovation. Video cameras are cheap and readily available, yet they are very rarely used in qualitative research. Advances have also been made with video analysis (Gylfe *et al.*, 2016; Liu and Maitlis, 2014; Wenzel and Koch, 2018), which provides new means to capture the role of socio-materiality (physical artifacts) and multimodality (e.g., video embedded in PowerPoint) in strategy work. This has the potential of enriching ethnographic analysis and opening up new perspectives on strategic communication. For an example, see Bencherki *et al.* (2020).

As strategizing migrates into digital platforms, it will leave digital trails. While traditional organizational ethnographers noted that scholars could not be everywhere at once in observing the organization (Czarniawska, 1997), this seemingly universal truth may be overturned in the age of surveillance capitalism (Vesa and Vaara, 2014). Video calls can be recorded with the press of a button, although the willingness of actors to accede to such obtrusive observation may be an obstacle. While digitalization involves new challenges for research ethics, it also opens new avenues of scholarship and unprecedented access to strategizing dynamics. We hope that future research will draw on these promising avenues. We also specifically want to encourage participant observation or action research approaches, which are still rare in this area (exceptions are Küpers *et al.*, 2013; Lüscher and Lewis, 2008), despite the fact that firsthand experience can offer a unique basis for qualitative case work.

Although quantitative research methods remain a minority in process and practice scholarship, the increasing prevalence of big data relevant to strategy formation creates space and demand for methodological innovation that is agnostic of orthodox boundaries between qualitative and quantitative research. There are many robust methods used in other areas of strategy research to draw from, which would also help cross-fertilize process and practice studies with other streams of research (Laamanen et al., 2015). This area would benefit greatly from the use of mixed methods where intensive qualitative case studies would be combined with specific statistical methods. For instance, analyses of inclusion, creativity, trust, and conflict are topics that could benefit from the combination of context-specific case studies with validated survey or experimental tools. Another particularly important approach is the use of large datasets (big data) with new methods (Simsek et al., 2019). While such analysis can take many forms, use of textual network analysis (e.g., structural topic modeling) could help to take the analysis of strategy discourses, narratives, and conversations to a new level.

Conclusion

Both strategy process research and strategy-as-practice research have come a long way since their origins, and both traditions continue to publish prolifically in the top strategy journals. Each has developed distinctive insights: strategy process research has given us a richer understanding of the emergence of strategies from throughout the organization and over extended periods of time; strategy-as-practice research has extended our understanding of the range of actors involved in strategy and the tools they draw on in their strategy work. These insights are highly complementary, both tending to take us beyond the conception of strategy as predominantly a matter of discrete choices by top managers.

Our argument in this chapter goes one step further. We call for a combinatory perspective, strategy as processes and practices, that unites the strengths of its two component traditions. Both traditions share a common interest in the complex social origins of strategy and both increasingly draw on a similar "strong process" ontology (Langley and Tsoukas, 2010) that prioritizes human activity rather than abstract organizations. Each tradition has developed effective methodologies for exploring the origins of strategy, mostly longitudinal case studies on the part of process researchers and various kinds of ethnography and discourse analysis on the part of strategy-as-practice researchers.

We suggest that the combined forces of the strategy process and strategy practice traditions can be applied to important contemporary themes, in particular temporality and spatiality, actors and agency, cognition and emotionality, and language and communication. These themes penetrate deeply into the complex realities of strategy creation. They warn strategy practitioners that strategies are not formed simply and abstractly by decision-takers in the executive suite. They give managers a pragmatic sense of who they need to enroll in the strategy process, what they can realistically expect to achieve, and where things might go wrong. Strategy is conceived as a tough kind of work, rather than a matter of abstract choice.

These themes are woven together by two increasingly important issues: the rising importance of strategy digitalization on the one hand and strategy inclusion on the other. Digitalization introduces a new fluidity to strategy processes and brings in new strategy tools, such as artificial intelligence and social media. Digitalization also potentially enhances the inclusivity of strategy, allowing greater participation in strategy-making from all around the organization and at different organizational levels. The potential acceleration of the strategy process raises new issues of temporality. The widening of participation poses intriguing questions about agency, cognition, and language. Together it is clear that digitalization and inclusivity set important challenges for strategy-making, ones that were barely conceivable at the original outset of both strategy process and strategy-as-practice research. We propose therefore that contemporary organizations provide an energizing context for strategy process and strategy-as-practice research and that many of the most compelling issues are best addressed together through the combinatory perspective of strategy as processes and practices.

Note

1. Our keyword search was carried out in the 12 highest-ranked journals publishing strategy articles. These included the *Academy of Management Journal, Academy of Management Review, Administrative Science Quarterly, Journal of Management, Journal of Management Studies, Long Range Planning, Management Science, Organization Science, Organization Studies*, the *Strategic Management Journal, Strategic Organization*, and *Strategy Science.*

References

Ahearne M., Lam SK, Kraus F. 2014. Performance impact of middle managers' adaptive strategy implementation: the role of social capital. *Strategic Management Journal* 35(1): 68–87.

Alcadipani R, Hassard J, Islam G. 2018. "I shot the sheriff": irony, sarcasm and the changing nature of workplace resistance. *Journal of Management Studies* 55(8): 1452–1487.

Andrews KR. 1971. *The Concept of Corporate Strategy*. R. D. Irwin: Homewood, IL.

Angwin D, Paroutis S, Mitson S. 2009. Connecting up strategy: are senior strategy directors a missing link? *California Management Review* 51(3): 74–94.

Ansoff HI. 1965. *Corporate Strategy: An Analytical Approach to Business Policy for Growth and Expansion*. McGraw-Hill: New York, NY.

Ateş NY, Tarakci M, Porck JP, van Knippenberg D, Groenen PJF. 2020. The dark side of visionary leadership in strategy implementation: strategic alignment, strategic consensus, and commitment. *Journal of Management* 46(5): 637–665.

Balogun J, Bartunek JM, Do B. 2015. Senior managers' sensemaking and responses to strategic change. *Organization Science* 26(4): 960–979.

Balogun J, Best K, Le J. 2015. Selling the object of strategy: how frontline workers realize strategy through their daily work. *Organization Studies* 36(10): 1285–1313.

Balogun J, Jacobs C, Jarzabkowski P, Mantere S, Vaara E. 2014. Placing strategy discourse in context: sociomateriality, sensemaking, and power. *Journal of Management Studies* 51(2): 175–201.

Balogun J, Johnson G. 2004. Organizational restructuring and middle manager sensemaking. *Academy of Management Journal* 47(4): 523–549.

Barnard CI. 1938. *The Functions of the Executive.* Harvard University Press: Cambridge, MA.

Bencherki N, Sergi V, Cooren F, Vasquez C. 2020. How strategy comes to matter: strategizing as the communicative materialization of matters of concern. *Strategic Organization.* https://doi.org/10.1177/1476127019890380.

Bower JL. 1970. *Managing the Resource Allocation Process.* Harvard Business School Press: Boston, MA.

Brauer M. 2006. What have we acquired and what should we acquire in divestiture research? A review and research agenda. *Journal of Management* 32(6): 751–785.

Burgelman RA. 1983. A model of the interaction of strategic behavior, corporate context, and the concept of strategy. *Academy of Management Review* 8(1): 61–70.

Burgelman RA. 1991. Intraorganizational ecology of strategy making and organizational adaptation: theory and field research. *Organization Science* 2: 239–262.

Burgelman RA. 2002. Strategy as vector and the inertia of coevolutionary lock-in. *Administrative Science Quarterly* 47(2): 325–357.

Burgelman RA. 2011. Bridging history and reductionism: a key role for longitudinal qualitative research. *Journal of International Business Studies* 42(5): 591–601.

Burgelman RA, Floyd SW, Laamanen T, Mantere S, Vaara E, Whittington R. 2018. Strategy processes and practices: dialogues and intersections. *Strategic Management Journal* 39(3): 531–558.

Burgelman RA, McKinney W, Meza PE. 2017. *Becoming Hewlett Packard: Why Strategic Leadership Matters.* Oxford University Press: Oxford, U.K.

Cabantous L, Gond JP, Wright A. 2018. The performativity of strategy: taking stock and moving ahead. *Long Range Planning* 51(3): 407–416.

Chandler AD Jr. 1962. *Strategy and Structure: Chapters in the History of American Industrial Enterprise.* MIT Press: Cambridge, MA.

Chia R. 1997. Essai: thirty years on: from organizational structures to the organization of thought. *Organization Studies* 18(4): 685–707.

Comi A, Whyte J. 2018. Future making and visual artefacts: an ethnographic study of a design project. *Organization Studies* 39(8): 1055–1083.

Curchod C, Patriotta G, Cohen L, Neysen N. 2020. Working for an algorithm: power asymmetries and agency in online work settings. *Administrative Science Quarterly* 65(3): 644–676.

Cyert RM, March JG. 1963. *A Behavioral Theory of the Firm.* Prentice Hall: Englewood Cliffs, NJ.

Czarniawska B. 1997. *Narrating the Organization: Dramas of Institutional Identity.* University of Chicago Press: Chicago, IL.

Dalpiaz E, Di Stefano G. 2018. A universe of stories: mobilizing narrative practices during transformative change. *Strategic Management Journal* 39(3): 664–696.

Dameron S, Lê JK, LeBaron C. 2015. Materializing strategy and strategizing material: why matter matters. *British Journal of Management* 26(S1): S1–S12.

Dick P, Collings DG. 2014. Discipline and punish? Strategy discourse, senior manager subjectivity and contradictory power effects. *Human Relations* 67(12): 1513–1536.

Dobusch L, Dobusch L, Muller-Seitz G. 2019. Closing for the benefit of openness? The case of Wikimedia's open strategy process. *Organization Studies* 40(3): 343–370.

Doz Y, Wilson K. 2018. *Ringtone: Exploring the Rise and Fall of Nokia in Mobile Phones*. Oxford University Press: New York, NY.

Ericson M, Melin L, Popp A. 2015. Studying strategy as practice through historical methods. In *Cambridge Handbook of Strategy as Practice*, Golsorkhi D, Rouleau L, Seidl D, Vaara E. (eds). Cambridge University Press: Cambridge, U.K.; 326–343.

Ezzamel M, Willmott H, Worthington F. 2001. Power, control and resistance in "the factory that time forgot." *Journal of Management Studies* **38**(8): 1053–1079.

Felin T, Foss NJ. 2005. Strategic organization: a field in search of micro-foundations. *Strategic Organization* **3**(4): 441–455.

Floyd SW, Lane PJ. 2000. Strategizing throughout the organization: managing role conflict in strategic renewal. *Academy of Management Review* **25**(1): 154–177.

Floyd SW, Wooldridge B. 1992. Middle management involvement in strategy and its association with strategy type—a research note. *Strategic Management Journal* **13**: 153–167.

Floyd SW, Wooldridge B. 2000. *Building Strategy from the Middle: Reconceptualizing Strategy Process*. Sage: Thousand Oaks, CA.

Fraser J, Ansari S. 2020. Pluralist perspectives and diverse responses: exploring multiplexed framing in incumbent responses to digital disruption. *Long Range Planning*: https://doi.org/10.1016/j.lrp.2020.102016.

Frey CB. 2019. *The Technology Trap: Capital, Labor, and Power in the Age of Automation*. Princeton University Press: Princeton, NJ.

Gabaldon P, Kanadli SB, Bankewitz M. 2018. How does job-related diversity affect boards' strategic participation? An information-processing approach. *Long Range Planning* **51**(6): 937–952.

Gaddis JL. 2002. *The Landscape of History: How Historians Map the Past*. Oxford University Press: Oxford, U.K.

Gavetti G. 2012. Toward a behavioral theory of strategy. *Organization Science* **23**(1): 267–285.

Gawer A. 2020. Digital platforms' boundaries: the interplay of firm scope, platform sides, and digital interfaces. *Long Range Planning*. https://doi.org/10.1016/j.lrp.2020.102045.

Geletkanycz MA, Hambrick DC. 1997. The external ties of top executives: implications for strategic choice and performance. *Administrative Science Quarterly* **42**(4): 654–681.

George G, Howard-Grenville J, Joshi A, Tihanyi L. 2016. Understanding and tackling societal grand challenges through management research. *Academy of Management Journal* **59**(6): 1880–1895.

Glaser BG, Strauss AL. 1967. *The Discovery of Grounded Theory: Strategies for Qualitative Research*. Aldine: New York, NY.

Gond JP, Cabantous L, Krikorian F. 2018. How do things become strategic? "Strategifying" corporate social responsibility. *Strategic Organization* **16**(3): 241–272.

Gulbrandsen IT, Plesner U, Raviola E. 2020. New media and strategy research: towards a relational agency approach. *International Journal of Management Reviews* **22**(1): 33–52.

Gylfe P, Franck H, LeBaron C, Mantere S. 2016. Video methods in strategy research: focusing on embodied cognition. *Strategic Management Journal* **37**(1): 133–148.

Hambrick DC, Lovelace JB. 2018. The role of executive symbolism in advancing new strategic themes in organizations: a social influence perspective. *Academy of Management Review* **43**(1): 110–131.

Hautz J, Seidl D, Whittington R. 2017. Open strategy: dimensions, dilemmas, dynamics. *Long Range Planning* **50**(3): 298–309.

Heavey C, Simsek Z, Kyprianou C, Risius M. 2020. How do strategic leaders engage with social media? A theoretical framework for research and practice. *Strategic Management Journal* **41**(8): 1490–1527.

Hitt MA, Tyler BB. 1991. Strategic decision models: integrating different perspectives. *Strategic Management Journal* **12**(5): 327–351.

Holstein J, Starkey K, Wright M. 2018. Strategy and narrative in higher education. *Strategic Organization* 16(1): 61–91.

Hutchins E. 1995. *Cognition in the Wild*. MIT Press: Cambridge, MA.

Hutzschenreuter T, Kleindienst I. 2006. Strategy-process research: what have we learned and what is still to be explored. *Journal of Management* 32(5): 673–720.

Jacobides MG, Cennamo C, Gawer A. 2018. Towards a theory of ecosystems. *Strategic Management Journal* 39(8): 2255–2276.

Jalonen K, Schildt H, Vaara E. 2018. Strategic concepts as micro-level tools in strategic sensemaking. *Strategic Management Journal* 39(10): 2794–2826.

Jarzabkowski P. 2004. Strategy as practice: recursiveness, adaptation, and practices-in-use. *Organization Studies* 25(4): 529–560.

Jarzabkowski P, Bednarek R. 2018. Toward a social practice theory of relational competing. *Strategic Management Journal* 39(3): 794–829.

Jarzabkowski P, Kaplan S. 2015. Strategy tools-in-use: a framework for understanding "technologies of rationality" in practice. *Strategic Management Journal* 36(4): 537–558.

Jarzabkowski P, Seidl D. 2008. The role of meetings in the social practice of strategy. *Organization Studies* 29(11): 1391–1426.

Jarzabkowski P, Spee AP. 2009. Strategy-as-practice: a review and future directions for the field. *International Journal of Management Reviews* 11(1): 69–95.

Johnson G, Melin L, Whittington R. 2003. Micro strategy and strategizing: towards an activity-based view—guest editors' introduction. *Journal of Management Studies* 40(1): 3–22.

Johnson G, Prashantham S, Floyd SW, Bourque N. 2010. The ritualization of strategy workshops. *Organization Studies* 31(12): 1589–1618.

Kannan-Narasimhan R, Lawrence BS. 2018. How innovators reframe resources in the strategy-making process to gain innovation adoption. *Strategic Management Journal* 39(3): 720–758.

Kaplan S. 2008. Framing contests: strategy making under uncertainty. *Organization Science* 19(5): 729–752.

Kaplan S. 2011. Strategy and PowerPoint: an inquiry into the epistemic culture and machinery of strategy making. *Organization Science* 22(2): 320–346.

Kaplan S, Henderson R. 2005. Inertia and incentives: bridging organizational economics and organizational theory. *Organization Science* 16(5): 509–521.

Karhu K, Ritala P. 2020. Slicing the cake without baking it: opportunistic platform entry strategies in digital markets. *Long Range Planning*. https://doi.org/10.1016/j.lrp.2020.101988.

Knight E, Paroutis S, Heracleous L. 2018. The power of PowerPoint: a visual perspective on meaning making in strategy. *Strategic Management Journal* 39(3): 894–921.

Kornberger M, Clegg S. 2011. Strategy as performative practice: the case of Sydney 2030. *Strategic Organization* 9(2): 136–162.

Kouame S, Langley A. 2018. Relating microprocesses to macro-outcomes in qualitative strategy process and practice research. *Strategic Management Journal* 39(3): 559–581.

Kunisch S, Bartunek J, Mueller J, Huy Q. 2017. Time in strategic change research. *Academy of Management Annals* 11(2): 1005–1064.

Küpers W, Mantere S, Statler M. 2013. Strategy as storytelling: a phenomenological collaboration. *Journal of Management Inquiry* 22(1): 83–100.

Laamanen T, Keil T. 2008. Performance of serial acquirers: toward an acquisition program perspective. *Strategic Management Journal* 29(6): 663–672.

Laamanen T, Maula M, Kajanto M, Kunnas P. 2018. The role of cognitive load in effective strategic issue management. *Long Range Planning* 51(4): 625–639.

Laamanen T, Reuter E, Schimmer M, Ueberbacher F, Guerra XW. 2015. Quantitative methods in strategy-as-practice research. In *Cambridge Handbook of Strategy as Practice*, Golsorkhi D, Seidl D, Vaara E, Rouleau L. (eds). 2nd edition. Cambridge University Press: Cambridge, U.K.; 520–544.

Laine PM, Vaara E. 2007. Struggling over subjectivity: a discursive analysis of strategic development in an engineering group. *Human Relations* 60(1): 29–58.

Langley A. 1999. Strategies for theorizing from process data. *Academy of Management Review* 24(4): 691–710.

Langley A, Smallman C, Tsoukas H, Van de Ven AH. 2013. Process studies of change in organization and management: unveiling temporality, activity, and flow. *Academy of Management Journal* 56(1): 1–13.

Langley A, Tsoukas H. 2010. Introducing perspectives on process organization studies. In *Process, Sensemaking, and Organizing*, Hernes T, Maitlis S (eds). Oxford University Press: Oxford, U.K.; 673–699.

Lechner C, Floyd SW. 2012. Group influence activities and the performance of strategic initiatives. *Strategic Management Journal* 33(5): 478–495.

Leonardi PM, Vaast E. 2017. Social media and their affordances for organizing: a review and agenda for research. *Academy of Management Annals* 11(1): 150–188.

Liu F, Maitlis S. 2014. Emotional dynamics and strategizing processes: a study of strategic conversations in top team meetings. *Journal of Management Studies* 51(2): 202–234.

Lorange P. 1980. *Corporate Planning: An Executive Viewpoint*. Prentice Hall: Englewood Cliffs, NJ.

Luoma J, Laamanen T, Lamberg J-A. 2020. Toward a routine-based view of interfirm rivalry. *Strategic Organization*. https://doi.org/10.1177/1476127020931359.

Lüscher LS, Lewis MW. 2008. Organizational change and managerial sensemaking: working through paradox. *Academy of Management Journal* 51(2): 221–240.

Ma SH, Seidl D. 2018. New CEOs and their collaborators: divergence and convergence between the strategic leadership constellation and the top management team. *Strategic Management Journal* 39(3): 606–638.

Mantere S. 2008. Role expectations and middle manager strategic agency. *Journal of Management Studies* 45(2): 294–316.

Mantere S, Vaara E. 2008. On the problem of participation in strategy: a critical discursive perspective. *Organization Science* 19(2): 341–358.

Mantere S, Whittington R. 2020. Becoming a strategist: the roles of strategy discourse and ontological security in managerial identity work. *Strategic Organization*. https://doi.org/10.1177/1476127020908781.

McLuhan M. 1964. *Understanding Media: The Extensions of Man*. McGraw-Hill: New York, NY.

Miller CC, McKee RA. 2020. Decision comprehensiveness and the outcomes of firms: reinterpreting and extending a recent meta-analysis. *Strategic Organization*. https://doi.org/10.1177/1476127020927483.

Mintzberg H. 1978. Patterns in strategy formation. *Management Science* 24: 934–948.

Mintzberg H, Etzion D, Mantere S. 2018. Worldly strategy for the global climate. *Stanford Social Innovation Review* 16(4): 42–47.

Mintzberg H, Waters JA. 1985. Of strategies, deliberate and emergent. *Strategic Management Journal* 6(3): 257–272.

Mirabeau L, Maguire S. 2014. From autonomous strategic behavior to emergent strategy. *Strategic Management Journal* 35(8): 1202–1229.

Mirabeau L, Maguire S, Hardy C. 2018. Bridging practice and process research to study transient manifestations of strategy. *Strategic Management Journal* 39(3): 582–605.

Morton J, Wilson AD, Cooke L. 2020. The digital work of strategists: using open strategy for organizational transformation. *Journal of Strategic Information Systems* 29(2): 101613.

Neeley TB, Leonardi PM. 2018. Enacting knowledge strategy through social media: passable trust and the paradox of nonwork interactions. *Strategic Management Journal* 39(3): 922–946.

Nell PC, Kappen P, Laamanen T. 2017. Reconceptualising hierarchies: the disaggregation and dispersion of headquarters in multinational corporations. *Journal of Management Studies* 54(8): 1121–1143.

Ocasio W. 1997. Towards an attention-based view of the firm. *Strategic Management Journal* 18: 187–206.

Ocasio W, Joseph J. 2005. An attention-based theory of strategy formulation: linking micro- and macroperspectives in strategy process. In *Strategy Process* (Advances in Strategic Management, Vol. 22), Szulanski G, Porac JF, Doz Y (eds). JAI Press / Emerald Publishing Group Limited, Bingley, U.K.; 39–61.

Ocasio W, Joseph J. 2008. Rise and fall—or transformation? The evolution of strategic planning at the general electric company, 1940–2006. *Long Range Planning* 41(3): 248–272.

Ocasio W, Laamanen T, Vaara E. 2018. Communication and attention dynamics: an attention-based view of strategic change. *Strategic Management Journal* 39(1): 155–167.

Palli P. 2018. Ascribing materiality and agency to strategy in interaction: a language-based approach to the material agency of strategy. *Long Range Planning* 51(3): 436–450.

Paroutis S, Heracleous L. 2013. Discourse revisited: dimensions and employment of first-order strategy discourse during institutional adoption. *Strategic Management Journal* 34(8): 935–956.

Pettigrew A. 1973. *The Politics of Organizational Decision-Making*. Tavistock: London, U.K.

Pettigrew A. 1985. *The Awakening Giant. Continuity and Changes in Imperial Chemical Industries*. Basil Blackwell: Oxford, U.K.

Pettigrew AM. 1992. The character and significance of strategy process research. *Strategic Management Journal* 13(S2): 5–16.

Pettigrew AM. 2012. Context and action in the transformation of the firm: a reprise. *Journal of Management Studies* 49(7): 1304–1328.

Phillips N, Sewell G, Jaynes S. 2008. Applying critical discourse analysis in strategic management research. *Organizational Research Methods* 11(4): 770–789.

Porck JP, van Knippenberg D, Tarakci M, Ates NY, Groenen PJF, de Haas M. 2020. Do group and organizational identification help or hurt intergroup strategic consensus? *Journal of Management* 46(2): 234–260.

Pratap S, Saha B. 2018. Evolving efficacy of managerial capital, contesting managerial practices, and the process of strategic renewal. *Strategic Management Journal* 39(3): 759–793.

Raisch S, Krakowski S. Forthcoming. Artificial intelligence and management: the automation-augmentation paradox. *Academy of Management Review*.

Rasche A, Chia R. 2009. Researching strategy practices: a genealogical social theory perspective. *Organization Studies* 30(7): 713–734.

Reger RK, Palmer TB. 1996. Managerial categorization of competitors: using old maps to navigate new environments. *Organization Science* 7(1): 22–39.

Ritvala T, Granqvist N, Piekkari R. 2021. A processual view of organizational stigmatization in foreign market entry: the failure of Guggenheim Helsinki. *Journal of International Business Studies* 52: 282–305.

Samra-Fredericks D. 2003. Strategizing as lived experience and strategists' everyday efforts to shape strategic direction. *Journal of Management Studies* 40(1): 141–174.

Sasaki I, Kotlar J, Ravasi D, Vaara E. 2020. Dealing with revered past: historical identity statements and strategic change in Japanese family firms. *Strategic Management Journal* 41(3): 590–623.

Schildt H. 2020. *The Data Imperative: How Digitalization is Reshaping Management, Organizing, and Work*. Oxford University Press: Oxford, U.K.

Schneider A, Bullinger B, Brandl J. 2020. Resourcing under tensions: how frontline employees create resources to balance paradoxical tensions. *Organization Studies*. https://doi.org/10.1177/0170840620926825.

Schubert T, Tavassoli S. 2020. Product innovation and educational diversity in top and middle management teams. *Academy of Management Journal* 63(1): 272–294.

Schwenk CR. 1984. Cognitive simplification processes in strategic decision-making. *Strategic Management Journal* 5(2): 111–128.

Seidl D, Werle F. 2018. Inter-organizational sensemaking in the face of strategic meta-problems: requisite variety and dynamics of participation. *Strategic Management Journal* 39(3): 830–858.

Seidl D, Whittington R. 2014. Enlarging the strategy-as-practice research agenda: towards taller and flatter ontologies. *Organization Studies* 35(10): 1407–1421.

Seidl D, Whittington R. 2020. How crisis reveals the structures of practices. *Journal of Management Studies*. https://doi.org/10.1111/joms.12650.

Shi WL, Sun J, Prescott JE. 2012. A temporal perspective of merger and acquisition and strategic alliance initiatives: review and future direction. *Journal of Management* 38(1): 164–209.

Simon HA. 1957. *Administrative Behavior*. 2nd edition. Macmillan: New York, NY.

Simsek Z, Heavey C, Fox BC. 2018. Interfaces of strategic leaders: a conceptual framework, review, and research agenda. *Journal of Management* 44(1): 280–324.

Simsek Z, Vaara E, Paruchuri S, Nadkarni S, Shaw JD. 2019. New ways of seeing big data. *Academy of Management Journal* 62(4): 971–978.

Snihur Y, Thomas LDW, Burgelman RA. 2018. An ecosystem-level process model of business model disruption: the disruptor's gambit. *Journal of Management Studies* 55(7): 1278–1316.

Spee AP, Jarzabkowski P. 2011. Strategic planning as communicative process. *Organization Studies* 32(9): 1217–1245.

Suominen K, Mantere S. 2010. Consuming strategy: the art and practice of managers everyday strategy usage. *Advances in Strategic Management* 27: 211–245.

Tarakci M, Ates NY, Floyd SW, Ahn Y, Wooldridge B. 2018. Performance feedback and middle managers' divergent strategic behavior: the roles of social comparisons and organizational identification. *Strategic Management Journal* 39(4): 1139–1162.

Vaara E, Lamberg J-A. 2016. Taking historical embeddedness seriously: three historical approaches to advance strategy process and practice research. *Academy of Management Review* 41(4): 633–657.

Vaara E, Monin P. 2010. A recursive perspective on discursive legitimation and organizational action in mergers and acquisitions. *Organization Science* 21(1): 3–22.

Vaara E, Whittington R. 2012. Strategy-as-practice: taking social practices seriously. *Academy of Management Annals* 6: 285–336.

van den Ende L, van Marrewijk A. 2018. The point of no return: ritual performance and strategy making in project organizations. *Long Range Planning* 51(3): 451–462.

Van den Steen E. 2018. Strategy and the strategist: how it matters who develops the strategy. *Management Science* 64(10): 4533–4551.

Vesa M, Vaara E. 2014. Strategic ethnography 2.0: four methods for advancing strategy process and practice research. *Strategic Organization* 12(4): 288–298.

Vidal E, Mitchell W. 2018. Virtuous or vicious cycles? The role of divestitures as a complementary Penrose effect within resource-based theory. *Strategic Management Journal* 39(1): 131–154.

Vogus TJ, Rerup C. 2018. Sweating the "small stuff": high-reliability organizing as a foundation for sustained superior performance. *Strategic Organization* 16(2): 227–238.

Vuori N, Vuori TO, Huy QN. 2018. Emotional practices: how masking negative emotions impacts the post-acquisition integration process. *Strategic Management Journal* 39(3): 859–893.

Vuori TO, Huy QN. 2016. Distributed attention and shared emotions in the innovation process: how Nokia lost the smartphone battle. *Administrative Science Quarterly* 61(1): 9–51.

Vuorinen T, Hakala H, Kohtamaki M, Uusitalo K. 2018. Mapping the landscape of strategy tools: a review on strategy tools published in leading journals within the past 25 years. *Long Range Planning* 51(4): 586–605.

Walsh JP. 1995. Managerial and organizational cognition—notes from a trip down memory lane. *Organization Science* 6(3): 280–321.

Weiser A-K. 2020. The role of substantive actions in sensemaking during strategic change. *Journal of Management Studies*. https://doi.org/10.1111/joms.12621.

Weiser A-K, Jarzabkowski P, Laamanen T. 2020. Completing the adaptive turn: an integrative view of strategy implementation. *Academy of Management Annals* 14(2): 969–1031.

Wenzel M, Koch J. 2018. Strategy as staged performance: a critical discursive perspective on keynote speeches as a genre of strategic communication. *Strategic Management Journal* 39(3): 639–663.

Whittington R. 1996. Strategy as practice. *Long Range Planning* 29(5): 731–735.

Whittington R. 2004. Strategy after modernism: recovering practice. *European Management Review* 1(1): 62–68.

Whittington R. 2006. Completing the practice turn in strategy research. *Organization Studies* 27(5): 613–634.

Whittington R. 2015. The massification of strategy. *British Journal of Management* 26(S1): S13–S16.

Whittington R. 2019. *Opening Strategy: Professional Strategists and Practice Change, 1960 to Today*. Oxford University Press: Oxford, U.K.

Whittington R, Cailluet L, Yakis-Douglas B. 2011. Opening strategy: evolution of a precarious profession. *British Journal of Management* 22(3): 531–544.

Whittington R, Yakis-Douglas B, Ahn K, Cailluet L. 2017. Strategic planners in more turbulent times: the changing job characteristics of strategy professionals, 1960–2003. *Long Range Planning* 50(1): 108–119.

Whittle A, Gilchrist A, Mueller F, Lenney P. 2020. The art of stage-craft: a dramaturgical perspective on strategic change. *Strategic Organization*. https://doi.org/10.1177/1476127020914225.

Wolf C, Floyd SW. 2017. Strategic planning research: toward a theory-driven agenda. *Journal of Management* 43(6): 1754–1788.

Wooldridge B, Floyd SW. 1990. The strategy process, middle management involvement, and organizational performance. *Strategic Management Journal* 11(3): 231–241.

Wooldridge B, Schmid T, Floyd SW. 2008. The middle management perspective on strategy process: contributions, synthesis, and future research. *Journal of Management* 34(6): 1190–1221.

Yates J, Orlikowski WJ. 1992. Genres of organizational communication: a structurational approach to studying communication and media. *Academy of Management Review* 17(2): 299–326.

Zilber TB. 2020. The methodology/theory interface: ethnography and the microfoundations of institutions. *Organization Theory* 1(2): 2631787720919439.

9.1

STRATEGIC DECISION-MAKING AND ORGANIZATIONAL ACTORS

Rhonda K. Reger and Michael D. Pfarrer

After a four-year wait, Apple on Wednesday announced an updated version of its smaller and lower priced iPhone SE model. (Pressman, 2020)

The business press, market watchers, and many strategic management scholars personify organizations, giving them agency to make decisions, such as in the chapter-opening quote. Strategic management researchers who are interested in how decisions are made in and around organizations, however, do not take such reification for granted. Instead, to understand organizational actions and performance, they focus on *who* influences *whom* and *how* and *why* organizations make specific strategic decisions. This branch of strategic management—which has come to be known alternatively as the sociocognitive perspective (Pfarrer *et al.*, 2019), behavioral strategy (Powell, Lovallo, and Fox, 2011), or the microfoundations of strategy (Felin, Foss, and Ployhart, 2015)—investigates how organizational actors' cognition, attention, motivation, personality, and other individual factors influence organizational actions and outcomes.

This perspective initially examined how the cognitive limitations of managerial actors within organizations biased their decisions away from the all-knowing, dispassionate rational actor assumptions of classical microeconomics (Cyert and March, 1963/1992; March and Simon, 1958). Within that tradition, decision-makers were initially viewed as intendedly rational, but with limited information processing capabilities and who advanced self-interested agendas that prevented optimally beneficial decisions for their organizations. While many working within the sociocognitive perspective still adopt those assumptions, many other sociocognitive researchers have embraced new forms of rationality, suggesting that human and organizational limits on cognition and attention can result in superior and more creative decisions than predicted by traditional economic rationality assumptions (Alvarez and Barney, 2007; Mintzberg, 1973; Weick, 1995).

Recent sociocognitive strategy research has also suggested that to understand strategic decision-making processes and outcomes more fully, both internal and external strategic actors beyond executives must be considered (see reviews by Huff and Reger, 1987; Rindova, Reger, and Dalpiaz, 2012; Wooldridge and Cowden, 2020). Strategic actors are broadly defined and diverse (Bundy and Pfarrer, 2015; Freeman, 2010). They include individuals and teams inside organizations such as CEOs and other executives, top management teams, middle managers, and boundary spanners such as boards of directors, as well as those outside of the organization's boundaries such as shareholders, customers, suppliers, information intermediaries, regulators, governments, stakeholders, and communities.

For example, predating the Apple new product announcement quoted earlier, potential customers, analysts, and journalists had long requested a lower-priced iPhone, putting pressure on Apple's top management team and board of directors to reconsider the firm's strategy. We know from research on strategic decision-making that such a decision would be hotly debated internally by middle managers (Floyd and Wooldridge, 1992) and the top management team (Cannella, Finkelstein, and Hambrick, 2008; Hambrick and Mason, 1984), as well as by the board of directors (Forbes and Milliken, 1999). Interested external actors, including the media, investors, activists, and consumer groups, might also seek to influence the nature and timing of such a strategic decision (Pfarrer, Pollock, and Rindova, 2010). Taken together, learning more about how views from disparate strategic actors lead to an organization's strategic actions is of paramount importance to scholars interested in the strategic decision-making processes that affect organizational outcomes.

This chapter briefly reviews the broad contours of this literature and its major contributions, with a focus on the current state of research and fruitful future research directions. The sociocognitive perspective on organizational decision-making (Pfarrer et al., 2019) focuses on how strategic actors (both internal and external to the organization) perceive, interpret, and react to create an organization's actions, performance, and other outcomes (Pfarrer et al., 2019). The "sociocognitive perspective, while varied in its theoretical framings, focuses on the roles of managers' and observers' attention; the bounded rationality of their cognitions, intuitions, and emotions; and the use of biases and heuristics to socially construct 'perceptual answers' to traditional strategic management questions about how firms obtain and sustain competitive advantage" (Rindova et al., 2012: 147).

A Brief Review of Foundational and Current Research

Today's sociocognitive strategy perspective can trace its origins to what is known as the Carnegie School (now, Carnegie Mellon University), whose researchers spawned the behavioral theory of the firm (Cyert and March, 1963/1992; March and Simon, 1958). Other important influences include the "cognitive revolution" in psychology (Barsalou, 2014), especially in social psychology (Fiske and Taylor, 2013), and behavioral decision-making (Tversky and Kahneman, 1992). Much of the early sociocognitive strategy work examined decision biases stemming from individuals' limited attention, memory, and cognitive capacity (Barr, Stimpert, and Huff, 1992; Duhaime and Schwenk, 1985) as well as ways in which groups mitigate or exacerbate these biases (Bazerman and Moore, 1994).

However, early work also focused on the distinct value that executives bring to their firms (Andrews, 1971; Mintzberg, 1973), spawning upper echelons theory (Hambrick and Mason, 1984), which has evolved and expanded into strategic leadership theory and encompasses not only top management teams but also boards of directors (Cannella et al., 2008). Likewise, managerial sensemaking (Weick, 1995) and sensegiving (Gioia and Chittipeddi, 1991) theories suggest that executives play prominent roles in framing and creating reality for themselves and others in and around their organizations. The resource-based view of the firm (Penrose, 1959; Barney, 1991) provides further theoretical underpinnings to the sociocognitive perspective by suggesting that managers' and firms' distinct ways of thinking may be sources of sustainable competitive advantages or disadvantages.[1]

Finally, early work on the external control of organizations (Pfeffer and Salancik, 1978/2003) foreshadowed and continues to influence today's work on social movements (King and Soule, 2007; Weber and King, 2014), organizational stakeholders (Freeman et al., 2010), information infomediaries (Ravasi et al., 2018; Westphal and Deephouse, 2011), and social evaluations (Bundy and Pfarrer, 2015). These streams of research conceptualize environments that affect organizations not in terms of abstract constructs like munificence and uncertainty (Dess and Beard, 1984), but rather in terms of individuals, groups, and other organizations. These actors have their own agendas and wherewithal to influence the actions of others, and they seek to influence the focal organization's decisions (Burgelman et al., 2018). From a sociocognitive perspective, the organization's environment is a social one, filled with sentient actors, not a physical one determined by economic axioms and the invisible hands of abstract markets.

Recognizing that external evaluators of organizations are influenced both by their own characteristics, experiences, and mental models as well as by the decisions and actions emanating from organizations, scholars have begun to consider this interplay of perceiver and perceived. For example, studies have contrasted various external stakeholder groups' reactions to high-reputation organizations' behaviors compared to their reactions to other types of organizations, including celebrity organizations (Pfarrer et al., 2010) and organizations with lower levels of reputation (Haleblian, Pfarrer, and Kiley, 2017; Zavyalova et al., 2012; Zavyalova et al., 2016).

Beyond examining individuals and groups inside and outside of organizations, sociocognitive researchers have also given attention to how organizational and supraorganizational cultures, systems, and structures, such as reward and communication systems, affect the scope of organizational actors' attention, awareness, motivation, and capability to utilize relevant information in strategic decision-making (Chen, Su, and Tsai, 2007; Daft and Weick, 1984; Ocasio, 1997; Reger and Huff, 1993). Others have examined the diffusion and evolution of societal and business practices across organizations, motivated by social and economic incentives (Busenbark *et al.*, 2019; Kennedy and Fiss, 2009; Maguire and Hardy, 2009).

Unlike more economically oriented perspectives that view organizational and environmental characteristics as natural outcomes of technological, economic, and other imperatives, a sociocognitive perspective makes no claims about optimality, natural selection, or equilibrium. Rather, from a sociocognitive perspective, an industry's structure is the result of motivated actions by diverse human actors. Current work continues to push the boundaries on which individual differences matter, such as examining how differences in regulatory focus among executives affect their motivation to pursue an acquisition strategy (Gamache *et al.*, 2015; Johnson *et al.*, 2015).

While motivation of actors is taken for granted within much of strategic management research (i.e., that all actors are self-interested to maximize returns), a sociocognitive perspective allows researchers to explore a range of motivations (Andrews, 1971; Livengood and Reger, 2010). Many sociocognitive strategists assume that these actors act rationally with the goal of improving their own situation, but often fall short, while others attribute more varied and even altruistic motives to at least some strategic actors (Haynes, Josefy, and Hitt, 2015; Schulze, Lubatkin, and Dino, 2002). Allowing motivation to vary across organizational actors permits sociocognitive researchers to explore additional reasons why actors hold different perceptions, take different actions, and achieve different performance levels. Certainly, there is much room for future work that examines the diversity of motivations and their effects on firm actions and outcomes. For instance, under what conditions do firms that pursue a triple-bottom-line strategy outperform firms that focus on maximizing shareholder wealth? Indeed, within the sociocognitive perspective, the very meaning of "outperform" can be contested, not only in terms of time frame, but also in terms of how performance is measured.

Following the practice in law to grant "personhood" to organizations, some sociocognitive researchers also apply agentic concepts such as motivation, goals, personality, preferences, and cognition at the organizational and even supraorganizational level (Daft and Weick, 1984; see also Walsh [1995] for an early comprehensive review and Burgelman *et al.* [2018] for a more recent review). Research from this perspective might contrast the cognitions and actions of Apple with those of Microsoft, or of the software industry compared to the biotechnology industry, or, implicitly ascribing morality to organizations, seek to explain why "good" firms do bad things (Mishina *et al.*, 2010).

All of the topics that we have touched upon so far in this chapter continue to attract research attention. The sociocognitive perspective continues to contribute important insights across the entire strategic management domain. Clearly, we have only begun to understand the implications of relaxing neoclassical microeconomic assumptions about individuals, groups, and organizations. Next, we focus on a few areas of research that we view as especially promising.

Promising Directions for Future Research

Taking a sociocognitive perspective seriously means that we believe the future of our field is shaped not only by those who have pioneered and currently work in the area, but also by daring newcomers. To those who wish to push the boundaries of socio-cognitive research, we find these three areas especially interesting and promising: (1) communication-based research on organizational actors; (2) alternative rationalities, especially those that focus on imagination, creativity, and vision; and (3) the digital revolution's effect on the strategic management process.

Communication among organizational actors

Whereas early work focused primarily on the "cognitive" end of sociocognitive approaches, newer work has begun to focus on the "socio" aspects of decision-making processes. The shift of focus from cognition of discrete actors to communications among disparate ones opens new investigations into many important phenomena. Notably, the shift to focusing on communications among actors has brought a number of new, interesting theoretical perspectives.

For instance, sociocognitive strategy theory is beginning to be influenced by many strands of communications-related work as part of the "linguistic turn in organizational research" (Vaara, 2010: 29), including discourse (Phillips, Lawrence, and Hardy, 2004; Kahl and Grodal, 2016; Paroutis and Heracleous, 2013), rhetoric (Green, 2004; Sinha *et al.*, 2020), conversation (Ford and Ford, 1995), narrative (Dalpiaz and Di Stefano, 2018; Greenstein, 2017), video (Gylfe *et al.*, 2016), multimodal (Meyer *et al.*, 2013), and impression management theories and methods (Busenbark, Lange, and Certo, 2017; Elsbach and Sutton, 1992; Whittington, Yakis-Douglas, and Ahn, 2016). While there are significant differences across sociocognitive research in their use of communication theories, they all explore the processes through which strategic actors use language to influence other actors (Ocasio, Laamanen, and Vaara, 2018).

Two recent studies suggest the promise of integrating communications theories into sociocognitive research. First, Cole and Chandler (2019) examine the symbolic competitive actions taken by Westinghouse and Edison to win constituents' support. Moving beyond the typical impression management study that examines how firms address specific threats emanating from a specific event, the authors chronicle and theorize about how two competitors strategically waged multiyear impression management campaigns to gain competitive advantage. Coining a new phrase that brings impression management solidly within the scope of strategic management, they define *competitive impression management* as "activity by a firm or its employees that is intended to alter the perceptions of a competing firm or its offerings in the eyes of a common audience" (Cole and Chandler, 2019: 1020). Future research could expand on this work to explore the claims and actions that sway modern audiences to support new firms and that aid in revitalization attempts by mature firms.

Second, Harmon (2019) utilizes rhetorical and sentiment analysis to uncover arguments and emotions in Federal Reserve Chair speeches and their effects on financial markets. He found a negative effect when the Fed Chair made taken-for-granted assumptions explicit, which was moderated when the speech provided an overall positive tone. Further, greater fear about the economy expressed in the media exacerbated the negative effect of the Fed leader's rhetoric on the market. This paper advances communications and impression management research by using rhetorical theory to dive deeply into the content and emotional tone of the regulatory leader's speeches and to provide analysis of a nuanced negative emotion among the audience, fear. In contrast, prior studies have generally utilized general measures of media positivity and negativity (Love, Lim, and Bednar, 2017; Pollock and Rindova, 2003). This and related work opens the door for more sophisticated content analyses of corporate and stakeholders' persuasive communications, including finer-grained examinations of specific emotions and rhetorical strategies.

Other exemplars of sociocognitive research that has applied communication-based theories to important issues in strategic management include work focusing on vague and concrete language in earnings calls (Guo, Yu, and Gimeno, 2017; Pan *et al.*, 2018), gestures and figurative language in entrepreneurial pitches (Clarke, Cornelissen, and Healey, 2019), and executives' use of metaphors to influence securities analysts and journalists (König *et al.*, 2018). This work has only begun to scratch the surface in understanding how managers and entrepreneurs influence stakeholders, providing opportunities to study which forms of communications have positive effects on different types of audiences and under what conditions.

Advances in content analysis (Duriau, Reger, and Pfarrer, 2007) should allow even greater understanding of the role of communication strategies in strategic decision processes. Using computerized content analysis—either dictionary-based or machine learning approaches—to analyze the voluminous corpus of digital records from and about organizations provides almost unlimited possibilities (Choudhury *et al.*, 2019). Data availability that is growing exponentially also allows for the study of previously difficult- or impossible-to-study phenomena. For example, digital records of subsidiaries' strategic decision processes provide fresh data sources to explore enduring questions relating to corporate strategy in multinational corporations.

We also expect future scholars will leverage advances in multimodal theorizing and analysis of video and pictures to better understand nonverbal influence (e.g., Meyer *et al.*, 2013). Constituents increasingly use videos and internet memes to share their approval and disapproval of firm actions such as the "tweet storms" that followed United Airlines forcibly removing a passenger and a Philadelphia Starbucks denying two Black men access to its bathroom (Wang, Reger, and Pfarrer, 2021). Better understanding of when such tactics have lasting effects on firms and when they are merely fleeting annoyances provides fertile ground for future research. While these techniques are gaining prominence (e.g., Petrenko *et al.*, 2016), technology continues to develop, lending itself to sociocognitive investigations that even recently were considered unimaginable (e.g., fMRI, eye scanners).

Similarly, a positive externality of the COVID-19 pandemic for researchers is the growing trove of Zoom meeting videos and other digitized records stored in collaborative software. These rich digital traces of meetings and working groups can provide valuable access to better understand who influences decisions and how they do it. Gaining access to sensitive meeting data will continue to be an issue in some domains, such as gaining access to board meeting videos from major corporations. With tenacity, time, and safeguards on corporate identities, we believe enough firms will allow access to provide unprecedented levels of detail on the inner workings of strategic decision-making. For example, does revealing personal information, such as including one's actual home and family members in Zoom meetings (as opposed to using a virtual background) provide greater or lesser weight to male and female executive proposals? Additionally, the COVID-19 pandemic provides a natural experiment to explore many interesting questions, such as why some firms banded together to support each other and their communities while others used supply chain disruptions for short-term gain, and which of these strategic responses to the pandemic foreshadow greater long-term success.

Alternative rationalities

The second major area we believe is especially promising is work that advances alternative ways of thinking beyond intendedly rational cognition. Recent work extolling the virtues of decision heuristics, or cognitive shortcuts (Bingham and Eisenhardt, 2011), and questioning whether normative decision-making standards are superior to the true complexity of human cognition (Porac and Tschang, 2013) are exemplars of this type of research. Rather than viewing cognitive shortcuts as a limitation of managerial decision-making, this work suggests that the benefits of heuristics might outweigh their downside; in short, "nonrational" ways of thinking might be more rational than economic theory predicts. For instance, the use of heuristics might allow firms to move faster into promising markets and to shape emerging markets to their advantage, which could result in greater overall returns, even if using the cognitive shortcut occasionally leads to a suboptimal decision.

Additionally, dual processing (conscious and automatic) work in social psychology (see Fiske and Taylor [2013] for a review), as well as work in strategic management on automaticity and intuition have begun to ask promising questions about how markets and industries develop (Dane and Pratt, 2007; Dane *et al.*, 2011; Hodgkinson and Sadler-Smith, 2018; Reger and Palmer, 1996; Simon, 1987). Much of the work questioning the rational model has focused on attributes of individual managerial cognition. As with sociocognitive research in general, there is a great opportunity to bring more attention to the effects of collective decision-making, such as how collective interpretations among actors shape the trajectory of an industry and the value of its products (Khaire and Wadhwani, 2010). This area of research has begun to challenge the previously taken-for-granted (almost sacred) belief that calculated, dispassionate decision-making is the standard against which managerial decision-making should be judged. Thus, finding new ways to more effectively measure managerial decision-making is a tremendous future research opportunity.

Sociocognitive research has also begun to unpack the importance of emotions in influencing strategic decisions, both by strategic decision-makers (Hodgkinson and Sadler-Smith, 2018; Huy, 2012) and those that influence them, both inside and outside the organization (Muller, Pfarrer, and Little, 2014; Wang et al., 2021). Concepts such as entrepreneurial passion (Cardon et al., 2009) might be applied more broadly within strategic management as, similar to entrepreneurs, managers can be passionate about their preferences. Similarly, future research can investigate how managers' emotional attachment to particular markets and their affective responses to some rivals can influence their choice of markets and other competitive actions (Chen, Su, and Tsai, 2007; Livengood and Reger, 2010). The digital records of strategic decision-making processes provide rich data to unpack these influences. Also within the realm of alternative rationalities is work on imagination and creativity (Cornelissen and Clarke, 2010; Ford and Gioia, 2000; Kauppila, Bizzi, and Obstfeld, 2018; Unsworth, 2001). For instance, Alvarez and Barney's (2007) theory of entrepreneurial creation of opportunities surely applies more broadly beyond entrepreneurship to other strategic management contexts.

Decision-making and the digital revolution

The major technological and societal changes associated with the rise of digital platforms, especially social media, alter which actors can influence strategic decision-making (Etter, Ravasi, and Colleoni, 2019; Wang et al., 2021). In particular, social media can empower secondary stakeholders and even previously "inactive" constituents—groups that had little voice or interest—to have greater influence in organizational decision-making processes (Pfarrer et al., 2008: 732; Toubiana and Zietsma, 2017; Wang et al., 2021). As such, investigating the role of "the public," "influencers," or "fans" on organizations' reputations and actions will continue to have greater prominence in sociocognitive research (Wang et al., 2021). Social media can also affect stakeholders and information infomediaries such as market analysts and the traditional media (Kim and Youm, 2017; Wang et al., 2021).

Additionally, social media provide new ways for organizations, members, and leaders to communicate directly with stakeholders without reliance on information intermediaries (Etter et al., 2019; Heavey et al., 2020; Neeley and Leonardi, 2018). Social media provide both opportunities and challenges for organizations and for sociocognitive theorists, because these are new communications platforms without established norms or regulations (Wang et al., 2021). How best to use them to gain competitive advantage (and to react to those who use them against a firm) is relatively unexplored territory. One particularly interesting area for future research is the role of social media in changing the power dynamics between firms and their constituents that previously were mediated by information gatekeepers such as investment analysts and the traditional business press.

Interesting research questions include who gains influence in a world that increasingly depends on social media for information about firms, and what communications and actions do the successful actors use to gain this influence? For example, the rhetorical styles adopted by effective financial analysts and influential news brokers in the pre–social media era may not bestow the same mantle of authoritative expertise today. As just one example of an interesting research question: what is it about the social media era that has led firms and their CEOs to weigh in more frequently on social issues like racial injustice and gun rights, when the received wisdom (pre–social media) was that these divisive issues should be avoided? Because social media increase the speed, emotionality, and commonality of communications among constituents (Wang *et al.*, 2021), we believe the social media era requires new theories about stakeholders, information intermediaries, the boundaries of firms and industries, and perhaps even new theories of competitive advantage and the growth of firms.

Conclusion

The sociocognitive perspective in strategic management has made great strides in the years since the publication of Schendel and Hofer's (1979) seminal volume. The very meaning of the term *strategic process* has been expanded to include more micro concerns such as investigating the use of strategic frameworks in decision-making meetings, to more macro foci on the roles of extra-organizational and collective actors in influencing firm actions and outcomes. The sociocognitive perspective provides almost unlimited possibilities for future research. Rather than being comprehensive of the field, our goal has been to provide a broad outline of the terrain sociocognitive researchers have covered to date and to suggest a few promising areas for future research. We have great confidence that many researchers will see the allure of treading in relatively virgin territory and will relish the opportunity to create new promising research directions. Our hope is that our thoughts on future research will spark interest among the next generation of strategy scholars to advance the frontiers of sociocognitive research in exciting directions.

A core sociocognitive belief in the agency of individuals to shape the future to their liking makes the field especially attractive to new researchers. The sociocognitive perspective not only celebrates how managers' unique perspectives provide competitive advantage to firms, it also applauds how researchers' unique perspectives provide advances to our field. New researchers will publish papers that they, editors, and reviewers believe are interesting, well done, and important, and readers will build upon those insights to take the field in directions of interest to them. That, we think, is exciting.

Note

1. For more details on these research streams, please see Parts 6 and 7 of this volume.

References

Alvarez SA, Barney JB. 2007. Discovery and creation: alternative theories of entrepreneurial action. *Strategic Entrepreneurship Journal* 1(1–2): 11–26.

Andrews KR. 1971. *The Concept of Corporate Strategy*. Dow Jones-Irwin: Homewood, IL.

Barney JB. 1991. The resource-based view of strategy: origins, implications, and prospects. *Journal of Management* 17(1): 97–211.

Barr PS, Stimpert JL, Huff AS. 1992. Cognitive change, strategic action, and organizational renewal. *Strategic Management Journal* 13(S1): 15–36.

Barsalou LW. 2014. *Cognitive Psychology: An Overview for Cognitive Scientists*. Psychology Press: New York, NY.

Bazerman MH, Moore DA. 1994. *Judgment in Managerial Decision Making*. Wiley: New York, NY.

Bingham CB, Eisenhardt KM. 2011. Rational heuristics: the "simple rules" that strategists learn from process experience. *Strategic Management Journal* 32(13): 1437–1464.

Bundy J, Pfarrer MD. 2015. A burden of responsibility: the role of social approval at the onset of a crisis. *Academy of Management Review* 40(3): 345–369.

Burgelman RA, Floyd SW, Laamanen T, Mantere S, Vaara E, Whittington R. 2018. Strategy processes and practices: dialogues and intersections. *Strategic Management Journal* 39(3): 531–558.

Busenbark JR, Lange D, Certo ST. 2017. Foreshadowing as impression management: illuminating the path for security analysts. *Strategic Management Journal* 38(12): 2486–2507.

Busenbark JR, Pfarrer MD, Miller BP, Marshall NT. 2019. How the severity gap influences the effect of top-actor performance on outcomes following a violation. *Strategic Management Journal* 40(12): 2078–2104.

Cannella B, Finkelstein S, Hambrick DC. 2008. *Strategic Leadership: Theory and Research on Executives, Top Management Teams, and Boards*. Oxford University Press: New York, NY.

Cardon MS, Wincent J, Singh J, Drnovsek M. 2009. The nature and experience of entrepreneurial passion. *Academy of Management Review* 34(3): 511–532.

Chen MJ, Su KH, Tsai W. 2007. Competitive tension: the awareness-motivation-capability perspective. *Academy of Management Journal* 50(1): 101–118.

Choudhury P, Wang D, Carlson NA, Khanna T. 2019. Machine learning approaches to facial and text analysis: discovering CEO oral communication styles. *Strategic Management Journal* 40(11): 1705–1732.

Clarke JS, Cornelissen JP, Healey MP. 2019. Actions speak louder than words: how figurative language and gesturing in entrepreneurial pitches influences investment judgments. *Academy of Management Journal* 62(2): 335–360.

Cole BM, Chandler D. 2019. A model of competitive impression management: Edison versus Westinghouse in the war of the currents. *Administrative Science Quarterly* 64(4): 1020–1063.

Cornelissen JP, Clarke JS. 2010. Imagining and rationalizing opportunities: inductive reasoning and the creation and justification of new ventures. *Academy of Management Review* 35(4): 539–557.

Cyert RM, March JG. 1963/1992. *A Behavioral Theory of the Firm*. Blackwell Publishers, Malden, MA.

Daft RL, Weick KE. 1984. Toward a model of organizations as interpretation systems. *Academy of Management Review* 9(2): 284–295.

Dalpiaz E, Di Stefano G. 2018. A universe of stories: mobilizing narrative practices during transformative change. *Strategic Management Journal* 39(3): 664–696.

Dane E, Pratt MG. 2007. Exploring intuition and its role in managerial decision making. *Academy of Management Review* 32(1): 33–54.

Dane E, Baer M, Pratt MG, Oldham GR. 2011. Rational versus intuitive problem solving: how thinking "off the beaten path" can stimulate creativity. *Psychology of Aesthetics, Creativity, and the Arts* 5(1): 3–12.

Dess GG, Beard DW. 1984. Dimensions of organizational task environments. *Administrative Science Quarterly* 29(1): 52–73.

Duhaime IM, Schwenk CR. 1985. Conjectures on cognitive simplification in acquisition and divestment decision making. *Academy of Management Review* 10(2): 287–295.

Duriau VJ, Reger RK, Pfarrer MD. 2007. A content analysis of the content analysis literature in organization studies: research themes, data sources, and methodological refinements. *Organizational Research Methods* 10(1): 5–34.

Elsbach KD, Sutton RI. 1992. Acquiring organizational legitimacy through illegitimate actions: a marriage of institutional and impression management theories. *Academy of Management Journal* 35(4): 699–738.

Etter M, Ravasi D, Colleoni E. 2019. Social media and the formation of organizational reputation. *Academy of Management Review* 44(1): 28–52.

Felin T, Foss NJ, Ployhart RE. 2015. The microfoundations movement in strategy and organization theory. *Academy of Management Annals* 9(1): 575–632.

Fiske ST, Taylor SE. 2013. *Social Cognition: From Brains to Culture*. SAGE: Thousand Oaks, CA.

Floyd SW, Wooldridge B. 1992. Middle management involvement in strategy and its association with strategic type: a research note. *Strategic Management Journal* 13(S1): 153–167.

Forbes DP, Milliken FJ. 1999. Cognition and corporate governance: understanding boards of directors as strategic decision-making groups. *Academy of Management Review* 24(3): 489–505.

Ford CM, Gioia DA. 2000. Factors influencing creativity in the domain of managerial decision making. *Journal of Management* 26(4): 705–732.

Ford JD, Ford LW. 1995. The role of conversations in producing intentional change in organizations. *Academy of Management Review* 20(3): 541–570.

Freeman RE. 2010. *Strategic Management: A Stakeholder Approach*. Cambridge University Press: New York, NY.

Freeman RE, Harrison JS, Wicks AC, Parmar BL, de Colle S. 2010. *Stakeholder Theory: The State of the Art*. Cambridge University Press: Cambridge, U.K.

Gamache DL, McNamara G, Mannor MJ, Johnson RE. 2015. Motivated to acquire? The impact of CEO regulatory focus on firm acquisitions. *Academy of Management Journal* 58(4): 1261–1282.

Gioia DA, Chittipeddi K. 1991. Sensemaking and sensegiving in strategic change initiation. *Strategic Management Journal* 12(6): 433–448.

Green SE Jr. 2004. A rhetorical theory of diffusion. *Academy of Management Review* 29(4): 653–669.

Greenstein S. 2017. The reference wars: Encyclopædia Britannica's decline and Encarta's emergence. *Strategic Management Journal* 38(5): 995–1017.

Guo W, Yu T, Gimeno J. 2017. Language and competition: communication vagueness, interpretation difficulties, and market entry. *Academy of Management Journal* 60(6): 2073–2098.

Gylfe P, Franck H, LeBaron C, Mantere S. 2016. Video methods in strategy research: focusing on embodied cognition. *Strategic Management Journal* 37(1): 133–148.

Haleblian JM, Pfarrer MD, Kiley JT. 2017. High-reputation firms and their differential acquisition behaviors. *Strategic Management Journal* 38(11): 2237–2254.

Hambrick DC, Mason PA. 1984. Upper echelons: the organization as a reflection of its top managers. *Academy of Management Review* 9(2): 193–206.

Harmon DJ. 2019. When the Fed speaks: arguments, emotions, and the microfoundations of institutions. *Administrative Science Quarterly* 64(3): 542–575.

Haynes KT, Josefy M, Hitt MA. 2015. Tipping point: managers' self-interest, greed, and altruism. *Journal of Leadership and Organizational Studies* 22(3): 265–279.

Heavey C, Simsek Z, Kyprianou C, Risius M. 2020. How do strategic leaders engage with social media? A theoretical framework for research and practice. *Strategic Management Journal* 41(8): 1490–1527.

Hodgkinson GP, Sadler-Smith E. 2018. The dynamics of intuition and analysis in managerial and organizational decision making. *Academy of Management Perspectives* 32(4): 473–492.

Huff AS, Reger RK. 1987. A review of strategic process research. *Journal of Management* 13(2): 211–236.

Huy QN. 2012. Emotions in strategic organization: opportunities for impactful research. *Strategic Organization* 10(3): 240–247.

Johnson PD, Smith MB, Wallace JC, Hill AD, Baron RA. 2015. A review of multilevel regulatory focus in organizations. *Journal of Management* 41(5): 1501–1529.

Kahl SJ, Grodal S. 2016. Discursive strategies and radical technological change: multilevel discourse analysis of the early computer 1947–1958). *Strategic Management Journal* 37(1): 149–166.

Kauppila OP, Bizzi L, Obstfeld, D. 2018. Connecting and creating: tertius iungens, individual creativity, and strategic decision processes. *Strategic Management Journal* 39(3): 697–719.

Kennedy MT, Fiss PC. 2009. Institutionalization, framing, and diffusion: the logic of TQM adoption and implementation decisions among U.S. hospitals. *Academy of Management Journal* 52(5): 897–918.

Khaire M, Wadhwani RD. 2010. Changing landscapes: the construction of meaning and value in a new market category—Modern Indian art. *Academy of Management Journal* 53(6): 1281–1304.

Kim EH, Youm YN. 2017. How do social media affect analyst stock recommendations? Evidence from S&P 500 electric power companies' Twitter accounts. *Strategic Management Journal* 38(13): 2599–2622.

King BG, Soule SA. 2007. Social movements as extra-institutional entrepreneurs: the effect of protests on stock price returns. *Administrative Science Quarterly* 52(3): 413–442.

König A, Mammen J, Luger J, Fehn A, Enders A. 2018. Silver bullet or ricochet? CEOs' use of metaphorical communication and infomediaries' evaluations. *Academy of Management Journal* 61(4): 1196–1230.

Livengood RS, Reger RK. 2010. That's our turf! Identity domains and competitive dynamics. *Academy of Management Review* 35(1): 48–66.

Love EG, Lim J, Bednar MK. 2017. The face of the firm: the influence of CEOs on corporate reputation. *Academy of Management Journal* 60(4): 1462–1481.

Maguire S, Hardy C. 2009. Discourse and deinstitutionalization: the decline of DDT. *Academy of Management Journal* 52(1): 148–178.

March JG, Simon HA. 1958. *Organizations*. John Wiley and Sons. New York, NY.

Meyer RE, Höllerer MA, Jancsary D, Van Leeuwen T. 2013. The visual dimension in organizing, organization, and organization research: core ideas, current developments, and promising avenues. *Academy of Management Annals* 7(1): 489–555.

Mintzberg H. 1973. *The Nature of Managerial Work*. Harper and Row: New York, NY.

Mishina Y, Dykes BJ, Block ES, Pollock TG. 2010. Why "good" firms do bad things: the effects of high aspirations, high expectations, and prominence on the incidence of corporate illegality. *Academy of Management Journal* 53(4): 701–722.

Muller AR, Pfarrer MD, Little LM. 2014. A theory of collective empathy in corporate philanthropy decisions. *Academy of Management Review* 39: 1–21.

Neeley TB, Leonardi PM. 2018. Enacting knowledge strategy through social media: passable trust and the paradox of nonwork interactions. *Strategic Management Journal* 39(3): 922–946.

Ocasio W. 1997. Towards an attention-based view of the firm. *Strategic Management Journal* 18(S1): 187–206.

Ocasio W, Laamanen T, Vaara E. 2018. Communication and attention dynamics: an attention-based view of strategic change. *Strategic Management Journal* 39(1): 155–167.

Pan L, McNamara G, Lee JJ, Haleblian J, Devers CE. 2018. Give it to us straight (most of the time): top managers' use of concrete language and its effect on investor reactions. *Strategic Management Journal* 39(8): 2204–2225.

Paroutis S, Heracleous L. 2013. Discourse revisited: dimensions and employment of first-order strategy discourse during institutional adoption. *Strategic Management Journal* 34(8): 935–956.

Penrose E. 1959. *The Theory of the Growth of the Firm*. Oxford University Press: Oxford, U.K.

Petrenko OV, Aime F, Ridge J, Hill A. 2016. Corporate social responsibility or CEO narcissism? CSR motivations and organizational performance. *Strategic Management Journal* 37(2): 262–279.

Pfarrer MD, DeCelles KA, Smith KG, Taylor MS. 2008. After the fall: reintegrating the corrupt organization. *Academy of Management Review* 33(3): 730–749.

Pfarrer MD, Devers CE, Corley K, Cornelissen JP, Lange D, Makadok R, Mayer K, Weber L. 2019. Sociocognitive perspectives in strategic management. *Academy of Management Review* 44(4): 767–774.

Pfarrer MD, Pollock TG, Rindova VP. 2010. A tale of two assets: the effects of firm reputation and celebrity on earnings surprises and investors' reactions. *Academy of Management Journal* 53(5): 1131–1152.

Pfeffer J, Salancik GR. 1978/2003. *The External Control of Organizations: A Resource Dependence Perspective*. Stanford University Press: Stanford, CA.

Phillips N, Lawrence TB, Hardy C. 2004. Discourse and institutions. *Academy of Management Review* 29(4): 635–652.

Pollock TG, Rindova VP. 2003. Media legitimation effects in the market for initial public offerings. *Academy of Management Journal* 46(5): 631–642.

Porac J, Tschang FT. 2013. Unbounding the managerial mind: it's time to abandon the image of managers as "small brains." *Journal of Management Inquiry* 22(2): 250–254.

Powell TC, Lovallo D, Fox CR. 2011. Behavioral strategy. *Strategic Management Journal* 32(13): 1369–1386.

Pressman A. 2020 Everything to know about Apple's iPhone SE—a new $400 phone amid the coronavirus pandemic. *Fortune*, April 15, https://fortune.com/2020/04/15/new-iphone-se-apple-screen-size-dimensions-price-cost-camera-coronavirus-announcement-2020/.

Ravasi D, Rindova V, Etter M, Cornelissen J. 2018. The formation of organizational reputation. *Academy of Management Annals* 12(2): 574–599.

Reger RK, Huff AS. 1993. Strategic groups: a cognitive perspective. *Strategic Management Journal* 14(2): 103–123.

Reger RK, Palmer TB. 1996. Managerial categorization of competitors: using old maps to navigate new environments. *Organization Science* 7(1): 22–39.

Rindova VP, Reger RK, Dalpiaz E. 2012. The mind of the strategist and the eye of the beholder: the socio-cognitive perspective in strategy research. In *Handbook of Research on Competitive Strategy*, Dagnino GB (ed). Edward Elgar: Cheltenham, U.K.; 147–164.

Schendel D, Hofer CW (eds). 1979. *Strategic Management: A New View of Business Policy and Planning.* Little, Brown: Boston, MA.

Schulze WS, Lubatkin MH, Dino RN. 2002. Altruism, agency, and the competitiveness of family firms. *Managerial and Decision Economics* 23(4–5): 247–259.

Simon HA. 1987. Making management decisions: the role of intuition and emotion. *Academy of Management Perspectives* 1(1): 57–64.

Sinha PN, Jaskiewicz P, Gibb J, Combs JG. 2020. Managing history: how New Zealand's Gallagher Group used rhetorical narratives to reprioritize and modify imprinted strategic guideposts. *Strategic Management Journal* 41(3): 557–589.

Toubiana M, Zietsma C. 2017. The message is on the wall? Emotions, social media and the dynamics of institutional complexity. *Academy of Management Journal* 60(3): 922–953.

Tversky A, Kahneman D. 1992. Advances in prospect theory: cumulative representation of uncertainty. *Journal of Risk and Uncertainty* 5(4): 297–323.

Unsworth K. 2001. Unpacking creativity. *Academy of Management Review* 26(2): 289–297.

Vaara E. 2010. Taking the linguistic turn seriously: strategy as a multifaceted and interdiscursive phenomenon. *Advances in Strategic Management* 27(1): 29–50.

Walsh JP. 1995. Managerial and organizational cognition: notes from a trip down memory lane. *Organization Science* 6(3): 280–321.

Wang X, Reger RK, Pfarrer MD. 2021. Faster, hotter, and more linked in: managing social disapproval in the social media era. *Academy of Management Review* 46: 1–24.

Weber K, King B. 2014. Social movement theory and organization studies. In *Oxford Handbook of Sociology, Social Theory and Organization Studies*, Adler PS, du Gay P, Morgan G, Reed M (eds). Oxford University Press: Oxford, U.K.; 487–509.

Weick KE. 1995. *Sensemaking in Organizations.* Sage: London, U.K.

Westphal JD, Deephouse DL. 2011. Avoiding bad press: interpersonal influence in relations between CEOs and journalists and the consequences for press reporting about firms and their leadership. *Organization Science* 22(4): 1061–1086.

Whittington R, Yakis-Douglas B, Ahn K. 2016. Cheap talk? Strategy presentations as a form of chief executive officer impression management. *Strategic Management Journal* 37(12): 2413–2424.

Wooldridge B, Cowden B. 2020. Strategic decision-making in business. In *Oxford Research Encyclopedia of Business and Management*, Hitt M (ed.). Oxford University Press: Oxford, U.K. Online publication date: January 2020. DOI: 10.1093/acrefore/9780190224851.013.1.

Zavyalova A, Pfarrer MD, Reger RK, Shapiro DL. 2012. Managing the message: the effects of firm actions and industry spillovers on media coverage following wrongdoing. *Academy of Management Journal* 55(5): 1079–1101.

Zavyalova A, Pfarrer MD, Reger RK, Hubbard TD. 2016. Reputation as a benefit and a burden? How stakeholders' organizational identification affects the role of reputation following a negative event. *Academy of Management Journal* 59(1): 253–276.

9.2
STRATEGIC CHANGE AND RENEWAL

Quy N. Huy and Daniel Z. Mack

Introduction

For as long as scholars have been interested in understanding how organizations compete and survive in their uncertain environment, strategic change and renewal have remained a central theme in the strategic management literature. Strategic change concerns a fundamental shift in priorities, norms, and goals, all of which are important elements of the organization's strategy (Gioia *et al.*, 1994). Strategic change is often associated with adjustments of the organization's allocation and deployment of resources to support this fundamental shift. Because major strategic change often entails structural changes to the organization, it is thus a risky activity that increases the probability of failure of the organization (Hannan and Freeman, 1984). Yet such endeavors are inevitable for the organization seeking to adapt its internal activities to maintain alignment with external demands from its environment (Rajagopalan and Spreitzer, 1997). Ultimately, whether such strategic changes lead to successful organizational renewal is contingent on the quality of the organization's strategy formulation and strategy execution (Hutzschenreuter and Kleindienst, 2006).

Notably, the processes of enacting strategic change within organizations are complex as they involve the actions and preferences of multiple stakeholder groups that are coevolving and interacting with another. Because of the many "moving parts," outcomes of attempts toward strategic change and renewal are difficult to predict. For instance, the process of formulating a change strategy is often uncertain. The extant literature has highlighted how the formulation of strategic changes originates not only from the upper echelons of the organization but could also arise unexpectedly from employees in a bottom-up fashion (Bower, 1970). Poor execution could undermine even the most well-formulated strategy, especially when the organization cannot obtain or maintain the support and commitment of its members during execution (Hambrick and Cannella, 1989). Because of its complexity, the phenomenon of strategic change and renewal is rich and presents ample research opportunities for scholars. Indeed, this phenomenon has been studied from multiple perspectives and under different theoretical lenses.

This chapter presents an overview of the current state of research in this domain and, based on gaps in current research, highlights some emerging themes that future research could focus on to enrich our understanding of strategic change and renewal in organizations.

State of Research and Current Issues

Given the complex nature of strategic change and renewal, scholars often constrain their scope of examination to remain tractable. However, relatively narrow scoping of research analyses can introduce simplifying assumptions about the behaviors and processes of the change event, undermining fuller understanding of these important organizational events. In this section, we highlight several approaches that have been dominant to date in the literature examining strategic change processes in organizations. We present the overview of researchers' focus grouped on three dimensions: (1) phases of the strategic change process, (2) roles in the strategic change process, and (3) theoretical lenses used by researchers in this area.

Phases: formulation versus execution

Despite the strong interdependence between the phases of strategy formulation and execution in the process of strategic change, most empirical studies fall into clusters that focus either on formulation or execution (for a review, see Hutzschenreuter and Kleindienst, 2006).

In the stream of research focusing on formulation, organizational renewal occurs when firms or managers as change agents can successfully make strategic decisions that allow the firm to maintain an internal and external fit with the environment (Gavetti and Levinthal, 2000). Examples include decisions to acquire or redeploy resources or personnel in response to environmental changes. These studies tend to adopt a cognitive perspective to elaborate on how firms engage in the process for renewal (e.g., Rajagopalan and Spreitzer, 1997). Information (or the access to information) is deemed important as it allows managers to derive the best plans that are comprehensive and most robust to contingencies. In the view of these studies, successful strategy change and renewal would rest on the quality of the strategy formulated. However, studies focusing on strategic formulation also share a common assumption that strategic execution will follow unproblematically. The premise is that a well-formulated plan for strategic change would have already accounted for various contingencies such that smooth execution of the strategic change will follow and generate the intended outcomes. Empirical studies on strategic formulation tend to overlook how the planned strategic change was actually executed and tend to attribute successful (or unsuccessful) outcomes of strategic change and renewal to the quality of the planned change (cf. Huy, Corley, and Kraatz, 2014).

In the stream of research focusing on strategic execution, by contrast, studies investigate how firms deal with the challenges of implementing the plans for strategic renewal (Weiser, Jarzabkowski, and Laamanen, 2020). These challenges include how to influence, motivate, or incentivize change recipients or other organizational members to adopt actions that facilitate organization-level changes (e.g., Huy, 2011; Huy et al., 2014). Successful strategic renewal occurs when firms overcome the barriers and challenges to implementing strategic change. Failing to resolve emerging roadblocks impeding the implementation of the strategic change could lead to the failure of the organization to renew itself (Floyd and Lane, 2000). Unlike research on strategic formulation, the stream of work focusing on strategic execution tends to have a distinct set of assumptions. Much of that literature has an underlying assumption that change recipients are actors who favor the status quo and thus tend to be highly resistant toward adopting strategic change. Moreover, the plan for strategic change is assumed to be exogenously imposed on change recipients, who have to manage around it with little or no involvement of the change agents. Hence, how strategy formulation as an iterative process is affected by downstream strategy execution, or how concerns about execution have an impact on upstream strategy formulation considerations, are potentially fruitful areas for future investigation.

Roles: change agents versus change recipients

Although the label is not specific to a functional role or expertise, in prior research change agents are often assumed to be organizational members of significant position or power—for example, CEOs, directors, or other top or middle managers (Balogun, Bartunek, and Do, 2015). This is unsurprising, given that most plans for strategic changes are typically formulated by the upper echelons of the organization. In certain cases, change agents have also been recognized as emerging from the ground or front line leading to strategic change and renewal from the bottom up (Burgelman, 1991). Change recipients are often assumed to be middle managers or front-line employees who have to deal with the planned change coming from their higher-level managers (Huy, 2011). Thus, change agents or change recipients could be general roles occupied by any organizational member, although in many studies they are highly correlated with their formal position within the organizational hierarchy. For example, Huy et al. (2014) studied how senior management, as change agents, had to grapple with increasing resistance from middle managers who were at the receiving end of change initiatives. Sonenshein and Dholakia (2012) examined how front-line employees, as change recipients, make sense and overcome challenges of change initiatives devised by top managers as change agents.

Parallel to researchers' focus on either strategic change formulation or its execution, studies on strategic change and renewal often focus on either change agents or change recipients. Because of the analytical focus around formulation or execution (assumed to be dominated by change agents and change recipients, respectively), most research isolates the story around the change agents or change recipients, treating the other entity as mostly exogenous and static (e.g., Balogun et al., 2015;

Sonenshein and Dholakia, 2012; Tripsas and Gavetti, 2000). There are, however, benefits to adopting such a role-focused approach, as it has enabled scholars to examine each role more richly, across different contexts and when enacted by distinct individuals. For instance, Balogun and colleagues (2015) have focused their examination on senior managers and how they enacted their role as change agents and found considerable heterogeneity within this seemingly homogeneous category. Huy's (2002) study on middle managers as change agents revealed the variety of actions that these managers adopted to manage continuity of changing operations. Hence these studies highlighted how the role of change agents or recipients could vary differently depending on who performs the role.

Despite the benefits of such role-specific focus in the literature, change agents and change recipients are important in their own right, and each plays a constituting role in facilitating change. Strategic change requires the coordination and effort of all organizational members for successful renewal to take place. Increasingly, studies are taking into account the juxtaposition of various roles in their examination of the change process (e.g., Huy et al., 2014; Sonenshein, 2010; Vuori and Huy, 2016). How change agents and change recipients jointly influence the evolution and outcomes of the change process through their interactions remains an underexamined area for future research.

Perspectives: cognitive lens versus other theoretical lenses

A dominant theoretical lens in the strategic change and renewal literature is the cognitive or information-processing perspective. This perspective focuses on how organizations and their managers acquire, process, and respond to information as they make decisions during change and renewal (Rajagopalan and Spreitzer, 1997; Schwenk, 1988). Broadly, this stream of research includes topics such as managerial beliefs and mental models (Corley and Gioia, 2004), learning and attention (Ocasio, 2011), heuristics and biases (Das and Teng, 1999), identity (Gioia, Schultz, and Corley, 2000), and framing and sensemaking (Kaplan, 2008).

In the early works on strategic change, the cognitive perspective burgeoned because of growing interest in explaining why some organizations could adapt to radical changes whereas others were less responsive. A common but implicit assumption was that decisions related to strategic changes were under the purview of top management (Hambrick and Mason, 1984). How managers perceive their environment was thought to be important to the extent that decisions about strategic change and renewal were based largely on managerial perceptions, beliefs, and mental models. The literature in this area suggests that organizations are more likely to engage in strategic change if managers were to revise their mental models (e.g., Eggers and Kaplan, 2009; Tripsas and Gavetti, 2000). One of the earlier works on managerial cognition demonstrated how the degree to which organizations could adapt to environmental changes is attributable to differences in managerial mindsets. Barr, Stimpert, and Huff (1992) showed that organizational renewal was strongly associated with a change in managers' mental models. Other studies in this stream of research also showed an association between managerial cognitive change and organizational renewal, and added how this relationship could be moderated by different conditions relating to various individual, organizational, and industry-level factors such as the pace of change in industries (Nadkarni and Barr, 2008).

Subsequent work from the cognitive perspective sought to explain why changes in mental models could occur or not. One line of inquiry at the individual level was to examine whether managers were biased and refrained from engaging in change. Because biases influence how managers interpret and potentially respond to external events in their environment (Tversky and Kahneman, 1974), biases could potentially explain why some managers are more receptive to change (e.g., Hambrick and Fukutomi, 1991; Henderson, Miller, and Hambrick, 2006). Several scholars theorized that some managers are more likely to exhibit higher levels of commitment to the status quo than others, and hence are less likely to take actions toward change (Hambrick, Geletkanycz, and Fredrickson, 1993). Other managers may be overly confident or hubristic if they are less likely to respond to the feedback of others during decision-making (Chen, Crossland, and Luo, 2015). At the community level, scholars also theorized how an existing identity could also constrain whether organizations perceive strategic change as relevant or even necessary (e.g., Porac, Thomas, and Baden-Fuller, 1989). When strategic changes were perceived to be inconsistent with the organization's identity, these changes—even if necessary—are less likely to be embraced (Tripsas, 2009). Conversely organizations are more likely to enact changes they view as central to their identity (Gioia et al., 2000).

In another line of inquiry, scholars have investigated when mental models are likely to change in the direction that favors strategic change. One view put forth by the attention-based view suggests that changes are more likely to occur if managers allocate greater attention to the issues that are associated with changes in the environment (Ocasio, 2011). When there is sufficient attention allocated to an issue, the organization is more likely to devote greater effort by channeling resources toward addressing the issue; however, when there is insufficient attention allocated to an issue, the issue is likely to be deemed unimportant by decision-makers (Ocasio, 1997; Ocasio and Joseph, 2005). Research has shown how the allocation of limited managerial attention to newly emerging issues can help the organization overcome inertia and implement strategic change (Cho and Hambrick, 2006) and adopt emerging technology more rapidly than their competitors (Eggers and Kaplan, 2009). Recent work on managerial attention has also speculated about the prospective nature of attention that encourages abductive thinking, which enables organizations to proactively manage strategic change rather than reacting to environmental changes (Shepherd, McMullen, and Ocasio, 2017).

More recent works have examined organizational change and renewal process using various theoretical perspectives that have traditionally been peripheral to the cognitive lens. Four areas seem to gain momentum in the change literature: (1) emotions, (2) temporality, (3) strategy-as-practice, and (4) discourse and narratives.

Emotions

One of such theoretical perspectives focuses on the role of emotions that introduces a more humanistic view of change actors rather than construing them as mere information processors. At the individual level, scholars have theorized about how the valence of emotions could influence the attitudes and responses of change recipients toward new initiatives (Lazarus, 1991). Change agents could elicit positive emotions such as anticipated pride and hope for the betterment of the organization to mobilize employees' support for their proposed change initiatives (Avey, Wernsing, and Luthans, 2008). Positive emotions also can create feelings of openness and playfulness that enable change recipients to adapt to changes (Ashkanasy and Ashton-James, 2007). Recent research suggests that negative emotions such as fear and cynicism can narrow recipients' thinking and receptivity to the proposed change and elicit their resistance toward change (Maitlis and Ozcelik, 2004; Oreg et al., 2018).

At the group level, group-focus emotions can reinforce or attenuate the extent to which personal emotions affect change recipients' support change initiatives. Research has shown how group-focus emotions (i.e., individual emotions that are felt on behalf of a group who experienced a specific event even if the focal individuals are not personally affected by it) could strongly influence how an individual should feel about particular issues (Smith, Seger, and Mackie, 2007). As a result, change recipients could develop shared, collective understandings about ongoing strategic changes and change the way they implement strategies (Huy, 2011).[1] Different shared emotions among various groups in the organization could lead to misaligned actions (such as failing to coordinate in a timely manner on a postmerger integration schedule) because these group-shared emotions could amplify differences in the level of attention and efforts they devote to addressing various organizational issues (Vuori and Huy, 2016). Beyond the role of emotions in mediating individual or collective action, the expression of emotions could also serve as an informative signal of the underlying issues surrounding organizational change (Clore et al., 2001). People who can adequately perceive or read the emotions of others are more likely to be sensitive to their needs and can enact more effective collective action toward change (Sanchez-Burks and Huy, 2009). As recent empirical works have noted, the emotional display of change recipients could be feedback to change agents that reflects the progress and intermediate success of change initiatives (Huy, 2011). The suppression of or lack of authentic emotional display among change recipients could hinder change execution by reducing the reliability of emotional signals for coordination (Vuori, Vuori, and Huy, 2017). Together, these recent studies highlight the importance of the need to manage personal and group emotions in the organization's strategic change process to ensure a precarious balance between continuity and change (Huy, 2002). Future work could examine in greater depth the various socioemotional-related aggregation mechanisms that could have an impact on the success of strategic renewal, such as collectively shared emotions stemming from differences in groups' identities, power asymmetries, formal structures, and informal networks.

Temporality

The role of temporality has also received increasing interest among strategic change scholars of late (Kunisch et al., 2017). A straightforward implication of bringing the concept of time to the foreground of strategic change research is to highlight how the subjectivity of time leads to a more nuanced understanding of why some organizations are more successful in renewing themselves than others. Time has both quantitative and qualitative aspects (Huy, 2001). Individuals and organizations could perceive time differently and ascribe different meanings to different events. The differences in time perceptions and interpretations create heterogeneity among individuals in terms of how they value the concept of time and influence the actions that the organization would adopt.

Recent empirical research seems to suggest that managing and reconciling unique interpretations of time can create opportunities to pursue organizational change and renewal (Kunisch et al., 2017). The reconciliation of different temporal structures can create flexibility among stakeholders, thus allowing the pursuit of changing goals (Reinecke and Ansari, 2015). The adoption of a certain time perspective could also help individuals or organizations overcome resource constraints by broadening the framing of an issue. For example, Kim, Bansal, and Haugh (2019) document how the enactment of a "long-present" perspective (i.e., viewing the present moment over a long duration that does not discriminate between the present and the future) can help individuals and organizations form better conceptions of resource flows and hence embrace temporal trade-offs, an occurrence common to organizations during strategic change. Conversely, leaving the differences in temporal interpretations unchecked can have drastic consequences. For example, McGivern et al. (2018) showed how failing to recognize and reconcile temporal differences could exacerbate covert tensions among stakeholders that exacerbate conflict and resistance toward change.

Beyond how different perceptions of time can influence strategic change, there is also research that examines how particular elements of time such as pacing (Gersick, 1994), rhythm (Klarner and Raisch, 2013), or temporal horizons (DesJardine and Bansal, 2019) affect how change is coordinated within organizations. However, in most of these studies, the discussion of temporality is embedded in the theorizing of other constructs such as firm growth, investment time frames, and organizational tenure (Kunisch et al., 2017).

Strategy-as-practice

The strategy-as-practice perspective introduces a more sociological approach toward the study of processes of strategic change and renewal (Vaara and Whittington, 2012; Whittington, 2007). Unlike conventional research that examines the relationships about the content and processes of strategic change, the strategy-as-practice perspective focuses on the activities and practices that managers engage in during strategic change. These practices could include how managers conduct strategy meetings, whether in the boardroom or during strategy retreats. The practice perspective also examines the tools—such as PowerPoint presentations or other facilitating information technologies—that managers used to orchestrate dialogues and conversations (Jarzabkowski and Kaplan, 2015). The fundamental idea underlying the practice perspective is that insights on how firms' managers approach the problem of strategy making during strategic change could inform why the strategic process of change unfolds in those firms. Also, unlike the conventional, more reductionist approach that explores macro-level properties in micro-level terms, the practice perspective adopts a more encompassing multilevel view of the ways of doing things that are shared among multi-actors and are routinized over time (Jarzabkowski, 2003). Hence, the practice perspective suggests that the role of strategy practices goes beyond the facilitation of decision-making to shape the concept of the organization itself (Vaara and Whittington, 2012).

This theoretical perspective for understanding strategic change has led to insights about the change process. For instance, Whittington and colleagues (2006) found that beyond the analytical skills that are assumed to be the most valuable during strategic planning, practices requiring managerial craft skills to shape materials and symbols (i.e., the deliberate attempt by change agents to create artifacts to represent their intentions) are also important when communicating strategic change to change recipients. Using strategy practices as the unit of analysis also helps reveal some of the underlying dynamism of the strategic change and renewal process. For example, strategy practices could be sources of both flexibility and rigidity, depending on the intentionality of practitioners who enable or constrain activities around some organizational issues during change (Giraudeau, 2008; Hendry, Kiel, and Nicholson, 2010). Practices such as masking negative emotions to avoid signaling disagreement can have negative consequences for the change process, especially when emotion expressions are essentially important feedback signals for the organization (Vuori et al., 2017).

Discourse and narratives

The discursive perspective of strategic change is closely aligned with and related to the practice view. The discursive perspective takes an interpretive approach, examining how the strategic change process unfolds as organizational actors interpret, give, and shape meanings of the ongoing narrative, artifacts, events, and actions constructed by others. This interpretive approach takes into account the historical context, frames of reference, and the collective memory of various organizational members to understand why and how strategic changes are enacted in ways that promote acceptance or resistance of change. Unlike studies that use other cognitive approaches, empirical studies that use the discursive approach place more focus on the actions and intentions of various actors rather than focusing only on the cognition of top managers. Studying organizational change involves investigating how managers construct meanings of ongoing organizational issues and disseminate these interpretations to change recipients to influence relevant others about a new strategic direction (Sonenshein, 2010). Thus, in contrast to conventional qualitative or quantitative approaches that work to explain social reality, discourse analysis focuses on the process of social construction to understand the origins of narratives.

Most empirical work applying the discourse perspective increasingly relies on discourse analysis as a method to examine the linguistic elements in the construction of the social phenomena (Vaara, Kleymann, and Seristo, 2004). Research using discourse as the unit of analysis in the context of organizational change highlights how the production and dissemination of texts or language influence how organizational change takes place (Ford and Ford, 1995; Sackmann, 1989). Findings in this stream of research reveal that the meanings actors construct during strategic change extend beyond the positive and negative (Sonenshein, 2010). For instance, Heracleous and Barrett (2001) found that diverse stakeholder groups can engender different discourses that were influenced in part by existing deep structures (such as stable and recurring metaphors that guide behaviors). In their study, brokers and underwriters were found to favor actions that resisted the change initiative of electronic trading championed by the market leaders. Their findings reveal how the process of strategic change can be characterized by the discursive shifts at both the communicative action and deep structure levels—not only are change recipients' interpretations of change affected by conveyed meanings, but are also influenced by underlying themes of the narrative. These studies highlight how adopting a discursive perspective can yield valuable insights into the nature of interactions among change agents and recipients.

Future Directions in Strategic Change and Renewal Process

Our overview of the state of the literature, while not intended to be exhaustive, highlights the disparate approaches taken by scholars in their investigation of the phenomenon of strategic change and renewal. Each of these approaches presents a different picture of the strategic change process; taken together, these approaches present a richer understanding of the phenomenon. In Figure 1, we present a summary model of the various theoretical perspectives covered in our review and the linkages we see between them. However, not all the linkages have been fully explored, and they represent promising future directions for researchers of strategic change and renewal. In this section, we discuss some of these linkages and the potential research questions that arise by weaving them together.

Recognizing the tight coupling between strategy formulation and execution

One approach to increase the theoretical richness of the strategic change phenomenon is to adopt a more holistic approach toward the strategic change process. For

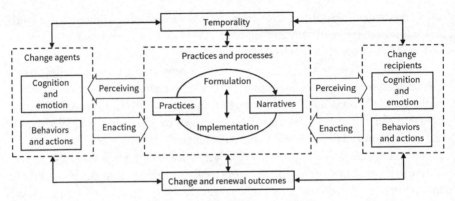

Figure 1 Integrative model of strategic change process and renewal

example, researchers could make their examination of the strong interdependence between strategy formulation and execution more explicit, rather than focusing on one phase or the other for analytical convenience. A holistic account of the strategic change process in regard to both formulation and execution will introduce many more interdependences and subtleties, enabling researchers to identify underexplored tensions, such as how the overemphasis on formulation could reduce managerial temporal and attentional resources for execution.

Investigating the processual interdependence between strategy formulation and execution could be further supported by using a practice perspective. A practice perspective could help bridge the knowledge gap between formulation and implementation by investigating the actual practices or activities that managers engage in to manage around the formulation-execution interdependencies. Research on communities of practice (e.g., Thompson, 2005; Wenger, 1999), for instance, highlights how practitioners share knowledge and learnings from their own experiences in their daily work. Similarly, research on the practice of using large-group interventions reveals managerial efforts to involve the entire system of key stakeholders in formulation to improve coordination and reduce errors during execution (e.g., Bartunek, Balogun, and Do, 2011; Worley, Mohrman, and Nevitt, 2011). Using practice as a unit of analysis could help reveal the intermediary microprocesses connecting the processes of strategy formulation and execution (see, e.g., Jarzabkowski, Lê, and Feldman, 2012; Vuori *et al.*, 2017).

A discursive perspective could also complement the practice-based approach. As highlighted by the strategy practice literature, how change recipients interpret change initiative influences how the change is executed. Although change agents can shape narratives during the process of change, narratives are also shaped by change recipients. For example, when change recipients perceive change narratives to be incompatible with current practices or routines, they may judge the narratives to be lacking legitimacy and diffuse their own narratives among their peer groups (Huy *et al.*, 2014). As practitioners perform various practices, emerging new narratives may impact how practices are performed over time (Feldman and Pentland, 2003). The interactions between interpretation, intentionality, and actions among actors can help us understand how change intentions evolve in response to their execution over time (Dittrich and Seidl, 2018). Future research investigating how practices and narratives intertwine to impact the process of change can generate new insights and help revise our understanding of how organizations renew themselves (Sonenshein, 2010). For instance, best practices intended to manage and implement strategic change could undermine the change narrative if these best practices fail to account for change recipients' emotional needs or expectations of change.

Interaction complexity between change agents and change recipients

More revelatory theoretical insights could be generated from a greater focus on the interactions between change agents and recipients. The process and outcomes of strategic change do not depend on the static demographics or are not reduced to actions of a particular actor or group of actors. Rather, the outcomes (whether successful or not) of strategic change partly result from the complex interactions between change agents and recipients. Understanding these complex interactions could reveal important but underexamined aggregation mechanisms in the strategic change process. For example, the study by Vuori and Huy (2016) revealed how Nokia failed to renew itself because responses from various groups (e.g., top versus middle managers) were misaligned because of misaligned shared fear: top managers were fearful of external competitors whereas middle managers were fearful of top managers and gave only optimistic but false news to them. This obviously hindered coordination efforts between the two powerful groups, suggesting that although change agents and recipients can be perceptive of their work environment and organizational issues, role-specific incentives and emotional responses could make coordination work during change unpredictable. Future work could examine the extent to which the differentiated roles and incentives of change agents and change recipients influence variations in how they perceive their environment and how they act during the change process.

Moreover, the interactions between change agents and change recipients may not be direct with one another but are mediated through various practices and narratives during the strategic change process. This likely occurs in large organizations where change agents and change recipients do not typically have proximate contact, and narratives could be one indirect approach through which change initiatives are translated from change agents to recipients (Sonenshein and Dholakia, 2012). Future research could also build on this stream of inquiry by investigating the extent to which actors could, intentionally or not, shape narratives or practices as soon as they receive them. For example, change agents and recipients may have personal cognitive and/or emotional responses that influence how they perceive common narratives. They could imbue these practices and narratives with their personal emotions or interpretations that impact their behaviors regarding strategy formulation and execution.

Temporality and emotionality among actors, processes, and practices

Addressing the role of temporality in strategic change and renewal could also enhance our understanding of how time influences processes of change. Building on recent research showing how organizational interpretations of time could affect change processes (e.g., Kim *et al.*, 2019; Reinecke and Ansari, 2015), future research could enrich how the diverse time perspectives of change agents and change recipients influence their behaviors during organizational change. One example of such a scenario occurs when change agents in their strategic planning of the organization's road map may pace the rate of strategic change using clock time (e.g., five years) as a reference, whereas change recipients may emphasize event time (e.g., milestones) to track the organization renewal process. These covert conflicts in time perspective not only hinder how change recipients respond and coordinate on information conveyed by change agents, but also impact the narratives that are shared among these organizational actors.

Explaining differences in time perspectives among change agents and recipients could also be a promising path for future research. Research in psychology suggests that different emotions are associated with different time perspectives. For example, future orientation is often associated with feelings of hope and optimism, whereas a backward orientation could be construed as a form of retrospection that can involve feelings of pride and despair. Future research could focus on whether practitioners dealing with more qualitative forms of time (e.g., social time) could influence various groups' emotions and identities and impact the outcome of change. As social time paces the ordering of events based on social interactions, such qualitative time may better account for and preserve the shared meanings of organizational members when pacing strategic change processes.

Finally, a temporal perspective could also help build theory about whether and how the interim outcomes of change initiatives influence the development of other events. Often change events are analyzed from a clock-time perspective, with the assumption that one event has to precede another to establish causality in the change process. However, such sequencing of events may not be consistent with other time perspectives experienced in practice. For example, integrating alternative interpretations of time into analyses of strategic change episodes could generate novel insights about how change agents and change recipients perceive the contemporaneous ordering of events, and the causality between two relational entities in practice.

Conclusion

In this chapter, we have suggested how future strategic change research could develop richer insights with a stronger focus on the whole than on the parts of the change process. This is potentially challenging, as researchers might need to combine several theoretical lenses rather than rely on one narrower focus. Nevertheless, we believe that taking a holistic approach moves the researcher of organizational change closer to a deeper understanding of the phenomenon.

A holistic approach could facilitate improvements in our understanding of critical topics that have hitherto remained inadequately addressed. One topic that could benefit from using a holistic approach would be the role of politics during strategic change and renewal. Because of its complexity, politics has traditionally been challenging to study (Pettigrew, 1973). As one can imagine, politics involves a myriad of conflicts, covert behaviors, and hidden intentions among actors from distinct groups (Hochwarter *et al.*, 2020). Without a broad understanding of the context and how each of these elements relates to one another, we could say little about how politics affects strategic change. Other topics such as pluralism of stakeholder groups, and how to manage change and renewal in organizations in which tensions about certain norms, goals, and values are constantly challenged by others, are also highly relevant in practice (Amis *et al.*, 2020; Denis, Lamothe, and Langley, 2001). For instance, future research should attempt to deepen our understanding of how hybrid organizations undergoing strategic change balance both economic and social performance. Managers striving to adopt an inclusive stakeholder approach may find it challenging to formulate and execute change while attending to the myriad of gender and ethnicity, religion, and spirituality issues in pluralistic organizations. In short, although much has been revealed, much remains to be investigated, and the phenomenon of strategic change and renewal still holds the promise of important discovery and intellectual excitement for future researchers.

Note

1. Group-focus emotions are distinct from collective emotions, which refer to emotions that are shared among many members of the group (e.g., Barsade, 2002).

References

Amis J, Barney J, Mahoney JT, Wang H. 2020. From the Editors—why we need a theory of stakeholder governance—and why this is a hard problem. *Academy of Management Review* 45(3): 499–503.

Ashkanasy NM, Ashton-James CE. 2007. Positive emotion in organizations: a multi-level framework. In *Positive Organizational Behavior*, Nelson DL, Cooper CL (eds). SAGE: London,

U.K.; 57–73. Available at: http://sk.sagepub.com/books/positive-organizational-behavior/n5.xml.

Avey JB, Wernsing TS, Luthans F. 2008. Can positive employees help positive organizational change? Impact of psychological capital and emotions on relevant attitudes and behaviors. *Journal of Applied Behavioral Science* 44(1): 48–70.

Balogun J, Bartunek JM, Do B. 2015. Senior managers' sensemaking and responses to strategic change. *Organization Science* 26(4): 960–979.

Barr PS, Stimpert JL, Huff AS. 1992. Cognitive change, strategic action, and organizational renewal. *Strategic Management Journal* 13: 15–36.

Barsade SG. 2002. The ripple effect: emotional contagion and its influence on group behavior. *Administrative Science Quarterly* 47(4): 644–675.

Bartunek JM, Balogun J, Do B. 2011. Considering planned change anew: stretching large group interventions strategically, emotionally, and meaningfully. *Academy of Management Annals* 5(1): 1–52.

Bower JL. 1970. *Managing the Resource Allocation Process: A Study of Corporate Planning and Investment*. Harvard Business School Press: Boston, MA.

Burgelman RA. 1991. Intraorganizational ecology of strategy-making and organizational adaptation. *Organization Science* 2(3): 239–262.

Chen G, Crossland C, Luo S. 2015. Making the same mistake all over again: CEO overconfidence and corporate resistance to corrective feedback. *Strategic Management Journal* 36(10): 1513–1535.

Cho TS, Hambrick DC. 2006. Attention as the mediator between top management team characteristics and strategic change: the case of airline deregulation. *Organization Science* 17(4): 453–469.

Clore GL, Wyer RS, Dienes B, Gasper K, Gohm C, Isbell L. 2001. Affective feelings as feedback: some cognitive consequences. In *Theories of Mood and Cognition: A User's Guidebook*, Martin LL, Clore GL (eds). Erlbaum: Mahwah, NJ; 27–62.

Corley KG, Gioia DA. 2004. Identity ambiguity and change in the wake of a corporate spin-off. *Administrative Science Quarterly* 49(2): 173–208.

Das TK, Teng BS. 1999. Cognitive biases and strategic decision processes: an integrative perspective. *Journal of Management Studies* 36(6): 757–778.

Denis J-L, Lamothe L, Langley A. 2001. The dynamics of collective leadership and strategic change in pluralistic organizations. *Academy of Management Journal* 44(4): 809–837.

DesJardine M, Bansal P. 2019. One step forward, two steps back: how negative external evaluations can shorten organizational time horizons. *Organization Science* 30(4): 761–780.

Dittrich K, Seidl D. 2018. Emerging intentionality in routine dynamics: a pragmatist view. *Academy of Management Journal* 61(1): 111–138.

Eggers JP, Kaplan S. 2009. Cognition and renewal: comparing CEO and organizational effects on incumbent adaptation to technical change. *Organization Science* 20(2): 461–477.

Feldman MS, Pentland BT. 2003. Reconceptualizing organizational routines as a source of flexibility and change. *Administrative Science Quarterly* 48(1): 94–118.

Floyd SW, Lane PJ. 2000. Strategizing throughout the organization: managing role conflict in strategic renewal. *Academy of Management Review* 25(1): 154–177.

Ford JD, Ford LW. 1995. The role of conversations in producing intentional change in organizations. *Academy of Management Review* 20(3): 541–570.

Gavetti G, Levinthal D. 2000. Looking forward and looking backward: cognitive and experiential search. *Administrative Science Quarterly* 45(1): 113–137.

Gersick CJG. 1994. Pacing strategic change: the case of a new venture. *Academy of Management Journal* 37(1): 9–45.

Gioia DA, Schultz M, Corley KG. 2000. Organizational identity, image, and adaptive instability. *Academy of Management Review* 25(1): 63–81.

Gioia DA, Thomas JB, Clark SM, Chittipeddi K. 1994. Symbolism and strategic change in academia: the dynamics of sensemaking and influence. *Organization Science* 5(3): 363–383.

Giraudeau M. 2008. The drafts of strategy: Opening up plans and their uses. *Long Range Planning* 41(3): 291–308.

Hambrick DC, Cannella AA. 1989. Strategy implementation as substance and selling. *Academy of Management Executive* 3(4): 178–285.

Hambrick DC, Fukutomi GDS. 1991. The seasons of a CEO's tenure. *Academy of Management Review* 16(4): 719–742.

Hambrick DC, Geletkanycz M, Fredrickson J. 1993. Top executive commitment to the status quo: some tests of its determinants. *Strategic Management Journal* 14(6): 401–418.

Hambrick DC, Mason PA. 1984. Upper echelons: the organization as a reflection of its top managers. *Academy of Management Review* 9(2): 193–206.

Hannan MT, Freeman J. 1984. Structural inertia and organizational change. *American Sociological Review* 49(2): 149–164.

Henderson AD, Miller D, Hambrick DC. 2006. How quickly do CEOs become obsolete? Industry dynamism, CEO tenure, and company performance. *Strategic Management Journal* 27(5): 447–460.

Hendry KP, Kiel GC, Nicholson G. 2010. How boards strategise: a strategy as practice view. *Long Range Planning* 43(1): 33–56.

Heracleous L, Barrett M. 2001. Organizational change as discourse: communicative actions and deep structures in the context of information technology implementation. *Academy of Management Journal* 44(4): 755–778.

Hochwarter WA, Rosen CC, Jordan SL, Ferris GR, Ejaz A, Maher LP. 2020. Perceptions of organizational politics research: past, present, and future. *Journal of Management* 46(6): 879–907.

Hutzschenreuter T, Kleindienst I. 2006. Strategy-process research: what have we learned and what is still to be explored. *Journal of Management* 32(5): 673–720.

Huy QN. 2001. Time, temporal capability, and planned change. *Academy of Management Review* 26(4): 601–623.

Huy QN. 2002. Emotional balancing of organizational continuity and radical change: the contribution of middle managers. *Administrative Science Quarterly* 47(1): 31–69.

Huy QN. 2011. How middle managers' group-focus emotions and social identities influence strategy implementation. *Strategic Management Journal* 32(13): 1387–1410.

Huy QN, Corley KG, Kraatz MS. 2014. From support to mutiny: shifting legitimacy judgments and emotional reactions impacting the implementation of radical change. *Academy of Management Journal* 57(6): 1650–1680.

Jarzabkowski P. 2003. Strategic practices: an activity theory perspective on continuity and change. *Journal of Management Studies* 40(1): 23–55.

Jarzabkowski P, Kaplan S. 2015. Strategy tools-in-use: a framework for understanding "technologies of rationality" in practice. *Strategic Management Journal* 36(4): 537–558.

Jarzabkowski PA, Lê JK, Feldman MS. 2012. Toward a theory of coordinating: creating coordinating mechanisms in practice. *Organization Science* 23(4): 907–927.

Kaplan S. 2008. Framing contests: strategy making under uncertainty. *Organization Science* 19(5): 729–752.

Kim A, Bansal P, Haugh H. 2019. No time like the present: how a present time perspective can foster sustainable development. *Academy of Management Journal* 62(2): 607–634.

Klarner P, Raisch S. 2013. Move to the beat—rhythms of change and firm performance. *Academy of Management Journal* 56(1): 160–184.

Kunisch S, Bartunek J, Mueller J, Huy QN. 2017. Time in strategic change research. *Academy of Management Annals* 11(2): 1005–1064.

Lazarus RS. 1991. Progress on a cognitive-motivational-relational theory of emotion. *American Psychologist* 46(8): 819–834.

Maitlis S, Ozcelik H. 2004. Toxic decision processes: a study of emotion and organizational decision making. *Organization Science* 15(4): 375–393.

McGivern G, Dopson S, Ferlie E, Fischer M, Fitzgerald L, Ledger J, Bennett C. 2018. The silent politics of temporal work: a case study of a management consultancy project to redesign public health care. *Organization Studies* 39(8): 1007–1030.

Nadkarni S, Barr PS. 2008. Environmental context, managerial cognition, and strategic action: an integrated view. *Strategic Management Journal* 29(13): 1395–1427.

Ocasio W. 1997. Towards an attention-based view of the firm. *Strategic Management Journal* 18: 187–206.

Ocasio W. 2011. Attention to attention. *Organization Science* 22(5): 1286–1296.

Ocasio W, Joseph J. 2005. An attention-based theory of strategy formulation: linking micro- and macroperspectives in strategy processes. *Advances in Strategic Management* 22: 39–61. Available at: https://www.emerald.com/insight/content/doi/10.1016/S0742-3322(05)22002-8/full/html.

Oreg S, Bartunek JM, Lee G, Do B. 2018. An affect-based model of recipients' responses to organizational change events. *Academy of Management Review* 43(1): 65–86.

Pettigrew AM. 1973. *The Politics of Organizational Decision-making*. Tavistock: London, U.K.

Porac JF, Thomas H, Baden-Fuller C. 1989. Competitive groups as cognitive communities: the case of Scottish knitwear manufacturers. *Journal of Management Studies* 26(4): 397–416.

Rajagopalan N, Spreitzer G. 1997. Toward a theory of strategic change: a multi-lens perspective and integrative framework. *Academy of Management Review* 22(1): 48–79.

Reinecke J, Ansari S. 2015. When times collide: temporal brokerage at the intersection of markets and developments. *Academy of Management Journal* 58(2): 618–648.

Sackmann S. 1989. The role of metaphors in organization transformation. *Human Relations* 42(6): 463–485.

Sanchez-Burks J, Huy QN. 2009. Emotional aperture and strategic change: the accurate recognition of collective emotions. *Organization Science* 20(1): 22–34.

Schwenk CR. 1988. The cognitive perspective on strategic decision making. *Journal of Management Studies* 25(1): 41–55.

Shepherd DA, McMullen JS, Ocasio W. 2017. Is that an opportunity? An attention model of top managers' opportunity beliefs for strategic action. *Strategic Management Journal* 38(3): 626–644.

Smith ER, Seger CR, Mackie DM. 2007. Can emotions be truly group level? Evidence regarding four conceptual criteria. *Journal of Personality and Social Psychology* 93(3): 431–446.

Sonenshein S. 2010. We're changing—or are we? Untangling the role of progressive, regressive, and stability narratives during strategic change implementation. *Academy of Management Journal* 53(3): 477–512.

Sonenshein S, Dholakia U. 2012. Explaining employee engagement with strategic change implementation: a meaning-making approach. *Organization Science* 23(1): 1–23.

Thompson M. 2005. Structural and epistemic parameters in communities of practice. *Organization Science* 16(2): 151–164.

Tripsas M. 2009. Technology, identity, and inertia through the lens of "The Digital Photography Company." *Organization Science* 20(2): 441–460.

Tripsas M, Gavetti G. 2000. Capabilities, cognition, and inertia: evidence from digital imaging. *Strategic Management Journal* 21: 1147–1161.

Tversky A, Kahneman D. 1974. Judgment under uncertainty: heuristics and biases. *Science* 185(4157): 1124–1131.

Vaara E, Kleymann B, Seristo H. 2004. Strategies as discursive constructions: the case of airline alliances. *Journal of Management Studies* 41(1): 1–35.

Vaara E, Whittington R. 2012. Strategy-as-practice: taking social practices seriously. *Academy of Management Annals* 6(1): 285–336.

Vuori N, Vuori TO, Huy QN. 2017. Emotional practices: how masking negative emotions impacts the post-acquisition integration process. *Strategic Management Journal* 39(3): 859–893.

Vuori TO, Huy QN. 2016. Distributed attention and shared emotions in the innovation process: how Nokia lost the smartphone battle. *Administrative Science Quarterly* 61(1): 9–51.

Weiser A-K, Jarzabkowski P, Laamanen T. 2020. Completing the adaptive turn: an integrative view of strategy implementation. *Academy of Management Annals* 14(2): 969–1031.

Wenger E. 1999. *Communities of Practice: Learning, Meaning, and Identity*. Cambridge University Press: Cambridge, U.K.

Whittington R. 2007. Strategy practice and strategy process: family differences and the sociological eye. *Organization Studies* 28(10): 1575–1586.

Whittington R, Molloy E, Mayer M, Smith A. 2006. Practices of strategising/organising: broadening strategy work and skills. *Long Range Planning* 39(6): 615–629.

Worley CG, Mohrman SA, Nevitt JA. 2011. Large group interventions: an empirical field study of their composition, process, and outcomes. *Journal of Applied Behavioral Science* 47(4): 404–431.

PART 10

MICROFOUNDATIONS AND BEHAVIORAL STRATEGY

Nicolai J. Foss, Lead

10.0

MICROFOUNDATIONS IN STRATEGY: CONTENT, CURRENT STATUS, AND FUTURE PROSPECTS

Nicolai J. Foss

Introduction

Strategy fundamentally revolves around *choice*. Thus, in their seminal essay, Rumelt, Schendel, and Teece (1991: 6) explained how firms

> have choices to make if they are to survive. Those which are strategic include: the selection of goals, the choice of products and services to offer; the design and configuration of policies determining how the firm positions itself to compete in product markets (e.g. competitive strategy); the choice of an appropriate level of scope and diversity; and the design of organization structure, administrative systems and policies used to define and coordinate work. It is a basic proposition of the strategy field that these choices have critical influence on the success or failure of the enterprise, and, that they must be integrated. It is the integration (or reinforcing pattern) among these choices that makes the set a strategy.

Of course, the domain of choice considered by this view is relatively restricted, as it is clear that the relevant choices are not those of "firms," whatever that may mean, but of top managers. This emphasis may have been forgotten for some time as strategy became fixated on a host of firm-level concepts such as (dynamic) capabilities, core competences, absorptive capacity, and so on, with an unclear relation to choice (Felin and Foss, 2005). Recently, however, the emphasis on choice as a central concept in strategy has returned. Thus, Leiblein, Reuer, and Zenger (2018: 559) propose that the "field of strategy [should] be defined by and unified around the study of strategic decisions—decisions that are interdependent with other decisions and therefore have the potential to guide other decisions" (see also Baer, Dirks, and Nickerson, 2013). Adding specific content to this focus on top manager choice, Zenger (2016) suggests focusing on the "theories" that strategists hold, that is, their reasoned instances of strategic "what-if" thinking concerning which combinations of resources and product markets will reach which strategic aims.

The return of choice reflects a number of developments in strategy and related fields since Rumelt *et al.* wrote, such as CEO and top management team research, strategic leadership research, behavioral strategy, research that stresses the interconnected, complementary nature of many strategic choices (e.g., as captured by the NK model in complex systems theory; Levinthal [1997]), cooperative game theory, strategic human capital theory, the greater availability of microdata—and *microfoundations*. In many ways, the microfoundations theme has served as a unifying label for those seeking to find more room for choice in strategy. Perhaps because of this inclusiveness, the term "microfoundations" has not always been used in a clear manner, and it is still advisable to proffer a definition when using the term. Among the potential sources of confusion are issues, such as, Whose choice matters? Only top managers'? Or other organizational members' also? Does "choice" mean "rational choice"? Isn't microfoundations just about applying organizational behavior theory to strategy?

While indeed choice is central in microfoundational research, microfoundations are fundamentally about understanding aggregate—which in strategy typically means firm- or industry-level—phenomena in terms of the actions and interactions of individuals, notably organizational members. The choices of CEOs and other top managers obviously matter a great deal, but to understand, for example, the nature of dynamic capabilities (Teece, Pisano, and Shuen, 1997) or of absorptive capacity (Foss, Laursen, and Pedersen, 2011), an isolated focus on top managers simply is not sufficient. It is also necessary to pay attention to middle managers, gatekeepers, research scientists, and indeed often also to organizational members on the shop floor.

Arguably the first use of microfoundations in this sense in strategy is in Felin and Foss (2005),[1] which was primarily an attack on what these authors saw as an excessive use of macro constructs without clear microfoundations, such as routines, capabilities, absorptive capacity, and the like. Felin and Foss argued that it was basically unclear how a construct such as (firm-level) "capability" relates to the skills, knowledge, actions, and interactions of organizational members. Microfoundations was quickly picked up and used as a framing device by prominent management scholars (e.g., Teece, 2007; Eisenhardt, Furr, and Bingham, 2010), and the methodological message of the "microfoundations movement" (Winter, 2013) has met with general acceptance in strategy (Aguinis and Molina-Azorin, 2015). However, microfoundational research represents challenges, particularly in the empirical dimension, as it requires sampling at minimum two levels and "proper" variation at these levels also, and raises difficult issues concerning the treatment of time and causality.

In this chapter, I briefly discuss the nature of microfoundations and then turn to a similarly brief exposition of the microfoundational currents in contemporary strategy thinking.[2] It is clear that rhetorically microfoundations has been successful; in other words, management scholars have found microfoundational arguments to be largely persuasive. Moreover, substantial theoretical and empirical microfoundational work has been made over the last decade. However, while much progress has already been made in the microfoundations space, perhaps the greatest challenge for microfoundations research in the context of strategy remains: developing models of decision-making that are particularly relevant in a strategy context. Significant parts of strategy research are based on a version of the expected utility model, or on behavioral models that at the end of the day rest on probabilistic foundations. However, these are ill-suited for dealing with unforeseen contingencies and in general with uncertainty that goes beyond probabilistic risk. The recent COVID-19 pandemic has underscored the importance of developing models of strategic choice under such conditions.

Microfoundations: Nature and Current Status

The nature of microfoundations

For starters, "microfoundations" is not a strategy theory, such as positioning, dynamic capabilities, or resource-based theory. Rather, it is an overarching approach to the explanation of social phenomena, such as firm profitability, firm capabilities, absorptive capacity, and so on, which can be expressed as a set of modeling heuristics. It is also an approach that starts from a basic ontological commitment, namely that the phenomena of interest in management are inherently multilevel in nature. The microfoundations project seeks to advance our understanding of management phenomena by ensuring that analysis explicitly considers this multilevel nature by locating (theoretically and empirically) the proximate causes of the phenomenon one seeks to explain at one or more levels of analysis lower than that of the phenomenon itself (Coleman, 1990; Foss and Linder, 2019).[3]

The details of microfoundational explanation have been outlined elsewhere (see, in particular, Foss and Linder, 2019: Chapter 3), so the following brief characterization will hopefully suffice. Microfoundational explanation is based on the notion of a *layered social ontology*, that is, levels are not theoretical abstractions, but exist in social reality (Little, 1998). It makes causal arguments rooted in *mechanistic explanation*, that is, it involves accounting for the mechanisms that are operative within as well as between levels (Machamer, Darden, and Craver, 2000), which also implies a commitment to account for time-dimensioned processes (Abell, Felin, and Foss, 2008). The emphasis on the *primacy of micro* (i.e., all explanation must always involve reference to micro) means that microfoundational explanation highlights the role of *actions/ behaviors and interactions*. Yet such explanation does not rule out the use of *collectives*, but does rule out explanation that proceeds only in terms of macro to macro relations as such relations are always mediated by micro.

This final prohibition against "methodological collectivism" in explanation may warrant some discussion. While as a matter of social ontology all macro-macro relations are indeed mediated by micro (how could it be otherwise?), does this necessarily mean that all our explanation must be macro-micro-macro? No. First, we can still say things like, "Firm A had superior capabilities which helped to do so and so and be more profitable," provided we can offer some account of how the effect of capabilities on performance was mediated by factors at the micro level. Second, there are indeed situations where we are entitled to disregard individuals in explanation. One is when individuals are so homogeneous that one randomly chosen individual is highly representative of the rest. Another is when organizations represent "strong situations" such that individuals, while perhaps initially heterogeneous, are also so malleable that the conditions in the first case obtain (Felin and Hesterly, 2007). Whether individuals are homogeneous and/or malleable and whether organizations (or other social entities) are indeed strong situations are not issues that can be settled on an a priori basis, but are ultimately empirical questions. However, a possible conclusion is that a meaningful microfoundational explanation presupposes individual-level heterogeneity, because otherwise little additional explanatory leverage is gained by including the micro level.

A diverse movement

In their keyword-based review of microfoundations papers in the top management journals, Foss and Linder (2019) document a marked increase since 2010 in research that is explicitly framed as microfoundational, in particular with respect to *empirical* microfoundational work that was basically absent from the literature until 2010. They also document a huge diversity with respect to (1) what is taken as the important entities and phenomena at the micro (e.g., individuals, teams, firms, routines, practices) and macro (e.g., groups, firms, industries, ecosystems) levels; (2) the models of action and behavior from which scholars build their microfoundations;[4] and (3) the degree to which contributions differ in terms of how the relevant explanation plays out over levels and causal mechanisms. Thus, some work focuses on how certain individual-level conditions affect the behavior of the respective individuals in question (what can be termed a "micro-micro" relation) and how this behavior then leads to certain organizational-level outcomes (and hence what is typically called a "micro-macro" relation). Other work, in turn, includes organizational-level antecedents to the individual-level conditions (a "macro-micro" relation), whereas some focus exclusively on the "micro-macro" relation. For example, Felin and Hesterly's (2007) provocative argument that organizational capabilities are fundamentally epiphenomena of individual-level heterogeneity is an argument that primarily invokes a micro-macro relation.

Very few strategy papers supply a "full" microfoundational explanation that accounts for both inter- and intralevel relations. An example is Distel (2019), which studies how formal and informal integration mechanisms are positively related to absorptive capacity at the organizational level through the mediation of microlevel process (employee perspective taking and creativity), explicitly estimating all relevant arrows of the Coleman diagram by means of structural equation modeling. A purely theoretical example is Lindenberg and Foss (2011), which examines the conditions under which organizational antecedents (e.g., task structure and rewards) may influence individual-level cognition and motivation such that the beneficial organizational consequences of what they call "joint production motivation" are realized.

Microfoundations as a course correction

While few strategy papers may be fully microfoundational in the sense that they account for macro to micro, micro to micro, and micro to macro links, a number of the theories that have been foundational in strategy certainly do this, and there is work that—without marketing itself as such—is in fact microfoundational, suggesting that the microfoundations movement is perhaps a course correction in a field that had increasingly focused on collective-level constructs with an unclear relation to individuals.

For example, transaction cost economics (TCE) (Williamson, 1985) is one of the foundational theories of strategy, shaping thinking on corporate strategy, alliance strategy, and much else (Rumelt et al., 1991; Leiblein and Reuer, 2020). What drives TCE predictions regarding governance structures is a subtle interplay between incentives (a property of an interaction context) and individual decisions (driven by opportunism and bounded rationality) that lead to simultaneous choice of transaction characteristics and governance structures. Thus, both macro and micro levels and relations between these are involved. Another important source theory is the behavioral theory of the firm (Cyert and March, 1963; Gavetti et al., 2012). This, too, ultimately rests on a sophisticated analysis of individual behaviors (March and Simon, 1958), but builds from that to analysis of standard operating procedures, coalitions, and firm-level behaviors, and how these feed back to coalitions and individuals. A third example is noncooperative game theory, which has influenced much thinking on competitive strategy (e.g., Ghemawat, 1991). Games specify the interdependence (collective level) of strategies (individual level) and identify equilibrium outcomes (collective level). Simulation approaches, increasingly influential in the understanding of how firms adapt strategies over time, similarly trace the interplay between micro and macro levels. In this sense, microfoundations is hardly a revolutionary movement, but is entirely in line with some of the main currents that have shaped strategy thinking.

New microfoundational insight in established concepts

Arguably, the microfoundations message has become influential not just because it represents an important course correction, but also because microfoundations seem particularly generative of new insight. Most theories have generative potential in the sense that they are capable of generating new insight beyond their original, intended context. For example, while TCE was originally intended as an alternative theory of the rationales of vertical integration, it developed into a general theory of the choice of efficient economic organization. Of course, the theory of evolution by natural selection has spread much beyond its original domain of application. Similarly, microfoundations has demonstrated a generative potential much beyond the original critical context of arguing that the firm-level capabilities had little real connection to individual behaviors and interaction (Felin and Foss, 2005).

In fact, over the last decade or so, much new insight into the workings of capabilities and routines has been obtained by being more explicit about their psychological underpinnings, and much of this is explicitly microfoundational (e.g., Helfat and Peteraf, 2015; Salvato and Rerup, 2018; for reviews and discussion, see further Felin and Foss, 2009; Felin et al., 2012; Heimeriks et al., 2012). Thus, Helfat and Peteraf (2015) further unpack Teece's notions of "sensing," "seizing," and "reconfiguring"— themselves (routine-based) microfoundations of dynamic capabilities—in terms of specific individual-level types of cognitive capabilities that reside at the level of top managers. They explain how these capabilities impact strategic change processes in firms. Salvato and Rerup (2018) examine routines in the context of product development and show how participants within a routine are capable of simultaneously balancing an explorative emphasis on design with an efficiency goal.

These are recent examples of how microfoundations have produced progress by supplying "missing parts." Thus, prior to 2005 very little work existed on the individual-level microfoundations of routines and capabilities; the microfoundations emphasis (along with the nonstrategy work of Feldman and Pentland, 2003) has prompted a spate of work on the microfoundations of routines and capabilities (Abell et al., 2008; Felin et al., 2012; Salvato and Rerup, 2018). However, a microfoundations focus has also brought new insight in phenomena where much theorizing already exists regarding microfoundations. Examples are the TCE analyses of the boundaries of the firm (e.g., Nickerson and Zenger, 2008) and the choice of hierarchical form (e.g., Foss and Weber, 2016). Specifically, theory has been advanced here, by adding to the behavioral repertoire of TCE or unpacking one of the behavioral assumptions of TCE. Thus, Nickerson and Zenger show how adding envy to TCE introduces a social comparison dimension that provides a new explanation of wage compression and hierarchical structure. Foss and Weber show that unpacking the bounded rationality component of TCE in terms of adding social comparison biases and framing effects produces new insight into the sources of hierarchical conflict, as transactions between hierarchical units (and organizational members) are influenced by the frames and biases these bring to the transaction. They show that hierarchical forms (e.g., M, U, and matrix forms) differ systematically in terms of social comparison and framing and therefore the level and kind of internal conflict with which they are associated.

Microfoundational streams

Thus, microfoundations may be generative of new insights to the extent that it "digs deeper" into the analysis of established constructs and relations, adding new detail to existing theorizing. However, there are also distinct theory streams in strategy that are properly microfoundational and have emerged and become successful roughly at the same time that microfoundations became a prominent theme in strategy. In particular, the fields of behavioral strategy and strategic human capital have become flourishing parts of the strategy theory landscape (each now has its own interest group in strategy's leading professional association, the Strategic Management Society).[5]

Behavioral strategy refers to the application of insights from psychology and behavioral economics to the research and practice of strategic management. In one definition of the field, "Behavioral strategy merges cognitive and social psychology with strategic management theory and practice. Behavioral strategy aims to bring realistic assumptions about human cognition, emotions, and social behavior to the strategic management of organizations and, thereby, to enrich strategy theory, empirical research, and real-world practice" (Powell, Lovallo, and Fox, 2011: 1371; see also Gavetti, 2012; Rindova, Reger, and Dalpiaz, 2012; Hambrick and Crossland, 2018).

More specifically, behavioral strategy is explicitly microfoundational (Felin, Foss, and Ployhart, 2015) in the sense that a psychology-based understanding of the actions and interactions of individuals is seen as important to adequately explain many traditional strategy phenomena (not only CEO and top management team behaviors, but also entry decisions, competitive interaction, and firm heterogeneity). In so doing, it draws in principle on all fields of psychology, even though cognitive and social psychology have been much more influential than, say, motivational psychology or the psychology of goals. Furthermore, behavioral strategy posits that microfoundational assumptions about behaviors and interactions are to be based in evidence (e.g., brought about by means of experiments) rather than the extent to which these allow for mathematical tractability, or are "elegant" or similar. Overall, behavioral strategy may be characterized as a commitment to understanding the (social, cognitive, motivational) psychology of strategists and other organizational members to the extent that these matter to the key dependent variables of strategy (ultimately, sustained competitive advantage).

Strategic human capital theory highlights one particular resource, namely "human capital"—that is, the skills, capabilities, experience, and so on.—as it is embodied in individual employees, managers, and entrepreneurs (Coff, 1997; Campbell *et al.*, 2010a, 2010b). Strategic human capital theory is surveyed in Coff and Rickley's (2021) chapter in this book. The interest in human capital stems from (at least) two considerations: first, the increasing general importance of human capital for value creation and growth (e.g., Barro, 2001); second, human capital is a unique resource in that it, unlike other resources, cannot be owned by the firm. In other words, an increasingly important resource presents unique management challenges. Strategic human capital theory examines firm and employee motivations to build or extend human capital in organizations under different assumptions about, for example, incentives, distribution of bargaining power, and the complementarity and specificity of the relevant human capital (e.g., Crook *et al.*, 2011).

For example, while employees who contribute much to firm-level creation may seem to be very attractive employees to hire, train, and maintain, this may not necessarily be so. If those employees are also highly mobile—that is, they can easily switch to employment in another firm without reducing their pay—they can leverage considerable bargaining power, in turn appropriating substantial parts of the value they create (with maximum bargain power, all such value). On the other hand, it may seem highly attractive from the point of view of firms that employees specialize to the firm (or, more precisely, other firm resources, Lippman and Rumelt, 2003), but this exposes employees to an appropriation risk. When employees specialize their human capital to their firm, they reduce their bargaining power. Thus, employees may be reluctant to engage in value-increasing human capital co-specialization without some kind of guarantee or commitment on the part of the firm (i.e., management) that its superior bargaining power will not be unfairly used in dealings with employees. As Kreps (1990) has argued, corporate culture may be one way in which firms signal their intentions to engage in fair dealings with employees. This will be a credible signal to the extent that corporate culture is a valuable reputational asset.

Challenges and Opportunities for Microfoundations Researchers

The first stage of the microfoundations movement in macro management was a basically philosophical and methodological critique of certain (verbal) modeling practices in strategy, specifically explaining firm-level outcomes in terms of firm-level variables (e.g., Felin and Foss, 2005; Felin and Hesterly, 2007). This message met with rather quick acceptance. Microfoundations then became increasingly constructive, and less critical, as theorizing began to explicitly refer to and heed microfoundational principles (e.g., Teece, 2007). However, in its third stage of development, the microfoundations movement faces some major challenges. The purpose of this section is to discuss them.

Making microfoundations come alive empirically

Microfoundations have been relatively slow to come alive in the empirical dimension. Perhaps because unfolding the empirical side of microfoundations is rather recent, there has so far been little discussion of the various empirical challenges of microfoundations (but see Aguinis and Molina-Azorin, 2015). However, this is an issue that cannot be neglected. Management research is a fundamentally empirical enterprise, which implies that theorizing eventually needs to demonstrate empirical support. If microfoundations cannot do this, enthusiasm about microfoundations will disappear.

The challenges in terms of empirical implementation that microfoundations face are relatively serious. Some are well known, such as the need for statistical techniques that are up to the job and the problem that sampling at both the micro and macro levels requires that the "right" variation is present at both levels and that selection issues stemming from the nested nature of multilevel data are kept at bay (for detailed discussion of these issues, see Foss and Linder, 2019: Chapter 4). However, there are additional pragmatic as well as problems-in-principle that may severely hamper the microfoundations project.

Micro-data availability

Empirical microfoundations requires analysis of micro-data, that is, individual-level data. As compared to the relatively easy availability of firm-level data, including financial data, individual-level datasets are scarce and often costly. Some countries (notably, the Nordic countries) hold public registers with very detailed individual-level information. For example, the statistics authorities of Denmark holds information on the current employment status, past job history, current job position, age, marital status, gender, education, income, car ownership, grades received by an individual throughout her educational history, even IQ (at least of the male part of the population as IQ tests are part of the annual draft) of each and every employee in the Danish economy. These are data with a high information content. They are useful for linking the individual level and the firm level in exploring how individual-level and firm-level characteristics interact in the production of outcomes at various levels. For example, Lyngsie and Foss (2017) explore how the proportion of women in top management is associated with innovation outcomes (positively), and how this is moderated by the proportion of women in the firm's workforce (negatively). Barney, Foss, and Lyngsie (2018) link these data to survey data to explore how the allocation of decision rights across the managerial hierarchy is associated with innovation outcomes. Dahl, Dezsö, and Ross (2012) use them to examine how the gender of a CEO's children help explain the firm's wage policy.

Individual behaviors and interaction

A fundamental issue concerning individual-level data is that even if the best demographic register data can be accessed, for many microfoundational purposes they are still inherently incomplete. In a microfoundational explanation, individual actions and behaviors as well as interactions, unfolding over time, are key. Thus, one would wish to observe such actions and interactions over time. Even if individual-level demographic data can be sampled at different points in time, they are at best proxies of behaviors. And even if such data may proxy for individual-level behaviors, at the CEO level, for example, they may be problematic as proxies for how such behaviors aggregate. An important reason is that interaction may cause new, unintended behaviors that are not related to individual-level demographics in any obvious way. This means that simply moving from micro to macro by averaging individual-level characteristics may be highly misspecified. Adding diversity indices may help somewhat, because they account for the dispersion of micro-level observations, but such indices still do not directly capture micro-to-macro effects based on micro-level actions. To better capture such effects and the underlying mechanisms it may be necessary to make use of less standard approaches.

Nonstandard approaches

Microfoundations highlight time, mechanisms, individual behaviors, and interactions. This challenges the application of conventional statistical techniques for the analysis of large datasets. However, microfoundations may, for the same reasons, help to stimulate the use of small-N, or "qualitative," research in strategy—for example, for purposes of examining the dynamics of strategic decision and TMT dynamics as a complement to investigation based on the analysis of panel data. For example, large-N inquiry into the role of dynamic capabilities in firm adaptation may benefit from careful small-N research on how the exercise of dynamic capabilities actually unfolds in terms of decision-making and interaction between managers.

Small-N research, and therefore also the combination of small- and large-N research, have not been used much in strategy research, although much strategy teaching makes use of narrative accounts ("cases") of the behaviors of top decision-makers and firms. In addition to their inherent unsuitability for purposes of statistical inference, small-N research may be seen as nonrigorous, because of the seeming absence of clear, formalized procedures and protocols for data sampling and analysis. Such perceived problems may overwhelm advantages in terms of allowing the researcher greater contextualization, detail, and, if not causal inference, then knowledge of the "causal grain" of reality.

However, these concerns may be partly exaggerated in light of the rigor of historical research approaches (cf. Argyres *et al.*, 2020), as well as the emergence of analytical approaches for the analysis of qualitative data. These approaches include basic tools for handling nonnumerical data, such as the NVivo software. But they also include analytical approaches such as comparative narratives constructed for the rigorous analysis and comparison of action-driven sequential events that can be described in terms of graphs such as the Coleman diagram (Abell and Engel, 2018). This requires description of states, actors, actions, and mapping of actions unto actors (making comparison possible, e.g., in terms of a formal treatment homogeneity of the relevant structures). The methodology of Bayesian narratives allows for the treatment of causality even if comparative cases are not available by using, for example, statements of the form "CEO N did x because of y" and "CEO N didn't do z because of t" to be treated as evidence that can be used as inputs into computations of Bayesian likelihood ratios of specific causal links (Abell, 2011).

A very different set of approaches allow for tracing actions and their consequences as these unfold over time, theoretically as well as empirically. Thus, agent-based modeling and simulation techniques can help in studying the emergent outcomes of the dynamics of simultaneously interacting agents (typically described in terms of the rules these follow), and how such outcomes feed back on actions and interactions. In other words, a simulation approach allows for connecting several Coleman bathtubs over time. Of course, simulation approaches have long been a staple of macro management theory, particularly in organizational learning (e.g., March, 1991). Empirically, simulation approaches allow for "history-friendly" modeling (cf. Capone *et al.*, 2019). This means that parameter values and initial conditions are not plucked "out of the blue" at the modeler's discretion, but are chosen, parameterized, and otherwise specified in the light of existing empirical evidence. Additionally, the modeling of the behaviors of agents may be responsive to microfoundational concerns. For example, small-N research may lend credence to adopting some rules rather than other ones as relevant for characterizing agents. For example, much research (starting in management research with Levinthal's [1997] application to organization learning and adaptation theory) has examined how firms search over "fitness landscapes." Small-N, microfoundational research may lend credibility to modeling, say, "long jumps" in such landscapes in one way rather than another. It may also provide insight into interactions, specifically, how interactions are clustered, interaction frequency, how dominant coalitions are formed and dissolved, and so on. In this context, an interesting question is how dominant strategy-making coalitions are shaped by reacting to various major events in the firm's environment.

Generative microfoundational theory

Because microfoundations has concrete implications for theory building, it has the potential to be generative—that is, productive of new theory. Thus, a microfoundational lens has been applied not just to routines and capabilities, the original targets of the microfoundations critique (Felin and Foss, 2005; Abell *et al.*, 2008), but also to organizational learning and absorptive capacity (Lewin, Massini, and Peeters, 2011), sustained competitive advantage (Campbell *et al.*, 2010a), and a host of other firm-level phenomena (see further, Felin *et al.*, 2015; Foss and Linder, 2019: Chapter 2). However, the microfoundations perspective has the potential to illuminate many other areas of strategy than those already covered in the literature. This may happen by continuing to problematize existing macro-to-macro relations, which may give rise to theorizing that fills the microfoundational holes. For example, how the link between firm-level absorptive capacity and innovation outcomes are mediated by processes and factors at the micro level is still ill-understood. However, there is another way in which microfoundations may be generative, namely by adding insights from an existing microfoundational perspective to a perspective that isn't currently microfoundational. In the following subsections, I identify two examples of this, and one example of making theoretical progress by drilling deeper and refining existing behavioral assumptions.

Strategic human capital microfoundations for open innovation

As mentioned above, the emerging strategic human capital approach can properly be described as microfoundational because of its emphasis on linking individual-level characteristics and behaviors to firm-level outcomes. It is also an approach that can be usefully deployed to other strategy contexts. In fact, in a recent paper, Laursen and Salter (2020) apply it to gain new insight into the role of employees in an "open innovation" context (Chesbrough, 2003), particularly with respect to the bargaining position and value of employees in an open innovation context. They point out that employees are needed to identify potentially useful knowledge in the firm's environment and bring it into the firm. Only then can it be deployed to an innovation context. Laursen and Salter (2020) call the employees who are most important in this process "OI employees." They argue that while it is desirable that OI employees get access to valuable knowledge in the firm's environment, there is also a potential penalty involved.

The problem is that even if OI employees share the knowledge they gathered from sources outside the firm to other employees, asymmetric information conditions are still likely to obtain in certain key respects. Thus, OI employees will have superior knowledge as compared to others in the firm concerning what kind of knowledge is likely to be in high demand now and in the future, why this is the case, and so on. This knowledge is obviously important not just to the employing firm but also to other firms. Moreover, because of their search efforts, OI employees become more visible to such other firms, which means a boost to their bargaining power. Of course, being able to appropriate more of the value they create strengthens the incentives of OI employees to engage in external knowledge search. Still, their increased bargaining power translates into diminished bargaining power of other employees, and the incentives of the latter to engage in actions that foster value creation are diminished. This classic trade-off only becomes visible in an OI context by taking an explicit micro-perspective.

Laursen and Salter's contribution is just one example of how microfoundations illuminates the understanding of innovation in strategy. Empirically, relatively little is known about how the characteristics and behaviors of employees and managers shape open innovation. There are many open research questions here related to the motivations, opportunities, and abilities of relevant actors to engage in actions that are conducive to successful open innovation. Such research may draw not only on the strategic human capital field but also on insights from human resource management.

TMT microfoundations for behavioral strategy

Behavioral strategy was highlighted earlier in this chapter as one of the microfoundational currents in contemporary strategy theory. Indeed, the attempt of behavioral strategy to link key strategy phenomena to cognitive and social-psychology sounds straight out of the microfoundational rulebook. And yet, not all of behavioral strategy is obviously microfoundational. Consider, for example, Greve's (1998) classic study of how divergences between realized performance and aspired-to performance influence organizational and strategic changes (Greve studies radio station format changes), a line of research that has been rather prominent in strategy (Gavetti *et al.*, 2012). He outlines various psychological mechanisms, such as framing and loss aversion, in describing firm reactions to such divergences. However, these are not explicitly linked to specific roles or persons in the relevant firms, so these micro mechanisms are blackboxed and unobserved, and firms are effectively seen as unitary decision-makers.

In contrast, the vast literature on top management teams (TMTs) that has followed Hambrick and Mason (1984) explicitly considers executive decision-making in a team context. Much of this literature also relies on demographic proxies for actual behaviors but it does drill deeper in terms of micro than most research on how performance feedback prompts strategic changes. For example, different team profiles in terms of age, gender, functional background, and so on may influence risk-taking behaviors (Hambrick and Mason, 1984). The extent of fault lines within the TMT (i.e., the extent to which the TMT manifests demographically defined subgroups) may influence the ability of the TMT to act in a coordinated way in the face of performance shortfalls. We currently know very little about this. However, adding TMT research on top management diversity, interaction, fault lines, and so on to the strategy literature on performance-aspiration divergences may be productive of new insight. In a recent example of such research, Kolev and McNamara (2020) draw on upper echelon theory to examine how key characteristics of the top management team— tenure and gender diversity, size, and pay disparity—influence how top managers deal with performance shortfalls. They find that top management teams with greater tenure diversity, smaller size, and smaller pay disparity among members make more risky strategic decisions in response to performance shortfalls. Many opportunities exist for extending this line of research in terms of characteristics and actions that are considered.

Bounded rationality microfoundations for comparative governance

Much of strategic management boils down to issues of comparative governance. Thus, executing business strategies requires an organization that is up to the task in terms of the right division of labor, allocation of authority, design of information channels, choice of reward structures, and other decisions. The choice of corporate strategies of vertical integration, diversification, horizontal integration, and so on requires matching hierarchical forms (Rumelt *et al.*, 1991). The perennial make-or-buy issue and associated issues of contracting are comparative governance issues. Thinking about these issues has been greatly assisted by theorizing such as transaction cost economics (TCE) (Williamson, 1985), a microfoundational theory that makes behavioral assumptions of bounded rationality and opportunism.

However, the theory is also quite vague about what bounded rationality actually means. Thus, Williamson (1985: 5) only cites Simon's definition that it means that a decision-maker is "intendedly rational, but boundedly so." However, as much cognitive psychology research suggests, decision-makers can be boundedly rational in a myriad of ways. Specifying what bounded rationality may mean in a TCE context may lead to new insights in comparative contracting. Thus, Weber and Mayer (2014) note that bounded rational decision-makers respond to uncertainty by adopting cognitive frames. When different parties to a transaction hold different frames, conflict may arise. Therefore, effective governance should also support the development of shared cognitive frames to assist transacting. Along similar lines, Foss and Weber (2016) argue that different hierarchical forms are associated with different cognitive frames and social comparison biases. This influences the level and type of conflict associated with different hierarchical forms, which is a factor that corporate strategy needs to consider. For example, future research may look into how this conflict potential shapes the ability of firms to adapt to major outside changes or to engage in strategies that require concerted efforts across business units.

Coming to grips with deep uncertainty

A final, but major opportunity for microfoundational research is building proper microfoundations for the understanding of how top management teams and firms deal with "deep" (aka "genuine" or "Knightian") uncertainty (or unknown unknowns, etc.). The ongoing COVID-19 pandemic has underscored the importance of this. While the pandemic may not have been a major surprise to, say, the infectious disease research community, it certainly came as a surprise, or unknown unknown, to the business community. As Ehrig and Foss (2020) argue, "unknown unknowns" may be thought of as future contingencies that lack an ex ante description for at least some decision-makers who are later affected by the contingencies. Such events often shake up and shape industries—redefining what are relevant strategic factors, creating new barriers to entry and imitation—and in general relate to core strategy issues.

The problem is that strategy theory lacks a good understanding of decision-making in the face of unknown unknowns and how fundamental uncertainty and ignorance are transformed into epistemically more stable conditions. Strategy has strong probabilistic models for analyzing the decisions of individuals, but the same cannot be said for those decision situations that escape a probabilistic (e.g., Bayesian) treatment. A microfoundational research effort here should focus on building models of decision-making for such decision situations. In a recent contribution, Ehrig and Schmidt (2020) draw on cognitive science research on belief revision to show how systematic insight may be developed into how strategists revise beliefs in the face of events that force them to drop some beliefs while new adding new ones (which is radically different from Bayesian updating). This highly promising line of research is illustrative of the generative potential of microfoundations in strategy.

Conclusions

Over the last one and a half decades, microfoundations has become an important part of the conversation in strategy research, partly because it has aligned well with other parallel developments (e.g., multilevel methods, the increasing availability of micro data, the emergence of behavioral strategy and strategic human capital approaches, etc.), and partly because a quest for microfoundations seems obviously right to many, as it embodies the general scientific attempt to gain insight by means of reduction (Elster, 1989).

While there is now a substantial body of microfoundational work in strategy, there are also stumbling blocks to the general acceptance and use of microfoundational approaches, notably in the areas of data and methods. However, research practices, data availability, and similar factors are to some extent endogenous to what is on the theoretical agenda of strategy scholars, so growing interest will lead to better practices and more data. Moreover, microfoundations have demonstrated a potent generative capability that makes them valuable for scholars interested in theory-building. Finally, microfoundations points to one of the deepest issues in strategy (and, more generally, management research): What is the proper model of the individual in strategy? Williamson (1985: 45) also cites Simon's claim that "Nothing is more fundamental in setting our research agenda and informing our research methods than our view of the nature of the human beings whose behavior we are studying." Perhaps the answer is that there isn't *a* best model, but that it depends on the research question. Even so, microfoundations points to the crucial importance of being clear about what is assumed about the cognition and motivation of individuals. As suggested in this chapter, such clarity of assumptions is essential to strategic management's continued theoretical progress.

Notes

1. "Microfoundations" also appear in Lippman and Rumelt (2003), but is used somewhat differently, namely as a call for insight into the bargaining process through which firm-level revenue is split between resources.
2. Microfoundations have also recently become important in institutional organization theory (e.g., Cardinale, 2018) and in international business (e.g., Foss and Pedersen, 2019). This discussion is not surveyed here.
3. This is the main difference from multilevel approaches as conventionally understood, as these do not privilege any particular level. Microfoundations do privilege a level, as signaled by the very name of the concept: "micro" is the foundation, not "macro."
4. Thus, Felin and Hesterly (2007) and Abell *et al.* (2008) build on rational choice models; Pentland *et al.* (2012) or Baer *et al.* (2013), in contrast, assume that individuals are bounded rational; Helfat and Peteraf (2015) specifically emphasize heuristics that help cope with bounded rationality; Lindenberg and Foss (2011) and Bridoux, Courderoy, and Durand

(2017) focus on motivational aspects, such as the difference between extrinsic and intrinsic motivation or egocentric and prosocial motivations.

5. Of course, the use of psychology insights to further research in the behavior and performance of firms has a long history that long precedes the microfoundations movement (e.g., Cyert and March, 1963; Staw, 1981).

References

Abell P. 2011. Singular mechanisms and Bayesian narratives. In *Analytical Sociology and Social Mechanisms*, Demeulenaere P (ed.). Cambridge University Press: Cambridge, U.K.; 121–135.

Abell P, Engel O. 2018. The Coleman Diagram, Small N Inquiry, and Ethnographic Causality. Working Paper, London School of Economics.

Abell P, Felin T, Foss N. 2008. Building microfoundations for the routines, capabilities, and performance links. *Managerial and Decision Economics* **29**: 489–502.

Abell P, Felin T, Foss N. 2010. Causal and constitutive relations, and the squaring of Coleman's Diagram: reply to Vromen. *Erkenntnis* **73**: 385–391.

Aguinis H, Molina-Azorin JF. 2015. Using multilevel modeling and mixed methods to make theoretical progress in microfoundations for strategy research. *Strategic Organization* **13**: 353–364.

Argyres N, De Massis A, Foss N, Frattini F, Jones G, Silverman B. 2020. History-informed strategy research: the promise of history and historical research methods in advancing strategy scholarship. *Strategic Management Journal* **41**: 343–368.

Baer M, Dirks, KT, Nickerson JA. 2013. Microfoundations of strategic problem formulation. *Strategic Management Journal* **34**: 197–214.

Barney JB, Foss NJ, Lyngsie J. 2018. The role of senior management in opportunity formation: direct involvement or reactive selection? *Strategic Management Journal* **39**: 1325–1349.

Barro RJ. 2001. Human capital and growth. *American Economic Review* **91**: 12–17.

Bridoux F, Courderoy R, Durand R. 2017. Heterogeneous social motives and interactions: the three predictable paths of capability development. *Strategic Management Journal* **38**: 1755–1773.

Campbell BA, Coff R, Kryscynski D. 2010a. Rethinking sustained competitive advantage from human capital. *Academy of Management Review* **37**: 376–395.

Campbell BA, Ganco M, Franco AM, Agarwal R. 2010b. Who leaves, where to, and why worry? Employee mobility, entrepreneurship, and effect on source firm performance. *Strategic Management Journal* **33**: 65–87.

Capone G, Malerba F, Nelson RR, Orsenigo L, Winter SG. 2019. History-friendly models: retrospective and future perspectives. *Eurasian Business Review* **9**: 1–23.

Cardinale I. 2018. Beyond constraining and enabling: toward new microfoundations for institutional theory. *Academy of Management Review* **43**: 132–155.

Chesbrough H. 2003. *Open Innovation: The New Imperative for Creating and Profiting from Technology*. Harvard Business School Press: Boston, MA.

Coff, R. 1997. Human assets and management dilemmas: coping with hazards on the road to resource-based theory. *Academy of Management Review* **22**(2): 374–402.

Coff R, Rickley M. 2021. Strategic human capital: Fit for the future. In *Strategic Management: State of the Field and Its Future*, Duhaime IM, Hitt MA, Lyles MA (eds). Oxford University Press: New York, NY; 579–593.

Coleman J. 1990. *Foundations of Social Theory*. Harvard University Press: Cambridge, MA.

Crook DJ, Combs JG, Woehr DJ, Ketchen DJ. 2011. Does human capital matter? A meta-analysis of the relationship between human capital and firm performance. *Journal of Applied Psychology* **96**: 443–456.

Cyert RM, March JG. 1963. *A Behavioral Theory of the Firm.* Oxford University Press: Oxford, U.K.

Dahl MS, Dezsö CL, Ross DG. 2012. Fatherhood and managerial style: how a male CEO's children affect the wages of his employees. *Administrative Science Quarterly* **57**: 669–693.

Distel AP. 2019. Unveiling the microfoundations of absorptive capacity: a study of Coleman's bathtub model. *Journal of Management* **45**: 2014–2044.

Ehrig T, Foss NJ. 2020. Unknown unknowns and the treatment of firm-level adaptation in strategy research. *Strategic Management Review* (forthcoming).

Ehrig T, Schmidt J. 2020. Theory-based learning and experimentation: how strategists can systematically generate knowledge under uncertainty. Working Paper.

Eisenhardt K, Furr NR, Bingham CB. 2010. Microfoundations of performance: balancing efficiency and flexibility in dynamic environments. *Organization Science* **21**: 1263–1273.

Elster J. 1989. *Nuts and Bolts for the Social Sciences.* Cambridge University Press: Cambridge, U.K.

Feldman MS, Pentland B. 2003. Reconceptualizing organizational routines as a source of flexibility and change. *Administrative Science Quarterly* **48**: 94–118.

Felin T, Foss N. 2005. Strategic organization: a field in search of micro-foundations. *Strategic Organization* **3**: 441–455.

Felin T, Foss N. 2009. Organizational routines and capabilities: historical drift and a course correction. *Scandinavian Journal of Management* **25**: 157–167.

Felin T, Foss N, Heimeriks K, Madsen, T. 2012. Microfoundations of routines and capabilities: individuals, processes, and structure. *Journal of Management Studies* **49**: 1351–1374.

Felin T, Foss, NJ, Ployhart R. 2015. The microfoundations movement in strategy and organization theory. *Academy of Management Annals* **9**: 575–632.

Felin T, Hesterly W. 2007. The knowledge-based view, nested heterogeneity, and new value creation: philosophical considerations on the locus of knowledge. *Academy of Management Review* **32**: 195–218.

Foss NJ, Laursen K, Pedersen T. 2011. Linking customer interaction and innovation: the mediating role of new organizational practices. *Organization Science* **22**: 980–999.

Foss NJ, Linder S. 2019. *Microfoundations.* Cambridge University Press: Cambridge, U.K.

Foss NJ, Pedersen T. 2019. Microfoundations in international management research: the case of knowledge sharing in multinational corporations. *Journal of International Business Studies* **50**: 1594–1621.

Foss NJ, Weber L. 2016. Putting opportunism in the back seat: bounded rationality, costly conflict, and hierarchical forms. *Academy of Management Review* **41**: 41–79.

Gavetti G. 2012. Toward a behavioral theory of strategy. *Organization Science* **23**: 267–285.

Gavetti G, Levinthal D, Greve H, Ocasio W. 2012. The behavioral theory of the firm: assessment and prospects. *Academy of Management Annals* **6**: 1–40.

Ghemawat P. 1991. *Commitment.* Free Press: New York, NY.

Greve H. 1998. Performance, aspirations, and risky organizational change. *Administrative Science Quarterly* **43**: 58–86.

Hambrick DC, Crossland C. 2018. A strategy for behavioral strategy: appraisal of small, mid-size, and large tent conceptions of this embryonic community. In *Behavioral Strategy in Perspective* (Advances in Strategic Management 39), Augier M, Fang C, Rindova V (eds). Emerald Group Publishing: Bingley, U.K.; 22–39.

Hambrick D, Mason P. 1984. Upper echelons: the organization as a reflection of its managers. *Academy of Management Review* **9**: 193–206.

Heimeriks K, Foss NJ, Winter M, Zollo S. 2012. A Hegelian dialogue on the micro-foundations of organizational routines and capabilities. *European Management Review* **8**: 173–197.

Helfat CE, Peteraf MA. 2015. Managerial cognitive capabilities and the microfoundations of dynamic capabilities. *Strategic Management Journal* **36**: 831–850.

Kolev KD, McNamara G. 2020. The role of top management teams in firm responses to performance shortfalls. *Strategic Organization* (forthcoming).

Kreps DM. 1990. Corporate culture and economic theory. In *Perspectives on Positive Political Economy*, Alt JE, Shepsle KA (eds). Cambridge University Press: Cambridge, U.K. ; 90–142.

Laursen K, Salter A. 2020. Who captures value from open innovation—the firm or its employees? *Strategic Management Review* (forthcoming).

Leiblein M, Reuer J. 2020. Foundations and futures of strategic management. *Strategic Management Review* **1**: 1–33.

Leiblein MJ, Reuer JJ, Zenger T. 2018. What makes a decision strategic? *Strategy Science* **3**(4): 558–573.

Levinthal DA. 1997. Adaptation on rugged landscapes. *Management Science* **43**: 934–950.

Lewin AY, Massini S, Peeters C. 2011. Microfoundations of internal and external absorptive capacity routines. *Organization Science* **22**: 81–98.

Lindenberg S, Foss N. 2011. Managing joint production motivation: the role of goal framing and governance mechanisms. *Academy of Management Review* **36**: 500–525.

Lippman SA, Rumelt RP. 2003. The payments perspective: micro-foundations of resource analysis. *Strategic Management Journal* **24**: 903–927.

Little D. 1998. *Microfoundations, Method, and Causation: On the Philosophy of the Social Sciences.* Transaction Publishers: New Brunswick, NJ:

Lyngsie J, Foss NJ. 2017. The more, the merrier? The role of gender in explaining entrepreneurial outcomes in established firms. *Strategic Management Journal* **38**: 487–505.

Machamer P, Darden L, Craver CF. 2000. Thinking about mechanisms. *Philosophy of Science* **67**: 1–25.

March JG. 1991. Exploration and exploitation in organizational learning. *Organization Science* **2**: 71–87.

March JG, Simon HA. 1958. *Organizations.* Wiley: New York, NY.

Nickerson JA, Zenger TR. 2008. Envy, comparison costs, and the theory of the firm. *Strategic Management Journal* **29**: 1429–1449.

Powell TC, Lovallo D, Fox CR. 2011. Behavioral strategy. *Strategic Management Journal* **32**: 1369–1382.

Rindova VP, Reger RK, Dalpiaz, E. 2012. The mind of the strategist and the eye of the beholder: the socio-cognitive perspective in strategy research. In *Handbook of Research on Competitive Strategy*, Dagnino GB (ed). Edward Elgar Publishing Ltd.: Cheltenham, U.K.; 147–164.

Rumelt RP, Schendel D, Teece DJ. 1991. Strategic management and economics. *Strategic Management Journal* **12**(S2): 5–29.

Salvato C, Rerup C. 2018. Routine regulation: balancing conflicting goals in organizational routines. *Administrative Science Quarterly* **63**: 170–209.

Staw BM. 1981. The escalation of commitment to a course of action. *Academy of Management Review* **6**: 577–587.

Teece DJ. 2007. Explicating dynamic capabilities: the nature and microfoundations of (sustainable) enterprise performance. *Strategic Management Journal* **28**: 1319–1350.

Teece DJ, Pisano G, Shuen A.1997. Dynamic capabilities and strategic management. *Strategic Management Journal* **18**: 509–533.

Weber L, Mayer K. 2014. Transaction cost economics and the cognitive perspective: investigating the sources and governance of interpretive uncertainty. *Academy of Management Review* **39**: 344–363.

Williamson OE. 1985. *The Economic Institutions of Capitalism*. Free Press: New York, NY.

Winter SG. 2013. Habit, deliberation, and action: Strengthening the microfoundations of routines and capabilities. *Academy of Management Perspectives* 27: 120–137.

Zenger T. 2016. *Beyond Competitive Advantage: How to Solve the Puzzle of Sustaining Growth While Creating Value*. Harvard Business Review Press: Boston, MA.

10.1

STRATEGIC HUMAN CAPITAL: FIT FOR THE FUTURE

Russell Coff and Marketa Rickley

Individual behavior is the essence of microfoundations that drive competitive advantage (Foss, 2011), and this movement has driven interest in strategic human capital (Coff and Kryscynski, 2011). Heightened attention has brought about a substantial shift in our understanding. Much of the early focus was on the differential impact of general and firm-specific human capital for generating and sustaining advantages (Coff, 1997; Wang, He, and Mahoney, 2009). We now see movement toward viewing individuals as having unique bundles of general human capital (Lazear, 2009), which underscores a complex matching process between human capital and organizations (Raffiee and Byun, 2020; Weller *et al.*, 2019). Our understanding of the relationships between human capital selection, development, mobility, compensation, and firm performance has become more nuanced (Campbell, Coff, and Kryscynski, 2012a) and is deviating from the central tenets of Becker's seminal work that suggested firms can capture value from investments into firm-specific but not general human capital (Becker, 1962, 1964). Traditionally held assumptions regarding what constitutes efficient matching between workers and firms are changing and inspiring new theoretical approaches.

Recognizing this shift holds implications for the broader field of strategy as well. As our understanding of individual behavior changes, this must also be reflected in our organization-level theories (Barney and Felin, 2013; Foss, 2011). While individual cognition, capabilities, and behavior have always played a central role in strategic management (Penrose, 1959), human capital—knowledge, skills, and abilities embedded in employees (Coff, 1997)—has become one of the most critical building blocks of unique firm-level capabilities. Indeed, assumptions regarding individuals and their human capital underlie a range of macro-level theories in strategy, including the resource-based view (Barney, 1991; Peteraf, 1993; Wernerfelt, 1984), knowledge-based view (Grant, 1996; Kogut and Zander, 1992), and behavioral theory of the firm (Cyert and March, 1992). This chapter therefore examines and assesses how thinking about human capital and firm outcomes has changed, and highlights advances in strategic human capital research that can affect the broader field of strategic management.

The chapter is organized around two major areas within strategic human capital research: human capital specificity and assortative matching in worker selection. We examine how each concept relates to competitive advantage and then briefly outline each stream's development, taking pause to identify areas of consensus and dissonance. Our emphasis is on identifying major unresolved issues and suggesting future opportunities.

What is the Role of Firm-Specific Human Capital?

Central to strategic management is the idea that performance among firms differs in large part due to heterogeneity in firm resources and capabilities (Barney, 1991; Leiblein and Madsen, 2009). In particular, firms enjoy sustained superior performance when isolating mechanisms, such as firm specificity, prevent rivals from imitating or accessing key resources (Rumelt, 1984).

Why past human capital research focuses on specificity

Firm-specific human capital has long been considered a critical type of human capital with potential to create value for firms (Jovanovic, 1979; Wang et al., 2009). Firm-specific human capital reflects knowledge and skills that are more applicable in the focal firm and are thereby less transferable, while general human capital can be applied across firms (Becker, 1962, 1964; Coff, 1997). By definition, there is a scarcity of individuals with capabilities that meet firm-specific needs. In addition, such skills may be causally ambiguous, socially complex, and/or tacit in nature (Coff, 1997; Hatch and Dyer, 2004). Accordingly, firm-specific human capital may be valuable and rare, and may hinder imitation by rival firms—a potential source of sustained competitive advantage (Barney and Wright, 1998).

For decades, the distinction between firm-specific and general human capital has been foundational in human capital research and provided a broadly accepted theoretical framing for mobility and compensation (Campbell et al., 2012a; Jovanovic, 1979; Mincer and Jovanovic, 1981), willingness to undertake firm-specific investments (Hashimoto, 1981; Wang et al., 2009), and how these interact to create value for firms (Campbell et al., 2012a; Kor and Leblebici, 2005).

In the classic human capital literature, the external labor market compensates workers for general human capital but not for firm-specific knowledge and skills from another firm. As a result, workers can expect to receive a discounted wage from other firms that may not reflect their full investment in human capital—reducing their willingness to leave the focal firm (Becker, 1964; Hashimoto, 1981; Jovanovic, 1979). The wage penalty associated with mobility serves two important purposes in this view. It allows the focal firm to retain essential knowledge (Peteraf, 1993), and to capture some of the differential between workers' use value in the focal firm and their next best external offer (Coff, 1999).

This argument sets the stage for a dilemma: workers may be unwilling to invest in firm-specific human capital if these are not fully compensated (Wang and Barney, 2006; Wang et al., 2009). Indeed, workers may perceive their firm-specific investments to be subject to *holdup hazard*—the risk that a firm may not follow through with promised compensation once workers invest. To address this concern, scholars explored corporate governance safeguards and incentives to motivate investment in firm-specific human capital (Mahoney and Kor, 2015).

However, empirical research has uncovered inconsistencies between theory and how employees and firms behaved (Kryscynski and Ulrich, 2015). For example, Somaya, Williamson, and Lorinkova (2008) showed that, not only can firms benefit from *hiring* workers from both cooperating firms (suppliers or buyers) and rivals, but they can even benefit from *losing* employees—though only to cooperating firms. Especially notable is the finding that employees' social capital from a previous employer, a form of firm-specific knowledge, can be leveraged by both cooperators and rivals. Indeed, there is evidence that firm-specific knowledge can be useful *across* firms despite barriers to transferability (Loewenstein and Spletzer, 1999). In practice, employers may not know what skills are applicable at other firms (Kryscynski and Ulrich, 2015).

Bias in perceptions of human capital specificity

Such inconsistencies between theory and observed behavior raise the question of whether the delineation between firm-specific and general human capital is as critical to sustained competitive advantage as traditional theory suggests. Although the claim is often taken for granted, a swell of recent work offers clarifications (Campbell et al., 2012a; Coff and Raffiee, 2015), caveats (Morris et al., 2017; Raffiee and Coff, 2016), reconceptualizations (Lazear, 2009; Lazear and Oyer, 2013), and critiques (Nyberg et al., 2018). However, it is important to acknowledge that it is still widely accepted that firms have heterogeneous capabilities and that these require them to deploy idiosyncratic skill sets. Thus, firm-specific human capital remains an important component of competitive advantage even if classical human capital theory is incorrect or incomplete.

Important recent developments in strategic human capital research highlight numerous implicit assumptions that underlie traditional human capital theory (Campbell et al., 2012a). For instance, in order for firm-specific human capital to function as an isolating mechanism, the external labor market (demand side) must have near perfect information about the value of applicants' skills at their current employer and the value these skills would provide for a different employer. Furthermore, it requires workers' (supply-side) assessments of the use and exchange value of their human capital to also be in alignment.

Thus, for human capital specificity to explain reduced labor mobility, compensation, and value capture, theories implicitly assume tight coupling between skills' use and exchange values in the market. Yet assuming near-perfect information is inconsistent not only with the way that employers and employees interact in practice (Coff and Raffiee, 2015) but also with information efficiency assumptions underlying resource-based theory (Mahoney and Pandian, 1992). Such inconsistent assumptions pose a fundamental problem for theory building (Foss and Hallberg, 2014) and warrant careful examination in future research.

These ideas have recently been extended in several ways. One such important contribution is the work of Morris *et al.* (2017), who proposed that workers' willingness to invest in firm-specific human capital may actually be perceived by hiring firms as a signal of workers' future willingness to invest in the firm-specific knowledge and skills required by the new employer. Taken this way, some might view workers' firm-specific human capital as a form of general human capital that could actually increase worker mobility.

To combat this and limit employee mobility, Morris *et al.* (2017) suggest that firms can muddy the signal that workers' investment in firm-specific human capital sends to the external labor market by providing incentives to workers for acquiring firm-specific human capital and creating a strong corporate culture. To avoid interference in the original signal, employees may, in turn, choose not to work for firms with such policies. However, questions remain regarding the relative efficacy of using extrinsic versus intrinsic incentives to weaken workers' signaling power. Also, does the positive signal value of worker investment in firm-specific human capital outweigh concerns about focal firms' potential postinvestment holdup?

On the supply side, recent research suggests that imperfect or biased perceptions of human capital specificity also abound (Groysberg, 2010), as evidenced by findings of negative or insignificant relationships between traditional proxies of firm-specific human capital (organizational commitment, firm tenure, and on-the-job training) and workers' perceptions of specificity (Raffiee and Coff, 2016). The implications of these findings could be significant, especially if future research uncovers that workers and firms make investment and mobility decisions based on perceived instead of objective firm-specific human capital.

Coff and Raffiee (2015) suggest that, if hiring firms perceive job candidates' human capital as general instead of as specific to another firm, firm-specific human capital would not hinder mobility. Indeed, the widely accepted use of skills-based résumés reflects the institutionalization of impression management to mask firm-specific skills. Furthermore, if employees perceive their human capital as general even though it is specific, they will be less reluctant to leave because they believe other firms will compensate them fully for their skills. Taken together, the resulting shift in the market equilibrium may push firms to share more of the surplus value created by the employer-employee relationship with employees (to retain them). This may have profound implications not only for employees' propensities to invest in firm-specific human capital, but also about the role of firm-specific human capital for human capital–based advantage (Coff and Raffiee, 2015). But Coff and Raffiee (2015) also highlight that firms can influence market perceptions of their employees' human capital. For example, firms can create reputations for having complementary assets that elevate productivity—without which workers would be less productive. They also may take actual and symbolic steps, like implementing noncompete agreements, to protect proprietary knowledge that may seem firm-specific. This underscores the significance of signaling and impression management in recruitment, hiring, and development.

Together, this line of inquiry raises several important questions for future research. To what extent are workers' and firms' perceptions of the specificity aligned? How do workers and firms manipulate perceptions of firm specificity? Finally, how do these perceptions affect critical outcomes (investments, mobility, wages, etc.)? This subjectivity prompts myriad questions.

The specific is general—and the general is specific

Recent developments are also changing conceptions of general human capital. Human capital theory posits that general human capital has homogeneous productivity across firms (Becker, 1962, 1964). General human capital has been conceptualized as equally valuable across firms. It was also presumed to be commonly available in the market—pervasive and abundant. Finally, individuals' stocks of general human capital were assumed to vary in level, but not in composition.

Lately, each of these assumptions has undergone scrutiny and criticism. First, because firms are heterogeneous (Weller et al., 2019), the productivity of individuals' general human capital may vary greatly across firms due to greater or lesser fit with firms' resources and capabilities (Ployhart et al., 2014). Second, it is evident that many skills are indeed generally applicable but are also quite rare. The available research on stars and their productivity highlights this point (e.g., Campbell et al. [2012b]; Kehoe, Lepak, and Bentley [2018]). For example, researchers who are highly successful at writing grant proposals will raise the profile of most research institutions. But these individuals are rare and thus provide a competitive advantage for only a limited number of institutions. Finally, individuals are not endowed with different levels of identical general human capital, but instead hold idiosyncratic combinations of general human capital (Campbell et al., 2012a; Lazear, 2009).

The conclusion is that firms choose unique combinations of general human capital based on their distinctive needs and preferences (Lazear, 2009), and it underlies the recent theoretical and empirically supported argument that competitive advantage can be derived from idiosyncratic bundles of general human capital (Molloy and Barney, 2015; Raffiee and Byun, 2020). Indeed, in their influential work, Campbell et al. (2012a) also noted that firm-specific human capital can only deter mobility through the wage mechanism if workers' idiosyncratic combinations of general human capital are not more valuable than their firm-specific knowledge and skills. This idea was recently empirically explored by Raffiee and Byun (2020), who found that new hires who possessed combinations of general human capital that the hiring firm lacked, experienced faster integration and utilization than new hires with general human capital already possessed by the hiring firm. This indicates that valuable general human capital eases workers' transition between firms, and lubricates potential frictions caused by transfer of irrelevant, firm-specific human capital.

A specific view of future human capital research

Taken together, recent research on human capital specificity offers important insights and paves the way for new inquiry. First, it is increasingly clear that the line of demarcation between general and specific human capital is blurred (Coff and Raffiee, 2015; Lazear, 2009). Not only are individuals' bundles of general human capital idiosyncratic (Lazear, 2009; Raffiee and Byun, 2020), but firms' and workers' perceptions of human capital may themselves be biased (Morris et al., 2017; Raffiee and Coff, 2016). This not only suggests that distinguishing between specific and general human capital is not as meaningful as prior theory suggests (Morris et al., 2017; Nyberg et al., 2018), but it also upends existing notions of firm-specific human capital as an isolating mechanism. Indeed, some recent work suggests that firm-specific human capital may not constrain mobility (Morris et al., 2017; Raffiee and Coff, 2016). To move forward, research can explore conditions under which workers consider firm specificity as a factor in investment or mobility decisions.

Second, perceptions of human capital specificity appear to play a powerful role in firm and worker mobility. This has implications not only for theory building, but also for how we measure constructs. For instance, using firm tenure as a proxy of firm-specific human capital is not useful where perceptions, and not objective assessments, guide behavior (Raffiee and Coff, 2016), because longer-tenured workers often perceive their skills as more general. Such proxies may fail to predict behavior, especially as perceptions of specificity diverge from objective measures.

These observations motivate several additional avenues of inquiry. First, the recent advances in human capital research underscore the importance of conceptualizing human capital as multidimensional, instead of as dichotomous (Nyberg et al., 2018). But what does such a multidimensional framework look like? What components, categories, and structure should it include? Scholars have previously suggested other types of specificity such as task-specific (Gibbons and Waldman, 2004), unit-specific (Ployhart, Van Iddekinge, and MacKenzie, 2011), industry-specific (Hatch and Dyer, 2004), and occupation-specific human capital (Mayer, Somaya, and Williamson, 2012) that can affect worker and firm behavior. Therefore, rethinking and expanding how we operationalize human capital may further our understanding of human capital–based advantages but may also advance research on employer-employee matching.

Second, although evidence of firm-specific human capital's limitations as a mobility deterrent is accumulating, the debate is not settled. One unexplored area regarding the relationship between firm-specific human capital and mobility is consideration of a worker's relative share of specific to human capital, and also whether the share of specific to general human capital is increasing or decreasing over time. This raises the question of whether mobility is perhaps constrained by the proportion of firm-specific to general human capital instead of the stock of firm-specific human capital. Another unexplored area is the role of human resource management (HRM) practices. HRM scholars argue that while firm-specific human capital is an ineffective deterrent to worker mobility, HRM practices (e.g., pay-for-performance, employment security, self-managed teams, etc.) can be constructed to constrain mobility (Delery and Roumpi, 2017). Delery and Roumpi (2017) argue that differentiated HRM practices can even be deployed within a single firm to influence different types of workers. Indeed, HRM practices often vary not only between but also within firms (Kehoe and Han, 2020), suggesting that future matching research needs to consider more nuanced HRM practices as an important firm attribute.

Assortative Matching: Finding Fit in the Dark

Given substantial differences in firms' resources and capabilities—and even greater differences in workers' abilities and skills—efficient matching between firms and workers is another key strategic choice with tremendous implications for value creation (Lazear and Oyer, 2013). Matches are the "meso-level building blocks" (Weller et al., 2019) linking micro-level firm and worker attributes to performance (Felin, Foss, and Ployhart, 2015). Yet despite the critical role of employer-employee matching for firm efficiency, we lack clarity for how the process unfolds or even what constitutes an ideal match. This is partly because understanding continues to evolve, but it is also an outcome of inconsistent conceptualizations of match efficacy between economics, strategy, and organizational behavior literatures.

The challenge of forming high-quality matches is threefold. First, workers' productivity is difficult to observe prior to hiring. Second, applicants may misrepresent their abilities and skills. Third, upon hiring, firms may engage in opportunistic behavior that limits worker mobility or compensation. Together, these factors have motivated a rich literature on incentive schemes that induce efficient self-selection (Oyer and Schaefer, 2011) through reliable and costly (e.g., hard-to-fake) signals of true worker ability (Bangerter, Roulin, and König, 2012; Spence, 1973).

What is a match made in heaven?

While economists and organizational behavior scholars agree on the above premises (difficult-to-observe productivity, misrepresentation by applicants, opportunistic behavior by firms), these disciplines differ in assessing match efficacy. Personnel economics uses the lens of productivity to determine match quality (Lazear and Oyer, 2013). Thus, an ideal match would be a high-performing worker going to an especially efficient firm to produce the greatest productivity. In contrast, organizational behavior research applies an expanded view of value creation that includes nonpecuniary outcomes, such as job satisfaction. While this is consistent with the economic notion of maximizing utility, it extends beyond traditional boundaries of production efficiency. Accordingly, whereas economists emphasize observable attributes (e.g., education and experience) to model match formation, organizational behavior scholars include subjective criteria (e.g., attitudes and behaviors) in assessing person-organization fit (Kristof-Brown, Zimmerman, and Johnson, 2005; Kristof, 1996).

These differences have led the two disciplines to focus on different aspects of the matching process. Although personnel economics recognizes that match efficiency can be influenced by training (Lazear and Oyer, 2013) and employment termination (Lazear, 1998), the assumption is that workers adapt to firms—and not vice versa (Lazear and Oyer, 2013). Overall, the research emphasis remains on understanding selection and hiring. Organizational behavior and HRM scholars, in contrast, expect match efficacy to evolve throughout the worker-firm relationship from selection to termination (Weller *et al.*, 2019), and they explore adaptation by both individuals and organizations (Follmer *et al.*, 2018).

How matches develop over time

These distinct approaches have brought numerous new insights about the matching process. Who drives the process, and how does it unfold? For example, match quality reflects more than the initial fit between individuals and firms; it is also a function of time (Weller *et al.*, 2019). Training (Mincer and Jovanovic, 1981) and socialization (Jones, 1986) improve fit between new hires and their employers over time. Furthermore, mobility through horizontal transfers and vertical promotions can strengthen match quality by aligning human capital with firm resources (Bidwell, 2011; Bidwell and Keller, 2014).

A second insight is that adaptation can be worker-led (as is often assumed) or firm-led. For instance, there is growing evidence of job crafting—worker-led changes in task or relational aspects of their jobs (Wrzesniewski and Dutton, 2001)—to improve fit between their skills and the firm's needs (Pieper *et al.*, 2019). Likewise, firms sometimes engage in job redesign to motivate and retain workers who may initially be a poor match (Follmer *et al.*, 2018).

These new avenues highlight the importance of signaling in all stages of human capital management. In selection, in addition to using reliable and costly (hard-to-fake) signals, realistic job previews (Weller *et al.*, 2019), referral networks (Granovetter, 1995), and intermediaries (Bonet, Cappelli, and Hamori, 2013) may help overcome imperfect information. These methods may deter job seekers from misleading or engaging in impression management (Stevens and Kristof, 1995), as they seek to align signals of their quality with the perceived demands of the hiring firm. Similarly, they may dissuade firms from exaggerating their qualities (Langer, König, and Scheuss, 2019).

The match of the future: a way forward for strategic management scholars

Conspicuously missing from the overview of recent literature on matching are studies firmly rooted in strategy. Contrasted with the ample person-organization fit literature in organizational behavior and the steady advances in personnel economics (e.g., Engborn and Moser, 2017; Fredriksson, Hensvik, and Skans, 2018), explorations of the determinants and consequences of employer-employee matching using a strategy-based lens are comparatively limited.

There are some important exceptions, including recent work by Campbell, Di Lorenzo, and Tartari (forthcoming) and Raffiee and Byun (2020). Specifically, Campbell *et al.* (forthcoming) showed that prior collaboration between individuals employed by separate firms facilitates match quality by enhancing postmobility job performance upon movement to the collaborator's firm. Importantly, given earlier discussion, match performance is driven by both selection (who moves) and adaptation (how new hires acclimate). Raffiee and Byun (2020) recently used matching logic to investigate hiring decisions in knowledge-intensive organizations. They found that job performance of newly hired workers was higher among those who possessed expertise that the firm lacked (complementary fit) than those workers whose expertise aligned with existing capabilities.

A challenge inhibiting further progress in this area is inadequate theory regarding which pairings of organizational and individual attributes constitute a high-quality match. At first glance, this difficulty appears banal because optimal pairings match the best workers with the best firms. Studies do indeed show assortative patterns in hiring, such as between managerial talent and firm size (Gabaix and Landier, 2008), and between education level and firm pay (Fredriksson *et al.*, 2018). But given the range of attributes along which firms and individuals vary, these findings are unsatisfying as they amount to a rather general conclusion: more resource-rich firms hire more talented workers (and more talented workers accept positions in more resource-rich firms). Future work might explicate *which* firm-level resources and capabilities match *which* individual-level knowledge and skills to add value.

Given the number of relevant attributes and the fact that organizations and individuals are themselves multifaceted, the question of optimal employer-employee matching is complex. There are many ways in which firms may differentiate themselves in factor markets since workers have varied preferences. Firms are characterized not only by size and status, but by industry, ownership (private/public), structure (focused/diversified), location (local/international), and product orientation (good/

service), to name a few observable attributes. Individuals differ in ability, personality, experience, and interpersonal connections, among many other attributes. Even though matched employer-employee datasets are increasingly accessible and empirical methods for modeling matching phenomena are becoming more common in strategy research (e.g., Honoré and Ganco, forthcoming; Mindruta, Moeen, and Agarwal, 2016; Rickley, 2018), the challenge now lies in developing more nuanced theory to understand how firm and worker characteristics drive the matching process.

This need for new theory invites deeper exploration into a new construct, firm-specific incentives, which provide a critical vehicle for differentiation in a strategic factor market (Kryscynski, Coff, and Campbell, 2021). Prior research focuses on wages and benefits that are relatively generic and are therefore easy for rival firms to imitate. In contrast, *firm-specific incentives* are defined as incentives that are more valuable to workers in the focal firm than similar incentives offered by other employers (Kryscynski et al., 2021). In this sense, they can be quite idiosyncratic and difficult to imitate. For example, the Walt Disney Company offers rich and highly valued employee discounts whose value draws heavily on the brand and product portfolio. A former cast member commented, "This discount was awesome, and I made use of it often. Not only a discount on park tickets, but also hotel rooms, merchandise, even cruises!" (Glassdoor. com, 2015). A rival, such as Six Flags, might offer a discount at similar levels, but its value to employees is likely substantially lower, because the products are less differentiated and reflect a narrower portfolio than Disney's. Similarly, companies like Google and 3M offer top employees the autonomy to work on ideas or projects of their choice. While this policy can be imitated, the complementary resources for these projects can vary widely and give this incentive unique value across companies.

Accordingly, firm-specific incentives may attract and motivate workers who become the basis for a competitive advantage. While the person-organization fit literature is not new, it does not focus on inimitable firm-specific attributes. In other words, applying a strategic human capital lens to this literature will unearth new insights and avenues of inquiry. For example, what attributes attract and motivate workers and thereby promote competitive advantages? A given attribute may attract all workers (or even those with low productivity), which may not generate a competitive advantage unless the firm has unusually strong screening capabilities to identify and hire the best employees. In this way, firm-specific incentives may confer an advantage in some contexts but certainly not always. This, in turn, may prompt exploration into the range of attributes that may confer a strategic factor market advantage, as well as how some firms develop them. For instance, do firm-specific incentives stem from rational decision-making (cost/benefit) or are they path-dependent—arising from environmental imprinting at founding or from managers' idiosyncratic experiences?

Since the construct is new, there has been relatively little research and opportunities abound. Firm-specific incentives range widely across existing incentive categories (tangible/intangible, extrinsic/intrinsic, high-powered/low-powered, etc.), opening new pathways for the incentives literature. Because these incentives are idiosyncratic, they may heavily depend on workers' perceived value, which implies a need for research on subjective value—a topic that seems unnecessary for traditional incentives (wages and benefits). Furthermore, some firm-specific incentives may be experience goods in the sense that workers may grow to value them more highly over time or the goods may instead decrease in value as their novelty wears off. For example, a unique organizational culture may accrue value to workers only after they have come to appreciate it over time. If so, these incentives may be more valuable for motivation and retention than for attraction and hiring. This gives rise to multiple research questions: Are firm-specific incentives equally potent for attraction, motivation, and retention? Can the utility of such incentives extend beyond a given employment relationship? How do sudden external shifts (like global financial crises or pandemics) affect firms' abilities to derive advantage from firm-specific incentives?

In sum, the field of strategic management is uniquely positioned to contribute theory for a more nuanced understanding of matching processes. Given strategy scholars' deep understanding of the firm side of the equation (e.g., organizational capabilities underlying competitive advantage), exploration into the determinants of match quality can begin by pairing critical firm-level factors for organizational performance with key individual-level factors for job performance. From this we can theorize why a particular combination matters for competitive advantage. Furthermore, as we gain insights into effective employer-employee matching, we will build microfoundational understanding of how individual- and firm-level heterogeneity interacts to impact organizational outcomes.

Given that matching is an endogenous process characterized by self-selection, subsequent theory testing would benefit from controlled environments where match quality is observable not only for realized matches, but also for all counterfactual matches between firms and workers that did not occur but could have. An example of one such controlled environment, where researchers have already explored the factors predicting successful matching, is in the field of medicine. Several studies have exploited medical school graduates' realized and unrealized (potential) matches to specialty residency programs to model matching (e.g., Loh et al., 2013; Rinard and Mahabir, 2010). However, the residency matching process is quite unique in that it is conducted in a closed environment that includes all eligible medical school graduates and all participating specialty programs in the United States (dermatology, general surgery, etc.). Other semiclosed hiring environments—like judicial clerkship appointments, professional sports drafts, or company-specific internship programs—may offer additional settings to explore this process. Exploration could then continue in other contexts to help understand the boundary conditions of a more nuanced matching theory.

Inquiring Minds: Groundwork for Microfoundations

Human capital theory had been relatively stable, even stodgy, for many years. Recent developments have exposed cracks in these foundations. We have described how this has played out with respect to firm specificity and matching as well as mapping an agenda for future inquiry. However, these are only a start, and there are many other promising areas. We have not touched upon human capital aggregation—how human capital combines with other resources to form organization-level capabilities. Nor have we explored value capture in any depth. Also, emergent technologies, like artificial intelligence, challenge the role of human capital in value creation as well as alter the dynamics of value capture. The opportunities are boundless.

References

Bangerter A, Roulin N, König CJ. 2012. Personnel selection as a signaling game. *Journal of Applied Psychology* 97(4): 719–738.

Barney JB. 1991. Firm resources and sustained competitive advantage. *Journal of Management* 17(1): 99–120.

Barney JB, Felin T. 2013. What are microfoundations? *Academy of Management Perspectives* 27: 138–155.

Barney JB, Wright PM. 1998. On becoming a strategic partner: the role of human resources in gaining competitive advantage. *Human Resource Management* 37(1): 31–46.

Becker GS. 1962. Investment in human capital: a theoretical analysis. *Journal of Political Economy* 70: 9–49.

Becker GS. 1964. *Human capital: a theoretical and empirical analysis with special reference to education.* University of Chicago Press: Chicago, IL.

Bidwell M. 2011. Paying more to get less: the effects of external hiring versus internal mobility. *Administrative Science Quarterly* 56(3): 369–407.

Bidwell M, Keller J. 2014. Within or without? How firms combine internal and external labor markets to fill jobs. *Academy of Management Journal* 57(4): 1035–1055.

Bonet R, Cappelli P, Hamori M. 2013. Labor market intermediaries and the new paradigm for human resources. *Academy of Management Annals* 7(1): 341–392.

Campbell BA, Coff R, Kryscynski D. 2012a. Rethinking sustained competitive advantage from human capital. *Academy of Management Review* 37(3): 376–395.

Campbell BA, Di Lorenzo F, Tartari V. Forthcoming. Employer-employee matching and complementary assets: the role of cross-organizational collaborations. *Academy of Management Journal.*

Campbell BA, Ganco M, Franco AM, Agarwal R. 2012b. Who leaves, where to, and why worry? Employee mobility, entrepreneurship, and effects on source firm performance. *Strategic Management Journal* 33: 65–87.

Coff R. 1997. Human assets and management dilemmas: coping with hazards on the road to resource-based theory. *Academy of Management Review* 22(2): 374–402.

Coff R. 1999. When competitive advantage doesn't lead to performance: the resource-based view and stakeholder bargaining power. *Organization Science* 10: 119–133.

Coff R, Kryscynski D. 2011. Drilling for microfoundations of human capital–based competitive advantages. *Journal of Management* 37(5): 1429.

Coff R, Raffiee J. 2015. Toward a theory of perceived firm-specific human capital. *Academy of Management Perspectives* 29(3): 326–341.

Cyert RM, March JG. 1992. *A Behavioral Theory of the Firm*. 2nd edition. Blackwell: Cambridge, MA.

Delery JE, Roumpi D. 2017. Strategic human resource management, human capital, and competitive advantage: Is the field going in circles? *Human Resource Management Journal* 27(1): 1–21.

Engborn N, Moser C. 2017. Returns to education through access to higher-paying firms: evidence from US matched employer-employee data. *American Economic Review: Papers and Proceedings* 107(5): 374–378.

Felin T, Foss NJ, Ployhart RE. 2015. The microfoundations movement in strategy and organization theory. *Academy of Management Annals* 9(1): 575–632.

Follmer EH, Talbot DL, Kristof-Brown AL, Astrove SL, Billsberry J. 2018. Resolution, relief, and resignation: a qualitative study of responses to misfit at work. *Academy of Management Journal* 61(2): 440–465.

Foss NJ. 2011. Why microfoundations for resource-based theory are needed and what they may look like. *Journal of Management* 37(5): 1413–1428.

Foss NJ, Hallberg NL. 2014. How symmetrical assumptions advance strategic management research. *Strategic Management Journal* 35: 903–913.

Fredriksson P, Hensvik L, Skans ON. 2018. Mismatch of talent: evidence on job match quality, entry wages, and job mobility. *American Economic Review* 108(11): 3303–3338.

Gabaix X, Landier A. 2008. Why has CEO compensation increased so much? *Quarterly Journal of Economics* 123(1): 49–100.

Gibbons R, Waldman M. 2004. Task-specific human capital. *American Economic Review* 94(2): 203.

Glassdoor.com. 2015. Walt Disney Company benefits [22 September 2020]. Mill Valley, CA.

Granovetter M. 1995. *Getting a Job: A Study of Contacts and Careers*. University of Chicago Press: Chicago, IL.

Grant R. 1996. Toward a knowledge-based theory of the firm. *Strategic Management Journal* 17: 109–122.

Groysberg B. 2010. *Chasing Stars: The Myth of Talent and the Portability of Performance*. Princeton University Press: Princeton, NJ.

Hashimoto M. 1981. Firm-specific human capital as a shared investment. *American Economic Review* 71(3): 475–482.

Hatch NW, Dyer JH. 2004. Human capital and learning as a source of sustainable competitive advantage. *Strategic Management Journal* 25(12): 1155–1178.

Honoré F, Ganco M. Forthcoming. Entrepreneurial teams' acquisition of talent: evidence from technology manufacturing industries using a two-sided approach. *Strategic Management Journal*.

Jones GR. 1986. Socialization tactics, self-efficacy, and newcomers' adjustments to organizations. *Academy of Management Journal* 29(2): 262–279.

Jovanovic B. 1979. Firm-specific capital and turnover. *Journal of Political Economy* 87(6): 1246–1260.

Kehoe RR, Han JH. 2020. An expanded conceptualization of line managers' involvement in human resource management. *Journal of Applied Psychology* 105(2): 111–129.

Kehoe RR, Lepak DP, Bentley FS. 2018. Let's call a star a star: task performance, external status, and exceptional contributors in organizations *Journal of Management* 44(5): 1848–1872.

Kogut B, Zander U. 1992. Knowledge of the firm, combinative capabilities, and the replication of technology. *Organization Science* 3(3): 383–397.

Kor YY, Leblebici H. 2005. How do interdependencies among human-capital deployment, development, and diversification strategies affect firms' financial performance? *Strategic Management Journal* 26: 967–985.

Kristof AL. 1996. Person-organization fit: an integrative review of its conceptualizations, measurement, and implications. *Personnel Psychology* 49(1): 1–49.

Kristof-Brown AL, Zimmerman RD, Johnson EC. 2005. Consequences of individual's fit at work: a meta-analysis of person-job, person-organization, person-group, and person-supervisor fit. *Personnel Psychology* 58(2): 281–342.

Kryscynski D, Coff R, Campbell BA. 2021. Charting a path between firm-specific incentives and human capital-based competitive advantage. *Strategic Management Journal* 42(2): 386–412.

Kryscynski D, Ulrich D. 2015. Making strategic human capital relevant: a time-sensitive opportunity. *Academy of Management Perspectives* 29(3): 357–369.

Langer M, König CJ, Scheuss AI. 2019. Love the way you lie: hiring managers' impression management in company presentation videos. *Journal of Personnel Psychology* 18(2): 84–94.

Lazear EP. 1998. Hiring risky workers. In *Internal Labour Market, Incentives, and Employment*. Ohashi I, Tachibanki R (eds), St. Martin's Press: New York, NY; 143–158.

Lazear EP. 2009. Firm-specific human capital: a skill-weights approach. *Journal of Political Economy* 117: 914–940.

Lazear EP, Oyer P. 2013. Personnel economics. In *The Handbook of Organizational Economics*. Gibbons R, Roberts J (eds), Princeton University Press: Princeton, NJ; 479–519.

Leiblein MJ, Madsen TL. 2009. Unbundling competitive heterogeneity: incentive structures and capability influences on technological innovation. *Strategic Management Journal* 30(7): 711–735.

Loewenstein MA, Spletzer JR. 1999. General and specific training: evidence and implications. *Journal of Human Resources* 34: 710–733.

Loh AR, Joseph D, Keenan JD, Lietman TM, Naseri A. 2013. Predictors of matching in ophthalmology residency program. *Ophthalmology* 120(4): 865–870.

Mahoney JT, Kor YY. 2015. Advancing the human capital perspective on value creation by joining capabilities and governance approaches. *Academy of Management Perspectives* 29(3): 296–308.

Mahoney JT, Pandian JR. 1992. The resource-based view of the firm within the conversation of strategic management. *Strategic Management Journal* 13: 363–380.

Mayer KJ, Somaya D, Williamson IO. 2012. Firm-specific, industry-specific, and occupational human capital and the sourcing of knowledge work. *Organization Science* 23: 1311–1329.

Mincer J, Jovanovic B. 1981. Labor mobility and wages. In *Studies in Labor Markets*, Rosen S (ed). National Bureau of Economic Research: New York; 21–64.

Mindruta D, Moeen M, Agarwal R. 2016. A two-sided matching approach for partner selection and assessing complementarities in partners' attributes in inter-firm alliances. *Strategic Management Journal* 37(1): 206–231.

Molloy JC, Barney JB. 2015. Who captures the value created with human capital? A market-based view. *Academy of Management Perspectives* 29: 309–325.

Morris SS, Alvarez SA, Barney JB, Molloy JC. 2017. Firm-specific human capital investments as a signal of general value: revisiting assumptions about human capital and how it is managed. *Strategic Management Journal* 38: 912–919.

Nyberg A, Reilly G, Essman S, Rodrigues J. 2018. Human capital resources: a call to retire settled debates and start a few new debates. *International Journal of Human Resource Management* 29(1): 68–86.

Oyer P, Schaefer S. 2011. Personnel economics: hiring and incentives. In *Handbook of labor economics*. Ashenfelter O, Card D (eds). Elsevier/North-Holland: Amsterdam; 1769–1823.

Penrose E. 1959. *The Theory of the Growth of the Firm*. Basil Blackwell: London, U.K.

Peteraf MA. 1993. The cornerstones of competitive advantage: a resource-based view. *Strategic Management Journal* 14(3): 179–191.

Pieper JR, Trevor CO, Weller I, Duchon D. 2019. Referral hire presence implications for referrer turnover and job performance. *Journal of Management* 45(5): 1858–1888.

Ployhart RE, Nyberg AJ, Reilly G, Maltarich MA. 2014. Human capital is dead; long live human capital resources! *Journal of Management* 40: 371–398.

Ployhart RE, Van Iddekinge CH, MacKenzie WI. 2011. Acquiring and developing human capital in service contexts: the interconnectedness of human capital resources. *Academy of Management Journal* 54: 353–368.

Raffiee J, Byun H. 2020. Revisiting the portability of performance paradox: employee mobility and the utilization of human social capital resources. *Academy of Management Journal* 63(1): 34–63.

Raffiee J, Coff R. 2016. Microfoundations of firm-specific human capital: when do employees perceive their skills to be firm-specific? *Academy of Management Journal* 59(3): 766–790.

Rickley M. 2018. Estimating the determinants of executive selection in multinational companies: a two-sided matching model. *European Journal of International Management* 12(5/6): 596–623.

Rinard JR, Mahabir RC. 2010. Successfully matching into surgical specialties: an analysis of national resident matching program data. *Journal of Graduate Medical Education* 2(3): 316–321.

Rumelt RP. 1984. Toward a strategic theory of the firm. In *Competitive Strategic Management*. Lamb R(ed). Prentice Hall: Englewood Cliffs, NJ; 556–570.

Somaya D, Williamson IO, Lorinkova N. 2008. Gone but not lost: the different performance impacts of employee mobility between cooperators versus competitors. *Academy of Management Journal* 51(5): 936–953.

Spence M. 1973. Job market signaling. *Quarterly Journal of Economics* 87: 355–374.

Stevens CK, Kristof AL. 1995. Making the right impression: a field study of applicant impression management during job interviews. *Journal of Applied Psychology* 80: 587–606.

Wang HC, Barney JB. 2006. Employee incentives to make firm-specific investments: implications for resource-based theories of corporate diversification. *Academy of Management Review* 31(2): 466–476.

Wang HC, He J, Mahoney JT. 2009. Firm-specific knowledge resources and competitive advantage: the roles of economic- and relationship-based employee governance mechanisms. *Strategic Management Journal* 30(12): 1265–1285.

Weller I, Hymer CB, Nyberg AJ, Ebert J. 2019. How matching creates value: cogs and wheels for human capital resources research. *Academy of Management Annals* 13(1): 188–214.

Wernerfelt B. 1984. The resource-based view of the firm. *Strategic Management Journal* 5(2): 171–180.

Wrzesniewski A, Dutton JE. 2001. Crafting a job: revisioning employees as active crafters of their work. *Academy of Management Review* 26(2): 179–201.

10.2

EXTENDING THE MICROFOUNDATIONS OF CAPABILITY DEVELOPMENT AND UTILIZATION: THE ROLE OF AGENTIC TECHNOLOGY AND IDENTITY-BASED COMMUNITY

David G. Sirmon

Introduction

Research on firm capabilities has held a dominant position in the strategic management literature for decades (Hoskisson *et al.*, 1999). Defined as an ability "to perform a coordinated set of tasks, utilizing organizational resources, for the purpose of achieving a particular end result" (Helfat and Peteraf, 2003: 999), a capability is an intricate construct. Thus, it is not surprising that scholars' treatment of capabilities has evolved over time. Early treatments illuminated capabilities with the broadest strokes by suggesting that management determined a firm's "distinctive competence" (Selznick, 1957). For instance, Penrose argued that "the experience of management will affect the productive services that all of [the organization's] other resources are capable of rendering" (1959: 5). It was not until strategic management turned its focus primarily to internal bases of competitive advantage (Hoskisson *et al.*, 1999) that more specific managerial actions and processes regarding capabilities were detailed. During this period and concurrent to the examination of capabilities effects on macro-level outcomes (i.e., firm performance, innovation, etc. [e.g., Henderson and Cockburn, 1994]), scholars undertook nuanced inquiry regarding the processes of how managers changed firm capabilities—what became known as the dynamic capabilities literature (e.g., Teece, Pisano, and Shuen, 1997).

The shift toward dynamics capabilities placed specific managerial actions of building and changing firm capabilities at the center of inquiry. Given that such actions do not exist in silos, it was suggested that such actions were contextually bounded—from both micro- and macro-level factors. For example, the basis of many firm capabilities is a group's collective human capital. However, the ability of the firm to utilize said capital is dependent on micro-level factors, such as individual cognition, and macro-level factors, such as group structure. As such, beyond examining managerial actions alone, scholarship began to holistically examine capabilities and their change with individuals, processes, structures, and their interactions in mind (Felin et al., 2012). This research occurs under the banner of *microfoundations*.

Microfoundations research endeavors to unpack "collective concepts to understand how individual-level factors impact organizations, how the interaction of individuals leads to emergent, collective, and organization-level outcomes and performance, and how relations between macro variables are mediated by micro actions and interactions" (Felin, Foss, and Ployhart, 2015: 576). To advance the microfoundation treatment of capabilities, I detail how scholars have previously treated capabilities and, more importantly, how they may treat capabilities in the future. This forward-looking sketch purposely engages novel factors that previously had not been explicitly considered within prior microfoundations work. While numerous factors could be included here, due to their novelty and increasing salience to contemporary organizations, I focus attention on two. First, I address *agentic technologies*. Agentic technologies are those that can constrain, complement, or substitute for human agency. With agency, these technologies are another "actor" within a capability, but with different properties and effects that require examination. Second, I discuss the role of *identity-based community*. Different from the traditional conceptualization of community being locale-based and due to very low levels of power being quickly dismissed from further discussion (Clarkson, 1995; Barney, 2018), identity-based community has both a legitimate claim on as well as influence over the firm. However, their claim is not profit-centric. An identity-based community maximizes its ideology-centric utility function by offering resources freely to the firm in exchange for support of the community's shared purpose (Murray, Kotha, and Fisher, 2020). However, if the firm violates the community's shared values, norms, or beliefs, the community can also maximize its utility by antagonistically responding to a previously supported firm. Thus, relationship with an identity-based community creates something of a double-edged sword for the firm.

The integration of these two factors—that is, agentic technologies and identity-based communities—into the microfoundations literature extends our understanding of capability development and utilization. But even more, including agentic technology and identity-based community within the microfoundations perspective offers intriguing new research opportunities—opportunities to ask novel research questions that are of relevance to contemporary organizations. Specific research questions are posed throughout the chapter to focus scholars' interest. As such, my hope is that this chapter supports yet another era in the study of capabilities that builds upon the foundations of prior literature but with the inclusion of agentic technologies and identity-based communities allows us to address futuristic issues such as capability autonomy or the development of community-driven platforms (as opposed to platforms dominated by a focal actor, like Amazon).

The chapter begins with a brief review of the microfoundation idea—what it is and is not. Here Felin et al.'s (2012) three-part treatment—individual, process, and structure—provides a clear basis to holistically conceive of interdependencies within the microfoundations literature, while also being amenable to broader inclusion of novel factors. Then I review how past and present capability-centric research has separately illuminated these three component parts. Here the advances of resource orchestration are emphasized with its process-heavy foci. Lastly, I turn toward a discussion of interdependence among microfoundational factors and future research.

Microfoundations

For much of organizational science, the interest in how lower-level actors and elements affect the formation of higher-level phenomena is not a concern. For the microfoundations literature, however, this is a central, but not its sole concern (Felin *et al.*, 2015). The term "microfoundation" may lead some to focus exclusively on psychological concerns of individuals, but the term reflects a broader focus. Specifically, microfoundation research unpacks "collective concepts to understand how individual-level factors impact organizations, how the interaction of individuals leads to emergent, collective, and organization-level outcomes and performance, and how relations between macro variables are mediated by micro actions and interactions" (Felin *et al.*, 2015: 576). Emphasizing this perspective, Barney and Felin (2013) argue that microfoundations are not limited to individuals' cognition, emotions, abilities, or skills, nor does this perspective reject context. Instead, this perspective attempts to richly detail how individuals, processes, and structures interactively (Felin *et al.*, 2012) affect salient organizational-level outcomes. Put differently, as understanding of the microfoundation literature improves, the importance of "foundations" grows to help contextualize the "micro."

Felin *et al.* (2012) and Felin *et al.* (2015) frame microfoundations around individual, process, and structural components, encouraging both depth and breadth in the investigation of capabilities. A deep focus explores the nuance reflected in each component. For instance, as discussed later, cognition and emotions have been identified as important factors of the individual component, but their effect on capability development and utilization is rather limited. On the other hand, increased breadth considers interactions among the three components. Indeed, a growing sentiment within the microfoundations literature is a call to explore the interdependence among these components. For instance, Felin *et al.* state that "going beyond the constituent individuals that make up the organization, there are questions about the utilization of individuals" (2015: 616). Even more explicitly, Raveendran, Silverstri, and Gulati (forthcoming) argue that the interdependence of microfoundations needs to be embraced to advance knowledge.

Before addressing future research related to the interdependence among a capability's microfoundations, I first review past and current capability research as it relates to Felin *et al.*'s (2012) three components of microfoundations—individuals, processes, and structure.

Past and Present Capabilities Research from a Microfoundational Perspective

While definitions abound for capabilities, they all invoke some logic regarding the use of assets or resources for a purpose. Herein, I rely on Helfat and Peteraf's definition of a *capability* as an ability "to perform a coordinated set of tasks, utilizing organizational resources, for the purpose of achieving a particular end result" (2003: 999). As such, capabilities are foundational to a firm's eventual performance outcomes as well as more proximal concerns, such as innovation, production, hiring, and so on.

Beyond these operational capabilities, significant thought has been focused on understanding how capabilities change. The capacity to change a capability has been specified as a dynamic capability—a construct that has captured the imagination of many practitioners and scholars alike. At its simplest description, a dynamic capability enables the changing of other capabilities. Indeed, Teece *et al.* refer to *dynamic capabilities* as "the firm's ability to integrate, build, and reconfigure internal and external competences" (1997: 516). Put differently, dynamic capabilities do not direct output as typical capabilities, but instead alter these "operational" capabilities.

The concept of dynamic capabilities was the first concerted effort to identify and understand capabilities from a microfoundational perspective. For instance, work on dynamic capabilities specified that managerial skills and cognitions are critical (Adner and Helfat, 2003). Specifically, Teece argued that "dynamic capabilities can be disaggregated into the capacity (1) to sense and shape opportunities and threats, (2) to seize opportunities, and (3) to maintain competitiveness through enhancing, combining, protecting, and, when necessary, reconfiguring the business enterprise's intangible and tangible assets" (Teece, 2007: 1319). In turn, Helfat and Peteraf (2015) argue that sensing, seizing, and reconfiguring are supported by individual-level cognitive factors such as perception, attention, reasoning, communication, and socially based comparisons. However, other individual-level factors are important too. For instance, Meyer-Doyle, Lee and Helfat (2019) document that such individual-level drivers—such as incentives, understanding, skills, and so on—can play an important role in the firm's acquisition capability. Moreover, this individual-level emphasis has been the focus of capability research regarding learning (Winter, 2000) and routines (Nelson and Winter, 1982; Zollo and Winter, 2002).

The next component of microfoundations is process. This component is arguably the most systematically studied microfoundation. Specifically, this stream focuses on managerial action/processes, and contributions come mainly from two independently conceived research efforts: asset orchestration (Helfat *et al.,* 2007) and resource management (Sirmon and Hitt, 2003; Sirmon, Hitt, and Ireland, 2007). Sirmon *et al.* (2011) called the integrated stream resource "orchestration." By integrating the related work of asset orchestration and resource management, Sirmon *et al.* (2011) provided a comprehensive treatment of the managerial actions and processes needed to understand capability building and deployment.

Specifically, resource orchestration focuses on how managers utilize resources for productive gains via structuring, bundling, and leveraging processes (e.g., Helfat *et al.*, 2007; Ndofor, Sirmon, and He, 2015; Sirmon *et al.*, 2007). Moreover, this literature has consistently focused on the synchronization of these orchestration choices (and their subprocesses), thereby holistically informing resource utilization (Sirmon *et al.*, 2011). Briefly, the first action, structuring the resource portfolio, provides the "working material" in the resource orchestration model. Here managers acquire or accumulate resources, which are defined as an "asset or input to production (tangible or intangible) that an organization owns, controls, or has access to on a semi-permanent basis" (Helfat and Peteraf, 2003: 999). Managers also act to divest resources, as appropriate, thereby freeing managerial attention and emotional bias, as well as financial capital. Second, managers bundle resources into capabilities. This occurs when they stabilize existing capabilities with slight improvements in the component resources, enrich existing capabilities with more substantial alterations, or lastly, pioneer (develop) new capabilities for the firm. Each bundling choice grows progressively more complicated and challenging to enact. The last action is leveraging. Here managers mobilize, coordinate, and deploy capabilities for specific market opportunities. This is the last step in the model and is where performance effects are realized. But this literature also argues that synchronizing these sets of actions with one another is crucial for favorable outcomes.

The empirical record for this stream provides credence to the importance of examining the managerial actions related to the subprocesses of structuring, bundling, and leveraging (D'Oria *et al.*, 2021). Indeed, evidence from this research indicates significant variance between firms' resource orchestration actions as well as documenting how these differences matter to important outcomes (Holcomb, Holmes, and Connelly, 2009; Kor and Leblebici 2005; Majumdar, 1998). For example, evidence shows that (1) managerial actions meditate the resource/performance relationship (Ndofor, Sirmon, and He, 2011); (2) managers need to attend to both capability strengths and weaknesses to optimize performance (Sirmon *et al.*, 2010); (3) managers are able to realize greater value from their resources when they effectively understand the environment in which they are leveraged (Sirmon, Gove, and Hitt, 2008); (4) managerial actions increase in importance as rivals' resource portfolios move toward parity (Sirmon *et al.*, 2008); (5) managers differ in the quality of their resource orchestration abilities (Holcomb *et al.*, 2009); and (6) synchronizing the various subprocesses of resource orchestration leads to successful outcomes, while the lack of synchronization produces negative results regardless of which action and subprocesses are selected (Sirmon and Hitt, 2009).

By synthesizing and extending these two models, resource orchestration provides a comprehensive view of managerial actions and processes in the realization of resource-based competitive advantage and resulting performance outcomes. However, this literature also touches on both the individual and structural components of microfoundations, but not at the same level of richness. In particular, research related to the "individual" component of microfoundations shows that performance norms originate from managers who "better understand technology and industry trends, reliably predict product demand, invest in higher-value projects, and manage their employees more efficiently" (Demerjian, Lev, and McVay, 2012: 1230). Helfat and Peteraf (2015) argue that managers' cognitive characteristics manifest differently in these processes, while Taylor and Helfat (2009) specifically identify middle-level managers' role in helping organization-wide shared understandings of these processes. Relatedly, Majumdar (1998: 811) argues that effective "orchestration of interaction between physical and human resources ... exploit[s] technical and behavioral interdependencies."

Next, structural issues are at least peripherally examined. For example, fault lines—subgroup divisions reflecting alignment of multiple member attributes (Lau and Murnighan, 1998)—and other group-related issues have been shown to affect orchestration actions. Specifically, Ndofor et al. (2015) found that differences among top management teams' (TMTs') fault lines affect their strategy formulation and implementation tasks differently. And more recently, Hitt et al. (forthcoming) empirically detail how resource orchestration actions and processes are nested within industry constraints, which themselves are influenced by institutions. These nested effects reflect context and a more general understanding of structure from a microfoundations perspective of capabilities.

Summarizing, these allied works suggest that substantive differences exist in how firms utilize resources, and that these differences, in turn, reflect variation among individual, process, and structural issues. But with resource orchestration's contribution to microfoundations largely based on processes, significant opportunity remains to more comprehensively address structural issues, like what has been done with fault lines (Ndofor et al., 2015) as well as individual-level issues, such as incentives and emotions. Indeed, incentives and emotions are important as they affect how managers act (Hodgkinson and Healey, 2011; Nickerson and Zenger, 2008) and likely affect the synchronization of resource orchestration's multiple processes over time. It is possible that managerial emotions, similar to skills, need to be more explicitly examined with a microfoundation framing. With regard to managerial skills, Teece argued that the "skills needed to sense are quite different from those needed to seize and those needed to reconfigure.... Since all three classes are unlikely to be found in an individual, they must be somewhere represented in top management" (2007: 1347). Likewise, it may be that a management team needs to robustly represent a broad representation of different emotional profiles—or the opposite might be true: that while different skills need to be present, a constrained emotional profile best suits the management team. As such, useful research question for future research include, How does a team's emotional profile heterogeneity affect the synchronization of resource orchestration processes, and How do incentives affect the synchronization of the resource orchestration processes?

While deeper examinations of any one component can be useful, the exploration of the interdependence among the three components of microfoundations can perhaps be even more fruitful. As such, we now turn our attention to an examination of the effects of the interaction of the three components of microfoundations on capability building and deployment.

Novel Considerations for Future Microfoundations Research

As the previous review shows, of the three components of microfoundations—individual, process, and structural—capabilities research has been predominantly focused on processes, with more limited focus on the individual or structural components and even less addressing multiple parts simultaneously. However, recent calls have identified the importance of the interdependencies among the microfoundations components of capabilities (Raveendran *et al.*, 2020).

Following prior research, Figure 1 graphically indicates that all three components inform and affect the others. In this figure, an arrow indicates a sequential path (a clockwise flow). This direction of flow is a simplification of what is likely complex and reciprocal in nature—the components affecting each other (Barney and Felin, 2013). For example, a structural choice may create constraints on processes that in turn affect individual-level concerns. Or two components may be jointly addressed as they are enabled by the third. We detail some of these specific potential effects shortly. Similarly, the same caution is warranted for the second flow arrow—the one shown in the resource orchestration processes. As this literature makes clear, while a structuring, bundling, and leveraging flow eases presentation, in fact the flow is complicated with reciprocal effects.

The broad treatment of microfoundations invites extensions beyond what may be traditionally thought of as the "individual" or "structural." For instance, Felin *et al.* (2012, 1355) clearly define the individual component with the term "actors," which purposefully allows researchers to identify lower-level drivers that are salient to the

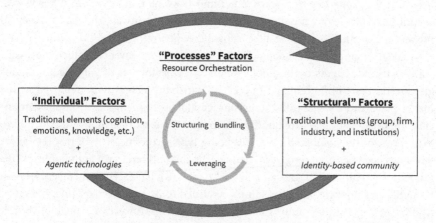

Figure 1 Novel individual and structural elements of capability microfoundations

outcome of interest. Likewise, Felin *et al.* (2015) suggest that wide-ranging structural elements combine to form important contextual factors that contribute to understanding microfoundations. As such, to extend microfoundational research, especially those addressing interdependencies, I introduce two novel factors—agentic technologies and identity-based community.

Agentic technologies as an individual component

Advanced technologies are moving beyond mere efficiency-producing tools. Some display agency of their own. As described by Murray, Rhymer, and Sirmon (forthcoming), agentic technologies are those that "possess a temporally embedded capacity to *intentionally* constrain, complement, and/or substitute for humans." These scholars point to three classes of agentic technologies. One class, arresting technologies, is exemplified by blockchain, "a shared, immutable ledger for recording transactions, tracking assets and building trust" (IBM, 2020), which allows for autonomous exchanges when precoded parameters are met (Murray *et al.*, 2021). The second and third classes are augmenting and automating technologies, which include, respectively, structured and unstructured machine learning. Both forms of machine learning identify complex patterns in data, but structured machine learning requires human engagement to provide training data after which the discovered patterns are then applied to new data sources, which helps augment decision-making. On the other hand, unstructured machine learning "independently seeks data and learns from it, formulates rules to guide how to act upon it," and ultimately enables autonomous execution (Murray *et al.*, forthcoming). Eventually, the bundling of these technologies into firm capabilities creates new forms of conjoined agency between human and technology (Murray *et al.*, forthcoming)—forms previously nonexistent. With agentic properties, when these technologies are bundled into a capability, it is, in effect, like adding another group member. However, each class of agentic technology has different properties from each other and from human actors. In other words, agentic technologies are not simple tools, nor are they identical to people, but they do possess agency and are likely to affect capabilities in novel ways.

While a single individual could form a complete firm-level capability, most capabilities include inputs beyond one employee. Typically, sets of tangible and intangible resources will be bundled to create a capability that is then deployed in the marketplace. More specifically, numerous "capitals"—human, social, physical, financial, and organizational—are bundled to create a capability (Sirmon and Hitt, 2003). With most of the combined resources being typical, the majority of theoretical interest has been on those resources deemed valuable and rare, such as individual skills (Sirmon and Hitt, 2009). As such, physical capital (e.g., tools, equipment, etc.), being thought of as nonrare, are often simply assumed to be available and thus not given significant theoretical treatment in capability building. However, the qualitative shift in advanced technologies—from efficiency-increasing tools to actors that act with purposeful intent—disrupt the validity of this approach. For instance, while block-chain technology (or other arresting technologies) is not rare—there are off-the-shelf options—it constrains human actors' agency such that organizational routines decrease in responsiveness, while the predictability of these routines increases (Murray et al., forthcoming). Thus, arresting technologies may impinge on the contributions of other valuable and rare resources. Even more, structured machine learning increases routine responsiveness and decreases predictability of change, while unstructured machine learning can fully supplant a human's role in a capability as well as in managerial processes of structuring, bundling, and leveraging. Here again, the inclusion of agentic technology in a capability has critical effects about which we know little. In fact, the impact of altering the locus of agency in a capability is difficult to overstate. While one class of agentic technology may impede or constrain the positive effects of human skill, others such as those reflected by structured and unstructured machine learning might increase a capability's effectiveness by complementing or substituting for human skills. Said differently, beyond the emotions and cognitive ability of human actors, capabilities involving agentic technology add new and compelling aspects to the "individual element" of microfoundations. Ranging from the constraining precision of blockchain to the black box of how unstructured machine learning optimizes data to find new creative solutions to problems, this class of technology presents wildly different parameters to consider in the individual-level component of microfoundations.

Likewise, the structural component of microfoundations can appropriately be broadened to include novel considerations. For instance, there are additional "structures" in which the firm and its members are embedded, such as partnerships with external stakeholders including identity-based communities.

Identity-based community as a structural component

Numerous firms are realizing the importance of identity-based community for firm survival and success (Afuah, 2018; Murray et al., 2020). For instance, online communities support firms by freely offering novel market information (Autio, Dahlander, and Frederiksen, 2013), product-enhancing feedback (Dahlander and Frederiksen, 2012), evangelism (Massa et al., 2017), brand commitment (Kim et al., 2008), and financial resources (Murray et al., 2020). However, an identity-based community is fundamentally different from traditional stakeholders, even locale-based community. Sirmon, Fisher, and Murray (2020) argue that, similar to traditional stakeholders (e.g., employees, owners, creditors, suppliers, etc.), identity-based community offers co-specialized assets to the firm (Barney, 2018). But they are unique in that they possess an identity-based affiliation as opposed to a profit-based affiliation with the firm. This difference allows the community to act swiftly and negatively against a previously supported firm when that firm threatens its shared identity. With a utility function focused on maximizing the community identity as opposed to maximizing a financial return, an identity-based community is a difficult stakeholder to control. Profit is simply not a motivating factor.

While research on control has waned, Cardinal, Kreutzer, and Miller (2017: 582) argue that the "planning, controlling, and coordinating" of resource bundles is at the heart of organizational control. So to the extent that identity-based community offers important resources, addressing control is salient, especially when both behavior-based controls (mandating, directing, and monitoring behaviors) and outcome-based controls (align an agent's self-interest with that of the principal) are irrelevant (Eisenhardt, 1985).

The curious case of identity-based community suggests that effective control need not be coercive in nature, but instead it can be enabling by promoting bidirectional information flows and mutual learning that in turn increases effectiveness, especially in complex task environments (Adler and Borys, 1996). Moreover, controls need not be formal, overt, or codified to be effective, but instead can be informal in nature (Kreutzer *et al.*, 2016)—or as Cardinal *et al.* (2017: 567) write, "even though informal control may not be explicitly stated or pre-specified, it still can be used intentionally and purposefully." When a firm accepts an identity-based community's contributions, it must reconsider how it might control this stakeholder from withdrawing or even antagonistically attacking the firm as the firm evolves. As such, identity-based community offers an interesting new structural factor to capability building and deployment.

Potential interdependencies for future research to consider

Constraints and requirements are two sides of the same coin with respect to the interdependencies among the microfoundations of capability building and deployment. In order for the three components to work in concert, choices in one component must complement the other components. That is, certain choices in one component may either constrain choices in the other components or require novel choices in other components. For instance, consider the microfoundational interdependencies among a young firm's community-enabling capability. More than merely marketing, a community-enabling capability endeavors to be a responsive, bidirectional, information processing mechanism (Murray *et al.*, 2020). Such a capability enables the firm to search for and secure resources from external actors (inflows) as well as inform, support, and enrich those same actors (outflows). For example, Propellerhead, a Swedish music software firm, created such a capability to identify and exploit their community's knowledge as well as stoke demand for rapid growth (Autio *et al.*, 2013). Similar capabilities have been identified in the Impossible Project (Hampel, Tracey, and Weber, 2020), and by Apple via Apple User Groups (Kim, 2010). Put simply, this type of capability couples both firm-to-market communications and support with crowdsourced-like inflows (Afuah and Tucci, 2012; Piezunka and Dahlander, 2015).

The benefits of such a capability are enormous. First, such a capability enhances the firm's research and development (R&D), product development, marketing, competitive intelligence, and even capital acquisition, while costing much less than traditional means. However, controlling a community is a novel challenge. Because community is not a single formal actor, contracts are not a viable mechanism for coordination or control. Instead, less formal mechanisms, such as relationship and trust building, are called for, but agentic technologies are likely needed to facilitate the nearly real-time interactions with an increasingly large, geographically dispersed community in a cost-effective manner.

For instance, Murray *et al.* (forthcoming) argue that in order to benefit from inputs from crowdsourced solutions, at least two problems need to be addressed—those of the firm as well as individuals in the crowd. Agentic technologies can overcome both. For the firm, agentic technology can be scaled less expensively than by increasing staff. And for crowd-based contributors, concerns regarding the lack of contracts and trust are mitigated by various aspects of the technology. For instance, blockchain technologies mitigate trust issues because once a preset condition is met, such as an accepted solution, the difficult-to-manipulate code triggers the release funds, access, or other awards autonomously, without any further involvement of an employee. However, this is a double-edged solution as blockchain technologies are arresting in nature. That is, they constrain human agency and responsiveness of which human actors are capable. Thus, once deployed, the firm faces increased costs to adjust to a blockchain-based capability. This then affects how the firm bundles blockchain with other firm resources to effectively utilize a community-enabling capability. This, in effect, reduces the evolutionary changes of a community-enabling capability after deployment. In this case, while the community remains a large solutions provider, it is not likely to become the vibrant evangelizing force that some communities become.

To enable an evangelizing community, other agentic technologies could be bundled into the capability. Instead of adding a greater number of employees to the community engagement capability to support and engaging in community-centric online forums, for example, the firm could utilize either structured or unstructured machine learning. These agentic technologies either supplement or even substitute for human agency. That is, instead of constraining, these technologies allow for change. However, important differences remain between these technologies. Employees can see into the black box of structured machine learning, while the black box of unstructured machine learning is obtuse. With unstructured machine learning, the objective is known, but the data, patterns, correlations, and so forth used to stipulate achievement of that objective are not well understood. Thus, unstructured data may lead to unexpected suggestions and behaviors that ultimately conflict with either the firm's or community's changing sentiments. As such, combining oversight in the form of additional technology (i.e., bundling blockchain with unstructured machine learning) or including more employees in the bundle/capability to oversee actual decisions the technology recommends are options. Regardless of the alternative chosen, the resource orchestration processes should be examined simultaneously.

All told, engaging an identity-based community with agentic technologies might be positive, from a microfoundation perspective, as it creates interdependencies among individuals, processes, and structure. The type of agentic technology may constrain the process by which community is cultivated as well as the type of community finally realized. In the opposite direction, choosing between engaging an organically grown community versus an existing community requires different processes as well as technologies.

These insights suggest a series of research questions that are open to examine. For example: When building and deploying a community-enabling capability, what roles can agentic technologies play? Do certain agentic technologies attract certain types of communities? Can multiple agentic technologies be bundled together to form an autonomous governance mechanism for platform-based industries? And how is the synchronization of resource orchestration processes ensured when human agency is constrained or substituted by agentic technology?

Conclusion

This chapter was developed to expand our understanding of the microfoundations of capability development and deployment. Two primary arguments were made to offer such a contribution. First, the three microfoundations components work in concert—that is, they are interdependent. Thus, choices for one (or more) component(s) creates constraints and/or requirements for the other components. While research on individual or structural components is warranted (processes is the most robustly investigated component to date), studying their interdependencies is novel and likely to be highly useful and can extend our knowledge beyond the recent contributions of Felin *et al.* (2012, 2015). Second, herein I endeavored to appropriately enlarge what is considered under the "individual" and "structural" components of the microfoundations focus. For example, agentic technology is reshaping our organizations and will do so even more in the future. With agentic properties, these technologies belong under the individual banner. Likewise, novelty in structures is changing the competitive landscape. Herein, identity-based communities were highlighted. But additional structures, such as distributed or location-independent organizational structures—those that have workers either synchronously or asynchronously engaged in work, but not co-located—are becoming increasingly prevalent (Rhymer, 2020). And, of course, the COVID-19 pandemic has hastened this structural choice as an imperative. Therefore, a broader consideration of structure is warranted for future microfoundations research.

In fact, both of these thrusts support future research to extend the microfoundation research stream. Deeper exploration of the individual or structural component—comparing and contrasting traditional to novel factors, for example—is encouraged. But I argue and offer examples of research questions that can act to spur research into the interdependencies among microfoundations components, especially as novel elements are introduced into firm capabilities. The example of a community-enabling capability was only for illustrative purposes. The interdependencies may differ depending on the type (dynamic or operational) or aim (creative, manufacturing, etc.) of the focal capability.

In conclusion, extending and enriching the microfoundations research stream within strategic management is likely one of the most opportune ways to maintain the field's relevance because it deeply connects phenomena and theory.

References

Adler PS, Borys B. 1996. Two types of bureaucracy: enabling and coercive. *Administrative Science Quarterly* 41: 61–89.

Adner R, Helfat C. 2003. Corporate effects and dynamic managerial capabilities. *Strategic Management Journal* 24: 1011–1025.

Afuah A. 2018. Crowdsourcing: a primer and framework. In *Creating and Capturing Value through Crowdsourcing*, Tucci C, Afuah A, Viscusi G (eds). Oxford University Press: Oxford, U.K.; 11–38.

Afuah A, Tucci CL. 2012. Crowdsourcing as a solution to distant search. *Academy of Management Review* 37(3): 355–375.

Autio E, Dahlander L, Frederiksen L. 2013. Information exposure, opportunity evaluation, and entrepreneurial action: an investigation of an online user community. *Academy of Management Journal* 56: 1348–1371.

Barney JB. 2018. Why resource-based theory's model of profit appropriation must incorporate a stakeholder perspective. *Strategic Management Journal* 39: 3305–3325.

Barney JB, Felin T. 2013. What are microfoundations? *Academy of Management Perspectives* 27(2): 138–155.

Cardinal LB, Kreutzer M, Miller CC. 2017. An aspirational view of organizational control research: re-invigorating empirical work to better meet the challenges of 21st-century organizations. *Academy of Management Annals* 11(2): 559–592.

Clarkson ME. 1995. A stakeholder framework for analyzing and evaluating corporate social performance. *Academy of Management Review* 20(1): 92–117.

Dahlander L, Frederiksen L. 2012. The core and cosmopolitans: a relational view of innovation and user communities. *Organization Science* 23: 988–1007.

Demerjian P, Lev B, McVay S. 2012. Quantifying managerial ability: a new measure and validity tests. *Management Science* 58(7): 1229–1248.

D'Oria L, Crook TR, Ketchen DJ Jr, Sirmon DG, Wright M. 2021. The evolution of Resource-Based inquiry: A review and meta-analytic integration of the strategic resources-action-performance pathway. *Journal of Management*, in press.

Eisenhardt KM. 1985. Control: organizational and economic approaches. *Management Science* 31(2): 134–149.

Felin T, Foss NJ, Heimeriks KH, Madsen TL. 2012. Microfoundation of routines and capabilities: individual, processes and structures. *Journal of Management Studies* 49: 1351–1374.

Felin T, Foss NJ, Ployhart RE. 2015. The microfoundations movement in strategy and organization theory. *Academy of Management Annals* 9: 575–632.

Hampel CE, Tracey P, Weber K. 2020. The art of the pivot: how new ventures manage identification relationships with stakeholders as they change direction. *Academy of Management Journal*, 63(2): 440-471 .

Helfat CE, Finkelstein S, Mitchell W, Peteraf M, Singh H, Teece D, Winter SG. 2007. *Dynamic Capabilities: Understanding Strategic Change in Organizations*. Blackwell: Malden, MA.

Helfat CE, Peteraf MA. 2003. The dynamic resource-based view: capability lifecycles. *Strategic Management Journal* 24: 997–1010.

Helfat CE, Peteraf, MA. 2015. Managerial cognitive capabilities and the microfoundations of dynamic capabilities. *Strategic Management Journal* 36: 831–850.

Henderson R, Cockburn I. 1994. Measuring competence: exploring firm effects in pharmaceutical research. *Strategic Management Journal* 15: 63–84.

Hitt MA, Sirmon DG, Li Y, Ghobadian A, Arregle JL, Xu K. Forthcoming. Institutions, industries, and entrepreneurial versus advantage-based strategies: how complex, nested environments affect strategic choice. *Journal of Management and Governance*, in press.

Hodgkinson GP, Healey MP. 2011. Psychological foundations of dynamic capabilities: reflexion and reflection in strategic management. *Strategic Management Journal* 32: 1500–1516.

Holcomb TR, Holmes RM, Connelly BL. 2009. Making the most of what you have: managerial ability as a source of resource value creation. *Strategic Management Journal* 30: 457–485.

Hoskisson RE, Hitt MA, Wan WP, Yiu D. 1999. Theory and research in strategic management: swings of a pendulum. *Journal of Management* 25(3): 417–456.

IBM. 2020. Retrieved from https://www.ibm.com/blockchain/what-is-blockchain#:~:text=-Blockchain%20is%20a%20shared%2C%20immutable%20ledger%20that%20facilitates%20the%20process,patents%2C%20copyrights%2C%20branding). 28 December 2020.

Kim JW, Choi J, Qualls W, Han K. 2008. It takes a marketplace community to raise brand commitment: the role of online communities. *Journal of Marketing Management* 24: 409–431.

Kim R. 2010. Apple passes Microsoft as top tech company. *SFGate*, 27 May. https://www.sfgate.com/business/article/Apple-passes-Microsoft-as-top-tech-company-3187136.php#ix-zz0pTkUBYj3 [28 December 2019].

Kor YY, Leblebici H. 2005. How interdependencies among human-capital deployment, development, and diversification strategies affect firms' financial performance. *Strategic Management Journal* 26(10): 967–985.

Kreutzer M., Cardinal LB, Walter J, Lechner C. 2016. Formal and informal control as complement or substitute? The role of the task environment. *Strategy Science* 1: 235–255.

Lau D, Murnighan JK. 1998. Demographic diversity and faultlines: the compositional dynamics of organizational groups. *Academy of Management Review* 23(2): 325–340.

Majumdar SK. 1998. On the utilization of resources: perspectives from the U.S. telecommunications industry. *Strategic Management Journal* 19(9): 809–831.

Massa FG, Helms WS, Voronov M, Wang L. 2017. Emotions uncorked: inspiring evangelism for the emerging practice of cool-climate winemaking in Ontario. *Academy of Management Journal* 60: 461–499.

Meyer-Doyle P, Lee S, Helfat CE. 2019. Disentangling the microfoundations of acquisition behavior and performance. *Strategic Management Journal* 40: 1733–1756.

Murray A, Kotha S, Fisher G. 2020. Community-based resource mobilization: how entrepreneurs acquire resources from distributed nonprofessionals via crowdfunding. *Organization Science* 31(4): 960–989.

Murray A, Kuban S, Josefy M, Anderson J. 2021. Contracting in the smart era: the implications of blockchain and decentralized autonomous organizations for contracting and corporate governance. *Academy of Management Perspectives*, in press.

Murray A, Rhymer J, Sirmon DG. Forthcoming. Humans and agentic technologies: toward a theory of conjoined agency in organizations. *Academy of Management Review*, in press.

Ndofor HA, Sirmon DG, He X. 2011. Firm resources, competitive actions, and performance: investigating a mediated model with evidence from the in-vitro diagnostics industry. *Strategic Management Journal* 32(6): 640–657.

Ndofor HA, Sirmon DG, He X. 2015. Utilizing the firm's resources: how TMT heterogeneity and resulting faultlines affect TMT tasks. *Strategic Management Journal* 36(11): 1656–1674.

Nelson RR, Winter SG. 1982. *An Evolutionary Theory of Economic Change*. Harvard University Press: Cambridge, MA.

Nickerson JA, Zenger TR. 2008. Envy, comparison costs, and the economic theory of the firm. *Strategic Management Journal* 29: 1429–1449.

Penrose ET. 1959. *The Theory of the Growth of the Firm*. John Wiley: New York, NY.

Piezunka H, Dahlander L. 2015. Distant search, narrow attention: how crowding alters organizations' filtering of suggestions in crowdsourcing. *Academy of Management Journal* 58(3): 856–880.

Raveendran M, Silvestri L, Gulati R. 2020. The role of interdependence in the microfoundations of organizational design: task, goals, and knowledge interdependence. *Academy of Management Annals* 14(2): 828–868.

Rhymer J. 2020. *Location Independent Organizations: Designing Work across Space and Time*. Dissertation, Graduate College, University of Washington, Seattle.

Selznick P. 1957. *Leadership in Administration: A Sociological Interpretation*. Row, Peterson: Evanston, IL.

Sirmon DG, Fisher G, Murray A. 2020. Volatility of community-based advantage: a resource-based view of community-driven performance gains and latent hazard. Working Paper, Foster School of Business, University of Washington.

Sirmon DG, Gove S, Hitt MA. 2008. Resource management in dyadic competitive rivalry: the effects of resource bundling and deployment. *Academy of Management Journal* 51(5): 919–935.

Sirmon DG, Hitt MA. 2003. Managing resources: linking unique resources, management, and wealth creation in family firms. *Entrepreneurship Theory and Practice* 27(4): 339–358.

Sirmon DG, Hitt MA. 2009. Contingencies within dynamic managerial capabilities: interdependent effects of resource investment and deployment on firm performance. *Strategic Management Journal* 30(13): 1375–1394.

Sirmon DG, Hitt MA, Arregle J-L, Campbell JT. 2010. The dynamic interplay of capability strengths and weaknesses: investigating the bases of temporary competitive advantage. *Strategic Management Journal* 31(13): 1386–1409.

Sirmon DG, Hitt MA, Ireland RD. 2007. Managing firm resources in dynamic environments to create value: looking inside the black box. *Academy of Management Review* 32(1): 273–292.

Sirmon DG, Hitt MA, Ireland RD, Gilbert BA. 2011. Resource orchestration to create competitive advantage: breadth, depth, and life cycle effects. *Journal of Management* 37(5): 1390–1412.

Taylor A, Helfat CE. 2009. Organizational linkages for surviving technological change: complementary assets, middle management, and ambidexterity. *Organization Science* 20(4): 718–739.

Teece DJ. 2007. Explicating dynamic capabilities: the nature and microfoundations of (sustainable) enterprise performance. *Strategic Management Journal* 28: 1319–1350.

Teece DJ, Pisano G, Shuen A. 1997. Dynamic capabilities and strategic management. *Strategic Management Journal* 18(7): 509–533.

Winter SG. 2000. The satisficing principle in capability learning. *Strategic Management Journal* 21(10–11): 981–996.

Zollo M, Winter SG. 2002. Deliberate learning and the evolution of dynamic capabilities. *Organization Science* 13(3): 339–351.

PART 11

CRITICAL FACTORS AFFECTING STRATEGY IN THE FUTURE

Phanish Puranam, Lead

11.0
CRITICAL FACTORS AFFECTING STRATEGY IN THE FUTURE

Phanish Puranam

As it defines the field, the fundamental research concern in strategic management is likely to remain that of understanding *the sources of interorganizational performance differentials, and their implications for managers and policymakers.* I deliberately used the words "organizational" and "performance" here. I think it is uncontroversial today to state that value creation, value capture, competition, and organizational capabilities are all concepts that have relevance even when no "firms" or "profits" are in sight, even though some of the founding texts in our field focused primarily on them (Rumelt, Schendel, and Teece, 1994).

Given the strong application orientation of the field, we are particularly concerned with *manipulable* sources of performance differences—things about which managers and other institutional actors can do something. When we study the strategic choices and behaviors of organizations, it is often with the intention that an enhanced understanding of these issues will eventually aid us in improving their performance. This normative or "design" stance (Simon, 1969) is a central feature of the field, though the field is by no means exclusively defined by it.

In my view, it is currently not possible to identify a single central theoretical paradigm in strategic management. This is not a source of discomfort; the track record of single-paradigm-driven approaches has not been very impressive in the social sciences in terms of scientific progress (setting aside the production of coherent tribal identity). Perhaps this is a consequence of the large variety of mechanisms that operate even within the simplest of phenomena in which we are interested. In any case, the lack of a single paradigm may well be the perpetual state of the strategic management field, given its problem-centric nature. For instance, theories from a range of (social and natural) sciences—economics, complex adaptive systems, psychology, sociology, anthropology, computer science, biology, political science—in addition to those seen as largely indigenous to the field, such as resource-based theory (Barney, 1991), positioning theory (Porter, 1980), the dynamic capabilities and knowledge-based perspectives (Kogut and Zander, 1996; Teece, Pisano, and Shuen, 1997), transaction cost economics (Williamson, 1975), and organizational design theory (Simon, 1947; Thompson, 1967, 2003)—all jostle to provide answers to the central question of strategy.

Table 1 Trends and theoretical developments

	Digitalization (Big data, machine learning / AI, connectivity)	Durability (Sustainability) (CSR, environment friendly business)	Diversity and inclusion (Gender and income inequality)	Deglobalization (Trade and mobility barriers)
The organization's objective function		Stakeholder view; sustainable or impact investment	How capital markets react to diversity and inclusion efforts	Business-government relations
Tools for analyzing market opportunities	Digitalized business models	Sustainable business models		
Rethinking the properties of resources	Seemingly unrelated diversification	Natural resources and externalities in the calculus of strategy	The business case for diversity	Global knowledge flows and integration
Nonhierarchical organization	Platforms, ecosystems	Nonmarket strategies, social movements	High-inclusion, high-equity organizations	Organization design dfferences across cultures

Note: Some cells are not filled today, but could be in the future.

Accordingly, when taking a forward-looking view of the field, perhaps a phenomenon-centric approach may bear more fruit than a theory-centric one. This is not to say that the menu of theories we currently work with will remain static. Rather, my point is that to anticipate the shape of future theoretical developments, focusing on novel phenomena may be useful, because theories (ideally) adapt to phenomena. I therefore first discuss some salient trends affecting our field, followed by a consideration of possible theoretical developments that might arise in response. A summary appears in Table 1, capturing important trends and associated theoretical questions. Note that not all cells in Table 1 have entries, but this does not rule out these blanks filling up going forward—indeed, this chapter invites researchers to take on that task.

Some Important Global Trends Affecting the Field of Strategy

Several trends affecting strategic management have been gathering strength at least for the last decade and possibly more.

The first among these is *deglobalization*, the process through which international trade barriers begin to reappear, making it harder for talent, goods, investment, and services to cross borders freely, and thereby reducing interdependence between countries (Witt, 2019). Much of the currently influential empirical work and theory in the field of strategic management was created in an era in which the forces of globalization were growing. Technological innovations in transportation and communication are forces that make globalization feasible, but not inevitable. As Witt (2019) observes, global politics needs to align in a way that enables these developments to translate into globalization, but the fact that they have done so in the post–World War II era does not guarantee that they will always do so. Trade tensions between the United States and China are likely to continue to define geopolitics. The rise of parochial forms of nationalism in many parts of the world (partly in reaction to the intracountry inequalities that globalization created) may continue.

This may lead not only to a multipolar world—with multiple focal points of political influence, such as the United States, Russia, and China—but also a multitrade-regime world—with the European Union, Association of Southeast Asian Nations (ASEAN) and the United States-Mexico-Canada Agreement (USMCA) (which replaced the North American Fair Trade Agreement [NAFTA] in 2020) each posing distinct challenges for firms attempting to develop a global strategy. Of course, this need not mean that our existing theories will become automatically less important. It may well be that in a world with strong barriers on the movement of goods and services, the ultimate advantage of multinationals will remain their capacity to move knowledge and innovation across boundaries (Bartlett and Ghoshal, 1989). However, to what extent legal regimes allow such actions, and what organizations might need to do in response, will likely pose important questions. For instance, how value chains should be distributed across locations, where research and development (R&D) should be located, and how to respond to localized competition are old questions that may yet demand new answers in a deglobalizing world.

A second important trend has been the growing realization that the *sustainability* or the durability of the natural world we live in matters, not just for policymakers but also for firms (Rangan, 2015). A magically self-regenerating natural environment is implicitly taken for granted in most current theories in strategy, with the onus being on policymakers to set the rules of the game in a manner that ensures the environment's protection. However, in a world in which such faith in the sufficiency of regulation increasingly seems naive, basic notions in strategy about competitive advantage, rents, economic profits, and the importance of the interests of shareholders versus stakeholders need to be reexamined carefully. Sustainability strategy is "a firm's detailed plan for achieving environmental integrity, social equity, and economic prosperity" (Barnett, Henriques, and Husted, 2021: 648). The central questions going forward are likely to be around what an organization will (or should) do when it can act in a legal manner that will help meet its stakeholders' expectations, but only at the expense of sustainability. For instance, an investment in a potentially profitable new factory that meets emission standards may nonetheless be opposed by some stakeholders because of the long-term negative consequences for the environment. How should firms balance possibly opposing pressures from their shareholders and other stakeholders who profess to guard the environment?

A third major trend involves *digitalization*—the trend that sees more and more of the economic sphere migrating to a digital format. Adner, Puranam, and Zhu (2019) argued that three basic processes—namely, digital representation, enhanced connectivity, and data aggregation—and the interactions among them are playing a key role in the digital transformation of the global economy. They considered the case of recorded digital music (Adner *et al*.: 253–254). The first major digital transition in this industry was from analog to digital formats. They term this a shift in *representation*—from the capture of physical markers such as grooves in a record, to digital markers such as ones and zeros. This shift occurred when the industry moved from LPs and cassette tapes to CDs. The shift from CDs to MP3 files distributed through technological platforms like iTunes was a shift in *connectivity*, as it enabled music content to be accessed through a digital network. The third transition that we are witnessing with services like Spotify entails a shift primarily in *aggregation*. More than streaming (which is just a particular refinement on digital delivery), they argued that what stands out here is the use of aggregated data on past requests and ratings to proactively customize suggestions for a specific user—through the use of advanced predictive analytics and data mining (for instance, through machine learning methods) (Adner *et al*., 2019).

Strategy scholars surely have well-attuned ears that can detect the background score to this terse libretto—a score rich in themes such as disruptive technologies, competence destruction, ambidexterity, and business model innovation—all of which may need to be reunderstood in the digital context. Does our current wisdom on these matters need refinement because of any unique properties that digital technologies have? At some level of extreme quantitative change, the effects can be qualitatively different. It may well be that ambidexterity—to take one instance—is a qualitatively different problem when the firm has to accommodate not just the old and new business models but a myriad of new business models at the same time.

A fourth trend involves the growing realization that *diversity* and *inclusion* are important agenda items for strategists and leaders. For leaders particularly in the Western world, it is viewed as increasingly important to have a clearly articulated statement on how they aim to improve diversity and inclusion in their organizations. At the same time, the capital markets seem unimpressed with these efforts, at least as far as board membership diversity is concerned. For instance, Solal and Snellman (2019) recently reported that in a sample of U.S. public firms, an increase in board diversity was met with a decline in market value. Apparently, investors interpret diversity expansion as a signal that the firm is not pursuing shareholder value maximization. How should firms deal with, and indeed avoid, such reactions?

Whether one sees efforts at improving diversity in organizations as a particular form of stakeholder management (also the topic of a chapter in this volume) or simply a self-enforced ethical norm, the implications for strategies and their implementation will very likely be important to understand. A broader perspective on diversity and inclusion might look beyond race and gender to consider economic inequality. An interesting related trend is the vocal expression of egalitarian norms by the post-millennial workforce, who appear eager to discover nonhierarchical alternatives to the traditional bureaucracy (Puranam, Alexy, and Reitzig, 2014) and to have their employers address social inequity (Bode and Singh, 2018). Should firms aim to meet such expectations? Do they have a choice if these expectations become widely held in the employment force?

The most prominent discontinuity in our current time that has affected the world of strategy is undoubtedly the COVID-19 pandemic. However, many of its effects can also be understood as amplifications of preexisting trends. For instance, attempts to curtail the spread of the virus produced outcomes that look very similar to policy decisions to curtail the flow of labor across national boundaries. In parallel, the need to work extensively through remote collaboration has sped up the digitalization of organizations. A widely circulating meme in the immediate aftermath of the COVID-19 outbreak was a multiple-choice question that asked, "Who has had the biggest impact on creating digital transformation in your organization?" The choices included the chief executive officer (CEO), the chief information officer (CIO), the chief technology officer (CTO), the board, and of course the correct answer—the COVID-19 pandemic.

One could keep the set of choices (and the purported "right answer") the same, and replace the question with, "Who or what has created the greatest awareness of the ecological footprint of our business activity?"[1] The pandemic may have given a new impetus to thinking about sustainability issues. Commuting and business travel affect our ecology in ways to which we have given limited consideration in the past. Finding out that we can in fact discharge many of our duties without either perhaps opens up the possibility of more responsible use of both. The impact of the pandemic has also highlighted social inequality and how far we are in terms of attaining inclusion, in sharp and sometimes tragic ways; the incidence of the disease and related negative implications have not been felt equally across class and economic strata. Even something as apparently neutral as remote collaboration poses significant risks for accentuating inequalities along the dimensions of gender. Working from home, it turns out, is not the same experience for men as it is for women if the latter shoulder the greater burden of supporting a family and home (Seitz et al., 2020). Existing inequalities can also be exacerbated between rich and poor, who differ in basic infrastructure for remote working, such as working space at home or high-bandwidth connectivity.

In addition to accentuating the trends noted here, the pandemic is of course also a classic recessionary shock. The differential effect of this shock on different industries, and the rise of possibly new business models to take advantage of the destruction of older industries and businesses and newer opportunities, will occupy strategy researchers for a significant amount of time. The topic of organizational resilience—which currently is the focus of the research not only of that name, but also of research on "ambidexterity" (Tushman and O'Reilly, 1996), "reconfiguration" (Agarwal and Helfat, 2009), and "dynamic capabilities" (Teece *et al.*, 1997)—will become even more relevant. Newer interests such as "agility" (Conboy, 2009) can usefully connect to these existing streams of work.

Strategy researchers may also see significant opportunities in using the shock created by the pandemic as a source of exogeneity for their empirical tests (Angrist and Pischke, 2008). This needs caution, however. The traditional case for the use of natural disasters as a source of exogeneity in empirical studies depends on the assumption that the factors that led to the disaster occurring in one location but not another are uncorrelated with the outcomes of interest. However, unobserved factors (such as location in a social network) that correlate with the incidence and impact of the pandemic for an organization may also be strongly correlated with its performance.

We may be on surer ground in leveraging the new data that the pandemic is generating. The forced move toward remote collaboration is creating a treasure trove of data on internal organizational processes. So far, we have had to rely on interviews, surveys, and participant observation, and none are very easy to scale. However, a consequence of having to work entirely remotely is the existence of significant "digital exhaust," which captures for the first time nearly all work-related interactions among individuals within an organization. For those interested in strategy implementation, organizational change, and more broadly organization design, we may be at the cusp of a unique opportunity to use these data to truly understand how organizations work, and how we can make them work better (Puranam, 2018).

Theoretical Implications

Turning from empirical phenomena and trends to their theoretical implications, what might occupy researchers in the field of strategy going forward? How would they respond to the trends identified above?

One overarching theme that seems inescapable is a questioning of the basic *objective function* of firms. So far, we have relied on a version of this function that was imported with relatively little reflection from the adjacent fields of finance and economics, and we have been content to assume that shareholder value maximization is the ultimate objective. As I noted earlier in the trends such as the increasing importance of sustainability and/or diversity-related goals, this assumption is now under serious question.

The legal properties of the firm, the doctrines of limited liability and legal forbearance, the ultimate accountability of the CEO, the employment contract, and the fact that shareholders primarily care about their economic interests are all properties of a particular cultural context. These are not eternal constants in the same sense as the speed of light or the gravitational constant are. For instance, the mainstreaming of sustainable investment and the rise of impact investment (Lee, Adbi, and Singh, forthcoming) clearly demonstrate that there exists at least a subset of shareholders who pay attention to intangible properties of the stocks they invest in, in addition to their financial returns and risks.

In an important sense, this is no different from the choice between different brands of bars of soap, with individual buyers making different choices about how much they care about the cleaning properties of the soap relative to the smell, the brand, and the image it evokes. If shares begin to be sold and marketed in much the same way that soap is, and the customers increasingly care about nonfinancial outcomes such as the preservation of the environment or enhanced social equity, then even a narrow pursuit of shareholder returns cannot save the leaders of firms from having to take a broader perspective of the outcomes of their strategies.

A related point is that in practice, many firms seem to already act as if shareholder value creation is a constraint to be satisfied rather than the objective function; this has been the animating theme in many recent discussions of corporate governance and its failures, as well as its variants across economic systems (Stern and James, 2016; Vissa, Greve, and Chen, 2010). We are now beginning to recognize good theoretical arguments for why shareholder value maximization may not always be the correct principle even on normative grounds.

A particularly persuasive argument comes from an old result in the property rights literature (Grossman and Hart, 1986; Holmström and Milgrom, 1991). Ownership of assets (in the sense of residual claimant rights) should optimally be held in the hands of the agent whose investments contributed the most to the joint product of their investments. This reasoning can be used to explain whether upstream supplier should buy downstream buyer or downstream buyer should buy upstream supplier in a vertical transaction. However, the same reasoning also seems applicable to the question of whether the providers of capital in the form of cash or in the form of human capital (or indeed some other form of capital) should be the ultimate residual claimants and owners of the firm.

An implication is that if cash or risk-bearing is a commodity, then it seems dubious to argue that shareholders should be the ultimate residual claimant. I am not arguing that they always will be—but in the contexts they are commodities, there is no obvious reason why their interest should be prioritized over those of other stakeholders—such as knowledgeable employees, the civic neighborhoods where facilities are located, or indeed even the state. Recent refinements in the resource-based view acknowledge these and related arguments, and are already moving to expand our conceptualization of the objective function of the firm, at least to increase the relevant set of residual claimants (Barney, 1991, 2018). For instance, Barney and Mackey (2021: 664) summarize the argument as follows: "In order for stakeholders to be willing to make profit-generating resources available to a firm, a firm must be willing to share some of the profits these resources help generate with the stakeholders that provide them (Lippman and Rumelt, 2003a, 2003b)." This highlights the crucial point that shareholders are not necessarily the stakeholders whose interests always have to be prioritized.

A second set of theoretical refinements will perhaps arise around the set of tools and frameworks that we currently use to do *industry analysis*. In their essay on digitalization and strategy, Adner *et al.* (2019) argued that the current progress of the digital revolution will almost certainly require a new conceptual apparatus. In addition to resources, capabilities, transaction costs, and the forces of competition including complementors, digitalization might require recognition of underlying drivers such as representation, connectivity, and aggregation. Additionally, there likely will be other and perhaps more refined ways of thinking about markets and business opportunities. The relevant unit of analysis may be a micro-segment, with its own competitive dynamics and resource requirements, suggesting that every firm effectively becomes a diversified, multibusiness firm, and that all strategy is ultimately corporate strategy (Puranam and Vanneste, 2016).

Of particular interest may be innovations in *business models*. As Amit and Zott (2021: 680) state, "*Business model innovation* (BMI) refers to the introduction of a novel system of interdependent activities in the product market space in which the focal firm competes (Amit and Zott, 2012; Chesbrough, 2010; Snihur and Zott, 2020)." Will the design of business models that respond to digitalization, or greater aspirations in terms of sustainability or diversity and inclusion, imply qualitatively different challenges? If so, what are these? Amit and Zott (2021) highlight a design perspective on business models, making explicit the point that there is room for strategic ingenuity in selecting a business model that provides cover from the forces of competition.

By symmetry, we may also need new conceptualizations of *resources* and *capabilities*. For instance, data are unquestionably a nonrivalrous resource—the use by one does not preclude the use by another, as is the case for most information. But when do data become a basis for competitive and corporate advantage (Barney, 1991)? Issues of ownership and reuse are perhaps far more salient for data than for other types of resources. For instance, even if data and algorithms are resources, their replication may be a qualitatively distinct phenomena from knowledge transfer among humans (Szulanski, 1996). On the one hand, *stickiness*—the challenge of transferring knowledge from one context to another—may be less relevant in replicating digital content. On the other hand, the property of stickiness may be even more important when humans attempt to understand the rationale of algorithms that use data to help make decisions. Many state-of-the art techniques in machine learning do not offer such causal understanding. Since they gain their predictive accuracy by fitting complex nonlinear functions to data (also see von Krogh, Ben-Menahem, and Shrestha [2021]) they are quite hard to interpret or explain. The *fungibility* of resources is another concept that is central to strategy thinking about corporate diversification. Digital assets are often usable with little decline in value in multiple markets. This implies that industry boundaries can become blurred, with an enhanced incidence of "seemingly unrelated diversification" (e.g., consider Amazon's portfolio of businesses).

Some of the new trends in deglobalization and digitalization may make the binary distinction between market and hierarchy perhaps even less useful. Transaction cost economics has had a very important influence on strategic management by offering a theoretical framework for understanding when activities are outsourced rather than conducted in-house. Yet, even in the heyday of this firm-versus-market dichotomy in strategy, Hennart observed the existence of a "swollen middle" nearly three decades ago (Hennart, 1993). By this he meant that, empirically, there seemed to be a lot more economic activity organized neither within firm boundaries nor in spot markets, but in some form of relational contracting. Far from being a temporary phenomenon, the swelling shows no signs of subsiding. That legal authority based on the employment contract (and undergirded by the doctrine of forbearance) is a powerful instrument to obtain cooperation and coordination does not mean that it is the only one. Relational contracting, leveraging both the "shadow of the past" (i.e., superior mutual understanding with partners) as well as the "shadow of the future" (i.e., the joint incentive to continue a productive relationship) is often enough superior to in-house production to contribute to that swollen middle.

It would also appear that such forms of organizing—neither firms nor markets, particularly as instantiated in digital formats—are here to stay. Interest in platforms and ecosystems is likely to remain high and be supplemented by interest in online communities, which offer a template for certain kinds of distributed collaboration even in the for-profit sector (Puranam *et al.*, 2014). In these different forms of "meta-organizations," legally autonomous entities—either individuals or firms—nonetheless act in a concerted manner without recourse to formal authority of the sort enshrined in employment contracts (Gulati, Puranam, and Tushman, 2012).

Conclusion

I have identified deglobalization, digitalization, diversity and durability (sustainability)- the "four D's" - as trends that are very likely to affect strategic management research and practice going forward, as well as highlighted how these trends may have been accentuated due to the COVID-19 pandemic. It would be foolhardy to attempt to foresee all the possible theoretical developments such trends may engender; however, I have identified a few areas that seem almost sure to be foci for theoretical development, with the proviso that they by no means represent a complete list.

These areas for theoretical development include the nature of the objective function for the strategist; the need for new tools and conceptualizations of industry analysis, business model innovation, and resources and capabilities; and the need to consider alternatives to hierarchy as the template for organizing nonmarket-based collaborative interaction. It is a wonderful time to enter the field of strategy—with such a wide canvas on which to paint. And the palette is as wonderful—strategy researchers are embracing cutting-edge methodologies such as computational modeling, experiments, and machine learning with enthusiasm, and the opportunities to make significant breakthroughs on these and other questions seem numerous.

Note

1. Or indeed "Who or what has helped us better understand the importance of preventing our work from becoming the sole source of meaning and connection in our lives"?

References

Adner R, Puranam P, Zhu F. 2019. What is different about digital strategy? From quantitative to qualitative change. *Strategy Science* 4: 251–342.

Agarwal R, Helfat CE. 2009. Strategic renewal of organizations. *Organization Science* 20(2): 281–293. doi:10.1287/orsc.1090.0423.

Amit R, Zott C. 2012. Creating value through business model innovation. *Sloan Management Review* 53(3): 41–49.

Amit R, Zott C. 2021. Business Model Innovation Strategy. In Strategic Management: State of the Field and Its Future, Duhaime IM, Hitt MA, Lyles MA (eds). Oxford University Press: New York, NY; 679–697.

Angrist JD, Pischke JS. 2008. *Mostly Harmless Econometrics: An Empiricist's Companion.* Princeton University Press: Princeton, NJ.

Barnett ML, Henriques I, Husted BW. 2021. Sustainability Strategy. In *Strategic Management: State of the Field and Its Future*, Duhaime IM, Hitt MA, Lyles MA (eds). Oxford University Press: New York, NY; 647–662.

Barney J. 1991. Firm resources and sustained competitive advantage. *Journal of Management* 17(1): 99–120. doi:10.1177/014920639101700108.

Barney JB. 2018. Why resource-based theory's model of profit appropriation must incorporate a stakeholder perspective. *Strategic Management Journal* 39: 3305–3325.

Barney JB, Mackey A. 2021. What would the field of strategic management look like if it took the stakeholder perspective seriously? In *Strategic Management: State of the Field and Its Future*, Duhaime IM, Hitt MA, Lyles MA (eds). Oxford University Press: New York, NY; 663–678.

Bartlett CA, Ghoshal S. 1989. *Managing Across Borders: The Transnational Solution.* Harvard Business School Press: Boston, MA.

Bode C, Singh J. 2018. Taking a hit to save the world? Employee participation in a corporate social initiative. *Strategic Management Journal* 39(4): 1003–1030.

Chesbrough H. 2010. Business model innovation: opportunities and barriers. *Long Range Planning* 43(2–3): 354–363.

Conboy K. 2009. Agility from first principles: reconstructing the concept of agility in information systems development. *Information System Research* 20(3): 329–354.

Grossman S, Hart O. 1986. The costs and benefits of ownership: a theory of vertical and lateral integration. *Journal of Political Economy* 94(4): 691–719.

Gulati R, Puranam P, Tushman M. 2012. Meta-organization design: rethinking design in inter-organizational and community contexts. *Strategic Management Journal* 33(6): 571–586. doi:10.1002/smj.1975.

Hennart JF. 1993. Explaining the swollen middle: why most transactions are a mix of "market" and "hierarchy." *Organization Science* 4(4): 529–547.

Holmström B, Milgrom P. 1991. Multitask principal-agent analyses: incentive contracts, asset ownership, and job design. *Journal of Law, Economics and Organization* 7(Spec. Issue): 24–52.

Kogut B, Zander U. 1996. What firms do? Coordination, identity, and learning. *Organization Science* 7(5): 502–518. doi:10.1287/orsc.7.5.502.

Lee M, Adbi A, Singh J. Forthcoming. Categorical cognition and outcome efficiency in impact investing decisions. *Strategic Management Journal*

Lippman SA, Rumelt RP. 2003a. A payments perspective: microfoundations of resource analysis. *Strategic Management Journal* 24(11): 903–927.

Lippman SA, Rumelt RP. 2003b. A bargaining perspective on resource advantage. *Strategic Management Journal* 24(11): 1069–1086.

Porter ME. 1980. *Competitive Strategy.* Free Press: New York, NY.

Puranam P. 2018. *The Microstructure of Organizations.* Oxford University Press: Oxford, U.K.

Puranam P, Alexy O, Reitzig M. 2014. What's "new" about new forms of organizing? *Academy of Management Review* 39(2): 162–180. doi:10.5465/amr.2011.0436.

Puranam P, Vanneste B. 2016. *Corporate Strategy: Tools for Analysis and Decision.* Cambridge University Press: Cambridge, U.K.

Rangan S. 2015. *Performance and Progress.* Oxford University Press: Oxford, U.K.

Rumelt R, Schendel DE, Teece D. 1994. *Fundamental Issues in Strategic Management: A Research Agenda.* Harvard Business School Press: Boston, MA.

Seitz BM, Aktipis A, Buss DM, Alcock J, Bloom P, Gelfand M, Harris S, *et al.* 2020. The pandemic exposes human nature: 10 evolutionary insights. *Proceedings of the National Academy of Sciences* 117(45): 27767–27776.

Simon HA. 1947. *Administrative Behavior.* Macmillan: New York, NY.

Simon HA. 1969. *The Sciences of the Artificial.* MIT Press: Cambridge, MA.

Snihur Y, Zott C. 2020. The genesis and metamorphosis of novelty imprints: how business model innovation emerges in young ventures. *Academy of Management Journal* 63(2): 554–583.

Solal I, Snellman K. 2019. Women don't mean business? Gender penalty in board composition. *Organization Science* 30(6): 1270–1288.

Stern I, James SD. 2016. Whom are you promoting? Positive voluntary public disclosures and executive turnover. *Strategic Management Journal* 37(7): 1413–1430.

Szulanski G. 1996. Exploring internal stickiness: impediments to the transfer of best practice within the firm. *Strategic Management Journal* 17(Suppl. Winter): 27–43.

Teece DJ, Pisano G, Shuen A. 1997. Dynamic capabilities and strategic management. *Strategic Management Journal* 18(7): 509–533. doi:10.1002/(sici)1097–0266(199708)18:7<509::aid-smj882>3.0.co;2-z.

Thompson JD. 1967. *Organizations in Action: Social Science Bases of Administrative Theory.* McGraw-Hill Book Company: New York, NY.

Thompson JD. 2003. *Organizations in Action: Social Science Bases of Administrative Theory.* Transaction Publishers: New Brunswick, NJ.

Tushman ML, O'Reilly CA III. 1996. Ambidextrous organizations: managing evolutionary and revolutionary change. *California Management Review* (4): 8–30.

Vissa B, Greve HR, Chen WR. 2010. Business group affiliation and firm search behavior in India: responsiveness and focus of attention. *Organization Science* 21(3): 696–712. doi:10.1287/orsc.1090.0475.

von Krogh G, Ben-Menahem SM, Shrestha YR. 2021. Artificial Intelligence in strategizing: prospects and challenges. In *Strategic Management: State of the Field and Its Future,* Duhaime IM, Hitt MA, Lyles MA (eds). Oxford University Press: New York, NY; 625–645.

Williamson OE. 1975. *Markets and Hierarchies: Analysis and Antitrust Implications.* Free Press: New York, NY.

Witt M. 2019. De-globalization: theories, predictions, and opportunities for international business research. *Journal of International Business Studies* 50: 1053–1077.

11.1

ARTIFICIAL INTELLIGENCE IN STRATEGIZING: PROSPECTS AND CHALLENGES

Georg von Krogh, Shiko M. Ben-Menahem, and Yash Raj Shrestha

Introduction

The past decade has seen momentous scientific advances in the field of *artificial intelligence* (*AI*), "a system's ability to interpret external data correctly, to learn from such data, and to use those learnings to achieve specific goals and tasks through flexible adaptation" (Haenlein and Kaplan, 2019). Powered by a surge in data generation and computing power, algorithms are becoming increasingly capable of digitally performing operations that efficiently and effectively emulate human learning, profound judgment, and decision-making across a wide range of application areas. Such applications include optimization of internal business operations, product design, the capture of scarce external knowledge, and the screening and recruiting of talent (Shrestha, Ben-Menahem, and von Krogh, 2019; Shrestha, Krishna, and von Krogh, 2021).

With these developments, management scholars have shown a growing interest in AI's potential to support or transform organizations (von Krogh, 2018). Yet, while the application of AI algorithms is by now widely studied across functional domains including engineering, human resource management, operations management, information systems, economics, finance, accounting, and marketing, much less attention has been devoted to understanding how the onset of AI changes the nature of strategizing—that is, the activities of people involved in the strategy process (Jarzabkowski, Balogun, and Seidl, 2007; Whittington, 2014).

In this chapter, we take stock of the promise and perils of AI in shaping the future of strategizing. We discuss applications known to us during the key stages in the strategy process and identify opportunities for future research on the strategy-AI nexus. Recognizing the historic diversity of definitions and approaches to strategic management (Nag, Hambrick, and Chen, 2007; Randall and Dent, 2019), we take a broad perspective and define the strategic management process as "the full set of commitments, decisions, and actions required for a firm to achieve strategic competitiveness and earn above-average returns" (Hitt, Ireland, and Hoskisson, 2015).

To structure our discussion, we discern two critical stages (Randall and Dent, 2019) in the strategy process: strategic *analysis* (the evaluation of an organization's external and internal context), as well as strategy *formulation* and *implementation* (the generation, evaluation, and selection of strategic options and choices). Our goal is not an all-inclusive treatment of how AI may be used in each of these stages, but to illustrate what we believe are central challenges and opportunities that AI poses for strategic leaders in the foreseeable future.

The chapter is organized as follows. The next section offers a very brief introduction to AI with a focus on machine learning (ML) algorithms. In the third section, we discuss applications of AI in strategic analysis, strategy formulation, and strategy implementation. The fourth section outlines research imperatives for strategy scholars, and the final section discusses risks and challenges to strategizing posed by AI. Table 1 displays selected key insights from this chapter.

What Is Artificial Intelligence?

John McCarthy first coined the term "artificial intelligence" in 1956 as "the science and engineering of making intelligent machines" (Hamet and Tremblay, 2017). During the 1950s, early advances in the study of AI coincided with progress in the areas of computer science and cognitive sciences. Pioneers such as Herbert Simon, Alan Newell, and Marvin Minsky pursued a strong ambition formulated by Alan Turing, to create a machine capable of emulating intelligent behavior on par with human beings. Turing's ambition is still preserved in the form of the Turing test, where programmers strive to create AI that passes this "imitation game."

The AI boom of the 1950s was followed by periods of reduced AI research and overall pessimism related to technology itself, popularly known as "AI winters" (McCorduck, 2004). Various problems in technical designs, the lack of processing power, and scarcity of high-quality data to train AI algorithms created severe obstacles in developing a useful form of AI (see von Krogh and Roos, 1995; McCarthy, 1981). During the past two decades, AI research and its applications in ML algorithms and deep learning have regained much scientific and practical attention (Franz, Shrestha, and Paudel, 2020). Four developments contributed to this renaissance: data generation and systematic storage and delivery, algorithm development, processing power, and open-source code (von Krogh, 2018).

Machine learning can be understood as a computer program's ability to learn from experience regarding a task in a way that it improves its performance with experience. Based on the data and the goal of use, ML algorithms can be broadly categorized into three classes: supervised learning, unsupervised learning, and reinforcement learning (see Shrestha *et al.*, forthcoming). Each of these ML classes holds different promise for strategists. Supervised ML algorithms excel at prediction and forecasting by learning from the outcomes of past experiences, similar to experiential learning in humans. Applications include demand forecasting and forecasting investment

Table 1 Strategists' core activities and AI augmentation in the strategy process

Stage of strategy process	Strategic analysis	Strategy formulation and implementation
Strategists' core activities	External analysis of macro environment (e.g., PESTEL, which refers to Political Economic Sociocultural Technological Environmental and Legal)	Formulating corporate and business strategy
	External analysis of competitive dynamics	Creating and selecting strategic options (e.g., mergers and acquisitions [M&As], cooperative strategies)
	Internal analysis of human, financial, and auxiliary resources and capabilities	Strategic innovation, entrepreneurship, and renewal
		Measuring and evaluating implementation and performance of strategic actions
AI augmentation	Continuous interaction with external environment to forage information from external data sources	Model business portfolio performance, synergies, and portfolio risks
	Interpreting data through identifying structures and patterns in high-dimensional data	Screen for novel and unobvious strategic options (e.g., M&As, collaboration partners, innovation projects)
	Predictive analysis	Increase speed of decision-making
		Monitor strategy implementation on online platforms and digital communication channels
Challenges and risks	Data privacy and data security	Limited variety and creativity in strategic options
	Data biases and lack of data variety	Perpetuating social, political, economic equalities
	Interruptions to data flows	Erratic strategic actions resulting from erratic data and analysis
	Cost of protecting access to privileged information and expertise	

returns. In contrast, unsupervised ML algorithms are useful for identifying robust patterns in data, by performing tasks such as clustering and dimension reduction. For example, by identifying clusters of companies following similar strategies and competing in similar markets, unsupervised ML can aid in strategic group analysis. Finally, reinforcement learning can be useful for strategists in running simulations and experimenting with innovation ideas or evaluating the outcome of a given strategic process. Such an application of reinforcement learning can be useful for strategists in evaluating various alternatives and their counterfactuals before taking a particular action, leading to organizational learning.

AI and Strategic Analysis

A starting point for exploring the role of AI in the strategy process is its potential for augmenting and transforming strategic analysis. While information systems have long assisted managers in gathering and organizing information for environmental scanning and decision-making purposes (Robinson, Ahmad, and Simmons, 2021), AI algorithms may have the potential for dramatically expanding the scale, scope, and speed of analysis of an organization's external and internal environment through its capacity for interacting with the environment and generating data. Specifically, AI can assist with (a) foraging information from internal and external data sources on a discrete or continuous basis, (b) analyzing and interpreting such data through pattern identification, and (c) assisting executives in decision-making through predictive analysis (Ferràs-Hernández, Tarrats-Pons, and Arimany-Serrat, 2017).

As a starting point for mapping how AI may support strategic analysis, we first discuss its applications for analyzing external (i.e., macro- and micro-environmental) factors. Next, we consider AI's role in competitor analysis, and subsequently in the internal analysis of human, financial, and auxiliary resources.

External analysis

AI applications have found their way into areas of strategic analysis across political, economic, social, technological, environmental, and legal factors.

Political scientists have developed various AI-based text analysis tools useful in inferring the "political climate" across regions. These systems analyze diverse data sources, including news outlets, legislative debates, and online political discourse. In particular, ML algorithms have proven effective in analyzing unstructured social media data (Zafarani, Abbasi, and Liu, 2014). Using such data, ML is increasingly useful for predicting outcomes of elections (e.g., Coletto *et al.*, 2015), policy changes (e.g., Chan and Zhong, 2018), and political bias and conflicts (Biessmann *et al.*, 2016). Early identification and prediction of political trends and developments with AI can help strategists understand how government and government policy may influence their organization. Doing so may provide an important source of competitive advantage.

Machine learning can also be applied to accurately and reliably measure economic trends, such as economic growth, the onset of economic recessions (e.g., Wu *et al.*, 2020), increasing poverty (Kshirsagar *et al.*, 2017), and bankruptcies (Cielen, Peeters, and Vanhoof, 2004). The adoption of ML tools by the financial services industry is an important precursor to applications by strategists. For example, institutional investors use ML to predict stock returns and thereby make better investment decisions (Avramov, Cheng, and Metzker, 2019) and estimate systemic financial risks (e.g., Kou *et al.*, 2019). Economists increasingly apply ML methods to unconventional data sources and questions, such as the use of satellite image data to predict spatial distribution of economic well-being across African countries (Jean *et al.*, 2016).

Strategists often need to include social factors in their analysis, such as changes in demographics and societal values. Some of these changes may be slow-moving (e.g., national culture), while others are subject to sudden jolts and rapid turns (e.g., fashion) that may pose significant opportunities or threats to the business. Scholars have proposed techniques such as automated text analysis to "map the contours of cultural fields, classify cultural elements and trace the evolution of culture over time" (Bail, 2014). New algorithms also enable systematic measurement of culture and modeling of its evolution within organizations and social groups (Doyle *et al.*, 2017). Such developments offer new opportunities for measuring difficult-to-capture concepts such as culture in strategy research.

Researchers tend to give technological factors an important role in most strategic analysis, whether for manufacturer or user firms. AI can assist companies in monitoring technological developments and anticipate any relevant technological changes. For example, ML is increasingly used to identify patterns of technology development by sifting through massive amounts of patent or publication data (e.g., Lee *et al.*, 2018). These uses of ML allow firms to construct "knowledge profiles" of their industry and major competitors (Suominen, Toivanen, and Seppänen, 2017).

With the growing awareness of climate change and the attention given to corporate sustainability responsibility (CSR), ecological and environmental factors rapidly gain importance in strategic analysis. Research on the use of AI in such analysis is still in its infancy, but there are promising examples, such as research into whether hydrogen electrical vehicles may become the dominant means of transportation for consumers (Ranaei *et al.*, 2016). Such applications are important for commercial investors, as well as for policymakers deciding on how and where to develop transportation infrastructures.

Traditionally, firms tend to invest significantly in legal consultants who often manually collect and analyze a large body of new laws and regulations that may alter the conditions for doing business across regions and legal regimes. AI applications may support firm internal collection and processing of such legal data, potentially reducing overall legal expenditures. For example, Yousfi-Monod, Farzindar, and Lapalme (2010) developed an ML algorithm that sifts through thousands of pages of legal documents and provides useful summaries relevant to a firm's strategy. AI is also increasingly being used for automating financial compliance monitoring and regulation (e.g., Treleaven and Batrinca, 2017).

Competitive analysis

A prime application of AI in strategic analysis concerns competitor analysis. As firms gather massive amounts of data on competitors and their industries, automated analysis can help cluster data, identify patterns in data, and even predict competitors' strategic moves.

Often before a strategic analysis may proceed, strategists need to identify relevant competitors, yet doing so remains one of the strategist's most challenging tasks (Haefliger, Jäger, and von Krogh, 2010; Hamel and Prahalad, 1994). New approaches, such as Pant and Sheng's (2015) analysis of web content to identify how firms' service and product offerings "link" or converge, offer new ways for identifying emerging competitors and predicting performance. In a similar vein, Shrestha *et al.* (forthcoming) propose that ML algorithms can be used to identify strategic groups consisting of firms that follow similar strategies, and also predict movements of firms between these groups.

Additionally, such tools offer a more dynamic approach to performing competitive analysis. Indeed, scholars have warned that assumptions about competitors need to be frequently reanalyzed and reexamined so as to judge the continuous validity of a firm's strategy (Ireland, Hitt, and Sirmon, 2003). The advantage of automated competitor analysis over traditional (manual and discrete) approaches is considerable: once plugged into market and competitor data generation machines (e.g., web crawlers, online sales), algorithms can perform competitor analysis on a continuous basis and help strategists dynamically gauge the validity of the firm's current strategy.

Internal analysis

AI may also augment strategic analysis of internal organizational factors, including human, financial, and auxiliary resources, such as supply chains or customer relationships.

Starting with human resources, AI applications can offer automated pattern recognition in such data and assist managers in identifying employee performance, predicting career trajectories, and revealing patterns of compensation and inequality, among others (see Strohmeier and Piazza [2013] for an overview). Careful assessment of skills, education, talent, and demographics enables the strategist to more adequately assess the extent to which a potential strategy can be implemented.

Firms also possess swaths of accurate, deep, and labeled accounting and financial data. Strategists tend to draw heavily on balance-sheet information, for example, when conducting analysis. ML algorithms may continuously or discretely cluster such data, performing analysis of patterns. In so doing, algorithms may boost the interpretation of what causes certain financial resource conditions (e.g., fluctuations in liquidity, exchange rate premiums at corporate treasuries) relevant to the type and timing of the firm's strategic commitments (Fethi and Pasiouras, 2010). AI can also be put to use in financial analyses less essential to the strategy process, such as tools used to monitor transactions performed throughout the firm. Applications can detect unusual amounts or frequency of transactions, and rapidly identify fraud. Using these tools, AI can aid in managing financial risk by augmenting compliance and risk management functions with improved data-driven insights, drawing on rapid and automated data analysis and reduced administrative loads, thereby saving finance and accounting employees' time for more creative activities.

Machine learning algorithms are increasingly providing efficient analysis on a range of other resources relevant to the strategy process, such as demand forecasting, production planning, resource allocation, and logistics. For example, ML can augment production planning decisions by automating the process of searching for potential suppliers by mining data from online catalogs and other repositories (Nissen and Sengupta, 2006), providing predictions on performance of prospective suppliers (Humphreys, McIvor, and Huang, 2002), and even estimating valuation and evaluating online bids (Cheung *et al.*, 2004).

Another auxiliary resource specifically relevant for ML-supported analysis concerns customer relationships. Customers are increasingly involved in a variety of product- and service-related discussions, consume digital content, and share knowledge among themselves on a diverse set of platforms such as YouTube, Facebook, Wikipedia, and TikTok (Hollebeek, Conduit, and Brodie, 2016). Observation of customer behavior by their digital traces can aid the strategist in better understanding trends and seasonality in customer needs related to their service and product offerings (Heinonen, 2011). Such insights can then be used to predict customer preferences, and eventually lead to analysis relevant for product innovation in the firm (Gomez-Uribe and Hunt, 2015).

AI in Strategy Formulation and Implementation

With AI's rapid emergence to general-purpose-technology status, numerous organizations are placing it at the center of their high-level strategy. Google CEO Sundar Pichai emphasized the company's strategy as "AI first" in his I/O 2017 keynote, emphasizing a new focus on ML and other AI technologies to increase organizational efficiency and improve customer experience. In the subsequent years, Google and its industry partners invested heavily in seemingly more "intelligent" products, such as Google Photos, which uses AI to detect people, places, and objects in images; RankBrain, which increases search speed; and Google Assistant as a personal virtual assistant—all decisions that markedly increased the overall valuation of the company.

AI is also reshaping the activities that constitute the formulation and implementation stages of the strategy process. In their pursuit of profitable growth, firms formulate business development and financial objectives and corresponding implementation plans at various levels of granularity. Regardless of whether such a process occurs regularly and formally or sporadically and informally, formulating and implementing a strategy is a lengthy and complex process that involves an extensive amount of varied data and draws on managerial analysis and decision-making at various levels of the organization. The cognitive limitations of strategists in processing data for the decision-making and problem-solving activities underlying strategy formulation and implementation are therefore well documented in the literature (March and Simon, 1958; Simon, 1947). The potential of AI to enhance human strategy formulation and implementation is a contentious subject that much resembles discussions following the advancement of previous generations of decision support systems since the 1950s (e.g., Yoo and Digman, 1987).

On one hand, researchers seem to agree that current applications of AI—combined with the availability of big data—exceed the capabilities of previous systems. Indeed, successful strategy *formulation* relies on in-depth knowledge of the organization, its environment, and the risk-reward profile of strategic options. In a similar vein, successful strategy *implementation* relies on a strategist's ability to effectively monitor operations and evaluate the performance of strategic actions. The potential of AI-powered systems to automate continuous data analysis, create new knowledge about strategic opportunities, and identify patterns to predict the payoff of choices thus stands to enhance the quality of the strategist's decisions where they concern formulation and implementation tasks requiring primarily explicit knowledge (Agrawal, Chatterjee, and Novotný, 2018; Keding, 2020).

On the other hand, concerns about the limitations of AI-based systems in the strategy process abound. For example, researchers have argued that while AI performs well in stable, context-specific settings, it underperforms in situations involving creativity, novelty, and uncertainty (Brynjolfsson and Mitchell, 2017; Jarrahi, 2018; von Krogh, 2018), and can even increase complexity in organizational decision-making (Lawrence, 1991). Rather than replacing automated formulation and implementation, AI can thus better be considered as a useful "assistant" that augments strategists' capacity to make judgments about external threats and opportunities, internal strengths and weaknesses, and strategic issues (Huang et al., 2019; Reeves, Levin, and Ueda, 2016; Shrestha, Krishna, and von Krogh, 2021).

AI and corporate strategy

To illustrate how AI can be applied in specific areas of strategy formulation and implementation, consider its role in the analysis of typical corporate-level strategy questions concerning a firm's business portfolio and decisions regarding growth and diversification. AI can be used to model the performance of a business portfolio;

evaluate the fit, risk, and performance of a firm's set of businesses; and analyze and propose potential synergies among them. For example, based on an analysis of market and product data across business units, AI can assist strategists in addressing portfolio risks, such as when fluctuations in demand are strongly correlated across the portfolio or when various businesses are exposed to similar currency risks. Davenport refers to such "sparring partner" activities by AI as "cognitive insight" (Davenport and Ronanki, 2018).

AI tools are also increasingly shaping the way in which companies identify and screen *merger and acquisition* (M&A) opportunities, as well as manage the deal cycle and postmerger integration (PMI) stage. Whereas traditional mergers and acquisitions require a host of resource-intensive analytic activities (due diligence, market analysis, valuation, pricing) and are thus limited to screening a small subset of potential targets, AI-based analytics allows companies to automatically and continuously screen a large pool of opportunities, as they arise. Natural language processing (NLP) methods such as automatic document summarization and topic modeling can be used to design a filter such that attractive cases can be preselected for further human consideration. The strength of AI in these scenarios derives from the technology's ability to integrate various data sources—such as patent databases, company financial records, historic data on M&A deals, social media (e.g., LinkedIn data to identify rare skill sets), news media, conference call transcript filings, and discussion fora—and dynamically adapt screening parameters to changing environmental conditions. Emerging financial-technology solution providers, such as San Francisco–based Refinitiv, use AI tools to develop predictive quantitative models on M&A targets that help decision-makers more accurately estimate synergies and assess deal value.[1]

Moreover, given the critical role of efficiency and speed in decision-making around M&A opportunities (Baum and Wally, 2003) and the postmerger integration stage (Homburg and Bucerius, 2006), AI can have important performance implications by automating acquisition process steps and shortening critical activities in the M&A cycle. These activities may also be performed at lower cost. For example, with respect to the preacquisition stage, recent years have seen consequential advancements in the use of AI in transactional law, where AI enables legal professionals to automate the labor-intensive M&A due-diligence process. Among the many opportunities for AI, automation can allow target firms to more efficiently collect and classify relevant documents and ensure that they meet disclosure requirements.

Postacquisition, AI and social analytics tools can support leaders in organizational integration by automating the process of mapping human resources and redeploying staff into new organizational structures, taking into consideration complex combinations of skills, remuneration, and job titles (see also the "AI and Strategic Analysis" section in this chapter). AI can further support and accelerate task integration and identify opportunities for cost reduction by combining large swaths of unstructured data from separate company systems, such as those found in customer databases and contract repositories.

In a similar way, AI may find applications in *cooperative strategies* such as the identification and selection of strategic alliance partners. For example, NLP of annual reports may help strategists identify relevant indicators such as a potential partner's business focus or strategic positioning (e.g., Menon, Choi, and Tabakovic, 2018).

Strategic innovation, entrepreneurship, and renewal

New insights are currently emerging on how the diffusion of AI technology across firms might create opportunities and challenges for new venture creation and strategic entrepreneurship. Cockburn, Henderson, and Stern (2018) argue that AI, and in particular deep learning, serves as a general-purpose technology (GPT) and a new "method of inventing" with the potential to reshape the nature of the innovation process and the organization of research and development (R&D). They argue that advancements in AI, much like the rise of other GPT such as the microprocessor, bring about a reinforcing cycle between innovation on the level of AI and its application areas.

Chalmers, MacKenzie, and Carter (2020) identify three ways in which AI can enhance information search and idea generation activities that lie at the basis of new venture opportunity identification and exploitation. First, the strength of deep-learning algorithms in identifying structures in high-dimensional data allows corporate and start-up entrepreneurs to search for and experiment with opportunities that were previously unobservable (e.g., Kucukkeles, Ben-Menahem, and von Krogh, 2019). Second, AI can support new venture activity through the identification and exploitation of consumer needs. Third, AI-based simulations and experiments promise investors and business leaders the ability to test innovations and new venture ideas. For example, simulations using real-world dynamic data can emulate the conditions new ventures may encounter in the future. Such tools, when fully developed, may not only benefit investment decisions but could one day be used to design innovations and make choices on critical product features such as pricing or promotions. Using AI-based simulations and experiments, entrepreneurs could thus test their ideas and predict how customers would react to particular product features and determine changes in product design and pricing (Chalmers *et al.*, 2020).

AI is also making inroads into augmenting and replacing human activities related to the exploitation of new venture ideas via the emerging conversational systems (e.g., drift.ai) and robo sales advisers (Chalmers *et al.*, 2020). The extent to which such solutions prove valuable in the long run remains an open question. Future research opportunities will arise from questions surrounding the implications of organizational de-skilling and loss of customer relationships as a result of robo-advisers, as well as questions concerning customer acceptance of interaction with AI-based systems. From a strategy perspective, important questions arise as to how AI-based technology changes strategic entrepreneurship when it comes to growing new ventures and managing the risk inherent in entrepreneurial activity.

Strategy control

Strategy control concerns the efforts of strategists to ensure that the implementation of strategic plans unfolds as intended and to measure progress on strategic goals. Research on the application of AI to strategy control has been limited thus far. Nonetheless, several promising areas can be identified, due to the possibility of automating identification of suitable performance criteria, monitoring and evaluating performance against standards, and proposing trajectories for corrective action based on predictive analysis. In addition to the AI applications we discussed in the "Internal Analysis" subsection, particularly compelling is the use of AI project management and internal communication. As more and more business activities are managed through increasingly integrated digital platforms, AI will become a salient tool for supporting strategists to evaluate strategy implementation and performance.

The Nexus of Strategizing and AI: Issues for Theory and Future Research

Future research imperatives

As mentioned earlier, AI may offer many attractive functions for strategists in conducting and orchestrating strategic processes. Strategy scholars need to continue to explore how such technologies may aid in strategy analysis, formulation, and implementation. At the same time, there is a particular need for scholars to take a prudent approach to AI and attempt to identify boundaries as well as challenges in implementing such systems in organizations. At the time of this writing, there is much enthusiasm expressed by scientists, consultants, technology companies, and managers about the potential of AI, but in our view much of AI's potential and advantages are overstated and lack solid grounding in an understanding of the technology itself. In the next subsection we address selected challenges for AI practice and research, but we first offer several imperatives that we believe can guide research in the nexus between strategizing and AI. We also identify elements of a research agenda that may help strategy scholars launch theoretical work and empirical inquiries.

First, it is key for scholars and strategists alike to understand that there is no magic bullet, single solution, or best practice for AI applications in strategy processes. The introduction of AI to organizational processes needs to be an iterative process that is based on trial-and-error learning. Like the functioning of ML algorithms, managers should be open-minded when exploring various technologies, learn from their own and others' experiences, and continuously improve their processes.

How strategists approach AI and how AI technology adoption unfolds in organizations offer many research opportunities. For example, in line with earlier research in technology adoption (King and He, 2006), scholars may ask which factors affect successful or failed implementation of AI in strategy processes. Critical in this respect are contextual factors (e.g., the need for accuracy and data) that relate to strategists' acceptance of AI, their perceptions of AI usefulness, and their behavioral intentions to utilize the technology.

Another important factor in the adoption of AI relates to strategists' cognitive and affective trust in such systems. Such trust may be shaped by AI's reliability, transparency, immediacy, and other factors (Glikson and Woolley, 2020). As trust may be related to a host of individual factors, as well as technological factors, it will be useful to explore what algorithms are best suited for which specific tasks or problems in the strategy process.

As we have shown in this chapter, AI is currently used to support strategizing, but in a somewhat piecemeal fashion. AI may be used during competitor analysis or legal analysis, or it may be aimed at supporting acquisition target assessment or strategy controls. A question of interest to strategy scholars is whether there exist technological architectures that can integrate and enable specific AI applications throughout the various tasks that make up strategy processes. A key rationale for examining this question is how to make AI more effective in supporting the firm's overall strategizing. This would require a study of architectural solutions, for example, by the methods of design science, similar to studies of enterprise architectures for resource planning (see Haki *et al.*, 2020). For example, while an isolated prediction algorithm tuned to market demand for certain product categories may give valuable information to the strategists, an open question is what added insights adjacent algorithms linked to this prediction algorithm could offer. Algorithms predicting factor costs / raw materials pricing, when linked with those predicting demand, may provide essential competitive insights to the strategists in planning product positioning on platforms. Scholars may want to investigate how such architectures may generate competitively valuable information to the firm, and more generally, if and how an AI architecture could become a new potential source of competitive advantage.

Generally, how AI can become a source of competitive advantage remains a critically important but ambiguous question. We expect that the answer to this question will depend on two factors: where and how AI is put to use, as well as the nature of data and the evolution of algorithms. Specifying the first factor would demand a step-by-step examination of what types of AI are utilized in strategy processes, where and how they are used, and with what intensity. In conjunction with these factors, researchers may aim to answer the following query: to what extent does AI augment and replace strategists? The overall motivation for analyzing AI in strategy processes is that such processes—if conducted efficiently and effectively, and they are based on the valuable and unique identification of a firm's strengths and weaknesses as well as novel opportunities and threats in the environment—can be a critical source of competitive advantage (Barney, 1991).

Specifying the second factor (the nature of data and the evolution of algorithms) would demand a much more detailed level of scrutiny of the chosen algorithms, available training data, and accuracy in predictions. The aim of this work would be to establish what are common and popular algorithms in use, and what types of data become input to machine learning. The combination of unique and rapidly updated data with efficient algorithms deployed in strategy processes may offer the firm substantial rents compared with those that use inferior algorithms and more constrained, dated, or flawed data—and that fail to continuously utilize AI in the strategy process (e.g., to investigate fundamental strategic assumptions). However, unless scholars successfully focus on this second factor connecting AI to competitive advantage, AI-oriented strategy research may suffer the same fate as much of the study of firm performance and information technology (e.g., Powell and Dent-Micallef, 1997), which consistently demonstrated weak correlations. It was not until the literature shifted its focus from IT investment to IT strategy or capabilities to build and utilize IT that relative performance effects of IT development and deployment could be discerned (Mithas and Rust, 2016).

As we discussed previously, modern AI drawing on big data, deep learning, or ML tools demands high levels of investments for a continued period of time (Shrestha *et al.*, 2021). Thus, it could be beneficial for adopting firms to forge partnerships on AI development and deployment. A large number of companies including Google, Intel, PwC, McKinsey, IBM, Samsung, Sony, and Amazon, have joined forces to form "partnership in AI" with the sole purpose of shaping best practices, research, and public dialogue about AI's benefits for business and society. Strategy scholars could investigate the drivers, processes, and outcomes of these partnerships and how they shape the adoption of AI in strategy processes.

Moreover, companies thinking of integrating AI applications in their strategy process are required to build an AI team composed of programmers and data scientists. Their knowledge of algorithms and their functioning is to be complemented with domain expertise, which requires the design of team structures that best benefit such complementarities. Scholars of strategy, organization theory, and organizational behavior can attempt to examine such team structures, antecedents for AI team performance, and team processes.

Finally, the rapid emergence of AI in the strategy process may have significant consequences for human creativity and ingenuity inextricably linked to successful process outcomes, and the politics surrounding corporate strategy. It is as of yet difficult to understand such consequences, which call for research from a broad set of perspectives rooted in organization behavior, organization theory, information systems, and strategic management. For example, with the increasing use of AI in strategic analysis, strategists may feel less inclined to introduce creative elements, such as novel and nontraditional data sources or radically different interpretations in strategic analysis. Moreover, those who control the deployment of algorithms and interpret analytical outcomes may also gain unprecedented power in the novel approach to strategizing. It will be critically important for scholars to investigate such power dynamics.

Finally, future research should explore the risks associated with reliance on AI in new venture activities, including the implications for the venture's ability to learn and develop critical capabilities. This is key, given the limited transparency that is currently inherent to many ML systems (Castelvecchi, 2016).

Besides these research questions, ML algorithms also generate useful avenues to investigate how algorithm-supported methods can be developed to conduct strategy research (He *et al.*, 2020; Shrestha, 2019).

Challenges and Risks for Strategizing

The application of AI for strategy analysis could lead to various social and organizational challenges. First, the application of AI requires the collection of vast amounts of personal and interactional data (e.g., on political sentiments or consumer behavior), which often interferes with individual privacy and data security. Firms should be highly cautious and aware of potential risks when using such data for strategic analysis. In particular, when using customer, employee, or client data for strategic analysis, firms must ensure that regulations or their code of conduct on privacy are not being violated unknowingly.

In recent years, the media have drawn the public's attention to various such high-profile privacy violations. Triggered by such cases, policymakers, investors, and the public are sensitized to the (mis)use of private information. As a consequence, various privacy regulations such as the General Data Protection Regulation (GDPR)—the European Union's regulation on data protection and privacy—will continue to be put in place, accompanying new standards relating to an individual's right to their own information. In addition to fulfilling ethical responsibilities to stakeholders regarding their information, firms will want to avoid hefty fines and/or reputational harm stemming from violations.

Second, with modern ML algorithms, information in the form of digital bits can be searched and replicated from terabytes of data at almost zero cost. With the reduced search, tracking, and verification costs in information acquisition, organizations of diverse size and scope have relatively similar access to information, reducing information asymmetry (Goldfarb and Tucker, 2019). As information searching forms an important constituent of strategy analysis, such lowered costs could have potentially mixed effects. On the one hand, they make it easier to rapidly find rare and potentially valuable strategic decision alternatives, resulting in the addition of variety in the alternative set (Yang, 2013; Zhang *et al.*, 2018). On the other, search algorithms (such as recommender systems) represent popularity bias, resulting in lack of variety with respect to information acquisition (Fleder and Hosanagar, 2009).

Third, and critically important, ML algorithms have been shown to produce results that are systematically prejudiced with respect to gender and ethnicity, among other factors. There are valid concerns that use of algorithms amplifies and perpetuates social inequalities (Barocas and Selbst, 2016; Starr, 2014). Scholars have identified various types of biases produced by algorithms, and the inherent trade-off between algorithm performance and algorithmic fairness makes correcting bias issues quite difficult

(Shrestha and Yang, 2019; Hardt, Price, and Srebro, 2016; Kleinberg, Mullainathan, and Raghavan, 2017). For instance, ML algorithms are trained on historic data, which can reflect social inequalities or biases contained in past human decisions. Flawed data collection or sampling procedures (either intentional or unintentional from the designer's perspective) could also lead to biases. Research in ML has also associated biases with the selection of the objective function or the algorithm itself (Arduini *et al.*, 2020; Mehrabi *et al.*, 2019). Thus, strategists are required to stay up to date with research on fair AI. Scholars suggest that the use of more transparent and interpretable AI models could assist in exposing and mitigating bias in algorithmic outcomes (Dodge *et al.*, 2020). Combining domain expertise with AI by "human-in-the loop" decision-making has also been shown to reduce algorithmic bias (Holstein *et al.*, 2019). In order to avoid detrimental consequences, strategists are well advised to put into place governance structures to deal with any unintentional biases produced by AI algorithms.

Fourth, as ML algorithms learn from past data to predict the future, their efficacy is contingent on the stability of data generation. That means, ML aimed at population prediction works well with relatively stable phenomena, such as consumer preferences, borrowing patterns, and demographic characteristics. Thus, relying on algorithmic predictions under conditions of disruption, crisis, or turbulence is misguided. Under these conditions the learning accumulated by algorithms loses relevance. Yet, when integrated into strategic processes, such as automated analysis of market demand, it may be difficult to "decouple" the algorithm from other strategy work. Moreover, putting in place an algorithm that performs complex learning with the intent to inform strategists, demands continuous data replenishment. Data flows may easily be interrupted, as we have seen with the disruptions in telecom infrastructures and other grids (e.g., energy). In general, it is worthwhile to recall that an algorithm's ability to make powerful predictions is only as strong as the quality of the data fed to it and the extent to which it fits the processing task. The strategist will likely be much worse off if she draws on flawed predictions based on low-quality data than if she uses her own good judgment.

Fifth, algorithms often feed off each other's behavior. Output from one algorithm often impacts the learning of another. This interconnectedness may sometimes lead to erratic behavior, as we have seen in the case of high-frequency trading, where algorithms have put significant financial assets at risk. Thus, in a market or industry where competitors are increasingly utilizing algorithms, their deployment demands careful human scrutiny, governance, and the enforcement of behavioral rules (e.g., a limit to the volume of assets exposed in high-frequency trading). Consider, for instance, the case of algorithms used for pricing, which are often misspecified and ignore effects that are outside their own control (e.g., market and competitors' prices). Research has shown that when competing sellers use ML for real-time dynamic pricing, it leads to overestimation of costs and market collusion, resulting in inflated prices (Harrington, 2018).

Finally, the use of AI-based technologies for strategic analysis requires and facilitates maintaining information within organizations in a central information system, cloud, or digital platform that can then be easily processed and used to train the predictive models. Such collected digital information when strategically relevant demands protective measures (Liebeskind, 1996), which in the case of modern digital technologies can become very costly. Traditionally, strategists have often held privileged access to information and expertise. With these technologies, maintaining such privileged access becomes increasingly costly.

Conclusion

We showed that AI holds great promise for the work of strategists and the effective and efficient conduct of strategic processes. The next few years will likely see a rapid adoption of ML algorithms that fundamentally alter the way we strategize. This opens up many important research opportunities for strategy scholars, some of which we discussed here. As practice begins to struggle with smart technologies, managers will urgently need our research findings to guide them.

Note

1. See https://www.refinitiv.com/perspectives/ai-digitalization/using-ai-to-predict-opportunity-in-m-and-a/.

References

Agrawal S, Chatterjee K, Novotný P. 2018. Lexicographic ranking supermartingales: an efficient approach to termination of probabilistic programs. *Proceedings of the ACM on Programming Languages* 2(POPL): 1–32. https://doi.org/10.1145/3158122.

Arduini M, Noci L, Pirovano F, Zhang C, Shrestha YR, Paudel B. 2020. Adversarial learning for debiasing knowledge graph embeddings. In *MLG 2020: 16th International Workshop on Mining and Learning with Graphs*—A Workshop at the KDD Conference, August 24, 2020, San Diego, CA: 7.

Avramov D, Cheng S, Metzker L. 2019. Machine learning versus economic restrictions: evidence from stock return predictability. *SSRN Electronic Journal*. https://doi.org/10.2139/ssrn.3450322.

Bail CA. 2014. The cultural environment: measuring culture with big data. *Theory and Society* 43(3/4): 465–482. http://www.jstor.org/stable/43694728.

Barney J. 1991. Firm resources and sustained competitive advantage. *Journal of Management* 17(1): 99–120. https://doi.org/10.1177/014920639101700108.

Barocas S, Selbst AD. 2016. Big data's disparate impact. *SSRN Electronic Journal*. https://doi.org/10.2139/ssrn.2477899.

Baum JR, Wally S. 2003. Strategic decision speed and firm performance. *Strategic Management Journal* 24(11): 1107–1129. https://doi.org/10.1002/smj.343.

Biessmann F, Lehmann P, Kirsch D, Schelter S. 2016. Predicting political party affiliation from text. *PolText*, 14–19. https://ssc.io/pdf/poltext.pdf.

Brynjolfsson E, Mitchell T. 2017. What can machine learning do? Workforce implications. *Science* **358**(6370): 1530–1534. https://doi.org/10.1126/science.aap8062.

Castelvecchi D. 2016. Can we open the black box of AI? *Nature* **538**(7623): 20–23. https://doi.org/10.1038/538020a.

Chalmers D, MacKenzie NG, Carter S. 2020. Artificial intelligence and entrepreneurship: implications for venture creation in the Fourth Industrial Revolution. *Entrepreneurship Theory and Practice*. https://doi.org/10.1177/1042258720934581.

Chan JT, Zhong W. 2018. Reading China: predicting policy change with machine learning. *SSRN Electronic Journal*. https://doi.org/10.2139/ssrn.3275687.

Cheung CF, Wang WM, Lo V, Lee WB. 2004. An agent-oriented and knowledge-based system for strategic e-procurement. *Expert Systems* **21**(1): 11–21.

Cielen A, Peeters L, Vanhoof K. 2004. Bankruptcy prediction using a data envelopment analysis. *European Journal of Operational Research* **154**(2): 526–532. https://doi.org/https://doi.org/10.1016/S0377-2217(03)00186-3.

Cockburn I, Henderson R, Stern S. 2018. The impact of artificial intelligence on innovation. NBER Working Paper Series 24449. National Bureau of Economic Research, Cambridge, MA. https://doi.org/10.3386/w24449.

Coletto M, Lucchese C, Orlando S, Perego R. 2015. Electoral predictions with Twitter: a machine-learning approach. *CEUR Workshop Proceedings*. http://eprints.imtlucca.it/3489/1/paper_19.pdf [1 August 2020].

Davenport TH, Ronanki R. 2018. Artificial intelligence for the real world. *Harvard Business Review* **96**(1): 108–116. https://hbr.org/2018/01/artificial-intelligence-for-the-real-world [1 August 2020].

Dodge J, Gururangan S, Card D, Schwartz R, Smith NA. 2020. Show your work: improved reporting of experimental results. *EMNLP-IJCNLP 2019: 2019 Conference on Empirical Methods in Natural Language Processing and 9th International Joint Conference on Natural Language Processing, Proceedings of the Conference*, 2185–2194.

Doyle G, Srivastava SB, Goldberg A, Frank MC. 2017. Alignment at work: using language to distinguish the internalization and self-regulation components of cultural fit in organizations. *ACL 2017—55th Annual Meeting of the Association for Computational Linguistics, Proceedings of the Conference (Long Papers)* **1**: 603–612.

Ferràs-Hernández X, Tarrats-Pons E, Arimany-Serrat N. 2017. Disruption in the automotive industry: a Cambrian moment. *Business Horizons* **60**(6): 855–863. https://doi.org/10.1016/j.bushor.2017.07.011.

Fethi MD, Pasiouras F. 2010. Assessing bank efficiency and performance with operational research and artificial intelligence techniques: a survey. *European Journal of Operational Research* **204**(2): 189–198.

Fleder D, Hosanagar K. 2009. Blockbuster culture's next rise or fall: the impact of recommender systems on sales diversity. *Management Science* **55**(5): 697–712. http://www.jstor.org/stable/40539182.

Franz L, Shrestha YR, Paudel B. 2020. A deep learning pipeline for patient diagnosis prediction using electronic health records. In *BioKDD 2020: 19th International Workshop on Data Mining in Bioinformatics*, August 24, 2020, San Diego, CA.

Glikson E, Woolley AW. 2020. Human trust in artificial intelligence: review of empirical research. *Academy of Management Annals* **14**(2), 627–660. https://doi.org/10.5465/annals.2018.0057.

Goldfarb A, Tucker C. 2019. Digital economics. *Journal of Economic Literature* **57**(1): 3–43.

Gomez-Uribe CA, Hunt N. 2015. The Netflix recommender system: algorithms, business value, and innovation. *ACM Transactions on Management Information Systems* **6**(4): 1–19. https://doi.org/10.1145/2843948.

Haefliger S, Jäger P, von Krogh G. 2010. Under the radar: industry entry by user entrepreneurs. *Research Policy* **39**(9): 1198–1213. https://ideas.repec.org/a/eee/respol/v39y2010i9p1198-1213.html.

Haenlein M, Kaplan A. 2019. A brief history of artificial intelligence: on the past, present, and future of artificial intelligence. *California Management Review* **61**(4): 5–14. https://doi.org/10.1177/0008125619864925.

Haki K, Beese J, Aier S, Winter R. 2020. The evolution of information systems architecture: an agent-based simulation model. *Management Information Systems Quarterly* **44**(1). https://aisel.aisnet.org/misq/vol44/iss1/8.

Hamel G, Prahalad CK. 1994. *Competing for the Future.* Harvard Business School Press: Boston, MA. http://www.books24x7.com/marc.asp?bookid=2420.

Hamet P, Tremblay J. 2017. Artificial intelligence in medicine. *Metabolism: Clinical and Experimental* **69**: S36–S40. https://doi.org/10.1016/j.metabol.2017.01.011.

Hardt M, Price E, Srebro N. 2016. Equality of opportunity in supervised learning. *Advances in Neural Information Processing Systems*, 3323–3331. https://arxiv.org/abs/1610.02413v1.

Harrington JE. 2018. Developing competition law for collusion by autonomous artificial agents. *Journal of Competition Law and Economics* **14**(3): 331–363. https://doi.org/10.1093/joclec/nhy016.

He VF, Puranam P, Shrestha YR, von Krogh G. 2020 Resolving governance disputes in communities: a study of software license decisions. *Strategic Management Journal* **41** (10): 1837–1868.

Heinonen K. 2011. Consumer activity in social media: Managerial approaches to consumers' social media behavior. *Journal of Consumer Behaviour* **10**(6): 356–364. https://doi.org/10.1002/cb.376.

Hitt MA, Ireland RD, Hoskisson RE. 2015. *Strategic Management: Competitiveness and Globalization--Concepts and Cases.* Cengage Learning Asia Pte Ltd.: Boston, MA.

Hollebeek LD, Conduit J, Brodie RJ. 2016. Strategic drivers, anticipated and unanticipated outcomes of customer engagement. *Journal of Marketing Management* **32**(5–6): 393–398.

Holstein K, Wortman Vaughan J, Daumé H, Dudik M, Wallach H. 2019. Improving fairness in machine learning systems: what do industry practitioners need? *Proceedings of the 2019 CHI Conference on Human Factors in Computing Systems*, 1–16. https://doi.org/10.1145/3290605.3300830.

Homburg C, Bucerius M. 2006. Is speed of integration really a success factor of mergers and acquisitions? An analysis of the role of internal and external relatedness. *Strategic Management Journal* **27**(4): 347–367. https://doi.org/10.1002/smj.520,

Huang AC, Jiang T, Liu YX, Bai YC, Reed J, Qu B, Goossens A, Nützmann HW, Bai Y, Osbourn A. 2019. A specialized metabolic network selectively modulates Arabidopsis root microbiota. *Science* **364**(6440). https://doi.org/10.1126/science.aau6389.

Humphreys P, McIvor R, Huang G. 2002. An expert system for evaluating the make-or-buy decision. *Computers and Industrial Engineering* **42**(2): 567–585.

Ireland RD, Hitt MA, Sirmon DG. 2003. A model of strategic entrepreneurship: the construct and its dimensions. *Journal of Management* **29**(6): 963–989. https://doi.org/10.1016/s0149-2063_03_00086-2.

Jarrahi MH. 2018. Artificial intelligence and the future of work: human-AI symbiosis in organizational decision making. *Business Horizons* **61**(4): 577–586. https://doi.org/10.1016/j.bushor.2018.03.007.

Jarzabkowski P, Balogun J, Seidl D. 2007. Strategizing: the challenges of a practice perspective. *Human Relations* **60**(1): 5–27. https://doi.org/10.1177/0018726707075703.

Jean N, Burke M, Xie M, Davis WM, Lobell DB, Ermon S. 2016. Combining satellite imagery and machine learning to predict poverty. *Science* **353**(6301): 790–794. https://doi.org/10.1126/science.aaf7894.

Keding C. 2020. Understanding the interplay of artificial intelligence and strategic management: four decades of research in review. *Management Review Quarterly* 71: 91–134. https://doi.org/10.1007/s11301-020-00181-x.

King WR, He J. 2006. A meta-analysis of the technology acceptance model. *Information and Management* 43(6): 740–755. https://doi.org/10.1016/j.im.2006.05.003.

Kleinberg J, Mullainathan S, Raghavan M. 2017. Inherent trade-offs in the fair determination of risk scores. *Leibniz International Proceedings in Informatics* (LIPIcs), 67. https://doi.org/10.4230/LIPIcs.ITCS.2017.43.

Kou G, Chao X, Peng Y, Alsaadi FE, Herrera-Viedma E. 2019. Machine learning methods for systemic risk analysis in financial sectors. *Technological and Economic Development of Economy* 25(5): 716–742. https://doi.org/10.3846/tede.2019.8740.

Kshirsagar V, Wieczorek J, Ramanathan S, Wells R. 2017. Household poverty classification in data-scarce environments: a machine learning approach. *ArXiv: Machine Learning.* https://arxiv.org/abs/1711.06813.

Kucukkeles B, Ben-Menahem SM, von Krogh G. 2019. Small numbers, big concerns: practices and organizational arrangements in rare disease drug repurposing. *Academy of Management Discoveries* 5(4): 415–437. https://doi.org/10.5465/amd.2018.0183.

Lawrence T. 1991. Impacts of artificial intelligence on organizational decision making. *Journal of Behavioral Decision Making* 4(3): 195–214. https://doi.org/10.1002/bdm.3960040306.

Lee C, Kwon O, Kim M, Kwon D. 2018. Early identification of emerging technologies: a machine learning approach using multiple patent indicators. *Technological Forecasting and Social Change* 127: 291–303. https://doi.org/10.1016/j.techfore.2017.10.002.

Liebeskind JP. 1996. Knowledge, strategy, and the theory of the firm. *Strategic Management Journal* 17(S2): 93–107.

March JG, Simon HA. 1958. *Organizations.* Wiley: New York, NY.

McCarthy J. 1981. Epistemological problems of artificial intelligence. In *Readings in Artificial Intelligence*, Webber BL, Nilsson NJ (eds). Elsevier: Burlington, MA; 459–465. https://doi.org/10.1016/b978-0-934613-03-3.50035-0.

McCorduck P. 2004. *Machines Who Think: A Personal Inquiry into the History and Prospects of Artificial Intelligence.* AK Peters / CRC Press: Natick, MA.

Mehrabi N, Morstatter F, Saxena N, Lerman K, Galstyan A. 2019. A survey on bias and fairness in machine learning. ArXiv, https://arxiv.org/pdf/1908.09635.pdf abs/1908.0.

Menon A, Choi J, Tabakovic H. 2018. What you say your strategy is and why it matters: natural language processing of unstructured text. *Academy of Management Proceedings* 2018(1). https://doi.org/10.5465/ambpp.2018.18319abstract.

Mithas S, Rust R. 2016. How information technology strategy and investments influence firm performance: conjecture and empirical evidence. *Management Information Systems Quarterly* 40(1). https://aisel.aisnet.org/misq/vol40/iss1/12.

Nag R, Hambrick DC, Chen MJ. 2007. What is strategic management, really? Inductive derivation of a consensus definition of the field. *Strategic Management Journal* 28(9): 935–955. https://doi.org/10.1002/smj.615.

Nissen ME, Sengupta K. 2006. Incorporating software agents into supply chains: experimental investigation with a procurement task. *MIS Quarterly: Management Information Systems* 30(1): 145–166. https://doi.org/10.2307/25148721.

Pant G, Sheng ORL. 2015. Web footprints of firms: using online isomorphism for competitor identification. *Information Systems Research* 26(1): 188–209. https://doi.org/10.1287/isre.2014.0563.

Powell TC, Dent-Micallef A. 1997. Information technology as competitive advantage: the role of human, business, and technology resources. *Strategic Management Journal* 18(5): 375–405. https://doi.org/10.1002/(SICI)1097-0266(199705)18:5<375::AID-SMJ876>3.0.CO;2-7.

Ranaei S, Karvonen M, Suominen, A, Kässi, T. 2016. Patent-based technology forecasting: case of electric and hydrogen vehicle. *International Journal of Energy Technology and Policy* 12(1): 20–40. https://doi.org/10.1504/IJETP.2016.074490.

Randall C, Dent EB. 2019. Reconciling the historical divide between strategy process and strategy content. *Journal of Management History* 25(3): 401–427. https://doi.org/10.1108/JMH-11-2018-0062.

Reeves M, Levin S, Ueda D. 2016. The biology of corporate survival. BCG Henderson Institute. https://hbr.org/2016/01/the-biology-of-corporate-survival.

Robinson CV, Ahmad F, Simmons JEL. 2021. Consolidation and fragmentation in environmental scanning: a review and research agenda. *Long Range Planning*, forthcoming. https://doi.org/10.1016/j.lrp.2020.101997.

Shrestha YR. 2019. Bridging data science and organization science: leveraging algorithmic induction to research online communities. Doctoral dissertation, ETH Zurich. https://doi.org/10.3929/ethz-b-000332700.

Shrestha YR, Ben-Menahem SM, von Krogh G. 2019. Organizational decision-making structures in the age of artificial intelligence. *California Management Review* 61(4): 66–83. https://doi.org/10.1177/0008125619862257.

Shrestha YR, He VF, Puranam P, von Krogh G. Forthcoming. Algorithmic induction through machine learning: opportunities for management and organization research. *Organization Science*.

Shrestha YR, Krishna V, von Krogh, G. 2021 Augmenting organizational decision-making with deep learning algorithms: principles, promises, and challenges. *Journal of Business Research* 123: 588–603.

Shrestha YR, Yang Y. 2019. Fairness in algorithmic decision-making: applications in multi-winner voting, machine learning, and recommender systems *Algorithms* 12 (9): 199–227.

Simon HA. 1947. *Administrative Behavior: A Study of Decision-Making Processes in Administrative Organization*. Macmillan: New York, NY.

Starr P. 2014. Is the past in our future? *Contemporary Sociology: A Journal of Reviews* 43(6): 795–800. https://doi.org/10.1177/0094306114553214b.

Strohmeier S, Piazza F. 2013. Domain driven data mining in human resource management: a review of current research. *Expert Systems with Applications* 40(7): 2410–2420. https://doi.org/10.1016/j.eswa.2012.10.059.

Suominen A, Toivanen H, Seppänen M. 2017. Firms' knowledge profiles: mapping patent data with unsupervised learning. *Technological Forecasting and Social Change* 115: 131–142. https://doi.org/10.1016/j.techfore.2016.09.028.

Treleaven P, Batrinca B. 2017. Algorithmic regulation: automating financial compliance monitoring and regulation using AI and blockchain. *Journal of Financial Transformation* 45: 14–21. https://econpapers.repec.org/RePEc:ris:jofitr:1586.

von Krogh G. 2018. Artificial intelligence in organizations: new opportunities for phenomenon-based theorizing. *Academy of Management Discoveries* 4(4): 404–409. https://doi.org/10.5465/amd.2018.0084.

von Krogh G, Roos J. 1995. *Organizational Epistemology*. St. Martin's Press: New York, NY.

Whittington, R. 2014. Information systems strategy and strategy-as-practice: a joint agenda. *Journal of Strategic Information Systems* 23(1): 87–91. https://doi.org/10.1016/j.jsis.2014.01.003.

Wu C-F, Huang SC, Chang T, Chiou C-C, Hsueh H-P. 2020. The nexus of financial development and economic growth across major Asian economies: evidence from bootstrap ARDL testing and machine learning approach. *Journal of Computational and Applied Mathematics* 372: 112660. https://doi.org/https://doi.org/10.1016/j.cam.2019.112660.

Yang H. 2013. Targeted search and the long tail effect. *RAND Journal of Economics* 44(4): 733–756. https://doi.org/10.1111/1756-2171.12036.

Yoo S, Digman LA. 1987. Decision support system: a new tool for strategic management. *Long Range Planning* 20(2): 114–124.

Yousfi-Monod M, Farzindar A, Lapalme G. 2010. Supervised machine learning for summarizing legal documents. Canadian AI 2010. In *Lecture Notes in Artificial Intelligence*, vol. 6085, Farzindar A, Keselj V (eds). Springer-Verlag: Berlin, Germany; 51–62. https://doi.org/10.1007/978-3-642-13059-5_8.

Zafarani R, Abbasi MA, Liu H. 2014. *Social Media Mining: An Introduction*. Cambridge University Press, Cambridge, U.K. https://doi.org/10.1017/CBO9781139088510.

Zhang S, Ke X, Frank Wang XH, Liu J. 2018. Empowering leadership and employee creativity: a dual-mechanism perspective. *Journal of Occupational and Organizational Psychology* 91(4): 896–917. https://doi.org/10.1111/joop.12219.

11.2
SUSTAINABILITY STRATEGY

Michael L. Barnett, Irene Henriques, and Bryan W. Husted

> *I want you to act as if the house is on fire, because it is.*
> —Greta Thunberg, World Economic Forum, Davos, January 24, 2019

Mainstream strategic management has been formulated and implemented with little concern for firms' influence on the sustainability of the environments in which they are embedded. This must change. The resource-based view of the firm becomes moot if essential resources are unavailable to firms. Strategizing how to minimize transaction costs proves exceedingly complex if society collapses. And no one will be around to strategically analyze general and industry environments if the natural environment is destroyed. Yet current resource usage is unsustainable, society is heavily stressed, and the natural environment is faltering. It is time to acknowledge that the house is on fire and that—to sustain themselves, and to help sustain all of us—firms must develop strategies to sustain their environments.

You've heard this before. The call to make sustainability central to strategy is not new. For example, a quarter-century ago, Shrivastava (1995: 957) noted that "current organizational concepts were developed when there were no severe ecological impacts of organizations" and argued that we need to rethink "the basic concepts of organizations, objectives, strategies, structures, performance and environments in order to accommodate the needs of ecological sustainability.... The question of central concern then becomes—what makes organizations ecologically sustainable, not simply what makes them grow or more profitable?"

The chapter-opening quote suggests that despite this and many other urgent calls, the need for firms to make a strategic shift to sustainability remains and is getting more urgent. How far have we come? What will push the field ahead? In this chapter, we define sustainability strategy, provide an overview of the literature, and identify the contributions and shortcomings of research to date. We then offer ideas on how strategy scholars can engage in meaningful research to advance sustainability strategy and thereby help to extinguish our house fire.

What Is Sustainability Strategy?

We combine a dictionary definition of strategy—"a detailed plan for achieving success" (Cambridge English Dictionary, 2020)—with the three dimensions of sustainable development put forth by the World Commission on Economic Development (WCED, 1987) and reiterated by leading sustainability practitioners (e.g., Elkington, 1998) and strategy scholars (e.g., Bansal, 2005)—environmental integrity, social equity, and economic prosperity—to define *sustainability strategy* as a firm's detailed plan for achieving environmental integrity, social equity, and economic prosperity.

Though we define sustainability strategy at the firm level, sustainability is a characteristic of a system, not of any individual firm within it (Ostrom, 2009). Firms are embedded in environmental, social, and economic environments and can develop strategies to have positive impacts on each, but firms cannot independently and directly ensure the sustainability of the broader social-ecological system. Nevertheless, firms have the responsibility and, increasingly, the strategic imperative to manage their interdependence with and influence on the environments in which they are embedded in ways that advance system sustainability.

Further complicating sustainability strategy, though they are often studied in separate disciplinary silos, environmental, social, and economic environments are intertwined. Environmental integrity, social equity, and economic prosperity each "represents a necessary, but not sufficient condition" (Bansal, 2005: 198) for bringing about sustainability of the broader social-ecological system—which constitutes the house that we collectively live in that is now on fire. A firm may have a detailed plan for ensuring "that human activities do not erode the earth's land, air, and water resources," or for ensuring "that all members of society have equal access to resources and opportunities," or for ensuring "the creation and distribution of goods and services that will help raise the standard of living around the world" (Bansal, 2005: 198), but the firm will not achieve its respective aims of environmental integrity, social equity, or economic prosperity without addressing the interdependence of these plans. Thus, our definition of sustainability strategy encompasses a firm's plans for achieving all three, not any subset thereof.

It is also important to note that sustainability strategy is *not* a firm's plan to sustain competitive advantage. Sustainable competitive advantage is a common term in the strategy literature and, like sustainability strategy, it is concerned with maintaining performance over time. However, sustainable competitive advantage is concerned with maintaining the firm's competitive advantage over rivals, while sustainability strategy looks beyond the firm, seeking to sustain the environments in which firms are embedded. Sustainability strategy can be a source of sustainable competitive advantage (Barnett, Darnall, and Husted, 2015). However, a firm's efforts to sustain its competitive advantage may also be to the detriment of the sustainability of the broader system—which is no small part of what has set our shared house ablaze.

We take the liberty of crafting a definition of sustainability strategy because the literature has not provided one. Through a search of the Web of Science, we found 83 articles that use the specific term. Some used sustainability strategy in ways consistent with our definition (e.g., Hengst *et al.*, 2020; Bansal, 2005; Tsai and Liao, 2017), but others focused on issues more akin to achieving sustainable competitive advantage (e.g., Lloret, 2016), not system sustainability. None of the articles directly defined sustainability strategy.

Though the exact terminology has limited presence in the literature, the concepts underpinning sustainability strategy are well represented. However, these many studies rarely address the critical aspect of system sustainability (cf. Whiteman, Walker, and Perego, 2013). We searched the Science Citation Index (SCI) and Social Science Citation Index (SSCI) from the Web of Science Core Collection from 1990 to 2019 for articles containing the keywords "sustainability strategy," "sustainability management," "environmental strategy," or "environmental management." The search returned 2,145 articles. We used bibliographic mapping software to make sense of this vast expanse of studies (Linnenluecke, Marrone, and Singh, 2019).

Our search revealed five clusters of related articles, which we note in order of cluster size, indicating relative importance in the literature. The largest cluster, which we label *Environmental Performance*, focuses on environmental pollution, emissions, degradation, and costs (e.g., King and Lenox, 2002; Li and Zhou, 2017). Impacts beyond the firm's boundaries are not addressed in the environmental performance cluster (Barnett, Henriques, and Husted, 2020). The second-largest cluster, *Environmental Capacity*, contains environmental initiatives, capabilities, and pressures (e.g., Darnall, Henriques, and Sadorsky, 2010; Sharma and Henriques, 2005). Here again the focus is on the environmental capacity of the firm, with little regard for the capacity of the planet (Rockström *et al.*, 2009). The third-largest cluster, *Greening Supply Chain*, contains sustainability practices and training, and reflects social responsibility across the firm and its supply chain (e.g., Delmas and Montiel, 2009; Sarkis, 2012). Promisingly, this cluster shows that some researchers are looking beyond the firm to upstream and downstream organizations when addressing environmental issues. The fourth-largest cluster, *Environmental Accounting*, contains terms such as reporting, life cycle analysis, and environmental accounting and reflects accountability and disclosure (e.g., Henri and Journeault, 2010; Reid and Toffel, 2009). Although accountability remains at the firm level, some recent research in this cluster looks long-term, analyzing the life cycle of products (Knauer and Moslang, 2018). Finally, the smallest cluster, *EMS*, contains studies that deal with environmental, health, and safety management systems (e.g., Christmann, 2000; Iatridis and Kesidou, 2018; Barnett and King, 2008). This literature assesses the performance—both financial and environmental—of environmental systems or practices. Unfortunately, the results are mixed and are often linked to the institutional environment in which the firm is located (Boiral, Guillaumie *et al.*, 2018).

We further examined the most highly cited of these articles to obtain more detailed insights about how the field is evolving. The Web of Science Core Collection employs a citation-based evaluation tool, InCites, to determine which papers are most influential in each field. Highly cited papers are the top 1 percent in each of the 22 Essential Science Indicators subject areas per year. As of October 2020, of the 2,145 articles we clustered, 58 received enough citations to place in the top 1 percent and so be considered Web of Science Highly Cited Papers for the business, management, business finance, and economics fields and publication year. Table 1 lists and categorizes these articles. Growing themes are *Environmental Capacity* and *Greening the Supply Chain*. We also identify two emerging areas: *Environmental Innovation* (Adams *et al.*, 2016; Demirel and Kesidou, 2019) and *Sustainable Business Models* (Schaltegger, Lüdeke-Freund, and Hansen, 2016). Consistent with the popular strategic management subfield of business model innovation (Teece, 2010; Zott, Amit, and Massa, 2011), these emerging areas focus on developing innovations and innovative business models to address our sustainability challenges (Pedersen *et al.*, 2020).

Though much work clearly remains to be done, our review revealed some positive developments in this burgeoning literature. We found several substantive studies that looked beyond the firm and incorporated concern for the constraints of our shared planet. Terms such as ecosystem, land, water, and conservation appear on the perimeter of our bibliographic map, indicating that some scholars have begun to heed the calls to address the social and ecological limitations of business behavior. For example, Whiteman, Walker, and Perego (2013: 324) argue that effective strategic options require managers to consider "symbiotic solutions for resource issues" to effectively govern within our planetary boundaries (Rockström *et al.*, 2009). They highlight the need to understand "how firms are connected to cumulative, systemic environmental problems" (Whiteman *et al.*, 2013: 326). To understand the interaction between human and natural systems, Winn and Pogutz (2013: 219) look to ecology and ecological economics to begin "to sketch the myriad interconnections between ecosystems and human, and thus organizational, life." Both papers underscore the need for multidisciplinary perspectives, cross-sector partnerships, and data collection and measurement across levels. Pogutz and Winn (2016) speak to the need for collaboration across stakeholders in order to derive new conceptions of multidisciplinary, multitier, sustainability-oriented knowledge. An exciting research area is emerging that examines cross-sector collaboration and partnership as a vehicle for sustainability transformations by co-creating the knowledge and momentum needed to address environmental problems (Pedersen *et al.*, 2020).

What Should Sustainability Strategy Be?

Overall, our review found that much of the current literature related to sustainability strategy views it as a plan to sustain and increase firm performance, subject to constraints imposed by the natural environment. Though many recent studies now model the natural environment as a constrained resource rather than as an open sink, developing strategies to buffer firms from the risks associated with ecological

Table 1 Highly cited sustainability strategy articles by theme

Environmental performance	Environmental capacity	Greening the supply chain	Environmental accounting	Environmental management systems	Environmental innovation	Sustainable business models
—Berrone et al. (2010)	—Baumgartner (2014)	—Azevedo et al. (2011)	—Clarkson et al. (2011)	—Albertini (2013)	—Adams et al. (2016)	—Dyllick and Muff (2016)
—Cadez et al. (2019)	—Cennamo et al. (2012)	—Carter and Easton (2011)	—Lyon and Maxwell (2011)	—Babiak et al. (2011)	—Albort-Morant et al. (2016)	—Schaltegger et al. (2016)
—Elmagrhi et al. (2019)	—Darnall et al. (2010)	—Dekker et al. (2012)		—Boiral et al. (2018)	—Dangelico (2016)	
—Filimonau and De Coteau (2019)	—Horisch et al. (2014)	—Devika et al. (2014)		—Chiou et al. (2011)	—Demirel and Kesidou (2019)	
—Fraj et al. (2015)	—Jansson et al. (2017)	—Gimenez et al. (2012)		—Iatridis and Kesidou (2018)	—Huang et al. (2017)	
—Montiel and Delgado-Ceballos (2014)	—Paille et al. (2014)	—Green et al. (2012)		—Kularatne et al. (2019)	—Melville (2010)	
	—Renwick et al. (2013)	—Lai et al. (2012)		—Molina-Azorin et al. (2015)	—Omerzel (2016)	
	—Schaltegger and Burritt (2018)	—Li et al. (2020)		—Testa et al. (2018)	—Triguero et al. (2013)	
	—Singh et al. (2019)	—Piercy and Rich (2015)			—Xie et al. (2019)	
	—Starik and Kanashiro (2013)	—Quarshie et al. (2016)				
	—Tang et al. (2018)	—Tate et al. (2010)				
	—Yang et al. (2019)	—Touboulic and Walker (2015)				
		—Varsei et al. (2014)				
		—Winter and Knemeyer (2013)				
		—Wolf (2014)				
		—Wu and Pagell (2011)				
		—Yang et al. (2013)				
		—Zhu et al. (2012)				
		—Zhu et al. (2013)				

constraints is not enough. Even developing plans to reduce or eliminate the harms that firms cause to the natural environment is inadequate to achieve sustainability (Barnett, Henriques, and Husted, 2018).

To put out our house fire, firms must treat the natural environment and all of their environment not as exogenous—to be strategically buffered from or even to do no harm to—but as key parts of an essential and vulnerable system that they have an active and critical role in sustaining. Because sustainability is achieved at the level of the system, while firms are only part of the subsystem of users (Ostrom, 2009; Young *et al.*, 2006), firms too easily can and often have ignored their role in resolving this larger problem. But rather than perfecting constrained optimization, firms must seek to understand and manage their interdependencies within the social-ecological system in which they are embedded (Williams *et al.*, 2017). For example, climate change, caused in large part by economic activity, has led to devastating forest fires in California, Australia, and elsewhere. Firms must do more than develop plans to safeguard and insure against the risks they now face from such events. They must understand how their activities contribute to these events and develop plans to counter the climate change that drives them.

Tragic consequences can arise when firms do not understand or manage their interdependence with the system. The coronavirus pandemic provides a too-salient example. Although the full COVID-19 causal chain has not yet been determined, the role of globalization in emerging infectious diseases has been traced (Frenk, Gómez-Dantés, and Knaul, 2011). The globalization of supply chains has made firms more efficient and brought work to millions of impoverished people, but it has also driven deforestation. Deforestation destroys ecosystems, which stresses animal species. As with humans, when animals are stressed, their immune systems are lowered, and they become susceptible to viruses. Once infected, animals can transmit viruses to humans. And, as we are experiencing, the result can be the deaths of millions globally, millions more returned to poverty, and unprecedented social upheaval.

Profitable firms and a roaring economy are not sustainable if they lead to global pandemics, irreversible climate change (Lenton *et al.*, 2019), or worse. Of course, not every shortsighted firm action leads to global devastation. Applying Rittel and Webber's (1973) distinction between tame and wicked problems, we define tame sustainability problems as those possessing scientific protocols that can guide solutions, are associated with low uncertainty as to the complex system components and outcomes, tend to be confined to one area, and do not change much across time. In contrast, wicked sustainability problems do not possess agreed-upon scientific protocols that can guide solutions, are associated with high uncertainty as to the complex system components and outcomes, tend not to be confined to one area, and change greatly across time (Barnett *et al.*, 2018; Batie, 2008). Examples of wicked problems include climate change and biodiversity loss.

Firms may pursue strategies in which they respond to either type of sustainability problem with a solution that addresses the firm level or the system level. For example, a firm could address the problem of income inequality, a wicked problem, by increasing its employee pay scale—a firm-level solution—or it could lobby state or federal governments to increase the minimum wage as a system-level solution (Grant, 2013). This creates a set of four sustainability strategies that populate the quadrants of Figure 1.

The *Calculative* strategy (Quadrant 1) is common in practice and represents the business case for sustainability, which holds that firms can profit from the implementation of sustainable business practices. For example, a firm may implement a "paperless office" practice that reduces its consumption of paper products, thereby helping to lessen the deforestation needed to supply paper while also saving the firm the costs of buying paper. Firms using this strategy have recognized that their activities cause harm and that they can create post-hoc solutions when the associated problems are tame. However, they act only when they calculate that it pays to do so. It is not feasible for firms to capture benefits that accrue to the system, so these calculations are confined to the firm level. As a result, many tame sustainability problems fail to produce a positive net present value or overcome a firm's hurdle rate for investment and so are not addressed by firms that follow this strategy.

In the *Cooperative* strategy (Quadrant 2), the problems remain tame but the firm develops solutions that account for the system and stakeholders affected, thereby increasing the ability of the solution to mitigate the damage or restore the system to its original state. These solutions may require the firm to organize agreements with other firms, nongovernmental organizations (NGOs), and governmental agencies.

Type of Problem	Level of Solution	
	Firm	**Social-Ecological System**
Tame	*Calculative* ⟶ Firm level calculation (e.g., local cost-benefit analysis) (King and Lenox, 2002) 1	*Cooperative* Compromise—government and firm (Reid and Toffel, 2009; Delmas and Pekovic, 2015) 2
Wicked	3 *Concerned* ⟶ Within-firm learning; create shared value to benefit firm but unable to find solutions (Reinhardt, 1998; Husted and Allen, 2007)	4 *Co-creative* Co-creation/collaboration/co-learning with multiple actors (Falkner, 2005; Dahlmann and Bullock, 2020)

Figure 1 Sustainability strategies

Examples include global, sectoral, and regional voluntary environmental programs to address environmental issues (Prakash and Potoski, 2012) such as the Responsible Care program developed by the chemical industry (Li, Khanna, and Vidovic, 2018), and certifiable standards such as ISO 14001 (Arimura, Darnall, and Katayama, 2011) and energy efficiency certifications (Delmas and Pekovic, 2015).

Firms attempt to address wicked problems at the firm level using the *Concerned* strategy (Quadrant 3). Though corporate concern for wicked problems represents an advance for sustainability over the *Calculative* strategy, decisions about which problems to pursue remain calculative, in favor of the firm. Firms seldom have both the desire and ability to assess the impacts of their social interventions on their targets. Thus the *Concerned* strategy often collapses into concern only for the firm, failing to achieve impact for the environment and society, as revealed in practice and academic research (Barnett *et al.*, 2020). Further research must go beyond analyzing firm-level impacts of corporate sustainability programs to determine how much difference such programs make in resolving social and environmental problems. Even with good intentions, the intractability of wicked problems suggests that firm-level solutions are symbolic at best or greenwashing at worst. Firms tend to deflect, deny, and blame others for wicked sustainability problems while lobbying government to not impose or to reduce regulation (Duchon and Drake, 2009).

Finally, in the *Co-Creative* strategy (Quadrant 4), firms spearhead system-level solutions to wicked sustainability problems. In this strategy, firms take seriously that problems involve many stakeholders with different values and priorities and have roots that are complex and tangled, dispersed among a host of actors and across borders, and so cannot be resolved by a single actor with any definitive solution. Thus, solutions here entail complex interactions among different sectors with a focus on "understanding connections, synergies and trade-offs" among different sustainability goals (Liu *et al.*, 2018: 466). Unfortunately, the sort of nexus thinking required to implement such a strategy has been found to be embryonic at best among firms (Dahlmann and Bullock, 2020). There is a significant need for more work on the creation of effective models of stakeholder collaboration toward system solutions. What role should government play in helping firms spearhead system-level solutions? Who should be at the table? What type of relationship is best for co-creating the knowledge necessary to bridge the social, environmental, and economic tensions that such collaborations inevitably entail?

Suggestions for Future Research

Like strategic management in general, sustainability strategy has been used to create advantages for firms while largely ignoring the consequences beyond the firm. How do we foster movement from firm-level to social-ecological sustainability strategies?

The literature has examined some of the pressures that might lead firms to move from a *Calculative* to a *Cooperative* strategy or from a *Concerned* to a *Co-Creative* strategy, but these pressures and processes need to be further studied. These include a firm's desire to reduce stakeholder pressure (Mitchell, Agle, and Wood, 1997), avoid more stringent environmental policies (Frondel, Horbach, and Rennings, 2008), increase its reputation insurance (Luo, Kaul, and Seo, 2018), reduce its liability of foreignness if a multinational (Crilly, Ni, and Jiang, 2016), or ingratiate itself with the community in which it does business (Dare, Schirmer, and Vanclay, 2011). How do these pressures lead firms to pursue sustainability strategy that has impacts beyond the firm?

To demonstrate the difference in sustainability strategy research when moving from a firm-level to a social-ecological solution, consider the example of the ozone depletion crisis. In 1985, British scientists discovered a shocking decline in atmospheric ozone concentrations high above Antarctica, known as the "ozone hole" and caused by ozone-destroying chemicals called chlorofluorocarbons (CFCs) (Farman, Gardiner, and Shanklin, 1985; Keating and Waugh, 2018). Public opinion was galvanized by the fact that depleted ozone led to increased health risks such as skin cancer, cataracts, and sunburn due to increased exposure to ultraviolet radiation. Then U.K. prime minister Margaret Thatcher and U.S. president Ronald Reagan both supported the international negotiations needed to ban CFCs. As a substitute technology was found and the CFC-using industries began moving away from CFCs, state-firm negotiations resulted in the 1987 Montreal Protocol.

Falkner (2005: 108) provides an excellent overview of the diverse corporate responses to the Montreal Protocol that, similar to the climate change debate, began with "the tried and tested strategy of denial and resistance, fighting the growing demands for regulation at the national and international level" (*Concerned*); as scientific evidence grew, DuPont declared support for the international controls on CFCs, where a fierce commercial battle to find a substitute for CFCs began (*Co-Creative*). Further research is needed to understand the social-ecological interactions that lead profit-maximizing firms to move from a position of denial to becoming an involved and leading partner in co-creating strategic solutions. Further research on how scientific evidence is interpreted, communicated, and incorporated into strategic decision-making is critical (e.g., Hunter, 2016).

Firms are naturally inclined toward firm-level solutions. The reluctance to move from the firm to the system is evidenced by the need for government to frequently enter the problem arena and use its powers to mandate collaborative actions through, for example, emissions regulation or prohibitions on overharvesting natural resources of various types (e.g., fish, forests, etc.). Although the tendency to focus on firm-level problems and solutions is understandable, it highlights the urgent need for business scholars to study what would motivate firms to voluntarily and effectively act with a system-level focus. Even the most common mechanisms developed to date, such as certifications and voluntary environmental programs, work best when there is governmental involvement to provide rewards for compliance (e.g., a temporary inspection moratorium) (Henriques, Husted, and Montiel, 2013). More research is needed on how firms can broaden their thinking beyond the firm level and embed themselves in social-ecological systems to co-create collaborative solutions to wicked problems.

The typology of sustainability strategies we developed helps to identify mismatches between problem types and firm strategies. Firms may be confronted by a wicked problem at the system level but treat it as a tame problem at the firm level, for example. These mismatches represent conflicts between what firms ought to be doing and what they are actually doing. Such tensions between the normative and the prescriptive provide fertile ground to analyze their causes and consequences. Why do firms choose to address wicked problems individually and eschew collaborative approaches with government and competitors? A myriad of micro-, macro-, and mezzo-level factors are likely at play and interacting in complex ways that have yet to be uncovered.

A nagging question raised by the typology is where science fits into sustainability strategies. Traditionally, firms' chief science officers have focused on the science relevant to the particular industrial processes that a firm may be innovating. However, science officers need to include within their routine duties the role of monitoring emerging issues and assessing how they might affect the ability of the firm to conduct business over time. Many sustainability problems were recognized by scientists much earlier than by private industry (Kowalok, 1993). Yet issues such as biodiversity management have been driven more by pressure for social legitimacy than by a keen awareness of the science. Deeper involvement of science in sustainability strategy could help to identify sustainability issues before they become sustainability crises (Boiral, Heras-Saizarbitoria, and Brotherton, 2018). We would all be better off if firms could see the smoke and act to extinguish fires while they are smoldering and before they fully engulf any environmental structures. Hence there is a need to explore the relationship of science to industry that goes beyond the specific chemistry or efficacy of firms' products to embrace a wider knowledge of the science of the social-ecological systems of which firms are a part.

Conclusion

Our house remains afire. Fighting this fire is not a solo undertaking. House fires cannot be extinguished by individuals attempting to suppress the flames in one or two rooms while the remainder remain engulfed. Likewise, a continued focus on the firm through calculative and concerned solutions will not be effective in addressing the greatest threats of our day. Our earnest hope is that this chapter will open the eyes of strategy researchers to the problems with current approaches to sustainability strategy and incite them to pursue work in this important area that can better address these critical issues. Let's act as if our house is on fire, because it is and has long been, and may not stand much longer if the fire is not soon brought under control.

References

Adams R, Jeanrenaud S, Bessant J, Denyer D, Overy, P. 2016. Sustainability-oriented innovation: a systematic review. *International Journal of Management Reviews* 18(2): 180–205.

Albertini E. 2013. Does environmental management improve financial performance? A meta-analytical review. *Organization & Environment* 26(4): 431–457.

Albort-Morant G, Leal-Millan A, Cepeda-Carrion G. 2016. The antecedents of green innovation performance: a model of learning and capabilities. *Journal of Business Research* 69(11): 4912–4917.

Arimura TH, Darnall N, Katayama H. 2011. Is ISO 14001 a gateway to more advanced voluntary action? The case of green supply chain management. *Journal of Environmental Economics and Management* 61(2): 170–182.

Azevedo SG, Carvalho H, Machado VC. 2011. The influence of green practices on supply chain performance: a case study approach. *Transportation Research Part E—Logistics and Transportation Review* 47(6): 850–871.

Babiak K, Trendafilova S. 2011. CSR and environmental responsibility: motives and pressures to adopt green management practices. *Corporate Social Responsibility and Environmental Management* 18(1): 11–24.

Bansal P. 2005. Evolving sustainably: a longitudinal study of corporate sustainable development. *Strategic Management Journal* 26(3): 197–218.

Barnett ML, Darnall N, Husted BW. 2015. Sustainability strategy in constrained economic times. *Long Range Planning* 48(2): 63–68.

Barnett ML, Henriques I, Husted BW. 2018. Governing the void between stakeholder management and sustainability. In *Sustainability, Stakeholder Governance, and Corporate Social Responsibility*, Dorobantu S, Aguilera RV, Luo J, Milliken FJ (eds). Emerald Group Publishing: Bingley, U.K.; 121–143.

Barnett ML, Henriques I, Husted BW. 2020. Beyond good intentions: Designing CSR initiatives for greater social impact. *Journal of Management* 46(6): 937–964.

Barnett M, King AA. 2008. Good fences make good neighbors: A longitudinal analysis of an industry self-regulatory institution. *Academy of Management Journal* 51(6): 1150–1170.

Batie SS. 2008. Wicked problems and applied economics. *American Journal of Agricultural Economics* 90(5): 1176–1191.

Baumgartner RJ. 2014. Managing corporate sustainability and CSR: a conceptual framework combining values, strategies, and instruments contributing to sustainable development. *Corporate Social Responsibility and Environmental Management* 21(5): 258–271.

Berrone P, Cruz C, Gomez-Mejia LR, Larraza-Kintana M. 2010. Socioemotional wealth and corporate responses to institutional pressures: do family-controlled firms pollute less? *Administrative Science Quarterly* 55(1): 82–113.

Boiral O, Guillaumie L, Heras-Saizarbitoria I, Tene CVT. 2018. Adoption and outcomes of ISO 14001: a systematic review. *International Journal of Management Reviews* 20(2): 411–432.

Boiral O, Heras-Saizarbitoria I, Brotherton MC. 2018. Corporate biodiversity management through certifiable standards. *Business Strategy and the Environment* 27(3): 389–402.

Cadez S, Czerny A, Letmathe P. 2019. Stakeholder pressures and corporate climate change mitigation strategies. *Business Strategy and the Environment* 28(1): 1–14.

Cambridge English Dictionary (CED). 2020. Strategy. https://dictionary.cambridge.org/us/dictionary/english/strategy [25 September 2020].

Carter CR, Easton PL. 2011. Sustainable supply chain management: evolution and future directions. *International Journal of Physical Distribution & Logistics Management* 41(1): 46–62.

Cennamo C, Berrone P, Cruz C, Gomez-Mejia LR. 2012. Socioemotional wealth and proactive stakeholder engagement: why family-controlled firms care more about their stakeholders. *Entrepreneurship Theory and Practice* **36**(6): 1153–1173.

Chiou TY, Chan HK, Lettice F, Chung SH. 2011. The influence of greening the suppliers and green innovation on environmental performance and competitive advantage in Taiwan. *Transportation Research Part E—Logistics and Transportation Review* **47**(6): 822–836.

Christmann P. 2000. Effects of "best practices" of environmental management on cost advantage: the role of complementary assets. *Academy of Management Journal* **43**(4): 663–680.

Clarkson PM, Li Y, Richardson GD, Vasvari FP. 2011. Does it really pay to be green? Determinants and consequences of proactive environmental strategies. *Journal of Accounting and Public Policy* **30**(2): 122–144.

Crilly D, Ni N, Jiang YW. 2016. Do-no-harm versus do-good social responsibility: attributional thinking and the liability of foreignness. *Strategic Management Journal* **37**(7): 1316–1329.

Dahlmann F, Bullock G. 2020. Nexus thinking in business: Analysing corporate responses to interconnected global sustainability challenges. *Environmental Science & Policy* **107**: 90–98.

Dangelico RM. 2016. Green product innovation: Where we are and where we are going. *Business Strategy and the Environment* **25**(8): 560–576.

Dare M, Schirmer J, Vanclay F. 2011. Does forest certification enhance community engagement in Australian plantation management? *Forest Policy and Economics* **13**(5): 328–337.

Darnall N, Henriques I, Sadorsky P. 2010. Adopting proactive environmental strategy: the influence of stakeholders and firm size. *Journal of Management Studies* **47**(6): 1072–1094.

Dekker R, Bloemhof J, Mallidis I. 2012. Operations research for green logistics—an overview of aspects, issues, contributions, and challenges. *European Journal of Operational Research* **219**(3): 671–679.

Delmas M, Montiel I. 2009. Greening the supply chain: when is customer pressure effective? *Journal of Economics & Management Strategy* **18**(1): 171–201.

Delmas MA, Pekovic S. 2015. Resource efficiency strategies and market conditions. *Long Range Planning* **48**(2): 80–94.

Demirel P, Kesidou E. 2019. Sustainability-oriented capabilities for eco-innovation: meeting the regulatory, technology, and market demands. *Business Strategy and the Environment* **28**(5): 847–857.

Devika K, Jafarian A, Nourbakhsh V. 2014. Designing a sustainable closed-loop supply chain network based on triple bottom line approach: a comparison of metaheuristics hybridization techniques. *European Journal of Operational Research* **235**(3): 594–615.

Duchon D, Drake B. 2009. Organizational narcissism and virtuous behavior. *Journal of Business Ethics* **85**(3): 301–308.

Dyllick T, Muff K. 2016. Clarifying the meaning of sustainable business: introducing a typology from business-as-usual to true business sustainability. *Organization & Environment* **29**(2): 156–174.

Elkington J. 1998. *Cannibals with Forks: The Triple Bottom Line of 21st-Century Business.* New Society: Stony Creek, CT.

Elmagrhi MH, Ntim CG, Elamer AA, Zhang QJ. 2019. A study of environmental policies and regulations, governance structures, and environmental performance: the role of female directors. *Business Strategy and the Environment* **28**(1): 206–220.

Falkner R. 2005. The business of ozone layer protection: corporate power in regime evolution. In *The Business of Global Environmental Governance*, Levy D, Newell PJ (eds). MIT Press: Cambridge, MA; 105–134.

Farman JC, Gardiner BG, Shanklin JD. 1985. Large losses of total ozone in Antarctica reveal seasonal ClOx/NOx interaction. *Nature* **315**(6016): 207–210.

Filimonau V, De Coteau DA. 2019. Food waste management in hospitality operations: a critical review. *Tourism Management* **71**: 234–245.

Fraj E, Matute J, Melero I. 2015. Environmental strategies and organizational competitiveness in the hotel industry: the role of learning and innovation as determinants of environmental success. *Tourism Management* 46: 30–42.

Frenk J, Gómez-Dantés O, Knaul FM. 2011. Globalization and infectious diseases. *Infectious Disease Clinics of North America* 25(3): 593–599.

Frondel M, Horbach J, Rennings K. 2008. What triggers environmental management and innovation? Empirical evidence for Germany. *Ecological Economics* 66(1): 153–160.

Gimenez C, Tachizawa EM. 2012. Extending sustainability to suppliers: a systematic literature review. *Supply Chain Management—An International Journal* 17(5): 531–543.

Grant, Tavia. 2013. How one company levels the pay slopes of executives and co-workers. *Globe and Mail.* 16 November. https://www.theglobeandmail.com/news/national/time-to-lead/how-one-company-levels-the-pay-slope-of-executives-and-workers/article15472738/.

Green KW, Zelbst PJ, Meacham J, Bhadauria VS. 2012. Green supply chain management practices: impact on performance. *Supply Chain Management—An International Journal* 17(3): 290–305.

Hengst I-A, Jarzabkowski P, Hoegl M, Muethel M. 2020. Toward a process theory of making sustainability strategies legitimate in action. *Academy of Management Journal* 63(1): 246–271.

Henri JF, Journeault M. 2010. Eco-control: the influence of management control systems on environmental and economic performance. *Accounting Organizations and Society* 35(1): 63–80.

Henriques I, Husted BW, Montiel I. 2013. Spillover effects of voluntary environmental programs on greenhouse gas emissions: lessons from Mexico. *Journal of Policy Analysis and Management* 32(2): 296–322.

Horisch J, Freeman RE, Schaltegger S. 2014. Applying stakeholder theory in sustainability management: links, similarities, dissimilarities, and a conceptual framework. *Organization & Environment* 27(4): 328–346.

Huang JW, Li YH. 2017. Green innovation and performance: the view of organizational capability and social reciprocity. *Journal of Business Ethics* 145(2): 309–324.

Hunter J. 2016. Final agreement reached to protect B.C.'s Great Bear Rainforest. *The Globe and Mail.* 1 February. https://www.theglobeandmail.com/news/british-columbia/final-agreement-reached-to-protect-bcs-great-bear-rainforest/article28475362/.

Iatridis K, Kesidou E. 2018. What drives substantive versus symbolic implementation of ISO 14001 in a time of economic crisis? Insights from Greek manufacturing companies. *Journal of Business Ethics* 148(4): 859–877.

Jansson J, Nilsson J, Modig F, Hed Vall G. 2017. Commitment to sustainability in small and medium-sized enterprises: the influence of strategic orientations and management values. *Business Strategy and the Environment* 26(1): 69–83.

Keating S, Waugh D. 2018. The ozone hole is both an environmental success story and an enduring global threat. *The Conversation*, July 29. https://theconversation.com/the-ozone-hole-is-both-an-environmental-success-story-and-an-enduring-global-threat-100524.

King A, Lenox M. 2002. Exploring the locus of profitable pollution reduction. *Management Science* 48(2): 289–299.

Knauer T, Moslang K. 2018. The adoption and benefits of life cycle costing. *Journal of Accounting and Organizational Change* 14(2): 188–215.

Kowalok ME. 1993. Common threads: research lessons from acid rain, ozone depletion, and global warming. *Environment: Science and Policy for Sustainable Development* 35(6): 12–38.

Kularatne T, Wilson C, Mansson J, Hoang V, Lee B. 2019. Do environmentally sustainable practices make hotels more efficient? A study of major hotels in Sri Lanka. *Tourism Management* 71: 213–225.

Lai KH, Wong CWV. 2012. Green logistics management and performance: some empirical evidence from Chinese manufacturing exporters. *Omega—International Journal of Management Science* 40(3): 267–282.

Lenton TM, Rockström J, Gaffney O, Rahmstorf S, Richardson K, Steffen W, Schellnhuber HJ. 2019. Climate tipping points—too risky to bet against. *Nature* 575 (7784): 592–595.

Li G, Li L, Choi TM, Sethi SP. 2020. Green supply chain management in Chinese firms: innovative measures and the moderating role of quick response technology. *Journal of Operations Management* 66(7–8): 958–988.

Li H, Khanna N, Vidovic M. 2018. The effects of third-party certification on voluntary self-regulation of accidents in the US chemical industry. *Journal of Regulatory Economics* 53(3): 327–356.

Li XY, Zhou YM. 2017. Offshoring pollution while offshoring production? *Strategic Management Journal* 38(11): 2310–2329.

Linnenluecke MK, Marrone M, Singh AK. 2019. Conducting systematic literature reviews and bibliometric analyses. *Australian Journal of Management*, in press.

Liu J, Hull V, Godfray HCJ, Tilman D, Gleick P, Hoff H, Pahl-Wostl C, *et al.* 2018. Nexus approaches to global sustainable development. *Nature Sustainability* 1(9): 466–476.

Lloret A. 2016. Modeling corporate sustainability strategy. *Journal of Business Research* 69(2): 418–425.

Luo J, Kaul A, Seo H. 2018. Winning us with trifles: adverse selection in the use of philanthropy as insurance. *Strategic Management Journal* 39(10): 2591–2617.

Lyon TP, Maxwell JW. 2011. Greenwash: corporate environmental disclosure under threat of audit. *Journal of Economics & Management Strategy* 20(1): 3–41.

Melville NP. 2010. Information systems innovation for environmental sustainability. *MIS Quarterly* 34(1): 1–21.

Mitchell RK, Agle BR, Wood DJ. 1997. Toward a theory of stakeholder identification and salience: defining the principle of who and what really counts. *Academy of Management Review* 22(4): 853–886.

Molina-Azorin JF, Tari JJ, Pereira-Moliner J, Lopez-Gamero MD, Pertusa-Ortega EM. 2015. The effects of quality and environmental management on competitive advantage: a mixed methods study in the hotel industry. *Tourism Management* 50: 41–54.

Montiel I, Delgado-Ceballos J. 2014. Defining and measuring corporate sustainability: are we there yet? *Organization & Environment* 27(2): 113–139.

Omerzel DG. 2016. A systematic review of research on innovation in hospitality and tourism. *International Journal of Contemporary Hospitality Management* 28(3): 516–558.

Ostrom E. 2009. A general framework for analyzing sustainability of social-ecological systems. *Science* 325(5939): 419–422.

Paille P, Chen Y, Boiral O, Jin JF. 2014. The impact of human resource management on environmental performance: an employee-level study. *Journal of Business Ethics* 121(3): 451–466.

Pedersen ER, Lüdeke-Freund F, Henriques I, Seitanidi MM. 2020. Toward collaborative cross-sector business models for sustainability. *Business & Society*, in press.

Piercy N, Rich N. 2015. The relationship between lean operations and sustainable operations. *International Journal of Operations & Production Management* 35(2): 282–315.

Pogutz S, Winn MI. 2016. Cultivating ecological knowledge for corporate sustainability: Barilla's innovative approach to sustainable farming. *Business Strategy and the Environment* 25(6): 435–448.

Prakash A, Potoski M. 2012. Voluntary environmental programs: a comparative perspective. *Journal of Policy Analysis and Management* 31(1): 123–138.

Quarshie AM, Salmi A, Leuschner R. 2016. Sustainability and corporate social responsibility in supply chains: the state of research in supply chain management and business ethics journals. *Journal of Purchasing and Supply Management* 22(2): 82–97.

Reid EM, Toffel MW. 2009. Responding to public and private politics: corporate disclosure of climate change strategies. *Strategic Management Journal* 30(11): 1157–1178.

Renwick DWS, Redman T, Maguire S. 2013. Green human resource management: a review and research agenda. *International Journal of Management Reviews* 15(1): 1–14.

Rittel HWJ, Webber MM. 1973. Dilemmas in a general theory of planning. *Policy Sciences* 4(2): 155–169.

Rockström J, Steffen W, Noone K, Persson, Å, Chapin FS III, Lambin EF, Lenton TM, et al. 2009. A safe operating space for humanity. *Nature* 461: 472–475.

Sarkis J. 2012. A boundaries and flows perspective of green supply chain management. *Supply Chain Management—An International Journal* 17(2): 202–216.

Schaltegger S, Burritt R. 2018. Business cases and corporate engagement with sustainability: differentiating ethical motivations. *Journal of Business Ethics* 147(2): 241–259.

Schaltegger S, Lüdeke-Freund F, Hansen EG. 2016. Business models for sustainability: A co-evolutionary analysis of sustainable entrepreneurship, innovation, and transformation. *Organization & Environment* 29(3): 264–289.

Sharma S, Henriques I. 2005. Stakeholder influences on sustainability practices in the Canadian forest products industry. *Strategic Management Journal* 26(2): 159–180.

Shrivastava P. 1995. The role of corporations in achieving ecological sustainability. *Academy of Management Review* 20(4): 936–960.

Singh SK, Chen J, Del Giudice M, El-Kassar AN. 2019. Environmental ethics, environmental performance, and competitive advantage: role of environmental training. *Technological Forecasting and Social Change* 146: 203–211.

Starik M, Kanashiro P. 2013. Toward a theory of sustainability management: uncovering and integrating the nearly obvious. *Organization & Environment* 26(1): 7–30.

Tang GY, Chen Y, Jiang Y, Paille P, Jia J. 2018. Green human resource management practices: scale development and validity. *Asia Pacific Journal of Human Resources* 56(1): 31–55.

Tate WL, Ellram LM, Kirchoff JF. 2010. Corporate social responsibility reports: a thematic analysis related to supply chain management. *Journal of Supply Chain Management* 46(1): 19–44.

Teece D. 2010. Business models, business strategy, and innovation. *Long Range Planning* 43(2): 172–194.

Testa F, Boiral O, Iraldo F. 2018. Internalization of environmental practices and institutional complexity: can stakeholders pressures encourage greenwashing? *Journal of Business Ethics* 147(2): 287–307.

Thunberg G. 2019. Forging a sustainable path towards a common future. World Economic Forum, Davos, January 24. https://www.weforum.org/agenda/2019/01/our-house-is-on-fire-16-year-old-greta-thunberg-speaks-truth-to-power/.

Touboulic A, Walker H. 2015. Theories in sustainable supply chain management: a structured literature review. *International Journal of Physical Distribution & Logistics Management* 45(1–2): 16–42.

Triguero A, Moreno-Mondejar L, Davia MA. 2013. Drivers of different types of eco-innovation in European SMEs. *Ecological Economics* 92: 25–33.

Tsai KH, Liao YC. 2017. Sustainability strategy and eco-innovation: A moderation model. *Business Strategy and the Environment* 26(4): 426–437.

Varsei M, Soosay C, Fahimnia B, Sarkis J. 2014. Framing sustainability performance of supply chains with multidimensional indicators. *Supply Chain Management—An International Journal* 19(3): 242–257.

WCED. 1987. *Our Common Future.* Oxford University Press: Oxford, U.K.

Whiteman G, Walker B, Perego P. 2013. Planetary boundaries: ecological foundations for corporate sustainability. *Journal of Management Studies* 50(2): 307–336.

Williams A, Kennedy S, Philipp F, Whiteman G. 2017. Systems thinking: a review of sustainability management research. *Journal of Cleaner Production* 148: 866–881.

Winn MI, Pogutz S. 2013. Business, ecosystems, and biodiversity. *Organization & Environment* 26(2): 203–229.

Winter M, Knemeyer AM. 2013. Exploring the integration of sustainability and supply chain management: current state and opportunities for future inquiry. *International Journal of Physical Distribution and Logistics Management* 43(1): 18–38.

Wolf J. 2014. The relationship between sustainable supply chain management, stakeholder pressure, and corporate sustainability performance. *Journal of Business Ethics* 119(3): 317–328.

Wu ZH, Pagell M. 2011. Balancing priorities: decision-making in sustainable supply chain management. *Journal of Operations Management* 29(6): 577–590.

Xie XM, Huo JG, Zou HL. 2019. Green process innovation, green product innovation, and corporate financial performance: a content analysis method. *Journal of Business Research* 101: 697–706.

Yang CS, Lu CS, Haider JJ, Marlow PB. 2013. The effect of green supply chain management on green performance and firm competitiveness in the context of container shipping in Taiwan. *Transportation Research Part E—Logistics and Transportation Review* 55: 55–73.

Yang DF, Wang AX, Zhou KZ, Jiang W. 2019. Environmental strategy, institutional force, and innovation capability: a managerial cognition perspective. *Journal of Business Ethics* 159(4): 1147–1161.

Young OR, Berkhout F, Gallopin CC, Janssen MA, Ostrom E, Van der Leeuw S. 2006. The globalization of socio-ecological systems: an agenda for scientific research. *Global Environmental Change* 16(3): 304–316.

Zhu QH, Sarkis J, Lai KH. 2012. Green supply chain management innovation diffusion and its relationship to organizational improvement: an ecological modernization perspective. *Journal of Engineering and Technology Management* 29(1): 168–185.

Zhu QH, Sarkis J, Lai KH. 2013. Institutional-based antecedents and performance outcomes of internal and external green supply chain management practices. *Journal of Purchasing and Supply Management* 19(2): 106–117.

Zott C, Amit RH, Massa L. 2011. The business model: recent developments and future research. *Journal of Management* 37(4): 1019–1042.

11.3

WHAT WOULD THE FIELD OF STRATEGIC MANAGEMENT LOOK LIKE IF IT TOOK THE STAKEHOLDER PERSPECTIVE SERIOUSLY?

Jay B. Barney and Alison Mackey

As Niels Bohr observed, "Prediction is hard, especially about the future" (Mencher, 1971: 37). Predicting how the field of strategic management will respond to recent calls to incorporate a stakeholder perspective is, indeed, difficult.[1] After all, the future of strategic management is not "out there" just waiting to be discovered but, instead, is being actively created by strategy scholars (Alvarez and Barney, 2007). About all that can be done is to examine how stakeholder thinking may impact some currently popular strategic management theories, while recognizing that the application of stakeholder logic in strategic management may generate new ideas and insights that cannot be fully anticipated.

Thus, this chapter has modest objectives: it concisely examines some of the implications of stakeholder logic for three currently popular strategic management theories—resource-based theory (RBT) (Barney, 1986, 1991), positioning theory (Porter, 1980), and the theory of the firm (Coase, 1931). No attempt is made to fully review the literatures associated with these theories—that is done elsewhere.[2] Nor does the chapter review the extensive literature on stakeholder theory (e.g., Freeman *et al.*, 2010; Harrison *et al.*, 2019) or attempt to address some of the limitations of this theory as it is currently constituted (e.g., stakeholder governance issues (Amis *et al.*, 2020).

Rather, the purpose of this chapter is to suggest how some of the central theories in the field of strategic management could be affected by stakeholder logic. Even in this limited effort, some of these effects are fundamental. For example, stakeholder logic implies that, in order for RBT's model of profit appropriation to be consistent with its model of profit generation, stakeholders in addition to shareholders must have residual claims on a firm's profits. Stakeholder considerations have the effect of changing positioning theory's traditional focus on threats to a focus on stakeholder-generated opportunities for profit generation. Finally, stakeholder logic brings into question the importance of a theory of the firm for strategic management theory.

After examining some of the implications of stakeholder thinking for these theories, implications for the study of specific strategic management topics are then discussed.

A Stakeholder Perspective and Three Strategic Management Theories

While there are a variety of other theories within the field of strategic management—besides RBT, positioning theory, and theories of the firm—these theories were chosen for three reasons. First, these theories are widely influential both in strategic management research and teaching. Second, they demonstrate some of the kinds of implications that stakeholder thinking might have on other strategic management theories. For example, incorporating a stakeholder perspective into the profit-generating process tends to expand how a theory links strategy and performance. Just as RBT, positioning, and theories of the firm are expanded from incorporating a stakeholder perspective, other theories such as agency theory, transaction cost economics, incomplete contracts, and so on are expanded as we discuss hereafter. Finally, these theories have been widely applied to the strategic management topics discussed at the end of this chapter.

Incorporating Stakeholder Thinking in Resource-Based Theory

Initially, RBT adopted—either implicitly (Barney, 1986) or explicitly (Denrell, Fang, and Winter, 2003)—the assumption of shareholder supremacy taken from finance—that is, that any profits generated by a firm would be appropriated by a firm's shareholders (Jensen, 2002). This was the case even though there was accumulating evidence—both in strategic management and finance—that stakeholders besides shareholders had residual claims on profits generated by a firm (e.g., Chacar and Hesterly, 2008; Lieberman and Chacar, 1997; Shleifer and Summers, 1988; Cen, Dasgupta, and Sen, 2015; and Johnson, Karpoff, and Yi, 2015).

Building on Asher, Mahoney, and Mahoney (2005) and Mahoney (2013), Barney (2018) showed that in order for RBT's model of profit appropriation to be logically consistent with its model of profit generation, stakeholders in addition to shareholders must have a residual claim on the profits that stakeholder resources help generate. The intuition behind this assertion is straightforward: in order for stakeholders to be willing to make profit-generating resources available to a firm, a firm must be willing to share some of the profits these resources help generate with the stakeholders that provide them (Lippman and Rumelt, 2003a, 2003b). If, instead, firms treat all their stakeholders as fixed claimants—that is, as stakeholders that have no claim on the profits generated by a firm—then firms will not be able to attract the kinds of resources needed to generate economic profits. It follows logically that the traditional assumption in RBT—that only shareholders have a residual claim on a firm's profits—is actually inconsistent with its model of profit generation. Thus, either RBT needs to abandon its well-established theory of profit generation or abandon its traditional shareholder supremacy assumption. The latter choice necessarily implies that RBT must incorporate a stakeholder perspective in its model of profit appropriation. Thus, the question for this chapter is: assuming Barney (2018) is correct, how does this conclusion change RBT as it currently exists in the field of strategic management?

Changes to the resource-based theory's model of profit generation

As noted, RBT's model of profit generation already adopts a stakeholder perspective. Consider the basic logic for how a firm can generate an economic profit as it builds its resource base (Barney, 1986). It is often the case that generating economic profits necessitates accessing resources from multiple stakeholders. Of course, the returns generated from these combined resources must exceed the expenses incurred to acquire access to these resources for the firm to generate profits (Brandenburger and Stuart, 1996). Co-specialized resources—that is, resources that are more productive in combination than in isolation—represent one way that this might occur (Milgrom and Roberts, 1992; Teece, 1986; Conner and Prahalad, 1991). Much of RBT already focuses on this scenario of how co-specialized resources generate economic profits (e.g., Barney, 1991; Rumelt, 1984; Adner and Helfat, 2003; Sirmon et al., 2011; Sirmon, Hitt, and Ireland, 2007). As such, the unit of profit generation, from a resource-based perspective, may in fact be the co-specialized resources and capabilities created in conjunction by a firm and its stakeholders (Amit and Schoemaker, 1993; Helfat and Peteraf, 2003) and not simply the resources (or bundles of resources) that exist within a firm (Barney, 1986) as is often concluded in resource-based work.

Research on economic value created through ecosystems (Adner, Oxley, and Silverman, 2013), network organizations (Hansen, 2002), multisided markets (Hagiu and Wright, 2015), value nets (Brandenburger and Nalebuff, 1996), open innovation (Chesbrough, 2003), and relations among firms (Dyer and Singh, 1998) suggests just this type of profit generation.

Changes to the resource-based theory's model of profit appropriation

While this stakeholder model of profit generation in RBT points the way for how firms can generate economic profits from collecting a set of co-specialized resources, an important question arises as to how profits will be allocated across these stakeholders who originally provided access to the resources.

Incomplete contract theory (Hart, 1988; Grossman and Hart, 1986; Hart and Moore, 1990) suggests that the stakeholder providing access to the resources creating the most value in the co-specialized resource should be allowed to appropriate the associated profits. Certainly, this stakeholder could appropriate all of the profits to him- or herself. The risk associated with this approach, of course, is that the other stakeholders involved would be unlikely to make (and sustain) the type of cooperative exchanges needed to produce the economic profits. Alternatively, the stakeholder could allocate at least some of the profits to other stakeholders who have provided access to resources combined in the co-specialized bundle. Allocations based on marginal contributions would be a reasonable approach (Hart, 1988; Grossman and Hart, 1986; Hart and Moore, 1990).

Unfortunately, complementarities across resources in a co-specialized bundle can make it difficult (if not impossible) to estimate these proportions for allocations (Conner and Prahalad, 1991; Alchian and Demsetz, 1972; Milgrom and Roberts, 1992). Further, stakeholders providing access to resources that are part of a co-specialized bundle may not fully understand the opportunity costs of doing so (Alchian, 1950; Lippman and Rumelt, 2003a, 2003b). How this allocation is likely to unfold in practice will be a function of factors such as expectations around the importance of a given resource, the economic value of the resource outside the bundle, and negotiation skills of those controlling access to these resources (e.g., Grossman and Hart, 1986; Molloy and Barney, 2015). In short, how the combination of resources evolves into co-specialized bundles directly impacts the bargaining power of stakeholders for appropriating the profits associated with the resources they control.

Highly valuable employees are one example of a class of stakeholders that have been shown (empirically) to appropriate a portion of the profits their human capital helped create (e.g., Molloy and Barney, 2015). Consistent with the model of profit appropriation from a stakeholder RBT, individuals with valuable *general* human capital are able to appropriate more of the profits their human capital generates (controlling for negotiation skills) compared to individuals with high levels of firm-specific human capital (Chacar and Hesterly, 2008; Groysberg, 2010). It should be expected that all of the stakeholders contributing to the bundle of co-specialized resources will expect to appropriate at least some of the profits associated with the resources that they provided (Castanias and Helfat, 1991). Their expectations could result in a situation in which a firm does not appropriate much (or any) of the profits associated with a bundle of co-specialized resources as the network of stakeholders providing access to these resources appropriates much (or all) of the profits generated. Thus, it may appear that the resources in question failed to generate profits, when in reality, the firm failed to appropriate those profits (Coff, 1999).

Incorporating Stakeholder Thinking in Positioning Theory

Positioning theory (Porter, 1979, 1980, 1985) builds on the structure-conduct-performance (SCP) paradigm (Bain, 1950) to explain how firms can generate economic profits by exercising market power in monopolies or oligopolies protected by barriers to entry. As such, positioning theory applies a very different model of profit generation (and appropriation) than RBT (Demsetz, 1973; Barney and Mackey, 2018). Yet, like RBT, SCP has not traditionally taken a stakeholder perspective and, instead, has assumed that any profits generated by a firm would be appropriated by a firm's shareholders as its only residual claimant (McGahan and Porter, 2002). This section considers at least one possible way that stakeholder thinking could influence positioning theory's current model of how firms both generate and appropriate economic profits.

Positioning theory and the Five Forces framework

Positioning theory became popular in strategic management as Porter turned traditional SCP logic upside down and observed that firms could earn economic profits in less competitive industries.[3] Porter developed the Five Forces framework to identify less competitive industries within which firms could position themselves in such a way as to earn economic profits. Firms could position themselves in such industries either through entry[4] or through increasing the concentration within an industry through consolidation (either through acquisitions or forcing rivals out of an industry). Once a firm had formed a concentrated industry, it could use its market power to keep supply below demand, thereby generating monopoly or oligopoly profits. Of course, these profits would have to be protected from increased competition by the erection of barriers to entry.

The Five Forces identified by Porter can be thought of as threats to an incumbent firm's profits and include threats of rivalry, substitutes, powerful buyers, powerful suppliers, and new entry. Profits in attractive industries are not threatened by these forces as much as in less attractive industries. However, these five forces also identify common categories of stakeholders that can affect, or be affected by, a firm's actions.

Stakeholders as threats or partners

Implicit in the Five Forces framework is the assumption that key stakeholders are threats to a firm's profits. This can often be the case as powerful buyers, suppliers, substitutes, rivals, and new entrants may dictate terms of how economic profits generated by a firm are appropriated.

However, this "threat" logic does not account for the possibility that these powerful stakeholders could, in fact, be the source of co-specialized resources in the profit-generating process in a firm. Most obviously, buyers and suppliers may not be just threats to a firm's ability to appropriate profits, but critical partners in the process of generating those profits. In addition, rivals, substitutes, and new entrants may be potential partners for a firm and can be a source of innovation and learning. If a firm treats its stakeholders solely as threats, it forgoes opportunities to work with those stakeholders as potential profit generators.

None of this suggests that firms will have a simple relationship with stakeholders who provide profit-generating resources. These stakeholders, and the firms with whom they interact, have at least two conflicting interests: On the one hand, they want to cooperate to generate economic profits, and on the other hand, they want to appropriate as much of the value they help create as possible. This conflicted relationship is likely to be difficult for firms (and stakeholders) to manage, and more complicated than simply treating all stakeholders as threats.

The emergence of complementors

Brandenburger and Nalebuff (1996) suggested a "sixth force" that can have an impact on a firm's profitability: complementors. Two firms complement each other when their economic value is greater when they are both operating than when one or the other is not operating. This most obviously occurs when the products of two firms are complements—movie and television production studios and streaming services complement each other, app developers and phone operating systems complement each other, tire manufacturers and automobile manufacturers complement each other. Supply partners, such as in these examples, are considered threats to a firm's profitability in positioning theory, yet they clearly play a complementary role in the creation of economic value. Of course, since complementors both affect and are affected by other firms, they can also be considered as one of a firm's stakeholders (Freeman, 1984).

Complementors have two important differences from the five forces identified by Porter. First, rather than assuming that complementors are a threat to a firm's profitability, complementors can help increase a firm's profitability. Thus, to the extent that complementors can be thought of as a "sixth force" in the Porter framework, their introduction already suggests the possibility of extending this framework beyond an emphasis on threats to include forces acting as a source of potential profits for a firm.

Second, each of the other five forces identified by Porter—including suppliers, buyers, substitutes, rivals, and new entrants—can be examples of complementors. For example, the value of firms and their suppliers is higher when they have made specific complementary investments in each other compared with firms and suppliers that maintain only arm's-length relationships. The same is true for firms and their buyers. Substitutes can act as complements when they provide an entry point for consumers into an industry and when, over time, these new consumers begin buying from other firms in the industry. Rivals and new entrants can be complements to a firm when they reduce the threat of antitrust action in an industry.

In this sense, the introduction of the idea of complements to the Five Forces framework has already brought stakeholder thinking into positioning theory. It is likely that understanding when and how threats can actually be opportunities for cooperation and economic profits will become increasingly important as positioning theory continues to evolve.

Incorporating Stakeholder Thinking in Theories of the Firm

In 1931, Ronald Coase posed a question that has puzzled economists ever since: Given how efficient markets are in coordinating the exchanges of thousands, and even millions, of independent economic actors, why do firms exist? Even the most efficient firm is not as efficient as an efficient market.

Three broad answers to this question have been proposed: (1) exchanges are organized in firms to reduce the threat of opportunism due to transaction-specific investments (transaction cost economics [TCE] [Williamson, 1975, 1985]), (2) exchanges are organized in firms to assign decision rights to parties in an exchange that cannot be assigned through an ex ante complete contracting (incomplete contract theory [Hart and Moore, 1990]), and (3) exchanges are *not* organized in firms in order for parties to an exchange to retain flexibility in the face of uncertainty associated with that exchange (real options theory [Kogut, 1991]). Theoretical and empirical work on this question continues even today.[5]

Stakeholders in theories of the firm

Questions of specific investment, opportunism, and governance are also important in a stakeholder theory applied in strategic management. For example, if a firm has a reputation of exploiting the specific investments of its stakeholders, then these stakeholders will have less incentive to make such investments in these firms. In this sense, the threat of opportunism can reduce the ability of firms to attract specific investments from their stakeholders, and thus forgo the economic value such specific investments would otherwise create (Clark *et al.*, 2020).

Stakeholder theory and the role of the theory of the firm in strategic management

However, from a broader perspective, incorporating stakeholder theory more completely into strategic management brings into question the entire "theory of the firm" enterprise that is central in TCE. It is quite easy to understand why a field—like economics—that focuses most of its attention on how markets operate would find the topic of why firms exist—as a clear exception to market forms of exchange governance—very interesting. Thus, firm boundaries—what kinds of exchanges should be managed within a firm and what kinds of exchanges should be managed through markets—are important in economics. It is less clear that firm boundaries are as important in strategic management, and especially in strategic management that takes stakeholder theory seriously.

Stakeholders, firms, and profit generation

Strategy as a field focuses on the generation and appropriation of economic profits—how profits are generated in an economy and who appropriates these profits (Brandenburger and Stuart, 1996). RBT's model of profit generation—summarized earlier in this chapter—suggests that profits are generated when stakeholders make resources available in an exchange that are co-specialized with the resources that other stakeholders make available in that exchange. If these jointly co-specialized resources meet the VRIN (valuable, rare, inimitable, and non-substitutable) criteria outlined in Barney (1991), then they can be a source of profits.

Of course, this theory of profit generation would require a new definition of the concept of "stakeholder." Prior definitions of this term assumed the existence of a firm: stakeholders influence and are influenced by firms (Freeman, 1984: 48). But, if stakeholders are thought of as those in an economy that control resources that can be combined with the resources from other stakeholders in co-specialized ways, then it is possible to have a theory of profit generation where the firm, per se, does not have to play a particularly important role. Indeed, as noted earlier, there is growing research on how ecosystems, network organizations, platforms, value nets, open innovation, and other ways of organizing economic exchanges can generate economic profits. Some of these new forms of exchange evolve as units within firms, yet others are strictly outside the traditional boundaries of the firm. This suggests that firms are not always a necessary actor in this profit-generating process.

Williamson (1975, 1985) has argued that these types of intermediate governance devices—between markets and firms (hierarchies)—are temporary: in the long run, exchanges tend towards markets or hierarchies. An alternative view is that these forms of exchange governance can provide unique sources of value that cannot be realized either through markets or hierarchies (Barney, 1999). And the observation that these nonhierarchical forms of governance are both increasing, and increasingly stable, seems inconsistent with the traditional TCE argument.

To be sure, arguing that firms are not necessary to a model of profit generation is not the same as suggesting that firms are *never* part of the profit-generating process. Firms, in fact, may be created for exactly the reasons identified in TCE and other theories of the firm. However, taking stakeholder theory seriously suggests that strategic management's quest should not be for a stakeholder or strategic theory of the firm, but rather for a stakeholder or strategic theory of profit generation.

Stakeholders, firms, and profit appropriation

Firms are also not necessarily central to questions of profit appropriation. As suggested earlier, these theories focus on the impact of a stakeholder's resources for generating profits, whether the resources in question are generic or firm specific, and the negotiation skills of those who control access to these resources. Thus, individual employees—as a stakeholders—may have enormous ability to appropriate the profits their human capital resources help generate. Consider, for example, the compensation of star athletes, star scientists, and star engineers (Groysberg, 2010).

None of this suggests that firms do not ever have an impact on how profits generated by co-specialized resources from stakeholders are appropriated. Indeed, some stakeholders may combine to form a firm to gain extra leverage in determining how the profits they helped generate are appropriated. As before, received theories of the firm can be used to explain when stakeholders will combine in this way. However, while firms *can* be part of this appropriation process, their existence is *not logically required* for an appropriation process to unfold.

Implications for Specific Strategic Management Topics

Not surprisingly, if incorporating a stakeholder perspective has a significant impact on these three theories in the field of strategic management, then it seems likely that stakeholder thinking will also have an impact on how these theories—and other strategic management theories—are applied in the study of a variety of strategic management topics. Several examples of how stakeholder logic is likely to affect research on specific topics in the field of strategic management are briefly discussed here.

Incorporating stakeholder thinking in the study of corporate diversification

Corporate diversification is among the most widely studied corporate strategies in the strategic management literature (see Erdorf *et al.* [2013] for a recent review). One of the central assumptions of this literature is that firms engaging in diversification strategies that could be enacted, at lower cost, by shareholders on their own will destroy shareholder value (Amihud and Lev, 1981). However, a stakeholder perspective would suggest that the interests of stakeholders, in addition to shareholders, need to be considered in making these decisions. For example, Wang and Barney (2006) argue that corporate diversification can reduce the risks associated with firm-specific investments made by stakeholders, including employees. And since these firm-specific investments are an important source of economic profits (Barney, 2018), it follows that diversification strategies that address the interests of nonshareholder stakeholders may also have a positive impact on shareholders (Clark *et al.*, 2020). Future research could examine the link between diversification and performance for diversification strategies that specifically address the needs of nonshareholder stakeholders. Is there a diversification discount for firms that consider the interests of nonshareholder stakeholders, or is it in fact, on average, a premium?

Incorporating stakeholder thinking in the study of mergers and acquisitions

Another common topic in the strategic management literature is mergers and acquisitions (M&As). Until recently, most of this work examined the short-term response of the stock market to the announcement of an acquisition. Results from the application of this "event study" methodology suggested that, on average, acquisitions do create economic value, the shareholders of target firms appropriate most of this value, and the shareholders of bidding firms about break even.

However, more recent research has examined the longer-term implications of acquisitions and paints a more nuanced story. In particular, firms that are able to acquire targets and then to retain the critical human capital and other specific resources in these target firms are able to generate economic profits (Shleifer and Summers, 1988; Johnson, Karpoff, and Yi, 2015). Put differently, this research suggests that focusing only on maximizing short-term shareholder profits—by, say, laying off large numbers of employees in acquired firms—can unintentionally jeopardize a firm's longer-term performance (Cen, Dasgupta, and Sen, 2015). Thus, incorporating stakeholder thinking into the study of mergers and acquisitions would broaden the viewpoint on value creation, looking beyond the immediate impact to shareholders to the long-term impacts to stakeholders and the subsequent economic performance of the firm. Future research should examine how various impacts on different stakeholder groups impact the long-term value created from mergers and acquisitions.

Incorporating stakeholder thinking in the study of corporate governance

To date, most work on corporate governance has focused on how governance can resolve potential conflicts of interest between a firm's senior managers and its shareholders in creating and distributing economic value. This work, based in agency theory (Alchian and Demsetz, 1972; Jensen and Meckling, 1976), has led to a variety of corporate governance mechanisms that have been widely implemented by many firms around the world (Williamson, 1996).

Theories of shareholder governance focus on how economic value is created by and distributed between two groups—shareholders and senior managers—that are relatively homogeneous with respect to their (sometimes) conflicting interests in how they would like to see a firm managed (Jensen and Meckling, 1976). Governance mechanisms structured to reconcile these potential conflicts are relatively straightforward to design, although not always easy to implement (Baysinger and Butler, 1985).

Stakeholder governance, however, requires dealing with and reconciling a much broader set of issues across stakeholders. For example, where shareholder governance has focused on the creation and distribution of economic value, stakeholders often have interests that go well beyond these narrow economic concerns (Campbell, Coff, and Kryscynski, 2012). Employees, for example, are likely to be concerned about appropriating some of the economic profits their human capital helps create, but may also have interests in work-life quality, internal and external pay equity, and employment stability. Customers generally want to purchase the highest-quality products at the lowest price possible but may also have concerns about exploiting child labor in developing countries, a firm's impact on global climate change, and rising economic inequality. The communities within which a firm operates will generally be interested in the taxes and other monetary benefits that can be generated by a firm in their midst, but may also have concerns about environmental pollution, traffic congestion, and urban sprawl.

Of course, many scholars have argued that firms can safely ignore the noneconomic interests of their stakeholders when making business decisions (Jensen, 2005). Some have suggested that these noneconomic issues can be best managed through political processes and are not part of a firm's sphere of operations—even though firms hope to obtain critical resources from stakeholders that have both economic and noneconomic interests. Others have suggested that if a firm maximizes the wealth of its shareholders, it will automatically address the interests of its other stakeholders (Friedman, 1970; Jensen, 2005). But this is not even true with respect to the economic interests of stakeholders—maximizing shareholder wealth does not necessarily address all the conflicting economic interests of employees, customers, communities, and so forth (Barney, 2018). And it certainly is not true with respect to the many noneconomic interests of a firm's stakeholders. Finally, others acknowledge the importance of the noneconomic interests of stakeholders but suggest that trying to incorporate these interests in a theory of business decision-making is simply too difficult (Jensen, 2005). Future research needs both theoretical and empirical work in this area. For theoretical work, qualitative work, such as inductive case studies, may be helpful to illustrate how some firms have successfully governed stakeholder relationships—balancing both economic and noneconomic interests across different stakeholder groups. Such work could identify important mechanisms that then could be tested empirically to deepen our understanding of how firms can achieve this difficult balancing act.

Conclusion

This chapter suggests that many of the core theories and topics researched in strategic management could be affected in fundamental ways if the field took the stakeholder perspective seriously. As strategic management's core theories and critical topics increasingly incorporate a stakeholder perspective, this will necessarily have implications for other fields of scholarship—fields that use and apply strategic management theories to develop applications and explain phenomena of interest in their own respective fields.

As just one example, human resource management scholars use strategic management theories to develop applications for acquiring, developing, and managing human capital (e.g., Lepak and Snell, 1999). Some of this work focuses on when to bring human capital "inside" the firm versus when to keep it "outside" the firm and access it through contracts, as well as how to manage and develop this capital. Yet human capital is unique among the various forms of resources and capabilities the firm needs to access in that human capital can never truly be owned (unless you allow for slavery).

Current strategic management theories work well to explain the governance of physical assets like machinery, equipment, land, and so on. However, extending these ideas to human capital is deeply problematic. The notion that human capital can be brought "inside" a firm in exchange for giving up the decision rights associated with use of the capital simply does not make sense. As explained earlier, stakeholder-type resource-based theory suggests that the residual rights of control should go to whomever is creating the most value in the exchange. Thus, in the case of human capital, valuable individuals creating co-specialized resources will create the most value for firms when they retain decision rights and have a residual claim on the value created.

Requiring that such valuable human capital relinquish decision rights could threaten the value creation from the relationship. Adopting a stakeholder perspective for human capital therefore shifts the conceptual space around human capital from a resource that can be "owned," "controlled," and "directed" to viewing human capital as a relationship—an important stakeholder relationship, requiring care, purpose, and co-specialized commitment. How firms access, manage, develop, govern, and compensate human capital is fundamentally altered when we, as strategy (and management) scholars, take the stakeholder perspective seriously.

In addition to this example within the human resource management literature, fields such as organizational behavior, organizational theory (i.e., institutional theory), entrepreneurship, finance, and accounting that draw on fundamental strategic management theories would all be impacted by incorporating a stakeholder perspective and taking it seriously. Strategic management scholars have the exciting opportunity to actively shape this future.

Notes

1. For a recent review, see Bosse and Sutton (2019).
2. For recent reviews of these theories, see Barney, Ketchen, and Wright (2011); Kraaijenbrink, Spender, and Groen (2010); McGahan and Porter (2002); and Zenger, Felin, and Bigelow (2017).

3. The SCP model was originally designed to identify industries where firms were earning high economic profits so that government regulators could implement remedies to increase industry competitiveness.
4. Although, ironically, the cost of entry is presumed to be very high in highly "attractive" industries.
5. This research has generated at least three Nobel Prizes in economics: Ronald Coase in 1991, Oliver Williamson in 2009, and Oliver Hart and Bengt Holmström in 2016.

References

Adner R, Helfat C. 2003. Corporate effects and dynamic managerial capabilities. *Strategic Management Journal* 24(10): 1011–1025.

Adner R, Oxley J, Silverman B. 2013. Collaboration and competition in business ecosystems. *Advances in Strategic Management* 31: 9–18.

Alchian AA. 1950. Uncertainty, evolution, and economic theory. *Journal of Political Economy* 58(3): 211–221.

Alchian AA, Demsetz H. 1972. Production, information costs, and economic organization. *American Economic Review* 62(5): 777–795.

Alvarez S, Barney JB. 2007. Discovery and creation: alternative theories of entrepreneurial action. *Strategic Entrepreneurship Journal* 1(1): 11–26.

Amihud Y, Lev B. 1981. Risk reduction as a managerial motive for conglomerate mergers. *Bell Journal of Economics* 12(2): 605–617.

Amis J, Barney J, Mahoney J, Wang H. 2020. Why we need a theory of stakeholder governance—and why this is a hard problem. *Academy of Management Review* 45(3): 499–503.

Amit R, Schoemaker PJH. 1993. Strategic assets and organizational rents. *Strategic Management Journal* 14: 33–46.

Asher CC, Mahoney JM, Mahoney JT. 2005. Towards a property rights foundation for a stakeholder theory of the firm. *Journal of Management and Governance* 9(1): 5–32.

Bain JB. 1950. Workable competition in oligopoly: theoretical considerations and some empirical evidence. *American Economic Review* 40(2): 35–47.

Barney JB. 1986. Strategic factor markets: expectations, luck, and business strategy. *Management Science* 32(10): 1231–1241.

Barney JB. 1991. Firm resources and sustained competitive advantage. *Journal of Management* 17(1): 99–120.

Barney JB. 1999. How a firm's capabilities affect boundary decisions. *Sloan Management Review* 40(3): 137–145.

Barney JB. 2018. Why resource-based theory's model of profit appropriation must incorporate a stakeholder perspective. *Strategic Management Journal* 39: 3305–3325.

Barney JB, Ketchen DJ Jr, Wright M. 2011. The future of resource-based theory: revitalization or decline? *Journal of Management* 37: 1299–1315.

Barney JB, Mackey A. 2018. Monopoly profits, efficiency profits, and teaching strategic management. *Academy of Management Learning and Education* 17(3): 359–373.

Baysinger BD, Butler HN. 1985. Corporate governance and the board of directors: performance effects of changes in board composition. *Journal of Law, Economics, and Organization* 1(1): 101–124.

Bosse D, Sutton T. 2019. The stakeholder perspective in strategic management. In *Cambridge Handbook of Stakeholder Theory*, Harrison JS, Barney JB, Freeman RE, Phillips RA (eds.) Cambridge University Press: Cambridge, U.K.; 189–207.

Brandenburger AM, Nalebuff BJ. 1996. *Co-opetition*. Doubleday: New York, NY.

Brandenburger AM, Stuart HW Jr. 1996. Value-based business strategy. *Journal of Economics and Management Strategy* 5(1): 5–24.

Campbell BA, Coff R, Kryscynski D. 2012. Rethinking sustained competitive advantage from human capital. *Academy of Management Review* 37(3): 376–395.

Castanias RP, Helfat CE. 1991. Managerial resources and rents. *Journal of Management* 17(1): 155–171.

Cen L, Dasgupta S, Sen R. 2015. Discipline or disruption: stakeholder relationships and the effect of takeover threat. *Management Science* 62(10): 2820–2841.

Chacar A, Hesterly W. 2008. Institutional settings and rent appropriation by knowledge based workers: the case of Major League Baseball. *Managerial and Decision Economics* 29(2-3): 117–136.

Chesbrough HW. 2003. *Open Innovation: The New Imperative for Creating and Profiting from Technology*. Harvard Business School Press: Boston, MA.

Clark A, Kofford S, Jones L, Barney JB. 2020. Stakeholder orientation and competitive advantage. Working Paper, University of Utah Working Paper Series.

Coase RH. 1931. The nature of the firm: origin. *Journal of, Law, Economics, and Organization* 4(1): 3–17.

Coff RW. 1999. When competitive advantage doesn't lead to performance: the resource-based view and stakeholder bargaining power. *Organization Science* 10(2): 119–133.

Conner K, Prahalad CK. 1991. A resource-based theory of the firm: knowledge versus opportunism. *Organization Science* 7(5): 477–501.

Demsetz H. 1973. Industry structure, market rivalry, and public policy. *Journal of Law and Economics* 16(1): 1–9.

Denrell J, Fang C, Winter S. 2003. The economics of strategic opportunity. *Strategic Management Journal* 24(10): 977–990.

Dyer JH, Singh H. 1998. The relational view: cooperative strategy and sources of interorganizational competitive advantage. *Academy of Management Review* 23(4): 660–679.

Erdorf S., Hartmann-Wendels T., Heinrichs N, Matz M. 2013. Corporate diversification and firm value: a survey of recent literature. *Financial Markets and Portfolio Management* 27: 187–215.

Freeman, RE. 1984. *Stakeholder Management: Framework and Philosophy*. Pitman: Mansfield, MA.

Freeman E, Harrison J, Wicks A, Parmar B, de Colle S. 2010. *Stakeholder Theory: The State of the Art*. Cambridge University Press: Cambridge, U.K.

Friedman M. 1970. A Friedman doctrine: the social responsibility of business is to increase its profits. *New York Times Magazine*, 13 September: 32–33.

Grossman SJ, Hart OD. 1986. The costs and benefits of ownership: a theory of vertical and lateral integration. *Journal of Political Economy* 94(4): 691–719.

Groysberg, B. 2010. *Chasing stars: the myth of talent and the portability of performance*. Princeton University Press: Princeton, NJ.

Hagiu A, Wright J. 2015. Multi-sided platforms. *International Journal of Industrial Organization* 43: 162–174.

Hansen M. 2002. Knowledge networks: Explaining effective knowledge sharing in multi-unit companies. *Organization Science* 13(3): 232–248.

Harrison JS Barney JB, Freeman RE, Phillips RA (eds). 2019. *The Cambridge Handbook of Stakeholder Theory*. Cambridge University Press: Cambridge, U.K.

Hart OD. 1988. Incomplete contracts and the theory of the firm. *Journal of Law, Economics, and Organization* 4(1): 119–139.

Hart O, Moore J. 1990. Property rights and the nature of the firm. *Journal of Political Economy* 98(6): 1119–1158.

Helfat C, Peteraf M. 2003. The dynamic resource-based view: capability lifecycles. *Strategic Management Journal* 24: 997–1016.

Jensen MC. 2002. Value maximization, stakeholder theory, and the corporate objective function. *Business Ethics Quarterly* 12(02): 235–256.

Jensen MC. 2005. Value maximization, stakeholder theory, and the corporate objective function. In *Corporate Governance at the Crossroads*, Chew DH Jr., Stuart L (eds). McGraw-Hill Irwin: New York, NY; 7–20.

Jensen MC, Meckling WH. 1976. Theory of the firm: managerial behavior, agency costs, and ownership structure. *Journal of Financial Economics* 3(4): 305–360.

Johnson WC, Karpoff JM, Yi S. 2015. The bonding hypothesis of takeover defense: evidence for IPO firms. *Journal of Financial Economics* 117(2): 307–332.

Kogut B. 1991. Joint ventures and the option to expand and acquire. *Management Science* 37(1): 19–33.

Kraaijenbrink J, Spender JC, Groen, AJ. 2010. The resource-based view: a review and assessment of its critiques. *Journal of Management* 36: 349–372.

Lepak DP, Snell SA. 1999. The human resource architecture: toward a theory of human capital allocation and development. *Academy of Management Review* 24: 31–48.

Lieberman M, Chacar A. 1997. Distribution of returns among stakeholders: method and application to US and Japanese auto companies. In *Strategic Discovery: Competing in New Arenas*, Thomas H, O'Neal D (eds). Wiley: New York, NY; 299–313.

Lippman SA, Rumelt RP. 2003a. A payments perspective: microfoundations of resource analysis. *Strategic Management Journal* 24(11): 903–927.

Lippman SA, Rumelt RP. 2003b. A bargaining perspective on resource advantage. *Strategic Management Journal* 24(11): 1069–1086.

Mahoney J. 2013. Toward a stakeholder theory of strategic management. In *Towards a New Theory of the Firm: Humanizing the Firm and the Management Profession*, Costa JER, Marti JMR (eds). BBVA: Bilbao, Spain; 153–182.

McGahan AM, Porter ME. 2002. What do we know about variance in accounting profitability? *Management Science* 48(7): 834–851.

Mencher AG. 1971. On the social deployment of science. *Bulletin of the Atomic Scientists* 27(10): 34–38.

Milgrom P, Roberts J. 1992. *Economics, Organization, and Management*. Prentice-Hall: New York, NY.

Molloy JC, Barney JB. 2015. Who captures the value created with human capital? A market-based view. *Academy of Management Perspectives* 29(3): 309–325.

Porter ME. 1979. The structure within industries and companies' performance. *Review of Economics and Statistics* 61(2): 214–227.

Porter ME. 1980. *Competitive Strategy*. Free Press: New York, NY.

Porter ME. 1985. *Competitive Advantage: Creating and Sustaining Competitive Advantage*. Free Press: New York, NY.

Rumelt R. 1984. Towards a strategic theory of the firm. In *Competitive Strategic Management*, Lamb R (ed.). Prentice Hall: Englewood Cliffs, NJ; 556–570.

Shleifer A, Summers L. 1988. Breach of trust in hostile takeovers. In *Corporate Takeovers: Causes and Consequences*, Auerbach A (ed). University of Chicago Press: Chicago, IL; 33–68.

Sirmon D, Hitt M, Ireland D. 2007. Managing resources in dynamic environments to create value: looking inside the black box. *Academy of Management Review* 32(1): 273–292.

Sirmon D, Hitt M, Ireland D, Gilbert B. 2011. Resource orchestration to create competitive advantage: breadth, depth, and life cycle effects. *Journal of Management* 37(5): 1390–1412.

Teece D. 1986. Profiting from technological innovation: implications for integration, collaboration, licensing, and public policy. *Research Policy* 15(6): 285–305.

Wang HC, Barney JB. 2006. Employee incentives to make firm-specific investments: implications for resource-based theories of corporate diversification. *Academy of Management Review* 31(2): 466–476.

Williamson OE. 1975. *Markets and Hierarchies: Analysis and Antitrust Implications*. Free Press: New York, NY.

Williamson OE. 1985. *The Economic Institutions of Capitalism*. Free Press: New York, NY.

Williamson OE. 1996. *The Mechanisms of Governance*. Oxford University Press: New York, NY.

Zenger T, Felin T, Bigelow L. 2017. Theories of the firm–market boundary. *Academy of Management Annals* 5(1): 89–133.

11.4
BUSINESS MODEL INNOVATION STRATEGY

Raphael Amit and Christoph Zott

Why business model innovation matters for strategic management

The business model has become one of the core strategic choices that general managers and entrepreneurs (and those who support and invest in them) need to consider (Zott, Amit, and Massa, 2011; Schneider and Spieth, 2013; Wirtz *et al.*, 2016; Massa, Tucci, and Afuah, 2017). It answers the question: How should the firm do business (Amit and Zott, 2001)? For decades, the key strategic decisions that managers and entrepreneurs were asked to address, which were also highlighted in classic strategy textbooks, centered on corporate strategy issues and business strategy issues. Corporate strategy issues concern the scope of the firm and include such questions as, What industries and product market segments should the firm be in? How should the firm enter these markets (i.e., through Mergers and Acquisitions [M&As], joint ventures, or de novo entry)? When should the firm enter these markets? Business strategy issues center on establishing and sustaining the competitive advantage of a firm through product market moves. They include such questions as how to compete in a particular product market (e.g., on the basis of product differentiation or cost leadership) and when to enter a market.

The advent of the internet in the 1990s did not undermine the importance of these classic choices; they remain as valid and relevant as ever. However, it added an essential strategic choice onto the entrepreneur's and general manager's plates—namely, the question of *how to do business*. This question does not replace, or diminish the importance of, any of the previously mentioned strategic issues. Rather, it complements them and thus expands the range of strategically relevant considerations for entrepreneurs and managers who are keen on pursuing and exploiting new business opportunities in addition to defending and securing their existing ones. In other words, addressing the business model question has become a strategic imperative for entrepreneurial leaders and managers (Amit and Zott, 2021).

A *business model* can be conceived of as a boundary-spanning activity system that centers on a focal firm, yet may encompass activities performed by its partners, suppliers, and customers in the pursuit of value creation and capture (Amit, Han, and Zott, 2020; Zott and Amit, 2010). *Business model innovation* (BMI) refers to the introduction of a novel system of interdependent activities in the product market space in which the focal firm competes (Amit and Zott, 2012; Chesbrough, 2010; Snihur and Zott, 2020).

BMI is a profoundly entrepreneurial task, as it centers on opportunity creation, development, and exploitation (Amit and Zott, 2001). At the same time, it is of high strategic importance (Snihur, Zott, and Amit, 2021). New and innovative business models explain why and how new entrants disrupt incumbents, and in turn offer a way for these same incumbents to invigorate their firms and mitigate the effects of disruption (Kim and Min, 2015). Emerging and established technologies—such as 5G, artificial intelligence, the internet of things, blockchain, cloud computing, and connected mobility, along with real-time digital data and data analytic tools—open a wide range of innovative ways for managers to conceive of, design, implement, and manage novel and transformative business models with new activities, business processes, ways of connecting activities, and/or ways of governing activities (Eggers and Park, 2018; Hacklin, Björkdahl, and Wallin, 2018). By purposefully designing their firm's boundary-spanning exchanges and activities, utilizing digital technologies, these managers create a purposeful networked system of interdependent activities— namely their business models (Zott and Amit, 2009). The business model has thus become an important lever for enhancing the focal firm's "ecological fitness," that is, for improving its fit with a continuously shifting technological and product-market environment, and for creating a competitive advantage (Amit and Zott, 2016; Helfat *et al.*, 2007).

As a result of the exponential decline in the costs of information processing and telecommunications, both direct and indirect transaction costs have decreased (Shapiro and Varian, 1999). This has shifted the balance from tangible resources and capabilities to intangible resources (such as knowledge resources anchored in human capital) and capabilities (see, e.g., Campbell, Coff, and Kryscynski, 2012). It has also opened up new possibilities for managers to conceive of, and implement, innovative business models. Since focal firms can now outsource almost anything to anyone, the combinatorial possibilities for constructing systems that combine in-house activities (i.e., those performed within focal firm boundaries) with those performed by other parties have exploded (Amit and Zott, 2016). In other words, the number of possible combinations of activities—which are enabled by different tangible and intangible resources—and capabilities—which are owned and controlled by different parties— has multiplied dramatically.

The question of whether and how to innovate the business model has therefore become a strategic imperative for incumbent firms digitizing their businesses, as well as for digital-native firms and start-ups that need to be mindful of changes in their competitive landscape along with technological changes (Karimi and Walter, 2016). A BMI perspective has indeed become a prerequisite for transformative innovation, and entrepreneurial leaders of all firms need a BMI strategy.

BMI Strategy Defined and Explained

A BMI strategy (Amit and Zott, 2021) aims at enabling an organization to generate a stream of business model innovations. It refers to the choices entrepreneurial leaders must make with respect to:

- The design of a new system of activities.
- The processes, including their antecedents, by which the new activity system is created and implemented.
- The management and ongoing adaptation of the new activity system to ensure coherence (i.e., internal, external, and strategic fit) with the objective of sustaining and improving the focal organization's competitive advantage.

The *design of a new system of activities* refers to the fact that entrepreneurial leaders need to choose and craft organizational activities, as well as the links that connect activities together, into a system. One important set of design parameters that characterize an activity system are the design elements of content (*What* activities should be performed?), structure (*How* should the activities be linked and sequenced?), governance (*Who* should perform the activities?), and value logic (*How* is value created and appropriated within the activity system?) (see Zott and Amit, 2010). An activity system can also be characterized through its design themes, which capture the system's main sources of value creation—namely, novelty, lock-in, complementarities, and efficiency (Amit and Zott, 2001).

The choices regarding the *processes* by which the new activity system will be created and implemented are shaped by several *antecedents*, such as goals to create and capture value, templates, stakeholder activities, and environmental constraints (Amit and Zott, 2015). These processes include multiple design stages that are linked iteratively, meaning that business model designers will have to cycle through the stages in an iterative manner before converging on a new business model design for the focal firm (Zott and Amit, 2015).

Lastly, the third component of our definition of BMI strategy takes into account that the business model not only represents a design artifact, but also a crucial intangible asset for the focal firm. Therefore, the management and ongoing adaptation of the new activity system to ensure coherence (i.e., internal, external, and strategic fit) should not be left to chance, but shaped by capabilities that combine organizational and managerial practices with creative insights at the individual level (Amit and Zott, 2016).

To illustrate the definition and highlight the importance of BMI strategy, consider Swedish company Inter Ikea Holding B.V., the holding company of furniture retailer IKEA. It has a well-established worldwide network of large furniture retail stores. The rapid changes in the retail landscape, however, coupled with the exponential growth of ecommerce prompted a radical rethinking by management about how IKEA does business and suggested the need for a BMI strategy. As a result of this process, IKEA's business model is currently undergoing a significant transformation. IKEA is testing new retail formats, such as opening smaller stores and pop-ups in city centers and experimenting with "circular economy"[1] initiatives such as refurbishing (Milne, 2018). New activities are being added to its business model, including ecommerce and services such as furniture assembly. These activities require resources and capabilities that are accessed through new partnerships. IKEA is also embracing partnerships with technology firms, which enable it to offer smart home products that are integrated into IKEA's traditional product line. One example is its partnership with Sonos, a California-based firm that makes smart speakers. Sonos speakers have been integrated into select IKEA products, creating, for instance, an innovative speaker lamp that can be controlled through a smartphone app (Milne, 2019).

A BMI strategy is not, however, only important for traditional, for-profit firms such as IKEA. It is relevant for both for-profit and non-for-profit firms, for organizations that pursue a primarily social objective (e.g., social entrepreneurs), for governmental as well as NonGovernmental Organizations (NGOs), and for organizations such as schools and hospitals. In non-for-profit, public service, and governmental contexts in particular, BMI is a vastly under-researched topic (Yunus, Moingeon, and Lehmann-Ortega, 2010; Saebi, Foss, and Linder, 2019). All firms and other organizations face unprecedented new threats and opportunities in the post-COVID-19 digital era (Wenzel, Stanske, and Lieberman, 2020; Dushnitsky, Graebner, and Zott, 2020). These threats and opportunities are anchored in the simple fact that innovations are no longer restricted to technological innovations (Chesbrough, 2020). Innovations may also hail from new combinations of resources and managerial choices, which are often (but not always) enabled by digital technologies (Amit and Han, 2017). These combinations can result in new business models, such as low-cost airlines, free newspapers that are only funded by advertising, or even hospitals for cataract surgery modeled after a fast-food chain.

Aravind Eye Hospitals is a chain of specialized eye hospitals that was founded in 1976, in the Indian state of Tamil Nadu. Inspired by the efficiency and replicability of the McDonald's fast-food business, Dr. Govindappa Venkataswamy (Dr. V), a retired ophthalmologist, founded the company by applying the template of the McDonald's business model to health care in order to ramp up the number of patients his organization could treat.[2] For example, Aravind allows two or more patients per operating room instead of just one (while one patient is having surgery, the other is being prepped by a team of assistants, so the surgeon can quickly move from one patient to the other), and has nurses who are trained to carry out specialized and repeatable tasks, such as preoperative anesthetic injections (McKinsey and Company, 2011).

In 2017–2018 alone, Aravind conducted over four million outpatient visits and close to half a million surgeries and laser procedures, as it works toward the goal of eradicating "needless blindness" in India (Aravind Eye Care System, 2018). Remarkably, through its revenue model that relies on cross-subsidies, half of its patients receive free or low-cost treatment (Aravind Eye Care website). Aravind is able to achieve all this by employing a novel approach to providing a large volume of high-quality eye surgeries while rigorously controlling costs. The uniqueness of the Aravind activity system lies in the scalability and efficiency that are enabled by the high level of standardization of quality surgical care to patients, regardless of their ability to pay for the services rendered. Key novel aspects of its business model are as follows:

- Aravind not only provides a high volume of specialized eye surgeries, but also performs vertically integrated manufacturing, training, and community outreach activities (i.e., innovations in the *What* dimension of the business model) that support its mission. For example, the organization's community outreach programs include eye camps in villages, as well as local vision centers that treat patients for more basic eye issues and provide screenings (McKinsey and Company, 2011). One of the aspects identified as important to the organization's impressive efficiency rate is having a "steady flow of patients" (Rangan and Thulasiraj, 2007: 45); through bringing in new patients via its local vision centers and eye camps, Aravind's community outreach activities help maintain this flow.

- Thus, a crucial aspect of its model has been adopting local communities as partners (i.e., innovation in the *Who* dimension of the business model)—for example, by training local women to become certified eye technicians. These technicians are qualified to perform many of the standardized tasks at the heart of its efficiency-centered model (McKinsey and Company, 2011). Aravind has also partnered with NGOs and nonprofits, such as the Lions Club, to expand its reach to poor and rural communities (Rangan and Thulasiraj, 2007).

Applying its innovative business model, Aravind has grown into a large, self-funded network of more than a dozen eye hospitals, as well as numerous outpatient and training facilities (Aravind Eye Care website). Furthermore, it has managed to do so adhering to best practices and achieving outstanding outcomes: Aravind's surgical complication rates are half the complication rates found in a survey of U.K. hospitals (McKinsey and Company, 2011). Aravind continues to rely on and deploy new technologies and innovative best practices; for example, to access an even greater number of people, Aravind has started to screen people for diabetic retinopathy, a serious degenerative condition related to diabetes, using an artificial intelligence system developed by Google (Metz, 2019).

Platform Business Models and BMI Strategy

The opportunities and threats presented by the emergence and growth of digitally enabled multisided platform business models (Cusumano, Gawer, and Yoffie, 2019; Greve and Song, 2017; Zhao *et al.*, 2019), which enable digital interactions, exchanges, and commercial transactions among multiple parties, further strengthen the case for having a BMI strategy. The online travel reservation platform Expedia, the social media platform Facebook, the dating platform Match.com, and the marketplace platform Amazon.com are examples of how advanced computing and communication technologies created new business opportunities that were captured by entrepreneurial leaders (Greve and Song, 2017). The innovative business models they crafted enabled the creation of value for the stakeholders of the platform, and the capture of value by the focal firm (the platform) (Täuscher and Laudien, 2018).

Each of these digital platform business models is robust and scalable and offers a compelling value proposition to the stakeholders incentivized to participate in it. Such digital platform business models can be standalone businesses, such as the music streaming service Spotify and video platform YouTube, where both the financial transactions (e.g., subscribing to the service) and the delivery of the service are digital. Alternatively, they can complement a brick-and-mortar retailing business; examples of this are ecommerce retail sites such as Walmart.com and Macys.com, where the financial transaction (e.g., purchasing the product) is digitally enabled but the delivery is physical.

In addition to considerations about how to organize the platform and combine it with the existing business, an important aspect of a BMI strategy is the alternative ways of monetizing the traffic on the digital platform. The value capture of digitally enabled business models is facilitated through a range of (often novel) revenue models (Tidhar and Eisenhardt, 2020; Casadesus-Masanell and Zhu, 2013). Examples of different revenue models include subscription-based revenue models, such as the *New York Times'* online media platform, music streaming platform Deezer, and movie streaming platform Netflix; advertising-based revenue models, such as search engines Google and Yahoo; or commission-based revenue models, such as different types of marketplace business models, including C2C (e.g., LendingClub.com), B2B (e.g., Faire.com), or B2C (e.g., Cars.com) companies. Commissions may also be generated through affiliate marketing programs, which are realized through digital referrals to an ecommerce site or digital marketplace; one example of this is Credit Karma, a personal finance digital platform that derives commissions from credit card issuers. Ecommerce platforms often use a range of revenue models, including sales revenue (e.g., Italian retailer Zegna's online site), transaction fees (e.g., parking payment app meterUp), razor and blade revenue models (e.g., the men's grooming companies Gillette and digital native Harrys.com), and more (Amit and Zott, 2021).

BMI Strategy: Questions for Research

The development of a BMI strategy starts by embracing a business model mindset. A business model mindset is a state of mind and perspective that help entrepreneurial leaders consider the firm's entire activity system as a way to capture business opportunities (see Amit and Zott, 2021: Chapter 3). Such a cognitive and holistic lens enables entrepreneurial leaders to proactively prepare their firms for disruptive changes that may occur in their ecosystems. As such, the business model mindset is a fertile area for future research.

Recall our definition of BMI strategy as the pattern of choices entrepreneurial leaders make with respect to (1) the design of a new system of activities; (2) the processes, including their antecedents, by which the new activity system is created and implemented; and (3) the management and ongoing adaptation of the activity system to ensure coherence (i.e., internal, external, and strategic fit) with the objective of sustaining and improving the focal organization's competitive advantage. All of these aspects have only been sparsely researched and offer many opportunities for future investigation.

Regarding the design of a new system of activities (part 1 of our definition), the development of a BMI strategy must be anchored on identifying needs in the market. Specifically, in order to effectively design an innovative business model, managers must recognize the perceived needs of customers, along with the needs of other potential stakeholders, and then address the following questions (see Amit and Zott, 2012):

- What activities are needed to create and deliver the solutions that satisfy customer needs and create value for them and for other stakeholders? Are there novel activities that can be used to provide the solutions?
- Who are the participants needed in the business model to create and deliver the value? What could be novel about the choice of participants?
- How should interactions among the business model participants and the activities that they perform and/or enable be structured? What could be novel about that structure?
- Why does the proposed business model create value for all stakeholders (partners, suppliers, and customers)? What could be novel about it? Why and how does the proposed business model enable value appropriation?

These are important questions that a manager must answer in order to design a value-creating business model. However, these questions can also serve to guide future research on BMI strategy. Adopting a design perspective to BMI can offer entrepreneurial leaders a content- and process-based framework for crafting their BMI strategy (Amit and Zott, 2015; Dunne, 2018; Liedtka and Kaplan, 2019). Mindful business model strategists think deeply and holistically about the design problem facing them. They should also be aware of their cognitive biases, the needs of stakeholders, and the constraints that must be considered in the design of the business model. A BMI strategy also needs to aim for business models that are strategically robust, namely, legitimate and difficult to imitate (Snihur *et al.*, 2021). These considerations suggest a number of interesting topics for future research, such as the following: How should mindfulness in the context of BMI design be conceptualized? How can the construct be measured? What cognitive biases are most harmful for BMI? How can these cognitive biases be mitigated, other than through mindfulness? What empirical evidence do we have about strategically robust business model design? What other dimensions of robustness in business model design could be important?

With respect to the processes, including the antecedents, by which the new activity system is created and implemented (part 2 of our definition), the development of a BMI strategy needs to consider the relevant internal and external factors that affect the design of a novel business model (Amit and Zott, 2015). First, a BMI strategy needs to consider the deployable resources (or internal constraints) at hand and the external environment (or external constraints) within which the focal firm operates. Deployable resources and the external environment present a creative challenge—and an opportunity—for innovation. Internal constraints include the resources and capabilities the focal firm can access to enable various activities. Such resources and capabilities may be internal to the firm or accessible in its ecosystem. An interesting question—both theoretically as well as empirically—in this context is whether the importance of ownership and/or control of valuable, rare, and difficult-to-imitate resources postulated by the resource-based view (RBV) of the firm (Wernerfelt, 1984; Barney, 1991; Amit and Schoemaker, 1993) for a firm's competitive advantage is somewhat diminished in the context of digitally enabled business models.

Second, a BMI strategy needs to consider stakeholders' activities—the activities in the business model that are performed by partners, customers, suppliers, and other stakeholders. Strategic collaborations with stakeholders need to be considered and forged, distinct value propositions need to be created, and incentives need to be aligned for each stakeholder to collaborate (with other stakeholders and with the focal firm) (Amit et al., 2020). How can this be best achieved? How can firms effectively build and maintain large portfolios of partnerships? How should managers decide, using the system-level perspective suggested by the business model, which activities to conduct in-house and which ones to outsource to partners (including customers)?

Third, a BMI strategy needs to consider incumbents' templates, namely the business models of incumbent firms in the same industry, or from another industry (like McDonald's serving as a business model template for Aravind Eye Hospitals). This entails considering a strategic trade-off between efficiency and novelty, as the dominant business model designs in a given industry are often associated with higher efficiency, but lower novelty. Yet what makes a template useful, and what are good or bad templates? And how can the right balance be struck between novelty and efficiency? What are the factors that influence the trade-off and tip the balance one way or another? Does the notion of "optimal distinctiveness" (Zhao et al., 2017), which is typically used to characterize a firm's products and services, also apply to business model innovation? How should it be determined in this context? How can novelty and efficiency in business model design be reconciled? Finally, how does the trade-off affect the firm's ability to overcome internal resistance to change to a new business model?

Fourth, a BMI strategy needs to define the strategic goals of business model innovation. These goals must be seen as closely related to the perceived and targeted needs of customers and of all the stakeholders in the business model. Balancing the needs of all stakeholders, and the dual goals of value creation and value appropriation, requires creativity, objectivity, and sound judgment. But how is this best done? What skills and decision-making processes are needed to ensure that the manifold needs of numerous stakeholders are simultaneously and dynamically satisfied over long periods of time? What screening mechanisms and actions can help managers detect shifts in those needs? And how can a new equilibrium be crafted?

A BMI strategy also needs to consider the design, testing, and implementation process of a novel business model (Zott and Amit, 2015). This process includes three iterative phases that we label BM*Ideate*, BM*Iterate*, and BM*Implement* (see Amit and Zott, 2021: Chapter 6). The first phase in the design of a new business model, BM*Ideate*, refers to:

(i) Observing and gaining a deep understanding of business models currently in use and their stakeholders' needs. The observation should be about the roles of stakeholders within a given business model. Observation for the purpose of designing new business models should be broad and deep; furthermore, it requires that the business model designers gain a profound understanding of the design drivers—but how much observation is needed, and with what kind of methods? This is still an open research question.

(ii) Synthesizing and organizing the data gathered in the observation phase to identify themes that emerge with respect to key design elements—but this is a profoundly creative and unstructured task, so how can business model designers maximize their chances to reach creative insights at this step?

(iii) Generating new business model solutions. This can be done by modifying one or more of the design elements of an existing business model or creating an entirely new activity system—but what creative processes work best in the context of BMI, given its holistic and systemic nature (and the challenges associated with these characteristics)?

The BM*Iterate* phase in the design process of a new business model includes:

(i) Consolidating the various ideas generated in the previous phase into a coherent whole to yield one or possibly several alternative new business model designs—but according to which principles?

(ii) Evaluating these alternatives according to relevant criteria—but what should these criteria be?

(iii) Prototyping the highest-ranked alternative(s) to the extent possible, that is, experimenting on a small scale and keeping expenditures low. In this design phase, the value proposition to each potential business model stakeholder must be formulated; that is, a hypothesis must be created about the value created for each business model stakeholder (net of any costs incurred). Note that the value proposition of a business model is separate from, but complementary to, the value proposition of a product.

When evaluating alternative business model designs, it is important to identify the drivers of value creation, namely novelty, lock-in, complementarities, and efficiency (Amit and Zott, 2001), which can be powerfully combined to maximize the value created for all stakeholders. That said, however, academic research on prototyping entire business models and crafting effective value propositions is scarce. How can complex activity systems be best prototyped? What are the trade-offs involved? How should value propositions be crafted, prototyped, and tested?

The BM*Implement* phase of the design process involves scaling the prototype business model and engaging in full-blown implementation. Business model implementation therefore refers to all the choices that need to be made to ensure that the new business model can be fully operational and fulfill its main objective(s) for the focal firm. As we pointed out earlier in this chapter, the design of a business model is a core element of a firm's strategy, which complements the firm's corporate and business unit strategies. Hence, the implementation issues associated with corporate and business unit strategies also apply to the implementation of a novel business model in a corporate setting. An interesting—and under-researched—issue is whether the systemic and holistic nature of business model innovation aggravates these challenges and poses new ones.

There are indeed many challenges associated with the implementation of a new business model. For incumbent firms, the implementation of a new business model often entails significant organizational challenges (see, e.g., Chesbrough, 2010; Markides and Charitou, 2004). These challenges are due in part to organizational inertia and in part to active resistance to change. Overcoming organizational barriers to the implementation of a novel business model requires managerial leadership (Doz and Kosonen, 2010; Lee and Puranam, 2016). It may also potentially demand structural changes to the organization, such as the creation of a new business unit. This unit would complement the existing organization and be staffed with new hires whose skills and experiences are relevant to the implementation of the new business model. As a result, there may be cultural and organizational challenges that need to be carefully managed, since organizational norms and compensation practices may differ between the new business unit and the existing organization.

There are also numerous challenges associated with the implementation of a new business model in a new firm. More research is needed on this important topic. In start-ups, the relevant resources must often be marshalled through partnerships that may create mission-critical dependencies on others. Weak governance structures and inexperienced senior leadership are also factors that may impede the successful implementation of novel business models in young companies. Similar to the case of an incumbent firm, the leadership of a young company must ensure that its business model fits tightly with the firm's ecosystem, its organizational structure, and its product market strategy (Foss and Saebi, 2017). Creating such multilateral fit is a new challenge that deserves to be addressed by research.

In a similar (and similarly under-researched) vein, a BMI strategy needs to consider the management and ongoing adaptation of the activity system (part 3 of our definition of a BMI strategy) to ensure coherence (i.e., internal, external, and strategic fit) with the objective of sustaining and improving the focal organization's key performance metrics. An innovation-oriented organizational culture and behavioral norms that embrace BMI as a continuous process may enable the organization to proactively recognize environmental trends and pivot its business model to ensure coherence. But how can such a culture and trends be created and nurtured? Firmly embedding the new business model into the ecosystem facilitates a tight fit between the new business model and all stakeholders' needs, ongoing technological change, social trends, the organization's strategic choices, and the firm's internal structure. Yet what ecosystem properties allow for creating tight fit? More generally speaking, how do business models and ecosystems interact? For example, how do business model properties influence ecosystem-level properties (and vice versa)? How do they coevolve? And what are the performance-enhancing organizational, business-, and corporate-strategy-level choices within these coevolutionary dynamics?

BMI Strategy and Managerial Capabilities

The capability to instill an innovation-oriented culture and behavioral norms in an organization—which enable it to innovate its business model regularly and adapt it to a continuously evolving external environment—resides to a large extent with individual managers and leaders (Adner and Helfat, 2003; Teece, 2014). Managerial insight, vision, and leadership play a pivotal role for developing a BMI strategy.

The distinctive function of entrepreneurial leaders lies in recognizing market and technological trends, then conceiving, designing, and implementing innovative, robust, and scalable business models (and revenue models that enable them to profit from their innovation) that create value for all stakeholders. As mentioned earlier, essential managerial tasks to ensure the business model's viability, feasibility, and desirability include firmly embedding new business models into the focal firm's ecosystem, ensuring their tight fit with the focal firm's product-market strategy and internal organizational structure, and providing for the ongoing orchestration and coordination of activities performed by the various stakeholders (Brown, 2007; Siggelkow, 2002).

More specifically, to successfully navigate through all the available possibilities, managers intent on continuously innovating their firms' business models need three essential types of capabilities: BMI design, BMI implementation, and management of the ongoing adaptation of the business model. Research has begun to address these capabilities, but much remains to be done.

BMI design capabilities

BMI design capabilities help managers conceive of a new business model that creates value for all stakeholders and ensures profit for the focal firm. These skills include the ability to think holistically, adopt a system-level perspective (focusing on the forest, not just the trees), look outside of the box of your firm and industry, and engage in analogical reasoning and conceptual combination (Snihur and Zott, 2020; Martins, Rindova, and Greenbaum, 2015). A quintessential prerequisite for all of this is a mindset focused on activities, not just on products, services, organizational functions, or operational processes.

The good news is that these cognitive skills can be learned and improved (Helfat and Peteraf, 2015). Importantly, business model designers need to focus on the problem before jumping (perhaps prematurely) to the conclusion. In order to understand the problem better, it is advantageous to adopt a design attitude, which means observing and listening carefully and empathetically to others. Finally, in designing performance-enhancing business model innovations, managers need to ensure that everybody will gain, and the value proposition for each business model stakeholder is adequate. In other words, they need to embrace a philosophy of total value creation, which accepts that value co-creation with others can only work if all stakeholders are compensated adequately, and one does not just focus on value capture for oneself (Barney, 2018; Brandenburger and Stuart, 1996).

Included among the many issues related to the development of a managerial BMI design capability that future work may address are such research questions as:

- What is the role of entrepreneurial mindset in the design of BMI?
- What is the role of managerial cognition, managerial attention, and top management team characteristics in BMI design?
- What are the roles of diversity, gender, education, and industry experience in determining BMI design choices?
- How can the learning capacities of the top management team influence BMI design choices?
- How does the interplay between leadership style and cognition influence BMI design capabilities?
- What methods and tools are most effective for BMI design, and what are their boundary conditions?
- When, and under which conditions, is an entrepreneur or a manager in an incumbent firm more likely to leverage opportunities for BMI?
- How do the cognitive schema and mental models of entrepreneurs compare to those of corporate managers in designing and implementing BMI?
- How can entrepreneurial leaders engage with others to sense new opportunities for BMI and enhance the co-creation of value together with other stakeholders?

BMI implementation capabilities

These skills will help managers bring the new model to life, integrate it with the old model (in the case of an established firm), and introduce the new business model into the marketplace. Since business models in the digital era typically span firm and industry boundaries, they often involve numerous third-party stakeholders that conduct key activities. Building, negotiating, and nurturing partnerships has therefore become a key competence that managers interested in BMI need to develop and perfect. The ability to build and project trust and credibility, which can be achieved through techniques such as symbolic management (Zott and Huy, 2007) or emotion regulation (Huy and Zott, 2019), helps with winning over partners, and also with acquiring many other kinds of valuable resources.

Other important skills for making BMI happen in new as well as established firms include recognizing, mitigating, and managing risks, for example, by having a business plan; adopting and adhering to sound governance standards, such as constituting a board of directors from the founding of the business (Westphal, 1999; Westphal and Zajac, 2013); identifying and adopting effective defense mechanisms against corporate "sharks" (Katila, Rosenberger, and Eisenhardt, 2008); and being strategic in your choice of revenue model.

Specifically in the context of an established organization, successful BMI strategists need to be able to guide and drive change. This can be through creating awareness about the need for business model change with other organization members by sharing one's vision, educating peers about the business model innovation so that they understand the vision, and anticipating and managing the doubts and fears that may stem from the uncertainty surrounding the new model. In general, managers should take others along with them on the BMI journey by communicating openly and clearly at each step of the journey (Finkelstein, Hambrick, and Cannella, 2009). In this context, managers also need to be able to build, coach, and lead cross-functional teams that are differentiated from the main organization, yet socially integrated with it, and properly governed and incentivized. Such teams are an important vehicle for developing a truly innovative new business model. More broadly speaking, managers need to help create an environment that encourages experimentation, tolerates failure, and promotes learning, so that organizational inertia and resistance to change can be successfully overcome (McDonald and Eisenhardt, 2020).

While some of the implementation capabilities that are described above apply to other situations, we draw on Spieth, Schneckenberg, and Ricart (2014); Wirtz *et al.* (2016); Spieth, Schneckenberg, and Matzler (2016); and Foss and Saebi (2017) to highlight numerous open research questions that relate to BMI implementation capabilities, such as:

- What is the role of employee resistance and inertia in BMI implementation, and how can they be overcome?
- What processes help managers anticipate and react to external and internal challenges to BMI implementation?
- What behaviors and processes help entrepreneurial leaders mitigate the risks and reduce the uncertainty associated with BMI implementation?
- What kind of leadership fosters effective BMI implementation?

- How do entrepreneurial activities, knowledge development, knowledge diffusion through networks, and mobilization of resources enhance BMI implementation?
- How does BMI implementation impact the focal firm's stakeholders and its eco-system network relationships?
- How can internal champions and stakeholders enhance the implementation of BMI?
- How should managers shape boundary-spanning intrafirm partnerships and cross-functional firm-level collaboration for effective BMI implementation?
- Which governance mechanisms and practices facilitate BMI implementation?
- How does corporate culture impact the implementation of business model innovation?

BMI management capabilities

From a research perspective, the management of the ongoing adaptation of the business model involves the continuous monitoring of the activities that encompass the business model and of the incentives of all the stakeholders who participate in the business model. It also involves the ongoing orchestration and coordination of activities performed by the various business model stakeholders, as well as the continuous adaptation of the entire system to changes in its environment (Sirmon, Hitt, and Ireland, 2007). For example, intangible assets and other resources need to be continuously coordinated within the new business model to enable and conduct activities, and thereby fully realize their potential for value creation (Amit and Han, 2017).

The acquisition and nurturing of these BMI capabilities come on top of the high demands placed on top managers by traditional management tasks, such as organization design or product management, and the requirements imposed on them to manage the interactions between internal and external stakeholders. In this sense, it has become significantly more complex and demanding to manage and lead modern organizations. In the past, the business model could be largely taken as a given. For example, banks, as financial service institutions, all basically functioned according to the same template, and taxi services essentially looked the same all over the world. This has profoundly changed, however. In the 21st century, the so-called digital age, the implementation and management of business model design has become a core strategic issue for entrepreneurial start-ups, as well as for incumbent firms. The issues that relate to BMI management capabilities are poorly understood and hence require an intense research effort to address such issues as:

- What capabilities can companies develop to manage continuous BMI?
- What are the risks associated with continuously updating the firm's business model?

- What is the desired level of organizational flexibility and resource reconfiguration for effective ongoing management of BMI?
- What organizational processes are needed to mitigate internal conflicts associated with the reallocation and restructuring of internal resources and corporate functions to embrace BMI?

Conclusion

A BMI strategy has become one of the core strategic choices that entrepreneurial leaders of all kinds of organizations need to consider. It is a relatively recent phenomenon and thus offers many opportunities for future research. For leaders of for-profit firms, BMI strategy complements the firm's corporate strategy—namely, issues that relate to the scope of the firm and include such questions as: What industries and product market segments should the firm be in? How and when should the firm enter or exit these markets (i.e., through mergers and acquisitions, joint ventures, or de novo entry)? A firm's BMI strategy also complements its business strategy, which centers on establishing and sustaining the competitive advantage of a firm in its product market(s). The focal firm's business strategy addresses such questions as how to compete in the firm's selected product market, and how to structure the organization of the firm in a manner that enables the profitable execution of its business strategy.

Entrepreneurial leaders are therefore faced with an indispensable and complementary strategic choice, namely the conceptualization, design, implementation, and management of potentially transformative, digitally enabled business models. The resulting business model is a strategic asset that contributes to a firm's sustained competitiveness and profitability (Amit and Schoemaker, 1993). The conception, introduction into the marketplace, and ongoing management of the business model should not be left to chance; rather, it must be guided by a BMI strategy, which is anchored in a rigorous design process that combines organizational practices (e.g., regular brainstorming sessions) with creative insight at the individual managerial level (e.g., the insight required for synthesizing the lessons learned from intense and comprehensive observation of stakeholders). In order to effectively navigate through the possibilities enabled in part by technological developments, the BMI strategy must depict the organizational processes of developing, implementing, managing, and continuously updating the firm's business model in a way that creates value for all the stakeholders in its activity system, while also capturing some of the value that is created.

The promise of innovative business models, however, goes beyond mere economic value creation and capture. Aravind Eye Hospitals in India and Grameen Bank in Bangladesh (a business model innovation in microlending to poor rural women, for which the founder, Muhammad Yunus, received the Nobel Peace Prize in 2006) serve as shining examples and sources of inspiration for entrepreneurs and leaders who want to make the world a better place (Yunus *et al.*, 2010). They remind us that the big problems facing humankind, such as poverty, inequality, hunger, disease, or climate change, can be tackled through scalable business model innovations. To address climate change, for example, we need more sustainable business models, not just cleaner technologies, products, services, and processes (Bocken *et al.*, 2014). Innovations in business models can help us chart a path into a better and brighter future for all.

Notes

1. The *circular economy* refers to a "regenerative system in which resource input and waste, emission, and energy leakage are minimized by slowing, closing, and narrowing material and energy loops. This can be achieved through long-lasting design, maintenance, repair, reuse, remanufacturing, refurbishing, and recycling" (Geissdoerfer *et al.*, 2017: 759).
2. According to Dr. V, "All I want to sell is good eyesight, and there are millions of people who need it.... If McDonald's can sell billions of burgers, why can't Aravind sell millions of sight-restoring operations, and, eventually, the belief in human perfection? With sight, people could be freed from hunger, fear, and poverty. You could perfect the body, then perfect the mind and the soul, and raise people's level of thinking and acting" (Fast Company Staff, 2006).

References

Adner R, Helfat CE. 2003. Corporate effects and dynamic managerial capabilities. *Strategic Management Journal* 24(10): 1011–1025.

Amit R, Han H. 2017. Value creation through novel resource configurations in a digitally enabled world. *Strategic Entrepreneurship Journal* 11(3): 228–242.

Amit R, Han H, Zott, C. 2020. Collaboration in business model innovation. In *The Oxford Handbook of Entrepreneurship and Collaboration*, Reuer J, Matusik S, Jones J (eds). Oxford University Press: New York, NY; 569–586.

Amit R, Schoemaker PJH. 1993. Strategic assets and organizational rent. *Strategic Management Journal* 14(1): 33–46.

Amit R, Zott C. 2001. Value creation in e-business. *Strategic Management Journal* 22(6–7): 493–520.

Amit R, Zott C. 2012. Creating value through business model innovation. *Sloan Management Review* 53(3): 41–49.

Amit R, Zott C. 2015. Crafting business architecture: the antecedents of business model design. *Strategic Entrepreneurship Journal* 9(4): 331–350.

Amit R, Zott C. 2016. Business model design: a dynamic capability perspective. In *The Oxford Handbook of Dynamic Capabilities*, Teece DJ, Heaton S (eds). Oxford University Press: Oxford, U.K.; 1–21.

Amit R, Zott C. 2021. *Business Model Innovation Strategy*. Wiley (forthcoming).

Aravind Eye Care System. 2018. Activity report 2017–18. Retrieved from https://aravind.org/wp-content/uploads/2019/04/Aravind_Annual-Report-2017-18.pdf [19 March 2021].

Aravind Eye Care System website. 2020. https://aravind.org/our-story/ [19 March 2021].

Barney J. 1991. Firm resources and sustained competitive advantage. *Journal of Management* 17(1): 99–120.

Barney J. 2018. Why resource-based theory's model of profit appropriation must incorporate a stakeholder perspective. *Strategic Management Journal* 39(13): 3305– 3325.

Bocken NM, Short SW, Rana P, Evans S. 2014. A literature and practice review to develop sustainable business model archetypes. *Journal of Cleaner Production* 65(2014): 42–56.

Brandenburger AM, Stuart H. 1996. Value-based business strategy. *Journal of Economics and Management Strategy* 5(1): 5–25.

Brown T. 2007. *Change by Design: How Design Thinking Transforms Organizations and Inspires Innovation.* HarperCollins: New York, NY.

Campbell B, Coff R, Kryscynski D. 2012. Re-thinking competitive advantage from human capital. *Academy of Management Review* 37(3): 376–395.

Casadesus-Masanell R, Zhu F. 2013. Business model innovation and competitive imitation: the case of sponsor-based business models. *Strategic Management Journal* 34(4): 464–482.

Chesbrough H. 2010. Business model innovation: opportunities and barriers. *Long Range Planning* 43(2–3): 354–363.

Chesbrough H. 2020. To recover faster from COVID-19, open up: managerial implications from an open innovation perspective. *Industrial Marketing Management* 88(2020): 410–413.

Cusumano MA, Gawer A, Yoffie DB. 2019. *The Business of Platforms: Strategy in the Age of Digital Competition, Innovation, and Power.* Harper Business: New York, NY.

Doz YL, Kosonen M. 2010. Embedding strategic agility: a leadership agenda for accelerating business model renewal. *Long Range Planning* 43(2–3): 370–382.

Dunne D. 2018. *Design Thinking at Work: How Innovative Organizations are Embracing Design.* University of Toronto Press: Toronto, Canada.

Dushnitsky G, Graebner M, Zott C. 2020. Entrepreneurial responses to crises. *Strategic Entrepreneurship Journal* (forthcoming).

Eggers JP, Park K. 2018. Incumbent adaptation to technological change: the past, present, and future of research on heterogeneous incumbent response. *Academy of Management Annals* 12(1): 357–389.

Fast Company Staff. 2006. And then there's Dr. V. *Fast Company.* July 20. https://www.fastcompany.com/675800/and-then-theres-dr-v [19 March 2020].

Finkelstein S, Hambrick DC, Cannella AA. 2009. *Strategic Leadership: Theory and Research on Executives, Top Management Teams, and Boards.* Oxford University Press: New York, NY.

Foss N, Saebi T. 2017. Fifteen years of research on business model innovation: how far have we come, and where should we go? *Journal of Management* 43(1): 200–227.

Geissdoerfer M, Savaget P, Bocken NM, Hultink EJ. 2017. The circular economy—a new sustainability paradigm? *Journal of Cleaner Production* 143(2017): 757–768.

Greve HR, Song SY. 2017. Amazon warrior: how a platform can restructure industry power and ecology. *Advances in Strategic Management* 37: 299–335.

Hacklin F, Bjorkdahl J, Wallin M. 2018. Strategies for business model innovation: how firms reel in migrating value. *Long Range Planning* 51(1): 82–110.

Helfat C, Finkelstein S, Mitchell W, Peteraf M, Singh H, Teece DJ, Winter S. 2007. *Dynamic Capabilities: Understanding Strategic Change in Organizations.* Blackwell: Malden, MA.

Helfat C, Peteraf M. 2015. Managerial cognitive capabilities and the microfoundations of dynamic capabilities. *Strategic Management Journal* 36(6): 831–850.

Huy Q, Zott C. 2019. Exploring the affective underpinnings of dynamic managerial capabilities: how managers' emotion regulation behaviors mobilize resources for their firms. *Strategic Management Journal* 40(1): 28–54.

Karimi J, Walter Z. 2016. Corporate entrepreneurship, disruptive business model innovation adoption, and its performance: The case of the newspaper industry. *Long Range Planning* 49 (2016): 342–360.

Katila R, Rosenberg JD, Eisenhardt KM. 2008. Swimming with sharks: technology ventures and corporate relationships. *Administrative Science Quarterly* 53(2): 295–332.

Kim SK, Min S. 2015. Business model innovation performance: when does adding a new business model benefit an incumbent? *Strategic Entrepreneurship Journal* 9(1): 34–57.

Lee E, Puranam P. 2016. The implementation imperative: why one should implement even imperfect strategies perfectly. *Strategic Management Journal* 37(8): 1529–1546.

Liedtka J, Kaplan S. 2019. How design thinking opens new frontiers for strategy development. *Strategy and Leadership* 47(2): 3–10.

Markides C, Charitou C. 2004. Competing with dual business models: a contingency approach. *Academy of Management Executive* 18(3): 22–36.

Martins LL, Rindova VP, Greenbaum BE. 2015. Unlocking the hidden value of concepts: a cognitive approach to business model innovation. *Strategic Entrepreneurship Journal* 9(1): 99–117.

Massa L, Tucci CL, Afuah A. 2017. A critical assessment of business model research. *Academy of Management Annals* 11(1): 73–104.

McDonald RM, Eisenhardt KM. 2020. Parallel play: startups, nascent markets, and effective business-model design. *Administrative Science Quarterly* 65(2): 483–523.

McKinsey and Company. 2011. Driving down the cost of high-quality care: Lessons from the Aravind Eye Care System. Retrieved from https://www.mckinsey.com/~/media/mckinsey/dotcom/client_service/healthcare%20systems%20and%20services/health%20international/issue%2011%20new%20pdfs/hi11_18%20aravindeyecaresys_noprint.ashx [19 March 2021].

Metz C. 2019. India fights diabetic blindness with help from A.I. *New York Times*. 10 March. Retrieved from https://www.nytimes.com/2019/03/10/technology/artificial-intelligence-eye-hospital-india.html [19 March 2021].

Milne R. 2018. Ikea unpacked: how the furniture giant is redesigning its future. *Financial Times*. 1 February. Retrieved from https://www.ft.com/content/8a8bb9a0-0613-11e8-9650-9c0ad2d7c5b5 [19 March 2021].

Milne R. 2019. Ikea assembles software engineers in smart home push. *Financial Times*. 2 October. Retrieved from https://www.ft.com/content/440249c8-e41e-11e9-9743-db5a370481bc [19 March 2021].

Rangan KV, Thulasiraj RD. 2007. Making sight affordable. *Innovations: Technology, Governance, Globalizations* 2(4): 35–49. Retrieved from http://www.bu.edu/ghblast/files/2012/10/Making-Sight-Affordable.pdf [19 March 2021].

Saebi T, Foss NJ, Linder S. 2019. Social entrepreneurship research: past achievements and future promises. *Journal of Management* 45(1): 70–95.

Schneider S, Spieth P. 2013. Business model innovation: towards an integrated future research agenda. *International Journal of Innovation Management* 17(1): 1340001.

Shapiro C, Varian HR. 1999. *Information Rules: A Strategic Guide to the Network Economy*. Harvard Business School Press: Boston, MA.

Siggelkow N. 2002. Evolution of fit. *Administrative Science Quarterly* 47(1): 125–159.

Sirmon DG, Hitt MA, Ireland RD. 2007. Managing firm resources in dynamic environments to create value: looking inside the black box. *Academy of Management Review* 32(1): 273–292.

Snihur Y, Zott C. 2020. The genesis and metamorphosis of novelty imprints: how business model innovation emerges in young ventures. *Academy of Management Journal* 63(2): 554–583.

Snihur Y, Zott C, Amit R. 2021. Managing the value appropriation dilemma in business model innovation. *Strategy Science* 6(1): 22–38.

Spieth P, Schneckenberg D, Matzler K. 2016. Exploring the linkage between business model (and) innovation and the strategy of the firm. *R&D Management* 46(3): 403–413.

Spieth P, Schneckenberg D, Ricart JE. 2014. Business model innovation—state of the art and future challenges for the field. *R&D Management* 44(3): 237–247.

Täuscher K, Laudien SM. 2018. Understanding platform business models: a mixed methods study of marketplaces. *European Management Journal* 36(3): 319–329.

Teece DJ. 2014. A dynamic capabilities-based entrepreneurial theory of multinational enterprise. *Journal of International Business Studies* 45(1): 8–37.

Tidhar R, Eisenhardt KM. 2020. Get rich or die trying … finding revenue model fit using machine learning and multiple cases. *Strategic Management Journal* (forthcoming).

Wenzel M, Stanske S, Lieberman MB. 2020. Strategic responses to crisis. *Strategic Management Journal* 41: V7–V18.

Wernerfelt B. 1984. A resource-based view of the firm. *Strategic Management Journal* 5(2): 171–180.

Westphal JD. 1999. Collaboration in the boardroom: behavioral and performance consequences of CEO-board social ties. *Academy of Management Journal* 42(1): 7–24.

Westphal JD, Zajac EJ. 2013. A behavioral theory of corporate governance: explicating the mechanisms of socially situated and socially constituted agency. *Academy of Management Annals* 7(1): 607–661.

Wirtz BW, Pistoia A, Ullrich S, Göttel V. 2016. Business models: origin, development and future research perspectives. *Long Range Planning* 49(1): 36–54.

Yunus M, Moingeon B, Lehmann-Ortega L. 2010. Building social business models: lessons from the Grameen experience. *Long Range Planning* 43(2–3): 308–325.

Zhao EY, Fisher G, Lounsbury M, Miller D. 2017. Optimal distinctiveness: broadening the interface between institutional theory and strategic management. *Strategic Management Journal* 38(1): 93–113.

Zhao Y, von Delft S, Morgan-Thomas A, Buck T. 2019. The evolution of platform business models: exploring competitive battles in the world of platforms. *Long Range Planning* 53(4): 101892.

Zott C, Amit R. 2009. The business model as the engine of network-based strategies. In *Network-Based Strategies and Competencies*, Kleindorfer PR, Wind Y (eds). Wharton School Publishing: Upper Saddle River, NJ; 259–275.

Zott C, Amit R. 2010. Business model design: an activity system perspective. *Long Range Planning* 43(2–3): 216–226.

Zott C, Amit R. 2015. Business model innovation: towards a process perspective. In *Oxford Handbook of Creativity, Innovation, and Entrepreneurship: Multilevel Linkages*, Shalley C, Hitt M, Zhou J (eds). Oxford University Press: New York, NY; 395–406.

Zott C, Amit R, Massa L. 2011. The business model: recent developments and future research. *Journal of Management* 37(4): 1019–1042.

Zott C, Huy Q. 2007. How entrepreneurs use symbolic management to acquire resources. *Administrative Science Quarterly* 52(1): 70–105.

Name Index

For the benefit of digital users, indexed terms that span two pages (e.g., 52–53) may, on occasion, appear on only one of those pages.

Subject Index

For the benefit of digital users, indexed terms that span two pages (e.g., 52–53) may, on occasion, appear on only one of those pages.